Oxf... Primary Dictionary

Compiled by Robert Allen

OXFORD
UNIVERSITY PRESS

OXFORD
UNIVERSITY PRESS

Great Clarendon Street, Oxford OX2 6DP

Oxford University Press is a department of the University of Oxford.
It furthers the University's objective of excellence in research, scholarship,
and education by publishing worldwide in
Oxford New York
Auckland Bangkok Buenos Aires Cape Town Chennai
Dar es Salaam Delhi Hong Kong Istanbul Karachi Kolkata
Kuala Lumpur Madrid Melbourne Mexico City Mumbai Nairobi
São Paulo Shanghai Taipei Tokyo Toronto
Oxford is a registered trade mark of Oxford University Press

in the UK and in certain other countries

First published 1993
Second edition 1998
Revised second edition 2002
This edition 2003

Database right Oxford University Press (maker)

British Library cataloguing in Publication Data available

ISBN 0-19-911122-7

4

Typeset in Univers and Century Schoolbook

Illustrations by Peter Bull and Hannah Cobley

Printed in Great Britain by

Clays Ltd, St Ives plc

Preface

This dictionary has been specially written for school children aged 8 to 11 years. Its aim is to explain the English words that they are most likely to meet in conversation and reading and through other media such as radio and television. Many features of the last edition have been retained and developed, in particular the spelling out of verb and noun inflections and the comparatives of adjectives and adverbs. Definitions are expressed clearly, and are supported by many examples of words in use.

Definitions of verbs are given in context to clarify the typical subject and object of the verb as well as its transitivity and other aspects of its use, without needing to use complex grammatical terms. For example, the first definition of *awake*, 'to awake is to wake up' is intransitive, while the second, 'to awake someone is to wake them up', is transitive with the object shown.

Definitions of some nouns are also given in contextualized form when this clarifies important aspects of their use, such as countability. This can be seen at *choice*, where one sense, 'choice is the process of choosing or the power to choose', is uncountable and another 'a choice is what someone chooses', is countable.

Definitions are given for all items, including derivative words added at the end of entries. There is nothing that the user has to work out from other definitions, which at this age level calls for unreasonable mental leaps (for example to work out what *provocative* means from the definition of *provoke*, or *qualification* from *qualify*).

Our watchwords in writing this dictionary have been clarity and interest, and we believe that as a result its users, teachers and children alike, will find exploring words and language to be stimulating, rewarding, and often entertaining.

I should like to thank Sara Hawker, Alan Spooner, and Jessica Feinstein, who have contributed to improving the text in many ways; and also the staff and pupils of Sciennes and St Ninian's Primary Schools in Edinburgh, from whom I learned much about dictionary use in the classroom.

Robert Allen

How to use the dictionary

Dictionary entries

Words defined are arranged in alphabetical order. The words derived from each word (derivatives) are often included at the end of an entry. These have their own short definitions, which seek principally to identify the basic type and function of the word, for example adverbs often have meanings conforming to the pattern 'in a ... way'.

Words with the same spelling but with a different meaning or origin (homographs) are given separate entries with space between them, and are numbered with a raised figure, e.g. *bat*¹ (a wooden implement) and *bat*² (a mammal).

Pronunciation

Help is given with pronouncing words when they are difficult in some way, when two words with the same spelling are pronounced differently (such as several words spelt *bow*), and when the same word is pronounced differently in its different word classes or parts of speech (as with *abstract* and *record*).

The pronunciation is given in brackets, introduced by 'rhymes with ...' (when possible) or 'pronounced...' followed by a simple scheme that uses ordinary letters, e.g.

draught *noun* (*plural* **draughts**)
(*rhymes with* craft)
a current of cold air indoors
draughty *adjective* having lots of draughts

acre *noun* (*plural* **acres**)
(*pronounced* **ay**-ker)
an acre is the area of a piece of land
containing 4,840 square yards

Words are divided into syllables, and the main stress is shown by bold type (thick black letters).

The following special sounds should be noted:

oo shows the sound as in s**oo**n
uu shows the sound as in b**oo**k
th shows the sound as in **th**in
th shows the sound as in ***th***is
zh shows the sound as in vi**zh**ion

Word classes (parts of speech)

These are printed in italic or sloping print (e.g. *noun*, *adjective*, *verb*) after the word and before its definition. When a word has more than one word class (part of speech), these are grouped together and the different word classes (parts of speech) are indicated by an arrow, e.g.

heap ➢ *noun* (*plural* **heaps**)
a pile, especially an untidy pile
heaps (*informal*) a large amount ♦ *We've got heaps of time*
heap ➢ *verb* (**heaps, heaping, heaped**)
1 to heap things is to make them into a heap
2 to heap something is to put large amounts on it ♦ *She heaped his plate with food*

Inflections and plurals

The parts of verbs, plurals of nouns, and some comparatives and superlatives of adjectives and adverbs are given after the word class (part of speech), e.g.

cancel (cancels, cancelling, cancelled)

camp (*plural* camps)

calm (calmer, calmest)

Meanings

Many words have more than one meaning. Each meaning is numbered separately and begins on a new line.

Labels

Words that are only used informally or in spoken English are marked informal or slang.

Examples

Examples of words in use are given in italic or sloping print *like this* to help make a meaning clearer, e.g.

choice *noun* (*plural* choices)
  1 choice is the process of choosing or the power to choose ♦ *I'm afraid we have no choice*
  2 a choice is what someone chooses ♦ *Let me know your choice of book*

Phrases

Phrases and idioms are listed and defined under the word class (part of speech) to which they belong, e.g.

jump ➤ *verb* (jumps, jumping, jumped)
  1 to jump is to move suddenly from the ground into the air 2 to jump a fence or other obstacle is to go over it by jumping
  3 to jump up or out is to move quickly or suddenly ♦ *He jumped out of his seat*
  4 to jump in or out of a vehicle is to get in or out quickly **to jump at something** (*informal*) is to accept it eagerly
  to jump the gun is to start something before the right time
  to jump the queue is to go ahead before it is your turn

jump ➤ *noun* (*plural* jumps)
  1 a sudden movement into the air 2 an obstacle to jump over

Dictionary features

Headword
the word that is
being looked up.

draught *noun* (*plural* **draughts**) (*rhymes with* **craft**)
a current of cold air indoors
draughty *adjective* having lots of draughts

Word class (part of speech)
noun, verb,
adjective,
adverb, etc.

draughts *noun*
a game played with 24 round pieces on a chessboard

draughtsman *noun* (*plural* **draughtsmen**)
1 someone who makes drawings **2** a piece used in the game of draughts

draw ➤ *verb* (**draws, drawing, drew, drawn**)
1 to draw a picture or outline is to form it with a pencil or pen **2** to draw something is to pull it ♦ *She drew her chair up to the table* **3** to draw people is to attract them ♦ *The fair drew large crowds* **4** to draw is to end a game or contest with the same score on both sides ♦ *They drew 2–2 last Saturday* **5** to draw near is to come nearer ♦ *The ship was drawing nearer*

Examples
shows how a
word is used.

draw ➤ *noun* (*plural* **draws**)
1 a raffle or similar competition in which the winner is chosen by picking tickets or numbers at random **2** a game that ends with the same score on both sides **3** an attraction

Number
used when a
word has more
than one
meaning.

drawback *noun* (*plural* **drawbacks**)
a disadvantage

drawbridge *noun* (*plural* **drawbridges**)
a bridge over a moat, hinged at one end so that it can be raised or lowered

dreary *adjective* (**drearier, dreariest**)
1 dull or boring **2** gloomy **drearily** *adverb* in a dreary way **dreariness** *noun* being dreary

dredge *verb* (**dredges, dredging, dredged**)
to dredge something is to drag it up, especially mud from the bottom of water
dredger *noun* a machine for dredging

Derivative
a word with a
meaning
connected with
the headword's
meaning.

Pronunciation
for some
difficult words
we give a
rhyming word,
or letters which
sound like the
headword.

Definition
the meaning of
the headword.

Verb forms
present tense,
present
participle, past
tense, past
participle.

Plural
all regular and
irregular
plurals are
given.

Adjective forms
all comparative
and superlative
forms of
adjectives are
given.

Aa

a *adjective* (called the *indefinite article*)
 1 one; any ♦ *I would like a holiday*
 2 each; every ♦ *I go there twice a month*

aback *adverb*
 taken aback surprised and slightly shocked
 ♦ *We were taken aback by their rudeness*

abacus *noun* (*plural* **abacuses**)
 a frame with rows of beads that slide on
 wires, used for counting and doing sums

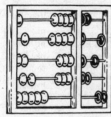

abandon *verb* (**abandons, abandoning,**
 abandoned)
 to abandon something or someone is to go
 away and leave them, without intending
 to go back for them ♦ *He abandoned his
 family and went off to Australia*
 abandon ship passengers abandon ship
 when they get into the lifeboats to save
 their lives

abbey *noun* (*plural* **abbeys**)
 1 a group of buildings where monks or
 nuns live and work 2 a community of
 monks or nuns 3 a church which is or was
 part of an abbey, such as Westminster
 Abbey in London

abbot *noun* (*plural* **abbots**)
 the head of an abbey of monks

abbreviate *verb* (**abbreviates, abbreviating,**
 abbreviated)
 to abbreviate a word or phrase is to write
 it in a shorter form

abbreviation *noun* (*plural* **abbreviations**)
 a word or group of letters that is a shorter
 form of something longer ♦ *BBC is an
 abbreviation of 'British Broadcasting
 Corporation'*

ABC *noun*
 a name for the alphabet ♦ *We know our
 ABC*

abdomen *noun* (*plural* **abdomens**)
 1 the part of the body that contains the
 stomach 2 the back part of the body of an
 insect or spider

abdominal *adjective*
 to do with the abdomen

abide *verb* (**abides, abiding, abode** or **abided**)
 1 you cannot abide something or someone
 when you cannot stand them
 ♦ *I can't abide noise* 2 (*old meaning*) to
 abide in a place is to be living or working
 in it
 to abide by a promise is to keep it

ability *noun* (*plural* **abilities**)
 the skill or talent to do something ♦ *They
 have a lot of ability at games*

ablaze *adjective*
 burning strongly; on fire

able *adjective* (**abler, ablest**)
 1 having the power or skill or opportunity
 to do something ♦ *They were not able to
 find our house* 2 having a special talent or
 skill ♦ *John is a very able musician*
 ably *adverb* in an able way, with talent

-able *suffix*
 meaning that something is possible or is
 allowed, as in *eatable* and *movable*

abnormal *adjective*
 unusual or peculiar, not normal
 abnormality *noun* something that is
 abnormal

aboard *adverb*
 on a ship or an aircraft

abode *noun* (*plural* **abodes**)
 a formal word for the place where someone
 lives

abolish *verb* (**abolishes, abolishing, abolished**)
 to get rid of a rule or custom ♦ *Some people
 would like to abolish homework*

abolition *noun* (*pronounced* ab-o-lish-on)
 getting rid of something

abominable *adjective*
 very shocking, dreadful ♦ *It was an
 abominable crime*

aboriginal *noun*
 one of the original inhabitants of a country

Aborigines *plural noun* (*pronounced*
 ab-er-ij-in-eez)
 the people who lived in Australia before
 the European settlers arrived there

abort *verb* (**aborts, aborting, aborted**)
 to abort a plan or mission is to cancel it
 after it has begun

abortion *noun* (*plural* **abortions**)
 an operation to remove an unborn child
 (foetus) from a woman's womb before it
 has developed fully enough to live

abound *verb* (**abounds, abounding, abounded**)
to abound is to be plentiful ♦ *Fish abound in the river*

about ➤ *preposition*
1 to do with, connected with ♦ *The story is about animals* 2 approximately, roughly ♦ *She's about five feet tall*

about ➤ *adverb*
1 in various directions or places ♦ *They were running about* 2 somewhere near by ♦ *There were wild animals about*
about to you are about to do something when you are just going to do it ♦ *He was about to leave*

above ➤ *preposition*
1 higher than, over ♦ *There was a window above the door* 2 more than ♦ *The temperature was just above freezing*

above ➤ *adverb*
at a higher point, or to a higher point ♦ *Look at the stars above*

abrasive *adjective*
an abrasive material is rough and is used to clean or scrape something hard

abreast *adverb*
side by side ♦ *They walked three abreast*
abreast of something you are abreast of something when you know all about it ♦ *We must be abreast of modern discoveries*

abroad *adverb*
in a foreign country ♦ *They live abroad now*

abrupt *adjective*
1 sudden and unexpected ♦ *It was the same for years and then there was an abrupt change* 2 rude and unfriendly ♦ *He gave an abrupt reply*

abscess *noun* (*plural* **abscesses**)
a painful swelling on the body containing pus

abseil *verb* (**abseils, abseiling, abseiled**)
to abseil is to lower yourself down a steep cliff or rock by sliding down a rope

absence *noun* (*plural* **absences**)
not being in a place where you are expected, for example school or work

absent *adjective*
not present; away

absentee *noun* (*plural* **absentees**)
someone who is away, for example not at school or work

absent-minded *adjective*
forgetting things easily
absent-mindedly *adverb* in an absent-minded way

absolute *adjective*
total, complete, not restricted ♦ *The king had absolute power*

absolutely *adverb*
1 completely 2 (*informal*) definitely ♦ *'Are you going to Beth's party?' 'Absolutely!'*

absorb *verb* (**absorbs, absorbing, absorbed**)
1 to absorb something like liquid is to soak it up 2 to be absorbed in something is to be interested in it and give it all your attention ♦ *He was very absorbed in his book*

absorption *noun* the process of absorbing something

absorbent *adjective*
an absorbent material soaks up liquid easily

abstract ➤ *adjective* (*pronounced* ab-strakt)
to do with ideas and not with physical things

abstract ➤ *verb* (**abstracts, abstracting, abstracted**) (*pronounced* ab-**strakt**)
to abstract something is to take it out of something else ♦ *Water is abstracted from the river*

abstract ➤ *noun* (*plural* **abstracts**) (*pronounced* **ab**-strakt)
a summary of a longer piece of writing

absurd *adjective*
silly or ridiculous ♦ *It was absurd to expect us to stay*

absurdity *noun* (*plural* **absurdities**)
something that is silly or ridiculous

abundance *noun*
a large amount, plenty ♦ *There was an abundance of good things*

abundant *adjective*
large in amount, plentiful

abuse ➤ *verb* (**abuses, abusing, abused**) (*pronounced* a-**bewz**)
1 to abuse something is to misuse it and harm it 2 to abuse someone is to say unpleasant things about them 3 to abuse someone also means to hurt them or treat them cruelly

abuse ➤ *noun* (*plural* **abuses**) (*pronounced* a-**bewss**)
1 misuse of something 2 unpleasant words said about someone 3 physical harm or cruelty done to someone

abusive *adjective*
saying unpleasant things about someone

abysmal *adjective*
(*informal*) very bad ♦ *The weather was abysmal*

abyss *noun* (*plural* **abysses**)
a deep dark hole that seems to go on for ever

acacia *noun* (*plural* **acacias**) (*pronounced* a-**kay**-sha)
a tree with small yellow or white flowers, which grows in warm countries

academic *adjective*
1 to do with learning in a school or university **2** not really important ♦ *It was academic who won now*

academy *noun* (*plural* **academies**)
1 a college or school **2** a society set up to deal with art or learning

accelerate *verb* (**accelerates, accelerating, accelerated**)
to accelerate is to go faster

acceleration *noun*
an increase of speed, going faster

accelerator *noun* (*plural* **accelerators**)
a pedal that you press down to make a motor vehicle go faster

accent ➤ *noun* (*plural* **accents**) (*pronounced* **ak**-sent)
1 your accent is the way you pronounce words **2** an accent is the way that people in different parts of a country pronounce words differently ♦ *He has a Yorkshire accent* **3** the accent in a word is the part you speak more strongly than the rest of it ♦ *The accent in 'dinner' is on the first syllable* **4** an accent is a special mark put over a letter, usually when it's a foreign word, to show its pronunciation ♦ *The word 'fiancé' has an accent on the 'e'*

accent ➤ *verb* (**accents, accenting, accented**) (*pronounced* ak-**sent**)
to accent part of a word is to speak it more strongly than the rest of it

accept *verb* (**accepts, accepting, accepted**)
1 to accept something is to take it when it is offered **2** to accept someone is to allow them to become a member of a college or society **3** to accept something is to agree that it is true or worth considering ♦ *I accept that idea*

acceptable *adjective*
1 worth accepting ♦ *We think it is an acceptable offer* **2** all right, satisfactory ♦ *Their behaviour was not acceptable*

acceptance *noun*
accepting something, or agreeing that something is true or worth considering

access ➤ *noun* (*plural* **accesses**)
a way to reach a place ♦ *This road is the only access to the house*

access ➤ *verb* (**accesses, accessing, accessed**)
(*in Computing*) to access data is to be able to use it

accessible *adjective*
easy to reach or approach
accessibility *noun* being accessible

accession *noun* (*plural* **accessions**)
the time when a new king or queen begins ruling ♦ *We saw a painting of Henry VIII at his accession*

accessory *noun* (*plural* **accessories**)
1 an extra or spare part that goes with something bigger **2** an item like a piece of jewellery or a handbag that goes with clothes

accident *noun* (*plural* **accidents**)
an unexpected event, especially one in which someone is hurt or killed
by accident by chance, not intentionally

accidental *adjective*
happening by chance, not intentionally ♦ *accidental damage*
accidentally *adverb* by accident

acclaim *verb* (**acclaims, acclaiming, acclaimed**)
to acclaim someone is to welcome or applaud them keenly

acclimatize *verb* (**acclimatizes, acclimatizing, acclimatized**)
to acclimatize someone is to make them get used to a new climate or a new situation
acclimatization *noun* getting used to something new

accommodate *verb* (**accommodates, accommodating, accommodated**)
1 to accommodate someone is to provide them with a room or a place to sleep **2** to accommodate someone also means to do what you can to please them

accommodation *noun*
accommodation is a place to live or stay ♦ *They were looking for cheap accommodation*

accompaniment *noun* (*plural* **accompaniments**)
the music played on a piano or another instrument while a singer sings

accompanist *noun* (*plural* **accompanists**)
a person who plays the piano or another instrument while a singer sings

accompany *verb* (**accompanies, accompanying, accompanied**)
1 to accompany someone is to go somewhere with them **2** to accompany a singer is to play the piano or another instrument while they sing

accomplish *verb* (**accomplishes, accomplishing, accomplished**)
to accomplish something is to do it successfully

accomplished *adjective*
skilful at something

accomplishment *noun* (*plural* **accomplishments**)
something you do well

accord *noun* (*plural* **accords**)
an accord is an agreement
of your own accord you do something of your own accord when you do it willingly and without being told to

according *adverb*
according to someone in their opinion, as stated by them ♦ *According to him, there is a party tomorrow*
according to something in a way that suits it ♦ *The shop has priced the apples according to their size*

accordingly *adverb*
1 consequently; therefore 2 in a way that is suitable ♦ *You are older now and must behave accordingly*

accordion *noun* (*plural* **accordions**)
a portable musical instrument like a large concertina with a set of piano-type keys at one end. It is played by squeezing it in and out and pressing the keys

account ➤ *noun* (*plural* **accounts**)
1 an account is a description or story
2 an account is also an amount of money kept in a bank or building society 3 an account is also a statement of money owed or received, a bill ♦ *We will send you an account next week*
on account of something because of it
on no account certainly not
take something into account to consider it along with other things

account ➤ *verb* (**accounts, accounting, accounted**)
to account for something is to be an explanation of it ♦ *They lost the match and that accounts for their bad mood*

accountant *noun* (*plural* **accountants**)
a person whose job is to prepare and analyse money accounts
accountancy *noun* the job of an accountant

accumulate *verb* (**accumulates, accumulating, accumulated**)
to accumulate things is to collect them or pile them up; things accumulate when they form a heap or pile

accumulation *noun*
1 a heap or pile, a collection
2 accumulating things

accuracy *noun*
exactness, correctness

accurate *adjective*
correct, done exactly and carefully ♦ *She does accurate work*
accurately *adverb* carefully and exactly

accusation *noun* (*plural* **accusations**)
a statement accusing someone of something

accuse *verb* (**accuses, accusing, accused**)
to accuse someone of doing something wrong is to say that they did it

accustomed *adjective*
be accustomed to something be used to it ♦ *I am accustomed to having lunch at twelve o'clock*

ace ➤ *noun* (*plural* **aces**)
1 the four aces in a pack of cards are the cards with an A in the corner and a large emblem of the suit in the centre
2 someone or something very clever or skilful

ace ➤ *adjective*
(*informal*) very good or clever

ache ➤ *noun* (*plural* **aches**)
a dull steady pain

ache ➤ *verb* (**aches, aching, ached**)
to ache is to feel a dull steady pain

achieve *verb* (**achieves, achieving, achieved**)
to achieve something is to succeed in doing it or getting it
achievement *noun* something achieved

acid ➤ *noun* (*plural* **acids**)
a substance that contains hydrogen and causes chemical change. Acids are the opposite of alkalis

acid ➤ *adjective*
sour or bitter to taste
acidic *adjective* containing acid **acidity** *noun* the level of acid in a substance

acid rain *noun*
rain that contains harmful acids because it has mixed with waste gases from the air

acknowledge *verb* (**acknowledges, acknowledging, acknowledged**)
1 to acknowledge something is to admit that it is true 2 to acknowledge a letter is to say that you have received it 3 to acknowledge a debt or favour is to express gratitude for it
acknowledgement *noun* acknowledging something; something that is acknowledged

acne *noun* (*pronounced* **ak**-ni)
a skin disease with red pimples on the face. It is common among teenagers

acorn *noun* (*plural* **acorns**)
the seed of the oak tree, an oval shape with a cup-shaped stem

acoustic *adjective* (*pronounced* a-**koo**-stik)
1 to do with sound or hearing **2** an acoustic guitar or other musical instrument uses its own shape to make the sound, without an electrical amplifier

acoustics *plural noun* (*pronounced* a-**koo**-stiks)
1 the acoustics of a place are the qualities that make it good or bad for sound
2 (*singular noun*) the science of sound

acquaint *verb* (**acquaints, acquainting, acquainted**)
1 to acquaint someone with something is to tell them about it **2** to be acquainted with someone is to know them slightly

acquaintance *noun* (*plural* **acquaintances**)
an acquaintance is someone you know slightly
to make someone's acquaintance is to get to know them

acquire *verb* (**acquires, acquiring, acquired**)
to acquire something is to obtain it, usually with some effort or difficulty

acquisition *noun* (*plural* **acquisitions**)
an acquisition is something you obtain. Usually it is something of value or interest

acquit *verb* (**acquits, acquitting, acquitted**)
to acquit someone is to decide that they are not guilty of a crime, especially in a law trial

acquittal *noun* (*plural* **acquittals**)
a decision that someone is not guilty

acre *noun* (*plural* **acres**) (*pronounced* **ay**-ker)
an acre is the area of a piece of land containing 4,840 square yards

acrobat *noun* (*plural* **acrobats**)
someone who entertains people with displays of jumping and balancing
acrobatic *adjective* to do with an acrobat
acrobatics *plural noun* the exercises that an acrobat does

acronym *noun* (*plural* **acronyms**) (*pronounced* **ak**-ron-im)
a word or name that is formed from the first letters of other words, for example *Nato* is an acronym of *North Atlantic Treaty Organization*

across *adverb and preposition*
1 from one side of a thing to the other
♦ *The table measures 1·5 metres across*
2 to the other side of something ♦ *How can we get across the busy road?*

act ➤ *noun* (*plural* **acts**)
1 something that someone does **2** an individual performance in a programme of entertainment, for example a juggling act or a comic act **3** one of the main sections of a play or opera **4** a government law
to put on an act is to show off or pretend to be something that you are not

act ➤ *verb* (**acts, acting, acted**)
1 to do something definite ♦ *We need to act straight away* **2** to act stupid or act clever is to behave stupidly or cleverly
3 to act in a play or film is to take part in it

action *noun* (*plural* **actions**)
1 an action is something that someone does **2** action is fighting in a battle ♦ *He was killed in action* **3** the action of a gun or a musical instrument is the part that makes it work
out of action not working properly
to take action is to do something decisive

activate *verb* (**activates, activating, activated**)
to activate a machine or device is to start it working

active *adjective*
1 busy, taking part in lots of activities
2 doing things, working ♦ *an active volcano* **3** (*in Grammar*) describing a verb in which the subject does the action, for example in the sentence *We made a cake,* the subject is *We* and *made* is an active verb

activity *noun* (*plural* **activities**)
1 activity is doing things **2** an activity is something special that someone does
♦ *They enjoy outdoor activities*

actor *noun* (*plural* **actors**)
someone who takes part in a play or film

actress *noun* (*plural* **actresses**)
a girl or woman who takes part in a play or film

actual *adjective*
really there or really happening

actually *adverb*
really, in fact ♦ *Actually, I think you are wrong*

acupuncture *noun*
a way of curing disease or taking away pain by pricking parts of the body with needles

acute *adjective*
1 sharp or intense ♦ *She has an acute pain* 2 severe ♦ *The explorers were suffering from an acute shortage of food* 3 clever, quick to understand something 4 an acute accent is the mark ´ put over a letter, as in *fiancé* 5 an acute angle is an angle of less than 90 degrees

AD short for *Anno Domini*, used with dates that come after the birth of Jesus Christ, for example AD 1492 is the year Columbus reached America

Adam's apple *noun* (*plural* **Adam's apples**)
the lump at the front of a man's neck

adapt *verb* (**adapts, adapting, adapted**)
1 to adapt something is to make it suitable for a new purpose 2 to adapt to something is to make yourself cope with it ♦ *They adapted to life in the country very quickly*
adaptation *noun* adapting something

adaptable *adjective*
able to adapt or become suitable for different things

adaptor *noun* (*plural* **adaptors**)
a device for connecting different pieces of equipment

add *verb* (**adds, adding, added**)
1 to add one number to another is to put them together to get a bigger number
2 to add one thing to another is to mix them together, for example the different things in a recipe
to add up is what numbers do to make a bigger number, called a total; **to add up** (*informal*) also means to make sense ♦ *The things they said just don't add up*
to add numbers up is to make them into a bigger number

adder *noun* (*plural* **adders**)
a small poisonous snake

addict *noun* (*plural* **addicts**)
someone with a habit they can't give up, for example taking drugs or drinking alcohol
addicted *adjective* being an addict **addictive** *adjective* forming a habit that people can't give up ♦ *They were taking addictive drugs*

addiction *noun* (*plural* **addictions**)
a habit that someone can't give up

addition *noun* (*plural* **additions**)
1 the process of adding numbers together, or adding other things 2 something or someone that has been added ♦ *James is an addition to the class*
in addition also, as well

additional *adjective*
extra, added on

additive *noun* (*plural* **additives**)
something that is added to food or to something else in small amounts

address ➤ *noun* (*plural* **addresses**)
1 the details of the place where someone lives ♦ *My address is 29 High Street, Newtown* 2 a speech

address ➤ *verb* (**addresses, addressing, addressed**)
1 to address a letter or parcel is to write the address on it before sending it 2 to address a person or a group of people is to make an important remark or speech to them ♦ *The judge addressed the prisoner*

adenoids *plural noun*
your adenoids are the spongy flesh at the back of your nose, which can become swollen making it difficult to breathe

adequate *adjective*
enough, sufficient

adhere *verb* (**adheres, adhering, adhered**)
to adhere to something is to stick to it ♦ *The stamp would not adhere easily to the envelope*

adhesive ➤ *noun* (*plural* **adhesives**)
something such as glue that you use to stick things together

adhesive ➤ *adjective*
causing things to stick together
adhesion *noun* sticking together

Adi Granth *noun* (*pronounced* ah-di **grunt**)
the holy book of the Sikhs

adjacent *adjective*
near or next to something ♦ *Her house is adjacent to the shop*

adjective *noun* (*plural* **adjectives**)
a word that describes a noun or adds to its meaning, for example *big, honest, red*

adjourn *verb* (**adjourns, adjourning, adjourned**) (*pronounced* a-**jern**)
1 to adjourn a meeting is to stop it for a time and start again later **2** to adjourn to a room is to go there for a while
adjournment *noun* a break in a meeting

adjudicate *verb* (**adjudicates, adjudicating, adjudicated**) (*pronounced* a-**joo**-di-kayt) to act as judge in a competition or disagreement
adjudication *noun* a judgement or decision
adjudicator *noun* a person who adjudicates

adjust *verb* (**adjusts, adjusting, adjusted**)
1 to adjust something is to change it slightly or change its position **2** to adjust to something is to try to get used to it ◆ *They found it hard to adjust to life in the city*

adjustment *noun* (*plural* **adjustments**) a small change you make to something

ad lib ➤ *adjective and adverb* without any rehearsal or preparation

ad lib ➤ *verb* (**ad libs, ad libbing, ad libbed**) to say or do something without any rehearsal or preparation

administer *verb* (**administers, administering, administered**)
1 to administer a country is to govern it **2** to administer something like a medicine is to give it to someone

administrate *verb* (**administrates, administrating, administrated**)
to administrate a country or business is to govern it
administrative *adjective* to do with administration **administrator** *noun* someone who administrates

administration *noun* (*plural* **administrations**)
1 administration is managing a business or governing a country **2** an administration is a government that is in office

admirable *adjective*
worth admiring; excellent ◆ *You have done an admirable piece of work*
admirably *adverb* in an admirable way

admiral *noun* (*plural* **admirals**) an officer of the highest rank in the navy

admire *verb* (**admires, admiring, admired**)
1 to admire someone or something is to think they are very good or very beautiful **2** to admire something is also to look at it and enjoy it ◆ *They went to the top of the hill to admire the view*
admiration *noun* admiring someone or something

admirer *noun* (*plural* **admirers**) someone who thinks that a particular person or thing is very good or beautiful ◆ *Madonna has many admirers*

admission *noun* (*plural* **admissions**)
1 an admission is something that someone admits or confesses ◆ *He is guilty by his own admission* **2** admission is being allowed to go into a place ◆ *Admission to the show is by ticket only*

admit *verb* (**admits, admitting, admitted**)
1 to admit someone is to let them come into a place **2** to admit something is to confess it or agree that it is true

admittance *noun*
being allowed to go into a private place

admittedly *adverb*
as an agreed fact; without denying it ◆ *Admittedly I was teasing the dog, but I didn't expect it to bite*

ado *noun*
without more ado without wasting any more time

adolescent *noun* (*plural* **adolescents**) an adolescent is a young person who is older than a child and not yet an adult
adolescence *noun* this time of someone's life

adopt *verb* (**adopts, adopting, adopted**)
1 to adopt someone is to take them into your family and treat them as your child **2** to adopt something like a system or method is to start using it
adoption *noun* adopting someone or something **adoptive** *adjective* adopting ◆ *They are his adoptive parents*

adorable *adjective*
lovely, worth adoring

adore *verb* (**adores, adoring, adored**)
to adore someone or something is to love them or admire them very much
adoration *noun* adoring someone or something

adorn *verb* (**adorns, adorning, adorned**)
to adorn something is to decorate it or make it pretty
adornment *noun* adorning something

adrenalin *noun*
a hormone that stimulates your nervous system and makes you feel ready to do something

adrift *adverb* and *adjective*
drifting ◆ *The boat was adrift*

adult *noun* (*plural* **adults**)
a fully grown person or animal

adultery *noun* (*pronounced* a-**dul**-ter-i) having a lover in addition to a husband or wife
adulterer *noun* someone who takes part in adultery

advance ➤ *noun* (*plural* **advances**)
  1 an advance is a forward movement
  2 advance is improvement or progress
  3 an advance of money is a loan **4** an advance warning is a warning given beforehand
  in advance beforehand

advance ➤ *verb* (**advances, advancing, advanced**)
  1 to advance is to move forward **2** to advance is also to make progress

advanced *adjective*
  1 a long way forward **2** an advanced course or exam is one at a higher level

advantage *noun* (*plural* **advantages**)
  an advantage is something useful or helpful
  to take advantage of someone is to treat them unfairly when they are not likely to complain
  to take advantage of something is to make good use of it
  advantageous *adjective* useful, giving an advantage

Advent *noun*
  in the Christian Church, the period before Christmas

adventure *noun* (*plural* **adventures**)
  1 an adventure is something exciting or interesting that someone does
  2 adventure is doing bold and exciting things ♦ *He likes adventure*
  adventurous *adjective* liking to do exciting things

adverb *noun* (*plural* **adverbs**)
  a word that tells you how or when or where or why something happens. In these sentences, the words in italics are adverbs: They moved *slowly*. Come back *soon*. I *only* want a drink.

adversary *noun* (*plural* **adversaries**)
  (*pronounced* ad-ver-sa-ri)
  an opponent or enemy

adverse *adjective*
  unfavourable; harmful ♦ *The drug had adverse effects*

adversity *noun* (*plural* **adversities**)
  bad fortune, trouble

advert *noun* (*plural* **adverts**)
  (*informal*) an advertisement

advertise *verb* (**advertises, advertising, advertised**)
  1 to advertise something you do or have made is to praise it in a newspaper or on television so that people will want it **2** to advertise an event is to tell people when it will take place ♦ *Have you advertised the concert?*

advertiser *noun* someone who advertises something

advertisement *noun* (*plural* **advertisements**)
  a public notice or short television film that tries to persuade people to buy something

advice *noun*
  something said to someone to help them decide what to do

advisable *adjective*
  sensible, worth doing
  advisability *noun* being advisable

advise *verb* (**advises, advising, advised**)
  to advise someone is to tell them what you think they should do
  adviser *noun* a person who gives advice
  advisory *adjective* offering advice

advocate ➤ *noun* (*plural* **advocates**)
  (*pronounced* ad-vo-kat)
  a person who speaks in favour of someone or something

advocate ➤ *verb* (**advocates, advocating, advocated**) (*pronounced* ad-vo-kayt)
  to advocate something is to speak in favour of it ♦ *We advocate changing the law*

aerial ➤ *noun* (*plural* **aerials**)
  a wire or metal rod for receiving or sending radio or television signals

aerial ➤ *adjective*
  from or in the air, or from aircraft ♦ *They showed us an aerial photograph of our school*

aerobatics *plural noun*
  an exciting display by flying aircraft
  aerobatic *adjective* to do with aerobatics

aerobics *plural noun*
  energetic exercises that strengthen your heart and lungs

aeronautics *plural noun*
  the study of aircraft and flying
  aeronautical *adjective* to do with aeronautics

aeroplane *noun* (*plural* **aeroplanes**)
  a flying machine with wings

aerosol *noun* (*plural* **aerosols**)
  a device that holds a liquid under pressure and lets it out in a fine spray

aesthetic *adjective*
  to do with beauty, especially in art or music

affair *noun* (*plural* **affairs**)
  1 something interesting that happens, an event **2** a temporary relationship between two people who are not married to each other **3** someone's affairs are their private business ♦ *She needs to sort out her business affairs*

affect *verb* (**affects, affecting, affected**)
to affect someone or something is to cause them to change or to harm them ♦ *The dampness might affect his health*

affected *adjective*
not real, pretended ♦ *He gave an affected smile*

affection *noun* (*plural* **affections**)
affection or an affection is love or fondness ♦ *I have a great affection for my nephew*

affectionate *adjective* showing love or fondness

afflict *verb* (**afflicts, afflicting, afflicted**)
to be afflicted by something unpleasant, like an illness, is to suffer from it

affliction *noun* something that someone suffers

affluent *adjective* (*pronounced* af-loo-ent)
having a lot of money or wealth

affluence *noun* wealth

afford *verb* (**affords, affording, afforded**)
1 to be able to afford something is to have enough money to pay for it **2** to be unable to afford the time to do something is not to have enough time for it **3** to afford someone pleasure is to please them

afforestation *noun*
the covering of an area with trees

afloat *adjective and adverb*
floating; on a boat ♦ *Do you enjoy life afloat?*

afraid *adjective*
frightened

I'm afraid I am sorry; I regret ♦ *I'm afraid I've burnt the cakes*

afresh *adverb*
again; in a new way ♦ *We must start afresh*

African ➢ *adjective*
coming from or to do with Africa

African ➢ *noun* (*plural* **Africans**)
a person from Africa

aft *adverb* (*pronounced* ahft)
at the back of a ship or aircraft

after *preposition and adverb*
meaning 'later' or 'later than' ♦ *Come after dinner* ♦ *I'll do it after*

afternoon *noun* (*plural* **afternoons**)
the time from midday or lunchtime until evening

afterwards *adverb*
at a later time

again *adverb*
1 once more; another time **2** as before ♦ *You will soon be well again*

again and again lots of times

against *preposition*
1 touching or hitting ♦ *He was leaning against the wall* **2** opposed to, not liking ♦ *Are you against smoking?*

age ➢ *noun* (*plural* **ages**)
1 how old someone or something is **2** a period of history ♦ *the Elizabethan age* **3** the last part of someone's life ♦ *She had the wisdom that comes with age*

ages (*informal*) a long time ♦ *We've been waiting ages*

age ➢ *verb* (**ages, ageing, aged**)
to age is to become old

aged *adjective*
1 (*pronounced* ayjd) having the age of ♦ *The girl was aged 9* **2** (*pronounced* ay-jid) very old ♦ *We saw an aged man*

age group *noun* (*plural* **age groups**)
people who are the same age

agency *noun* (*plural* **agencies**)
the office or business of someone who organizes things

agenda *noun* (*plural* **agendas**) (*pronounced* a-jen-da)
a list of things to be done or discussed, for example at a business meeting

agent *noun* (*plural* **agents**)
1 someone whose job is to organize things for other people ♦ *We booked our holiday with a travel agent* **2** a spy ♦ *He is a secret agent*

aggravate *verb* (**aggravates, aggravating, aggravated**)
1 to aggravate something is to make it worse **2** (*informal*) to aggravate someone is to annoy them

aggravation *noun*
1 (*informal*) trouble or difficulty
2 making something worse

aggression *noun*
starting a war or attack; being aggressive

aggressor *noun* someone who starts an attack

aggressive *adjective*
1 likely to attack or use violence
2 strong, forceful ♦ *They began an aggressive sales campaign*

agile *adjective*
able to move quickly and easily

agility *noun* being agile

agitate *verb* (**agitates, agitating, agitated**)
1 to agitate someone is to make them feel worried and anxious **2** to agitate is to make a fuss so that something gets done **3** to agitate something is to shake it about

agitation *noun* agitating someone or something

agitator *noun* (*plural* **agitators**)
a person who makes a lot of fuss to get
something done

agnostic *noun* (*plural* **agnostics**)
(*pronounced* ag-nos-tik)
someone who believes that we cannot
know if there is a God

ago *adverb*
in the past ♦ *She died long ago*

agony *noun* (*plural* **agonies**)
severe pain or suffering
agonizing *adjective* causing severe pain

agree *verb* (**agrees, agreeing, agreed**)
1 to agree with someone is to think the
same as them **2** to agree to do something
is to say that you are willing ♦ *She agreed
to go with him* **3** to agree with someone
also means to suit them ♦ *Spicy food
doesn't agree with her*

agreeable *adjective*
1 willing ♦ *We shall go if you are agreeable*
2 (*rather old use*) pleasant ♦ *It is a very
agreeable little place*

agreement *noun* (*plural* **agreements**)
1 agreement is thinking the same ♦ *Are
we in agreement?* **2** an agreement is an
arrangement that people have agreed on

agriculture *noun*
farming, cultivating the land
agricultural *adjective* to do with agriculture

aground *adverb*
stuck on the bottom of a river or the sea in
shallow water ♦ *The ship has run aground*

ah *interjection*
a word you shout out when you are
surprised or pleased

ahead *adverb*
forwards, in front ♦ *Sheila went ahead to
show us the way*

ahoy *interjection*
a shout used by seamen to attract
attention

aid ➤ *noun* (*plural* **aids**)
1 help **2** money or food or other help sent
to another country **3** something that
helps ♦ *He was wearing a hearing aid*
in aid of something or **someone** so as to help
them

aid ➤ *verb* (**aids, aiding, aided**)
to aid someone is to help them

Aids or **AIDS** *noun*
a disease caused by a virus, which
destroys the body's immunity to other
diseases

ailing *adjective*
suffering, in a bad way

ailment *noun* (*plural* **ailments**)
a minor illness

aim ➤ *verb* (**aims, aiming, aimed**)
1 to aim to do something is to try to do it
2 to aim a gun at someone is to point it at
them so as to shoot them **3** to aim
something like a ball is to throw it or kick
it in a particular direction

aim ➤ *noun* (*plural* **aims**)
1 a person's aim is what they intend to do
2 aim is also pointing a weapon in a
particular direction

aimless *adjective*
not having any aim or purpose ♦ *He led an
aimless life*
aimlessly *adverb* in an aimless way

air ➤ *noun* (*plural* **airs**)
1 air is the mixture of gases which
surrounds the earth and which everyone
breathes **2** an air is a tune **3** an air of
mystery or secrecy is a feeling that things
are mysterious or secret
by air in an aircraft
in the air just an idea, not certain ♦ *Our
plans are still in the air*
on the air on radio or television
to put on airs is to behave grandly, as if you
are important

air ➤ *verb* (**airs, airing, aired**)
1 to air clothes or washing is to put them
in a warm place to finish drying **2** to air a
room is to let fresh air into it **3** to air
views or opinions is to say them

airborne *adjective*
1 flying in an aircraft **2** carried by the air

air-conditioning *noun*
a system for controlling the temperature
and freshness of the air in a building
air-conditioned *adjective* equipped with
air-conditioning

aircraft *noun* (*plural* **aircraft**)
an aeroplane or a helicopter ♦ *The two
aircraft landed together*

aircraft carrier *noun* (*plural* **aircraft carriers**)
a large ship with a flat deck on which
aircraft can take off and land

Airedale *noun* (*plural* **Airedales**)
a large rough-haired terrier

airfield *noun* (*plural* **airfields**)
a place where aircraft can take off and
land

air force *noun* (*plural* **air forces**)
the branch of a country's fighting force
that uses aircraft

airgun *noun* (*plural* **airguns**)
a gun that works with compressed air

airline *noun* (*plural* **airlines**)
a company that provides a regular
transport service by aircraft

airliner *noun* (*plural* **airliners**)
a large aircraft for carrying passengers

airlock *noun* (*plural* **airlocks**)
1 a bubble of air that stops liquid flowing
through a pipe 2 a compartment with
airtight doors at each end

airmail *noun*
airmail is mail that is sent by air

airman *noun* (*plural* **airmen**)
a man who is a member of an air force or
one of the crew of an aircraft

airport *noun* (*plural* **airports**)
a place where aircraft land and take off,
with passenger terminals and other
buildings

air raid *noun* (*plural* **air raids**)
an attack by bombs dropped from aircraft

airship *noun* (*plural* **airships**)
a large balloon with engines, designed to
carry passengers or cargo

airstream *noun* (*plural* **airstreams**)
a current of air, especially one that affects
the weather

airstrip *noun* (*plural* **airstrips**)
a strip of land prepared for aircraft to take
off and land

airtight *adjective*
not letting air get in or out

airy *adjective* (**airier, airiest**)
1 with plenty of fresh air 2 vague and
insincere ♦ *They were just airy promises*
3 like air
airily *adverb* in a casual or light-hearted
way ♦ *He replied airily that he didn't want
to know*

aisle *noun* (*plural* **aisles**) (*rhymes with*
mile)
1 a part at the side of a church 2 a
passage between or beside rows of seats or
pews

ajar *adverb and adjective*
slightly open ♦ *Please leave the door ajar*

akela *noun* (*plural* **akelas**) (*pronounced*
ah-**kay**-la)
an adult leader of a group of Cub Scouts

alarm ➤ *verb* (**alarms, alarming, alarmed**)
to alarm someone is to make them
frightened or anxious

alarm ➤ *noun* (*plural* **alarms**)
1 a warning sound or signal 2 a feeling of
fear or anxiety ♦ *He cried out in alarm*
3 an alarm clock

alarm clock *noun* (*plural* **alarm clocks**)
a clock with a loud ring or bleep, which can
be set to wake someone who is asleep

alas *interjection*
(*old use*) something you say when you are
sad

albatross *noun* (*plural* **albatrosses**)
a large seabird with long wings

album *noun* (*plural* **albums**)
1 a book in which you keep things like
photographs or stamps or autographs 2 a
collection of songs on a CD, record, or tape

alcohol *noun*
1 a colourless liquid made by fermenting
sugar or starch 2 drinks containing this
liquid (for example beer, wine, gin), which
affects people's behaviour and can make
them drunk if they have too much

alcoholic ➤ *adjective*
containing alcohol

alcoholic ➤ *noun* (*plural* **alcoholics**)
someone who is constantly ill from
drinking too much alcohol
alcoholism *noun* being an alcoholic

alcove *noun* (*plural* **alcoves**)
a part of a room where the wall is set back
from the main part

ale *noun* (*plural* **ales**)
ale is a kind of beer, especially when it is
made and stored in a traditional way

alert ➤ *adjective*
watching for something; ready to act

alert ➤ *verb* (**alerts, alerting, alerted**)
to alert someone to a danger or problem is
to warn them about it

alert ➤ *noun* (*plural* **alerts**)
an alarm
on the alert on the lookout for danger or
attack

A level *noun* (*plural* **A levels**)
a higher standard of examination that is
taken after the GCSE, especially by pupils
who want to go to university

algebra *noun* (*pronounced* al-ji-bra)
mathematics in which letters and symbols
are used to represent numbers
algebraic *adjective* to do with algebra

alias ➤ *noun* (*plural* **aliases**) (*pronounced*
ay-li-as)
a false or different name that someone
uses instead of their real name

alias ➤ *adverb*
also named ♦ *Clark Kent, alias Superman*

alibi *noun* (*plural* **alibis**) (*pronounced*
al-i-by)
evidence that someone accused of a crime
was not there when the crime was
committed

alien ➤ *noun* (*plural* **aliens**) (*pronounced*
ay-li-en)
1 someone who is not a citizen of the
country where they are living **2** in science
fiction, a being from another world

alien ➤ *adjective*
1 foreign **2** not in keeping, quite unlike
♦ *Lying was alien to his nature*

alienate *verb* (**alienates**, **alienating**, **alienated**)
to alienate someone is to make them
unfriendly to you
alienation *noun* alienating someone

alight *adjective*
on fire, burning

alike ➤ *adjective*
similar, like each other

alike ➤ *adverb*
in the same way ♦ *He treats everybody
alike*

alimentary canal *noun* (*plural* **alimentary
canals**)
the tube along which food passes through
the body

alive *adjective*
living, existing ♦ *Is he alive?*
alive to something well aware of it ♦ *She is
alive to all the dangers*

alkali *noun* (*plural* **alkalis**) (*pronounced*
al-ka-ly)
a substance that neutralizes acids or that
combines with acids to form salts
alkaline *adjective* to do with alkalis **alkalinity**
noun the amount of an alkali in something

all *adjective and adverb and noun*
meaning 'everything' or 'everyone' ♦ *That
is all I know* ♦ *All my books are in the desk*
♦ *She was dressed all in white*
all in (*informal*) exhausted ♦ *I'm all in after
that run*

all out (*informal*) using all your ability ♦ *Go
all out to win*

all there (*informal*) mentally alert;
intelligent

all the same nevertheless; making no
difference ♦ *It was raining but I went out
all the same*

Allah the Muslim name of God

all-clear *noun*
a signal that a danger has passed

allege *verb* (**alleges**, **alleging**, **alleged**)
(*pronounced* a-lej)
to allege that someone has done something
is to accuse them of it, usually without
proof ♦ *He alleged that I stole his ring*
allegation *noun* an accusation

allegedly *adverb* (*pronounced* a-lej-idli)
so it is claimed ♦ *The statue was allegedly
damaged by a tractor*

allegiance *noun* (*plural* **allegiances**)
(*pronounced* a-lee-jans)
loyalty shown to a person or organization

allegory *noun* (*plural* **allegories**)
a story or poem with made-up people and
places that are meant to stand for real
people and places
allegorical *adjective* to do with allegory

allergic *adjective*
very sensitive to something, so that it may
make you ill ♦ *He is allergic to pollen,
which gives him hay fever*
allergy *noun* being allergic to something

alley *noun* (*plural* **alleys**)
1 a narrow street or passage **2** a place
where you can play at skittles or tenpin
bowling

alliance *noun* (*plural* **alliances**)
an agreement between countries to
support each other and have the same
enemies

allied *adjective*
having an alliance; on the same side ♦ *The
allied countries declared war*

alligator *noun* (*plural* **alligators**)
a large reptile like a crocodile

all-in *adjective*
including or allowing everything ♦ *This is the all-in price*

allot *verb* (**allots, allotting, allotted**)
to allot shares or jobs is to give them to various people

allotment *noun* (*plural* **allotments**)
a small rented piece of ground used for growing vegetables

allow *verb* (**allows, allowing, allowed**)
1 to allow someone to do something is to let them do it ♦ *We will allow you to leave now* ♦ *Smoking is not allowed* **2** to allow an amount of money is to provide it for some reason ♦ *She was allowed £10 for books*

allowance *noun* (*plural* **allowances**)
a sum of money given regularly to someone
to make allowances is to be considerate ♦ *We must make allowances for his age*

alloy *noun* (*plural* **alloys**)
a metal formed from a mixture of other metals

all right *adjective*
satisfactory; in good condition ♦ *She fixed my bike, so it's all right*

all-round *adjective*
having many skills ♦ *She's a good all-round athlete*
all-rounder *noun* a person with many skills

ally ➣ *noun* (*plural* **allies**) (*pronounced* al-I)
1 a country in alliance with another country **2** a person who helps or cooperates with you

ally ➣ *verb* (**allies, allying, allied**)
to ally oneself with someone else is to form an alliance with them

almighty *adjective*
1 having a lot of power **2** (*informal*) very great ♦ *They were making an almighty din*

almond *noun* (*plural* **almonds**) (*pronounced* ah-mond)
an oval nut that you can eat

almost *adverb*
very close to but not quite ♦ *I am almost ready*

aloft *adverb*
high up ♦ *The sailors climbed aloft*

alone *adjective and adverb*
without any other people or other things ♦ *The food alone took us all morning to prepare*

along *preposition and adverb*
1 from one end of something to the other **2** on; onwards ♦ *Move along, please!* **3** accompanying someone ♦ *I have brought my brother along*

alongside *preposition and adverb*
next to something

aloud *adverb*
in a voice that can be heard

alphabet *noun* (*plural* **alphabets**)
the letters used in a language, usually arranged in a set order
alphabetical *adjective* to do with the alphabet **alphabetically** *adverb* in the order of the alphabet

alpine *adjective*
to do with the Alps in Switzerland

already *adverb*
by or before now ♦ *I've already told you once*

Alsatian *noun* (*plural* **Alsatians**) (*pronounced* al-say-shan)
a large strong dog

also *adverb*
as an extra, besides ♦ *We also need some bread*

altar *noun* (*plural* **altars**)
a table or raised surface used in religious ceremonies

alter *verb* (**alters, altering, altered**)
to alter something is to change it
alteration *noun* a change you make to something

alternate ➣ *adjective* (*pronounced* ol-ter-nat)
1 happening on every other one ♦ *They work on alternate days* **2** coming in turns, one after the other ♦ *alternate laughter and tears*
alternately *adverb* one after the other in turn

alternate ➣ *verb* (**alternates, alternating, alternated**) (*pronounced* ol-ter-nayt)
to alternate is to happen in turns
alternation *noun* happening one after the other in turns

alternating current *noun*
electric current that continually reverses its direction

alternative ➣ *noun* (*plural* **alternatives**) (*pronounced* ol-ter-na-tiv)
something you can choose instead of something else ♦ *If you don't like this book there is an alternative*

alternative ➣ *adjective*
for you to choose instead of something else ♦ *The café has an alternative menu for vegetarians*

alternator *noun* (*plural* **alternators**)
a generator that produces alternating current

although *conjunction*
in spite of the fact that ♦ *Although they like parties, they prefer a trip to the zoo*

altitude *noun* (*plural* **altitudes**)
the height of something, especially above sea level

alto *noun* (*plural* **altos**)
1 a female singer with a low voice 2 a male singer with a voice higher than a tenor's

altogether *adverb*
1 completely ♦ *He is altogether wrong*
2 on the whole ♦ *Altogether, it wasn't a bad holiday*

aluminium *noun*
a silver-coloured metal that is light in weight

always *adverb*
1 all the time, at all times 2 often, constantly ♦ *You are always crying*
3 whatever happens ♦ *You can always sleep on the floor*

am 1st person singular present tense of **be**

a.m. short for Latin *ante meridiem* which means 'before midday'

amalgamate *verb* (**amalgamates, amalgamating, amalgamated**)
1 to amalgamate things is to mix them or join them together 2 to amalgamate is to join together to form one thing
amalgamation *noun* joining things together

amateur ➤ *noun* (*plural* **amateurs**)
(*pronounced* am-a-ter)
someone who does something because they like it, without being paid for it

amateur ➤ *adjective*
done by amateurs

amateurish *adjective*
1 not done very well ♦ *It was an amateurish piece of work* 2 not very good at something ♦ *He was rather amateurish at swimming*

amaze *verb* (**amazes, amazing, amazed**)
to amaze someone is to surprise them greatly
amazement *noun* a feeling of great surprise

ambassador *noun* (*plural* **ambassadors**)
someone sent to a foreign country to represent their own government

amber *noun*
1 a hard, clear, yellowish substance used for making ornaments 2 a yellowish colour, the one used in traffic lights as a signal for caution

ambiguous *adjective*
having more than one possible meaning, uncertain ♦ *His reply was ambiguous*
ambiguity *noun* being ambiguous

ambition *noun* (*plural* **ambitions**)
1 ambition is a strong desire to be successful in life 2 an ambition is something you want to do very much ♦ *His ambition is to run his own airline*
ambitious *adjective* having a lot of ambition

amble *verb* (**ambles, ambling, ambled**)
to amble along is to walk slowly

ambulance *noun* (*plural* **ambulances**)
a vehicle for carrying sick or injured people

ambush ➤ *noun* (*plural* **ambushes**)
a surprise attack from a hidden place

ambush ➤ *verb* (**ambushes, ambushing, ambushed**)
to ambush someone is to attack them suddenly from a hidden place

amen *interjection*
a word used by Christians at the end of a prayer or hymn, meaning 'may it be so'

amend *verb* (**amends, amending, amended**)
to amend something like a piece of writing is to change or improve it
amendment *noun* a change to a piece of writing or a law

amenity *noun* (*plural* **amenities**)
a pleasant or useful feature ♦ *The town has many amenities, including a skating rink*

American ➤ *adjective*
coming from America, or to do with America

American ➤ *noun* (*plural* **Americans**)
a person from America

amiable *adjective*
friendly, good-tempered
amiability *noun* friendliness **amiably** *adverb* in a friendly way

amicable *adjective*
friendly
amicably *adverb* in a friendly way

amid or **amidst** *preposition*
in the middle of, among

amidships *adverb*
in the middle of a ship

amino acid *noun* (*plural* **amino acids**)
an acid found in proteins

ammeter *noun* (*plural* **ammeters**)
an instrument for measuring electric current

ammonia *noun*
a gas or liquid with a strong smell

ammunition *noun*
bullets, bombs, and other explosive objects used in fighting

amnesty *noun* (*plural* **amnesties**)
a decision to pardon people who have broken the law

amoeba *noun* (*plural* **amoebas**) (*pronounced* a-**mee**-ba)
a tiny creature made of one cell. It can change shape and split itself in two

among or **amongst** *preposition*
1 surrounded by, in the middle of ♦ *She was hiding among the bushes* **2** between ♦ *Let's divide the money amongst ourselves*

amount ➤ *noun* (*plural* **amounts**)
a quantity or total

amount ➤ *verb* (**amounts, amounting, amounted**)
to amount to something is to reach it as a total ♦ *The bill amounted to £55*

ampere *noun* (*plural* **amperes**) (*pronounced* am-**pair**)
a unit for measuring the rate of flow of an electric current

ampersand *noun* (*plural* **ampersands**)
the sign &, which means 'and'

amphibious *adjective*
able to live or travel on land and in water
amphibian *noun* an amphibious animal or vehicle

ample *adjective* (**ampler, amplest**)
1 large, having plenty of space ♦ *This car has an ample boot* **2** more than enough ♦ *We had ample provisions*
amply *adverb* generously; in full ♦ *They were amply rewarded*

amplifier *noun* (*plural* **amplifiers**)
an electronic device for making music or other sounds louder

amplify *verb* (**amplifies, amplifying, amplified**)
1 to amplify sounds is to make them louder or stronger **2** to amplify something you say is to give more details about it
amplification *noun* making something louder

amputate *verb* (**amputates, amputating, amputated**)
to amputate an arm or a leg is to cut it off when it is diseased
amputation *noun* cutting off an arm or a leg

amuse *verb* (**amuses, amusing, amused**)
1 to amuse someone is to make them laugh or smile **2** to amuse yourself is to find pleasant things to do

amusement *noun* (*plural* **amusements**)
1 an amusement is something that amuses you **2** amusement is being amused; laughing or smiling

amusing *adjective*
making you laugh or smile ♦ *It was an amusing story*

an *adjective* (called the *indefinite article*)
a word used instead of **a** when the next word begins with a vowel-sound or a silent h ♦ *Take an apple* ♦ *You can hire boats for £5 an hour*

anaemia *noun* (*pronounced* a-**nee**-mi-a)
a poor condition of the blood that makes someone look pale
anaemic *adjective* suffering from anaemia

anaesthesia *noun* (*pronounced* an-iss-**thee**-zi-a)
having no feeling of pain

anaesthetic *noun* (*plural* **anaesthetics**) (*pronounced* an-iss-**thet**-ik)
a drug or gas that makes you unable to feel pain

anaesthetize *verb* (**anaesthetizes, anaesthetizing, anaesthetized**) (*pronounced* an-**ees**-thit-ize)
to anaesthetize a person or an animal is to give them an anaesthetic
anaesthetist *noun* a doctor who gives patients anaesthetics

anagram *noun* (*plural* **anagrams**)
a word or phrase made by rearranging the letters of another word or phrase, for example *carthorse* is an anagram of *orchestra*

analogue *adjective*
an analogue clock or watch has hands and a dial to indicate numbers (the opposite of *digital*)

analogy *noun* (*plural* **analogies**)
a comparison or similarity between two things that are fairly like each other ♦ *There is an analogy between the human heart and a pump*
analogous *adjective* like something else

analyse *verb* (**analyses, analysing, analysed**)
1 to analyse something is to examine it carefully **2** to analyse a substance is to divide it into its parts
analytic or **analytical** *adjective* to do with analysis

analysis *noun* (*plural* **analyses**)
a detailed study or examination of something

analyst *noun* (*plural* **analysts**)
a person who is skilled at making analyses

anarchist *noun* (*plural* **anarchists**)
someone who thinks that governments and laws are bad and should be abolished
anarchism *noun* having no government or laws

anarchy *noun*
1 disorder; confusion 2 lack of
government or control

anatomy *noun*
the study of the parts of the body
anatomical *adjective* to do with anatomy
anatomist *noun* someone who studies
anatomy

ancestor *noun* (*plural* **ancestors**)
a person who lived in the past and was in
the same family as someone alive now
ancestral *adjective* to do with ancestors
ancestry *noun* a person's ancestors

anchor *noun* (*plural* **anchors**)
a heavy object joined to a ship by a chain
or rope and dropped to the bottom of the
sea to stop the ship from moving

anchorage *noun* (*plural* **anchorages**)
a place where ships can stay, held by their
anchors

ancient *adjective*
1 belonging to times that were long ago
2 very old ♦ *They came from an ancient
family*

and *conjunction*
linking words and phrases ♦ *We had cakes
and lemonade* ♦ *Touch that and you'll get
burnt* ♦ *Go and buy a pen*

anemone *noun* (*plural* **anemones**)
(*pronounced* a-**nem**-on-i)
1 a small flower with the shape of a cup
2 a sea anemone

angel *noun* (*plural* **angels**)
1 a being that some people believe in, who
is a messenger or attendant of God 2 a
very kind or beautiful person

angelic *adjective*
kind and beautiful, like an angel

anger *noun*
a strong feeling that you want to quarrel
or fight with someone

angle ➤ *noun* (*plural* **angles**)
1 the space between two lines or surfaces
that meet 2 a point of view ♦ *What is your
angle on this?*

angle ➤ *verb* (**angles, angling, angled**)
1 to angle something is to put it in a
slanting position 2 to angle news or a
story is to tell it in a special way ♦ *The
report was angled so that the robbers
looked like heroes*

angler *noun* (*plural* **anglers**)
someone who fishes with a fishing rod

Anglican ➤ *adjective*
belonging to the Church of England
Anglican ➤ *noun* (*plural* **Anglicans**)
a member of the Church of England

Anglo-Saxon *noun* (*plural* **Anglo-Saxons**)
1 an English person, especially of the time
before the Norman Conquest in 1066
2 the old form of English spoken before
1066

angry *adjective* (**angrier, angriest**)
feeling or showing anger
angrily *adverb* in an angry way

anguish *noun*
severe suffering; great sorrow or pain
anguished *adjective* suffering in this way

angular *adjective*
1 having sharp corners 2 bony ♦ *She has
a thin, angular face*

animal *noun* (*plural* **animals**)
a being that is alive and can move and feel

animate *adjective* (*pronounced* **an**-im-at)
having life

animated *adjective*
1 lively and excited 2 an animated film is
one made by photographing a series of still
pictures and showing them rapidly one
after another, so they appear to move

animation *noun*
1 being lively or excited 2 a way of
making films from still pictures so they
appear to move

animosity *noun* (*plural* **animosities**)
a feeling of being an enemy towards
someone ♦ *There was a lot of animosity in
his voice*

aniseed *noun*
a seed with a strong sweet taste like
liquorice

ankle *noun* (*plural* **ankles**)
the part of your leg where it is joined to
your foot

annex *verb* (**annexes, annexing, annexed**)
(*pronounced* a-**neks**)
1 to annex something is to add it to
something larger 2 to annex territory is to
take it from someone else and add it to
your own
annexation *noun* annexing or adding
something

annexe *noun* (*plural* **annexes**) (*pronounced*
an-**eks**)
a building added to a larger building

annihilate *verb* (**annihilates, annihilating,
annihilated**) (*pronounced* a-**ny**-il-ayt)
to annihilate something is to destroy it
completely
annihilation *noun* destroying something
completely

anniversary *noun* (*plural* **anniversaries**)
a day when you remember something special that happened on the same date in an earlier year

announce *verb* (**announces, announcing, announced**)
to announce something is to say it publicly
announcer *noun* someone who announces something, especially on radio or television

announcement *noun* (*plural* **announcements**)
something that is made known publicly, especially in a newspaper or on radio or television

annoy *verb* (**annoys, annoying, annoyed**)
to annoy someone is to give them a feeling of not being pleased

annoyance *noun* (*plural* **annoyances**)
1 annoyance is the feeling of being annoyed **2** an annoyance is something that annoys you ♦ *Wasps are a great annoyance at a picnic*

annual ➤ *adjective*
happening or coming every year
annually *adverb* every year

annual ➤ *noun* (*plural* **annuals**)
1 a book that comes out once a year **2** a plant that dies when winter comes

anon. short for **anonymous**

anonymous *adjective*
an anonymous book or letter is one with the name of the writer unknown
anonymity *noun* not having your name known to other people **anonymously** *adverb* with the name unknown

anorak *noun* (*plural* **anoraks**)
a thick warm jacket with a hood

anorexia *noun* (*pronounced* an-er-**eks**-ee-a)
an illness that makes someone not want to eat
anorexic *adjective* suffering from anorexia

another *adjective* and *pronoun*
a different person or thing ♦ *Have another look* ♦ *May I have another?*

answer ➤ *noun* (*plural* **answers**)
1 an answer is what you say back when someone asks you a question **2** the answer to a problem is the thing that solves it

answer ➤ *verb* (**answers, answering, answered**)
1 to answer someone is to give or find them an answer **2** to answer a telephone is to pick it up when it rings
to answer back is to say something rude or cheeky as an answer
to answer for something is to be responsible for it

ant *noun* (*plural* **ants**)
a tiny insect

antagonism *noun*
antagonism is a feeling of being someone's enemy
antagonistic *adjective* feeling antagonism

antagonize *verb* (**antagonizes, antagonizing, antagonized**)
to antagonize someone is to make them feel you are their enemy

Antarctic or **Antarctica** *noun*
the area round the South Pole

anteater *noun* (*plural* **anteaters**)
an animal with a long tongue that lives by eating ants

antelope *noun* (*plural* **antelope** or **antelopes**)
an animal like a deer, found in Africa and parts of Asia

antenna *noun*
1 (*plural* **antennae**) a feeler on the head of an insect or shellfish **2** (*plural* **antennas**) an aerial

anthem *noun* (*plural* **anthems**)
a religious or patriotic song, usually sung by a choir or group of people

anthill *noun* (*plural* **anthills**)
a mound of earth over an ants' nest

anthology *noun* (*plural* **anthologies**)
a collection of poems, stories, or songs in one book

anthracite *noun*
a kind of hard coal

anthrax *noun*

a disease of sheep and cattle that people can also catch.

anthropology *noun*

the study of human beings and the way they live

anthropological *adjective* to do with anthropology **anthropologist** *noun* someone who studies anthropology

anti- *prefix*

against something or someone, as in *antibiotic* and *anti-school*

antibiotic *noun* (*plural* **antibiotics**)

a drug such as penicillin which destroys bacteria

anticipate *verb* (**anticipates, anticipating, anticipated**)

1 to anticipate something is to expect it and be ready for it ♦ *The police were anticipating trouble* **2** to anticipate someone is to act before they do ♦ *They anticipated us in getting the early train*

anticipation *noun*

looking forward to doing something

anticlimax *noun* (*plural* **anticlimaxes**)

a disappointing ending or result after something exciting

anticlockwise *adverb and adjective*

moving in the opposite direction to the hands of a clock

anticyclone *noun* (*plural* **anticyclones**)

an area where air pressure is high, usually causing fine weather

antidote *noun* (*plural* **antidotes**)

something which takes away the bad effects of a poison or disease

antifreeze *noun*

a liquid added to water to make it less likely to freeze

antipodes *plural noun* (*pronounced* an-ti-po-deez)

the Antipodes Australia and New Zealand in relation to Britain and Europe

antiquated *adjective*

old-fashioned

antique *noun* (*plural* **antiques**) (*pronounced* an-teek*)

something that is valuable because it is very old

antiseptic *noun* (*plural* **antiseptics**)

a chemical that kills germs

antler *noun* (*plural* **antlers**)

the horn of a deer, which divides into several branches

anus *noun* (*plural* **anuses**)

the opening at the lower end of the intestines, through which solid waste leaves the body

anvil *noun* (*plural* **anvils**)

a large block of iron on which a blacksmith hammers metal into shape

anxiety *noun* (*plural* **anxieties**)

1 anxiety is a feeling of being worried **2** an anxiety is something that worries you

anxious *adjective*

1 worried and nervous **2** eager to do something ♦ *They were anxious to help us*

any ➢ *adjective*

1 one or some ♦ *Have you any wool?* **2** no matter which ♦ *Come any day you like* **3** every ♦ *Any fool knows that!*

any ➢ *adverb*

at all; in some degree ♦ *Is it any good?*

anybody *noun and pronoun*

anyone

anyhow *adverb*

1 anyway **2** (*informal*) carelessly, without much thought ♦ *He does his work anyhow*

anyone *noun and pronoun*

any person

anything *noun and pronoun*

any thing

anyway *adverb*

whatever happens; whatever the situation may be ♦ *If it rains, we'll go anyway*

anywhere *adverb*

in any place or to any place

apart *adverb*

1 away from each other; separately ♦ *Keep your desks apart* **2** into pieces ♦ *It fell apart* **3** excluded ♦ *Joking apart, what do you think?*

apartment *noun* (*plural* **apartments**)

1 a set of rooms **2** (*in America*) a flat

apathy *noun*
not having much interest in something
apathetic *adjective* uninterested

ape *noun* (*plural* **apes**)
a monkey without a tail, such as a gorilla
or a chimpanzee

aphid or **aphis** *noun* (*plural* **aphids**)
a tiny insect that sucks juices from plants

apiece *adverb*
(*old use*) each ♦ *She gave us an apple
apiece*

apologetic *adjective*
saying you are sorry for something
apologetically *adverb* in an apologetic way
♦ *He replied apologetically*

apologize *verb* (**apologizes, apologizing,
apologized**)
to apologize to someone is to tell them you
are sorry

apology *noun* (*plural* **apologies**)
a statement that you are sorry for doing
something wrong

apostle *noun* (*plural* **apostles**)
in Christianity, one of the twelve men sent
out by Christ to tell people about God

apostrophe *noun* (*plural* **apostrophes**)
(*pronounced* a-**pos**-tro-fi)
a punctuation mark (') used to show that
letters have been left out, as in *can't* and
he'll. It is also used with *s* to show who
owns something, as in *the boy's books* (one
boy), *the boys' books* (more than one boy)

appal *verb* (**appals, appalling, appalled**)
to appal someone is to shock them a lot
♦ *The violence appalled everyone*

appalling *adjective*
dreadful, shocking ♦ *The room was in an
appalling mess*

apparatus *noun* (*plural* **apparatuses**)
an apparatus is a set of equipment for a
special use

apparent *adjective*
1 clear, obvious ♦ *He burst out laughing
for no apparent reason* 2 appearing to be
true ♦ *They were not put off by their
apparent failure*

apparently *adverb*
as it seems, so it appears ♦ *The door had
apparently been locked*

appeal ➤ *verb* (**appeals, appealing, appealed**)
1 to appeal for something is to ask for it
when you need it badly ♦ *They are
appealing for money to rebuild the church
roof* 2 to appeal to someone is to interest
or attract them ♦ *Football appeals to them*
3 to appeal against a decision is to ask for
it to be changed ♦ *He decided to appeal
against his prison sentence*

appeal ➤ *noun* (*plural* **appeals**)
1 an appeal is asking for something you
need 2 appeal is what makes something
interesting ♦ *Adventure stories have a lot
of appeal for older children* 3 an appeal is
asking for a decision to be changed

appear *verb* (**appears, appearing, appeared**)
1 to appear is to become visible 2 to
appear is also to seem ♦ *They appeared
very anxious* 3 to appear in a film or play
is to take part in it

appearance *noun* (*plural* **appearances**)
1 coming into sight 2 taking part in a
play, film, show, etc. 3 what someone
looks like 4 what something seems to be

appease *verb* (**appeases, appeasing, appeased**)
to appease someone is to make them
peaceful or calm, often by giving them
what they want
appeasement *noun* appeasing someone

appendicitis *noun*
an inflammation or disease of the
appendix

appendix *noun*
1 (*plural* **appendixes**) a small tube leading
off from the intestines in the body
2 (*plural* **appendices**) an extra section at
the end of a book

appetite *noun* (*plural* **appetites**)
a desire for something, especially for food

appetizer *noun* (*plural* **appetizers**)
something you eat or drink before a meal,
to give you an appetite

appetizing *adjective*
looking good to eat

applaud *verb* (**applauds, applauding, applauded**)
to applaud someone or something is to
show that you like them, especially by
clapping
applause *noun* clapping or cheering

apple *noun* (*plural* **apples**)
a round fruit with skin that is red, green,
or yellow

appliance *noun* (*plural* **appliances**)
a device or gadget

applicable *adjective*
1 that applies to someone ♦ *This rule is
now applicable to everyone* 2 relevant
♦ *Ignore any questions which are not
applicable*

applicant *noun* (*plural* **applicants**)
someone who applies for something, for
example a job

application *noun* (*plural* **applications**)
1 an application is a letter or form you use
to ask for something important, such as a
job 2 application is when you make a lot of
effort to do something

applied *adjective*
used for something practical
♦ *Engineering is an applied science*

apply *verb* (**applies, applying, applied**)
1 to apply something is to put it on something else ♦ *You need to apply a patch to the puncture* **2** to apply for a job is to write formally and ask for it **3** to apply to someone is to concern them ♦ *These rules apply to everybody* **4** to apply yourself to something is to give it all your attention

appoint *verb* (**appoints, appointing, appointed**)
1 to appoint someone is to choose them for a job **2** to appoint a time and place for a meeting is to decide when and where to have it

appointment *noun* (*plural* **appointments**)
1 an arrangement to meet or visit someone **2** choosing someone for a job **3** a job or position

apposition *noun*
apposition is placing a word next to one that it describes. In the phrase *Elizabeth, our Queen, our Queen* is in apposition to *Elizabeth*

appraise *verb* (**appraises, appraising, appraised**)
to appraise something or someone is to estimate their quality or value
appraisal *noun* estimating or valuing something

appreciate *verb* (**appreciates, appreciating, appreciated**)
1 to appreciate something is to enjoy or value it **2** to appreciate a fact is to understand it ♦ *You don't seem to appreciate how lucky we are* **3** to appreciate is to increase in value
appreciation *noun* appreciating something; an increase in value

appreciative *adjective*
enjoying or valuing something ♦ *I enjoy playing to an appreciative audience*

apprehension *noun* (*plural* **apprehensions**)
nervous fear or worry
apprehensive *adjective* nervous and fearful

apprentice *noun* (*plural* **apprentices**)
someone who is learning a trade or craft
apprenticeship *noun* the time when someone is an apprentice

approach ➤ *verb* (**approaches, approaching, approached**)
1 to approach a place is to come near to it **2** to approach someone is to go to them with a request or offer **3** to approach a problem or difficulty is to start solving it

approach ➤ *noun* (*plural* **approaches**)
1 coming near to a place **2** going to someone with a request or offer **3** a way of tackling a problem **4** a way or road leading up to a building ♦ *The approach to the house had trees on each side* **5** the final part of an aircraft's flight as it comes in to land

approachable *adjective*
friendly and easy to talk to

appropriate *adjective*
suitable

approval *noun*
thinking well of someone or something

approve *verb* (**approves, approving, approved**)
to approve of someone or something is to think they are good or suitable

approximate *adjective*
not exact ♦ *The approximate size of the playground is half an acre*
approximately *adverb* roughly

approximation *nóoun* (*plural* **approximations**)
something that is a rough estimate and not exact

apricot *noun* (*plural* **apricots**)
a juicy, orange-coloured fruit like a small peach, with a stone in it

April *noun*
the fourth month of the year

April fool *noun*
someone who is fooled on April Fool's Day (1 April)

apron *noun* (*plural* **aprons**)
1 a piece of clothing worn over the front of your body to protect your clothes **2** the part of an airfield where aircraft are loaded and unloaded

apt *adjective*
1 likely to do something ♦ *He is apt to be careless* **2** suitable ♦ *I need to find an apt quotation* **3** quick at learning ♦ *She is an apt pupil*

aptitude *noun* (*plural* **aptitudes**)
aptitude or an aptitude is a talent in something

aquarium *noun* (*plural* **aquariums**)
a tank or building for keeping live fish

aquatic *adjective*
to do with water and swimming ♦ *They enjoy aquatic sports*

aqueduct *noun* (*plural* **aqueducts**)
a bridge that carries water across a valley

Arab *noun* (*plural* **Arabs**)
a member of a people inhabiting Arabia and other parts of the Middle East and North Africa
Arabian *adjective* to do with the Arabs
Arabic *noun*
the language of the Arabs
arabic figures or **arabic numerals** *plural noun*
the figures 1, 2, 3, 4, and so on (compare *Roman numerals*)
arable *adjective*
to do with the growing of crops
arbitrary *adjective* (*pronounced* ar-bi-trer-i)
done or chosen at random or without a proper reason ♦ *It was an arbitrary decision*
arbitrate *verb* (**arbitrates, arbitrating, arbitrated**)
to arbitrate is to settle someone else's quarrel
arbitration *noun*
settling a quarrel between two people or two sides by someone who is impartial
arbitrator *noun* someone who settles a quarrel
arc *noun* (*plural* **arcs**)
part of the circumference of a circle, a curve
arcade *noun* (*plural* **arcades**)
a covered place to walk, with shops down each side
arch ➤ *noun* (*plural* **arches**)
a curved structure that helps to support a bridge or building
arch ➤ *verb* (**arches, arching, arched**)
to curve
archaeology *noun* (*pronounced* ar-ki-ol-o-ji)
the study of ancient people from the remains of their buildings
archaeological *adjective* to do with archaeology **archaeologist** *noun* someone who studies archaeology
archbishop *noun* (*plural* **archbishops**)
the chief bishop of a region

archer *noun* (*plural* **archers**)
someone who shoots with a bow and arrows

archery *noun*
the sport of shooting with a bow and arrows
architect *noun* (*plural* **architects**) (*pronounced* ar-ki-tekt)
someone whose work is to design buildings
architecture *noun*
1 the work of designing buildings 2 a style of building ♦ *Victorian architecture*
Arctic *noun*
the area round the North Pole
are plural and 2nd person singular present tense of **be**
area *noun* (*plural* **areas**)
1 part of a country, place, etc. 2 the space occupied by something ♦ *The area of this room is 20 square metres*
arena *noun* (*plural* **arenas**) (*pronounced* a-ree-na)
1 the level space in the middle of a stadium or sports ground 2 the place where a sports event takes place
aren't short for *am not* or *are not*
argue *verb* (**argues, arguing, argued**)
1 to argue with someone is to quarrel with them 2 to argue is also to give reasons for something ♦ *She argued that the housework should be shared*
argument *noun* (*plural* **arguments**)
1 a quarrel 2 a reason someone gives for something
arid *adjective*
dry and barren
aridity *noun* being arid
arise *verb* (**arises, arising, arose, arisen**)
1 to arise is to appear or to come into existence 2 (*old meaning*) to rise; to stand up
aristocracy *noun* (*plural* **aristocracies**)
the aristocracy are the people from important families who often have titles like *Lord* and *Lady*
aristocrat *noun* (*plural* **aristocrats**) (*pronounced* a-ris-to-krat)
a nobleman or noblewoman

aristocratic *adjective* to do with aristocrats

arithmetic *noun*
the study of using numbers and working things out with them
arithmetical *adjective* to do with arithmetic

ark *noun* (*plural* **arks**)
1 in the Bible, the ship in which Noah and his family escaped the Flood **2** a model of Noah's ark

arm ➤ *noun* (*plural* **arms**)
1 the part of your body between your shoulder and your hand **2** the sleeve of a coat or dress **3** the side part of a chair, on which you can rest your arm

arm ➤ *verb* (**arms, arming, armed**)
1 to arm people is to give them weapons
2 to arm is to prepare for war

armada *noun* (*plural* **armadas**) (*pronounced* ar-mah-da)
a fleet of warships, especially the Spanish Armada which attacked England in 1588

armadillo *noun* (*plural* **armadillos**)
a South American animal whose body is covered with a shell of bony plates

armaments *plural noun*
weapons

armchair *noun* (*plural* **armchairs**)
a chair with parts on either side to rest your arms on

armed forces *plural noun*
the army, navy, and air force of a country

armful *noun* (*plural* **armfuls**)
as much of something as you can hold in your arms ♦ *He had an armful of hay*

armistice *noun* (*plural* **armistices**)
an agreement to stop fighting in a war or battle

armour *noun*
armour is a metal covering to protect people or things in battle
armoured *adjective* having armour

armpit *noun* (*plural* **armpits**)
the hollow part under your arm at your shoulder

arms *plural noun*
1 weapons ♦ *Lay down your arms* **1**
2 a coat of arms

army *noun* (*plural* **armies**)
1 a large number of soldiers ready to fight
2 a large group ♦ *They had an army of supporters*

aroma *noun* (*plural* **aromas**) (*pronounced* a-roh-ma)
a pleasant smell, for example of food
aromatic *adjective* having a pleasant smell

arose past tense of **arise**

around *adverb* and *preposition*
1 round ♦ *They stood around the pond*
2 about ♦ *Stop running around*

arouse *verb* (**arouses, arousing, aroused**)
1 to arouse someone is to make them wake up **2** to arouse feelings in someone is to cause them to have those feelings

arrange *verb* (**arranges, arranging, arranged**)
1 to arrange things is to put them all in the position you want **2** to arrange a meeting or event is to organize it **3** to arrange to do something is to make sure someone does it
arrangement *noun* arranging something or the way you arrange something

array *noun* (*plural* **arrays**)
a display of things for people to see
♦ *There was a huge array of books*

arrears *plural noun*
money that someone owes and ought to have paid earlier
in arrears owing money ♦ *He's in arrears with his rent*

arrest ➤ *verb* (**arrests, arresting, arrested**)
1 to arrest someone is to take hold of them by the power of the law **2** to arrest something is to stop it ♦ *The doctors were trying to arrest the spread of disease*

arrest ➤ *noun* (*plural* **arrests**)
taking hold of someone by the power of the law
under arrest taken by the police into custody

arrive *verb* (**arrives, arriving, arrived**)
1 to arrive at a place is to get there at the end of a journey **2** to arrive is also to happen ♦ *The great day arrived*
arrival *noun* arriving at a place

arrogant *adjective*
unpleasantly proud and self-important
arrogance *noun* being arrogant

arrow *noun* (*plural* **arrows**)
1 a pointed stick shot from a bow **2** a sign used to show direction or position

arsenal *noun* (*plural* **arsenals**)
a place where bullets, shells, and weapons are made or stored

arsenic *noun*
a strong poison made from a metallic element and used in insecticides

arson *noun*
the crime of deliberately setting fire to a building

art *noun* (*plural* **arts**)
1 art is producing something by drawing or painting or sculpture **2** the arts are subjects such as history and languages, as distinct from the sciences such as physics and chemistry **3** an art is also a skill in something, such as sewing or public speaking

artefact *noun* (*plural* **artefacts**)
an object made by humans, especially one from the past that is studied by archaeologists

artery *noun* (*plural* **arteries**)
a tube carrying blood from the heart to parts of the body

artful *adjective*
clever at deceiving people
artfully *adverb* in an artful way

arthritic *adjective* (*pronounced* arth-rit-ik)
suffering from arthritis

arthritis *noun* (*pronounced* arth-ry-tiss)
a disease that makes joints in the body painful and stiff

article *noun* (*plural* **articles**)
1 an object or thing that you can touch or pick up **2** a piece of writing published in a newspaper or magazine **3** (*in Grammar*) the word 'a' or 'an' (called the *indefinite article*) or the word 'the' (called the *definite article*)

articulate ➤ *adjective* (*pronounced* ar-tik-yoo-lat)
able to speak clearly and fluently

articulate ➤ *verb* (**articulates, articulating, articulated**) (*pronounced* ar-tik-yoo-layt)
to articulate a word or phrase is to pronounce it clearly
articulation *noun* clear speaking or pronunciation

articulated lorry *noun* (*plural* **articulated lorries**)
a large lorry with a cab that is connected to the main part by a joint that bends, so that it can turn more easily

artificial *adjective*
made by human beings and not by nature
artificially *adverb* in an artificial way

artificial intelligence *noun*
the use of computers to do things that humans do, for example thinking and making decisions

artificial respiration *noun*
helping someone to start breathing again, especially after an accident

artillery *noun* (*plural* **artilleries**)
1 artillery is a collection of large guns **2** the artillery is the part of the army that uses large guns

artist *noun* (*plural* **artists**)
1 someone who produces art, especially a painter **2** an entertainer

artiste *noun* (*plural* **artistes**)
someone whose work is to entertain people, especially by singing, dancing, or telling stories

artistic *adjective*
1 to do with art and artists **2** showing skill and beauty ♦ *an artistic flower arrangement*

artistry *noun*
the skill of an artist ♦ *The carving showed great artistry*

as *conjunction, adverb, and preposition*
linking words and phrases ♦ *As you were late, you had better stay behind* ♦ *Leave it as it is* ♦ *She slipped as she got off the bus* ♦ *It is not as hard as you think* ♦ *He was dressed as a sailor*

asbestos *noun*
a fireproof material that is made up of fine soft fibres

ascend *verb* (**ascends, ascending, ascended**)
to ascend something like a hill or staircase is to go up it

ascent *noun* (*plural* **ascents**)
an ascent is a climb, usually a hard or long one

ash¹ *noun* (*plural* **ashes**)
ash is the powder that is left after something has been burned

ash² *noun* (*plural* **ashes**)
an ash or ash tree is a tree with silvery bark and winged seeds

ashamed *adjective*
feeling shame
ashamed of something is feeling shame because of something

ashen *adjective*
grey and pale ♦ *Her face was ashen*

ashore *adverb*
on the shore

ashtray *noun* (*plural* **ashtrays**)
a small bowl for putting cigarette ash in

Asian ➤ *adjective*
to do with Asia

Asian ➤ *noun* (*plural* **Asians**)
a person from Asia

aside ➤ *adverb*
to or at one side; away ♦ *Step aside and let them pass*

aside ➤ *noun* (*plural* **asides**)
something said so that only some people will hear

ask *verb* (**asks, asking, asked**)
1 to ask someone something is to speak to them so as to find out or get something
2 to ask someone to something like a party is to invite them
to ask for it or **to ask for trouble** (*informal*) is to do something that will bring trouble

asleep *adverb* and *adjective*
sleeping

aspect *noun* (*plural* **aspects**)
1 one way of looking at a problem or situation ♦ *Perhaps the worst aspect of winter is the dark mornings* 2 the appearance of someone or something
3 the direction a building faces ♦ *This room has a southern aspect*

asphalt *noun* (*pronounced* ass-falt)
a sticky black stuff like tar. It is mixed with gravel to make a surface for roads and areas such as playgrounds

aspirin *noun* (*plural* **aspirins**)
1 aspirin is a drug used to relieve pain or reduce fever 2 an aspirin is a tablet of this drug

ass *noun* (*plural* **asses**)
1 a donkey 2 (informal) a fool ♦ *Shaun, you are an ass!*

assassin *noun* (*plural* **assassins**)
a person who assassinates someone

assassinate *verb* (**assassinates, assassinating, assassinated**)
to assassinate someone such as a ruler or leader is to murder them to stop them having power

assassination *noun* (*plural* **assassinations**)
the murder of a ruler or leader

assault ➤ *noun* (*plural* **assaults**)
a violent or illegal attack on someone

assault ➤ *verb* (**assaults, assaulting, assaulted**)
to assault someone is to attack them violently

assemble *verb* (**assembles, assembling, assembled**)
1 to assemble people or things is to bring them together in one place 2 to assemble is to come together in one place ♦ *Please assemble in the playground*

assembly *noun* (*plural* **assemblies**)
1 an assembly is when a lot of people come together and someone speaks to them, for example in a school 2 an assembly is also a group of people who meet together, such as a parliament 3 assembly of a machine or piece of furniture is putting the parts together to make it

assent *noun*
assent is agreement or permission to do something ♦ *Have your parents given their assent?*

assert *verb* (**asserts, asserting, asserted**)
to assert something is to say it strongly and clearly
assertion *noun* something you say clearly

assertive *adjective*
speaking or behaving firmly and with authority

assess *verb* (**assesses, assessing, assessed**)
to assess someone or something is to decide how good or useful they are
assessment *noun* assessing or valuing someone or something **assessor** *noun* a person who assesses someone or something

asset *noun* (*plural* **assets**)
something useful or valuable to someone

assets *plural noun*
the property of a person or company that they could sell to raise money

assign *verb* (**assigns, assigning, assigned**)
to assign something to someone is to give it to them as their share or duty
♦ *Teachers assign homework to their pupils every day*

assignment *noun* (*plural* **assignments**)
a piece of work that someone is given to do

assist *verb* (**assists, assisting, assisted**)
to assist someone is to help them, usually in a practical way
assistance *noun* practical help

assistant *noun* (*plural* **assistants**)
1 someone whose job is to help another person in their work 2 someone who serves in a shop

associate ➤ *verb* (**associates, associating, associated**) (*pronounced* a-soh-shi-ayt)
1 to associate one thing with another is to connect them in your mind ♦ *I associate Christmas with ice and snow* 2 to associate with someone is to be friendly with them or work together ♦ *The people we associate with all have young children*

associate ➤ *noun* (*plural* **associates**)
(*pronounced* a-soh-shi-at)
someone you are friendly with or work with

association *noun* (*plural* **associations**)
1 an association is an organization for people sharing an interest or doing the same work **2** association is being friendly with someone

Association Football *noun*
a game played on a field between two teams of eleven players using a round ball that may only be handled by the goalkeepers

assorted *adjective*
of various sorts; mixed
assortment *noun* a mixture

assume *verb* (**assumes, assuming, assumed**)
to assume something is to think it is true or likely without being sure of it ♦ *I assume you will be coming tomorrow*
assumed *adjective* an assumed name is a name someone uses that is not their real one

assumption *noun* (*plural* **assumptions**)
something you assume or take for granted

assurance *noun* (*plural* **assurances**)
1 assurance is a feeling of certainty about something **2** an assurance is a promise or guarantee **3** assurance is also a kind of life insurance

assure *verb* (**assures, assuring, assured**)
to assure someone is to tell someone something definite ♦ *I can assure you that we will make every effort to help*

asterisk *noun* (*plural* **asterisks**)
a star-shaped sign * used in printing and writing to draw attention to something

asteroid *noun* (*plural* **asteroids**)
one of the small planets found mainly between the orbits of Mars and Jupiter

asthma *noun* (*pronounced* **ass-ma**)
a disease which makes breathing difficult

asthmatic ➢ *adjective*
suffering from asthma

asthmatic ➢ *noun* (*plural* **asthmatics**)
someone who is suffering from asthma

astonish *verb* (**astonishes, astonishing, astonished**)
to astonish someone is to surprise them very much
astonishment *noun* a feeling of great surprise

astound *verb* (**astounds, astounding, astounded**)
to astound someone is to amaze or shock them very much

astride *adverb*
with one leg on each side of something
♦ *She was sitting astride a big horse*

astrology *noun*
astrology is studying how the planets and stars may affect people's lives

astrologer *noun* someone who studies astrology **astrological** *adjective* to do with astrology

astronaut *noun* (*plural* **astronauts**)
someone who travels in a spacecraft

astronomical *adjective*
1 to do with astronomy **2** (*informal*) extremely large ♦ *The cost of the party was astronomical*

astronomy *noun*
astronomy is studying the sun, moon, planets, and stars
astronomer *noun* someone who studies astronomy

at *preposition*
showing where someone or something is
♦ *I was at the hospital* ♦ *They are looking at their new books*

ate past tense of **eat**

atheist *noun* (*plural* **atheists**)
someone who does not believe in a God
atheism *noun* not believing in a God

athlete *noun* (*plural* **athletes**)
someone who is good at athletics or other sports

athletic *adjective*
1 to do with athletics ♦ *an athletic competition* **2** good at sports; strong

athletics *plural noun*
physical exercises and sports such as running and jumping

atlas *noun* (*plural* **atlases**)
a book of maps

atmosphere *noun* (*plural* **atmospheres**)
1 the earth's atmosphere is the air around it **2** an atmosphere is a feeling you get in a room or at a place ♦ *There was a happy atmosphere at the fairground*

atmospheric *adjective*
1 to do with the earth's atmosphere
2 having a strong atmosphere

atoll *noun* (*plural* **atolls**)
a ring-shaped island of coral in the sea

atom *noun* (*plural* **atoms**)
1 the smallest possible part of a chemical element **2** a tiny part of something

atom bomb or **atomic bomb** noun (plural **atom bombs** or **atomic bombs**)
a bomb that uses atomic energy to make the explosion, and has nuclear fallout

atomic adjective
involving atoms; nuclear

at once adverb
immediately ♦ *Come here at once!*

atrocious adjective (pronounced a-**troh**-shus)
awful, terrible

atrocity noun (plural **atrocities**)
a terrible and cruel act, such as the killing of a large number of people

attach verb (attaches, attaching, attached)
to attach one thing to another is to fix or fasten it

attached adjective
to be attached to someone is to be fond of them

attachment noun (plural **attachments**)
1 an extra part you fix to a device so that it can do a special kind of work ♦ *The garden hose has an attachment for washing cars* 2 a fondness or friendship ♦ *The boys felt a real attachment to their pet hamster*

attack ➤ noun (plural **attacks**)
1 an attempt to hurt someone with violence 2 an attempt to harm someone or something by using unfriendly words 3 a sudden illness or pain

attack ➤ verb (attacks, attacking, attacked)
to attack someone is to try to hurt them with violence, or to harm them with unfriendly words

attain verb (attains, attaining, attained)
to attain something is to reach or achieve it ♦ *I have attained Grade 3 on the violin*
attainment noun something you have achieved

attempt ➤ verb (attempts, attempting, attempted)
to attempt to do something is to make an effort to do it

attempt ➤ noun (plural **attempts**)
an attempt at something is making an effort to do it

attend verb (attends, attending, attended)
1 to attend something like a meeting or a wedding is to be there 2 to attend school or college is to be a pupil or student there 3 to attend to someone is to look after them, especially when they are ill 4 to attend to something is to spend time dealing with it ♦ *She had some business to attend to*

attendance noun (plural **attendances**)
1 attendance is being somewhere where you are supposed to be 2 the attendance at an event is the number of people who are there to see it

attendant noun (plural **attendants**)
someone who helps or goes with another person

attention noun
giving care or thought to someone or something
to stand to attention is to stand with your feet together and your arms straight down, like soldiers on parade

attentive adjective
listening closely

attic noun (plural **attics**)
a room or space under the roof of a house

attitude noun (plural **attitudes**)
1 your attitude is the way you think or feel about something, and the way you behave 2 your attitude is also the position of your body

attract verb (attracts, attracting, attracted)
1 to attract someone is to seem pleasant to them and get their attention or interest 2 to attract something unwelcome is to make it come ♦ *Empty bottles of drink attract wasps* 3 to attract something is also to pull it by a physical force like magnetism ♦ *Magnets attract metal pins*

attraction noun (plural **attractions**)
1 attraction is the power to attract someone 2 an attraction is something pleasant that people like to see, such as a fair or a rock concert

attractive adjective
1 interesting or welcome ♦ *They made us an attractive offer of a free holiday* 2 pleasant, good-looking

auburn adjective
auburn hair is a reddish-brown colour

auction noun (plural **auctions**)
a sale at which things are sold to the person who offers the most money for them
auctioneer noun someone in charge of an auction

audible adjective
loud enough to be heard
audibility noun being audible

audience noun (plural **audiences**)
1 the people who have come to see or hear an event like a concert or film 2 a formal interview with an important person

audiovisual adjective
using both sound and pictures to give information ♦ *Audiovisual aids include films and video recordings*

audition *noun* (*plural* **auditions**)
a test to see if a performer is suitable to act in a play or sing in a choir

auditorium *noun* (*plural* **auditoriums**)
(*pronounced* aw-dit-or-i-um)
the part of a building where the audience sits

August *noun*
the eighth month of the year

aunt *noun* (*plural* **aunts**)
1 the sister of your mother or father
2 your uncle's wife

auntie or **aunty** *noun* (*plural* **aunties**)
(*informal*) an aunt

au pair *noun* (*plural* **au pairs**) (*pronounced* oh-**pair**)
a person from another country, usually a girl or young woman, who works for a time in someone's home

aural *adjective*
using the sense of hearing ♦ *The children had an aural comprehension test*

austere *adjective*
1 not having much comfort or luxury
2 an austere person is severe and strict
austerity *noun* lacking comfort; strictness

Australian ➤ *adjective*
to do with Australia

Australian ➤ *noun* (*plural* **Australians**)
a person from Australia

authentic *adjective*
real, genuine
authenticity *noun* being authentic

author *noun* (*plural* **authors**)
the writer of a book or something like a poem or article
authorship *noun* being an author

authority *noun* (*plural* **authorities**)
1 authority is the power to give orders to other people 2 the authorities are the people who have the power to make decisions 3 an authority on a subject is an expert on it or a book that gives you reliable information about it

authorize *verb* (**authorizes, authorizing, authorized**)
1 to authorize something is to give official permission for it 2 to authorize someone to do something is to give them permission to do it

autistic *adjective*
having a disability that makes someone unable to communicate with other people

autobiography *noun* (*plural* **autobiographies**)
the story of someone's life that they have written themselves
autobiographical *adjective* to do with autobiography

autograph *noun* (*plural* **autographs**)
the signature of a famous person

automate *verb* (**automates, automating, automated**)
to automate something is to make it work by an automatic process

automatic *adjective*
1 working on its own; not needing continuous attention or control by human beings 2 done without thinking
automatically *adverb* by automatic means

automation *noun* (*pronounced* aw-tom-**ay**-shun)
making processes automatic, and using machines instead of people to do work

automobile *noun* (*plural* **automobiles**)
(*in America*) a motor car

autumn *noun* (*plural* **autumns**) (*pronounced* **aw**-tum)
the season when leaves fall off the trees, between summer and winter

autumnal *adjective* (*pronounced* aw-**tum**-nal)
in autumn; to do with autumn

auxiliary ➤ *adjective*
helping, extra ♦ *The boat had an auxiliary engine*

auxiliary ➤ *noun* (*plural* **auxiliaries**)
(*in Grammar*) a type of verb that is used in forming parts of other verbs ♦ *In 'I have finished', the auxiliary is 'have'*

available *adjective*
able to be found or used ♦ *Fresh strawberries are available in June*
availability *noun* being available

avalanche *noun* (*plural* **avalanches**) (*pronounced* av-a-**lahnsh**)
a sudden heavy fall of rocks or snow down the side of a mountain

avenue *noun* (*plural* **avenues**)
a wide street, usually with trees along each side

average ➤ *noun* (*plural* **averages**)
1 an average is the number you get by adding several amounts together and dividing the total by the number of amounts ♦ *The average of 2, 4, 6, and 8 is 5*
2 the average is the usual or ordinary standard ♦ *Their work is well above the average*

average ➤ *adjective*
of the usual or ordinary standard

average ➤ *verb* (**averages, averaging, averaged**)
to average is to have as an average ♦ *We averaged 50 runs last season*

avert *verb* (**averts, averting, averted**)
 1 to avert something is to turn it away ♦ *People averted their eyes from the accident* **2** to avert something is also to stop it happening ♦ *The train driver's quick reaction had averted a disaster*

aviary *noun* (*plural* **aviaries**)
 a place where birds are kept

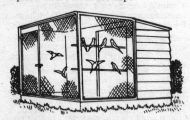

aviation *noun*
 aviation is flying in aircraft

avid *adjective*
 keen, eager ♦ *She is an avid reader*

avocado *noun* (*plural* **avocados**)
 (*pronounced* av-o-kah-doh)
 a fruit like a pear, with a rough skin and thick smooth flesh

avoid *verb* (**avoids, avoiding, avoided**)
 1 to avoid something or someone is to keep yourself away from them ♦ *They try to avoid their relations at Christmas* **2** to avoid something is also to find a way of not doing it ♦ *They wanted to avoid extra homework*
 avoidance *noun* avoiding something

await *verb* (**awaits, awaiting, awaited**)
 to await someone or something is to wait for them

awake ➤ *adjective*
 not sleeping

awake ➤ *verb* (**awakes, awaking, awoke, awoken**)
 1 to awake is to wake up **2** to awake someone is to wake them up

awaken *verb* (**awakens, awakening, awakened**)
 1 to awaken is to wake up **2** to awaken someone is to wake them up

award ➤ *noun* (*plural* **awards**)
 something such as a prize given to a person who has done something successful

award ➤ *verb* (**awards, awarding, awarded**)
 to award something to someone is to give it to them as an award

aware *adjective*
 to be aware of something is to know about it or realize it is there ♦ *They soon became aware of the danger*
 awareness *noun* being aware

awash *adjective*
 flooded with waves or water ♦ *The sink has overflowed, and the kitchen floor is awash!*

away ➤ *adverb*
 at a distance or somewhere else ♦ *I wish those people would go away* ♦ *The ice cream melted so I threw it away*

away ➤ *adjective*
 an away match is one that is played at the opponents' ground

awe *noun*
 fear and wonder ♦ *The mountains filled him with awe*
 awed filled with fear and wonder

awful *adjective*
 1 (*informal*) very bad; very great ♦ *I've been an awful fool* **2** causing fear or horror ♦ *It was an awful sight*

awfully *adverb*
 (*informal*) very, extremely ♦ *It's awfully hot in June*

awhile *adverb*
 for a short time

awkward *adjective*
 1 difficult to use or cope with ♦ *The box was an awkward shape* **2** embarrassed and uncomfortable ♦ *The boy felt awkward in the smart hotel*

awoke past tense of **awake** *verb*

awoken past participle of **awake** *verb*

axe ➤ *noun* (*plural* **axes**)
 a tool for chopping

axe ➤ *verb* (**axes, axing, axed**)
 (*informal*) to axe something is to cancel or abolish it

axis *noun* (*plural* **axes**)
 1 a line through the centre of a spinning object **2** a line dividing something in half

axle *noun* (*plural* **axles**)
 the rod through the centre of a wheel, on which it turns

ay or **aye** *interjection* (*pronounced* I)
 (*in dialects or old uses*) yes

azalea *noun* (*plural* **azaleas**) (*pronounced* a-**zay**-li-a)
 a flowering shrub like a rhododendron

Aztec *noun* (*plural* **Aztecs**)
 one of a native Indian people who lived in Mexico before the Spanish conquest of 1521

azure *adjective*
 sky-blue

Bb

babble *verb* (**babbles, babbling, babbled**)
1 to babble is to talk in a silly or meaningless way **2** to babble is also to make a murmuring sound ♦ *They came across a babbling brook*

baboon *noun* (*plural* **baboons**)
a large kind of monkey

baby *noun* (*plural* **babies**)
a very young child

babyish *adjective*
silly and childish

babysit *verb* (**babysits, babysitting, babysat**)
to babysit is to look after a child while the parents are out

babysitter *noun* (*plural* **babysitters**)
someone who babysits

bachelor *noun* (*plural* **bachelors**)
a man who is not married

back ➢ *noun* (*plural* **backs**)
1 the part of your body between your shoulders and your bottom **2** the upper part of a four-legged animal's body **3** the part of a thing that faces away from the front ♦ *The back of the house faces a river*

back ➢ *adjective*
placed at the back ♦ *Let's sit in the back row*

back ➢ *adverb*
1 backwards or towards the back ♦ *Go back!* **2** to an earlier time ♦ *Put the clock back* **3** at a distance ♦ *The house stands back from the road*

back ➢ *verb* (**backs, backing, backed**)
1 to back a vehicle is to move it backwards **2** to back a horse is to bet on it winning a race **3** to back someone is to support them or give them help **4** to back a singer is to play or sing music to support them
to back out is to decide not to get involved in something

to back someone up is to give them support or help

backache *noun* (*plural* **backaches**)
a pain in your back, usually lasting for a long time

backbone *noun* (*plural* **backbones**)
your backbone is your spine

background *noun* (*plural* **backgrounds**)
1 the background of a picture or view is the part that is farthest away from you
2 the background to an event or situation is what helped to cause it **3** a person's background is their family and education
in the background not noticeable, not obvious

backing *noun*
1 backing is support or help ♦ *Our firm will give you financial backing* **2** backing is also the material that forms a support or back for something **3** a backing is a musical accompaniment, especially for a singer

backlash *noun* (*plural* **backlashes**)
a strong and often angry reaction

backlog *noun* (*plural* **backlogs**)
a backlog is work that should have been finished but still has to be done

backside *noun* (*plural* **backsides**)
(*informal*) your backside is your bottom

backstroke *noun*
a stroke you use when swimming on your back

backward ➢ *adjective*
1 facing the back **2** slow in learning

backward ➢ *adverb*
backwards

backwards *adverb*
1 towards the back **2** from the end to the beginning ♦ *Count backwards from 10 to 1*

backwater *noun* (*plural* **backwaters**)
1 a branch of a river that comes to a dead end **2** a place that is remote from other people ♦ *They thought the village was a bit of a backwater*

backyard *noun* (*plural* **backyards**)
an open area at the back of a building

bacon *noun*
smoked or salted meat from the back or sides of a pig

bacteria *plural noun*
tiny organisms that can cause diseases
bacterial *adjective* to do with bacteria

bad *adjective* (**worse, worst**)
1 something you do not want or like, the opposite of 'good' ♦ *Eating fatty foods is*

bad for you ♦ *I've got a bad leg* ♦ *We were watching a very bad film on television*
2 someone who is bad is wicked or naughty
not bad fairly good, all right

baddy *noun* (*plural* **baddies**)
(*informal*) a bad person, especially in a story or a film

badge *noun* (*plural* **badges**)
a small piece of metal or cloth sewn or pinned on your clothes to tell people something about you, such as a club you belong to

badger ➤ *noun* (*plural* **badgers**)
a grey animal with a white stripe along its nose, which lives underground and is active at night

badger ➤ *verb* (**badgers, badgering, badgered**)
to badger someone is to pester them ♦ *He kept badgering his mother for his pocket money*

badly *adverb*
1 in a bad way ♦ *They did the work badly*
2 very much ♦ *I need a drink badly*
badly off poor or unfortunate

badminton *noun*
a game in which a lightweight object called a *shuttlecock* is hit backwards and forwards with rackets across a high net

baffle *verb* (**baffles, baffling, baffled**)
to baffle someone is to puzzle them completely

bag ➤ *noun* (*plural* **bags**)
a container made of soft material
bags of something (*informal*) plenty ♦ *There's bags of room*

bag ➤ *verb* (**bags, bagging, bagged**)
to bag something is to get hold of it or take it ♦ *I bagged the best seat*

bagel *noun* (*plural* **bagels**)
a hard ring-shaped bread roll

baggage *noun*
the luggage you take on a journey

baggy *adjective* (**baggier, baggiest**)
hanging loosely

bagpipes *plural noun*
bagpipes are a musical instrument with air squeezed out of a bag into a set of pipes

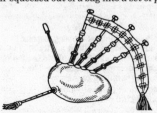

bail [1] *noun*
money paid or promised so that an accused person will not be kept in prison before coming to trial

bail [2] *noun* (*plural* **bails**)
one of the two small pieces of wood placed on top of the stumps in cricket

bail *verb* (**bails, bailing, bailed**)
to bail water out of a boat is to scoop it over the side

Bairam *noun* (*plural* **Bairams**) (*pronounced* by-**ram**)
either of two Muslim festivals, one in the tenth month and one in the twelfth month of the Islamic year

Baisakhi *noun*
a Sikh festival held in April

bait ➤ *noun*
bait is food put on a hook or in a trap to catch fish or animals

bait ➤ *verb* (**baits, baiting, baited**)
1 to bait an animal is to torment it **2** to bait a hook or trap is to put the bait on it or in it, to catch fish or animals

bake *verb* (**bakes, baking, baked**)
1 to bake food is to cook it in an oven **2** to bake something like clay is to make it hard by heating it in an oven **3** to bake is to become very hot, especially in the sun

baker *noun* (*plural* **bakers**)
someone who makes or sells bread and cakes

bakery *noun* (*plural* **bakeries**)
a place where bread is made or sold

baking powder *noun*
baking powder is a special powder used to make cakes rise

balance ➤ *noun* (*plural* **balances**)
1 a balance is a device for weighing things, with two trays hanging from the ends of a horizontal bar **2** a person's balance is their feeling of being steady ♦ *He lost his balance and fell over* **3** the balance of a bank account is the difference between the

money paid into it and the money taken out of it **4** a balance is also an amount of money that someone owes ♦ *I will pay you the balance on Saturday*

balance ➤ *verb* (**balances, balancing, balanced**)
1 to balance something is to make it steady ♦ *He was balancing a tray on one hand* **2** a balanced diet is one that has all the right kinds of food for being healthy

balcony *noun* (*plural* **balconies**)
1 a platform built out from the wall of a building, with a railing round it **2** the upstairs part of a cinema or theatre

bald *adjective* (**balder, baldest**)
not having much hair or any hair

bale [1] *noun* (*plural* **bales**)
a large bundle of something like hay or straw, usually tied up tightly

bale [2] *verb* (**bales, baling, baled**)
to bale out is to jump out of an aircraft with a parachute

ball *noun* (*plural* **balls**)
1 a round object used in many games **2** something such as string wound round to form a ball **3** a grand or formal dance

ballad *noun* (*plural* **ballads**)
a simple song or poem that tells a story

ballerina *noun* (*plural* **ballerinas**)
(*pronounced* bal-e-ree-na)
a female ballet dancer

ballet *noun* (*plural* **ballets**) (*pronounced* bal-ay)
a type of entertainment performed on stage, telling a story or expressing an idea in dancing and mime

ballet dancer *noun* (*plural* **ballet dancers**)
someone who performs ballet

ballistic missile *noun* (*plural* **ballistic missiles**)
a type of rocket that goes up into the air by its own power and falls freely

balloon *noun* (*plural* **balloons**)
1 a small rubber pouch that you fill up with air or gas and use as a toy or for decoration **2** a large round or pear-shaped bag inflated with a light gas or hot air, so that it can carry people into the air **3** an outline in a strip cartoon containing the words the characters are saying

ballot *noun* (*plural* **ballots**) (*pronounced* bal-ot)
a method of voting in secret by writing your vote on a piece of paper

ballpoint *noun* (*plural* **ballpoints**)
a pen that writes with a tiny ball round which the ink flows

ballroom *noun* (*plural* **ballrooms**)
a large room where dances are held

balsa *noun* (*pronounced* bol-sa)
a kind of lightweight wood used to make models

bamboo *noun* (*plural* **bamboos**)
1 a tall plant with hard hollow stems **2** a stem of this kind of plant

ban *verb* (**bans, banning, banned**)
to ban something is to forbid people to do it

banana *noun* (*plural* **bananas**)
a tropical fruit with a yellow skin

band ➤ *noun* (*plural* **bands**)
1 an organized group of people **2** a group of musicians **3** a circular strip of something

band ➤ *verb* (**bands, banding, banded**)
to band together is to be friends or form a group

bandage *noun* (*plural* **bandages**)
(*pronounced* ban-dij)
a strip of material for binding a wound

bandit *noun* (*plural* **bandits**)
an outlaw

bandstand *noun* (*plural* **bandstands**)
a platform for a band playing music outdoors

bandwagon *noun* (*plural* **bandwagons**)
a wagon for a band playing music in a parade
to jump or **climb on the bandwagon** (*informal*) is to join in something that looks like being successful

bandy *adjective* (**bandier, bandiest**)
having legs that curve outwards at the knees; bow-legged

bang ➤ *noun* (*plural* **bangs**)
1 a sudden loud noise **2** a heavy blow or knock

bang ➤ *verb* (**bangs, banging, banged**)
1 to bang something is to hit or shut it noisily **2** to bang is to make a loud noise

banger *noun* (*plural* **bangers**)
1 (*informal*) a firework that explodes **2** (*slang*) a sausage **3** (*slang*) a noisy old car

banish *verb* (**banishes, banishing, banished**)
to banish someone is to send them away as a punishment
banishment *noun* being banished

banisters *plural noun*
banisters are a rail with upright supports at the side of a staircase

banjo *noun* (*plural* **banjos**)
an instrument like a small guitar with a round body

bank ➤ *noun* (*plural* **banks**)
1 a business which looks after people's money 2 the ground beside a river or lake 3 a piece of raised or sloping ground 4 a mass of clouds 5 a row of lights or switches

bank ➤ *verb* (**banks, banking, banked**)
1 to bank money is to put it in a bank 2 to bank is to lean over while changing direction ♦ *The plane banked as it turned to land*
to bank on something is to rely on it ♦ *We're banking on the weather being good*

bank holiday *noun* (*plural* **bank holidays**)
a public holiday, when the banks are closed

banknote *noun* (*plural* **banknotes**)
a piece of paper money

bankrupt *adjective*
unable to pay your debts
bankruptcy *noun* being bankrupt

banner *noun* (*plural* **banners**)
a large flag or piece of cloth carried on a pole or between two poles in a procession

banquet *noun* (*plural* **banquets**)
(*pronounced* **bank**-wit)
a large formal dinner, often with speeches

baobab *noun* (*plural* **baobabs**) (*pronounced* **bay**-oh-bab)
an African tree with a large trunk and fruit that can be eaten

baptism *noun* (*plural* **baptisms**)
baptism is the ceremony of baptizing someone

Baptist *noun* (*plural* **Baptists**)
a Christian who believes that people should be baptized when they are adults

baptize *verb* (**baptizes, baptizing, baptized**)
to baptize someone is to sprinkle them with water, or dip them in water, in a ceremony receiving them into a Christian Church

bar ➤ *noun* (*plural* **bars**)
1 a long piece of a hard substance 2 a counter or room where drinks and refreshments are served 3 one of the small equal sections into which music is divided ♦ *A waltz has three beats in a bar*

bar ➤ *verb* (**bars, barring, barred**)
1 to bar something is to fasten it with a bar 2 to bar someone from something is to prevent them from taking part in it

barb *noun* (*plural* **barbs**)
a backward-curving point on a fish-hook or spear, which makes it stick in more firmly

barbarian *noun* (*plural* **barbarians**)
an uncivilized or savage person

barbaric or **barbarous** *adjective*
savage and cruel
barbarism *noun* or **barbarity** *noun* savage cruelty

barbecue *noun* (*plural* **barbecues**)
1 a party at which food is cooked outdoors 2 a place or device for cooking food outdoors

barbed wire *noun*
wire with sharp twisted spikes on it, used to make fences

barber *noun* (*plural* **barbers**)
a men's hairdresser

bar chart *noun* (*plural* **bar charts**)
a diagram showing amounts as bars of equal width but different heights

bar code *noun* (*plural* **bar codes**)
a code made up of a series of lines and spaces, which is printed on goods so that they can be identified by a computer

bard *noun* (*plural* **bards**)
(*old use*) a poet or minstrel

bare *adjective* (**barer, barest**)
1 not having any clothing or covering ♦ *The trees were bare* 2 empty or almost empty ♦ *The cupboard was bare* 3 only just enough ♦ *They just had the bare necessities of life*

bareback *adjective* and *adverb*
riding on a horse without a saddle

barely *adverb*
only just; with difficulty ♦ *They were barely able to see in the fog*

bargain ➤ *noun* (*plural* **bargains**)
1 an agreement to buy or sell something 2 something bought at a surprisingly low cost
into the bargain as well ♦ *He lost all his money and got lost into the bargain*

bargain ➤ *verb* (**bargains, bargaining, bargained**)
to bargain over something is to argue over its price
to get more than you bargained for is to get an unwelcome surprise

barge ➤ *noun* (*plural* **barges**)
a long flat-bottomed boat used especially on canals

barge ➤ *verb* (**barges, barging, barged**)
to barge into someone is to rush or bump clumsily into them

baritone *noun* (*plural* **baritones**)
a male singer with a voice between a tenor and a bass

bark ➤ *noun* (*plural* **barks**)
1 a bark is the sound made by a dog or a fox **2** bark is the outer covering of a tree's branches or trunk

bark ➤ *verb* (**barks, barking, barked**)
to make the sound of a dog or fox

barley *noun*
a kind of grain from which malt is made

barley sugar *noun*
a sweet made from boiled sugar

barman *noun* (*plural* **barmen**)
a man who serves drinks in a bar

bar mitzvah *noun* (*plural* **bar mitzvahs**)
a religious ceremony for Jewish boys when they reach the age of 13

barn *noun* (*plural* **barns**)
a building on a farm used to store things such as grain or hay

barnacle *noun* (*plural* **barnacles**)
a shellfish that attaches itself to rocks and the bottoms of ships

barn dance *noun* (*plural* **barn dances**)
a type of country dance, or an informal gathering of people for dancing

barnyard *noun* (*plural* **barnyards**)
a farmyard

barometer *noun* (*plural* **barometers**)
(*pronounced* ba-rom-it-er)
an instrument that measures air pressure, used in forecasting the weather

barometric *adjective* to do with air pressure

baron *noun* (*plural* **barons**)
a member of the lowest rank of noblemen

baronial *adjective* belonging to a baron

baroness *noun* (*plural* **baronesses**)
1 a female baron **2** a baron's wife or widow

barrack *verb* (**barracks, barracking, barracked**)
to barrack someone is to jeer at them in public

barracks *noun* (*plural* **barracks**)
a place where soldiers live

barrage *noun* (*plural* **barrages**) (*pronounced* ba-rah*z*h)
1 a round of heavy gunfire **2** a dam or barrier across a river to make the water deeper

barrel *noun* (*plural* **barrels**)
1 a large cylindrical container with flat ends **2** the metal tube of a gun, through which the shot is fired

barrel organ *noun* (*plural* **barrel organs**)
a musical instrument which you play by turning a handle

barren *adjective*
not able to produce any crops or fruit

barricade ➤ *noun* (*plural* **barricades**)
a barrier, especially one put up quickly to block a street

barricade ➤ *verb* (**barricades, barricading, barricaded**)
to barricade a place is to block or defend it with a barrier

barrier *noun* (*plural* **barriers**)
1 a fence or railing put up to stop people getting past 2 something that stops you doing something ♦ *Lack of money is often a barrier to happiness*

barrister *noun* (*plural* **barristers**)
a lawyer who argues legal cases in the higher courts

barrow *noun* (*plural* **barrows**)
1 a small cart 2 an ancient mound of earth over a grave

barter *verb* (**barters, bartering, bartered**)
to barter is to exchange goods for other goods, without using money

base ➤ *noun* (*plural* **bases**)
1 the bottom part of something, or the part on which something stands 2 a place from which military or police operations are controlled 3 (*in Science*) a substance (such as an alkali) that combines with an acid to form a salt

base ➤ *verb* (**bases, basing, based**)
to base one thing on another thing is to use the second thing as the starting point for the first ♦ *She based the story on an event in her own childhood*

baseball *noun* (*plural* **baseballs**)
1 baseball is an American game like rounders, in which the players run round a series of four 'bases' to score points 2 a baseball is a ball used in this game

basement *noun* (*plural* **basements**)
a part of a building at the lowest level, usually below the ground

bash ➤ *verb* (**bashes, bashing, bashed**)
(*informal*) to bash someone or something is to hit them hard

bash ➤ *noun* (*plural* **bashes**)
(*informal*) 1 a hard hit 2 an attempt ♦ *Have a bash at it*

bashful *adjective*
shy

basic *adjective*
forming the first or most important part ♦ *He has a basic knowledge of French* ♦ *Food is a basic human need*

basically *adverb*
essentially, mainly ♦ *She is basically lazy*

basin *noun* (*plural* **basins**)
1 a deep round dish 2 a large container to hold water for washing in 3 an enclosed area of water where ships can stay safely 4 the area of land where a river's water comes from

basis *noun* (*plural* **bases**)
1 something to start from or add to ♦ *These players will be the basis of a new team* 2 the way in which something is arranged or organized ♦ *You will be paid on a monthly basis*

bask *verb* (**basks, basking, basked**)
to bask is to lie or sit comfortably warming yourself

basket *noun* (*plural* **baskets**)
a container, often made of woven strips of wood

basketball *noun* (*plural* **basketballs**)
1 basketball is a team game in which players try to throw a ball through a hoop fixed 3 metres above the ground 2 a basketball is a ball used in this game

basketful *noun* (*plural* **basketfuls**)
as much of something as you can hold in a basket ♦ *They brought her a basketful of apples*

bass ➤ *adjective* (*pronounced* bayss)
forming the lowest sounds in music

bass ➤ *noun* (*plural* **basses**) (*pronounced* bayss)
a bass singer or instrument

bassoon *noun* (*plural* **bassoons**)
a woodwind instrument that plays low notes

bastard *noun* (*plural* **bastards**)
1 (*informal*) a person, especially an unpleasant or unfortunate person 2 an old word for a person whose parents were not married

bat [1] ➤ *noun* (*plural* **bats**)
a wooden implement used to hit the ball in cricket, baseball, and other games

off your own bat (*informal*) without any help from other people

bat ➤ *verb* (**bats**, **batting**, **batted**)
to bat is to use a bat in a ball game

bat [2] *noun* (*plural* **bats**)
a flying mammal that looks like a mouse with wings

batch *noun* (*plural* **batches**)
a set of things made at one time

bated *adjective*
with bated breath waiting anxiously

bath ➤ *noun* (*plural* **baths**)
1 a bath is a large container you fill with water and get into to wash **2** a bath sometimes means the water in a bath
♦ *Your bath is getting cold* **3** the baths are also a swimming bath

bath ➤ *verb* (**baths**, **bathing**, **bathed**)
1 to bath someone is to give them a bath
2 to bath is to have a bath

bathe ➤ *verb* (**bathes**, **bathing**, **bathed**)
1 to bathe is to swim in the sea or a river
2 to bathe something is to wash it gently

bathe ➤ *noun* (*plural* **bathes**)
a bathe is a swim

bathroom *noun* (*plural* **bathrooms**)
a room for having a bath or wash in

baton *noun* (*plural* **batons**)
a short stick, especially one used to conduct an orchestra or one used in a relay race

batsman *noun* (*plural* **batsmen**)
someone who uses a bat in cricket or another ball game

battalion *noun* (*plural* **battalions**)
an army unit consisting of two or more companies

batten *noun* (*plural* **battens**)
a flat strip of wood

batter ➤ *verb* (**batters**, **battering**, **battered**)
to batter someone is to hit them hard and often, so that they suffer physically

batter ➤ *noun*
batter is a beaten mixture of flour, eggs, and milk, used in cooking pancakes

battering ram *noun* (*plural* **battering rams**)
(*historical*) a heavy pole used to break through the walls and gateways of a city or fort

battery *noun* (*plural* **batteries**)
1 a portable device for storing and supplying electricity **2** a series of cages in which animals are kept close together on a farm ♦ *Free-range hens are not kept in batteries* **3** a set of devices, especially a group of large guns

battle *noun* (*plural* **battles**)
a fight between armies

battlefield *noun* (*plural* **battlefields**)
a place where a battle is or was fought

battlements *plural noun*
the top of a castle wall, usually with notches through which arrows could be shot

battleship *noun* (*plural* **battleships**)
a large heavily armed warship

bawl *verb* (**bawls**, **bawling**, **bawled**)
to bawl is to shout or cry loudly

bay *noun* (*plural* **bays**)
1 a place by the sea or a lake where the shore curves inwards **2** an alcove or compartment

to keep someone at bay is to prevent them from coming near you

bayonet *noun* (*plural* **bayonets**)
a steel blade fixed to the muzzle of a rifle and used for jabbing

bay window *noun* (*plural* **bay windows**)
a window that sticks out from the wall of a house and forms a bay in the room

bazaar *noun* (*plural* **bazaars**)
1 a sale to raise money **2** an oriental market

BBC short for *British Broadcasting Corporation*

BC short for *before Christ*, used with dates that come before the birth of Jesus Christ ♦ *Julius Caesar came to Britain in 55 BC*

be *verb* (I am; you are; he, she, or it is; they are; I, he, she, or it was; you were; they were; I, you, or they have been; he, she, or it has been)
1 to live or exist ♦ *Three boys were in the classroom* ♦ *There is a bus stop at the corner* 2 to have a particular description ♦ *She is my teacher* ♦ *You are very tall*

beach *noun* (*plural* **beaches**)
the pebbly or sandy part of the seashore

beacon *noun* (*plural* **beacons**)
a light used as a warning signal

bead *noun* (*plural* **beads**)
1 a small piece of something hard with a hole through it, threaded on a string or wire to make a necklace 2 a small drop of liquid ♦ *She had beads of sweat on her face*

beady *adjective* (**beadier, beadiest**)
like beads, especially describing eyes that are small and bright

beagle *noun* (*plural* **beagles**)
a small hound used for hunting hares

beak *noun* (*plural* **beaks**)
the hard, horny part of a bird's mouth

beaker *noun* (*plural* **beakers**)
1 a tall mug, usually without handles, for drinking 2 (*in Science*) a glass container for pouring liquids

beam ➤ *noun* (*plural* **beams**)
1 a long, thick bar of wood or metal 2 a ray of light or other radiation

beam ➤ *verb* (**beams, beaming, beamed**)
1 to smile very happily 2 to send out a beam of light or radio waves

bean *noun* (*plural* **beans**)
1 a kind of plant with seeds growing in pods 2 the seed or pod of this kind of plant, eaten as food

bear[1] *verb* (**bears, bearing, bore, born** or **borne**)
1 to bear something is to carry or support it 2 to bear something such as a signature is to have or show it ♦ *The letter bore her signature* 3 not to bear something is to be unable to endure or tolerate it ♦ *I can't bear this noise* 4 to bear children is to give birth to them ♦ *She was born in 1950. She has borne three sons*

bear[2] *noun* (*plural* **bears**)
a heavy animal with thick fur and sharp hooked claws

bearable *adjective*
able to be endured; tolerable ♦ *His toothache was hardly bearable*

beard *noun* (*plural* **beards**)
hair on the lower part of a man's face
bearded *adjective* having a beard

bearing *noun* (*plural* **bearings**)
1 your bearing is the way you stand and move 2 the direction or relative position of something
to lose your bearings is to forget where you are in relation to other things

beast *noun* (*plural* **beasts**)
1 any large four-footed animal
2 (*informal*) a person you think is horrid or unkind

beastly *adjective*
(*informal*) horrid, unkind ♦ *I think you are being beastly to me*

beat ➤ *verb* (**beats, beating, beat, beaten**)
1 to beat someone is to hit them repeatedly, especially with a stick 2 to beat someone in a game or match is to do better than them and win it 3 to beat a cooking mixture is to stir it briskly so that it becomes thicker 4 to beat something is to shape or flatten it by hitting it many times 5 to beat is also to make regular movements like your heart does
to beat someone up is to attack them very violently

beat ➤ *noun* (*plural* **beats**)
1 a regular rhythm or stroke, like your heart makes 2 a strong rhythm in pop music 3 the regular route of a police officer

Beaufort scale *noun* (*pronounced* boh-fert skayl)
a scale for wind speed ranging from 0 (calm) to 12 (hurricane)

beautiful *adjective*
very pleasing to look at

beautifully *adverb* in a beautiful or pleasing way

beautify *verb* (**beautifies, beautifying, beautified**) to beautify something or someone is to make them look beautiful

beauty *noun* (*plural* **beauties**)
1 beauty is a quality that gives delight or pleasure, especially to your senses ♦ *They enjoyed the beauty of the sunset* 2 a beauty is a particularly beautiful person or thing

beauty queen *noun* (*plural* **beauty queens**) a woman chosen as the most beautiful in a contest

beaver *noun* (*plural* **beavers**)
1 a brown furry animal with strong teeth and a long flat tail, which builds dams in rivers 2 a member of the most junior section of the Scout Association

becalmed *adjective* unable to sail on because the wind has dropped

became past tense of **become**

because *conjunction* for the reason that ♦ *We were happy because it was a holiday* **because of someone** or **something** for that reason; on account of them ♦ *He limped because of his bad leg*

beckon *verb* (**beckons, beckoning, beckoned**) to beckon to someone is to make a sign asking them to come to you

become *verb* (**becomes, becoming, became, become**)
1 to become is to start being something described ♦ *It gradually became darker* 2 to become someone is to make them look attractive ♦ *That dress becomes you* to ask **what became of someone** or **something** is to wonder what happened to them in the end ♦ *Whatever became of Jim?*

bed *noun* (*plural* **beds**)
1 a bed is a piece of furniture for sleeping on 2 bed is the place where you sleep ♦ *I'm going to bed now* 3 a bed is also a part of a garden where plants are grown 4 the bed of the sea or of a river is the bottom of it

bedclothes *plural noun* sheets and blankets for using on a bed

bedding *noun* things for making a bed, such as sheets and blankets

bedlam *noun* a loud noise or disturbance ♦ *There was bedlam at the playgroup*

bedraggled *adjective* (*pronounced* bi-**drag**-uld) wet and dirty

bedridden *adjective* (*pronounced* bed-rid-en) too ill or injured to get out of bed

bedroom *noun* (*plural* **bedrooms**) a room where you sleep

bedside *noun* the space beside a bed, especially the bed of someone who is ill ♦ *He sat by his son's bedside all night*

bedspread *noun* (*plural* **bedspreads**) a covering put over the top of a bed

bedstead *noun* (*plural* **bedsteads**) the framework of a bed

bedtime *noun* the time when you are supposed to go to bed

bee *noun* (*plural* **bees**) a stinging insect that makes honey

beech *noun* (*plural* **beeches**) a tree with smooth bark and glossy leaves

beef *noun* the meat of an ox, bull, or cow

beefburger *noun* (*plural* **beefburgers**) a hamburger

beefeater *noun* (*plural* **beefeaters**) a guard at the Tower of London

beefy *adjective* (**beefier, beefiest**)
(*informal*) a beefy person is big, with
strong muscles

beehive *noun* (*plural* **beehives**)
a container for bees to live in

beeline *noun*
to make a beeline for something is to go quickly
and directly towards it

been past participle of **be**

beer *noun* (*plural* **beers**)
beer is an alcoholic drink made from malt
and hops

beet *noun* (*plural* **beet** or **beets**)
beet is a plant used as a vegetable or for
making sugar

beetle *noun* (*plural* **beetles**)
an insect with hard, shiny covers over its
wings

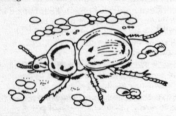

beetroot *noun* (*plural* **beetroot**)
the crimson root of beet used as a
vegetable

before *adverb* and *preposition*
1 earlier; already ♦ *Have you been here
before?* ♦ *They came the day before
yesterday* 2 in front of ♦ *He stood up
before the whole school*

beforehand *adverb*
earlier, or before something else happens
♦ *She had tried to phone me beforehand*
♦ *Let me know beforehand if you want to
come on the picnic*

beg *verb* (**begs, begging, begged**)
1 to beg is to ask people to give you money
2 to beg someone is to ask them seriously
or desperately ♦ *He begged me not to tell
the teacher*
I beg your pardon I didn't hear or understand
what you said; I apologize

began past tense of **begin**

beggar *noun* (*plural* **beggars**)
1 someone who lives by begging
2 (*informal*) a person ♦ *You lucky beggar!*

begin *verb* (**begins, beginning, began, begun**)
to begin something is to start doing it

beginner *noun* (*plural* **beginners**)
someone who is just starting to learn or is
still learning a subject

beginning *noun* (*plural* **beginnings**)
the start of something

begrudge *verb* (**begrudges, begrudging,
begrudged**)
to begrudge something is to grudge or
envy it ♦ *She begrudged her brother's good
luck*

begun past participle of **begin**

behalf *noun*
on behalf of something to help a cause ♦ *They
were collecting money on behalf of cancer
research*
on someone's behalf for them; for their sake
♦ *I have a lawyer acting on my behalf*

behave *verb* (**behaves, behaving, behaved**)
1 to behave well or badly is to act in a good
or bad way ♦ *They behaved very badly at
the party* 2 to show good manners ♦ *Why
can't you behave?*
behaviour *noun* how someone behaves

behead *verb* (**beheads, beheading, beheaded**)
to behead someone is to cut off their head,
as a form of execution

behind ➤ *adverb* and *preposition*
1 at or to the back ♦ *The others are a long
way behind* 2 She hid behind a tree* 2 not
making good progress; late ♦ *I'm behind
with my rent* ♦ *He's behind the rest of the
class in French* 3 supporting ♦ *We're all
behind you*
behind someone's back without them
knowing or approving

behind ➤ *noun* (*plural* **behinds**)
your behind is your bottom ♦ *He kicked me
on the behind*

beige *noun* and *adjective* (*pronounced*
bay*zh*)
a fawn colour

being *noun* (*plural* **beings**)
1 a being is a person or creature of any
kind 2 being is existence ♦ *Experience the
joy of being*

belch ➤ *verb* (**belches, belching, belched**)
1 to belch is to let wind noisily out of your
stomach through your mouth 2 to belch
smoke or fumes is to send out thick smoke
or fumes

belch ➤ *noun* (*plural* **belches**)
the act or sound of belching

belfry *noun* (*plural* **belfries**)
the top part of a tower or steeple, in which
bells hang

belief *noun* (*plural* **beliefs**)
1 a belief is something you believe ♦ *They
have very few beliefs* 2 belief is when you
believe something

believe *verb* (**believes, believing, believed**)
1 to believe something is to think that it is true **2** to believe someone is to think that they are telling the truth **3** to believe in something is to think it is real or important ♦ *Do you believe in ghosts?*
believable *adjective* able to be believed
believer *noun* someone who believes, especially in God

bell *noun* (*plural* **bells**)
a device that makes a ringing sound, especially a cup-shaped metal device with a clapper

bellow *verb* (**bellows, bellowing, bellowed**)
to bellow is to roar or shout

bellows *plural noun*
a device for blowing out air, especially into a fire to make it burn more strongly

belly *noun* (*plural* **bellies**)
1 the abdomen or the stomach of a human **2** the under part of a four-legged animal

belong *verb* (**belongs, belonging, belonged**)
1 to belong to someone is to be their property ♦ *The pencil belongs to me* **2** to belong somewhere is to have a special place where it goes ♦ *The butter belongs in the fridge*

belongings *plural noun*
your belongings are the things that you own

beloved *adjective* (*pronounced* bi-**luvd** or bi-**luv**-id)
greatly loved

below ➤ *preposition*
lower than, under ♦ *We have nice neighbours in the flat below us*

below ➤ *adverb*
at a lower point, or to a lower point ♦ *I'll have the top bunk, and you can sleep below*

belt ➤ *noun* (*plural* **belts**)
1 a strip of material, often leather or cloth, worn round the waist **2** a long narrow area ♦ *As we went further north we met a belt of rain*

belt ➤ *verb* (**belts, belting, belted**)
(*informal*) **1** to belt someone is to hit them hard **2** to belt along is to move very fast

bench *noun* (*plural* **benches**)
1 a long seat **2** a long table for working at

bend ➤ *verb* (**bends, bending, bent**)
1 to bend something is to make it curved or crooked **2** to bend is to become curved or crooked ♦ *The trees were bending in the wind* **3** to bend is also to move the top of your body downwards ♦ *She bent to pick up the cat*

bend ➤ *noun* (*plural* **bends**)
1 a part where something curves or turns **2** a sailor's knot

beneath *preposition* and *adverb*
under ♦ *Beneath the soil there is clay*

benefactor *noun* (*plural* **benefactors**)
someone who gives money or other help
benefaction *noun* a gift of money or other help

benefit *noun* (*plural* **benefits**)
1 a benefit is something that is useful or helpful ♦ *Television is one of the benefits of modern science* **2** benefit is money paid by the government to help people who are poor, sick, or out of work **3** a benefit concert or match is one organized to raise money for a good cause
to give someone the benefit of the doubt is to believe them even though you cannot be sure
beneficial *adjective* useful; giving a benefit

benevolent *adjective*
kind or helpful
benevolence *noun* kindness or being helpful

bent ➤ *adjective*
1 curved or crooked **2** (*slang*) dishonest
to be bent on something is to be determined to do it

bent ➤ *noun*
a bent is a liking or talent for something ♦ *She has quite a bent for acting*

bequeath *verb* (**bequeaths, bequeathing, bequeathed**) (*rhymes with* breathe)
to bequeath something to someone is to leave it to them in a will
bequest *noun* something bequeathed in a will

bereaved *adjective*
a bereaved person is someone with a close relative who has recently died
bereavement *noun* being bereaved

bereft *adjective*
deprived of something ♦ *He was bereft of speech*

beret *noun* (*plural* **berets**) (*pronounced* bair-ay)
a soft, round, flat cap

berry *noun* (*plural* **berries**)
a small, juicy fruit

berserk *adjective*
to go berserk is to become extremely angry or lose control ♦ *The man went berserk and started flinging things around*

berth *noun* (*plural* **berths**)
1 a sleeping place on a ship or train **2** a place where a ship is tied up

beside *preposition*

next to; close to ♦ *A house beside the sea*

to be beside the point is to have nothing to do with what is being talked about ♦ *All your excuses are beside the point*

to be beside yourself is to be very excited or upset ♦ *He was beside himself with anger*

besides ➣ *preposition*

in addition to ♦ *Who came besides you?*

besides ➣ *adverb*

also; in addition to this ♦ *The coat cost too much. Besides, it's the wrong colour*

besiege *verb* (besieges, besieging, besieged) (*pronounced* bi-**seej**)

1 to besiege a place is to surround it with troops until the inhabitants surrender

2 to besiege someone famous is to crowd round them ♦ *The rock group was besieged by hundreds of fans*

best ➣ *adjective* superlative of **good** and **well**

most excellent; most able to do something ♦ *She's the best swimmer in the class*

best ➣ *adverb*

1 in the best way; most ♦ *We'll do what suits you best* **2** most usefully; most wisely ♦ *He is best ignored*

best ➣ *noun*

the best person or thing, or the best people or things ♦ *She was the best at tennis* ♦ *These apples are the best you can buy*

to get the best of someone is to defeat or outwit them

best man *noun*

someone who helps and supports the bridegroom at his wedding

best-seller *noun* (*plural* best-sellers)

a book or other product that has sold in very large numbers

bet ➣ *noun* (*plural* bets)

1 an agreement that you will receive money if you are correct in choosing the winner of a race or in saying something will happen, and will lose money if you are not correct **2** the money you risk losing in a bet

bet ➣ *verb* (bets, betting, bet or betted)

1 to bet, or to bet money, is to make a bet

2 (*informal*) to bet something is to say you are sure about it ♦ *I bet I'm right*

betray *verb* (betrays, betraying, betrayed)

1 to betray someone is to do them harm when they are expecting your support

2 to betray something like a secret is to give it away

betrayal *noun* betraying someone

better ➣ *adjective* comparative of **good** and **well**

1 more excellent ♦ *I need a better bike*

2 to be better is to feel well again after an illness ♦ *Are you better?*

better ➣ *noun* (*plural* betters)

a better person or thing

to get the better of someone is to defeat or outwit them

better ➣ *adverb*

in a better way ♦ *Try to do it better next time*

I had better do something it would be better for me to do it (you can use **we, you**, and so on, instead of **I**)

to be better off is to be more fortunate in some way, for example by having more money

better ➣ *verb* (betters, bettering, bettered)

to better something is to improve on it ♦ *She hopes to better her own record time*

between *preposition and adverb*

within two or more points; among ♦ *Call me between Tuesday and Friday* ♦ *The train runs between London and Glasgow* ♦ *What is the difference between butter and margarine?* ♦ *Divide the sweets between the children* ♦ *The two houses are side by side with a fence between*

beware *verb* (*only in the form* beware)

be careful ♦ *Beware of pickpockets*

bewilder *verb* (bewilders, bewildering, bewildered)

to bewilder someone is to puzzle them completely

bewilderment *noun* being bewildered

bewitch *verb* (bewitches, bewitching, bewitched)

1 to bewitch someone is to put a spell on them **2** to bewitch someone is also to delight them very much ♦ *Sarah's beauty completely bewitched him*

beyond *preposition and adverb*

farther on ♦ *Don't go beyond the end of the street* ♦ *You can see the next valley and the mountains beyond*

bias *noun* (*plural* biases)

1 bias is a preference for one person or side over another ♦ *The referee was accused of bias* **2** bias is also a tendency for a ball to swerve, especially in a game of bowls

biased *adjective* having a bias or preference

bib *noun* (*plural* bibs)

a piece of cloth or plastic put under a baby's chin during meals to protect its clothes from stains

Bible *noun* (*plural* Bibles)

the holy book of Christianity and Judaism

biblical *adjective* to do with the Bible

bicycle *noun* (*plural* **bicycles**)
a two-wheeled vehicle driven by pedals

bid ➤ *noun* (*plural* **bids**)
1 offering an amount you will pay for something, especially at an auction **2** an attempt ♦ *He will make a bid for the world record*

bid ➤ *verb* (**bids, bidding, bid**)
to bid an amount of money is to offer it for something at an auction

bide *verb* (**bides, biding, bided**)
to bide your time is to wait, expecting something to happen that will help you

big *adjective* (**bigger, biggest**)
1 more than the normal size; large
2 important ♦ *This is a big decision*
3 elder ♦ *Have you met my big sister?*

bigamy *noun*
the crime of having two or more wives or husbands at the same time
bigamist *noun* someone who commits bigamy **bigamous** *adjective* to do with bigamy

bike *noun* (*plural* **bikes**)
(*informal*) a bicycle or motor cycle

bikini *noun* (*plural* **bikinis**)
a woman's two-piece bathing costume

bile *noun*
a bitter greenish-brown fluid produced in the liver, that helps the body to digest fat

bilge *noun* (*plural* **bilges**)
1 the bilge is the bottom of a ship **2** bilge is the water that collects inside the bottom of a ship **3** (*slang*) bilge also means nonsense

bilingual *adjective*
speaking two languages well

bill¹ *noun* (*plural* **bills**)
1 an account showing how much money someone owes for something **2** a plan for a new law in parliament **3** a poster **4** a programme of entertainment ♦ *There's a conjurer on the bill*

bill² *noun* (*plural* **bills**)
a bird's beak

billiards *noun*
a game played with long sticks (called *cues*) and three balls on a cloth-covered table

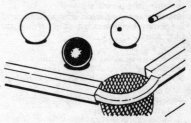

billion *noun* (*plural* **billions**)
a thousand millions (1,000,000,000)
billionth *adjective* and *noun* a thousand-millionth

billow ➤ *noun* (*plural* **billows**)
billows are the large waves on the sea

billow ➤ *verb* (**billows, billowing, billowed**)
to billow is to rise up or move like waves on the sea ♦ *The washing was billowing in the wind*

billy or **billycan** *noun* (*plural* **billies** or **billycans**)
a can with a lid, used by campers, etc. for making hot drinks or cooking food

billy goat *noun* (*plural* **billy goats**)
a male goat

bin *noun* (*plural* **bins**)
a large or deep container

binary *adjective*
involving sets of two; consisting of two parts

binary system *noun*
a system of expressing numbers by using the digits 0 and 1 only. For example, 21 is written 10101

bind *verb* (**binds, binding, bound**)
1 to bind things is to tie them up or tie them together **2** to bind something is to fasten material round it **3** to bind a book is to fasten the pages inside a cover **4** to bind someone is to make them do something or promise something

bingo *noun*
a game played with cards with numbered squares. These are covered or crossed out as the numbers are called out, and the first person to complete the card wins the game

binoculars *plural noun*
a device with lenses for both eyes, for making distant objects seem nearer

biodegradable *adjective*
able to be broken down by bacteria in the environment

biography *noun* (*plural* **biographies**)
the story of a person's life
biographer *noun* a person who writes a biography **biographical** *adjective* to do with biography

biology *noun*
the science or study of living things
biological *adjective* to do with biology
biologist *noun* a person who studies biology

bionic *adjective*
worked by electronic devices, and imitating a living being

biosphere *noun*
the parts of the earth's surface and its atmosphere where living things are found

birch *noun* (*plural* **birches**)
a thin tree with shiny bark and slender branches

bird *noun* (*plural* **birds**)
a feathered animal with two wings and two legs

birdseed *noun*
seeds for caged birds to eat

bird's-eye view *noun*
a general view of something, seen from above

Biro *noun* (*plural* **Biros**)
(*trademark*) a kind of ballpoint pen

birth *noun* (*plural* **births**)
birth is the beginning of a person's life, when they come from their mother's womb

birth certificate *noun* (*plural* **birth certificates**)
a document showing where and when you were born

birth control *noun*
the use of contraceptives to control pregnancies

birthday *noun* (*plural* **birthdays**)
the anniversary of the day someone was born

birthmark *noun* (*plural* **birthmarks**)
a mark which has been on someone's body since they were born

birthplace *noun* (*plural* **birthplaces**)
the place where someone was born

birth rate *noun*
the number of children born in one year for every 1,000 of the population

biscuit *noun* (*plural* **biscuits**)
a flat thin piece of crisp baked pastry like a hard cake

bisect *verb* (**bisects**, **bisecting**, **bisected**)
to bisect something is to divide it into two equal parts

bishop *noun* (*plural* **bishops**)
1 a senior member of the clergy who is in charge of all the churches in a city or district 2 a chess piece shaped like a bishop's mitre

bison *noun* (*plural* **bison**)
a wild ox with shaggy hair

bit *noun* (*plural* **bits**)
1 a small piece or amount of something 2 the part of a horse's bridle that is put into its mouth 3 the part of a tool that cuts or grips
a bit slightly ♦ *I'm a bit worried*
bit by bit gradually
bits and pieces oddments

bit past tense of **bite** *verb*

bitch *noun* (*plural* **bitches**)
1 a female dog, fox, or wolf 2 (*offensive slang*) a spiteful or unpleasant woman

bitchy *adjective* (**bitchier**, **bitchiest**)
spiteful ♦ *Stop making bitchy remarks about Rebecca!*

bite ➤ *verb* (**bites**, **biting**, **bit**, **bitten**)
1 to bite something is to cut it or hold it with your teeth 2 to bite into something is to penetrate it ♦ *The tyres bit into the mud* 3 to accept bait ♦ *The fish are biting* 4 to sting or hurt ♦ *a biting wind*

bite ➤ *noun* (*plural* **bites**)
1 an act of biting 2 a mark or spot made by biting ♦ *You've had an insect bite* 3 a snack ♦ *Would you like a bite?*

bitter *adjective*
1 tasting sour and unpleasant 2 feeling resentful and envious ♦ *They felt bitter about their spoilt holiday* 3 extremely cold ♦ *There was a bitter wind*

black ➤ *adjective* (**blacker**, **blackest**)
1 of the darkest colour, like coal or soot 2 having dark skin 3 dismal; not hopeful ♦ *The outlook is black* 4 very dirty

black ➤ *noun* (*plural* **blacks**)
1 a black colour 2 a person with dark skin

blackberry *noun* (*plural* **blackberries**)
a sweet black berry

blackbird *noun* (*plural* **blackbirds**)
a dark European songbird

blackboard *noun* (*plural* **blackboards**)
a dark board for writing on with chalk

blacken *verb* (**blackens, blackening, blackened**)
1 to blacken something is to make it black
2 to blacken someone's name is to say bad things about them

black eye *noun* (*plural* **black eyes**)
an eye with heavy bruises round it

black hole *noun* (*plural* **black holes**)
(*in Astronomy*) a region in space with such strong gravity that no light escapes

black ice *noun*
thin transparent ice on roads

blackmail *verb* (**blackmails, blackmailing, blackmailed**)
to get money from someone by threatening to reveal something that they want to keep secret

black market *noun*
a black market in goods is illegal trading in them

blackout *noun* (*plural* **blackouts**)
1 losing consciousness or memory for a short time **2** a time when lights are kept hidden or turned off

blacksmith *noun* (*plural* **blacksmiths**)
someone who makes and repairs things made of iron, and fits shoes on horses

bladder *noun* (*plural* **bladders**)
1 the bladder is the bag-like part of the body in which urine collects **2** a bladder is also an inflatable bag inside a football

blade *noun* (*plural* **blades**)
1 the sharp part of a device for cutting, such as a knife or sword **2** the flat, wide part of an oar or propeller **3** a long narrow leaf of grass

blame ➤ *verb* (**blames, blaming, blamed**)
to blame someone is to say that they have done something wrong ◆ *My brother broke the window but they blamed me*

blame ➤ *noun* to get the blame for something is to be blamed for it
to be to blame is to be the person who has done something wrong

blancmange *noun* (*plural* **blancmanges**) (*pronounced* bla-**monj**)
blancmange is a pudding like a jelly made with milk

blank ➤ *adjective*
1 not written, drawn, or printed on ◆ *The piece of paper was blank* **2** without interest or expression ◆ *His face looked blank*
to go blank is to suddenly forget everything ◆ *When he asked me the way, my mind went blank*

blank ➤ *noun* (*plural* **blanks**)
1 an empty space **2** a blank cartridge
to draw a blank is to fail to achieve what you wanted

blank cartridge *noun* (*plural* **blank cartridges**)
a cartridge which makes a noise but does not fire a bullet

blanket *noun* (*plural* **blankets**)
a large piece of thick cloth, used as a warm covering for a bed

blank verse *noun*
verse which does not rhyme at the ends of lines

blare *verb* (**blares, blaring, blared**)
to blare is to make a harsh, loud sound

blaspheme *verb* (**blasphemes, blaspheming, blasphemed**)
to blaspheme is to talk without respect about sacred things
blasphemous *adjective* disrespectful about sacred things **blasphemy** *noun* blaspheming

blast ➤ *noun* (*plural* **blasts**)
1 a strong rush of wind or air **2** a sharp or loud noise ◆ *The referee gave a long blast of his whistle*

blast ➤ *verb* (**blasts, blasting, blasted**)
to blast something is to blow it up with explosives

blast-off *noun*
the launch of a spacecraft

blaze ➤ *noun* (*plural* **blazes**)
a very bright flame, fire, or light

blaze ➤ *verb* (**blazes, blazing, blazed**)
1 to blaze is to burn or shine brightly **2** to blaze with a feeling is to feel it very strongly ◆ *He was blazing with anger*
to blaze a trail is to show the way for others to follow

blazer *noun* (*plural* **blazers**)
a kind of jacket, often with a badge on the front

bleach ➤ *noun* (*plural* **bleaches**)
a substance used to clean things or make clothes white

bleach ➤ *verb* (**bleaches, bleaching, bleached**)
to bleach something is to make it white

bleak *adjective* (**bleaker, bleakest**)
1 bare and cold ♦ *They were walking up a bleak hillside* **2** dreary and miserable ♦ *The future looks bleak*

bleary *adjective* (**blearier, bleariest**)
having eyes that are sore and do not see clearly
blearily *adverb* with bleary eyes ♦ *He looked at me blearily*

bleat ➤ *noun* (*plural* **bleats**)
the cry of a sheep or goat

bleat ➤ *verb* (**bleats, bleating, bleated**)
to make a bleat

bleed *verb* (**bleeds, bleeding, bled**)
1 to lose blood **2** to draw blood from someone or an animal **3** to draw fluid from something ♦ *You will need to bleed the radiators*

bleep *noun* (*plural* **bleeps**)
a small, high sound such as some digital watches make

blemish *noun* (*plural* **blemishes**)
a flaw or imperfection

blend ➤ *verb* (**blends, blending, blended**)
to blend things is to mix them together smoothly or easily

blend ➤ *noun* (*plural* **blends**)
a smooth mixture

bless *verb* (**blesses, blessing, blessed**)
1 to bless someone is to wish or bring them happiness **2** to bless someone is also to call them holy

blessing *noun* (*plural* **blessings**)
1 a prayer or act of blessing someone
2 something you are glad of or happy about ♦ *It's a blessing that they are safe*

blew past tense of **blow** *verb*

blight *noun* (*plural* **blights**)
1 blight is a plant disease **2** a blight is an evil influence

blind ➤ *adjective* (**blinder, blindest**)
1 unable to see **2** without thought or understanding

blind ➤ *verb* (**blinds, blinding, blinded**)
to blind someone is to make them blind

blind ➤ *noun* (*plural* **blinds**)
1 a screen for a window **2** something used to hide the truth ♦ *His story of missing the train was just a blind*

blind alley *noun* (*plural* **blind alleys**)
a road which is closed at one end

blindfold ➤ *noun* (*plural* **blindfolds**)
a piece of cloth used to cover someone's eyes so that they cannot see where they are or what is happening

blindfold ➤ *verb* (**blindfolds, blindfolding, blindfolded**)
to blindfold someone is to cover their eyes with a blindfold

blindfold ➤ *adjective*
with a blindfold over the eyes

blink *verb* (**blinks, blinking, blinked**)
to blink is to shut and open your eyes quickly

bliss *noun*
bliss is great happiness
blissful *adjective* very happy **blissfully** *adverb* very happily

blister *noun* (*plural* **blisters**)
a swelling like a bubble on the skin

blitz *noun* (*plural* **blitzes**)
a sudden violent attack, especially from aircraft

blizzard *noun* (*plural* **blizzards**)
a severe snowstorm

bloated *adjective*
swollen or puffed out

blob *noun* (*plural* **blobs**)
a small round lump of something like paint or ice cream

block ➤ *noun* (*plural* **blocks**)
1 a solid piece of something hard such as wood **2** an obstruction in a pipe or on a road **3** a large building or group of buildings with streets all around it

block ➤ *verb* (**blocks, blocking, blocked**)
1 to block something is to get in the way of it ♦ *Tall buildings blocked our view* **2** to block something like a pipe or drain is to prevent water flowing through it

blockade *noun* (*plural* **blockades**)
a kind of siege, especially of a seaport

blockage *noun* (*plural* **blockages**)
1 something that stops up a pipe or drain
2 a blocked state ♦ *Roadworks are causing blockages in the traffic*

block capitals or **block letters** *plural noun*
large capital letters

blond or **blonde** *adjective* (**blonder, blondest**)
fair-haired

blonde *noun* (*plural* **blondes**)
a fair-haired girl or woman

blood *noun*
1 blood is the red liquid that flows through the veins and arteries **2** something like noble or royal blood means ancestors who were noble or royal
to do something in cold blood is to do it deliberately and cruelly

blood donor *noun* (*plural* **blood donors**)
someone who gives some blood for use in
transfusions

bloodhound *noun* (*plural* **bloodhounds**)
a large breed of dog which can track people
over long distances by following their
scent

bloodshed *noun*
bloodshed is the killing and injuring of
people

bloodshot *adjective*
eyes are bloodshot when they are streaked
with red from being strained or tired

bloodstream *noun* the bloodstream is the
blood flowing round your body

bloodthirsty *adjective* (**bloodthirstier,
bloodthirstiest**)
enjoying bloodshed or killing

bloody *adjective* (**bloodier, bloodiest**)
1 bleeding **2** involving bloodshed

bloody-minded *adjective*
deliberately awkward or unhelpful

bloom ➤ *verb* (**blooms, blooming, bloomed**)
to bloom is to produce flowers ♦ *Look! The
roses have bloomed!*

bloom ➤ *noun* (*plural* **blooms**)
a bloom is a flower
in bloom producing flowers

blossom ➤ *noun* (*plural* **blossoms**)
1 a blossom is a flower, especially on a
fruit tree **2** blossom is a mass of flowers on
a tree

blossom ➤ *verb* (**blossoms, blossoming,
blossomed**)
1 to blossom is to produce flowers **2** to
blossom is also to develop into something
very fine or good ♦ *She has blossomed into
a lovely singer*

blot ➤ *noun* (*plural* **blots**)
1 a spot or blob of ink **2** a flaw or fault

blot ➤ *verb* (**blots, blotting, blotted**)
1 to blot something is to make a blot on it
2 to blot paper is to dry it with blotting
paper
to blot something out is to remove it or make
it invisible
to blot your copybook is to spoil your good
reputation

blotch *noun* (*plural* **blotches**)
an untidy patch of colour
blotchy *adjective* having lots of blotches

blotting paper *noun*
blotting paper is thick, soft paper for
soaking up ink blots on paper

blouse *noun* (*plural* **blouses**)
a loose piece of clothing like a shirt, worn
by girls and women

blow ➤ *noun* (*plural* **blows**)
1 a hard knock or hit **2** a shock or setback
♦ *Losing so much money was a great blow*
3 the action of blowing

blow ➤ *verb* (**blows, blowing, blew, blown**)
1 to blow is to force out air from your
mouth or nose ♦ *He blew on his painting to
dry it* **2** to blow something is to form it by
blowing ♦ *Let's blow bubbles* **3** to blow
something such as a whistle is to make a
sound with it **4** to blow is to melt or break,
as a fuse or light bulb does
to blow away or **to blow off** is to be driven away
in the wind
to blow something up is to destroy it with an
explosion
to blow up is to be destroyed in an explosion

blowlamp or **blowtorch** *noun* (*plural*
blowlamps or **blowtorches**)
a device for directing a strong flame at a
surface, especially to remove old paint

blue ➤ *adjective* (**bluer, bluest**)
1 of the colour of a bright cloudless sky
2 sad and miserable ♦ *I'm feeling blue*
3 rude or obscene ♦ *They were telling blue
jokes*

blue ➤ *noun* (*plural* **blues**)
a blue colour
out of the blue with no warning ♦ *My friend
turned up out of the blue*

bluebell *noun* (*plural* **bluebells**)
a blue wild flower

bluebottle *noun* (*plural* **bluebottles**)
a large fly that makes a loud buzz

blueprint *noun* (*plural* **blueprints**)
a detailed plan of something

blues *plural noun*
blues is a type of music that is often sad
to get the blues is to feel sad and miserable

bluff ➤ *verb* (**bluffs, bluffing, bluffed**)
to bluff someone is to make them think
something that is not true

bluff ➤ *noun* (*plural* **bluffs**)
a bluff is something that someone says or does to bluff someone else, for example an empty promise or threat ♦ *He said he'd report us, but that was just a bluff*

to call someone's bluff is to challenge them to do what they have threatened to do

blunder *noun* (*plural* **blunders**)
a careless mistake

blunt *adjective* (**blunter, bluntest**)
1 having an edge that is smooth and not good for cutting 2 saying what you mean without being very tactful

blur ➤ *verb* (**blurs, blurring, blurred**)
to blur something is to make it unclear or smeared

blur ➤ *noun* (*plural* **blurs**)
a smudge or smear

blush *verb* (**blushes, blushing, blushed**)
to have a strong pink tinge in the face, especially when you are embarrassed

bluster *verb* (**blusters, blustering, blustered**)
1 to bluster is to blow in gusts, as the wind does 2 to bluster is to boast or make threats that don't mean very much

blustery *adjective*
blowing like the wind; windy

boa or **boa constrictor** *noun* (*plural* **boas** or **boa constrictors**)
a large South American snake that crushes its prey

boar *noun* (*plural* **boars**)
1 a wild pig 2 a male pig

board ➤ *noun* (*plural* **boards**)
1 a board is a flat piece of wood, used in building 2 a board is also a flat piece of wood or cardboard used to play games with, for example a dartboard or a chess board 3 board is daily meals supplied in return for money or work 4 a board is a group of people who run an organization
on board aboard a ship

board ➤ *verb* (**boards, boarding, boarded**)
1 to board a ship or train or aircraft is to get on it for a journey 2 to board is to get meals and accommodation

to board something up is to cover it with boards

boarder *noun* (*plural* **boarders**)
1 a child who lives at a boarding school during the term 2 a lodger

board game *noun* (*plural* **board games**)
a game played on a board, such as chess or draughts

boarding house *noun* (*plural* **boarding houses**)
a house where people rent rooms to live in

boarding school *noun* (*plural* **boarding schools**)
a school in which the pupils live during the term

boast *verb* (**boasts, boasting, boasted**)
to boast about something that you own or that you have done is to talk proudly about it

boastful *adjective* liking to boast **boastfully** *adverb* in a boasting way

boat *noun* (*plural* **boats**)
a vehicle designed to float and travel on water

to be in the same boat is to share the same problems or difficulties

boating *noun*
going out in a boat for fun

boat people *plural noun*
refugees who leave their country by sea

bob *verb* (**bobs, bobbing, bobbed**)
to move gently up and down, like something floating on water

bobble *noun* (*plural* **bobbles**)
a small round ornament made of something soft such as wool

bobsled or **bobsleigh** *noun* (*plural* **bobsleds** or **bobsleighs**)
a large sledge with two sets of runners

bodice *noun* (*plural* **bodices**)
the upper part of a woman's dress

bodily ➤ *adjective*
to do with your body

bodily ➤ *adverb*
with your whole body; as a whole ♦ *He was picked up bodily and bundled into the car*

body *noun* (*plural* **bodies**)
1 the body is the flesh and bones and other parts of a person or animal 2 a body is a dead person or corpse 3 the body of something is the main part of it 4 a body of people is a group of them in one place 5 a body is a distinct object or piece of matter ♦ *Stars and planets are heavenly bodies*

bodyguard *noun* (*plural* **bodyguards**)
a guard who protects someone's life

bog *noun* (*plural* **bogs**)
bog or a bog is an area of wet, spongy ground

boggy *adjective* wet and spongy, like a bog

bogus *adjective*
false; not genuine ♦ *He gave a name that turned out to be bogus*

boil[1] *verb* (**boils, boiling, boiled**)
1 to boil a liquid is to heat it until it starts to bubble and give off vapour **2** to boil is to start bubbling, like water **3** to boil something such as potatoes or eggs is to cook them in boiling water
to be boiling (*informal*) is to be very hot, like the weather ♦ *It was boiling when we reached our hotel*
to bring a liquid to the boil is to heat it until it boils
boil[2] *noun* (*plural* **boils**)
an inflamed spot on the skin
boiler *noun* (*plural* **boilers**)
a container for heating water or making steam
boiling point *noun* (*plural* **boiling points**)
the temperature at which something boils
boisterous *adjective*
noisy and lively
bold *adjective* (**bolder, boldest**)
1 brave and adventurous **2** clear and easy to see
bollard *noun* (*plural* **bollards**)
1 a short thick post to direct or keep out traffic **2** a short thick post on a ship or quay, to which ropes are tied
bolster ➤ *noun* (*plural* **bolsters**)
a long pillow
bolster ➤ *verb* (**bolsters, bolstering, bolstered**)
to bolster something such as a feeling is to increase it ♦ *Their success has bolstered their confidence*
to bolster something up is to support it when it is weak
bolt ➤ *noun* (*plural* **bolts**)
1 a sliding bar for fastening a door or window **2** a thick metal pin for fastening things together **3** a sliding bar that opens and closes the breech of a rifle **4** a flash of lightning
a bolt from the blue an unwelcome surprise
bolt ➤ *verb* (**bolts, bolting, bolted**)
1 to bolt a door or window is to fasten it with a bolt **2** to bolt is to run away in panic, as a horse does **3** to bolt food is to swallow it too quickly
bomb ➤ *noun* (*plural* **bombs**)
a container with explosives, which blows up when it is detonated
bomb ➤ *verb* (**bombs, bombing, bombed**)
to bomb people or a place is to attack them with bombs
bombard *verb* (**bombards, bombarding, bombarded**)
1 to bombard a place is to attack it with heavy gunfire **2** to bombard someone with questions or complaints is to direct a large number of questions or complaints at them
bombardment *noun* a heavy attack with guns
bomber *noun* (*plural* **bombers**)
1 an aircraft built to drop bombs **2** a person who throws or plants bombs
bond *noun* (*plural* **bonds**)
1 something that binds or restrains people **2** something that brings people together, such as a common interest
bondage *noun*
bondage is being a slave
bone *noun* (*plural* **bones**)
a bone is one of the hard pieces of a skeleton
to have a bone to pick with someone is to have a reason to argue with them about something
bonfire *noun* (*plural* **bonfires**)
a large fire lit out of doors
bonnet *noun* (*plural* **bonnets**)
1 the hinged cover over the front part of a car **2** a round hat usually tied under someone's chin
bonus *noun* (*plural* **bonuses**)
1 an extra payment that someone gets for their work **2** an extra advantage or reward
bony *adjective* (**bonier, boniest**)
1 thin and hard, like a bone **2** having bones without much flesh on them
boo *verb* (**boos, booing, booed**)
to shout disapproval
booby *noun* (*plural* **boobies**)
a stupid or childish person
booby prize *noun* (*plural* **booby prizes**)
a prize given to someone who comes last in a contest
booby trap *noun* (*plural* **booby traps**)
something designed to hit or injure someone when they do not expect it
book ➤ *noun* (*plural* **books**)
a set of sheets of paper, usually with printing or writing on, fastened together inside a cover
book ➤ *verb* (**books, booking, booked**)
1 to book a place in a theatre, or hotel, or a seat on a train, is to reserve it **2** to book something is to record it in a book or list
to book in is to record that you have arrived in a place such as a hotel
bookcase *noun* (*plural* **bookcases**)
a piece of furniture with shelves for holding books
bookkeeping *noun*
bookkeeping is recording details of money you receive and spend

booklet *noun* (*plural* **booklets**)
a small book with paper covers

bookmaker *noun* (*plural* **bookmakers**)
a person whose business is taking bets,
especially bets made on horse races

bookmark *noun* (*plural* **bookmarks**)
something to mark a place in a book

boom ➤ *noun* (*plural* **booms**)
1 a deep hollow sound **2** a time when
people are well off **3** a long pole at the
bottom of a sail to keep it stretched **4** a
long pole carrying a microphone

boom ➤ *verb* (**booms, booming, boomed**)
1 to boom is to make a deep hollow sound,
like a heavy gun **2** to boom is also to be
prosperous ♦ *Business is booming*

boomerang *noun* (*plural* **boomerangs**)
a curved stick which returns to its thrower
if it misses the target. It is used as a
hunting weapon by Australian
Aboriginals

boost *verb* (**boosts, boosting, boosted**)
to boost something is to increase its size or
value or power ♦ *Their success has boosted
their reputation*

booster *noun* (*plural* **boosters**)
1 something that increases the power of a
system, especially a radio or television
transmitter **2** an additional engine or
rocket for a spacecraft **3** an additional
dose of a vaccine

boot ➤ *noun* (*plural* **boots**)
1 a tall shoe that covers the ankle or leg
2 the space for luggage at the back of a car

boot ➤ *verb* (**boots, booting, booted**)
1 to boot someone is to kick them hard
2 to boot a computer is to switch it on and
start it

booth *noun* (*plural* **booths**)
a small compartment for a special
purpose, such as making a telephone call

border *noun* (*plural* **borders**)
1 the border between two countries is the
line where they meet ♦ *We're about to
cross the Scottish border* **2** an edge
♦ *There is a black border around the
poster* **3** a flower bed

borderline *adjective*
only just acceptable or valid

bore[1] ➤ *verb* (**bores, boring, bored**)
1 to bore a hole is to drill it through
something **2** to bore someone is to make
them feel tired and uninterested

bore ➤ *noun* (*plural* **bores**)
a tedious or uninteresting person or thing

bore[2] past tense of **bear** *verb*

boredom *noun*
a feeling of tiredness and lack of interest

borehole *noun* (*plural* **boreholes**)
a deep narrow hole that engineers make in
the ground when they are looking for
water or oil.

boring *adjective*
tedious and uninteresting ♦ *The book was
really boring*

born or **borne** past participle of **bear** *verb*

borough *noun* (*plural* **boroughs**)
(*pronounced* **bu**-ro)
an important town or district with its own
local council

borrow *verb* (**borrows, borrowing, borrowed**)
to borrow something is to have it for a time
and then return it to its owner

bosom *noun* (*plural* **bosoms**)
a woman's breasts

boss ➤ *noun* (*plural* **bosses**)
(*informal*) a person who runs a business or
group of workers

boss ➤ *verb* (**bosses, bossing, bossed**)
(*informal*) to boss someone is to order
them around

bossy *adjective* (**bossier, bossiest**)
(*informal*) fond of ordering people about

botany *noun*
botany is the study of plants
botanical *adjective* to do with botany or
plants **botanist** *noun* someone who studies
plants

both ➤ *adjective* and *pronoun*
all of two, not just one ♦ *I want them both*

both ➤ *adverb*
you use **both** with **and** to say two things
about something or someone ♦ *He is both
friendly and helpful*

bother ➤ *verb* (**bothers, bothering, bothered**)
1 to bother someone is to cause them
trouble or worry **2** to be bothered to do
something is to take trouble over it

bother ➤ *noun*
bother is trouble or worry

bottle ➤ *noun* (*plural* **bottles**)
a glass or plastic container with a narrow
neck for holding liquids

bottle ➤ *verb* (**bottles, bottling, bottled**)
to bottle something is to put it in a bottle
to bottle something up is to keep something
you are worried about to yourself

bottle bank *noun* (*plural* **bottle banks**)
a large tank or drum for putting glass
bottles and jars in for recycling

bottleneck *noun* (*plural* **bottlenecks**)
a place where traffic is slowed down or
stuck by a blockage or hazard

bottom *noun* (*plural* **bottoms**)
1 the bottom of something is its lowest
point 2 the bottom of a garden is the
farther end of it, away from the house
3 your bottom is the part of you that you
sit on, also called your buttocks

bottomless *adjective*
1 very deep 2 not seeming to have any
limit ♦ *I don't have a bottomless purse*

bougainvillea *noun* (*plural* **bougainvilleas**)
(*pronounced* boo-gan-**vil**-ia)
a brightly coloured tropical shrub

bough *noun* (*plural* **boughs**) (*rhymes with*
cow)
a large branch of a tree that reaches out
from the trunk

bought past tense and past participle of **buy**
verb

boulder *noun* (*plural* **boulders**)
a large smooth stone

bounce ➤ *verb* (**bounces, bouncing, bounced**)
1 to bounce is to spring back when thrown
against something, like a rubber ball 2 to
bounce something like a ball is to throw it
so that it bounces

bounce ➤ *noun* (*plural* **bounces**)
1 a bounce is the action of bouncing
2 bounce is liveliness, such as a young
child or puppy has
bouncy *adjective* lively, energetic

bouncing *adjective*
lively and healthy ♦ *She has a bouncing
baby brother*

bound [1] past tense and past participle of
bind *verb*

bound [2] *adjective*
to be bound for a place is to be travelling
towards it ♦ *This train is bound for
London*
to be bound to do something is to have to do it
or be likely to do it ♦ *He is bound to come*

bound [3] ➤ *verb* (**bounds, bounding, bounded**)
to bound is to leap or to run with leaping
steps

bound ➤ *noun* (*plural* **bounds**)
a leaping movement

boundary *noun* (*plural* **boundaries**)
1 a line that marks a limit 2 a hit to the
outer edge of a cricket field

bounds *plural noun*
out of bounds a place where you are not
allowed to go ♦ *The teachers' common
room is out of bounds to pupils*

bouquet *noun* (*plural* **bouquets**)
(*pronounced* boo-**kay** or boh-**kay**)
a smartly arranged bunch of flowers

bout *noun* (*plural* **bouts**) (*pronounced* bowt)
1 a period of illness ♦ *I've just had a bout
of flu* 2 a boxing or wrestling fight

boutique *noun* (*plural* **boutiques**)
(*pronounced* boo-**teek**)
a small shop, especially one that sells
fashionable clothes

bow [1] *noun* (*plural* **bows**) (*rhymes with* go)
1 a knot made with loops 2 the stick used
for playing a stringed instrument such as
a violin or cello 3 a device for shooting
arrows

bow [2] *noun* (*plural* **bows**) (*rhymes with* cow)
the front part of a ship

bow [3] ➤ *verb* (**bows, bowing, bowed**) (*rhymes
with* cow)
to bow is to bend your body forwards to
show respect or submission

bow ➤ *noun* (*plural* **bows**) (*rhymes with*
cow)
a movement of bowing your body ♦ *The
pianist gave a bow*

bowels *plural noun*
the bowels are the intestines

bowl [1] *noun* (*plural* **bowls**)
1 a deep round dish for eating from 2 the
rounded part of a spoon 3 a wooden or
hard rubber ball used in the game of bowls

bowl [2] *verb* (**bowls, bowling, bowled**)
(*in Cricket*) 1 to bowl is to send the ball
towards the batsman 2 to bowl someone
is to get them out by hitting the wicket
with the ball

bow-legged *adjective*
having legs that curve outwards at the
knees; bandy

bowler *noun* (*plural* **bowlers**)
1 someone who bowls in cricket 2 a hat
with a rounded top

bowling *noun*
1 bowling is the game of bowls 2 bowling
is also another game, in which you have to
knock down skittles with a ball you roll
down an alley 3 the action of throwing a
cricket ball

bowls *plural noun*
a game played on a smooth piece of grass, in which you roll heavy balls towards a white target ball called the 'jack'

bow tie *noun* (*plural* **bow ties**)
a tie in the form of a bow, worn by men as part of formal dress

box ➤ *noun* (*plural* **boxes**)
1 a container made of wood or cardboard 2 a compartment or special place in a theatre or lawcourt ♦ *The policeman got into the witness box* 3 a hut or shelter ♦ *There was a soldier in the sentry box* 4 an evergreen shrub

box ➤ *verb* (**boxes, boxing, boxed**)
1 to box is to fight with the fists 2 to box something is to put it into a box

boxer *noun* (*plural* **boxers**)
1 someone who boxes 2 a breed of dog that looks like a bulldog

Boxing Day *noun* (*plural* **Boxing Days**)
the first weekday after Christmas Day

box number *noun* (*plural* **box numbers**)
a number used as an address in replying to newspaper advertisements

box office *noun* (*plural* **box offices**)
a place where you can buy seats for the theatre or cinema

boy *noun* (*plural* **boys**)
a male child
boyhood *noun* the time of being a boy **boyish** *adjective* like a boy

boycott *verb* (**boycotts, boycotting, boycotted**)
to boycott something is to refuse to have anything to do with it ♦ *They boycotted the buses when the fares went up*

boyfriend *noun* (*plural* **boyfriends**)
a person's regular male friend or lover

bra *noun* (*plural* **bras**)
(*informal*) a piece of underwear worn by women to support their breasts

brace *noun* (*plural* **braces**)
1 a device for holding something in place 2 a wire device for straightening the teeth

bracelet *noun* (*plural* **bracelets**)
a small band or chain worn round the wrist

braces *plural noun*
braces are a pair of stretching straps worn over the shoulders to hold trousers up

bracken *noun*
bracken is a kind of large fern that grows in open country

bracket *noun* (*plural* **brackets**)
1 a kind of punctuation mark used in pairs round words or figures to separate them from what comes before and after. Brackets are round ( ) or square [ ] 2 a support attached to a wall to hold up a shelf or light fitting

brag *verb* (**brags, bragging, bragged**)
to brag is to boast

braid *noun* (*plural* **braids**)
1 a plait 2 a decorative ribbon or band

braille *noun*
braille is a system of writing or printing using raised dots, which blind people can read by touch

brain *noun* (*plural* **brains**)
1 your brain is the part inside the top of your head that controls your body 2 brain also means a person's mind or intelligence ♦ *They really didn't have much brain*

brainy *adjective* (**brainier, brainiest**)
(*informal*) clever, intelligent ♦ *She's the brainiest child in the school*

brake *noun* (*plural* **brakes**)
a device for making a vehicle stop or slow down

bramble *noun* (*plural* **brambles**)
a bramble is a blackberry bush or a prickly bush like it

branch ➤ *noun* (*plural* **branches**)
1 a part that sticks out from the trunk of a tree 2 a part of a railway or river or road that leads off from the main part 3 a part of a large organization

branch ➤ *verb* (**branches, branching, branched**)
to branch is to form a branch
to branch out is to start doing something new

brand ➤ *noun* (*plural* **brands**)
a particular make or kind of goods ♦ *Just get a cheap brand of tea*

brand ➤ *verb* (**brands, branding, branded**)
to brand sheep or cattle is to mark them with a hot iron

brandish *verb* (**brandishes, brandishing, brandished**)
to brandish something is to wave it about

brand-new *adjective*
completely new

brandy *noun* (*plural* **brandies**)
brandy is a kind of strong alcoholic drink

brass *noun*
1 brass is an alloy made from copper and zinc 2 brass also means the wind instruments made of brass, such as trumpets and trombones

brass band *noun* (*plural* **brass bands**)
a musical band made up of brass instruments

brassière *noun* (*plural* **brassières**) (*pronounced* **braz**-i-er)
a piece of underwear worn by women to support their breasts

brassy *adjective* (**brassier, brassiest**)
1 having the colour of brass 2 loud and harsh ♦ *We heard a brassy laugh* 3 cheeky and showy

brave ➤ *adjective* (**braver, bravest**)
ready to face danger or suffering

brave ➤ *noun* (*plural* **braves**)
a Native American warrior
bravery *noun* being brave

brawl *noun* (*plural* **brawls**)
a noisy quarrel or fight

brawn *noun*
brawn is physical strength

brawny *adjective* (**brawnier, brawniest**)
having a strong body and muscles

bray *verb* (**brays, braying, brayed**)
to bray is to make a noise like a donkey

brazen *adjective*
1 made of brass 2 impudent, shameless

brazier *noun* (*plural* **braziers**) (*pronounced* **bray-zi-er**)
a metal container holding hot coals

breach *noun* (*plural* **breaches**)
1 the breaking of an agreement or rule 2 a gap

bread *noun*
1 bread is food made by baking flour and water, usually with yeast 2 (*slang*) bread is also money

breadth *noun* (*plural* **breadths**)
a thing's breadth is its width from side to side

breadwinner *noun* (*plural* **breadwinners**)
the member of a family who earns most of the money

break ➤ *verb* (**breaks, breaking, broke, broken**)
1 to break something is to make it go into several pieces by hitting it or dropping it 2 to break is to stop working properly ♦ *I think my watch must have broken* 3 to break a law or rule or promise is to fail to keep it or observe it 4 the weather breaks when it changes after being hot 5 waves break over rocks when they fall and froth over them 6 a boy's voice breaks when it

starts to go deeper at about the age of 14 7 to break a record is to do better than the previous holder, for example in athletics

to break down is to stop working properly, as a machine does

to break off is to stop doing something for a time ♦ *We broke off for lunch*

to break out is to start and spread rapidly, like a disease

to break the news is to make it known

to break up 1 is to separate, when friends leave one another 2 is to finish school at the end of term

break ➤ *noun* (*plural* **breaks**)
1 a broken place; a gap 2 a sudden dash 3 a short rest from work 4 (*informal*) a piece of luck; a fair chance ♦ *Give me a break*

breakable *adjective*
easy to break ♦ *Be careful with that box – there are breakable things in it*

breakage *noun* (*plural* **breakages**)
something that is broken ♦ *All breakages must be paid for*

breakdown *noun* (*plural* **breakdowns**)
1 a sudden failure to work, especially by a car ♦ *We had a breakdown on the motorway* 2 a failure or collapse of an organization or arrangement ♦ *There has been a breakdown of communications* 3 a collapse from mental exhaustion 4 a detailed look at the parts of something to make it easier to understand ♦ *The paper had a breakdown of the season's football results*

breaker *noun* (*plural* **breakers**)
a wave breaking on the shore

breakfast *noun* (*plural* **breakfasts**)
breakfast is the first meal of the day

breakneck *adjective*
dangerously fast ♦ *He drove at breakneck speed*

breakthrough *noun* (*plural* **breakthroughs**)
an important piece of progress, for example in medical research

breakwater *noun* (*plural* **breakwaters**)
a wall built out into the sea to protect a harbour or coast against heavy waves

breast *noun* (*plural* **breasts**)
1 one of the two parts of a woman's body where milk is produced 2 a person's or animal's chest

breaststroke *noun*
a stroke you use when swimming on your front, by pushing the arms forward and bringing them round and back

breath noun (plural **breaths**) (pronounced breth)
the air that you breathe
to be out of breath is to gasp for air after exercise
to take someone's breath away is to surprise or delight them

breathalyser noun (plural **breathalysers**)
a device to measure the amount of alcohol in someone's breath
breathalyse verb to breathalyse someone is to test their breath with a breathalyser

breathe verb (**breathes, breathing, breathed**) (pronounced breeth)
to breathe is to take air into your lungs through your nose or mouth and send it out again

breather noun (plural **breathers**)
(informal) a pause for a rest ♦ We all need a breather

breathless adjective
short of breath

breathtaking adjective
extremely beautiful or delightful

bred past tense and past participle of **breed** verb

breech noun (plural **breeches**)
the part of a gun barrel where the bullets are put in

breeches plural noun (pronounced brich-iz)
trousers, especially trousers that fit tightly at the knee

breed ➤ verb (**breeds, breeding, bred**)
1 to breed is to produce offspring 2 to breed animals is to keep them so as to get young ones from them 3 to breed something like illness or poverty is to cause it

breed ➤ noun (plural **breeds**)
a variety of similar animals

breeder noun (plural **breeders**)
someone who breeds animals

breeder reactor noun (plural **breeder reactors**)
a nuclear reactor that creates more radioactive material than it uses

breeze noun (plural **breezes**)
a gentle wind

breeze-block noun (plural **breeze-blocks**)
a lightweight building-block made of cinders and cement

breezy adjective (**breezier, breeziest**)
1 slightly windy 2 bright and cheerful

brethren plural noun
(old use) brothers

brevity noun
being brief or short

brew verb (**brews, brewing, brewed**)
1 to brew beer or tea is to make it 2 to be brewing is to start or develop ♦ Trouble is brewing

brewer noun (plural **brewers**)
someone whose work is to make beer

brewery noun (plural **breweries**)
a place where beer is made

briar noun (plural **briars**)
another spelling of brier

bribe ➤ noun (plural **bribes**)
a bribe is money or a gift offered to someone to make them do something

bribe ➤ verb (**bribes, bribing, bribed**)
to bribe someone is to give them a bribe
bribery noun bribing someone

brick noun (plural **bricks**)
1 a small hard block of baked clay used in building 2 a rectangular block of something

bricklayer noun (plural **bricklayers**)
a worker who builds with bricks

bride noun (plural **brides**)
a woman on her wedding day
bridal adjective to do with brides

bridegroom noun (plural **bridegrooms**)
a man on his wedding day

bridesmaid noun (plural **bridesmaids**)
a girl or unmarried woman who attends the bride at a wedding

bridge noun (plural **bridges**)
1 a bridge is a structure built over a river, railway, or road, to allow people to cross it 2 the bridge of a ship is the high platform above the deck, from where the ship is controlled 3 the bridge of your nose is the bony upper part of your nose 4 bridge is a card game rather like whist

bridle noun (plural **bridles**)
the part of a horse's harness that controls its head

bridle path noun (plural **bridle paths**)
a path for people on horseback

brief ➤ adjective (**briefer, briefest**)
lasting a short time
in brief in a few words

brief ➤ *noun* (*plural* **briefs**)
a brief is a set of instructions about a job to be done, especially one given to a lawyer about a case

brief ➤ *verb* (**briefs, briefing, briefed**)
to brief someone is to give them instructions about a job to be done

briefcase *noun* (*plural* **briefcases**)
a flat case for keeping documents and papers in

briefs *plural noun*
short underpants

brier *noun* (*plural* **briers**)
1 a thorny bush, especially a wild rose bush 2 a hard root used especially for making tobacco pipes

brigade *noun* (*plural* **brigades**)
1 an army unit usually consisting of three battalions 2 a group of people in uniform, for example the fire brigade

brigadier *noun* (*plural* **brigadiers**)
an army officer who commands a brigade and is higher in rank than a colonel

brigand *noun* (*plural* **brigands**)
an old word for a robber or outlaw

bright *adjective* (**brighter, brightest**)
1 giving a strong light; shining 2 clever
♦ *He's a bright lad* 3 cheerful

brighten *verb* (**brightens, brightening, brightened**)
1 to brighten something is to make it brighter 2 to brighten is to become brighter, like the sky when the weather improves

brilliant *adjective*
1 very bright and sparkling 2 very clever
3 (*informal*) really good or enjoyable
♦ *That was a brilliant film!*
brilliance *noun* brightness

brim *noun* (*plural* **brims**)
1 the edge round the top of a container
2 the projecting edge of a hat

brimming *adjective*
completely full
brimming over overflowing

brine *noun*
brine is salt water

bring *verb* (**brings, bringing, brought**)
to bring someone or something is to make them come with you to a place
to bring someone round is to make them conscious again after they have fainted
to bring someone up is to look after them and educate them as a child
to bring something about is to make it happen
to bring something off is to achieve something difficult or unexpected

brink *noun*
the edge of a steep or dangerous place

brisk *adjective* (**brisker, briskest**)
quick and lively

bristle *noun* (*plural* **bristles**)
a short, stiff hair
bristly *adjective* having many bristles

British *adjective*
to do with Great Britain

Briton *noun* (*plural* **Britons**)
someone born in Great Britain

brittle *adjective* (**brittler, brittlest**)
hard and likely to break or snap

broad *adjective* (**broader, broadest**)
1 wide and open ♦ *They walked down a broad avenue* 2 broad daylight is clear and full daylight 3 general, not detailed
♦ *a broad outline*

broad bean *noun* (*plural* **broad beans**)
a large flat bean

broadcast ➤ *noun* (*plural* **broadcasts**)
a radio or television programme

broadcast ➤ *verb* (**broadcasts, broadcasting, broadcast**)
to broadcast a radio or television programme is to transmit it or take part in it
broadcaster *noun* a person who takes part in a broadcast

broaden *verb* (**broadens, broadening, broadened**)
to broaden something is to make it broader

broadly *adverb*
in general terms ♦ *They were broadly right*

broad-minded *adjective*
tolerant of other people's views and opinions

broadside *noun* (*plural* **broadsides**)
a round of firing by all the guns on one side of a ship

brochure *noun* (*plural* **brochures**)
a pamphlet containing information, especially about a place

brogue *noun* (*plural* **brogues**)
1 a strong kind of shoe 2 a strong accent
♦ *He spoke with an Irish brogue*

broke [1] past tense of **break** *verb*

broke [2] *adjective*
(*informal*) not having any money

broken ➤ past participle of **break** *verb*

broken ➤ *adjective*
1 broken English is English spoken with a strong foreign accent and lots of mistakes
2 a broken home is a home in which the parents have separated

bronchitis *noun* (*pronounced* brong-**ky**-tiss)
bronchitis is a disease of the lungs

bronze *noun*
1 bronze is an alloy of copper and tin
2 bronze is also a yellowish-brown colour

bronze medal *noun* (*plural* bronze medals)
a medal made of bronze, usually awarded
as the third prize

brooch *noun* (*plural* brooches) (*rhymes with* coach)
an ornament pinned on to clothes

brood ➤ *noun* (*plural* broods)
a brood is a number of young birds
hatched together

brood ➤ *verb* (broods, brooding, brooded)
1 to brood is to sit on eggs to hatch them,
as chickens do **2** to brood over something
is to keep on thinking and worrying about
it

broody *adjective* (broodier, broodiest)
1 a broody hen is one that wants to hatch
its eggs **2** a broody person is one who
keeps on thinking and worrying about
things

brook *noun* (*plural* brooks)
a small stream

broom *noun* (*plural* brooms)
1 a broom is a brush with a long handle,
for sweeping **2** broom is a shrub with
yellow, white, or pink flowers

broomstick *noun* (*plural* broomsticks)
the handle of a broom

broth *noun* (*plural* broths)
broth is a thin kind of soup

brother *noun* (*plural* brothers)
your brother is a man or boy who has the
same parents as you
brotherly *adjective* like a brother

brother-in-law *noun* (*plural* brothers-in-law)
a person's brother-in-law is the brother of
their husband or wife, or the husband of
their sister

brought past tense and past participle of
bring

brow *noun* (*plural* brows)
1 your brow is your forehead **2** your brow
can also mean your eyebrow **3** the brow of
a hill is the top of it

brown ➤ *adjective* (browner, brownest)
1 of the colour of earth or toast
2 suntanned

brown ➤ *noun*
a brown colour

brownie *noun* (*plural* brownies)
a small chocolate cake with nuts

Brownie *noun* (*plural* Brownies)
a junior member of the Guides

browse *verb* (browses, browsing, browsed)
1 to browse is to read or look at something
casually **2** to browse is to feed on grass or
leaves, as animals do

bruise ➤ *noun* (*plural* bruises)
a dark mark that appears on your skin
when it is hit or hurt

bruise ➤ *verb* (bruises, bruising, bruised)
to bruise your skin or a part of your body
is to get a bruise on it

brunette *noun* (*plural* brunettes)
a woman with dark brown or black hair

brush ➤ *noun* (*plural* brushes)
1 a device with hairs or bristles for
sweeping, painting, or arranging the hair
2 a fox's bushy tail

brush ➤ *verb* (brushes, brushing, brushed)
1 to brush something is to use a brush on
it ♦ *Have you brushed your hair yet?* **2** to
brush against someone is to touch them
gently as you pass them
to brush something aside is to ignore it
to brush something up is to improve your
knowledge of it

Brussels sprout *noun* (*plural* Brussels
sprouts)
a green vegetable like a tiny cabbage

brutal *adjective*
savage and cruel
brutality *noun* savage cruelty **brutally** *adverb*
with savage cruelty

brute *noun* (*plural* brutes)
1 a cruel person **2** an animal

BSE short for **bovine spongiform
encephalopathy**, a fatal disease of cattle that
attacks their nervous system and makes
them stagger about. Also called **mad cow
disease**

bubble ➤ *noun* (*plural* bubbles)
1 a thin transparent ball of liquid filled
with air or gas **2** a small ball of air in a
liquid or a solid

bubble ➤ *verb* (bubbles, bubbling, bubbled)
to bubble is to produce bubbles, as a
boiling liquid does

bubble gum *noun*
bubble gum is a kind of chewing gum that
you can blow into a bubble out of the front
of your mouth

bubbly *adjective* (bubblier, bubbliest)
1 full of bubbles, like fizzy water **2** a
bubbly person is cheerful and lively

buccaneer *noun* (*plural* **buccaneers**)
an old word for a pirate

buck ➤ *noun* (*plural* **bucks**)
a male deer, rabbit, or hare

buck ➤ *verb* (**bucks, bucking, bucked**)
to buck is to jump with the back arched as
a horse does
to buck up (*informal*) is to start hurrying

bucket *noun* (*plural* **buckets**)
a container with a handle, for carrying
liquids or something such as sand

bucketful *noun* (*plural* **bucketfuls**)
as much of something as you can carry in
a bucket

buckle ➤ *noun* (*plural* **buckles**)
a clip at the end of a belt or strap for
fastening it

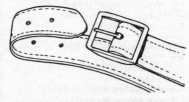

buckle ➤ *verb* (**buckles, buckling, buckled**)
1 to buckle something is to fasten it with a
buckle **2** to buckle is to bend or give way
under a strain ♦ *The arm of the crane was
beginning to buckle*
to buckle down is to start work

bud *noun* (*plural* **buds**)
a flower or leaf before it has opened

Buddhism *noun* (*pronounced* **buud**-izm)
Buddhism is a religion that started in Asia
and follows the teachings of Buddha
Buddhist *noun* someone who practises
Buddhism

budding *adjective*
showing great promise ♦ *The new class
had several budding musicians*

budge *verb* (**budges, budging, budged**)
to budge is to move slightly ♦ *The door
was stuck and wouldn't budge*

budgerigar *noun* (*plural* **budgerigars**)
(*pronounced* **bud**-jer-i-gar)
an Australian bird often kept as a pet in a
cage

budget ➤ *noun* (*plural* **budgets**)
1 the money someone plans to spend on
something **2** a plan for earning and
spending money

budget ➤ *verb* (**budgets, budgeting, budgeted**)
to budget is to plan how much you are
going to spend

budgie *noun* (*plural* **budgies**)
(*informal*) a budgerigar

buff *adjective*
of a dull yellow colour

buffalo *noun* (*plural* **buffalo** or **buffaloes**)
a wild ox with long curved horns

buffer *noun* (*plural* **buffers**)
1 something that softens a blow or
collision, especially a device on a railway
engine or wagon or at the end of a railway
line **2** (*in Computing*) a memory in which
data can be stored temporarily, especially
while being sent from one device to
another

buffet *noun* (*plural* **buffets**) (*pronounced*
buu-fay)
1 a café or place for buying drinks and
snacks **2** a meal where guests serve
themselves

bug ➤ *noun* (*plural* **bugs**)
1 a tiny insect **2** (*informal*) a germ that
causes illness ♦ *I may have a tummy bug*
3 (*informal*) a hidden microphone **4** a
fault or problem in a computer program
that stops it working properly

bug ➤ *verb* (**bugs, bugging, bugged**)
1 (*informal*) to bug a place is to put a
hidden microphone into it **2** (*slang*) to bug
someone is to annoy them ♦ *The noise of
the burglar alarm was really bugging me*

bugle *noun* (*plural* **bugles**) (*pronounced*
byoo-gul)
a brass instrument like a small trumpet

bugler *noun* someone who plays the bugle

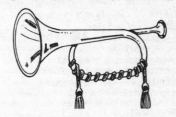

build ➤ *verb* (**builds, building, built**)
to build something is to make it by putting
the parts together
to build something up is to make it larger or
stronger ♦ *Regular exercise will build up
your health*
to build up is to become larger or stronger
♦ *The work was starting to build up*

build ➤ *noun* (*plural* **builds**)
your build is the shape of your body

builder *noun* (*plural* **builders**)
someone who puts up buildings

building *noun* (*plural* **buildings**)
1 building is the business of making houses and other structures **2** a building is a structure that someone has built, such as a house or a block of flats

building society *noun* (*plural* **building societies**)
an organization that lends money to people for them to buy houses

built-in *adjective*
made into a permanent part of something ♦ *The house had built-in kitchen units*

built-up *adjective*
a built-up area is one with lots of houses and other buildings

bulb *noun* (*plural* **bulbs**)
1 the glass part of an electric light, with a wire inside that glows when you switch it on **2** a thing like an onion, which grows into a plant or flower when it is put in the ground

bulge ➤ *noun* (*plural* **bulges**)
a part that sticks out; a swelling

bulge ➤ *verb* (**bulges, bulging, bulged**)
to bulge is to stick out or swell

bulk *noun*
1 a thing's bulk is its size, especially when it is large **2** the bulk of something is most of it ♦ *They spent the bulk of their time practising their recorders*
in bulk in large quantities

bulky *adjective* (**bulkier, bulkiest**)
taking up a lot of space

bull *noun* (*plural* **bulls**)
1 a large and powerful male animal, such as an ox **2** a male seal, whale, or elephant

bulldog *noun* (*plural* **bulldogs**)
a breed of dog with a short thick neck

bulldozer *noun* (*plural* **bulldozers**)
a heavy vehicle with caterpillar tracks and a wide metal blade in front, used to clear or flatten land
bulldoze *verb* to bulldoze land is to clear it with a bulldozer

bullet *noun* (*plural* **bullets**)
a piece of shaped metal shot from a rifle or pistol

bulletin *noun* (*plural* **bulletins**)
a short announcement of news on radio or television

bulletproof *adjective*
able to stop bullets getting through

bullfight *noun* (*plural* **bullfights**)
in Spain, a public entertainment in which people challenge bulls, and sometimes kill them
bullfighter *noun* someone who takes part in a bullfight

bullion *noun*
gold or silver in the form of bars

bullock *noun* (*plural* **bullocks**)
a young bull

bull's-eye *noun* (*plural* **bull's-eyes**)
1 the centre of a target **2** a hard peppermint sweet

bully ➤ *verb* (**bullies, bullying, bullied**)
to bully someone is to hurt or frighten them when they are weaker

bully ➤ *noun* (*plural* **bullies**)
someone who bullies people

bulrush *noun* (*plural* **bulrushes**)
a tall reed which grows in water or on boggy land

bulwark *noun* (*plural* **bulwarks**) (*pronounced* buul-werk)
a strong defending wall

bulwarks *plural noun*
a ship's side above the level of the deck

bum *noun* (*plural* **bums**)
(*slang*) **1** your bum is your bottom **2** (*in America*) a bum is a tramp

bumble-bee *noun* (*plural* **bumble-bees**)
a large kind of bee with a loud buzz

bump ➤ *verb* (**bumps, bumping, bumped**)
1 to bump something is to knock against it accidentally **2** to bump along is to move along unsteadily, like an old car
to bump into someone (*informal*) is to meet them unexpectedly
to bump someone off (*slang*) is to kill them

bump ➤ *noun* (*plural* **bumps**)
1 an accidental knock **2** a swelling or lump

bumper[1] *noun* (*plural* **bumpers**)
a bar along the front or back of a motor vehicle to protect it in collisions

bumper[2] *adjective*
unusually large or fine ♦ *The comic had a bumper annual at Christmas*

bumpy *adjective* (**bumpier, bumpiest**)
having lots of bumps

bun *noun* (*plural* **buns**)
1 a small sweet roll made of egg and dough **2** a round bunch of hair that some women make at the back of their head

bunch *noun* (*plural* **bunches**)
a number of things joined or tied together, such as fruit or flowers or keys ♦ *Why not give your Mum a nice bunch of daffodils?*

bundle ➤ *noun* (*plural* **bundles**)
a number of things tied or wrapped loosely together, such as clothes or papers

bundle ➤ *verb* (**bundles, bundling, bundled**)
1 to bundle things together is to tie or wrap them loosely 2 to bundle someone into a room or car is to push them there hurriedly ◆ *They had to get him home so they bundled him into the back of a taxi*

bung ➤ *verb* (**bungs, bunging, bunged**)
(*slang*) to bung something somewhere is to throw or pass it carelessly ◆ *Bung that pencil over here*
to bung something up is to block it

bung ➤ *noun* (*plural* **bungs**)
a stopper for a bottle or barrel

bungalow *noun* (*plural* **bungalows**)
a house with all the rooms on one floor

bungle *verb* (**bungles, bungling, bungled**)
to bungle something is to do it badly and clumsily
bungler *noun* someone who bungles something

bunk *noun* (*plural* **bunks**)
a bed like a shelf, as on a ship
to do a bunk (*slang*) is to run away

bunk bed *noun* (*plural* **bunk beds**)
a single bed with another bed above it or below it

bunker *noun* (*plural* **bunkers**)
1 a container for storing fuel 2 a hollow filled with sand, made as an obstacle on a golf course 3 an underground shelter

bunny *noun* (*plural* **bunnies**)
(*informal*) a rabbit

bunsen burner *noun* (*plural* **bunsen burners**)
a gas burner with an adjustable flame used in laboratories

buoy *noun* (*plural* **buoys**) (*pronounced* boi)
a floating object anchored to the bottom of the sea and used to mark a channel or a stretch of shallow water

buoyant *adjective*
1 able to float 2 lively and cheerful ◆ *He was in a buoyant mood*
buoyancy *noun* being able to float

bur *noun* (*plural* **burs**)
part of a plant that clings to your clothes or hair

burden *noun* (*plural* **burdens**)
1 a heavy load 2 something unwelcome that you have to put up with
burdensome *adjective* hard to put up with

bureau *noun* (*plural* **bureaux**) (*pronounced* bewr-oh)
1 a writing desk 2 an office or department ◆ *They will tell you at the Information Bureau*

burglar *noun* (*plural* **burglars**)
someone who breaks into a building to steal things
burglary *noun* the crime of stealing things from a building

burgle *verb* (**burgles, burgling, burgled**)
to burgle someone is to steal from their house

burial *noun* (*plural* **burials**)
putting a dead body in a grave

burly *adjective* (**burlier, burliest**)
big and strong

burn[1] ➤ *verb* (**burns, burning, burnt** or **burned**)
1 to burn something is to damage or destroy it by fire or strong heat 2 to burn is to be damaged or destroyed by fire or heat 3 to be burning is to be on fire 4 to be burning is also to feel very hot

burn ➤ *noun* (*plural* **burns**)
1 an injury caused by fire or strong heat 2 the firing of a spacecraft's rocket

burn[2] *noun* (*plural* **burns**)
(*in Scotland*) a small stream

burner *noun* (*plural* **burners**)
the part of a lamp or cooker that forms the flame

burning *adjective*
a burning wish or desire is one that is very strong

burp ➤ *noun* (*plural* **burps**)
a belch

burp ➤ *verb* (**burps, burping, burped**)
to burp is to belch

burrow ➤ *noun* (*plural* **burrows**)
a hole dug by an animal such as a rabbit or fox

burrow ➤ *verb* (**burrows, burrowing, burrowed**)
1 to burrow is to dig a burrow 2 to burrow is also to dig or search deeply ◆ *He burrowed in his pockets to find a pound coin*

burst ➤ *verb* (**bursts, bursting, burst**)
1 to burst is to break apart suddenly 2 to burst something is to make it break apart 3 to be bursting with energy or excitement is to have a lot of energy or to be very excited
to burst in is to rush in noisily or clumsily
to burst into tears is to suddenly start crying
to burst out laughing is to start laughing noisily

burst ➤ *noun* (*plural* **bursts**)
1 a split caused by something bursting ◆ *There's a burst in one of the pipes*
2 something short and quick ◆ *a burst of gunfire*

bury *verb* (**buries, burying, buried**)
1 to bury something is to put it under the ground **2** to bury someone is to put them in a grave when they are dead
to bury the hatchet is to agree to stop quarrelling or fighting

bus *noun* (*plural* **buses**)
a large road vehicle for carrying passengers

bus stop *noun* (*plural* **bus stops**)
a place where a bus regularly stops

bush *noun* (*plural* **bushes**)
1 a bush is a plant like a small tree with a lot of stems or branches **2** the bush is wild land, especially in Australia or Africa

bushy *adjective* (**bushier, bushiest**)
thick and hairy ♦ *His dad has bushy eyebrows*

busily *adverb*
in a busy way

business *noun* (*plural* **businesses**)
(*pronounced* **biz-niss**)
1 a business is an organization that makes money by selling goods or services ♦ *His uncle worked in a garage business* **2** business is what an organization does to make money ♦ *She has made a career in business* **3** a person's business is what concerns them and no one else ♦ *He said that was his business* **4** a business is also an affair or subject ♦ *I am tired of the whole business*
to get down to business is to start working or talking seriously
to go out of business is to stop trading because you are not making enough money

businesslike *adjective*
efficient and practical

busker *noun* (*plural* **buskers**)
someone who plays music in the street, hoping for money from people passing by

bust [1] *noun* (*plural* **busts**)
1 a woman's bosom **2** a sculpture of a person's head and shoulders

bust [2] *adjective*
(*informal*) **1** broken or burst **2** bankrupt

bustle *verb* (**bustles, bustling, bustled**)
to bustle is to be in a hurry or rushing about busily

busy *adjective* (**busier, busiest**)
1 a busy person is one with a lot to do **2** a busy place is one with a lot going on **3** a busy telephone line is one that someone is already using

busybody *noun* (*plural* **busybodies**)
someone who interferes in other people's affairs

but ➤ *conjunction*
linking two statements ♦ *I wanted to go but I couldn't*

but ➤ *preposition*
except ♦ *There's no one here but me*

butcher *noun* (*plural* **butchers**)
1 someone who runs a shop that cuts and sells meat **2** a person who kills people cruelly

butchery *noun*
butchery is the cruel killing of many people

butler *noun* (*plural* **butlers**)
a male servant in charge of other servants in a large private house

butt [1] *noun* (*plural* **butts**)
1 the thicker end of a weapon or tool **2** a large barrel **3** someone people often make fun of ♦ *James always seems to be the butt of your jokes*

butt [2] *verb* (**butts, butting, butted**)
to butt someone is to hit them hard with your head
to butt in is to interrupt suddenly or rudely

butter *noun*
butter is a fatty yellow food made from cream

buttercup *noun* (*plural* **buttercups**)
a yellow wild flower

butter-fingers *noun* (*plural* **butter-fingers**)
(*informal*) someone who is clumsy and keeps dropping things

butterfly *noun* (*plural* **butterflies**)
1 an insect with large white or coloured wings **2** a stroke you use when swimming on your front, by raising both arms together over your head

butterscotch *noun* (*plural* **butterscotches**)
butterscotch is a kind of hard toffee

buttocks *plural noun*
your buttocks are the part of the body on which you sit, your bottom

button ➤ *noun* (*plural* **buttons**)
1 a flat plastic or metal disc sewn on clothes and passed through a buttonhole to fasten them **2** a small knob you press to work an electric device

button ➤ *verb* (**buttons, buttoning, buttoned**)
to button clothes or to button up clothes is
to fasten them with buttons

buttonhole *noun* (*plural* **buttonholes**)
1 a slit for a button to pass through **2** a
flower worn on a lapel

buttress *noun* (*plural* **buttresses**)
a support built against a wall

buy ➤ *verb* (**buys, buying, bought**)
to get something by paying for it ♦ *I
bought a CD yesterday*
buyer *noun* someone who buys something

buy ➤ *noun* (*plural* **buys**)
something you buy ♦ *That was a good buy*

buzz ➤ *noun* (*plural* **buzzes**)
a sharp humming sound, like bees make
to get a buzz from something (*slang*) is to find
it exciting

buzz ➤ *verb* (**buzzes, buzzing, buzzed**)
to make a buzz
to buzz off (*slang*) is to go away

buzzard *noun* (*plural* **buzzards**)
a bird of prey like a large hawk

buzzer *noun* (*plural* **buzzers**)
an alarm or signalling device that makes a
buzzing noise

by *preposition* and *adverb*
1 near, close ♦ *Sit by me* **2** using; by
means of ♦ *I fixed the tyre by sticking on a
patch* **3** before ♦ *Do your homework by
tomorrow* **4** past ♦ *She went by the
window* ♦ *I can't get by*
by and large mostly, on the whole
by the way a phrase you use to begin a new
topic

bye *noun* (*plural* **byes**)
a run scored in cricket when the batsman
has not touched the ball

bye-bye *interjection*
(*informal*) goodbye

by-election *noun* (*plural* **by-elections**)
an election in one district only, when an
MP has died or resigned

by-law *noun* (*plural* **by-laws**)
a law which only applies to a particular
town, district, etc.

bypass *noun* (*plural* **bypasses**)
a road that takes traffic past a congested
area

by-product *noun* (*plural* **by-products**)
something useful that is made while
something else is being made

bystander *noun* (*plural* **bystanders**)
someone who sees something happening
but takes no part in it

byte *noun*
(*in Computing*) a unit that measures data
or memory

Cc

C 1 short for centigrade **2** 100 in Roman
numerals

CAB short for *Citizens' Advice Bureau*

cab *noun* (*plural* **cabs**)
1 a taxi **2** the place for the driver in a
lorry, bus, train, or crane

cabaret *noun* (*plural* **cabarets**) (*pronounced
kab-a-ray*)
an entertainment, especially performed in
a restaurant or nightclub

cabbage *noun* (*plural* **cabbages**)
a round green vegetable

cabin *noun* (*plural* **cabins**)
1 a hut or shelter **2** a room for sleeping on
a ship **3** the part of an aircraft where the
passengers sit

cabinet *noun* (*plural* **cabinets**)
1 a cupboard with shelves and doors
2 the group of chief ministers who control
the government ♦ *The Prime Minister is
going to choose a new cabinet*

cable *noun* (*plural* **cables**)
1 a thick rope, wire, or chain **2** a
telegram sent overseas

cable television *noun*
a television system in which programmes
are transmitted by underground cable

cackle *noun* (*plural* **cackles**)
1 a cackle is the clucking of a hen **2** a
cackle is also a loud, silly laugh **3** cackle
is stupid chattering

cactus *noun* (*plural* **cacti**)
a fleshy plant that grows in hot, dry places

caddie *noun* (*plural* **caddies**)
someone who helps a golfer by carrying
the clubs

caddy *noun* (*plural* **caddies**)
a small container for tea leaves

cadet *noun* (*plural* **cadets**)
a young person being trained for the armed forces or the police

cadge *verb* (**cadges, cadging, cadged**)
to cadge something is to get it by asking for it in a blunt or direct way

cafe *noun* (*plural* **cafes**) (*pronounced* **kaf**-ay)
a place that sells hot and cold drinks and light meals

cafeteria *noun* (*plural* **cafeterias**) (*pronounced* kaf-e-teer-i-a)
a café where customers serve themselves from a counter

caffeine *noun*
a drug found in tea and coffee which keeps you awake and makes you feel active

caftan *noun* (*plural* **caftans**)
a long loose jacket or dress with wide sleeves

cage *noun* (*plural* **cages**)
a container made of bars or wires, in which birds or animals are kept

cagey *adjective* (**cagier, cagiest**)
(*informal*) cautious about what you say

cagoule *noun* (*plural* **cagoules**)
a lightweight waterproof jacket

cake *noun* (*plural* **cakes**)
1 a baked mixture of flour, eggs, fat, and sugar 2 something made into a lump rather like a cake, such as soap
a piece of cake (*informal*) something very easy to do
to have your cake and eat it is to get the benefit of two things that are normally alternatives

caked *adjective*
covered with something that has dried hard, like mud

calamine *noun*
a pink powder used to make a soothing liquid to put on your skin

calamity *noun* (*plural* **calamities**)
a disaster
calamitous *adjective* disastrous

calcium *noun*
a greyish-white element contained in teeth, bones, and lime

calculate *verb* (**calculates, calculating, calculated**)
1 to calculate something is to work it out by arithmetic or with a calculator 2 to calculate on something is to plan round it ♦ *They were calculating on a fine day for the picnic*
calculation *noun* something you calculate; a sum

calculator *noun* (*plural* **calculators**)
a machine for doing sums

calendar *noun* (*plural* **calendars**)
a chart or display that shows the days of the year

calf[1] *noun* (*plural* **calves**)
1 a young cow or ox 2 a young seal, whale, or elephant

calf[2] *noun* (*plural* **calves**)
the back part of your leg below your knee

calico *noun*
calico is a kind of cotton cloth

call ➤ *noun* (*plural* **calls**)
1 a shout or cry 2 a short visit 3 a telephone conversation with someone 4 a request or invitation

call ➤ *verb* (**calls, calling, called**)
1 to call is to shout out 2 to call someone is to telephone them ♦ *I'll call you on Wednesday* 3 to call someone near you is to ask them to come to you 4 to call on someone is to visit them 5 to be called something is to have it as your name ♦ *His friend was called Damon* 6 to call something a certain thing is to describe it that way ♦ *I call that a swindle*
to call it a day is to stop working for a while
to call someone names is to insult them
to call something off is to cancel it

calling *noun* (*plural* **callings**)
someone's calling is their profession or trade

callipers *plural noun*
a device for measuring the width of tubes or of round objects

callous *adjective*
not caring about other people's feelings; cruel

calm *adjective* (**calmer, calmest**)
1 quiet and still, like the sea or the weather 2 someone is calm when they are not excited or agitated ♦ *Please keep calm*
calmly *adverb* in a calm way **calmness** *noun* being calm

calorie *noun* (*plural* **calories**)
a unit for measuring the amount of heat or the energy produced by food

calves plural of **calf**

calypso *noun* (*plural* **calypsos**)
a West Indian folk song which is made up as the singer goes along

camcorder *noun* (*plural* **camcorders**)
a video camera and sound recorder in one machine

came past tense of **come**

camel *noun* (*plural* **camels**)
a large animal with a long neck and one or two humps on its back ♦ *Arabian camels have one hump, and Bactrian camels have two*

camera *noun* (*plural* **cameras**)
a device for taking photographs, films, or television pictures
cameraman *noun* someone who works a film or television camera

camouflage *noun* (*pronounced* kam-o-flah*zh*)
a way of hiding things by making them look like part of their surroundings

camp ➤ *noun* (*plural* **camps**)
a place where people live in tents or huts for a short time

camp ➤ *verb* (**camps, camping, camped**)
1 to camp or go camping is to have a holiday in a tent 2 to camp is also to put up a tent or tents ♦ *Let's camp here for the night*
camper *noun* a person who goes camping

campaign ➤ *noun* (*plural* **campaigns**)
1 a planned series of actions, especially to arouse interest in something ♦ *a campaign for human rights* 2 a series of battles in one area or with one aim

campaign ➤ *verb* (**campaigns, campaigning, campaigned**)
to campaign is to carry out a plan of action to arouse interest in something such as a good cause ♦ *They are campaigning to stop the destruction of the rain forest*

campsite *noun* (*plural* **campsites**)
a place for camping

campus *noun* (*plural* **campuses**)
the buildings of a college or university and the land around them

can [1] *verb* (*present tense* **can**; *past tense* **could**)
1 to be able to do something or to know how to do it ♦ *Can you lift this stone?* ♦ *They can speak French* 2 (*informal*) to be allowed to do something ♦ *Can I go home?*

can [2] ➤ *noun* (*plural* **cans**)
a sealed metal container holding food or drink

can ➤ *verb* (**cans, canning, canned**)
to can something like food is to put it into cans

canal *noun* (*plural* **canals**)
1 an artificially made channel for boats 2 a tube in a human's or animal's body ♦ *The canals in your ears help you balance*

canary *noun* (*plural* **canaries**)
a small yellow bird that sings

cancel *verb* (**cancels, cancelling, cancelled**)
1 to cancel something planned is to say that it will not be done or not take place after all 2 to cancel an order or instruction is to stop it 3 to cancel a stamp or ticket is to mark it so that it cannot be used again
cancellation *noun* something cancelled

cancer *noun* (*plural* **cancers**)
1 a serious disease in which a harmful growth forms in the body 2 a harmful growth in the body

candidate *noun* (*plural* **candidates**)
1 someone who applies for a job or position 2 someone taking an examination

candle *noun* (*plural* **candles**)
a stick of wax with a wick through it, giving light when it is burning

candlelight *noun*
light given by a candle

candlestick *noun* (*plural* **candlesticks**)
a holder for a candle or candles

candy *noun* (*plural* **candies**)
1 candy is crystallized sugar 2 a candy is a sweet

candyfloss *noun*
a fluffy mass of sugar that has been spun into fine threads

cane ➤ *noun* (*plural* **canes**)
a cane is the hollow stem of a reed or tall grass

cane ➤ *verb* (**canes, caning, caned**)
to cane someone is to beat them with a cane

canine *adjective*
to do with dogs

canine tooth *noun* (*plural* **canine teeth**)
a pointed tooth at the front of the mouth

cannabis *noun* (*pronounced* kan-a-bis)
a drug made from the plant that also produces hemp

canned music *noun*
light recorded music played in the background

cannibal *noun* (*plural* **cannibals**)
1 a person who eats human flesh 2 an animal that eats animals of its own kind
cannibalism *noun* being a cannibal

cannon *noun* (*plural* **cannon** or **cannons**)
a large heavy gun

cannonball *noun* (*plural* **cannonballs**)
a large ball fired from a cannon

cannot can not ♦ *I cannot believe it*

canoe ➤ *noun* (*plural* **canoes**)
a light narrow boat driven with paddles

canoe ➤ *verb* (**canoes, canoeing, canoed**)
to canoe is to travel in a canoe
canoeist *noun* someone who uses a canoe

can-opener *noun* (*plural* **can-openers**)
a device for opening cans of food

canopy *noun* (*plural* **canopies**)
an overhanging cover

can't short for *can not*

canteen *noun* (*plural* **canteens**)
1 a restaurant for workers in a factory or
office **2** a box containing a set of cutlery
3 a soldier's or camper's water flask or set
of eating utensils

canter *verb* (**canters, cantering, cantered**)
to canter is to go at a gentle gallop

canton *noun* (*plural* **cantons**)
each of the districts into which
Switzerland is divided

canvas *noun* (*plural* **canvases**)
1 canvas is strong, coarse cloth **2** a
canvas is a piece of this kind of cloth used
for painting on

canvass *verb* (**canvasses, canvassing,
canvassed**)
to canvass people is to visit them to ask
them for their support, especially in an
election

canyon *noun* (*plural* **canyons**)
a deep valley with a river running through
it

cap ➤ *noun* (*plural* **caps**)
1 a soft hat without a brim but often with
a peak **2** a cover or top

cap ➤ *verb* (**caps, capping, capped**)
1 to cap something is to cover it **2** to cap
a story or joke is to tell one that is better

capable *adjective*
able to do something
capability *noun* being capable **capably** *adverb*
in a capable way

capacity *noun* (*plural* **capacities**)
1 ability to do something ♦ *He has a great
capacity for work* **2** the amount that
something can hold **3** the position
someone occupies ♦ *He was there in his
capacity as our leader*

cape [1] *noun* (*plural* **capes**)
a piece of high land sticking out into the
sea

cape [2] *noun* (*plural* **capes**)
a cloak

caper ➤ *verb* (**capers, capering, capered**)
to jump about playfully

caper ➤ *noun* (*plural* **capers**)
1 jumping about playfully **2** (*slang*) an
activity or adventure

capital *noun* (*plural* **capitals**)
1 the capital of a country is the most
important city in it **2** capital is money or
property that can be used to make more
wealth **3** a capital is the top part of a pillar

capitalism *noun* (*pronounced* **kap**-i-ta-lizm)
a system in which the wealth of a country
is owned by private individuals and not by
the state
capitalist *noun* someone who supports
capitalism

capital letter *noun* (*plural* **capital letters**)
a large letter of the kind used at the start
of a name or a sentence, such as A, B, C

capital punishment *noun*
punishment by putting someone to death

capsize *verb* (**capsizes, capsizing, capsized**)
to capsize is to overturn in a boat in the
water

capsule *noun* (*plural* **capsules**)
1 a hollow pill containing medicine **2** a
small spacecraft or pressurized cabin

captain *noun* (*plural* **captains**)
1 an officer in charge of a ship or aircraft
2 an officer in the army or navy **3** the
leader in a sports team

caption *noun* (*plural* **captions**)
1 the words printed beside a picture to
describe it **2** a heading in a newspaper or
magazine

captivating *adjective*
charming and attractive

captive ⊳ *noun* (*plural* **captives**)
a prisoner

captive ⊳ *adjective*
imprisoned; unable to escape
captivity *noun* being held prisoner

captor *noun* (*plural* **captors**)
someone who has captured a person or
animal

capture ⊳ *verb* (**captures, capturing, captured**)
1 to capture an animal or person is to
catch or imprison them **2** (*in Computing*)
to capture data is to put it into a form that
a computer can accept

capture ⊳ *noun*
catching or imprisoning an animal or
person

car *noun* (*plural* **cars**)
1 a private motor vehicle **2** a railway
carriage ♦ *The train has a dining car*

caramel *noun* (*plural* **caramels**)
1 caramel is burnt sugar used to give a
sweet taste to food **2** a caramel is a sweet
made from butter, milk, and sugar

carat *noun* (*plural* **carats**)
1 a measure of weight for precious stones
2 a measure of the purity of gold

caravan *noun* (*plural* **caravans**)
1 a vehicle towed by a car and used for
living in, especially by people on holiday
2 a large number of people travelling
together, especially across a desert

carbohydrate *noun* (*plural* **carbohydrates**)
a compound of carbon, oxygen, and
hydrogen ♦ *Sugar and starch are*
carbohydrates

carbon *noun*
carbon is an element found in charcoal,
graphite, diamonds, and other substances

carbon copy *noun* (*plural* **carbon copies**)
1 a copy made with carbon paper **2** an
exact copy ♦ *The attack was a carbon copy*
of one carried out last month

carbon dioxide *noun*
a colourless gas made by humans and
animals breathing

carbon monoxide *noun*
a colourless, poisonous gas found
especially in the exhaust fumes of motor
vehicles

carbon paper *noun*
thin coated paper put between sheets of
paper to make a copy on the bottom sheet
of what is typed or written on the top sheet

car-boot sale *noun* (*plural* **car-boot sales**)
an outdoor sale where people sell things
which have brought by car

carburettor *noun* (*plural* **carburettors**)
a device for mixing fuel and air in an
internal-combustion engine

carcass *noun* (*plural* **carcasses**)
the dead body of an animal or bird

card *noun* (*plural* **cards**)
1 a card is a small and usually oblong
piece of stiff paper **2** a card is also a
playing card **3** card is cardboard **4** a card
is a small, oblong piece of plastic issued to
a customer by a bank or building society,
giving details of their account
cards is a game with playing cards
something is on the cards when it is likely or
possible

cardboard *noun*
cardboard is thick stiff paper

cardigan *noun* (*plural* **cardigans**)
a knitted jumper fastened with buttons
down the front

cardinal *noun* (*plural* **cardinals**)
one of the leading priests in the Roman
Catholic Church

cardinal number *noun* (*plural* **cardinal**
numbers)
a number for counting things, for example
1, 2, 3 (compare *ordinal number*)

cardphone *noun* (*plural* **cardphones**)
a public telephone that needs a special
plastic card (a *phonecard*) to make it work

care ⊳ *noun* (*plural* **cares**)
1 care is worry or trouble ♦ *She was free*
from care **2** care is also serious thought or
attention ♦ *Take more care with your*
homework **3** care is also protection or
supervision ♦ *Leave the child in my care*
to take care is to be especially careful
to take care of someone or **something** is to look
after them ♦ *Please could you take care of*
the cat while I'm away?
to write to someone care of someone else is to
write to the first person at the address of
the second ♦ *While I'm away, write to me*
care of my father

care ⊳ *verb* (**cares, caring, cared**)
to care about something or someone is to
feel interested or concerned about them
to care for someone is to look after them ♦ *He*
cared for his wife when she was ill

career ⊳ *noun* (*plural* **careers**)
a person's career is the way they earn a
living and make progress in their job

career ➤ *verb* (**careers, careering, careered**)
to career along or down somewhere is to
rush along wildly

carefree *adjective*
without worries or responsibilities

careful *adjective*
1 giving serious thought and attention to
something ♦ *She is a careful worker*
2 avoiding damage or danger ♦ *Be careful
with that knife!*
carefully *adverb* with care

careless *adjective*
not taking care; clumsy
carelessly *adverb* in a careless way
carelessness *noun* not taking care

caress ➤ *noun* (*plural* **caresses**)
(*pronounced* ka-ress)
a gentle and loving touch
caress ➤ *verb* (**caresses, caressing, caressed**)
to caress someone is to touch them gently
and fondly

caretaker *noun* (*plural* **caretakers**)
someone who looks after a large building

cargo *noun* (*plural* **cargoes**)
cargo or a cargo is the goods carried in a
ship or aircraft

Caribbean *adjective* (*pronounced*
ka-ri-bee-an)
to do with the West Indies

caricature *noun* (*plural* **caricatures**)
an amusing or exaggerated picture or
description of someone

carnation *noun* (*plural* **carnations**)
a garden flower with a sweet smell

carnival *noun* (*plural* **carnivals**)
a festival, usually with a procession of
people in fancy dress

carnivore *noun* (*plural* **carnivores**)
an animal that eats meat
carnivorous *adjective* that eats meat

carol *noun* (*plural* **carols**)
a hymn, especially a Christmas hymn
caroller *noun* someone who sings carols
carolling *noun* singing carols

carp *noun* (*plural* **carp**)
a freshwater fish

carpenter *noun* (*plural* **carpenters**)
someone who makes things, especially
parts of buildings, out of wood

carpentry *noun*
the work of a carpenter; things made by a
carpenter

carpet *noun* (*plural* **carpets**)
a thick soft covering for a floor

car phone *noun* (*plural* **car phones**)
a mobile telephone fitted to a car

carriage *noun* (*plural* **carriages**)
1 one of the separate parts of a train
where passengers sit 2 a passenger
vehicle pulled by horses 3 carrying goods
from one place to another ♦ *You will have
to pay extra for carriage*

carriageway *noun* (*plural* **carriageways**)
the part of a road that vehicles travel on

carrier *noun* (*plural* **carriers**)
someone or something that carries things

carrier bag *noun* (*plural* **carrier bags**)
a large bag for holding shopping

carrier pigeon *noun* (*plural* **carrier pigeons**)
a pigeon used to carry messages

carrot *noun* (*plural* **carrots**)
an orange-coloured vegetable

carry *verb* (**carries, carrying, carried**)
1 to carry something is to lift it and take it
somewhere 2 to carry something is also to
have it with you ♦ *He is carrying a gun*
3 a sound carries when it can be heard a
long way away
to be carried away is to become very excited
to carry on is to continue doing something
to carry something out is to put it into practice
♦ *Will you please carry out my orders?*

cart ➤ *noun* (*plural* **carts**)
a small vehicle for carrying loads
to put the cart before the horse is to do things in
the wrong order
cart ➤ *verb* (**carts, carting, carted**)
(*informal*) to cart something somewhere is
to carry or transport it, especially when it
is heavy or tiring ♦ *I've been carting these
books around the school all afternoon*

carthorse *noun* (*plural* **carthorses**)
a large heavy horse

cartilage *noun* (*pronounced* kar-ti-lij)
cartilage is tough and flexible tissue
attached to a bone

carton *noun* (*plural* **cartons**)
a lightweight cardboard box

cartoon *noun* (*plural* **cartoons**)
1 a drawing that is funny or tells a joke
2 a series of drawings that tell a story
3 an animated film
cartoonist *noun* someone who draws
cartoons

cartridge *noun* (*plural* **cartridges**)
1 the case containing the explosive for a
bullet or shell 2 a container holding film
to be put into a camera or ink to be put into
a pen

cartridge paper *noun*
strong white paper used for drawing

cartwheel *noun* (*plural* **cartwheels**)
1 the wheel of a cart 2 a somersault done
sideways, with your arms and legs spread
wide

carve *verb* (**carves, carving, carved**)
1 to carve wood or stone is to make something artistic by cutting it carefully
2 to carve meat is to cut it into slices

cascade *noun* (*plural* **cascades**)
a waterfall or a series of waterfalls

case[1] *noun* (*plural* **cases**)
1 a container 2 a suitcase

case[2] *noun* (*plural* **cases**)
1 an example of something existing or happening ♦ *We've had four cases of chickenpox* 2 something investigated by the police or by a lawcourt ♦ *The detective's next case was a murder* 3 the facts or arguments used to support something ♦ *She made a good case for abolishing homework* 4 the form of a word that shows how it is related to other words, for example *John's* is the possessive case of *John*
in any case anyway
in case because something may happen ♦ *Take an umbrella in case it rains*

cash > *noun*
1 cash is money in coins and banknotes
2 cash is also immediate payment for goods ♦ *I got a discount for paying cash*

cash > *verb* (**cashes, cashing, cashed**)
to cash a cheque is to exchange it for coins and banknotes
to cash in on something (*informal*) is to take advantage of it

cash dispenser *noun* (*plural* **cash dispensers**)
a machine from which customers of a bank or building society can get money

cashew *noun* (*plural* **cashews**) (*pronounced* kash-oo)
a small nut with a curved shape, which grows on a tropical tree

cashier *noun* (*plural* **cashiers**)
someone in charge of the money in a bank, office, or shop

cash register *noun* (*plural* **cash registers**)
a machine that records and stores money received in a shop

cask *noun* (*plural* **casks**)
a barrel

casket *noun* (*plural* **caskets**)
a small box for jewellery or other small objects

cassava *noun* (*plural* **cassavas**) (*pronounced* ka-sah-va)
a fleshy root from a tropical tree, used for food

casserole *noun* (*plural* **casseroles**)
1 a covered dish in which food is cooked
2 food cooked in a dish of this kind

cassette *noun* (*plural* **cassettes**)
a small sealed case containing recording tape or film

cassette recorder *noun* (*plural* **cassette recorders**)
a tape recorder that uses cassettes

cast > *verb* (**casts, casting, cast**)
1 to cast something is to throw it 2 to cast something is to shed it or throw it off
3 to cast a vote is to make your vote in an election 4 to cast something made of metal or plaster is to make it in a mould
5 to cast a play or film is to choose the performers for it
to cast off is to untie a boat and start sailing in it

cast > *noun* (*plural* **casts**)
1 a shape made by pouring liquid metal or plaster into a mould 2 the performers in a play or film

castanets *plural noun*
two pieces of wood or ivory held in one hand and clapped together to make a clicking sound, as in Spanish dancing

castaway *noun* (*plural* **castaways**)
a shipwrecked person

castle *noun* (*plural* **castles**)
1 a large, old building made to protect people in it from attack 2 a piece in chess, also called a *rook*

castor *noun* (*plural* **castors**) (*pronounced* kah-ster)
a small wheel on the leg of a piece of furniture

castor sugar *noun*
finely ground white sugar

casual *adjective*
1 not deliberate or planned ♦ *It was just a casual remark* 2 informal; suitable for leisure time ♦ *They were all wearing casual clothes* 3 not regular or permanent ♦ *His dad was doing casual work*
casually *adverb* in a casual way

casualty *noun* (*plural* **casualties**)
someone killed or injured in war or in an accident

cat *noun* (*plural* **cats**)
1 a small furry animal, usually kept as a pet and known for catching mice **2** a larger member of the same family, for example a lion, tiger, or leopard
to let the cat out of the bag is to give away a secret

catalogue *noun* (*plural* **catalogues**)
a list of goods for sale or of books in a library

catalyst *noun* (*plural* **catalysts**) (*pronounced* kat-a-list)
1 something that starts or speeds up a chemical reaction **2** something important that results in a change

catamaran *noun* (*plural* **catamarans**)
a boat with two hulls fixed side by side

catapult *noun* (*plural* **catapults**)
a forked stick with elastic attached, used for shooting pellets or small stones

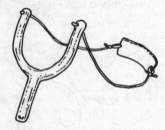

catastrophe *noun* (*plural* **catastrophes**) (*pronounced* ka-**tas**-tro-fi)
a great or sudden disaster

catastrophic *adjective* disastrous, dreadful

catch ➤ *verb* (**catches, catching, caught**)
1 to catch something is to get hold of it
2 to catch someone is to discover them doing something wrong ♦ *He was caught smoking in the playground* **3** to catch an illness is to get it from someone else **4** to catch a bus or train is to get on it before it leaves **5** to catch something someone says is to manage to hear it ♦ *I'm afraid I didn't catch your question* **6** to catch your clothes is to get them entangled in something ♦ *I've caught my sleeve on a bramble*

to catch fire is to start burning

to catch on (*informal*) is to become popular, as a craze or fashion does

to catch someone out is to show that they are wrong or mistaken

to catch up with someone is to reach them after you have been behind

catch ➤ *noun* (*plural* **catches**)
1 something caught or worth catching ♦ *They had a large catch of fish* **2** a hidden difficulty or snag ♦ *The car was so cheap there had to be a catch* **3** a device for fastening a door or window

catching *adjective*
a disease is catching when it is easily caught, and liable to spread quickly

catchphrase *noun* (*plural* **catchphrases**)
a phrase that a lot of people use

catchy *adjective* (**catchier, catchiest**)
pleasant and easy to remember, like a tune

category *noun* (*plural* **categories**)
a group or division of similar people or things ♦ *I'm going to enter the competition in the under-twelves category*

cater *verb* (**caters, catering, catered**)
to cater for someone or something is to give them what they need

caterer *noun* (*plural* **caterers**)
someone whose job is to provide food for people, especially at an important function

caterpillar *noun* (*plural* **caterpillars**)
a long, creeping creature that turns into a butterfly or moth

cathedral *noun* (*plural* **cathedrals**)
a large and important church in a major city, with a bishop as its chief priest

Catherine wheel *noun* (*plural* **Catherine wheels**)
a wheel-shaped firework that spins round

cathode *noun* (*plural* **cathodes**)
the electrode by which electric current leaves a device (the opposite of *anode*)

Catholic ➤ *adjective*
belonging to the Roman Catholic Church

Catholic ➤ *noun* (*plural* **Catholics**)
a member of the Roman Catholic Church

catkin *noun* (*plural* **catkins**)
a tiny flower hanging down from a willow or hazel

Cat's-eye *noun* (*plural* **Cat's-eyes**)
(*trademark*) a stud containing small pieces of glass or plastic that reflect the lights of vehicles, set in a row in the road to help drivers see their way at night

cattle *plural noun*
cattle are cows and bulls

caught past tense and past participle of **catch** *verb*

cauldron *noun* (*plural* **cauldrons**)
a large round iron cooking pot used especially by witches in stories

cauliflower *noun* (*plural* **cauliflowers**)
a kind of cabbage with a large head of white flowers

cause ➤ *noun* (*plural* **causes**)
1 what makes something happen, a reason ♦ *You have no cause for complaint*
2 the aim or purpose that a group of people are working for ♦ *They were raising money for a good cause*

cause ➤ *verb* (**causes, causing, caused**)
to cause something is to make it happen

caution *noun* (*plural* **cautions**)
1 caution is being careful 2 a caution is a warning

cautious *adjective*
careful
cautiously *adverb* in a careful way

Cavalier *noun* (*plural* **Cavaliers**)
a supporter of King Charles I in the English Civil War

cavalry *noun*
soldiers who fight on horseback or in armoured vehicles

cave ➤ *noun* (*plural* **caves**)
a large hole in the side of a hill or cliff, or under the ground

cave ➤ *verb* (**caves, caving, caved**)
to cave or go caving is to explore caves
to cave in is to collapse

caveman *noun* (*plural* **cavemen**)
a person who lived in a cave in prehistoric times

cavern *noun* (*plural* **caverns**)
a cave, especially a deep or dark cave

cavity *noun* (*plural* **cavities**)
a hollow or hole

CD short for
compact disc

CD-ROM short for *compact disc read-only memory*, a system for storing information to be displayed on a VDU screen

cease *verb* (**ceases, ceasing, ceased**)
to cease doing something is to stop doing it

ceasefire *noun* (*plural* **ceasefires**)
an agreement to stop using weapons, made by people who are fighting a war

ceaseless *adjective*
going on all the time

cedar *noun* (*plural* **cedars**)
an evergreen tree with hard sweet-smelling wood

ceiling *noun* (*plural* **ceilings**) (*pronounced* see-ling)
1 the flat surface that covers the top of a room 2 the highest limit that something can reach ♦ *They agreed to put a ceiling on taxes*

celebrate *verb* (**celebrates, celebrating, celebrated**)
to celebrate is to do something to show that a day or an event is important

celebrated *adjective*
famous, well known ♦ *He won a prize to meet a celebrated film star*

celebration *noun* (*plural* **celebrations**)
a celebration is a party or other event to celebrate something

celebrity *noun* (*plural* **celebrities**)
a famous person, especially in show business or on television

celery *noun*
a vegetable with crisp white or green stems

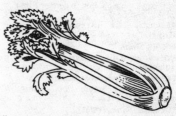

cell *noun* (*plural* **cells**)
1 a small room, especially in a prison 2 a tiny part of a living creature or plant 3 a device for producing electric current chemically

cellar *noun* (*plural* **cellars**)
an underground room for storing things

cello *noun* (*plural* **cellos**) (*pronounced* chel-oh)
a large stringed musical instrument, placed between the knees of the player

cellular *adjective*
1 made of cells ♦ *the cellular structure of living things* 2 a cellular telephone is one that uses a network of radio stations to allow messages to be sent over a wide area

celluloid *noun*
celluloid is a transparent plastic

cellulose *noun*
cellulose is a tissue that forms the main part of all plants and trees

Celsius *adjective*
using a scale for measuring temperature that gives 0 degrees for freezing water and 100 degrees for boiling water

Celt *noun* (*plural* **Celts**) (*pronounced* kelt)
one of the people who lived in Britain before the Romans came

Celtic *adjective* (*pronounced* kel-tik)
to do with the Celts, or the people descended from them and now living in Wales, Scotland, and Ireland

cement *noun*
1 cement is a mixture of lime and clay used in building to make floors and join bricks together 2 cement is also a strong glue

cemetery *noun* (*plural* **cemeteries**)
(*pronounced* sem-e-tri)
a place where dead people are buried

censor ➤ *verb* (**censors, censoring, censored**)
to censor films, plays, and books is to look at them to make sure that they are suitable for people to see

censor ➤ *noun* (*plural* **censors**)
someone whose job is to censor films, plays, and books
censorship *noun* the process of censoring things

censure *noun*
criticizing or disapproving of something or someone

census *noun* (*plural* **censuses**)
an official count or survey of the number of people or the volume of traffic in a place

cent *noun* (*plural* **cents**)
a coin and unit of money in America and some other countries
not to have a cent (*informal*) to have no money

centenary *noun* (*plural* **centenaries**)
the hundredth anniversary of something

centigrade *adjective*
a non-technical word for **Celsius**

centimetre *noun* (*plural* **centimetres**)
one-hundredth of a metre, about four-tenths of an inch

centipede *noun* (*plural* **centipedes**)
a small, long creature with many legs

central *adjective*
1 at or near the centre of something
2 most important ♦ *She will have a central role in our plans*
centrally *adverb* in a central position

central heating *noun*
a system of heating a building by sending hot water, hot air, or steam round it in pipes

centre *noun* (*plural* **centres**)
1 the middle of something 2 an important place ♦ *Vienna is one of the great music centres of Europe* 3 a building or place for a special purpose, such as a sports centre or a shopping centre

centre forward *noun* (*plural* **centre forwards**)
the middle player in the front line of a team in football or hockey

centre of gravity *noun* (*plural* **centres of gravity**)
the point in an object around which its mass is perfectly balanced

centrifugal force *noun*
a force that appears to make something revolving move out from the centre

centurion *noun* (*plural* **centurions**)
an officer in the ancient Roman army, originally commanding a hundred men

century *noun* (*plural* **centuries**)
1 a period of a hundred years 2 a hundred runs scored by one batsman in an innings at cricket

ceramic *adjective*
to do with pottery

ceramics *plural noun*
ceramics is the art of making pottery

cereal *noun* (*plural* **cereals**)
1 a grass that produces seeds which are used as food 2 a breakfast food made from seeds of this kind

ceremony *noun* (*plural* **ceremonies**)
(*pronounced* se-ri-mo-ni)
the solemn actions carried out at a wedding, funeral, or other important occasion
ceremonial *adjective* to do with a ceremony

certain *adjective*
1 sure, not having any doubt 2 you refer to a certain person or thing when you know them but don't want to name them ♦ *I met a certain person in town this morning*
for certain for sure
to make certain is to make sure

certainly *adverb*
as a fact, without any doubt ♦ *They were certainly here last night*

certainty *noun* (*plural* **certainties**)
1 a certainty is something that is sure to happen 2 certainty is being sure

certificate *noun* (*plural* **certificates**)
an official document that records an important event or achievement, such as someone's birth or passing an exam

certify *verb* (**certifies, certifying, certified**)
to certify something is to say in writing that it is true

CFC short for *chlorofluorocarbon*, a chemical formerly used in refrigerators and aerosols, now thought to be harmful to the ozone layer

chaffinch *noun* (*plural* **chaffinches**) a small bird

chain *noun* (*plural* **chains**)
1 a row of metal rings fastened together
2 a line of people 3 a connected series of things ♦ *The story told of a strange chain of events*

chain letter *noun* (*plural* **chain letters**) a letter someone sends you asking you to copy it and send it to several other people, who are supposed to do the same

chain reaction *noun* (*plural* **chain reactions**) a series of happenings, each causing the next

chain saw *noun* (*plural* **chain saws**) a saw with teeth on a chain that is rotated by a motor

chair *noun* (*plural* **chairs**)
1 a seat with a back for one person 2 the person who is in charge of a meeting

chairlift *noun* (*plural* **chairlifts**) a set of seats hanging from a moving cable, carrying people up the side of a mountain

chairman or **chairperson** *noun* (*plural* **chairmen** or **chairpersons**) the person who is in charge of a meeting

chalet *noun* (*plural* **chalets**) (*pronounced* **shal**-ay) a small house, usually built of wood

chalk *noun* (*plural* **chalks**)
1 a kind of soft white rock 2 a soft white or coloured stick of a similar rock, used for writing on blackboards

chalky *adjective* white or powdery like chalk

challenge ➤ *verb* (**challenges, challenging, challenged**) to challenge someone is to demand that they perform some feat or take part in a fight

challenger *noun* a person who makes a challenge, especially for a sports title

challenge ➤ *noun* (*plural* **challenges**) something difficult that someone has to do

chamber *noun* (*plural* **chambers**)
1 (*old use*) a room 2 a hall used for meetings of a parliament or council

chamber music *noun* classical music for a small group of players

champagne *noun* (*pronounced* sham-**payn**) a bubbly white French wine

champion *noun* (*plural* **champions**)
1 the best person in a sport or competition
2 someone who supports a cause by fighting or speaking for it ♦ *Martin Luther King was a champion of human rights*

championship *noun* (*plural* **championships**) a contest to decide who is the best player or competitor in a game or sport

chance *noun* (*plural* **chances**)
1 a chance is a possibility or opportunity ♦ *This is your only chance to see them*
2 chance is the way things happen accidentally ♦ *It was pure chance that we met*

by chance accidentally, without any planning ♦ *We found the place by chance*
to take a chance is to take a risk

chancel *noun* (*plural* **chancels**) the part of a church round the altar

chancellor *noun* (*plural* **chancellors**)
1 an important government or legal official 2 the chief minister of the government in some European countries

Chancellor of the Exchequer *noun* the minister in charge of a country's finances and taxes

chandelier *noun* (*plural* **chandeliers**) (*pronounced* shan-de-**leer**) a hanging support for several lights

change ➤ *verb* (**changes, changing, changed**)
1 to change something or someone is to make them different 2 to change is to become different ♦ *My gran said I'd changed since she'd last seen me* 3 to change one thing for another is to exchange them ♦ *I'm going to change my bike for a new one* 4 to change money is to give coins or notes of small values in exchange for higher value money ♦ *Can you change a £5 note?* 5 to change trains or buses is to get off one and get on another ♦ *Change at York for the train to Durham*

change ➤ *noun* (*plural* **changes**)
1 change is the process of changing
2 your change is the money you get back when you give more money than is needed to pay for something **3** a change of clothes is a set of fresh clothes
for a change as something different ♦ *Let's walk home for a change*

changeable *adjective*
likely to change, often changing ♦ *The weather has been very changeable*

channel *noun* (*plural* **channels**)
1 a stretch of water joining two seas, like the English Channel between Britain and France **2** a broadcasting wavelength **3** a way for water to flow along **4** the part of a river or sea that is deep enough for ships to sail on

chant ➤ *noun* (*plural* **chants**)
a tune, especially one that is often repeated

chant ➤ *verb* (**chants, chanting, chanted**)
to chant words is to say them or call them out in a special rhythm

chaos *noun* (*pronounced* **kay-**oss)
complete disorder or confusion ♦ *The room was in chaos*

chaotic *adjective* (*pronounced* kay-ot-ik)
completely confused or in a mess

chap *noun* (*plural* **chaps**)
(*informal*) a man or boy ♦ *What a funny chap he is*

chapatti *noun* (*plural* **chapattis**)
a flat thin cake of bread made without yeast, eaten with Indian food

chapel *noun* (*plural* **chapels**)
1 a place in a church or large house, used for Christian worship **2** a small church

chapped *adjective*
having rough, cracked skin

chapter *noun* (*plural* **chapters**)
a section of a book

char *verb* (**chars, charring, charred**)
to char something is to scorch it or blacken it with fire

character *noun* (*plural* **characters**)
1 the special nature and qualities of a person or thing **2** a person in a story or play

characteristic ➤ *noun* (*plural* **characteristics**)
something that makes a person or thing noticeable or different from others

characteristic ➤ *adjective*
typical, what you would expect of someone

characterize *verb* (**characterizes, characterizing, characterized**)
1 to characterize something is to provide it with its special character or qualities

♦ *Stony beaches and grey seas characterize the south coast of England* **2** to characterize someone is to describe their character in a certain way ♦ *His friends characterized him as boastful*

charades *noun* (*pronounced* sha-**rahdz**)
charades is a game in which people have to guess a word from other people's acting

charcoal *noun*
charcoal is a black substance made by burning wood slowly

charge ➤ *noun* (*plural* **charges**)
1 the price asked for something **2** an accusation that someone committed a crime ♦ *He is facing three charges of burglary* **3** an attack in a battle **4** the amount of explosive needed to fire a weapon **5** the amount of an electric current
to be in charge of something or **someone** is to be the one who decides what will happen to them

charge ➤ *verb* (**charges, charging, charged**)
1 to charge a price for something is to ask people to pay it **2** to charge someone is to accuse them of committing a crime **3** to charge in a battle is to rush to attack the enemy

chariot *noun* (*plural* **chariots**)
a horse-drawn vehicle with two wheels, used in ancient times for fighting and racing

charioteer *noun* someone who drove a chariot

charity *noun* (*plural* **charities**)
1 charity is giving money and help to other people **2** a charity is an organization that helps those in need

charitable *adjective* involving charity; kind and generous

charm ➤ *noun* (*plural* **charms**)
1 charm is being pleasant and attractive
2 a charm is a magic spell **3** a charm is also something small worn or carried to bring good luck

charm ➤ *verb* (**charms, charming, charmed**)
1 to charm someone is to give them pleasure or delight **2** to charm someone is also to put a spell on them

charming *adjective*
pleasant and attractive

chart *noun* (*plural* **charts**)
1 a large plan or map **2** a diagram or list with information set out in columns or rows
the charts (*informal*) a list of the records that are most popular

charter ➤ *noun* (*plural* **charters**)
1 an official document explaining someone's rights or privileges 2 the hire of an aircraft or vehicle for a special purpose

charter ➤ *verb* (**charters, chartering, chartered**)
to charter an aircraft or vehicle is to hire it

charter flight *noun* (*plural* **charter flights**)
a flight by an aircraft specially hired by the holiday companies

charwoman *noun* (*plural* **charwomen**)
(*old use*) a woman paid to clean a house or office

chase ➤ *verb* (**chases, chasing, chased**)
to chase someone is to go quickly after them to try to catch them up

chase ➤ *noun* (*plural* **chases**)
a chase is when you chase someone

chasm *noun* (*plural* **chasms**) (*pronounced* ka-zum)
a deep opening in the ground

chassis *noun* (*plural* **chassis**) (*pronounced* shass-i)
the frame and wheels of a vehicle, which support the body

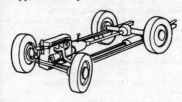

chat ➤ *noun* (*plural* **chats**)
a friendly or informal talk with someone

chat ➤ *verb* (**chats, chatting, chatted**)
to chat to someone is to talk to them in a friendly or informal way

chatty *adjective* liking to chat with people

château *noun* (*plural* **châteaux**) (*pronounced* shat-oh)
a castle or large house in France

chatter *verb* (**chatters, chattering, chattered**)
1 to talk quickly or stupidly; to talk too much 2 to make a rattling noise

chauffeur *noun* (*plural* **chauffeurs**) (*pronounced* shoh-fer)
someone who is paid to drive a car for someone

chauvinism *noun* (*pronounced* shoh-vin-izm)
1 chauvinism is believing your country is always better than any other 2 male chauvinism is believing men are always better than women

chauvinist *noun* someone who shows chauvinism

cheap *adjective* (**cheaper, cheapest**)
1 low in price; not expensive 2 shoddy or inferior

cheat ➤ *verb* (**cheats, cheating, cheated**)
1 to cheat someone is to trick them so they lose something 2 to cheat is to try to do well in an examination or game by breaking the rules

cheat ➤ *noun* (*plural* **cheats**)
someone who cheats

check ➤ *verb* (**checks, checking, checked**)
1 to check something is to make sure that it is correct or all right 2 to check someone or something is to make them stop or slow down

to check in is to sign your name to show you have arrived at a hotel or to show your ticket at an airport

to check on something or **check up on something** is to look at it carefully to see if it is correct or suitable

to check out is to pay your bill and leave a hotel

check ➤ *noun* (*plural* **checks**)
1 a check is when you check something 2 check in chess is when the king is threatened by another piece 3 a check is a pattern of squares

checkmate *noun* (*plural* **checkmates**)
checkmate in chess is when one side wins by trapping the other side's king

checkout *noun* (*plural* **checkouts**)
the place where you pay for your shopping in a supermarket or a large shop

check-up *noun* (*plural* **check-ups**)
a careful check or examination

cheek ➤ *noun* (*plural* **cheeks**)
1 your cheek is the side of your face below your eye 2 cheek is being rude or impolite

cheek ➤ *verb* (**cheeks, cheeking, cheeked**)
to cheek someone is to be rude to them

cheeky *adjective* (**cheekier, cheekiest**)
rude or impolite

cheekily *adverb* in a cheeky way

cheer ➤ *noun* (*plural* **cheers**)
a shout praising or supporting someone

cheer ➤ *verb* (**cheers, cheering, cheered**)
1 to cheer someone is to support them by cheering 2 to cheer someone is to comfort or encourage them

to cheer someone up is to make them more cheerful

to cheer up is to become more cheerful

cheerful *adjective*
happy and bright

cheerio *interjection*
(*informal*) goodbye

cheese *noun* (*plural* **cheeses**)
a solid food made from milk curds
cheesy *adjective* like cheese

cheetah *noun* (*plural* **cheetahs**)
a large spotted animal of the cat family,
which can run very fast

chef *noun* (*plural* **chefs**) (*pronounced* shef)
the chief cook in a hotel or restaurant

chemical ➤ *noun* (*plural* **chemicals**)
a substance used in or made by chemistry

chemical ➤ *adjective*
to do with chemistry or made by chemistry

chemist *noun* (*plural* **chemists**)
1 someone who makes or sells medicines
2 an expert in chemistry

chemistry *noun*
chemistry is the study of the way
substances combine and react with one
another

cheque *noun* (*plural* **cheques**)
a written form instructing a bank to pay
money out of an account

chequebook *noun* (*plural* **chequebooks**)
a book of blank cheques for filling in

chequered *adjective*
marked with a pattern of squares

cherish *verb* (**cherishes, cherishing, cherished**)
to cherish something is to look after it
lovingly

cherry *noun* (*plural* **cherries**)
a small bright red fruit with a stone

chess *noun*
a game for two players played with sixteen
pieces each (called **chessmen**) on a board of
64 squares (called a **chessboard**)

chest *noun* (*plural* **chests**)
1 a chest is a large strong box 2 your
chest is the front part of your body
between your neck and your waist
to get something off your chest (*informal*) is to
admit something you are worried about

chestnut *noun* (*plural* **chestnuts**)
1 a hard brown nut 2 the tree that
produces this kind of nut

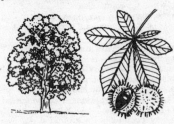

chest of drawers *noun* (*plural* **chests of
drawers**)
a piece of furniture with drawers for
holding clothes

chew *verb* (**chews, chewing, chewed**)
to chew food is to grind it into pieces
between your teeth
chewy *adjective* tough and needing a lot of
chewing

chewing gum *noun*
a sticky flavoured gum for chewing

chic *adjective* (*pronounced* sheek)
smart and elegant

chick *noun* (*plural* **chicks**)
a young bird, especially a young chicken

chicken ➤ *noun* (*plural* **chickens**)
1 a young hen 2 a hen's flesh used as food

chicken ➤ *adjective*
(*informal*) cowardly

chicken ➤ *verb* (**chickens, chickening,
chickened**)
to chicken out of something (*informal*) is to
avoid it because you are afraid

chickenpox *noun*
a disease that produces red spots on your
skin

chief ➤ *noun* (*plural* **chiefs**)
1 a leader, especially of a Native
American tribe 2 the most important
person, the boss

chief ➤ *adjective*
most important

chiefly *adverb*
mainly, mostly ♦ *Peter is the one who is
chiefly to blame*

chieftain *noun* (*plural* **chieftains**)
the chief of a tribe or clan

chilblain *noun* (*plural* **chilblains**)
a sore place, usually on a hand or foot, caused by cold weather

child *noun* (*plural* **children**)
1 a young person; a boy or girl
2 someone's son or daughter ♦ *Whose child is that?*

childhood *noun* (*plural* **childhoods**)
the time when you are a child

childish *adjective*
silly and immature ♦ *Don't be childish!*

childminder *noun* (*plural* **childminders**)
a person who is paid to look after children while their parents are out at work

childproof *adjective*
not able to be opened or operated by small children ♦ *The car has childproof door locks*

chill ➤ *noun* (*plural* **chills**)
1 chill is coldness **2** a chill is a cold that makes you shiver

chill ➤ *verb* (**chills, chilling, chilled**)
to chill something or someone is to make them cold

chilli *noun* (*plural* **chillies**)
the hot-tasting pod of a red pepper

chilly *adjective* (**chillier, chilliest**)
1 slightly cold **2** unfriendly ♦ *They went to see the head and got a chilly reception*

chime ➤ *noun* (*plural* **chimes**)
a sound made by a bell

chime ➤ *verb* (**chimes, chiming, chimed**)
to chime is to ring ♦ *The clock chimes every quarter-hour*

chimney *noun* (*plural* **chimneys**)
a tall pipe or passage that carries away smoke from a fire

chimney pot *noun* (*plural* **chimney pots**)
the piece of pipe at the top of a chimney

chimney sweep *noun* (*plural* **chimney sweeps**)
someone who cleans the soot out of chimneys

chimpanzee *noun* (*plural* **chimpanzees**)
a type of African ape

chin *noun* (*plural* **chins**)
your chin is the part of your face under your mouth

china *noun*
china is thin and delicate pottery

chink *noun* (*plural* **chinks**)
1 a narrow opening ♦ *He looked through a chink in the curtains* **2** a clinking sound ♦ *They heard the chink of coins*

chip ➤ *noun* (*plural* **chips**)
1 a small piece of something **2** a place where a small piece has been knocked off something **3** a small piece of fried potato **4** a small counter used in gambling games **5** a silicon chip
to have a chip on your shoulder is to feel defensive and resentful about something ♦ *He's got a chip on his shoulder about rich people*

chip ➤ *verb* (**chips, chipping, chipped**)
to chip something is to knock a small piece off it by accident

chirp *verb* (**chirps, chirping, chirped**)
to chirp is to make short sharp sounds like a small bird

chirpy *adjective* (**chirpier, chirpiest**)
(*informal*) lively and cheerful

chisel ➤ *noun* (*plural* **chisels**)
a tool with a sharp end for shaping wood or stone

chisel ➤ *verb* (**chisels, chiselling, chiselled**)
to chisel wood or stone is to shape or cut it with a chisel

chivalrous *adjective*
ready to help people who are less strong than you are
chivalry *noun* being chivalrous

chlorine *noun*
a chemical used to disinfect water

chlorophyll *noun*
the substance that makes plants green

choc *noun* (*plural* **chocs**)
(*informal*) a chocolate

choc ice *noun* (*plural* **choc ices**)
an ice cream covered with chocolate

chock-a-block or **chock-full** *adjective* and *adverb*
completely full

chocolate *noun* (*plural* **chocolates**)
1 chocolate is a sweet brown food **2** a chocolate is a sweet made of or covered with chocolate **3** chocolate is also a sweet powder used for making drinks

choice *noun* (*plural* **choices**)
1 choice is the process of choosing or the power to choose ♦ *I'm afraid we have no choice* **2** a choice is what someone chooses ♦ *Let me know your choice of book*

choir *noun* (*plural* **choirs**)
a group of singers, especially in a church
choirboy or **choirgirl** *noun* a boy or girl singer in a choir

choke ➤ *verb* (**chokes, choking, choked**)
1 to choke someone is to stop them breathing properly **2** to choke is to be unable to breathe properly **3** to choke something is to block it up

choke ➤ *noun* (*plural* **chokes**)
a device in a motor vehicle to control the mixture of air and petrol

cholera *noun* (*pronounced* **kol**-er-a)
cholera is a severe infectious disease that affects the intestines

cholesterol *noun* (*pronounced* ko-**less**-te-rol)
cholesterol is a substance found in the cells of your body which helps to carry fat in the bloodstream

choose *verb* (**chooses, choosing, chose, chosen**)
1 to choose something or someone is to decide to take them instead of another **2** to choose is to make a decision about something ♦ *Do hurry up and choose*

choosy *adjective* (**choosier, choosiest**)
(*informal*) fussy and difficult to please

chop ➤ *verb* (**chops, chopping, chopped**)
1 to chop something up is to cut it into small pieces **2** to chop something is to cut or hit it with a heavy blow

chop ➤ *noun* (*plural* **chops**)
1 a chopping blow **2** a small thick slice of meat
to get the chop (*slang*) is to be sacked from a job

chopper *noun* (*plural* **choppers**)
1 a small axe **2** (*informal*) a helicopter

choppy *adjective* (**choppier, choppiest**)
a choppy sea is fairly rough with small waves

chopsticks *plural noun*
a pair of thin sticks used for eating Chinese or Japanese food

choral *adjective* (*pronounced* **kor**-al)
for a choir or chorus

chord *noun* (*plural* **chords**) (*pronounced* kord)
a number of musical notes sounded together

chore *noun* (*plural* **chores**) (*pronounced* chor)
a tedious or difficult task

chorister *noun* (*plural* **choristers**) (*pronounced* **kor**-is-ter)
someone who sings in a choir

chorus *noun* (*plural* **choruses**) (*pronounced* **kor**-us)
1 a group of people singing or speaking together **2** a piece of music sung by a group of people **3** the words repeated after every verse of a song or poem

chose past tense of **choose**

chosen past participle of **choose**

christen *verb* (**christens, christening, christened**)
to christen someone is to baptize them
christening *noun* the ceremony of baptizing someone

Christian ➤ *noun* (*plural* **Christians**)
someone who believes in Christ

Christian ➤ *adjective*
to do with Christ or Christians

Christianity *noun*
the religion of Christians

Christian name *noun* (*plural* **Christian names**)
a first name, for example *John* and *Mary*

Christmas *noun* (*plural* **Christmases**)
the time of celebrating the birth of Christ on 25 December

chrome or **chromium** *noun*
a shiny silvery metal

chromosome *noun* (*plural* **chromosomes**)
the part of an animal cell that carries the genes

chronic *adjective*
1 lasting for a long time ♦ *She's suffering from chronic diabetes* **2** (*informal*) very bad or unpleasant ♦ *He was telling us chronic stories about his holidays*
chronically *adverb* for a long time

chronicle *noun* (*plural* **chronicles**)
a list of events with their dates

chronological *adjective*
arranged in the order in which things happen
chronologically *adverb* in the order things happen

chronology *noun*
the arrangement of events in the order in which they happened, especially in history or geology

chrysalis *noun* (*plural* **chrysalises**) (*pronounced* **kris**-a-lis)
the hard cover a caterpillar makes round itself before it turns into a butterfly or moth

chrysanthemum *noun* (*plural* **chrysanthemums**)
a garden flower that blooms in autumn

chubby *adjective* (**chubbier, chubbiest**)
plump and healthy

chuck *verb* (**chucks, chucking, chucked**)
(*informal*) to chuck something is to throw it

chuckle ➤ *verb* (**chuckles, chuckling, chuckled**)
to chuckle is to laugh quietly

chuckle ➤ *noun* (*plural* **chuckles**)
a quiet laugh

chug *verb* (**chugs, chugging, chugged**)
to chug is to move with the sound of a slow-running engine

chum *noun* (*plural* **chums**)
(*informal*) a friend
chummy *adjective* friendly

chunk *noun* (*plural* **chunks**)
a thick lump
chunky *adjective* big and thick

church *noun* (*plural* **churches**)
1 a church is a building where Christians worship 2 a church is also a particular Christian religion, for example the Church of England

churchyard *noun* (*plural* **churchyards**)
the ground round a church, usually used as a graveyard

churn ➤ *noun* (*plural* **churns**)
1 a large container for milk 2 a machine for making butter

churn ➤ *verb* (**churns, churning, churned**)
1 to churn butter is to make it in a churn 2 to churn something is to stir it vigorously
to churn something out (*informal*) is to produce lots of it

chute *noun* (*plural* **chutes**) (*pronounced* shoot)
a steep channel for people or things to slide down

chutney *noun*
chutney is a strong-tasting mixture of fruit and peppers in a sauce, eaten with meat

cider *noun* (*plural* **ciders**)
cider is an alcoholic drink made from apples

cigar *noun* (*plural* **cigars**)
a roll of compressed tobacco leaves for smoking

cigarette *noun* (*plural* **cigarettes**)
a small, thin roll of shredded tobacco in thin paper for smoking

cinder *noun* (*plural* **cinders**)
a small piece of coal or wood that is partly burned

cine camera *noun* (*plural* **cine cameras**)
a camera used for taking moving pictures on film

cinema *noun* (*plural* **cinemas**)
a place where people go to see films

cinnamon *noun*
a yellowish-brown spice

circle ➤ *noun* (*plural* **circles**)
1 a round flat shape, the shape of a coin or wheel 2 a balcony in a cinema or theatre 3 a number of people with similar interests ♦ *She belongs to a writers' circle*

circle ➤ *verb* (**circles, circling, circled**)
1 to circle is to move in a circle ♦ *Vultures circled overhead* 2 to circle a place is go round it ♦ *The space probe circled Mars*

circuit *noun* (*plural* **circuits**) (*pronounced* ser-kit)
1 a circular line or journey 2 a racecourse 3 the path of an electric current

circular ➤ *adjective*
round like a circle

circular ➤ *noun* (*plural* **circulars**)
a letter or advertisement sent to a lot of people

circulate *verb* (**circulates, circulating, circulated**)
1 to circulate is to move around and come back to the beginning ♦ *Blood circulates in the body* 2 to circulate something like a letter or notice is to send it to a lot of people

circulation *noun* (*plural* **circulations**)
1 the movement of blood around your body 2 the number of copies of each issue of a newspaper or magazine that are sold

circumference *noun* (*plural* **circumferences**)
the line or distance round something, especially round a circle

circumstance *noun* (*plural* **circumstances**)
a fact or event that affects something ♦ *He won under difficult circumstances*

circus *noun* (*plural* **circuses**)
an entertainment with clowns, acrobats, and animals, usually performed in a large tent

cistern *noun* (*plural* **cisterns**)
a water tank

citizen *noun* (*plural* **citizens**)
a citizen of a place is someone who was born there or lives there
citizenship *noun* the rights of a citizen

citric acid *noun*
a weak acid found in fruits like lemons and limes

citrus *adjective*
to do with fruits like oranges, lemons, and grapefruit

city *noun* (*plural* **cities**)
a large and important town, often having a cathedral

civic *adjective*
to do with a city or its citizens

civil *adjective*
1 concerning the citizens of a place 2 to do with the ordinary people and not those who are in the armed forces 3 polite, courteous

civil engineering *noun*
designing and making roads, bridges, and large buildings

civilian *noun* (*plural* civilians)
someone who is an ordinary citizen and not in the armed forces

civilization *noun* (*plural* civilizations)
1 a civilization is a society or culture at a particular time in history ♦ *They were learning about the Bronze Age civilization* 2 civilization is a developed or organized way of life ♦ *We are studying a primitive society with little civilization*

civilize *verb* (civilizes, civilizing, civilized)
to civilize someone is to improve their education and manners

civil rights *plural noun*
the rights of citizens to have freedom and equality, and to vote

civil service *noun*
the paid administrators of a country

civil war *noun* (*plural* civil wars)
a war fought between people of the same country, such as the English Civil War (1642–51) or the American Civil War (1861–65)

clad *adjective*
clothed ♦ *The story was about a knight clad in shining armour*

claim ➤ *verb* (claims, claiming, claimed)
1 to claim something is to ask for it when you think it belongs to you ♦ *I'd like to claim the three weeks' pocket money you owe me* 2 to claim something is to state or assert it ♦ *They claimed they had been at home all evening*

claim ➤ *noun* (*plural* claims)
1 an act of claiming 2 something claimed

claimant *noun* (*plural* claimants)
someone who makes a claim, especially for a right or benefit

clam *noun* (*plural* clams)
a large shellfish

clamber *verb* (clambers, clambering, clambered)
to clamber is to climb with difficulty ♦ *We clambered over the slippery rocks*

clammy *adjective* (clammier, clammiest)
damp and slimy

clamp ➤ *noun* (*plural* clamps)
a device for holding things together

clamp ➤ *verb* (clamps, clamping, clamped)
to clamp something is to fit a clamp on it
to clamp down on something is to be strict about it ♦ *The teachers decided to clamp down on homework*

clan *noun* (*plural* clans)
a number of families with the same ancestor ♦ *The Scottish clans include the Campbells and the MacDonalds*

clang *verb* (clangs, clanging, clanged)
to clang is to make a loud ringing sound

clanger *noun* (*plural* clangers)
(*slang*) a blunder
to drop a clanger is to make a blunder

clank *verb* (clanks, clanking, clanked)
to clank is to make a loud sound like heavy pieces of metal banging together

clap ➤ *verb* (claps, clapping, clapped)
to clap is to make a noise by hitting the palms of your hands together, especially as applause

clap ➤ *noun* (*plural* claps)
1 a round of clapping, especially as applause ♦ *They gave the winners a loud clap* 2 a clap of thunder is a sudden sound of loud thunder

clapper *noun* (*plural* clappers)
the piece that swings inside a bell and makes it ring when the bell is moved
like the clappers (*slang*) very quickly or very hard ♦ *They were running like the clappers to get the bus*

clarify *verb* (clarifies, clarifying, clarified)
to clarify something is to explain it and make it clear
clarification *noun* making something clear

clarinet *noun* (*plural* clarinets)
a woodwind instrument with a low tone
clarinettist *noun* someone who plays a clarinet

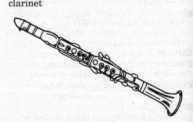

clarity *noun*
clearness ♦ *Try to speak with clarity*

clash ➤ *verb* (clashes, clashing, clashed)
1 to clash is to make a loud sound like cymbals banging together 2 two events clash when they happen inconveniently at

the same time ♦ *My favourite TV programmes clash at 8 o'clock tonight* **3** two or more people clash when they have a fight or argument ♦ *Gangs of rival supporters clashed outside the ground*

clash ➤ *noun* (*plural* **clashes**)
1 a clashing sound **2** a fight or argument

clasp ➤ *verb* (**clasps, clasping, clasped**)
to clasp someone or something is to hold them tightly

clasp ➤ *noun* (*plural* **clasps**)
1 a device for fastening things **2** a tight grasp

class ➤ *noun* (*plural* **classes**)
1 a class is a group of similar people, animals, or things **2** a class is also a group of children or students who are taught together **3** class is a system of different ranks in society
to have class (*informal*) is to look smart or behave elegantly

class ➤ *verb* (**classes, classing, classed**)
to class things is to put them in classes or groups

classic ➤ *noun* (*plural* **classics**)
a book, film, or story that is well known and thought to be very good and important

classic ➤ *adjective*
generally thought to be very good and important
classics is the study of Greek and Latin

classical *adjective*
1 to do with Greek and Latin literature **2** classical music is serious music, often written in the past and still played

classified *adjective*
1 put into classes or groups **2** officially secret ♦ *That is classified information*

classified advertisements *plural noun*
brief newspaper advertisements arranged in subjects

classify *verb* (**classifies, classifying, classified**)
to classify things is to put them in classes or groups
classification *noun* a system of classifying things

classmate *noun* (*plural* **classmates**)
someone in the same class at school

classroom *noun* (*plural* **classrooms**)
a room where a class is taught

clatter ➤ *noun*
a loud noise of things being rattled or banged

clatter ➤ *verb* (**clatters, clattering, clattered**)
to clatter is to make a clatter

clause *noun* (*plural* **clauses**)
1 a part of a contract, treaty, or law **2** (*in Grammar*) part of a sentence with its own verb

claw ➤ *noun* (*plural* **claws**)
one of the hard sharp nails that some birds and animals have on their feet

claw ➤ *verb* (**claws, clawing, clawed**)
to claw something is to grasp or scratch it with a claw or hand

clay *noun*
clay is a sticky kind of earth, and is used for making bricks and pottery
clayey *adjective* like clay

clean ➤ *adjective* (**cleaner, cleanest**)
1 free of dirt and stains **2** fresh, not yet used ♦ *Start on a clean page* **3** not rude or offensive ♦ *I hope your jokes are clean ones* **4** fair and honest ♦ *They wanted a clean fight*

clean ➤ *verb* (**cleans, cleaning, cleaned**)
to clean something is to make it clean

clean ➤ *adverb*
(*informal*) completely ♦ *I clean forgot*

cleaner *noun* (*plural* **cleaners**)
1 someone who cleans rooms or offices **2** something used for cleaning
the cleaners a firm which cleans clothes

cleanliness *noun* (*pronounced* **klen**-li-nes)
the practice of keeping things clean

cleanly *adverb*
neatly, exactly ♦ *He cut the brick cleanly in two*

cleanse *verb* (**cleanses, cleansing, cleansed**) (*pronounced* klenz)
to cleanse something is to clean it and make it pure
cleanser *noun* something that cleanses

clear ➤ *adjective* (**clearer, clearest**)
1 easy to see or hear or understand ♦ *He spoke with a clear voice* **2** free from things that get in the way or aren't wanted ♦ *Make sure the table's clear for dinner*

clear ➤ *adverb*
1 clearly ♦ *Speak loud and clear* **2** completely ♦ *He got clear away* **3** at a distance from something ♦ *You'd better stand clear of the gates*

clear ➤ *verb* (**clears, clearing, cleared**)
1 to clear something is to make it free of unwanted things ♦ *Will you clear the table for dinner?* **2** to clear is to become clearer ♦ *After the storm, the sky slowly cleared* **3** to clear someone is to find out that they are not to blame for something they were suspected of **4** to clear something is to jump over it without touching it
to clear off or **clear out** (*informal*) is to go away
to clear something out is to empty or tidy it
to clear up is to make things tidy

clearance *noun* (*plural* **clearances**)
1 getting rid of unwanted goods **2** the space between two things ♦ *There was not much clearance between the bridge and the top of the bus*

clearing *noun* (*plural* **clearings**)
an open space in a wood or forest

clearly *adverb*
in a clear way; obviously ♦ *He was clearly an idiot*

clef *noun* (*plural* **clefs**)
a sign that shows the pitch of a stave in music

clench *verb* (**clenches, clenching, clenched**)
to clench your teeth or fingers is to close them tightly

clergy *plural noun*
the clergy are the priests and other officials of a Christian Church

clergyman *noun* (*plural* **clergymen**)
a male member of the clergy

clergywoman *noun* (*plural* **clergywomen**)
a female member of the clergy

clerical *adjective*
1 to do with the routine work in an office, such as filing and writing letters **2** to do with the clergy

clerk *noun* (*plural* **clerks**) (*pronounced* klark)
someone employed to keep records and accounts and deal with the papers in an office

clever *adjective* (**cleverer, cleverest**)
quick to learn and understand things; skilful

cliché *noun* (*plural* **clichés**) (*pronounced* klee-shay)
a phrase that people use a lot, so that it doesn't mean very much

click *noun* (*plural* **clicks**)
a short sharp sound ♦ *She heard a click as someone turned on the light*

client *noun* (*plural* **clients**)
someone who gets help or advice from a professional person such as a lawyer or architect; a customer

cliff *noun* (*plural* **cliffs**)
a steep rock face, especially on the coast

cliffhanger *noun* (*plural* **cliffhangers**)
something like a story or a sports match that is exciting because you do not know how it will finish

climate *noun* (*plural* **climates**)
the normal weather in a particular area
climatic *adjective* to do with the climate

climax *noun* (*plural* **climaxes**)
the most important part of a story or series of events

climb ➤ *verb* (**climbs, climbing, climbed**)
1 to climb or climb up something is go up it **2** to climb down something is to go down it **3** to climb is to grow or rise upwards, like a tall plant or a building
to climb down is to admit that you have been wrong

climb ➤ *noun* (*plural* **climbs**)
an act of climbing

climber *noun* (*plural* **climbers**)
someone who climbs hills and mountains for sport

cling *verb* (**clings, clinging, clung**)
to cling to someone or something is to hold on tightly ♦ *The child was clinging to its mother*

clingfilm *noun*
a thin clear plastic material that sticks to itself easily and is used for wrapping food

clinic *noun* (*plural* **clinics**)
a place where people see doctors for treatment or advice

clink *verb* (**clinks, clinking, clinked**)
to clink is to make a short ringing sound, like a coin being dropped

clip ➤ *noun* (*plural* **clips**)
a fastener for keeping things together

clip ➤ *verb* (**clips, clipping, clipped**)
1 to clip things together is to fasten them with a clip **2** to clip something is to cut it with shears or scissors

clipboard *noun* (*plural* **clipboards**)
a board that you can carry around, with a clip at the top to hold papers

clipper *noun* (*plural* **clippers**)
an old type of fast sailing ship

clippers *plural noun*
large scissors for clipping

clipping *noun* (*plural* **clippings**)
a piece cut from a newspaper or magazine

cloak *noun* (*plural* **cloaks**)
a piece of outdoor clothing, usually without sleeves, that hangs loosely from your shoulders

cloakroom *noun* (*plural* **cloakrooms**)
1 a place where you can leave coats and bags while you are visiting a building **2** a lavatory

clobber *verb* (**clobbers, clobbering, clobbered**)
(*slang*) to clobber someone is to hit them hard

clock *noun* (*plural* **clocks**)
a device that shows what the time is

clockwise *adverb* and *adjective*
moving round a circle in the same direction as the hands of a clock

clockwork *adjective*
worked by a spring which you wind up

clog ➤ *verb* (**clogs, clogging, clogged**)
to clog something is to block it up accidentally

clog ➤ *noun* (*plural* **clogs**)
a shoe made entirely or mostly of wood

cloister *noun* (*plural* **cloisters**)
a covered path round a courtyard or along the side of a cathedral or monastery

clone ➤ *noun* (*plural* **clones**)
an animal or plant made from the cells of another animal or plant

clone ➤ *verb* (**clones, cloning, cloned**)
to clone something is to produce a clone of it

close[1] ➤ *adjective* (**closer, closest**)
(*pronounced* klohss)
1 near, either in time or place ♦ *They were close to finding the answer* ♦ *The shops were quite close to their new house*
2 careful and detailed ♦ *Please pay close attention* **3** tight; with little empty space ♦ *They got the wardrobe in but it was a close fit* **4** in which competitors are nearly equal ♦ *The race was very close* **5** stuffy; without fresh air ♦ *It's very close in this room*

close ➤ *adverb* (**closer, closest**) (*pronounced* klohss)
at a close distance ♦ *The children were following close behind*

close ➤ *noun* (*plural* **closes**) (*pronounced* klohss)
1 a street that is closed at one end **2** an enclosed area, especially round a cathedral

close[2] *verb* (**closes, closing, closed**)
(*pronounced* klohz)
1 to close something is to shut it **2** to close an event or meeting is to finish it
to close down is to stop trading ♦ *Several shops in the High Street have closed down recently*
to close in is to get nearer ♦ *The police closed in around the house*

closely *adverb* (*pronounced* klohss-li)
1 carefully, with attention ♦ *His friends were watching closely* **2** tightly ♦ *The box was closely packed with toys*

close-up *noun* (*plural* **close-ups**)
(*pronounced* klohss-up)
a photograph or film taken at short range

closure *noun* (*plural* **closures**) (*pronounced* kloh-zher)
the closure of a business is when it closes down

clot ➤ *noun* (*plural* **clots**)
1 a mass of thick liquid like blood or cream that has become nearly solid **2** (*informal*) a stupid person

clot ➤ *verb* (**clots, clotting, clotted**)
to clot is to form into clots, like blood or cream

cloth *noun* (*plural* **cloths**)
1 cloth is material woven from wool, cotton, or some other fabric **2** a cloth is a piece of this material **3** a cloth is also a tablecloth

clothe *verb* (**clothes, clothing, clothed**)
to clothe someone is to put clothes on them

clothes *plural noun*
clothes are things like shirts and coats worn to cover your body

clothes line *noun* (*plural* **clothes lines**)
a line on which clothes are hung to dry or air

clothing *noun*
clothing is clothes

cloud ➤ *noun* (*plural* **clouds**)
1 a mass of water vapour floating in the air **2** a mass of smoke or something else dense in the air

cloud ➤ *verb* (**clouds, clouding, clouded**)
to cloud or cloud over is to become full of clouds ♦ *In the afternoon the sky clouded over*

cloudless *adjective* not having any clouds

cloudy *adjective* (**cloudier, cloudiest**)
1 full of clouds **2** hard to see through ♦ *The glass contained a cloudy liquid*

clout *verb* (**clouts, clouting, clouted**)
to clout someone is to give them a hard blow

clove *noun* (*plural* **cloves**)
the dried bud of a tropical tree used as a spice, especially to flavour apples

clover *noun*
a small wild plant, usually with leaves in three parts

clown ➤ *noun* (*plural* **clowns**)
1 a circus comedian who dresses up and wears bright face paint **2** an amusing or silly person

clown ➤ *verb* (**clowns, clowning, clowned**)
to clown is to behave like a clown

club ➤ *noun* (*plural* **clubs**)
1 a heavy stick **2** a stick for playing golf **3** a group of people who meet together because they are interested in the same thing **4** a playing card with a black cloverleaf printed on it

club ➤ *verb* (**clubs, clubbing, clubbed**)
to club someone is to hit them hard with a heavy stick
to club together is to join with other people in doing something, especially raising money

cluck *verb* (**clucks, clucking, clucked**)
to cluck is to make a noise like a hen

clue *noun* (*plural* **clues**)
something that helps you to solve a puzzle or a mystery

clueless *adjective*
(*informal*) stupid; having no idea of how to do something

clump *noun* (*plural* **clumps**)
a cluster of trees or plants

clumsy *adjective* (**clumsier, clumsiest**)
a clumsy person is careless and awkward, and likely to knock things over or drop things
clumsily *adverb* in a clumsy way **clumsiness** *noun* being clumsy

clung past tense and past participle of **cling**

cluster *noun* (*plural* **clusters**)
a group of people or things close together

clutch[1] ➤ *verb* (**clutches, clutching, clutched**)
to clutch something or clutch at something is to grab hold of it

clutch ➤ *noun* (*plural* **clutches**)
1 a tight grasp **2** a device for disconnecting the engine of a motor vehicle from its gears and wheels

clutch[2] *noun* (*plural* **clutches**)
a set of eggs in a nest

clutter ➤ *verb* (**clutters, cluttering, cluttered**)
to clutter a place up is to make it untidy or messy

clutter ➤ *noun*
clutter is a lot of things left around untidily

cm short for **centimetre** or **centimetres**

Co. short for **company**

c/o short for **care of**

coach ➤ *noun* (*plural* **coaches**)
1 a comfortable bus, usually with one deck, used for long journeys **2** a carriage of a railway train **3** a carriage pulled by horses **4** a sports instructor

coach ➤ *verb* (**coaches, coaching, coached**)
to coach someone is to instruct or train them in a sport

coal *noun*
coal is a hard black mineral used as fuel

coarse *adjective* (**coarser, coarsest**)
1 rough, not delicate or smooth **2** rude or offensive ♦ *You have a very coarse sense of humour*

coast ➤ *noun* (*plural* **coasts**)
the seashore and the land close to it

coast ➤ *verb* (**coasts, coasting, coasted**)
to coast is to ride downhill without using power ♦ *They stopped pedalling and coasted down the slope*

coastal *adjective*
near the coast

coastguard *noun* (*plural* **coastguards**)
someone whose job is to keep watch on coasts to prevent smuggling

coastline *noun*
the edge of the land by the sea

coat ➤ *noun* (*plural* **coats**)
1 a piece of clothing with sleeves, worn over other clothes **2** a coating

coat ➤ *verb* (**coats, coating, coated**)
to coat something is to cover it with a coating

coating *noun* (*plural* **coatings**)
a covering or layer, especially of paint

coat of arms *noun* (*plural* **coats of arms**)
a design on a shield or building, representing a historic family or town

coax *verb* (**coaxes, coaxing, coaxed**)
to coax someone is to persuade them gently or patiently

cobalt *noun*
cobalt is a silvery-white metal

cobbled *adjective*
paved with cobblestones

cobbler *noun* (*plural* **cobblers**)
someone who mends shoes
cobblers (*slang*) nonsense

cobbles *plural noun*
cobbles are a surface of cobblestones

cobblestone *noun* (*plural* **cobblestones**)
a small smooth and rounded stone sometimes used in large numbers to pave streets in towns

cobra *noun* (*plural* **cobras**) (*pronounced* koh-bra)
a poisonous snake

cobweb *noun* (*plural* **cobwebs**)
a thin, sticky net spun by a spider to trap insects

cock ➤ *noun* (*plural* **cocks**)
a male bird, especially a male fowl

cock ➤ *verb* (**cocks, cocking, cocked**)
1 to cock your eye or ear is to turn it in a particular direction **2** to cock a gun is to make it ready to fire

cockerel *noun* (*plural* **cockerels**)
a young male fowl

cocker spaniel *noun* (*plural* **cocker spaniels**)
a kind of small spaniel

cockle *noun* (*plural* **cockles**)
an edible shellfish

cockney *noun* (*plural* **cockneys**)
1 a cockney is someone born in the East End of London **2** cockney is a kind of English spoken by cockneys

cockpit *noun* (*plural* **cockpits**)
the place in an aircraft where the pilot sits

cockroach *noun* (*plural* **cockroaches**)
a dark brown insect

cocky *adjective* (**cockier, cockiest**)
(*informal*) conceited and cheeky

cocoa *noun* (*plural* **cocoas**)
1 a hot drink that tastes of chocolate
2 the powder from which you make this
drink

coconut *noun* (*plural* **coconuts**)
a large round nut containing a milky juice,
that grows on palm trees

cocoon *noun* (*plural* **cocoons**)
the covering round a chrysalis

cod *noun* (*plural* **cod**)
a large edible sea fish

code ➤ *noun* (*plural* **codes**)
1 a set of signs and letters for sending
messages secretly 2 a set of rules ♦ *the
Highway Code*

code ➤ *verb* (**codes, coding, coded**)
1 to code a message is to use special signs
and letters, so that other people cannot
understand it 2 to code data is to put it
into a form that can be accepted by a
computer

coeducation *noun*
educating boys and girls together
coeducational *adjective* to do with
coeducation

coffee *noun* (*plural* **coffees**)
1 a hot drink made from the roasted and
crushed beans of a tropical shrub 2 the
powder from which you make this drink

coffin *noun* (*plural* **coffins**)
a long box in which a corpse is buried or
cremated

cog *noun* (*plural* **cogs**)
one of a number of pieces sticking out from
the edge of a wheel and allowing it to drive
another wheel

cohort *noun* (*plural* **cohorts**)
in the ancient Roman army, any one of the
ten parts of a legion

coil ➤ *noun* (*plural* **coils**)
a circle or spiral of rope or wire

coil ➤ *verb* (**coils, coiling, coiled**)
to coil something is to wind it into circles
or spirals

coin ➤ *noun* (*plural* **coins**)
a piece of metal money

coin ➤ *verb* (**coins, coining, coined**)
1 to coin money is to manufacture it 2 to
coin a new word is to invent it

coinage *noun* (*plural* **coinages**)
1 coinage is manufacturing money 2 a
coinage is a system of money

coincide *verb* (**coincides, coinciding, coincided**)
to coincide is to happen at the same time
as something else ♦ *The end of term
coincides with my birthday*

coincidence *noun* (*plural* **coincidences**)
the way that two things can happen
accidentally at the same time; a case of
this happening

coke *noun*
a solid fuel made out of coal

cola *noun* (*plural* **colas**)
a sweet brown fizzy drink

colander *noun* (*plural* **colanders**)
(*pronounced* **kul-an-der**)
a strainer for vegetables

cold ➤ *adjective* (**colder, coldest**)
1 low in temperature, not hot or warm
2 a cold person is unfriendly and distant

cold ➤ *noun* (*plural* **colds**)
1 cold weather or temperature 2 a cold is
an illness that makes your nose run and
gives you a sore throat
coldly *adverb* in an unfriendly way **coldness**
noun being unfriendly

cold-blooded *adjective*
1 having blood that changes temperature
according to the surroundings 2 cruel,
ruthless

coleslaw *noun*
a salad made of chopped cabbage covered
in mayonnaise

collaborate *verb* (**collaborates, collaborating, collaborated**)
1 to collaborate with someone is to work
with them on a job 2 to collaborate with
an enemy is to work secretly on their side
collaboration *noun* collaborating with
someone **collaborator** *noun* someone who
works with an enemy

collage *noun* (*plural* **collages**) (*pronounced*
kol-ah*zh* or kol-ah*zh*)
a picture made by arranging scraps of
paper and other things on a card

collapse ➤ *verb* (**collapses, collapsing, collapsed**)
1 to collapse is to break or fall to pieces
2 to collapse is to become very weak or ill

collapse ➤ *noun* (*plural* **collapses**)
1 an act of collapsing 2 a breakdown

collapsible *adjective*
able to be folded up

collar *noun* (*plural* **collars**)
1 the part of a piece of clothing that goes round your neck 2 a band that goes round the neck of a dog, cat, or other animal

collate *verb* (**collates, collating, collated**)
to collate things such as pieces of information is to collect and arrange them in an organized way ♦ *They had to collate the results in the form of a graph*

colleague *noun* (*plural* **colleagues**)
someone you work with

collect *verb* (**collects, collecting, collected**)
1 to collect things is to get them together from various places, especially as a hobby ♦ *She collects stamps, and I collect coins*
2 to collect someone or something is to go and get them

collector *noun* someone who collects things for a hobby

collection *noun* (*plural* **collections**)
1 things you have collected as a hobby
2 money given by people at a meeting or concert or church service

collective *adjective*
involving several people or things ♦ *It was a collective decision*

collective noun *noun* (*plural* **collective nouns**)
a singular noun that is a name for a group of things or people, for example *choir, flock, government*

college *noun* (*plural* **colleges**)
a place where people can continue to study after they have left school

collide *verb* (**collides, colliding, collided**)
to collide with something is to hit it while moving ♦ *The bicycle collided with the car*

collie *noun* (*plural* **collies**)
a breed of dog with a long, pointed muzzle and long hair

collision *noun* (*plural* **collisions**)
a crash between moving vehicles

colloquial *adjective*
suitable for conversation but not for formal speech or writing ♦ *'Chuck' is a colloquial word for 'throw'*

colon *noun* (*plural* **colons**)
a punctuation mark (:)
See the entry for **punctuation**

colonel *noun* (*plural* **colonels**) (*pronounced* ker-nel)
an army officer, usually in charge of a regiment

colonial *adjective*
from or to do with colonies

colonist *noun* (*plural* **colonists**)
a person who settles in a place and lives in a colony there

colony *noun* (*plural* **colonies**)
1 a country controlled by another country
2 a group of people or animals living together

colossal *adjective*
huge, great

colour ➤ *noun* (*plural* **colours**)
1 the quality of being red, green, blue, and so on, produced by rays of light of different wavelengths 2 the use of all colours, not just black and white ♦ *Is this film in colour?* 3 the colour of someone's skin 4 a substance used to give colour to things
5 the special flag of a ship or regiment

colour ➤ *verb* (**colours, colouring, coloured**)
1 to colour something is to give it a colour or colours, especially by using paints 2 to colour a story or description is to make it more interesting or amusing 3 to colour is to blush

colour-blind *adjective*
unable to see or distinguish between some colours

coloured *adjective*
1 having a particular colour 2 having a dark skin

colourful *adjective*
1 having a lot of colour 2 lively ♦ *The film was a colourful story of life on board a pirate ship*

colouring *noun*
shade or complexion

colourless *adjective*
not having any colour ♦ *Many gases are colourless*

colt *noun* (*plural* **colts**)
a young male horse

column *noun* (*plural* **columns**)
1 a pillar 2 something long and narrow ♦ *They could see a column of smoke in the distance* 3 a strip of printing in a book or newspaper 4 a regular feature in a newspaper ♦ *He always read the sports column*

coma *noun* (*plural* **comas**) (*pronounced* koh-ma)
a state in which someone is unconscious for a long time

comb ➤ *noun* (*plural* **combs**)
1 a tool with teeth for making the hair tidy
2 the red, fleshy crest on a fowl's head

comb ➤ *verb* (**combs, combing, combed**)
1 to comb the hair is to tidy it with a comb
2 to comb an area is to search it carefully for something lost ♦ *We combed the woods all day but couldn't find the cat*

combat ➤ *noun* (*plural* **combats**)
a fight or contest

combat ➤ *verb* (**combats, combating, combated**)
to combat something is to try and reduce it or get rid of it ♦ *The government has been combating unemployment without much success*

combatant *noun* (*plural* **combatants**)
(*pronounced* **komb**-e-tent)
someone who takes part in a fight

combination *noun* (*plural* **combinations**)
1 combination is combining things **2** a combination is a series of numbers or letters used to open a combination lock

combination lock *noun* (*plural* **combination locks**)
a lock that is opened by setting a dial to positions shown by numbers or letters

combine ➤ *verb* (**combines, combining, combined**) (*pronounced* kom-**byn**)
to combine things is to join them or mix them together

combine ➤ *noun* (*plural* **combines**)
(*pronounced* kom-**byn**)
a combine is a group of people working together in business

combine harvester *noun* (*plural* **combine harvesters**)
a machine that reaps and threshes grain

combustion *noun*
combustion is what happens when something burns

come *verb* (**comes, coming, came, come**)
1 to come is to move towards the person or place that is here, and is the opposite of **go** ♦ *Do you want to come to my house?* ♦ *Has that letter come yet?* **2** to come is also to occur or be present ♦ *The pictures come at the end of the book*

to come about is to happen

to come across someone is to meet them by chance

to come by something is to get it ♦ *How did you come by that watch?*

to come round or **come to** is to revive after being unconscious

to come to something is to add up to it ♦ *The bill came to £10*

to come true is to actually happen ♦ *Their holiday was a dream come true*

comeback *noun* (*plural* **comebacks**)
a return to an activity in which you have been successful before ♦ *Some rock stars have had several comebacks*

comedian *noun* (*plural* **comedians**)
someone who entertains people with humour and jokes

comedy *noun* (*plural* **comedies**)
1 a comedy is a play or film that makes people laugh **2** comedy is humour

comet *noun* (*plural* **comets**)
an object moving across the sky with a bright tail of light

comfort ➤ *noun*
comfort is a feeling of relief from worry or pain

comfort ➤ *verb* (**comforts, comforting, comforted**)
to comfort someone is to give them comfort

comfortable *adjective*
1 pleasant to use or wear ♦ *Who gets the comfortable chair?* **2** free from worry or pain ♦ *The nurse made the patient comfortable*
comfortably *adverb* in a comfortable way

comic ➤ *noun* (*plural* **comics**)
1 a children's paper with illustrated stories **2** a comedian

comic or **comical** ➤ *adjective*
funny, making people laugh
comically *adverb* in a funny way

comic strip *noun* (*plural* **comic strips**)
a series of drawings telling a story

comings and goings *plural noun*
people arriving and leaving, bustle

comma *noun* (*plural* **commas**)
a punctuation mark (,) used to mark a pause in a sentence or between items in a list

command ➤ *noun* (*plural* **commands**)
1 a command is telling someone to do something **2** command is authority or control ♦ *Who has command of these soldiers?* **3** a command of a subject is skill or ability in it ♦ *She has a good command of Spanish*

command ➤ *verb* (**commands, commanding, commanded**)
1 to command someone is to tell them to do something **2** to command a group of people is to be in charge of them ♦ *A centurion commanded a hundred soldiers*

commander *noun* (*plural* **commanders**)
someone who commands, especially a
naval officer below captain

commandment *noun* (*plural* **commandments**)
a sacred command, especially one of the
Ten Commandments of Moses

commando *noun* (*plural* **commandos**)
a soldier trained for making dangerous
raids

commemorate *verb* (**commemorates,
commemorating, commemorated**)
to commemorate a past event is to do
something special so that people
remember it
commemoration *noun* an act of
commemorating something

commence *verb* (**commences, commencing,
commenced**)
to commence something is to begin it
commencement *noun* a beginning

commend *verb* (**commends, commending,
commended**)
to commend someone is to praise them
♦ *He was commended for bravery*
commendable *adjective* worthy of praise
commendation *noun* praise for something
someone has done

comment *noun* (*plural* **comments**)
a remark or opinion

commentary *noun* (*plural* **commentaries**)
a description of an event by someone who
is watching it, especially for radio or
television

commentator *noun* (*plural* **commentators**)
a person who gives a commentary,
especially of a sports event
commentate *verb* to give a commentary

commerce *noun*
commerce is trade, or buying and selling
goods

commercial ➤ *adjective*
1 connected with trade and making
money **2** financed by advertisements
♦ *They set up a commercial radio station*

commercial ➤ *noun* (*plural* **commercials**)
an advertisement, especially on television
or radio
commercially *adverb* in a commercial or
profitable way

commercialized *adjective*
changed so as to make more money ♦ *A lot
of holiday resorts are becoming very
commercialized*

commit *verb* (**commits, committing, committed**)
1 to commit a crime is to do it **2** to
commit a person is to send them to a

particular place ♦ *The judge committed
them all to prison*
to commit yourself to something is to promise or
decide to do it

commitment *noun* (*plural* **commitments**)
1 commitment is being determined to do
something **2** a commitment is something
you have agreed to do

committee *noun* (*plural* **committees**)
a group of people who meet to organize or
discuss something

commodity *noun* (*plural* **commodities**)
a product that is bought and sold

common ➤ *adjective* (**commoner, commonest**)
1 ordinary or usual ♦ *The dandelion is a
common plant* **2** happening or used often
♦ *Street markets are common where we
live* **3** shared by many people ♦ *The story
was common knowledge* ♦ *Music was their
common interest* **4** vulgar ♦ *She said it
was common to pick your nose*

common ➤ *noun* (*plural* **commons**)
a piece of land that anyone can use

commonplace *adjective*
ordinary, familiar

common room *noun* (*plural* **common rooms**)
an informal room for teachers or pupils at
a school or college

commonwealth *noun* (*plural* **commonwealths**)
a group of countries cooperating together
the Commonwealth an association of Britain
and various other countries, such as
Canada, Australia, and New Zealand

commotion *noun* (*plural* **commotions**)
an uproar

communal *adjective*
shared by several people

commune *noun* (*plural* **communes**)
a group of people sharing a home and way
of life

communicate *verb* (**communicates,
communicating, communicated**)
to communicate news or information is to
pass it on to other people
communicative *adjective* willing to give
information

communication *noun* (*plural* **communications**)
1 communication is telling people things
2 a communication is something that is
told to someone, a message
3 communication is also a form of
technology for passing on information, for
example television and telephones

communion *noun* (*plural* **communions**)
1 communion is sharing of religious
feeling **2** Communion is the Christian
ceremony in which holy bread and wine
are given to worshippers

communism *noun*
a political system in which the state controls property and industry

communist *noun* (*plural* **communists**)
someone who believes in communism

community *noun* (*plural* **communities**)
the people living in one area

commuter *noun* (*plural* **commuters**)
someone who travels to work, especially by train or bus

commute *verb* to travel to work

compact ➤ *adjective*
small and neat

compact ➤ *noun* (*plural* **compacts**)
a small flat container for face powder

compact disc *noun* (*plural* **compact discs**)
a small plastic disc on which music or information is stored as digital signals and is read by a laser beam. Usually called **CD**

companion *noun* (*plural* **companions**)
someone who is with you a lot, and whose company you enjoy

companionship *noun* friendship

company *noun* (*plural* **companies**)
1 a company is a group of people, especially a business firm **2** company is having people with you ♦ *Jill was lonely and longed for some company* **3** a company is an army unit consisting of two or more platoons

comparable *adjective* (*pronounced* kom-per-a-bul)
able to be compared, similar

comparative ➤ *adjective*
using or connected with comparisons

comparative ➤ *noun* (*plural* **comparatives**)
the form of an adjective or adverb that expresses 'more' ♦ *The comparative of 'big' is 'bigger', and the comparative of 'bad' is 'worse'*

comparatively *adverb*
in comparison, relatively ♦ *They all went to bed comparatively late*

compare *verb* (**compares, comparing, compared**)
1 to compare things is to see how they are similar ♦ *Compare your answers* **2** to compare with something is to be as good as it ♦ *Our football pitch cannot compare with Wembley Stadium*

comparison *noun* (*plural* **comparisons**)
the act of comparing

compartment *noun* (*plural* **compartments**)
a part or division of something, especially of a railway carriage

compass *noun* (*plural* **compasses**)
an instrument with a magnetized needle that shows direction

compasses or **pair of compasses** a device for drawing circles

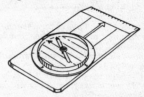

compassion *noun*
compassion is pity or mercy

compassionate *adjective* merciful

compatible *adjective*
1 able to live or exist together without trouble **2** machines and devices are compatible when they can be used together

compel *verb* (**compels, compelling, compelled**)
to compel someone to do something is to force them to do it

compensate *verb* (**compensates, compensating, compensated**)
to compensate someone is to give them something to make up for a loss or injury

compensation *noun* something given to compensate someone

compère *noun* (*plural* **compères**)
(*pronounced* kom-pair)
someone who introduces the performers in a show or broadcast

compete *verb* (**competes, competing, competed**)
to compete in a competition is to take part in it

competent *adjective*
able to do something ♦ *He is not competent to teach French*

competence *noun* ability

competition *noun* (*plural* **competitions**)
a game or race in which you try to do better than other people

competitive *adjective* enjoying competing

competitor *noun* someone who competes in a game or race, or a rival in business

compile *verb* (**compiles, compiling, compiled**)
to compile information is to collect and arrange it, especially in a book ♦ *She compiled a collection of children's poems*

compilation *noun* something that someone compiles **compiler** *noun* someone who compiles something

complacent *adjective*
smugly satisfied with the way things are, without wanting to improve them

complain *verb* (**complains, complaining, complained**)
to complain about something is to say that you are not pleased about it

complaint *noun* (*plural* **complaints**)
1 something someone complains about 2 a minor illness

complement *noun* (*plural* **complements**)
1 the amount needed to fill or complete something ♦ *This ship has a full complement of sailors* 2 (*in Grammar*) a word or words used after a verb to complete the meaning ♦ *In 'She is brave' and 'He was made king', the complements are 'brave' and 'king'*
complementary *adjective* acting as a complement

complete ➤ *adjective*
1 having all its parts ♦ *I hope the tool kit is complete* 2 finished, achieved ♦ *By evening the jigsaw puzzle was complete* 3 utter, total ♦ *It came as a complete surprise*

complete ➤ *verb* (**completes, completing, completed**)
to complete something is to finish it or make it complete
completion *noun* completing something

completely *adverb*
totally, utterly ♦ *You are completely wrong*

complex ➤ *adjective*
difficult and complicated
complexity *noun* being complex

complex ➤ *noun* (*plural* **complexes**)
1 a group of buildings, such as a sports centre 2 something that someone has a strange attitude or obsession about ♦ *He has a complex about winning*

complexion *noun* (*plural* **complexions**)
the colour or appearance of your skin, especially of your face

complicated *adjective*
difficult to understand or cope with because it has so many parts or details

complication *noun* (*plural* **complications**)
1 a difficult or awkward situation 2 a difficulty that makes something worse

compliment *noun* (*plural* **compliments**)
words or actions that show you approve of a person or thing
complimentary *adjective* praising

component *noun* (*plural* **components**)
a part, especially of a machine

compose *verb* (**composes, composing, composed**)
1 to compose music or poetry is to write it 2 to be composed of several people or things is to be made up of them ♦ *The*
class is composed of children up to the age of 8

composer *noun* someone who writes music

composition *noun* (*plural* **compositions**)
1 composition is composing or writing something 2 a composition is a piece of music or an essay

compost *noun*
manure made of decayed leaves, grass, and other natural refuse

compound[1] ➤ *adjective*
made of two or more parts or ingredients

compound ➤ *noun* (*plural* **compounds**)
a compound substance ♦ *Water is a compound of hydrogen and oxygen*

compound[2] *noun* (*plural* **compounds**)
a fenced area containing buildings

comprehend *verb* (**comprehends, comprehending, comprehended**)
to comprehend something is to understand it

comprehension *noun* (*plural* **comprehensions**)
1 comprehension is understanding 2 a comprehension is an exercise that tests or helps your understanding of a language

comprehensive ➤ *adjective*
including all or many kinds of people or things

comprehensive ➤ *noun* (*plural* **comprehensives**)
a comprehensive school

comprehensive school *noun* (*plural* **comprehensive schools**)
a secondary school for all or most of the children in an area

compress *verb* (**compresses, compressing, compressed**)
1 to compress something is to press it or squeeze it together 2 to be compressed is to be forced into a small space
compression *noun* pressing or squeezing something

comprise *verb* (**comprises, comprising, comprised**)
to comprise several people or things is to include them ♦ *A football team comprises eleven players*

compromise ➤ *noun* (*plural* **compromises**) (*pronounced* kom-pro-myz)
accepting less than you really wanted

compromise ➤ *verb* (**compromises, compromising, compromised**) (*pronounced* kom-pro-myz)
to compromise is to accept less than you really wanted, especially so as to settle a dispute

compulsory *adjective*
that you have to do ♦ *Wearing seat belts is compulsory*

compute *verb* (**computes, computing, computed**)
to compute something is to calculate it
computation *noun* calculation

computer *noun* (*plural* **computers**)
an electronic machine that does word processing, sorts data, and does rapid calculations

comrade *noun* (*plural* **comrades**)
a friend or companion
comradeship *noun* friendship

con *verb* (**cons, conning, conned**)
(*slang*) to con someone is to swindle them

concave *adjective*
curved like the inside of a circle or ball

conceal *verb* (**conceals, concealing, concealed**)
to conceal something is to hide it
concealment *noun* hiding something

conceit *noun*
vanity or pride
conceited *adjective* vain and proud

conceive *verb* (**conceives, conceiving, conceived**)
1 to conceive an idea or plan is to form it in your mind 2 to conceive is to become pregnant

concentrate *verb* (**concentrates, concentrating, concentrated**)
1 to concentrate on something is to think hard about it 2 to concentrate people or things is to bring them together in one place

concentrated *adjective*
a liquid is concentrated when it is made stronger by having water removed from it

concentration *noun*
concentration is thinking hard about something

concentric *adjective*
having the same centre

concept *noun* (*plural* **concepts**)
a new idea about something

conception *noun* (*plural* **conceptions**)
1 forming an idea 2 becoming pregnant

concern ➤ *verb* (**concerns, concerning, concerned**)
1 to concern someone is to be important or interesting to them 2 to concern something is to be about a particular subject ♦ *This story concerns a shipwreck* 3 to worry someone

concern ➤ *noun* (*plural* **concerns**)
1 something that matters to someone ♦ *I think that is my concern* 2 a business

concerning *preposition*
on the subject of; in connection with ♦ *They wrote to us concerning our refuse collection*

concert *noun* (*plural* **concerts**)
a performance of music

concertina *noun* (*plural* **concertinas**)
a portable musical instrument that you squeeze to push air past reeds

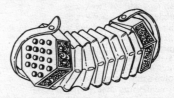

concerto *noun* (*plural* **concertos**)
(*pronounced* kon-**cher**-toh)
a piece of music for a solo instrument and an orchestra

concession *noun* (*plural* **concessions**)
something that someone lets you have or do ♦ *As a special concession, parents may park in the teachers' car park on Sports Day*

concise *adjective*
giving a lot of information in a few words

conclude *verb* (**concludes, concluding, concluded**)
1 to conclude something is to end it 2 to conclude something is also to decide about it ♦ *The jury concluded that he was not guilty*

conclusion *noun* (*plural* **conclusions**)
1 an ending 2 a decision
in conclusion lastly

concrete ➤ *noun*
cement mixed with water and gravel or
sand and used in building

concrete ➤ *adjective*
real, definite ♦ *We must have concrete
evidence*

concussion *noun*
a temporary injury to the brain caused by
a hard knock

condemn *verb* (**condemns, condemning,
condemned**)
1 to condemn someone or something is to
say that you strongly disapprove of them
2 to condemn criminals is to sentence
them to a punishment ♦ *He was
condemned to death* 3 to condemn a
building is to declare that it is not fit to be
used

condemnation *noun* strong blame or
disapproval

condensation *noun*
drops of liquid formed from vapour that
has condensed

condense *verb* (**condenses, condensing,
condensed**)
1 to condense a piece of writing is to make
it shorter 2 to condense is to change into
water or other liquid ♦ *Steam condenses
on cold windows*

condensed *adjective*
a condensed liquid, such as milk, is one
that is made stronger or thicker

condition *noun* (*plural* **conditions**)
1 the state in which a person or thing is
♦ *This bike is in good condition* 2 being
physically fit ♦ *Get in condition*
3 something that must happen if
something else is to happen ♦ *Learning to
swim is a condition of going sailing*
on condition or **on condition that** only if ♦ *You
can come on condition that you behave*

condom *noun* (*plural* **condoms**)
a rubber covering that a man can wear on
his penis during sexual intercourse, as a
contraceptive and as protection against
disease

conduct ➤ *verb* (**conducts, conducting,
conducted**) (*pronounced* kon-dukt)
1 to conduct someone is to lead or guide
them 2 to conduct something is to
organize or manage it 3 to conduct an
orchestra or band is to direct it in a piece
of music 4 to conduct electricity or heat is
to allow it to pass along ♦ *Copper conducts
electricity well*

conduct ➤ *noun* (*pronounced* kon-dukt)
a person's conduct is their behaviour

conduction *noun*
the conducting of electricity or heat

conductor *noun* (*plural* **conductors**)
1 someone who sells tickets on a bus or
coach 2 someone who conducts an
orchestra 3 something that conducts
electricity or heat

cone *noun* (*plural* **cones**)
1 an object which is circular at one end
and pointed at the other end 2 an ice
cream cornet 3 the fruit of a pine, fir, or
cedar

confectioner *noun* (*plural* **confectioners**)
someone who makes or sells sweets
confectionery *noun* sweets

confer *verb* (**confers, conferring, conferred**)
1 to confer a title or honour on someone is
to give it to them 2 to confer is to have a
discussion

conference *noun* (*plural* **conferences**)
a meeting for discussion

confess *verb* (**confesses, confessing, confessed**)
to confess to something wrong is to admit
that you have done it

confession *noun* (*plural* **confessions**)
1 an act of admitting that you have done
wrong ♦ *The burglar made a confession of
all his crimes* 2 (*in the Roman Catholic
Church*) an act of telling a priest that you
have sinned

confetti *plural noun*
tiny bits of coloured paper thrown at the
bride and bridegroom after their wedding

confide *verb* (**confides, confiding, confided**)
to confide in someone is to tell them a
secret

confidence *noun*
1 trust or faith 2 believing that you are
right or that you can do something
in confidence as a secret ♦ *He told me all
this in confidence*

confidence trick *noun* (*plural* **confidence
tricks**)
a trick to get money out of someone by
gaining their trust

confident *adjective*
showing or feeling confidence

confidential *adjective*
that should be kept secret ♦ *This information is confidential*
confidentially *adverb* in secret

confine *verb* (**confines, confining, confined**)
1 to confine something is to restrict or limit it ♦ *Please confine your comments to points of fact* **2** to confine someone is to shut them in a place
confinement *noun* being confined or shut in

confirm *verb* (**confirms, confirming, confirmed**)
1 to confirm something is to prove that it is true **2** to confirm an arrangement is to make it definite ♦ *Please write to confirm your booking* **3** to confirm someone is to make them a full member of a Christian Church
confirmation *noun* confirming something or someone

confiscate *verb* (**confiscates, confiscating, confiscated**)
to confiscate something is to take it away from someone as a punishment
confiscation *noun* confiscating something

conflict ➤ *noun* (*plural* **conflicts**) (*pronounced* **kon**-flikt)
a fight, struggle, or disagreement

conflict ➤ *verb* (**conflicts, conflicting, conflicted**) (*pronounced* kon-**flikt**)
to conflict is to contradict or disagree with one another ♦ *The two accounts of the incident conflict*

conform *verb* (**conforms, conforming, conformed**)
to conform with something is to follow other people's rules or ideas about it ♦ *The older girls like to conform with adult fashions*
conformity *noun* conforming with something

confront *verb* (**confronts, confronting, confronted**)
1 to confront someone is to oppose them face to face ♦ *The policeman decided to confront the criminals there and then* **2** to confront a problem or difficulty is to face up to it
confrontation *noun* meeting someone, especially an opponent, face to face

confuse *verb* (**confuses, confusing, confused**)
1 to confuse someone is to make them puzzled or muddled **2** to confuse things is to mistake one thing for another
confusion *noun* being confused or muddled

congested *adjective*
crowded, especially with people or traffic
congestion *noun* being crowded

congratulate *verb* (**congratulates, congratulating, congratulated**)
to congratulate someone is to tell them how pleased you are about something they have done
congratulations *plural noun* words congratulating someone

congregation *noun* (*plural* **congregations**)
the people who take part in a church service

congress *noun* (*plural* **congresses**)
a large meeting or conference
Congress the parliament or government of the USA

congruent *adjective*
(*in Mathematics*) having exactly the same shape and size ♦ *The two triangles are congruent*
congruence *noun* being congruent

conical *adjective*
shaped like a cone

conifer *noun* (*plural* **conifers**) (*pronounced* kon-i-fer)
an evergreen tree with cones
coniferous *adjective* having cones

conjunction *noun* (*plural* **conjunctions**)
a joining word ♦ *Conjunctions are words like 'and', 'but', and 'whether'*

conjure *verb* (**conjures, conjuring, conjured**)
to conjure is to perform tricks that look like magic
conjurer *noun* someone who performs tricks

conker *noun* (*plural* **conkers**)
a hard and shiny brown nut that grows on a horse chestnut tree
conkers a game played with conkers threaded on pieces of string

connect *verb* (**connects, connecting, connected**)
to connect things is to join them together

connection *noun* (*plural* **connections**)
1 a link between things **2** joining together

conning tower *noun* (*plural* **conning towers**)
the part on top of a submarine, containing the periscope

conquer *verb* (**conquers, conquering, conquered**)
to conquer someone or something is to defeat them ♦ *William I conquered England* ♦ *He managed to conquer all his fears*
conqueror *noun* someone who conquers a place

conquest *noun* (*plural* **conquests**)
a victory over someone

conscience *noun* (*pronounced* **kon**-shens)
a feeling people have about what is right or wrong

conscientious *adjective* (*pronounced* kon-shee-en-shus)
careful and hard-working
conscientiously *adverb* carefully

conscious *adjective* (*pronounced* **kon**-shus)
1 awake and knowing what is happening
2 aware of something ♦ *Are you conscious of the danger you are in?* 3 deliberate ♦ *She has made a conscious effort to improve*
consciously *adverb* deliberately
consciousness *noun* being conscious

conscription *noun*
a system of making young people join the army for a time

consecutive *adjective*
following one after another

consensus *noun*
an agreement between most people about something ♦ *There was a consensus that the law should be changed*

consent ➢ *noun*
consent is agreement or permission

consent ➢ *verb* (**consents, consenting, consented**)
to consent to something is to agree to it or permit it

consequence *noun* (*plural* **consequences**)
1 a consequence is something which happens because of an event or action ♦ *His illness was the consequence of smoking* 2 consequence is importance ♦ *It is of no consequence*
consequences a game in which a story is built up by two or more people
consequently *adverb* as a result

conservation *noun*
keeping buildings and natural surroundings in a good state
conservationist *noun* someone who supports conservation

conservative ➢ *adjective*
1 wanting things to stay the same
2 cautious, prudent ♦ *It was a conservative estimate*

Conservative ➢ *noun* (*plural* **Conservatives**)
someone who supports the Conservative Party, a British political party

conservatory *noun* (*plural* **conservatories**)
a room with glass walls and a glass roof, usually built on to the back of a house, where plants can be grown

conserve *verb* (**conserves, conserving, conserved**)
to conserve something is to keep it from being changed or spoilt

consider *verb* (**considers, considering, considered**)
1 to consider something is to think carefully about it 2 to consider something is also to believe it ♦ *We consider that people should be allowed to follow their own religion*

considerable *adjective*
large or important
considerably *adverb* very much ♦ *The new dictionary is considerably larger*

considerate *adjective*
kind and thoughtful

consideration *noun* (*plural* **considerations**)
1 consideration is careful thought or attention 2 a consideration is a serious thought or reason ♦ *Money is a major consideration in this plan*

considering *preposition*
in view of ♦ *This car runs well, considering its age*

consist *verb* (**consists, consisting, consisted**)
to consist of something is to be made of it

consistency *noun* (*plural* **consistencies**)
1 thickness, especially of a liquid 2 being consistent

consistent *adjective*
1 always the same, regular 2 always acting in the same way
consistently *adverb* in a regular way

consolation *noun* (*plural* **consolations**)
comfort or sympathy given to someone

consolation prize *noun* (*plural* **consolation prizes**)
a prize given to someone who does not win a main prize

console *verb* (**consoles, consoling, consoled**)
to console someone is to give them comfort or sympathy

consonant *noun* (*plural* **consonants**)
a letter that is not a vowel

conspicuous *adjective*
noticeable, remarkable

conspiracy *noun* (*plural* **conspiracies**)
a plot to do something bad or illegal
conspirator *noun* someone involved in a conspiracy

conspire *verb* (**conspires, conspiring, conspired**)
to conspire is to plot together

constable *noun* (*plural* **constables**)
an ordinary member of the police

constant ➢ *adjective*
1 not changing; continual 2 a constant person is loyal and faithful

constant ➢ *noun* (*plural* **constants**)
(*in Science and Mathematics*) a number or quantity that does not change
constancy *noun* loyalty **constantly** *adverb* continually, always

constellation *noun* (*plural* **constellations**)
a group of stars

constipated *adjective*
unable to empty the bowels easily or
regularly

constipation *noun* being constipated

constituency *noun* (*plural* **constituencies**)
a district that elects a Member of
Parliament

constituent *noun* (*plural* **constituents**)
1 a part of something **2** someone who
lives in the district of a particular Member
of Parliament

constitute *verb* (**constitutes, constituting,
constituted**)
to constitute something is to form it or
make it up ♦ *50 states constitute the USA*

constitution *noun* (*plural* **constitutions**)
1 the set of principles or laws by which a
country is governed **2** a person's condition
or state of health

constitutional *adjective* to do with a
constitution

construct *verb* (**constructs, constructing,
constructed**)
to construct something is to build it

construction *noun* (*plural* **constructions**)
1 construction is the process of building
2 a construction is something built

constructive *adjective*
helpful and positive ♦ *Their criticism was
very constructive*

consul *noun* (*plural* **consuls**)
1 an official representative of one country,
living in another country **2** in ancient
Rome, an elected chief ruler

consult *verb* (**consults, consulting, consulted**)
to consult a person or book is to look for
information or advice

consultation *noun* an act of consulting
someone or something

consultant *noun* (*plural* **consultants**)
1 a person who provides professional
advice **2** a senior hospital doctor

consume *verb* (**consumes, consuming,
consumed**)
1 to consume food or drink is to eat or
drink it **2** to consume something is to use
it up or destroy it ♦ *The building was
consumed by fire*

consumer *noun* (*plural* **consumers**)
someone who buys goods or services

consumption *noun*
using up food or fuel ♦ *The consumption of
oil has increased*

contact ➤ *noun* (*plural* **contacts**)
1 contact is touching someone or
something **2** contact is also
communication ♦ *I've lost contact with my
uncle* **3** a contact is a person to
communicate with

contact ➤ *verb* (**contacts, contacting, contacted**)
to contact someone is to get in touch with
them

contact lens *noun* (*plural* **contact lenses**)
a small plastic lens worn against the
eyeball instead of glasses

contagious *adjective* (*pronounced*
kon-tay-jus)
a contagious disease is caught by contact
with infected people or things

contain *verb* (**contains, containing, contained**)
to contain something is to have it inside
♦ *This book contains a great deal of
information*

container *noun* (*plural* **containers**)
1 something that is designed to contain
things **2** a large box-shaped container for
transporting goods by sea

contaminate *verb* (**contaminates, contaminating,
contaminated**)
to contaminate something is to make it
dirty, impure, or diseased

contamination *noun* contaminating
something

contemplate *verb* (**contemplates, contemplating,
contemplated**)
1 to contemplate something is to look hard
at it or think about it **2** to contemplate
doing something is to plan or intend to do
it

contemplation *noun* thinking about
something

contemporary *adjective*
1 belonging to the same time ♦ *Florence
Nightingale was contemporary with Queen
Victoria* **2** modern or up to date ♦ *We like
contemporary furniture*

contempt *noun*
a feeling of strong disapproval

contemptible *adjective* deserving contempt

contemptuous *adjective*
strongly disapproving

contend *verb* (**contends, contending, contended**)
1 to contend is to struggle or compete
2 to contend something is to claim or
assert it ♦ *We contend that the company
was guilty of negligence*

contender *noun* a contestant

content[1] *noun* (*pronounced* **kon-tent**)
1 the contents of something **2** the amount of a substance found in something ♦ *Drink milk with a low fat content*

content[2] *adjective* (*pronounced* **kon-tent**)
happy and willing ♦ *Are you content to stay behind?*
contentment *noun* being happy

contented *adjective* (*pronounced* **kon-tent-id**)
happy and satisfied ♦ *After his big dinner he looked very contented*
contentedly *adverb* happily

contents *plural noun* (*pronounced* **kon-tents**)
what something contains

contest ➤ *noun* (*plural* **contests**)
(*pronounced* **kon-test**)
a competition

contest ➤ *verb* (**contests, contesting, contested**)
(*pronounced* **kon-test**)
to contest something is to argue about it ♦ *After her death, relatives contested her will*

contestant *noun* (*plural* **contestants**)
(*pronounced* **kon-test-ant**)
someone taking part in a contest

context *noun* (*plural* **contexts**)
the words that come before or after a particular word or phrase and help to tell you what it means

continent *noun* (*plural* **continents**)
one of the main masses of land in the world
the Continent the mainland of Europe, not including the British Isles

continental *adjective*
on a continent, especially Europe ♦ *We thought we'd have a continental holiday this year*

continual *adjective*
happening repeatedly ♦ *I get fed up with his continual shouting*
continually *adverb* repeatedly, often

continue *verb* (**continues, continuing, continued**)
to continue something, or to do something, is to go on doing it
continuation *noun* continuing something

continuous *adjective*
going on all the time; without a break ♦ *We could hear a continuous hum from the fridge*
continuity *noun* being continuous
continuously *adverb* all the time

contour *noun* (*plural* **contours**)
1 an outline **2** a line on a map joining points that are the same height above sea level

contraception *noun*
preventing women from becoming pregnant

contraceptive *noun* (*plural* **contraceptives**)
something that is used to prevent women from becoming pregnant

contract ➤ *noun* (*plural* **contracts**)
(*pronounced* **kon-trakt**)
a legal agreement

contract ➤ *verb* (**contracts, contracting, contracted**) (*pronounced* **kon-trakt**)
1 to contract is to become smaller ♦ *Heated metal contracts as it cools* **2** to contract to do something is to make a contract about it **3** to contract an illness is to get it ♦ *She contracted pneumonia*
contraction *noun* getting smaller; contracting

contractor *noun* (*plural* **contractors**)
a company or firm that does a piece of work for someone else, especially in the building industry

contradict *verb* (**contradicts, contradicting, contradicted**)
to contradict someone or something is to say they are wrong
contradiction *noun* contradicting someone or something **contradictory** *adjective* saying the opposite

contraflow *noun* (*plural* **contraflows**)
a special arrangement of traffic when a motorway is being repaired, with some traffic using the carriageway on the other side

contralto *noun* (*plural* **contraltos**)
a female singer with a low voice

contraption *noun* (*plural* **contraptions**)
a strange-looking device or machine

contrary ➤ *adjective*
1 (*pronounced* **kon-tra-ri**) opposite
2 (*pronounced* **kon-trair-i**) obstinate or awkward

contrary ➤ *noun* (*pronounced* **kon-tra-ri**)
the contrary is the opposite
on the contrary the opposite is true ♦ *Are you pleased? On the contrary, I'm furious*

contrast ➤ *verb* (**contrasts, contrasting, contrasted**) (*pronounced* **kon-trahst**)
1 to contrast two things is to show they are different **2** one thing contrasts with another when it is clearly different

contrast ➤ *noun* (*plural* **contrasts**)
(*pronounced* **kon-trahst**)
1 the action of contrasting **2** a clear difference **3** the amount of difference between colours or tones

contribute *verb* (**contributes, contributing, contributed**)
1 to contribute to something is to give money for it **2** to contribute to a result is to help cause it ♦ *His tiredness contributed to the accident* **3** to contribute to a magazine or newspaper is to write an article for it
contribution *noun* something you give
contributor *noun* someone who contributes

contrivance *noun* (*plural* **contrivances**)
a weird or unusual device or machine

contrive *verb* (**contrives, contriving, contrived**)
to contrive something is to plan or invent it

control ➤ *noun* (*plural* **controls**)
1 control is the power to make someone or something do what you want **2** the controls of a machine are the switches and levers that make it work
in control having power; controlling things

control ➤ *verb* (**controls, controlling, controlled**)
to control something or someone is to have power over what they do
controller *noun* someone who controls something

control tower *noun* (*plural* **control towers**)
the building at an airport where people control air traffic by radio

controversial *adjective*
likely to cause disagreement

controversy *noun* (*plural* **controversies**)
(*pronounced* **kon**-tro-ver-si or kon-**trov**-er-si)
a long argument or disagreement

conundrum *noun* (*plural* **conundrums**)
a riddle

convalescent *adjective*
recovering from an illness
convalescence *noun* a period of recovery

convection *noun*
heating by moving air or liquid
convector *noun* a heater that works by convection

convenience *noun* (*plural* **conveniences**)
1 convenience is usefulness and comfort **2** a convenience is something that is useful, such as central heating **3** a convenience is also a public lavatory
at your convenience as it suits you

convenience food *noun* (*plural* **convenience foods**)
food that is easy to use and partly prepared in a factory

convenient *adjective*
easy to use or reach
conveniently *adverb* in a convenient way

convent *noun* (*plural* **convents**)
a group of buildings where nuns live and work

convention *noun* (*plural* **conventions**)
an accepted way of doing things

conventional *adjective*
done in the accepted way; usual, traditional
conventionally *adverb* in a conventional way

converge *verb* (**converges, converging, converged**)
to converge is to come together ♦ *The two roads converge at the pub* ♦ *Thousands of fans converged on the football ground*

conversation *noun* (*plural* **conversations**)
conversation or a conversation is when you talk to someone
conversational *adjective* to do with conversation

converse [1] *verb* (**converses, conversing, conversed**) (*pronounced* kon-**verss**)
to converse is to talk ♦ *They conversed in low voices*

converse [2] *noun* (*pronounced* **kon**-verss)
the converse is the opposite ♦ *The converse is true*

conversion *noun* (*plural* **conversions**)
conversion or a conversion is changing or converting something

convert ➤ *verb* (**converts, converting, converted**) (*pronounced* kon-**vert**)
1 to convert something is to change it for a new purpose **2** to convert someone is to persuade them to change their beliefs **3** (*in Rugby Football*) to convert a try is to kick a goal after scoring

convert ➤ *noun* (*plural* **converts**) (*pronounced* **kon**-vert)
someone who has changed their beliefs
convertible *adjective* able to be converted

convex *adjective*
curved like the outside of a circle or ball

convey *verb* (**conveys, conveying, conveyed**)
1 to convey someone or something is to take them somewhere **2** to convey a message or idea is to get someone to understand it

conveyor belt noun (plural **conveyor belts**)
a long belt or chain for carrying goods in a factory

convict ➤ noun (plural **convicts**)
(pronounced **kon**-vikt)
a criminal in prison

convict ➤ verb (**convicts, convicting, convicted**)
(pronounced kon-**vikt**)
to convict someone of a crime is to declare them guilty of it

conviction noun (plural **convictions**)
1 being convicted of a crime 2 being convinced of something; a strong opinion

convince verb (**convinces, convincing, convinced**)
to convince someone is to persuade them about something

convoy noun (plural **convoys**)
a group of ships or vehicles travelling together

cook ➤ verb (**cooks, cooking, cooked**)
to cook food is to make it ready to eat by heating it
to cook something up (informal) is to make it up hurriedly ♦ They cooked up a clever excuse for being late

cook ➤ noun (plural **cooks**)
someone who cooks, especially as their job

cooker noun (plural **cookers**)
a device with an oven and hotplates for cooking food

cookery noun
the art or skill of cooking food

cool ➤ adjective (**cooler, coolest**)
1 not very warm; fairly cold 2 a cool person is calm and not easily excited
3 fashionable, chic ♦ He's wearing sunglasses so as to look cool
coolly adverb calmly **coolness** noun being cool

cool ➤ verb (**cools, cooling, cooled**)
1 to cool something is to make it cool 2 to cool is to become cool
cooler noun a device for making something cool

coop noun (plural **coops**)
a cage for poultry

cooped up adjective
having to stay in a place which is small and uncomfortable ♦ The children felt cooped up in their tiny classroom

cooperate verb (**cooperates, cooperating, cooperated**)
to cooperate with people is to work helpfully with them
cooperation noun working helpfully together **cooperative** adjective willing to cooperate

coordinate ➤ verb (**coordinates, coordinating, coordinated**) (pronounced koh-or-din-ayt)
to coordinate people or things is to get them to work well together

coordinate ➤ noun (plural **coordinates**)
(pronounced koh-or-din-at)
a quantity used to fix the position of something ♦ The coordinates of point P are (4,2)
coordination noun coordinating people or things **coordinator** noun someone who coordinates people or things

coot noun (plural **coots**)
a waterbird with a horny white plate on its forehead

cop ➤ verb (**cops, copping, copped**)
(slang) to cop something is to get or catch it, especially when you don't want it ♦ Her brother copped most of the blame
to cop it is to get into trouble
to cop out of something is to avoid it because you are afraid

cop ➤ noun (plural **cops**)
(slang) a police officer
not much cop not very good

cope verb (**copes, coping, coped**)
to cope with something awkward or difficult is to deal with it successfully
♦ How did you cope with that awful homework?

copper noun (plural **coppers**)
1 copper is a reddish-brown metal used for making wire and pipes 2 copper is also a reddish-brown colour 3 a copper is a coin made of copper or bronze 4 (slang) a copper is a police officer
coppery adjective like copper

copper sulphate noun
blue-green crystals that are a compound of copper and sulphur

copy ➤ noun (plural **copies**)
1 something made to look exactly like something else 2 something written out a second time 3 one newspaper, magazine, or book ♦ We each have a copy of 'Alice in Wonderland'

copy ➤ verb (**copies, copying, copied**)
1 to copy something is to make a copy of it
2 to copy someone is to do the same as them
copier noun a machine for copying pages

coral noun
coral is a hard substance made of the skeletons of tiny sea creatures

cord noun (plural **cords**)
a cord is a piece of thin rope

cordial ➤ *adjective*
warm and friendly ♦ *We got a cordial welcome*
cordiality *noun* being cordial **cordially** *adverb* in a friendly way

cordial ➤ *noun* (*plural* **cordials**)
a sweet drink

corduroy *noun* (*pronounced* **kor**-der-oi)
thick cotton cloth with ridges along it

core *noun* (*plural* **cores**)
the part in the middle of something

corgi *noun* (*plural* **corgis**)
a small breed of dog with short legs and large upright ears

cork *noun* (*plural* **corks**)
1 cork is the lightweight bark of a kind of oak tree 2 a cork is a piece of this bark used to close a bottle

corkscrew *noun* (*plural* **corkscrews**)
1 a device for removing corks from bottles 2 a spiral

cormorant *noun* (*plural* **cormorants**)
a large black seabird

corn [1] *noun*
grain ♦ *a field of corn*

corn [2] *noun* (*plural* **corns**)
a small, hard lump on your toe or foot

corned beef *noun*
tinned beef preserved with salt

corner ➤ *noun* (*plural* **corners**)
1 the point where two lines, roads, or walls meet 2 a kick from the corner of a football field; a hit from the corner of a hockey field

corner ➤ *verb* (**corners, cornering, cornered**)
1 to corner someone is to trap them ♦ *The police cornered the escaped prisoner* 2 to corner is to go round a corner ♦ *The car cornered slowly and accelerated up the road*

cornet *noun* (*plural* **cornets**)
1 a long cone-shaped biscuit open at the top for ice cream 2 a musical instrument like a trumpet

cornfield *noun* (*plural* **cornfields**)
a field where corn grows

cornflakes *plural noun*
toasted maize flakes eaten for breakfast

cornflour *noun*
fine flour used for making puddings

cornflower *noun* (*plural* **cornflowers**)
a blue wild flower

Cornish *adjective*
from or to do with Cornwall

Cornish pasty *noun* (*plural* **Cornish pasties**)
a small pie containing meat and vegetables

corny *adjective* (**cornier, corniest**)
(*informal*) a corny joke is one that is feeble and often repeated

coronation *noun* (*plural* **coronations**)
the ceremony of crowning a king or queen

coroner *noun* (*plural* **coroners**)
an official who holds an inquiry into the cause of an unnatural death

corporal ➤ *noun* (*plural* **corporals**)
a soldier just below sergeant in rank

corporal ➤ *adjective*
to do with the human body

corporal punishment *noun*
punishment by hitting or beating someone

corporation *noun* (*plural* **corporations**)
a group of people elected to govern a town

corps *noun* (*plural* **corps**) (*pronounced* kor)
1 a large unit of soldiers 2 a special army unit ♦ *He is in the Medical Corps*

corpse *noun* (*plural* **corpses**)
a dead body

corpuscle *noun* (*plural* **corpuscles**)
(*pronounced* **kor**-pu-sul)
one of the many red or white cells in the blood

corral *noun* (*plural* **corrals**) (*pronounced* ko-**rahl**)
an enclosure for horses or cattle

correct ➤ *adjective*
1 true or accurate; without any mistakes ♦ *Your answers are all correct* 2 proper, suitable ♦ *Is that the correct way to talk to your parents?*
correctly *adverb* in a correct way **correctness** *noun* being correct

correct ➤ *verb* (**corrects, correcting, corrected**)
to correct a piece of work is to mark the mistakes in it, or to put them right

correction *noun* (*plural* **corrections**)
1 correction is correcting something 2 a correction is a change made to something in order to correct it

correspond *verb* (**corresponds, corresponding, corresponded**)
1 to correspond with something is to agree with it or match it ♦ *Your story corresponds with what I heard* 2 to correspond with someone is to exchange letters with them

correspondence *noun*
1 similarity or agreement 2 letters or writing letters

correspondent *noun* (*plural* **correspondents**)
1 someone who writes letters 2 someone employed to send news or articles to a newspaper or magazine

corridor *noun* (*plural* **corridors**)
1 a long narrow passage from which doors open into rooms or compartments **2** a route an aircraft follows

corrode *verb* (**corrodes, corroding, corroded**)
to corrode is to wear away by rust or chemical action
corrosion *noun* corroding **corrosive** *adjective* likely to corrode

corrugated *adjective*
shaped into folds or ridges ♦ *The roof was made of corrugated iron*

corrupt *adjective*
1 wicked **2** likely to give or accept bribes
corruption *noun* being corrupt

corset *noun* (*plural* **corsets**)
a tight piece of underwear worn round the hips and waist

cosmetics *plural noun*
substances like lipstick and face powder, for making the skin or hair look beautiful or different

cosmic *adjective* (*pronounced* **koz**-mik)
to do with the universe

cosmonaut *noun* (*plural* **cosmonauts**)
a Russian astronaut

cost ➤ *verb* (**costs, costing, cost**)
to cost a certain amount is to have that amount as its price ♦ *The book only cost £5 last year*

cost ➤ *noun* (*plural* **costs**)
what you have to spend to do or get something
at all costs or **at any cost** no matter what the cost or difficulty may be

costly *adjective* (**costlier, costliest**)
expensive

cost of living *noun*
the average amount each person in a country spends on food, clothing, and housing

costume *noun* (*plural* **costumes**)
clothes, especially for a particular purpose or of a particular period

cosy ➤ *adjective* (**cosier, cosiest**)
warm and comfortable

cosy ➤ *noun* (*plural* **cosies**)
a cover put over a teapot or boiled egg to keep it hot

cot *noun* (*plural* **cots**)
a baby's bed with high sides

cottage *noun* (*plural* **cottages**)
a small house, especially in the country

cottage cheese *noun*
soft white cheese made from skimmed milk

cottage pie *noun* (*plural* **cottage pies**)
minced meat covered with mashed potato and baked

cotton *noun*
1 a soft white substance covering the seeds of a tropical plant **2** thread made from this substance **3** cloth made from cotton thread

couch *noun* (*plural* **couches**)
a long soft seat or sofa

couch potato *noun* (*plural* **couch potatoes**)
(*slang*) a person who spends a lot of time watching television

cough ➤ *verb* (**coughs, coughing, coughed**) (*pronounced* kof)
to cough is to push air suddenly out of your lungs with a harsh noise
to cough up (*slang*) is to give someone money or information

cough ➤ *noun* (*plural* **coughs**)
1 the action or sound of coughing **2** an illness which makes you cough a lot

could past tense of **can**[1] *verb*

couldn't short for *could not*

council *noun* (*plural* **councils**)
a group of people chosen to organize or discuss something, especially to plan the affairs of a town

council house *noun* (*plural* **council houses**)
a house owned and let by a council

councillor *noun* (*plural* **councillors**)
a member of a council

council tax *noun*
a tax paid to the local council by owners of houses

counsel ➤ *noun* (*plural* **counsels**)
1 advice **2** the barrister or barristers involved in a case in a lawcourt

counsel ➤ *verb* (**counsels, counselling, counselled**)
to counsel someone is to give them advice

counsellor *noun* (*plural* **counsellors**)
someone who gives advice, especially as their job

count[1] ➤ *verb* (**counts, counting, counted**)
1 to count is to use numbers to find out how many people or things there are in a place **2** to count or count out is to say numbers in their proper order **3** to count someone or something is to include them in a total ♦ *There are 30 in the class, counting the teacher* **4** to count is to have a particular value or importance
♦ *Playing well counts a lot even if you lose*
to count on someone or **something** is to rely on them

count ➤ *noun* (*plural* **counts**)
1 the total reached by counting **2** one of the things that someone is accused of ♦ *He was found guilty on all counts*

count[2] *noun* (*plural* **counts**)
a foreign nobleman

countable *adjective*
able to be counted

countdown *noun* (*plural* **countdowns**)
a counting down to 0, especially before launching a rocket

countenance *noun* (*plural* **countenances**)
someone's face or the expression on their face

counter *noun* (*plural* **counters**)
1 a long table where customers are served in a shop or café **2** a small plastic disc used in board games

counterfeit *adjective* (*pronounced* **kown**-ter-fit)
faked to deceive or swindle people ♦ *They were using counterfeit money*

countess *noun* (*plural* **countesses**)
the wife or widow of a count or earl; a female earl

countless *adjective*
too many to count; very many

country *noun* (*plural* **countries**)
1 a country is a part of the world where a particular nation of people lives **2** the country is the countryside

countryman or **countrywoman** *noun* (*plural* **countrymen** or **countrywomen**)
1 a man or woman who lives in the countryside **2** a fellow countryman is someone who lives in the same country

countryside *noun*
an area with fields, woods, and villages, away from towns

county *noun* (*plural* **counties**)
one of the areas that a country is divided into, for example Kent in England, Fife in Scotland, and Powys in Wales

couple ➤ *noun* (*plural* **couples**)
a couple is two people or things

couple ➤ *verb* (**couples, coupling, coupled**)
to couple things is to join them together

coupling *noun* (*plural* **couplings**)
a link or fastening, especially for vehicles

coupon *noun* (*plural* **coupons**)
a piece of paper that gives you the right to receive or do something

courage *noun*
being courageous

courageous *adjective*
ready to face danger or pain

courgette *noun* (*plural* **courgettes**)
a kind of vegetable like a small marrow

courier *noun* (*plural* **couriers**) (*pronounced* **koor**-i-er)
1 someone who carries a message **2** someone employed to guide and help holidaymakers, especially abroad

course *noun* (*plural* **courses**)
1 the direction in which something moves along ♦ *The ship's course was to the west* **2** a series of lessons or exercises in learning something ♦ *My Mum's starting a cookery course at last* **3** a part of a meal, such as the meat course or the pudding course **4** a racecourse or golf course
in due course eventually; at the right time
in the course of something while it is happening
of course naturally; certainly ♦ *Of course they will help us* ♦ *'Will you help us?' 'Of course!'*

court ➤ *noun* (*plural* **courts**)
1 a lawcourt **2** an enclosed place for games like tennis or netball **3** a courtyard **4** the place where a king or queen lives **5** the people who are usually at a king's or queen's court

court ➤ *verb* (**courts, courting, courted**)
to court someone is to try to win their love or support

courteous *adjective* (*pronounced* **ker**-ti-us)
friendly and polite

courteously *adverb* in a courteous way

courtesy *noun* being courteous

court martial *noun* (*plural* **courts martial**)
1 a court for trying offenders against military law **2** a trial in this court

courtship *noun*
courting someone, especially a boyfriend or girlfriend

courtyard *noun* (*plural* **courtyards**)
a paved area surrounded by walls or buildings

cousin *noun* (*plural* **cousins**)
your cousin is a child of your uncle or aunt

cove *noun* (*plural* **coves**)
a small bay

cover ➤ *verb* (**covers, covering, covered**)
1 to cover something is to put something else over it to hide or protect it **2** to cover a distance is to travel over it ♦ *We managed to cover ten miles a day* **3** to cover a subject is to deal with it or include it ♦ *This book covers everything you need to know about stamp collecting* **4** to cover something is to be enough money for it ♦ *I expect £2 will cover my fare* **5** to cover someone is to aim a gun at or near them ♦ *I've got you covered*
to cover something up is to make sure no one knows about something wrong or illegal

cover ➤ *noun* (*plural* **covers**)
1 a cover is something used for covering something else; a lid or wrapper **2** cover is a place where someone can hide or take shelter

coverage *noun*
the amount of time or space given to reporting an event on radio, on television, or in a newspaper

cover-up *noun* (*plural* **cover-ups**)
a cover-up is when people in power prevent other people knowing about something wrong or illegal ♦ *The government were accused of a cover-up of their mistakes*

cow *noun* (*plural* **cows**)
a female animal kept by farmers for its milk and beef

coward *noun* (*plural* **cowards**)
someone who avoids difficulty or danger

cowardice *noun* being a coward **cowardly** *adjective* like a coward

cowboy *noun* (*plural* **cowboys**)
1 a man who rides round looking after the cattle on a large farm in America
2 (*informal*) a person who uses dishonest methods in business, especially in building

cowslip *noun* (*plural* **cowslips**)
a wild plant that has yellow flowers in spring

cox *noun* (*plural* **coxes**)
someone who steers a racing boat

coxswain *noun* (*plural* **coxswains**)
(*pronounced* **kok**-swayn or **kok**-sun)
a person who steers a boat or is in charge of the crew of a small ship

coy *adjective*
shy; pretending to be shy or modest

coyly *adverb* in a coy way **coyness** *noun* being coy

crab *noun* (*plural* **crabs**)
a shellfish with ten legs

crab apple *noun* (*plural* **crab apples**)
a small sour apple

crack ➤ *noun* (*plural* **cracks**)
1 a line on the surface of something where it has broken but not come completely

apart; a narrow gap ♦ *There's a crack in this cup* 2 a sudden sharp noise ♦ *They heard the crack of a pistol shot* 3 a sudden sharp blow ♦ *He got a crack on the head*

crack ➤ *verb* (**cracks, cracking, cracked**)
1 to crack something is to make a crack in it 2 something cracks when it splits without breaking ♦ *The plate has cracked*
3 to crack is to make a sudden sharp noise
4 to crack a joke is to tell it
to get cracking (*informal*) is to start work

cracker *noun* (*plural* **crackers**)
1 a pretty paper tube with a small gift inside it, which bangs when two people pull it apart 2 a thin biscuit

crackle *verb* (**crackles, crackling, crackled**)
to crackle is to make small cracking sounds, like a fire

crackling *noun*
the hard skin of roast pork

cradle *noun* (*plural* **cradles**)
1 a cot for a baby 2 a supporting frame for something

craft *noun* (*plural* **crafts**)
1 a craft is an activity which needs skill with the hands 2 a boat 3 craft is cunning or trickery

craftsman *noun* (*plural* **craftsmen**)
someone who is good at a craft

craftsmanship *noun* the skill of a craftsman

crafty *adjective* (**craftier, craftiest**)
cunning and clever

craftily *adverb* in a crafty way **craftiness** *noun* being crafty

crag *noun* (*plural* **crags**)
a steep piece of rough rock

craggy *adjective* steep and rocky

cram *verb* (**crams, cramming, crammed**)
1 to cram things is to force them into a small space 2 to cram is to study very hard for an examination

cramp ➤ *noun* (*plural* **cramps**)
pain caused by a muscle tightening suddenly

cramp ➤ *verb* (**cramps, cramping, cramped**)
to cramp someone is to hinder their freedom or growth

cramped *adjective*
in a space that is too small or tight ♦ *We felt very cramped sleeping three in the same room*

crane ➤ *noun* (*plural* **cranes**)
1 a machine for lifting and moving heavy objects **2** a large bird with long legs and neck

crane ➤ *verb* (**cranes, craning, craned**)
to crane your neck is to stretch it so that you can see something

crane-fly *noun* (*plural* **crane-flies**)
an insect with long thin legs

crank ➤ *noun* (*plural* **cranks**)
1 an L-shaped rod used to turn or control something **2** a person with weird or unusual ideas

crank ➤ *verb* (**cranks, cranking, cranked**)
to crank something like an engine is to turn it by using an L-shaped rod

cranky *adjective* (**crankier, crankiest**)
weird or unusual

cranny *noun* (*plural* **crannies**)
a crevice; a narrow hole or space

crash ➤ *noun* (*plural* **crashes**)
1 the loud noise of something falling or breaking **2** a collision between road vehicles, causing damage

crash ➤ *verb* (**crashes, crashing, crashed**)
1 to crash is to collide or fall violently **2** to crash a vehicle is to have a crash while driving it **3** to crash along or through something is to move violently and loudly

crash helmet *noun* (*plural* **crash helmets**)
a padded helmet worn by cyclists and motorcyclists

crash landing *noun* (*plural* **crash landings**)
an emergency landing of an aircraft, causing it damage

crate *noun* (*plural* **crates**)
a container in which goods are transported

crater *noun* (*plural* **craters**)
1 the mouth of a volcano **2** a hole in the ground made by a bomb

crave *verb* (**craves, craving, craved**)
to crave something is to want it very badly

crawl ➤ *verb* (**crawls, crawling, crawled**)
1 to crawl is to move along on your hands and knees **2** to crawl is also to move slowly in a vehicle **3** to be crawling with something unpleasant is to be full of it or covered in it ♦ *This room's crawling with cockroaches*

crawl ➤ *noun*
1 a crawling movement **2** a powerful swimming stroke with the arms hitting the water alternately

crayon *noun* (*plural* **crayons**)
a coloured pencil for drawing or writing

craze *noun* (*plural* **crazes**)
a brief enthusiasm for something

crazy *adjective* (**crazier, craziest**)
mad or weird
crazily *adverb* in a crazy way **craziness** *noun* being crazy

crazy paving *noun*
paving made of odd pieces of stone fitted together

creak ➤ *noun* (*plural* **creaks**)
a sound like the noise made by a stiff door opening

creak ➤ *verb* (**creaks, creaking, creaked**)
to make a creak
creaky *adjective* old and creaking

cream *noun* (*plural* **creams**)
1 the rich fatty part of milk **2** a yellowish-white colour **3** a food containing or looking like cream **4** something that looks like cream, for example face cream
creamy *adjective* smooth and thick like cream

crease ➤ *noun* (*plural* **creases**)
1 a line made in something by folding or pressing it **2** a line on a cricket pitch showing where the batsman should stand

crease ➤ *verb* (**creases, creasing, creased**)
to crease something is to make a crease in it

create *verb* (**creates, creating, created**)
to create something is to make it exist
creation *noun* creating something

creative *adjective*
showing imagination and thought as well as skill ♦ *The older children have started some creative writing*
creativity *noun* being creative

creator *noun* (*plural* **creators**)
someone who creates something
the Creator a name for God

creature *noun* (*plural* **creatures**)
a living animal or person

crèche *noun* (*plural* **crèches**) (*pronounced* **kresh**)
a place where babies or small children are looked after while their parents are busy

credibility *noun*
being credible

credible *adjective*
able to be believed; trustworthy
credibly *adverb* in a credible way

credit ➤ *noun*
  1 honour or approval ◆ *Give her credit for her honesty* **2** a system of allowing someone to pay for something later on ◆ *Do you want cash now or can I have it on credit?* **3** an amount of money in an account at a bank or building society
  credits the list of people who have helped to produce a film, television programme, etc.
  to do someone credit is to earn them praise ◆ *Your topic work does you credit*

credit ➤ *verb* (**credits, crediting, credited**)
  1 to credit something is to believe it ◆ *Can you credit that?* **2** to credit someone with something is to enter it as a credit in their bank account ◆ *We will credit you with a £50 refund*

creditable *adjective*
  deserving praise
  creditably *adverb* in a creditable way

credit card *noun* (*plural* **credit cards**)
  a card allowing someone to buy goods on credit

creditor *noun* (*plural* **creditors**)
  someone to whom you owe money

creed *noun* (*plural* **creeds**)
  a set or statement of beliefs

creek *noun* (*plural* **creeks**)
  1 a narrow inlet **2** (*in Australia, New Zealand, or America*) a small stream
  up the creek (*slang*) in trouble

creep ➤ *verb* (**creeps, creeping, crept**)
  1 to creep is to move along with the body close to the ground **2** to creep about is to move quietly or secretly
  to creep up on someone is to go up to them quietly from behind

creep ➤ *noun* (*plural* **creeps**)
  1 a creeping movement **2** (*slang*) a nasty or unpleasant person
  the creeps (*informal*) a feeling of fear or disgust

creeper *noun* (*plural* **creepers**)
  a plant that grows close to the ground or up walls

creepy *adjective* (**creepier, creepiest**)
  (*informal*) weird and slightly frightening

cremate *verb* (**cremates, cremating, cremated**)
  to cremate a body is to burn it into ashes
  cremation *noun* cremating a body

crematorium *noun* (*plural* **crematoria**)
  (*pronounced* krem-a-**tor**-i-um)
  a place where dead bodies are cremated

creosote *noun* (*pronounced* **kree**-o-soht)
  a brown oily liquid painted on wood to prevent it from rotting

crêpe *noun* (*plural* **crêpes**) (*pronounced* krayp)
  1 cloth or paper with a wrinkled surface **2** a kind of thin French pancake

crept past tense and past participle of **creep** *verb*

crescendo *noun* (*plural* **crescendos**) (*pronounced* kri-**shen**-doh)
  music that gets gradually louder

crescent *noun* (*plural* **crescents**)
  1 a narrow curved shape, pointed at both ends, like a new moon **2** a curved street

cress *noun*
  a green plant used in salads and sandwiches

crest *noun* (*plural* **crests**)
  1 a tuft of hair, feathers, or skin on an animal's head **2** the top of a hill or wave

crevasse *noun* (*plural* **crevasses**)
  a deep crack in a glacier

crevice *noun* (*plural* **crevices**)
  a crack in rock or in a wall

crew *noun* (*plural* **crews**)
  the people who work on a ship or aircraft

crib ➤ *noun* (*plural* **cribs**)
  1 a baby's cot **2** a framework containing fodder for animals **3** a translation of a book written in another language **4** something copied

crib ➤ *verb* (**cribs, cribbing, cribbed**)
  to crib someone else's work is to copy it

cricket [1] *noun*
  a game played outdoors by two teams with a ball, two bats, and two wickets
  cricketer *noun* someone who plays cricket

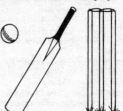

cricket [2] *noun* (*plural* **crickets**)
  an insect like a grasshopper

cried past tense and past participle of **cry** *verb*

crime *noun* (*plural* **crimes**)
  an act that breaks the law

criminal ➤ *noun* (*plural* **criminals**)
  someone who has committed one or more crimes

criminal ➤ *adjective*
  to do with crime or criminals

crimson *noun* and *adjective*
a dark red colour

crinkle *verb* (**crinkles, crinkling, crinkled**)
to crinkle something is to crease or wrinkle it
crinkly *adjective* wrinkled

cripple ➤ *noun* (*plural* **cripples**)
someone who cannot walk properly

cripple ➤ *verb* (**cripples, crippling, crippled**)
1 to cripple someone is to make them a cripple **2** to cripple something is to damage it so it won't work properly

crisis *noun* (*plural* **crises**) (*pronounced* kry-sis)
an important or difficult time or situation

crisp ➤ *adjective* (**crisper, crispest**)
1 very dry so that it breaks easily **2** firm and fresh ♦ *I'd like a nice crisp apple* **3** cold and frosty ♦ *We woke up to a crisp winter morning*

crisp ➤ *noun* (*plural* **crisps**)
a thin fried slice of potato, sold in packets

criss-cross *adjective* and *adverb*
with crossing lines

critic *noun* (*plural* **critics**)
1 a person who criticizes someone or something **2** someone who gives opinions on books, plays, films, music, or other performances

critical *adjective*
1 criticizing **2** to do with critics or criticism **3** serious, amounting to a crisis
critically *adverb* in a critical way; seriously

criticism *noun* (*plural* **criticisms**) (*pronounced* krit-i-si-zum)
an opinion or judgement about something, usually pointing out its faults

criticize *verb* (**criticizes, criticizing, criticized**) (*pronounced* krit-i-syz)
to criticize something or someone is to give an opinion pointing out their faults

croak ➤ *noun* (*plural* **croaks**)
a deep sound, like a frog makes

croak ➤ *verb* (**croaks, croaking, croaked**)
to make a croak

crochet *noun* (*pronounced* kroh-shay)
a kind of needlework done with a hooked needle

crock *noun* (*plural* **crocks**)
(*informal*) an old or worn-out person or thing

crockery *noun*
dishes, plates, and cups and saucers used for eating

crocodile *noun* (*plural* **crocodiles**)
a large reptile living in hot countries, with a thick skin, long tail, and huge jaws

crocodile tears *plural noun*
sorrow that is not genuine

crocus *noun* (*plural* **crocuses**)
a small spring flower that is yellow, purple, or white

croft *noun* (*plural* **crofts**)
a small farm in Scotland
crofter *noun* someone who works on a croft

croissant *noun* (*plural* **croissants**) (*pronounced* krwa-sahn)
a crescent-shaped roll of rich pastry, first made in France and usually eaten for breakfast

crook ➤ *noun* (*plural* **crooks**)
1 (*informal*) someone who cheats or robs people; a criminal **2** a shepherd's or bishop's stick with a curved end

crook ➤ *verb* (**crooks, crooking, crooked**)
to crook something is to bend it into a hook shape

crooked *adjective* (*pronounced* kruuk-id)
1 bent or twisted **2** (*informal*) dishonest or criminal

croon *verb* (**croons, crooning, crooned**)
to croon is to sing softly or sentimentally

crop ➤ *noun* (*plural* **crops**)
1 something grown for food, especially in a field ♦ *They had a good crop of wheat last year* **2** a riding whip with a loop instead of a lash

crop ➤ *verb* (**crops, cropping, cropped**)
to crop something is to cut or bite the top off it ♦ *They could see sheep in a field, cropping the grass*
to crop up is to happen or appear unexpectedly

cross ➤ *noun* (*plural* **crosses**)
1 a mark or shape like + or × **2** an upright post with another post across it, used in ancient times for crucifixions **3** an animal produced by mixing one breed with another ♦ *A mule is a cross between a donkey and a horse*
the Cross the cross on which Christ was crucified, used as a symbol of Christianity

cross ➤ *verb* (**crosses, crossing, crossed**)
1 to cross something is to go across it ♦ *She crossed the room to meet him* **2** to cross your fingers or legs is to put one over the other
to cross something out is to draw a line across something because it is unwanted or wrong

cross ➤ *adjective*
1 angry or bad-tempered **2** going from one side to another ♦ *There were cross winds on the bridge*
crossly *adverb* angrily **crossness** *noun* being cross

crossbar *noun* (*plural* **crossbars**)
a horizontal bar between two upright bars

crossbow *noun* (*plural* **crossbows**)
a kind of bow used for shooting arrows, held like a gun and fired by pulling a trigger

cross-country *noun*
a running race through fields and country

cross-examine *verb* (**cross-examines, cross-examining, cross-examined**)
to cross-examine someone is to question them about information they have given **cross-examination** *noun* cross-examining someone

cross-eyed *adjective*
having eyes that appear to look in different directions

crossing *noun* (*plural* **crossings**)
a place where people can cross a road or railway

cross-legged *adverb* and *adjective*
having crossed legs

crossroads *noun* (*plural* **crossroads**)
a place where two or more roads cross one another

cross-section *noun* (*plural* **cross-sections**)
1 a drawing of something as if it has been cut through 2 a typical sample ♦ *A cross-section of parents said they wanted an after-school club*

crosswise *adverb* and *adjective*
with one thing crossing another

crossword *noun* (*plural* **crosswords**)
a puzzle with blank squares in which you put the letters of words worked out from clues

crotchet *noun* (*plural* **crotchets**)
(*pronounced* **kroch**-it)
a musical note equal to half a minim, written ♩

crouch *verb* (**crouches, crouching, crouched**)
to crouch is to lower your body, with your arms and legs bent

crow ➤ *noun* (*plural* **crows**)
a large black bird
as the crow flies in a straight line

crow ➤ *verb* (**crows, crowing, crowed**)
1 to make a noise like a cock 2 to boast; to be proudly triumphant

crowbar *noun* (*plural* **crowbars**)
an iron bar used as a lever

crowd ➤ *noun* (*plural* **crowds**)
a large number of people in one place

crowd ➤ *verb* (**crowds, crowding, crowded**)
1 to crowd or crowd round is to form a crowd 2 to crowd a place is to make it uncomfortably full of people ♦ *The town is crowded with tourists in summer*

crown ➤ *noun* (*plural* **crowns**)
1 a crown is an ornamental headdress worn by a king or queen 2 the crown is the king or queen of a country ♦ *This land belongs to the crown* 3 the top of the head 4 the middle part of a road, which is higher than the sides

crown ➤ *verb* (**crowns, crowning, crowned**)
1 to crown someone is to make them king or queen 2 to crown something is to form the top of it 3 to crown an achievement is to finish it happily ♦ *Their efforts were crowned with success*

crow's-nest *noun* (*plural* **crow's-nests**)
a look-out position at the top of a ship's mast

crucial *adjective* (*pronounced* **kroo**-shal)
extremely important

crucifix *noun* (*plural* **crucifixes**)
a model of the Cross or of Christ on the Cross

crucify *verb* (**crucifies, crucifying, crucified**)
to crucify someone is to execute them by fixing their hands and feet to a cross **crucifixion** *noun* crucifying someone

crude *adjective* (**cruder, crudest**)
1 natural; not purified ♦ *The country exported crude oil* 2 rough and simple ♦ *They stayed in a crude hut in the mountains* 3 rude or dirty ♦ *The boys were telling each other crude jokes*

cruel *adjective* (**crueller, cruellest**)
causing pain and suffering to others
♦ *They were ruled by a cruel tyrant* ♦ *War is cruel*
cruelly *adverb* in a cruel way **cruelty** *noun* being cruel

cruise ➤ *noun* (*plural* **cruises**)
a holiday on a ship, usually visiting different places

cruise ➤ *verb* (**cruises, cruising, cruised**)
1 to cruise is to sail or travel at a gentle speed 2 to cruise is also to have a cruise on a ship

cruiser *noun* (*plural* **cruisers**)
1 a fast warship 2 a large motor boat

crumb *noun* (*plural* **crumbs**)
a tiny piece of bread or cake

crumble *verb* (**crumbles, crumbling, crumbled**)
1 to crumble something is to break it into small pieces 2 to crumble is to be broken into small pieces
crumbly *adjective* soft and likely to crumble

crumpet *noun* (*plural* **crumpets**)
a soft flat cake made with yeast, toasted and eaten with butter

crumple *verb* (**crumples, crumpling, crumpled**)
1 to crumple something is to make it creased 2 to crumple is to become creased

crunch ➤ *noun* (*plural* **crunches**)
the noise made by chewing hard food or walking on gravel
the crunch (*informal*) a crucial event; a crisis

crunch ➤ *verb* (**crunches, crunching, crunched**)
to crunch something is to chew or crush it with a crunch
crunchy *adjective* making a crunch

crusade *noun* (*plural* **crusades**)
1 a military expedition to Palestine made by Christians in the Middle Ages **2** a campaign against something that you think is bad
crusader *noun* someone who takes part in a crusade

crush ➤ *verb* (**crushes, crushing, crushed**)
1 to crush something is to press it so that it gets broken or damaged **2** to crush an enemy is to defeat them

crush ➤ *noun* (*plural* **crushes**)
1 a crowd; a crowded place **2** a fruit-flavoured drink **3** (*informal*) a sudden liking you have for someone

crust *noun* (*plural* **crusts**)
1 the hard outside part of something, especially of a loaf **2** the rocky outer part of a planet

crustacean *noun* (*plural* **crustaceans**)
(*pronounced* krus-**tay**-shan)
a shellfish

crutch *noun* (*plural* **crutches**)
a stick that fits under the arm, used as a support in walking

cry ➤ *verb* (**cries, crying, cried**)
1 to cry is to shout **2** to cry is also to let tears fall from your eyes
to cry off is to change your mind and not do something you were going to do ◆ *George was going to come on holiday with us, but he cried off at the last minute*

cry ➤ *noun* (*plural* **cries**)
1 a loud shout **2** a period of weeping

crypt *noun* (*plural* **crypts**)
a large room underneath a church

crystal *noun* (*plural* **crystals**)
1 a clear mineral rather like glass **2** a small solid piece of a substance with a symmetrical shape, such as snow and ice
crystalline *adjective* made of crystals

crystallize *verb* (**crystallizes, crystallizing, crystallized**)
to crystallize is to form into crystals

cub *noun* (*plural* **cubs**)
a young animal, especially a lion, tiger, fox, or bear
Cub a junior Scout

cubbyhole *noun* (*plural* **cubbyholes**)
a small compartment or snug place

cube ➤ *noun* (*plural* **cubes**)
1 an object that has six square sides, like a box or dice **2** the result of multiplying something by itself twice ◆ *The cube of 3 is $3 \times 3 \times 3 = 27$*

cube ➤ *verb* (**cubes, cubing, cubed**)
1 to cube a number is to multiply it by itself twice ◆ *4 cubed is $4 \times 4 \times 4 = 64$* **2** to cube something is to cut it into small cubes

cube root *noun* (*plural* **cube roots**)
a number that gives another number if it is multiplied by itself twice ◆ *2 is the cube root of 8*

cubic *adjective*
1 shaped like a cube **2** a cubic metre or foot is the volume of a cube with sides that are one metre or foot long

cubicle *noun* (*plural* **cubicles**)
a small division of a room

cuboid *noun* (*plural* **cuboids**)
an object with six rectangular sides

cuckoo *noun* (*plural* **cuckoos**)
a bird that makes a sound like 'cuck-oo', and lays its eggs in other birds' nests

cucumber *noun* (*plural* **cucumbers**)
a long green vegetable, eaten raw

cud *noun*
half-digested food that a cow brings back from its first stomach to chew again

cuddle *verb* (**cuddles, cuddling, cuddled**)
to cuddle someone is to put your arms closely round them
cuddly *adjective* nice to cuddle

cue [1] *noun* (*plural* **cues**)
something that tells an actor when to start speaking or come on the stage

cue [2] *noun* (*plural* **cues**)
a long stick used to strike the ball in billiards or snooker

cuff ➤ *noun* (*plural* **cuffs**)
1 the end of a sleeve that fits round your wrist **2** a blow given to someone with your hand

cuff ➤ *verb* (**cuffs, cuffing, cuffed**)
to cuff someone is to hit them with the hand

cul-de-sac *noun* (*plural* **cul-de-sacs**)
a street that is closed at one end

culminate *verb* (**culminates, culminating, culminated**)
to reach the end or the most important part ◆ *Their long struggle for freedom culminated in victory*
culmination *noun* the end or most important part

culprit *noun* (*plural* **culprits**)
someone who is to blame for something

cult *noun* (*plural* **cults**)
1 a religion 2 being extremely keen on someone or something ♦ *They enjoyed the cult of rock music*

cultivate *verb* (**cultivates, cultivating, cultivated**)
1 to cultivate land is to grow crops on it
2 to cultivate something is to try to make it grow or develop
cultivation *noun* cultivating land

cultivated *adjective*
having good manners and education

culture *noun* (*plural* **cultures**)
1 culture is the development of the mind by education and learning 2 a culture is the customs and traditions of a people ♦ *They were studying Greek culture*
cultural *adjective* to do with culture **cultured** *adjective* educated

cunning *adjective*
clever at deceiving people

cup ➤ *noun* (*plural* **cups**)
1 a small container with a handle, from which you drink liquid 2 a prize in the form of a silver cup, usually with two handles

cup ➤ *verb* (**cups, cupping, cupped**)
to cup your hands is to form them into the shape of a cup

cupboard *noun* (*plural* **cupboards**)
(*pronounced* kub-erd)
a compartment or piece of furniture with a door, for storing things

cupful *noun* (*plural* **cupfuls**)
as much as a cup will hold

curate *noun* (*plural* **curates**) (*pronounced* kewr-at)
a member of the clergy who helps a vicar

curator *noun* (*plural* **curators**) (*pronounced* kewr-ay-ter)
someone in charge of a museum or art gallery

curb *verb* (**curbs, curbing, curbed**)
to curb a feeling is to restrain it ♦ *You must curb your anger*

curd *noun* (*plural* **curds**)
a thick substance formed when milk turns sour

curdle *verb* (**curdles, curdling, curdled**)
to curdle is to form into curds

cure ➤ *verb* (**cures, curing, cured**)
1 to cure someone who is ill is to make them better 2 to cure something bad is to stop it 3 to cure food is to treat it so as to preserve it ♦ *Fish can be cured in smoke*

cure ➤ *noun* (*plural* **cures**)
something that cures a person or thing ♦ *They are still trying to find a cure for cancer*

curfew *noun* (*plural* **curfews**)
a time or signal after which people must stay indoors until the next day

curiosity *noun* (*plural* **curiosities**)
1 curiosity is being curious 2 a curiosity is something strange or interesting

curious *adjective*
1 wanting to find out about things
2 strange or unusual
curiously *adverb* in a curious way

curl ➤ *noun* (*plural* **curls**)
a curve or coil, especially of hair

curl ➤ *verb* (**curls, curling, curled**)
to curl is to form into curls
to curl up is to sit or lie with your knees drawn up

curly *adjective* (**curlier, curliest**)
full of curls

currant *noun* (*plural* **currants**)
1 a small black fruit made from dried grapes 2 a small juicy berry, or the bush that produces it

currency *noun* (*plural* **currencies**)
money that is in use in a place ♦ *You can pay with French currency*

current ➤ *noun* (*plural* **currents**)
a flow of water, air, or electricity

current ➤ *adjective*
happening or used now
currently *adverb* now, at the moment

curriculum *noun* (*plural* **curriculums** or **curricula**)
a course of study

curry [1] *noun* (*plural* **curries**)
food cooked with spices that make it taste hot

curry [2] *verb* (**curries, currying, curried**)
to curry a horse is to groom it
to curry favour is to try to win favour or approval

curse ➤ *noun* (*plural* **curses**)
1 a call or prayer for someone to be harmed or killed 2 something very unpleasant 3 an angry word or words

curse ➤ *verb* (**curses, cursing, cursed**)
to curse someone is to use a curse against them

cursor *noun* (*plural* **cursors**)
a movable flashing signal on a VDU screen, showing where new data will go

curtain *noun* (*plural* **curtains**)
a piece of material hung at a window or door, or at the front of a stage

curtsy ➤ *noun* (*plural* **curtsies**)
a bow made by bending the knees, done by women as a mark of respect

curtsy ➤ *verb* (**curtsies, curtsying, curtsied**)
to curtsy is to make a curtsy

curvature *noun* (*plural* **curvatures**)
a curving or bending, especially of the earth's horizon

curve ➤ *noun* (*plural* **curves**)
a line that bends smoothly

curve ➤ *verb* (**curves, curving, curved**)
to curve is to bend smoothly

cushion ➤ *noun* (*plural* **cushions**)
a fabric cover filled with soft material so that it is comfortable to sit on or rest against

cushion ➤ *verb* (**cushions, cushioning, cushioned**)
to cushion someone is to protect them from harm ♦ *When he fell down the stairs, the rug at the bottom cushioned his fall*

custard *noun*
a sweet yellow sauce eaten with puddings

custom *noun* (*plural* **customs**)
1 the usual way of doing things ♦ *It is the custom to go on holiday in the summer*
2 regular business from customers ♦ *That rude man at the corner shop won't get my custom any more*
customs are the group of officials at a port or airport to whom people coming into a country declare what goods they have with them

customary *adjective*
usual
customarily *adverb* usually

customer *noun* (*plural* **customers**)
someone who uses a shop, bank, or business

customize *noun* (**customizes, customizing, customized**)
to customize something is to alter it for a special use

cut ➤ *verb* (**cuts, cutting, cut**)
1 to cut something is to divide it or make a slit in it with a knife or scissors 2 to cut something like prices or taxes is to reduce them 3 to cut a pack of playing cards is to divide it 4 to cut a corner is to go across it rather than round it 5 to cut a meeting or lesson is to stay away from it 6 a baby cuts a tooth when it has a new tooth coming
to cut someone off is to interrupt them ♦ *She cut me off before I could finish my sentence*
to cut something out (*informal*) is to stop doing it ♦ *Cut out the talking!*

cut ➤ *noun* (*plural* **cuts**)
1 an act of cutting; the result of cutting ♦ *Your hair could do with a cut* 2 a small wound caused by something sharp
3 (*informal*) a share ♦ *I want a cut of the profits*

cut and dried *adjective*
already organized or decided ♦ *By the time we arrived the plans were all cut and dried*

cute *adjective* (**cuter, cutest**)
(*informal*) attractive in a quaint or simple way

cutlass *noun* (*plural* **cutlasses**)
a short sword with a wide curved blade

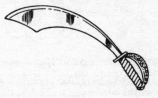

cutlery *noun*
knives, forks, and spoons used for eating

cutlet *noun* (*plural* **cutlets**)
a thick slice of meat still on the bone

cut-out *noun* (*plural* **cut-outs**)
something cut out of paper or cardboard

cut-price *adjective*
sold at a reduced price

cutter *noun* (*plural* **cutters**)
a sailing ship with one mast

cutting *noun* (*plural* **cuttings**)
1 something cut from a newspaper or magazine 2 a piece cut off a plant to grow as a new plant 3 a deep passage cut through high ground for a railway or road

cycle ➤ *noun* (*plural* **cycles**)
1 a bicycle 2 a series of events that are regularly repeated ♦ *Rainfall is part of the water cycle*

cycle ➤ *verb* (**cycles, cycling, cycled**)
to cycle is to ride a bicycle

cyclist *noun* someone who rides a bicycle

cyclone *noun* (*plural* **cyclones**)
a strong wind rotating round a calm central area

cyclonic *adjective* like a cyclone

cygnet *noun* (*plural* **cygnets**) (*pronounced* **sig-nit**)
a young swan

cylinder *noun* (*plural* **cylinders**)
1 an object with straight sides and circular ends **2** part of an engine in which a piston moves

cylindrical *adjective*
shaped like a cylinder

cymbal *noun* (*plural* **cymbals**)
a cymbal is a round, slightly hollowed metal plate that you hit to make a ringing sound in music

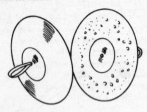

cynic *noun* (*plural* **cynics**) (*pronounced* sin-ik)
someone who doubts that anything is good or worthwhile

cynical *adjective* doubting that anything is good **cynically** *adverb* in a cynical way **cynicism** *noun* being cynical

cypress *noun* (*plural* **cypresses**)
an evergreen tree with dark leaves

Dd

dab ➤ *noun* (*plural* **dabs**)
a gentle touch with something soft

dab ➤ *verb* (**dabs, dabbing, dabbed**)
to dab something is to touch it gently with something soft ♦ *I dabbed my eyes with a handkerchief*

dabble *verb* (**dabbles, dabbling, dabbled**)
1 to dabble something is to splash it about in water **2** to dabble in something is to do it as a hobby ♦ *She likes to dabble in photography*

dachshund *noun* (*plural* **dachshunds**)
(*pronounced* **daks**-huund or **daks**-huunt)
a small dog with a long body and short legs

dad *noun* (*plural* **dads**)
(*informal*) father

daddy *noun* (*plural* **daddies**)
(*informal*) father

daddy-long-legs *noun* (*plural* **daddy-long-legs**)
a crane-fly

daffodil *noun* (*plural* **daffodils**)
a yellow flower that grows from a bulb

daft *adjective* (**dafter, daftest**)
silly or stupid

dagger *noun* (*plural* **daggers**)
a pointed knife with two sharp edges, used as a weapon

dahlia *noun* (*plural* **dahlias**) (*pronounced* **day**-li-a)
a garden plant with brightly-coloured flowers

daily *adjective* and *adverb*
every day

dainty *adjective* (**daintier, daintiest**)
small and delicate

daintily *adverb* in a dainty way **daintiness** *noun* being dainty

dairy *noun* (*plural* **dairies**)
a place where milk, butter, cream, and cheese are made or sold

daisy *noun* (*plural* **daisies**)
a small flower with white petals and a yellow centre

dale *noun* (*plural* **dales**)
a valley

Dalmatian *noun* (*plural* **Dalmatians**)
a large dog that is white with black or brown spots

dam ➤ *noun* (*plural* **dams**)
a wall built to hold water back

dam ➤ *verb* (**dams, damming, dammed**)
to dam water is to build a dam across it

damage ➤ *verb* (**damages, damaging, damaged**)
to damage something is to injure or harm it

damage ➤ *noun*
injury or harm

damages *plural noun*
money paid to someone to make up for an injury or loss

Dame *noun* (*plural* **Dames**)
the title of a lady who has been given the equivalent of a knighthood

dame *noun* (*plural* **dames**)
a comic middle-aged woman in a pantomime, usually played by a man

damn *verb* (**damns, damning, damned**)
to damn something is to say it is bad or wrong
damn! is a swear word

damned *adjective*
(*informal*) hateful or annoying

damp ➤ *adjective* (**damper, dampest**)
slightly wet; not quite dry

damp ➤ *noun*
damp or the damp is wetness in the air or on something

dampen *verb* (**dampens, dampening, dampened**)
1 to dampen something is to make it damp
2 to dampen sound or noise is to make it softer

damson *noun* (*plural* **damsons**)
a small purple plum

dance ➤ *verb* (**dances, dancing, danced**)
to dance is to move about in time to music

dance ➤ *noun* (*plural* **dances**)
1 a piece of music or set of movements for dancing 2 a party or gathering where people dance

dancer *noun* someone who dances

dandelion *noun* (*plural* **dandelions**)
a yellow wild flower with jagged leaves

dandruff *noun*
small white flakes of dead skin in a person's hair

danger *noun* (*plural* **dangers**)
something that is dangerous

dangerous *adjective*
likely to harm you

dangle *verb* (**dangles, dangling, dangled**)
to dangle is to hang or swing loosely

dappled *adjective*
marked with patches of different colours

dare ➤ *verb* (**dares, daring, dared**)
1 to dare to do something is to be brave or bold enough to do it 2 to dare someone to do something is to challenge them to do it
♦ *I dare you to climb that tree*

dare ➤ *noun* (*plural* **dares**)
(*informal*) a challenge to do something risky

daredevil *noun* (*plural* **daredevils**)
a reckless or brave person

daring *adjective*
bold or brave

dark ➤ *adjective* (**darker, darkest**)
1 with little or no light 2 deep and rich in colour ♦ *She wore a dark green coat*

dark ➤ *noun*
1 dark or the dark is when there is no light
♦ *Cats can see in the dark* 2 dark is also sunset ♦ *She went out after dark*

darkness *noun* being dark

darken *verb* (**darkens, darkening, darkened**)
to darken something is to make it dark

darkroom *noun* (*plural* **darkrooms**)
a room kept dark for developing and printing photographs

darling *noun* (*plural* **darlings**)
someone who is loved very much

darn *verb* (**darns, darning, darned**)
to darn a hole is to mend it by sewing across it

dart *noun* (*plural* **darts**)
an object with a sharp point, thrown at a dartboard in the game of **darts**

dartboard *noun* (*plural* **dartboards**)
a round target at which you throw darts

dash ➤ *noun* (*plural* **dashes**)
1 a quick rush or a hurry ♦ *They made a dash for the door* 2 a dash of something is a small amount of it 3 a short line (—) used in writing or printing

dash ➤ *verb* (**dashes, dashing, dashed**)
1 to dash is to rush 2 to dash something is to hurl it and smash it ♦ *In her anger she dashed the cup against the wall*

dashboard *noun* (*plural* **dashboards**)
a panel with dials and controls in front of the driver of a car

data *plural noun* (*pronounced* **day**-ta)
items of information

database *noun* (*plural* **databases**)
a store of information held in a computer

date [1] ➤ *noun* (*plural* dates)
1 the day of the month, or the year, when something happens or happened **2** an appointment to meet someone

date ➤ *verb* (dates, dating, dated)
1 to date something that happened is to give it a date **2** to date from a time is to have existed from then ♦ *The church dates from 1684* **3** to date is also to seem old-fashioned ♦ *Some fashions date very quickly*

date [2] *noun* (*plural* dates)
a sweet brown fruit that grows on a palm tree

daughter *noun* (*plural* daughters)
a girl or woman who is someone's child

dawdle *verb* (dawdles, dawdling, dawdled)
to dawdle is to go or act too slowly

dawn ➤ *noun* (*plural* dawns)
the time when the sun rises

dawn ➤ *verb* (dawns, dawning, dawned)
1 to dawn is to begin to become light in the morning **2** something dawns on you when you begin to realize it

day *noun* (*plural* days)
1 the 24 hours between midnight and the next midnight **2** the light part of the day **3** a period in time ♦ *Write about what it was like in Queen Victoria's day*

daybreak *noun*
the first light of day; dawn

daydream *verb* (daydreams, daydreaming, daydreamed)
to daydream is to have pleasant thoughts about things you would like to happen

daylight *noun*
1 the light of day **2** dawn ♦ *We must start before daylight*

day-to-day *adjective*
ordinary; happening every day

daze *noun*
in a daze unable to think or see clearly

dazed *adjective*
unable to think or see clearly

dazzle *verb* (dazzles, dazzling, dazzled)
to dazzle someone is to make them dazed with bright light

de- *prefix*
meaning removing something, as in *debug* and *de-ice*

dead *adjective*
1 no longer alive **2** not lively or active ♦ *This place is dead at the weekend* **3** complete, sure ♦ *It was a dead loss*

deaden *verb* (deadens, deadening, deadened)
to deaden pain or noise is to make it weaker

dead end *noun* (*plural* dead ends)
a road or passage with one end closed

dead heat *noun* (*plural* dead heats)
a race in which two or more winners finish exactly together

deadline *noun* (*plural* deadlines)
a time limit

deadlock *noun*
a situation in which people cannot agree

deadly *adjective* (deadlier, deadliest)
likely to kill ♦ *The liquid in the glass was a deadly poison*

deaf *adjective* (deafer, deafest)
unable to hear
deafness *noun* being deaf

deafen *verb* (deafens, deafening, deafened)
to be deafening is to be very loud ♦ *The noise from the party upstairs was deafening*

deal [1] ➤ *verb* (deals, dealing, dealt)
1 to deal something is to hand it out **2** to deal in something is to buy and sell it ♦ *He deals in scrap metal* **3** to deal playing cards is to give them to players in a card game
to deal with someone or **something** is to attend to them ♦ *I'll deal with you later*
to deal with something is to be concerned with it ♦ *This book deals with cacti*

deal ➤ *noun* (*plural* deals)
1 an agreement or bargain **2** someone's turn to deal at cards
a good deal or **a great deal** a large amount

deal [2] *noun*
sawn fir or pine wood

dealer *noun* (*plural* dealers)
1 someone who buys and sells things **2** the person dealing at cards

dean *noun* (*plural* deans)
1 an important member of the clergy in a cathedral or large church **2** a senior official in a college or university

dear *adjective* (dearer, dearest)
1 loved very much **2** the usual way of beginning a letter ♦ *Dear Mary* **3** expensive

death *noun* (*plural* deaths)
dying; the end of life

deathly *adjective*
like death; very quiet or spooky

debatable *adjective*
uncertain; that can be argued about

debate ➤ *noun* (*plural* debates)
a formal discussion

debate ➤ *verb* (debates, debating, debated)
to debate is to have a debate or to discuss something

debris *noun* (*pronounced* deb-ree)
scattered fragments or wreckage

debt *noun* (*plural* debts) (*pronounced* det)
something that someone owes

debtor *noun* (*plural* **debtors**) (*pronounced* det-er)
someone who owes money

debug *verb* (**debugs, debugging, debugged**) (*informal*) **1** to remove faults from a computer program **2** to remove listening devices from a room

début *noun* (*plural* **débuts**) (*pronounced* day-bew or day-boo)
someone's first public appearance

decade *noun* (*plural* **decades**)
a period of ten years

decant *verb* (**decants, decanting, decanted**)
to pour a liquid from one container into another without disturbing any solid matter that was in the first container

decathlon *noun* (*plural* **decathlons**) (*pronounced* dek-ath-lon)
an athletics competition that has ten events

decay ➤ *verb* (**decays, decaying, decayed**)
to rot or go bad

decay ➤ *noun*
decaying; the result of decaying

deceased *adjective* (*pronounced* di-**seest**)
a formal word for dead

deceit *noun* (*pronounced* di-**seet**)
deceiving someone
deceitful *adjective* using deceit **deceitfully** *adverb* in a deceitful way

deceive *verb* (**deceives, deceiving, deceived**) (*pronounced* di-**seev**)
to deceive someone is to make them believe something that is not true

December *noun*
the last month of the year

decent *adjective*
1 respectable and honest **2** proper or suitable ♦ *We'd like to buy a decent car*
decency *noun* being decent **decently** *adverb* in a decent way

deception *noun* (*plural* **deceptions**)
something that deceives someone

deceptive *adjective*
not what it seems to be ♦ *The sunshine was deceptive and the wind made it very cold*

decibel *noun* (*plural* **decibels**)
a unit for measuring the loudness of sound

decide *verb* (**decides, deciding, decided**)
1 to decide something is to make up your mind about it or make a choice **2** to decide a contest or argument is to settle it **decided** *adjective* definite or clear **decidedly** *adverb* definitely

deciduous *adjective*
a deciduous tree loses its leaves in autumn

decimal ➤ *adjective*
using tens or tenths

decimal ➤ *noun* (*plural* **decimals**)
a decimal fraction

decimal fraction *noun* (*plural* **decimal fractions**)
a fraction with tenths shown as numbers after a dot ($\frac{3}{10}$ is 0·3; $1\frac{1}{2}$ is 1·5)

decimalize *verb* (**decimalizes, decimalizing, decimalized**)
to decimalize measurements or currency is to change them to a decimal system
decimalization *noun* changing to a decimal system

decimal point *noun* (*plural* **decimal points**)
the dot in a decimal fraction

decipher *verb* (**deciphers, deciphering, deciphered**) (*pronounced* di-sy-fer)
to decipher writing is to work out its meaning when it is in code or difficult to read

decision *noun* (*plural* **decisions**)
a decision is what someone has decided

decisive *adjective*
1 ending or deciding something important ♦ *The decisive battle of the war was fought here* **2** a decisive person decides things quickly and firmly
decisively *adverb* in a decisive way

deck *noun* (*plural* **decks**)
1 a floor on a ship or bus **2** the part of a record player where the record is put for playing

deckchair *noun* (*plural* **deckchairs**)
a folding chair with a seat of canvas or plastic material

declaration *noun* (*plural* **declarations**)
an official or public statement

declare *verb* (**declares, declaring, declared**)
1 to declare something is to say it clearly and openly **2** to declare is to end a cricket innings before all the batsmen are out
to declare war is to announce a state of war with someone

decline *verb* (**declines, declining, declined**)
1 to decline is to become weaker or smaller **2** to decline an offer is to refuse it politely **3** to decline a noun or adjective is to give its grammatical forms

decode *verb* (decodes, decoding, decoded)
to decode something written in code is to
work out its meaning

decompose *verb* (decomposes, decomposing,
decomposed)
to decompose is to decay or rot
decomposition *noun* decomposing

decompression *noun*
a process of reducing air pressure

decontamination *noun*
removing poisonous chemicals or
radioactive material from a place

decorate *verb* (decorates, decorating, decorated)
1 to decorate something is to make it look
more beautiful or colourful **2** to decorate
someone is to give them a medal for
bravery
decorative *adjective* colourful, pretty

decoration *noun* (*plural* decorations)
1 decorations are the paint, wallpaper,
and ornaments that make a place look
more attractive **2** decoration is making
something look more attractive or
colourful **3** a decoration is a medal

decorator *noun* (*plural* decorators)
a person whose job is to paint rooms and
buildings and to put up wallpaper

decoy *noun* (*plural* decoys) (*pronounced*
dee-koi *or* di-koi)
something used to tempt a person or
animal into a trap

decrease ➤ *verb* (decreases, decreasing,
decreased) (*pronounced* di-kreess)
1 to decrease something is to make it
smaller or fewer **2** to decrease is to
become smaller or fewer

decrease ➤ *noun* (*plural* decreases)
(*pronounced* dee-kreess)
the amount by which something decreases

decree ➤ *noun* (*plural* decrees)
an official order or decision

decree ➤ *verb* (decrees, decreeing, decreed)
to decree something is to make a decree
about it

decrepit *adjective* (*pronounced* dik-rep-it)
old and weak

dedicate *verb* (dedicates, dedicating, dedicated)
1 to dedicate yourself or your life to
something is to spend all your time doing
it ♦ *She dedicated her life to nursing* **2** to
dedicate a book to someone is to name
them at the beginning, as a sign of
friendship or thanks
dedication *noun* dedicating something or
oneself

deduce *verb* (deduces, deducing, deduced)
to deduce a fact or answer is to work it out
by reasoning ♦ *She deduced from my smile
that I had won the prize*

deduct *verb* (deducts, deducting, deducted)
to deduct something is to subtract it from
a total ♦ *His Dad deducted 50 pence from
his pocket money for breaking a window*
deductible *adjective* able to be deducted

deduction *noun* (*plural* deductions)
1 something worked out by reasoning
2 something subtracted

deed *noun* (*plural* deeds)
1 something that someone has done **2** a
legal document

deep *adjective* (deeper, deepest)
1 going down or back a long way from the
top or front **2** measured from top to
bottom or from front to back ♦ *The hole
was two metres deep* **3** intense or strong
♦ *The room was painted a deep blue*
deeply *adverb* very, extremely

deepen *verb* (deepens, deepening, deepened)
to deepen is to become deeper ♦ *The pool
deepened to 2 metres half way along*

deep-freeze *noun* (*plural* deep-freezes)
a freezer for food

deer *noun* (*plural* deer)
a fast-running, graceful animal. The male
has antlers

deface *verb* (defaces, defacing, defaced)
to deface something is to spoil its
appearance

default *noun* (*plural* defaults)
(*in Computing*) what a computer does
unless you give it another command

defeat ➤ *verb* (defeats, defeating, defeated)
to defeat someone is to beat them in a
game or battle

defeat ➤ *noun* (*plural* defeats)
1 defeat is losing a game or battle **2** a
defeat is a lost game or battle

defecate *verb* (defecates, defecating, defecated)
to defecate is a formal word for getting rid
of faeces from the body
defecation *noun* defecating

defect ➤ *noun* (*plural* defects) (*pronounced*
dee-fekt)
a flaw or weakness

defect ➤ *verb* (defects, defecting, defected)
(*pronounced* di-fekt)
to defect is to desert a country or cause and
join the enemy
defection *noun* defecting **defector** *noun* a
person who defects

defective *adjective*
having flaws or faults

defence *noun* (*plural* defences)
1 defending something **2** something that
defends or protects
defenceless *adjective* having no defences

defend *verb* (defends, defending, defended)
1 to defend someone or something is to protect them from an attack or accusation 2 to defend an accused person is to try to prove that they are innocent
defender *noun* someone who defends something **defensible** *adjective* able to be defended

defendant *noun* (*plural* defendants)
a person accused of something in a lawcourt

defensive *adjective*
1 used to defend something 2 a defensive person is anxious about being criticized

defer *verb* (defers, deferring, deferred)
to defer something is to postpone it ♦ *She deferred her departure until Saturday*
deferment *noun* deferring something

defiant *adjective*
openly disobedient or defying someone
defiance *noun* being defiant **defiantly** *adverb* in a defiant way

deficiency *noun* (*plural* deficiencies)
a lack or shortage
deficient *adjective* not being enough

deficit *noun* (*plural* deficits) (*pronounced* def-i-sit)
the amount by which a sum of money is too small

defile *verb* (defiles, defiling, defiled)
to defile something is to make it dirty or impure

define *verb* (defines, defining, defined)
1 to define a word is to explain what it means 2 to define an idea or problem is to show exactly what it is

definite *adjective*
fixed or certain ♦ *Is it definite that we are going to move?*

definite article *noun* (*plural* definite articles)
the word *the*

definitely *adverb* and *interjection*
certainly, without doubt ♦ *We are definitely going to the party*

definition *noun* (*plural* definitions)
an explanation of what a word means

deflate *verb* (deflates, deflating, deflated)
1 to deflate a tyre or balloon is to let air out of it 2 to deflate someone is to make them less proud or confident

deflect *verb* (deflects, deflecting, deflected)
to deflect something that is moving is to make it turn aside
deflection *noun* movement to one side

deforestation *noun*
the loss of trees from an area

deformed *adjective*
not properly shaped
deformity *noun* something that is deformed

defrost *verb* (defrosts, defrosting, defrosted)
1 to defrost a refrigerator or windscreen is to remove the ice and frost from it 2 to defrost frozen food is to unfreeze it

deft *adjective* (defter, deftest)
skilful and quick
deftly *adverb* in a deft way

defuse *verb* (defuses, defusing, defused)
1 to defuse a bomb is to remove its fuse so that it won't blow up 2 to defuse a situation is to make it less dangerous or tense

defy *verb* (defies, defying, defied)
1 to defy someone is to refuse to obey them 2 to defy someone to do something is to challenge them ♦ *I defy you to do that* 3 to defy something is to prevent it happening ♦ *The door defied all attempts to open it*

degenerate *verb* (degenerates, degenerating, degenerated)
to degenerate is to become worse ♦ *The game degenerated into a succession of fouls*
degeneration *noun* becoming worse

degrade *verb* (degrades, degrading, degraded)
to degrade someone is to humiliate them
degradation *noun* humiliation

degree *noun* (*plural* degrees)
1 a unit for measuring temperature ♦ *Water boils at 100 degrees centigrade, or 100°C* 2 a unit for measuring angles ♦ *There are 90 degrees (90°) in a right angle* 3 extent ♦ *We are to a large degree responsible* 4 an award to someone at a university or college who has successfully finished a course ♦ *She has a degree in English*

dehydrated *adjective*
dried up, with all moisture removed
dehydration *noun* having moisture removed

de-ice *verb* (de-ices, de-icing, de-iced)
to de-ice a windscreen is to remove ice from its surface
de-icer *noun* a substance that de-ices

deity *noun* (*plural* deities) (*pronounced* dee-i-ti or day-i-ti)
a god or goddess

dejected *adjective*
sad or depressed
dejection *noun* being dejected

delay ➤ *verb* (delays, delaying, delayed)
1 to delay someone is to make them late 2 to delay something is to postpone it 3 to delay is to wait before doing something

delay ➤ *noun* (*plural* delays)
1 delaying or waiting ♦ *Do it without delay* 2 a period of waiting ♦ *There will be a delay of 20 minutes*

delegate ➤ noun (plural **delegates**)
(pronounced del-i-gat)
a person who represents other people and
acts on their instructions
delegate ➤ verb (**delegates, delegating,**
delegated) (pronounced del-i-gayt)
to delegate someone is to choose them to
be a delegate
delegation noun delegating; a group of
delegates
delete verb (**deletes, deleting, deleted**)
to delete something is to cross it out or
erase it
deletion noun deleting; something deleted
deliberate ➤ adjective (pronounced
di-lib-er-at)
1 done on purpose ♦ It was a deliberate lie
2 slow and careful ♦ He has a deliberate
way of talking
deliberately adverb on purpose
deliberate ➤ verb (**deliberates, deliberating,**
deliberated) (pronounced di-lib-er-ayt)
to deliberate is to think carefully about
something
deliberation noun deliberating about
something
delicacy noun (plural **delicacies**)
1 delicacy is being delicate 2 a delicacy is
something small and tasty to eat
delicate adjective
1 fine and graceful ♦ The cloth had
delicate embroidery 2 fragile and easily
damaged 3 becoming ill easily 4 using or
needing great care ♦ It was a delicate
situation
delicately adverb in a delicate way
delicatessen noun (plural **delicatessens**)
a shop that sells cooked or prepared food
such as meat and cheese
delicious adjective
tasting or smelling very pleasant
deliciously adverb in a delicious way
delight ➤ verb (**delights, delighting, delighted**)
to delight someone is to please them a lot
delight ➤ noun (plural **delights**)
great pleasure
delightful adjective causing great pleasure
delightfully adverb in a delightful way
delinquent noun (plural **delinquents**)
a young person who breaks the law
delinquency noun being a delinquent
delirious adjective
1 affected with delirium 2 extremely
excited or enthusiastic
deliriously adverb in a delirious way
delirium noun (plural **deliriums**)
1 the confused state of mind of people who
are drunk or who have a high fever
2 wild excitement

deliver verb (**delivers, delivering, delivered**)
1 to deliver letters, milk, or newspapers is
to take them to a house or office 2 to
deliver a speech or lecture is to give it to an
audience 3 to deliver a baby is to help with
its birth
delivery noun delivering something
delphinium noun (plural **delphiniums**)
a garden plant with tall spikes of flowers,
usually blue
delta noun (plural **deltas**)
1 a triangular area at the mouth of a river
where it spreads into branches 2 a
triangular shape
delude verb (**deludes, deluding, deluded**)
to be deluded is to think that something
isn't true when it is
deluge ➤ noun (plural **deluges**)
1 a large flood 2 a heavy fall of rain
3 something coming in great numbers
♦ After the speech there was a deluge of
questions
deluge ➤ verb (**deluges, deluging, deluged**)
to be deluged with something is to get a
huge amount of it ♦ He was deluged with
questions
delusion noun (plural **delusions**)
a false belief
de luxe adjective
of very high quality
demand ➤ verb (**demands, demanding,**
demanded)
to demand something is to ask for it
forcefully
demand ➤ noun (plural **demands**)
1 a demand is what someone demands
2 demand is a desire to have something
♦ There's a great demand for old furniture
in demand wanted; popular
demanding adjective
1 asking for many things ♦ Toddlers can
be very demanding 2 needing skill or
effort ♦ She has a demanding job
demerara noun (pronounced dem-er-air-a)
light-brown cane sugar
demist verb (**demists, demisting, demisted**)
to demist a window or windscreen is to
remove misty condensation from it
demo noun (plural **demos**)
(informal) a demonstration
democracy noun (plural **democracies**)
1 democracy is government by leaders
elected by the people 2 a democracy is a
country governed in this way
democrat noun (plural **democrats**)
a person who believes in or supports
democracy
Democrat a supporter of the Democratic
Party in the USA

democratic *adjective*
believing in democracy
democratically *adverb* by democracy

demolish *verb* (**demolishes, demolishing, demolished**)
to demolish a building is to knock it down and break it up
demolition *noun* demolishing a building

demon *noun* (*plural* **demons**)
1 a devil or evil spirit **2** a fierce or forceful person

demonstrate *verb* (**demonstrates, demonstrating, demonstrated**)
1 to demonstrate something is to show or prove it **2** to demonstrate is to take part in a demonstration

demonstration *noun* (*plural* **demonstrations**)
1 showing how to do or work something **2** a march or meeting to show everyone what you think about something ♦ *There will be a demonstration against the new motorway*

demonstrator *noun* (*plural* **demonstrators**)
1 someone who takes part in a demonstration or meeting **2** someone who demonstrates something

demoralize *verb* (**demoralizes, demoralizing, demoralized**)
to demoralize someone is to make them lose confidence or courage
demoralization *noun* being demoralized

demote *verb* (**demotes, demoting, demoted**)
to demote someone is to reduce them to a lower position or rank

den *noun* (*plural* **dens**)
1 an animal's lair **2** a place where something illegal happens ♦ *a gambling den* **3** a hiding place, especially for children

denial *noun* (*plural* **denials**)
denying or refusing something

denim *noun*
strong cotton cloth, used to make jeans

denominator *noun* (*plural* **denominators**)
the number below the line in a fraction ♦ *In $\frac{1}{4}$ the 4 is the denominator*

denote *verb* (**denotes, denoting, denoted**)
to denote something is to indicate or mean it ♦ *In road signs, P denotes a car park*

denounce *verb* (**denounces, denouncing, denounced**)
to denounce someone or something is to speak strongly against them, or accuse them of something
denunciation *noun* denouncing someone or something

dense *adjective* (**denser, densest**)
1 thick ♦ *The fog was getting very dense* **2** packed close together ♦ *They walked through a dense forest* **3** (*informal*) stupid
densely *adverb* thickly, close together

density *noun* (*plural* **densities**)
1 thickness **2** (*in Science*) the proportion of mass to volume ♦ *Water has greater density than air*

dent *noun* (*plural* **dents**)
an impression or hollow made in a surface by hitting it or pressing it

dental *adjective*
to do with the teeth or dentistry

dentist *noun* (*plural* **dentists**)
a person who is trained to treat teeth, fill them or take them out, and fit false ones
dentistry *noun* the work of a dentist

denture *noun* (*plural* **dentures**)
a set of false teeth

deny *verb* (**denies, denying, denied**)
1 to deny something is to say that it is not true **2** to deny a request is to refuse it

deodorant *noun* (*plural* **deodorants**)
a powder or liquid that removes unpleasant smells

depart *verb* (**departs, departing, departed**)
to depart is to go away or leave
departure *noun* leaving a place

department *noun* (*plural* **departments**)
one part of a large organization or shop

department store *noun* (*plural* **department stores**)
a large shop that sells many different kinds of goods

depend *verb* (**depends, depending, depended**)
to depend on someone or **something** is to rely on them ♦ *We depend on you for help*
to depend on something is to be decided by it ♦ *Whether we can have a picnic depends on the weather*

dependable *adjective*
that you can depend on; reliable

dependant *noun* (*plural* **dependants**)
a person who depends on someone else, especially for money ♦ *She has two dependants, a son and a daughter*

dependent *adjective*
depending or relying on someone ♦ *He was dependent on his father* ♦ *She has two dependent children*
dependence *noun* being dependent on someone

depict *verb* (**depicts, depicting, depicted**)
1 to depict something is to show it in a painting or drawing **2** to depict a scene is to describe it ♦ *The story depicted a small village in Austria*

deplorable *adjective*
extremely bad; shocking ♦ *Their rudeness was deplorable*
deplorably *adverb* in a deplorable way

deplore *verb* (**deplores, deploring, deplored**)
to deplore something is to be very upset or annoyed by it

deport *verb* (**deports, deporting, deported**)
to deport someone is to send them out of a country
deportation *noun* deporting someone

deposit *noun* (*plural* **deposits**)
1 an amount of money paid into a bank or building society **2** a sum of money paid as a first instalment **3** a layer of solid matter in or on the earth

depot *noun* (*plural* **depots**) (*pronounced* dep-oh)
1 a place where things are stored **2** a place where buses or trains are kept and repaired **3** a headquarters

depress *verb* (**depresses, depressing, depressed**)
to depress someone is to make them very sad

depressed *adjective*
very sad

depression *noun* (*plural* **depressions**)
1 a feeling of great sadness and hopelessness **2** an area of low air pressure which may bring rain **3** a long period when there is less trade and business than usual and many people have no work **4** a shallow hollow in the ground

deprive *verb* (**deprives, depriving, deprived**)
to deprive someone of something is to take it away from them ♦ *Prisoners are deprived of their freedom*
deprivation *noun* being deprived

depth *noun* (*plural* **depths**)
how deep something is ♦ *They were measuring the depth of the river*
in depth thoroughly
out of your depth 1 in water that is too deep to stand in **2** trying to do something that is too difficult for you

deputize *verb* (**deputizes, deputizing, deputized**)
to deputize for someone is to act as their deputy

deputy *noun* (*plural* **deputies**)
a substitute or chief assistant for someone

derail *verb* (**derails, derailing, derailed**)
to derail a train is to cause it to leave the track

derby *noun* (*plural* **derbies**)
a sporting event between two teams from the same city or area

derelict *adjective* (*pronounced* de-re-likt)
abandoned and left to fall into ruin

deride *verb* (**derides, deriding, derided**)
to deride someone or something is to treat them with scorn ♦ *They derided him for his silly jokes*

derision *noun*
scorn or ridicule ♦ *They treated him with derision*

derivation *noun* (*plural* **derivations**)
where a word comes from

derive *verb* (**derives, deriving, derived**)
to get something from another person or thing ♦ *She derived a lot of pleasure from music* ♦ *Many English words are derived from Latin*

derrick *noun* (*plural* **derricks**)
1 a kind of large crane for lifting things **2** a tall framework that holds the machinery used for drilling an oil well

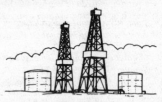

derv *noun*
diesel fuel for heavy vehicles

descant *noun* (*plural* **descants**)
a tune sung or played above another tune

descend *verb* (**descends, descending, descended**)
to descend is to go down
to be descended from someone is to be in the same family as them but living at a later time

descent *noun* descending

descendant *noun* (*plural* **descendants**)
a person who is descended from someone

describe *verb* (**describes, describing, described**)
to describe something or someone is to say what they are like
description *noun* describing; something that describes **descriptive** *adjective* describing

desert ➤ *noun* (*plural* **deserts**) (*pronounced* dez-ert)
a large area of very dry, often sandy, land

desert ➤ *verb* (**deserts, deserting, deserted**) (*pronounced* di-zert)
to desert someone or something is to leave them without intending to return
desertion *noun* deserting someone

deserter *noun* (*plural* **deserters**)
someone who leaves the armed forces without permission

desert island *noun* (*plural* **desert islands**)
a tropical island where nobody lives

deserts *plural noun* (*pronounced* di-**zerts**)
someone's deserts are what they deserve
♦ *He got his deserts*

deserve *verb* (**deserves, deserving, deserved**)
to deserve something is to be worthy of it
or to have a right to it
deservedly *adverb* in a way that deserves
something

design ➢ *noun* (*plural* **designs**)
1 the way that something is made or
arranged **2** a drawing that shows how
something is to be made **3** lines and
shapes forming a pattern

design ➢ *verb* (**designs, designing, designed**)
to design something is to make a design or
plan for it
designer *noun* someone who designs things,
especially clothes

designate *verb* (**designates, designating,
designated**)
to designate something is to give it a
special purpose ♦ *The meadow was
designated a picnic area*

desirable *adjective*
1 worth having **2** worth doing; advisable
♦ *It is desirable for you to come with us*
desirability *noun* being desirable

desire ➢ *verb* (**desires, desiring, desired**)
to desire something is to want it very
much

desire ➢ *noun* (*plural* **desires**)
a feeling of wanting something very much

desk *noun* (*plural* **desks**)
1 a piece of furniture with a flat top and
drawers, used for writing and reading **2** a
counter at which a cashier or receptionist
sits

desktop *adjective*
small enough to use on a desk ♦ *I've
bought a desktop computer*

desolate *adjective*
1 lonely and sad **2** uninhabited ♦ *a
desolate island*
desolation *noun* feeling desolate

despair *noun*
despair is a feeling of hopelessness

despatch *noun* (*plural* **despatches**)
and *verb* (**despatches, despatching,
despatched**)
a different spelling of *dispatch*

desperate *adjective*
1 extremely serious or hopeless ♦ *We were
in a desperate situation* **2** ready to do
anything to get out of a difficulty ♦ *There
are three desperate criminals at large*
desperately *adverb* seriously; recklessly
desperation *noun* being desperate

despicable *adjective*
deserving to be despised; contemptible

despise *verb* (**despises, despising, despised**)
to despise someone is to think they are
inferior or worthless

despite *preposition*
in spite of ♦ *They went out despite the rain*

dessert *noun* (*plural* **desserts**) (*pronounced*
di-**zert**)
fruit or a sweet food eaten at the end of a
meal

dessertspoon *noun* (*plural* **dessertspoons**)
a medium-sized spoon used for eating
puddings

destination *noun* (*plural* **destinations**)
the place you are travelling to

destined *adjective*
intended by fate ♦ *They felt they were
destined to win*

destiny *noun* (*plural* **destinies**)
what is intended for someone; fate ♦ *His
destiny was to travel the world*

destroy *verb* (**destroys, destroying, destroyed**)
to destroy something is to ruin it or put an
end to it
destruction *noun* destroying something
destructive *adjective* causing things to be
destroyed

destroyer *noun* (*plural* **destroyers**)
a fast warship

detach *verb* (**detaches, detaching, detached**)
to detach something is to remove it or
separate it
detachable *adjective* able to be detached

detached *adjective*
1 impartial; not involved ♦ *I was just a
detached observer* **2** a detached house is
one that is not joined to another house

detachment *noun* (*plural* **detachments**)
1 detachment is being impartial **2** a
detachment is a special group of people,
especially soldiers

detail *noun* (*plural* **details**)
1 a small part of a design or picture or
piece of decoration **2** a small piece of
information
in detail describing or dealing with
everything fully

detain *verb* (**detains, detaining, detained**)
1 to detain someone is to keep them in a
place **2** to detain someone is also to keep
them waiting ♦ *I'll try not to detain you for
long*

detect *verb* (**detects, detecting, detected**)
to detect something is to discover it
detection *noun* detecting something **detector**
noun a device that detects something

detective *noun* (*plural* **detectives**)
a person who investigates crimes

detention noun (plural **detentions**)
being made to stay in a place, especially being made to stay late in school as a punishment

deter verb (**deters, deterring, deterred**)
to deter someone is to put them off doing something

detergent noun (plural **detergents**)
a kind of washing powder or liquid

deteriorate verb (**deteriorates, deteriorating, deteriorated**)
to deteriorate is to become worse
♦ Paintwork deteriorates when it is exposed to the weather
deterioration noun becoming worse

determination noun
a strong intention to achieve something

determine verb (**determines, determining, determined**)
to determine something is to decide it or work it out ♦ The task was to determine the height of the mountain

determined adjective
having your mind firmly made up

deterrent noun (plural **deterrents**)
something that may deter people, such as a powerful weapon
deterrence noun being a deterrent

detest verb (**detests, detesting, detested**)
to detest something is to dislike it very much ♦ He detested noise
detestable adjective horrid **detestation** noun detesting something

detonate verb (**detonates, detonating, detonated**)
to detonate a bomb is to make it explode
detonation noun detonating a bomb **detonator** noun a device that detonates a bomb

detour noun (plural **detours**)
a roundabout route used instead of the normal route

deuce noun
a tennis score when each side has 40 points and needs two more points in a row to win

devastate verb (**devastates, devastating, devastated**)
to devastate a place is to ruin or destroy it, making it impossible to live in
devastation noun destruction

develop verb (**develops, developing, developed**)
1 to develop something is to make it bigger or better 2 to develop is to become bigger or better 3 to develop land is to put up new buildings on it 4 to develop photographic film is to treat it with chemicals so that pictures appear on it

developing country noun (plural **developing countries**)
a poor country that is building up its industry and trying to improve its living conditions

development noun (plural **developments**)
1 a development is something interesting that has happened ♦ Have there been any further developments since I last saw you? 2 development is putting up new buildings ♦ Extensive development has taken place around the village

device noun (plural **devices**)
something made for a particular purpose ♦ We need a device for opening tins
to leave someone to their own devices is to leave them to do as they wish

devil noun (plural **devils**)
an evil spirit or person
devilish adjective like a devil **devilment** noun mischief

devious adjective
1 using unfair and dishonest methods
♦ They thought he had been devious with them 2 roundabout; not direct ♦ The coach took us by a devious route to avoid the traffic jams

devise verb (**devises, devising, devised**)
to devise a plan or idea is to think it up

devolution noun
giving authority to a local or regional government

devote verb (**devotes, devoting, devoted**)
to devote yourself or your time to something is to spend all your time doing it ♦ They devote all their free time to sport
devotee noun an enthusiast for something **devotion** noun great love or loyalty

devoted adjective
loving and loyal ♦ They are devoted parents

devour verb (**devours, devouring, devoured**)
to devour something is to eat or swallow it greedily

devout adjective
religious; sincere

dew noun
tiny drops of water that form during the night on surfaces out of doors
dewy adjective like dew

dhoti noun (plural **dhotis**) (pronounced doh-ti)
a long piece of cloth worn by Hindu men around the lower part of their bodies

diabetes noun (pronounced dy-a-**bee**-teez)
a disease in which there is too much sugar in a person's blood
diabetic noun someone suffering from diabetes

diabolical *adjective*
like a devil; very wicked

diagnose *verb* (**diagnoses, diagnosing, diagnosed**)
to diagnose a disease is to find out what it is and what treatment is needed
diagnosis *noun* deciding what disease someone has

diagonal *noun* (*plural* **diagonals**)
a straight line joining opposite corners
diagonally *adverb* across from one corner to another

diagram *noun* (*plural* **diagrams**)
a drawing or picture that shows the parts of something or how it works

dial ➤ *noun* (*plural* **dials**)
a circular piece of plastic or card with numbers or letters round it

dial ➤ *verb* (**dials, dialling, dialled**)
to dial a telephone number is to choose it by turning a dial or by pressing numbered buttons

dialect *noun* (*plural* **dialects**)
the words used by people in one district but not in the rest of the country

dialogue *noun* (*plural* **dialogues**)
a conversation

diameter *noun* (*plural* **diameters**)
1 a line drawn from one side of a circle to the other, passing through the centre
2 the length of this line

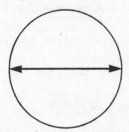

diamond *noun* (*plural* **diamonds**)
1 a very hard jewel that looks like clear glass 2 a shape which has four equal sides but which is not a square 3 a playing card with red diamond shapes on it

diaphragm *noun* (*plural* **diaphragms**)
(*pronounced* **dy**-a-fram)
1 the muscular layer inside the body between the chest and the abdomen, used in breathing 2 a thin sheet or membrane that keeps things apart

diarrhoea *noun* (*pronounced* dy-a-**ree**-a)
too frequent and too watery emptying of the bowels

diary *noun* (*plural* **diaries**)
a book giving the days of the year, in which someone writes down their appointments or what happens each day

dice *noun* (*plural* **dice**)
a small cube marked with one to six dots on each side, thrown to give a number in games

dictate *verb* (**dictates, dictating, dictated**)
1 to dictate something is to speak or read it aloud for someone else to write down
2 to dictate to someone is to give them orders in a bossy way
dictation *noun* an exercise in writing down what someone reads out

dictator *noun* (*plural* **dictators**)
a ruler who has unlimited power
dictatorial *adjective* like a dictator
dictatorship *noun* the powers of a dictator

dictionary *noun* (*plural* **dictionaries**)
a book with words listed in alphabetical order, so that you can find out what a word means and how to spell it

did past tense of **do**

diddle *verb* (**diddles, diddling, diddled**)
(*informal*) to cheat someone ♦ *We've been diddled! He's charged us £10 too much*

didn't short for *did not*

die *verb* (**dies, dying, died**)
to die is to stop living
to die out is to gradually disappear ♦ *The tiger is beginning to die out*

diesel *noun* (*plural* **diesels**)
1 a diesel is an engine that works by burning oil in compressed air 2 diesel is fuel for this kind of engine

diet ➤ *noun* (*plural* **diets**)
1 a diet is special meals that someone eats to be healthy or to lose weight ♦ *Mum's on a diet* 2 someone's diet is the food they normally eat

diet ➤ *verb* (**diets, dieting, dieted**)
to diet is to keep to a special diet

differ *verb* (**differs, differing, differed**)
1 to differ from something is to be not the same as it 2 to differ is to disagree ♦ *The two writers differ on this point*

difference *noun* (*plural* **differences**)
the way in which something is different from something else

different *adjective*
one person or thing is different from another when they are not the same
differently *adverb* in a different way

differential *noun* (*plural* **differentials**)
1 a difference in wages between groups of workers 2 a system of gears that allows a vehicle's driving wheels to turn at slightly different speeds when going round corners

difficult *adjective*
needing a lot of effort or skill; not easy

difficulty *noun* (*plural* **difficulties**)
1 difficulty is not being easy, trouble
♦ *I had difficulty in climbing up the slippery slope* **2** a difficulty is something that causes a problem ♦ *We had a lot of difficulties selling our house*

diffuse *verb* (**diffuses, diffusing, diffused**)
to diffuse something is to spread it widely or thinly ♦ *The building had diffused lighting*
diffusion *noun* spreading something

dig ➤ *verb* (**digs, digging, dug**)
1 to dig soil or the ground is to break it up and move it **2** to dig a hole is to make it **3** to dig someone is to poke them ♦ *He dug me in the ribs*
digger *noun* a machine for digging

dig ➤ *noun* (*plural* **digs**)
1 a place of digging, especially where archaeologists are looking for ancient remains **2** a sharp thrust or poke ♦ *She gave me a dig in the ribs with her elbow* **3** an unpleasant remark ♦ *What he said was clearly a dig at me*

digest *verb* (**digests, digesting, digested**)
to digest food is to soften and change it in the stomach and intestine so that the body can absorb it
digestible *adjective* easy to digest **digestion** *noun* digesting

digestive *adjective*
to do with digesting food

digit *noun* (*plural* **digits**) (*pronounced* dij-it)
1 any of the numbers from 0 to 9 **2** a finger or toe

digital *adjective*
1 to do with or using digits **2** a digital clock or watch has a row of digits to indicate numbers (the opposite of *analogue*) **3** a digital computer or recording stores the data or sound as a series of binary digits

dignified *adjective*
having dignity

dignity *noun*
a calm and serious manner

digs *plural noun*
(*informal*) rented rooms in a house

dike *noun* (*plural* **dikes**)
1 a long wall or embankment to hold back water and prevent flooding **2** a ditch for draining water from land

dilemma *noun* (*plural* **dilemmas**)
an awkward choice between two possible actions, either of which would cause difficulties

dilute *verb* (**dilutes, diluting, diluted**)
to dilute a liquid is to make it weaker by mixing it with water
dilution *noun* diluting a liquid

dim *adjective* (**dimmer, dimmest**)
only faintly lit and difficult to see
dimly *adverb* faintly

dimension *noun* (*plural* **dimensions**)
1 a measurement such as length, width, area, or volume **2** size or extent

diminish *verb* (**diminishes, diminishing, diminished**)
1 to diminish something is to make it smaller **2** to diminish is to become smaller

dimple *noun* (*plural* **dimples**)
a small hollow on the skin

din *noun*
a loud noise

dine *verb* (**dines, dining, dined**)
to dine is to have dinner
diner *noun* someone who has dinner

dinghy *noun* (*plural* **dinghies**) (*pronounced* ding-i)
a kind of small boat

dingy *adjective* (**dingier, dingiest**) (*pronounced* din-ji)
shabby and dirty-looking

dinner *noun* (*plural* **dinners**)
the main meal of the day, either at midday or in the evening

dinosaur *noun* (*plural* **dinosaurs**)
a prehistoric animal, often of enormous size

dioxide *noun* (*plural* **dioxides**)
an oxide with two atoms of oxygen and one atom of another element, as in carbon dioxide

dip ≻ *verb* (**dips, dipping, dipped**)
1 to dip something is to put it into a liquid ♦ *Dip the brush in the paint* **2** to dip is to go downwards ♦ *The road dips steeply after the hill* **3** to dip a vehicle's headlights is to lower the beam so as not to dazzle other drivers

dip ≻ *noun* (*plural* **dips**)
1 dipping **2** a downward slope **3** a quick swim **4** a mixture into which things are dipped

diphtheria *noun* (*pronounced* dif-**theer**-i-a)
a serious disease of the throat

diploma *noun* (*plural* **diplomas**)
a certificate awarded for skill in a particular subject

diplomacy *noun*
keeping friendly with other nations or other people

diplomatic *adjective*
1 to do with diplomacy **2** tactful and courteous
diplomat *noun* someone who works in diplomacy **diplomatically** *adverb* in a diplomatic way

dire *adjective* (**direr, direst**)
dreadful or serious ♦ *The refugees are in dire need of food and shelter*

direct ≻ *adjective*
1 as straight or quick as possible **2** frank and honest
directness *noun* being frank

direct ≻ *verb* (**directs, directing, directed**)
1 to direct someone is to show them the way **2** to direct something is to control or manage it

direct current *noun*
electric current flowing only in one direction

direction *noun* (*plural* **directions**)
1 a direction is the way you go to get somewhere **2** direction is directing something
directions information on how to use or do something

directly *adverb*
1 by a direct route ♦ *Go directly to the shop* **2** immediately ♦ *I want you to come directly*

direct object *noun* (*plural* **direct objects**)
the word that receives the action of the verb. In *she hit him*, the direct object is *him*

director *noun* (*plural* **directors**)
1 a person who is in charge of something, especially one of a group of people managing a company **2** a person who decides how a film or play should be made or performed

directory *noun* (*plural* **directories**)
a book containing a list of people with their telephone numbers and addresses

direct speech *noun*
someone's words written down exactly in the way they were said

dirt *noun*
earth or soil; anything that is not clean

dirty *adjective* (**dirtier, dirtiest**)
1 covered with dirt; not clean **2** rude or offensive ♦ *Someone has written dirty words on the wall* **3** unfair or mean ♦ *It was a dirty trick to steal my sweets*
dirtily *adverb* in a dirty way **dirtiness** *noun* being dirty

dis- *prefix*
1 showing the opposite of something, as in *dishonest* **2** showing that something has been taken away or apart, as in *disarm* or *dismantle*

disability *noun* (*plural* **disabilities**)
something that prevents someone from using their body in the usual way

disabled *adjective*
having a disease or injury that makes it difficult for someone to use their body properly

disadvantage *noun* (*plural* **disadvantages**)
something that hinders you or makes things difficult

disagree *verb* (**disagrees, disagreeing, disagreed**)
1 to disagree with someone is to have or express a different opinion from them **2** to disagree with someone is also to have a bad effect on them ♦ *Rich food disagrees with me*
disagreement *noun* thinking differently

disagreeable *adjective*
unpleasant

disappear *verb* (**disappears, disappearing, disappeared**)
to disappear is to stop being visible; to vanish
disappearance *noun* disappearing

disappoint *verb* (**disappoints, disappointing, disappointed**)
to disappoint someone is to fail to do what they want
disappointing *adjective* causing someone to be disappointed **disappointment** *noun* a feeling of being disappointed

disapprove *verb* (**disapproves, disapproving, disapproved**)
to disapprove of someone or something is to have a bad opinion of them
disapproval *noun* having a bad opinion

disarm *verb* (**disarms, disarming, disarmed**)
1 to disarm is to reduce the size of armed forces 2 to disarm someone is to take away their weapons
disarmament *noun* disarming, or disarming someone

disaster *noun* (*plural* **disasters**)
a very bad accident or misfortune
disastrous *adjective* causing great misfortune **disastrously** *adverb* in a disastrous way

disc *noun* (*plural* **discs**)
1 a round flat object 2 a round, flat piece of plastic on which sound or data is recorded; a CD

discard *verb* (**discards, discarding, discarded**)
to discard something is to throw it away

discharge *verb* (**discharges, discharging, discharged**)
1 to release someone 2 to send something out ♦ *Vehicles must not discharge excessive smoke*

disciple *noun* (*plural* **disciples**)
a follower of a political or religious leader, especially one of Christ's first followers

discipline *noun*
orderly and obedient behaviour

disc jockey *noun* (*plural* **disc jockeys**)
someone who introduces and plays records, especially on radio

disclose *verb* (**discloses, disclosing, disclosed**)
to disclose something is to tell someone about it
disclosure *noun* disclosing information

disco *noun* (*plural* **discos**)
a place or party where records are played for dancing

discolour *verb* (**discolours, discolouring, discoloured**)
to discolour something is to spoil its colour

discomfort *noun*
being uncomfortable

disconnect *verb* (**disconnects, disconnecting, disconnected**)
to disconnect something is to break its connection or detach it
disconnection *noun* disconnecting something

discontented *adjective*
not contented; dissatisfied
discontent *noun* feeling discontented

discotheque *noun* (*plural* **discotheques**) (*pronounced* **dis**-ko-tek)
a disco

discount *noun* (*plural* **discounts**)
an amount by which a price is reduced

discourage *verb* (**discourages, discouraging, discouraged**)
1 to discourage someone is to take away their enthusiasm or confidence 2 to discourage someone from doing something is to try to persuade them not to do it
discouragement *noun* a feeling of being discouraged

discover *verb* (**discovers, discovering, discovered**)
to discover something is to find it, especially by chance or for the first time
discovery *noun* finding something

discreet *adjective*
being careful in what you say and do, especially when you have a secret to keep
discreetly *adverb* in a discreet way

discriminate *verb* (**discriminates, discriminating, discriminated**)
1 to discriminate between things is to notice the differences between them, or to prefer one thing to another 2 to discriminate between people is to treat them differently or unfairly because of their race, sex, or religion
discrimination *noun* discriminating between people or things

discus *noun* (*plural* **discuses**) (*pronounced* **dis**-kuss)
a thick heavy disc thrown in an athletic contest

discuss *verb* (**discusses, discussing, discussed**) (*pronounced* **dis**-kuss)
to discuss a subject is to talk with other people about it
discussion *noun* discussing a subject

disease *noun* (*plural* **diseases**)
1 a disease is an illness or sickness 2 disease is unhealthy conditions ♦ *They introduced new measures to reduce disease*
diseased *adjective* having a disease

disembark *verb* (**disembarks, disembarking, disembarked**)
to disembark is to get out of a boat or aircraft

disgrace ➤ *noun*
1 shame ♦ *It's no disgrace to be poor* 2 a person or thing that causes shame or disapproval ♦ *The slums are a disgrace*
disgraceful *adjective* deserving disgrace
disgracefully *adverb* in a disgraceful way

disgrace ➤ *verb* (**disgraces, disgracing, disgraced**)
to disgrace someone or something is to bring them shame

disguise ➤ *verb* (disguises, disguising, disguised)
to disguise someone or something is to make them look different so as to deceive people

disguise ➤ *noun* (*plural* disguises)
something used for disguising

disgust ➤ *noun*
a strong feeling of dislike or contempt

disgust ➤ *verb* (disgusts, disgusting, disgusted)
to disgust someone is to cause them disgust

disgusted *adjective* feeling disgust **disgusting** *adjective* causing disgust

dish ➤ *noun* (*plural* dishes)
1 a plate or bowl for food 2 an item of food prepared for eating

dish ➤ *verb* (dishes, dishing, dished)
to dish something out (*informal*) is to give it to people

dishcloth *noun* (*plural* dishcloths)
a cloth for washing or drying dishes

dishevelled *adjective*
untidy in appearance

dishonest *adjective*
not honest

dishonesty *noun* being dishonest

dishwasher *noun* (*plural* dishwashers)
a machine for washing dishes automatically

disinfect *verb* (disinfects, disinfecting, disinfected)
to disinfect something is to treat it to destroy germs in it

disinfectant *noun* (*plural* disinfectants)
a liquid used to disinfect things

disintegrate *verb* (disintegrates, disintegrating, disintegrated)
to disintegrate is to break up into small pieces

disintegration *noun* disintegrating

disinterested *adjective*
not favouring one side more than the other; impartial

disk *noun* (*plural* disks)
a disc, especially one used to store computer data

dislike ➤ *noun* (*plural* dislikes)
a feeling of not liking someone or something

dislike ➤ *verb* (dislikes, disliking, disliked)
to dislike someone or something is not to like them

dislocate *verb* (dislocates, dislocating, dislocated)
1 to dislocate a part of the body is to dislodge a bone in it 2 to dislocate something is to upset it ♦ *The fog has dislocated rail services*

dislocation *noun* dislocating something

dislodge *verb* (dislodges, dislodging, dislodged)
to dislodge something is to move it from its right place

disloyal *adjective*
not loyal

dismal *adjective*
gloomy

dismally *adverb* in a dismal way

dismantle *verb* (dismantles, dismantling, dismantled)
to dismantle something is to take it to pieces

dismay *noun*
a feeling of strong disappointment and surprise

dismayed *adjective* feeling dismay

dismiss *verb* (dismisses, dismissing, dismissed)
1 to dismiss someone is to send them away, especially from their job 2 to dismiss an idea or suggestion is to reject it

dismissal *noun* being dismissed

dismount *verb* (dismounts, dismounting, dismounted)
to dismount is to get off a horse or bicycle

disobey *verb* (disobeys, disobeying, disobeyed)
to disobey someone is to do the opposite of what they tell you

disobedience *noun* disobeying someone **disobedient** *adjective* tending to disobey someone

disorder *noun* (*plural* disorders)
1 disorder is confusion or disturbance 2 a disorder is an illness

disorderly *adjective* behaving badly

dispatch ➤ *noun* (*plural* dispatches)
a report or message

dispatch ➤ *verb* (dispatches, dispatching, dispatched)
1 to dispatch something or someone is to send them somewhere 2 to dispatch someone is to kill them

dispense *verb* (dispenses, dispensing, dispensed)
1 to dispense something is to distribute it 2 to dispense medicine is to prepare it for patients

to dispense with something is to do without it

dispenser *noun* (*plural* dispensers)
a device that gives you things, especially in special amounts ♦ *There is a soap dispenser above each washbasin*

disperse *verb* (**disperses, dispersing, dispersed**)
1 to disperse people is to send them away
in various directions ♦ *The police
dispersed the crowd* **2** to disperse is to go
off in various directions
dispersal *noun* dispersing, or dispersing
people

displace *verb* (**displaces, displacing, displaced**)
1 to displace something is to move it from
its place **2** to displace someone is to take
their place

displacement *noun*
1 displacing **2** the amount of water
displaced by a ship

display ➤ *verb* (**displays, displaying, displayed**)
to display something is to arrange it so
that it can be clearly seen

display ➤ *noun* (*plural* **displays**)
1 the displaying of something; an
exhibition **2** the showing of information
on a VDU screen

displease *verb* (**displeases, displeasing,
displeased**)
to displease someone is to annoy them

disposable *adjective*
made to be thrown away after it has been
used

disposal *noun*
getting rid of something
at your disposal for you to use; ready for you

dispose *verb* (**disposes, disposing, disposed**)
to be disposed to do something is to be
ready and willing to do it ♦ *They were not
at all disposed to help us*
to dispose of something is to get rid of it

disposition *noun* (*plural* **dispositions**)
a person's nature or qualities

disprove *verb* (**disproves, disproving, disproved**)
to disprove something is to prove that it is
not true

dispute *noun* (*plural* **disputes**)
a quarrel or disagreement

disqualify *verb* (**disqualifies, disqualifying,
disqualified**)
to disqualify someone is to remove them
from a race or competition because they
have broken the rules
disqualification *noun* being disqualified

disregard *verb* (**disregards, disregarding,
disregarded**)
to disregard someone or something is to
take no notice of them

disrespect *noun*
lack of respect; rudeness
disrespectful *adjective* showing disrespect
disrespectfully *adverb* in a disrespectful way

disrupt *verb* (**disrupts, disrupting, disrupted**)
to disrupt something is to cause confusion
or disorder ♦ *Floods have disrupted local
traffic*
disruption *noun* being disrupted **disruptive**
adjective causing disruption

dissatisfied *adjective*
not satisfied
dissatisfaction *noun* being dissatisfied

dissect *verb* (**dissects, dissecting, dissected**)
to dissect something is to cut it up so as to
examine it
dissection *noun* dissecting something

dissolve *verb* (**dissolves, dissolving, dissolved**)
1 to dissolve something is to mix it with a
liquid so that it becomes part of the liquid
2 to dissolve is to melt or become liquid

dissuade *verb* (**dissuades, dissuading,
dissuaded**)
to dissuade someone is to persuade them
not to do something

distance *noun* (*plural* **distances**)
the amount of space between two places
in the distance far away but visible

distant *adjective*
1 far away **2** a person who is distant is not
friendly or sociable

distil *verb* (**distils, distilling, distilled**)
to distil a liquid is to purify it by boiling it
and condensing the vapour

distillery *noun* (*plural* **distilleries**)
a place where spirits such as whisky are
produced
distiller *noun* a person or firm that makes
spirits

distinct *adjective*
1 easily heard or seen; definite ♦ *You have
made a distinct improvement* **2** clearly
separate or different ♦ *A rabbit is distinct
from a hare*
distinctly *adverb* clearly, noticeably

distinction *noun* (*plural* **distinctions**)
1 a distinction is a difference
2 distinction is excellence or honour, or a
high mark in an examination

distinctive *adjective*
clearly distinguishing something from all
the others ♦ *The school has a distinctive
blue football strip*

distinguish *verb* (**distinguishes, distinguishing,
distinguished**)
1 to distinguish things is to notice the
differences between them **2** to distinguish
something is to see or hear it clearly

distinguished *adjective*
famous or outstanding ♦ *There was a
distinguished writer staying at the same
hotel*

distort *verb* (**distorts, distorting, distorted**)
1 to distort something is to change it into
a strange shape ♦ *His face was distorted
with anger* **2** to distort facts is to change
them so that they are untrue

distortion *noun* distorting something

distract *verb* (**distracts, distracting, distracted**)
to distract someone is to take their
attention away from what they are doing
♦ *Don't distract me from my work*

distraction *noun* being distracted

distress ➣ *noun*
great sorrow or trouble

distress ➣ *verb* (**distresses, distressing,
distressed**)
to distress someone is to cause them
distress

distribute *verb* (**distributes, distributing,
distributed**)
1 to distribute things is to give them out
♦ *The teacher distributed textbooks to the
class* **2** to distribute something is to
spread or scatter it around ♦ *She
distributed the seed over the soil*

distribution *noun* distributing things
distributor *noun* someone who distributes things

district *noun* (*plural* **districts**)
part of a town or country

distrust *noun*
lack of trust; suspicion

distrustful *adjective* not trusting people

disturb *verb* (**disturbs, disturbing, disturbed**)
1 to disturb someone is to spoil their peace
or worry them **2** to disturb something is to
move it from its right position

disturbance *noun* something that disturbs
someone

disused *adjective*
no longer used ♦ *The house was next to a
disused warehouse*

ditch *noun* (*plural* **ditches**)
a narrow trench to hold or carry away
water

dither *verb* (**dithers, dithering, dithered**)
to dither is to hesitate nervously

ditto *noun*
the same again

divan *noun* (*plural* **divans**)
a bed or couch without a raised back or
sides

dive *verb* (**dives, diving, dived**)
1 to dive is to go into water head first
2 to dive is also to move downwards
quickly ♦ *The aeroplane then dived*

diver *noun* (*plural* **divers**)
1 a swimmer who dives **2** someone who
works under water in a special suit called
a **diving suit 3** a bird that dives for its food

diverse *adjective*
varied; of several different kinds

diversity *noun* variety

diversify *verb* (**diversifies, diversifying,
diversified**)
to diversify is to try out different things

diversion *noun* (*plural* **diversions**)
1 a different way for traffic to go when the
usual road is closed **2** something amusing
or entertaining

divert *verb* (**diverts, diverting, diverted**)
1 to divert something is to change the
direction it is moving in **2** to divert
someone is to amuse or entertain them

divide *verb* (**divides, dividing, divided**)
1 to divide something is to separate it into
smaller parts or shares **2** (*in
Mathematics*) to divide a number by
another number is to find out how many
times the second number is contained in
the first ♦ *Divide six by two and you get
three (6 ÷ 2 = 3)*

dividend *noun* (*plural* **dividends**)
1 (*in Mathematics*) an amount to be
divided **2** a share in the profit a business
makes

dividers *plural noun*
dividers are a pair of compasses for
measuring distances

divine ➣ *adjective*
1 belonging to God or coming from God
2 like a god **3** (*informal*) excellent;
extremely beautiful

divinely *adverb* in a divine or excellent way
divinity *noun* being divine

divine ➣ *verb* (**divines, divining, divined**)
to divine is to find hidden water or metal
by holding a Y-shaped stick called a
divining rod

division *noun* (*plural* **divisions**)
1 dividing numbers or things 2 a dividing line or partition 3 one of the parts into which something is divided
divisible *adjective* able to be divided, or divided exactly

divorce ➤ *noun* (*plural* **divorces**)
the legal ending of a marriage

divorce ➤ *verb* (**divorces, divorcing, divorced**)
to divorce a husband or wife is to end a marriage to them by law

Diwali *noun* (*pronounced* di-wah-li)
a Hindu festival held in October or November

DIY short for **do-it-yourself**

dizzy *adjective* (**dizzier, dizziest**)
giddy and feeling confused
dizzily *adverb* in a dizzy way **dizziness** *noun* feeling dizzy

DJ short for **disc jockey**

do *verb* (**does, doing, did, done**)
1 to do something is to perform it or deal with it ♦ *Are you doing your work?* ♦ *I can't do this sum* 2 to do well is to manage; to do badly is not to manage very well 3 you say that something will do when it is all right or suitable ♦ *I'd really like some football boots but trainers will do* 4 you also use **do** with other verbs in special ways ♦ *Do you want this?* ♦ *He does not want it* ♦ *I do like crisps* ♦ *We work as hard as they do*
to do away with something or **someone** (*informal*) is to get rid of them or kill them
to do something up is to fasten it ♦ *Do up your coat*
to do without something is to manage without having it

docile *adjective*
gentle and obedient

dock[1] ➤ *noun* (*plural* **docks**)
a part of a harbour where ships are loaded, unloaded, or repaired

dock ➤ *verb* (**docks, docking, docked**)
1 a ship docks when it comes into a dock 2 spacecraft dock when they join together in orbit

dock[2] *noun* (*plural* **docks**)
a place for the prisoner on trial in a lawcourt

dock[3] *verb* (**docks, docking, docked**)
1 to dock an animal's tail is to cut it short 2 to dock someone's pay is to take something off it as a penalty

dock[4] *noun*
a weed with broad leaves

docker *noun* (*plural* **dockers**)
a labourer who loads and unloads ships

dockyard *noun* (*plural* **dockyards**)
an open area with docks and equipment for building or repairing ships

doctor *noun* (*plural* **doctors**)
a person trained to heal sick or injured people

doctrine *noun* (*plural* **doctrines**)
a religious or political belief
doctrinal *adjective* to do with doctrine

document *noun* (*plural* **documents**)
something important that is written or printed
documentation *noun* a collection of documents

documentary *noun* (*plural* **documentaries**)
a film or a television programme showing real events or situations

doddery *adjective*
shaking or unsteady because of being old

doddle *noun*
(*informal*) something that is very easy to do

dodge ➤ *verb* (**dodges, dodging, dodged**)
to dodge something is to move quickly to avoid it

dodge ➤ *noun* (*plural* **dodges**)
1 a dodging movement 2 a trick; a clever way of doing something

dodgem *noun* (*plural* **dodgems**)
a small electrically driven car at a funfair, in which you drive round an enclosure, dodging and bumping other cars

dodgy *adjective* (**dodgier, dodgiest**)
(*informal*) 1 awkward or tricky 2 dishonest or unreliable

doe *noun* (*plural* **does**)
a female deer, rabbit, or hare

does 3rd singular present tense of **do**
♦ *She does what she likes*

doesn't short for *does not* ♦ *He doesn't understand*

dog *noun* (*plural* **dogs**)
a four-legged animal that barks, often kept as a pet

dog-eared *adjective*
a dog-eared book has the corners of its pages bent or worn from use

dogged *adjective* (*pronounced* **dog**-id)
not giving up in spite of difficulties; obstinate
doggedly *adverb* in a dogged way

do-it-yourself *adjective*
suitable for anyone to make or use at home

doldrums *plural noun*
the ocean regions near the equator, where there is little or no wind
in the doldrums bored and unhappy

dole *noun*
(*informal*) the dole is money paid by the State to unemployed people

doll *noun* (*plural* **dolls**)
a toy model of a person, especially a baby or child

dollar *noun* (*plural* **dollars**)
a unit of money in the United States and some other countries

dolly *noun* (*plural* **dollies**)
(*informal*) a doll

dolphin *noun* (*plural* **dolphins**)
a sea animal like a small whale with a snout like a beak

domain *noun* (*plural* **domains**)
a kingdom

dome *noun* (*plural* **domes**)
a roof shaped like the top half of a ball

domestic *adjective*
1 to do with the home 2 a domestic animal is tame and kept at home

domesticated *adjective*
1 a domesticated animal is trained to live with people 2 a domesticated person enjoys household work and home life

dominant *adjective*
most powerful or important
dominance *noun* being dominant

dominate *verb* (**dominates, dominating, dominated**)
to dominate people is to control them by being the most powerful
domination *noun* dominating people

dominion *noun* (*plural* **dominions**)
1 rule or authority 2 an area ruled by one ruler

domino *noun* (*plural* **dominoes**)
a small flat oblong piece of wood or plastic with dots (1 to 6) or a blank space at each end, used in the game of **dominoes**

donate *verb* (**donates, donating, donated**)
to donate something, especially money, is to give it to a charity or organization
donation *noun* something that is donated

done past participle of do

donkey *noun* (*plural* **donkeys**)
an animal that looks like a small horse with long ears

donor *noun* (*plural* **donors**)
someone who gives something ♦ *I think I'll be a blood donor*

don't short for *do not* ♦ *Don't cycle on the pavement*

doodle ➤ *noun* (*plural* **doodles**)
a quick drawing or scribble

doodle ➤ *verb* (**doodles, doodling, doodled**)
to doodle is to draw a doodle

doom ➤ *noun*
a grim fate like ruin or death

doom ➤ *verb* (**dooms, dooming, doomed**)
to be doomed to something is to have a grim fate you cannot avoid

door *noun* (*plural* **doors**)
a movable panel that opens and closes the entrance to a room, building, or cupboard

doorstep *noun* (*plural* **doorsteps**)
the step or piece of ground outside a door

doorway *noun* (*plural* **doorways**)
the opening into which a door fits

dope *noun* (*plural* **dopes**)
(*informal*) 1 dope is a narcotic drug 2 a dope is a fool

dopey *adjective* (**dopier, dopiest**)
(*informal*) 1 half asleep 2 stupid

dormitory *noun* (*plural* **dormitories**)
a room for several people to sleep in, especially in a school

dose *noun* (*plural* **doses**)
an amount of medicine taken at one time

dossier *noun* (*plural* **dossiers**) (*pronounced* **doss-i-er** or **doss-i-ay**)
a set of documents with information about a person or event

dot ➤ *noun* (*plural* **dots**)
a tiny spot

dot ➤ *verb* (**dots, dotting, dotted**)
to dot something is to mark it with dots

dotty *adjective* (**dottier, dottiest**)
(*informal*) crazy or silly
dottiness *noun* being dotty

double ➤ *adjective*
1 twice as much or twice as many 2 having two of something ♦ *a double-barrelled shotgun* 3 suitable for two people ♦ *a double bed*

double ➤ *noun* (*plural* **doubles**)
1 double is twice the amount or cost 2 a double is someone who looks like someone else

double ➤ *verb* (**doubles, doubling, doubled**)
1 to double something is to make it twice as big **2** to double is to become twice as big **3** to double something flat is to fold it in two

double bass *noun* (*plural* **double basses**)
a musical instrument with strings, like a large cello

double-cross *verb* (**double-crosses, double-crossing, double-crossed**)
to double-cross someone is to cheat or betray them when you are supposed to be supporting them

double-decker *noun* (*plural* **double-deckers**)
a bus with two floors, one above the other

doubly *adverb*
twice as much ♦ *It's doubly important that you should go*

doubt ➤ *noun* (*plural* **doubts**)
not feeling sure about something

doubt ➤ *verb* (**doubts, doubting, doubted**)
to doubt something is to feel unsure about it ♦ *I doubt whether he is telling the truth*

doubtful *adjective*
1 having doubts ♦ *She looked doubtful* **2** making you feel doubt ♦ *Their story was very doubtful*
doubtfully *adverb* in a doubtful way

doubtless *adverb*
certainly; without any doubt

dough *noun*
1 a thick mixture of flour and water used for making bread or pastry **2** (*slang*) money
doughy *adjective* like dough

doughnut *noun* (*plural* **doughnuts**)
a round bun that has been fried and covered with sugar

dove *noun* (*plural* **doves**)
a kind of pigeon

dovetail ➤ *noun* (*plural* **dovetails**)
a wedge-shaped joint used to join two pieces of wood

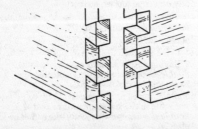

dovetail ➤ *verb* (**dovetails, dovetailing, dovetailed**)
1 to dovetail two pieces of wood is to join them with a dovetail **2** to dovetail is to fit neatly together ♦ *My plans dovetailed with hers*

dowel *noun* (*plural* **dowels**)
a headless wooden or metal pin for holding together two pieces of wood or stone

down[1] *adverb and preposition*
1 to or in a lower place ♦ *It fell down* ♦ *Run down the hill* **2** along ♦ *Go down to the shops*

down[2] *noun*
very soft feathers or hair ♦ *Ducks are covered with down*
downy *adjective* like down

downcast *adjective*
1 looking downward ♦ *Her eyes were downcast* **2** sad or dejected

downfall *noun* (*plural* **downfalls**)
1 ruin or fall from power **2** a heavy fall of rain or snow

downhill *adverb*
down a slope

downpour *noun* (*plural* **downpours**)
a heavy fall of rain

downright *adjective and adverb*
very, completely ♦ *I felt downright angry about it*

downs *plural noun*
grass-covered hills ♦ *Let's have a picnic on the downs*

downstairs *adverb and adjective*
to or on a lower floor

downstream *adverb*
in the direction that a river or stream flows

downward or **downwards** *adverb*
towards a lower place

doze *verb* (**dozes, dozing, dozed**)
to doze is to sleep lightly
dozy *adjective* feeling sleepy

dozen *noun* (*plural* **dozens**)
a set of twelve
dozens (*informal*) lots

Dr short for **Doctor**

drab *adjective* (**drabber, drabbest**)
1 dull and without colour ♦ *His clothes were drab* **2** dreary and uninteresting

draft ➤ *noun* (*plural* **drafts**)
a rough sketch or plan

draft ➤ *verb* (**drafts, drafting, drafted**)
to draft something is to make a sketch or plan of it

drag ➤ *verb* (**drags, dragging, dragged**)
1 to drag something heavy is to pull it along **2** to drag a river or lake is to search it with nets and hooks
drag ➤ *noun*
(*informal*) something annoying or tedious
dragon *noun* (*plural* **dragons**)
a monster that breathes fire in stories

dragonfly *noun* (*plural* **dragonflies**)
an insect with a long body and two pairs of transparent wings
drain ➤ *noun* (*plural* **drains**)
1 a pipe or ditch for taking away water or sewage **2** something that uses up your strength ♦ *Looking after her friend's children has been a real drain on her*
drain ➤ *verb* (**drains, draining, drained**)
1 to drain water is to take it away with drains **2** to drain is to flow or trickle away **3** to drain a glass or bottle is to empty liquid out of it **4** to drain someone is to exhaust them
drainage *noun* a system of drains
draining board *noun* (*plural* **draining boards**)
a sloping surface beside a sink where washed dishes are put
drake *noun* (*plural* **drakes**)
a male duck
drama *noun* (*plural* **dramas**)
1 drama is writing or performing plays **2** a drama is a play **3** a drama is also a series of exciting events
dramatic *adjective*
1 to do with drama **2** exciting and impressive ♦ *A dramatic change has taken place*
dramatically *adverb* in a dramatic way
dramatics *plural noun*
performing plays
dramatist *noun* (*plural* **dramatists**)
someone who writes plays
dramatize *verb* (**dramatizes, dramatizing, dramatized**)
1 to dramatize a story is to make it into a play **2** to dramatize is to exaggerate
dramatization *noun* making a play

drank past tense of **drink** *verb*
drape *verb* (**drapes, draping, draped**)
to drape something like cloth is to hang it loosely over something
drastic *adjective*
having a strong or violent effect
drastically *adverb* in a drastic way
draught *noun* (*plural* **draughts**) (*rhymes with* craft)
a current of cold air indoors
draughty *adjective* having lots of draughts
draughts *noun*
a game played with 24 round pieces on a chessboard
draughtsman *noun* (*plural* **draughtsmen**)
1 someone who makes drawings **2** a piece used in the game of draughts
draw ➤ *verb* (**draws, drawing, drew, drawn**)
1 to draw a picture or outline is to form it with a pencil or pen **2** to draw something is to pull it ♦ *She drew her chair up to the table* **3** to draw people is to attract them ♦ *The fair drew large crowds* **4** to draw is to end a game or contest with the same score on both sides ♦ *They drew 2–2 last Saturday* **5** to draw near is to come nearer ♦ *The ship was drawing nearer*
draw ➤ *noun* (*plural* **draws**)
1 a raffle or similar competition in which the winner is chosen by picking tickets or numbers at random **2** a game that ends with the same score on both sides **3** an attraction
drawback *noun* (*plural* **drawbacks**)
a disadvantage
drawbridge *noun* (*plural* **drawbridges**)
a bridge over a moat, hinged at one end so that it can be raised or lowered
drawer *noun* (*plural* **drawers**)
a sliding box-like container in a piece of furniture
drawing *noun* (*plural* **drawings**)
something drawn with a pencil or pen
drawing pin *noun* (*plural* **drawing pins**)
a short pin with a large flat top, for fixing paper to a surface
drawing room *noun* (*plural* **drawing rooms**)
a sitting room
drawl *verb* (**drawls, drawling, drawled**)
to drawl is to speak very slowly or lazily
dread ➤ *noun*
great fear
dread ➤ *verb* (**dreads, dreading, dreaded**)
to dread something is to fear it very much
dreadful *adjective*
very bad ♦ *We've had dreadful weather*
dreadfully *adverb* very badly

dreadlocks *plural noun*
hair in long tightly-curled ringlets, worn especially by Rastafarians

dream ➤ *noun* (*plural* **dreams**)
1 things a person seems to see while sleeping **2** something imagined; an ambition or ideal ♦ *His dream is to go to China*
dreamy *adjective* like a dream; not real

dream ➤ *verb* (**dreams, dreaming, dreamt** or **dreamed**)
1 to dream is to have a dream **2** to dream is also to want something badly ♦ *She dreams of being a ballet dancer* **3** to dream something is to think it may happen ♦ *I never dreamt she would leave*

dreary *adjective* (**drearier, dreariest**)
1 dull or boring **2** gloomy
drearily *adverb* in a dreary way **dreariness** *noun* being dreary

dredge *verb* (**dredges, dredging, dredged**)
to dredge something is to drag it up, especially mud from the bottom of water
dredger *noun* a machine for dredging

drench *verb* (**drenches, drenching, drenched**)
to drench someone or something is to soak them ♦ *They got drenched in the rain*

dress ➤ *noun* (*plural* **dresses**)
1 a dress is a woman's or girl's piece of clothing, having a top and skirt in one
2 dress is clothes or costume ♦ *We have to wear fancy dress*

dress ➤ *verb* (**dresses, dressing, dressed**)
1 to dress is to put clothes on **2** to dress a wound is to bandage it **3** to dress food is to prepare it for cooking or eating

dresser *noun* (*plural* **dressers**)
a sideboard with shelves at the top

dressing *noun* (*plural* **dressings**)
1 a sauce of oil, vinegar, and spices for a salad **2** a covering for a wound; a plaster

dressing gown *noun* (*plural* **dressing gowns**)
a loose light indoor coat worn over pyjamas or a nightdress

dressmaker *noun* (*plural* **dressmakers**)
a person whose job is to make clothes for women

drew past tense of **draw** *verb*

dribble *verb* (**dribbles, dribbling, dribbled**)
1 to dribble is to let saliva trickle out of your mouth **2** to dribble is also to kick a ball gently in front of you as you run forward

dried past tense and past participle of **dry** *verb*

drier *noun* (*plural* **driers**)
a device for drying hair or washing

drift ➤ *verb* (**drifts, drifting, drifted**)
1 to drift is to be carried gently along by water or air **2** to drift is also to live casually without any real aims

drift ➤ *noun* (*plural* **drifts**)
1 a drifting movement **2** a mass of snow or sand piled up by the wind **3** the general meaning of what someone says ♦ *I don't follow your drift*

driftwood *noun*
wood floating on the sea or washed ashore

drill ➤ *noun* (*plural* **drills**)
1 a tool for making holes **2** repeated exercises in military training, gymnastics, or sport **3** a set way of doing something ♦ *Do you know the drill?*

drill ➤ *verb* (**drills, drilling, drilled**)
1 to drill a hole is to make a hole with a drill **2** to drill is to do repeated exercises

drink ➤ *verb* (**drinks, drinking, drank, drunk**)
1 to drink is to swallow liquid **2** to drink can also mean to have a lot of alcohol ♦ *Don't drink and drive*
drinker *noun* someone who drinks

drink ➤ *noun* (*plural* **drinks**)
1 a liquid for drinking **2** an alcoholic drink

drip ➤ *noun* (*plural* **drips**)
a falling drop of liquid

drip ➤ *verb* (**drips, dripping, dripped**)
1 to drip is to fall in drops **2** to drip is also to let liquid fall in drops ♦ *The tap was dripping*

dripping *noun*
fat melted from roasted meat and allowed to set

drive ➤ *verb* (**drives, driving, drove, driven**)
1 to drive someone or something is to make them move **2** to drive a vehicle is to operate it **3** to drive someone into a state or feeling is to force them into it ♦ *They will drive me crazy!*
to be driving at something is to be trying to say it ♦ *What is he driving at?*
driver *noun* someone who drives a vehicle

drive ➤ *noun* (*plural* **drives**)
1 a drive is a journey in a vehicle **2** drive is energy and enthusiasm **3** a drive is a road leading to a house **4** a drive is a powerful stroke of the ball in cricket, golf and other games

drizzle ➤ *noun*
gentle rain

drizzle ➤ *verb* (**drizzles, drizzling, drizzled**)
to rain gently

drone ➤ *verb* (**drones, droning, droned**)
1 to drone is to make a low humming sound **2** to drone is also to talk in a boring voice

drone ➤ *noun* (*plural* **drones**)
1 a droning sound **2** a male bee

drool *verb* (**drools, drooling, drooled**)
to drool is to dribble continuously
to drool over something is to look at it with longing ♦ *He's been drooling over car catalogues all afternoon*

droop *verb* (**droops, drooping, drooped**)
to droop is to hang down weakly

drop ➤ *noun* (*plural* **drops**)
1 a tiny amount of liquid **2** a fall or decrease ♦ *There has been a sharp drop in prices*
droplet *noun* a small drop

drop ➤ *verb* (**drops, dropping, dropped**)
1 to drop is to fall **2** to drop something is to let it fall
to drop in is to visit someone casually
to drop out is to stop taking part in something

drought *noun* (*plural* **droughts**) (*rhymes with* out)
a long period of dry weather

drove past tense of **drive** *verb*

drown *verb* (**drowns, drowning, drowned**)
1 to drown is to die from being under water and unable to breathe **2** to drown a person or animal is to kill them by forcing them to stay under water **3** to drown sounds is to make so much noise that they cannot be heard

drowsy *adjective* (**drowsier, drowsiest**)
sleepy
drowsily *adverb* in a drowsy way **drowsiness** *noun* being drowsy

drug ➤ *noun* (*plural* **drugs**)
1 a substance that kills pain or cures a disease **2** a substance that affects your senses or your mind, such as heroin

drug ➤ *verb* (**drugs, drugging, drugged**)
to drug someone is to make them unconscious with drugs

druid *noun* (*plural* **Druids**)
a priest of an ancient Celtic religion in Britain and France

drum ➤ *noun* (*plural* **drums**)
1 a musical instrument made of a cylinder with a thin skin stretched over one end or both ends **2** a cylindrical container
♦ *There was a row of oil drums along the side of the road*

drum ➤ *verb* (**drums, drumming, drummed**)
1 to drum is to play a drum or drums **2** to drum on something is to tap it repeatedly
♦ *He drummed his fingers on the table*
drummer *noun* someone who plays the drums

drumstick *noun* (*plural* **drumsticks**)
1 a stick used for hitting a drum **2** the lower part of a cooked bird's leg

drunk[1] ➤ *adjective*
not able to control your behaviour through drinking too much alcohol

drunk ➤ *noun* (*plural* **drunks**)
someone who is drunk
drunkard *noun* a person who is often drunk

drunk[2] past participle of **drink** *verb*

dry ➤ *adjective* (**drier, driest**)
1 not wet or damp **2** boring and dull
♦ *The book I'm reading is rather dry*
3 sarcastic ♦ *He has a very dry sense of humour*
drily *adverb* sarcastically **dryness** *noun* being dry

dry ➤ *verb* (**dries, drying, dried**)
1 to dry is to become dry **2** to dry something is to make it dry
to dry up (*informal*) is to stop talking

dry-cleaning *noun*
a method of cleaning clothes without using water

dry dock *noun*
a dock which can be emptied of water, for repairing ships

dual *adjective*
having two parts; double

dual carriageway *noun* (*plural* **dual carriageways**)
a road with several lanes in each direction

dub *verb* (**dubs, dubbing, dubbed**)
1 to change or add new sound to the sound on a film or magnetic tape 2 to give someone a name or title

duchess *noun* (*plural* **duchesses**)
a duke's wife or widow

duck ➤ *noun* (*plural* **ducks**)
1 a web-footed bird with a flat beak 2 a batsman's score of nought at cricket

duck ➤ *verb* (**ducks, ducking, ducked**)
1 to duck is to bend down quickly to avoid something 2 to duck someone is to push them under water quickly

duckling *noun* (*plural* **ducklings**)
a young duck

duct *noun* (*plural* **ducts**)
a tube or channel

dud *noun* (*plural* **duds**)
(*slang*) something that is useless or that fails to work

due ➤ *adjective*
1 expected ◆ *The train is due in five minutes* 2 needing to be paid ◆ *Payment for the trip is due next week*
due to something or **someone** because of something or someone ◆ *He was in a muddle due to being late*
in due course eventually; at the expected time

due ➤ *adverb*
directly ◆ *The camp is due north*

duel *noun* (*plural* **duels**)
a fight between two people, especially with pistols or swords

duet *noun* (*plural* **duets**)
a piece of music for two players or two singers

duff *adjective*
(*slang*) useless or broken

duffel coat *noun* (*plural* **duffel coats**)
a thick overcoat with a hood

dug past tense and past participle of **dig** *verb*

dugout *noun* (*plural* **dugouts**)
1 an underground shelter 2 a canoe made by hollowing out a tree trunk

duke *noun* (*plural* **dukes**)
a member of the highest rank of noblemen

dull *adjective* (**duller, dullest**)
1 not bright or clear; gloomy ◆ *It was a dull day* 2 not sharp ◆ *I had a dull pain* 3 stupid ◆ *You are a dull boy* 4 boring ◆ *What a dull programme*
dully *adverb* in a dull way **dullness** *noun* being dull

duly *adverb*
rightly; as expected ◆ *They promised to come, and later they duly arrived*

dumb *adjective* (**dumber, dumbest**)
1 unable to speak; silent 2 (*informal*) stupid

dumbfounded *adjective*
unable to say anything because you are so astonished

dummy *noun* (*plural* **dummies**)
1 something made to look like a person or thing; an imitation 2 an imitation teat for a baby to suck

dump ➤ *noun* (*plural* **dumps**)
1 a place where something, especially rubbish, is left or stored 2 (*informal*) a place you don't like

dump ➤ *verb* (**dumps, dumping, dumped**)
1 to dump something is to get rid of it when you don't want it 2 to dump something somewhere is to put it down carelessly

dumpling *noun* (*plural* **dumplings**)
a lump of boiled or baked dough

dumpy *adjective* (**dumpier, dumpiest**)
short and fat

dune *noun* (*plural* **dunes**)
a mound of loose sand formed by the wind

dung *noun*
solid waste matter from an animal

dungarees *plural noun*
trousers with a piece in front covering your chest, held up by straps over your shoulders

dungeon *noun* (*plural* **dungeons**)
(*pronounced* **dun**-jon)
an underground prison cell

duo *noun* (*plural* **duos**)
a pair of people, especially playing music

duplicate ➤ *noun* (*plural* **duplicates**)
(*pronounced* **dew**-pli-kat)
something that is exactly the same as something else; an exact copy

duplicate ➤ *verb* (**duplicates, duplicating, duplicated**) (*pronounced* **dew**-pli-kayt)
to duplicate something is to make another copy of it
duplication *noun* duplicating something

durable *adjective*
lasting and strong

durability *noun* being durable

duration *noun*
the time something lasts

during *preposition*
while something else is going on ♦ *Let's meet in the café during the interval*

dusk *noun*
twilight in the evening

dust ➤ *noun*
tiny particles of dry earth or other material

dust ➤ *verb* (**dusts, dusting, dusted**)
1 to dust things is to clear the dust off them **2** to dust something is to sprinkle it with dust or powder

dustbin *noun* (*plural* **dustbins**)
a bin for household rubbish

duster *noun* (*plural* **dusters**)
a cloth for dusting things

dustman *noun* (*plural* **dustmen**)
a person whose job is to empty dustbins

dustpan *noun* (*plural* **dustpans**)
a pan into which dust is brushed

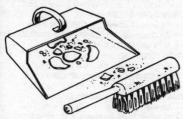

dusty *adjective* (**dustier, dustiest**)
1 covered with dust **2** like dust

dutiful *adjective*
doing your duty; obedient
dutifully *adverb* in a dutiful way

duty *noun* (*plural* **duties**)
1 your duty is what you have to do **2** a duty is a kind of tax

duvet *noun* (*plural* **duvets**) (*pronounced* doo-vay)
a kind of quilt used instead of other bedclothes

dwarf ➤ *noun* (*plural* **dwarfs** or **dwarves**)
a very small person or thing

dwarf ➤ *verb* (**dwarfs, dwarfing, dwarfed**)
to dwarf something is to make it seem very small ♦ *The skyscraper dwarfs all the buildings round it*

dwell *verb* (**dwells, dwelling, dwelt**)
to dwell in a place is to live there
to dwell on something is to think or talk about it constantly

dwelling *noun* (*plural* **dwellings**)
a house or other place to live in

dwindle *verb* (**dwindles, dwindling, dwindled**)
to dwindle is to get smaller gradually

dye ➤ *verb* (**dyes, dyeing, dyed**)
to dye something is to colour it by putting it in a special liquid

dye ➤ *noun* (*plural* **dyes**)
a liquid used to dye things

dying present participle of **die** *verb*

dyke *noun* (*plural* **dykes**)
another spelling of **dike**

dynamic *adjective*
energetic and active

dynamite *noun*
1 a powerful explosive **2** (*informal*) something that will make people angry or excited

dynamo *noun* (*plural* **dynamos**)
a machine that makes electricity

dynasty *noun* (*plural* **dynasties**) (*pronounced* din-a-sti)
a series of kings and queens from the same family

dyslexia *noun* (*pronounced* dis-lek-si-a)
special difficulty in being able to read and spell words
dyslexic *adjective* having dyslexia

dystrophy *noun* (*pronounced* dis-tro-fi)
a disease that badly weakens the muscles

Ee

each *adjective* and *pronoun*
every; every one ♦ *Each child had a cake* ♦ *I'll give each of you a new book* ♦ *They were yelling at each other*

eager *adjective*
badly wanting to do something; enthusiastic
eagerly *adverb* in an eager way **eagerness** *noun* being eager

eagle *noun* (*plural* **eagles**)
a large bird of prey with strong eyesight

ear[1] *noun* (*plural* **ears**)
1 the organ of the body that you hear with
2 hearing ability ♦ *She has a good ear for music*

ear[2] *noun* (*plural* **ears**)
the spike of seeds at the top of a stalk of corn

earache *noun*
a pain in the ear

eardrum *noun* (*plural* **eardrums**)
a membrane in the ear that vibrates when sound reaches it

earl *noun* (*plural* **earls**)
a British nobleman

early *adverb* and *adjective* (**earlier, earliest**)
1 before the usual or expected time
2 near the beginning ♦ *The robbery comes early in the story*
earliness *noun* being early

earmark *verb* (**earmarks, earmarking, earmarked**)
to earmark something, especially money, is to put it aside for a special purpose

earn *verb* (**earns, earning, earned**)
to earn something is to get it by working for it or as a reward

earnest *adjective*
serious; determined
earnestly *adverb* in an earnest way

earnings *plural noun*
earnings are money that someone earns

earphones *plural noun*
a listening device that fits over or into your ears

earring *noun* (*plural* **earrings**)
an ornament worn on the ear

earth *noun* (*plural* **earths**)
1 the earth is the planet that we live on
2 earth is soil or the ground 3 an earth is a hole where a fox or badger lives 4 an earth is also a connection to the ground to complete an electric circuit
on earth used for emphasis ♦ *What on earth are you doing?*
to cost the earth (*informal*) is to cost a lot

earthenware *noun*
crockery made of baked clay

earthly *adjective*
to do with life on earth

earthquake *noun* (*plural* **earthquakes**)
a violent movement of part of the earth's surface

earthworm *noun* (*plural* **earthworms**)
a worm that lives in the soil

earthy *adjective* (**earthier, earthiest**)
1 like earth or soil 2 crude or vulgar

earwig *noun* (*plural* **earwigs**)
a crawling insect with pincers at the end of its body

ease ➤ *noun*
freedom from difficulty or trouble

ease ➤ *verb* (**eases, easing, eased**)
1 to ease something is to make it easier or less troublesome 2 to ease is to become less severe or troublesome ♦ *Later the pain began to ease* 3 to ease something is to move it gently into position

easel *noun* (*plural* **easels**)
a stand for holding a blackboard or a painting

easily *adverb*
1 without difficulty; with ease 2 by far
♦ *This one is easily the best* 3 very likely
♦ *He could easily be lying*

east ➤ *noun*
1 the direction in which the sun rises
2 the part of a country or city that is in this direction

east ➤ *adjective* and *adverb*
1 towards the east or in the east
2 coming from the east ♦ *An east wind made the day very cold*

Easter *noun*
the day or period when the resurrection of Christ is remembered

easterly *adjective*
an easterly wind is one that blows from the east

eastern *adjective*
from or to do with the east

eastward or **eastwards** *adjective* and *adverb*
towards the east

easy ➤ *adjective* (**easier, easiest**)
able to be done or understood without trouble

easy ➤ *adverb* (**easier, easiest**)
with ease; comfortably ♦ *Easy does it*
take it easy relax; go carefully

eat *verb* (**eats, eating, ate, eaten**)
to eat food is to chew it and swallow it
to eat something up or **eat something away** is to use it up or destroy it ♦ *The sea air has eaten away the ironwork*

eatable *adjective*
fit to be eaten

eaves *plural noun*
the overhanging edges of a roof

ebb ➤ *noun*
the movement of the tide when it is going out

at a low ebb in a poor or weak condition

ebb ➤ *verb* (**ebbs, ebbing, ebbed**)
1 the tide ebbs when it goes away from the land 2 to ebb or ebb away is to weaken or lessen ♦ *His strength ebbed away*

ebony *noun*
a hard black wood

EC short for **European Community**

eccentric *adjective* (*pronounced* ik-**sen**-trik)
behaving strangely
eccentricity *noun* being eccentric

echo ➤ *noun* (*plural* **echoes**)
a sound that is heard again as it is reflected off something

echo ➤ *verb* (**echoes, echoing, echoed**)
1 to echo is to make an echo 2 to echo something said is to repeat it

éclair *noun* (*plural* **éclairs**) (*pronounced* ay-**klair**)
a finger-shaped cake of pastry with a cream filling

eclipse *noun* (*plural* **eclipses**)
the blocking of light from the sun or moon when the moon or the earth is in the way

ecology *noun* (*pronounced* ee-**kol**-o-ji)
the study of living creatures and plants in their surroundings
ecological *adjective* to do with ecology
ecologist *noun* someone who studies ecology

economic *adjective* (*pronounced* eek-o-**nom**-ik or ek-o-**nom**-ik)
1 to do with economics 2 profitable ♦ *It is not normally economic to get drinking water from the sea*

economical *adjective* (*pronounced* eek-o-**nom**-ik-al)
careful in using money and resources
economically *adverb* in an economical way

economics *noun* (*pronounced* eek-o-**nom**-iks or ek-o-**nom**-iks)
the study of how money is used and how goods and services are provided and used

economist *noun* (*plural* **economists**) (*pronounced* i-**kon**-o-mist)
someone who studies economics

economize *verb* (**economizes, economizing, economized**) (*pronounced* i-**kon**-o-myz)
to economize is to use less money

economy *noun* (*plural* **economies**) (*pronounced* i-**kon**-o-mi)
1 an economy is a country's or family's income and the way it is spent 2 economy is being careful with money 3 economies are ways of saving money

ecstasy *noun* (*plural* **ecstasies**)
1 a feeling of great delight or joy 2 an illegal drug that gives people extra energy and can cause hallucinations
ecstatic *adjective* joyful

eczema *noun* (*pronounced* ek-si-ma)
a skin disease that causes rough itching patches

edge ➤ *noun* (*plural* **edges**)
1 the part along the side or end of something 2 the sharp part of a knife or other cutting device

to be on edge is to feel nervous and irritable

edge ➤ *verb* (**edges, edging, edged**)
1 to edge is to move gradually ♦ *She edged towards the door* 2 to edge something is to form a border to it

edgeways *adverb*
with the edge outwards or forwards

edgy *adjective* (**edgier, edgiest**)
nervous and irritable

edible *adjective*
suitable for eating; not poisonous

edit *verb* (**edits, editing, edited**)
1 to edit a book, newspaper, or magazine is to get it ready for publishing 2 to edit a film or tape recording is to choose parts of it and put them in the right order

edition *noun* (*plural* **editions**)
1 the form in which something is published ♦ *Is there a paperback edition?*
2 all the copies of a newspaper, magazine, or book issued at the same time

editor *noun* (*plural* **editors**)
someone who edits a book, newspaper, or magazine

editorial *noun* (*plural* **editorials**)
a newspaper article giving the editor's opinion on current affairs

educate *verb* (**educates, educating, educated**)
to educate someone is to give them knowledge or skill
educator *noun* someone who educates people

education *noun*
the process of training people's minds and abilities so that they can learn things and develop skills ♦ *She has had a good education*
educational *adjective* to do with education

eel *noun* (*plural* **eels**)
a long fish that looks like a snake

eerie *adjective* (**eerier, eeriest**)
weird and frightening
eerily *adverb* in an eerie way **eeriness** *noun*
being eerie
effect *noun* (*plural* **effects**)
1 something that happens because of
something else ♦ *The drink had a strange
effect on Alice* 2 a general impression
♦ *The lights made a cheerful effect*
effective *adjective*
producing what you want; successful
effectively *adverb* in an effective way
effectiveness *noun* being effective
effeminate *adjective* (*pronounced*
i-**fem**-in-at)
an effeminate man has some of the
characteristics of a woman
effervescent *adjective* (*pronounced*
ef-er-**vess**-ent)
fizzy; giving off bubbles
effervescence *noun* being effervescent
efficient *adjective*
doing work well; effective
efficiency *noun* being efficient **efficiently**
adverb in an efficient way
effort *noun* (*plural* **efforts**)
1 effort is using energy or hard work
2 an effort is an attempt
effortless *adjective* not needing much effort;
easy
e.g. for example ♦ *He teaches lots of
subjects, e.g. music, geography, and maths*
egg¹ *noun* (*plural* **eggs**)
1 an oval or round object with a thin shell,
laid by birds, fish, reptiles, and insects, in
which their offspring develop 2 a hen's or
duck's egg used as food
egg² *verb* (**eggs, egging, egged**)
to egg someone on is to encourage them with
taunts or dares
eh *interjection* (*pronounced* ay)
an exclamation of surprise or doubt
Eid *noun* (*pronounced* eed)
a Muslim festival that marks the end of
the fast of Ramadan

eiderdown *noun* (*plural* **eiderdowns**)
(*pronounced* I-der-down)
a quilt stuffed with soft material
eight *noun* (*plural* **eights**)
the number 8
eighteen *noun* (*plural* **eighteens**)
the number 18
eighteenth *adjective* and *noun* 18th
eighth *adjective* and *noun*
the next after the seventh
eighthly *adverb* in the eighth place; as the
eighth one
eighty *noun* (*plural* **eighties**)
the number 80
eightieth *adjective* and *noun* 80th
either ➤ *adjective* and *pronoun*
1 one of two ♦ *Either team could win* ♦ *I
haven't seen either of them* 2 both of two
♦ *There are fields on either side of the river*
either ➤ *adverb*
also; similarly ♦ *If you won't go, I won't
either*
either ➤ *conjunction*
either … or … one thing or another, but not
both ♦ *You can choose either red or blue*
♦ *Either come in or go out*
eject *verb* (**ejects, ejecting, ejected**)
1 to eject something is to send it out with
force 2 to eject someone is to make them
leave
ejection *noun* being ejected
elaborate ➤ *adjective* (*pronounced*
i-**lab**-er-at)
complicated or detailed
elaborate ➤ *verb* (**elaborates, elaborating,
elaborated**) (*pronounced* i-**lab**-er-ayt)
to elaborate something is to describe it or
work it out in detail
elaboration *noun* elaborating something
elastic ➤ *noun*
cord or material with strands of rubber in
it so that it can stretch
elastic ➤ *adjective*
able to be stretched and then return to its
original shape or length
elasticity *noun* ability to stretch
elated *adjective*
very pleased
elation *noun* feeling elated
elbow ➤ *noun* (*plural* **elbows**)
the joint in the middle of your arm
elbow ➤ *verb* (**elbows, elbowing, elbowed**)
to elbow someone is to push them with
your elbow
elder¹ *adjective*
older ♦ *This is my elder brother*
elder² *noun* (*plural* **elders**)
a tree with white flowers and black berries

elderberry *noun* a berry from an elder

elderly *adjective*
rather old

eldest *adjective*
oldest ♦ *Jane is my eldest sister*

elect *verb* (**elects, electing, elected**)
to elect someone is to choose them by voting

election *noun* (*plural* **elections**)
the process of voting for people, especially for Members of Parliament

electorate *noun*
the people who vote in an election

electric or **electrical** *adjective*
to do with electricity, or worked by electricity
electrically *adverb* by electricity

electrician *noun* (*plural* **electricians**)
someone whose job is to fit and repair electrical equipment

electricity *noun*
a kind of energy used for lighting, heating, and making machines work

electrify *verb* (**electrifies, electrifying, electrified**)
1 to electrify something is to make it work by electricity, or to give it an electric charge 2 to electrify someone is to excite or startle them ♦ *Her singing electrified the audience*
electrification *noun* making something work by electricity

electrocute *verb* (**electrocutes, electrocuting, electrocuted**)
to electrocute someone is to kill them by electricity
electrocution *noun* electrocuting someone

electromagnet *noun* (*plural* **electromagnets**)
a magnet worked by electricity

electron *noun* (*plural* **electrons**)
a particle of matter that is smaller than an atom and has a negative electric charge

electronic *adjective*
using devices such as transistors and silicon chips, which are worked by electrons
electronically *adverb* by means of electronic devices

electronic mail *noun*
a system of sending messages from one computer to another by means of a network

electronics *plural noun*
electronics are the use or study of electronic devices

elegant *adjective*
graceful and smart
elegance *noun* being elegant **elegantly** *adverb* in an elegant way

element *noun* (*plural* **elements**)
1 (*in Science*) a substance that cannot be split up into simpler substances, for example copper and oxygen 2 a part of something 3 the elements of a subject are the basic facts to do with it ♦ *Next term you will learn the elements of algebra* 4 the elements are forces that make the weather, such as rain and wind 5 a wire or coil that gives out heat in an electric heater or cooker
to be in your element is to be doing something you enjoy

elementary *adjective*
dealing with the simplest stages of something; easy

elephant *noun* (*plural* **elephants**)
a very large animal with a trunk and tusks

elevate *verb* (**elevates, elevating, elevated**)
to elevate something is to lift it or raise it to a higher position

elevation *noun* (*plural* **elevations**)
1 lifting or raising something 2 the height of something 3 a drawing of something seen from the side

eleven *noun* (*plural* **elevens**)
1 the number 11 2 a team of eleven people in cricket, football, and other sports
eleventh *adjective* and *noun* 11th

elf *noun* (*plural* **elves**)
a small or mischievous fairy in stories

eligible *adjective*
qualified or suitable for something
eligibility *noun* being eligible

eliminate *verb* (**eliminates, eliminating, eliminated**)
to eliminate someone or something is to get rid of them
elimination *noun* eliminating someone or something

élite *noun* (*plural* **élites**)
a group of people with special privileges

elk *noun* (*plural* **elk** or **elks**)
a large kind of deer

ellipse *noun* (*plural* **ellipses**)
an oval shape

elliptical *adjective*
oval-shaped

elm *noun* (*plural* **elms**)
a tall tree with rough leaves

elocution *noun*
the art of speaking clearly and correctly

elongated *adjective*
made longer; lengthened
elongation *noun* making something longer

eloquent *adjective*
speaking well and expressing ideas clearly
eloquence *noun* being eloquent

else *adverb*
besides; instead ♦ *Nobody else knows*
or else otherwise ♦ *Run or else you'll be late*

elsewhere *adverb*
somewhere else

elude *verb* (**eludes, eluding, eluded**)
to elude someone is to escape from them or
avoid being caught by them

elusive *adjective*
difficult to find or catch ♦ *Deer are elusive
animals*

elves plural of **elf**

e-mail short for **electronic mail**

emancipate *verb* (**emancipates, emancipating,
emancipated**)
to emancipate someone is to set them free
emancipation *noun* setting people free

embankment *noun* (*plural* **embankments**)
a long wall or bank of earth to hold back
water or support a road or railway

embark *verb* (**embarks, embarking, embarked**)
to embark is to go on board a ship
to embark on something is to begin something
important
embarkation *noun* going on board a ship

embarrass *verb* (**embarrasses, embarrassing,
embarrassed**)
to embarrass someone is to make them
feel shy or awkward
embarrassment *noun* feeling embarrassed

embassy *noun* (*plural* **embassies**)
the building where an ambassador lives
and has an office

embedded *adjective*
fixed firmly into something

embers *plural noun*
small pieces of burning coal or wood in a
dying fire

emblem *noun* (*plural* **emblems**)
a symbol that stands for something ♦ *The
dove is an emblem of peace*

embrace *verb* (**embraces, embracing, embraced**)
1 to embrace someone is to hold them
closely in your arms **2** to embrace a cause
or belief is to adopt it ♦ *Many Roman
soldiers embraced Christianity* **3** to
embrace several things is to include them
♦ *The questionnaire embraces all the main
subjects done at school*

embroider *verb* (**embroiders, embroidering,
embroidered**)
to embroider cloth is to decorate it with
sewn designs or pictures
embroidery *noun* the art of embroidering

embryo *noun* (*plural* **embryos**)
a baby or young animal that is growing in
the womb

emerald *noun* (*plural* **emeralds**)
1 a green jewel **2** a bright green colour

emerge *verb* (**emerges, emerging, emerged**)
to emerge is to come out or appear
emergence *noun* emerging

emergency *noun* (*plural* **emergencies**)
a sudden dangerous or serious happening
that needs prompt action

emery paper *noun*
a gritty paper like sandpaper

emigrant *noun* (*plural* **emigrants**)
someone who goes to live in another
country

emigrate *verb* (**emigrates, emigrating, emigrated**)
to emigrate is to go and live in another
country
emigration *noun* emigrating

eminent *adjective*
famous and respected ♦ *We met an
eminent scientist*
eminence *noun* being eminent

emission *noun* (*plural* **emissions**)
1 the action of sending something out
2 something that is emitted, especially
fumes or radiation

emit *verb* (**emits, emitting, emitted**)
to emit something such as smoke or fumes
is to send it out

emotion *noun* (*plural* **emotions**)
1 an emotion is a strong feeling in your
mind, such as love or fear **2** emotion is
being excited or upset ♦ *Her voice
trembled with emotion*
emotional *adjective* to do with emotion;
having strong feelings **emotionally** *adverb* in
an emotional way

emperor *noun* (*plural* **emperors**)
a man who rules an empire

emphasis *noun* (*plural* **emphases**)
special importance given to something
emphatic *adjective* using emphasis; definite
emphatically *adverb* in an emphatic way

emphasize *verb* (**emphasizes, emphasizing, emphasized**)
to emphasize something is to give it special importance

empire *noun* (*plural* **empires**)
1 a group of countries ruled by one person or group of people 2 a large group of businesses or shops under the control of one person or group of people

employ *verb* (**employs, employing, employed**)
1 to employ someone is to pay them to work for you 2 to employ something is to use it

employee *noun* (*plural* **employees**) (*pronounced* im-**ploi**-ee)
someone who is employed by someone else

employer *noun* (*plural* **employers**)
someone who employs people

employment *noun*
1 employment is having paid work 2 an employment is a paid job

empress *noun* (*plural* **empresses**)
a female emperor, or the wife of an emperor

empties *plural noun*
(*informal*) empty bottles or containers

empty ➤ *adjective* (**emptier, emptiest**)
having nothing or no one in it
emptiness *noun* being empty

empty ➤ *verb* (**empties, emptying, emptied**)
1 to empty something is to make it empty 2 to empty is to become empty ♦ *After the show the room quickly emptied*

emu *noun* (*plural* **emus**) (*pronounced* **ee**-mew)
a large Australian bird rather like an ostrich

emulsion *noun* (*plural* **emulsions**)
1 a creamy or slightly oily liquid 2 a kind of paint

enable *verb* (**enables, enabling, enabled**)
to enable someone to do something is to make it possible for them ♦ *A calculator will enable you to multiply and divide quickly*

enamel *noun* (*plural* **enamels**)
1 a shiny glassy substance for coating metal or pottery 2 a hard shiny paint 3 the hard shiny surface of teeth

encampment *noun* (*plural* **encampments**)
a military camp

enchant *verb* (**enchants, enchanting, enchanted**)
1 to enchant someone is to delight them
2 to enchant someone is also to put a magic spell on them in stories
enchantment *noun* a feeling of delight

encircle *verb* (**encircles, encircling, encircled**)
to encircle something or someone is to surround them ♦ *The pond was encircled by trees*

enclose *verb* (**encloses, enclosing, enclosed**)
1 to enclose something is to put it in a box or envelope 2 to enclose an area is to put a fence or wall round it
enclosure *noun* an enclosed piece of ground

encore *noun* (*plural* **encores**) (*pronounced* on-kor)
an extra item performed at a concert or show after the applause for the main items

encounter *verb* (**encounters, encountering, encountered**)
1 to encounter someone is to meet them unexpectedly 2 to encounter something is to experience it ♦ *We have encountered some problems*

encourage *verb* (**encourages, encouraging, encouraged**)
1 to encourage someone is to give them confidence or hope ♦ *We were encouraged by your support* 2 to encourage something is to help it happen ♦ *We need to encourage healthy eating*
encouragement *noun* encouraging or supporting someone or something

encyclopedia *noun* (*plural* **encyclopedias**)
a book or set of books containing many kinds of information
encyclopedic *adjective* giving a lot of information

end ➤ *noun* (*plural* **ends**)
1 the end of something is the last part of it or the point where it stops 2 each end of a sports pitch is the part defended by one team or player 3 an end is an aim or purpose
on end 1 upright ♦ *His hair stood on end* **2** continuously ♦ *She spoke for two hours on end*

end ➤ *verb* (**ends, ending, ended**)
1 to end something is to finish it 2 to end is to finish

endanger *verb* (**endangers, endangering, endangered**)
to endanger someone or something is to cause them danger, especially of being injured or becoming extinct

endeavour *verb* (**endeavours, endeavouring, endeavoured**)
to endeavour to do something is to try hard ♦ *He endeavoured to please her*

ending *noun* (*plural* **endings**)
the last part of something

endless *adjective*
never stopping ♦ *Teachers need endless patience*
endlessly *adverb* without ending

endure *verb* (**endures, enduring, endured**)
1 to endure pain or suffering is to put up with it 2 to endure is to continue or last
endurance *noun* enduring something

enemy *noun* (*plural* **enemies**)
1 someone who is opposed to someone else and wants to harm them 2 a nation or army that is at war with another country

energetic *adjective*
1 full of energy 2 done with energy ♦ *They then performed an energetic dance*
energetically *adverb* with energy

energy *noun* (*plural* **energies**)
1 strength to do things; liveliness 2 the ability to do work, for example electrical energy

enforce *verb* (**enforces, enforcing, enforced**)
to enforce a law or order is to make people obey it
enforceable *adjective* able to be enforced
enforcement *noun* enforcing laws

engage *verb* (**engages, engaging, engaged**)
1 to engage someone is to give them a job 2 to engage someone in conversation is to talk to them 3 to engage the enemy is to start a battle

engaged *adjective*
1 having promised to marry someone 2 already being used ♦ *Her telephone number is engaged*

engagement *noun* (*plural* **engagements**)
1 being engaged 2 an appointment to meet someone or do something 3 a battle

engine *noun* (*plural* **engines**)
1 a machine that turns energy into motion 2 a vehicle that pulls a railway train

engineer *noun* (*plural* **engineers**)
an expert in engineering

engineering *noun*
the designing and building of machines, roads, bridges, and other large buildings

engrave *verb* (**engraves, engraving, engraved**)
to engrave a surface is to carve figures or words on it
engraver *noun* someone who is skilled in engraving

engrossed *adjective*
having all your attention taken up ♦ *They were all engrossed in their work*

engulf *verb* (**engulfs, engulfing, engulfed**)
to engulf something is to flow over it and swamp it ♦ *Several villages near the coast were engulfed by0 the sea*

enhance *verb* (**enhances, enhancing, enhanced**)
to enhance something is to make it more valuable or attractive ♦ *The school show was enhanced by the beautiful costumes*
enhancement *noun* something that enhances

enjoy *verb* (**enjoys, enjoying, enjoyed**)
to enjoy something is to get pleasure from it
enjoyable *adjective* able to be enjoyed
enjoyment *noun* a feeling of great pleasure

enlarge *verb* (**enlarges, enlarging, enlarged**)
to enlarge something is to make it bigger
enlargement *noun* making something bigger

enlist *verb* (**enlists, enlisting, enlisted**)
to enlist is to join the armed forces
enlistment *noun* enlisting

enmity *noun* (*plural* **enmities**)
being someone's enemy; hostility

enormity *noun*
great wickedness ♦ *They admitted the enormity of their crimes*

enormous *adjective*
very large; huge
enormously *adverb* hugely **enormousness** *noun* great size

enough *adjective, noun,* and *adverb*
as much or as many as people need

enquire *verb* (**enquires, enquiring, enquired**)
to enquire about something is to ask for information ♦ *He enquired if I was well*
enquiry *noun* a question

enrage *verb* (**enrages, enraging, enraged**)
to enrage a person or animal is to make them very angry

enrich *verb* (**enriches, enriching, enriched**)
to enrich something is to make it richer
enrichment *noun* making something richer

enrol *verb* (**enrols, enrolling, enrolled**)
1 to enrol in a society or class is to become a member of it 2 to enrol someone is to make them a member
enrolment *noun* becoming a member or making someone a member

ensemble *noun* (*plural* **ensembles**)
(*pronounced* ahn-sahmbl)
1 a set of matching clothes, or a group of other things that go together 2 a group of musicians

ensue *verb* (**ensues, ensuing, ensued**)
to ensue is to happen or come afterwards

ensure *verb* (**ensures, ensuring, ensured**)
to ensure something is to make sure of it
♦ *Please ensure that you leave the room tidy when you go*

entangle *verb* (**entangles, entangling, entangled**)
to entangle something is to get it tangled
entanglement *noun* being tangled

enter *verb* (**enters, entering, entered**)
1 to enter is to come in or go in **2** to enter something in a list or book is to put it there **3** to enter data in a computer is to key it in **4** to enter for a competition or examination is to take part in it

enterprise *noun* (*plural* **enterprises**)
1 enterprise is being adventurous **2** an enterprise is a difficult or important task or project

enterprising *adjective*
adventurous; courageous

entertain *verb* (**entertains, entertaining, entertained**)
1 to entertain someone is to amuse them or give them pleasure, as a singer or comedian does **2** to entertain people is to have them as guests and give them food and drink
entertainer *noun* someone such as a singer or comedian who entertains people
entertainment *noun* something that entertains people

enthusiasm *noun* (*plural* **enthusiasms**)
a strong liking or interest

enthusiast *noun* (*plural* **enthusiasts**)
a person who has an enthusiasm for something ♦ *Her brother is a football enthusiast*

enthusiastic *adjective*
full of enthusiasm ♦ *She is very enthusiastic about breeding mice*
enthusiastically *adverb* in an enthusiastic way

entire *adjective*
whole or complete ♦ *The entire school gathered in the field for a photograph*
entirely *adverb* completely **entirety** *noun* the whole of something

entitle *verb* (**entitles, entitling, entitled**)
to entitle someone to something is to give them a right to it ♦ *The voucher entitles you to a free drink with your pizza*

entitled *adjective*
having as a title ♦ *Dickens wrote a book entitled 'Oliver Twist'*

entrance[1] *noun* (*plural* **entrances**)
(*pronounced* en-transs)
1 the way into a place **2** coming into a room or on to a stage or arena ♦ *Everyone clapped when the clowns made their entrance*

entrance[2] *verb* (**entrances, entrancing, entranced**) (*pronounced* in-trahnss)
to entrance someone is to delight or enchant them

entrant *noun* (*plural* **entrants**)
someone who goes in for a competition or examination

entreat *verb* (**entreats, entreating, entreated**)
to entreat someone is to ask them seriously or earnestly
entreaty *noun* an earnest request

entrust *verb* (**entrusts, entrusting, entrusted**)
to entrust someone with something, or to entrust something to someone, is to give it to them to look after

entry *noun* (*plural* **entries**)
1 an entrance **2** something written in a list or diary

envelop *verb* (**envelops, enveloping, enveloped**)
(*pronounced* in-vel-op)
to envelop something is to cover or wrap it completely ♦ *The mountain was enveloped in mist*

envelope *noun* (*plural* **envelopes**)
(*pronounced* en-ve-lohp or on-ve-lohp)
a wrapper or covering, especially for a letter

envious *adjective*
feeling envy
enviously *adverb* in an envious way

environment *noun* (*plural* **environments**)
1 surroundings, especially as they affect people and other living things ♦ *Some animals and plants can die out if their environment is damaged* **2** the environment is the natural world of the land and sea and air
environmental *adjective* to do with the environment

environmentalist *noun* (*plural* **environmentalists**)
a person who wants to protect the environment

envy ➤ *noun*
a discontented feeling you have when you want something that someone else has got

envy ➤ *verb* (**envies, envying, envied**)
to envy someone is to feel envy about them

enzyme *noun* (*plural* **enzymes**)
a chemical substance that the body produces and that causes changes such as those involved in digesting food

epic *noun* (*plural* **epics**)
1 a story or poem about heroes **2** an exciting or spectacular film

epidemic *noun* (*plural* **epidemics**)
a disease that spreads quickly among the people of an area

epilepsy *noun*
a disease of the nervous system, which causes convulsions

epileptic ➤ *adjective*
to do with epilepsy

epileptic ➤ *noun* (*plural* **epileptics**)
someone with epilepsy

epilogue *noun* (*plural* **epilogues**)
(*pronounced* **ep**-i-log)
words written or spoken at the end of a story or a play

episode *noun* (*plural* **episodes**)
1 one event in a series of happenings
2 one programme in a radio or television serial

epistle *noun* (*plural* **epistles**)
a letter, especially one forming part of the New Testament

epitaph *noun* (*plural* **epitaphs**)
words written on a tomb or describing a person who has died

epoch *noun* (*plural* **epochs**) (*pronounced* **ee**-pok)
an era

equal ➤ *adjective*
the same in amount, size, or value
to be equal to something is to have the strength or ability to do it ♦ *She was equal to the task*

equal ➤ *noun* (*plural* **equals**)
a person or thing that is equal to another ♦ *He thought he was his sister's equal at maths*

equal ➤ *verb* (**equals, equalling, equalled**)
to equal something is to be the same in amount, size, or value

equality *noun*
being equal

equalize *verb* (**equalizes, equalizing, equalized**)
to equalize things is to make them equal

equalizer *noun* (*plural* **equalizers**)
a goal or point that makes the scores in a game equal

equally *adverb*
in the same way or to the same extent
♦ *You are all equally to blame*

equation *noun* (*plural* **equations**)
(*pronounced* i-**kway**-zhon)
(*in Mathematics*) a statement that two amounts are equal, for example $3 + 4 = 2 + 5$

equator *noun* (*pronounced* i-**kway**-ter)
an imaginary line round the earth at an equal distance from the North and South Poles

equatorial *adjective* to do with the equator or near the equator

equestrian *adjective*
to do with horse-riding

equilateral *adjective* (*pronounced* ee-kwi-**lat**-er-al)
an equilateral triangle has all its sides equal

equilibrium *noun* (*plural* **equilibria**)
(*pronounced* ee-kwi-**lib**-ri-um)
a state of even balance

equinox *noun* (*plural* **equinoxes**)
the time of year when day and night are equal in length (about 20 March in spring and about 22 September in autumn)

equip *verb* (**equips, equipping, equipped**)
to equip someone or something is to supply them with what is needed ♦ *Are you equipped for mountaineering?*

equipment *noun*
the things needed for a special purpose

equivalent *adjective*
equal in value, importance, or meaning
equivalence *noun* being equivalent

era *noun* (*plural* **eras**) (*pronounced* **eer**-a)
a period of history

erase *verb* (**erases, erasing, erased**)
1 to erase something written is to rub it out **2** to erase a recording on magnetic tape is to wipe it out

eraser *noun* a piece of rubber or plastic for erasing writing

erect ➤ *adjective*
standing straight up

erect ➤ *verb* (**erects, erecting, erected**)
to erect something is to set it up or build it
erection *noun* erecting something; something that has been erected

ermine *noun* (*plural* **ermine**)
1 a kind of weasel with brown fur that turns white in winter 2 this white fur

erode *verb* (**erodes, eroding, eroded**)
to erode something is to wear it away ♦ *Water has eroded the rocks*

erosion *noun*
the wearing away of the earth's surface by the action of water and wind

errand *noun* (*plural* **errands**)
a short journey to take a message or fetch something

erratic *adjective* (*pronounced* i-**rat**-ik)
not reliable or regular
erratically *adverb* in an erratic way

erroneous *adjective* (*pronounced* ir-**oh**-nee-us)
wrong; incorrect

error *noun* (*plural* **errors**)
a mistake
in error by mistake

erupt *verb* (**erupts, erupting, erupted**)
1 to erupt is to burst out 2 a volcano erupts when it shoots out lava
eruption *noun* erupting

escalate *verb* (**escalates, escalating, escalated**)
to escalate is to become gradually greater or more serious ♦ *The riots escalated into a war*
escalation *noun* escalating

escalator *noun* (*plural* **escalators**)
a staircase with a revolving band of steps moving up or down

escape ➤ *verb* (**escapes, escaping, escaped**)
1 to escape is to get free or get away 2 to escape something is to avoid it ♦ *He escaped the washing-up*

escape ➤ *noun* (*plural* **escapes**)
1 escaping 2 a way to escape

escort ➤ *noun* (*plural* **escorts**) (*pronounced* **ess**-kort)
1 a person or group who accompanies someone, especially to give protection 2 a group of vehicles, ships, or aircraft accompanying someone or something

escort ➤ *verb* (**escorts, escorting, escorted**) (*pronounced* i-**skort**)
to escort someone or something is to act as an escort to them

Eskimo *noun* (*plural* **Eskimos** or **Eskimo**)
one of the people who live in very cold parts of North America, Greenland, and Siberia

especially *adverb*
chiefly; more than anything else ♦ *I like buns, especially cream buns*

espionage *noun* (*pronounced* **ess**-pi-on-ah*z*h)
spying

esplanade *noun* (*plural* **esplanades**)
a flat open area for walking, especially by the sea

Esq. a title sometimes put after a man's surname on letters, when no title is used before his name, for example John Smith Esq.

-ess *suffix*
used to make feminine forms of words, for example *lioness* and *actress*

essay *noun* (*plural* **essays**)
a short piece of writing on one subject

essence *noun* (*plural* **essences**)
1 the most important quality or ingredient of something 2 a concentrated liquid

essential ➤ *adjective*
that you must have or do
essentially *adverb* basically; necessarily

essential ➤ *noun* (*plural* **essentials**)
something you must have or do

establish *verb* (**establishes, establishing, established**)
1 to establish a business, government, or relationship is to start it on a firm basis 2 to establish a fact is to show that it is true ♦ *He managed to establish his innocence*

establishment *noun* (*plural* **establishments**)
1 establishing something 2 a place where business is carried on; an organization
the Establishment the people in positions of power and influence

estate *noun* (*plural* **estates**)
1 an area of land with a set of houses or factories on it 2 a large area of land belonging to one person 3 everything that a person owns when they die

estate agent *noun* (*plural* **estate agents**)
someone whose business is selling or letting buildings and land

estate car *noun* (*plural* **estate cars**)
a car with a door or doors at the back, and
rear seats that can be removed or folded
away

esteem *verb* (**esteems, esteeming, esteemed**)
to esteem someone or something is to
think they are excellent

estimate ➢ *noun* (*plural* **estimates**)
(*pronounced* **ess**-ti-mat)
a rough calculation or guess about an
amount or value

estimate ➢ *verb* (**estimates, estimating,
estimated**) (*pronounced* **ess**-ti-mayt)
to estimate is to make an estimate

estimation *noun*

  1 making an estimate **2** opinion ♦ *It is
very good in my estimation*

estuary *noun* (*plural* **estuaries**) (*pronounced*
ess-tew-er-i)
the mouth of a large river where it flows
into the sea

etc. short for **et cetera**

et cetera and other similar things; and so on

etch *verb* (**etches, etching, etched**)
to etch a picture is to make it by engraving
on a metal plate with an acid
  etching *noun* a picture made in this way

eternal *adjective*
lasting for ever; not ending or changing
  eternally *adverb* for ever **eternity** *noun* a
state in which time has no end

ether *noun* (*pronounced* **ee**-ther)
  1 ether is a colourless liquid that
evaporates easily, and is used as an
anaesthetic or a solvent **2** the ether is the
upper air

ethnic *adjective*
belonging to a particular national or racial
group

etymology *noun* (*plural* **etymologies**)
  1 etymology is the study of words and
where they come from **2** a word's
etymology is a description of where it came
from

EU short for **European Union**

eucalyptus *noun* (*plural* **eucalyptuses**)
  (*pronounced* yoo-ka-**lip**-tus)
an evergreen tree from which an oil is
obtained

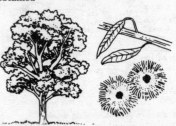

euphemism *noun* (*plural* **euphemisms**)
a word or phrase which is used instead of
an impolite or less tactful one; 'pass away'
is a euphemism for 'die'
  euphemistic *adjective* serving as a
euphemism

Eurasian *adjective*
having European and Asian parents or
ancestors

euro *noun* (*plural* **euros** or **euro**)
the single currency introduced in the
European Union in 1999.

European ➢ *adjective*
coming from Europe or to do with Europe

European ➢ *noun* (*plural* **Europeans**)
a European person

euthanasia *noun* (*pronounced*
yooth-an-**ay**-zi-a)
causing someone to die gently and without
pain when they are suffering from an
incurable disease

evacuate *verb* (**evacuates, evacuating,
evacuated**)
to evacuate people is to move them away
from a dangerous place
  evacuation *noun* evacuating people **evacuee**
noun someone who is evacuated

evade *verb* (**evades, evading, evaded**)
to evade someone or something is to make
an effort to avoid them

evaluate *verb* (**evaluates, evaluating, evaluated**)
to evaluate something is to estimate its
value
  evaluation *noun* evaluating something

evangelist *noun* (*plural* **evangelists**)
someone who tells people about the
Christian gospel
  evangelical *adjective* to do with preaching
the gospel **evangelism** *noun* preaching the
gospel

evaporate *verb* (**evaporates, evaporating, evaporated**)
to evaporate is to change from liquid into steam or vapour
evaporation *noun* the process of evaporating

evasion *noun* (*plural* **evasions**)
1 evasion is evading something **2** an evasion is an answer that tries to avoid the question being asked

evasive *adjective*
trying to avoid answering something; not honest or straightforward

eve *noun* (*plural* **eves**)
the day or evening before an important day, for example Christmas Eve

even ➢ *adjective*
1 level and smooth **2** calm and stable ♦ *He has a very even temper* **3** equal ♦ *Our scores were even* **4** (*in Mathematics*) able to be divided exactly by two ♦ *6 and 14 are even numbers*
to get even with someone is to take revenge on them
evenly *adverb* in an even way **evenness** *noun* being even

even ➢ *verb* (**evens, evening, evened**)
1 to even something is to make it even **2** to even or even out is to become even

even ➢ *adverb*
used to emphasize another word ♦ *You haven't even started your work!* ♦ *I ran fast, but she ran even faster* ♦ *She even ignored her mother*
even so although that is correct

evening *noun* (*plural* **evenings**)
the time at the end of the day before night time

event *noun* (*plural* **events**)
1 something that happens, especially something important **2** an item in an athletics contest ♦ *The next event will be the long jump*
at all events or **in any event** anyway

eventful *adjective*
full of happenings, especially remarkable or exciting ones ♦ *They had an eventful train journey across the USA*

eventual *adjective*
happening at last or as a result ♦ *Many failures preceded his eventual success*

eventually *adverb*
finally, in the end ♦ *We eventually managed to get the door open*

ever *adverb*
1 at any time ♦ *It's the best present I've ever had* **2** always ♦ *ever hopeful* **3** (*informal*) used for emphasis ♦ *Why ever didn't you tell me?*

ever so or **ever such** (*informal*) very much ♦ *I'm ever so pleased* ♦ *She's ever such a nice girl*

evergreen ➢ *adjective*
having green leaves all through the year

evergreen ➢ *noun* (*plural* **evergreens**)
an evergreen tree

everlasting *adjective*
lasting for ever or for a long time

every *adjective*
all the people or things of a particular kind; each ♦ *Every child should learn to swim*
every other each alternate one; every second one ♦ *Every other house had a garage*

everybody *pronoun*
everyone

everyday *adjective*
happening or used every day; ordinary ♦ *Just wear your everyday clothes*

everyone *pronoun*
every person; all people ♦ *Everyone likes her*

everything *pronoun*
1 all things; all ♦ *Everything you need is here* **2** the only or most important thing ♦ *Beauty is not everything*

everywhere *adverb*
in all places

evict *verb* (**evicts, evicting, evicted**)
to evict someone is to make them move out of a house
eviction *noun* evicting someone

evidence *noun*
anything that gives people reason to believe something

evident *adjective*
obvious; clearly seen ♦ *It is evident that he is lying*
evidently *adverb* clearly; obviously

evil ➢ *adjective*
wicked and harmful
evilly *adverb* in an evil way

evil ➢ *noun* (*plural* **evils**)
something evil or harmful

evolution *noun* (*pronounced* ee-vo-loo-shon)
1 gradual change into something different **2** the development of animals and plants from earlier or simpler forms of life
evolutionary *adjective* to do with evolution

evolve *verb* (**evolves, evolving, evolved**)
to develop gradually or naturally

ewe *noun* (*plural* **ewes**) (*pronounced* yoo)
a female sheep

ex- *prefix*
meaning something or someone that used to be, as in *ex-husband*

exact *adjective*
1 completely correct **2** giving all the details ♦ *He gave an exact description of the robbers*
exactly *adverb* in an exact way; correctly
exactness *noun* being correct

exaggerate *verb* (**exaggerates, exaggerating, exaggerated**)
to exaggerate something is to make it seem bigger or better or worse than it really is
exaggeration *noun* exaggerating

exalt *verb* (**exalts, exalting, exalted**)
1 to exalt someone is to make them higher in rank **2** to exalt someone is also to praise them highly

exam *noun* (*plural* **exams**)
(*informal*) an examination

examination *noun* (*plural* **examinations**)
1 a test of someone's knowledge or skill **2** a close inspection of something

examine *verb* (**examines, examining, examined**)
to examine something is to look at it closely or in detail

examiner *noun* (*plural* **examiners**)
a person who sets and marks an examination to test students' knowledge

example *noun* (*plural* **examples**)
1 a single thing or event that shows what others of the same kind are like **2** a person or thing that you should copy or learn from
for example as an example

exasperate *verb* (**exasperates, exasperating, exasperated**)
to exasperate someone is to make them very annoyed
exasperation *noun* a feeling of being exasperated

excavate *verb* (**excavates, excavating, excavated**)
to excavate a piece of land is to dig in it, especially in building or archaeology
excavation *noun* excavating land **excavator** *noun* a person or machine that excavates

exceed *verb* (**exceeds, exceeding, exceeded**)
1 to exceed an amount or achievement is to be more than it or do better than it **2** to exceed a rule or limit is to go beyond it when you are not supposed to ♦ *The driver was exceeding the speed limit*

exceedingly *adverb*
extremely; very much

excel *verb* (**excels, excelling, excelled**)
to excel at something is to be very good at it, and better than everyone else

excellent *adjective*
very good; of the best kind
excellence *noun* being excellent

except *preposition*
not including; apart from ♦ *Everyone got a prize except me*

exception *noun* (*plural* **exceptions**)
1 something or someone that does not follow the normal rule **2** something that is left out
to take exception to something is to complain about it

exceptional *adjective*
unusual ♦ *She has exceptional skill*
exceptionally *adverb* to an unusual degree

excerpt *noun* (*plural* **excerpts**)
a piece taken from a book or story or film

excess *noun* (*plural* **excesses**)
too much of something ♦ *We have an excess of food*

excessive *adjective*
too much or too great
excessively *adverb* too ♦ *They are excessively greedy*

exchange ➤ *verb* (**exchanges, exchanging, exchanged**)
to exchange something is to give it and receive something else for it

exchange ➤ *noun* (*plural* **exchanges**)
1 exchanging **2** a place where telephone lines are connected to each other when a call is made **3** a place where company shares are bought and sold

excite *verb* (**excites, exciting, excited**)
to excite someone is to make them eager and enthusiastic about something ♦ *The thought of the outing excited them*
excitable *adjective* easily excited **excitedly** *adverb* in an excited way

excitement *noun* (*plural* **excitements**)
1 excitement is being excited **2** an excitement is something that excites you

exclaim *verb* (**exclaims, exclaiming, exclaimed**)
to exclaim is to shout or cry out

exclamation *noun* (*plural* **exclamations**)
1 shouting or crying out **2** a word or phrase you say out loud that expresses a strong feeling such as surprise or pain

exclamation mark *noun* (*plural* **exclamation marks**)
the punctuation mark (!) placed after an exclamation

exclude *verb* (**excludes, excluding, excluded**)
1 to exclude someone or something is to keep them out **2** to exclude something is to leave it out ♦ *Do not exclude the possibility of rain*
exclusion *noun* excluding someone or something

exclusive *adjective*
1 not shared with others ♦ *Today's newspaper has an exclusive report about the match* **2** allowing only a few people to be involved ♦ *They joined an exclusive club*
exclusively *adverb* in an exclusive way

excrement *noun*
waste matter excreted from the body

excrete *verb* (**excretes, excreting, excreted**)
to excrete is to pass waste matter out of your body
excretion *noun* excreting waste matter

excursion *noun* (*plural* **excursions**)
a short journey or outing made for pleasure

excuse ➤ *noun* (*plural* **excuses**)
(*pronounced* iks-**kewss**)
a reason given to explain why something wrong has been done

excuse ➤ *verb* (**excuses, excusing, excused**)
(*pronounced* iks-**kewz**)
1 to excuse someone is to forgive them
2 to excuse someone something is to allow them not to do it ♦ *Please may I be excused swimming?*
excuse me a polite apology for interrupting or disagreeing
excusable *adjective* able to be excused

execute *verb* (**executes, executing, executed**)
1 to execute someone is to put them to death as a punishment **2** to execute something is to perform or produce it ♦ *She executed the somersault perfectly*
execution *noun* executing someone or something **executioner** *noun* someone who executes people

executive *noun* (*plural* **executives**)
a senior person with authority in a business or government organization

exempt *adjective*
not having to do something that others have to do ♦ *Old people are sometimes exempt from paying bus fares*
exemption *noun* being exempt

exercise ➤ *noun* (*plural* **exercises**)
1 exercise is using your body to make it strong and healthy **2** an exercise is a piece of work done for practice

exercise ➤ *verb* (**exercises, exercising, exercised**)
1 to exercise is to do exercises **2** to exercise an animal is to give it exercise **3** to exercise something is to use it ♦ *You will have to exercise patience*

exercise book *noun* (*plural* **exercise books**)
a book for writing in

exert *verb* (**exerts, exerting, exerted**)
to exert oneself or one's ability is to make an effort to get something done ♦ *He exerted all his strength to bend the bar*
exertion *noun* exerting yourself; effort

exhale *verb* (**exhales, exhaling, exhaled**)
to exhale is to breathe out
exhalation *noun* breathing out

exhaust ➤ *noun* (*plural* **exhausts**)
1 the waste gases from an engine **2** the pipe these gases are sent out through

exhaust ➤ *verb* (**exhausts, exhausting, exhausted**)
1 to exhaust someone is to make them very tired **2** to exhaust something is to use it up completely
exhaustion *noun* being very tired

exhibit ➤ *verb* (**exhibits, exhibiting, exhibited**)
to exhibit something is to show it in public, especially in a gallery or museum
exhibitor *noun* someone who exhibits something

exhibit ➤ *noun* (*plural* **exhibits**)
something displayed in a gallery or museum

exhibition *noun* (*plural* **exhibitions**)
a collection of things put on display for people to look at

exile ➤ *verb* (**exiles, exiling, exiled**)
to exile someone is to send them away from their country

exile ➤ *noun* (*plural* **exiles**)
1 exile is having to live away from your own country ♦ *He was in exile for ten years* **2** an exile is a person who is exiled

exist *verb* (**exists, existing, existed**)
1 to exist is to have life or be real ♦ *Do ghosts exist?* **2** to exist is also to stay alive ♦ *They existed on biscuits and water*

existence *noun* (*plural* **existences**)
1 existing or being **2** staying alive ♦ *It was a real struggle for existence*

exit ➤ *noun* (*plural* **exits**)
1 the way out of a place **2** going out of a room or going off a stage or arena ♦ *The clowns then made their exit*

exit ➤ *verb* (**exits, exiting, exited**)
to exit is to leave a stage or arena

exorcize *verb* (**exorcizes, exorcizing, exorcized**)
to exorcize a spirit is to get rid of it, usually with a special ceremony
exorcism *noun* exorcizing a spirit **exorcist** *noun* someone who exorcizes a spirit

exotic *adjective*
unusual and colourful, especially because it comes from another part of the world

expand *verb* (**expands, expanding, expanded**)
1 to expand something is to make it larger
2 to expand is to become larger
expansion *noun* becoming larger or making something larger

expanse *noun* (*plural* **expanses**)
a wide area

expect *verb* (**expects, expecting, expected**)
1 to expect something is to think that it will probably happen ♦ *We expected it would rain* 2 to be expecting someone is to be waiting for them to arrive 3 to expect something is to think that it ought to happen ♦ *She expects us to be quiet*

expectant *adjective*
1 full of expectation or hope 2 an expectant mother is a woman who is pregnant
expectantly *adverb* in an expectant way

expectation *noun* (*plural* **expectations**)
1 expectation is expecting something or being hopeful 2 an expectation is something you hope to get

expecting *adjective*
a woman is expecting when she is pregnant

expedition *noun* (*plural* **expeditions**)
a journey made in order to do something
♦ *They are going on a climbing expedition*

expel *verb* (**expels, expelling, expelled**)
1 to expel something is to send or force it out ♦ *The fan expels stale air and fumes*
2 to expel someone is to make them leave a school or country ♦ *He was expelled for bullying*

expenditure *noun*
the spending of money or use of effort
♦ *We must reduce our expenditure*

expense *noun* (*plural* **expenses**)
the cost of doing something

expensive *adjective*
costing a lot of money

experience ➤ *noun* (*plural* **experiences**)
1 experience is what you learn from doing and seeing things 2 an experience is something that has happened to you

experience ➤ *verb* (**experiences, experiencing, experienced**)
to experience something is to have it happen to you

experienced *adjective*
having skill or knowledge from much experience

experiment ➤ *noun* (*plural* **experiments**)
a test made in order to study what happens
experimental *adjective* to do with experiments **experimentally** *adverb* as an experiment

experiment ➤ *verb* (**experiments, experimenting, experimented**)
to experiment is to carry out experiments
experimentation *noun* doing experiments

expert ➤ *noun* (*plural* **experts**)
someone who has skill or special knowledge in something

expert ➤ *adjective*
having great knowledge or skill

expertise *noun*
expert ability or knowledge

expire *verb* (**expires, expiring, expired**)
1 to expire is to come to an end or to stop being usable ♦ *Your TV licence has expired* 2 to expire is also to die
expiry *noun* the time when something expires

explain *verb* (**explains, explaining, explained**)
1 to explain something is to make it clear to someone else 2 to explain a fact or event is to show why it happens ♦ *That explains his absence*
explanation *noun* explaining something; something that explains **explanatory** *adjective* that explains something

explode *verb* (**explodes, exploding, exploded**)
1 to explode is to burst or suddenly release energy with a loud bang 2 to explode a bomb is to set it off 3 to explode is to increase suddenly or quickly ♦ *The city's population exploded to 3 million in a year*

exploit ➤ *noun* (*plural* **exploits**) (*pronounced* **eks**-ploit)
a brave or exciting deed

exploit ➤ *verb* (**exploits, exploiting, exploited**) (*pronounced* iks-**ploit**)
1 to exploit resources is to use or develop them 2 to exploit someone is to use them selfishly
exploitation *noun* exploiting something or someone

explore *verb* (**explores, exploring, explored**)
1 to explore a place is to travel through it to find out more about it 2 to explore a subject is to examine it carefully ♦ *We need to explore all the possibilities*

exploration *noun* exploring a place
exploratory *adjective* for the purpose of exploring **explorer** *noun* someone who explores a country

explosion *noun* (*plural* **explosions**)
1 the exploding of a bomb or other weapon
2 a sudden or quick increase ♦ *There was a population explosion after the war*

explosive ➤ *noun* (*plural* **explosives**)
a substance that can explode

explosive ➤ *adjective*
likely to explode; able to cause an explosion

export ➤ *verb* (**exports, exporting, exported**) (*pronounced* iks-**port**)
to export goods is to send them abroad to be sold
exporter *noun* someone who exports goods

export ➤ *noun* (*plural* **exports**) (*pronounced* **eks**-port)
something that is sent abroad to be sold

expose *verb* (**exposes, exposing, exposed**)
1 to expose something is to reveal or uncover it 2 to expose someone is to show that they are to blame for something 3 to expose a photographic film is to let light reach it in a camera, so as to take a picture

exposure *noun* (*plural* **exposures**)
1 exposure is being harmed by the weather when in the open without enough protection 2 an exposure is a single photograph or frame on a film

express ➤ *adjective*
going or sent quickly

express ➤ *noun* (*plural* **expresses**)
a fast train stopping at only a few stations

express ➤ *verb* (**expresses, expressing, expressed**)
to express an idea or feeling is to put it into words

expression *noun* (*plural* **expressions**)
1 the look on a person's face that shows what they are thinking or feeling 2 a word or phrase 3 a way of speaking or performing music that expresses feelings
expressive *adjective* showing a person's feelings

expulsion *noun* (*plural* **expulsions**)
expelling or being expelled

exquisite *adjective*
very delicate or beautiful
exquisitely *adverb* in an exquisite way

extend *verb* (**extends, extending, extended**)
1 to extend is to stretch out 2 to extend something is to make it longer or larger 3 to extend a greeting or welcome is to offer it

extension *noun* (*plural* **extensions**)
1 extension is extending or being extended 2 an extension is something added on, especially to a building 3 an extension is also an extra telephone in an office or house

extensive *adjective*
covering a large area ♦ *The house has extensive gardens*
extensively *adverb* over a large area

extent *noun* (*plural* **extents**)
1 the area or length of something 2 an amount or level ♦ *The extent of the damage was enormous*

exterior *noun* (*plural* **exteriors**)
the outside of something

exterminate *verb* (**exterminates, exterminating, exterminated**)
to exterminate a people or breed of animal is to kill all the members of it
extermination *noun* exterminating people or animals

external *adjective*
outside
externally *adverb* on the outside

extinct *adjective*
1 not existing any more ♦ *The dodo is an extinct bird* 2 not burning or active ♦ *We saw an extinct volcano*
extinction *noun* being extinct

extinguish *verb* (**extinguishes, extinguishing, extinguished**)
to extinguish a fire or light is to put it out
extinguisher *noun* a device for putting out a fire

extra ➤ *adjective*
more than usual; added ♦ *There is an extra charge for taking a bicycle on the train*

extra ➤ *noun* (*plural* **extras**)
1 an extra person or thing 2 someone acting as part of the crowd in a film or play

extra- *prefix*
1 more than usual, as in *extra-special*
2 outside or beyond something, as in *extraterrestrial*

extract ➤ *noun* (*plural* **extracts**) (*pronounced* **eks**-trakt)
1 a piece taken from a book, play, or film
2 something obtained from something else ♦ *a plant extract*

extract ➤ *verb* (**extracts, extracting, extracted**) (*pronounced* iks-**trakt**)
to extract something is to remove it or take it out of something else

extraction *noun*
1 taking something out 2 the place or people that someone comes from ♦ *She is of Indian extraction*

extraordinary *adjective*
unusual or very strange
extraordinarily *adverb* in an extraordinary way

extrasensory *adjective*
beyond the range of the ordinary senses

extraterrestrial ➤ *adjective*
existing in or coming from another planet

extraterrestrial ➤ *noun* (*plural* **extraterrestrials**)
a living thing from another planet, especially in science fiction

extravagant *adjective*
spending or using too much of something
extravagance *noun* being extravagant
extravagantly *adverb* in an extravagant way

extreme ➤ *adjective*
1 very great or strong ◆ *They were suffering from extreme cold* 2 farthest away ◆ *She lives in the extreme north of the country*

extreme ➤ *noun* (*plural* **extremes**)
1 something very great, strong, or far away 2 either end of something

extremely *adverb*
as much or as far as possible; very much ◆ *They are extremely pleased*

extremity *noun* (*plural* **extremities**) (*pronounced* iks-trem-it-ee)
an extreme point; the very end of something

exuberant *adjective*
very cheerful or lively
exuberance *noun* being exuberant

exult *verb* (**exults, exulting, exulted**)
to exult is to rejoice or be very pleased
exultant *adjective* rejoicing **exultation** *noun* a feeling of rejoicing

eye ➤ *noun* (*plural* **eyes**)
1 the organ of your body used for seeing 2 the small hole in a needle 3 the centre of a storm

eye ➤ *verb* (**eyes, eyeing, eyed**)
to eye someone or something is to look at them closely

eyeball *noun* (*plural* **eyeballs**)
the ball-shaped part of your eye, inside your eyelids

eyebrow *noun* (*plural* **eyebrows**)
the curved fringe of hair growing above each eye

eyelash *noun* (*plural* **eyelashes**)
one of the short hairs that grow on your eyelids

eyelid *noun* (*plural* **eyelids**)
the upper or lower fold of skin that can close over your eyeball

eyepiece *noun* (*plural* **eyepieces**)
the lens of a telescope or microscope that you put to your eye

eyesight *noun*
the ability to see

eyesore *noun* (*plural* **eyesores**)
something that is ugly to look at

eyewitness *noun* (*plural* **eyewitnesses**)
someone who actually saw something happen, especially an accident or crime

Ff

F short for
Fahrenheit

fable *noun* (*plural* **fables**)
a story which teaches a lesson about behaviour, often with animals as characters

fabric *noun* (*plural* **fabrics**)
cloth

fabricate *verb* (**fabricates, fabricating, fabricated**)
1 to fabricate something is to make it, especially in a factory 2 to fabricate a story or excuse is to make it up

fabulous *adjective*
1 very great, as in stories ◆ *The prince enjoyed fabulous wealth* 2 (*informal*) wonderful; marvellous 3 spoken of or described in fables and myths ◆ *Dragons are fabulous creatures*

face ➤ *noun* (*plural* **faces**)
1 the front part of your head 2 the look on a person's face ◆ *She had a friendly face* 3 the front or upper side of something ◆ *Put the cards face down* 4 a surface ◆ *A cube has six faces*
face to face looking directly at someone
facial *adjective* to do with the face

face ➤ *verb* (**faces, facing, faced**)
1 to face in a certain direction is to look there or have the front in that direction ◆ *Please face the front* ◆ *The church faces the school* 2 to face a problem or danger is to meet or deal with it confidently or bravely

facet *noun* (*plural* **facets**) (*pronounced* fass-it)
1 one aspect or view of something 2 one side of a many-sided object like a diamond

facetious *adjective* (*pronounced* fa-see-shus)
trying to be funny at an unsuitable time
facetiously *adverb* in a facetious way

facilitate *verb* (**facilitates, facilitating, facilitated**)
to facilitate something is to make it easier

facility *noun* (*plural* **facilities**) (*pronounced* fa-sil-i-ti*)
1 something that helps you to do things
♦ *The youth club has facilities for dancing and sport* **2** easiness ♦ *She played the piano with amazing facility*

fact *noun* (*plural* **facts**)
something that is true or certain
as a matter of fact or **in fact** really
the facts of life knowledge of how humans have sex and produce babies

factor *noun* (*plural* **factors**)
1 something that helps to bring about a result or situation ♦ *Hard work has been a factor in her success* **2** a number by which a larger number can be divided exactly ♦ *2 and 3 are factors of 6*

factory *noun* (*plural* **factories**)
a large building where machines are used to make things

factual *adjective*
based on fact; real
factually *adverb* in a factual way

fad *noun* (*plural* **fads**)
1 a craze or fashion ♦ *The fad for jogging has largely died away* **2** someone's particular like or dislike ♦ *He has a fad about the food he eats*

fade *verb* (**fades, fading, faded**)
1 to fade is to lose colour, freshness, or strength **2** to fade or fade away is to disappear gradually **3** to fade in a sound is to make it gradually louder, and to fade out a sound is to make it gradually softer

faeces *plural noun* (*pronounced* fee-seez*)
solid waste that is passed out of the body

fag *noun* (*plural* **fags**)
(*informal*) **1** something that is tiring or boring **2** a cigarette

fagged or **fagged out** *adjective*
(*informal*) very tired

faggot *noun* (*plural* **faggots**)
a meat ball made of baked chopped liver

Fahrenheit *adjective* (*pronounced* fa-ren-hyt*)
using a scale for measuring temperature that gives 32 degrees for freezing water and 212 degrees for boiling water

fail ➤ *verb* (**fails, failing, failed**)
1 to fail is to try to do something but not be able to do it **2** to fail is also to become weak or useless or to come to an end ♦ *The batteries are failing* ♦ *The crops failed last year* **3** to fail to do something is not to do it when you should ♦ *He failed to warn me of the danger*

fail ➤ *noun* (*plural* **fails**)
not being successful in an examination
♦ *She has five passes and one fail*
without fail definitely ♦ *I'll be there without fail*

failing *noun* (*plural* **failings**)
a fault or weakness

failure *noun* (*plural* **failures**)
1 failure is not being successful **2** a failure is someone or something that has failed

faint ➤ *adjective* (**fainter, faintest**)
1 weak; not clear or distinct **2** nearly unconscious; exhausted
faintly *adverb* softly; not clearly **faintness** *noun* being faint

faint ➤ *verb* (**faints, fainting, fainted**)
to faint is to become unconscious for a short time

faint-hearted *adjective*
not having much courage or confidence

fair[1] *adjective* (**fairer, fairest**)
1 right or just; honest ♦ *It was a fair fight* **2** light in colour ♦ *The sisters both had fair hair* **3** moderate; quite good ♦ *I've got a fair idea of what is needed* **4** fine; favourable ♦ *The weather turned out fair after all*
fairness *noun* being fair

fair[2] *noun* (*plural* **fairs**)
1 a group of outdoor entertainments like roundabouts, sideshows, and stalls **2** an exhibition or market

fairground *noun* (*plural* **fairgrounds**)
a place where a fair is held

fairly *adverb*
1 honestly; justly **2** moderately; quite ♦ *It is fairly hard*

fairy *noun* (*plural* **fairies**)
an imaginary small creature with magic powers

fairyland *noun*
a place where fairies live; an imaginary place

fairy story or **fairy tale** *noun* (*plural* **fairy stories** or **fairy tales**)
a story about fairies; an unbelievable story

faith *noun* (*plural* **faiths**)
1 faith is strong belief or trust **2** a faith is a religion
in good faith with honest intentions

faithful *adjective*
reliable; trustworthy
faithfully *adverb* in a faithful way **faithfulness** *noun* being faithful

fake ➤ *noun* (*plural* **fakes**)
a copy of something made to deceive people

fake ➤ *verb* (fakes, faking, faked)
1 to fake something is to make it look real so as to deceive people 2 to fake something is also to pretend to have it
♦ *He faked illness so as to miss games*
faker *noun* someone who fakes something

falcon *noun* (*plural* falcons)
a small kind of hawk
falconry *noun* using falcons to hunt other birds

fall ➤ *verb* (falls, falling, fell, fallen)
1 to fall is to come down quickly towards the ground 2 numbers or prices fall when they get lower or smaller 3 a city or stronghold falls when it is captured
4 soldiers fall when they die in battle
5 when silence falls it becomes quiet 6 to fall sick or ill is to become ill 7 a look or glance falls on someone when it is directed at them
to fall back on something or **someone** is to rely on them in a difficulty
to fall for someone or **something** is to like them a lot
to fall in is to collapse
to fall out is to quarrel
to fall through is to fail to happen ♦ *Our plans have fallen through*

fall ➤ *noun* (*plural* falls)
1 the action of falling 2 (*in America*) autumn

fallacy *noun* (*plural* fallacies)
a false idea or belief
fallacious *adjective* false

fallout *noun*
radioactive material carried in the air after a nuclear explosion

fallow *adjective*
ploughed but not sown with crops ♦ *The field was left fallow every three years*

falls *plural noun*
a waterfall

false *adjective* (falser, falsest)
1 untrue or incorrect 2 faked; not genuine
3 treacherous or deceitful
falsely *adverb* in a false way **falseness** *noun* being false

falsehood *noun* (*plural* falsehoods)
1 falsehood is telling lies 2 a falsehood is a lie

falter *verb* (falters, faltering, faltered)
1 to falter is to hesitate when you move or speak 2 to falter is also to become weaker
♦ *His courage began to falter*

fame *noun*
being famous
famed *adjective* having fame

familiar *adjective*
1 well-known; often seen or experienced
♦ *It was a familiar sight* 2 knowing something well ♦ *Are you familiar with this story?* 3 very friendly
familiarity *noun* being familiar **familiarly** *adverb* in a familiar way

family *noun* (*plural* families)
1 parents and their children, sometimes including grandchildren and other relations 2 a group of things that are alike in some way

family planning *noun*
the use of contraceptives to control pregnancies

family tree *noun* (*plural* family trees)
a diagram showing how people in a family are related

famine *noun* (*plural* famines)
a severe shortage of food

famished *adjective*
extremely hungry

famous *adjective*
known to a lot of people ♦ *Her uncle is a famous scientist*

fan[1] ➤ *noun* (*plural* fans)
a device for making the air move about, so as to cool people or things

fan ➤ *verb* (fans, fanning, fanned)
to fan something is to send a draught of air at it ♦ *She fanned her face with her hand*
to fan out is to spread out (in the shape of a fan)

fan[2] *noun* (*plural* fans)
an enthusiast or supporter

fanatic *noun* (*plural* **fanatics**) (*pronounced* fa-nat-ik)
someone who is too enthusiastic about something
fanatical *adjective* too enthusiastic **fanatically** *adverb* in a fanatical way

fan belt *noun* (*plural* **fan belts**)
a belt driving the fan that cools a vehicle's radiator

fanciful *adjective*
1 imaginary; not real 2 having a strong imagination

fancy ➤ *noun* (*plural* **fancies**)
1 fancy is imagination 2 a fancy is a liking or desire for something

fancy ➤ *adjective* (**fancier, fanciest**)
decorated; not plain

fancy ➤ *verb* (**fancies, fancying, fancied**)
1 to fancy something is to want it ♦ *I fancied an ice cream* 2 to fancy something unusual is to imagine or think of it ♦ *Just fancy him riding a horse!*

fancy dress *noun*
unusual costume worn to a party or dance, often to make you look like someone else

fanfare *noun* (*plural* **fanfares**)
a short burst of music, often with trumpets and to announce something

fang *noun* (*plural* **fangs**)
a long, sharp tooth

fantastic *adjective*
1 strange or unusual 2 (*informal*) excellent
fantastically *adverb* strangely or unusually

fantasy *noun* (*plural* **fantasies**)
something imaginary or fantastic

far ➤ *adverb* (**farther, farthest**)
1 a long way ♦ *We didn't go far* 2 much; by a great amount ♦ *She's a far better singer than I am*
so far up to now

far ➤ *adjective* (**farther, farthest**)
distant; opposite ♦ *She swam to the far side of the river*

far-away *adjective*
distant ♦ *I'd love to go to far-away places*

farce *noun* (*plural* **farces**)
1 a farce is a far-fetched or absurd kind of comedy 2 farce, or a farce, is a series of ridiculous events ♦ *The meeting ended up in farce* ♦ *The trial was a complete farce*
farcical *adjective* absurd, like farce

fare ➤ *noun* (*plural* **fares**)
the money you pay to travel on a bus, train, ship, or aircraft

fare ➤ *verb* (**fares, faring, fared**)
to fare is to get on or make progress ♦ *How did you fare in your exam?*

farewell *interjection*
goodbye

far-fetched *adjective*
unlikely; difficult to believe

farm ➤ *noun* (*plural* **farms**)
1 an area of land where someone grows crops and keeps animals for food 2 the buildings on land of this kind 3 a farmhouse

farm ➤ *verb* (**farms, farming, farmed**)
1 to farm is to grow crops and raise animals for food 2 to farm land is to use it for growing crops

farmer *noun* (*plural* **farmers**)
someone who owns or looks after a farm

farmhouse *noun* (*plural* **farmhouses**)
the house where a farmer lives

farmyard *noun* (*plural* **farmyards**)
the open area surrounded by farm buildings

farther *adverb* and *adjective*
at or to a greater distance; more distant ♦ *She lives farther from the school than I do*

farthest *adverb* and *adjective*
at or to the greatest distance; most distant

farthing *noun* (*plural* **farthings**)
an old British coin that was worth a quarter of a penny

fascinate *verb* (**fascinates, fascinating, fascinated**)
to fascinate someone is to attract or interest them very much
fascination *noun* being fascinated by someone or something

Fascist *noun* (*plural* **Fascists**) (*pronounced* fash-ist)
a person who supports a dictatorial type of government
Fascism *noun* this type of government

fashion ➤ *noun* (*plural* **fashions**)
1 the style of clothes or other things that most people like at a particular time 2 a way of doing something ♦ *Please continue in the same fashion*

fashion ➤ *verb* (**fashions, fashioning, fashioned**)
to fashion something is to make it in a particular shape or style
fashionable *adjective* following the fashion of the time

fast [1] ➤ *adjective* (**faster, fastest**)
1 moving or done quickly ♦ *He's a fast runner* 2 allowing fast movement ♦ *This is a fast road* 3 firmly fixed ♦ *Make the boat fast* 4 showing a time later than the correct time ♦ *Your watch is fast* 5 a fast colour is one that is not likely to fade

fast ➤ *adverb*
1 quickly 2 firmly
fast asleep deeply asleep

fast[2] *verb* (**fasts, fasting, fasted**)
to fast is to go without food

fasten *verb* (**fastens, fastening, fastened**)
to fasten something is to join it firmly to
something else
fastener or **fastening** *noun* a device that
fastens something

fat ➤ *noun* (*plural* **fats**)
1 the white greasy part of meat 2 an oily
or greasy substance used in cooking

fat ➤ *adjective* (**fatter, fattest**)
1 having a very thick round body 2 thick
♦ *What a fat book!* 3 fat meat is meat
with a lot of fat

fatal *adjective*
causing death or disaster ♦ *There has been
a fatal accident on the motorway*
fatally *adverb* so as to cause death

fatality *noun* (*plural* **fatalities**)
a death caused by war or an accident

fate *noun* (*plural* **fates**)
1 a power that is thought to make things
happen 2 someone's fate is what has
happened or will happen to them

father *noun* (*plural* **fathers**)
a male parent

father-in-law *noun* (*plural* **fathers-in-law**)
the father of your husband or wife

fathom ➤ *noun* (*plural* **fathoms**)
a unit used in measuring the depth of
water, equal to 1·83 metres or 6 feet

fathom ➤ *verb* (**fathoms, fathoming, fathomed**)
to fathom something difficult or tricky is to
work it out ♦ *I can't fathom how you did it*

fatigue *noun* (*pronounced* fa-**teeg**)
1 extreme tiredness 2 weakness in
metals, caused by stress
fatigued *adjective* extremely tired

fatten *verb* (**fattens, fattening, fattened**)
1 to fatten something is to make it fat
2 to fatten is to become fat

fattening *adjective*
fattening food is food that is likely to make
you fat

fatty *adjective* (**fattier, fattiest**)
1 like fat 2 full of fat

fault ➤ *noun* (*plural* **faults**)
something wrong that spoils a person or
thing; a flaw or mistake
at fault wrong; responsible for a mistake
faultless *adjective* having no faults; perfect

fault ➤ *verb* (**faults, faulting, faulted**)
to fault something is to find faults in it

faulty *adjective* (**faultier, faultiest**)
having a fault or faults; not working
properly

fauna *noun* (*pronounced* **faw**-na)
the animals of an area or of a period of
time

favour ➤ *noun* (*plural* **favours**)
1 a favour is something kind that you do
for someone ♦ *Will you do me a favour?*
2 favour is approval or goodwill
to be in favour of someone or **something** is to
like or support them

favour ➤ *verb* (**favours, favouring, favoured**)
to favour someone or something is to like
or support them, or prefer them to others

favourable *adjective*
1 helpful or advantageous 2 showing
approval
favourably *adverb* in a favourable way

favourite ➤ *adjective*
liked more than others ♦ *This is my
favourite book*

favourite ➤ *noun* (*plural* **favourites**)
a person or thing that someone likes most
♦ *This book is my favourite*

favouritism *noun*
unfairly being kinder to one person than to
others

fawn *noun* (*plural* **fawns**)
1 a young deer 2 a light brown colour

fax ➤ *noun* (*plural* **faxes**)
1 a machine that sends copies of
documents by electronic means through a
telephone line 2 a copy made by this
process

fax ➤ *verb* (**faxes, faxing, faxed**)
to fax a document is to send a copy of it by
means of a fax

fear ➤ *noun* (*plural* **fears**)
a feeling that something unpleasant may
happen

fear ➤ *verb* (**fears, fearing, feared**)
1 to fear someone or something is to be
afraid of them 2 to fear something is also
to be anxious or sad about it ♦ *I fear we
may be too late*

fearful *adjective*
1 frightened 2 (*informal*) awful or horrid
♦ *They had a fearful quarrel*
fearfully *adverb* in a fearful way

fearless *adjective*
having no fear
fearlessly *adverb* in a fearless way

fearsome *adjective*
frightening

feasible *adjective*
able to be done; possible or likely

feast ➤ noun (plural **feasts**)
a large and splendid meal

feast ➤ verb (**feasts, feasting, feasted**)
to feast is to have a feast
to feast your eyes on something is to gaze at it with pleasure

feat noun (plural **feats**)
a brave or clever deed

feather noun (plural **feathers**)
one of the very light coverings that grow from a bird's skin
feathery adjective soft or light like feathers

feature ➤ noun (plural **features**)
1 any part of the face ♦ *He has rugged features* 2 an important or noticeable part of something; a characteristic 3 a special film or programme or newspaper article

feature ➤ verb (**features, featuring, featured**)
1 to feature something is to make it an important part of something 2 to feature in something is to be an important part of it ♦ *Sport features a lot in the Sunday papers*

February noun
the second month of the year

fed past tense and past participle of **feed** verb

federal adjective
to do with a system in which several States are ruled by a central government but make some of their own laws
federation noun a group of federal States

fed up adjective
(informal) depressed or unhappy

fee noun (plural **fees**)
a payment or charge

feeble adjective (**feebler, feeblest**)
weak; not having much strength or force
feebly adverb in a feeble way

feed ➤ verb (**feeds, feeding, fed**)
1 to feed a person or animal is to give them food 2 to feed on something is to eat it ♦ *Sheep feed on grass* 3 to feed a machine is to put coins or other things into it

feed ➤ noun (plural **feeds**)
1 a feed is a meal 2 feed is food for animals

feedback noun
information from someone about something you have done for them

feel ➤ verb (**feels, feeling, felt**)
1 to feel something is to touch it to find out what it is like 2 to feel a feeling or emotion is to experience it ♦ *I feel very angry about it*
to feel like something is to want it

feel ➤ noun
what something feels like ♦ *Her dress has a funny feel about it*

feeler noun (plural **feelers**)
1 one of two long thin parts that extend from the front of an insect's body and are used for feeling 2 a cautious question or suggestion

feeling noun (plural **feelings**)
1 feeling is the ability to feel or touch things ♦ *She lost the feeling in her right hand* 2 feeling is also what a person feels in the mind, such as love or fear ♦ *I have hurt her feelings* 3 a feeling is what you think about something ♦ *My feeling is that he's right*

feet plural of **foot**

feline adjective
to do with cats; like a cat

fell[1] past tense of **fall** verb

fell[2] verb (**fells, felling, felled**)
1 to fell a tree is to cut it down 2 to fell someone is to knock them down

fell[3] noun (plural **fells**)
a piece of wild hilly country in the north of England

fellow ➤ noun (plural **fellows**)
1 a friend or companion; someone who belongs to the same group 2 (informal) a man or boy ♦ *He's a clever fellow*

fellow ➤ adjective
of the same group or kind ♦ *She arranged a meeting with her fellow teachers*

fellowship noun (plural **fellowships**)
1 fellowship is friendship 2 a fellowship is a group of friends; a society

felt[1] past tense and past participle of **feel**

felt[2] noun
thick woollen material

felt-tip pen or **felt-tipped pen** noun (plural **felt-tip pens** or **felt-tipped pens**)
a pen with a tip made of felt or fibre

female ➤ adjective
of the sex that can produce offspring

female ➤ noun (plural **females**)
a female person or animal

feminine adjective
1 to do with women or like women; suitable for women 2 in some languages, belonging to the class of words that includes words referring to women
femininity noun being feminine

feminist noun (plural **feminists**)
someone who believes that women should have the same rights as men
feminism noun belief in women's rights

fen *noun* (*plural* **fens**)
an area of low-lying marshy or flooded
land

fence ➤ *noun* (*plural* **fences**)
1 a wooden or metal barrier round an area
of land **2** (*slang*) someone who buys stolen
goods and sells them again
to sit on the fence is to avoid saying anything
definite in an argument

fence ➤ *verb* (**fences, fencing, fenced**)
1 to fence something or to fence it in is to
put a fence round it **2** to fence is to fight
with long narrow swords called *foils*, as a
sport
fencer *noun* someone who fences **fencing**
noun the sport of someone who fences

fend *verb* (**fends, fending, fended**)
to fend for yourself is to take care of yourself
to fend someone or **something off** is to keep
them away from yourself

fender *noun* (*plural* **fenders**)
1 a low guard placed round a fireplace to
stop coal from falling into the room
2 something hung over the side of a boat
to protect it from knocks

fender

ferment ➤ *verb* (**ferments, fermenting, fermented**)
(*pronounced* fer-**ment**)
to ferment is to bubble and change
chemically by the action of a substance
such as yeast
fermentation *noun* the process of fermenting

ferment ➤ *noun* (*pronounced* **fer**-ment)
1 fermenting **2** an excited or agitated
condition ♦ *The crowd was in a ferment*

fern *noun* (*plural* **ferns**)
a plant with feathery leaves and no
flowers

ferocious *adjective*
fierce or savage
ferociously *adverb* in a ferocious way **ferocity**
noun fierceness

ferret ➤ *noun* (*plural* **ferrets**)
a small animal like a weasel, used for
catching rabbits and rats

ferret ➤ *verb* (**ferrets, ferreting, ferreted**)
to ferret, or ferret about, is to search busily
for something

ferry ➤ *noun* (*plural* **ferries**)
a ship or aircraft used for taking people or
things across a river or other stretch of
water

ferry ➤ *verb* (**ferries, ferrying, ferried**)
to ferry people or things is to take them in
a ship or aircraft or car

fertile *adjective*
1 producing good crops **2** able to produce
offspring
fertility *noun* being fertile

fertilize *verb* (**fertilizes, fertilizing, fertilized**)
1 to fertilize the soil is to add chemicals or
manure to make it more fertile **2** to
fertilize an egg or plant is to put sperm or
pollen into it so that it develops its young
or seeds
fertilization *noun* fertilizing the soil or an
egg or plant

fertilizer *noun* (*plural* **fertilizers**)
chemicals or manure added to the soil to
make it more fertile

fervent *adjective*
very enthusiastic or passionate ♦ *He is a
fervent supporter of reform*
fervently *adverb* in a fervent way **fervour**
noun a fervent feeling

festival *noun* (*plural* **festivals**)
a time when people arrange special shows
and celebrations

festive *adjective*
to do with a festival; joyful
festivity *noun* festive activity

festoon *verb* (**festoons, festooning, festooned**)
to festoon a place is to decorate it with
chains of flowers or ribbons

fetch *verb* (**fetches, fetching, fetched**)
1 to fetch something or someone is to go
and get them **2** to fetch a particular price
is to be sold for it ♦ *My old bike fetched £10*

fête *noun* (*plural* **fêtes**) (*pronounced* fayt)
an outdoor entertainment with stalls and
sideshows

fetlock *noun* (*plural* **fetlocks**)
the part of a horse's leg above and behind
its hoof

fetters *plural noun*
chains put round a prisoner's ankles

feud *noun* (*plural* **feuds**) (*pronounced* fewd)
a long-lasting quarrel or feeling of hatred

feudal *adjective* (*pronounced* **few**-dal)
to do with the system used in the Middle Ages, in which people could farm land in exchange for work done for the owner
feudalism *noun* the feudal system

fever *noun* (*plural* **fevers**)
1 a fever is an unusually high body-temperature, usually with an illness **2** fever is excitement or agitation
fevered *adjective* having a fever

feverish *adjective*
1 having a slight fever **2** excited or frantic ♦ *There was feverish activity getting the hall ready for the show*
feverishly *adverb* in a feverish way

few ➤ *adjective* (**fewer**, **fewest**)
not many

few ➤ *noun*
a small number of people or things
a good few or **quite a few** a fairly large number

fez *noun* (*plural* **fezzes**)
a tall round hat with a flat top and a tassel, worn especially by Muslim men

fiancé *noun* (*plural* **fiancés**) (*pronounced* fee-**ahn**-say)
a man who is engaged to be married

fiancée *noun* (*plural* **fiancées**) (*pronounced* fee-**ahn**-say)
a woman who is engaged to be married

fiasco *noun* (*plural* **fiascos**) (*pronounced* fi-**ass**-koh)
a complete failure ♦ *The party turned into a fiasco*

fib *noun* (*plural* **fibs**)
a lie about something unimportant
fibber *noun* someone who tells fibs

fibre *noun* (*plural* **fibres**) (*pronounced* **fy**-ber)
1 a fibre is a very thin thread **2** fibre is a substance made up of thin threads **3** fibre is also a substance in food that helps you to digest it
fibrous *adjective* like fibre

fibreglass *noun*
a kind of lightweight plastic containing glass fibres

fickle *adjective*
often changing; not loyal to one person or group

fiction *noun* (*plural* **fictions**)
1 fiction is writings about events that have not really happened; stories and novels **2** a fiction is something untrue or made up
fictional *adjective* to do with fiction; not real
fictitious *adjective* not true; made up

fiddle ➤ *noun* (*plural* **fiddles**)
1 a violin **2** (*informal*) a swindle

fiddle ➤ *verb* (**fiddles**, **fiddling**, **fiddled**)
1 to fiddle is to play the violin **2** to fiddle with something is to play with it with your fingers **3** (*informal*) to fiddle something is to be dishonest about it ♦ *Her dad was fiddling his company's expenses*
fiddler *noun* someone who fiddles; someone dishonest

fiddling *adjective*
unimportant but tedious ♦ *The job involves a lot of fiddling details*

fiddly *adjective*
(*informal*) small and awkward to handle or use

fidelity *noun* (*pronounced* fi-**del**-i-ti)
1 being faithful **2** the exactness with which sound is reproduced

fidget *verb* (**fidgets**, **fidgeting**, **fidgeted**)
to fidget is to make small restless movements
fidgety *adjective* fidgeting a lot

field ➤ *noun* (*plural* **fields**)
1 a piece of land with crops or grass growing on it, often surrounded by a hedge or fence **2** an area of interest or study ♦ *The book describes important developments in the field of science* **3** those taking part in a race or hunt

field ➤ *verb* (**fields**, **fielding**, **fielded**)
1 to field a ball in cricket or other games is to stop it or catch it **2** to be fielding in cricket is to be on the side that is not batting
fielder or **fieldsman** *noun* a player who is fielding

Field Marshal *noun* (*plural* **Field Marshals**)
an army officer of the highest rank

fieldwork *noun*
practical work or research done in various places, not in a school, library, or laboratory ♦ *We went to the coast to do some geography fieldwork*

fiend *noun* (*plural* **fiends**) (*pronounced* feend)
  1 a devil **2** a wicked or cruel person
fiendish *adjective* like a fiend; dreadful
fiendishly *adverb* in a fiendish way

fierce *adjective* (**fiercer**, **fiercest**)
  1 angry and violent or cruel **2** strong or intense ♦ *They felt a fierce heat*
fiercely *adverb* in a fierce way **fierceness** *noun* being fierce

fiery *adjective* (**fierier**, **fieriest**)
  1 full of flames or heat **2** easily made angry ♦ *He had a fiery temper*

fife *noun* (*plural* **fifes**)
  a small shrill flute

fifteen *noun* (*plural* **fifteens**)
  1 the number 15 **2** a team in Rugby Union football
fifteenth *adjective* and *noun* 15th

fifth *adjective* and *noun*
  the next after the fourth
fifthly *adverb* in the fifth place; as the fifth one

fifty *noun* (*plural* **fifties**)
  the number 50
fiftieth *adjective* and *noun* 50th

fifty-fifty *adjective* and *adverb*
  shared equally between two people or groups ♦ *Let's split the money fifty-fifty*

fig *noun* (*plural* **figs**)
  a soft fruit full of small seeds

fight ➤ *noun* (*plural* **fights**)
  1 a struggle against someone, using hands or weapons **2** an attempt to achieve or overcome something ♦ *They joined the fight against poverty*

fight ➤ *verb* (**fights**, **fighting**, **fought**)
  1 to fight someone is to have a fight with them **2** to fight something is to try to stop it ♦ *They fought the fire all night*
fighter *noun* someone who fights

figurative *adjective*
  using words for special effect and not in their literal meanings, for example *flood* in *a flood of letters*

figure ➤ *noun* (*plural* **figures**)
  1 one of the symbols that stand for numbers, such as 1, 2, and 3 **2** the shape of someone's body **3** a diagram or illustration **4** a pattern or shape ♦ *He drew a figure of eight*

figure ➤ *verb* (**figures**, **figuring**, **figured**)
  1 to appear or take part in something ♦ *His name does not figure in the list of entrants* **2** to imagine ♦ *I figure he'll turn up later* **3** to work out ♦ *We figured that we had enough money for the holiday*

figure of speech *noun* (*plural* **figures of speech**)
  a special way of using words that makes what you say or write interesting, such as a metaphor or a simile

filament *noun* (*plural* **filaments**)
  a thread or thin wire

file[1] ➤ *noun* (*plural* **files**)
  a metal tool with a rough surface that is rubbed on things to shape them or make them smooth

file ➤ *verb* (**files**, **filing**, **filed**)
  to file something is to shape it or make it smooth with a file

file[2] ➤ *noun* (*plural* **files**)
  1 a box or folder for keeping papers in **2** a line of people one behind the other **3** (*in Computing*) a set of data that has been stored under one name in a computer

file ➤ *verb* (**files**, **filing**, **filed**)
  1 to file a paper or document is to put it in a box or folder **2** to file is to walk one behind the other

filings *plural noun*
  tiny pieces of metal

fill ➤ *verb* (**fills**, **filling**, **filled**)
  1 to fill something is to make it full **2** to fill is to become full **3** to fill a tooth is to put a filling in it
to fill something in is to put answers or other writing in a form or document
to fill something up is to fill it completely

fill ➤ *noun* (*plural* **fills**)
  enough to fill a person or thing ♦ *Eat your fill*

filler *noun* (*plural* **fillers**)
  1 filler is material used to fill holes in wood or plaster **2** a filler is a device for filling things, such as a funnel

fillet *noun* (*plural* **fillets**)
  a piece of fish or meat without bones

filling *noun* (*plural* **fillings**)
  something used to fill a hole or gap, especially a piece of metal put in a tooth to replace a decayed part

filling station *noun* (*plural* **filling stations**)
  a place where petrol is sold

filly *noun* (*plural* **fillies**)
a young female horse

film ➤ *noun* (*plural* **films**)
1 a moving picture that tells a story, such as those shown in cinemas **2** a roll or piece of thin plastic coated with a chemical that is sensitive to light, put in a camera for taking photographs **3** a very thin layer ♦ *The table was covered in a film of grease*
filmy *adjective* thin and transparent, like a film

film ➤ *verb* (**films, filming, filmed**)
to film a book or story is to make a film of it

filter ➤ *noun* (*plural* **filters**)
1 a device for removing dirt or other unwanted things from a liquid or gas that passes through it **2** a system allowing a line of traffic to move in one direction while other lines are held up

filter ➤ *verb* (**filters, filtering, filtered**)
1 to filter something is to pass it through a filter **2** to filter is to move gradually ♦ *They filtered into the hall* **3** traffic filters when it moves in one direction while other traffic is held up

filth *noun*
disgusting dirt
filthy *adjective* extremely dirty

fin *noun* (*plural* **fins**)
1 a thin flat part that sticks out from a fish's body and helps it to swim **2** a small part that sticks out from an aircraft or rocket and helps it to balance

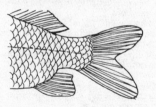

final ➤ *adjective*
1 coming at the end; last **2** that puts an end to argument or doubt ♦ *You must not go, and that's final!*
finality *noun* being final or last **finally** *adverb* as the last thing

final ➤ *noun* (*plural* **finals**)
the last of a series of contests, that decides the overall winner

finale *noun* (*plural* **finales**) (*pronounced* fin-ah-li)
the last part of a show or piece of music

finalist *noun* (*plural* **finalists**)
a person or team taking part in a final

finance ➤ *noun*
the use and control of money
finances *noun* money or funds

finance ➤ *verb* (**finances, financing, financed**)
to finance something is to provide money for it
financier *noun* someone who provides money

financial *adjective*
to do with money

finch *noun* (*plural* **finches**)
a small bird with a short thick beak

find *verb* (**finds, finding, found**)
1 to find something is to see or get it by chance or by looking for it **2** to find something is also to learn it by experience ♦ *He found that digging is hard work*
to find someone out is to discover them doing wrong
to find something out is to get information about it
finder *noun* someone who finds something

findings *plural noun*
things someone has found out

fine [1] *adjective* (**finer, finest**)
1 of high quality; excellent ♦ *They saw some fine pictures at the show* **2** dry and sunny; bright ♦ *The day turned out fine* **3** very thin; delicate ♦ *The curtains were made of a fine material* **4** made of small particles ♦ *The sand on the beach was very fine*
finely *adverb* into fine or small parts ♦ *Slice the tomato finely*

fine [2] ➤ *noun* (*plural* **fines**)
money which has to be paid as a punishment

fine ➤ *verb* (**fines, fining, fined**)
to fine someone is to make them pay money as a punishment

finger ➤ *noun* (*plural* **fingers**)
1 one of the separate parts of your hand **2** something with a similar shape

finger ➤ *verb* (**fingers, fingering, fingered**)
to finger something is to touch it with your fingers

fingernail *noun* (*plural* **fingernails**)
the hard covering at the end of a finger

fingerprint *noun* (*plural* **fingerprints**)
a mark made by the tip of a person's finger

finicky *adjective*
fussy or hard to please

finish ➤ *verb* (**finishes, finishing, finished**)
1 to finish something is to bring it to an end **2** to finish is to come to an end

finish ➤ *noun* (*plural* **finishes**)
the end of something

fiord *noun* (*plural* **fiords**) (*pronounced* fi-ord)
in Norway, an inlet of the sea between high cliffs

fir *noun* (*plural* **firs**)
an evergreen tree with leaves like needles

fire ➤ *noun* (*plural* **fires**)
1 burning; the heat and bright light that come from burning things **2** coal or wood burning in a grate or furnace to give heat **3** a device using electricity or gas to heat a room **4** the shooting of guns ♦ *Hold your fire!*
on fire burning
to set fire to something is to start it burning

fire ➤ *verb* (**fires, firing, fired**)
1 to fire something is to start it burning **2** to fire pottery or bricks is to bake them in an oven to make them hard **3** to fire a gun is to shoot it **4** (*informal*) to fire someone is to dismiss them from their job

firearm *noun* (*plural* **firearms**)
a gun or rifle

fire brigade *noun* (*plural* **fire brigades**)
a team of people organized to fight fires

fire drill *noun* (*plural* **fire drills**)
a practice of what to do if a fire breaks out

fire engine *noun* (*plural* **fire engines**)
a large vehicle that carries firefighters and equipment to fight fires

fire escape *noun* (*plural* **fire escapes**)
a special staircase or exit for use if there is a fire

fire extinguisher *noun* (*plural* **fire extinguishers**)
a metal cylinder containing water or foam for spraying over a fire to put it out

firefighter *noun* (*plural* **firefighters**)
a member of a fire brigade

fireman *noun* (*plural* **firemen**)
a man who is a member of a fire brigade

fireplace *noun* (*plural* **fireplaces**)
the part of a room where the fire and hearth are

fireproof *adjective*
able to stand great heat without burning

fireside *noun* (*plural* **firesides**)
the part of a room near the fire

fire station *noun* (*plural* **fire stations**)
the headquarters of a fire brigade

firewood *noun*
wood suitable for fuel

firework *noun* (*plural* **fireworks**)
a cardboard tube containing chemicals that give off pretty sparks and lights and sometimes make loud noises

firm ➤ *noun* (*plural* **firms**)
a business organization ♦ *She works for a clothing firm*

firm ➤ *adjective* (**firmer, firmest**)
1 fixed or solid so that it will not move **2** definite; not likely to change ♦ *She has a firm belief in the power of fate*
firmly *adverb* so as to be firm **firmness** *noun* being firm

first ➤ *adjective*
1 coming before all others **2** the most important ♦ *He plays in the First Eleven*

first ➤ *adverb*
before everything else ♦ *Finish your work first*

first ➤ *noun*
a person or thing that is first
at first at the beginning; to start with

first aid *noun*
treatment given to an injured person before a doctor comes

first-class *adjective*
1 belonging to the best part of a service ♦ *Send the letter by first-class post* **2** excellent

first floor *noun* (*plural* **first floors**)
the next floor above the ground floor

first-hand *adjective and adverb*
got directly, rather than from other people or from books ♦ *We have first-hand information*

firstly *adverb*
as the first thing ♦ *Firstly, let me tell you about our holiday*

first-rate *adjective*
excellent

fish ➤ *noun* (*plural* **fish** or **fishes**)
an animal that lives and breathes in water

fish ➤ *verb* (**fishes, fishing, fished**)
1 to fish is to try to catch fish **2** to fish for something is to try and get it ♦ *He is only fishing for praise*
to fish something out is to get it out of something with some difficulty

fisherman *noun* (*plural* **fishermen**)
someone who tries to catch fish

fishmonger *noun* (*plural* **fishmongers**)
a shopkeeper who sells fish

fishy *adjective* (**fishier, fishiest**)
1 smelling or tasting of fish **2** (*informal*) suspicious or doubtful ♦ *His excuse was rather fishy*

fission *noun* (*pronounced* **fish-on**)
splitting something, especially the nucleus of an atom to produce energy

fist *noun* (*plural* **fists**)
a tightly closed hand with the fingers bent into the palm

fit[1] ➤ *adjective* (**fitter, fittest**)
1 suitable or good enough ♦ *It was a meal fit for a king* **2** healthy and strong ♦ *Keep fit with exercises* **3** ready or likely ♦ *They worked till they were fit to collapse*
to see fit or **think fit to do something** is to decide or choose to do it

fit ➤ *verb* (**fits, fitting, fitted**)
1 to fit someone or something is to be the right size and shape for them **2** to fit something is to put it into place ♦ *We need to fit a new lock on the door* **3** to fit something is to be suitable for it ♦ *Her speech fitted the occasion perfectly*
to fit in is to be suitable or agreeable

fit ➤ *noun*
the way something fits ♦ *The coat is a good fit*

fit[2] *noun* (*plural* **fits**)
1 a sudden illness, especially one that makes you move violently or become unconscious **2** (*informal*) an outburst ♦ *He rushed off in a fit of rage*
in fits and starts in short bursts; now and then

fitness *noun*
being fit and healthy

fitted *adjective*
made to fit something exactly ♦ *The room has a fitted carpet*

fitter *noun* (*plural* **fitters**)
someone who fits clothes or machinery

fitting ➤ *adjective*
suitable or proper

fitting ➤ *noun* (*plural* **fittings**)
something fixed or fitted in a room or building

five *noun* (*plural* **fives**)
the number 5

fiver *noun* (*plural* **fivers**)
(*informal*) a five-pound note; £5

fives *noun*
a game in which a ball is hit with gloved hands or a bat against the walls of a court

fix ➤ *verb* (**fixes, fixing, fixed**)
1 to fix something is to join it firmly to something else or to put it where it will not move **2** to fix something is also to decide or settle it ♦ *We have fixed a date for the party* **3** (*informal*) to fix something that is broken is to mend it ♦ *He's fixing my bike*
to fix something up is to arrange or organize something

fix ➤ *noun* (*plural* **fixes**)
1 (informal) an awkward situation ♦ *I'm in a fix* **2** finding the position of something, especially by using a compass

fixture *noun* (*plural* **fixtures**)
1 something fixed in its place **2** a sports event planned for a particular day

fizz *verb* (**fizzes, fizzing, fizzed**)
1 to fizz is to make a hissing or spluttering sound **2** liquid fizzes when it produces a lot of small bubbles
fizzy *adjective* having a lot of bubbles

fizzle *verb* (**fizzles, fizzling, fizzled**)
to fizzle is to make a slight hissing sound
to fizzle out is to end in a disappointing or unsuccessful way

flabbergasted *adjective*
(*informal*) completely astonished

flabby *adjective* (**flabbier, flabbiest**)
fat and soft; not firm

flag[1] ➤ *noun* (*plural* **flags**)
1 a piece of material with a coloured pattern or shape on it, used as a sign or signal **2** a small piece of paper that looks like a flag, especially sold in aid of charity

flag ➤ *verb* (**flags, flagging, flagged**)
1 to flag is to become weak or droop **2** to flag a signal is to send a signal with flags, especially from ships at sea

flag[2] *noun* (*plural* **flags**)
a flat slab of paving stone

flagpole *noun* (*plural* **flagpoles**)
a pole to which a flag is attached

flagship *noun* (*plural* **flagships**)
a ship that has the commander of the fleet on board and flies his flag

flagstaff *noun* (*plural* **flagstaffs**)
a flagpole

flagstone *noun* (*plural* **flagstones**)
a flat slab of paving stone

flake ➤ *noun* (*plural* **flakes**)
1 a very light thin piece of something **2** a piece of falling snow
flaky *adjective* made of flakes or like flakes

flake ➤ *verb* (**flakes, flaking, flaked**)
to flake is to come off in light thin pieces
to flake out (*informal*) is to faint or fall asleep

flame ➤ *noun* (*plural* **flames**)
a bright strip of fire that flickers and leaps

flame ➤ *verb* (flames, flaming, flamed)
to flame is to produce flames or become
bright red

flamingo *noun* (*plural* flamingos)
a wading bird with long legs, a long neck,
and pale pink feathers

flan *noun* (*plural* flans)
a pie without any pastry on top

flank *noun* (*plural* flanks)
the side of something, especially an
animal's body or an army

flannel *noun* (*plural* flannels)
1 a flannel is a piece of soft cloth used for
washing yourself 2 flannel is a soft
woollen material

flap ➤ *noun* (*plural* flaps)
1 a part that hangs down from one edge of
something, usually to cover an opening
2 the action or sound of flapping
3 (*informal*) a panic or fuss ♦ *Don't get in
a flap*

flap ➤ *verb* (flaps, flapping, flapped)
1 to flap something is to move it up and
down or from side to side ♦ *The bird
flapped its wings* 2 to flap is to wave
about ♦ *The sails were flapping in the
breeze* 3 (*informal*) to panic or fuss

flapjack *noun* (*plural* flapjacks)
a cake made from oats and syrup

flare ➤ *noun* (*plural* flares)
1 a sudden bright flame 2 a bright light
fired into the sky as a signal 3 a gradual
widening, especially in skirts or trousers

flare ➤ *verb* (flares, flaring, flared)
1 to flare is to burn with a sudden bright
flame 2 to flare is also to become suddenly
angry 3 things flare when they get
gradually wider

flash ➤ *noun* (*plural* flashes)
1 a sudden bright burst of light 2 a
device for making a brief bright light by
which to take photographs 3 a sudden
display of anger or humour 4 a brief item
of news
in a flash immediately; very quickly

flash ➤ *verb* (flashes, flashing, flashed)
1 to flash is to make a sudden bright burst
of light 2 to flash past or across is to
approach and go past very fast ♦ *The train
flashed past into the distance*

flashback *noun* (*plural* flashbacks)
going back in a film or story to something
that happened earlier ♦ *The hero's
childhood was shown in flashbacks*

flashy *adjective* (flashier, flashiest)
showy and bright

flask *noun* (*plural* flasks)
1 a bottle with a narrow neck 2 a vacuum
flask

flat ➤ *adjective* (flatter, flattest)
1 having no curves or bumps; smooth and
level 2 spread out; lying at full length
♦ *Lie flat on the ground* 3 dull or
uninteresting ♦ *He spoke in a flat voice*
4 complete; not changing ♦ *We got a flat
refusal* 5 a liquid is flat when it is no
longer fizzy 6 a tyre is flat when it is
punctured and has lost its air 7 feet are
flat when they do not have the normal
arch underneath 8 below the proper
musical pitch ♦ *The clarinet was flat*
flatness *noun* being flat

flat ➤ *adverb*
exactly and no more ♦ *He did it in ten
seconds flat*
flat out as fast as possible

flat ➤ *noun* (*plural* flats)
1 a set of rooms for living in, usually on
one floor of a building 2 (*in Music*) the
note that is a semitone lower than the
natural note; the sign (♭) that indicates
this

flatly *adverb*
in a definite way, leaving no room for
doubt ♦ *They flatly refused to go*

flatten *verb* (flattens, flattening, flattened)
1 to flatten something is to make it flat
2 to flatten is to become flat

flatter *verb* (flatters, flattering, flattered)
1 to flatter someone is to praise them
more than they deserve 2 to flatter
someone is also to make them seem better
or more attractive than they really are
♦ *The portrait flatters him, don't you
think?*
flatterer *noun* someone who is often
flattering people **flattery** *noun* flattering
people

flaunt *verb* (flaunts, flaunting, flaunted)
to flaunt something is to show it off too
proudly ♦ *He is always flaunting his
expensive clothes*

flavour ➤ *noun* (*plural* flavours)
the taste and smell of something

flavour ➤ *verb* (**flavours, flavouring, flavoured**)
to flavour something is to give it a particular taste and smell
flavouring *noun* something that gives a flavour

flaw *noun* (*plural* **flaws**)
something that makes a person or thing imperfect ♦ *The diamond had a flaw*
flawed *adjective* having a flaw **flawless** *adjective* perfect

flax *noun*
a plant that produces fibres from which cloth is made and seeds from which oil is obtained

flea *noun* (*plural* **fleas**)
a small jumping insect that sucks blood

fleck *noun* (*plural* **flecks**)
a small piece or speck ♦ *There were flecks of dirt on the table*

flee *verb* (**flees, fleeing, fled**)
to flee is to run away from something

fleece ➤ *noun* (*plural* **fleeces**)
the wool that covers a sheep's body
fleecy *adjective* soft like a fleece

fleece ➤ *verb* (**fleeces, fleecing, fleeced**)
1 to fleece a sheep is to shear it 2 to fleece someone is to swindle them

fleet *noun* (*plural* **fleets**)
a number of ships, aircraft, or vehicles owned by one country or company

fleeting *adjective*
very brief; passing quickly ♦ *I caught a fleeting glimpse of him*

flesh *noun*
the soft substance of the bodies of people and animals, made of muscle and fat
fleshy *adjective* like flesh

flew past tense of **fly** *verb*

flex ➤ *noun* (*plural* **flexes**)
flexible insulated wire for electric current

flex ➤ *verb* (**flexes, flexing, flexed**)
to flex something is to move or bend it
♦ *Try flexing your muscles*

flexible *adjective*
1 easy to bend or stretch 2 able to be changed ♦ *Our plans are flexible*
flexibility *noun* being flexible

flick ➤ *noun* (*plural* **flicks**)
a quick light hit or movement

flick ➤ *verb* (**flicks, flicking, flicked**)
to flick something is to hit or move it with a flick

flicker *verb* (**flickers, flickering, flickered**)
to flicker is to burn or shine unsteadily

flight[1] *noun* (*plural* **flights**)
1 flight is flying 2 a flight is a journey in an aircraft or rocket 3 a flight is also a group of flying birds or aircraft 4 a flight of stairs is one set of stairs 5 a flight on a dart or arrow is its feathers or fins

flight[2] *noun* (*plural* **flights**)
running away; escape

flimsy *adjective* (**flimsier, flimsiest**)
light and thin; fragile

flinch *verb* (**flinches, flinching, flinched**)
to flinch is to feel or show fear, or to wince

fling *verb* (**flings, flinging, flung**)
to fling something is to throw it violently or carelessly ♦ *He flung his shoes under the bed*

flint *noun* (*plural* **flints**)
1 flint is a very hard kind of stone 2 a flint is a piece of this stone or hard metal used to produce sparks
flinty *adjective* hard like flint

flip *verb* (**flips, flipping, flipped**)
to flip something is to flick it

flippant *adjective*
not showing proper seriousness ♦ *Don't be flippant about his illness*
flippancy being flippant **flippantly** in a flippant way

flipper *noun* (*plural* **flippers**)
1 a limb that water animals use for swimming 2 a flat rubber shoe shaped like a duck's foot, that you wear on your feet to help you swim

flirt *verb* (**flirts, flirting, flirted**)
to flirt with someone is to treat them as if you wanted to gain their love, to amuse yourself
flirtation *noun* flirting with someone

flit *verb* (flits, flitting, flitted)
to flit is to fly or move lightly and quickly
♦ *A moth flitted across the room*

float ➤ *verb* (floats, floating, floated)
1 to float is to stay or move on the surface of a liquid or in the air **2** to float something is to make it stay on the surface of a liquid

float ➤ *noun* (*plural* floats)
1 a device designed to float **2** a vehicle with a platform used for delivering milk or for carrying a display in a parade **3** a small amount of money kept for paying small bills or giving change

flock ➤ *noun* (*plural* flocks)
a group of sheep, goats, or birds

flock ➤ *verb* (flocks, flocking, flocked)
to flock is to gather or move in a crowd

flog *verb* (flogs, flogging, flogged)
1 to flog someone is to beat them severely with a whip or stick **2** (*slang*) to flog something is to sell it

flood ➤ *noun* (*plural* floods)
1 a large amount of water spreading over a place that is usually dry **2** a great amount of something ♦ *They received a flood of letters* **3** the tide when it is coming in

flood ➤ *verb* (floods, flooding, flooded)
1 to flood something is to cover it with a large amount of water **2** a river floods when it flows over its banks **3** to arrive in large amounts ♦ *Letters flooded in*

floodlight *noun* (*plural* floodlights)
a lamp that gives a broad bright beam
floodlit *adjective* lit by floodlights

floor ➤ *noun* (*plural* floors)
1 the part of a room that people walk on **2** all the rooms on the same level in a building ♦ *The sports department is on the top floor*

floor ➤ *verb* (floors, flooring, floored)
1 to floor a room or building is to provide it with a floor **2** to floor someone is to knock them down **3** to floor someone is also to baffle them ♦ *One of the exam questions floored everyone*

floorboard *noun* (*plural* floorboards)
one of the boards forming the floor of a room

flop ➤ *verb* (flops, flopping, flopped)
1 to flop, or flop down, is to fall or sit down heavily **2** to flop is also to fall or hang loosely or heavily ♦ *Her hair flopped over her eyes* **3** (*informal*) to flop is to be a failure

flop ➤ *noun* (*plural* flops)
1 the movement or sound of sudden falling or sitting down **2** (*informal*) a failure or disappointment

floppy *adjective* (floppier, floppiest)
hanging loosely or heavily ♦ *They saw a dog with huge floppy ears*

floppy disk *noun* (*plural* floppy disks)
a flexible disc used to store data for use in a computer

flora *noun* (*pronounced* flor-a)
the plants of an area or of a period of time

floral *adjective*
made of flowers or to do with flowers

florist *noun* (*plural* florists)
a shopkeeper who sells flowers

floss *noun*
silky thread or fibres

flounder *verb* (flounders, floundering, floundered)
to flounder is to move or behave awkwardly or clumsily when in difficulty

flour *noun*
a fine powder made from corn or wheat and used for making bread, cakes, and pastry
floury *adjective* powdery like flour

flourish *verb* (flourishes, flourishing, flourished)
1 to flourish is to grow or develop strongly; to be successful **2** to flourish something is to wave it about

flow ➤ *verb* (flows, flowing, flowed)
1 to flow is to move along smoothly **2** to flow is also to hang loosely ♦ *She had golden flowing hair*

flow ➤ *noun* (*plural* flows)
1 a flowing movement or mass **2** the movement of the tide when it is coming in

flower ➤ *noun* (*plural* flowers)
1 the part of a plant from which the seed or fruit develops **2** a plant with a flower in flower producing flowers

flower ➤ *verb* (flowers, flowering, flowered)
to flower is to produce flowers

flowerpot *noun* (*plural* flowerpots)
a pot in which plants are grown

flowery *adjective*
1 decorated with flowers or pictures of them ♦ *The room had flowery wallpaper* **2** using fancy words ♦ *He had a flowery style of writing*

flown past participle of **fly** *verb*

flu *noun*
influenza

fluctuate *verb* (fluctuates, fluctuating, fluctuated)
to fluctuate is to change irregularly
♦ *Prices fluctuated*
fluctuation *noun* irregular change

flue *noun* (*plural* **flues**)
a pipe that takes smoke and fumes away
from a stove or boiler

fluent *adjective*
skilful at speaking, especially a foreign
language
fluency *noun* being fluent **fluently** *adverb* in a
fluent way

fluff *noun*
soft stuff like feathers or bits that come off
wool and cloth
fluffy *adjective* soft like fluff

fluid *noun* (*plural* **fluids**)
a substance that flows easily, like liquids
and gases

fluke *noun* (*plural* **flukes**)
a success that you achieve by unexpected
good luck

flung past tense and past participle of **fling**

fluorescent *adjective*
a fluorescent light or lamp is one that
creates light from radiation

fluoridation *noun*
adding fluoride to drinking water

fluoride *noun*
a chemical that is thought to help prevent
tooth-decay

flurry *noun* (*plural* **flurries**)
a sudden gust of wind or rain or snow

flush[1] ➣ *verb* (**flushes, flushing, flushed**)
1 to flush is to blush slightly **2** to flush
something is to clean or remove it with a
fast flow of liquid

flush ➣ *noun* (*plural* **flushes**)
1 a slight blush **2** a fast flow of water

flush[2] *adjective*
1 level; without any part sticking out
♦ *The doors are flush with the walls*
2 (*slang*) having a lot of money

flustered *adjective*
nervous and confused

flute *noun* (*plural* **flutes**)
a musical instrument consisting of a long
pipe with holes that are covered by fingers
or keys

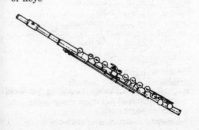

flutter ➣ *verb* (**flutters, fluttering, fluttered**)
1 to flutter is to move with a quick
flapping of wings ♦ *A butterfly fluttered in
through the window* **2** to flutter is to move
or flap quickly and irregularly ♦ *The flags
fluttered in the breeze*

flutter *noun* (*plural* **flutters**)
1 a fluttering movement **2** a feeling of
nervous excitement ♦ *We were all in a
flutter about our holiday in Spain*
3 (*informal*) a small bet ♦ *Let's have a
flutter*

fly ➣ *verb* (**flies, flying, flew, flown**)
1 to fly is to move through the air with
wings or in an aircraft **2** to fly is also to
wave in the air ♦ *Flags were flying* **3** to
fly something is to make it move through
the air ♦ *They were flying model aircraft*
4 to fly is to move or pass quickly ♦ *Time
flies* ♦ *I must fly!*

fly ➣ *noun* (*plural* **flies**)
1 a small flying insect with two wings **2** a
real or artificial insect used as bait in
fishing **3** the front opening of a pair of
trousers

flying saucer *noun* (*plural* **flying saucers**)
a saucer-shaped flying object believed to
come from outer space, especially in
science fiction stories

flyleaf *noun* (*plural* **flyleaves**)
a blank page at the beginning or end of a
book

flyover *noun* (*plural* **flyovers**)
a bridge that carries one road over another

flywheel *noun* (*plural* **flywheels**)
a heavy wheel fixed to a turning part of a
machine, helping it to run smoothly

foal *noun* (*plural* **foals**)
a young horse

foam ➣ *noun*
1 a mass of tiny bubbles on a liquid; froth
2 a spongy kind of rubber or plastic
foamy *adjective* like foam

foam ➣ *verb* (**foams, foaming, foamed**)
to foam is to form bubbles or froth

focus ➣ *noun* (*plural* **focuses** or **foci**)
1 the distance at which something
appears most clearly to your eye or in a
lens **2** the point at which rays seem to
meet **3** the most important or interesting
part of something
in focus appearing clearly
out of focus appearing blurred
focal *adjective* to do with a focus; at a focus

focus ➣ *verb* (**focuses, focusing, focused**)
1 to focus a lens is to use it or adjust it so
that objects appear clearly **2** to focus your
attention on something is to concentrate
on it

fodder *noun*
food for horses and farm animals

foe *noun* (*plural* **foes**)
(*old use*) an enemy

foetus *noun* (*plural* **foetuses**) (*pronounced* fee-tus)
a developing embryo, especially an unborn human baby
foetal *adjective* to do with a foetus

fog *noun* (*plural* **fogs**)
thick mist
foggy *adjective* having a lot of fog

foghorn *noun* (*plural* **foghorns**)
a loud horn for warning ships in fog

fogy *noun* (*plural* **fogies**)
a person with old-fashioned ideas

foil[1] *noun* (*plural* **foils**)
1 a very thin sheet of metal 2 a person or thing that makes another look better in comparison

foil[2] *noun* (*plural* **foils**)
a long narrow sword used in fencing

foil[3] *verb* (**foils, foiling, foiled**)
to foil someone or something is to prevent them from succeeding ♦ *We managed to foil his wicked plan*

fold[1] ➤ *verb* (**folds, folding, folded**)
1 to fold something is to bend it so that one part lies on another part 2 to fold is to bend or move in this way 3 to fold ingredients in cooking is to blend them together

fold ➤ *noun* (*plural* **folds**)
a line where something is folded

fold[2] *noun* (*plural* **folds**)
an enclosure for sheep

folder *noun* (*plural* **folders**)
a folding cover to keep loose papers in

foliage *noun*
the leaves of a tree or plant

folk *plural noun*
ordinary people

folk dance *noun* (*plural* **folk dances**)
a dance in the traditional style of a country

folklore *noun*
old beliefs and legends

folk song *noun* (*plural* **folk songs**)
a song in the traditional style of a country

follow *verb* (**follows, following, followed**)
1 to follow someone or something is to go or come after them, or to do something after they have 2 to follow someone is also to take them as a guide or example 3 to follow a sport or team is to take an interest

in them or support them ♦ *Which football team do you follow?* 4 to follow someone is to understand them ♦ *Do you follow me?* 5 to follow is to happen as a result ♦ *Who knows what trouble may follow*

follower *noun* (*plural* **followers**)
a person who follows or supports someone or something

following *preposition*
after or as a result of ♦ *Following the break-in we had new locks fitted*

fond *adjective* (**fonder, fondest**)
1 loving ♦ *He gave me a fond goodbye kiss*
2 unwisely hopeful ♦ *They had fond hopes*
to be fond of someone or **something** is to like them very much
fondly *adverb* in a fond way **fondness** *noun* love or liking

font *noun* (*plural* **fonts**)
a stone or wooden basin in a church, to hold water for baptism

food *noun* (*plural* **foods**)
anything that a plant or animal can take into its body to make it grow or give it energy

food chain *noun* (*plural* **food chains**)
a series of plants and animals, each of which serves as food for the one above in the series

fool ➤ *noun* (*plural* **fools**)
1 a silly person 2 a jester or clown ♦ *Stop playing the fool* 3 a pudding made of fruit mixed with custard or cream

fool ➤ *verb* (**fools, fooling, fooled**)
1 to fool is to behave like a fool 2 to fool someone is to trick or deceive them
to fool about or **fool around** is to behave stupidly

foolhardy *adjective* (**foolhardier, foolhardiest**)
bold but foolish; reckless
foolhardiness *noun* being foolhardy

foolish *adjective*
stupid or unwise
foolishly *adverb* in a foolish way **foolishness** *noun* being foolish

foolproof *adjective*
easy to use or do correctly

foot *noun* (*plural* **feet**)
1 the lower part of your leg below your ankle 2 the lowest part of something
♦ *They met up at the foot of the hill* 3 a measure of length, 12 inches or about 30 centimetres
on foot walking

football *noun* (*plural* **footballs**)
1 a game played by two teams which try to kick an inflated ball into their opponents' goal 2 the ball used in this game
footballer *noun* someone who plays football

foothill noun (plural **foothills**)
a low hill near the bottom of a mountain or range of mountains

foothold noun (plural **footholds**)
1 a place to put your foot when climbing 2 a good start in achieving something
♦ Our win has given us a foothold in the championship

footing noun
1 having your feet placed on something; what your feet are standing on ♦ He lost his footing and slipped 2 a position or status ♦ We must try to get on a more friendly footing with them

footlights plural noun
a row of lights along the front of the stage in a theatre

footnote noun (plural **footnotes**)
a note printed at the bottom of the page of a book

footpath noun (plural **footpaths**)
a path for people to walk along

footprint noun (plural **footprints**)
a mark made by a foot or shoe

footstep noun (plural **footsteps**)
a step taken in walking, or the sound it makes

for ➤ preposition
used to show 1 purpose or direction
♦ This letter is for you ♦ We set out for home ♦ Let's go for a walk 2 length of time or distance ♦ We've been waiting for hours ♦ They walked for three miles 3 price or cost ♦ She bought it for £2 4 an alternative ♦ New lamps for old! 5 cause or reason ♦ He was rewarded for bravery
♦ I only did it for the money 6 reference
♦ She has a good ear for music 7 support
♦ Are you for us or against us?
for ever always

for ➤ conjunction
because ♦ They paused, for they heard a noise

forbid verb (**forbids, forbidding, forbade, forbidden**)
1 to forbid someone to do something is to tell them not to do it 2 to forbid something is not to allow it

forbidding adjective
looking stern or unfriendly

force ➤ noun (plural **forces**)
1 strength or power 2 (in Science) an influence that can be measured and that tends to cause things to move 3 an organized body of soldiers or police
in force having effect ♦ Is the rule still in force?

force ➤ verb (**forces, forcing, forced**)
1 to force someone to do something is to use your power or strength to make them do it 2 to force something is to break it open with force

forceful adjective
strong and effective
forcefully adverb in a forceful way

forceps plural noun (pronounced **for**-seps)
pincers or tongs used by a dentist or surgeon

forcible adjective
done by force
forcibly adverb with force

ford noun (plural **fords**)
a shallow place where you can wade or drive across a river

fore ➤ adjective
at or towards the front

fore ➤ noun
the front part
to the fore to or at the front; in a leading position

forecast ➤ noun (plural **forecasts**)
a statement about what is likely to happen, especially what the weather is likely to be

forecast ➤ verb (**forecasts, forecasting, forecast** or **forecasted**)
to forecast something is to say what is likely to happen

forecourt noun (plural **forecourts**)
an area in front of a petrol station or large building

forefathers plural noun
ancestors

forefinger noun (plural **forefingers**)
the finger next to your thumb

foregone conclusion noun
a result that can be foreseen

foreground noun (plural **foregrounds**)
the part of a scene or view that is nearest to you

forehead noun (plural **foreheads**)
(pronounced **for**-hed or **fo**-rid)
the part of your face above your eyes

foreign adjective
1 belonging to or coming from another country 2 strange or unnatural ♦ Lying is foreign to her nature

foreigner noun (plural **foreigners**)
a person from another country

foreman noun (plural **foremen**)
someone in charge of a group of workers

foremost adjective
most important

forename noun (plural **forenames**)
a person's first name

foresee *verb* (**foresees, foreseeing, foresaw, foreseen**)
to foresee something is to realize that it is likely to happen
foreseeable *adjective* able to be foreseen

foresight *noun*
the ability to foresee future needs and prepare for them

forest *noun* (*plural* **forests**)
a large area of trees growing close together
forester *noun* a worker in a forest

forestry *noun*
the science of planting forests and looking after them

foretell *verb* (**foretells, foretelling, foretold**)
to foretell something is to say it will happen

forever *adverb*
continually ♦ *He is forever complaining*

forfeit ➤ *noun* (*plural* **forfeits**)
something that you lose or have to pay as a penalty

forfeit ➤ *verb* (**forfeits, forfeiting, forfeited**)
to forfeit something is to lose it as a penalty

forgave past tense of **forgive**

forge[1] ➤ *noun* (*plural* **forges**)
a place where metal is heated and shaped; a blacksmith's workshop

forge ➤ *verb* (**forges, forging, forged**)
1 to forge metal is to shape it by heating and hammering 2 to forge money or a signature is to copy it in order to deceive people

forge[2] *verb* (**forges, forging, forged**)
to forge ahead is to make progress with a strong effort

forgery *noun* (*plural* **forgeries**)
1 forgery is copying something in order to deceive people 2 a forgery is a copy made by forging it

forget *verb* (**forgets, forgetting, forgot, forgotten**)
1 to forget something is to fail to remember it 2 to forget something is also to stop thinking about it ♦ *Try to forget your worries*
to forget yourself is to behave rudely or thoughtlessly

forgetful *adjective*
tending to forget things
forgetfulness *noun* being forgetful

forget-me-not *noun* (*plural* **forget-me-nots**)
a plant with small blue flowers

forgive *verb* (**forgives, forgiving, forgave, forgiven**)
to forgive someone is to stop being angry with them for something they have done
forgiveness *noun* forgiving someone

fork ➤ *noun* (*plural* **forks**)
1 a small device with prongs for lifting food to your mouth 2 a large device with prongs used for digging or lifting things 3 a place where a road or river divides into two or more parts

fork ➤ *verb* (**forks, forking, forked**)
1 to fork something is to dig or lift it with a fork 2 to fork is to divide into two or more branches ♦ *Go left where the road forks*
to fork out (*informal*) is to pay out money

fork-lift truck *noun* (*plural* **fork-lift trucks**)
a truck with two metal bars at the front for lifting and moving heavy loads

forlorn *adjective*
left alone and unhappy

form ➤ *noun* (*plural* **forms**)
1 the form of something is its shape and general appearance ♦ *The dark form of a tree stood out on the brow of the hill* 2 a form is the way in which something exists; a kind of thing ♦ *Ice is a form of water* 3 a form is also a class in a school 4 a form is also a piece of paper with printed questions and spaces for the answers

form ➤ *verb* (**forms, forming, formed**)
1 to form something is to shape or make it 2 to form is to come into existence or develop ♦ *Icicles formed on the window*

formal *adjective*
1 strictly following the accepted rules or customs ♦ *You will receive a formal invitation to the wedding* 2 ceremonial ♦ *The formal opening of the bridge takes place tomorrow*
formally *adverb* in a formal way

formality *noun* (*plural* **formalities**)
1 formality is formal behaviour 2 a formality is something done to obey a rule or custom

format *noun* (*plural* **formats**)
1 the shape and size of a book or magazine
2 the way something is organized ♦ *What will the format of the lesson be?*

formation *noun* (*plural* **formations**)
1 the action of forming something
2 something formed ♦ *We were studying formations of rock* 3 a special pattern or arrangement ♦ *The aircraft were flying in formation*

former *adjective*
earlier; of past times ♦ *The house had been an inn in former days*
the former the first of two people or things just mentioned ♦ *If it's a choice between a picnic or a swim I prefer the former*
See also **latter**

formerly *adverb*
once; previously

formidable *adjective* (*pronounced* for-mid-a-bul)
1 frightening or alarming ♦ *She is a formidable woman* 2 very difficult to deal with or do ♦ *This is a formidable task*
formidably *adverb* in a formidable way

formula *noun* (*plural* **formulas** or **formulae**)
1 a set of chemical symbols showing what a substance consists of ♦ *H_2O is the formula for water* 2 a rule or statement expressed in symbols or numbers 3 a list of what is needed for making something
4 one of the groups into which racing cars are placed according to their engine size, for example Formula 1

formulate *verb* (**formulates, formulating, formulated**)
to formulate an idea or plan is to express it clearly and exactly

forsake *verb* (**forsakes, forsaking, forsook, forsaken**)
to forsake someone is to abandon them

fort *noun* (*plural* **forts**)
a fortified building

forth *adverb*
forwards or onwards

fortification *noun* (*plural* **fortifications**)
a place that is built with strong defences against attack

fortify *verb* (**fortifies, fortifying, fortified**)
1 to fortify a place is to make it strong against attack 2 to fortify someone is to make them strong and fit ♦ *A good breakfast will fortify you*

fortnight *noun* (*plural* **fortnights**)
a period of two weeks
fortnightly *adverb* and *adjective* every two weeks

fortress *noun* (*plural* **fortresses**)
a large fort or fortified town

fortunate *adjective*
lucky
fortunately *adverb* luckily

fortune *noun* (*plural* **fortunes**)
1 fortune is luck or chance 2 a fortune is a large amount of money

fortune-teller *noun* (*plural* **fortune-tellers**)
someone who tells you what will happen to you in the future

forty *noun* (*plural* **forties**)
the number 40
fortieth *adjective* and *noun* 40th

forward ➤ *adjective*
1 going forwards 2 placed in the front
3 having made more than normal progress; clever 4 too eager or bold

forward ➤ *adverb*
forwards

forward ➤ *noun* (*plural* **forwards**)
a player in the front line of a team at football, hockey, and other games

forwards *adverb*
to or towards the front; in the direction you are facing

fossil *noun* (*plural* **fossils**)
the remains of a prehistoric animal or plant that has been in the ground for a very long time and become hardened in rock

fossilized *adjective* formed into a fossil

foster *verb* (**fosters, fostering, fostered**)
to foster someone is to bring up someone else's child as if they were your own

foster child *noun* (*plural* **foster children**)
a child brought up by foster parents

foster parent *noun* (*plural* **foster parents**)
a parent who is fostering a child

fought past tense and past participle of **fight** *verb*

foul ➤ *adjective* (**fouler, foulest**)
1 disgusting; tasting or smelling unpleasant **2** unfair; breaking the rules of a game
foully *adverb* in a foul way **foulness** *noun* being foul

foul ➤ *noun* (*plural* **fouls**)
an action that breaks the rules of a game

foul ➤ *verb* (**fouls, fouling, fouled**)
to foul a player in a game is to commit a foul against them

found[1] *verb* (**founds, founding, founded**)
to found an organization or society is to start it or set it up ♦ *They founded a hospital*

found[2] past tense and past participle of **find**

foundation *noun* (*plural* **foundations**)
1 the solid base on which a building is built **2** the basis for something **3** the founding of something

founder[1] *noun* (*plural* **founders**)
someone who founds something ♦ *Guru Nanak was the founder of the Sikh religion*

founder[2] *verb* (**founders, foundering, foundered**)
1 to founder is to fill with water and sink ♦ *The ship foundered* **2** to founder is to fail completely ♦ *Their plans have foundered*

foundry *noun* (*plural* **foundries**)
a factory or workshop where metal or glass is made

fountain *noun* (*plural* **fountains**)
an outdoor structure in which jets of water shoot up into the air

fountain pen *noun* (*plural* **fountain pens**)
a pen that can be filled with a cartridge or a supply of ink

four *noun* (*plural* **fours**)
the number 4
on all fours on hands and knees

fourteen *noun* (*plural* **fourteens**)
the number 14
fourteenth *adjective* and *noun* 14th

fourth *adjective* and *noun*
the next after the third
fourthly *adverb* in the fourth place; as the fourth one

fowl *noun* (*plural* **fowl** or **fowls**)
a bird that is kept for its eggs or meat

fox ➤ *noun* (*plural* **foxes**)
a wild animal that looks like a dog with a long furry tail
foxy *adjective* like a fox; cunning

fox ➤ *verb* (**foxes, foxing, foxed**)
to fox someone is to puzzle them

foxglove *noun* (*plural* **foxgloves**)
a tall plant with flowers like the fingers of gloves

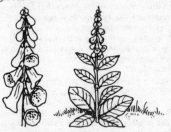

foyer *noun* (*plural* **foyers**) (*pronounced* foi-ay)
the entrance hall of a cinema, theatre, or hotel

fraction *noun* (*plural* **fractions**)
1 a number that is not a whole number, for example $\frac{1}{2}$ and 0·5 **2** a tiny part

fractionally *adverb*
by a small amount; very slightly ♦ *Their new house is fractionally larger*

fracture ➤ *verb* (**fractures, fracturing, fractured**)
to fracture something, especially a bone, is to break it

fracture ➤ *noun* (*plural* **fractures**)
the breaking of something, especially a bone

fragile *adjective* (*pronounced* fra-jyl)
easy to break or damage
fragility *noun* being fragile

fragment *noun* (*plural* **fragments**)
1 a small piece broken off something **2** a small part ♦ *She overheard fragments of conversation*
fragmentary *adjective* consisting of small pieces; not whole **fragmentation** *noun* making something into fragments

fragrant *adjective* (*pronounced* fray-grant)
having a sweet or pleasant smell
fragrance *noun* being fragrant

frail *adjective* (**frailer, frailest**)
weak or fragile
frailty *noun* being frail

frame ➤ *noun* (*plural* **frames**)
1 a set of wooden or metal strips that fit round the outside of a picture to hold it **2** a rigid structure that supports something ♦ *I've broken the frame of my glasses* **3** a human body ♦ *He has a small frame*
your frame of mind is the way you think or feel for a while ♦ *Wait till he's in a better frame of mind*

frame ➤ *verb* (**frames, framing, framed**)
1 to frame a picture is to put a frame round it 2 to frame laws or proposals is to put them together 3 (*slang*) to frame someone is to make them seem guilty when they are innocent

framework *noun* (*plural* **frameworks**)
1 a frame supporting something 2 a basic plan or system

franc *noun* (*plural* **francs**)
a unit of money in France, Switzerland, and some other countries

franchise *noun* (*plural* **franchises**)
1 the franchise is the right to vote in elections 2 a franchise is a licence to sell a firm's goods or services in a certain area

frank ➤ *adjective* (**franker, frankest**)
honest; making your thoughts and feelings clear to people
frankly *adverb* in a frank way **frankness** *noun* being frank

frank ➤ *verb* (**franks, franking, franked**)
to frank a letter or parcel is to mark it with a postmark

frantic *adjective*
wildly agitated or excited
frantically *adverb* in a frantic way

fraud *noun* (*plural* **frauds**)
1 fraud is the crime of swindling people; a fraud is a swindle 2 a fraud is also someone who is not what they pretend to be
fraudulent *adjective* dishonest

fraught *adjective*
tense or upset

frayed *adjective*
1 worn and ragged at the edge ♦ *Your shirt collar is frayed* 2 strained or upset ♦ *Tempers became frayed*

freak *noun* (*plural* **freaks**)
1 a very strange or abnormal person, animal, or thing 2 (*informal*) someone who is a keen fan of something ♦ *She is a fitness freak*
freakish *adjective* unusual

freckle *noun* (*plural* **freckles**)
a small brown spot on the skin
freckled *adjective* having freckles

free ➤ *adjective* (**freer, freest**)
1 able to do what you want to do or go where you want to go 2 not costing anything ♦ *Entrance to the museum is free* 3 available; not being used or occupied ♦ *Our afternoons are free* 4 generous ♦ *She is very free with her money*
to be free of something is not to have it or be affected by it ♦ *The roads are free of ice*
freely *adverb* in a free way; as you want

free ➤ *verb* (**frees, freeing, freed**)
to free someone or something is to make them free

freedom *noun*
being free; independence

freehand *adjective* and *adverb*
without using a ruler or compasses when drawing ♦ *Draw a circle freehand*

free-range *adjective*
1 free-range hens are allowed to move about freely in the open instead of being caged 2 free-range eggs are those laid by free-range hens

freewheel *verb* (**freewheels, freewheeling, freewheeled**)
to freewheel is to ride a bicycle without pedalling

freeze *verb* (**freezes, freezing, froze, frozen**)
1 to freeze is to turn into ice or another solid, or to become covered with ice ♦ *The pond froze last night* 2 to be freezing or to be frozen is to be very cold ♦ *My hands are frozen* 3 to freeze food is to store it at a low temperature to preserve it 4 to freeze wages or prices is to keep them at a fixed level 5 a person or animal freezes when they suddenly stand still with fright

freezer *noun* (*plural* **freezers**)
a large refrigerator for keeping food frozen

freezing point *noun* (*plural* **freezing points**)
the temperature at which a liquid freezes

freight *noun* (*pronounced* frayt)
goods carried by road or in a ship or aircraft

freighter *noun* (*plural* **freighters**)
a ship or aircraft for carrying goods

French window *noun* (*plural* **French windows**)
a long window that reaches down to the ground and serves as a door

frenzy *noun* (*plural* **frenzies**)
wild excitement; madness
frenzied *adjective* wildly excited

frequency *noun* (*plural* **frequencies**)
1 how often something happens 2 being frequent 3 the number of vibrations made each second by a wave of sound or light

frequent ➤ *adjective* (*pronounced* free-kwent)
happening often
frequently *adverb* often

frequent ➤ *verb* (**frequents, frequenting, frequented**) (*pronounced* fri-kwent)
to frequent a place is to visit it often
♦ *They frequented the youth club*

fresh *adjective* (**fresher, freshest**)
1 newly made or produced; not old or used ♦ *We need fresh bread* 2 not tinned or preserved ♦ *Would you like some fresh fruit?* 3 cool and clean ♦ *It's nice to be in the fresh air* 4 fresh water is water that is not salty
freshly *adverb* newly, recently **freshness** *noun* being fresh

freshen *verb* (**freshens, freshening, freshened**)
1 to freshen something is to make it fresh
2 to freshen is to become fresh

freshwater *adjective*
freshwater fish live in rivers or lakes and not the sea

fret *verb* (**frets, fretting, fretted**)
to fret is to worry or be upset about something
fretful *adjective* worried and upset **fretfully** *adverb* in a fretful way

fretsaw *noun* (*plural* **fretsaws**)
a narrow saw used for making fretwork

fretwork *noun*
1 the skill of cutting decorative patterns in wood 2 wood cut in this way

friar *noun* (*plural* **friars**)
a man who is a member of a Roman Catholic order and has vowed to live a life of poverty
friary *noun* a house of friars

friction *noun*
1 rubbing of one thing against another
2 disagreement; quarrelling

Friday *noun* (*plural* **Fridays**)
the sixth day of the week

fridge *noun* (*plural* **fridges**)
(*informal*) a refrigerator

friend *noun* (*plural* **friends**)
1 someone you like and who likes you 2 a helpful or kind person
friendless *adjective* without friends

friendly *adjective* (**friendlier, friendliest**)
behaving like a friend; kind and helpful
friendliness *noun* being friendly

friendship *noun* (*plural* **friendships**)
being friends

frieze *noun* (*plural* **friezes**) (*pronounced* freez)
a strip of designs or pictures along the top of a wall

frigate *noun* (*plural* **frigates**)
a small fast warship

fright *noun* (*plural* **frights**)
1 sudden great fear 2 (*informal*) a person or thing that looks ridiculous

frighten *verb* (**frightens, frightening, frightened**)
to frighten someone is to make them afraid

frightful *adjective*
awful; very great or bad ♦ *It's a frightful shame*
frightfully *adverb* awfully; very

frill *noun* (*plural* **frills**)
1 a decorative pleated edging on a dress or curtain 2 an unnecessary extra ♦ *We lead a simple life with no frills*
frilled *adjective* having a frill **frilly** *adjective* like a frill; having frills

fringe *noun* (*plural* **fringes**)
1 a decorative edging with many threads hanging down loosely 2 a straight line of short hair hanging down over the forehead 3 the edge of something ♦ *He stood on the fringe of the crowd*
fringed *adjective* having a fringe

frisk *verb* (**frisks, frisking, frisked**)
1 to frisk is to jump or run around playfully 2 (*informal*) to frisk someone is to search them by moving the hands over their body

frisky *adjective* (**friskier, friskiest**)
playful or lively
friskily *adverb* in a frisky way **friskiness** *noun* being frisky

fritter[1] *noun* (*plural* **fritters**)
a slice of meat, potato, or fruit fried in batter

fritter[2] *verb* (**fritters, frittering, frittered**)
to fritter something or fritter it away is to waste it gradually ♦ *He frittered all his money on comics*

frivolous *adjective*
1 light-hearted and playful 2 trivial ♦ *We all enjoy frivolous pleasures*
frivolity *noun* playfulness **frivolously** *adverb* in a frivolous way

frizzy *adjective* (**frizzier, frizziest**)
tightly curled ♦ *She has frizzy hair*

fro *adverb*
to and fro backwards and forwards

frock *noun* (*plural* **frocks**)
a girl's or woman's dress

frog *noun* (*plural* **frogs**)
a small jumping animal that can live both
in water and on land

to have a frog in your throat is to be hoarse

frogman *noun* (*plural* **frogmen**)
a swimmer equipped with a rubber suit
and flippers and breathing apparatus for
swimming under water

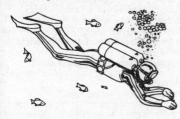

frolic ➤ *noun* (*plural* **frolics**)
a lively cheerful game or pastime

frolicsome *adjective* lively and cheerful

frolic ➤ *verb* (**frolics, frolicking, frolicked**)
to frolic is to spend time in lively cheerful
games or activities

from *preposition*
used to show 1 a beginning or starting
point ♦ *She comes from London* ♦ *Buses
run from 8 o'clock* 2 distance ♦ *We are a
mile from home* 3 separation ♦ *Get the
gun from him* 4 origin or source ♦ *Get
water from the tap* 5 cause ♦ *I suffer from
headaches* 6 difference ♦ *Can you tell
margarine from butter?*

front *noun* (*plural* **fronts**)
1 the part of a person or thing that faces
forwards; the most important side of
something ♦ *The front of the house is
blue* 2 the part of a thing or place that is
furthest forward ♦ *Go to the front of the
class* 3 a road or promenade along the
seashore 4 the place where fighting is
happening in a war ♦ *More troops were
moved to the front* 5 in weather systems,
the forward edge of an approaching mass

of air ♦ *There is a warm front out in the
Atlantic*

in front at or near the front

frontier *noun* (*plural* **frontiers**)
the boundary between two countries or
regions

frost ➤ *noun* (*plural* **frosts**)
1 powdery ice that forms on things in
freezing weather 2 weather with a
temperature below freezing point

frost ➤ *verb* (**frosts, frosting, frosted**)
to frost something is to cover it with frost
or frosting

frostbite *noun*
harm done to the body by very cold
weather

frostbitten *adjective* suffering from frostbite

frosted glass *noun*
glass that is made cloudy so that you
cannot see clearly through it

frosting *noun*
sugar icing for cakes

frosty *adjective*
1 like frost; covered in frost 2 unfriendly
♦ *She gave us a frosty look*

froth ➤ *noun*
a white mass of tiny bubbles on or in a
liquid

frothy *adjective*

froth ➤ *verb* (**froths, frothing, frothed**)
to froth is to form a froth

frown ➤ *verb* (**frowns, frowning, frowned**)
to frown is to wrinkle your forehead
because you are angry or worried

frown ➤ *noun* (*plural* **frowns**)
the wrinkling of your forehead when you
frown

froze past tense of **freeze**

frozen past participle of **freeze**

frugal *adjective* (*pronounced* **froo**-gal)
1 spending very little money ♦ *The girls
tried to be frugal with their pocket money*
2 costing little money ♦ *They ate a frugal
meal*

frugality *noun* being frugal

fruit *noun* (*plural* **fruit** or **fruits**)
1 the seed-container that grows on a tree
or plant and is often used as food, such as
apples, oranges, and bananas 2 the result
of doing something ♦ *He lived to see the
fruits of his efforts*

fruitful *adjective*
1 successful; having good results ♦ *Their
talks were fruitful* 2 producing fruit

fruitfully *adverb* in a fruitful way

fruitless *adjective*
unsuccessful; having no results
fruitlessly *adverb* without success

fruity *adjective* (**fruitier, fruitiest**)
1 tasting like fruit 2 full and rich ♦ *She sang with a fruity voice*

frustrate *verb* (**frustrates, frustrating, frustrated**)
to frustrate someone is to prevent them from doing something or from succeeding in something
frustration *noun* being frustrated

fry *verb* (**fries, frying, fried**)
to fry food is to cook it in hot fat

frying pan *noun* (*plural* **frying pans**)
a shallow pan in which things are fried
out of the frying pan into the fire from a bad situation to something worse

fudge *noun*
a soft sweet made with milk, sugar, and butter

fuel ➤ *noun* (*plural* **fuels**)
something that is burnt to make heat or power, such as coal and oil

fuel ➤ *verb* (**fuels, fuelling, fuelled**)
to fuel something is to provide it with material to burn to make heat or power

fug *noun* (*plural* **fugs**)
(*informal*) a stuffy atmosphere in a room
fuggy *adjective* stuffy

fugitive *noun* (*plural* **fugitives**) (*pronounced* few-ji-tiv)
a person who is running away from something, especially from the law

-ful *suffix*
meaning 'full of', as in the adjectives *plentiful* and *truthful* and the nouns *handful* and *spoonful*

fulcrum *noun* (*plural* **fulcra** or **fulcrums**)
the point on which a lever rests

fulfil *verb* (**fulfils, fulfilling, fulfilled**)
1 to fulfil something is to achieve it 2 to fulfil a prophecy is to make it come true
fulfilment *noun* fulfilling something; achievement

full ➤ *adjective*
1 containing as much or as many as possible ♦ *The cinema was full* 2 having many people or things ♦ *They are full of ideas* 3 complete ♦ *We want the full story* 4 the greatest possible ♦ *They drove at full speed* 5 fitting loosely; having many folds ♦ *She's wearing a full skirt*
in full not leaving anything out
to the full completely; thoroughly
fullness *noun* being full **fully** *adverb* completely

full ➤ *adverb*
completely; very ♦ *You knew full well what I wanted*

full moon *noun* (*plural* **full moons**)
the moon when you can see the whole of it as a bright disc

full stop *noun* (*plural* **full stops**)
the dot used as a punctuation mark at the end of a sentence or an abbreviation

full-time *adjective* and *adverb*
for all the normal working hours of the day ♦ *She has a full-time job* ♦ *She works full-time*

fumble *verb* (**fumbles, fumbling, fumbled**)
to fumble something is to hold or handle it clumsily

fume *verb* (**fumes, fuming, fumed**)
1 to fume is to give off strong-smelling smoke or gas 2 to be fuming is to be very angry

fumes *plural noun*
strong-smelling smoke or gas

fun *noun*
amusement or enjoyment
to make fun of someone or **something** is to make them look silly or funny

function ➤ *noun* (*plural* **functions**)
1 what someone or something does or ought to do ♦ *The function of a doctor is to cure sick people* 2 an important event or party 3 a basic operation of a computer or calculator

function ➤ *verb* (**functions, functioning, functioned**)
to function is to work properly or perform a function ♦ *The chair also functions as a small table*

functional *adjective*
1 working properly ♦ *The drinks machine is fully functional again* 2 practical ♦ *I need a car with a simple functional design*
functionally *adverb* in a functional way

fund *noun* (*plural* **funds**)
a fund is money collected or kept for a special purpose ♦ *They started a fund for refugees*

fundamental *adjective*
basic
fundamentally *adverb* basically

funeral *noun* (*plural* **funerals**)
the ceremony where a dead person is
buried or cremated

fungus *noun* (*plural* **fungi**)
a plant without leaves or flowers that
grows on other plants or on decayed
material, such as mushrooms and
toadstools

funk *verb* (**funks, funking, funked**)
(*informal*) to funk something is to be
afraid of it and avoid it

funnel *noun* (*plural* **funnels**)
1 a chimney on a ship or steam engine
2 a tube that is wide at the top and narrow
at the bottom, to help you pour things into
bottles or other containers

funny *adjective* (**funnier, funniest**)
1 that makes you laugh or smile ♦ *We
heard a funny joke* 2 strange or odd
♦ *There's a funny smell in here*
funnily *adverb* in a funny way

funny bone *noun* (*plural* **funny bones**)
part of your elbow which gives you a
strange tingling feeling if you knock it

fur *noun* (*plural* **furs**)
1 the soft hair that covers some animals
2 animal skin with the hair on it, used for
clothing; fabric that looks like animal skin
with hair on it

furious *adjective*
1 very angry 2 violent or extreme ♦ *They
were travelling at a furious speed*
furiously *adverb* angrily; extremely

furl *verb* (**furls, furling, furled**)
to furl a sail or flag or umbrella is to roll it
up and fasten it

furlong *noun* (*plural* **furlongs**)
one-eighth of a mile, 220 yards or about
201 metres

furnace *noun* (*plural* **furnaces**)
an oven in which great heat can be
produced for making glass or heating
metals

furnish *verb* (**furnishes, furnishing, furnished**)
to furnish a room or building is to provide
it with furniture

furniture *noun*
tables, chairs, beds, cupboards, and other
movable things that you need inside a
building

furrow *noun* (*plural* **furrows**)
1 a long cut in the ground made by a
plough 2 a deep wrinkle on the skin

furry *adjective* (**furrier, furriest**)
1 soft and hairy like fur 2 covered with
fur

further ➤ *adverb* and *adjective*
1 at or to a greater distance; more distant
♦ *I can't walk any further* 2 more ♦ *We
need further information*

further ➤ *verb* (**furthers, furthering, furthered**)
to further something is to help it make
progress ♦ *We want to further the cause of
peace*

further education *noun*
education for people above school age

furthermore *adverb*
also; moreover

furthest *adverb* and *adjective*
at or to the greatest distance; most distant

furtive *adjective*
cautious, trying not to be seen ♦ *He gave a
furtive glance and helped himself to the
biscuits*

fury *noun* (*plural* **furies**)
wild anger or rage

fuse[1] ➤ *noun* (*plural* **fuses**)
a safety device containing a short piece of
wire that melts if too much electricity
passes through it

fuse ➤ *verb* (**fuses, fusing, fused**)
1 to fuse is to stop working because a fuse
has melted ♦ *The lights have fused* 2 to
fuse things is to blend them together,
especially through melting

fuse[2] *noun* (*plural* **fuses**)
a device for setting off an explosive

fuselage *noun* (*plural* **fuselages**)
(*pronounced* few-ze-lah*zh*)
the body of an aircraft

fusion *noun* (*pronounced* few-zh*o*n)
1 the action of blending or joining together
2 the joining together of the nuclei of
atoms, usually releasing energy

fuss ➤ *noun* (*plural* **fusses**)
unnecessary excitement or worry about
something that is not important
to make a fuss of someone is to treat them
with great kindness and attention

fuss ➤ *verb* (**fusses, fussing, fussed**)
to fuss is to be excited or worried about
something that is not important

fussy *adjective* (**fussier, fussiest**)
1 fussing; inclined to make a fuss 2 full of
unnecessary details or decorations
fussily *adverb* in a fussy way **fussiness** *noun*
being fussy

futile *adjective* (*pronounced* few-tyl)
useless; having no result
futility *noun* being futile

futon *noun* (*plural* **futons**) (*pronounced* **foo**-ton)
a seat with a mattress that rolls out to form a bed

future *noun*
1 the time that will come 2 what is going to happen in the time that will come
in future from now onwards

future tense *noun*
the form of a verb that shows that something is going to happen in the time that will come. In English, the future tense uses 'will' and 'shall' in front of the verb, for example *I shall come tomorrow*

fuzz *noun*
something soft and fluffy like soft hair

fuzzy *adjective* (**fuzzier, fuzziest**)
1 blurred; not clear 2 covered in fuzz
fuzzily *adverb* in a fuzzy way **fuzziness** *noun* being fuzzy

Gg

g short for **gram** or **grams**

gabardine *noun* (*plural* **gabardines**)
a coat made of a smooth heavy fabric

gabble *verb* (**gabbles, gabbling, gabbled**)
to gabble is to talk so quickly that it is difficult to hear the words

gable *noun* (*plural* **gables**)
the three-sided part of a wall between two sloping roofs
gabled *adjective* having a gable

gadget *noun* (*plural* **gadgets**) (*pronounced* **gaj**-it)
a small useful device or tool

Gaelic *noun* (*pronounced* **gay**-lik (in Ireland) or **gal**-ik (in Scotland))
a Celtic language that is spoken in Ireland and (in a different form) in the Highlands of Scotland

gag ➤ *noun* (*plural* **gags**)
1 something put over someone's mouth to stop them from speaking 2 (*informal*) a joke

gag ➤ *verb* (**gags, gagging, gagged**)
to gag someone is to put a gag over their mouth

gaiety *noun*
being cheerful; amusement

gaily *adverb*
in a cheerful way

gain ➤ *verb* (**gains, gaining, gained**)
1 to gain something is to get it when you did not have it before 2 a clock or watch gains when it goes ahead of the correct time
to gain on someone is to come closer to them when you are following them

gain ➤ *noun* (*plural* **gains**)
something you have got that you did not have before; profit

gala *noun* (*plural* **galas**) (*pronounced* **gah**-la)
1 a festival 2 a series of sports contests, especially in swimming

galaxy *noun* (*plural* **galaxies**) (*pronounced* **gal**-ak-si)
a very large group of stars
galactic *adjective* to do with a galaxy

gale *noun* (*plural* **gales**)
a very strong wind

gallant *adjective*
brave or courteous
gallantly *adverb* in a gallant way **gallantry** *noun* being gallant

galleon *noun* (*plural* **galleons**)
a large Spanish sailing ship used in the 16th and 17th centuries

gallery *noun* (*plural* **galleries**)
1 a platform sticking out from the inside wall of a building 2 the highest set of seats in a cinema or theatre 3 a long room or passage 4 a building or room for showing works of art

galley *noun* (*plural* **galleys**)
1 an ancient type of long ship driven by oars 2 the kitchen in a ship

gallon *noun* (*plural* **gallons**)
a measure of liquid, 8 pints or about 4·5 litres

gallop ➤ *noun* (*plural* **gallops**)
1 the fastest pace that a horse can go 2 a fast ride on a horse

gallop ➤ *verb* (**gallops, galloping, galloped**)
to gallop is to ride fast on a horse

gallows *plural noun*
a framework with a noose for hanging
criminals

galore *adjective*
in large amounts ♦ *There was food galore
at the party*

galvanize *verb* (**galvanizes, galvanizing,
galvanized**)
1 to galvanize iron is to coat it with zinc to
protect it from rust 2 to galvanize
someone is to stimulate or shock them into
doing something

gamble ➤ *verb* (**gambles, gambling, gambled**)
1 to gamble is to play a betting game for
money 2 to gamble with something is to
take great risks ♦ *He was gambling with
his life*
gambler *noun* someone who gambles

gamble ➤ *noun* (*plural* **gambles**)
1 a bet or chance ♦ *Let's have a gamble on
the lottery* 2 a risk ♦ *Having our holiday
in March is a bit of a gamble*

game ➤ *noun* (*plural* **games**)
1 something that you can play, usually
with rules ♦ *They had a game of football*
♦ *Do you like computer games?* 2 a
section of a long game like tennis or whist
3 a trick or scheme ♦ *What's his game, I
wonder?* 4 wild animals or birds hunted
for sport or food
to give the game away is to reveal a secret

game ➤ *adjective*
1 able and willing to do something ♦ *Are
you game for a swim?* 2 brave ♦ *She's a
game lass*

gamekeeper *noun* (*plural* **gamekeepers**)
someone whose job is to protect game birds
and animals, especially from poachers

gammon *noun*
a kind of ham or thick bacon

gander *noun* (*plural* **ganders**)
a male goose

gang ➤ *noun* (*plural* **gangs**)
1 a group of people who do things together
2 a group of criminals

gang ➤ *verb* (**gangs, ganging, ganged**)
to gang up on someone is to form a group to
oppose them or frighten them

gangplank *noun* (*plural* **gangplanks**)
a plank for walking on to or off a ship

gangster *noun* (*plural* **gangsters**)
a member of a gang of violent criminals

gangway *noun* (*plural* **gangways**)
1 a gap left for people to move along
between rows of seats or through a crowd
2 a movable bridge for getting on or off a
ship

gaol *noun* and *verb*
a different spelling of
jail

gaoler *noun*
a different spelling of
jailer

gap *noun* (*plural* **gaps**)
1 an opening or break in something 2 an
interval

gape *verb* (**gapes, gaping, gaped**)
1 to gape is to open your mouth wide 2 to
gape is also to stare in amazement

garage *noun* (*plural* **garages**) (*pronounced*
ga-rah*zh* or **ga-rij**)
1 a building for keeping motor vehicles in
2 a place where motor vehicles are
serviced and repaired and where petrol is
sold

garbage *noun*
household refuse or rubbish

garden *noun* (*plural* **gardens**)
a piece of ground where flowers, fruit, or
vegetables are grown

gardener *noun* (*plural* **gardeners**)
someone who looks after gardens,
especially as a job

gardening *noun*
looking after a garden

gargle *verb* (**gargles, gargling, gargled**)
to gargle is to wash your throat by holding
liquid at the back of your mouth and
breathing air through it

gargoyle *noun* (*plural* **gargoyles**)
an ugly or comical carving of a face on a
building, especially one that sticks out
from a gutter and sends out rainwater
through its mouth

garland *noun* (*plural* **garlands**)
a wreath of flowers worn as a decoration

garlic *noun*
a plant with a bulb divided into sections
(called cloves), which have a strong smell
and taste and are used in cooking

garment *noun* (*plural* **garments**)
a piece of clothing

garnish verb (garnishes, garnishing, garnished)
to garnish a dish of food is to decorate it
with extra items such as salad

garrison noun (plural garrisons)
troops who stay in a town or fort to defend
it

garter noun (plural garters)
a band of elastic to hold up a sock or
stocking

gas ➤ noun (plural gases)
1 a substance, such as oxygen, that can
move freely and is not liquid or solid at
normal temperatures 2 a gas that burns
and is used for heating or cooking ♦ Gas is
used for gas cookers and gas fires
gaseous adjective in the form of a gas

gas ➤ verb (gasses, gassing, gassed)
to gas someone is to kill or injure them
with a poisonous gas

gash noun (plural gashes)
a long deep cut or wound

gasket noun (plural gaskets)
a flat ring or strip of soft material for
sealing a joint between metal surfaces

gasoline noun
(in America) petrol

gasometer noun (plural gasometers)
(pronounced gas-om-it-er)
a large round tank in which gas is stored

gasp verb (gasps, gasping, gasped)
1 to gasp is to breathe in suddenly when
you are shocked or surprised 2 to gasp is
also to struggle to breathe when you are ill
or tired 3 to gasp something is to say it in
a breathless way

gastric adjective
to do with the stomach

gate noun (plural gates)
1 a movable barrier, usually on hinges,
used as a door in a wall or fence 2 a
barrier used to control the flow of water in
a dam or lock 3 a place where you wait
before you board an aircraft 4 the
number of people attending a football
match

gateau noun (plural gateaux) (pronounced
gat-oh)
a rich cream cake

gateway noun (plural gateways)
an opening containing a gate

gather verb (gathers, gathering, gathered)
1 to gather is to come together 2 to
gather people or things is to bring them
together 3 to gather flowers or fruit is to
pick them 4 to gather a piece of
information is to hear or read about it ♦ I
gather you've been on holiday
to gather speed is to move gradually faster

gathering noun (plural gatherings)
an assembly or meeting of people; a party

gaudy adjective (gaudier, gaudiest)
very showy and bright

gauge ➤ noun (plural gauges) (pronounced
gayj)
1 a measuring instrument, such as a fuel
gauge 2 one of the standard sizes of
something 3 the distance between a pair
of railway lines

gauge ➤ verb (gauges, gauging, gauged)
to gauge something is to measure it or
estimate it ♦ We need to gauge the likely
size of the audience

gaunt adjective
a gaunt person is thin and tired-looking

gauntlet[1] noun (plural gauntlets)
a glove with a wide covering for the wrist
to throw down the gauntlet is to offer a
challenge

gauntlet[2] noun
to run the gauntlet is to face a lot of criticism
or risks

gauze noun
thin transparent material

gave past tense of **give**

gay adjective (gayer, gayest)
1 cheerful 2 brightly coloured
3 (informal) homosexual

gaze ➤ verb (gazes, gazing, gazed)
to gaze at something or someone is to look
at them hard for a long time

gaze ➤ noun (plural gazes)
a long steady look

gazetteer noun (plural gazetteers)
a list of place names

GCSE short for **General Certificate of Secondary
Education**

gear noun (plural gears)
1 a gear is a set of toothed wheels working
together in a machine, especially those
connecting the engine to the wheels of a
vehicle 2 gear is equipment or clothes
♦ We'll need our rain gear
in gear with the gears connected
out of gear with the gears not connected

gee interjection
1 a command to a horse to go on or go
faster ♦ Gee up! 2 an exclamation of
surprise or disappointment

geese plural of **goose**

Geiger counter noun (plural Geiger counters)
a device that detects and measures
radioactivity

gel noun (plural gels)
a substance like jelly, especially one used
to give a style to hair

gelatine *noun*
a clear tasteless substance used to make jellies

gelding *noun* (*plural* **geldings**)
a male horse that has been neutered

gem *noun* (*plural* **gems**)
1 a precious stone or jewel **2** an excellent person or thing ♦ *Her auntie's a real gem*

gender *noun* (*plural* **genders**) (*pronounced* jen-der)
the group to which a noun or pronoun belongs in some languages (masculine, feminine, and neuter)

gene *noun* (*plural* **genes**) (*pronounced* jeen)
the part of a living cell that controls which characteristics (such as the colour of your hair or eyes) you inherit from your parents

genealogy *noun* (*plural* **genealogies**) (*pronounced* jeen-ee-al-o-jee)
1 genealogy is the study of the history of families **2** a genealogy is a list or diagram of the members of a family

general ➤ *adjective*
1 to do with most people or things ♦ *The general rule is that we leave after lunch* **2** not detailed or specialized ♦ *That is the general idea*
in general usually; to do with most people

general ➤ *noun* (*plural* **generals**)
an army officer of high rank

general election *noun* (*plural* **general elections**)
an election of Members of Parliament for the whole country

generalize *verb* (**generalizes, generalizing, generalized**)
to generalize is to say things about people or things generally
generalization *noun* a general statement

generally *adverb*
usually; to do with most people

general practitioner *noun* (*plural* **general practitioners**)
a doctor who treats all kinds of diseases and sends people to specialists if necessary

generate *verb* (**generates, generating, generated**)
to generate something is to produce or create it

generation *noun* (*plural* **generations**)
1 generating something **2** a single stage in a family ♦ *Three generations were included: children, parents, and grandparents* **3** all the people born about the same time ♦ *His generation grew up during the war*

generator *noun* (*plural* **generators**)
a machine for producing electricity

generous *adjective*
ready to give or share what you have
generosity *noun* being generous **generously** *adverb* in a generous way

genetic *adjective* (*pronounced* ji-net-ik)
to do with genes and with characteristics inherited from parents
genetically *adverb* by means of genes

genetics *plural noun*
the study of genes and genetic behaviour

genial *adjective*
kind and pleasant
genially *adverb* in a genial way

genie *noun* (*plural* **genies**)
a magical being in stories who can grant wishes

genitals *plural noun*
the parts of the body used for sexual intercourse

genius *noun* (*plural* **geniuses**)
1 an unusually clever person **2** an unusually great ability

gent *noun* (*plural* **gents**)
(*informal*) a gentleman; a man

gentle *adjective* (**gentler, gentlest**)
kind and quiet; not rough or severe
gentleness *noun* being gentle **gently** *adverb* in a gentle way

gentleman *noun* (*plural* **gentlemen**)
1 a man **2** a well-mannered or honest man ♦ *He's a real gentleman*
gentlemanly *adjective* polite and courteous

genuine *adjective*
real; not faked or pretending
genuinely *adverb* really; in a genuine way

genus *noun* (*plural* **genera**) (*pronounced* jee-nus)
a group of similar animals or plants

geography *noun*
the science or study of the world and its climate, peoples, and products
geographer *noun* an expert in geography
geographical *adjective* to do with geography
geographically *adverb* as regards geography

geology *noun* (*pronounced* ji-ol-o-ji)
the study of the earth's crust and its layers
geological *adjective* to do with geology
geologically *adverb* as regards geology
geologist *noun* an expert in geology

geometry *noun*
the study of lines, angles, surfaces, and solids in mathematics
geometric or **geometrical** *adjective* to do with geometry **geometrically** *adverb* as regards geometry

geranium *noun* (*plural* **geraniums**)
(*pronounced* je-ray-ni-um)
a plant with red, pink, or white flowers

gerbil *noun* (*plural* **gerbils**) (*pronounced*
jer-bil)
a small brown animal with long back
legs

germ *noun* (*plural* **germs**)
a tiny living thing, especially one that
causes a disease

germinate *verb* (**germinates, germinating,
germinated**)
a seed germinates when it starts growing
and developing
germination *noun* the process of germinating

gesticulate *verb* (**gesticulates, gesticulating,
gesticulated**)
to gesticulate is to make movements with
your hands and arms while you are
talking

gesture *noun* (*plural* **gestures**) (*pronounced*
jes-cher)
a movement or action which expresses
what you feel

get *verb* (**gets, getting, got**)
This word has many meanings, depending
on the words that go with it **1** to get
something is to obtain or receive it ♦ *I got
a new bike yesterday* **2** to get (for
example) angry or upset is to become
angry or upset **3** to get to a place is to
reach it ♦ *We'll get there by midnight*
4 to get something (for example) on or
off is take it on or off ♦ *I can't get my shoe
on* **5** to get (for example) a meal is to
prepare it **6** to get an illness is to catch it
♦ *I think she's got measles* **7** to get
someone to do something is to persuade or
order them to do it ♦ *I'll get him to take the
dog for a walk* **8** (*informal*) to get
something is to understand it ♦ *Do you get
what I mean?*
to get by is to manage
to get on is to make progress, or to be
friendly with someone
to get out of something is to avoid having to do
it
to get over something is to recover from an
illness or shock
to get your own back is to have your revenge
have got to must

getaway *noun* (*plural* **getaways**)
an escape

geyser *noun* (*plural* **geysers**) (*pronounced*
gee-zer or gy-zer)
a natural spring that shoots up columns of
hot water

ghastly *adjective* (**ghastlier, ghastliest**)
horrible; awful

ghetto *noun* (*plural* **ghettos**) (*pronounced*
get-oh)
an area of a city, often a slum area, where
a group of people live who are treated
unfairly compared with other people

ghost *noun* (*plural* **ghosts**)
the spirit of a dead person seen by a living
person
ghostly *adjective* like a ghost

ghoulish *adjective* (*pronounced* gool-ish)
enjoying looking at things to do with death
and suffering

giant ➤ *noun* (*plural* **giants**)
1 a creature in stories, like a huge man
2 something that is much larger than the
usual size

giant ➤ *adjective*
huge

giddy *adjective* (**giddier, giddiest**)
feeling unsteady or dizzy
giddily *adverb* in a giddy way **giddiness** *noun*
being giddy

gift *noun* (*plural* **gifts**)
1 a present **2** a talent ♦ *She has a gift for
music*

gifted *adjective*
having a special talent

gigantic *adjective*
huge

giggle ➤ *verb* (**giggles, giggling, giggled**)
to giggle is to laugh in a silly way

giggle ➤ *noun* (*plural* **giggles**)
1 a silly laugh **2** (*informal*) something
amusing; a joke ♦ *We did it for a giggle*
the giggles (*informal*) a fit of giggling

gild *verb* (**gilds, gilding, gilded**)
to gild something is to cover it with a thin
layer of gold paint or gold

gills *plural noun*
the part of a fish's body that it breathes
through

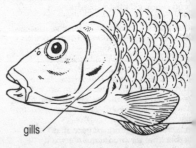

gills

gimmick *noun* (*plural* **gimmicks**)
something unusual done or used to attract people's attention

gin *noun*
a colourless alcoholic drink

ginger *noun*
1 a hot-tasting tropical root, used as a flavouring for food **2** a reddish-yellow colour **3** liveliness or energy
gingery *adjective* like ginger

gingerbread *noun*
a cake or biscuit flavoured with ginger

gingerly *adverb*
cautiously

gipsy *noun* (*plural* **gipsies**)
a different spelling of **gypsy**

giraffe *noun* (*plural* **giraffes**)
a tall African animal with a very long neck

girder *noun* (*plural* **girders**)
a metal beam supporting part of a building or bridge

girdle *noun* (*plural* **girdles**)
a belt or cord worn around your waist

girl *noun* (*plural* **girls**)
1 a female child **2** a young woman
girlhood *noun* the time of being a girl **girlish** *adjective* like a girl

girlfriend *noun* (*plural* **girlfriends**)
a person's regular female friend or lover

giro *noun* (*plural* **giros**)
a system of sending money directly from one bank account or Post Office account to another

girth *noun* (*plural* **girths**)
1 the measurement round something **2** a band fastened round a horse's belly to keep its saddle in place

gist *noun* (*pronounced* jist)
the main points or general meaning of a speech or conversation

give *verb* (**gives, giving, gave, given**)
1 to give someone something is to let them have it ♦ *She gave me a sweet* **2** to give (for example) a laugh or shout is to laugh or shout out **3** to give a performance is to present or perform something ♦ *They gave a concert to raise money* **4** something gives if it bends or goes down under a strain ♦ *Will this branch give if I sit on it?*

to give in is to surrender

to give up is to stop doing or trying something

to give way is to break or collapse

giver *noun* a person who gives something

given *adjective*
stated or agreed in advance ♦ *We had to meet at a given time*

glacial *adjective* (*pronounced* glay-shal)
made of ice or formed by glaciers

glacier *noun* (*plural* **glaciers**) (*pronounced* glas-i-er)
a mass of ice moving slowly along a valley

glad *adjective* (**gladder, gladdest**)
pleased; happy

to be glad of something is to be grateful for it

gladly *adverb* with pleasure **gladness** *noun* being glad

gladden *verb* (**gladdens, gladdening, gladdened**)
to gladden someone is to make them glad

gladiator *noun* (*plural* **gladiators**)
a man who fought with a sword or other weapons at public shows in ancient Rome

glamorize *verb* (**glamorizes, glamorizing, glamorized**)
to glamorize something is to make it attractive and exciting

glamorous *adjective*
attractive and exciting

glamour *noun*
1 the attractive exciting appearance of something ♦ *He liked the glamour of working in television* **2** a person's beauty or attractiveness

glance ➤ *verb* (**glances, glancing, glanced**)
1 to glance at something is to look at it quickly **2** to glance off something is to hit it and slide off ♦ *The ball glanced off his bat*

glance ➤ *noun* (*plural* **glances**)
a quick look

gland *noun* (*plural* **glands**)
an organ of the body that separates substances from the blood, so that they can be used or passed out of the body

glandular *adjective*
to do with the glands

glare ➤ *verb* (**glares, glaring, glared**)
1 to glare is to shine with a bright or dazzling light 2 to glare at someone is to look angrily at them

glare ➤ *noun* (*plural* **glares**)
1 a strong light 2 an angry stare

glaring *adjective*
1 very bright 2 very obvious ♦ *They made several glaring errors*

glass *noun* (*plural* **glasses**)
1 glass is a hard brittle substance that lets light through 2 a glass is a container made of glass, for drinking out of 3 a glass is also a mirror or a lens

glasses *plural noun*
spectacles or binoculars

glassful *noun* (*plural* **glassfuls**)
as much as a glass will hold

glassy *adjective* (**glassier, glassiest**)
1 like glass 2 dull; without liveliness or expression ♦ *He gave a glassy stare*

glaze ➤ *verb* (**glazes, glazing, glazed**)
1 to glaze something is to cover or fit it with glass 2 to glaze pottery is to give it a shiny surface 3 to glaze is to become glassy ♦ *Her eyes glazed and she fainted*

glaze ➤ *noun* (*plural* **glazes**)
a shiny surface

glazier *noun* (*plural* **glaziers**)
someone whose job is to fit glass into windows and doors

gleam ➤ *noun* (*plural* **gleams**)
1 a beam of soft light, especially one that comes and goes 2 a small amount ♦ *There was a gleam of hope*

gleam ➤ *verb* (**gleams, gleaming, gleamed**)
to gleam is to shine with beams of soft light

glee *noun*
delight; joy

gleeful *adjective* full of joy **gleefully** *adverb* in a gleeful way

glen *noun* (*plural* **glens**)
a narrow valley, especially in Scotland

glide *verb* (**glides, gliding, glided**)
1 to glide is to fly or move smoothly 2 to glide is also to fly without using an engine

glider *noun* (*plural* **gliders**)
an aircraft that does not use an engine and floats on air currents

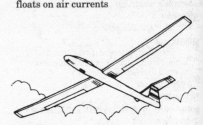

glimmer ➤ *noun* (*plural* **glimmers**)
a faint light

glimmer ➤ *verb* (**glimmers, glimmering, glimmered**)
to glimmer is to shine with a faint light

glimpse ➤ *verb* (**glimpses, glimpsing, glimpsed**)
to glimpse something is to see it briefly

glimpse ➤ *noun* (*plural* **glimpses**)
a brief view of something

glint ➤ *verb* (**glints, glinting, glinted**)
to glint is to shine with a flash of light

glint ➤ *noun* (*plural* **glints**)
a brief flash of light

glisten *verb* (**glistens, glistening, glistened**)
to glisten is to shine like something wet or oily

glitter *verb* (**glitters, glittering, glittered**)
to glitter is to shine with tiny flashes of light

gloat *verb* (**gloats, gloating, gloated**)
to gloat is to be pleased in an unkind way that you have succeeded or that someone else has been hurt or upset

global *adjective*
to do with the whole world

globally *adverb* all over the world

global warming *noun*
a gradual increase in the average temperature of the earth's climate, caused by the greenhouse effect

globe *noun* (*plural* **globes**)
1 a globe is something shaped like a ball, especially one with a map of the world on it 2 the globe is the world

gloom *noun*
a depressed condition or feeling

gloomy *adjective* (**gloomier, gloomiest**)
1 almost dark; not well lit 2 sad or depressed

gloomily *adverb* in a gloomy way **gloominess** *noun* being gloomy

glorify *verb* (**glorifies, glorifying, glorified**)
1 to glorify someone is to praise them highly **2** to glorify something is to make it seem splendid
glorification *noun* glorifying someone or something

glorious *adjective*
splendid or magnificent
gloriously *adverb* in a glorious way

glory *noun* (*plural* **glories**)
1 fame and honour; praise **2** splendour or beauty

gloss *noun* (*plural* **glosses**)
the shine on a smooth surface

glossary *noun* (*plural* **glossaries**)
a list of words with their meanings explained ♦ *Your Science book has a glossary at the back*

glossy *adjective* (**glossier, glossiest**)
smooth and shiny

glove *noun* (*plural* **gloves**)
a covering for the hand, with a separate division for each finger

glow ➤ *noun*
1 a brightness and warmth without flames **2** a warm or cheerful feeling ♦ *We felt a glow of pride*

glow ➤ *verb* (**glows, glowing, glowed**)
to glow is to shine with a soft light

glower *verb* (**glowers, glowering, glowered**)
(*rhymes with* **flower**)
to glower is to stare with an angry look

glow-worm *noun* (*plural* **glow-worms**)
an insect with a tail that gives out a green light

glucose *noun*
a type of sugar found in fruits and honey

glue ➤ *noun* (*plural* **glues**)
a thick liquid for sticking things together
gluey *adjective* sticky like glue

glue ➤ *verb* (**glues, gluing, glued**)
to glue something is to stick it with glue

glum *adjective* (**glummer, glummest**)
sad or depressed
glumly *adverb* in a glum way

glutton *noun* (*plural* **gluttons**)
someone who eats too much
gluttonous *adjective* like a glutton **gluttony** *noun* being a glutton

gnarled *adjective* (*pronounced* **narld**)
twisted and knobbly, like an old tree

gnash *verb* (**gnashes, gnashing, gnashed**)
(*pronounced* **nash**)
to gnash your teeth is to grind them together

gnat *noun* (*plural* **gnats**) (*pronounced* **nat**)
a tiny fly that bites

gnaw *verb* (**gnaws, gnawing, gnawed**)
(*pronounced* **naw**)
to gnaw something hard is to keep biting it

gnome *noun* (*plural* **gnomes**) (*pronounced* **nohm**)
a kind of dwarf in fairy tales that usually lives underground

gnu (*pronounced* **noo**)
noun (*plural* **gnus gnu**)
a large African antelope with a head like an ox.

go ➤ *verb* (**goes, going, went, gone**)
1 to go is to move or lead from one place to another ♦ *Where are you going?* ♦ *We shall go in a minute* ♦ *This road goes to Bristol* **2** **Go** also has many special uses shown in these examples ♦ *The milk went sour* ♦ *My watch isn't going* ♦ *The plates go on that shelf* ♦ *The party went well* ♦ *The gun went bang* ♦ *My money has gone*
to be going to do something is to be ready to do it
to go in for something is to take part in it
to go off is to explode
to go off someone or **something** is to stop liking them
to go on is to happen or continue ♦ *What's going on?*

go ➤ *noun* (*plural* **goes**)
1 a go is a turn or try ♦ *May I have a go?* **2** (*informal*) a go is also a successful try ♦ *They made a go of it* **3** (*informal*) go is energy or liveliness ♦ *She's full of go*
on the go always working or moving

go-ahead ➤ *noun*
permission to do something ♦ *We have got the go-ahead to organize a class outing*

go-ahead ➤ *adjective*
adventurous and keen to try out new methods

goal *noun* (*plural* **goals**)
1 the two posts that the ball must go between to score a point in football, hockey, and other games **2** a point scored in football, hockey, netball, and other games **3** something that you try to do or to achieve ♦ *Her goal was to become the Prime Minister*

goalie *noun* (*plural* **goalies**)
(*informal*) a goalkeeper

goalkeeper *noun* (*plural* **goalkeepers**)
the player who guards the goal in football and hockey

goalpost *noun* (*plural* **goalposts**)
each of the upright posts of a goal in sports

goat *noun* (*plural* **goats**)
an animal with horns, belonging to the
same family as sheep

gobble *verb* (**gobbles, gobbling, gobbled**)
to gobble something is to eat it quickly and
greedily

gobbledegook or **gobbledygook** *noun*
the pompous technical language used by
officials that is difficult to understand

goblet *noun* (*plural* **goblets**)
a drinking glass with a long stem and a
base

goblin *noun* (*plural* **goblins**)
an evil or mischievous fairy in stories

God *noun*
the creator of the Universe in Christian,
Jewish, and Muslim belief

god *noun* (*plural* **gods**)
a male being that is worshipped

godchild *noun* (*plural* **godchildren**)
a child that a godparent promises to see
brought up as a Christian. A boy is a
godson and a girl is a **god-daughter**

goddess *noun* (*plural* **goddesses**)
a female being that is worshipped

godparent *noun* (*plural* **godparents**)
a person at a child's christening who
promises to see that it is brought up as a
Christian. A man is a **godfather** and a
woman is a **godmother**

goggles *plural noun*
large spectacles you wear to protect your
eyes from wind, water, or dust

going *noun*
good going is quick progress ♦ *It was good
going to get home before dark*

gold *noun*
1 a precious yellow metal **2** a bright
yellow colour

golden *adjective*
1 made of gold **2** coloured like gold
3 precious or excellent ♦ *It was a golden
opportunity*

golden wedding *noun* (*plural* **golden
weddings**)
the 50th anniversary of a wedding

goldfinch *noun* (*plural* **goldfinches**)
a small, brightly-coloured bird with yellow
feathers in its wings

goldfish *noun* (*plural* **goldfish**)
a small red or orange fish, often kept as a
pet

golf *noun*
an outdoor game played on a prepared
course by hitting a small ball into a series
of small holes, using a club
golfer *noun* a player of golf **golfing** *noun*
playing golf

golf course *noun* (*plural* **golf courses**)
an area of land where golf is played

gondola *noun* (*plural* **gondolas**)
(*pronounced* **gon**-do-la)
a boat with high pointed ends, used on the
canals in Venice
gondolier *noun* the person who moves a
gondola along with a pole

gone past participle of **go** *verb*

gong *noun* (*plural* **gongs**)
a large metal disc that makes a deep
hollow sound when it is hit

good ➤ *adjective* (**better, best**)
1 of the kind that people like, want, or
praise ♦ *I like a good book* **2** kind ♦ *It
was good of you to help us* **3** well-behaved
♦ *Be a good boy* **4** healthy; giving benefit
♦ *Exercise is good for you* **5** thorough;
large enough ♦ *Give it a good clean*
6 quite large ♦ *It's a good distance to the
station*

good ➤ *noun*
1 something good or right ♦ *Do good to
others* **2** benefit or advantage ♦ *I'm telling
you for your own good*
for good for ever
no good useless

goodbye *interjection*
a word you use when you leave someone or
at the end of a telephone call

Good Friday *noun*
the Friday before Easter, when Christians
remember Christ's death on the Cross

good-looking *adjective*
attractive or handsome

good-natured *adjective*
kind

goodness *noun*
1 being good **2** the good part of something

goods *plural noun*
1 things that are bought and sold
2 things that are carried on trains or
lorries

goodwill *noun*
a kindly feeling; approval

gooey *adjective*
sticky or slimy

goose *noun* (*plural* **geese**)
a water bird with webbed feet, larger than a duck

gooseberry *noun* (*plural* **gooseberries**)
a small green fruit that grows on a prickly bush

goose pimples *plural noun*
skin when it is covered in small bumps, when you are cold or afraid

gore *verb* (**gores, goring, gored**)
to gore someone is to wound them with a horn or tusk ♦ *The bull was about to gore the matador*

gorge *noun* (*plural* **gorges**)
a narrow valley with steep sides

gorgeous *adjective*
magnificent; beautiful
gorgeously *adverb* in a gorgeous way

gorilla *noun* (*plural* **gorillas**)
a large strong African ape

gorse *noun*
a prickly bush with small yellow flowers

gory *adjective* (**gorier, goriest**)
1 covered in blood **2** involving a lot of killing

gosh *interjection*
(*informal*) an exclamation of surprise

gosling *noun* (*plural* **goslings**)
a young goose

gospel *noun* (*plural* **gospels**)
1 the gospel is the teachings of Jesus Christ **2** gospel is something you can safely believe ♦ *You can take what she says as gospel*
the Gospels the first four books of the New Testament

gossip ➤ *verb* (**gossips, gossiping, gossiped**)
to gossip is to talk a lot about other people

gossip ➤ *noun* (*plural* **gossips**)
1 gossip is talk or rumours about other people **2** a gossip is someone who likes talking about other people

got past tense and past participle of **get**

gouge *verb* (**gouges, gouging, gouged**)
(*pronounced* gowj)
to gouge something is to press or scoop it out

gourd *noun* (*plural* **gourds**)
1 the hard-skinned fruit of a climbing plant **2** this fruit hollowed out to make a bowl or container

govern *verb* (**governs, governing, governed**)
to govern a country or organization is to be in charge of it

government *noun* (*plural* **governments**)
the group of people who are in charge of a country

governor *noun* (*plural* **governors**)
someone who governs or runs a place

gown *noun* (*plural* **gowns**)
a loose flowing piece of clothing

GP short for **general practitioner**

grab *verb* (**grabs, grabbing, grabbed**)
to grab something is to take hold of it firmly or suddenly

grace *noun* (*plural* **graces**)
1 beauty, especially in movement
2 goodwill or favour **3** a short prayer before or after a meal

graceful *adjective*
beautiful and elegant in movement or shape
gracefully *adverb* in a graceful way
gracefulness *noun* being graceful

gracious *adjective*
1 kind and pleasant to other people
2 merciful
graciously *adverb* in a gracious way

grade ➤ *noun* (*plural* **grades**)
a step in a scale of quality, value, or rank

grade ➤ *verb* (**grades, grading, graded**)
to grade things is to sort or divide them into grades

gradient *noun* (*plural* **gradients**)
(*pronounced* gray-di-ent)
1 a slope **2** the amount that a road or railway slopes

gradual *adjective*
happening slowly but steadily
gradually *adverb* slowly but steadily

graduate ➤ *noun* (*plural* **graduates**)
(*pronounced* grad-yoo-at)
someone who has a degree from a university or college

graduate ➤ *verb* (**graduates, graduating, graduated**) (*pronounced* grad-yoo-ayt)
1 to graduate is to get a university degree
2 to graduate something is to divide it into graded sections, or to mark it so that it can be used for measuring ♦ *The ruler was graduated in millimetres*
graduation *noun* graduating from a university or college

graffiti *plural noun* (*pronounced* gra-fee-tee)
words or drawings scribbled on a wall

grain *noun* (*plural* **grains**)
1 grain is cereals when they are growing or after they have been harvested **2** a grain is the hard seed of a cereal
3 a grain of something is a small amount of it ♦ *The story had a grain of truth in it*
4 the grain on a piece of wood is the pattern of lines going through it
grainy *adjective* having a distinct grain

gram *noun* (*plural* **grams**)
a unit of weight in the metric system, a thousandth of a kilogram

grammar noun (plural **grammars**)
  1 grammar is the rules for using words
  2 a grammar is a book that gives the rules for using words

grammar school noun (plural **grammar schools**)
  a kind of secondary school

grammatical adjective
  following the rules of grammar
  grammatically adverb in a grammatical way

gramophone noun (plural **gramophones**)
  (old use) a record player

grand adjective (**grander**, **grandest**)
  1 great or splendid **2** including everything ♦ I've worked out the grand total
  grandly adverb in a grand way

grandad noun (plural **grandads**)
  (informal) grandfather

grandchild noun (plural **grandchildren**)
  a child of a person's son or daughter. A girl is a **granddaughter**, and a boy is a **grandson**

grandeur noun
  greatness; splendour

grandfather noun (plural **grandfathers**)
  the father of a person's mother or father

grandfather clock noun (plural **grandfather clocks**)
  a clock in a tall wooden case

grandma noun (plural **grandmas**)
  (informal) grandmother

grandmother noun (plural **grandmothers**)
  the mother of a person's mother or father

grandpa noun (plural **grandpas**)
  (informal) grandfather

grandparent noun (plural **grandparents**)
  a grandmother or grandfather

grand piano noun (plural **grand pianos**)
  a large piano that extends at the back and has its strings arranged horizontally

grandstand noun (plural **grandstands**)
  a building at a racecourse or sports ground, that is open at the front with rows of seats for spectators

granite noun
  a very hard kind of rock

granny noun (plural **grannies**)
  (informal) grandmother

granny knot noun (plural **granny knots**)
  a reef knot with the strings crossed the wrong way

grant ➤ verb (**grants**, **granting**, **granted**)
  to grant someone something is to give or allow them what they have asked for
  to take something for granted is to assume that it is true or will happen

grant ➤ noun (plural **grants**)
  something given, especially a sum of money

granulated sugar noun
  sugar in the form of hard grains

grape noun (plural **grapes**)
  a small green or purple fruit that grows in bunches on a vine

grapefruit noun (plural **grapefruit**)
  a large round yellow citrus fruit with a soft juicy pulp

grapevine noun (plural **grapevines**)
  1 a climbing plant on which grapes grow **2** a way in which you hear information or rumours ♦ I heard it on the grapevine

graph noun (plural **graphs**)
  a diagram that shows how two amounts are related

graphic adjective
  1 short and lively ♦ He gave a graphic account of the race **2** to do with drawing or painting ♦ She is a graphic artist
  graphically adverb in a graphic way

graphics plural noun
  diagrams, lettering, and drawings, especially pictures that are produced by a computer

graphite noun
  a soft kind of carbon used for the lead in pencils

graph paper noun
  paper covered with small squares, used for making graphs

grapple verb (**grapples**, **grappling**, **grappled**)
  1 to grapple someone or grapple with someone is to fight them **2** to grapple something is to hold it tightly **3** to grapple with a problem is to try to deal with it

grasp ➤ verb (**grasps**, **grasping**, **grasped**)
  1 to grasp someone or something is to hold them tightly **2** to grasp something is to understand it

grasp ➤ noun
  1 a firm hold **2** the power to understand things ♦ She has a good grasp of mathematics

grasping *adjective*
greedy for money or possessions

grass *noun* (*plural* **grasses**)
1 a green plant with thin stalks 2 ground covered with grass
grassy *adjective* covered with grass

grasshopper *noun* (*plural* **grasshoppers**)
a jumping insect that makes a shrill noise

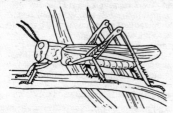

grate[1] *noun* (*plural* **grates**)
1 a metal framework that keeps fuel in the fireplace 2 a fireplace

grate[2] *verb* (**grates, grating, grated**)
1 to grate something is to shred it into small pieces 2 to grate is to make an unpleasant noise by rubbing something ♦ *The chalk grated on the blackboard*

grateful *adjective*
feeling glad that someone has done something for you ♦ *I am grateful for your help*
gratefully *adverb* in a grateful way

grating *noun* (*plural* **gratings**)
a framework of metal bars placed across an opening

gratitude *noun*
being grateful

grave[1] *noun* (*plural* **graves**)
the place where a dead body is buried

grave[2] *adjective* (**graver, gravest**)
serious or solemn ♦ *We've had grave news*
gravely *adverb* solemnly

gravel *noun*
small stones mixed with coarse sand, used to make paths
gravelled *adjective* covered with gravel
gravelly *adjective* like gravel; stony

gravestone *noun* (*plural* **gravestones**)
a stone monument over a grave

graveyard *noun* (*plural* **graveyards**)
a place where dead bodies are buried

gravity *noun*
1 the force that pulls all objects in the universe towards each other 2 the force that pulls everything towards the earth 3 seriousness
gravitation *noun* the force of gravity
gravitational *adjective* to do with gravity

gravy *noun*
a hot brown sauce made from meat juices

graze ➤ *verb* (**grazes, grazing, grazed**)
1 to graze is to feed on growing grass 2 to graze your skin is to scrape it slightly against something rough

graze ➤ *noun* (*plural* **grazes**)
a sore place where skin has been scraped

grease *noun*
thick fat or oil
greasy *adjective* oily like grease

great *adjective* (**greater, greatest**)
1 very large 2 very important or distinguished ♦ *He was a great writer* 3 (*informal*) very good or enjoyable ♦ *It's great to see you again* 4 older or younger by one generation, as in *great-grandmother* and *great-grandson*
greatly *adverb* very much **greatness** *noun* fame or importance

greed *noun*
being greedy

greedy *adjective* (**greedier, greediest**)
wanting more food or money than you need
greedily *adverb* in a greedy way **greediness** *noun* being greedy

green ➤ *adjective* (**greener, greenest**)
1 of the colour of grass and leaves 2 concerned with protecting the natural environment

green ➤ *noun* (*plural* **greens**)
1 green is a green colour 2 a green is an area of grass

greenery *noun*
green leaves or plants

greengage *noun* (*plural* **greengages**)
a green kind of plum

greengrocer *noun* (*plural* **greengrocers**)
someone who keeps a shop that sells fruit and vegetables
greengrocery *noun* a greengrocer's shop

greenhouse *noun* (*plural* **greenhouses**)
a glass building that is kept warm inside for growing plants

greenhouse effect *noun*
the warming of the earth's surface by gases (called **greenhouse gases**) such as methane and carbon dioxide, which trap heat in the earth's atmosphere

greens *plural noun*
green vegetables, such as cabbage and spinach

greet *verb* (**greets, greeting, greeted**)
1 to greet someone is to welcome them when they arrive 2 to greet something is to respond to it in a certain way ♦ *They greeted the song with loud applause*

greeting *noun* (*plural* **greetings**)
a greeting is the words or actions used to greet someone
greetings good wishes

grenade *noun* (*plural* **grenades**)
a small bomb, usually thrown by hand

grew past tense of **grow**

grey ➤ *adjective* (**greyer, greyest**)
of the colour between black and white, like ashes or dark clouds

grey ➤ *noun*
a grey colour

greyhound *noun* (*plural* **greyhounds**)
a slim dog with smooth hair, used in racing

grid *noun* (*plural* **grids**)
a framework or pattern of bars or lines crossing each other

grief *noun*
deep sadness or sorrow, especially when someone has died
to come to grief is to have an accident or misfortune

grievance *noun* (*plural* **grievances**)
something that people are unhappy or angry about

grieve *verb* (**grieves, grieving, grieved**)
1 to grieve is to feel sad or sorrowful **2** to grieve someone is to make them feel very sad ♦ *It grieves me to have to tell you this*

grievous *adjective*
1 causing great sadness **2** serious ♦ *We have suffered a grievous injury*
grievously *adverb* in a grievous way

grill ➤ *noun* (*plural* **grills**)
1 an element or burner on a cooker, that sends heat downwards **2** grilled food **3** a grating

grill ➤ *verb* (**grills, grilling, grilled**)
1 to grill food is to cook it under a grill **2** to grill someone is to question them closely and severely ♦ *The police grilled him for several hours*

grim *adjective* (**grimmer, grimmest**)
1 stern or severe **2** frightening or unpleasant ♦ *They had a grim experience*
grimly *adverb* in a grim way **grimness** *noun* being grim

grimace *noun* (*plural* **grimaces**)
a strange or twisted expression on your face

grime *noun*
grime is a layer of dirt on a surface
grimy *adjective* dirty

grin ➤ *noun* (*plural* **grins**)
a smile showing your teeth

grin ➤ *verb* (**grins, grinning, grinned**)
to grin is to smile showing your teeth
to grin and bear it is to put up with something without complaining

grind *verb* (**grinds, grinding, ground**)
1 to grind something is to crush it into a powder **2** to grind something hard is to sharpen or polish it by rubbing it on a rough surface
to grind to a halt is to stop suddenly with a lot of noise
grinder *noun* something that grinds things

grindstone *noun* (*plural* **grindstones**)
a rough round revolving stone used for grinding things
to keep your nose to the grindstone is to keep working hard

grip ➤ *verb* (**grips, gripping, gripped**)
1 to grip something is to hold it tightly **2** to grip someone is to interest them and keep their attention ♦ *The film gripped me for hours*

grip ➤ *noun* (*plural* **grips**)
1 a firm hold on something **2** a handle

grisly *adjective* (**grislier, grisliest**)
disgusting or horrible ♦ *They came across the grisly remains of a dead sheep*

gristle *noun*
the tough rubbery part of meat
gristly *adjective* tough like gristle

grit ➤ *noun*
1 tiny pieces of stone or sand **2** courage or determination
gritty *adjective* rough like grit

grit ➤ *verb* (**grits, gritting, gritted**)
1 to grit your teeth is to clench them tightly when in pain or trouble **2** to grit a road or path is to put grit on it

grizzly bear *noun* (*plural* **grizzly bears**)
a large bear of North America

groan ➤ *verb* (**groans, groaning, groaned**)
to groan is to make a long deep sound when in pain or distress

groan ➤ *noun* (*plural* **groans**)
a long deep sound of pain or distress

grocer *noun* (*plural* **grocers**)
someone who keeps a shop that sells food, drink, and other goods for the house

grocery *noun* (*plural* **groceries**)
a grocer's shop
groceries goods sold by a grocer

groggy *adjective* (**groggier, groggiest**)
dizzy or unsteady, especially from illness or injury

groin *noun* (*plural* **groins**)
the flat part between your thighs and your trunk

groom ➤ *noun* (*plural* **grooms**)
1 someone whose job is to look after horses 2 a bridegroom

groom ➤ *verb* (**grooms, grooming, groomed**)
1 to groom a horse or other animal is to clean and brush it 2 to groom something is to make it neat and trim ♦ *He enjoyed grooming his beard*

groove *noun* (*plural* **grooves**)
a long narrow channel cut in the surface of something

grope *verb* (**gropes, groping, groped**)
to grope for something is to feel about for it when you cannot see it

gross ➤ *adjective* (**grosser, grossest**)
1 fat and ugly 2 having bad manners; crude or vulgar 3 very bad or shocking ♦ *You showed gross stupidity* 4 total; without anything deducted ♦ *What is your gross income?*
grossly *adverb* extremely; crudely **grossness** *noun* being gross

gross ➤ *noun* (*plural* **gross**)
a gross is twelve dozen or 144

grotesque *adjective* (*pronounced* groh-**tesk**)
strange and ugly
grotesquely *adverb* in a grotesque way

grotty *adjective* (**grottier, grottiest**)
(*informal*) unpleasant or dirty

ground[1] *noun* (*plural* **grounds**)
1 the ground is the surface of the earth 2 a ground is a sports field

ground[2] past tense and past participle of **grind**

grounded *adjective*
1 aircraft are grounded when they are prevented from flying, for example because of the weather 2 (*informal*) someone is grounded when they are not allowed to go out

ground floor *noun* (*plural* **ground floors**)
in a building, the floor that is level with the ground

groundnut *noun* (*plural* **groundnuts**)
a peanut

grounds *plural noun*
1 reasons ♦ *There are grounds for suspicion* 2 the gardens of a large house 3 bits of coffee or dregs at the bottom of a cup

groundsheet *noun* (*plural* **groundsheets**)
a piece of waterproof material for spreading on the ground, especially in a tent

groundsman *noun* (*plural* **groundsmen**)
someone whose job is to look after a sports ground

group ➤ *noun* (*plural* **groups**)
a number of people, animals, or things that belong together in some way

group ➤ *verb* (**groups, grouping, grouped**)
to group people or things is to make them into a group

grouse[1] *verb* (**grouses, grousing, groused**)
to grouse is to grumble or complain

grouse[2] *noun* (*plural* **grouse**)
a large bird with feathered feet, hunted as game

grove *noun* (*plural* **groves**)
a group of trees; a small wood

grovel *verb* (**grovels, grovelling, grovelled**)
1 to grovel is to crawl on the ground 2 to grovel is to be extremely humble and obedient towards someone, usually because you want something from them

grow *verb* (**grows, growing, grew, grown**)
1 to grow is to become bigger ♦ *You have grown a lot* 2 to grow is to develop in the ground ♦ *The seeds are growing now* 3 to grow something is to plant it in the ground and look after it ♦ *She grows lovely roses* 4 to grow is also to become ♦ *He grew richer and richer*
to grow on someone is to become more attractive to them ♦ *This music grows on you*
to grow out of something is to become too big or too old for it
to grow up is to become an adult
grower *noun* someone who grows things

growl ➤ *verb* (**growls, growling, growled**)
to growl is to make a deep rough sound, like an angry dog

growl ➤ *noun* (*plural* **growls**)
a deep rough sound

grown-up *noun* (*plural* **grown-ups**)
an adult

growth *noun* (*plural* **growths**)
1 growth is growing or development 2 a growth is something that has grown, especially something unwanted in the body such as a tumour

grub *noun* (*plural* **grubs**)
1 a grub is a tiny creature that will become an insect; a larva 2 (*slang*) grub is food

grubby *adjective* (**grubbier, grubbiest**)
rather dirty

grudge ➤ *noun* (*plural* **grudges**)
a dislike of someone because you think they have harmed you, or because you are jealous

grudge ➤ *verb* (**grudges, grudging, grudged**)
to grudge someone something is to feel unwilling to let them have it
grudgingly *adverb* unwillingly

gruelling *adjective*
exhausting ♦ *It was a long gruelling journey*

gruesome *adjective*
horrible or disgusting to look at

gruff *adjective* (**gruffer, gruffest**)
having a rough unfriendly voice or manner
gruffly *adverb* in a gruff way

grumble *verb* (**grumbles, grumbling, grumbled**)
to grumble is to complain in a bad-tempered way
grumbler *noun* someone who grumbles

grumpy *adjective* (**grumpier, grumpiest**)
bad-tempered
grumpily *adverb* in a grumpy way **grumpiness** *noun* being grumpy

grunt ➤ *verb* (**grunts, grunting, grunted**)
to grunt is to make a snorting sound like a pig

grunt ➤ *noun* (*plural* **grunts**)
a snort like that of a pig

guarantee ➤ *noun* (*plural* **guarantees**)
a formal promise to do something, especially to repair something you have sold someone if it goes wrong

guarantee ➤ *verb* (**guarantees, guaranteeing, guaranteed**)
to guarantee something is to make a promise to do it

guard ➤ *verb* (**guards, guarding, guarded**)
1 to guard something or someone is to keep them safe **2** to guard a prisoner is to prevent them from escaping
to guard against something is to be careful to prevent it happening

guard ➤ *noun* (*plural* **guards**)
1 guard is protecting or guarding ♦ *Keep the prisoners under close guard* **2** a guard is someone who protects a person or place, or a group of people guarding a prisoner **3** a guard is also an official in charge of a railway train **4** a guard is a shield or device protecting people from the dangers of a fire or machinery
on guard protecting; acting as a guard

guardian *noun* (*plural* **guardians**)
1 someone who protects something **2** someone who is legally in charge of a child instead of the child's parents
guardianship *noun* being a guardian

guava *noun* (*plural* **guavas**) (*pronounced* gwah-va)
an orange-coloured fruit with pink juicy flesh, from a tropical American tree

guerrilla *noun* (*plural* **guerrillas**) (*pronounced* ge-ril-a)
a member of a small army or band that fights by means of surprise attacks

guess ➤ *noun* (*plural* **guesses**)
an opinion or answer that you give without working it out in detail or being sure of it

guess ➤ *verb* (**guesses, guessing, guessed**)
to guess is to make a guess

guesswork *noun*
guesswork is something you do by guessing ♦ *I got it right, but it was only guesswork*

guest *noun* (*plural* **guests**) (*pronounced* gest)
1 a person who is invited to visit or stay at someone's house **2** someone staying at a hotel **3** a performer in a show in which someone else is the main performer

guest house *noun* (*plural* **guest houses**)
a kind of small hotel

guidance *noun*
guiding or giving help

guide ➤ *noun* (*plural* **guides**)
1 someone who shows people the way, helps them, or points out interesting sights **2** a book that tells you about a place
Guide a member of the Girl Guides Association, an organization for girls

guide ➤ *verb* (**guides, guiding, guided**)
to guide someone is to show them the way or help them do something

guide dog *noun* (*plural* **guide dogs**)
a dog specially trained to lead a blind person

guided missile *noun* (*plural* **guided missiles**)
an explosive rocket that is guided to its target from the ground

guidelines *plural noun*
the main rules or guidance about how something should be done

guild *noun* (*plural* **guilds**) (*pronounced* gild)
a society of people, especially in the Middle Ages, with similar skills or interests

guillotine *noun* (*plural* **guillotines**) (*pronounced* gil-o-teen)
1 a machine once used in France for beheading people **2** a device with a sharp blade for cutting paper

guilt *noun*
1 the fact of having done something wrong ♦ *Their guilt was obvious* **2** a feeling that you have done something wrong

guilty *adjective* (**guiltier, guiltiest**)
1 someone is guilty when they have done wrong 2 someone feels guilty when they know they have done wrong

guinea *noun* (*plural* **guineas**)
a British gold coin worth 21 shillings or £1·05, no longer in use

guinea pig *noun* (*plural* **guinea pigs**)
1 a small furry animal without a tail, kept as a pet 2 a person who is used in an experiment

guitar *noun* (*plural* **guitars**)
a musical instrument played by plucking its strings

guitarist *noun* someone who plays the guitar

gulf *noun* (*plural* **gulfs**)
a large area of sea partly surrounded by land

gull *noun* (*plural* **gulls**)
a seagull

gullet *noun* (*plural* **gullets**)
the tube from the throat to the stomach

gullible *adjective*
easily deceived

gully *noun* (*plural* **gullies**)
a narrow channel that carries water

gulp ➤ *verb* (**gulps, gulping, gulped**)
1 to gulp something is to swallow it quickly or greedily 2 to gulp is to make a loud swallowing noise, especially out of fear

gulp ➤ *noun* (*plural* **gulps**)
a loud swallowing noise

gum[1] *noun* (*plural* **gums**)
the firm fleshy part of the mouth that holds the teeth

gum[2] ➤ *noun* (*plural* **gums**)
1 a sticky substance used as glue
2 chewing gum
gummy *adjective* sticky like gum

gum ➤ *verb* (**gums, gumming, gummed**)
to gum something is to cover it or stick it with gum

gum tree *noun* (*plural* **gum trees**)
a eucalyptus tree

up a gum tree (*slang*) in great difficulties

gun ➤ *noun* (*plural* **guns**)
1 a weapon that fires shells or bullets from a metal tube 2 a pistol fired to signal the start of a race 3 a device that forces a substance such as grease out of a tube

gun ➤ *verb* (**guns, gunning, gunned**)
to gun someone down is to shoot them with a gun

gunboat *noun* (*plural* **gunboats**)
a small warship

gunfire *noun*
the firing or sound of guns

gunman *noun* (*plural* **gunmen**)
a man armed with a gun

gunner *noun* (*plural* **gunners**)
someone who works with guns, especially in the army

gunnery *noun* the skill of making guns

gunpowder *noun*
a type of explosive

gunshot *noun* (*plural* **gunshots**)
the shot of a gun

gurdwara *noun* (*plural* **gurdwaras**)
a building where Sikhs worship

gurgle *verb* (**gurgles, gurgling, gurgled**)
to gurgle is to make a bubbling sound
♦ *The water gurgled as it flowed out of the bath*

guru *noun* (*plural* **gurus**)
1 a Hindu religious teacher 2 a wise and respected teacher

Guru Granth Sahib *noun*
the holy book of the Sikh religion

gush *verb* (**gushes, gushing, gushed**)
1 to gush is to flow quickly 2 to gush is also to talk quickly and with excitement

gust *noun* (*plural* **gusts**)
a sudden rush of wind or rain
gusty *adjective* windy

gut ➤ *noun* (*plural* **guts**)
the lower part of the digestive system; the
intestine

gut ➤ *verb* (**guts, gutting, gutted**)
1 to gut a dead fish or animal is to remove
its insides before cooking it **2** to gut a
place is to remove or destroy the inside of
it ♦ *Fire has completely gutted the factory*

guts *plural noun*
1 the guts are the digestive system; the
insides of a person or thing **2** (*informal*)
guts are courage ♦ *I must say you have
guts*

gutter *noun* (*plural* **gutters**)
a long narrow channel at the side of a
street or along the edge of a roof, to carry
away rainwater

guy[1] *noun* (*plural* **guys**)
1 a figure in the form of Guy Fawkes,
burnt on or near 5 November in memory of
the Gunpowder Plot to blow up
Parliament in 1605 **2** (*informal*) a man

guy[2] or **guy-rope** *noun* (*plural* **guys** or
guy-ropes)
a rope used to hold something in place,
especially a tent

guzzle *verb* (**guzzles, guzzling, guzzled**)
to guzzle food or drink is to eat or drink it
greedily

gym *noun* (*plural* **gyms**) (*pronounced* jim)
(*informal*) **1** a gym is a gymnasium
2 gym is gymnastics

gymkhana *noun* (*plural* **gymkhanas**)
(*pronounced* jim-kah-na)
a show of horse-riding contests and other
events

gymnasium *noun* (*plural* **gymnasiums**)
a place equipped for gymnastics

gymnast *noun* (*plural* **gymnasts**)
an expert in gymnastics

gymnastics *plural noun*
exercises and movements that
demonstrate the body's agility and
strength

gypsy *noun* (*plural* **gypsies**)
a member of a community of people, also
called **travellers**, who live in caravans or
similar vehicles and travel from place to
place

gyroscope *noun* (*plural* **gyroscopes**)
a device used in navigation, that keeps
steady because of a heavy wheel spinning
inside it

Hh

habit *noun* (*plural* **habits**)
something that you do without thinking,
because you have done it so often
habitual *adjective* done as a habit; usual
habitually *adverb* in a habitual way

habitat *noun* (*plural* **habitats**)
the natural living place of an animal or
plant

hack *verb* (**hacks, hacking, hacked**)
to hack something is to chop or cut it
roughly

hacker *noun* (*plural* **hackers**)
someone who uses a computer to get
access to a company's or government's
computer system without permission

hacksaw *noun* (*plural* **hacksaws**)
a saw for cutting metal

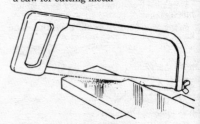

had past tense and past participle of **have**

haddock *noun* (*plural* **haddock**)
a sea fish used for food

hadn't short for *had not*

hag *noun* (*plural* **hags**)
an ugly old woman

haggard *adjective*
looking ill or very tired

haggis *noun* (*plural* **haggises**)
a Scottish food made from parts of a sheep
and oatmeal

haggle *verb* (**haggles, haggling, haggled**)
to haggle is to argue about a price or
agreement

haiku *noun* (*plural* **haiku**) (*pronounced*
hy-koo)
a Japanese short poem, usually with three
lines

hail[1] ➤ *noun*
frozen drops of rain

hail ➤ *verb* (**hails, hailing, hailed**)
it hails or it is hailing when hail falls

hail[2] *verb* (hails, hailing, hailed)
to hail someone is to call out to them

hailstone *noun* (*plural* hailstones)
a piece of hail

hair *noun* (*plural* hairs)
1 hair is the soft covering that grows on the heads and bodies of people and animals **2** a hair is one of the threads that makes up this soft covering

hairbrush *noun* (*plural* hairbrushes)
a brush for tidying your hair

haircut *noun* (*plural* haircuts)
cutting a person's hair when it gets too long

hairdresser *noun* (*plural* hairdressers)
someone whose job is to cut and arrange people's hair

hairpin *noun* (*plural* hairpins)
a pin for keeping your hair in place

hairpin bend *noun* (*plural* hairpin bends)
a very sharp bend in a road

hair-raising *adjective*
terrifying or dangerous

hairstyle *noun* (*plural* hairstyles)
a way or style of arranging the hair

hairy *adjective* (hairier, hairiest)
1 having a lot of hair **2** (*slang*) dangerous or risky

hake *noun* (*plural* hake)
a sea fish used for food

halal *noun*
meat prepared according to Muslim law

half ➤ *noun* (*plural* halves)
each of the two equal parts that something is or can be divided into

half ➤ *adverb*
partly; not completely ♦ *This meat is only half cooked*
not half (*slang*) very much ♦ *Was she cross? Not half!*

half-baked *adjective*
(*informal*) not properly planned; foolish ♦ *It was only a half-baked idea*

half-hearted *adjective*
not very enthusiastic
half-heartedly *adverb* in a half-hearted way

half-life *noun* (*plural* half-lives)
the time it takes for radioactivity to fall to half the original amount

half-mast *noun*
a flag is at half-mast when it is lowered to halfway down its flagpole, as a sign that someone important has died

halfpenny *noun* (*plural* halfpennies or halfpence) (*pronounced* hayp-ni)
an old British coin that was worth half a penny

half-term *noun* (*plural* half-terms)
a short holiday in the middle of a school term

half-time *noun* (*plural* half-times)
the time halfway through a game

halfway *adverb* and *adjective*
at a point half the distance or amount between two places or times

halibut *noun* (*plural* halibut)
a large flat sea fish used for food

hall *noun* (*plural* halls)
1 a space or passage inside the front door of a house **2** a very large room for meetings, concerts, or other large gatherings of people **3** a large important building or house, such as a town hall

hallo *interjection*
a word used to greet someone or to attract their attention

Hallowe'en *noun*
the night of 31 October, when some people think that ghosts and witches might appear

hallucination *noun* (*plural* hallucinations)
something you think you can see or hear when it is not really there

halo *noun* (*plural* haloes)
a circle of light, especially shown round the head of a saint in a picture

halt ➤ *verb* (halts, halting, halted)
to halt is to stop

halt ➤ *noun*
to call a halt is to stop something
to come to a halt is to stop

halter *noun* (*plural* halters)
a rope or strap put round a horse's head so that it can be controlled

halting *adjective*
slow and uncertain ♦ *He has a halting walk*

halve *verb* (halves, halving, halved)
1 to halve something is to divide it into halves **2** to halve something large is to reduce it by a lot ♦ *If the shop had another checkout it would halve the queues*

halves plural of **half** *noun*

ham *noun* (*plural* hams)
1 ham is meat from a pig's leg **2** (*slang*) a ham is an actor or performer who is not very good **3** (*informal*) a ham is also someone who sends and receives radio messages as a hobby

hamburger *noun* (*plural* hamburgers)
a round flat cake of minced beef that is fried and usually eaten in a bread roll

hammer ➤ *noun* (*plural* **hammers**)
a tool with a heavy metal head, used for
hitting nails or beating out things

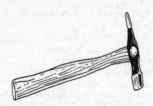

hammer ➤ *verb* (**hammers**, **hammering**,
hammered)
1 to hammer something is to hit it with a
hammer **2** to hammer is to knock loudly
♦ *We heard someone hammering on the
door* **3** (*informal*) to hammer an opponent
is to defeat them completely

hammock *noun* (*plural* **hammocks**)
a bed made of a strong net or piece of cloth
hung up above the ground or floor

hamper¹ *noun* (*plural* **hampers**)
a large box-shaped basket with a lid

hamper² *verb* (**hampers**, **hampering**, **hampered**)
to hamper someone or something is to get
in their way or make it difficult for them to
work

hamster *noun* (*plural* **hamsters**)
a small furry animal with cheek pouches,
kept as a pet

hand ➤ *noun* (*plural* **hands**)
1 the part of your body at the end of your
arm **2** a pointer on a clock or dial **3** a
worker, especially a member of a ship's
crew **4** the cards held by one player in a
card game **5** side or direction ♦ *on the
other hand*
at hand near or close by
by hand using your hand or hands
to give someone a hand is to help them
hands down winning easily or completely
on hand available
out of hand out of control

hand ➤ *verb* (**hands**, **handing**, **handed**)
to hand something to someone is to give or
pass it to them
something is handed down when it is passed
on from one generation to the next

handbag *noun* (*plural* **handbags**)
a small bag for holding money and
personal items

handbook *noun* (*plural* **handbooks**)
a book that gives useful facts about
something

handcuffs *plural noun*
a pair of metal rings joined by a chain,
used for locking a person's wrists together

handful *noun* (*plural* **handfuls**)
1 as much as you can carry in one hand
2 a small number of people or things
3 (*informal*) a troublesome person

handicap *noun* (*plural* **handicaps**)
1 a disadvantage **2** a disability affecting a
person

handicapped *adjective*
1 suffering from a disadvantage
2 suffering from a disability

handicraft *noun* (*plural* **handicrafts**)
artistic work done with your hands, such
as woodwork and pottery

handiwork *noun*
something done or made by your hands

handkerchief *noun* (*plural* **handkerchiefs**)
(*pronounced* **hang-ker-cheef**)
a square piece of material for wiping your
nose

handle ➤ *noun* (*plural* **handles**)
the part of a thing by which you can hold
or control it

handle ➤ *verb* (**handles**, **handling**, **handled**)
1 to handle something is to touch or feel it
with your hands **2** to handle a task or
problem is to deal with it

handlebars *plural noun*
a bar with a handle at each end, used to
steer a bicycle or motor cycle

handrail *noun* (*plural* **handrails**)
a rail for holding on to for support

handsome *adjective* (**handsomer**, **handsomest**)
1 attractive or good-looking **2** generous
♦ *They have made a handsome offer*
handsomely *adverb* in a handsome way

hands-on *adjective*
involving actual experience of doing
something

handstand *noun* (*plural* **handstands**)
an exercise in which you balance on your
hands with your feet in the air

handwriting *noun*
writing done by hand
handwritten *adjective* written by hand

handy *adjective* (**handier, handiest**)
useful or convenient

handyman *noun* (*plural* **handymen**)
someone who does small jobs or repairs in
the house

hang *verb* (**hangs, hanging, hung**)
1 to hang something is to fix the top part
of it to a hook or nail **2** to hang wallpaper
is to paste it in strips on to a wall **3** to
hang is to float in the air **4** (in this
meaning, the past tense and past
participle are **hanged**) to hang someone is
to execute them by hanging them from a
rope that tightens around the neck ♦ *He
was hanged in 1950*
to hang about or **hang around** is to loiter or
wait around doing nothing
to hang on (*informal*) is to wait ♦ *Hang on!
I'm not ready yet*
to hang on to something is to hold it tightly
to hang up is to end a telephone
conversation by putting back the receiver

hangar *noun* (*plural* **hangars**)
a large shed where aircraft are kept

hanger *noun* (*plural* **hangers**)
a device on which you hang things,
especially a coat or other clothing

hang-glider *noun* (*plural* **hang-gliders**)
a device on which a person can glide
through the air
hang-gliding *noun* the sport of using a
hang-glider

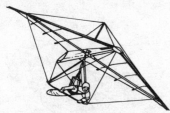

hangman *noun* (*plural* **hangmen**)
a person whose job is to execute people by
hanging them

hangover *noun* (*plural* **hangovers**)
an unpleasant feeling after drinking too
much alcohol

hank *noun* (*plural* **hanks**)
a coil or piece of wool or thread

hanker *verb* (**hankers, hankering, hankered**)
to hanker after something is to want it
badly ♦ *They're always hankering after
trips to the sea*

hanky *noun* (*plural* **hankies**)
(*informal*) a handkerchief

Hanukkah *noun*
a Jewish festival held in December

haphazard *adjective* (*pronounced*
hap-**haz**-erd)
done or chosen at random
haphazardly *adverb* in a haphazard way

happen *verb* (**happens, happening, happened**)
to happen is to take place or occur
to happen to do something is to do it by chance
without planning it ♦ *I happened to see
him in the street*

happening *noun* (*plural* **happenings**)
something that happens; an unusual
event

happy *adjective* (**happier, happiest**)
1 pleased or contented **2** lucky, fortunate
♦ *It was a happy chance they were still at
home*
happily *adverb* in a happy way **happiness**
noun being happy

happy-go-lucky *adjective*
being cheerful and not worrying about the
future

harass *verb* (**harasses, harassing, harassed**)
(*pronounced* **ha**-ras)
to harass someone is to annoy or trouble
them a lot
harassment *noun* being harassed

harbour ➤ *noun* (*plural* **harbours**)
a place where ships can shelter or unload

harbour ➤ *verb* (**harbours, harbouring,
harboured**)
to harbour someone, especially a criminal,
is to give them shelter

hard ➤ *adjective* (**harder, hardest**)
1 firm or solid; not soft ♦ *The ground was
hard* **2** difficult ♦ *These sums are quite
hard* **3** severe or harsh ♦ *There has been a
hard frost* **4** energetic; using great effort
♦ *She is a hard worker*
hard up short of money
hardness *noun* being hard

hard ➤ *adverb* (**harder, hardest**)
with great effort ♦ *We must work hard*

hardboard *noun*
stiff board made of compressed wood pulp

hard-boiled *adjective*
a hard-boiled egg is one that has been
boiled until it is hard

hard disk *noun* (*plural* **hard disks**)
a disk fitted inside a computer, able to
store large amounts of data

harden *verb* (**hardens, hardening, hardened**)
1 to harden something is to make it hard
2 to harden is to become hard

hardly *adverb*
only just; only with difficulty ♦ *She was
hardly able to walk*

hardship *noun* (*plural* **hardships**)
1 hardship is suffering or difficulty 2 a hardship is something that causes suffering

hardware *noun*
1 metal implements and tools; machinery
2 the machinery of a computer

hard-wearing *adjective*
able to stand a lot of wear

hardwood *noun* (*plural* **hardwoods**)
hard heavy wood from deciduous trees, such as oak and teak

hardy *adjective* (**hardier, hardiest**)
able to endure cold or difficult conditions

hare *noun* (*plural* **hares**)
a fast-running animal like a large rabbit

hark *verb* (**harks, harking, harked**)
(*old-fashioned use*) to hark is to listen
to hark back is to return to an earlier subject

harm ➤ *verb* (**harms, harming, harmed**)
to harm someone or something is to hurt or damage them

harm ➤ *noun*
injury or damage
harmful *adjective* causing harm **harmless** *adjective* not doing any harm

harmonica *noun* (*plural* **harmonicas**)
a mouth organ

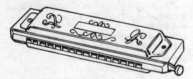

harmonize *verb* (**harmonizes, harmonizing, harmonized**)
to harmonize is to combine together in an effective or pleasant way
harmonization *noun* harmonizing

harmony *noun* (*plural* **harmonies**)
1 a pleasant combination of musical notes
2 agreement; friendship
harmonic *adjective* to do with musical harmony **harmonious** *adjective* sounding pleasant **harmoniously** *adverb* in a harmonious way

harness ➤ *noun* (*plural* **harnesses**)
the straps put over a horse's head and round its neck to control it

harness ➤ *verb* (**harnesses, harnessing, harnessed**)
1 to harness a horse is to put a harness on it 2 to harness something is to control it and make use of it ♦ *They tried to harness the power of the wind to make electricity*

harp ➤ *noun* (*plural* **harps**)
a musical instrument made of strings stretched across a frame and plucked with the fingers
harpist *noun* someone who plays the harp

harp ➤ *verb* (**harps, harping, harped**)
to harp on is to keep on talking about something in a tiresome way ♦ *He keeps harping on about all the work he has to do*

harpoon *noun* (*plural* **harpoons**)
a spear attached to a rope, fired from a gun to catch whales and other large sea-animals

harpsichord *noun* (*plural* **harpsichords**)
a musical instrument like a piano but with the strings plucked and not struck

harrow *noun* (*plural* **harrows**)
a heavy device pulled over the ground to break up the soil

harsh *adjective* (**harsher, harshest**)
1 rough and unpleasant 2 cruel or severe
harshly *adverb* in a harsh way **harshness** *noun* being harsh

harvest ➤ *noun* (*plural* **harvests**)
1 the time when farmers gather in the corn, fruit, or vegetables they have grown
2 the crop that is gathered in

harvest ➤ *verb* (**harvests, harvesting, harvested**)
to harvest crops is to gather them in

has 3rd person singular of **have**

hash *noun* (*plural* **hashes**)
a mixture of small pieces of meat and vegetables, usually fried
to make a hash of something is to mess it up or bungle it

hasn't short for *has not*

hassle *noun* (*plural* **hassles**)
(*informal*) hassle or a hassle is something that is difficult or troublesome

haste *noun*
hurry

hasten *verb* (**hastens, hastening, hastened**)
1 to hasten something is to speed it up
2 to hasten is to hurry

hasty *adjective* (**hastier, hastiest**)
hurried; done too quickly
hastily *adverb* in a hasty way **hastiness** *noun* being hasty

hat *noun* (*plural* **hats**)
a covering for the head
to keep something under your hat is to keep it as a secret

hatch[1] *noun* (*plural* **hatches**)
an opening in a floor, wall, or door, usually with a covering

hatch[2] *verb* (**hatches, hatching, hatched**)
1 to hatch is to break out of an egg **2** to hatch an egg is to keep it warm until a young bird hatches from it **3** to hatch a plan is to form it

hatchback *noun* (*plural* **hatchbacks**)
a car with a sloping rear door hinged at the top

hatchet *noun* (*plural* **hatchets**)
a small axe

hate ➤ *verb* (**hates, hating, hated**)
to hate someone or something is to dislike them very much

hate ➤ *noun* (*plural* **hates**)
1 hate is great dislike **2** (*informal*) a hate is someone or something that you dislike very much

hateful *adjective*
hated; very nasty
hatefully *adverb* in a hateful way

hatred *noun* (*pronounced* hay-trid)
a great dislike

hat trick *noun* (*plural* **hat tricks**)
getting three goals, wickets, or victories one after another

haughty *adjective* (**haughtier, haughtiest**) (*pronounced* haw-ti)
proud of yourself and looking down on other people
haughtily *adverb* in a haughty way
haughtiness *noun* being haughty

haul ➤ *verb* (**hauls, hauling, hauled**)
to haul something is to pull it using a lot of power or strength

haul ➤ *noun* (*plural* **hauls**)
an amount that someone has gained; a catch or booty ♦ *The thieves made a haul of over £1 million* ♦ *The trawler brought home a large haul of fish*

haunt *verb* (**haunts, haunting, haunted**)
1 a ghost haunts a place or person when it appears often **2** to haunt a place is to visit it often **3** an idea or memory haunts someone when they are always thinking of it

have *verb* (**has, having, had**)
This word has many meanings, depending on the words that go with it **1** to have something is to own or possess it ♦ *We haven't any money* **2** to have something in it is to contain it ♦ *I thought this tin had biscuits in it* **3** to have (for example) a party is to organize it **4** to have (for example) a shock or accident is to experience it ♦ *I'm afraid she has had an accident* **5** to have to do something is to be obliged or forced to do it ♦ *We really have to go now* **6** to have something (for example) mended or built is to get someone to mend or build it ♦ *I'm having my watch mended* **7** to have (for example) a letter is to receive it ♦ *I had a letter from my cousin*
to have someone on (*informal*) is to fool them

haven *noun* (*plural* **havens**) (*pronounced* hay-ven)
1 a harbour **2** a safe place

haven't short for *have not*

haversack *noun* (*plural* **haversacks**)
a strong bag carried on your back

hawk[1] *noun* (*plural* **hawks**)
a bird of prey with very strong eyesight

hawk[2] *verb* (**hawks, hawking, hawked**)
to hawk things is to go round selling them
hawker *noun* someone who calls at houses to sell things

hawthorn *noun* (*plural* **hawthorns**)
a thorny tree with small red berries

hay *noun*
dried grass for feeding to animals

hay fever *noun*
irritation of the nose, throat, and eyes caused by pollen or dust

haymaking *noun*
spreading grass to dry after mowing it

haystack *noun* (*plural* **haystacks**)
a large neat pile of stored hay

hazard *noun* (*plural* **hazards**)
a risk or danger
hazardous *adjective* dangerous

haze *noun* (*plural* **hazes**)
thin mist

hazel *noun* (*plural* **hazels**)
1 a type of small nut tree 2 a nut from this tree 3 a light brown colour

hazy *adjective* (**hazier, haziest**)
1 misty or unclear 2 obscure; uncertain **hazily** *adverb* in a hazy way **haziness** *noun* being hazy

H-bomb *noun* (*plural* **H-bombs**)
a hydrogen bomb

he *pronoun* and *noun*
a male person or animal: used as the subject of a verb

head ➤ *noun* (*plural* **heads**)
1 the part of the body containing the brains, eyes, and mouth 2 brains or intelligence ♦ *Use your head!* 3 a talent or ability ♦ *He has a head for sums* 4 the side of a coin on which someone's head is shown 5 a person ♦ *It costs £3 per head* 6 the top or front of something, such as a pin or nail 7 the person in charge ♦ *She's the head of this school*
to come to a head is to reach a point of crisis **to keep your head** is to stay calm **off the top of your head** (*informal*) without preparation or thinking carefully ♦ *He gave an estimate off the top of his head*

head ➤ *verb* (**heads, heading, headed**)
1 to head something is to be at the top or front of it 2 to head a ball is to hit it with your head 3 to head in a particular direction is to start going there ♦ *They headed for home*
to head someone off is to get in front of them in order to turn them aside

headache *noun* (*plural* **headaches**)
1 a pain in the head that goes on hurting 2 (*informal*) a problem or difficulty

headdress *noun* (*plural* **headdresses**)
a decorative covering for the head

header *noun* (*plural* **headers**)
1 the act of hitting the ball with your head in football 2 a dive headfirst

head first *adverb*
with your head at the front ♦ *I dived in head first*

heading *noun* (*plural* **headings**)
a word or words at the top of a piece of printing or writing

headland *noun* (*plural* **headlands**)
a piece of high land sticking out into the sea

headlight *noun* (*plural* **headlights**)
a strong light at the front of a vehicle or railway engine

headline *noun* (*plural* **headlines**)
a heading in a newspaper

headlong *adverb* and *adjective*
1 falling head first 2 in a hasty or thoughtless way

headmaster *noun* (*plural* **headmasters**)
a male headteacher

headmistress *noun* (*plural* **headmistresses**)
a female headteacher

head-on *adverb* and *adjective*
with the front parts hitting each other ♦ *They had a head-on collision*

headphones *plural noun*
a listening device that fits over the top of your head

headquarters *noun* (*plural* **headquarters**)
the place from which an organization is controlled

headteacher *noun* (*plural* **headteachers**)
the person in charge of a school

headway *noun*
progress ♦ *They've made some headway in their talks*

heal *verb* (**heals, healing, healed**)
1 to heal someone is to make them healthy 2 to heal is to become healthy 3 to heal a disease is to cure it
healer *noun* someone who heals a disease

health *noun*
1 the condition of a person's body or mind ♦ *His health is bad* 2 being healthy ♦ *in sickness and in health*

health food *noun* (*plural* **health foods**)
food that contains only natural substances and is thought to be good for your health

healthy *adjective* (**healthier, healthiest**)
1 free from illness; having good health 2 producing good health ♦ *Fresh air is healthy*
healthily *adverb* in a healthy way **healthiness** *noun* being healthy

heap ➤ *noun* (*plural* **heaps**)
a pile, especially an untidy pile
heaps (*informal*) a large amount ♦ *We've got heaps of time*

heap ➤ *verb* (**heaps, heaping, heaped**)
1 to heap things is to make them into a heap 2 to heap something is to put large amounts on it ♦ *She heaped his plate with food*

hear *verb* (**hears, hearing, heard**)
1 to hear is to take in sounds through the ears 2 to hear something is to take in its sound through the ear 3 to hear news or information is to receive it
hear! hear! something you say when you strongly agree with something said

hearing *noun* (*plural* **hearings**)
1 the ability to hear 2 a chance to be heard 3 a trial in court

hearing aid *noun* (*plural* **hearing aids**)
a device to help a deaf person to hear

hearse *noun* (*plural* **hearses**)
a vehicle for taking a coffin to a funeral

heart *noun* (*plural* **hearts**)
1 the part of the body that makes the blood circulate **2** a person's feelings or emotions; sympathy **3** courage or enthusiasm ♦ *We must take heart* **4** the middle or most important part of something **5** a curved shape representing a heart, or a playing card with this shape on it

to break someone's heart is to make them very unhappy

by heart by using your memory

heart attack *noun* (*plural* **heart attacks**)
a sudden failure of the heart to work properly, causing pain and sometimes death

hearth *noun* (*plural* **hearths**) (*pronounced* harth)
the floor of a fireplace or near it

heartless *adjective*
cruel or without pity

hearty *adjective* (**heartier, heartiest**)
1 strong and vigorous **2** enthusiastic; sincere ♦ *Hearty congratulations!*
heartily *adverb* in a hearty way **heartiness** *noun* being hearty

heat ➤ *noun* (*plural* **heats**)
1 being hot; great warmth **2** a race or contest to decide who will take part in the final

heat ➤ *verb* (**heats, heating, heated**)
1 to heat something, or heat something up, is to make it hot **2** to heat, or heat up, is to become hot

heater *noun* (*plural* **heaters**)
a device for heating something, especially a room or a car

heath *noun* (*plural* **heaths**)
wild flat land often covered with heather or bushes

heathen *noun* (*plural* **heathens**)
someone who does not believe in any of the world's chief religions

heather *noun*
a low bush with small purple, pink, or white flowers

heatwave *noun* (*plural* **heatwaves**)
a long period of hot weather

heave *verb* (**heaves, heaving, heaved** or, in the last phrase given below, **hove**)
1 to heave something is to lift or move it with great effort **2** (*informal*) to heave something is to throw it

to heave a sigh is to sigh deeply

to heave to is what a ship does when it stops without anchoring or mooring

heaven *noun*
1 the place where God and the angels are thought to live **2** a very pleasant place or condition

the heavens the sky

heavenly *adjective*
1 to do with the sky or in the sky
2 (*informal*) pleasing or delicious ♦ *The cake is heavenly*

heavy *adjective* (**heavier, heaviest**)
1 weighing a lot; hard to lift or carry
2 strong or severe ♦ *Heavy rain was falling* **3** hard or difficult ♦ *It was heavy work getting the roof repaired*

with a heavy heart unhappily ♦ *I left my home town with a heavy heart*

heavily *adverb* strongly; seriously **heaviness** *noun* being heavy

heavyweight *noun* (*plural* **heavyweights**)
1 a heavy person **2** a boxer or wrestler of the heaviest weight

Hebrew *noun*
the language of the ancient Jews, with a modern form used in Israel

hectare *noun* (*plural* **hectares**) (*pronounced* hek-tar)
a unit of area equal to 10,000 square metres or nearly $2\frac{1}{2}$ acres

hectic *adjective*
very active or busy

he'd short for *he had, he should,* or *he would*

hedge ➤ *noun* (*plural* **hedges**)
a row of bushes forming a barrier or boundary

hedge ➤ *verb* (**hedges, hedging, hedged**)
1 to hedge a field or other area is to surround it with a hedge **2** to hedge is to make or trim a hedge **3** to hedge is also to avoid giving a definite answer ♦ *He wasn't sure, so he tried to hedge*

hedgehog *noun* (*plural* **hedgehogs**)
a small animal covered with prickles

hedgerow *noun* (*plural* **hedgerows**)
a row of bushes forming a hedge

heed ➤ *verb* (**heeds, heeding, heeded**)
to heed something is to pay attention to it

heed ➤ *noun*
attention given to something
heedless *adjective* taking no notice

heel ➤ *noun* (*plural* **heels**)
1 the back part of your foot **2** the part of a sock or shoe round or under the back part of your foot

to take to your heels is to run away

heel ➣ *verb* (heels, heeling, heeled)
1 to heel a shoe is to mend its heel **2** to heel a ball is to kick it with your heel

hefty *adjective* (heftier, heftiest)
big and strong

heifer *noun* (*plural* heifers) (*pronounced* hef-er)
a young cow

height *noun* (*plural* heights)
1 how high someone or something is **2** a high place **3** the highest or most important part of something ♦ *We shall be going at the height of the holiday season*

heighten *verb* (heightens, heightening, heightened)
1 to heighten something is to make it higher or more intense **2** to heighten is to become higher or more intense ♦ *Their excitement heightened as the kick-off approached*

heir *noun* (*plural* heirs) (*pronounced* air)
someone who inherits something
heiress *noun* a female heir

held past tense and past participle of **hold** *verb*

helicopter *noun* (*plural* helicopters)
a kind of aircraft without wings, lifted by a large horizontal propeller on top

helium *noun* (*pronounced* hee-li-um)
a light colourless gas that does not burn

helix *noun* (*plural* helices)
a three-dimensional spiral

hell *noun*
1 a place where, in some religions, wicked people are thought to be punished after they die **2** a very unpleasant place or situation
hell for leather at great speed

he'll short for *he will*

hellish *adjective*
very unpleasant or difficult

hello *interjection*
a word used to greet someone or to attract their attention

helm *noun* (*plural* helms)
the handle or wheel used to steer a ship

helmsman *noun* someone who steers a ship

helmet *noun* (*plural* helmets)
a strong covering worn to protect the head

help ➣ *verb* (helps, helping, helped)
1 to help someone is to do something useful for them **2** when you cannot help doing something, you cannot avoid doing it ♦ *I can't help coughing* **3** to help someone to food is to give them some
helper *noun* someone who helps

help ➣ *noun* (*plural* helps)
1 doing something useful for someone **2** someone who does something, especially housework, for someone

helpful *adjective*
giving help; useful
helpfully *adverb* in a helpful way

helping *noun* (*plural* helpings)
a portion of food

helpless *adjective*
not able to do things or look after yourself
helplessly *adverb* in a helpless way

helter-skelter *noun* (*plural* helter-skelters)
a spiral slide at a fair

hem ➣ *noun* (*plural* hems)
the edge of a piece of cloth that is folded over and sewn down

hem ➣ *verb* (hems, hemming, hemmed)
to hem material is to fold it over and sew down its edge in making clothes
to hem someone in is to surround them or restrict their movements

hemisphere *noun* (*plural* hemispheres)
1 half a sphere **2** half the earth ♦ *Australia is in the southern hemisphere*

hemp *noun*
a plant that produces coarse fibres from which cloth and ropes are made

hen *noun* (*plural* hens)
a female bird, especially a fowl

hence *adverb*
1 from this time on **2** therefore

henceforth *adverb*
from now on; from this time on

her ➤ *pronoun*
a word used for *she* when it is the object of
a verb, or when it comes after a
preposition ♦ *I can see her* ♦ *He took the
books from her*

her ➤ *adjective*
belonging to her ♦ *That is her book*

herald ➤ *noun* (*plural* **heralds**)
1 an official who in earlier times used to
make announcements or carry messages
for a king or queen **2** someone or
something that is a sign of things to come

herald ➤ *verb* (**heralds, heralding, heralded**)
to herald something or someone is to say
or show that they are coming

heraldry *noun*
the study of coats of arms
heraldic *adjective* to do with heraldry

herb *noun* (*plural* **herbs**)
a plant used for flavouring or for making
medicines
herbal *adjective* to do with herbs

herbivore *noun* (*plural* **herbivores**)
an animal that eats plants

herd ➤ *noun* (*plural* **herds**)
1 a group of cattle that feed together **2** a
mass of people; a mob

herd ➤ *verb* (**herds, herding, herded**)
to herd animals is to gather them together
or move them in a large group

here *adverb*
in or to this place
here and there in various places or directions

heredity *noun* (*pronounced* hi-**red**-i-ti)
inheriting characteristics from your
parents or ancestors
hereditary *adjective* inherited

heritage *noun* (*plural* **heritages**)
1 the things that someone has inherited
2 things that have been passed from one
generation to another ♦ *Music is part of
our cultural heritage*

hermit *noun* (*plural* **hermits**)
someone who lives alone and keeps away
from people
hermitage *noun* a hermit's home

hero *noun* (*plural* **heroes**)
1 a man or boy who has done something
very brave **2** the most important man or
boy in a story or play
heroic *adjective* brave like a hero **heroically**
adverb bravely **heroism** *noun* being a hero

heroine *noun* (*plural* **heroines**)
1 a woman or girl who has done something
very brave **2** the most important woman
or girl in a story or play

heron *noun* (*plural* **herons**)
a wading bird with long legs and a long
neck

herring *noun* (*plural* **herring** or **herrings**)
a sea fish used for food

hers *pronoun*
belonging to her ♦ *Those books are hers*

herself *pronoun*
she or her and nobody else, used to refer
back to the subject of a verb ♦ *She has
hurt herself*
by herself on her own; alone ♦ *She did the
work all by herself*

he's short for *he is* and (before a verb in the
past tense) *he has*

hesitant *adjective*
hesitating
hesitantly *adverb* in a hesitant way

hesitate *verb* (**hesitates, hesitating, hesitated**)
to hesitate is to be slow or uncertain in
speaking or moving
hesitation *noun* hesitating

hexagon *noun* (*plural* **hexagons**)
a flat shape with six sides
hexagonal *adjective* having six sides

hey *interjection*
an exclamation used to express surprise or
to call someone's attention

hi *interjection*
an exclamation used to greet someone or
to call their attention

hibernate *verb* (**hibernates, hibernating,
hibernated**) (*pronounced* hy-ber-nayt)
to hibernate is to sleep for a long time, as
animals do during cold weather
hibernation *noun* hibernating

hiccup *noun* (*plural* **hiccups**)
a high gulping sound made when your
breath is briefly interrupted

hide *verb* (**hides, hiding, hidden, hid, hidden**)
1 to hide is to get into a place where you
cannot be seen ♦ *I hid behind a tree* **2** to
hide someone or something is to keep them
from being seen ♦ *The gold was hidden in
a cave* **3** to hide information is to keep it
secret ♦ *Are you hiding the truth from me?*

hide-and-seek *noun*
a game in which one person looks for
others who are hiding

hideous *adjective*
very ugly or unpleasant
hideously *adverb* in a hideous way

hideout *noun* (*plural* **hideouts**)
a place where someone hides

hiding[1] *noun*
being hidden ♦ *She went into hiding*

hiding[2] *noun* (*plural* **hidings**)
a thrashing or beating

hieroglyphics *plural noun* (*pronounced* hyr-o-glif-iks)
pictures or symbols used in ancient Egypt to represent words

hi-fi *noun* (*plural* **hi-fis**) (*pronounced* hy-fy) (*informal*) **1** good reproduction of sound **2** equipment that reproduces sound well

higgledy-piggledy *adverb* and *adjective*
in disorder; completely mixed up

high *adjective* (**higher, highest**)
1 reaching a long way up ♦ *They could see a high building* **2** far above the ground or above sea level ♦ *The clouds were high in the sky* **3** measuring from top to bottom ♦ *The post is two metres high* **4** above average in amount or importance ♦ *They are people of a high rank* ♦ *Prices are high* **5** lively; happy ♦ *They are in high spirits* **6** a high note is one at the top end of a musical scale **7** going bad ♦ *This meat is high*

high time when you should do something at once ♦ *It's high time you started work*

higher education *noun*
education at a university or college

high explosive *noun* (*plural* **high explosives**)
a very strong explosive

high jump *noun*
an athletic contest in which competitors jump over a high bar

highland *adjective*
in the highlands; to do with the highlands

highlands *plural noun*
mountainous country, especially in Scotland

highlander *noun* someone who lives in the highlands

highlight *noun* (*plural* **highlights**)
the most interesting part of something

highlighter *noun* (*plural* **highlighters**)
a pen with bright coloured ink that you spread over words on paper to draw attention to them

highly *adverb*
1 extremely ♦ *He is highly amusing* **2** favourably ♦ *He thinks highly of her*

highly-strung *adjective*
very sensitive or nervous

Highness *noun* (*plural* **Highnesses**)
a title of a prince or princess ♦ *His Royal Highness, the Prince of Wales*

high-pitched *adjective*
high in sound

high-rise *adjective*
a high-rise building is one having many storeys

high school *noun* (*plural* **high schools**)
a secondary school

high tea *noun* (*plural* **high teas**)
a cooked meal eaten in the early evening

highway *noun* (*plural* **highways**)
an important road or route

highwayman *noun* (*plural* **highwaymen**)
a man who in earlier times robbed travellers on highways

hijack *verb* (**hijacks, hijacking, hijacked**)
to hijack an aircraft or vehicle is to seize control of it during a journey

hijacker *noun* someone who hijacks an aircraft or vehicle

hike ➤ *noun* (*plural* **hikes**)
a long walk in the country

hike ➤ *verb* (**hikes, hiking, hiked**)
to hike is to go for a hike

hiker *noun* someone who hikes

hilarious *adjective*
very funny

hilariously *adverb* in a hilarious way **hilarity** *noun* being hilarious

hill *noun* (*plural* **hills**)
a piece of ground that is higher than the ground around it

hillside *noun* the side of a hill **hilly** *adjective* having lots of hills

hilt *noun* (*plural* **hilts**)
the handle of a sword or dagger

up to the hilt completely

him *pronoun*
a word used for *he* when it is the object of a verb, or when it comes after a preposition ♦ *I like him* ♦ *I gave it to him*

himself *pronoun*
he or him and nobody else, used to refer back to the subject of a verb ♦ *He has hurt himself*

by himself on his own; alone ♦ *He did the work all by himself*

hind[1] *adjective* (*pronounced* hynd)
at the back ♦ *The donkey had hurt one of its hind legs*

hind[2] *noun* (*plural* **hinds**) (*pronounced* hynd)
a female deer

hinder *verb* (**hinders, hindering, hindered**) (*pronounced* hin-der)
to hinder someone is to get in their way, or to make it difficult for them to do something

hindrance *noun* something that hinders someone

Hindi *noun*
a language spoken in northern India

Hindu *noun* (*plural* **Hindus**)
someone who believes in **Hinduism**, one of the religions of India

hinge ➤ *noun* (*plural* **hinges**)
a joining device on which a door, gate, or lid swings when it opens

hinge ➤ *verb* (**hinges, hinging, hinged**)
to hinge a door or window is to fix it on a hinge
to hinge on something is to depend on it ♦ *It all hinges on the weather*

hint ➤ *noun* (*plural* **hints**)
1 a slight indication or suggestion ♦ *Give me a hint of what you want* **2** a useful idea ♦ *He was always giving us household hints*

hint ➤ *verb* (**hints, hinting, hinted**)
to hint is to make a hint or suggestion

hip¹ *noun* (*plural* **hips**)
the bony part at the side of the body between the waist and the thigh

hip² *noun* (*plural* **hips**)
the fruit of the wild rose

hip³ *interjection*
a word that you say when you give a cheer ♦ *Hip, hip, hooray!*

hippo *noun* (*plural* **hippos**)
(*informal*) a hippopotamus

hippopotamus *noun* (*plural* **hippopotamuses**)
a very large African animal that lives near water

hire *verb* (**hires, hiring, hired**)
to hire something is to pay to use it for a time

hire purchase *noun*
buying something by paying for it in instalments

his *adjective*
belonging to him ♦ *That is his book*

hiss *verb* (**hisses, hissing, hissed**)
to hiss is to make a sound like a continuous *s*, as some snakes do

histogram *noun* (*plural* **histograms**)
a chart showing amounts as bars of different heights and widths

historian *noun* (*plural* **historians**)
someone who writes or studies history

historic *adjective*
famous or important in history

historical *adjective*
1 to do with history **2** that really happened ♦ *The story is based on historical events*

history *noun* (*plural* **histories**)
1 what happened in the past **2** the study of past events **3** a description of important events

hit ➤ *verb* (**hits, hitting, hit**)
1 to hit someone or something is to come up against them with force, or to give them a blow **2** to hit a place or people is to have a bad effect on them ♦ *Famine hit the poorer countries* **3** to hit a note is to reach it in singing
to hit it off with someone is to become quickly friendly with them
to hit on something is to think of an idea suddenly

hit ➤ *noun* (*plural* **hits**)
1 a knock or stroke **2** a shot that hits the target **3** a successful song or show

hitch ➤ *verb* (**hitches, hitching, hitched**)
1 to hitch something is to fasten it with a loop or hook **2** (*informal*) to hitch a lift is to hitch-hike
to hitch something up is to pull it up quickly or with a jerk ♦ *He hitched up his trousers*

hitch ➤ *noun* (*plural* **hitches**)
1 the movement that you make when you hitch something up **2** a knot **3** a slight difficulty or delay

hitch-hike *verb* (**hitch-hikes, hitch-hiking, hitch-hiked**)
to hitch-hike is to travel by getting lifts in other people's vehicles
hitch-hiker *noun* someone who hitch-hikes

hi-tech *adjective*
(*informal*) using the most advanced technology, such as computers

hither *adverb*
(*old use*) to or towards this place

hitherto *adverb*
up to now

HIV short for *human immunodeficiency virus*, a virus that weakens a person's resistance to disease

hive *noun* (*plural* **hives**)
1 a beehive **2** a very busy place ♦ *The office was a hive of activity*

HMS short for *His* or *Her Majesty's Ship*

ho *interjection*
an exclamation of triumph or surprise, etc.

hoard ➤ *noun* (*plural* **hoards**)
a secret store of something valuable

hoard ➤ *verb* (**hoards, hoarding, hoarded**)
to hoard things is to store them away
hoarder *noun* someone who hoards things

hoarding *noun* (*plural* **hoardings**)
a tall fence covered with advertisements

hoar frost *noun*
white frost

hoarse *adjective* (**hoarser, hoarsest**)
having a rough or croaking voice ♦ *He was hoarse from shouting*

hoax ➤ *noun* (*plural* **hoaxes**)
a trick played on someone

hoax ➤ *verb* (**hoaxes, hoaxing, hoaxed**)
to hoax someone is to play a hoax on them

hobble *verb* (**hobbles, hobbling, hobbled**)
to hobble is to limp or walk with difficulty

hobby *noun* (*plural* **hobbies**)
something that you do for pleasure in your spare time

hockey *noun*
an outdoor game played by two teams with curved sticks and a small hard ball

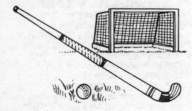

hoe ➤ *noun* (*plural* **hoes**)
a tool for scraping up weeds

hoe ➤ *verb* (**hoes, hoeing, hoed**)
to hoe ground is to scrape it or dig it with a hoe

hog ➤ *noun* (*plural* **hogs**)
1 a male pig **2** (*informal*) a greedy person
to go the whole hog (*informal*) is to do something completely or thoroughly

hog ➤ *verb* (**hogs, hogging, hogged**)
(*informal*) to hog something is to take more than your fair share of it

Hogmanay *noun*
New Year's Eve in Scotland

hoist *verb* (**hoists, hoisting, hoisted**)
to hoist something is to lift it up using ropes or pulleys

hold ➤ *verb* (**holds, holding, held**)
1 to hold something is to have it in your hands **2** to hold something is also to possess it or be the owner of it ♦ *She holds the world high jump record* **3** to hold someone is to restrain them or stop them

getting away ♦ *They held the thief until help arrived* **4** a container holds an amount when that is what you can put in it ♦ *This jug holds a litre* **5** to hold someone or something is to support them ♦ *This plank won't hold my weight* **6** something like the weather holds when it stays the same ♦ *Will this good weather hold?* **7** to hold an opinion is to believe it
hold it (*informal*) stop; wait a minute
to hold on (*informal*) is to wait ♦ *Hold on! I'm not ready yet*
to hold on to something is to keep holding it
to hold out is to last or continue
to hold someone up is to rob them with threats of force
to hold someone or **something up** is to hinder them ♦ *Roadworks in the town centre are holding up the traffic*

hold ➤ *noun* (*plural* **holds**)
1 holding something; a way of holding something **2** something to hold on to
3 the part of a ship where cargo is stored
to get hold of someone is to make contact with them ♦ *I want to invite Jane to the party but I can't get hold of her*
to get hold of something is to grasp it

holdall *noun* (*plural* **holdalls**)
a large portable bag or case

holder *noun* (*plural* **holders**)
a person or thing that holds something

hold-up *noun* (*plural* **hold-ups**)
1 a delay **2** a robbery with threats or force

hole *noun* (*plural* **holes**)
1 a gap or opening made in something
2 an animal's burrow
holey *adjective* having lots of holes

Holi *noun*
a Hindu festival held in the spring

holiday *noun* (*plural* **holidays**)
a day or time when you do not go to work or school; a time when you go away to enjoy yourself
on holiday having a holiday

hollow ➤ *adjective*
having an empty space inside; not solid

hollow ➤ *adverb*
(*informal*) by a lot; completely ♦ *We beat them hollow*

hollow ➤ *verb* (**hollows, hollowing, hollowed**)
to hollow something is to make it hollow

hollow ➤ *noun* (*plural* **hollows**)
1 a hollow or sunken place; a hole **2** a small valley

holly *noun*
an evergreen bush with shiny prickly leaves and red berries

holocaust *noun* (*plural* **holocausts**)
(*pronounced* hol-o-kawst)
an immense destruction, especially by fire
the Holocaust the mass murder of Jews by
the Nazis from the 1930s until 1945

hologram *noun* (*plural* **holograms**)
a type of photograph made by laser beams,
that appears to have depth as well as
height and width

holster *noun* (*plural* **holsters**)
a leather case for a pistol, usually attached
to a belt

holy *adjective* (**holier, holiest**)
1 to do with God and treated with
religious respect 2 a holy person is
devoted to God or a religion
holiness *noun* being holy

home ➤ *noun* (*plural* **homes**)
1 the place where you live 2 the place
where you were born or where you feel you
belong 3 a place where people are looked
after ♦ *She went to a home for the elderly*
4 the place that you try to reach in a game
♦ *The far end of the gym is home*
to feel at home is to feel comfortable and
happy

home ➤ *adverb*
1 to or at the place where you live ♦ *Go
home! Is she home yet?* 2 to the place
aimed at ♦ *Push the bolt home*
to bring something home to someone is to make
them realize it

home ➤ *verb* (**homes, homing, homed**)
to home in on something is to aim for it

home economics *plural noun*
studying how to run a home

homeless *adjective*
not having a place to live

homely *adjective*
simple or ordinary

home-made *adjective*
made at home and not bought from a shop

homesick *adjective*
sad or upset because you are away from
home
homesickness *noun* being homesick

homestead *noun* (*plural* **homesteads**)
a farmhouse and the land around it

homeward or **homewards** *adverb*
towards home

homework *noun*
school work that has to be done at home

homing *adjective*
trained to fly home ♦ *He kept homing
pigeons*

homosexual ➤ *adjective* (*pronounced*
hoh-mo-**seks**-yoo-al or hom-o-**seks**-yoo-al)
loving or attracted to people of the same
sex

homosexual ➤ *noun* (*plural* **homosexuals**)
a homosexual person

honest *adjective*
1 truthful and just; not stealing, cheating,
or telling lies 2 fair ♦ *We want honest
dealings* 3 truthful ♦ *It was an honest
reply*
honestly *adverb* in an honest way **honesty**
noun being honest

honey *noun*
a sweet sticky food made by bees

honeycomb *noun* (*plural* **honeycombs**)
a wax framework made by bees to hold
their honey and eggs

honeymoon *noun* (*plural* **honeymoons**)
a holiday spent together by a
newly-married couple

honeysuckle *noun*
a climbing plant with sweet-smelling
yellow or pink flowers

honk ➤ *noun* (*plural* **honks**)
a loud sound like the one made by a car
horn or a wild goose

honk ➤ *verb* (**honks, honking, honked**)
to make a honking sound

honour ➤ *noun* (*plural* **honours**)
1 honour is great respect or reputation
2 an honour is something given to a
deserving person 3 an honour is also
something a person is proud to do ♦ *It is
an honour to meet you*

honour ➤ *verb* (**honours, honouring, honoured**)
1 to honour someone is to feel or show
honour for them 2 to honour a promise or
agreement is to keep it

honourable *adjective*
honest or loyal
honourably *adverb* in an honourable way

hood *noun* (*plural* **hoods**)
1 a covering of soft material for the head
and neck 2 a folding roof or cover
hooded *adjective* having a hood

-hood *suffix*
forming nouns meaning a state or time of
life, for example *childhood*

hoof *noun* (*plural* **hoofs**)
the horny part of the foot of horses, cattle,
or deer

hook ➤ *noun* (*plural* **hooks**)
a piece of bent or curved metal for hanging
things on or catching hold of something
hooked *adjective* having a hook

hook ➤ *verb* (**hooks, hooking, hooked**)
1 to hook something is to fasten it with or
on a hook 2 to hook a fish is to catch it
with a hook

hooligan *noun* (*plural* **hooligans**)
a rough or noisy person

hoop *noun* (*plural* **hoops**)
a large ring made of metal, wood, or plastic

hoopla *noun*
a game in which you try to throw hoops round an object, which you then win as a prize

hooray *interjection*
a shout of joy or approval; a cheer

hoot ➤ *noun* (*plural* **hoots**)
1 a sound like the one made by an owl or a train whistle **2** a jeer

hoot ➤ *verb* (**hoots, hooting, hooted**)
to hoot is to make a sound like an owl or a train whistle

hooter *noun* (*plural* **hooters**)
a horn or other device that makes a hoot

hop[1] ➤ *verb* (**hops, hopping, hopped**)
1 to hop is to jump on one foot, or to move in jumps **2** (*informal*) to hop is also to move quickly ♦ *Here's the car; hop in!*
hop it (*slang*) go away

hop ➤ *noun* (*plural* **hops**)
a jump made on one foot

hop[2] *noun* (*plural* **hops**)
a climbing plant used to give beer its flavour

hope ➤ *noun* (*plural* **hopes**)
1 the feeling of wanting something to happen, and thinking that it will happen **2** a person or thing that makes you feel like this ♦ *Our big hope is that someone will give us the money*

hope ➤ *verb* (**hopes, hoping, hoped**)
to hope for something is to want it and expect it to happen

hopeful *adjective*
1 having hope **2** likely to be good or successful ♦ *The future did not seem very hopeful*

hopefully *adverb*
1 in a hopeful way ♦ *'Can I come too?' she asked hopefully* **2** I hope that ...
♦ *Hopefully we can all go to the sea tomorrow*

hopeless *adjective*
1 without hope **2** very bad at something ♦ *I'm hopeless at cricket*
hopelessly *adverb* in a hopeless way

hopscotch *noun*
a game in which you hop into squares drawn on the ground

horde *noun* (*plural* **hordes**)
a large group or crowd

horizon *noun* (*plural* **horizons**) (*pronounced* ho-**ry**-zon)
the line where the sky appears to meet the land or sea

horizontal *adjective* (*pronounced* ho-ri-**zon**-tal)
level or flat; going across from left to right
horizontally *adverb* in a horizontal direction

hormone *noun* (*plural* **hormones**)
a substance made in glands in the body and sent directly into the blood to stimulate other organs in the body

horn *noun* (*plural* **horns**)
1 a kind of pointed bone that grows on the head of a bull, cow, ram, and other animals **2** a brass musical instrument that you blow **3** a device for making a warning sound

hornet *noun* (*plural* **hornets**)
a large kind of wasp

horoscope *noun* (*plural* **horoscopes**)
an astrologer's forecast of future events

horrible *adjective*
very unpleasant or nasty; horrifying
horribly *adverb* in a horrible way

horrid *adjective*
horrible

horrific *adjective*
horrifying
horrifically *adverb* in a horrific way

horrify *verb* (**horrifies, horrifying, horrified**)
to horrify someone is to make them feel very afraid or disgusted

horror *noun* (*plural* **horrors**)
1 horror is great fear or disgust **2** a horror is a horrifying person or thing

horse *noun* (*plural* **horses**)
1 a four-legged animal used for riding on or pulling carts **2** a framework to hang clothes on to dry **3** a tall box for jumping over in gymnastics

horseback *noun*
on horseback riding a horse

horse chestnut *noun* (*plural* **horse chestnuts**)
a large tree that produces dark brown nuts called conkers

horseman *noun* (*plural* **horsemen**)
a man who rides a horse, especially a skilful rider

horsemanship *noun* the art of riding

horsepower *noun* (*plural* **horsepower**)
a unit for measuring the power of an engine, equal to 746 watts

horseshoe *noun* (*plural* **horseshoes**)
a U-shaped piece of metal nailed as a shoe to a horse's hoof

horsewoman *noun* (*plural* **horsewomen**)
a woman who rides a horse, especially a skilful rider

horticulture *noun*
the art of planning and looking after gardens

hose *noun* (*plural* **hoses**)
a long flexible tube through which liquids or gases can travel

hospitable *adjective*
welcoming; liking to give hospitality

hospitably *adverb* in a hospitable way

hospital *noun* (*plural* **hospitals**)
a place where sick or injured people are given medical treatment

hospitality *noun*
welcoming people and giving them food and entertainment

host[1] *noun* (*plural* **hosts**)
someone who has guests and looks after them

host[2] *noun* (*plural* **hosts**)
a large number of people or things

hostage *noun* (*plural* **hostages**)
someone who is held prisoner until the captor's demands are met

hostel *noun* (*plural* **hostels**)
a building with rooms for students or other people

hostess *noun* (*plural* **hostesses**)
a woman who has guests and looks after them

hostile *adjective*
1 opposed to someone or something
2 unfriendly ♦ *The audience was hostile*

hostility *noun* being hostile

hot ➤ *adjective* (**hotter, hottest**)
1 having a high temperature; very warm
2 having a burning taste like pepper or mustard 3 excited or angry ♦ *He has a hot temper*
in hot water (*informal*) in trouble or difficulty

hot ➤ *verb* (**hots, hotting, hotted**)
to hot up (*informal*) is to become hotter or more exciting
to hot something up (*informal*) is to make it hotter or more exciting

hot cross bun *noun* (*plural* **hot cross buns**)
a spicy bun with a cross marked on it, eaten at Easter

hot dog *noun* (*plural* **hot dogs**)
a hot sausage in a bread roll

hotel *noun* (*plural* **hotels**)
a building where people pay to have meals and stay for the night

hothouse *noun* (*plural* **hothouses**)
a heated greenhouse

hotly *adverb*
strongly or forcefully ♦ *He hotly denied that he'd done it*

hotpot *noun* (*plural* **hotpots**)
a kind of stew

hot-water bottle *noun* (*plural* **hot-water bottles**)
a container that you fill with hot water to make a bed warm

hound ➤ *noun* (*plural* **hounds**)
a dog used in hunting or racing

hound ➤ *verb* (**hounds, hounding, hounded**)
to hound someone is to chase or harass them ♦ *The family was hounded by newspaper reporters*

hour *noun* (*plural* **hours**)
1 one of the twenty-four parts into which a day is divided 2 a particular time
♦ *Why are you up at this hour?*

hourglass *noun* (*plural* **hourglasses**)
an old-fashioned device for telling the time, with sand running from one half of a glass container into the other through a narrow middle part

hourly *adjective* and *adverb*
every hour; done once an hour

house ➤ *noun* (*plural* **houses**) (*pronounced* howss)
1 a building where people live, usually designed for one family 2 a building used for a special purpose ♦ *They passed the opera house* 3 a building for a government assembly, or the assembly itself, for example the Houses of Parliament and the House of Commons 4 one of the divisions in some schools for sports competitions and other events

house ➤ *verb* (**houses, housing, housed**) (*pronounced* howz)
to house someone or something is to provide a house or room for them

houseboat *noun* (*plural* **houseboats**)
a boat for living in

household *noun* (*plural* **households**)
all the people who live together in the same house

householder *noun* (*plural* **householders**)
someone who owns or rents a house

housekeeper *noun* (*plural* **housekeepers**)
a person employed to look after a household

housekeeping *noun*
1 looking after a household 2 the money for a household's food and other supplies

house-proud *adjective*
very careful to keep a house clean and tidy

house-trained *adjective*
an animal that is house-trained is trained to be clean in the house

house-warming *noun* (*plural* **house-warmings**)
a party to celebrate moving into a new home

housewife *noun* (*plural* **housewives**)
a woman who does the housekeeping for her family

housework *noun*
the work like cooking and cleaning that has to be done in a house

housing *noun* (*plural* **housings**)
1 housing is accommodation or houses 2 a housing is a cover or guard for a piece of machinery

hove see **heave**

hover *verb* (**hovers, hovering, hovered**)
1 to hover is to stay in one place in the air
2 to hover round someone is to wait near them to watch what they do

hovercraft *noun* (*plural* **hovercraft**)
a vehicle that travels just above the surface of water or land, supported by a strong current of air sent downwards by its engines

how *adverb*
1 in what way ♦ *How did you do it?* 2 to what extent ♦ *How much do you want?* 3 in what condition ♦ *How are you?*
how about ... would you like ... ? ♦ *How about a game of football?*
how do you do? a more formal greeting when you meet someone

however ➤ *adverb*
1 in whatever way; to whatever extent ♦ *You will never catch him, however hard you try* 2 nevertheless ♦ *It was snowing; however, he went out*

however ➤ *conjunction*
in any way ♦ *You can do it however you like*

howl ➤ *noun* (*plural* **howls**)
a long loud cry like an animal in pain

howl ➤ *verb* (**howls, howling, howled**)
to howl is to make a howl, or to weep loudly

howler *noun* (*plural* **howlers**)
(*informal*) a silly mistake

HQ short for **headquarters**

hub *noun* (*plural* **hubs**)
the centre of a wheel

huddle *verb* (**huddles, huddling, huddled**)
to huddle is to crowd together with other people for warmth or comfort

hue[1] *noun* (*plural* **hues**)
a colour or tint

hue[2] *noun*
hue and cry a general alarm or protest

huff *noun*
in a huff annoyed or offended

hug ➤ *verb* (**hugs, hugging, hugged**)
1 to hug someone is to clasp them tightly in your arms **2** to hug something is to keep close to it ♦ *The ship hugged the shore*

hug ➤ *noun* (*plural* **hugs**)
clasping someone tightly in your arms

huge *adjective* (**huger, hugest**)
extremely large
hugely *adverb* greatly; very

hulk *noun* (*plural* **hulks**)
1 the remains of an old decaying ship **2** a large clumsy person or thing
hulking *adjective* large and clumsy

hull *noun* (*plural* **hulls**)
the main part or framework of a ship

hullabaloo *noun* (*plural* **hullabaloos**)
an uproar

hullo *interjection*
a word used to greet someone or to attract their attention

hum ➤ *verb* (**hums, humming, hummed**)
1 to hum is to sing a tune with your lips closed **2** to hum is also to make a low continuous sound like a bee

hum ➤ *noun* (*plural* **hums**)
a humming sound

human ➤ *noun* (*plural* **humans**)
a man, woman, or child; a human being

human ➤ *adjective*
to do with humans

human being *noun* (*plural* **human beings**)
a man, woman, or child; a human

humane *adjective* (*pronounced* hew-**mayn**)
kind or merciful
humanely *adverb* in a humane way

humanitarian *adjective* (*pronounced* hew-man-i-**tair**-i-an)
concerned with helping humanity and relieving suffering

humanity *noun*
1 all the people in the world **2** being human **3** being humane
humanities *plural noun* arts subjects such as history and English, not sciences

humble *adjective* (**humbler, humblest**)
modest; not proud
humbly *adverb* in a humble way

humid *adjective* (*pronounced* hew-mid)
damp or moist in the air
humidity *noun* being humid

humiliate *verb* (**humiliates, humiliating, humiliated**)
to humiliate someone is to make them feel ashamed or disgraced
humiliation *noun* a feeling of shame or disgrace

humility *noun*
being humble

hummingbird *noun* (*plural* **hummingbirds**)
a small tropical bird that makes a humming sound by beating its wings rapidly

humorous *adjective*
full of humour; amusing or funny

humour ➤ *noun*
1 being amusing; what makes people laugh **2** being able to enjoy comical things ♦ *He has a good sense of humour* **3** a person's mood ♦ *Keep him in a good humour*

humour ➤ *verb* (**humours, humouring, humoured**)
to humour someone is to keep them happy by doing what they want

hump ➤ *noun* (*plural* **humps**)
1 a rounded lump or mound **2** a lump on a person's back

hump ➤ *verb* (**humps, humping, humped**)
to hump something heavy is to carry it with difficulty on your back

humpback bridge *noun* (*plural* **humpback bridges**)
a small bridge that rises steeply in the middle

humus *noun* (*pronounced* hew-mus)
rich earth made by decayed plants

hunch[1] *noun* (*plural* **hunches**)
a feeling that you can guess what will happen ♦ *I have a hunch that she won't come*

hunch[2] *verb* (**hunches, hunching, hunched**)
to hunch your shoulders is to bend them upward so that your back is rounded

hunchback *noun* (*plural* **hunchbacks**)
someone with a hump on their back
hunchbacked *adjective* having a hunchback

hundred *noun* (*plural* **hundreds**)
the number 100
hundredth *adjective* and *noun* 100th

hundredweight *noun* (*plural* **hundredweights**)
a unit of weight equal to 112 pounds or 50·8 kilograms

hung past tense and past participle of **hang**

hunger *noun*
the feeling that you want to eat; a need for food

hunger strike *noun* (*plural* **hunger strikes**)
refusing to eat, as a way of making a protest

hungry *adjective* (**hungrier, hungriest**)
feeling hunger; needing to eat
hungrily *adverb* in a hungry way

hunk *noun* (*plural* **hunks**)
a large piece or chunk of something

hunt ➤ *verb* (**hunts, hunting, hunted**)
1 to hunt animals is to chase and kill them for food or sport 2 to hunt for something is to look hard for it

hunt ➤ *noun* (*plural* **hunts**)
1 hunting, especially for foxes 2 a group of people who go hunting

hunter or **huntsman** *noun* (*plural* **hunters** or **huntsmen**)
someone who hunts for sport

hurdle *noun* (*plural* **hurdles**)
1 an upright frame that runners jump over in hurdling 2 a problem or difficulty

hurdling *noun*
racing in which the runners run and jump over hurdles
hurdler *noun* someone who does hurdling

hurl *verb* (**hurls, hurling, hurled**)
to hurl something is to throw it as far as you can

hurrah or **hurray** *interjection*
a shout of joy or approval; a cheer

hurricane *noun* (*plural* **hurricanes**)
a severe storm with a strong wind

hurry ➤ *verb* (**hurries, hurrying, hurried**)
1 to hurry is to move or act quickly 2 to hurry someone is to try to make them be quick
hurriedly *adverb* in a hurry

hurry ➤ *noun*
moving quickly; doing something quickly
in a hurry hurrying or impatient ♦ *They were in a hurry to catch their train*

hurt ➤ *verb* (**hurts, hurting, hurt**)
1 to hurt a person or animal is to harm them or cause them pain 2 to hurt someone is also to upset or offend them

hurt ➤ *noun*
pain or injury

hurtle *verb* (**hurtles, hurtling, hurtled**)
to hurtle is to move quickly or dangerously ♦ *The train was hurtling along*

husband *noun* (*plural* **husbands**)
the man that a woman has married

hush ➤ *verb* (**hushes, hushing, hushed**)
to hush someone is to make them quiet
to hush something up is to prevent people knowing about it

hush ➤ *noun*
silence; quiet ♦ *Let's have a bit of hush*

hush-hush *adjective*
(*informal*) very secret

husk *noun* (*plural* **husks**)
the dry outer covering of a seed

husky[1] *adjective* (**huskier, huskiest**)
1 hoarse ♦ *She has a husky voice* 2 big and strong
huskily *adverb* with a husky voice **huskiness** *noun* being husky

husky[2] *noun* (*plural* **huskies**)
a large strong dog used in the Arctic for pulling sledges

hustle *verb* (**hustles, hustling, hustled**)
1 to hustle is to hurry 2 to hustle someone is to push them rudely

hut *noun* (*plural* **huts**)
a small roughly made house or shelter

hutch *noun* (*plural* **hutches**)
a box or cage for a rabbit or other pet animal

hyacinth *noun* (*plural* **hyacinths**)
a sweet-smelling flower that grows from a bulb

hybrid *noun* (*plural* **hybrids**)
1 an animal or plant that combines two different species ♦ *A mule is a hybrid of a donkey and a mare* 2 something that is a mixture of two things

hydrangea *noun* (*plural* **hydrangeas**) (*pronounced* hy-**drayn**-ja)
a shrub with large pink, blue, or white flowers

hydrant *noun* (*plural* **hydrants**)
an outdoor water-tap for fixing a hose to

hydraulic *adjective*
worked by the movement of water or other liquid

hydroelectric *adjective*
using water-power to make electricity

hydrofoil *noun* (*plural* **hydrofoils**)
a boat designed to skim over the surface of the water

hydrogen *noun*
a very light gas which with oxygen makes water

hydrogen bomb *noun* (*plural* **hydrogen bombs**)
a very powerful bomb using energy from the joining of hydrogen nuclei

hydrophobia *noun*
an abnormal fear of water, as experienced by someone with rabies

hyena *noun* (*plural* **hyenas**) (*pronounced* hy-**ee**-na)
a wild animal that looks like a wolf and makes a shrieking howl

hygiene *noun* (*pronounced* hy-**jeen**)
keeping clean and healthy

hygienic *adjective*
clean and healthy
hygienically *adverb* in a hygienic way

hymn *noun* (*plural* **hymns**)
a religious song, especially one praising God

hymn book *noun* (*plural* **hymn books**)
a book of hymns

hyperactive *adjective*
unable to relax and always moving about or doing things

hypermarket *noun* (*plural* **hypermarkets**)
a very large supermarket, usually outside a town

hyphen *noun* (*plural* **hyphens**)
a short dash used to join words or parts of words together, for example in *house-proud*
hyphenated spelt with a hyphen

hypnosis *noun* (*pronounced* hip-**noh**-sis)
a condition like a deep sleep in which a person follows the instructions of another person

hypnotism *noun* (*pronounced* **hip**-no-tizm)
hypnotizing people
hypnotist *noun* someone who hypnotizes people

hypnotize *verb* (**hypnotizes, hypnotizing, hypnotized**)
to hypnotize someone is to put them to sleep by hypnosis

hypocrite *noun* (*plural* **hypocrites**) (*pronounced* **hip**-o-krit)
someone who pretends to be a better person than they really are
hypocrisy *noun* being a hypocrite **hypocritical** *adjective* to do with a hypocrite

hypodermic *adjective* (*pronounced* hy-po-**der**-mik)
injecting something under the skin ♦ *The doctor used a hypodermic syringe*

hypotenuse *noun* (*plural* **hypotenuses**) (*pronounced* hy-**pot**-i-newz)
the side opposite the right angle in a right-angled triangle

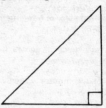

hypothermia *noun*
having a body temperature well below normal

hypothesis *noun* (*plural* **hypotheses**) (*pronounced* hy-**poth**-i-sis)
a suggestion or theory that tries to explain something but has not been proved right

hypothetical *adjective*
based on a theory; not proved or certain

hysteria *noun*
wild uncontrollable excitement or emotion

hysterical *adjective*
1 suffering from hysteria 2 very excited 3 (*informal*) very funny
hysterically *adverb* in a hysterical way

hysterics *plural noun*
a fit of hysteria
in hysterics (*informal*) laughing a lot

Ii

I *pronoun*
a word used by someone to speak about himself or herself

ice ➤ *noun* (*plural* **ices**)
1 ice is frozen water 2 an ice is an ice cream

ice ➤ *verb* (**ices, icing, iced**)
1 to ice or ice up is to become covered in ice 2 to ice a cake is to put icing on it

ice age *noun*
a time in the past when ice covered large areas of the earth's surface

iceberg *noun* (*plural* **icebergs**)
a large mass of ice floating in the sea, with most of it under water

ice cream *noun* (*plural* **ice creams**)
1 ice cream is a sweet creamy frozen food 2 an ice cream is a portion of this

ice hockey *noun*
a game like hockey played on ice

ice lolly *noun* (*plural* **ice lollies**)
a piece of flavoured ice on a stick

icicle *noun* (*plural* **icicles**)
a thin pointed piece of hanging ice formed
from dripping water

icing *noun*
a sugary substance for decorating cakes

icon *noun* (*plural* **icons**)
1 a small picture or symbol standing for a
program on a computer screen **2** a
painting of a holy person

icy *adjective* (**icier, iciest**)
1 like ice; very cold **2** very unfriendly;
hostile ♦ *He gave them an icy stare*
icily *adverb* in an icy or unfriendly way

I'd short for *I had, I should,* or *I would*

idea *noun* (*plural* **ideas**)
something that someone has thought of;
a plan

ideal ➣ *adjective*
exactly what you want; perfect
ideally *adverb* in an ideal way

ideal ➣ *noun* (*plural* **ideals**)
something that is perfect or the best thing
to have; a very high standard

identical *adjective*
exactly the same
identically *adverb* in exactly the same way

identification *noun*
1 identification is any document, such as a
passport, that proves who you are
2 identification is the process of
identifying someone or something

identify *verb* (**identifies, identifying, identified**)
to identify someone or something is to
discover who or what they are ♦ *The police
have identified the car used in the robbery*
to identify with someone is to understand or
share their feelings or opinions

identity *noun* (*plural* **identities**)
who someone is or what something is
♦ *They had no way of proving their
identity*

idiom *noun* (*plural* **idioms**) (*pronounced*
id-i-om)
a phrase or group of words that together
have a special meaning that is not obvious
from the words themselves, for example *to
be in hot water* means to be in trouble or
difficulty

idiomatic *adjective*
a person's language is idiomatic when it is
natural and uses a lot of idioms

idiot *noun* (*plural* **idiots**)
(*informal*) a stupid or foolish person
idiocy *noun* being stupid or foolish

idiotic *adjective*
(*informal*) stupid or foolish ♦ *It was an
idiotic thing to do*
idiotically *adverb* in an idiotic way

idle ➣ *adjective* (**idler, idlest**)
1 a person is idle when they are lazy or
doing nothing **2** a machine is idle when it
is not being used **3** idle talk or gossip is
talk that is silly or pointless

idle ➣ *verb* (**idles, idling, idled**)
a machine or engine idles when it is
working slowly
idly *adverb* in an idle way

idol *noun* (*plural* **idols**)
1 a statue or image that people worship as
a god **2** a famous person whom many
people admire
idolatry *noun* the worship of idols

idolize *verb* (**idolizes, idolizing, idolized**)
to idolize someone is to admire them very
much

i.e. short for the Latin *id est*, which means
that is, used to explain something ♦ *The
world's highest mountain (i.e. Mount
Everest) is in the Himalayas*

if *conjunction*
1 on condition that ♦ *I'll tell you what
happened if you promise to keep it secret*
2 although; even though ♦ *I'll finish this
job if it kills me!* **3** whether ♦ *Do you
know if lunch is ready?*
if only ... I wish ... ♦ *If only I could go with
you!*

igloo *noun* (*plural* **igloos**)
an Inuit round house made of blocks of
hard snow

igneous *adjective* (*pronounced* ig-ni-us)
igneous rocks are formed by the action of a
volcano

ignite *verb* (**ignites, igniting, ignited**)
1 to ignite something is to set fire to it
2 to ignite is to catch fire

ignition *noun*
1 igniting **2** the system in a motor engine
that starts the fuel burning

ignorant *adjective*
not knowing about something; knowing
very little
ignorance *noun* being ignorant

ignore *verb* (**ignores, ignoring, ignored**)
to ignore someone or something is to take no notice of them

I'll short for *I shall* or *I will*

ill ➢ *adjective*
1 not well; in bad health 2 bad or harmful
♦ *There were no ill effects*

ill ➢ *adverb*
badly ♦ *She was ill-treated*

illegal *adjective*
not legal; against the law
illegally *adverb* in an illegal way

illegible *adjective* (*pronounced* i-lej-i-bul)
not clear enough to read
illegibly *adverb* so as to be illegible

illegitimate *adjective* (*pronounced* il-i-jit-i-mat)
(*old use*) born of parents who were not married to each other

illiterate *adjective* (*pronounced* i-lit-er-at)
unable to read or write
illiteracy *noun* being illiterate

illness *noun* (*plural* **illnesses**)
1 illness is being ill 2 an illness is something that makes people ill; a disease

illogical *adjective*
not logical or having any good reason
illogically *adverb* in an illogical way

illuminate *verb* (**illuminates, illuminating, illuminated**)
1 to illuminate a place or street is to light it up or decorate it with lights 2 to illuminate something difficult is to make it clearer
illumination *noun* illuminating something or making it bright

illusion *noun* (*plural* **illusions**)
something that you think is real or happening but is not; an imaginary thing

illustrate *verb* (**illustrates, illustrating, illustrated**)
1 to illustrate something is to show it with pictures or examples 2 to illustrate a book is to put pictures in it

illustration *noun* (*plural* **illustrations**)
1 an illustration is a picture in a book
2 an illustration is also an example that explains something 3 illustration is explaining something by pictures or examples

illustrious *adjective* (*pronounced* i-lus-tri-us)
famous

I'm short for *I am*

image *noun* (*plural* **images**)
1 a picture or statue of a person or thing
2 what you see in a mirror or through a lens 3 a person who looks very much like another ♦ *She is the image of her mother*
4 the way that people think of a person or thing

imagery *noun*
the use of words to produce pictures in the mind of the reader

imaginary *adjective*
not real; only in someone's mind

imagination *noun* (*plural* **imaginations**)
being able to imagine things

imaginative *adjective*
able to imagine things; showing an ability to imagine things ♦ *They wrote an imaginative story about a train journey*

imagine *verb* (**imagines, imagining, imagined**)
to imagine something or someone is to form a picture of them in your mind
imaginable *adjective* able to be imagined

imam *noun* (*plural* **imams**)
a Muslim religious leader

imbecile *noun* (*plural* **imbeciles**)
(*pronounced* im-bi-seel)
(*informal*) a very stupid person

imitate *verb* (**imitates, imitating, imitated**)
to imitate someone or something is to do the same as them
imitation *noun* imitating or copying someone or something **imitator** *noun* someone who imitates

immature *adjective*
not fully grown or developed
immaturity *noun* being immature

immediate *adjective*
1 happening or done without any delay
2 nearest; with nothing or no one between
♦ *The Smiths are our immediate neighbours*

immediately *adverb*
without any delay; at once

immense *adjective*
huge
immensely *adverb* extremely **immensity** *noun* being immense

immerse *verb* (**immerses, immersing, immersed**)
1 to immerse something is to put it completely into a liquid 2 to be immersed in something is to be very interested or involved in it
immersion *noun* immersing something

immersion heater *noun* (*plural* **immersion heaters**)
a device that heats water with an electric element immersed in the water in a tank

immigrant *noun* (*plural* **immigrants**)
someone who has come into a country to
live there

immigrate *verb* (**immigrates, immigrating,
immigrated**)
to immigrate is to come into a country to
live there
immigration *noun* immigrating

immobile *adjective*
not moving
immobility *noun* being immobile

immobilize *verb* (**immobilizes, immobilizing,
immobilized**)
to immobilize something is to stop it
moving or working

immoral *adjective*
not following the usual standards of right
and wrong
immorality *noun* being immoral

immortal *adjective*
living for ever; never dying
immortality *noun* being immortal

immune *adjective*
safe from danger or attack, especially from
disease
immunity *noun* being immune

immunize *verb* (**immunizes, immunizing,
immunized**)
to immunize someone is to make them safe
from disease
immunization *noun* immunizing someone

imp *noun* (*plural* **imps**)
1 a small devil **2** a naughty child
impish *adjective* naughty, like an imp

impact *noun* (*plural* **impacts**)
1 a collision, or the force of a collision **2** a
strong influence or effect ♦ *Computers are
making a big impact on our lives*

impair *verb* (**impairs, impairing, impaired**)
to impair something is to harm or weaken
it ♦ *The accident has impaired his health*

impale *verb* (**impales, impaling, impaled**)
to impale something is to fix it on to a
sharp pointed object

impartial *adjective*
not favouring one side more than the
other; fair
impartiality *noun* being impartial **impartially**
adverb in an impartial way

impassable *adjective*
an impassable road is one that you cannot
get through

impatient *adjective*
not patient; in a hurry
impatience *noun* being impatient **impatiently**
adverb in an impatient way

impede *verb* (**impedes, impeding, impeded**)
to impede someone or something is to
hinder them or get in their way

imperative *adjective*
1 essential ♦ *Speed is imperative* **2** in
grammar, an imperative word expresses a
command, like *come* in *Come here!*

imperceptible *adjective*
too small or gradual to be noticed ♦ *The
change in the weather was imperceptible*
imperceptibly *adverb* in an imperceptible
way

imperfect *adjective*
not perfect; not complete
imperfection *noun* being imperfect **imperfectly**
adverb in an imperfect way

imperial *adjective*
1 belonging to an empire or its rulers
2 an imperial unit or measure is one fixed
by British law, such as an imperial gallon.
These are non-metric units

impersonal *adjective*
1 not affected by personal feelings;
showing no emotion **2** not referring to a
particular person
impersonally *adverb* in an impersonal way

impersonate *verb* (**impersonates, impersonating,
impersonated**)
to impersonate someone is to pretend to be
them
impersonation *noun* impersonating someone
impersonator *noun* someone who
impersonates someone else

impertinent *adjective*
not respectful; rude
impertinence *noun* being impertinent

implement ➤ *noun* (*plural* **implements**)
(*pronounced* im-pli-ment)
a tool or device for working with

implement ➤ *verb* (**implements, implementing,
implemented**) (*pronounced* im-pli-ment)
to implement a plan or idea is to put it into
action

implore *verb* (**implores, imploring, implored**)
to implore someone to do something is to
beg them to do it

imply *verb* (**implies, implying, implied**)
to imply something is to suggest it without
actually saying it ♦ *His comment on my
work implied that I was lazy*
implication *noun* something that someone
implies

impolite *adjective*
not having good manners; not respectful
and thoughtful towards other people

import ➤ *verb* (**imports, importing, imported**)
(*pronounced* im-**port**)
to import goods is to bring them in from
another country to sell them
importer *noun* someone who imports goods

import ➤ *noun* (*plural* **imports**) (*pronounced* im-port)
something brought in from another country to be sold

important *adjective*
1 needing to be taken seriously; having a great effect ♦ *This is an important decision* 2 powerful or influential ♦ *They are important people*
importance *noun* being important **importantly** *adverb* in an important way

impose *verb* (**imposes, imposing, imposed**)
1 to impose something on someone is to make them have to put up with it ♦ *The building plans were imposed on the village against everyone's wishes* 2 to impose a charge or tax is to make people pay it
to impose on someone is to take unfair advantage of them

imposing *adjective*
looking important; impressive

imposition *noun* (*plural* **impositions**)
something that someone is made to suffer, especially as a punishment

impossible *adjective*
1 not possible 2 (*informal*) very annoying ♦ *He is impossible!*
impossibility *noun* something that is impossible **impossibly** *adverb* in an impossible way

impostor *noun* (*plural* **impostors**)
someone who is not what he or she pretends to be

impracticable *adjective*
not able to be done or used

impractical *adjective*
1 not good at making or doing things 2 not likely to work or be useful ♦ *Their ideas are impractical*

impress *verb* (**impresses, impressing, impressed**)
1 to impress someone is to make them admire you 2 to impress something on someone is to make them realize or remember it

impression *noun* (*plural* **impressions**)
1 a vague idea 2 an effect on someone's mind or feelings 3 an imitation of a person or a sound

impressive *adjective*
making a good impression
impressively *adverb* in an impressive way

imprison *verb* (**imprisons, imprisoning, imprisoned**)
to imprison someone is to put them in prison
imprisonment *noun* being put in prison

improbable *adjective*
unlikely
improbability *noun* being improbable

impromptu *adjective* and *adverb* (*pronounced* im-**promp**-tew)
done without any rehearsal or preparation

improper *adjective*
1 not proper; wrong 2 indecent
improperly *adverb* in an improper way
impropriety *noun* something improper

improve *verb* (**improves, improving, improved**)
to improve something is to make it better; to improve is to become better
improvement *noun* something that is better or makes a thing better

improvise *verb* (**improvises, improvising, improvised**)
1 to improvise is to do something without any rehearsal or preparation, especially to play music without rehearsing 2 to improvise something is to make it quickly with what is to hand
improvisation *noun* improvising something

impudent *adjective*
not respectful; rude
impudence *noun* being impudent

impulse *noun* (*plural* **impulses**)
1 a sudden desire to do something 2 a push; a driving force 3 (*in Science*) a force acting for a very short time

impulsive *adjective*
acting from impulse, without much thought
impulsively *adverb* in an impulsive way

impure *adjective*
not pure
impurity *noun* being impure

in *preposition* and *adverb*
1 showing position at or inside something ♦ *They live in London* ♦ *Please come in* ♦ *She fell in the water* ♦ *Then the others fell in* 2 **In** also has some special uses, shown by the following examples ♦ *We came in April* ♦ *I paid in cash* ♦ *They are watching a serial in four parts* ♦ *He is in the army* ♦ *We knocked on the door but no one was in*
in all including everything ♦ *The bill comes to £120 in all*
to be in for something is to be likely to get it ♦ *You're in for a shock*
to be in on something is to take part in something ♦ *I want to be in on this game*

in- *prefix*
meaning 'not', as in *inefficient*

inability *noun*
being unable to do something

inaccessible *adjective*
not able to be reached

inaccurate *adjective*
not accurate

inaccuracy *noun* being inaccurate **inaccurately** *adverb* in an inaccurate way

inaction *noun*
lack of action

inactive *adjective*
not working or doing anything
inactivity *noun* being inactive

inadequate *adjective*
not enough
inadequacy *noun* being inadequate
inadequately *adverb* in an inadequate way

inanimate *adjective* (*pronounced* in-an-im-at)
not living or moving

inappropriate *adjective*
not appropriate or suitable
inappropriately *adverb* in an inappropriate way

inattentive *adjective*
not listening or paying attention
inattention *noun* being inattentive

inaudible *adjective*
not able to be heard
inaudibly *adverb* so as not to be heard

incapable *adjective*
unable to do something ♦ *They are incapable of understanding the problem*

incapacity *noun*
inability; disability

incendiary *adjective*
an incendiary bomb or device is one that starts a fire

incense ➤ *noun* (*pronounced* in-senss)
a substance that makes a spicy smell when it is burnt

incense ➤ *verb* (**incenses, incensing, incensed**) (*pronounced* in-**senss**)
to incense someone is to make them very angry

incentive *noun* (*plural* **incentives**)
something that encourages a person to do something or to work harder

incessant *adjective*
going on without stopping, usually in an annoying way ♦ *They were bothered by the incessant noise*
incessantly *adverb* without stopping

inch *noun* (*plural* **inches**)
a measure of length, one twelfth of a foot or about $2\frac{1}{2}$ centimetres

incident *noun* (*plural* **incidents**)
an event, usually a strange or unusual one

incidental *adjective*
happening along with something else; not so important
incidentally *adverb* by the way

incinerator *noun* (*plural* **incinerators**)
a device for burning rubbish

inclination *noun* (*plural* **inclinations**)
a tendency ♦ *He had an inclination to eat too many sweets*

incline ➤ *verb* (**inclines, inclining, inclined**) (*pronounced* in-**klyn**)
to incline is to lean or bend
to be inclined to do something is to feel like doing it ♦ *I'm inclined to wait until later*

incline ➤ *noun* (*plural* **inclines**) (*pronounced* **in**-klyn)
a slope

include *verb* (**includes, including, included**)
to include something or someone is to make or consider them as part of a group of things ♦ *Did you include Peter in the party?*
inclusion *noun* being included

inclusive *adjective*
including everything; including all the things mentioned ♦ *We want to stay from Monday to Thursday inclusive*

income *noun* (*plural* **incomes**)
the money that a person earns regularly

income tax *noun*
a tax people have to pay on their income

incompatible *adjective*
1 not able to live or exist together without trouble **2** machines and devices are incompatible when they cannot be used together

incompetent *adjective*
unable to do something properly
incompetence *noun* being incompetent
incompetently *adverb* in an incompetent way

incomplete *adjective*
not complete
incompletely *adverb* not completely

incomprehensible *adjective*
not able to be understood

incongruous *adjective* (*pronounced* in-**kong**-roo-us)
not suitable; out of place
incongruity *noun* being incongruous
incongruously *adverb* in an incongruous way

inconsiderate *adjective*
not thinking of other people

inconsistent *adjective*
not consistent
inconsistency *noun* being inconsistent
inconsistently *adverb* in an inconsistent way

inconspicuous *adjective*
not noticeable or remarkable

inconvenient *adjective*
not convenient; awkward
inconvenience *noun* being inconvenient

incorporate *verb* (**incorporates, incorporating, incorporated**)
to incorporate something is to include it as a part of something else

incorporation *noun* incorporating something

incorrect *adjective*
not correct; wrong
incorrectly *adverb* wrongly

increase ➢ *verb* (**increases, increasing, increased**) (*pronounced* in-**kreess**)
1 to increase something is to make it bigger **2** to increase is to become bigger
increasingly *adverb* more and more ♦ *They were becoming increasingly angry*

increase ➢ *noun* (*plural* **increases**) (*pronounced* in-kreess)
1 increasing **2** the amount by which something increases

incredible *adjective*
unbelievable
incredibly *adverb* in an incredible way

incredulous *adjective*
finding it difficult to believe someone
incredulity *noun* disbelief

incubate *verb* (**incubates, incubating, incubated**)
to incubate eggs is to hatch them by keeping them warm
incubation *noun* incubating

incubator *noun* (*plural* **incubators**)
1 a specially heated container for keeping newly born babies warm and well supplied with oxygen **2** a container for hatching eggs

indebted *adjective*
owing something to someone

indecent *adjective*
not decent; improper
indecency *noun* being indecent **indecently** *adverb* in an indecent way

indeed *adverb*
used for emphasis ♦ *He was very wet indeed*

indefinite *adjective*
not definite; vague

indefinite article *noun* (*plural* **indefinite articles**)
the word *a* or *an*

indefinitely *adverb*
for an indefinite or unlimited time

indelible *adjective*
impossible to rub out or remove

indelibly *adverb* so as to be indelible

indent *verb* (**indents, indenting, indented**)
1 to indent something is to make notches or recesses in it **2** to indent a line of print or writing is to begin it further to the right than usual

indentation *noun* a mark or dent caused by indenting

independent *adjective*
free to act; not controlled by another person or country
independence *noun* being independent
independently *adverb* in an independent way

index *noun* (*plural* **indexes**)
1 a list of names or topics, usually in alphabetical order at the end of a book
2 a number showing how much prices or wages have changed

index finger *noun* (*plural* **index fingers**)
the finger next to the thumb

Indian summer *noun* (*plural* **Indian summers**)
a period of warm weather in early autumn

indicate *verb* (**indicates, indicating, indicated**)
to indicate something is to point it out or show that it is there
indication *noun* a sign of something

indicative *adjective*
being a sign of something

indicator *noun* (*plural* **indicators**)
1 something that tells you what is happening **2** a flashing light on a vehicle, to show that it is turning left or right

indifferent *adjective*
1 not caring about something; not interested **2** not very good; ordinary
♦ *He is an indifferent cricketer*
indifference *noun* not caring **indifferently** *adverb* in an indifferent way

indigestible *adjective*
not easy to digest

indigestion *noun*
pain caused by difficulty in digesting food

indignant *adjective*
angry at something that seems wrong or unjust
indignantly *adverb* in an indignant way
indignation *noun* a feeling of being indignant

indigo *noun*
a deep blue colour

indirect *adjective*
not direct or straight
indirectly *adverb* in an indirect way

indirect speech *noun*
someone's words given in a changed form reported by someone else, as in *He said that he would come* (reporting the words 'I will come')

indispensable *adjective*
essential

indistinct *adjective*
not clear
indistinctly *adverb* in an indistinct way

indistinguishable *adjective*
impossible to see or hear, or to tell apart
from something else

individual ➤ *adjective*
1 of or for one person 2 single or separate
individually *adverb* separately; one by one

individual ➤ *noun* (*plural* **individuals**)
an individual is one person

individuality *noun*
the things that make one person or thing
different from another

indoctrinate *verb* (**indoctrinates, indoctrinating,
indoctrinated**)
to indoctrinate someone is to fill their
mind with particular ideas or beliefs, so
that they accept them without thinking
indoctrination *noun* indoctrinating someone

indoor *adjective*
placed or done inside a building ◆ *We like
indoor sports*

indoors *adverb*
inside a building

induce *verb* (**induces, inducing, induced**)
1 to induce someone to do something is to
persuade them to do it 2 to induce a
pregnant woman is to start the birth of her
baby artificially
inducement *noun* inducing someone;
persuasion

indulge *verb* (**indulges, indulging, indulged**)
to indulge someone is to let them have or
do what they want
to indulge in something is to have or do
something that you like

indulgent *adjective*
kind and allowing people to do what they
want
indulgence *noun* being indulgent

industrial *adjective*
to do with industry

industrial action *noun*
ways for workers to protest, such as
striking or working to rule

industrialist *noun* (*plural* **industrialists**)
someone who runs an industry

industrialize *verb* (**industrializes, industrializing,
industrialized**)
to industrialize a country is to increase or
develop its industry
industrialization *noun* industrializing a
country

industrious *adjective*
hard-working
industriously *adverb* in an industrious way

industry *noun* (*plural* **industries**)
1 industry is making or producing goods
to sell, especially in factories 2 an
industry is a branch of this, such as the
motor industry 3 industry is also working
hard

ineffective *adjective*
not effective; not working well
ineffectively *adverb* in an ineffective way

ineffectual *adjective*
not achieving anything
ineffectually *adverb* in an ineffectual way

inefficient *adjective*
not doing work well; wasteful of energy
inefficiency *noun* being inefficient **inefficiently**
adverb in an inefficient way

inequality *noun* (*plural* **inequalities**)
not being equal

inert *adjective*
not moving or reacting

inertia *noun* (*pronounced* in-er-sha)
1 being inert or slow to take action 2 (*in
Science*) the tendency for a moving thing
to keep moving in a straight line

inevitable *adjective*
unavoidable
inevitability *noun* being inevitable **inevitably**
adverb in an inevitable way

inexhaustible *adjective*
that you cannot use up completely;
never-ending

inexpensive *adjective*
not expensive; cheap
inexpensively *adverb* cheaply

inexperience *noun*
lack of experience
inexperienced *adjective* not having
experience

inexplicable *adjective*
impossible to explain
inexplicably *adverb* in an inexplicable way

infallible *adjective*
1 never wrong 2 always working ◆ *They
have an infallible way of winning the
lottery*
infallibility *noun* being infallible **infallibly**
adverb in an infallible way

infamous *adjective* (*pronounced* in-fa-mus)
having a bad reputation; thought to be
wicked
infamy *noun* being infamous

infant *noun* (*plural* **infants**)
a baby or young child
infancy *noun* the time of being an infant

infantile *adjective*
1 to do with babies or young children
2 childish and silly

infantry *noun*
soldiers trained to fight on foot

infect *verb* (**infects, infecting, infected**)
to infect someone is to pass on a disease to
them
infection *noun* (*plural* **infections**)
1 infection is infecting someone **2** an
infection is an infectious disease
infectious *adjective*
1 an infectious disease is one that can
spread from one person to another
2 something like laughter or fear is
infectious when it spreads to other people
infer *verb* (**infers, inferring, inferred**)
to infer something is to work it out from
what someone says or does ♦ *I infer from
your uniform that you are the postman*
inference *noun* something inferred or
guessed
inferior ➤ *adjective*
less good or important; lower in position or
quality
inferiority *noun* being inferior
inferior ➤ *noun* (*plural* **inferiors**)
a person who is lower in position or rank
than someone else
infernal *adjective*
1 like hell or to do with hell **2** (*informal*)
awful; very annoying ♦ *What an infernal
nuisance*
infernally *adverb* in an infernal way
inferno *noun* (*plural* **infernos**) (*pronounced*
in-fer-noh)
a fierce fire
infested *adjective*
full of troublesome things like insects or
rats
infiltrate *verb* (**infiltrates, infiltrating, infiltrated**)
to infiltrate a place or organization is to
get into it without being noticed
infiltration *noun* infiltrating a place
infinite *adjective* (*pronounced* in-fi-nit)
endless; too large to be measured or
imagined
infinitely *adverb* to an infinite extent
infinitive *noun* (*plural* **infinitives**)
(*pronounced* in-fin-i-tiv)
the form of a verb that does not change to
indicate a particular person or tense. In
English it often comes after *to*, as in *to go*
and *to hit*
infinity *noun* (*pronounced* in-fin-i-ti)
an infinite number or distance
infirm *adjective*
weak because of illness or old age
infirmity *noun* being infirm
infirmary *noun* (*plural* **infirmaries**)
a place for sick people; a hospital

inflame *verb* (**inflames, inflaming, inflamed**)
1 a part of the body is inflamed when it
has become red and sore **2** to inflame
someone is to make them angry
inflammable *adjective*
that can be set alight
inflammation *noun* (*plural* **inflammations**)
a painful swelling or sore place on the body
inflammatory *adjective*
likely to make people angry
inflate *verb* (**inflates, inflating, inflated**)
1 to inflate something is to fill it with air
or gas **2** a claim or statement is inflated
when it is exaggerated
inflatable *adjective* able to be filled with air
inflation *noun*
1 filling something with air or gas **2** a
general rise in prices
inflect *verb* (**inflects, inflecting, inflected**)
1 (*in Grammar*) to inflect a word is to
change it slightly to make it fit with other
words, for example *make, makes, making*
2 to inflect your voice is to change the
sound of it when you speak
inflection *noun* (*plural* **inflections**)
(*in Grammar*) the change you make to a
word when you inflect it
inflexible *adjective*
that you cannot bend or change ♦ *There
are a lot of inflexible rules*
inflexibility *noun* being inflexible **inflexibly**
adverb in an inflexible way
inflict *verb* (**inflicts, inflicting, inflicted**)
to inflict something on someone is to make
them suffer it ♦ *She inflicted a severe blow
on him*
influence ➤ *noun* (*plural* **influences**)
the power to affect someone or something
influence ➤ *verb* (**influences, influencing,
influenced**)
to influence someone or something is to
have an effect on what they are or do
♦ *The tides are influenced by the moon*
influential *adjective*
having a big influence; important
influenza *noun* (*pronounced* in-floo-en-za)
an infectious disease that causes fever,
catarrh, and pain
inform *verb* (**informs, informing, informed**)
to inform someone of something is to tell
them about it
to inform against or **on someone** is to give
information about them, especially to the
police
informal *adjective*
not formal; relaxed
informality *noun* being informal **informally**
adverb in an informal way

informant *noun* (*plural* **informants**)
a person who gives information

information *noun*
facts; knowledge; what someone tells you

information technology *noun*
ways of storing, arranging, and giving out
information, especially the use of
computers and telecommunications

informative *adjective* (*pronounced*
in-**form**-a-tiv)
containing a lot of helpful information

informed *adjective*
knowing about something

informer *noun* (*plural* **informers**)
a person who tells the police about
someone else

infrequent *adjective*
not frequent
infrequency *noun* being infrequent
infrequently *adverb* not often

infuriate *verb* (**infuriates, infuriating, infuriated**)
to infuriate someone is to make them very
angry

ingenious *adjective*
1 clever at doing things 2 cleverly made
or done
ingeniously *adverb* in an ingenious way
ingenuity *noun* being ingenious

ingot *noun* (*plural* **ingots**)
a lump of gold or silver that has been cast
in the form of a brick

ingrained *adjective*
deeply fixed ♦ *She was accused of
ingrained idleness*

ingredient *noun* (*plural* **ingredients**)
(*pronounced* in-**greed**-i-ent)
1 one of the parts of a mixture 2 one of
the things used in a recipe

inhabit *verb* (**inhabits, inhabiting, inhabited**)
to inhabit a place is to live in it
inhabitant *noun* someone who lives in a
place

inhale *verb* (**inhales, inhaling, inhaled**)
1 to inhale is to breathe in 2 to inhale
something is to breathe it in

inhaler *noun* (*plural* **inhalers**)
a device for taking medicine by inhaling it

inherent *adjective* (*pronounced* in-**heer**-ent)
naturally or permanently part of
something
inherently *adverb* in an inherent way

inherit *verb* (**inherits, inheriting, inherited**)
1 to inherit money, property, or a title is to
receive it when its previous owner dies
2 to inherit qualities or characteristics is
to get them from your parents or ancestors
inheritance *noun* something you inherit

inhibited *adjective*
resisting or holding back emotions,
instincts, or impulses

inhospitable *adjective* (*pronounced*
in-hos-**pit**-a-bul or in-**hos**-pit-a-bul)
1 unfriendly to visitors 2 giving no
shelter ♦ *They reached an inhospitable
rocky island*

inhuman *adjective*
cruel; without pity or kindness
inhumanity *noun* being inhuman

initial ➤ *noun* (*plural* **initials**)
the first letter of a word or name,
especially of someone's forename

initial ➤ *adjective*
first; of the beginning ♦ *the initial stages
of the work*
initially *adverb* at the beginning

initiate *verb* (**initiates, initiating, initiated**)
(*pronounced* in-**ish**-i-ayt)
1 to initiate something is to start it 2 to
initiate someone is to admit them as a
member of a society or group, often with
special ceremonies
initiation *noun* being initiated

initiative *noun* (*plural* **initiatives**)
(*pronounced* in-**ish**-a-tiv)
1 the action that starts something ♦ *She
took the initiative in planning the party*
2 ability or power to start things or to get
them done on your own

inject *verb* (**injects, injecting, injected**)
1 to inject someone is to put a medicine or
drug through their skin using a hollow
needle 2 to inject something is to add it
♦ *Try to inject some humour into the story*
injection *noun* injecting someone with
medicine

injure *verb* (**injures, injuring, injured**)
to injure someone is to harm or hurt them

injury *noun* (*plural* **injuries**)
harm or damage done to someone
injurious *adjective* causing injury

injustice *noun* (*plural* **injustices**)
unjust action or treatment

ink *noun* (*plural* **inks**)
a black or coloured liquid used for writing
and printing
inky *adjective* like ink; covered in ink

inkling *noun*
a slight idea or suspicion ♦ *I had an
inkling that we'd find them in here*

inland *adverb*
in or towards a place on land and away
from the coast

in-laws *plural noun*
the relatives of someone's husband or wife
♦ *We're going to visit the in-laws at Easter*

inlet *noun* (*plural* **inlets**)
a strip of water reaching into the land
from a sea or lake

inn *noun* (*plural* **inns**)
a hotel or public house, especially in the
country
innkeeper *noun* someone who runs an inn

inner *adjective*
inside; nearer the centre
innermost *adjective* furthest inside

innings *noun* (*plural* **innings**)
the time when a cricket team or player is
batting

innocent *adjective*
1 not guilty; not wicked 2 harmless
innocence *noun* being innocent **innocently**
adverb in an innocent way

innocuous *adjective*
harmless

innovation *noun* (*plural* **innovations**)
1 innovation is inventing or using new
things 2 an innovation is something new
that you have just invented or started
using
innovative *adjective* new and interesting
innovator *noun* someone who innovates
something

innumerable *adjective*
too many to be counted

inoculate *verb* (**inoculates, inoculating,
inoculated**)
to inoculate someone is to inject them as
protection against a disease
inoculation *noun* being inoculated

in-patient *noun* (*plural* **in-patients**)
someone who stays at a hospital for
treatment

input ➤ *noun* (*plural* **inputs**)
what you put into something, especially
data put into a computer

input ➤ *verb* (**inputs, inputting, input**)
(*in Computing*) to input data or programs
is to put them into a computer

inquest *noun* (*plural* **inquests**)
an official investigation to decide why
someone died

inquire *verb* (**inquires, inquiring, inquired**)
1 to inquire about something is to ask
about it 2 to inquire into something is to
make an official investigation of it

inquiry *noun* (*plural* **inquiries**)
an official investigation

inquisitive *adjective*
always trying to find out things, especially
about other people
inquisitively *adverb* in an inquisitive way

insane *adjective*
not sane; mad

insanely *adverb* in an insane way **insanity**
noun being insane

insanitary *adjective*
not clean or healthy

inscribe *verb* (**inscribes, inscribing, inscribed**)
to inscribe something is to write or carve it
on a surface

inscription *noun* (*plural* **inscriptions**)
words written or carved on a monument,
stone, or coin, or written in the front of a
book

insect *noun* (*plural* **insects**)
a small animal with six legs and a body
divided into three parts

insecticide *noun* (*plural* **insecticides**)
a poison for killing insects

insecure *adjective*
1 not secure or safe 2 not feeling safe or
confident
insecurely *adverb* in an insecure way
insecurity *noun* being insecure

insensitive *adjective*
not sensitive or thinking about the
feelings of others
insensitively *adverb* in an insensitive way
insensitivity *noun* being insensitive

inseparable *adjective*
1 unable to be separated 2 always
together ♦ *The friends are inseparable*
inseparably *adverb* so as to be inseparable

insert *verb* (**inserts, inserting, inserted**)
to insert something is to put it into
something else
insertion *noun* inserting something

inshore *adjective and adverb*
on the sea near or nearer to the shore

inside ➤ *noun* (*plural* **insides**)
1 the middle or centre of something; the
part nearest to the middle 2 (*informal*)
your insides are your stomach or abdomen
inside out with the inside turned so that it
faces outwards

inside ➤ *adjective*
placed on the inside of something ♦ *Look
on an inside page*

inside ➤ *adverb and preposition*
in or to the inside of something ♦ *Come
inside* ♦ *It's inside that box*

insight *noun* (*plural* **insights**)
1 being able to see the truth about things
2 an understanding of something

insignificant *adjective*
not important or influential
insignificance *noun* being insignificant

insincere *adjective*
not sincere
insincerely *adverb* in an insincere way
insincerity *noun* being insincere

insist *verb* (insists, insisting, insisted)
to insist something is to be very firm in
saying it ♦ *He insisted that he was
innocent*
to insist on something is to demand it ♦ *We
insist on seeing the manager*

insistent *adjective*
insisting on doing or having something
insistence *noun* being insistent

insolent *adjective*
very rude and insulting
insolence *noun* being insolent

insoluble *adjective*
1 impossible to solve ♦ *It is an insoluble
problem* **2** impossible to dissolve ♦ *Some
chemicals are insoluble*
insolubility *noun* being insoluble

insomnia *noun* (*pronounced* in-som-ni-a)
being unable to sleep

inspect *verb* (inspects, inspecting, inspected)
to inspect something or someone is to look
carefully at them, especially to check them
inspection *noun* inspecting

inspector *noun* (*plural* inspectors)
1 someone employed to inspect things or
people **2** a police officer next in rank above
a sergeant

inspire *verb* (inspires, inspiring, inspired)
to inspire someone is to fill them with
ideas or enthusiasm
inspiration *noun* being inspired

install *verb* (installs, installing, installed)
1 to install something is to put it in
position ready for use ♦ *We want to install
central heating* **2** to install someone is to
put them into an important position with
a ceremony ♦ *He was installed as pope*
installation *noun* being installed; something
that is installed

instalment *noun* (*plural* instalments)
one of the parts into which something is
divided so as to spread it over a period of
time ♦ *He is paying for his bike in monthly
instalments*

instance *noun* (*plural* instances)
an example
for instance for example

instant ⊱ *adjective*
1 happening immediately ♦ *It has been an
instant success* **2** that can be made very
quickly ♦ *Do you like instant coffee?*

instant ⊱ *noun* (*plural* instants)
a moment ♦ *I don't believe it for an instant*
this instant at once ♦ *Come here this instant!*

instantaneous *adjective*
happening or done in an instant, or
without any delay
instantaneously *adverb* in an instant;
immediately

instantly *adverb*
without any delay

instead *adverb*
in place of something else; as a substitute
♦ *There were no potatoes, so we had rice
instead*

instep *noun* (*plural* insteps)
the top of the foot between the toes and the
ankle

instinct *noun* (*plural* instincts)
a natural tendency to do or feel something
♦ *Spiders spin webs by instinct*
instinctive *adjective* following instinct
instinctively *adverb* in an instinctive way

institute ⊱ *noun* (*plural* institutes)
a society or organization, or the building
used by it

institute ⊱ *verb* (institutes, instituting, instituted)
to institute something is to establish it or
start it

institution *noun* (*plural* institutions)
1 an organization or institute
2 something that is an established habit
or custom ♦ *Going for a swim on Sunday
was a family institution*

instruct *verb* (instructs, instructing, instructed)
1 to instruct someone is to teach them a
subject or skill **2** to instruct someone is
also to give them information or orders

instruction *noun* (*plural* instructions)
1 instruction is teaching a subject or skill
2 an instruction is an order or piece of
information ♦ *Follow the instructions
carefully*

instrument *noun* (*plural* instruments)
1 a device for making musical sounds **2** a
device for delicate or scientific work

instrumental *adjective*
1 of or using musical instruments
2 being one of the causes of something
♦ *She was instrumental in getting him a
job*

insufficient *adjective*
not enough

insulate *verb* (insulates, insulating, insulated)
to insulate something is to cover it so as to
stop heat, cold, or electricity from passing
in or out
insulation *noun* insulating something

insulin *noun*
a chemical that controls how much sugar
there is in the blood

insult ⊱ *verb* (insults, insulting, insulted)
(*pronounced* in-**sult**)
to insult someone is to speak or behave in
a way that hurts their feelings or pride

insult ⊱ *noun* (*plural* insults) (*pronounced*
in-sult)
a remark or action that insults someone

insurance *noun*
a business agreement to receive money or compensation if you suffer a loss or injury, in return for a regular payment called a premium

insure *verb* (**insures, insuring, insured**)
to insure yourself or your goods is to protect them with insurance

intact *adjective*
complete and undamaged ♦ *Despite the storm our tent was still intact*

intake *noun* (*plural* **intakes**)
1 taking something in 2 the number of people or things taken in ♦ *The school had a high intake of pupils this year*

integer *noun* (*plural* **integers**) (*pronounced* in-ti-jer)
a whole number, such as 0, 1, 24, and not a fraction

integral *adjective* (*pronounced* in-ti-gral)
1 that is an essential part of something ♦ *Your heart is an integral part of your body* 2 whole or complete

integrate *verb* (**integrates, integrating, integrated**) (*pronounced* in-ti-grayt)
1 to integrate different things or parts is to make them into a whole 2 to integrate people, especially of different origins, is to bring them together into a single community
integration *noun* being integrated

integrity *noun* (*pronounced* in-teg-ri-ti)
honesty

intellect *noun* (*plural* **intellects**)
the ability to think and work things out with the mind

intellectual ➤ *adjective*
1 involving the intellect 2 able to think effectively; keen to study and learn
intellectually *adverb* in an intellectual way

intellectual ➤ *noun* (*plural* **intellectuals**)
an intellectual person

intelligence *noun*
1 being intelligent 2 information, especially of military value 3 the people who collect and study this information

intelligent *adjective*
good at thinking and learning
intelligently *adverb* in an intelligent way

intelligible *adjective*
able to be understood ♦ *The message was barely intelligible*
intelligibility *noun* being intelligible **intelligibly** *adverb* so as to be intelligible

intend *verb* (**intends, intending, intended**)
1 to intend to do something is to have it in mind as a plan ♦ *She was intending to go swimming* 2 to intend someone to do something is to want them to do it

intense *adjective*
1 very strong or great ♦ *The heat was intense* 2 having or showing strong feelings
intensely *adverb* very strongly

intensify *verb* (**intensifies, intensifying, intensified**)
1 to intensify something is to make it more intense 2 to intensify is to become more intense
intensification *noun* intensifying something or becoming more intense

intensity *noun* (*plural* **intensities**)
how strong or great something is

intensive *adjective*
using a lot of effort; thorough ♦ *We have made an intensive search*
intensively *adverb* in an intensive way

intent ➤ *adjective*
eager; very interested
intent on something eager or determined to do it
intently *adverb* eagerly

intent ➤ *noun* (*plural* **intents**)
intention

intention *noun* (*plural* **intentions**)
what you intend to do; a plan

intentional *adjective*
deliberate or planned
intentionally *adverb* deliberately; on purpose

inter- *prefix*
meaning between two or more people or things, as in *interchangeable* and *inter-school*

interact *verb* (**interacts, interacting, interacted**)
two people or things interact when they have an effect on one another ♦ *It is interesting to watch how young children interact*
interaction *noun* the process of interacting

interactive *adjective*
(*in Computing*) allowing information to be sent in either direction between a computer system and its user

intercept *verb* (**intercepts, intercepting, intercepted**)
to intercept someone or something is to stop them going from one place to another
interception *noun* intercepting someone or something

interchange *noun* (*plural* **interchanges**)
a place where you can move from one main road or motorway to another

interchangeable *adjective*
able to be changed or swapped round

intercom *noun* (*plural* **intercoms**)
a device for communicating by radio or telephone

intercourse *noun*
1 communication or dealings between people 2 sexual intercourse

interest ➤ *verb* (interests, interesting, interested)
to interest someone is to make them want to look or listen or take part in something

interest ➤ *noun* (*plural* interests)
1 interest is being interested; curiosity 2 an interest is a thing that interests someone 3 interest is also money a borrower has to pay regularly for a loan

interface *noun* (*plural* interfaces)
a connection between two parts of a computer system

interfere *verb* (interferes, interfering, interfered)
1 to interfere in something is to become involved in it when it has nothing to do with you 2 to interfere is to get in the way

interference *noun*
1 interfering in something 2 a crackling or distorting of a radio or television signal

interior *noun* (*plural* interiors)
the inside of something

interjection *noun* (*plural* interjections)
an exclamation, such as *oh!*

interlock *verb* (interlocks, interlocking, interlocked)
to interlock is to fit into one another ♦ *The gearwheels interlocked*

interlude *noun* (*plural* interludes)
1 an interval 2 music played during an interval

intermediate *adjective*
coming between two things in place, order, or time

interminable *adjective* (*pronounced* in-ter-min-a-bul)
seeming to go on for ever
interminably *adverb* in an interminable way

intermission *noun* (*plural* intermissions)
an interval in a play or film

intermittent *adjective*
happening at intervals
intermittently *adverb* at intervals

intern *verb* (interns, interning, interned)
to intern someone is to imprison them in a special camp or building, usually during a war
internee *noun* someone who is interned
internment *noun* being interned

internal *adjective*
of or in the inside of something
internally *adverb* on the inside

internal-combustion engine *noun* (*plural* internal-combustion engines)
an engine that produces power by burning fuel inside the engine itself

international *adjective*
to do with more than one country ♦ *Interpol is an international police organization*
internationally *adverb* for or in more than one country

internet *noun*
a computer network that allows people all over the world to share information and send messages

interplanetary *adjective*
between planets

interpret *verb* (interprets, interpreting, interpreted)
1 to interpret something is to explain what it means 2 to interpret a foreign language is to translate it into another language
interpretation *noun* deciding what something means

interpreter *noun* (*plural* interpreters)
a person who translates what someone says into another language

interrogate *verb* (interrogates, interrogating, interrogated)
to interrogate someone is to question them closely
interrogation *noun* interrogating someone
interrogator *noun* someone who interrogates

interrogative *adjective*
expressing a question ♦ *'Are they here?' is an interrogative sentence*

interrupt *verb* (interrupts, interrupting, interrupted)
1 to interrupt someone is to stop them talking 2 to interrupt something is to stop it continuing
interruption *noun* interrupting someone or something

intersect *verb* (intersects, intersecting, intersected)
to intersect something is to cross or divide it ♦ *The cloth had a design of intersecting lines*

intersection *noun* (*plural* intersections)
a place where lines or roads cross each other

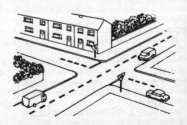

interval *noun* (*plural* **intervals**)
1 a time between two events or between two parts of a play or film **2** a space between two things
at intervals with some time or distance between each one; not continuously

intervene *verb* (**intervenes, intervening, intervened**)
1 to intervene is to come between two events ♦ *During the intervening years they went abroad* **2** to intervene is also to interrupt an argument or fight so as to stop it or affect the result
intervention *noun* the act of intervening

interview ➤ *noun* (*plural* **interviews**)
a meeting with someone to ask them questions or discuss something
interview ➤ *verb* (**interviews, interviewing, interviewed**)
to interview someone is to have an interview with them
interviewer *noun* (*plural* **interviewers**)
a person who interviews someone, especially on radio or television

intestine *noun* or **intestines** *plural noun*
the long tube along which food passes from the stomach to the anus
intestinal *adjective* to do with the intestine

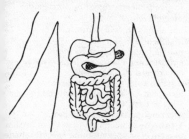

intimate ➤ *adjective* (*pronounced* in-ti-mat)
1 very friendly with someone **2** intimate thoughts are thoughts that are private or personal **3** detailed ♦ *They have an intimate knowledge of the town*
intimacy *noun* being intimate **intimately** *adverb* in an intimate way
intimate ➤ *verb* (**intimates, intimating, intimated**)
(*pronounced* in-ti-mayt)
to intimate something is to hint at it or suggest it ♦ *He has not yet intimated what his plans are*
intimation *noun* a hint or suggestion
intimidate *verb* (**intimidates, intimidating, intimidated**)
to frighten a person with threats into doing something

intimidation *noun* intimidating someone
into *preposition*
1 expressing movement to the inside of something ♦ *Go into the house* **2** **Into** also has some special uses, shown by the following examples ♦ *He got into trouble* ♦ *She went into acting* ♦ *3 into 12 goes 4 times*

intolerable *adjective*
unbearable ♦ *The noise outside was intolerable*
intolerably *adverb* to an intolerable degree
intolerant *adjective*
not tolerant or willing to put up with people
intolerance *noun* being intolerant **intolerantly** *adverb* in an intolerant way

intonation *noun* (*plural* **intonations**)
1 the pitch or tone of a voice or musical instrument **2** (*in Grammar*) using the pitch of your voice to alter the meaning of what you are saying, for example when asking a question

intoxicate *verb* (**intoxicates, intoxicating, intoxicated**)
1 a person is intoxicated when they are drunk **2** a person is intoxicated by something when they are very excited by it
intoxication *noun* intoxicating someone

intransitive *adjective*
(*in Grammar*) a verb is intransitive when it is used without a direct object, for example *ran* in *they ran away* (but not in *they ran a paper shop*)

intrepid *adjective*
brave or fearless
intrepidly *adverb* in an intrepid way

intricate *adjective*
complicated
intricacy *noun* being intricate **intricately** *adverb* in an intricate way

intrigue *verb* (**intrigues, intriguing, intrigued**)
(*pronounced* in-**treeg**)
1 to intrigue someone is to interest them very much **2** to intrigue is to make secret plans

introduce *verb* (**introduces, introducing, introduced**)
1 to introduce someone is to make them known to other people **2** to introduce something is to get it into general use

introduction *noun* (*plural* **introductions**)
1 introducing someone or something **2** a piece at the beginning of a book, explaining what it is about
introductory *adjective* serving as an introduction

intrude *verb* (intrudes, intruding, intruded)
to intrude is to come in or join in without being wanted
intrusion *noun* intruding **intrusive** *adjective* getting in the way

intruder *noun* (*plural* intruders)
1 someone who intrudes 2 a burglar

intuition *noun* (*pronounced* in-tew-ish-on)
the power to know or understand things without having to think hard
intuitive *adjective* using intuition

Inuit *noun* (*plural* Inuit or Inuits)
one of the people who live in very cold parts of North America

inundate *verb* (inundates, inundating, inundated)
to inundate something is to flood it
inundation *noun* flooding or a flood

invade *verb* (invades, invading, invaded)
to invade a country or place is to attack and enter it
invader *noun* someone who invades a place

invalid[1] *noun* (*plural* invalids) (*pronounced* in-va-leed or in-va-lid)
someone who is ill or weakened by a long illness

invalid[2] *adjective* (*pronounced* in-val-id)
not valid ♦ *This passport is invalid*

invaluable *adjective*
very valuable

invariable *adjective*
never changing; always the same
invariably *adverb*
always

invasion *noun* (*plural* invasions)
the act of attacking and entering a place

invent *verb* (invents, inventing, invented)
1 to invent something is to be the first person to make it or think of it 2 to invent a story or excuse is to make it up
invention *noun* something invented **inventive** *adjective* good at inventing things **inventor** *noun* someone who invents things

inverse ➤ *adjective*
reversed or opposite
inversely *adverb* in an inverse or opposite way

inverse ➤ *noun*
the opposite of something

invert *verb* (inverts, inverting, inverted)
to invert something is to turn it upside down
inversion *noun* inverting things

invertebrate *noun* (*plural* invertebrates) (*pronounced* in-vert-i-brat)
an animal without a backbone, such as a worm or an amoeba

inverted commas *plural noun*
punctuation marks (" ") or (' ') put round spoken words and quotations

invest *verb* (invests, investing, invested)
1 to invest money is to use it to earn interest or make a profit 2 to invest someone is to give them an honour or medal or special title ♦ *He was invested as Prince of Wales*
investor *noun* someone who invests money

investigate *verb* (investigates, investigating, investigated)
to investigate something or someone is to find out as much as you can about them
investigation *noun* a formal inquiry
investigator *noun* a person who investigates someone or something

investiture *noun* (*plural* investitures)
a ceremony in which someone is given an official title

investment *noun* (*plural* investments)
1 money someone invests 2 something someone invests money in ♦ *Houses are a safe investment*

invigilate *verb* (invigilates, invigilating, invigilated)
to supervise candidates at an examination
invigilation *noun* invigilating candidates
invigilator *noun* someone who invigilates

invigorate *verb* (invigorates, invigorating, invigorated)
to give someone vigour or courage

invincible *adjective*
not able to be defeated

invisible *adjective*
not visible; not able to be seen
invisibility *noun* being invisible **invisibly** *adverb* so as to be invisible

invitation *noun* (*plural* invitations)
a request for someone to do something, such as come to a party

invite *verb* (invites, inviting, invited)
1 to invite someone is to ask them to come to a party or do something special 2 to invite something unwelcome is to cause it to happen by your actions ♦ *You are inviting trouble by doing that*

inviting *adjective*
attractive or tempting
invitingly *adverb* in an inviting way

invoice *noun* (*plural* invoices)
a list of goods sent or of work done, with the prices charged

involuntary *adjective*
not deliberate; done without thinking

involve *verb* (involves, involving, involved)
1 to involve something is to need it or result in it ♦ *The job involved a lot of effort* 2 to be involved in something is to take part in it ♦ *We are involved in charity work*

involvement *noun* being involved in something

involved *adjective*
long and complicated

inward ➤ *adjective*
on the inside, or facing the inside

inward ➤ *adverb*
inwards

inwardly *adverb*
in one's thoughts; privately

inwards *adverb*
towards the inside

iodine *noun* (*pronounced* I-o-deen or I-o-dyn)
a chemical used to kill germs

ion *noun* (*plural* ions) (*pronounced* I-on)
an electrically-charged particle

IQ *noun* (*plural* IQs)
a measure of someone's intelligence, calculated from the results of a test

iris *noun* (*plural* irises)
1 the coloured part of the eyeball
2 a flower with long pointed leaves

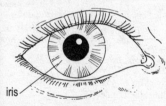
iris

iron ➤ *noun* (*plural* irons)
1 a strong heavy metal 2 a device that is heated for smoothing clothes or cloth 3 a tool made of iron

iron ➤ *verb* (irons, ironing, ironed)
to iron clothes or cloth is to smooth them with an iron
to iron something out is to solve a difficulty gradually and carefully

ironic or **ironical** *adjective* (*pronounced* I-ron-ik or I-ron-ikal)
using irony; full of irony
ironically *adverb* in an ironic way

ironmonger *noun* (*plural* ironmongers)
someone who keeps a shop that sells tools, nails, and other metal things
ironmongery *noun* things an ironmonger sells

irony *noun* (*plural* ironies) (*pronounced* I-ro-ni)
1 irony is saying the opposite of what you mean so as to emphasize it, for example *What a lovely day* when it is pouring with rain 2 an irony is an unexpected or strange event or situation ♦ *The irony is that she had sold all her jewels the day before the burglars broke in*

irrational *adjective*
not rational
irrationally *adverb* in an irrational way

irregular *adjective*
1 not regular; not usual 2 against the rules
irregularity *noun* being irregular or unusual
irregularly *adverb* in an irregular way

irrelevant *adjective* (*pronounced* i-rel-i-vant)
not relevant; not having anything to do with what is being considered
irrelevance *noun* something irrelevant
irrelevantly *adverb* in an irrelevant way

irresistible *adjective*
too strong or good or tempting to resist

irresponsible *adjective*
not trustworthy; not sensible
irresponsibility *noun* being irresponsible
irresponsibly *adverb* in an irresponsible way

irreverent *adjective*
not reverent or respectful
irreverence *noun* being irreverent **irreverently** *adverb* in an irreverent way

irrigate *verb* (irrigates, irrigating, irrigated)
to irrigate land is to supply it with water so that crops can grow
irrigation *noun* irrigating land

irritable *adjective*
easily annoyed; bad-tempered
irritability *noun* being irritable **irritably** *adverb* in an irritable way

irritate *verb* (irritates, irritating, irritated)
1 to irritate someone is to annoy them
2 to irritate a part of your body is to make it itch or feel sore
irritant *noun* something that makes you sore **irritation** *noun* something that annoys you

is 3rd person singular present tense of **be**

-ish *suffix*
meaning 'somewhat; rather like something', as in *boyish* and *reddish*

Islam *noun* (*pronounced* iz-lahm)
the religion of Muslims
Islamic *adjective* to do with Islam

island *noun* (*plural* islands)
a piece of land surrounded by water
islander *noun* someone who lives on an island

isle *noun* (*plural* isles)
an island

-ism *suffix*
meaning a belief or a system of thought,
such as *Hinduism*

isn't short for *is not*

isobar *noun* (*plural* **isobars**) (*pronounced*
I-so-bar)
a line on a map connecting places that
have the same atmospheric pressure

isolate *verb* (**isolates, isolating, isolated**)
to isolate someone or something is to put
them apart from others
isolation *noun* being isolated or alone

isosceles triangle *noun* (*plural* **isosceles
triangles**) (*pronounced* I-**sos**-i-leez)
a triangle with two sides the same length

isotope *noun* (*plural* **isotopes**) (*pronounced*
I-so-tohp)
(*in Science*) a form of an element that is
different from other forms in the structure
of its nucleus, but has the same chemical
properties as the other forms

issue ➤ *verb* (**issues, issuing, issued**)
1 to issue something is to send it or give it
out to people ♦ *They issued blankets to the
refugees* 2 to issue a book or piece of
information is to publish it 3 to issue is to
come out of something ♦ *Smoke was
issuing from the chimney*

issue ➤ *noun* (*plural* **issues**)
1 an issue is a subject for discussion or
concern ♦ *What are the most important
issues?* 2 an issue of a magazine or
newspaper is the edition sold on a
particular day ♦ *Have you got Tuesday's
issue of The Daily Mirror?* 3 the issue of
documents is making them available to
people 4 the issue of some process is its
result ♦ *We are waiting for the issue of the
trial*

-ist *suffix*
meaning someone who does a particular
job, such as *anaesthetist*

isthmus *noun* (*plural* **isthmuses**)
(*pronounced* iss-mus)
a narrow strip of land connecting two
larger pieces of land

it *pronoun*
1 the thing being talked about, used as the
subject or object of a verb 2 It also has
some special uses, as in ♦ *It is raining*
♦ *We must go it alone*

italics *plural noun* (*pronounced* it-al-iks)
letters printed with a slant, *like this*

itch ➤ *noun* (*plural* **itches**)
1 a tickling feeling in your skin that
makes you want to scratch it 2 a longing
to do something ♦ *He has an itch to go to
America*
itchy *adjective* making you itch

itch ➤ *verb* (**itches, itching, itched**)
to itch is to have an itch

item *noun* (*plural* **items**)
one thing in a list or group of things

itinerary *noun* (*plural* **itineraries**)
(*pronounced* I-tin-er-er-i)
a list of places to be visited on a journey; a
route

-itis *suffix*
used in names of diseases in which part of
the body is inflamed, such as *bronchitis*

it'll short for *it will*

its *pronoun*
of it; belonging to it ♦ *The cat hurt its paw*

it's short for *it is* and (before a verb in the
past tense) *it has* ♦ *It's raining* ♦ *It's been
raining*

itself *pronoun*
it and nothing else, used to refer back to
the subject of a verb ♦ *I think the cat has
hurt itself*
by itself on its own, alone ♦ *The house
stands by itself in a wood*

ITV short for *Independent Television*

I've short for *I have*

ivory *noun*
1 the hard creamy-white substance that
forms elephants' tusks 2 a creamy-white
colour

ivy *noun*
a climbing evergreen plant with shiny
leaves

Jj

jab ➤ *verb* (**jabs, jabbing, jabbed**)
1 to jab someone or something is to poke
them roughly 2 to jab something is to
push it roughly into something else

jab ➤ *noun* (*plural* **jabs**)
1 a jabbing movement 2 (*informal*) an
injection

jabber *verb* (**jabbers, jabbering, jabbered**)
to jabber is to chatter a lot or to speak
quickly and not clearly

jack ➤ *noun* (*plural* **jacks**)
  1 a device for lifting something heavy off the ground **2** a playing card with a picture of a young man **3** a small white ball that you aim at in the game of bowls

jack ➤ *verb* (**jacks, jacking, jacked**)
  to jack something is to lift it with a jack

jackal *noun* (*plural* **jackals**)
  a wild animal rather like a dog

jackass *noun* (*plural* **jackasses**)
  1 a male donkey **2** a stupid person

jackdaw *noun* (*plural* **jackdaws**)
  a bird like a small crow

jacket *noun* (*plural* **jackets**)
  1 a short coat covering the top half of the body **2** a paper cover for a book **3** a wrapping round a boiler to insulate it

jacket potato *noun* (*plural* **jacket potatoes**)
  a potato that is baked without being peeled

jack-in-the-box *noun* (*plural* **jack-in-the-boxes**)
  a toy figure that springs out of a box when you lift the lid

jackknife *verb* (**jackknifes, jackknifing, jackknifed**)
  an articulated lorry jackknifes when it goes out of control, with the trailer skidding round towards the cab

jackpot *noun* (*plural* **jackpots**)
  an amount of prize money that increases until someone wins it

jacuzzi *noun* (*plural* **jacuzzis**) (*pronounced* ja-koo-zi)
  a large bath with jets of water that massage the body under the water

jade *noun*
  a green stone which is carved to make ornaments

jaded *adjective*
  tired and bored

jagged *adjective* (*pronounced* jag-id)
  having an uneven edge with sharp points

jaguar *noun* (*plural* **jaguars**)
  a large fierce South American animal rather like a leopard

jail ➤ *noun* (*plural* **jails**)
  a prison

jail ➤ *verb* (**jails, jailing, jailed**)
  to jail someone is to put them in prison

jailer *noun* (*plural* **jailers**)
  a person in charge of a jail

Jain *noun* (*plural* **Jains**) (*rhymes with* main)
  a believer in an Indian religion rather like Buddhism

jam ➤ *noun* (*plural* **jams**)
  1 a sweet food made of fruit boiled with sugar until it is thick **2** a lot of people or cars or other things crowded together so that it is difficult to move
  in a jam (*informal*) in a difficult situation

jam ➤ *verb* (**jams, jamming, jammed**)
  1 to jam something is to make it stuck and difficult to move **2** to jam is to become stuck ♦ *The door has jammed* **3** to jam something is to push or squeeze it with force ♦ *I jammed on the brakes*

jamboree *noun* (*plural* **jamborees**)
  1 a large party or celebration **2** a rally of Scouts

jammy *adjective* (**jammier, jammiest**)
  1 smeared or sticky with jam
  2 (*informal*) very easy or lucky

jangle *verb* (**jangles, jangling, jangled**)
  to jangle is to make a harsh ringing sound

January *noun*
  the first month of the year

jar[1] *noun* (*plural* **jars**)
  a container made of glass or pottery

jar[2] *verb* (**jars, jarring, jarred**)
  1 to jar is to cause an unpleasant shock or jolt **2** to jar is also to sound harshly

jaundice *noun*
  a disease that makes the skin yellow

jaunt *noun* (*plural* **jaunts**)
  a short trip for fun

jaunty *adjective* (**jauntier, jauntiest**)
  lively and cheerful
  jauntily *adverb* in a jaunty way **jauntiness** *noun* being jaunty

javelin *noun* (*plural* **javelins**)
  a light spear used for throwing in athletics

jaw *noun* (*plural* **jaws**)
  1 one of the two bones that hold the teeth **2** the lower part of the face **3** the part of a tool that grips something

jay *noun* (*plural* **jays**)
  a noisy brightly-coloured bird

jazz *noun*
  a kind of music with strong rhythm
  jazzy *adjective* like jazz

jealous *adjective*
  unhappy or resentful because you feel that someone is better or luckier than you
  jealously *adverb* in a jealous way **jealousy** *noun* being jealous

jeans *plural noun*
casual trousers made of denim

Jeep *noun* (*plural* **Jeeps**)
(*trademark*) a small sturdy motor car used
on rough ground

jeer *verb* (jeers, jeering, jeered)
to jeer is to laugh or shout at someone
rudely or scornfully

jelly *noun* (*plural* **jellies**)
1 a soft sweet food with a fruit flavour
2 any soft slippery substance
jellied *adjective* made of jelly

jellyfish *noun* (*plural* **jellyfish**)
a sea animal with a body like jelly

jerk ➤ *verb* (jerks, jerking, jerked)
1 to jerk is to make a sudden sharp
movement **2** to jerk something is to pull it
suddenly

jerk ➤ *noun* (*plural* **jerks**)
1 a sudden sharp movement **2** (*slang*) a
fool

jerky *adjective* (jerkier, jerkiest)
moving with jerks
jerkily *adverb* in a jerky way

jersey *noun* (*plural* **jerseys**)
a pullover with sleeves

jest ➤ *noun* (*plural* **jests**)
a joke

jest ➤ *verb* (jests, jesting, jested)
to jest is to make jokes
in jest joking; not seriously

jester *noun* (*plural* **jesters**)
a professional entertainer at a royal court
in the Middle Ages

jet[1] ➤ *noun* (*plural* **jets**)
1 a stream of liquid, gas, or flame forced
out of a narrow opening **2** a narrow
opening from which a jet comes out **3** an
aircraft driven by jet engines

jet ➤ *verb* (jets, jetting, jetted)
1 to jet is to come out in a strong stream
2 (*informal*) to jet around is to travel a lot
in jet aircraft

jet[2] *noun*
1 a hard black mineral **2** a deep glossy
black colour

jet engine *noun* (*plural* **jet engines**)
an engine that sends out a powerful jet of
hot gas at the back

jet lag *noun*
extreme tiredness that someone feels after
a long air journey because they have not
got used to the different time zones

jet-propelled *adjective*
driven by jet engines

jetty *noun* (*plural* **jetties**)
a small landing stage

Jew *noun* (*plural* **Jews**)
1 a member of the race of people
descended from the ancient tribes of Israel
2 someone who believes in Judaism
Jewish *adjective* to do with the Jews

jewel *noun* (*plural* **jewels**)
1 a precious stone **2** an ornament
containing precious stones
jewelled *adjective* decorated with jewels

jeweller *noun* (*plural* **jewellers**)
someone who sells or makes jewellery

jewellery *noun*
jewels or ornaments for wearing

jib *noun* (*plural* **jibs**)
1 a triangular sail of a ship, stretching
forward from the mast **2** the projecting
arm of a crane

jiffy *noun*
(*informal*) a moment ♦ *I won't be a jiffy*

jig ➤ *noun* (*plural* **jigs**)
1 a lively jumping dance **2** a device that
holds something in place while you work
on it with tools

jig ➤ *verb* (jigs, jigging, jigged)
1 to jig is to dance a jig **2** to jig is also to
move up and down with quick jerks

jigsaw *noun* (*plural* **jigsaws**)
1 a saw that can cut curved shapes **2** a
jigsaw puzzle

jigsaw puzzle *noun* (*plural* **jigsaw puzzles**)
a puzzle made of shapes that you fit together to make a picture

jingle ➤ *verb* (**jingles, jingling, jingled**)
to jingle is to make a tinkling or clinking sound

jingle ➤ *noun* (*plural* **jingles**)
1 a tinkling or clinking sound **2** a simple tune or song, especially one used in an advertisement

job *noun* (*plural* **jobs**)
1 work that someone does regularly to earn a living ♦ *He got a job as a postman* **2** a piece of work to be done ♦ *We'll have tea when we've finished this job* **3** (*informal*) a difficult task ♦ *You'll have a job to lift that box* **4** (*informal*) a situation or state of affairs ♦ *It's a good job you're here*
just the job (*informal*) exactly what you want

jobcentre *noun* (*plural* **jobcentres**)
a government office with information about jobs that are available

jockey *noun* (*plural* **jockeys**)
someone who rides horses in races

jodhpurs *plural noun* (*pronounced* jod-perz)
trousers for riding a horse, fitting closely from the knee to the ankle

jog *verb* (**jogs, jogging, jogged**)
1 to jog is to run slowly, especially for exercise **2** to jog someone is to give them a slight knock or push
to jog someone's memory is to help them remember something
jogger *noun* someone who goes jogging

jogtrot *noun* (*plural* **jogtrots**)
a slow steady trot

join ➤ *verb* (**joins, joining, joined**)
1 to join things together, or join one thing to another, is to put or fix them together **2** two or more things join when they come together **3** to join a society or group is to become a member of it
to join in is to take part in something

join ➤ *noun* (*plural* **joins**)
a place where things join

joiner *noun* (*plural* **joiners**)
someone whose job is to make furniture and other things out of wood
joinery *noun* the work of a joiner

joint ➤ *noun* (*plural* **joints**)
1 a place where things are fixed together **2** the place where two bones fit together **3** a large piece of meat

joint ➤ *adjective*
shared or done by two or more people or countries
jointly *adverb* together

joist *noun* (*plural* **joists**)
a long beam supporting a floor or ceiling

jojoba *noun* (*pronounced* hoh-hoh-ba)
oil from the seeds of a desert plant, used in making shampoo and cosmetics

joke ➤ *noun* (*plural* **jokes**)
1 something said or done to make people laugh **2** a trick

joke ➤ *verb* (**jokes, joking, joked**)
to joke is to make jokes, or to talk in a way that is not serious

joker *noun* (*plural* **jokers**)
1 someone who makes jokes **2** an extra playing card with a picture of a jester

jollity *noun*
being jolly or merry; enjoyment

jolly ➤ *adjective* (**jollier, jolliest**)
happy and cheerful

jolly ➤ *adverb*
(*informal*) very ♦ *That film was jolly good!*

jolly ➤ *verb* (**jollies, jollying, jollied**)
to jolly someone along is to make them more cheerful

jolt ➤ *verb* (**jolts, jolting, jolted**)
1 to jolt something or someone is to hit them or move them suddenly and sharply **2** to jolt is to move along with sudden sharp movements

jolt ➤ *noun* (*plural* **jolts**)
1 a sudden sharp movement **2** a surprise or shock

jostle *verb* (**jostles, jostling, jostled**)
to jostle someone is to push them roughly

jot ➤ *noun*
a tiny amount ♦ *I don't care a jot*

jot ➤ *verb* (**jots, jotting, jotted**)
to jot something down is to write it quickly

jotter *noun* (*plural* **jotters**)
a notebook

joule *noun* (*plural* **joules**)
(*in Science*) a unit of work or energy

journal *noun* (*plural* **journals**)
1 a newspaper or magazine **2** a diary

journalist *noun* (*plural* **journalists**)
someone whose job is to write for a newspaper or magazine
journalism *noun* the work of a journalist

journey ➤ *noun* (*plural* **journeys**)
1 going from one place to another **2** the distance or time taken to travel somewhere ♦ *The town is a day's journey away*

journey ➤ *verb* (**journeys, journeying, journeyed**)
to journey is to go from one place to another

joust *verb* (**jousts, jousting, jousted**)
to joust is to fight on horseback with lances, as knights did in medieval times

jovial *adjective*
cheerful and jolly
joviality *noun* being jovial **jovially** *adverb* in a jovial way

joy *noun* (*plural* **joys**)
1 great happiness or pleasure
2 something that gives happiness

joyful *adjective*
very happy
joyfully *adverb* in a joyful way

joyous *adjective*
full of joy; causing joy
joyously *adverb* in a joyous way

joyride *noun* (*plural* **joyrides**)
(*informal*) a ride in a stolen car for amusement

joystick *noun* (*plural* **joysticks**)
1 (*informal*) the lever that controls the movement of an aircraft 2 a lever for controlling the cursor on a VDU screen, especially in computer games

jubilant *adjective* (*pronounced* joo-bi-lant)
rejoicing; joyful
jubilantly *adverb* in a jubilant way **jubilation** *noun* being jubilant

jubilee *noun* (*plural* **jubilees**)
a special anniversary of an important event

Judaism *noun* (*pronounced* joo-day-izm)
the religion of the Jewish people

judge ➤ *noun* (*plural* **judges**)
1 someone appointed to hear cases in a lawcourt and decide what should be done 2 someone appointed to decide who has won a contest or competition 3 someone who is good at forming opinions or making decisions about things ♦ *She's a good judge of musical ability*

judge ➤ *verb* (**judges, judging, judged**)
1 to judge something is to act as judge in a law case or a competition 2 to judge an amount is to estimate or guess what it is 3 to judge something is to form an opinion about it

judgement *noun* (*plural* **judgements**)
1 judgement is acting as judge for a law case or a contest 2 a judgement is the decision made by a lawcourt 3 judgement is also the ability to make decisions wisely 4 someone's judgement is their opinion ♦ *In my judgement, the food is too salty* 5 a judgement is something considered as a punishment from God

judicial *adjective* (*pronounced* joo-**dish**-al)
to do with lawcourts, judges, or decisions made in lawcourts
judicially *adverb* in a judicial way

judicious *adjective* (*pronounced* joo-**dish**-us)
showing good sense or judgement

judiciously *adverb* in a judicious way

judo *noun* (*pronounced* joo-doh)
a Japanese form of unarmed combat for sport

jug *noun* (*plural* **jugs**)
a container for liquids, with a handle and lip

juggernaut *noun* (*plural* **juggernauts**)
a very large articulated lorry

juggle *verb* (**juggles, juggling, juggled**)
to juggle objects is to toss them and keep them in the air without dropping any
juggler *noun* someone who juggles at a fair or circus

juice *noun* (*plural* **juices**)
1 the liquid from fruit, vegetables, or other food 2 a liquid produced by the body, such as the digestive juices
juicy *adjective* full of juice

jukebox *noun* (*plural* **jukeboxes**)
a machine that automatically plays a record of your choice when you put a coin in

July *noun*
the seventh month of the year

jumble ➤ *verb* (**jumbles, jumbling, jumbled**)
to jumble things is to mix them up in a confused way

jumble ➤ *noun*
a confused mixture of things; a muddle

jumble sale *noun* (*plural* **jumble sales**)
a sale of second-hand goods to raise money

jumbo jet *noun* (*plural* **jumbo jets**)
a large jet aircraft, especially a Boeing 747

jump ➤ *verb* (**jumps, jumping, jumped**)
1 to jump is to move suddenly from the ground into the air 2 to jump a fence or other obstacle is to go over it by jumping 3 to jump up or out is to move quickly or suddenly ♦ *He jumped out of his seat* 4 to jump in or out of a vehicle is to get in or out quickly
to jump at something (*informal*) is to accept it eagerly
to jump the gun is to start something before the right time
to jump the queue is to go ahead before it is your turn

jump ➤ *noun* (*plural* **jumps**)
1 a sudden movement into the air 2 an obstacle to jump over

jumper *noun* (*plural* **jumpers**)
a jersey

jump suit *noun* (*plural* **jump suits**)
a piece of clothing made in one piece and covering the whole body

jumpy *adjective* (**jumpier, jumpiest**)
nervous and edgy

junction *noun* (*plural* **junctions**)
a place where roads or railway lines join

June *noun*
the sixth month of the year

jungle *noun* (*plural* **jungles**)
a thick tangled forest, especially in
tropical countries
jungly *adjective* like jungle

junior ➤ *adjective*
1 younger **2** for young children ♦ *She
goes to a junior school* **3** lower in rank or
importance

junior ➤ *noun* (*plural* **juniors**)
1 a younger person ♦ *Peter is my junior*
2 a person of lower rank or importance

junk[1] *noun*
1 rubbish **2** things that are worthless

junk[2] *noun* (*plural* **junks**)
a Chinese sailing boat

junket *noun* (*plural* **junkets**)
1 junket is a sweet runny food made from
milk **2** a junket is a feast or entertainment

junk food *noun*
food that is not nourishing, usually
containing a lot of sugar and starch

juror *noun* (*plural* **jurors**)
a member of a jury

jury *noun* (*plural* **juries**)
a group of people (usually twelve)
appointed to make a decision about a case
in a lawcourt

just ➤ *adjective*
1 fair and right; giving proper thought to
everybody **2** deserved ♦ *He got his just
reward*
justly *adverb* in a just or fair way

just ➤ *adverb*
1 exactly ♦ *It's just what I wanted* **2** only;
simply ♦ *I just wanted another cake*
3 barely; by only a short amount ♦ *The
ball hit her just below the knee* **4** a short
time ago ♦ *They had just gone*

justice *noun* (*plural* **justices**)
1 justice is being just or having fair
treatment **2** justice is also the actions of
the law ♦ *They were tried in a court of
justice* **3** a justice is a judge or magistrate

justify *verb* (**justifies, justifying, justified**)
to justify something is to show that it is
fair or reasonable ♦ *Do you think that you
were justified in taking such a risk?*
justifiable *adjective* able to be justified
justification *noun* good reason

jut *verb* (**juts, jutting, jutted**)
to jut, or to jut out, is to stick out

juvenile *adjective* (*pronounced* **joo**-vi-nyl)
to do with young people

juvenile delinquent *noun* (*plural* **juvenile
delinquents**)
a young person who has broken the law

Kk

kaleidoscope *noun* (*plural* **kaleidoscopes**)
(*pronounced* kal-l-dos-kohp)
a tube that you look through to see
brightly-coloured patterns which change
as you turn the end of the tube

kangaroo *noun* (*plural* **kangaroos**)
an Australian animal that moves by
jumping on its strong hind legs

karaoke *noun* (*pronounced* ka-ri-oh-ki)
a party entertainment in which people
sing songs with a recorded background
played from a special machine

karate *noun* (*pronounced* ka-rah-ti)
a Japanese method of self-defence using
the hands, arms, and feet

kayak *noun* (*plural* **kayaks**) (*pronounced*
ky-ak)
a small canoe with a covering that fits
round the canoeist's waist

kebab *noun* (*plural* **kebabs**)
small pieces of meat or vegetables grilled on a skewer

keel ➤ *noun* (*plural* **keels**)
the long piece of wood or metal along the bottom of a boat
on an even keel steady

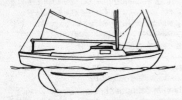

keel ➤ *verb* (**keels, keeling, keeled**)
to keel over is to fall sideways or overturn

keen *adjective* (**keener, keenest**)
1 enthusiastic or eager ♦ *She is keen on swimming* ♦ *We are keen to go* **2** strong or sharp ♦ *The knife had a keen edge* ♦ *There was a keen wind*
keenly *adverb* eagerly **keenness** *noun* being keen

keep ➤ *verb* (**keeps, keeping, kept**)
1 to keep something is to have it and not get rid of it **2** to keep (for example) well or still is to continue to be well or still **3** to keep someone (for example) warm or happy is to cause them to continue to be warm or happy **4** something keeps when it lasts without going bad ♦ *Will the milk keep until tomorrow?* **5** to keep doing something is to continue to do it ♦ *They kept laughing at her* **6** to keep one's word or promise is to honour it and not break it **7** to keep animals or pets is to have them and look after them
to keep something up is to continue doing it ♦ *Keep up the good work!*
to keep up with someone is to go as fast as them

keep ➤ *noun* (*plural* **keeps**)
1 someone's keep is the food or money they need to live ♦ *They have to earn their keep* **2** a keep is a strong tower in a castle
for keeps (*informal*) to keep; permanently ♦ *Is this football mine for keeps?*

keeper *noun* (*plural* **keepers**)
1 someone who looks after an animal or place **2** a goalkeeper

keeping *noun*
care; looking after something ♦ *They are in safe keeping*
in keeping with something agreeing with it or suiting it

keg *noun* (*plural* **kegs**)
a small barrel

kennel *noun* (*plural* **kennels**)
a shelter for a dog

kept past tense and past participle of **keep** *verb*

kerb *noun* (*plural* **kerbs**)
the edge of a pavement

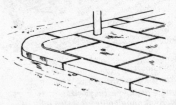

kerbstone *noun* (*plural* **kerbstones**)
a long square stone used to make a kerb

kernel *noun* (*plural* **kernels**)
the part inside the shell of a nut

kestrel *noun* (*plural* **kestrels**)
a kind of small falcon

ketchup *noun*
a thick sauce made from tomatoes

kettle *noun* (*plural* **kettles**)
a container with a spout and handle, used for boiling water in

kettledrum *noun* (*plural* **kettledrums**)
a drum made of skin stretched over a large metal bowl

key *noun* (*plural* **keys**)
1 a piece of metal shaped so that it opens a lock **2** a device for winding up a clock or clockwork toy **3** a small lever that you press with your finger, on a piano or keyboard **4** a scale of musical notes ♦ *It is played in the key of C major* **5** something that solves a problem or mystery ♦ *Police think they have found the key to the crime*

keyboard *noun* (*plural* **keyboards**)
a set of keys on a piano, typewriter, or computer

keyhole *noun* (*plural* **keyholes**)
the hole through which a key is put into a lock

keynote *noun* (*plural* **keynotes**)
1 the note on which a key in music is based ♦ *The keynote of C major is C* **2** the main idea in something said, written, or done

kg short for
kilogram or **kilograms**

khaki *noun* (*pronounced* kah-ki)
a dull yellowish-brown colour, used for army uniforms

kibbutz *noun* (*plural* **kibbutzim**)
a farming commune in Israel

kick ➤ *verb* (**kicks, kicking, kicked**)
1 to kick someone or something is to hit them with your foot **2** to kick is to move your legs about vigorously **3** a gun kicks when it moves back sharply on being fired
to kick off is to start a football match, or (*informal*) to start doing something
to kick someone out is to get rid of them
to kick up a fuss or row (*informal*) is to make a loud fuss or noise

kick ➤ *noun* (*plural* **kicks**)
1 a kicking movement **2** the sudden backwards movement a gun makes when it is fired **3** (*informal*) a thrill
4 (*informal*) an interest or activity ♦ *He's on a health kick*

kick-off *noun* (*plural* **kick-offs**)
the start of a football match

kid ➤ *noun* (*plural* **kids**)
1 a young goat **2** (*informal*) a child

kid ➤ *verb* (**kids, kidding, kidded**)
(*informal*) to kid someone is to deceive or tease them

kidnap *verb* (**kidnaps, kidnapping, kidnapped**)
to kidnap someone is to capture them by force, usually to get a ransom
kidnapper *noun* a person who kidnaps someone

kidney *noun* (*plural* **kidneys**)
each of two organs in the body that remove waste products from the blood and send them as urine to the bladder

kill *verb* (**kills, killing, killed**)
1 to kill a person or animal is to make them die **2** to kill something like an idea or plan is to make sure it doesn't happen
killer *noun* a person who kills someone

kiln *noun* (*plural* **kilns**)
an oven for hardening or drying pottery or bricks, or for drying hops

kilo *noun* (*plural* **kilos**)
a kilogram

kilogram *noun* (*plural* **kilograms**)
a unit of weight equal to 1,000 grams or about 2·2 pounds

kilometre *noun* (*plural* **kilometres**)
(*pronounced* kil-o-mee-ter or kil-om-i-ter)
a unit of length equal to 1,000 metres or about $\frac{5}{8}$ of a mile

kilowatt *noun* (*plural* **kilowatts**)
a unit of electrical power equal to 1,000 watts

kilt *noun* (*plural* **kilts**)
a kind of pleated skirt worn as traditional Scottish dress
kilted *adjective* wearing a kilt

kin *noun*
a person's family or relatives
next of kin a person's closest relative

kind[1] *noun* (*plural* **kinds**)
a type or sort of something ♦ *What kind of food do you like?*
kind of (*informal*) in a way, to some extent ♦ *We kind of hoped you would come*

kind[2] *adjective* (**kinder, kindest**)
helpful and friendly
kindness *noun* being kind

kindergarten *noun* (*plural* **kindergartens**)
(*pronounced* kin-der-gar-ten)
a school or class for very young children

kind-hearted *adjective*
kind and generous

kindle *verb* (**kindles, kindling, kindled**)
1 to kindle something is to get it to burn
2 to kindle is to start burning

kindling *noun*
small pieces of wood for lighting fires

kindly ➤ *adverb*
1 in a kind way **2** please ♦ *Kindly close the door*

kindly ➤ *adjective* (**kindlier, kindliest**)
kind ♦ *She gave a kindly smile*
kindliness *noun* being kindly

kinetic *adjective* (*pronounced* kin-et-ik)
to do with movement, or produced by movement, as in ♦ *kinetic energy*

king *noun* (*plural* **kings**)
1 a man who has been crowned as the ruler of a country **2** a piece in chess that has to be captured to win the game **3** a playing card with a picture of a king
kingly *adjective* like a king

kingdom *noun* (*plural* **kingdoms**)
a country that is ruled by a king or queen

kingfisher *noun* (*plural* **kingfishers**)
a brightly-coloured bird that lives near water and catches fish

king-size or **king-sized** *adjective*
larger than the usual size

kink *noun* (*plural* **kinks**)
1 a short twist in a rope, wire, or piece of hair 2 something peculiar or eccentric

kinky *adjective* (**kinkier, kinkiest**)
1 having kinks or twists 2 having odd sexual habits

kiosk *noun* (*plural* **kiosks**) (*pronounced* kee-osk)
1 a telephone box 2 a small hut or stall where newspapers, sweets, and tobacco are sold

kipper *noun* (*plural* **kippers**)
a smoked herring

kiss ➤ *noun* (*plural* **kisses**)
touching someone with your lips as a sign of affection or greeting

kiss ➤ *verb* (**kisses, kissing, kissed**)
to kiss someone is to give them a kiss

kiss of life *noun*
blowing air from your mouth into someone else's to help them to start breathing again, especially after an accident

kit *noun* (*plural* **kits**)
1 equipment or clothes for a special purpose 2 a set of parts sold to be fitted together

kitchen *noun* (*plural* **kitchens**)
a room where food is prepared and cooked

kite *noun* (*plural* **kites**)
a light frame covered with cloth or paper and flown in the wind at the end of a long piece of string

kitten *noun* (*plural* **kittens**)
a very young cat

kitty¹ *noun* (*plural* **kitties**)
1 an amount of money that you can win in a card game 2 an amount of money put aside for a special purpose

kitty² *noun* (*plural* **kitties**)
(*informal*) a kitten

kiwi *noun* (*plural* **kiwis**) (*pronounced* kee-wee)
a New Zealand bird that cannot fly

kiwi fruit *noun* (*plural* **kiwi fruits**)
a fruit with thin hairy skin, soft green flesh, and black seeds

km short for
  kilometre or kilometres

knack *noun*
a special skill or ability ♦ *There's a knack to putting up a deckchair*

knapsack *noun* (*plural* **knapsacks**)
a bag carried on the back by hikers or soldiers

knave *noun* (*plural* **knaves**)
(*old use*) 1 a dishonest man 2 a jack in a pack of playing cards

knead *verb* (**kneads, kneading, kneaded**)
to knead dough or something else soft is to press and stretch it with your hands

knee *noun* (*plural* **knees**)
the joint in the middle of your leg

kneecap *noun* (*plural* **kneecaps**)
the bony part at the front of your knee

kneel *verb* (**kneels, kneeling, knelt**)
to kneel is to be or get into a position on your knees

knew past tense of **know**

knickers *plural noun*
underpants worn by women or girls

knife ➤ *noun* (*plural* **knives**)
a cutting instrument made of a short blade set in a handle

knife ➤ *verb* (**knifes, knifing, knifed**)
to knife someone is to stab them with a knife

knight ➤ *noun* (*plural* **knights**)
1 a man who has been given the honour that lets him put 'Sir' before his name 2 a warrior who had been given the rank of a nobleman, in the Middle Ages 3 a piece in chess, with a horse's head
knighthood *noun* the honour of being a knight

knight ➤ *verb* (**knights, knighting, knighted**)
to knight someone is to make them a knight

knit *verb* (**knits, knitting, knitted**)
to knit something is to make it by looping together threads of wool or other material, using long needles or a machine
knitter *noun* a person who knits things

knitting needle *noun* (*plural* **knitting needles**)
a long large needle used in knitting

knives plural of **knife** *noun*

knob *noun* (*plural* **knobs**)
1 the round handle of a door or drawer 2 a lump or swelling 3 a control to adjust a radio or television set
knobbly *adjective* having many knobs or bumps

knock ➤ *verb* (**knocks, knocking, knocked**)
1 to knock something is to hit it hard so as to make a noise 2 (*slang*) to knock someone or something is to criticize them unfavourably
to knock off (*informal*) is to stop working
to knock someone out is to hit them so as to make them unconscious
to knock something off (*slang*) is to steal it

knock ➤ *noun* (*plural* **knocks**)
the act or sound of hitting something

knocker *noun* (*plural* **knockers**)
a device for knocking on a door

knockout *noun* (*plural* **knockouts**)
1 knocking someone out 2 a game or contest in which the loser in each round has to drop out 3 (*slang*) an amazing person or thing

knot ➤ *noun* (*plural* **knots**)
1 a fastening made with string, rope, or ribbon 2 a tangle; a lump 3 a round spot on a piece of wood where a branch once joined it 4 a cluster of people or things 5 a unit for measuring the speed of ships and aircraft, 2,025 yards (or 1,852 metres) per hour

knot ➤ *verb* (**knots, knotting, knotted**)
to knot something is to tie or fasten it with a knot

knotty *adjective* (**knottier, knottiest**)
1 full of knots 2 difficult or puzzling ♦ *It's a knotty problem*

know *verb* (**knows, knowing, knew, known**)
1 to have something in your mind that you have learned or discovered 2 to know a person or place is to recognize it or be familiar with it ♦ *I've known him for years*

know-all *noun* (*plural* **know-alls**)
someone who behaves as if they know everything

know-how *noun*
skill; ability for a particular job

knowing *adjective*
showing that you know something ♦ *He gave me a knowing look*

knowingly *adverb*
1 in a knowing way ♦ *He winked at me knowingly* 2 deliberately ♦ *She would never have done such a thing knowingly*

knowledge *noun* (*pronounced* **nol-ij**)
what someone or everybody knows

knowledgeable *adjective* (*pronounced* **nol-ij-a-bul**)
having much knowledge; clever
knowledgeably *adverb* in a knowledgeable way

knuckle *noun* (*plural* **knuckles**)
a joint in the finger

koala *noun* (*plural* **koalas**) (*pronounced* koh-ah-la)
a furry Australian animal that looks like a small bear

kookaburra *noun* (*plural* **kookaburras**) (*pronounced* kuuk-a-bu-ra)
a large Australian kingfisher that makes a laughing or shrieking noise

Koran *noun* (*pronounced* kor-ahn)
the holy book of Islam, believed by Muslims to contain the words of Allah

kosher *adjective* (*pronounced* koh-sher)
kosher food is food prepared according to Jewish religious law

kung fu *noun* (*pronounced* kuung-foo)
a Chinese method of self-defence rather like karate

Ll

L short for **learner**

label ➤ *noun* (*plural* **labels**)
a piece of paper, cloth, or metal fixed on or beside something to show what it is or to give other information about it such as its price

label ➤ *verb* (**labels, labelling, labelled**)
to label something is to put a label on it

laboratory *noun* (*plural* **laboratories**) (*pronounced* la-bo-ra-ter-i)
a room or building equipped for scientific work

laborious *adjective*
needing a lot of effort; very hard
laboriously *adverb* in a laborious way

labour *noun*
  1 hard work **2** the movements of a woman's womb when a baby is born
  Labour the Labour Party, a socialist political party

labourer *noun* (*plural* **labourers**)
  someone who does hard work with their hands, especially outdoors

Labrador *noun* (*plural* **Labradors**)
  a large black or light-brown dog

laburnum *noun* (*plural* **laburnums**)
  a tree with hanging yellow flowers

labyrinth *noun* (*plural* **labyrinths**)
  a complicated set of passages or paths; a maze

lace ➤ *noun* (*plural* **laces**)
  1 lace is thin material with decorative patterns of holes in it **2** a lace is a piece of thin cord used to tie up a shoe or boot
  lacy *adjective* like lace

lace ➤ *verb* (**laces, lacing, laced**)
  1 to lace a shoe or boot is to fasten it with a lace **2** to lace a drink is to add strong spirits to it

lack ➤ *noun*
  being without something ♦ *There was a lack of water for the crops*

lack ➤ *verb* (**lacks, lacking, lacked**)
  to lack something is to be without it ♦ *He lacks courage*

lacquer *noun*
  a kind of varnish

lacrosse *noun*
  a game using a stick with a net on it (called a *crosse*) to catch and throw a ball

lad *noun* (*plural* **lads**)
  a boy or youth

ladder *noun* (*plural* **ladders**)
  1 a device to help you climb up or down something, made of upright pieces of wood, metal, or rope with crosspieces called rungs **2** a run of damaged stitches in tights or a stocking

laden *adjective*
  carrying a heavy load

ladle *noun* (*plural* **ladles**)
  a large deep spoon with a long handle, used for serving soup or other liquids

lady *noun* (*plural* **ladies**)
  1 a polite name for a woman **2** a well-mannered woman, or a woman of high social standing
  Lady the title of a noblewoman

ladybird *noun* (*plural* **ladybirds**)
  a small flying beetle, usually red with black spots

ladylike *adjective*
  suitable for a lady

ladyship *noun*
  a title for a woman of high social standing

lag[1] *verb* (**lags, lagging, lagged**)
  to lag is to go too slowly and not keep up with others

lag[2] *verb* (**lags, lagging, lagged**)
  to lag pipes or boilers is to wrap them with insulating material to keep in the heat

lager *noun* (*plural* **lagers**) (*pronounced* lah-ger)
  a light beer

lagoon *noun* (*plural* **lagoons**)
  1 a lake separated from the sea by sandbanks or reefs **2** (*in Australia and New Zealand*) a pond, often a stagnant pond

laid past tense and past participle of **lay** *verb*

lain past participle of **lie**[1] *verb*

lair *noun* (*plural* **lairs**)
  the place where a wild animal lives

lake *noun* (*plural* **lakes**)
  a large area of water completely surrounded by land

lama *noun* (*plural* **lamas**)
  a Buddhist priest or monk in Tibet and Mongolia

lamb *noun* (*plural* **lambs**)
  1 a lamb is a young sheep **2** lamb is the meat from young sheep

lame *adjective* (**lamer, lamest**)
  1 unable to walk normally **2** weak; not convincing ♦ *That's a lame excuse*
  lamely *adverb* weakly **lameness** *noun* being lame

lament ➤ *verb* (**laments, lamenting, lamented**)
  to lament something is to express grief about it
  lamentation *noun* lamenting something

lament ➤ *noun* (*plural* **laments**)
  a song or poem expressing grief or regret

laminated *adjective*
  1 made of layers joined together
  2 permanently covered in a kind of plastic for protection

lamp *noun* (*plural* **lamps**)
  a device for producing light from electricity, gas, or oil

lamp-post *noun* (*plural* **lamp-posts**)
  a tall post in a street or public place, with a lamp at the top

lampshade *noun* (*plural* **lampshades**)
  a cover for the bulb of an electric lamp, to soften the light

lance *noun* (*plural* **lances**)
  a long spear

lance corporal *noun* (*plural* **lance corporals**)
  a soldier between a private and a corporal in rank

land ➤ *noun* (*plural* **lands**)
  1 a land is a country or nation **2** land or the land is all the dry parts of the world's surface **3** land is the ground or soil

land ➤ *verb* (**lands, landing, landed**)
  1 to land someone or something is to bring them to a place by means of a ship or aircraft **2** to land is to arrive in a ship or aircraft **3** to land is also to reach the ground after jumping or falling
  4 (*informal*) to land someone in difficulty or trouble is to cause them difficulty or trouble

to land up (*informal*) is to get to a particular place or situation ♦ *They landed up in France*

landing *noun* (*plural* **landings**)
  the floor at the top of a flight of stairs

landing stage *noun* (*plural* **landing stages**)
  a platform used for taking people and things on or off a boat

landlady *noun* (*plural* **landladies**)
  1 a woman who lets rooms to lodgers **2** a woman who looks after a pub

landlord *noun* (*plural* **landlords**)
  1 a person who rents a house or land to someone else, or lets rooms to lodgers **2** a person who looks after a pub

landmark *noun* (*plural* **landmarks**)
  an object on land that you can easily see from a distance

landowner *noun* (*plural* **landowners**)
  a person who owns a large amount of land

landscape *noun* (*plural* **landscapes**)
  1 a view of a particular area of town or countryside **2** a picture of the countryside

landscape gardening *noun*
  laying out gardens to imitate natural scenery

landslide *noun* (*plural* **landslides**)
  1 earth or rocks sliding down the side of a hill **2** an overwhelming victory in an election

lane *noun* (*plural* **lanes**)
  1 a narrow road, especially in the country
  2 a strip of road for a single line of traffic
  3 a strip of track or water for one runner or swimmer in a race

language *noun* (*plural* **languages**)
  1 language is the use of words in speech and writing **2** a language is the words used in a particular country or by a particular group of people **3** a language is also a system of signs or symbols giving information, especially in computing

lanky *adjective* (**lankier, lankiest**)
  awkwardly tall and thin
  lankiness *noun* being lanky

lantern *noun* (*plural* **lanterns**)
  a transparent case for holding a light and shielding it from the wind

lap[1] ➤ *noun* (*plural* **laps**)
  1 the level part from the waist to the knees of a person sitting down **2** going once round a racecourse

lap ➤ *verb* (**laps, lapping, lapped**)
  to lap someone in a race is to be more than one lap ahead of them

lap[2] *verb* (**laps, lapping, lapped**)
  1 to lap liquid is to drink it with the tongue, as a cat or dog does **2** waves lap when they make a gentle splash on rocks or the shore

lapel *noun* (*plural* **lapels**) (*pronounced* la-**pel**)
  the flap folded back at each front edge of a coat or jacket

lapse ➤ *noun* (*plural* **lapses**)
  1 a slight mistake or fault **2** the passing of time ♦ *After a lapse of three months work began again*

lapse ➤ *verb* (**lapses, lapsing, lapsed**)
1 to lapse into a state is to pass gradually into it ♦ *He lapsed into unconsciousness*
2 a contract or document lapses when it is no longer valid ♦ *My passport has lapsed*

laptop *noun* (*plural* **laptops**)
a computer small enough to be held and used on your lap, especially while you are travelling

lapwing *noun* (*plural* **lapwings**)
a black and white bird with a crest on its head and a shrill cry

larch *noun* (*plural* **larches**)
a tall deciduous tree that bears small cones

lard *noun*
white greasy fat from pigs, used in cooking

larder *noun* (*plural* **larders**)
a cupboard or small room for storing food

large *adjective* (**larger, largest**)
more than the ordinary or average size; big
at large free and dangerous ♦ *The escaped prisoners were still at large*
largeness *noun* being large

largely *adverb*
mainly; mostly ♦ *We are largely to blame for the mistake*

lark[1] *noun* (*plural* **larks**)
a small sandy-brown bird; a skylark

lark[2] ➤ *noun* (*plural* **larks**)
(*informal*) something amusing; a bit of fun ♦ *They just did it for a lark*

lark ➤ *verb* (**larks, larking, larked**)
to lark about is to have fun or play tricks

larva *noun* (*plural* **larvae**)
an insect in the first stage of its life, after it comes out of the egg

lasagne *noun* (*pronounced* la-**zan**-ya)
pasta in the form of flat sheets, cooked with minced meat or vegetables and a white sauce

laser *noun* (*plural* **lasers**) (*pronounced* **lay**-zer)
a device that makes a very strong narrow beam of light

lash ➤ *noun* (*plural* **lashes**)
1 a stroke with a whip **2** the cord of a whip **3** an eyelash

lash ➤ *verb* (**lashes, lashing, lashed**)
1 to lash someone or something is to hit them with a whip or like a whip ♦ *Rain lashed the window* **2** to lash something is to tie it tightly ♦ *During the storm they lashed the boxes to the mast*
to lash out is to speak or hit out angrily
to lash out on something (*informal*) is to spend a lot of money on it

lass *noun* (*plural* **lasses**)
a girl or young woman

lasso *noun* (*plural* **lassos**) (*pronounced* la-**soo**)
a rope with a loop at the end which tightens when you pull the rope, used for catching cattle

last[1] ➤ *adjective*
1 coming after all the others; final ♦ *Try not to miss the last bus* **2** most recent or latest ♦ *Where were you last night?*
the last straw a final or added thing that makes a problem unbearable

last ➤ *adverb*
at the end; after everything else ♦ *I'll do the washing last*

last ➤ *noun*
a person or thing that is last ♦ *I think I was the last to arrive*
at last finally; at the end

last[2] *verb* (**lasts, lasting, lasted**)
1 to continue ♦ *The journey lasts for two hours* **2** to go on without being used up ♦ *How long will our supplies last?*

lastly *adverb*
in the last place; finally

latch *noun* (*plural* **latches**)
a small bar fastening a gate or door

late *adjective* and *adverb* (**later, latest**)
1 after the proper or expected time
2 near the end of a period of time ♦ *They came late in the afternoon* **3** recent ♦ *Do you have the latest news?* **4** no longer alive ♦ *They saw the tomb of the late king*
lateness *noun* being late

lately *adverb*
recently ♦ *She has been very tired lately*

latent *adjective* (*pronounced* **lay**-tent)
existing but not yet active, developed, or visible

lateral *adjective*
to do with the sides of something

lateral thinking *noun*
thinking of unusual ways to solve problems or achieve things

lathe *noun* (*plural* **lathes**) (*pronounced* lay*th*)
a machine for holding and turning pieces of wood or metal while you shape them

lather *noun* (*plural* **lathers**)
a thick soapy froth

Latin *noun*
the language of the ancient Romans

latitude *noun* (*plural* **latitudes**)
1 the distance of a place from the equator, measured in degrees 2 freedom to do what you want or make decisions

latter *adjective*

later ♦ *We'd like a holiday in the latter part of the year*

the latter the second of two people or things just mentioned ♦ *If it's a choice between a picnic or a swim I prefer the latter*

See also **former**

latterly *adverb*

recently

lattice *noun* (*plural* **lattices**)
a framework of crossed strips with spaces between

laugh ➤ *verb* (**laughs, laughing, laughed**)
to laugh is to make sounds that show you are happy or that you think something is funny

laugh ➤ *noun* (*plural* **laughs**)
1 an act or sound of laughing
2 (*informal*) something that is fun or amusing ♦ *Yesterday's party was quite a laugh*

laughable *adjective*
deserving to be laughed at; silly or absurd

laughter *noun*
laughing or the sound of laughing

launch[1] ➤ *verb* (**launches, launching, launched**)
1 to launch a ship is to send it into the water for the first time 2 to launch a rocket is to send it into space 3 to launch a new idea or product is to make it available for the first time

launch ➤ *noun* (*plural* **launches**)
the launching of a ship or spacecraft

launch[2] *noun* (*plural* **launches**)
a large motor boat

launch pad *noun* (*plural* **launch pads**)
a platform from which rockets are sent into space

launder *verb* (**launders, laundering, laundered**)
to launder clothes is to wash and iron them

launderette *noun* (*plural* **launderettes**)
a shop with washing machines that people pay to use

laundry *noun* (*plural* **laundries**)
1 clothes to be washed 2 a place where clothes are sent or taken to be washed and ironed

laurel *noun* (*plural* **laurels**)
an evergreen bush with smooth shiny leaves

lava *noun*
molten rock that flows from a volcano, or the solid rock formed when it cools

lavatory *noun* (*plural* **lavatories**)
a place for getting rid of waste from the body

lavender *noun*
1 a shrub with pale purple flowers that smell very sweet 2 a pale purple colour

lavish *adjective*
1 generous ♦ *They are lavish with their gifts* 2 plentiful ♦ *What a lavish meal!*

law *noun* (*plural* **laws**)
1 a rule or set of rules that everyone must keep 2 something that always happens, for example the law of gravity

lawcourt *noun* (*plural* **lawcourts**)
a room or building where a judge and jury or a magistrate decide whether someone has broken the law

lawful *adjective*
allowed or accepted by the law
lawfully *adverb* in a lawful way

lawless *adjective*
having no proper laws ♦ *It was a lawless country*

lawn *noun* (*plural* **lawns**)
an area of mown grass in a garden

lawnmower *noun* (*plural* **lawnmowers**)
a machine with revolving blades for cutting grass

lawsuit *noun* (*plural* **lawsuits**)
a dispute or claim that is brought to a lawcourt to be settled

lawyer *noun* (*plural* **lawyers**)
an expert on law; someone whose job is to help people with the law

lax *adjective*
not strict; tolerant ♦ *Discipline was very lax*

laxative *noun* (*plural* **laxatives**)
a medicine that causes your bowels to empty

lay[1] *verb* (**lays, laying, laid**)
1 to lay something somewhere is to put it down in a particular place or in a particular way **2** to lay a table or other surface is to arrange things on it, especially for a meal **3** to lay an egg is to produce it **4** to lay plans is to form or prepare them
to lay someone off is to stop employing them for a while
to lay something on is to supply or provide it
to lay something out is to arrange or prepare it

lay[2] past tense of **lie**[1] *verb*

layabout *noun* (*plural* **layabouts**)
a lazy person

layer *noun* (*plural* **layers**)
something flat that lies on or under something else ♦ *The cake had a layer of icing on top and a layer of jam inside*

layman *noun* (*plural* **laymen**)
a person without special knowledge in a subject

layout *noun* (*plural* **layouts**)
the arrangement or design of something

laze *verb* (**lazes, lazing, lazed**)
to laze is to spend time in a lazy way

lazy *adjective* (**lazier, laziest**)
not wanting to work; doing little work
lazily *adverb* in a lazy way **laziness** *noun* being lazy

lb. short for **pound** or **pounds** in weight ♦ *I bought 5 lb. of potatoes*

l.b.w. short for **leg before wicket**

lead[1] ➤ *verb* (**leads, leading, led**) (*pronounced* leed)
1 to lead a person or animal is to guide them, especially by going in front **2** to lead an activity is to be in charge of it
3 to lead in a race or contest is to be winning **4** a road or path leads somewhere when it goes in that direction ♦ *This road leads to the beach* **5** to lead is to play the first card in a card game
to lead to something is to cause it ♦ *Their carelessness led to the accident*

lead ➤ *noun* (*plural* **leads**) (*pronounced* leed)
1 leading or guidance ♦ *Give us a lead*
2 a leading place or position ♦ *She took the lead* **3** a strap or cord for leading a dog **4** an electric wire ♦ *Don't trip over that lead*

lead[2] *noun* (*plural* **leads**) (*pronounced* led)
1 a soft heavy grey metal **2** the writing substance (graphite) in the middle of a pencil

leader *noun* (*plural* **leaders**)
1 someone who leads or is in charge **2** an article in a newspaper, giving the editor's opinion
leadership *noun* being a leader

leaf *noun* (*plural* **leaves**)
1 a flat and usually green growth on a tree or plant, growing from its stem **2** a page of a book **3** a very thin sheet of metal, such as gold leaf **4** a flap that makes a table larger
leafy *adjective* having many leaves
to turn over a new leaf is to make a fresh start and improve your behaviour

leaflet *noun* (*plural* **leaflets**)
a piece of paper printed with information

league *noun* (*plural* **leagues**) (*pronounced* leeg)
1 a group of teams that play matches against each other **2** a group of countries that have agreed to work together for a particular reason
to be in league with someone is to work or plot together

leak ➤ *noun* (*plural* **leaks**)
1 a hole or crack through which liquid or gas escapes **2** the revealing of some secret information
leaky *adjective* having leaks

leak ➤ *verb* (**leaks, leaking, leaked**)
1 something leaks when it lets something out through a hole or crack ♦ *The sink is leaking* **2** liquid or gas leaks out when it escapes from a container **3** to leak secret information is to reveal it
leakage *noun* leaking

lean[1] *verb* (**leans, leaning, leaned** or **leant**)
1 to lean is to bend your body towards something or over it **2** to lean something is to put it into a sloping position ♦ *Do not lean bicycles against the window* **3** to lean against something is to rest against it

lean[2] *adjective* (**leaner, leanest**)
1 lean meat has little fat **2** a lean person is thin

leap ➤ *noun* (*plural* **leaps**)
1 a vigorous jump **2** a sudden increase or advance

leap ➤ *verb* (**leaps, leaping, leapt** or **leaped**)
1 to leap is to make a vigorous jump **2** to leap is also to increase or advance suddenly

leapfrog *noun*
a game in which each player jumps with legs apart over another player who is bending down

leap year *noun* (*plural* **leap years**)
a year with an extra day in it, on 29 February

learn *verb* (**learns, learning, learnt** or **learned**)
to learn something is to find out about it, and be knowledgeable or skilful in it

learned *adjective* (*pronounced* **ler**-nid)
clever and knowledgeable

learner *noun* (*plural* **learners**)
someone who is learning something, especially how to drive a car

learning *noun*
knowledge got by studying

lease *noun* (*plural* **leases**)
an agreement to let someone use a building or land for a fixed period in return for a payment

a new lease of life a chance to go on being active or useful

leash *noun* (*plural* **leashes**)
a strap or cord for leading a dog

least ➤ *adjective* and *adverb*
smallest; less than all the others ♦ *I'll get the least expensive bike* ♦ *I like this one least*

at least 1 not less than what is mentioned ♦ *It will cost at least £50* **2** anyway ♦ *He's at home; at least I think he is*

least ➤ *noun*
the smallest amount

leather *noun* (*plural* **leathers**)
a strong material made from animals' skins

leathery *adjective* tough like leather

leave ➤ *verb* (**leaves, leaving, left**)
1 to leave a person, place, or group is to go away from them **2** to leave something is to let it stay where it is or remain as it is ♦ *I've left my book at home* **3** to leave something to someone is to give it to them in a will

to leave something or **someone out** is not to include them

to be left over is to remain when other things have been used

leave ➤ *noun*
1 permission, especially to be away from work **2** the time when someone is allowed to be away from work ♦ *They get 30 days' leave*

leaves plural of **leaf**

lectern *noun* (*plural* **lecterns**)
a stand to hold a Bible or other large book from which you read

lecture ➤ *noun* (*plural* **lectures**)
1 a talk about a subject to an audience or a class **2** a long or serious warning given to someone ♦ *We got a lecture about closing the windows*

lecture ➤ *verb* (**lectures, lecturing, lectured**)
to lecture is to give a lecture

lecturer *noun* someone who gives a lecture

led past tense and past participle of **lead** *verb*

ledge *noun* (*plural* **ledges**)
a narrow shelf

lee *noun*
the sheltered side of something, away from the wind

leek *noun* (*plural* **leeks**)
a long green and white vegetable like an onion with broad leaves

leer *verb* (**leers, leering, leered**)
to leer at someone is to look unpleasantly or evilly at them

leeward *adjective*
facing away from the wind

left[1] ➤ *adjective* and *adverb*
1 on or towards the west if you think of yourself as facing north **2** in favour of political and social change

left ➤ *noun*
the left side

left[2] past tense and past participle of **leave** *verb*

left-hand *adjective*
on the left side of something

left-handed *adjective*
using the left hand more than the right hand

leftovers *plural noun*
food not eaten by the end of a meal

leg *noun* (*plural* **legs**)
 1 one of the parts of a human's or animal's body on which they stand or move **2** the part of a piece of clothing that covers a leg **3** each of the supports of a chair or other piece of furniture **4** one part of a journey **5** each of a pair of matches between the same teams in a competition
 on your last legs exhausted

legacy *noun* (*plural* **legacies**)
 something given to someone in a will

legal *adjective*
 1 lawful **2** to do with the law or lawyers
 legality *noun* being legal **legally** *adverb* in a legal way

legalize *verb* (**legalizes, legalizing, legalized**)
 to legalize something is to make it legal

legend *noun* (*plural* **legends**) (*pronounced* lej-end)
 an old story handed down from the past
 legendary *adjective* belonging to a legend

legible *adjective*
 clear enough to read ♦ *Make sure your writing is legible*
 legibility *noun* being legible **legibly** *adverb* in a legible way

legion *noun* (*plural* **legions**)
 1 a division of the ancient Roman army **2** a group of soldiers, or men who used to be soldiers

legislate *verb* (**legislates, legislating, legislated**)
 to legislate is to make laws
 legislation *noun* making laws **legislator** *noun* someone who makes laws

legitimate *adjective* (*pronounced* li-jit-i-mat)
 1 lawful **2** (*old use*) born of parents who were married to each other
 legitimacy *noun* being legitimate **legitimately** *adverb* in a legitimate way

leisure *noun*
 time that is free from work, when you can do what you like
 at leisure having leisure; not hurried

leisurely *adjective*
 done with plenty of time; unhurried
 ♦ *They took a leisurely stroll down to the river*

lemon *noun* (*plural* **lemons**)
 1 a yellow citrus fruit with a sour taste **2** a pale yellow colour

lemonade *noun* (*plural* **lemonades**)
 a drink with a lemon flavour

lend *verb* (**lends, lending, lent**)
 1 to lend something to someone is to let them have it for a short time **2** to lend someone money is to give them money which they must pay back plus an extra amount called interest
 to lend a hand is to help someone

length *noun* (*plural* **lengths**)
 1 how long something is **2** a piece of something cut from a longer piece, for example rope, wire, or cloth **3** the distance of a swimming pool from one end to the other
 at length after a while; eventually

lengthen *verb* (**lengthens, lengthening, lengthened**)
 1 to lengthen something is to make it longer **2** to lengthen is to become longer

lengthways or **lengthwise** *adverb*
 from end to end; along the longest part of something

lengthy *adjective* (**lengthier, lengthiest**)
 going on for a long time ♦ *He gave a lengthy speech*

lenient *adjective* (*pronounced* lee-ni-ent)
 merciful; not severe
 lenience *noun* being lenient **leniently** *adverb* in a lenient way

lens *noun* (*plural* **lenses**)
 1 a curved piece of glass or plastic used to focus images of things, or to concentrate light **2** the transparent part of the eye, behind the pupil

Lent *noun*
 a time of fasting observed by Christians for about six weeks before Easter

lent past tense and past participle of **lend**

lentil *noun* (*plural* **lentils**)
 a kind of small bean

leopard *noun* (*plural* **leopards**) (*pronounced* lep-erd)
 a large spotted wild animal of the cat family

leotard *noun* (*plural* **leotards**) (*pronounced* lee-o-tard)
 a close-fitting piece of clothing worn by acrobats and dancers

leper *noun* (*plural* **lepers**)
 someone who has leprosy

leprosy *noun*
 an infectious disease that affects the skin and nerves, and causes parts of the body to waste away
 leprous *adjective* suffering from leprosy

ess ➤ *adjective* and *adverb*
smaller; not so much ♦ *Make less noise*
♦ *It is less important*

ess ➤ *noun*
a smaller amount ♦ *I have less than you*

ess ➤ *preposition*
minus; deducting ♦ *She earned £100, less tax*

less *suffix*
forming adjectives meaning 'lacking something' or 'free from something', such as *smokeless* and *useless*

essen *verb* (**lessens, lessening, lessened**)
1 to lessen something is to make it smaller or not so much 2 to lessen is to become smaller or not so much

esser *adjective*
the smaller or less great of two things
♦ *This is the lesser evil*

esson *noun* (*plural* **lessons**)
1 the time when someone is teaching you 2 something that you have to learn 3 a passage from the Bible read aloud as part of a church service

est *conjunction*
so that something should not happen ♦ *He ran away lest he should be seen*

et *verb* (**lets, letting, let**)
1 to let someone do something is to allow them to do it 2 to let something happen is to cause it or not prevent it ♦ *Don't let your bike slide into the ditch* 3 to let a house or room or building is to allow someone to use it in return for payment 4 to let someone in or out is to allow them to go in or out
to let on (*informal*) is to reveal a secret ♦ *If I tell you, don't let on*
to let someone down is to disappoint them
to let someone off is to excuse them from a punishment or duty
to let something off is to make it explode
to let up is to relax or do less work

ethal *adjective*
deadly; causing death
lethally *adverb* in a lethal way

et's *verb*
(*informal*) shall we? ♦ *Let's go to the park*

etter *noun* (*plural* **letters**)
1 one of the symbols used for writing words, such as a, b, or c 2 a written message sent to another person

etter box *noun* (*plural* **letter boxes**)
a box or slot into which letters are delivered or posted

ettering *noun*
letters drawn or painted

ettuce *noun* (*plural* **lettuces**)
a green vegetable with crisp leaves used in salads

leukaemia *noun* (*pronounced* lew-kee-mi-a)
a disease in which there are too many white cells in the blood

level ➤ *adjective*
1 flat or horizontal ♦ *The ground is level near the house* 2 at the same height or position ♦ *He was level with the others*

level ➤ *verb* (**levels, levelling, levelled**)
1 to level something is to make it flat or horizontal 2 to level, or to level out, is to become horizontal 3 to level a gun at a target is to aim it

level ➤ *noun* (*plural* **levels**)
1 height or position ♦ *Fix the shelf at eye level* 2 a device that shows if something is horizontal 3 a flat or horizontal surface 4 a standard or grade of achievement
♦ *She has reached level 3 in gymnastics*
on the level (*informal*) honest

level crossing *noun* (*plural* **level crossings**)
a place where a road crosses a railway at the same level

lever *noun* (*plural* **levers**)
a bar that is pushed or pulled to lift something heavy, force something open, or make a machine work

leverage *noun*
the force you need when you use a lever

lexical *adjective*
to do with the words of a language

liability *noun* (*plural* **liabilities**)
1 liability is being legally liable for something 2 a liability is a debt or obligation 3 a liability is also a disadvantage or handicap

liable *adjective*
1 likely to do or get something ♦ *Parking on the yellow lines makes you liable to a fine* 2 responsible for something

liar *noun* (*plural* **liars**)
someone who tells lies

liberal *adjective*
1 generous; ample 2 not strict; tolerant
Liberal a supporter of the Liberal Party, now part of the Liberal Democrats
liberally *adverb* in a liberal way; generously

liberate *verb* (**liberates, liberating, liberated**)
to liberate someone is to set them free
liberation *noun* liberating someone

liberty *noun* (*plural* **liberties**)
freedom
to take liberties is to behave too casually or informally

librarian *noun* (*plural* **librarians**)
someone who looks after a library or works in one
librarianship *noun* the work of a librarian

library *noun* (*plural* **libraries**)
a place where books are kept for people to use or borrow

lice plural of **louse**

licence *noun* (*plural* **licences**)
an official document allowing someone to do or use or own something

license *verb* (**licenses, licensing, licensed**)
to license someone to do something is to give them a licence to do it ♦ *We are not licensed to sell alcoholic drinks*

lichen *noun* (*plural* **lichens**) (*pronounced* ly-ken)
a dry-looking plant that grows on rocks, walls, trees, and other surfaces

lick ➤ *verb* (**licks, licking, licked**)
1 to lick something is to move your tongue over it **2** (*informal*) to lick someone is to defeat them

lick ➤ *noun* (*plural* **licks**)
the act of moving your tongue over something
at a lick (*informal*) very fast

lid *noun* (*plural* **lids**)
1 a cover for a box or jar **2** an eyelid

lie[1] *verb* (**lies, lying, lay, lain**)
1 to lie is to be in or get into a flat position, especially to rest with your body flat as it is in bed ♦ *He lay on the grass* ♦ *The cat has lain here all night* **2** to lie is also to be or remain a certain way ♦ *The castle was lying in ruins* ♦ *The valley lay before us*
to lie low is to keep yourself hidden

lie[2] ➤ *verb* (**lies, lying, lied**)
to lie is to say something that you know is not true

lie ➤ *noun* (*plural* **lies**)
something you say that you know is not true

lieutenant *noun* (*plural* **lieutenants**)
(*pronounced* left-ten-ant)
an officer in the army or navy

life *noun* (*plural* **lives**)
1 a person's or animal's life is the time between their birth and death **2** life is being alive and able to grow **3** life is also all living things ♦ *Is there life on Mars?* **4** life is also liveliness ♦ *She is full of life* **5** the life of a famous person is the story of what they have done

lifebelt *noun* (*plural* **lifebelts**)
a circle of material that will float, used to support someone's body in water

lifeboat *noun* (*plural* **lifeboats**)
a boat for rescuing people at sea

life cycle *noun* (*plural* **life cycles**)
the series of changes in the life of a living thing

lifeguard *noun* (*plural* **lifeguards**)
someone whose job is to rescue swimmers who are in difficulty

life jacket *noun* (*plural* **life jackets**)
a jacket of material that will float, used to support a person in water

lifeless *adjective*
1 without life **2** unconscious

lifelike *adjective*
looking exactly like a real person or thing

lifelong *adjective*
lasting throughout someone's life

lifespan *noun* (*plural* **lifespans**)
how long a person or animal or plant lives

lifestyle *noun* (*plural* **lifestyles**)
the way of life of a person or a group of people

lifetime *noun* (*plural* **lifetimes**)
the time for which someone is alive

lift ➤ *verb* (**lifts, lifting, lifted**)
1 to lift something is to pick it up or raise it **2** to lift is to rise or go upwards
3 (*informal*) to lift something is to steal it

lift ➤ *noun* (*plural* **lifts**)
1 the act of lifting **2** a device for taking people or goods from one floor to another in a building **3** a ride in someone else's car or other vehicle

lift-off *noun* (*plural* **lift-offs**)
the vertical take-off of a rocket or spacecraft

light[1] ➤ *noun* (*plural* **lights**)
1 light is the form of energy that makes things visible, the opposite of darkness ♦ *There was not enough light to see the garden* **2** a light is something that provides light or a flame, especially an electric lamp ♦ *Switch on the light*

light ➤ *adjective* (**lighter, lightest**)
1 full of light; not dark **2** pale ♦ *The house was painted light blue*

light ➤ *verb* (**lights, lighting, lit or lighted**)
1 to light something is to start it burning
2 to light is to begin to burn ♦ *The fire won't light* **3** to light a place is to give it light ♦ *The streets were lit by gaslamps*

to **light up** is to become bright with lights
to light something up is to make it bright with lights

light[2] *adjective* (**lighter, lightest**)
1 not heavy; weighing little 2 not large or strong ♦ *There is a light wind* 3 not needing much effort ♦ *They were doing some light work in the garden* 4 pleasant and entertaining rather than serious ♦ *We prefer light music*

lightly *adverb* gently; pleasantly

lighten *verb* (**lightens, lightening, lightened**)
1 to lighten something is to make it lighter or brighter 2 to lighten is to become lighter

lighter *noun* (*plural* **lighters**)
a device for lighting something like a cigarette or a fire

light-hearted *adjective*
1 cheerful; free from worry 2 not serious
light-heartedly *adverb* in a light-hearted way
light-heartedness *noun* being light-hearted

lighthouse *noun* (*plural* **lighthouses**)
a tower with a bright light at the top to guide ships and warn them of danger

lighting *noun*
lamps, or the light they provide

lightning *noun*
a flash of bright light in the sky during a thunderstorm

lightning conductor *noun* (*plural* **lightning conductors**)
a metal wire or rod fixed on a building to divert lightning into the earth

light-pen *noun* (*plural* **light-pens**)
a device shaped like a pen, connected to a computer and used to read bar codes

lightweight *adjective*
less than average weight

light year *noun* (*plural* **light years**)
the distance that light travels in one year (about 9.5 million million km or 6 million million miles)

like[1] *verb* (**likes, liking, liked**)
to like someone or something is to think they are pleasant or satisfactory
should like or **would like** to want ♦ *I should like to see him*

like[2] ➤ *preposition*
1 resembling; similar to; in the manner of ♦ *He cried like a baby* 2 such as ♦ *We need things like knives and forks* 3 typical of ♦ *It was like her to forgive him*
like anything (*informal*) very much ♦ *She wanted like anything to become a doctor*

like ➤ *adjective*
similar ♦ *They are as like as two peas*

likeable *adjective*
pleasant and easy to like

likely *adjective* (**likelier, likeliest**)
probable; expected to happen or to be true or suitable

liken *verb* (**likens, likening, likened**)
to liken one thing to another is to compare them or show that they are similar

likeness *noun* (*plural* **likenesses**)
a resemblance

likewise *adverb*
similarly; in the same way

liking *noun* (*plural* **likings**)
a feeling that you like something or someone ♦ *She has a great liking for chocolate*
to someone's liking what they like

lilac *noun* (*plural* **lilacs**)
1 a bush with sweet-smelling purple or white flowers 2 a pale purple colour

lily *noun* (*plural* **lilies**)
a garden flower grown from a bulb

limb *noun* (*plural* **limbs**)
a leg, arm, or wing

limber *verb* (**limbers, limbering, limbered**)
to limber up is to do exercises to be ready for a sport or athletic activity

lime[1] *noun*
a white chalky powder (calcium oxide) used in making cement or as a fertilizer

lime[2] *noun* (*plural* **limes**)
a green fruit like a small round lemon

lime[3] *noun* (*plural* **limes**)
a tree with yellow blossom

limelight *noun*
in the limelight getting a lot of publicity and attention

limerick *noun* (*plural* **limericks**) (*pronounced* lim-er-ik)
an amusing poem with five lines and a strong rhythm

limestone *noun*
rock from which lime (calcium oxide) is made

limit ➤ *noun* (*plural* **limits**)
1 a line or point that you cannot or should not pass ♦ *You must obey the speed limit*
2 a line or edge where something ends ♦ *The white line marks the limit of the road*
limitless *adjective* having no limit

limit ➤ *verb* (**limits, limiting, limited**)
to limit something or someone is to keep them within a limit
limitation *noun* something that limits something or someone

limited *adjective*
kept within limits; not great ♦ *The choice was limited*

limited company *noun* (*plural* **limited companies**)
a business company whose members are responsible for only some of its debts

limp[1] ➤ *verb* (**limps, limping, limped**)
to limp is to walk with difficulty because something is wrong with your leg or foot

limp[1] ➤ *noun* (*plural* **limps**)
a limping movement

limp[2] *adjective* (**limper, limpest**)
not stiff or firm; without much strength ♦ *He gave me a limp handshake*
limply *adverb* in a limp way

limpet *noun* (*plural* **limpets**)
a small shellfish that attaches itself firmly to rocks

line[1] ➤ *noun* (*plural* **lines**)
1 a long thin mark made on a surface 2 a row or series of people or things 3 a length of something long and thin like rope, string, or wire 4 a railway or a length of railway track 5 a company operating a transport service of ships, aircraft, or buses 6 a way of working or behaving; a type of business ♦ *What line are you in?*
in line 1 forming a straight line **2** obeying or behaving well

line ➤ *verb* (**lines, lining, lined**)
1 to line something is to mark it with lines
2 to line a place is to form an edge or border along it ♦ *The streets are lined with trees*
to line up is to form lines or rows ♦ *The children lined up in the playground*
to line things up is to set them up in a line or row

line[2] *verb* (**lines, lining, lined**)
to line material or a piece of clothing is to put a lining on it

linen *noun*
1 cloth made from flax, used to make shirts, sheets, tablecloths, and so on
2 things made of this cloth

liner *noun* (*plural* **liners**)
a large ship or aircraft, usually carrying passengers

linesman *noun* (*plural* **linesmen**)
an official in football, tennis, and other games who decides whether the ball has crossed a line

linger *verb* (**lingers, lingering, lingered**)
to linger is to stay for a long time or be slow to leave

lingerie *noun* (*pronounced* lan-zher-ee)
women's underclothes

linguist *noun* (*plural* **linguists**)
an expert in languages, or someone who can speak several languages well
linguistic *adjective* to do with languages

linguistics *noun*
the study of language

lining *noun* (*plural* **linings**)
a layer covering the inside of something

link ➤ *noun* (*plural* **links**)
1 one of the rings in a chain 2 a connection

link ➤ *verb* (**links, linking, linked**)
to link things is to join them together
to link up is to become connected

lino *noun*
linoleum

linoleum *noun* (*pronounced* lin-oh-li-um)
a stiff shiny floor covering

lint *noun*
a soft material for covering wounds

lion *noun* (*plural* **lions**)
a large strong flesh-eating animal found in Africa and India

lioness *noun* (*plural* **lionesses**)
a female lion

lip *noun* (*plural* **lips**)
1 each of the two fleshy edges of the mouth
2 the edge of something hollow such as a cup or a crater **3** the pointed part at the top of a jug or saucepan, for pouring from

lip-read *verb* (**lip-reads, lip-reading, lip-read**)
to lip-read is to understand what someone is saying by watching the movements of their lips, not by hearing their voice

lipstick *noun* (*plural* **lipsticks**)
a stick of a waxy substance for colouring the lips

liquid ➤ *noun* (*plural* **liquids**)
a substance (such as water or oil) that can flow but is not a gas

liquid ➤ *adjective*
in the form of a liquid; flowing freely

liquidizer *noun* (*plural* **liquidizers**)
a device for making food into a pulp or a liquid

liquor *noun* (*plural* **liquors**) (*pronounced* lik-er)
alcoholic drink

liquorice *noun* (*pronounced* lik-er-iss)
a soft black sweet with a strong taste, which comes from the root of a plant

lisp ➤ *noun* (*plural* **lisps**)
a fault in speaking, in which *s* and *z* are pronounced like *th*

lisp ➤ *verb* (**lisps, lisping, lisped**)
to lisp is to speak with a lisp

list[1] ➤ *noun* (*plural* **lists**)
a number of names or figures or items written or printed one after another

list ➤ *verb* (**lists, listing, listed**)
to list things is to make a list of them

list[2] *verb* (**lists, listing, listed**)
a ship lists when it leans over to one side in the water

listen *verb* (**listens, listening, listened**)
to listen to someone or something is to pay attention in order to hear them
listener *noun* someone who is listening

listless *adjective*
too tired to be active or enthusiastic
listlessly *adverb* in a listless way

lit past tense and past participle of **light** *verb*

literacy *noun* (*pronounced* lit-er-a-si)
the ability to read and write

literal *adjective*
1 meaning exactly what it says **2** word for word ♦ *Write out a literal translation*

literally *adverb*
really; exactly as stated ♦ *The noise made me literally jump out of my seat*

literary *adjective* (*pronounced* lit-er-er-i)
to do with literature; interested in literature

literate *adjective* (*pronounced* lit-er-at)
able to read and write

literature *noun*
books or writings, especially the best or most famous

litmus *noun*
a blue substance used to show whether something is an acid or an alkali

litmus paper *noun*
paper stained with litmus

litre *noun* (*plural* **litres**) (*pronounced* lee-ter)
a measure of liquid, 1,000 cubic centimetres or about $1\frac{3}{4}$ pints

litter ➤ *noun* (*plural* **litters**)
1 litter is rubbish or untidy things left lying about **2** a litter is a number of young animals born to one mother at one time

litter ➤ *verb* (**litters, littering, littered**)
to litter a place is to make it untidy with litter

little ➤ *adjective* (**less** or **littler, least** or **littlest**)
1 small; not great or not much ♦ *She brought a little boy* ♦ *We have very little time* **2** a small amount of something ♦ *Have a little sugar*
little by little gradually

little ➤ *adverb*
not much ♦ *They go swimming very little now*

live[1] *verb* (**lives, living, lived**) (*rhymes with* give)
1 to live is to be alive **2** to live in a particular place is to have your home there ♦ *She is living in Glasgow* **3** to live in a certain way is to pass your life in that way ♦ *He lived as a hermit*
to live on something is to have it as food or income ♦ *The islanders lived mainly on fish* ♦ *No one can live on £50 a week*

live[2] *adjective* (*rhymes with* hive)
1 alive **2** carrying electricity **3** broadcast while it is actually happening, not from a recording

livelihood *noun* (*plural* **livelihoods**)
(*pronounced* **lyv**-li-huud)
the way in which you earn a living

lively *adjective* (**livelier, liveliest**)
full of life and energy; cheerful
liveliness *noun* being lively

liver *noun* (*plural* **livers**)
1 a large organ in the body that produces
bile and helps keep the blood clean 2 an
animal's liver used as food

livery *noun* (*plural* **liveries**)
the special colours used by a railway or
bus company or airline

lives plural of **life**

livestock *noun*
farm animals

livid *adjective*
1 very angry 2 of a dark blue-grey colour,
like bruised skin

living *noun* (*plural* **livings**)
1 the way that a person lives ♦ *They have
a good standard of living* 2 a means of
earning money ♦ *What do you do for a
living?*

living room *noun* (*plural* **living rooms**)
a room for general use during the day

lizard *noun* (*plural* **lizards**)
a reptile with a scaly skin, four legs, and a
long tail

llama *noun* (*plural* **llamas**) (*pronounced*
lah-ma)
a South American animal with woolly fur

load ➤ *noun* (*plural* **loads**)
1 something to be carried 2 an amount
that can be carried 3 (*informal*) a large
amount ♦ *It's a load of nonsense*

load ➤ *verb* (**loads, loading, loaded**)
1 to load something is to put a load on it
♦ *I'll go and load the back of the car* 2 to
load dice is to put a weight into them to
make them fall in a special way 3 to load
someone with something is to give them
large amounts of it ♦ *They loaded him
with gifts* 4 to load a gun is to put a bullet
or shell into it 5 to load a machine is to
put something it needs into it, such as a
film in a camera or a cassette in a tape
recorder 6 to load a computer is to enter
programs or data on it

loaf[1] *noun* (*plural* **loaves**)
a shaped mass of bread baked in one piece

loaf[2] *verb* (**loafs, loafing, loafed**)
to loaf or loaf about is to loiter or waste
time

loafer *noun* someone who loafs about

loam *noun*
rich fertile soil
loamy *adjective* like loam

loan ➤ *noun* (*plural* **loans**)
something that has been lent to someone,
especially money
on loan being lent ♦ *The books are on loan
from the library*

loan ➤ *verb* (**loans, loaning, loaned**)
to loan something is to lend it

loath *adjective* (*rhymes with* both)
unwilling ♦ *I was loath to go*

loathe *verb* (**loathes, loathing, loathed**) (*rhymes
with* clothe)
to loathe something or someone is to
dislike them very much

loathsome *adjective*
making you feel disgusted; horrible

loaves plural of **loaf** *noun*

lob *verb* (**lobs, lobbing, lobbed**)
to lob something is to throw or hit it high
into the air

lobby ➤ *noun* (*plural* **lobbies**)
an entrance hall

lobby ➤ *verb* (**lobbies, lobbying, lobbied**)
to lobby politicians or officials is to try to
influence them or persuade them of
something

lobe *noun* (*plural* **lobes**)
the rounded part at the bottom of the ear

lobster *noun* (*plural* **lobsters**)
a large shellfish with eight legs and two claws

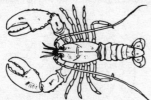

lobster pot *noun* (*plural* **lobster pots**)
a basket for catching lobsters

local ➤ *adjective*
1 belonging to a particular place or area
2 affecting a special part of the body
♦ *You'll need a local anaesthetic*
locally *adverb* nearby; in a particular district

local ➤ *noun* (*plural* **locals**)
(*informal*) 1 a local is someone who lives in a particular district 2 someone's local is the pub near their home

locality *noun* (*plural* **localities**)
a district or location

locate *verb* (**locates, locating, located**)
1 to locate something is to discover where it is ♦ *I have located the fault* 2 to be located in a place is to be situated there
♦ *The cinema is located in the High Street*

location *noun* (*plural* **locations**)
the place where something is
on location filmed in natural surroundings, not in a studio

loch *noun* (*plural* **lochs**)
a lake in Scotland

lock¹ ➤ *noun* (*plural* **locks**)
1 a fastening that is opened with a key or other device 2 a section of a canal or river with gates at each end, so that the level of water can be raised or lowered to allow boats to pass from one level to another
3 the distance that a vehicle's front wheels can turn
lock, stock, and barrel completely

lock ➤ *verb* (**locks, locking, locked**)
1 to lock a door or window or lid is to fasten or secure it with a lock 2 to lock is to become fixed in one place, or to jam

lock² *noun* (*plural* **locks**)
a few strands of hair formed into a loop

locker *noun* (*plural* **lockers**)
a small cupboard for keeping things safe

locket *noun* (*plural* **lockets**)
a small case holding a photograph or lock of hair, worn on a chain round the neck

locomotive *noun* (*plural* **locomotives**)
a railway engine

locus *noun* (*plural* **loci**)
(*in Mathematics*) the line made by a moving point or by points placed in a certain way

locust *noun* (*plural* **locusts**)
an insect like a large grasshopper, that flies in swarms which eat all the plants in an area

lodge ➤ *noun* (*plural* **lodges**)
1 a small house 2 a room or small house at the entrance to a large house or building

lodge ➤ *verb* (**lodges, lodging, lodged**)
1 to lodge somewhere is to stay there as a lodger 2 to lodge someone is to give them a place to sleep 3 to lodge is to become fixed ♦ *The ball lodged in the branches*
to lodge a complaint is to make an official complaint

lodger *noun* (*plural* **lodgers**)
someone who pays to live in someone else's house

lodgings *plural noun*
a room or set of rooms that a person rents in someone else's house

loft *noun* (*plural* **lofts**)
the room or space under the roof of a house

lofty *adjective* (**loftier, loftiest**)
1 tall 2 noble and proud ♦ *They have lofty ideas*
loftily *adverb* in a lofty way

log¹ ➤ *noun* (*plural* **logs**)
1 a large piece of a tree that has fallen or been cut down 2 a detailed record kept of a voyage or flight

log ➤ *verb* (**logs, logging, logged**)
to log information is to put it in a log
to log in is to gain access to a computer
to log out is to finish using a computer

log² *noun* (*plural* **logs**)
a logarithm

logarithm *noun* (*plural* **logarithms**)
one of a series of numbers set out in tables, used to help you do arithmetic

logbook *noun* (*plural* **logbooks**)
1 a book in which a log of a voyage is kept
2 the registration document of a motor vehicle

logic *noun*
a system of thinking and working out ideas

logical *adjective*
using logic or worked out by logic
logically *adverb* in a logical way

logo *noun* (*plural* **logos**)
a printed symbol used by a business company or other organization as its emblem

loiter *verb* (**loiters, loitering, loitered**)
to loiter is to stand about with nothing to do
loiterer *noun* someone who loiters

loll *verb* (**lolls, lolling, lolled**)
to loll is to sit or lie in an untidy and lazy way

lollipop *noun* (*plural* **lollipops**)
a hard sticky sweet on the end of a stick

lollipop woman or **lollipop man** *noun*
(*plural* **lollipop women** or **lollipop men**)
an official who uses a circular sign on a stick to signal traffic to stop so that children can cross the road

lolly *noun* (*plural* **lollies**)
1 (*informal*) a lolly is a lollipop or an ice lolly 2 (*slang*) lolly is money

lone *adjective*
solitary ♦ *a lone rider*

lonely *adjective* (**lonelier, loneliest**)
1 unhappy because you are on your own 2 far from other inhabited places; not often used or visited ♦ *They passed through a lonely village*
loneliness *noun* being lonely

long[1] ➤ *adjective* (**longer, longest**)
1 big when measured from one end to the other ♦ *They walked up a long path* 2 taking a lot of time ♦ *I'd like a long holiday* 3 measuring from one end to the other ♦ *A cricket pitch is 22 yards long*

long[2] ➤ *adverb* (**longer, longest**)
1 for a long time ♦ *Have you been waiting long?* 2 a long time before or after ♦ *They left long ago*
as long as or **so long as** provided that; on condition that ♦ *I'll come as long as I can bring my dog*

long[2] *verb* (**longs, longing, longed**)
to long for something is to want it very much

long division *noun*
dividing one number by another and writing down all the calculations

longitude *noun* (*plural* **longitudes**)
(*pronounced* long-i-tewd or lon-ji-tewd)
the distance of a place east or west, measured in degrees from an imaginary

line that passes through Greenwich in London
longitudinal *adjective* to do with longitude

long jump *noun*
an athletic contest of jumping as far as possible along the ground with one leap

long-range *adjective*
covering a long distance or period of time

long-sighted *adjective*
able to see things clearly when they are at a distance but not when they are close

long-term *adjective*
to do with a long period of time

loo *noun* (*plural* **loos**)
(*informal*) a lavatory

look ➤ *verb* (**looks, looking, looked**)
1 to look is to use your eyes to see something, or to turn your eyes towards something 2 to look in a particular direction is to face it ♦ *Look right and left before you cross* 3 to look (for example) happy or sad is to appear that way
to look after something or **someone** is to protect them or take care of them
to look down on someone is to despise them
to look for something or **someone** is to try to find them
to look forward to something is to be waiting eagerly for it to happen
to look out is to be careful
to look up to someone is to admire or respect them

look ➤ *noun* (*plural* **looks**)
1 a look is the act of looking 2 the look of someone or something is their appearance, or what they seem to be

look-alike *noun* (*plural* **look-alikes**)
someone who looks very like a famous person

looking-glass *noun* (*plural* **looking-glasses**)
(*old use*) a glass mirror

lookout *noun* (*plural* **lookouts**)
1 a place from which you watch for
something **2** someone whose job is to keep
watch **3** watching or being watchful
♦ *Keep a lookout for snakes* **4** (*informal*) a
person's fault or concern ♦ *It's your
lookout if you get hurt* **5** what is likely to
happen ♦ *It's a poor lookout for us*

loom¹ *noun* (*plural* **looms**)
a machine for weaving cloth

loom² *verb* (**looms, looming, loomed**)
to loom or loom up is to appear large and
threatening ♦ *An iceberg loomed up
through the fog*

loop ➤ *noun* (*plural* **loops**)
the shape made by a curve crossing itself;
a piece of string, ribbon, or wire made into
this shape

loop ➤ *verb* (**loops, looping, looped**)
to loop something is to make it into a loop

loophole *noun* (*plural* **loopholes**)
1 a narrow opening **2** a way of getting
round a law or rule without quite breaking
it

loose ➤ *adjective* (**looser, loosest**)
1 not tight; not firm ♦ *a loose tooth* **2** not
tied up or shut in ♦ *The dog got loose*
at a loose end with nothing to do
loosely *adverb* in a loose way **looseness**
noun being loose

loose ➤ *verb* (**looses, loosing, loosed**)
to loose something is to make it less tight,
or to untie or release it

loose-leaf *adjective*
having a cover that allows pages to be put
in or taken out

loosen *verb* (**loosens, loosening, loosened**)
1 to loosen something is to make it loose
2 to loosen is to become loose

loot ➤ *noun*
stolen things

loot ➤ *verb* (**loots, looting, looted**)
to loot a place is to rob it violently,
especially in a time of war or disorder
looter *noun* someone who loots a place

lopsided *adjective*
with one side lower than the other; uneven

lord *noun* (*plural* **lords**)
1 a nobleman, especially one who is
allowed to use the title 'Lord' in front of his
name **2** (*old use*) a master or ruler
Our Lord a name used by Christians for
Jesus Christ
the Lord a name for God

lordly *adjective*
1 relating to a lord **2** proud; haughty

Lord Mayor *noun*
the mayor of a large city

lordship *noun*
a title for a lord or a man of high social
standing

lorry *noun* (*plural* **lorries**)
a large motor vehicle for carrying goods

lose *verb* (**loses, losing, lost**)
1 to lose something is to no longer have it,
especially because you cannot find it ♦ *I've
lost my hat* **2** to lose a contest or game is
to be beaten in it ♦ *We lost last Friday's
match* **3** a clock or watch loses when it
gives a time that is later than the correct
time
to be lost or **to lose your way** is not to know
where you are

loser *noun* someone who loses a game

loss *noun* (*plural* **losses**)
1 losing something **2** something you have
lost
at a loss puzzled; unable to do something

lot *noun* (*plural* **lots**)
1 a lot is a large number of people or
things **2** a lot is a piece of land **3** at an
auction, a lot is one item or group of items
for sale
to draw lots is to choose one person or thing
from a group by a method that depends on
chance
the lot or **the whole lot** everything

lotion *noun* (*plural* **lotions**)
a liquid that you put on your skin

lottery *noun* (*plural* **lotteries**)
a way of raising money by selling
numbered tickets and giving prizes to
people who have the winning tickets

lotto *noun*
a game like bingo

loud *adjective* (**louder, loudest**)
1 noisy; easily heard **2** bright or gaudy
♦ *The room was painted in loud colours*
loudly *adverb* in a loud way **loudness** *noun*
being loud

loudspeaker *noun* (*plural* **loudspeakers**)
a device that changes electrical impulses
into sound, for reproducing music or voices

lounge ➤ *noun* (*plural* **lounges**)
a sitting room

lounge ➤ *verb* (**lounges, lounging, lounged**)
to lounge is to sit or stand in a relaxed or
lazy way

louse *noun* (*plural* **lice**)
a small insect that sucks the blood of
animals or the juices of plants

lousy *adjective* (**lousier, lousiest**)
1 full of lice **2** (*slang*) very bad or
unpleasant

lout *noun* (*plural* **louts**)
a bad-mannered man

love ➤ *noun* (*plural* **loves**)
1 a feeling of liking someone or something very much; great affection or kindness
2 sexual feelings and great affection between two people 3 a person that you like very much 4 in games, a score of nothing
to be in love is to love another person very deeply
to make love is to have sexual intercourse

love ➤ *verb* (**loves, loving, loved**)
to love someone or something is to like them very much
lovable *adjective* easy to love **lovingly** *adverb* in a way that shows love

lovely *adjective* (**lovelier, loveliest**)
1 fine or beautiful 2 (*informal*) very pleasant or enjoyable
loveliness *noun* being lovely

lover *noun* (*plural* **lovers**)
1 someone who loves something ♦ *I am a lover of milk chocolate* 2 a person who is having a sexual affair with someone without being married to them

low[1] *adjective* (**lower, lowest**)
1 only reaching a short way up; not high
2 below average in amount or importance
♦ *They are people of a low rank* ♦ *Prices are low* 3 unhappy ♦ *I'm feeling low* 4 a low note is one at the bottom end of a musical scale
lowness *noun* being low

low[2] *verb* (**lows, lowing, lowed**)
to low is to make a sound like a cow

lower *verb* (**lowers, lowering, lowered**)
1 to lower something is to make it less, or less high 2 to lower is to become less, or less high

lowland *adjective*
to do with the lowlands

lowlands *plural noun*
low-lying country, especially the south of Scotland
lowlander *noun* someone who lives in the lowlands

lowly *adjective* (**lowlier, lowliest**)
humble
lowliness *noun* being lowly

loyal *adjective*
always true to your friends; faithful
loyally *adverb* in a loyal way **loyalty** *noun* being loyal

lozenge *noun* (*plural* **lozenges**)
1 a small sweet tablet, especially one that contains medicine 2 a diamond-shaped design

Ltd. in names of companies, short for **limited**

lubricant *noun* (*plural* **lubricants**)
oil or grease for lubricating machinery

lubricate *verb* (**lubricates, lubricating, lubricated**)
to lubricate something like machinery is to put oil or grease on it so that it moves smoothly
lubrication *noun* lubricating something

lucid *adjective* (*pronounced* loo-sid)
1 something is lucid when it is clear and easy to understand 2 someone is lucid when they are sane and can be understood
lucidity *noun* being lucid **lucidly** *adverb* in a lucid way

luck *noun*
1 the way things happen by chance, without being planned 2 good fortune

luckily *adverb*
by a lucky chance; fortunately ♦ *Luckily it stayed warm all day*

lucky *adjective* (**luckier, luckiest**)
having or bringing good luck

ludicrous *adjective* (*pronounced* loo-di-krus)
extremely silly or absurd
ludicrously *adverb* in a ludicrous way

ludo *noun*
a game played with dice and counters on a board

lug *verb* (**lugs, lugging, lugged**)
to lug something heavy is to carry it or drag it with difficulty

luggage *noun*
suitcases and bags taken on a journey

lukewarm *adjective*
1 slightly warm 2 not very keen or enthusiastic ♦ *They got a lukewarm response*

lull ➤ *verb* (**lulls, lulling, lulled**)
to lull someone is to soothe or calm them

lull ➤ *noun* (*plural* **lulls**)
a short period of quiet or rest

lullaby *noun* (*plural* **lullabies**)
a song that is sung to send a baby to sleep

lumber ➤ *noun*
junk or old unwanted furniture or other things

lumber ➤ *verb* (**lumbers, lumbering, lumbered**)
1 to lumber is to move along clumsily or noisily 2 (*informal*) to lumber someone is to leave them with something unpleasant or difficult to do

lumberjack *noun* (*plural* **lumberjacks**)
someone whose job is to cut down trees or transport them

luminous *adjective* (*pronounced* loo-mi-nus)
shining or glowing in the dark
luminosity *noun* being luminous

lump[1] ➤ *noun* (*plural* **lumps**)
1 a solid piece of something **2** a swelling
lumpy *adjective* having lots of lumps

lump ➤ *verb* (**lumps, lumping, lumped**)
to lump things together is to combine them
awkwardly or clumsily

lump[2] *verb* (**lumps, lumping, lumped**)
to lump it (*informal*) is to put up with
something you do not like ♦ *You'll have to
like it or lump it*

lunacy *noun* (*plural* **lunacies**) (*pronounced*
loo-na-si)
madness

lunar *adjective*
to do with the moon

lunar month *noun* (*plural* **lunar months**)
a period of four weeks between one new
moon and the next

lunatic *noun* (*plural* **lunatics**) (*pronounced*
loo-na-tik)
a mad person

lunch *noun* (*plural* **lunches**)
a meal eaten in the middle of the day

lung *noun* (*plural* **lungs**)
each of the two organs in the chest, used
for breathing

lunge *verb* (**lunges, lunging, lunged**)
to lunge is to thrust or move the body
forward suddenly

lupin *noun* (*plural* **lupins**)
a garden plant with tall spikes of flowers

lurch ➤ *verb* (**lurches, lurching, lurched**)
to lurch is to stagger or lean suddenly
♦ *The passengers lurched forward as the
bus stopped*

lurch ➤ *noun* (*plural* **lurches**)
a sudden staggering or leaning movement

lurch[2] *noun*
to leave someone in the lurch is to desert them
when they are in difficulty

lure *verb* (**lures, luring, lured**)
to lure a person or animal is to tempt them
into a trap or difficulty

lurk *verb* (**lurks, lurking, lurked**)
to lurk is to wait threateningly where you
cannot be seen

luscious *adjective* (*pronounced* lush-us)
tasting or smelling delicious

lush *adjective* (**lusher, lushest**)
1 growing abundantly **2** luxurious
lushly *adverb* in a lush way **lushness** *noun*
being lush

lust *noun* (*plural* **lusts**)
a powerful or greedy desire

lustful *adjective*
having a greedy desire for something

lustre *noun* (*plural* **lustres**) (*pronounced*
lus-ter)
brightness or brilliance
lustrous *adjective* having a lustre

lute *noun* (*plural* **lutes**)
a musical instrument rather like a guitar
but with a deeper and rounder body. It
was used a lot in the Middle Ages

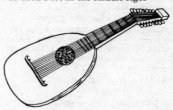

luxury *noun* (*plural* **luxuries**)
1 a luxury is something expensive that
you enjoy but do not really need **2** luxury
is having many such things ♦ *They led a
life of luxury*
luxurious *adjective* having a lot of luxury

Lycra *noun*
(*trademark*) a thin stretchy material used
especially for sports clothing

lying present participle of **lie**[1] *verb* and **lie**[2]
verb

lynch *verb* (**lynches, lynching, lynched**)
to lynch someone is to execute them
without a proper trial

lyre *noun* (*plural* **lyres**)
an ancient musical instrument like a
small harp

lyric *noun* (*plural* **lyrics**) (*pronounced* li-rik)
a short poem expressing feelings and
emotions

lyrical *adjective*
like a song

lyrics *plural noun*
the words of a popular song

Mm

m short for
  metre, metres, miles, or millions

ma *noun* (*plural* **mas**)
  (*informal*) mother

mac *noun* (*plural* **macs**)
  (*informal*) a mackintosh

macabre *adjective* (*pronounced* mak-**ahbr**)
  strange and horrible

macaroni *noun*
  pasta in the form of short tubes

machine *noun* (*plural* **machines**)
  a set of parts that work together to do a job

machine-gun *noun* (*plural* **machine-guns**)
  a gun that can keep firing bullets quickly
  one after another

machinery *noun*
  1 machinery is machines generally
  2 machinery is a mechanism ♦ *The lift's
  machinery is faulty* **3** machinery is also a
  system for doing something ♦ *They are
  studying the machinery of local
  government*

mackerel *noun* (*plural* **mackerel**)
  a sea fish used as food

mackintosh *noun* (*plural* **mackintoshes**)
  a raincoat

mad *adjective* (**madder, maddest**)
  1 having something wrong with your
  mind; not sane **2** very keen ♦ *She's mad
  about rock music* **3** (*informal*) very
  excited or annoyed
  like mad (*informal*) with great speed,
  energy, or enthusiasm
  madness *noun* being mad; insanity

madam *noun*
  a word sometimes used when speaking or
  writing politely to a woman, instead of her
  name ♦ *Can I help you, madam?*

mad cow disease *noun*
  a name for BSE

madden *verb* (**maddens, maddening, maddened**)
  to madden someone is to make them mad
  or angry

made past tense and past participle of
  make *verb*

madly *adverb*
  extremely; very much ♦ *They are madly in
  love*

madman *noun* (*plural* **madmen**)
  a man who is mad

magazine *noun* (*plural* **magazines**)
  1 a paper-covered publication with
  articles or stories, which comes out
  regularly **2** the part of a gun that holds
  the cartridges **3** a store for weapons and
  ammunition or for explosives **4** a device
  that holds film for a camera or slides for a
  projector

maggot *noun* (*plural* **maggots**)
  the larva of some kinds of fly

magic *noun*
  the power to do wonderful things or clever
  tricks that people cannot usually do

magical *adjective*
  1 done by magic or as if by magic
  2 wonderful; marvellous
  magically *adverb* in a magical way

magician *noun* (*plural* **magicians**)
  1 someone who does magic tricks **2** a
  wizard

magistrate *noun* (*plural* **magistrates**)
  a judge in a local court

magma *noun*
  a molten substance beneath the earth's
  crust

magnesium *noun*
  a silvery-white metal that burns with a
  very bright flame

magnet *noun* (*plural* **magnets**)
  a piece of metal that can attract iron or
  steel and that points north and south
  when it is hung in the air
  magnetism *noun* the attraction of a magnet

magnetic *adjective*
  having or using the powers of a magnet
  magnetically *adverb* by magnetism

magnetic tape *noun*
  a plastic strip coated with a magnetic
  substance for recording sound

magnetize *verb* (**magnetizes, magnetizing,
  magnetized**)
  1 to magnetize something is to make it
  into a magnet **2** to magnetize someone is
  to attract them or influence them very
  strongly ♦ *Jane magnetized the audience
  when she began to sing*

magnificent *adjective*
  1 looking grand or splendid **2** excellent
  ♦ *We had a magnificent meal*
  magnificence *noun* being magnificent
  magnificently *adverb* in a magnificent way

magnify *verb* (**magnifies, magnifying, magnified**)
to magnify something is to make it look bigger than it really is
magnification *noun* magnifying **magnifier** *noun* something that magnifies things

magnifying glass *noun* (*plural* **magnifying glasses**)
a lens that magnifies things

magnitude *noun* (*plural* **magnitudes**)
how large or important something is

magnolia *noun* (*plural* **magnolias**)
a tree with large white or pale pink flowers

magpie *noun* (*plural* **magpies**)
a black and white bird, related to the crow

mahogany *noun* (*pronounced* ma-hog-a-ni)
a hard brown wood

maid *noun* (*plural* **maids**)
1 a female servant **2** (*old use*) a girl

maiden ➤ *noun* (*plural* **maidens**)
(*old use*) a girl

maiden ➤ *adjective*
not married ♦ *He had a maiden aunt*

maiden name *noun* (*plural* **maiden names**)
a woman's family name before she gets married

maiden over *noun* (*plural* **maiden overs**)
a cricket over in which no runs are scored

maiden voyage *noun* (*plural* **maiden voyages**)
a ship's first voyage

mail[1] ➤ *noun*
letters and parcels sent by post

mail ➤ *verb* (**mails, mailing, mailed**)
to mail something is to send it by post

mail[2] *noun*
armour made of metal rings joined together

mail order *noun*
a system of buying goods through the post

maim *verb* (**maims, maiming, maimed**)
to maim someone is to injure them so that they are disabled

main ➤ *adjective*
largest or most important

main or **mains** ➤ *noun*
the main pipe or cable in a system carrying water, gas, or electricity to a building

main clause *noun* (*plural* **main clauses**)
a clause which can be used as a complete sentence

mainland *noun*
the main part of a country or continent, not the islands around it

mainly *adverb*
chiefly or usually; almost completely

maintain *verb* (**maintains, maintaining, maintained**)
1 to maintain something is to keep it in good condition **2** to maintain a belief is to have it or state it ♦ *I maintain that animals should not be hunted* **3** to maintain someone is to provide money for them

maintenance *noun*
1 maintaining or keeping something in good condition **2** money for food and clothing

maisonette *noun* (*plural* **maisonettes**)
a small flat or house

maize *noun*
a tall kind of corn with large seeds

majestic *adjective*
stately and dignified
majestically *adverb* in a majestic way

majesty *noun* (*plural* **majesties**)
1 being stately and dignified **2** the title of a king or queen

major ➤ *adjective*
1 more important; main ♦ *Use the major roads* **2** of the musical scale that has a semitone between the 3rd and 4th notes and between the 7th and 8th notes

major ➤ *noun* (*plural* **majors**)
an army officer above captain in rank

majority *noun* (*plural* **majorities**)
(*pronounced* ma-jo-ri-ti)
1 the greatest part of a group of people or things ♦ *The majority of the class wanted a quiz* **2** the amount by which the winner in an election beats the loser ♦ *She had a majority of 25 over her opponent* **3** the age at which a person becomes legally an adult, now usually 18

make ➤ *verb* (**makes, making, made**)
1 to make something is to build or produce it ♦ *They are making a raft out of logs* **2** to make someone or something do something is to cause it to happen ♦ *The bang made him jump* **3** to make money is to get it or earn it ♦ *She makes £10,000 a year* **4** in a game, to make a score is to achieve it ♦ *He has made 20 runs so far* **5** to make a certain point is to reach it ♦ *The swimmer just made the shore* **6** to make something is to estimate it or reckon it ♦ *What do you make the time?* **7** several numbers make a total when they add up to it ♦ *4 and 6 make 10* **8** to make an offer or promise is to give it to someone **9** to make a bed is to tidy it or arrange it for use
to make someone's day is to cause them to be happy or successful
to make do is to manage with something that is not what you really want
to make for a place is to go towards it
to make off is to leave quickly
to make something or **someone out** is to manage to see or hear or understand them
to make something up is to invent a false story or excuse
to make up is to be friendly again after a disagreement
to make up for something is to give or do something in return for a loss or difficulty
to make up your mind is to decide

make ➤ *noun* (*plural* **makes**)
1 how something is made **2** a brand of goods; something made by a particular firm ♦ *What make of car is that?*

make-believe *noun*
pretending or imagining things

maker *noun* (*plural* **makers**)
the person or firm that has made something

makeshift *adjective*
used because you have nothing better ♦ *We'll use the bed as a makeshift table*

make-up *noun*
1 substances for making your skin look beautiful or different **2** a person's character

maladjusted *adjective*
a person is maladjusted when they cannot cope with their life or with other people

malaria *noun* (*pronounced* ma-lair-i-a)
a feverish disease spread by mosquitoes

male ➤ *adjective*
of the sex that produces young by fertilizing the female's egg cells

male ➤ *noun* (*plural* **males**)
a male person or animal

male chauvinist *noun* (*plural* **male chauvinists**)
a man who believes that men are always better than women

malevolent *adjective* (*pronounced* ma-lev-o-lent)
wanting to harm other people
malevolence *noun* being malevolent
malevolently *adverb* in a malevolent way

malice *noun*
a desire to harm other people

malicious *adjective*
intending to do harm
maliciously *adverb* in a malicious way

mallet *noun* (*plural* **mallets**)
a large wooden hammer

malnutrition *noun*
bad health caused by not having enough food
malnourished *adjective* suffering from malnutrition

malt *noun*
dried barley used in brewing and making vinegar
malted *adjective* made with malt

mammal *noun* (*plural* **mammals**)
any animal of which the female gives birth to live young and can feed them with her own milk

mammoth ➤ *noun* (*plural* **mammoths**)
an extinct kind of hairy elephant with long curved tusks

mammoth ➤ *adjective*
huge

man ➤ *noun* (*plural* **men**)
1 a man is a grown-up male human being
2 a man is also any individual person
♦ *No man is perfect* 3 man is all the people in the world 4 a man is one of the pieces used in a board game

man ➤ *verb* (**mans, manning, manned**)
to man something is to supply people to work it ♦ *Man the pumps!*

manage *verb* (**manages, managing, managed**)
1 to manage something is to be able to do it although it is difficult 2 to manage a shop or factory or other business is to be in charge of it

manageable *adjective*
able to be managed or done

management *noun*
1 management is being in charge of something 2 the management of a business is the people in charge of it

manager *noun* (*plural* **managers**)
a person who manages a business or part of it

manageress *noun* (*plural* **manageresses**)
a woman manager of a shop or restaurant

mane *noun* (*plural* **manes**)
the long hair along the back of the neck of a horse or lion

manger *noun* (*plural* **mangers**) (*pronounced* **mayn**-jer)
a trough in a stable for animals to feed from

mangle *verb* (**mangles, mangling, mangled**)
to mangle something is to crush it or cut it up roughly

mango *noun* (*plural* **mangoes**)
a juicy tropical fruit with yellow pulp

manhandle *verb* (**manhandles, manhandling, manhandled**)
to manhandle someone or something is to handle them or move them roughly

manhole *noun* (*plural* **manholes**)
a hole, usually with a cover, through which a person can get into a sewer or boiler to inspect or repair it

mania *noun* (*plural* **manias**)
1 mania is violent madness 2 a mania is a strong enthusiasm ♦ *They have a mania for sport*

maniac *noun* (*plural* **maniacs**)
a person with mania

manic *adjective*
suffering from mania

manifesto *noun* (*plural* **manifestos**)
a public statement of a group's or person's policy or principles

manipulate *verb* (**manipulates, manipulating, manipulated**)
1 to manipulate something is to handle it skilfully 2 to manipulate someone is to get them to do what you want by treating them cleverly

manipulation *noun* manipulating something or someone **manipulator** *noun* a person who manipulates something or someone

mankind *noun*
all the people in the world

manly *adjective* (**manlier, manliest**)
1 strong or brave 2 suitable for a man
manliness *noun* being manly

manner *noun* (*plural* **manners**)
the way that something happens or is done

manners *plural noun*
how you behave with other people; behaving politely

manoeuvre ➤ *noun* (*plural* **manoeuvres**) (*pronounced* ma-**noo**-ver)
a skilful or clever action

manoeuvre ➤ *verb* (**manoeuvres, manoeuvring, manoeuvred**)
1 to manoeuvre is to move skilfully or cleverly 2 to manoeuvre something is to move it skilfully into position
manoeuvrable *adjective* easy to manoeuvre

man-of-war *noun* (*plural* **men-of-war**)
in earlier times, a warship

manor *noun* (*plural* **manors**)
a large important house in the country

mansion *noun* (*plural* **mansions**)
a large stately house

manslaughter *noun* (*pronounced* **man**-slaw-ter)
the crime of killing someone without meaning to

mantelpiece *noun* (*plural* **mantelpieces**)
a shelf above a fireplace

mantle *noun* (*plural* **mantles**)
1 (*old use*) a cloak 2 a covering ♦ *There was a mantle of snow on the hills*

manual ➤ *adjective*
done with the hands ♦ *He does manual work*
manually *adverb* with the hands

manual ➤ *noun* (*plural* **manuals**)
a handbook or book of instructions

manufacture ➤ *verb* (**manufactures, manufacturing, manufactured**)
to manufacture things is to make them with machines

manufacture ➤ *noun*
the process of making things with machines, especially in large quantities for sale

manufacturer *noun* a business that manufactures things

manure *noun*
animal dung added to the soil to make it more fertile

manuscript *noun* (*plural* **manuscripts**)
something written or typed but not printed

Manx *adjective*
to do with the Isle of Man

Manx cat *noun* (*plural* **Manx cats**)
a breed of cat without a tail

many ➤ *adjective* (**more, most**)
large in number ♦ *There were many people at the party*

many ➤ *noun*
a large number of people or things ♦ *Many were found*

Maori *noun* (*plural* **Maoris**) (*pronounced* mow-ri)
1 a member of the aboriginal people of New Zealand 2 their language

map ➤ *noun* (*plural* **maps**)
a diagram of part or all of the earth's surface, showing features such as towns, mountains, and rivers

to put someone on the map is to make them famous or important

map ➤ *verb* (**maps, mapping, mapped**)
to map an area is to make a map of it

to map something out is to arrange it or organize it

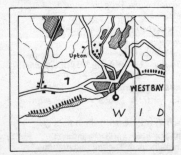

maple *noun* (*plural* **maples**)
a tree with broad leaves

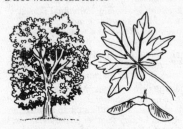

mar *verb* (**mars, marring, marred**)
to mar something is to spoil it

marathon *noun* (*plural* **marathons**)
a long-distance race for runners, usually 26 miles long

marauder *noun* (*plural* **marauders**)
someone who attacks a place and steals things from it

marauding *adjective* attacking and plundering

marble *noun* (*plural* **marbles**)
1 a marble is a small glass ball used in games 2 marble is a hard kind of limestone that is polished and used for building or sculpture

March *noun*
the third month of the year

march ➤ *verb* (**marches, marching, marched**)
1 to march is to walk with regular steps 2 to march someone is to make them walk somewhere ♦ *He marched them up the hill*

marcher *noun* someone who marches

march ➤ *noun* (*plural* **marches**)
1 a march is a movement or walk by marching 2 a march is also a piece of music suitable for marching to

mare *noun* (*plural* **mares**)
a female horse or donkey

margarine *noun* (*pronounced* mar-ja-reen)
a soft creamy substance used like butter, made from animal or vegetable fats

margin *noun* (*plural* **margins**)
1 the empty space between the edge of a page and the writing or pictures 2 the small difference between two scores or prices ♦ *She won by a narrow margin*

marginal *adjective*
very small or slight ♦ *The difference was marginal*

marginally *adverb* by a small amount

marigold *noun* (*plural* **marigolds**)
a yellow or orange garden flower

marijuana *noun* (*pronounced* ma-ri-hwahna)
a drug made from hemp

marina *noun* (*plural* **marinas**) (*pronounced* ma-ree-na)
a harbour for yachts and motor boats

marine ➤ *adjective* (*pronounced* ma-reen)
to do with the sea

marine ➤ *noun* (*plural* **marines**)
a soldier trained to serve on land and sea

mariner *noun* (*plural* **mariners**)
(*old use*) a sailor

marionette *noun* (*plural* **marionettes**)
a puppet worked by strings or wires

mark[1] ➤ *noun* (*plural* **marks**)
1 a spot, dot, line, or stain on something 2 a number or letter put on a piece of work to show how good it is 3 a distinguishing feature or sign of something ♦ *They kept a minute's silence as a mark of respect* 4 a target aimed at 5 the place from which you start a race

mark ➤ *verb* (**marks, marking, marked**)
1 to mark something is to put a mark on it 2 to mark a piece of work is to give it a number or letter to show how good it is 3 to mark something said is to take note of it ♦ *Mark my words!*

mark[2] *noun* (*plural* **marks**)
a German unit of money

market ➤ *noun* (*plural* **markets**)
1 a place where things are bought and sold, usually from stalls in the open air 2 a demand for goods ♦ *There is hardly any market for typewriters now*

market ➤ *verb* (**markets, marketing, marketed**)
to market a product is to put it on sale

marksman *noun* (*plural* **marksmen**)
an expert in shooting at a target
marksmanship *noun* the skill of a marksman

marmalade *noun*
jam made from oranges or lemons

maroon[1] *verb* (**maroons, marooning, marooned**)
to maroon someone is to abandon them in a place far away from other people

maroon[2] *adjective*
dark red

marquee *noun* (*plural* **marquees**) (*pronounced* mar-kee)
a large tent used for a party or exhibition

marriage *noun* (*plural* **marriages**)
1 marriage is the state of being married 2 a marriage is a wedding

marrow *noun* (*plural* **marrows**)
1 a marrow is a large green or yellow vegetable with a hard skin 2 marrow is the soft substance inside bones

marry *verb* (**marries, marrying, married**)
1 to marry someone is to become their husband or wife 2 to marry two people is to declare them to be husband and wife

marsh *noun* (*plural* **marshes**)
a low-lying area of very wet ground
marshy *adjective* like a marsh

marshal *noun* (*plural* **marshals**)
1 an official who supervises a contest or ceremony 2 a high-ranking officer ♦ *He is a Field Marshal* 3 a police official in the USA

marshmallow *noun* (*plural* **marshmallows**)
a soft spongy sweet

marsupial *noun* (*plural* **marsupials**) (*pronounced* mar-soo-pi-al)
an animal such as a kangaroo or wallaby. The female has a pouch for carrying her young

martial *adjective*
to do with war or fighting

martial arts *plural noun*
fighting sports such as karate and judo

martial law *noun*
government of a country by the army during a crisis

Martian *noun* (*plural* **Martians**)
in stories, a creature from the planet Mars

martin *noun* (*plural* **martins**)
a bird rather like a swallow

martyr *noun* (*plural* **martyrs**) (*pronounced* mar-ter)
someone who is killed or suffers because of their beliefs
martyrdom *noun* being a martyr

marvel ➤ *noun* (*plural* **marvels**)
a wonderful thing

marvel ➤ *verb* (**marvels, marvelling, marvelled**)
to marvel at something is to be filled with wonder or astonishment by it

marvellous *adjective*
wonderful
marvellously *adverb* in a marvellous way

Marxism *noun*
the Communist ideas of the German writer Karl Marx (1818–83)
Marxist *noun* a believer in Marxism

marzipan *noun*
a soft sweet food made from almonds and sugar

mascot *noun* (*plural* **mascots**)
a person, animal, or object that is believed to bring good luck

masculine *adjective*
1 to do with men or like men; suitable for men **2** in some languages, belonging to the class of words that includes words referring to men
masculinity *noun* being masculine

mash ➤ *verb* (**mashes, mashing, mashed**)
to mash something is to crush it into a soft mass

mash ➤ *noun*
(*informal*) mashed potatoes

mask ➤ *noun* (*plural* **masks**)
a covering worn over your face to disguise or protect it

mask ➤ *verb* (**masks, masking, masked**)
1 to mask your face is to cover it with a mask **2** to mask something is to hide it

Mason *noun* (*plural* **Masons**)
a member of a secret society called the Freemasons

mason *noun* (*plural* **masons**)
someone who builds or works with stone

masonry *noun*
the stone parts of a building

Mass *noun* (*plural* **Masses**)
the Communion service in a Roman Catholic church

mass ➤ *noun* (*plural* **masses**)
1 a large amount of something **2** a lump or heap **3** (*in Science*) the amount of matter in an object
the masses the ordinary people

mass ➤ *verb* (**masses, massing, massed**)
to mass is to collect into a mass ♦ *People were massing in the square*

massacre ➤ *verb* (**massacres, massacring, massacred**) (*pronounced* mas-a-ker)
to massacre people is to kill a large number of them

massacre ➤ *noun* (*plural* **massacres**)
the killing of a large number of people

massage ➤ *verb* (**massages, massaging, massaged**) (*pronounced* mas-ahzh)
to massage the body is to rub and press it to make it less stiff or less painful

massage ➤ *noun*
massaging the body

massive *adjective*
very big; large and heavy
massively *adverb* hugely

mass production *noun*
producing goods in large quantities

mast *noun* (*plural* **masts**)
a tall pole that holds up a ship's sails or a flag or aerial

master ➤ *noun* (*plural* **masters**)
1 a man who is in charge of something **2** a male teacher **3** someone who is very good at what they do, such as a great artist or composer **4** something from which copies are made
Master (*old use*) a title put before a boy's name

master ➤ *verb* (**masters, mastering, mastered**)
1 to master a subject or skill is to learn it completely **2** to master a fear or difficulty is to control it ♦ *She succeeded in mastering her fear of heights*

masterly *adjective*
very clever or skilful

mastermind *noun* (*plural* **masterminds**)
1 a very clever person **2** someone who organizes a scheme or crime

masterpiece *noun* (*plural* **masterpieces**)
1 an excellent piece of work **2** someone's best piece of work

mastery *noun*
complete control or knowledge of something ♦ *He has a complete mastery of French*

mat *noun* (*plural* **mats**)
1 a small piece of material that partly covers a floor **2** a small piece of material put on a table to protect the surface

matador *noun* (*plural* **matadors**)
someone who fights and kills the bull in a bullfight

match[1] *noun* (*plural* **matches**)
a small thin stick with a small amount of chemical at one end that gives a flame when rubbed on something rough

match[2] ➤ *noun* (*plural* **matches**)
1 a game or contest between two teams or players **2** one person or thing that is equal or similar to another **3** a marriage

match ➤ *verb* (**matches, matching, matched**)
1 to match another person or thing is to be equal to them **2** one thing matches another when it goes well with it **3** to match one person with another is to put them in competition

mate[1] ➤ *noun* (*plural* **mates**)
1 a friend or companion **2** one of a pair of animals that have come together to have offspring **3** one of the officers on a ship

mate ➤ *verb* (**mates, mating, mated**)
1 to mate is to come together so as to have offspring **2** to mate animals is to put them together so that they will have offspring

mate[2] *noun* (*plural* **mates**)
checkmate in chess

material *noun* (*plural* **materials**)
1 anything used for making something else **2** cloth or fabric

materialistic *adjective*
liking possessions, money, and comfort most of all

maternal *adjective*
to do with a mother; motherly
maternally *adverb* in a maternal way

maternity *noun*
having a baby; motherhood

mathematician *noun* (*plural* **mathematicians**) (*pronounced* math-em-a-**tish**-an)
an expert in mathematics

mathematics *noun*
the study of numbers, measurements, and shapes
mathematical *adjective* to do with mathematics

maths *noun*
(*informal*) mathematics

matinée *noun* (*plural* **matinées**) (*pronounced* mat-i-nay)
an afternoon performance at a theatre or cinema

matrimony *noun* (*pronounced* mat-ri-mo-ni)
marriage
matrimonial *adjective* to do with marriage

matrix *noun* (*plural* **matrices**)
(*in Mathematics*) a set of numbers or quantities arranged in rows and columns

matron *noun* (*plural* **matrons**)
1 an older married woman **2** a woman in charge of health in a school

matt *adjective*
not shiny ♦ *The wall was decorated with matt paint*

matted *adjective*
tangled

matter ➤ *noun* (*plural* **matters**)
1 something you need to think about or do ♦ *It is a serious matter* **2** a substance ♦ *Peat consists mainly of vegetable matter*
a matter of fact something true
no matter it is not important
what's the matter? what is wrong?

matter ➤ *verb* (**matters, mattering, mattered**)
to matter is to be important

matting *noun*
mats; rough material for covering a floor

mattress *noun* (*plural* **mattresses**)
a thick layer of soft or springy material covered in cloth and used on a bed

mature *adjective*
fully grown or developed; grown-up
maturity *noun* being mature

mauve *adjective* (*pronounced* mohv)
pale purple

maximum ➤ *noun* (*plural* **maxima**)
the greatest number or amount ♦ *The maximum is 10*

maximum ➤ *adjective*
greatest ♦ *The maximum speed is 60 miles per hour*

May *noun*
the fifth month of the year

may[1] *verb* (*past tense* **might**)
1 may means to be allowed to ♦ *May I have a sweet?* **2** may also means that something will possibly happen or has possibly happened ♦ *He may come tomorrow* ♦ *He might have missed the train*

may[2] *noun*
hawthorn blossom

maybe *adverb*
perhaps

May Day *noun*
the first day of May, often celebrated with sport and dancing

mayday *noun* (*plural* **maydays**)
an international radio signal calling for help

mayonnaise *noun* (*pronounced* may-on-**ayz**)
a creamy sauce made from eggs, oil, and vinegar, and used on salads

mayor *noun* (*plural* **mayors**)
the person in charge of the council in a town or city

mayoress *noun* (*plural* **mayoresses**)
a woman who is a mayor

maypole *noun* (*plural* **maypoles**)
a decorated pole round which people dance
on May Day

maze *noun* (*plural* **mazes**)
a complicated arrangement of paths or
lines to follow as a game or puzzle

me *pronoun*
a word used for *I*, usually when it is the
object of a sentence, or when it comes after
a preposition ♦ *She likes me* ♦ *She gave it
to me*

meadow *noun* (*plural* **meadows**)
a field of grass

meagre *adjective* (*pronounced* **meeg**-er)
very little; barely enough

meal[1] *noun* (*plural* **meals**)
a meal is the food eaten at one time, as at
breakfast or lunch or dinner

meal[2] *noun*
meal is grain coarsely ground to a powder

mean[1] *verb* (**means, meaning, meant**)
1 to mean something is to have that as its
explanation or equivalent, or to convey
that as its sense ♦ *'Maybe' means 'perhaps'*
2 to mean to do something is to intend to
do it ♦ *I meant to tell him, but I forgot*

mean[2] *adjective* (**meaner, meanest**)
1 not generous; selfish ♦ *What a mean
man* **2** unkind; spiteful ♦ *That was a
mean trick*
meanly *adverb* in a mean way **meanness**
noun being mean

mean[3] *adjective*
average ♦ *Work out the mean temperature*

meander *verb* (**meanders, meandering,
meandered**) (*pronounced* mee-**an**-der)
to meander is to wander about or take a
winding course or route

meaning *noun* (*plural* **meanings**)
what something means
meaningful *adjective* having a meaning
meaningless *adjective* having no meaning

means ➤ *noun*
a way of doing something; a method
by all means certainly
by means of something using something or
with something
by no means not at all

means ➤ *plural noun*
money or other resources for doing things

meantime *noun*
in the meantime meanwhile

meanwhile *adverb*
while something else is happening ♦ *I'll
finish my book; meanwhile, you can do
your homework*

measles *plural noun*
an infectious disease that causes small red
spots on the skin

measly *adjective* (**measlier, measliest**)
(*informal*) very small or poor ♦ *All I got
was a measly T-shirt*

measure ➤ *verb* (**measures, measuring,
measured**)
1 to measure something is to find out how
big it is **2** to measure (for example) six
feet is to be six feet long

measure ➤ *noun* (*plural* **measures**)
1 a unit used for measuring **2** a device
used for measuring **3** the size of
something **4** something done for a
particular purpose; a law or rule

measurement *noun*   (*plural* **measurements**)
1 a measurement is the size or length of
something **2** measurement is when you
measure something

meat *noun* (*plural* **meats**)
animal flesh used as food
meaty *adjective* full of meat

mechanic *noun* (*plural* **mechanics**)
someone who maintains and repairs
machinery

mechanical *adjective*
1 to do with machines **2** automatic; done
without thought
mechanically *adverb* with machines; in a
mechanical way

mechanics *noun*
1 the study of movement and force **2** the
study or use of machines

mechanism *noun* (*plural* **mechanisms**)
1 the moving parts of a machine **2** the
way a machine works

medal *noun* (*plural* **medals**)
a piece of metal shaped like a coin, star, or
cross, given to someone for bravery or for
achieving something

medallist *noun* (*plural* **medallists**)
a winner of a medal

meddle *verb* (**meddles, meddling, meddled**)
to meddle in something is to interfere in ▶

meddler *noun* someone who meddles
meddlesome *adjective* liking to meddle

media *plural noun* (*pronounced* **mee**-di-a)
the plural of **medium** *noun*
the media newspapers and radio and
television, which provide information
about current events to the public

median *noun* (*plural* **medians**)
(*in Mathematics*) the middle number in a
set of numbers that have been arranged in
order ♦ *The median of 2, 3, 5, 8, 9, 14, and
15 is 8*

medical *adjective*
to do with the treatment of disease
medically *adverb* by medical means

medicine *noun* (*plural* **medicines**)
1 a medicine is a substance, usually
swallowed, used to try to cure a disease
2 medicine is the treatment of disease
medicinal *adjective* to do with medicine

medieval *adjective* (*pronounced*
med-i-**ee**-val)
to do with the Middle Ages

mediocre *adjective* (*pronounced*
meed-i-**oh**-ker)
only fairly good
mediocrity *noun* being mediocre

meditate *verb* (**meditates, meditating, meditated**)
to meditate is to think deeply and
seriously
meditation *noun* meditating

Mediterranean *adjective* (*pronounced*
med-i-ter-**ay**-ni-an)
to do with the Mediterranean Sea, which
is between Europe and Africa, or the
countries round it

medium¹ *adjective*
average; of middle size

medium² *noun* (*plural* **media** or **mediums**)
1 a thing in which something exists,
moves, or is expressed ♦ *Air is the medium
in which sound travels* **2** someone who
claims to communicate with the dead

meek *adjective* (**meeker, meekest**)
quiet and obedient
meekly *adverb* in a meek way **meekness** *noun*
being meek

meet *verb* (**meets, meeting, met**)
1 to meet is to come together from
different places ♦ *We all met in London*
2 to meet someone is to come in contact
with them, especially for the first time or
by an arrangement ♦ *I met her at a party*
♦ *I'll meet you at the station* **3** to meet a
bill or cost is to be able to pay it ♦ *He is
finding it difficult to meet all his debts*

meeting *noun* (*plural* **meetings**)
a time when people come together for a
special purpose

megaphone *noun* (*plural* **megaphones**)
a funnel-shaped device for making
someone's voice sound louder

melancholy *adjective*
sad and gloomy

mellow *adjective* (**mellower, mellowest**)
having a soft rich sound or colour

melodious *adjective*
sounding sweet; pleasant to listen to

melodrama *noun* (*plural* **melodramas**)
a play full of excitement and emotion
melodramatic *adjective* exciting and
dramatic

melody *noun* (*plural* **melodies**)
a tune, especially a pleasing tune
melodic *adjective* having a pleasing melody

melon *noun* (*plural* **melons**)
a large juicy fruit with yellow or green
skin

melt *verb* (**melts, melting, melted**)
1 to melt something is to make it liquid by
heating **2** to melt is to become liquid by
heating **3** to melt, or to melt away, is to go
away or disappear slowly

member *noun* (*plural* **members**)
someone who belongs to a society or group
membership *noun* being a member

Member of Parliament *noun* (*plural* **Members
of Parliament**)
someone who has been elected by the
people of an area to speak for them in
Parliament

membrane *noun* (*plural* **membranes**)
a thin skin or covering

memoirs *plural noun*
a person's account of their own life and
experiences

memorable *adjective*
1 worth remembering ♦ *It was a
memorable holiday* **2** easy to remember
♦ *He has a memorable name*
memorably *adverb* in a memorable way

memorial *noun* (*plural* **memorials**)
something set up to remind people of a person or an event ♦ *They passed a war memorial in the High Street*

memorize *verb* (**memorizes, memorizing, memorized**)
to memorize something is to get it into your memory

memory *noun* (*plural* **memories**)
1 memory is the ability to remember things **2** a memory is something that you remember, usually something interesting or special **3** memory is also the part of a computer where information is stored
in memory of someone or **something** as a memorial to a person or an event

men plural of **man** *noun*

menace ➤ *verb* (**menaces, menacing, menaced**)
to menace someone is to threaten them with harm or danger

menace ➤ *noun* (*plural* **menaces**)
1 something menacing **2** an annoying person or thing

menagerie *noun* (*plural* **menageries**)
(*pronounced* min-aj-er-i)
a small zoo

mend *verb* (**mends, mending, mended**)
to mend something that is broken or damaged is to make it as good as it was before
on the mend getting better after an illness
mender *noun* someone who mends something

meningitis *noun* (*pronounced* men-in-jl-tiss)
a serious disease caused by a virus, in which the covering of the brain becomes inflamed.

menstruation *noun*
the natural flow of blood from a woman's womb, normally happening every 28 days
menstrual *adjective* to do with menstruation

-ment *suffix*
used to make nouns, as in *amusement* and *oddments*

mental *adjective*
1 to do with the mind **2** (*informal*) mad or crazy
mentally *adverb* with regard to the mind

mention ➤ *verb* (**mentions, mentioning, mentioned**)
to mention someone or something is to speak about them or refer to them

mention ➤ *noun* (*plural* **mentions**)
when someone or something is mentioned ♦ *Our school got a mention in the local paper*

menu *noun* (*plural* **menus**) (*pronounced* men-yoo)
1 a list of the food that is available in a restaurant or served at a meal **2** (*in Computing*) a list of possible actions, displayed on a screen, from which you choose what you want a computer to do

MEP short for *Member of the European Parliament*

mercenary ➤ *adjective*
working only for money or some other reward

mercenary ➤ *noun* (*plural* **mercenaries**)
a soldier hired to serve in a foreign country

merchandise *noun*
goods for buying or selling

merchant *noun* (*plural* **merchants**)
someone involved in trade

merchant navy *noun* (*plural* **merchant navies**)
the ships and sailors that carry goods for trade

merciful *adjective*
showing mercy
mercifully *adverb* in a merciful way

merciless *adjective*
showing no mercy; cruel
mercilessly *adverb* in a merciless way

mercury *noun*
a heavy silvery metal that is usually liquid, used in thermometers

mercy *noun* (*plural* **mercies**)
1 mercy is kindness or pity shown towards someone instead of harming them or punishing them **2** a mercy is something to be thankful for ♦ *Thank God for small mercies*

mere[1] *adjective*
not more than ♦ *He's a mere child*

mere[2] *noun* (*plural* **meres**)
(*poetical use*) a lake

merely *adverb*
only; simply ♦ *She was merely joking*

merge *verb* (**merges, merging, merged**)
1 to merge things is to combine or blend them **2** to merge is to be combined

merger *noun* (*plural* **mergers**)
making two businesses or companies into one

meridian *noun* (*plural* **meridians**)
(*pronounced* mer-rid-i-an)
a line on a map or globe from the North Pole to the South Pole

meringue *noun* (*plural* **meringues**)
(*pronounced* mer-rang)
a crisp cake made from the whites of eggs mixed with sugar and baked

merit ➤ *noun* (*plural* **merits**)
1 a merit is something that deserves praise **2** merit is being good or excellent

merit ➤ *verb* (**merits, meriting, merited**)
to merit something is to deserve
something good

mermaid *noun* (*plural* **mermaids**)
a mythical sea creature with a woman's
body and a fish's tail instead of legs

merry *adjective* (**merrier, merriest**)
happy and cheerful
merrily *adverb* in a merry way **merriment**
noun being merry

merry-go-round *noun* (*plural*
merry-go-rounds)
a large roundabout with horses and other
things to ride on

mesh *noun* (*plural* **meshes**)
1 mesh is material made like a net, or a
network **2** a mesh is one of the spaces in a
net, sieve, or other criss-cross structure

mess ➤ *noun* (*plural* **messes**)
1 an untidy or dirty condition or thing
2 a difficult or confused situation **3** a
place where soldiers or sailors eat their
meals
to make a mess of something is to do it very
badly

mess ➤ *verb* (**messes, messing, messed**)
to mess about is to behave stupidly or idly
to mess something up is to do it very badly

message *noun* (*plural* **messages**)
a question or piece of information sent
from one person to another

messenger *noun* (*plural* **messengers**)
someone who carries a message

Messiah *noun* (*pronounced* mi-sy-a)
1 the person that the Jews expect to come
as their saviour **2** Jesus Christ, who
Christians believe was their saviour

messy *adjective* (**messier, messiest**)
1 untidy or dirty **2** difficult or
complicated
messily *adverb* in a messy way **messiness**
noun being messy

met past tense and past participle of **meet**

metal *noun* (*plural* **metals**)
a hard substance that melts when it is
heated, such as gold, silver, copper, and
iron
metallic *adjective* made of metal; shining
like metal

metallurgy *noun* (*pronounced* mi-tal-er-ji)
1 the study of metals **2** the craft of
making and using metals
metallurgical *adjective* to do with metallurgy
metallurgist *noun* an expert in using metals

metamorphosis *noun* (*plural* **metamorphoses**)
a complete change made by some living
things, such as a caterpillar changing into
a butterfly

metaphor *noun* (*plural* **metaphors**)
(*pronounced* met-a-fer)
using words in a way that does not mean
exactly what they say, as in *the lion, the
king of beasts*, in which *king* is a metaphor
metaphorical *adjective* used as a metaphor
metaphorically *adverb* in a metaphorical way

meteor *noun* (*plural* **meteors**) (*pronounced*
meet-i-er)
a piece of rock or metal that moves
through space and burns up as it enters
the earth's atmosphere

meteoric *adjective*
very fast and sudden, like a meteor
♦ *They've had a meteoric rise to fame*

meteorite *noun* (*plural* **meteorites**)
(*pronounced* meet-i-er-ryt)
the remains of a meteor that has landed on
the earth

meteorology *noun* (*pronounced*
meet-i-er-ol-o-ji)
the study of the weather
meteorological *adjective* to do with
meteorology **meteorologist** *noun* an expert
on the weather

meter *noun* (*plural* **meters**)
a device for measuring something,
especially for measuring how much of
something has been used

methane *noun*
an inflammable gas produced when plants
rot away, found mainly in mines and
marshes

method *noun* (*plural* **methods**)
1 a method is a way of doing something
2 method is good organization or orderly
behaviour ♦ *There is method in everything
she does*

methodical *adjective* (*pronounced*
mi-thod-i-kal)
done carefully; well organized
methodically *adverb* in a methodical way

Methodist *noun* (*plural* **Methodists**)
someone who believes in Methodism, a
Christian religious movement started by
John and Charles Wesley in the 18th
century

meths *noun*
(*informal*) methylated spirit

methylated spirit or **spirits** *noun*
a liquid fuel made from alcohol

meticulous *adjective*
very careful and precise
meticulously *adverb* in a meticulous way

metre *noun* (*plural* **metres**) (*pronounced*
meet-er)
1 the main unit of length in the metric
system, equal to about $39\frac{1}{2}$ inches **2** a
particular type of rhythm in poetry

metric *adjective*
1 to do with the metric system 2 to do with metre in poetry

metrical *adjective*
written as poetry rather than prose

metric system *noun*
a measuring system based on decimal units (the metre, litre, and gram)

metronome *noun* (*plural* **metronomes**) (*pronounced* **met**-ro-nohm)
a device that makes a regular clicking noise to help you keep in time when practising music

mettle *noun*
to be on your mettle is to be ready to do your best

mew *verb* (mews, mewing, mewed)
to make a sound like a cat

miaow *verb* (miaows, miaowing, miaowed) (*pronounced* mee-**ow**)
to mew

mice plural of mouse

microbe *noun* (*plural* **microbes**) (*pronounced* **my**-krohb)
a tiny organism only visible with a microscope

microchip *noun* (*plural* **microchips**)
a very small piece of silicon working as an electric circuit

microcomputer *noun* (*plural* **microcomputers**)
a small computer that uses a microprocessor as its central processing unit

microfilm *noun* (*plural* **microfilms**)
film on which printing or writing is photographed in greatly reduced size

microphone *noun* (*plural* **microphones**)
an electrical device that picks up sound waves for amplifying, broadcasting, or recording

microprocessor *noun* (*plural* **microprocessors**)
a set of microchips that form the central processing unit of a computer

microscope *noun* (*plural* **microscopes**) (*pronounced* **my**-kro-skohp)
a device with lenses that make tiny objects appear larger

microscopic *adjective* (*pronounced* my-kro-**skop**-ik)
too small to be seen without a microscope; tiny

microwave ➤ *noun* (*plural* **microwaves**)
1 energy moving in very short waves 2 a microwave oven

microwave ➤ *verb* (microwaves, microwaving, microwaved)
to microwave food is to cook it in a microwave oven

microwave oven *noun* (*plural* **microwave ovens**)
a kind of oven which heats things by using energy in very short waves

mid *adjective*
in the middle of ♦ *The holiday is from mid-July to mid-August*

midday *noun*
the middle of the day; noon

middle ➤ *noun* (*plural* **middles**)
1 the place or part of something that is at the same distance from all its sides or edges or from both its ends 2 someone's waist

middle ➤ *adjective*
placed in the middle

middle-aged *adjective*
aged between about forty and sixty

Middle Ages *noun*
the period in history from about AD 1100 to 1500

middle class *noun* or **middle classes** *plural noun*
the class of people between the upper class and the working class, including business and professional people such as teachers, doctors, and lawyers
middle-class *adjective* belonging to the middle class

Middle East *noun*
the countries to the east of the Mediterranean Sea, from Egypt to Iran

middle school *noun* (*plural* middle schools)
a school for children aged from about
9 to 13

midge *noun* (*plural* midges)
a small insect like a gnat

midget *noun* (*plural* midgets)
an unusually short person

midland *adjective*
of the middle part of a country; of the
middle part of England

Midlands *plural noun*
the central part of England

midnight *noun*
twelve o'clock at night

midst *noun*
in the midst of something in the middle of it

midsummer *noun*
the middle of summer, about 21 June in
the northern hemisphere

midway *adverb*
halfway

midwife *noun* (*plural* midwives)
a person trained to look after a woman
who is giving birth to a baby
midwifery *noun* the job of a midwife

might[1] past tense of **may** *verb*

might[2] *noun*
great power or strength

mighty *adjective* (mightier, mightiest)
very strong or powerful
mightily *adverb* in a mighty way **mightiness**
noun being mighty

migraine *noun* (*plural* migraines)
(*pronounced* mee-grayn)
a severe kind of headache

migrant *noun* (*plural* migrants) (*pronounced*
my-grant)
a person or animal that goes to live in
another country

migrate *verb* (migrates, migrating, migrated)
(*pronounced* my-**grayt**)
1 to migrate is to go to live in another
country **2** birds migrate when they fly to a
warmer region for the winter
migration *noun* migrating to another
country **migratory** *adjective* that migrate
every year

mike *noun* (*plural* mikes)
(*informal*) a microphone

mild *adjective* (milder, mildest)
gentle; not harsh or severe
mildly *adverb* in a mild way **mildness** *noun*
being mild

mile *noun* (*plural* miles)
a measure of distance, equal to 1,760
yards or about 1·6 kilometres

mileage *noun* (*plural* mileages)
the number of miles travelled

milestone *noun* (*plural* milestones)
1 a stone of a kind that used to be placed
beside a road to mark the distance
between towns **2** an important event in
history or in a person's life

militant *adjective*
aggressive; eager to fight
militancy *noun* being militant

militarism *noun*
belief in the use of military strength and
methods
militaristic *adjective* using military strength

military *adjective*
to do with soldiers or the armed forces

milk ➤ *noun*
a white liquid that female mammals
produce in their bodies to feed to their
young

milk ➤ *verb* (milks, milking, milked)
to milk a cow or other animal is to get milk
from it

milkman *noun* (*plural* milkmen)
a man who delivers milk to people's houses

milk shake *noun* (*plural* milk shakes)
a frothy drink of milk mixed with a sweet
fruit flavouring

milk tooth *noun* (*plural* milk teeth)
one of the first set of teeth a child or
animal has, which are later replaced by
adult teeth

milky *adjective* (milkier, milkiest)
1 like milk; white **2** made with a lot of
milk

Milky Way *noun*
a faintly shining band of light from the
stars in our galaxy

mill ➤ *noun* (*plural* mills)
1 a building with machinery for grinding
corn to make flour **2** a factory for
processing materials, such as a paper mill
3 a grinding machine for coffee or pepper

mill ➤ *verb* (mills, milling, milled)
1 to mill something is to grind or crush it
in a mill **2** to mill or mill about is to move
in a confused crowd

millennium *noun* (*plural* millenniums)
a period of 1,000 years

miller *noun* (*plural* millers)
someone who runs a flour mill

millet *noun*
a kind of cereal with tiny seeds

milligram *noun* (*plural* milligrams)
one thousandth of a gram

millilitre *noun* (*plural* millilitres)
one thousandth of a litre

millimetre *noun* (*plural* millimetres)
one thousandth of a metre

million *noun* (*plural* **millions**)
a thousand thousands (1,000,000)
millionth *adjective* and *noun* 1,000,000th

millionaire *noun* (*plural* **millionaires**)
an extremely rich person

millstone *noun* (*plural* **millstones**)
a large heavy stone used in grinding corn
a millstone round someone's neck a heavy
burden or responsibility

milometer *noun* (*plural* **milometers**)
(*pronounced* my-lom-it-er)
a device for measuring how far a vehicle
has travelled

mime ➤ *verb* (**mimes, miming, mimed**)
to mime is to tell a story by using
movements of the body without speaking

mime ➤ *noun* (*plural* **mimes**)
acting by miming

mimic ➤ *verb* (**mimics, mimicking, mimicked**)
to mimic someone is to imitate them,
especially to amuse people
mimicry *noun* mimicking someone

mimic ➤ *noun* (*plural* **mimics**)
a person who mimics someone

minaret *noun* (*plural* **minarets**)
a tall tower on a mosque

mince ➤ *verb* (**minces, mincing, minced**)
to mince food is to cut it into very small
pieces
not to mince matters is to speak frankly or
bluntly
mincer *noun* a device for mincing food

mince ➤ *noun*
minced meat

mincemeat *noun*
a sweet mixture of currants, raisins, and
chopped fruit, used in pies

mince pie *noun* (*plural* **mince pies**)
a pie containing mincemeat

mind ➤ *noun* (*plural* **minds**)
the function of the brain to think, feel,
understand, and remember; your thoughts
and feelings
to change your mind is to have a new opinion
or intention about something
to have a good mind to do something is to intend
to do it

mind ➤ *verb* (**minds, minding, minded**)
1 to mind someone or something is to look
after them for a time ♦ *He was minding
the baby* 2 to mind, or to mind out, is to be
careful or watch out for something ♦ *Mind
the doors!* 3 to mind something is to be
sad or upset about it ♦ *I don't mind
missing the party*

mindless *adjective*
done without thinking; stupid or pointless

mine [1] *adjective* and *pronoun*
belonging to me ♦ *That book is mine*

mine [2] ➤ *noun* (*plural* **mines**)
1 a place where coal, metal, or precious
stones are dug out of the ground 2 an
explosive hidden under the ground or in
the sea to destroy people and things that
come close to it

mine ➤ *verb* (**mines, mining, mined**)
1 to mine something is to dig it from a
mine 2 to mine a place is to lay explosives
in it

minefield *noun* (*plural* **minefields**)
1 an area where explosive mines have
been laid 2 an activity or place that has
many dangers

miner *noun* (*plural* **miners**)
someone who works in a mine

mineral *noun* (*plural* **minerals**)
1 a hard substance that can be dug out of
the ground, such as coal and iron ore 2 a
cold fizzy drink

mingle *verb* (**mingles, mingling, mingled**)
1 to mingle is to mix or blend 2 to mingle
things is to mix or blend them

mingy *adjective* (**mingier, mingiest**)
(*pronounced* min-ji)
(*informal*) mean or stingy

miniature *adjective* (*pronounced* min-i-cher)
very small, especially copying something
larger ♦ *A piccolo looks like a miniature
flute*

minibus *noun* (*plural* **minibuses**)
a small bus with seats for about ten people

minim *noun* (*plural* **minims**)
a musical note equal to two crotchets or
half a semibreve, written ♩

minimal *adjective*
very little; as little as possible

minimize *verb* (minimizes, minimizing, minimized)
to minimize something is to make it as small as possible

minimum ➤ *noun* (*plural* minima)
the smallest number or amount ♦ *We want the minimum of fuss*

minimum ➤ *adjective*
least or smallest ♦ *The minimum number is 3*

minister *noun* (*plural* ministers)
1 a member of the government who is in charge of a department **2** a member of the clergy

ministry *noun* (*plural* ministries)
1 a government department **2** the work of a minister in the church

mink *noun* (*plural* minks)
1 a small animal rather like a stoat
2 this animal's valuable brown fur

minnow *noun* (*plural* minnows)
a tiny freshwater fish

minor *adjective*
1 not very important, especially when compared to something else **2** of the musical scale that has a semitone between the 2nd and 3rd notes

minority *noun* (*plural* minorities) (*pronounced* myn-o-ri-ti)
1 the smaller part of a group of people or things ♦ *There was a minority who wanted to leave* **2** a small group that is different from others

minstrel *noun* (*plural* minstrels)
a travelling singer and musician in the Middle Ages

mint [1] *noun*
1 mint is a green plant with sweet-smelling leaves used for flavouring
2 a mint is a sweet flavoured with peppermint

mint [2] ➤ *noun* (*plural* mints)
a place where a country's coins are made
in mint condition new, as if it had just been made

mint ➤ *verb* (mints, minting, minted)
to mint coins is to make them

minus *preposition*
1 less; with the next number taken away
♦ *Eight minus two equals six* $(8-2=6)$
2 less than zero ♦ *The temperature is minus 5 degrees*

minute [1] *noun* (*plural* minutes) (*pronounced* min-it)
1 one-sixtieth of an hour **2** (*informal*) a short time ♦ *I'll be ready in a minute!*

minute [2] *adjective* (*pronounced* my-newt)
1 tiny ♦ *The insect was minute* **2** very detailed ♦ *He gave it a minute examination*
minutely *adverb* in a minute or detailed way

miracle *noun* (*plural* miracles)
a wonderful or magical happening that is unexpected
miraculous *adjective* wonderful or magical
miraculously *adverb* in a miraculous way

mirage *noun* (*plural* mirages) (*pronounced* mi-rahzh)
something that seems to be visible but is not really there, like a lake in a desert

mirror *noun* (*plural* mirrors)
a glass or metal device or surface that reflects things clearly

mirth *noun*
laughter or cheerfulness

mis- *prefix*
meaning 'wrong, wrongly', as in *misbehave* and *misunderstanding*

misbehave *verb* (misbehaves, misbehaving, misbehaved)
to behave badly
misbehaviour *noun* misbehaving

miscarriage *noun* (*plural* miscarriages)
the birth of a baby before it is old enough to survive

miscellaneous *adjective* (*pronounced* mis-el-ay-ni-us)
of various kinds; mixed

miscellany *noun* (*plural* miscellanies) (*pronounced* mis-el-an-ee)
a mixture of different things

mischief *noun*
naughty or troublesome behaviour
mischievous *adjective* naughty or troublesome

miser *noun* (*plural* misers)
someone who stores money away and spends as little as they can
miserly *adjective* like a miser

miserable *adjective*
1 unhappy or wretched ♦ *He felt miserable* **2** unpleasant ♦ *What miserable weather!*
miserably *adverb* in a miserable way

misery *noun* (*plural* miseries)
1 misery is great unhappiness or suffering
2 (*informal*) a misery is someone who is always unhappy or complaining

misfire *verb* (misfires, misfiring, misfired)
1 a gun misfires when it fails to fire **2** a plan or idea or joke misfires when it goes wrong

misfit *noun* (*plural* misfits)
someone who does not fit in well with other people

misfortune *noun* (*plural* **misfortunes**)
1 a misfortune is an unlucky event or an accident 2 misfortune is bad luck

mishap *noun* (*plural* **mishaps**) (*pronounced* mis-hap)
an unfortunate accident

misjudge *verb* (**misjudges, misjudging, misjudged**)
to misjudge someone or something is to form a wrong idea or opinion about them

mislay *verb* (**mislays, mislaying, mislaid**)
to mislay something is to lose it for a short time

mislead *verb* (**misleads, misleading, misled**)
to mislead someone is to give them a wrong idea or impression deliberately

misprint *noun* (*plural* **misprints**)
a mistake in printing

Miss *noun* (*plural* **Misses**)
a title put before the name of a girl or unmarried woman

miss ➤ *verb* (**misses, missing, missed**)
1 to miss something is to fail to hit, reach, catch, see, hear, or find it 2 to miss someone or something is to be sad because they are not with you ♦ *I missed my sister when she was in hospital* 3 to miss something is also to notice that it has gone ♦ *When I got home I missed my gloves*

miss ➤ *noun* (*plural* **misses**)
not hitting, reaching, or catching something ♦ *Was that shot a hit or a miss?*

missile *noun* (*plural* **missiles**)
a weapon fired or thrown at a target

missing *adjective*
lost, or not in the proper place

mission *noun* (*plural* **missions**)
1 an important job that someone is sent to do or that someone feels they must do 2 a place or building where missionaries work

missionary *noun* (*plural* **missionaries**)
someone who goes to another country to spread a religious faith

misspell *verb* (**misspells, misspelling, misspelt or misspelled**)
to misspell a word is to spell it wrongly

mist *noun* (*plural* **mists**)
1 damp cloudy air like a thin fog 2 condensed water vapour on a window or mirror

mistake ➤ *noun* (*plural* **mistakes**)
something done or said wrongly

mistake ➤ *verb* (**mistakes, mistaking, mistook, mistaken**)
1 to mistake something is to misunderstand it 2 to mistake one person or thing for another is to confuse them

mistaken *adjective*
incorrect; wrong ♦ *You are mistaken if you believe that*

mistakenly *adverb* incorrectly; wrongly

mister *noun*
1 Mr 2 (*informal*) sir ♦ *Can you tell me the time, mister?*

mistletoe *noun*
a plant with green leaves and white berries in winter

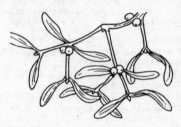

mistreat *verb* (**mistreats, mistreating, mistreated**)
to mistreat someone is to treat them badly or unfairly

mistreatment *noun* mistreating someone

mistress *noun* (*plural* **mistresses**)
1 a woman who is in charge of something 2 a woman who teaches in a school 3 the woman owner of a dog or other animal 4 a woman who is a man's lover, although he is married to someone else

mistrust *verb* (**mistrusts, mistrusting, mistrusted**)
to mistrust someone or something is not to trust them

misty *adjective* (**mistier, mistiest**)
1 full of mist 2 not clear

mistily *adverb* in a misty way **mistiness** *noun* being misty

misunderstand *verb* (**misunderstands, misunderstanding, misunderstood**)
to misunderstand something is to get a wrong idea or impression about it ♦ *You misunderstood what I said*

misunderstanding *noun* a wrong idea or impression

misuse ➤ *verb* (**misuses, misusing, misused**) (*pronounced* mis-**yooz**)
to misuse something is to use it wrongly or treat it badly

misuse ➤ *noun* (*pronounced* mis-**yooss**)
misusing something

mite *noun* (*plural* **mites**)
1 a tiny insect found in food 2 a small child

mitre *noun* (*plural* **mitres**) (*pronounced* **my**-ter)
1 the tall tapering hat worn by a bishop
2 a joint of two tapering pieces of wood or cloth, forming a right angle

mitten *noun* (*plural* **mittens**)
a kind of glove without separate parts for the fingers

mix *verb* (**mixes, mixing, mixed**)
1 to mix different things is to stir or shake them together to make one thing 2 to mix is to get on well with other people ♦ *She mixes well*
to mix up people or things is to confuse them
mixer *noun* a machine for mixing food

mixed *adjective*
containing two or more kinds of things or people

mixture *noun* (*plural* **mixtures**)
something made of different things mixed together

mix-up *noun* (*plural* **mix-ups**)
a muddle or confused situation, especially one that ruins a plan

mm short for **millimetre** or **millimetres**

moan ➤ *noun* (*plural* **moans**)
1 a long low sound, usually of suffering
2 a grumble

moan ➤ *verb* (**moans, moaning, moaned**)
1 to moan is to make a long low sound
2 to moan is also to grumble

moat *noun* (*plural* **moats**)
a deep ditch round a castle, usually filled with water

mob ➤ *noun* (*plural* **mobs**)
1 a large disorderly crowd of people 2 a gang

mob ➤ *verb* (**mobs, mobbing, mobbed**)
to mob someone is to crowd round them

mobile ➤ *adjective*
able to be moved or carried about easily
mobility *noun* being mobile

mobile ➤ *noun* (*plural* **mobiles**)
1 a decoration made to be hung up so that it moves about in the air 2 (*informal*) a mobile telephone

mobilize *verb* (**mobilizes, mobilizing, mobilized**)
to mobilize people or things is to get them ready for a particular purpose, especially for war
mobilization *noun* mobilizing people

moccasin *noun* (*plural* **moccasins**)
(*pronounced* **mok**-a-sin)
a soft leather shoe like those worn by Native Americans

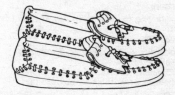

mock ➤ *adjective*
not real; imitation ♦ *The cakes had mock cream in them*

mock ➤ *verb* (**mocks, mocking, mocked**)
to mock someone or something is to make fun of them
mockery *noun* mocking people or things

mock-up *noun* (*plural* **mock-ups**)
a model of something, especially to study it or test it

mode *noun* (*plural* **modes**)
1 the way that something is done ♦ *Flying is the fastest mode of transport* 2 what is fashionable 3 (*in Mathematics*) the value that occurs most often in a set of values ♦ *The mode of 6, 5, 4, 4, 5, 4 and 3 is 4*

model ➤ *noun* (*plural* **models**)
1 a small copy of an object ♦ *He makes models of aircraft* 2 a particular version or design of something ♦ *We saw the new models at the motor show* 3 someone who poses for an artist or photographer or displays clothes by wearing them
4 someone or something worth copying or imitating

model ➤ *adjective*
1 miniature ♦ *I'd like a model railway*
2 being a good example for people to follow ♦ *She was a model pupil*

model ➤ *verb* (**models, modelling, modelled**)
1 to model something is to make a small copy of it 2 to model one thing on another is to use the second thing as a pattern for the first ♦ *The building is modelled on an Egyptian temple* 3 to model, or to model clothes, is to work as an artist's model or a fashion model

modem *noun* (*plural* **modems**)
(*in Computing*) a device that links a computer to a telephone line

moderate ➤ *adjective* (*pronounced* **mod**-er-at)
not too little and not too much; medium
moderately *adverb* in a moderate way
moderation *noun* being moderate

moderate ➤ *verb* (**moderates, moderating, moderated**) (*pronounced* **mod-er-ayt**)
to moderate something is to make it less strong or severe

modern *adjective*
belonging to the present day or recent times

modernity *noun* being modern

modernize *verb* (**modernizes, modernizing, modernized**)
to modernize something is to make it modern, or suitable for modern tastes

modernization *noun* making things modern

modest *adjective*
1 not thinking too much of how good you are 2 moderate ♦ *Their needs were modest*

modestly *adverb* in a modest way **modesty** *noun* being modest

modify *verb* (**modifies, modifying, modified**)
to modify something is to change it slightly

modification *noun* modifying something

module *noun* (*plural* **modules**) (*pronounced* **mod-yool**)
1 an independent part of a spacecraft or building 2 a part of a course of learning ♦ *This term I'm doing a Maths module* 3 a unit used in measuring

moist *adjective*
damp

moisture *noun* dampness

moisten *verb* (**moistens, moistening, moistened**) (*pronounced* **moi-sen**)
1 to moisten something is to make it moist 2 to moisten is to become moist

molar *noun* (*plural* **molars**) (*pronounced* **moh-ler**)
one of the wide teeth at the back of the mouth

mole *noun* (*plural* **moles**)
1 a small furry animal that digs holes under the ground 2 a small dark spot on the skin

molecule *noun* (*plural* **molecules**) (*pronounced* **mol-i-kewl**)
1 a very small particle of matter 2 (*in Science*) the smallest part into which a substance can be divided without changing its chemical nature; a group of atoms

molecular *adjective* to do with molecules

molehill *noun* (*plural* **molehills**)
a small pile of earth thrown up by a mole

to make a mountain out of a molehill is to give something too much importance

molest *verb* (**molests, molesting, molested**)
1 to molest someone is to annoy or pester them in an unfriendly or violent way 2 to molest someone is also to abuse them sexually

mollusc *noun* (*plural* **molluscs**)
an animal with a soft body and usually a hard shell, such as a snail or an oyster

molten *adjective*
melted; made into liquid by great heat

moment *noun* (*plural* **moments**)
1 a very short period of time ♦ *Wait a moment* 2 a particular time ♦ *He arrived at the last moment*

at the moment now

momentary *adjective* (*pronounced* **moh-men-ter-i**)
lasting for only a moment

momentarily *adverb* for only a moment

momentous *adjective* (*pronounced* **moh-ment-us**)
very important

momentum *noun* (*pronounced* **moh-ment-um**)
the amount or force of movement ♦ *The stone gained momentum as it rolled down the hill*

monarch *noun* (*plural* **monarchs**)
a king, queen, emperor, or empress ruling a country

monarchy *noun* (*plural* **monarchies**)
1 rule by a monarch 2 a country ruled by a monarch

monastery *noun* (*plural* **monasteries**) (*pronounced* **mon-a-ster-i**)
a building where monks live and work

monastic *adjective* to do with a monastery

Monday *noun* (*plural* **Mondays**)
the second day of the week

money *noun*
coins and notes used by people to buy things

mongoose *noun* (*plural* mongooses)
a small animal like a large weasel, that
can kill snakes

mongrel *noun* (*plural* mongrels)
(*pronounced* mung-rel)
a dog of mixed breeds

monitor ➤ *noun* (*plural* monitors)
1 a device used for checking how
something is working **2** (*in Computing*) a
computer or television screen **3** a pupil
who is given a special job to do at school

monitor ➤ *verb* (**monitors, monitoring,
monitored**)
to monitor something or someone is to
watch or test them to see how they are
working

monk *noun* (*plural* monks)
a member of a religious community of men

monkey *noun* (*plural* monkeys)
1 an animal with long arms, hands with
thumbs, and a tail **2** a mischievous
person, especially a child

mono- *prefix*
meaning 'having one of something', as in
monorail

monogram *noun* (*plural* monograms)
a design made up of a letter or a group of
letters

monologue *noun* (*plural* monologues)
(*pronounced* mon-o-log)
a long speech by one person or performer

monopolize *verb* (**monopolizes, monopolizing,
monopolized**)
to monopolize something is to have
complete control of it and keep out
everyone else

monopoly *noun* (*plural* monopolies)
control of a business or activity by one
person or group

monorail *noun* (*plural* monorails)
a railway that runs on a single rail

monotonous *adjective* (*pronounced*
mon-ot-on-us)
boring because it does not change ♦ *This is
monotonous work*
monotonously *adverb* in a monotonous way
monotony *noun* being monotonous

monsoon *noun* (*plural* monsoons)
a strong wind in and around the Indian
Ocean, bringing heavy rain in summer

monster ➤ *noun* (*plural* monsters)
a huge frightening creature

monster ➤ *adjective*
(*informal*) huge

monstrous *adjective*
1 like a monster; huge **2** very shocking or
cruel ♦ *It was a monstrous crime*
monstrosity *noun* a monstrous thing

month *noun* (*plural* months)
one of the twelve parts into which a year is
divided

monthly *adjective* and *adverb*
every month

monument *noun* (*plural* monuments)
a statue, building, or column put up as a
memorial of some person or event

monumental *adjective*
1 built as a monument **2** great or huge
♦ *It was a monumental achievement*

moo *verb* (**moos, mooing, mooed**)
to make the sound of a cow

mood *noun* (*plural* moods)
the way someone feels ♦ *She is in a
cheerful mood*

moody *adjective* (**moodier, moodiest**)
1 gloomy **2** likely to have sudden changes
of mood
moodily *adverb* in a moody way **moodiness**
noun being moody

moon *noun* (*plural* moons)
1 the natural satellite which orbits the
earth and shines in the sky at night **2** a
similar object which orbits another planet

moonlight *noun*
the light reflected from the moon
moonlit *adjective* lit by the moonlight

moor [1] *noun* (*plural* moors)
an area of rough land covered with
bracken and bushes

moor [2] *verb* (**moors, mooring, moored**)
to moor a boat or other thing in the water
is to tie it up or secure it

moorhen *noun* (*plural* moorhens)
a small water bird

mooring *noun* (*plural* moorings)
a place where a boat can be moored

moose *noun* (*plural* **moose**)
a North American elk

mop ➤ *noun* (*plural* **mops**)
a piece of soft material on the end of a
stick, used for cleaning floors or dishes

mop ➤ *verb* (**mops, mopping, mopped**)
to mop something is to clean it with a mop
to mop something up is to clear away spilt
liquid

mope *verb* (**mopes, moping, moped**)
to mope is to be sad and moody

moped *noun* (*plural* **mopeds**) (*pronounced*
moh-ped)
a kind of small motorcycle with pedals

moraine *noun* (*plural* **moraines**)
a mass of stones and earth carried down
by a glacier

moral ➤ *adjective*
1 to do with people's behaviour and what
is right and wrong **2** being or doing good
♦ *We are expected to lead moral lives*
morality *noun* moral behaviour or standards
morally *adverb* in a moral way

moral ➤ *noun* (*plural* **morals**)
a lesson taught by a story or event

morale *noun* (*pronounced* mo-**rahl**)
confidence or courage

morals *plural noun*
standards of behaviour

morbid *adjective*
thinking about gloomy or unpleasant
things
morbidly *adverb* in a morbid way

more ➤ *adjective*
greater in number or amount ♦ *We need
more money* ♦ *She is more beautiful*

more ➤ *noun*
a larger number or amount ♦ *I want more*

more ➤ *adverb*
1 to a greater extent ♦ *You must work
more* **2** again ♦ *I'll tell you once more*
more or less almost; approximately ♦ *I've
more or less finished the work* ♦ *The
repairs cost £100, more or less*

moreover *adverb*
also; in addition to what has been said

Mormon *noun* (*plural* **Mormons**)
a member of a religious group founded in
the USA

morning *noun* (*plural* **mornings**)
the early part of the day before noon or
before lunchtime

moron *noun* (*plural* **morons**)
(*informal*) a stupid person
moronic *adjective* stupid

morose *adjective*
bad-tempered and miserable

morphine *noun* (*pronounced* mor-feen)
a drug made from opium, used to relieve
pain

morris dance *noun* (*plural* **morris dances**)
a traditional English dance performed by
people in costume with ribbons and bells

Morse code *noun*
a code for sending radio signals, using dots
and dashes to represent letters and
numbers

morsel *noun* (*plural* **morsels**)
a small piece of food

mortal *adjective*
1 certain to die ♦ *All men are mortal*
2 causing death ♦ *He received a mortal
wound*
mortally *adverb* fatally; so as to cause death

mortality *noun*
1 the number of people who die over a
period of time ♦ *There is a low rate of
infant mortality* **2** being mortal

mortar *noun*
1 a mixture of sand, cement, and water
used in building to stick bricks together
2 a small thick bowl for pounding food
with a tool called a pestle **3** a small
cannon

mortgage *noun* (*plural* **mortgages**)
(*pronounced* mor-gij)
an arrangement to borrow money to buy a
house, repaid over many years

mortuary *noun* (*plural* **mortuaries**)
a place where dead bodies are kept before
they are buried or cremated

mosaic *noun* (*plural* **mosaics**) (*pronounced*
moh-**zay**-ik)
a picture or design made from small
coloured pieces of glass or stone

mosque *noun* (*plural* **mosques**)
(*pronounced* mosk)
a building where Muslims worship

mosquito *noun* (*plural* **mosquitoes**)
(*pronounced* mos-**kee**-toh)
an insect that sucks blood and carries
disease

moss *noun* (*plural* **mosses**)
a plant that grows in damp places and has
no flowers

mossy *adjective* covered in moss; soft like
moss

most ➤ *adjective*
greatest in number or amount ♦ *Most
people came by bus*

most ➤ *noun*
the greatest number or amount ♦ *They've
eaten most of the food*

most ➤ *adverb*
1 more than any other ♦ *I liked this book
most* **2** very; extremely ♦ *It was most
amusing*

mostly *adverb*
mainly

MOT or **MOT test** *noun* (*plural* **MOTs** or **MOT
tests**)
a safety check that has to be made every
year on road vehicles

motel *noun* (*plural* **motels**) (*pronounced*
moh-**tel**)
a hotel near a main road, with parking and
rooms for motorists

moth *noun* (*plural* **moths**)
an insect rather like a butterfly, that
usually flies around at night

mother *noun* (*plural* **mothers**)
a female parent

motherhood *noun*
being a mother and looking after children

mother-in-law *noun* (*plural* **mothers-in-law**)
the mother of your husband or wife

motherly *adjective*
kind or tender like a mother

motion *noun* (*plural* **motions**)
a way of moving; movement
to go through the motions is to do or say
something because you have to, without
much interest
motionless *adjective* not moving; still

motivate *verb* (**motivates, motivating, motivated**)
to motivate someone is to make them keen
to achieve something ♦ *She is good at
motivating her team*

motive *noun* (*plural* **motives**)
what makes a person do something

motor *noun* (*plural* **motors**)
a machine that provides power to drive
machinery

motorbike *noun* (*plural* **motorbikes**)
(*informal*) a motorcycle

motor boat *noun* (*plural* **motor boats**)
a boat driven by a motor

motor car *noun* (*plural* **motor cars**)
a motor vehicle able to carry several
people inside it

motorcycle *noun* (*plural* **motorcycles**)
a motor vehicle with two wheels and a
saddle for the riders

motorcyclist *noun* someone who rides a
motorcycle

motorist *noun* (*plural* **motorists**)
someone who drives a motor car

motor vehicle *noun* (*plural* **motor vehicles**)
a vehicle driven by a motor, for use on
roads

motorway *noun* (*plural* **motorways**)
a wide road for fast long-distance traffic

mottled *adjective*
marked with spots or patches of colour

motto *noun* (*plural* **mottoes**)
1 a short saying used as a guide for behaviour ♦ *His motto was 'Do your best'*
2 a short verse or riddle found inside a cracker

mould[1] ➤ *noun* (*plural* **moulds**)
a mould is a container for making things like jelly or plaster set in a special shape

mould ➤ *verb* (**moulds, moulding, moulded**)
to mould something is to make it have a particular shape or character

mould[2] *noun* (*plural* **moulds**)
mould is a furry growth that appears on some moist surfaces, especially on something decaying

mouldy *adjective* (**mouldier, mouldiest**)
having mould on it; decaying

moult *verb* (**moults, moulting, moulted**) (*pronounced* mohlt)
to moult is to lose feathers or hair, as some animals do

mound *noun* (*plural* **mounds**)
a pile of earth or stones; a small hill

mount ➤ *verb* (**mounts, mounting, mounted**)
1 to mount a horse or bicycle is to get on it so that you can ride it 2 to mount is to increase in amount ♦ *The cost of running a car is mounting* 3 to mount a picture or photograph is to put it in a frame or album so as to display it

mount ➤ *noun* (*plural* **mounts**)
1 a mountain, especially in names such as *Mount Everest* 2 something on which a picture or photograph is mounted 3 an animal for someone to ride on

mountain *noun* (*plural* **mountains**)
1 a very high hill 2 a large amount ♦ *We've got a mountain of work to do*

mountainous *adjective* having a lot of mountains

mountaineer *noun* (*plural* **mountaineers**)
someone who climbs mountains

mountaineering *noun*
the sport of climbing mountains

mourn *verb* (**mourns, mourning, mourned**)
to mourn is to be sad, especially because someone has died

mourner *noun* someone who mourns

mournful *adjective*
sad and sorrowful

mournfully *adverb* in a mournful way

mouse *noun* (*plural* **mice**)
1 a small animal with a long tail and a pointed nose 2 (*in Computing*) a small device that you move around on a mat to control the movements of a cursor on a VDU screen

mousetrap *noun* (*plural* **mousetraps**)
a trap for catching and killing mice

mousse *noun* (*plural* **mousses**) (*pronounced* mooss)
1 a creamy pudding flavoured with chocolate or fruit 2 a frothy creamy substance used for holding hair while styling it

moustache *noun* (*plural* **moustaches**) (*pronounced* mus-**tahsh**)
a strip of hair left to grow above a man's upper lip

mousy *adjective* (**mousier, mousiest**)
1 light brown in colour 2 timid and feeble

mouth *noun* (*plural* **mouths**)
1 the part of the face that opens for eating and speaking 2 the place where a river enters the sea 3 an opening or outlet

mouthful *noun* (*plural* **mouthfuls**)
an amount of food you put in your mouth

mouth organ *noun* (*plural* **mouth organs**)
a small musical instrument you play by blowing and sucking while passing it along your lips

mouthpiece *noun* (*plural* **mouthpieces**)
the part of a musical instrument or other device that you put to your mouth

movable *adjective*
able to be moved

move ➤ *verb* (**moves, moving, moved**)
1 to move something is to take it from one place to another 2 to move is to go from one place to another 3 to move someone is to affect their feelings ♦ *Their story moved us deeply*

move ➤ *noun* (*plural* **moves**)
1 a movement 2 a player's turn in a game **to get a move on** (*informal*) is to hurry up **on the move** moving or making progress

movement *noun* (*plural* **movements**)
1 movement is moving or being moved
2 a movement is a group of people working together to achieve something 3 in music, a movement is one of the main parts of a long piece such as a symphony

movie *noun* (*plural* **movies**)
a cinema film

moving *adjective*
causing someone to feel strong emotion, especially sadness or joy

mow *verb* (**mows, mowing, mowed, mown**)
to mow grass is to cut it with a machine **to mow people down** is to knock them down and kill them

mower *noun* a machine for mowing grass

MP short for
Member of Parliament

m.p.h. short for *miles per hour*

Mr *noun* (*plural* **Messrs**) (*pronounced* mis-ter)
a title put before a man's name

Mrs *noun* (*plural* **Mrs** or **Mesdames**) (*pronounced* mis-iz)
a title put before a married woman's name

Ms *noun* (*pronounced* miz)
a title put before a woman's name

much ➤ *adjective*
existing in a large amount ♦ *There is much work to do*

much ➤ *noun*
a large amount of something ♦ *£5 is not very much*

much ➤ *adverb*
1 greatly; considerably ♦ *They came, much to my surprise* **2** about; approximately ♦ *It's much the same*

muck ➤ *noun*
1 muck is farmyard manure **2** (*informal*) muck is dirt or filth
to make a muck of something is to make a mess of it

muck ➤ *verb* (**mucks, mucking, mucked**) (*informal*)
to muck about or **muck around** is to behave stupidly or idly
to muck something up is to do it very badly

mucky *adjective* (**muckier, muckiest**)
dirty, messy

mud *noun*
wet soft earth
muddy *adjective* covered with mud

muddle ➤ *verb* (**muddles, muddling, muddled**)
1 to muddle things is to mix them up **2** to muddle someone is to confuse them
muddler *noun* someone who muddles things

muddle ➤ *noun* (*plural* **muddles**)
a confusion or mess

mudguard *noun* (*plural* **mudguards**)
a curved cover fixed over a bicycle wheel to stop mud and water being thrown up on to the rider

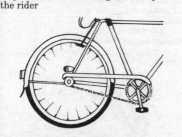

muesli *noun* (*pronounced* mooz-li)
a breakfast food made of cereals, nuts, and dried fruit

muezzin *noun* (*plural* **muezzins**)
a man who calls Muslims to prayer from a minaret

muffle *verb* (**muffles, muffling, muffled**)
1 to muffle something is to cover or wrap it to protect it or keep it warm **2** to muffle a sound is to deaden it or reduce it

mug ➤ *noun* (*plural* **mugs**)
1 a large cup, usually used without a saucer **2** (*slang*) a fool; someone who is easily fooled or cheated **3** (*slang*) a person's face

mug ➤ *verb* (**mugs, mugging, mugged**)
to mug someone is to attack and rob them in the street
mugger *noun* someone who attacks or mugs people

muggy *adjective* (**muggier, muggiest**)
unpleasantly warm and damp

mule *noun* (*plural* **mules**)
an animal that is the offspring of a donkey and a mare

multi- *prefix*
meaning 'having many of something', as in *multiracial*

multiple ➤ *adjective*
having many parts

multiple ➤ *noun* (*plural* **multiples**)
a number that can be divided exactly by another number ♦ *30 and 50 are multiples of 10*

multiply *verb* (**multiplies, multiplying, multiplied**)
1 to multiply a number is to add it to itself a certain number of times ♦ *Five multiplied by four equals twenty (5 ×4 =20)*
2 to multiply is to increase or become many
multiplication *noun* multiplying numbers

multiracial *adjective* (*pronounced* mul-ti-ray-shal)
having people of many different races

multitude *noun* (*plural* **multitudes**)
a very large number of people or things

mum *noun* (*plural* **mums**)
(*informal*) mother

mumble *verb* (**mumbles, mumbling, mumbled**)
to mumble is to speak softly and unclearly

mummify *verb* (**mummifies, mummifying, mummified**)
in ancient Egypt, to mummify a dead body was to prepare it as a mummy

mummy[1] *noun* (*plural* **mummies**)
(*informal*) mother

mummy[2] *noun* (*plural* **mummies**)
in ancient Egypt, a dead body wrapped in
cloth and treated with oils for burial

mumps *noun*
an infectious disease that makes the neck
swell painfully

munch *verb* (**munches, munching, munched**)
to munch food is to chew it noisily

mundane *adjective*
ordinary or dull

municipal *adjective* (*pronounced*
mew-nis-i-pal)
to do with a town or city

mural *noun* (*plural* **murals**)
a picture painted on a wall

murder ➤ *verb* (**murders, murdering, murdered**)
to murder someone is to kill them
deliberately

murder ➤ *noun* (*plural* **murders**)
1 the deliberate killing of someone
2 (*informal*) something very difficult or
unpleasant ♦ *It was murder changing the
wheel in the dark*

murderer *noun* (*plural* **murderers**)
someone who commits murder

murderous *adjective*
likely to commit murder; violent and
wicked

murky *adjective* (**murkier, murkiest**)
dark and gloomy

murmur ➤ *noun* (*plural* **murmurs**)
a low or soft continuous sound, especially
of people speaking

murmur ➤ *verb* (**murmurs, murmuring, murmured**)
to murmur is to make a low continuous
sound, especially of speaking

muscle ➤ *noun* (*plural* **muscles**)
a bundle of fibres that can stretch to cause
movement of a part of the body

muscle ➤ *verb* (**muscles, muscling, muscled**)
to muscle in on something (*informal*) is to try
to take part in something that does not
concern you

muscular *adjective*
having a lot of muscles; powerful

museum *noun* (*plural* **museums**)
a place where interesting old or valuable
objects are displayed for people to see

mushroom ➤ *noun* (*plural* **mushrooms**)
a fast-growing edible fungus with a
dome-shaped top

mushroom ➤ *verb* (**mushrooms, mushrooming, mushroomed**)
to mushroom is to grow or appear
suddenly like mushrooms ♦ *Blocks of flats
mushroomed in the city*

music *noun*
1 pleasant or interesting sounds made by
instruments or by the voice **2** a system of
printed or written symbols for making this
kind of sound

musical ➤ *adjective*
1 to do with music **2** good at music or
interested in it
musically *adverb* in a musical way

musical ➤ *noun* (*plural* **musicals**)
a play or film with music and songs

musician *noun* (*plural* **musicians**)
someone who plays a musical instrument,
especially for a living

musket *noun* (*plural* **muskets**)
an old type of rifle

musketeer *noun* (*plural* **musketeers**)
a soldier armed with a musket

Muslim *noun* (*plural* **Muslims**) (*pronounced*
muuz-lim)
someone who follows the religious
teachings of Muhammad, as set out in the
Koran

muslin *noun*
fine cotton cloth

mussel *noun* (*plural* **mussels**)
a black shellfish, often found sticking to
rocks

must *verb*
a word used with another verb to show
1 that someone has to do something ♦ *I must go home soon* **2** that something is certain ♦ *You must be joking!*

mustard *noun*
a yellow paste or powder used to give food a hot taste

mustard and cress *plural noun*
small green plants eaten in salads

muster *verb* (musters, mustering, mustered)
to muster is to assemble or gather together

musty *adjective* (mustier, mustiest)
smelling or tasting mouldy or stale
mustiness *noun* being musty

mutation *noun* (*plural* mutations)
a change in the form of a living creature because of changes in its genes

mute ➤ *adjective*
1 silent; not speaking or able to speak
2 not pronounced ♦ *The k in 'knife' is mute*
mutely *adverb* in a mute or silent way

mute ➤ *noun* (*plural* mutes)
1 a person who cannot speak **2** a device fitted to a musical instrument to soften the sound

muted *adjective*
silent or quiet ♦ *She gave a muted reply*

mutilate *verb* (mutilates, mutilating, mutilated)
to mutilate something is to damage it by breaking or cutting off part of it
mutilation *noun* mutilating something

mutineer *noun* (*plural* mutineers)
(*pronounced* mew-tin-eer)
someone who takes part in a mutiny

mutiny ➤ *noun* (*plural* mutinies)
(*pronounced* mew-tin-i)
a rebellion by sailors or soldiers against their officers
mutinous *adjective* rebellious **mutinously** *adverb* in a mutinous way

mutiny ➤ *verb* (mutinies, mutinying, mutinied)
(*pronounced* mew-tin-i)
to mutiny is to take part in a mutiny

mutter *verb* (mutters, muttering, muttered)
to mutter is to murmur or grumble in a low voice

mutton *noun*
meat from a sheep

mutual *adjective* (*pronounced* mew-tew-al)
given or done to each other ♦ *They gave mutual help*
mutually *adverb* in a mutual way

muzzle ➤ *noun* (*plural* muzzles)
1 an animal's nose and mouth **2** a cover put over an animal's nose and mouth so that it cannot bite **3** the open end of a gun

muzzle ➤ *verb* (muzzles, muzzling, muzzled)
1 to muzzle an animal is to put a muzzle on it **2** to muzzle someone is to prevent them from saying what they think

my *adjective*
belonging to me ♦ *This is my book*

myself *pronoun*
me and nobody else, used to refer back to the person who is speaking ♦ *I have hurt myself*
by myself on my own; alone ♦ *I did the work all by myself*

mysterious *adjective*
full of mystery; puzzling
mysteriously *adverb* in a mysterious way

mystery *noun* (*plural* mysteries)
something strange or puzzling

mystify *verb* (mystifies, mystifying, mystified)
to mystify someone is to puzzle them very much
mystification *noun* being mystified

myth *noun* (*plural* myths)
1 an old story about gods and heroes in ancient times **2** an untrue story or belief
♦ *It is a myth that carrots make you see better*

mythical *adjective*
imaginary; only found in myths

mythology *noun*
the study of myths
mythological *adjective* to do with mythology or myths

Nn

nab *verb* (nabs, nabbing, nabbed)
(*informal*) to nab someone is to catch or grab them

nag[1] *verb* (nags, nagging, nagged)
to nag someone is to keep criticizing them or complaining to them

nag[2] *noun* (*plural* nags)
(*informal*) a horse

nail ➤ *noun* (*plural* nails)
1 the hard covering on the end of a finger or toe **2** a small, sharp piece of metal used to fix pieces of wood together

nail ➤ *verb* (nails, nailing, nailed)
1 to nail something is to fasten it with a nail or nails **2** to nail someone is to catch or trap them

naïve *adjective* (*pronounced* ny-eev)
1 innocent and trusting **2** too ready to believe what you are told; showing a lack of experience
naïvely *adverb* in a naïve way
naïvety *noun* being naïve

naked *adjective* (*pronounced* nay-kid)
without any clothes or coverings on
the naked eye your eye when it is not helped by a telescope or microscope
nakedness *noun* being naked

name ➤ *noun* (*plural* **names**)
what you call a person or thing

name ➤ *verb* (**names, naming, named**)
1 to name someone or something is to give them a name **2** to name someone or something is to say what they are called
♦ *Can you name these plants?*

nameless *adjective*
1 not having a name **2** not named or identified ♦ *The culprit shall be nameless*

namely *adverb*
that is to say ♦ *I will invite two friends, namely Vicky and Tom*

nanny *noun* (*plural* **nannies**)
1 a woman whose job is to look after small children **2** (*informal*) a grandmother

nanny goat *noun* (*plural* **nanny goats**)
a female goat

nap *noun* (*plural* **naps**)
a short sleep

napkin *noun* (*plural* **napkins**)
1 a piece of cloth or paper to keep your clothes clean or wipe your lips at meals **2** (*old use*) a nappy

nappy *noun* (*plural* **nappies**)
a piece of cloth or a paper pad put round a baby's bottom

narcissus *noun* (*plural* **narcissi**)
(*pronounced* nar-**sis**-us)
a garden flower like a daffodil

narcotic *noun* (*plural* **narcotics**)
(*pronounced* nar-**kot**-ik)
a drug that makes you sleepy or unconscious

narrate *verb* (**narrates, narrating, narrated**)
to narrate a story or experiences is to tell them to someone ♦ *She narrated her adventures in South America*
narration *noun* telling a story **narrator** *noun* someone who tells a story

narrative *noun* (*plural* **narratives**)
a story or account that someone tells

narrow *adjective* (**narrower, narrowest**)
1 not wide **2** with only a small margin of error or safety ♦ *We all had a narrow escape*
narrowly *adverb* closely; barely

narrow-minded *adjective*
not liking or understanding other people's ideas or beliefs

nasal *adjective*
to do with the nose

nasturtium *noun* (*plural* **nasturtiums**)
(*pronounced* na-**ster**-shum)
a garden flower with round leaves

nasty *adjective* (**nastier, nastiest**)
not pleasant; unkind
nastily *adverb* in a nasty way
nastiness *noun* being nasty

nation *noun* (*plural* **nations**)
1 a large number of people who have the same history, language, and customs, and live in the same part of the world under one government **2** a country and the people who live there

national *adjective*
to do with a nation or country
nationally *adverb* with regard to a nation

nationalism *noun*
supporting one's country and wanting it to be independent
nationalist *noun* someone who believes in nationalism

nationality *noun* (*plural* **nationalities**)
the nation someone belongs to ♦ *What is her nationality?*

nationalize *verb* (**nationalizes, nationalizing, nationalized**)
to nationalize an industry or organization is to put it under government control
nationalization *noun* nationalizing industries and organizations

nationwide *adjective* and *adverb*
over the whole of a country

native ➤ *noun* (*plural* **natives**)
a person born in a particular place ♦ *He is a native of Sweden*

native ➤ *adjective*
1 natural; belonging to someone from birth ♦ *He has plenty of native ability*
2 of the country where you were born
♦ *English is my native language*

Native American *noun* (*plural* **Native Americans**)
one of the original inhabitants of North or South America

nativity *noun* (*plural* **nativities**) (*pronounced* na-**tiv**-i-ti)
someone's birth
the Nativity the birth of Jesus Christ

natural ➣ *adjective*
1 made or done by nature, not by people or machines 2 normal; not surprising 3 in music, not sharp or flat

natural ➣ *noun* (*plural* **naturals**)
1 a natural note in music; a sign ♮ that shows a note is natural 2 someone who is naturally good at something ♦ *She's a natural at juggling*

natural gas *noun*
gas that is found underground or under the sea, not made from coal

natural history *noun*
the study of plants and animals

naturalist *noun* (*plural* **naturalists**)
someone who studies natural history

naturalize *verb* (**naturalizes, naturalizing, naturalized**)
1 to naturalize a person is to make them a full citizen of a country 2 to naturalize a plant or animal is to cause it to grow or live in a place where it is not normally found

naturalization *noun* naturalizing someone or something

naturally *adverb*
1 in a natural way ♦ *The gas is produced naturally* 2 the qualities of ♦ *Naturally I will pay your train fare*

nature *noun* (*plural* **natures**)
1 everything in the universe that was not made by people 2 the qualities or characteristics of a person or thing ♦ *She has a loving nature* 3 a kind or sort of thing ♦ *He likes things of that nature*

nature reserve *noun* (*plural* **nature reserves**)
an area of land set aside to keep wild life

nature trail *noun* (*plural* **nature trails**)
a path in the country with signs telling you about the plants and wildlife

naughty *adjective* (**naughtier, naughtiest**)
not behaving as you should; disobedient or rude

naughtily *adverb* in a naughty way
naughtiness *noun* being naughty

nausea *noun*
a feeling of sickness or disgust

nautical *adjective*
connected with ships or sailors

naval *adjective*
to do with a navy

nave *noun* (*plural* **naves**)
the main central part of a church

navel *noun* (*plural* **navels**)
the small hollow at the front of your stomach, where the umbilical cord was attached

navigable *adjective*
suitable for ships to sail in

navigate *verb* (**navigates, navigating, navigated**)
1 to navigate a sea or river is to sail a ship on it 2 to navigate is to make sure that an aircraft or vehicle is going in the right direction

navigation *noun* navigating on land or water or in the air **navigator** *noun* someone who navigates

navy *noun* (*plural* **navies**)
1 a fleet of ships and the people trained to use them 2 navy blue

navy blue *noun* and *adjective*
dark blue

Nazi *noun* (*plural* **Nazis**) (*pronounced* nah-tsi)
a member of the German National Socialist Party in Hitler's time
Nazism *noun* the Fascist beliefs of the Nazis

near ➣ *adverb* and *adjective* (**nearer, nearest**)
not far away
near by at a place not far away ♦ *They live near by*

near ➣ *preposition*
not far away from something ♦ *She lives near the town*

near ➣ *verb* (**nears, nearing, neared**)
to near a place is to come close to it ♦ *The ships were nearing the harbour*

nearby *adjective*
near; not far away ♦ *We live in a nearby town*

nearly *adverb*
1 almost ♦ *It was nearly midnight*
2 closely ♦ *They are nearly related*
not nearly not at all ♦ *There is not nearly enough food*

neat *adjective* (**neater, neatest**)
1 tidy; simple and pleasant to look at
2 skilfully done 3 without water added
♦ *They were drinking neat orange juice*
neatly *adverb* in a neat way **neatness** *noun* being neat

necessarily *adverb*
for certain; definitely ♦ *It won't necessarily cost you a lot*

necessary *adjective*
needed very much; essential

necessity *noun* (*plural* **necessities**)
1 a necessity is a need ♦ *There is a necessity to buy food and clothing*
2 something needed ♦ *We have brought all the necessities for a picnic*

neck *noun* (*plural* **necks**)
1 the part of the body that joins the head to the shoulders 2 a narrow part of something, especially of a bottle
neck and neck almost exactly together in a race or contest
to stick your neck out is to say or do something that could get you into trouble

neckerchief *noun* (*plural* **neckerchiefs**)
a square of cloth worn round the neck, for example by Scouts and Cubs

necklace *noun* (*plural* **necklaces**)
an ornament worn round the neck

nectar *noun*
a sweet liquid collected by bees from flowers

nectarine *noun* (*plural* **nectarines**)
a kind of peach with a smooth skin

need > *verb* (**needs, needing, needed**)
1 to need something is to be without it when you should have it 2 to need to do something is to have to do it ♦ *I needed to get a haircut*

need > *noun* (*plural* **needs**)
1 a need is something that you need
2 need is a situation in which something is necessary ♦ *There is no need to cry*
in need needing money or help
needless *adjective* unnecessary **needlessly** *adverb* without being necessary

needle *noun* (*plural* **needles**)
1 a very thin pointed piece of metal used for sewing 2 something long, thin, and sharp, such as a knitting needle or a pine needle 3 the pointer of a meter or compass

needlework *noun*
sewing or embroidery

needy *adjective* (**needier, neediest**)
very poor; not having what you need to live properly

negative > *adjective*
1 a negative statement or answer is one that says 'no' 2 not definite or helpful 3 a negative number is one that is less than nought 4 a negative electric charge is one that carries electrons
negatively *adverb* in a negative way

negative > *noun* (*plural* **negatives**)
1 something that means 'no' 2 a photograph or film with the dark parts light and the light parts dark, from which prints are made

neglect > *verb* (**neglects, neglecting, neglected**)
1 to neglect something or someone is to fail to look after them or deal with them
2 to neglect to do something is to fail to do it

neglect > *noun*
neglect is failing to look after someone or do something

neglectful *adjective*
tending not to do things you should
neglectfully *adverb* in a neglectful way

negligent *adjective*
not taking proper care or paying enough attention ♦ *The cleaners had been negligent and left the windows open*
negligence *noun* being negligent

negligible *adjective* (*pronounced* **neg-li-ji-bul**)
not big enough or important enough to bother about ♦ *The damage was negligible*

negotiate *verb* (**negotiates, negotiating, negotiated**) (*pronounced* **nig-oh-shi-ayt**)
1 to negotiate is to try to reach agreement about something by discussing it 2 to negotiate an obstacle or difficulty is to get past it or over it
negotiation *noun* negotiating about something **negotiator** *noun* someone who negotiates an agreement

neigh > *verb* (**neighs, neighing, neighed**)
to make a high-pitched cry like a horse

neigh > *noun* (*plural* **neighs**)
the sound of a horse neighing

neighbour *noun* (*plural* **neighbours**)
someone who lives next door or near to you
neighbouring *adjective* next door or nearby

neighbourhood *noun* (*plural* **neighbourhoods**)
the surrounding district

neighbourly *adjective*
friendly and helpful to people who live near you

neither > *adjective* and *pronoun* (*pronounced* **ny-th**er or **nee-th**er)
not either ♦ *Neither parent was there* ♦ *Neither of them likes cabbage*

neither > *conjunction*
neither ... nor ... not one thing and not the other ♦ *I neither know nor care*

neon *noun* (*pronounced* **nee-on**)
a gas that glows when electricity passes through it, used in street lighting

nephew *noun* (*plural* **nephews**)
the son of a person's brother or sister

nerve *noun* (*plural* **nerves**)
1 a nerve is one of the fibres inside the body that carry messages to and from the

brain, so that parts of the body can feel
and move **2** nerve is courage and
calmness in a dangerous situation ♦ *Don't
lose your nerve* **3** (*informal*) nerve is cheek
or impudence ♦ *He had the nerve to ask for
more*

to get on someone's nerves is to irritate them
nerves nervousness ♦ *I was suffering from
nerves before my exam*

nerve-racking *adjective*
difficult and worrying ♦ *We had a
nerve-racking time trying to get out*

nervous *adjective*
1 easily upset or agitated; timid **2** to do
with the nerves
nervously *adverb* in a nervous way
nervousness *noun* being nervous

nervous breakdown *noun* (*plural* **nervous
breakdowns**)
a mental illness in which a person is
depressed and anxious, and unable to cope
with life

nest ➤ *noun* (*plural* **nests**)
1 the place where a bird lays its eggs and
feeds its young **2** a warm place where
some small animals live

nest ➤ *verb* (**nests, nesting, nested**)
to nest is to make or have a nest ♦ *Birds
were nesting in the roof*

nestle *verb* (**nestles, nestling, nestled**)
to nestle is to curl up comfortably

nestling *noun* (*plural* **nestlings**)
a young bird before it can leave the nest

net[1] *noun* (*plural* **nets**)
1 net is material made of pieces of thread,
cord, or wire joined together in a
criss-cross pattern with holes between
2 a net is a piece of this material

net[2] *adjective*
left over after everything has been taken
away ♦ *The net weight, without the box, is
100 grams*

netball *noun*
a game in which two teams try to throw a
ball through a high net hanging from a
ring

nettle *noun* (*plural* **nettles**)
a wild plant with leaves that sting when
they are touched

network *noun* (*plural* **networks**)
1 a criss-cross arrangement **2** a system
with many connections or parts, such as a
railway or broadcasting system

neuter ➤ *adjective* (*pronounced* **new**-ter)
1 neither male nor female **2** in some
languages, belonging to the class of words
that are neither masculine nor feminine

neuter ➤ *verb* (**neuters, neutering, neutered**)
(*pronounced* **new**-ter)
to neuter an animal is to remove its sexual
organs so that it cannot breed

neutral *adjective* (*pronounced* **new**-tral)
1 not supporting either side in a war or
quarrel **2** not distinct or distinctive ♦ *The
room was painted in neutral colours* **3** a
neutral gear is one that is not connected to
the driving parts of an engine
neutrality *noun* being neutral **neutrally** *adverb*
in a neutral way

neutralize *verb* (**neutralizes, neutralizing,
neutralized**)
to neutralize something is to take away its
use or effect

neutron *noun* (*plural* **neutrons**)
a particle of matter with no electric charge

never *adverb*
at no time; not ever; not at all

nevertheless *conjunction* and *adverb*
in spite of this; although that is a fact

new *adjective* (**newer, newest**)
1 not existing before; just bought, made,
or received **2** different or unfamiliar
♦ *That's a new idea*
newly *adverb* recently **newness** *noun* being
new

newcomer *noun* (*plural* **newcomers**)
someone who has recently arrived in a
place

new moon *noun* (*plural* **new moons**)
the moon at the beginning of its cycle,
when it appears as a thin crescent

news *noun*
  1 new information about people or recent events **2** a radio or television report about important events

newsagent *noun* (*plural* **newsagents**)
  a shopkeeper who sells newspapers and magazines

newsletter *noun* (*plural* **newsletters**)
  a short informal report sent regularly to members of an organization or club

newspaper *noun* (*plural* **newspapers**)
  1 a newspaper is a daily or weekly publication of large sheets of printed paper folded together, containing news reports and articles **2** newspaper is the paper these are printed on ♦ *Wrap it in newspaper*

newt *noun* (*plural* **newts**)
  a small animal rather like a lizard, that lives near or in water

New Testament *noun*
  the second part of the Bible, which describes the life and teachings of Jesus Christ

newton *noun* (*plural* **newtons**)
  a unit for measuring force

next ➤ *adjective*
  the nearest; following immediately after

next ➤ *adverb*
  1 in the nearest place **2** at the nearest time ♦ *What comes next?*

next door *adverb* and *adjective*
  in the next house or room

nib *noun* (*plural* **nibs**)
  the pointed metal part at the end of a pen

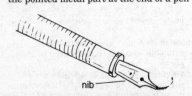

nib

nibble *verb* (**nibbles, nibbling, nibbled**)
  to nibble something is to take small or gentle bites at it

nice *adjective* (**nicer, nicest**)
  1 pleasant or kind **2** delicate or precise ♦ *There is a nice difference between stealing and borrowing*
  nicely *adverb* in a nice way **niceness** *noun* being nice

nicety *noun* (*plural* **niceties**)
  a small detail or feature

nick ➤ *noun* (*plural* **nicks**)
  1 a small cut or notch **2** (*slang*) a prison or police station
  in good nick (*informal*) in good condition
  in the nick of time only just in time

nick ➤ *verb* (**nicks, nicking, nicked**)
  1 to nick something is to make a small cut in it **2** (*slang*) to nick something is to steal it **3** (*slang*) to nick someone is to arrest them

nickel *noun* (*plural* **nickels**)
  1 a silvery-white metal **2** (*in America*) a 5-cent coin

nickname *noun* (*plural* **nicknames**)
  a name given to someone instead of their real name

nicotine *noun* (*pronounced* nik-o-teen)
  a poisonous substance found in tobacco

niece *noun* (*plural* **nieces**)
  the daughter of a person's brother or sister

night *noun* (*plural* **nights**)
  the time when it is dark, between sunset and sunrise

nightclub *noun* (*plural* **nightclubs**)
  a club or restaurant where there is entertainment at night

nightdress *noun* (*plural* **nightdresses**)
  a loose light dress that girls and women wear in bed

nightfall *noun*
  the time when it becomes dark just after sunset

nightingale *noun* (*plural* **nightingales**)
  a small brown bird that sings sweetly

nightly *adjective*
  happening every night

nightmare *noun* (*plural* **nightmares**)
  a frightening or unpleasant dream
  nightmarish *adjective* terrifying

nil *noun*
  nothing ♦ *Our team's score was nil*

nimble *adjective* (**nimbler, nimblest**)
  moving quickly or easily
  nimbly *adverb* in a nimble way

nine *noun* (*plural* **nines**)
  the number 9

nineteen *noun* (*plural* **nineteens**)
the number 19
nineteenth *adjective* and *noun* 19th

ninety *noun* (*plural* **nineties**)
the number 90
ninetieth *adjective* and *noun* 90th

ninth *adjective* and *noun*
the next after the eighth
ninthly *adverb* in the ninth place; as the
ninth one

nip ➤ *verb* (**nips, nipping, nipped**)
1 to nip someone is to pinch or bite them
sharply 2 (*informal*) to nip somewhere is to
go quickly there ♦ *I'll just nip into the
supermarket*

nip ➤ *noun* (*plural* **nips**)
1 a quick pinch or bite 2 a cold feeling
♦ *There's a nip in the air*

nipple *noun* (*plural* **nipples**)
the small part that sticks out at the front of
a person's breast

nippy *adjective* (*nippier, nippiest*)
(*informal*) 1 quick or nimble 2 cold

nit *noun* (*plural* **nits**)
a louse or its egg

nit-picking *noun*
pointing out small faults or mistakes

nitrate *noun* (*plural* **nitrates**)
a chemical compound containing nitrogen

nitric acid *noun* (*pronounced* ny-trik)
a very strong acid containing nitrogen

nitrogen *noun* (*pronounced* ny-tro-jen)
a gas that makes up about four-fifths of the
air

nitty-gritty *noun*
(*slang*) the important or practical details or
facts about something

nitwit *noun* (*plural* **nitwits**)
(*informal*) a stupid person

no ➤ *adjective* and *adverb*
not any ♦ *We have no money* ♦ *She is no
better*

no ➤ *interjection*
a word used to deny or refuse something

nobility *noun*
1 the nobility is the nobles or the
aristocracy 2 nobility is being noble

noble ➤ *adjective* (**nobler, noblest**)
1 of high social rank; aristocratic 2 having
a good and generous nature ♦ *He is a noble
king* 3 stately or impressive ♦ *It was a
noble building*
nobly *adverb* in a noble way

noble ➤ *noun* (*plural* **nobles**)
a person of high social rank

nobleman or **noblewoman** *noun* (*plural*
noblemen or **noblewomen**)
a man or woman of high rank

nobody ➤ *pronoun*
no person; not anyone ♦ *Nobody knows*

nobody ➤ *noun* (*plural* **nobodies**)
an unimportant person ♦ *He's just a
nobody*

nocturnal *adjective* (*pronounced* nok-ter-nal)
1 active at night ♦ *Badgers are nocturnal
animals* 2 happening at night

nod *verb* (**nods, nodding, nodded**)
1 to nod, or nod your head, is to move your
head up and down as a way of agreeing
with someone or as a greeting 2 to nod is
also to be drowsy

noise *noun* (*plural* **noises**)
a loud sound, especially one that is
unpleasant or unwanted
noiseless *adjective* without noise, silent
noiselessly *adverb* in a noiseless way

noisy *adjective* (**noisier, noisiest**)
making a lot of noise
noisily *adverb* in a noisy way
noisiness *noun* being noisy

nomad *noun* (*plural* **nomads**) (*pronounced*
noh-mad)
a member of a tribe that moves from place
to place looking for pasture for their
animals
nomadic *adjective* moving from place to
place

no man's land *noun*
land that does not belong to anyone,
especially the land between two armies at
war

nominate *verb* (**nominates, nominating,
nominated**)
to nominate someone is to propose that
they should be a candidate in an election
nomination *noun* nominating someone

non- *prefix*
meaning 'not', as in *non-existent*

none ➤ *pronoun*
not any; not one ♦ *None of us went*

none ➤ *adverb*
not at all ♦ *He's none too pleased*
none the less nevertheless

non-existent *adjective*
not existing

non-fiction *noun*
writings that are not fiction; books about
real things and true events

non-flammable *adjective*
not able to be set on fire

nonsense *noun*
1 words that do not mean anything or
make any sense 2 absurd or silly ideas or
behaviour
nonsensical *adjective* not making any sense

non-stop *adverb* and *adjective*
1 not stopping ♦ *They talked non-stop all morning* 2 not stopping until the end of a journey ♦ *There's a non-stop train to London*

noodles *plural noun*
pasta made in narrow strips, used in soups

noon *noun*
twelve o'clock midday

no one *pronoun*
no person; not anyone

noose *noun* (*plural* **nooses**)
a loop in a rope that gets smaller when the rope is pulled

nor *conjunction*
and not ♦ *She cannot do it; nor can I*

normal *adjective*
1 usual or ordinary ♦ *It's normal to want a holiday* 2 natural and healthy; not suffering from an illness
normality *noun* being normal **normally** *adverb* in a normal way; usually

north ➤ *noun*
1 the direction to the left of a person facing east 2 the part of a country or city that is in this direction

north ➤ *adjective* and *adverb*
1 towards the north or in the north 2 coming from the north ♦ *A north wind was blowing*

north-east *noun*, *adjective*, and *adverb*
midway between north and east

northerly *adjective*
a northerly wind is one that blows from the north

northern *adjective*
from or to do with the north

northerner *noun* (*plural* **northerners**)
someone who lives in the north of a country

northward or **northwards** *adjective* and *adverb*
towards the north

north-west *noun*, *adjective*, and *adverb*
midway between north and west

nose ➤ *noun* (*plural* **noses**)
1 the part of the face that is used for breathing and smelling 2 the front part of something, especially a vehicle or aircraft

nose ➤ *verb* (**noses, nosing, nosed**)
to nose forward or through is to make progress cautiously ♦ *The ship nosed through the ice*
to nose about or **nose around** is to pry or interfere in someone else's affairs

nosedive ➤ *noun* (*plural* **nosedives**)
a steep dive, especially in an aircraft

nosedive ➤ *verb* (**nosedives, nosediving, nosedived**)
to go suddenly downward

nostalgia *noun* (*pronounced* nos-**tal**-ja)
a fond remembering of or longing for the past
nostalgic *adjective* thinking fondly about the past

nostril *noun* (*plural* **nostrils**)
each of the two openings in your nose

nosy *adjective* (**nosier, nosiest**)
(*informal*) prying into other people's business
nosily *adverb* in a nosy way **nosiness** *noun* being nosy

not *adverb*
a word used to change the meaning of something to its opposite

notable *adjective*
remarkable or famous
notably *adverb* in a notable way

notch *noun* (*plural* **notches**)
a small V-shaped cut or mark

note ➤ *noun* (*plural* **notes**)
1 something written down as a reminder or help 2 a short letter 3 a single sound in music 4 a sound or tone that indicates something ♦ *There was a note of anger in his voice* 5 a banknote ♦ *Have you got a five-pound note?*
to take note of something is to listen to it and understand it

note ➤ *verb* (**notes, noting, noted**)
to note something is to pay attention to it, or to write it down as a reminder or help

notebook *noun* (*plural* **notebooks**)
a book in which you write things down

notepaper *noun*
paper for writing letters

nothing *noun*
not anything

notice ➤ *noun* (*plural* **notices**)
1 a notice is something written or printed and displayed for people to see 2 notice is attention ♦ *It escaped my notice* 3 a warning that something is going to happen

notice ➤ *verb* (**notices, noticing, noticed**)
to notice something is to see it or become aware of it

noticeable *adjective*
easy to see or notice
noticeably *adverb* in a noticeable way

noticeboard *noun* (*plural* **noticeboards**)
a board on which notices can be displayed

notion *noun* (*plural* **notions**)
an idea, especially one that is vague or uncertain ♦ *The notion that the earth is flat was disproved long ago*

notorious *adjective* (*pronounced* noh-**tor**-i-us)
well-known for doing something bad
notoriety *noun* being notorious **notoriously** *adverb* in a notorious way

nougat *noun* (*pronounced* **noo**-gah)
a chewy sweet made from nuts and sugar or honey

nought *noun* (*plural* **noughts**) (*pronounced* nawt)
1 the figure 0 2 nothing

noun *noun* (*plural* **nouns**)
a word that stands for a person, place, or thing

nourish *verb* (**nourishes, nourishing, nourished**)
to nourish someone is to give them enough good food to keep them alive and well
nourishment *noun* food to nourish someone

novel ➤ *adjective*
unusual ♦ *What a novel idea*

novel ➤ *noun* (*plural* **novels**)
a story that fills a whole book

novelist *noun* (*plural* **novelists**) (*pronounced* nov-el-ist)
someone who writes novels

novelty *noun* (*plural* **novelties**)
1 novelty is being new or novel 2 a novelty is something new and unusual 3 a novelty is also a cheap toy or ornament

November *noun*
the eleventh month of the year

novice *noun* (*plural* **novices**)
a beginner

now ➤ *adverb*
1 at this time ♦ *I am now living in Glasgow* 2 without any delay ♦ *Do it now!* **for now** until a later time ♦ *Goodbye for now* **now and again** or **now and then** occasionally; sometimes

now ➤ *conjunction*
since or as ♦ *I do remember, now you mention it*

now ➤ *noun*
this moment ♦ *They should be home by now*

nowadays *adverb*
at the present time

nowhere *adverb*
not anywhere; in no place or to no place

nozzle *noun* (*plural* **nozzles**)
the part at the end of a hose or pipe from which something flows

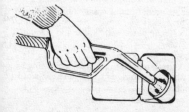

nuclear *adjective* (*pronounced* **new**-kli-er)
1 to do with a nucleus, especially of an atom 2 using the energy that is created by reactions in the nuclei of atoms

nucleus *noun* (*plural* **nuclei**) (*pronounced* **new**-kli-us)
1 the part in the centre of something, round which other things are grouped ♦ *The queen bee is the nucleus of the hive* 2 the central part of an atom or cell

nude ➤ *adjective*
not wearing any clothes

nude ➤ *noun* (*plural* **nudes**)
a nude person, especially in a work of art **nudity** *noun* being nude

nudge *verb* (**nudges, nudging, nudged**)
to nudge someone is to touch or push them with your elbow

nudist *noun* (*plural* **nudists**)
a person who believes that going naked is enjoyable and good for the health

nugget *noun* (*plural* **nuggets**)
a rough lump of gold from the ground

nuisance *noun* (*plural* **nuisances**)
an annoying person or thing

numb *adjective*
unable to feel or move
numbly *adverb* in a numb way **numbness** *noun* being numb

number ➤ *noun* (*plural* **numbers**)
1 a symbol or word that tells you how many of something there are 2 a quantity of people or things ♦ *Do you know the number of people at the game?* 3 one issue of a magazine or newspaper 4 a song or piece of music

number ➤ *verb* (**numbers, numbering, numbered**)
1 to number things is to count them or mark them with numbers 2 to number a certain amount is to reach it ♦ *The crowd numbered 10,000*

numeral *noun* (*plural* **numerals**)
a symbol or figure that stands for a number

numerate *adjective*
having a good basic knowledge of mathematics
numeracy *noun* being numerate

numerator *noun* (*plural* **numerators**)
the number above the line in a fraction ♦ *In $\frac{1}{4}$ the 1 is the numerator*

numerical *adjective*
to do with numbers
numerically *adverb* by numbers; as a number

numerous *adjective*
many ♦ *There are numerous kinds of cat*

nun *noun* (*plural* **nuns**)
a member of a religious community of
women

nunnery *noun* (*plural* **nunneries**)
a group of nuns; a convent

nurse ➤ *noun* (*plural* **nurses**)
a person trained to look after people who
are ill or injured

nurse ➤ *verb* (**nurses, nursing, nursed**)
1 to nurse someone is to look after them
when they are ill or injured **2** to nurse
someone or something is to hold them
carefully in your arms ♦ *He was nursing a
puppy* **3** to nurse a baby is to feed it from
the breast

nursery *noun* (*plural* **nurseries**)
1 a place where young children are looked
after or play **2** a place where young plants
are grown and usually offered for sale

nursery rhyme *noun* (*plural* **nursery rhymes**)
a simple poem or song that young children
like

nursery school *noun* (*plural* **nursery schools**)
a school for very young children

nursing home *noun* (*plural* **nursing homes**)
a small or private hospital

nurture *verb* (**nurtures, nurturing, nurtured**)
to nurture children is to look after them
and educate them

nut *noun* (*plural* **nuts**)
1 a fruit with a hard shell **2** the eatable
part of this kind of fruit **3** a hollow piece
of metal for screwing on to a bolt
4 (*slang*) the head **5** (*slang*) a mad or
eccentric person
nutty *adjective* full of nuts

nutcrackers *plural noun*
pincers for cracking the shells of nuts

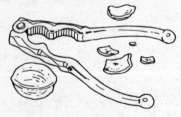

nutmeg *noun* (*plural* **nutmegs**)
a hard seed that is made into a powder and
used as a spice

nutrient *noun* (*plural* **nutrients**) (*pronounced*
new-tri-ent)
something nourishing

nutrition *noun* (*pronounced* new-**trish**-on)
1 food that keeps people well;
nourishment **2** the study of what
nourishes people
nutritional *adjective* to do with nutrition

nutritious *adjective* (*pronounced*
new-**trish**-us)
nourishing ♦ *They ate a nutritious meal*

nutshell *noun* (*plural* **nutshells**)
the shell of a nut
in a nutshell stated very briefly

nuzzle *verb* (**nuzzles, nuzzling, nuzzled**)
to nuzzle someone is to rub gently against
them with the nose, as some animals do

nylon *noun*
a lightweight synthetic cloth or fibre

nymph *noun* (*plural* **nymphs**)
in myths, a young goddess living in trees
or rivers or the sea

Oo

oak *noun* (*plural* **oaks**)
a large tree with seeds called acorns

oar *noun* (*plural* **oars**)
a pole with a flat blade at one end, used for
rowing a boat

oarsman or **oarswoman** *noun* (*plural*
oarsmen or **oarswomen**)
a man or woman who rows a boat

oasis *noun* (*plural* **oases**) (*pronounced*
oh-**ay**-sis)
a fertile place with water and trees in a
desert

oath *noun* (*plural* **oaths**)
1 a solemn promise to do something or
that something is true **2** a swear word

oatmeal *noun*
ground oats

oats *plural noun*
a cereal used to make food for humans and animals

obedient *adjective*
obeying; willing to obey
obedience *noun* being obedient **obediently** *adverb* in an obedient way

obey *verb* (**obeys, obeying, obeyed**)
1 to obey someone is to do what they tell you **2** to obey a rule or law is to do what it says

obituary *noun* (*plural* **obituaries**)
(*pronounced* o-**bit**-yoo-er-i)
an announcement in a newspaper that someone has died, often with a short account of their life

object ➣ *noun* (*plural* **objects**) (*pronounced* **ob**-jikt)
1 something that can be seen or touched
2 the purpose of something **3** (*in Grammar*) the word naming the person or thing that the action of the verb affects, for example *him* in the sentence *I chased him*

object ➣ *verb* (**objects, objecting, objected**)
(*pronounced* ob-**jekt**)
to object to something or someone is to say that you do not like them or do not agree with them
objector *noun* someone who objects to something

objection *noun* (*plural* **objections**)
1 objecting to something **2** a reason for objecting ♦ *I have three objections to your plan*

objectionable *adjective*
unpleasant or nasty

objective ➣ *noun* (*plural* **objectives**)
what you are trying to reach or do; an aim

objective ➣ *adjective*
1 having a real existence outside someone's mind ♦ *No objective evidence has yet been found to prove his claims*
2 not influenced by your own beliefs or ideas ♦ *He gave an objective account of the incident*

obligation *noun* (*plural* **obligations**)
a duty

obligatory *adjective*
having to be done; compulsory ♦ *Games are obligatory*

oblige *verb* (**obliges, obliging, obliged**)
1 to oblige someone is to help and please them ♦ *Can you oblige me with a loan?*
2 to oblige someone to do something is to force them to do it
to be obliged to someone is to be grateful to them for helping you

oblique *adjective* (*pronounced* o-**bleek**)
1 slanting **2** not straightforward or direct
♦ *They gave an oblique reply*
obliquely *adverb* in an oblique way

oblong ➣ *noun* (*plural* **oblongs**)
a rectangle that is longer than it is wide

oblong ➣ *adjective*
having the shape of an oblong

oboe *noun* (*plural* **oboes**) (*pronounced* oh-boh)
a high-pitched woodwind instrument
oboist *noun* someone who plays the oboe

obscene *adjective* (*pronounced* ob-**seen**)
offensive to people's feelings, especially because of being connected with sex, violence, or cruelty
obscenely *adverb* in an obscene way
obscenity *noun* being obscene

obscure *adjective* (**obscurer, obscurest**)
1 difficult to see or understand; very unclear **2** not well-known
obscurely *adverb* in an obscure way **obscurity** *noun* being obscure

observance *noun* (*plural* **observances**)
obeying a law or keeping a custom

observant *adjective*
quick at observing or noticing things
observantly *adverb* in an observant way

observation *noun* (*plural* **observations**)
1 observation is observing or watching
2 an observation is a comment or remark
♦ *He made a few observations about the weather*

observatory *noun* (*plural* **observatories**)
(*pronounced* ob-**zerv**-a-ter-i)
a building equipped with telescopes for looking at the stars or weather

observe *verb* (**observes, observing, observed**)
1 to observe someone or something is to watch them carefully **2** to observe something is to notice it **3** to observe a law or custom is to obey it or keep it **4** to observe a fact is to state it ♦ *She observed that she did not like ice in her drinks*
observer *noun* someone who observes something

obsessed *adjective*
always thinking about something ♦ *He is obsessed with his work*
obsession *noun* being obsessed

obsolete *adjective*
not used any more; out of date

obstacle *noun* (*plural* **obstacles**)
something that gets in your way or makes it difficult for you to do something

obstinate *adjective*
not willing to change your ideas or ways, even though they may be wrong
obstinacy *noun* being obstinate **obstinately** *adverb* in an obstinate way

obstruct *verb* (**obstructs, obstructing, obstructed**)
to obstruct someone or something is to stop them from getting past, or to hinder them
obstruction *noun* obstructing someone or something **obstructive** *adjective* causing difficulties or obstructions

obtain *verb* (**obtains, obtaining, obtained**)
to obtain something is to get it or be given it
obtainable *adjective* able to be bought or got

obtuse *adjective* (**obtuser, obtusest**)
1 slow to understand; stupid **2** an obtuse angle is an angle of between 90 and 180 degrees
obtusely *adverb* in an obtuse way

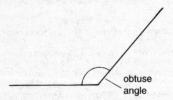

obtuse angle

obvious *adjective*
easy to see or understand
obviously *adverb* in an obvious way; clearly

occasion *noun* (*plural* **occasions**)
1 the time when something happens ♦ *On this occasion, we will not take any action* **2** a special event ♦ *The wedding was a grand occasion*

occasional *adjective*
happening from time to time, but not often and not regularly
occasionally *adverb* from time to time

occupant *noun* (*plural* **occupants**)
someone who occupies a place

occupation *noun* (*plural* **occupations**)
1 a person's job or profession **2** the occupying of territory

occupy *verb* (**occupies, occupying, occupied**)
1 to occupy a place or building is to live in it **2** to occupy a space or position is to fill it **3** in a war, to occupy territory is to capture it and keep an army in it **4** to occupy someone is to keep them busy or interested

occur *verb* (**occurs, occurring, occurred**)
1 an event occurs when it happens or takes place ♦ *An earthquake occurred on the island in 1953* **2** something occurs when it exists or is found somewhere ♦ *These plants occur in ponds* **3** to occur to someone is to come into their mind ♦ *An idea suddenly occurred to me*
occurrence *noun* something that occurs or happens

ocean *noun* (*plural* **oceans**)
1 the ocean is the area of salt water surrounding the land of the earth **2** an ocean is a large part of this water, such as the Pacific Ocean

o'clock *adverb*
by the clock ♦ *Lunch is at one o'clock*

octagon *noun* (*plural* **octagons**)
a flat shape with eight sides
octagonal *adjective* having eight sides

octave *noun* (*plural* **octaves**)
1 the interval between one musical note and the next note of the same name above or below it **2** these two notes played together

October *noun*
the tenth month of the year

octopus *noun* (*plural* **octopuses**)
a sea creature with eight arms (called *tentacles*)

odd *adjective* (**odder, oddest**)
1 strange or unusual 2 an odd number is one that cannot be divided by 2, such as 5 and 31 3 left over or spare ♦ *I've got an odd sock* 4 of various kinds; occasional ♦ *He's doing odd jobs*
oddity *noun* something that is odd or strange **oddly** *adverb* in an odd way **oddness** *noun* being odd

oddments *plural noun*
small things of various kinds

odds *plural noun*
1 the chances that something will happen 2 the proportion of money that you will win if a bet is successful ♦ *When the odds are 10 to 1, you will win £10 if you bet £1*
odds and ends small things of various kinds

odour *noun* (*plural* **odours**)
a smell, usually an unpleasant one
odorous *adjective* having an odour

oesophagus *noun* (*plural* **oesophagi** or **oesophaguses**) (*pronounced* ee-**sof**-a-gus) the tube leading from the throat to the stomach

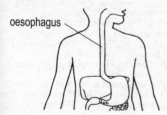

oesophagus

of *preposition*
1 belonging to ♦ *She is the mother of the child* 2 coming from ♦ *He is a native of Italy* 3 away from ♦ *The supermarket is two miles north of the town* 4 about; concerning ♦ *Is there any news of your father?* 5 from; out of ♦ *The house is built of stone*

off ➤ *adverb*
1 not on; away ♦ *His hat blew off* 2 not working or happening ♦ *The heating is off* ♦ *The match is off because of snow* 3 behind or at the side of a stage ♦ *There were noises off* 4 beginning to go bad ♦ *I think the milk is off*

off ➤ *preposition*
1 not on; away or down from ♦ *He fell off his chair* 2 not taking or wanting ♦ *She is off her food* 3 taken away from ♦ *There is £5 off the normal price*

offence *noun* (*plural* **offences**)
1 an offence is a crime or illegal action ♦ *When was the offence committed?*
2 offence is a feeling of annoyance or hurt **to give offence** is to hurt someone's feelings **to take offence** is to be upset by what someone has said or done

offend *verb* (**offends, offending, offended**)
1 to offend someone is to hurt their feelings or be unpleasant to them 2 to offend is to break a law or do wrong
offender *noun* someone who breaks a law or does wrong

offensive *adjective*
1 insulting or causing offence 2 used for attacking; aggressive ♦ *They found a supply of offensive weapons*
offensively *adverb* in an offensive way

offer ➤ *verb* (**offers, offering, offered**)
1 to offer something is to hold it out so that someone can take it if they want it
2 to offer to do something is to say that you are willing to do it 3 to offer a sum of money is to say how much you are willing to pay for something

offer ➤ *noun* (*plural* **offers**)
1 the action of offering something 2 an amount of money that you are willing to pay for something

offhand *adjective*
1 said without much thought 2 rude or curt

office *noun* (*plural* **offices**)
1 a room or building for business, where people do typing and administration and hold meetings 2 a government department, for example the Foreign and Commonwealth Office 3 an important job or position ♦ *He wanted the office of Lord Mayor*

officer *noun* (*plural* **officers**)
1 someone who is in charge of other people, especially in the armed forces; an official 2 a policeman or policewoman

official ➤ *adjective*
1 done or said by someone with authority 2 connected with a job of authority or trust ♦ *She has considerable official responsibilities*
officially *adverb* in an official way

official ➤ *noun* (*plural* **officials**)
someone who does a job of authority or trust

officious *adjective* (*pronounced* o-**fish**-us) too ready to order people about; bossy and unpleasant
officiously *adverb* in an officious way

off-licence noun (plural **off-licences**)
a shop with a licence to sell alcoholic
drinks for people to take away

offset verb (**offsets, offsetting, offset**)
one thing offsets another when it balances
it out ♦ *The failures were offset by some*
successes

offshore adjective and adverb
1 from the land towards the sea ♦ *There is*
an offshore breeze 2 in the sea some
distance from the shore ♦ *They swam to*
an offshore island

offside adjective
(*in Sport*) in a position which is not
allowed by the rules

offspring noun (plural **offspring**)
a child or young animal

often adverb
many times; in many cases

ogre noun (plural **ogres**)
1 a cruel giant in stories 2 a frightening
person

oh interjection
a cry of surprise, pain, or delight

ohm noun (plural **ohms**) (*rhymes with*
home)
a unit of electrical resistance

oil ➤ noun (plural **oils**)
1 a thick slippery liquid that does not mix
with water 2 a kind of petroleum used as
fuel

oil ➤ verb (**oils, oiling, oiled**)
to oil something is to put oil on it to make
it work smoothly

oilfield noun (plural **oilfields**)
an area where oil is found under the
ground or under the sea

oil painting noun (plural **oil paintings**)
a painting done using paints made with oil

oil rig noun (plural **oil rigs**)
a structure set up to support the
equipment for drilling for oil

oilskin noun (plural **oilskins**)
a waterproof piece of clothing worn
especially by fishermen

oil well noun (plural **oil wells**)
a hole drilled in the ground or under the
sea to get oil

oily adjective (**oilier, oiliest**)
1 like oil or covered in oil 2 unpleasantly
over-polite ♦ *She didn't like his oily*
manner

ointment noun (plural **ointments**)
a cream for putting on sore skin and cuts

OK adverb and adjective
(*informal*) all right

old adjective (**older, oldest**)
1 not new; born or made a long time ago
2 of a particular age ♦ *I'm ten years old*
3 former or original ♦ *Put it back in its old*
place

old age noun
the time when a person is old

old-fashioned adjective
of the kind that was usual a long time ago;
out of date

Old Norse noun
the language of the Vikings, from which
the modern Scandinavian languages come

Old Testament noun
the first part of the Bible, which is the holy
book of the Jewish and Christian religions

olive noun (plural **olives**)
1 an evergreen tree with a small bitter
fruit 2 the fruit of this tree, used for
eating and to make olive oil

olive branch noun (plural **olive branches**)
something you do or say that shows you
want to make peace

Olympic Games or **Olympics** plural noun
(*pronounced* o-lim-pik)
a series of international sports contests
held every four years in different countries

ombudsman noun (plural **ombudsmen**)
(*pronounced* om-budz-man)
an official who looks into people's
complaints against government
departments

omelette noun (plural **omelettes**)
(*pronounced* om-lit)
eggs beaten together and fried, often with
a filling or flavouring

omen noun (plural **omens**)
an event that some people see as a sign
that something is going to happen

ominous adjective
suggesting that trouble is coming
ominously adverb in an ominous way

omission noun (plural **omissions**)
something left out or not done

omit verb (**omits, omitting, omitted**)
1 to omit something is to leave it out 2 to
omit to do something is to fail to do it

omnivorous adjective
feeding on plants as well as the flesh of
animals

on ➤ *preposition*
1 at or over the top or surface of something ♦ *Sit on the floor* 2 at the time of ♦ *Come on Monday* 3 about; concerning ♦ *We went to a talk on butterflies* 4 towards or near ♦ *They advanced on the town*

on ➤ *adverb*
1 so as to be on something ♦ *Put your hat on* 2 forwards ♦ *Move on* 3 working; in action ♦ *Is the heater on?*

once ➤ *adverb*
1 at one time ♦ *I once lived in Leeds* 2 ever ♦ *They never once offered to pay*

once ➤ *conjunction*
as soon as ♦ *We can get out once I open this door*

one ➤ *noun* (*plural* ones)
the smallest whole number, 1

one ➤ *pronoun*
a person or thing on their own ♦ *One likes to help* ♦ *One of my friends is ill*
one another each other

one ➤ *adjective*
single ♦ *I have one packet left*

oneself *pronoun*
one's own self; yourself ♦ *One should not always think of oneself*

one-sided *adjective*
with one side having a big advantage ♦ *It will be a very one-sided game*

one-way *adjective*
where traffic is only allowed to go in one direction ♦ *Is this a one-way street?*

ongoing *adjective*
continuing to exist or make progress ♦ *It's an ongoing project*

onion *noun* (*plural* onions)
a round vegetable with a strong flavour

onlooker *noun* (*plural* onlookers)
a spectator

only ➤ *adjective*
being the one person or thing of a kind ♦ *He's the only person we can trust*

only ➤ *adverb*
no more than ♦ *There are only three cakes*

only ➤ *conjunction*
but then; however ♦ *I want to come, only I'm busy that night*

onshore *adjective*
from the sea towards the land ♦ *There is an onshore breeze*

onto *preposition*
to a position on ♦ *They fell onto the floor*

onward or **onwards** *adverb*
forward or forwards

ooze *verb* (**oozes, oozing, oozed**)
to ooze is to flow out slowly, especially through a narrow opening ♦ *Blood oozed from his wound*

opaque *adjective* (*pronounced* oh-**payk**)
not allowing light through or able to be seen through

open ➤ *adjective*
1 allowing people or things to pass through; not shut ♦ *The door is open* ♦ *The bottles need to be open* 2 not enclosed ♦ *There were miles of open land* 3 not folded; spread out ♦ *She greeted us with open arms* 4 honest; not secret or secretive ♦ *We all want open government* 5 not settled or finished ♦ *That is still an open question*
in the open air outdoors; not inside a house or building

open ➤ *verb* (**opens, opening, opened**)
1 to open something is to make it open 2 to open is to become open 3 to open is also to start ♦ *The jumble sale opens at 2 o'clock*

opener *noun* (*plural* openers)
a device for opening a bottle or can

opening *noun* (*plural* openings)
1 a space or gap in something 2 the beginning of something 3 an opportunity, especially for a job

openly *adverb*
not secretly; publicly

open-minded *adjective*
ready to listen to other people's ideas and opinions; not having fixed ideas

opera *noun* (*plural* operas)
opera, or an opera, is a form of drama in which the characters sing all or most of the words, with an orchestra
operatic *adjective* to do with opera

operate *verb* (**operates, operating, operated**)
1 to operate something is to make it work 2 to operate is to work or be in action 3 to operate on someone is to perform a surgical operation on them

operation *noun* (*plural* operations)
1 making something work; working 2 something done to a patient's body by a surgeon to remove or repair a part of it 3 a planned military activity

operator *noun* (*plural* operators)
someone who works something, especially a telephone switchboard or exchange

opinion *noun* (*plural* opinions)
what you think of something; a belief or judgement

opinion poll *noun* (*plural* opinion polls)
an estimate of what people think, made by questioning a certain number of them

opium *noun*
a drug made from poppies, used to calm people and to make them unable to feel pain

opponent *noun* (*plural* **opponents**)
someone who is against you in a contest, war, or argument

opportunity *noun* (*plural* **opportunities**)
a good time to do something

oppose *verb* (**opposes, opposing, opposed**)
to oppose someone or something is to be against them or disagree with them
as opposed to in contrast with ♦ *We want some action, as opposed to mere talking*
to be opposed to something is to disagree strongly with it ♦ *We are opposed to parking in the town centre*

opposite ➤ *adjective* and *adverb*
1 on the other side; facing ♦ *She lives on the opposite side of the road to me* ♦ *I'll sit opposite* 2 completely different ♦ *They went in opposite directions*

opposite ➤ *noun* (*plural* **opposites**)
something that is opposite to something else ♦ *'Happy' is the opposite of 'sad'*

opposition *noun*
opposing something; resistance
the Opposition the chief political party opposing the one that has formed the government

oppress *verb* (**oppresses, oppressing, oppressed**)
1 to oppress people is to govern them or treat them cruelly or unjustly 2 to oppress someone is to trouble them with worry or sadness
oppression *noun* treating people cruelly
oppressor *noun* someone who oppresses people

oppressive *adjective*
1 harsh and cruel ♦ *They live under an oppressive regime* 2 hot and tiring ♦ *The weather can be very oppressive in July*

opt *verb* (**opts, opting, opted**)
to opt for something or to do something is to choose it ♦ *I opted for the cash prize* ♦ *We opted to go abroad*
to opt out is to decide not to join in

optical *adjective*
to do with sight or the eyes
optically *adverb* as far as sight or the eyes are concerned

optical illusion *noun* (*plural* **optical illusions**)
something you think you see that is not really there

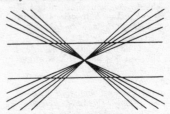

optician *noun* (*plural* **opticians**)
(*pronounced* op-**tish**-an)
someone who tests your eyesight and supplies spectacles

optimist *noun* (*plural* **optimists**)
someone who usually expects things to turn out well
optimism *noun* being an optimist

optimistic *adjective*
expecting things to turn out well
optimistically *adverb* in an optimistic way

option *noun* (*plural* **options**)
1 the right to choose; choice ♦ *You have the option of staying* 2 something that is or can be chosen ♦ *Your options are to travel by bus or by train*

optional *adjective*
that you can choose; not compulsory
optionally *adverb* as a choice or option

opulent *adjective* (*pronounced* **op**-yoo-lent)
1 wealthy or luxurious 2 abundant or plentiful ♦ *The garden had plants with opulent foliage*
opulence *noun* being opulent **opulently** *adverb* in an opulent way

or *conjunction*
used to show that there is a choice or alternative ♦ *Do you want a cake or a biscuit?*

oral *adjective*
1 spoken, not written 2 to do with the mouth or using your mouth
orally *adverb* by speaking, not writing

orange ➤ *noun* (*plural* **oranges**)
1 a round juicy fruit with thick reddish-yellow peel 2 a reddish-yellow colour

orange ➤ *adjective*
reddish-yellow

orangeade *noun* (*plural* **orangeades**)
a drink with a flavour of oranges

orang-utan *noun* (*plural* **orang-utans**)
(*pronounced* o-rang-u-**tan**)
a large kind of ape found in Borneo and
Sumatra

oration *noun* (*plural* **orations**)
a long formal speech

orator *noun* (*plural* **orators**) (*pronounced*
o-ra-ter)
someone who makes formal speeches

oratorio *noun* (*plural* **oratorios**) (*pronounced*
o-ra-**tor**-i-oh)
a piece of music for voices and orchestra,
usually on a religious subject

oratory *noun*
the art of making speeches in public
oratorical *adjective* to do with oratory

orbit ➢ *noun* (*plural* **orbits**)
the curved path taken by something
moving round a planet or other body in
space

orbit ➢ *verb* (**orbits, orbiting, orbited**)
to orbit a planet or other body in space is
to move round it ♦ *The satellite orbited the
earth*
orbital *adjective* going round something;
forming an orbit

orchard *noun* (*plural* **orchards**)
a piece of ground with fruit trees

orchestra *noun* (*plural* **orchestras**)
a group of musicians playing various
instruments together
orchestral *adjective* to do with an orchestra

orchid *noun* (*plural* **orchids**) (*pronounced*
or-kid)
a brightly coloured flower

ordeal *noun* (*plural* **ordeals**)
a difficult or unpleasant experience

order ➢ *noun* (*plural* **orders**)
1 a command **2** a request for something to
be supplied **3** obedience or good behaviour
4 tidiness; neatness **5** the way things are
arranged ♦ *The words are in alphabetical
order* **6** a kind or sort of thing ♦ *They
showed courage of the highest order* **7** a
group of religious monks, priests, or nuns
in order that or **in order to** for the purpose of

order ➢ *verb* (**orders, ordering, ordered**)
1 to order someone to do something is to
tell them to do it **2** to order something is
to ask for it to be supplied to you

orderly *adjective*
1 arranged tidily or well; methodical
2 well-behaved; obedient
orderliness *noun* being orderly

ordinal number *noun* (*plural* **ordinal numbers**)
a number that shows where something
comes in a series, for example 1st, 2nd, 3rd
(compare *cardinal number*)

ordinary *adjective*
normal or usual; not special
ordinarily *adverb* usually

ore *noun* (*plural* **ores**)
rock with metal in it, such as iron ore

organ *noun* (*plural* **organs**)
1 a musical instrument from which
sounds are produced by air forced through
pipes, played by keys and pedals **2** a part
of the body with a particular function, for
example the digestive organs

organic *adjective*
1 to do with the organs of the body
2 made by or found in living things
3 organic food is grown or produced
without using artificial chemicals to act as
fertilizers or pesticides

organism *noun* (*plural* **organisms**)
a living animal or plant

organist *noun* (*plural* **organists**)
someone who plays the organ

organization *noun* (*plural* **organizations**)
1 an organization is an organized group of
people **2** organization is organizing things
such as getting people together to do
something

organize *verb* (**organizes, organizing, organized**)
1 to organize people is to get them
together to do something **2** to organize
something is to plan or arrange it ♦ *We
organized a picnic* **3** to organize things is
to put them in order
organizer *noun* someone who organizes
something

oriental *adjective*
to do with the countries east of the
Mediterranean Sea, especially China and
Japan

orienteering *noun* (*pronounced*
or-i-en-**teer**-ing)
the sport of finding your way across rough
country with a map and compass

origami noun (pronounced o-ri-gah-mi)
folding pieces of paper to make decorative
shapes

origin noun (plural **origins**)
the start of something; the point where
something began

original adjective
1 existing from the start; earliest ♦ They
were the original inhabitants 2 new; not a
copy or an imitation ♦ It is an original
design 3 producing new ideas; inventive
♦ He was an original thinker.
originality noun being original or inventive
originally adverb in the beginning

originate verb (**originates, originating, originated**)
1 to originate something is to create it or
develop it 2 to originate is to start in a
certain way ♦ The war originated in a
dispute over fishing rights
origination noun originating something
originator noun someone who originates
something

ornament noun (plural **ornaments**)
an object worn or displayed as a decoration
ornamental adjective used as an ornament
ornamentation noun decoration

ornithology noun (pronounced
or-ni-thol-o-ji)
the study of birds
ornithological adjective to do with birds
ornithologist noun an expert on birds

orphan noun (plural **orphans**)
a child whose parents are dead

orphanage noun (plural **orphanages**)
a home for orphans

orthodox adjective
having beliefs that are correct or generally
accepted
orthodoxy noun being orthodox

Orthodox Church noun
the Christian Churches of eastern Europe

oscillate verb (**oscillates, oscillating, oscillated**)
(pronounced **oss**-il-ate)
to oscillate is to vibrate or move to and fro
oscillation noun oscillating

ostrich noun (plural **ostriches**)
a large long-legged bird that can run fast
but cannot fly

other ➤ adjective
not the same as this; different ♦ Play some
other tune ♦ Try the other shoe
every other day every second day, for
example Monday, Wednesday, and Friday
other than except ♦ They have no belongings
other than what they are carrying
the other day or **the other week** a few days or
weeks ago

other ➤ noun (plural **others**)
the other person or thing ♦ Where are the
others?

otherwise adverb
1 if you do not; if things happen
differently ♦ Write it down, otherwise
you'll forget it 2 in other ways ♦ It rained
a lot but otherwise the holiday was good
3 differently ♦ We could not do otherwise

otter noun (plural **otters**)
an animal with thick fur, webbed feet, and
a flat tail, that lives near water

ouch interjection
a cry of pain

ought verb
used with other words to show 1 what
you should or must do ♦ You ought to do
your music practice 2 what is likely to
happen ♦ With all these dark clouds it
ought to rain

ounce noun (plural **ounces**)
a unit of weight equal to $\frac{1}{16}$ of a pound or
about 28 grams

our adjective
belonging to us ♦ This is our house

ours pronoun
belonging to us ♦ This house is ours

ourselves pronoun
us and nobody else, used to refer back to
the subject of a verb ♦ We have hurt
ourselves
by ourselves on our own; alone ♦ We did the
work all by ourselves

out *adverb*
1 away from a place or not in it; not at home 2 into the open or outdoors ♦ *Are you going out today?* 3 not burning or working ♦ *The fire has gone out* 4 loudly ♦ *She cried out* 5 completely ♦ *They have sold out* 6 dismissed from a game ♦ *Another batsman is out*
to be out for something is to want it badly
to be out of something is to have no more of it left
out of date old-fashioned; not used any more
out of doors in the open air
out of the way remote or distant

out and out *adjective*
complete or thorough ♦ *He is an out and out villain*

outback *noun*
the remote inland areas of Australia

outboard motor *noun* (*plural* **outboard motors**)
a motor fitted to the outside of a boat's stern

outbreak *noun* (*plural* **outbreaks**)
the sudden start of a disease, war, or show of anger

outburst *noun* (*plural* **outbursts**)
the sudden beginning of anger or laughter

outcast *noun* (*plural* **outcasts**)
someone who has been rejected by family, friends, or society

outcome *noun* (*plural* **outcomes**)
the result of what happens or has happened

outcry *noun* (*plural* **outcries**)
a strong protest from many people ♦ *There was an outcry over the rise in rail fares*

outdated *adjective*
out of date

outdo *verb* (**outdoes, outdoing, outdid, outdone**)
to outdo someone else is to do better than them

outdoor *adjective*
done or used outdoors ♦ *You'll need your outdoor clothes*

outdoors *adverb*
in the open air ♦ *It is cold outdoors*

outer *adjective*
nearer the outside; external

outer space *noun*
the universe beyond the earth's atmosphere

outfit *noun* (*plural* **outfits**)
1 a set of clothes worn together 2 a set of things needed for doing something

outgrow *verb* (**outgrows, outgrowing, outgrew, outgrown**)
1 to outgrow something such as clothes or a habit is to grow out of them 2 to outgrow someone is to grow faster or taller than them

outhouse *noun* (*plural* **outhouses**)
a small building attached to a larger building or close to it

outing *noun* (*plural* **outings**)
a trip or short journey for pleasure

outlast *verb* (**outlasts, outlasting, outlasted**)
to outlast something else is to last longer than it

outlaw ➢ *noun* (*plural* **outlaws**)
a person who is punished by being no longer protected by the law, especially a robber or bandit

outlaw ➢ *verb* (**outlaws, outlawing, outlawed**)
1 to outlaw someone is to make them an outlaw 2 to outlaw something is to make it illegal

outlet *noun* (*plural* **outlets**)
1 a way for something to get out ♦ *The tank has an outlet at the bottom* 2 a place to sell goods ♦ *We need to find fresh outlets for our products*

outline ➢ *noun* (*plural* **outlines**)
1 a line round the outside of something; a line showing the shape of a thing 2 a summary

outline ➢ *verb* (**outlines, outlining, outlined**)
1 to outline something is to draw a line round it to show its shape 2 to outline a story or account is to summarize or describe it briefly

outlook *noun* (*plural* **outlooks**)
1 a view on which people look out 2 the way that someone looks at and thinks about things 3 what seems likely to happen in the future ♦ *The outlook is bright*

outlying *adjective*
far from a town or city; distant ♦ *We need to visit the outlying districts*

outnumber *verb* (**outnumbers, outnumbering, outnumbered**)
to outnumber something else is to be greater in number than it

outpatient *noun* (*plural* **outpatients**)
a patient who visits a hospital for treatment but does not stay there

outpost *noun* (*plural* **outposts**)
a distant settlement

output ➢ *noun* (*plural* **outputs**)
1 the amount produced, especially by a factory or business 2 (*in Computing*) information produced by a computer

output ➤ *verb* (**outputs, outputting, output**)
(*in Computing*) to output information is to get it from a computer

outrage ➤ *noun* (*plural* **outrages**)
something very shocking or cruel

outrage ➤ *verb* (**outrages, outraging, outraged**)
to outrage someone is to make them very shocked and angry

outrageous *adjective*
causing shock or outrage; dreadful

outright *adverb*
1 completely ♦ *We won outright* 2 all at once; in one go ♦ *They were able to buy their house outright*

outset *noun*
at or **from the outset** at or from the beginning of something

outside ➤ *noun* (*plural* **outsides**)
the outer side or surface of a thing; the part furthest from the middle

outside ➤ *adjective*
1 on or coming from the outside 2 the greatest possible ♦ *£100 is the outside price* 3 slight or remote ♦ *There is an outside chance that he will come*

outside ➤ *adverb* and *preposition*
on or to the outside of something ♦ *Go outside* ♦ *It's outside the house*

outside broadcast *noun* (*plural* **outside broadcasts**)
a broadcast made where something is happening and not in a studio

outsider *noun* (*plural* **outsiders**)
1 someone who is not a member of a particular group of people 2 a horse or person thought to have no chance of winning a race or contest

outskirts *plural noun*
the parts on the outside edge of an area; the suburbs of a town

outspoken *adjective*
speaking frankly; not tactful

outstanding *adjective*
1 extremely good or distinguished ♦ *She is an outstanding athlete* 2 not yet dealt with ♦ *What are your outstanding debts?*

outward *adjective*
1 going outwards 2 on the outside

outwardly *adverb*
on the outside; for people to see ♦ *They were outwardly calm*

outwards *adverb*
towards the outside

outweigh *verb* (**outweighs, outweighing, outweighed**)
to outweigh something is to be more important than it ♦ *The benefits of the plan outweigh its drawbacks*

outwit *verb* (**outwits, outwitting, outwitted**)
to outwit someone is to deceive or defeat them by being more clever

oval ➤ *adjective*
shaped like an egg or a number 0

oval ➤ *noun* (*plural* **ovals**)
an oval shape

ovary *noun* (*plural* **ovaries**)
1 part of a female body where egg-cells (*ova*) are produced 2 the part of a flowering plant that produces seeds

oven *noun* (*plural* **ovens**)
a closed space in which things are cooked or heated

over ➤ *adverb*
1 down or sideways; out and down from the top or edge ♦ *He fell over* 2 across to a place ♦ *We walked over to the house* 3 so that a different side shows ♦ *Turn it over* 4 finished ♦ *The lesson is over* 5 left or remaining ♦ *There are a few apples over* 6 through or thoroughly ♦ *Think it over*
over and over repeatedly; many times

over ➤ *preposition*
1 above or covering ♦ *There's a light over the door* ♦ *I'll put a cloth over the table* 2 across ♦ *They ran over the road* 3 more than ♦ *The house is over a mile away* 4 concerning; about ♦ *They quarrelled over money* 5 during ♦ *We can talk over dinner* 6 being better than ♦ *They won a victory over their opponents*

over ➤ *noun* (*plural* **overs**)
in cricket, a series of six balls bowled by one person

over- *prefix*
meaning 'too much', as in *over-excited*

overall *adjective* and *adverb*
including everything; total ♦ *What is the overall cost?*

overalls *plural noun*
a kind of light coat worn over other clothes to protect them when working

overarm *adjective* and *adverb*
with the arm lifted above shoulder level and coming down in front of the body

overboard *adverb*
over the side of a boat into the water ♦ *He jumped overboard*

overcast *adjective*
covered with cloud ♦ *The sky is grey and overcast*

overcoat *noun* (*plural* **overcoats**)
a warm outdoor coat

overcome *verb* (**overcomes, overcoming, overcame, overcome**)
1 to overcome someone is to gain a victory over them **2** to overcome a problem or difficulty is to succeed in spite of it **3** to be overcome by something is to become helpless from it ♦ *She was overcome by the fumes*

overdo *verb* (**overdoes, overdoing, overdid, overdone**)
1 to overdo something is to do it too much **2** to overdo food is to cook it for too long

overdose *noun* (*plural* **overdoses**)
too large a dose of a drug or medicine

overdue *adjective*
later than it should be ♦ *The train is overdue*

overflow *verb* (**overflows, overflowing, overflowed**)
to overflow is to flow over the edges or limits of something

overgrown *adjective*
covered with weeds or unwanted plants

overhang *verb* (**overhangs, overhanging, overhung**)
to overhang something is to stick out beyond and above it ♦ *The second storey of the old house overhung the first*

overhaul *verb* (**overhauls, overhauling, overhauled**)
1 to overhaul a machine or vehicle is to check it thoroughly and repair it if necessary **2** to overhaul someone or something is to overtake it

overhead *adjective* and *adverb*
above your head; in the sky

overheads *plural noun*
the expenses of running a business

overhear *verb* (**overhears, overhearing, overheard**)
to overhear something is to hear it accidentally or without the speaker knowing

overland *adjective* and *adverb*
travelling over the land, not by sea or air

overlap *verb* (**overlaps, overlapping, overlapped**)
to overlap something is to lie across part of it ♦ *The carpet overlapped the fireplace*

overlook *verb* (**overlooks, overlooking, overlooked**)
1 to overlook something is not to notice it **2** to overlook a mistake or offence is not to punish it **3** to overlook a place is to have a view over it ♦ *The hotel overlooks the city park*

overnight *adverb* and *adjective*
of or during a night ♦ *We stayed overnight in a hotel* ♦ *There will be an overnight stop in Paris*

overpower *verb* (**overpowers, overpowering, overpowered**)
to overpower someone is to overcome them by force

overpowering *adjective* very strong

overrun *verb* (**overruns, overrunning, overran, overrun**)
1 to overrun an area is to spread harmfully over it ♦ *The place is overrun with mice* **2** to overrun is to go on longer than it should ♦ *The programme overran by ten minutes*

overseas ➢ *adverb*
abroad ♦ *They travelled overseas*

overseas ➢ *adjective*
from abroad; foreign ♦ *We met some overseas students*

oversight *noun* (*plural* **oversights**)
a mistake made by not noticing something

oversleep *verb* (**oversleeps, oversleeping, overslept**)
to sleep longer than you intended to

overtake *verb* (**overtakes, overtaking, overtook, overtaken**)
to overtake a moving vehicle or person is to catch them up or pass them in the same direction

overthrow ➢ *verb* (**overthrows, overthrowing, overthrew, overthrown**)
1 to overthrow something is to abolish it or make it fail **2** to overthrow someone is to defeat them

overthrow ➢ *noun* (*plural* **overthrows**)
overthrowing or defeating someone or something

overtime *noun*
time spent working outside the normal hours

overture *noun* (*plural* **overtures**)
a piece of music played at the start of a concert, opera, or ballet
overtures a friendly attempt to start a discussion with someone

overturn *verb* (**overturns, overturning, overturned**)
1 to overturn something is to make it turn over or fall over **2** to overturn is to turn over ♦ *The car went out of control and overturned*

overwhelm *verb* (**overwhelms, overwhelming, overwhelmed**)
1 to overwhelm someone or something is to bury or drown them under a huge mass ♦ *The sea overwhelmed several coastal villages* **2** to overwhelm someone is to overcome them completely

overwork ➤ *verb* (**overworks, overworking, overworked**)
1 to overwork is to become exhausted from working too hard **2** to overwork something is to use it too much ♦ *Don't overwork the word 'nice'*

overwork ➤ *noun*
too much work, causing exhaustion

ovum *noun* (*plural* **ova**) (*pronounced* oh-vum)
a female cell that can develop into offspring of plants and animals

owe *verb* (**owes, owing, owed**)
1 to owe something, especially money, is to have a duty to pay or give it to someone ♦ *I owe you a pound* **2** to owe something to someone is to have it thanks to them ♦ *They owed their lives to the pilot's skill*
owing to something because of it ♦ *The train was late owing to leaves on the line*

owl *noun* (*plural* **owls**)
a bird of prey with large eyes, usually flying at night

own ➤ *adjective*
belonging to yourself or itself
to get your own back (*informal*) is to have your revenge
on your own by yourself; alone ♦ *I did it all on my own* ♦ *I sat on my own in the empty room*

own ➤ *verb* (**owns, owning, owned**)
to own something is to have it as your property
to own up to something (*informal*) is to admit that you did it

owner *noun* (*plural* **owners**)
the person who owns something
ownership *noun* owning something

ox *noun* (*plural* **oxen**)
a neutered bull kept for its meat and for pulling carts

oxide *noun* (*plural* **oxides**)
a compound of oxygen and one other element

oxidize *verb* (**oxidizes, oxidizing, oxidized**)
1 to oxidize something is to cause it to combine with oxygen **2** to oxidize is to be combined with oxygen
oxidation *noun* oxidizing

oxygen *noun*
one of the gases in the air that people need to stay alive

oyster *noun* (*plural* **oysters**)
a kind of shellfish whose shell sometimes contains a pearl

oz. short for **ounce** or **ounces**

ozone *noun*
a gas that is a form of oxygen

ozone layer *noun*
a layer of ozone high in the atmosphere, that absorbs harmful radiation from the sun

Pp

p short for **penny** or **pence**

pa *noun* (*plural* **pas**)
(*informal*) father

pace ➤ *noun* (*plural* **paces**)
1 one step in walking, marching, or running **2** speed ♦ *He set a fast pace*

pace ➤ *verb* (**paces, pacing, paced**)
to pace is to walk with slow or regular steps ♦ *He was pacing across the room as he spoke*
to pace something off or **pace something out** is to measure a distance in paces

pacemaker *noun* (*plural* **pacemakers**)
1 a person who sets the speed for someone else in a race **2** an electrical device put into a person by surgery, that keeps the heart beating regularly

pacifist *noun* (*plural* **pacifists**) (*pronounced* pas-i-fist)
someone who believes that war is always wrong
pacifism *noun* being a pacifist

pacify *verb* (**pacifies, pacifying, pacified**)
(*pronounced* **pas**-i-fy)
1 to pacify someone is to calm them down
2 to pacify a people or country is to bring
them peace
pacification *noun* pacifying someone or a
country

pack ➤ *noun* (*plural* **packs**)
1 a bundle or collection of things wrapped
or tied together **2** a set of playing cards
3 a haversack **4** a group of hounds,
wolves, or other animals **5** a group of
people, especially a group of Brownies or
Cub Scouts

pack ➤ *verb* (**packs, packing, packed**)
1 to pack a suitcase, bag, or box is to put
things in it so as to store them or take
them somewhere **2** to pack a room or
building is to fill it ♦ *The hall was packed*

package *noun* (*plural* **packages**)
1 a parcel or packet **2** a number of things
offered or accepted together

package holiday *noun* (*plural* **package
holidays**)
a holiday with all travel and
accommodation arranged and included in
the price

packet *noun* (*plural* **packets**)
a small parcel

pad¹ ➤ *noun* (*plural* **pads**)
1 a piece of soft material used to protect or
shape something **2** a piece of soft material
worn to protect your leg in cricket and
other games **3** a flat surface from which
helicopters take off or rockets are
launched **4** a number of sheets of blank or
lined paper joined together along one edge

pad ➤ *verb* (**pads, padding, padded**)
to pad something is to put a piece of soft
material on it or into it so as to protect or
shape it
to pad something out is to make a book or
story longer than it needs to be

pad² *verb* (**pads, padding, padded**)
to pad is to walk softly

padding *noun*
soft material used to pad things

paddle ➤ *verb* (**paddles, paddling, paddled**)
1 to paddle is to walk about with bare feet
in shallow water **2** to paddle a boat is to
move it along with a short oar

paddle ➤ *noun* (*plural* **paddles**)
1 a time spent paddling in water **2** a
short oar with a broad blade

paddock *noun* (*plural* **paddocks**)
a small field for keeping horses

paddy *noun* (*plural* **paddies**)
a field where rice is grown

padlock *noun* (*plural* **padlocks**)
a lock with a metal loop that you can use
to fasten a gate or lock a bicycle

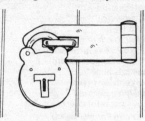

pagan *noun* (*plural* **pagans**)
a person who does not believe in any
religion; a heathen

page¹ *noun* (*plural* **pages**)
a piece of paper that is part of a book or
newspaper; one side of this piece of paper

page² *noun* (*plural* **pages**)
a boy who acts as an attendant or runs
errands

pageant *noun* (*plural* **pageants**)
(*pronounced* **paj**-ent)
1 a play or entertainment about historical
events and people **2** a procession of people
in costume
pageantry *noun* elaborate display

pagoda *noun* (*plural* **pagodas**) (*pronounced*
pa-**goh**-da)
a Buddhist tower or Hindu temple in the
Far East

paid past tense and past participle of **pay**
verb

pail *noun* (*plural* **pails**)
a bucket

pain ➤ *noun* (*plural* **pains**)
 1 pain or a pain is an unpleasant feeling caused by injury or disease **2** pain is also mental suffering
 to take pains is to make a careful effort or take trouble over something

pain ➤ *verb* (**pains, paining, pained**)
 to pain someone is to cause them pain, usually mental pain

painful *adjective*
 causing pain
 painfully *adverb* in a painful way

painkiller *noun* (*plural* **painkillers**)
 a drug that reduces pain

painless *adjective*
 not causing any pain

painstaking *adjective*
 making a careful effort

paint ➤ *noun* (*plural* **paints**)
 a liquid substance put on something to colour or cover it

paint ➤ *verb* (**paints, painting, painted**)
 1 to paint something is to put paint on it **2** to paint a picture is to make it with paints **3** to paint someone or something is to make a picture of them

paintbox *noun* (*plural* **paintboxes**)
 a box of coloured paints used in art

paintbrush *noun* (*plural* **paintbrushes**)
 a brush used in painting

painter[1] *noun* (*plural* **painters**)
 someone who paints

painter[2] *noun* (*plural* **painters**)
 a rope used to tie up a boat

painting *noun* (*plural* **paintings**)
 1 painting is using paints to make a picture ♦ *She likes painting* **2** a painting is a painted picture

pair *noun* (*plural* **pairs**)
 1 two things or people that go together or are the same kind ♦ *I need a new pair of shoes* **2** something made of two parts joined together ♦ *Have you got a pair of scissors?*

pal *noun* (*plural* **pals**)
 (*informal*) a friend

palace *noun* (*plural* **palaces**)
 a mansion where a king or queen or other important person lives

palate *noun* (*plural* **palates**) (*pronounced* pal-at)
 1 the roof of your mouth **2** a person's sense of taste ♦ *She has a refined palate*

pale *adjective* (**paler, palest**)
 1 almost white ♦ *He had a pale face* **2** not bright in colour; faint ♦ *The sky was a pale blue*
 paleness *noun* being pale

palette *noun* (*plural* **palettes**) (*pronounced* pal-it)
 a board on which an artist mixes colours

paling *noun* (*plural* **palings**)
 a wooden fence

palisade *noun* (*plural* **palisades**)
 a fence made of wooden posts or railings

pall *verb* (**palls, palling, palled**)
 to pall is to become dull or uninteresting after a time ♦ *The novelty of the new computer game soon began to pall*

pallid *adjective*
 pale, especially because of illness

pallor *noun*
 paleness in a person's face, especially from illness

palm ➤ *noun* (*plural* **palms**)
 1 the inner part of your hand, between your fingers and wrist **2** a tropical tree with large leaves and no branches

palm ➤ *verb* (**palms, palming, palmed**)
 to palm something off on someone is to fool them into taking something they don't want

palmistry *noun*
 fortune-telling by looking for signs in the markings of a person's hand

Palm Sunday *noun*
 the Sunday before Easter, when Christians celebrate Christ's entry into Jerusalem on a path of palm leaves

paltry *adjective*
 not very much or not very valuable ♦ *His reward was a paltry 50 pence*

pampas *plural noun*
 pampas are wide grassy plains in South America

pampas grass *noun*
 a tall grass with long feathery flowers

pamper *verb* (**pampers, pampering, pampered**)
 to pamper someone is to treat them too kindly and let them have whatever they want

pamphlet *noun* (*plural* **pamphlets**)
 a thin book with a paper cover

pan *noun* (*plural* **pans**)
 1 a pot or dish with a flat base, used for cooking **2** the bowl of a lavatory

pancake *noun* (*plural* **pancakes**)
 a flat round cake of batter fried on both sides

panda *noun* (*plural* **pandas**)
a large black-and-white animal found in China

panda car *noun* (*plural* **panda cars**)
a police patrol car, which was originally white with black stripes on the sides

pandemonium *noun*
a loud noise or disturbance

pander *verb* (**panders, pandering, pandered**)
to pander to someone is to let them have whatever they want

pane *noun* (*plural* **panes**)
a sheet of glass in a window

panel *noun* (*plural* **panels**)
1 a long flat piece of wood, metal, or other material that is part of a door, wall, or piece of furniture 2 a group of people appointed to discuss or decide something
♦ *He was tried by a panel of judges*

pang *noun* (*plural* **pangs**)
a sudden feeling of pain or strong emotion

panic ➤ *noun*
sudden fear that makes you behave wildly
panicky *adjective* feeling panic

panic ➤ *verb* (**panics, panicking, panicked**)
to panic is to be overcome with fear or anxiety and behave wildly

pannier *noun* (*plural* **panniers**)
a bag or basket hung on one side of a bicycle or horse

panorama *noun* (*plural* **panoramas**)
a view or picture of a wide area
panoramic *adjective* covering a wide area

pansy *noun* (*plural* **pansies**)
a small brightly-coloured garden flower

pant *verb* (**pants, panting, panted**)
to pant is to take short quick breaths, usually after running or working hard

panther *noun* (*plural* **panthers**)
a leopard

panties *plural noun*
(*informal*) short knickers worn by women and girls

pantomime *noun* (*plural* **pantomimes**)
a Christmas entertainment based on a fairy tale

pantry *noun* (*plural* **pantries**)
a cupboard or small room for storing food

pants *plural noun*
1 (*informal*) underpants or knickers 2 (*in America*) trousers

paper ➤ *noun* (*plural* **papers**)
1 paper is a thin substance made in sheets and used for writing or printing or drawing on, or for wrapping things 2 a paper is a newspaper 3 a paper is also a document

paper ➤ *verb* (**papers, papering, papered**)
to paper a wall or room is to cover it with wallpaper

paperback *noun* (*plural* **paperbacks**)
a book with thin flexible covers

papier mâché *noun* (*pronounced* pap-yay mash-ay)
paper made into pulp and used to make models or ornaments

papyrus *noun* (*plural* **papyri**) (*pronounced* pa-py-rus)
1 papyrus is a kind of paper made from the stems of reeds, used in ancient Egypt
2 a papyrus is a document written on this paper

parable *noun* (*plural* **parables**)
a story told to teach people something, especially one of the stories told by Jesus Christ

parachute *noun* (*plural* **parachutes**)
an umbrella-shaped device on which people or things can float slowly down to the ground from an aircraft
parachutist *noun* someone who uses a parachute

parade ➤ *noun* (*plural* **parades**)
1 a procession that displays people or things 2 an assembly of troops for inspection or drill 3 a public square or row of shops

parade ➤ *verb* (**parades, parading, paraded**)
1 to parade is to move in a public procession 2 to parade is also to assemble for inspection or drill, as soldiers do

paradise *noun*
 1 heaven; a heavenly place 2 in the Bible, the Garden of Eden

paradox *noun* (*plural* **paradoxes**)
 (*pronounced* pa-ra-doks)
 a statement which does not seem to make sense but may still be true, for example 'More haste, less speed'

paradoxical *adjective*
 seeming to make no sense; like a paradox
 paradoxically *adverb* in a paradoxical way

paraffin *noun*
 a kind of oil used as fuel

paragraph *noun* (*plural* **paragraphs**)
 a group of sentences forming a division of a piece of writing, and beginning on a new line

parallel *adjective*
 parallel lines are lines that are the same distance apart for their whole length, like railway lines

parallelogram *noun* (*plural* **parallelograms**)
 a four-sided figure with its opposite sides parallel to each other and equal in length

paralyse *verb* (**paralyses, paralysing, paralysed**)
 1 to paralyse someone is to make them unable to feel anything or to move 2 to paralyse something is to make it unable to move or work properly ◆ *Train services were paralysed by the strike*

paralysis *noun* (*pronounced* pa-ral-i-sis)
 being unable to move or feel anything
 paralytic *adjective* suffering from paralysis

parapet *noun* (*plural* **parapets**)
 a low wall along the edge of a balcony, bridge, or roof

paraphernalia *noun* (*pronounced* pa-ra-fer-nay-li-a)
 various pieces of equipment or small possessions

paraphrase *verb* (**paraphrases, paraphrasing, paraphrased**)
 to paraphrase something said or written is to give its meaning by using different words

parasite *noun* (*plural* **parasites**)
 an animal or plant that lives in or on another, from which it gets its food
 parasitic *adjective* like a parasite

parasol *noun* (*plural* **parasols**)
 a lightweight umbrella used to shade yourself from the sun

paratroops *plural noun*
 troops trained to be dropped from aircraft by using parachutes
 paratrooper *noun* a soldier in the paratroops

parcel *noun* (*plural* **parcels**)
 something wrapped up to be posted or carried

parched *adjective*
 very dry or thirsty

parchment *noun*
 a kind of heavy paper originally made from animal skins

pardon ➤ *verb* (**pardons, pardoning, pardoned**)
 to pardon someone is to forgive or excuse them

pardon ➤ *noun* (*plural* **pardons**)
 1 forgiveness; an act of pardoning someone 2 used as an exclamation to mean 'I didn't hear or understand what you said', or 'I apologize'

pardonable *adjective*
 able to be forgiven ◆ *Their mistake was pardonable*

parent *noun* (*plural* **parents**)
 a father or mother; a living thing that has produced offspring
 parental *adjective* to do with parents
 parenthood *noun* being a parent

parentage *noun*
 who your parents are

parenthesis *noun* (*plural* **parentheses**)
 (*pronounced* pa-ren-thi-sis)
 1 something extra put in a sentence between brackets or dashes 2 one of a pair of brackets (like these) used in the middle of a sentence

parish *noun* (*plural* **parishes**)
 a district that has its own church
 parishioner *noun* a member of a parish

park ➤ *noun* (*plural* **parks**)
 1 a large area with grass and trees, for public use 2 a piece of ground belonging to a large country house

park ➤ *verb* (**parks, parking, parked**)
 to park a vehicle is to leave it somewhere for a time

parka *noun* (*plural* **parkas**)
 a warm jacket with a hood attached

parking meter *noun* (*plural* **parking meters**)
 a device that shows how long a vehicle has been parked in a street ◆ *When you park your car, you put a coin in the parking meter*

parliament *noun* (*plural* **parliaments**)
 the group of people that make a country's laws
 parliamentary *adjective* to do with a parliament

parody *noun* (*plural* **parodies**)
 a play or poem that makes fun of people or things by imitating them

parole *noun* (*pronounced* pa-rohl)
 letting someone out of prison before they have finished their sentence, on condition that they behave well ◆ *He was on parole*

parrot *noun* (*plural* **parrots**)
a brightly-coloured bird that can learn to repeat words or sounds

parsley *noun*
a plant with crinkled green leaves used to flavour and decorate food

parsnip *noun* (*plural* **parsnips**)
a pale yellow vegetable

parson *noun* (*plural* **parsons**)
a member of the clergy

parsonage *noun* (*plural* **parsonages**)
a rectory or vicarage

part ➤ *noun* (*plural* **parts**)
1 some but not all of a thing or a number of things; anything that belongs to something bigger **2** the character played by an actor or actress; the words spoken by a character in a play

part ➤ *verb* (**parts**, **parting**, **parted**)
1 to part people or things is to separate them or divide them **2** to part is to separate **3** to part hair is to divide it so that it goes in two different directions
to part with something is to give it away or get rid of it

part exchange *noun* (*plural* **part exchanges**)
giving something you own as well as some money as part of the price for something else

partial *adjective*
1 not complete or total ♦ *There will be a partial eclipse of the sun* **2** favouring one person or side more than another; unfair
to be partial to something is to like it
partiality *noun* being partial **partially** *adverb* partly

participate *verb* (**participates**, **participating**, **participated**)
to participate in something is to take part or have a share in it
participant *noun* someone who participates in something **participation** *noun* participating

participle *noun* (*plural* **participles**)
a word formed from a verb and used as part of the verb or as an adjective, for example 'going', 'gone', 'sailed', 'sailing'

particle *noun* (*plural* **particles**)
a very small piece or amount

particular ➤ *adjective*
1 only this one and no other; special; individual ♦ *Are you looking for a particular book?* **2** fussy; hard to please ♦ *He is very particular about his clothes*
in particular especially; chiefly
particularly *adverb* especially

particular ➤ *noun* (*plural* **particulars**)
a detail or single fact

parting *noun* (*plural* **partings**)
1 leaving or separation **2** the line where hair is combed in different directions

partition *noun* (*plural* **partitions**)
1 partition is dividing something into parts **2** a partition is a thin dividing wall

partly *adverb*
not completely; somewhat

partner *noun* (*plural* **partners**)
1 one of a pair of people who do something together, especially in business, dancing, or playing a game **2** someone who is married to someone else or living with them
partnership *noun* being a partner

part of speech *noun* (*plural* **parts of speech**)
each of the groups (also called **word classes**) into which words can be divided in grammar: noun, adjective, verb, pronoun, adverb, preposition, conjunction, interjection

partridge *noun* (*plural* **partridges**)
a game bird with brown feathers

part-time *adjective* and *adverb*
working for only some of the normal hours
part-timer *noun* someone who works part-time

party *noun* (*plural* **parties**)
1 a time when people get together to enjoy themselves ♦ *Come to my birthday party* **2** a group of people working or travelling together ♦ *They organized a search party* **3** an organized group of people with similar political beliefs ♦ *The Labour Party won the election* **4** a person who is involved in an action or legal case ♦ *He is the guilty party*

pass ➤ *verb* (**passes, passing, passed**)
1 to pass something or someone is to go past them **2** to pass in a certain direction is to move or go that way ♦ *They passed over the bridge* **3** to pass something to someone is to give it or hand it to them ♦ *Please pass the jam* **4** to pass an examination is to be successful in it **5** to pass time is to use time doing something **6** to pass is to finish or no longer be there ♦ *His opportunity passed* **7** to pass a law or rule is to approve or accept it

pass ➤ *noun* (*plural* **passes**)
1 going by something **2** a success in an examination ♦ *She got several GCSE passes* **3** a permit to go in or out of a place **4** a narrow way between hills

passable *adjective*
just about acceptable or all right

passage *noun* (*plural* **passages**)
1 a way through something ♦ *The police forced a passage through the crowd* **2** a corridor **3** a journey by sea or air **4** a section of a piece of writing or music **5** passing ♦ *the passage of time*

passageway *noun* (*plural* **passageways**)
a passage or way through, especially between buildings

passenger *noun* (*plural* **passengers**)
someone who is driven in a car or travels by public transport

passer-by *noun* (*plural* **passers-by**)
someone who happens to be going past

passion *noun* (*plural* **passions**)
1 passion is strong feeling or emotion **2** a passion is a great enthusiasm for something
the Passion the suffering of Jesus Christ at the Crucifixion

passionate *adjective*
full of passion or strong feeling
passionately *adverb* in a passionate way

passion fruit *noun* (*plural* **passion fruits**)
a fruit that grows on a climbing plant in warm countries. Some people think its flowers look like the crown of thorns and other things associated with the Passion of Christ

passive *adjective*
1 not active; not resisting or fighting against something **2** (*in Grammar*) describing a verb in which the subject receives the action, for example in the sentence *She was hit by a car* the subject is *She* and *was hit* is a passive verb
passively *adverb* in a passive way

Passover *noun*
a Jewish religious festival, celebrating the escape of the ancient Jews from slavery in Egypt

passport *noun* (*plural* **passports**)
an official document that allows you to travel abroad

password *noun* (*plural* **passwords**)
a secret word or phrase used to distinguish friends from enemies, or to gain access to a computer system

past ➤ *noun*
the time gone by ♦ *Try to forget the past*

past ➤ *adjective*
of the time gone by ♦ *He was thinking about his past achievements*

past ➤ *preposition*
1 beyond ♦ *Go past the school and turn right* **2** later than ♦ *It is past midnight*
to be past it (*slang*) is to be too old to be able to do something

pasta *noun*
an Italian food made as a dried paste of flour, water, and often eggs, formed into various shapes such as macaroni and lasagne

paste ➤ *noun* (*plural* **pastes**)
a soft and moist or gluey substance

paste ➤ *verb* (**pastes, pasting, pasted**)
to paste something is to stick it to a surface with paste

pastel *noun* (*plural* **pastels**)
1 a crayon that is like a slightly greasy chalk **2** a light delicate colour

pasteurize *verb* (**pasteurizes, pasteurizing, pasteurized**) (*pronounced* **pahs**-cher-ryz)
to pasteurize milk is to purify it by heating and then cooling it
pasteurization *noun* the process of pasteurizing milk

pastille *noun* (*plural* **pastilles**)
a small flavoured sweet for sucking

pastime *noun* (*plural* **pastimes**)
something you do to pass time pleasantly; a hobby or game

pastoral *adjective*
to do with the country

past participle *noun* (*plural* **past participles**)
a form of a verb used after *has, have, had, was, were*, to describe an action that happened at a time before now, for example *done, overtaken*, and *written*

pastry *noun* (*plural* **pastries**)
1 pastry is dough made from flour, fat, and water rolled flat and baked **2** a pastry is something made from this dough

past tense *noun*
a form of a verb used to describe an action that happened at a time before now, for example *took* is the past tense of *take*

pasture *noun* (*plural* **pastures**)
land covered with grass that cattle, sheep, or horses can eat

pasty[1] *noun* (*plural* **pasties**) (*pronounced* pas-ti)
a pastry filled with meat and vegetables, like a small pie

pasty[2] *adjective* (**pastier, pastiest**) (*pronounced* pay-sti)
pale or white like paste

pat ➤ *verb* (**pats, patting, patted**)
to pat something or someone is to tap them gently with your open hand or with something flat

pat ➤ *noun* (*plural* **pats**)
1 a patting movement or sound 2 a small piece of butter
a pat on the back congratulations or praise

patch ➤ *noun* (*plural* **patches**)
1 a piece of material put over a hole or damaged place 2 an area that is different from its surroundings ♦ *We have a black cat with a white patch on its chest* 3 a small area of land 4 a small piece of something ♦ *There are patches of ice on the road*

patch ➤ *verb* (**patches, patching, patched**)
to patch something is to put a piece of material on it to repair it
to patch something up is to repair it roughly
to patch things up is to be friendly again after a quarrel

patchwork *noun*
needlework using small pieces of different cloth which are sewn together

patchy *adjective* (**patchier, patchiest**)
occurring in some areas but not others; uneven ♦ *There may be some patchy rain*

patent ➤ *noun* (*plural* **patents**) (*pronounced* pay-tent or pat-ent)
an official authority given to someone to make something they have invented and to stop other people from copying it

patent ➤ *adjective* (*pronounced* pay-tent)
1 protected by a patent 2 obvious ♦ *What they say is a patent lie*

patent ➤ *verb* (**patents, patenting, patented**) (*pronounced* pay-tent or pat-ent)
to patent an idea or invention is to get a patent for it

patent leather *noun*
leather with a special glossy surface

patently *adverb*
clearly; obviously ♦ *They were patently lying*

paternal *adjective*
to do with a father, or like a father

path *noun* (*plural* **paths**)
1 a narrow way to walk or ride along 2 the line along which something moves ♦ *They were tracing the path of the meteor*

pathetic *adjective*
1 sad and pitiful 2 sadly or comically weak or useless ♦ *He made a pathetic attempt to climb the tree*
pathetically *adverb* in a pathetic way

patience *noun* (*pronounced* pay-shens)
1 being patient 2 a card game for one person

patient ➤ *adjective* (*pronounced* pay-shent)
1 able to wait for a long time without getting anxious or angry 2 able to bear pain or trouble
patiently *adverb* in a patient way

patient ➤ *noun* (*plural* **patients**) (*pronounced* pay-shent)
a person who is getting treatment from a doctor or dentist

patio *noun* (*plural* **patios**) (*pronounced* pat-i-oh)
a paved area beside a house

patriot *noun* (*plural* **patriots**) (*pronounced* pay-tri-ot or pat-ri-ot)
someone who loves and supports their country
patriotic *adjective* loyal to your country
patriotism *noun* being a patriot

patrol ➤ *verb* (**patrols, patrolling, patrolled**)
to walk or travel regularly round a place or a thing to guard it and make sure that all is well

patrol ➤ *noun* (*plural* **patrols**)
1 a patrolling group of people or vehicles 2 a group of Scouts or Guides
on patrol patrolling

patron *noun* (*plural* **patrons**) (*pronounced* pay-tron)
1 someone who supports a person or cause with money or encouragement 2 a regular customer of a shop or business
patronage *noun* being a patron

patronize *verb* (**patronizes, patronizing, patronized**)
1 to patronize a shop or business is to be one of its regular customers 2 to patronize someone is to treat them as an inferior

patron saint *noun* (*plural* **patron saints**)
a saint who is thought of as protecting a
place or activity

patter[1] ➤ *noun* (*plural* **patters**)
a series of light tapping sounds

patter ➤ *verb* (**patters, pattering, pattered**)
to patter is to make light tapping sounds
♦ *The rain was pattering on the glass roof*

patter[2] *noun*
the quick talk of a performer or
salesperson

pattern *noun* (*plural* **patterns**)
1 a decorative arrangement of lines or
shapes **2** a thing that you copy so as to
make something, such as a piece of
clothing

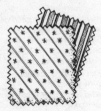

pause ➤ *noun* (*plural* **pauses**)
a short stop before continuing

pause ➤ *verb* (**pauses, pausing, paused**)
1 to pause is to make a short stop before
continuing **2** to pause a video recorder,
cassette recorder, CD player is to make
the tape or disc stop for a short time

pave *verb* (**paves, paving, paved**)
to pave a road or path is to put a hard
surface on it
to pave the way is to prepare for something

pavement *noun* (*plural* **pavements**)
a path with a hard surface, along the side
of a street

pavilion *noun* (*plural* **pavilions**)
a building at a sports ground for players
and spectators to use

paw ➤ *noun* (*plural* **paws**)
an animal's foot

paw ➤ *verb* (**paws, pawing, pawed**)
to paw something is to touch or scrape it
clumsily with a hand or foot

pawn ➤ *noun* (*plural* **pawns**)
1 one of the sixteen pieces in chess that
are at the front on each side and are the
least valuable **2** a person who is
controlled by someone else

pawn ➤ *verb* (**pawns, pawning, pawned**)
to pawn something is to leave it with a
pawnbroker while borrowing money ♦ *He
had to pawn his watch*

pawnbroker *noun* (*plural* **pawnbrokers**)
a shopkeeper who lends money to people
in return for objects that they leave and
which are sold if the money is not paid
back

pay ➤ *verb* (**pays, paying, paid**)
1 to pay for something is to give money in
return for it ♦ *Have you paid for your
lunch?* **2** to pay is to be profitable or
worthwhile ♦ *It pays to be honest* **3** to pay
(for example) attention or a compliment is
to give someone your attention or make
them a compliment **4** to pay for
something you have done wrong is to
suffer for it ♦ *I'll make you pay for this!*
to pay someone back is to pay money that you
owe them, or to get revenge on them

pay ➤ *noun*
wages or salary

payment *noun* (*plural* **payments**)
1 payment is when you pay someone **2** a
payment is money you pay

PC short for
personal computer,
police constable

PE short for
physical education

pea *noun* (*plural* **peas**)
a small round green seed of a climbing
plant, growing inside a pod and used as a
vegetable

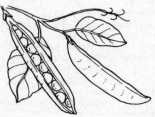

peace *noun*
1 a time when there is no war or violence
2 quietness and calm

peaceful *adjective*
quiet and calm
peacefully *adverb* in a peaceful way

peach *noun* (*plural* **peaches**)
a soft round juicy fruit with a slightly
furry skin and a large stone

peacock *noun* (*plural* **peacocks**)
a large male bird with a long brightly coloured tail that it can spread out like a fan

peak ➤ *noun* (*plural* **peaks**)
1 the top of a mountain **2** the highest or best point of something ♦ *Traffic reaches its peak at 5 o'clock* **3** the part of a cap that sticks out in front
peaked *adjective* having a peak

peak ➤ *verb* (**peaks, peaking, peaked**)
to reach the highest point or amount ♦ *Prices peaked in March*

peal ➤ *verb* (**peals, pealing, pealed**)
to peal is to make a loud ringing sound

peal ➤ *noun* (*plural* **peals**)
a loud ringing sound

peanut *noun* (*plural* **peanuts**)
a small round nut that grows in a pod in the ground

peanut butter *noun*
a paste made from crushed roasted peanuts

pear *noun* (*plural* **pears**)
a juicy fruit that gets narrower near the stalk

pearl *noun* (*plural* **pearls**)
a small shiny white ball found in the shells of some oysters and used as a jewel
pearly *adjective* white and shiny like a pearl

peasant *noun* (*plural* **peasants**)
a person who belongs to a farming community, especially in poor areas of the world
peasantry *noun* the peasants of a place

peat *noun*
rotted plant material that can be dug out of the ground and used as fuel or fertilizer

pebble *noun* (*plural* **pebbles**)
a small round stone
pebbly *adjective* having lots of pebbles

peck ➤ *verb* (**pecks, pecking, pecked**)
1 when a bird pecks something, it bites it or eats it with its beak **2** (*informal*) to peck someone is to give them a quick kiss

peck ➤ *noun* (*plural* **pecks**)
1 a short sharp bite with a bird's beak
2 (*informal*) a quick kiss

peckish *adjective*
(*informal*) hungry

peculiar *adjective*
strange; unusual
peculiar to someone or **something** restricted to them ♦ *The custom is peculiar to this tribe*
peculiarly *adverb* in a peculiar or special way

peculiarity *noun* (*plural* **peculiarities**)
something peculiar or special

pedal ➤ *noun* (*plural* **pedals**)
a lever pressed by the foot to operate a bicycle, car, or machine, or to play some musical instruments

pedal ➤ *verb* (**pedals, pedalling, pedalled**)
to pedal is to push or turn the pedals of a bicycle or other device

peddle *verb* (**peddles, peddling, peddled**)
to peddle things is to sell them as a pedlar

pedestal *noun* (*plural* **pedestals**)
the base that supports a statue or pillar

pedestrian ➤ *noun* (*plural* **pedestrians**)
someone who is walking

pedestrian ➤ *adjective*
ordinary and dull

pedigree *noun* (*plural* **pedigrees**)
a list of a person's or animal's ancestors, especially to show how well an animal has been bred

pedlar *noun* (*plural* **pedlars**)
someone who goes from house to house selling small things

peel ➤ *noun* (*plural* **peels**)
the skin of some fruit and vegetables

peel ➤ *verb* (**peels, peeling, peeled**)
1 to peel a piece of fruit or a vegetable is to remove the peel or covering from it **2** to peel is to lose a covering or skin ♦ *My skin is peeling*

peep ➤ *verb* (**peeps, peeping, peeped**)
1 to peep is to look quickly or secretly, or through a narrow opening **2** to peep or peep out is to come slowly or briefly into view ♦ *The moon peeped out through the clouds*

peep ➤ *noun* (*plural* **peeps**)
a quick look

peer¹ *verb* (**peers, peering, peered**)
to peer at something or someone is to look at them closely or with difficulty

peer² *noun* (*plural* **peers**)
1 a noble **2** someone who is equal to another in rank, age, or ability

peerless *adjective*
not having an equal; best

peewit *noun* (*plural* **peewits**)
a kind of wading bird

peg ➤ *noun* (*plural* **pegs**)
a clip or pin for fixing things in place or for hanging things on

peg ➤ *verb* (**pegs, pegging, pegged**)
1 to peg something is to fix it with pegs ♦ *We pegged out the tent* **2** to peg prices or wages is to keep them at a fixed amount
to peg out (*slang*) is to die

Pekingese or **Pekinese** *noun* (*plural* **Pekingese** or **Pekinese**) (*pronounced* peek-i-neez)
a small breed of dog with short legs and long silky hair

pelican *noun* (*plural* **pelicans**)
a large bird with a pouch in its long beak for storing fish

pelican crossing *noun* (*plural* **pelican crossings**)
a place where pedestrians can cross a street by operating lights that signal the traffic to stop

pellet *noun* (*plural* **pellets**)
a tiny ball of metal, food, wet paper, or other substance

pelt [1] *verb* (**pelts, pelting, pelted**)
1 to pelt things is to throw a lot of them at someone ♦ *We pelted him with snowballs* **2** to pelt is to run fast **3** it pelts down when it is raining very hard

pelt [2] *noun* (*plural* **pelts**)
an animal skin, especially with the fur or hair still on it

pen [1] *noun* (*plural* **pens**)
a device with a metal point for writing with ink

pen [2] *noun* (*plural* **pens**)
an enclosure for cattle or other animals

penalize *verb* (**penalizes, penalizing, penalized**)
1 to penalize someone is to punish them **2** in a game, to penalize someone is to award a penalty against them

penalty *noun* (*plural* **penalties**)
1 a punishment **2** a point or advantage given to one side in a game when a member of the other side breaks a rule

pence *plural noun*
pennies

pencil ➤ *noun* (*plural* **pencils**)
a device for drawing or writing, made of a thin stick of graphite or coloured chalk inside a cylinder of wood or metal

pencil ➤ *verb* (**pencils, pencilling, pencilled**)
to pencil something is to draw or write it with a pencil

pendant *noun* (*plural* **pendants**)
an ornament hung round the neck on a long chain or string

pendulum *noun* (*plural* **pendulums**)
a weight hung at the end of a rod so that it swings to and fro, especially in the works of a clock

penetrate *verb* (**penetrates, penetrating, penetrated**)
to penetrate something is to find a way through it or into it
penetration *noun* penetrating something

penfriend *noun* (*plural* **penfriends**)
someone in another country you write to, usually without meeting them

penguin *noun* (*plural* **penguins**)
an Antarctic sea bird that cannot fly but uses its wings as flippers for swimming

penicillin *noun*
a drug that kills bacteria, made from mould

peninsula *noun* (*plural* **peninsulas**)
a long piece of land that is almost
surrounded by water
peninsular *adjective* to do with a peninsula

penis *noun* (*plural* **penises**)
the part of the body with which a male
person or animal urinates and has sexual
intercourse

penitence *noun*
regret for having done wrong
penitent *adjective* sorry for what you have
done

penknife *noun* (*plural* **penknives**)
a small folding knife

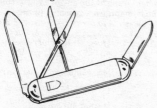

pennant *noun* (*plural* **pennants**)
a long pointed flag

penniless *adjective*
having no money; very poor

penny *noun* (*plural* **pennies** or **pence**)
a British coin worth a hundredth of a
pound

pension *noun* (*plural* **pensions**)
an income of regular payments made to
someone who has retired or been widowed

pensioner *noun* (*plural* **pensioners**)
someone who receives a pension

pentagon *noun* (*plural* **pentagons**)
a flat shape with five sides
the Pentagon a five-sided building in
Washington, headquarters of the leaders
of the American armed forces

pentathlon *noun* (*plural* **pentathlons**)
(*pronounced* pent-**ath**-lon)
an athletic competition that has five events

peony *noun* (*plural* **peonies**) (*pronounced*
pee-o-ni)
a plant with large round red, pink, or
white flowers

people ➤ *plural noun*
1 people are human beings; men, women,
and children **2** the people of a particular
country or area are the men, women, and
children who live there

people ➤ *noun* (*plural* **peoples**)
a people is a community or nation ◆ *They
are a peaceful people*

pepper *noun* (*plural* **peppers**)
1 a hot-tasting powder used to flavour
food **2** a bright green, red, or yellow
vegetable
peppery *adjective* hot-tasting like pepper

peppermint *noun* (*plural* **peppermints**)
1 a kind of mint used for flavouring **2** a
sweet flavoured with this mint

per *preposition*
for each ◆ *The charge is £2 per person*

per annum *adverb*
each year ◆ *£15,000 per annum*

per capita *adjective* and *adverb*
for each person ◆ *The daily water
consumption was thirty litres per capita*

perceive *verb* (**perceives, perceiving, perceived**)
to perceive something is to see or notice it
or understand it

per cent *adverb*
for every hundred ◆ *We pay interest at 5
per cent (5%)*

percentage *noun* (*plural* **percentages**)
an amount or rate expressed as a
proportion of 100 ◆ *Out of £300 he spent
£60, a percentage of 20*

perceptible *adjective*
able to be seen or noticed
perceptibly *adverb* in a perceptible way

perception *noun*
the ability to see, notice, or understand
something

perceptive *adjective*
quick to notice or understand things

perch[1] ➤ *noun* (*plural* **perches**)
a place where a bird sits or rests

perch ➤ *verb* (**perches, perching, perched**)
to perch is to sit or stand on the edge of
something or on something small

perch[2] *noun* (*plural* **perch**)
a freshwater fish used for food

percolator *noun* (*plural* **percolators**)
a device for making coffee

percussion *noun*
musical instruments played by striking
them or shaking them, such as drums and
cymbals
percussive *adjective* making a sound by
being struck

perennial ➤ *adjective*
lasting or recurring for many years ◆ *It is
a perennial problem*

perennial ➤ *noun* (*plural* **perennials**)
a plant that lives for many years
perennially *adverb* year after year

perfect ➤ *adjective* (*pronounced* per-fikt)
1 so good that it cannot be made any better; without any faults **2** complete ♦ *The man is a perfect stranger*
perfection *noun* being perfect **perfectly** *adverb* in a perfect way; completely

perfect ➤ *noun*
a form of a verb that describes a completed action or event in the past, in English formed with *has* and *have*, for example *I have lost my pen*

perfect ➤ *verb* (**perfects, perfecting, perfected**) (*pronounced* per-fekt)
to perfect something is to make it perfect

perforate *verb* (**perforates, perforating, perforated**)
to perforate something is to make tiny holes in it, especially so that it can be torn off easily
perforation *noun* being perforated

perform *verb* (**performs, performing, performed**)
1 to perform something is to present it in front of an audience ♦ *They performed a play in the school hall* **2** to perform something is also to do something you have to do or ought to do ♦ *The surgeon performed the operation on Tuesday*
performance *noun* performing something, or something performed **performer** *noun* someone who performs an entertainment

perfume *noun* (*plural* **perfumes**)
1 a sweet or pleasant smell **2** a sweet-smelling liquid put on the skin

perhaps *adverb*
it may be; possibly

peril *noun* (*plural* **perils**)
danger ♦ *She was in great peril*
perilous *adjective* dangerous **perilously** *adverb* dangerously

perimeter *noun* (*plural* **perimeters**) (*pronounced* per-im-it-er)
1 a boundary ♦ *A fence marks the perimeter of the airfield* **2** the distance round the edge of something

period *noun* (*plural* **periods**)
1 a length of time **2** the time every month when a woman or girl bleeds from the womb in menstruation

periodic *adjective*
occurring at regular intervals
periodically *adverb* from time to time

periodical *noun* (*plural* **periodicals**)
a magazine published regularly (for example, monthly)

periscope *noun* (*plural* **periscopes**)
a device with a tube and mirrors that lets you see things at a higher level, used for example in submarines

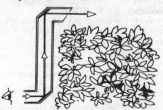

perish *verb* (**perishes, perishing, perished**)
1 to perish is to die or be destroyed **2** to perish is also to rot ♦ *The tyres have perished* **3** (*informal*) to be perished is to feel extremely cold ♦ *I was perished after the long walk in the hills*
perishable *adjective* liable to perish or rot quickly

perm ➤ *noun*
(*informal*) a permanent wave

perm ➤ *verb* (**perms, perming, permed**)
to perm hair is to give it a permanent wave

permanent *adjective*
lasting for ever or for a long time
permanence *noun* being permanent
permanently *adverb* for ever or for a long time

permanent wave *noun* (*plural* **permanent waves**)
treatment of the hair to give it long-lasting waves

permissible *adjective*
allowable; permitted

permission *noun*
the right to do something, given by someone in authority

permissive *adjective*
letting people do what they wish; tolerant or liberal
permissively *adverb* in a permissive way
permissiveness *noun* being permissive

permit ➤ *verb* (**permits, permitting, permitted**) (*pronounced* per-mit)
1 to permit someone to do something is to allow them to do it **2** to permit something is to allow it to be done

permit ➤ *noun* (*plural* **permits**) (*pronounced* per-mit)
a written or printed statement that something is permitted

perpendicular *adjective*
upright, or at a right angle to a line or surface

perpetual *adjective*
lasting for a long time; permanent
perpetually *adverb* continually

perpetuate *verb* (**perpetuates, perpetuating, perpetuated**)
to perpetuate something is to cause it to continue or be remembered for a long time

perplex *verb* (**perplexes, perplexing, perplexed**)
to perplex someone is to puzzle them very much
perplexity *noun* being perplexed

persecute *verb* (**persecutes, persecuting, persecuted**)
to persecute someone is to be continually cruel to them, especially because you disagree with their beliefs
persecution *noun* being persecuted **persecutor** *noun* someone who persecutes people

persevere *verb* (**perseveres, persevering, persevered**)
to persevere is to go on in spite of difficulties
perseverance *noun* persevering

persist *verb* (**persists, persisting, persisted**)
1 to persist is to keep on firmly or obstinately doing something ♦ *She persists in breaking the rules* **2** to persist is also to continue or survive ♦ *The custom persists in some countries*
persistence *noun* persisting in something
persistent *adjective* determined to keep trying **persistently** *adverb* in a persistent way

person *noun* (*plural* **persons** or **people**)
1 a human being; a man, woman, or child **2** (*in Grammar*) each of the parts of a verb and the pronouns that go with the verb. The **first person** (= *I, me, we, us*) refers to the person or people speaking; the **second person** (= *you*) refers to the person or people spoken to; and the **third person** (= *he, him, she, her, it, they, them*) refers to the person or people spoken about

personal *adjective*
1 belonging to, done by, or concerning a particular person ♦ *The film star made a personal appearance at the gala* **2** private ♦ *We have personal business to discuss*

personal computer *noun* (*plural* **personal computers**)
a small computer designed for a single user

personality *noun* (*plural* **personalities**)
1 a person's nature and characteristics ♦ *She has a cheerful personality* **2** a well-known person ♦ *There were several TV personalities at the party*

personally *adverb*
1 in person; being actually there ♦ *The head thanked me personally* **2** as far as I am concerned ♦ *Personally, I'd rather stay here*

personnel *noun* (*pronounced* per-so-nel)
the people employed by a business or in a particular place

perspective *noun* (*plural* **perspectives**)
the impression of depth and space in a picture or scene
in perspective giving a balanced view of things ♦ *Try to see the problem in perspective*

perspire *verb* (**perspires, perspiring, perspired**)
to perspire is to sweat
perspiration *noun* perspiring

persuade *verb* (**persuades, persuading, persuaded**)
to persuade someone is to get them to agree about something
persuasion *noun* persuading someone
persuasive *adjective* good at persuading people

perverse *adjective* (*pronounced* per-verss)
obstinate or unreasonable in what you do or say
perversely *adverb* in a perverse way
perversity *noun* being perverse

pervert ➤ *verb* (**perverts, perverting, perverted**) (*pronounced* per-vert)
1 to pervert something is to make it go wrong **2** to pervert someone is to make them behave wickedly or abnormally
perversion *noun* being perverted

pervert ➤ *noun* (*plural* **perverts**) (*pronounced* per-vert)
someone with odd or unnatural sexual behaviour

Pesach *noun*
the Hebrew name for Passover

pessimist *noun* (*plural* **pessimists**)
someone who usually expects things to turn out badly
pessimism *noun* being a pessimist

pessimistic *adjective*
expecting things to turn out badly
pessimistically *adverb* in a pessimistic way

pest *noun* (*plural* **pests**)
1 a destructive insect or animal, such as a locust or a mouse **2** a nuisance

pester *verb* (**pesters, pestering, pestered**)
to pester someone is to annoy them with frequent questions or interruptions

pesticide *noun* (*plural* **pesticides**)
a chemical used to kill insects and grubs

pestle *noun* (*plural* **pestles**)
a tool with a heavy rounded end for pounding food in a bowl called a mortar

pet *noun* (*plural* **pets**)
1 a tame animal kept for companionship and pleasure **2** a person treated as a favourite ♦ *She seems to be teacher's pet*

petal *noun* (*plural* **petals**)
each of the separate coloured outer parts of a flower

petition *noun* (*plural* **petitions**)
a written request for something, usually signed by a large number of people

petrify *verb* (**petrifies, petrifying, petrified**)
to petrify someone is to make them so terrified or surprised that they cannot act or move

petrochemical *noun* (*plural* **petrochemicals**)
a chemical substance made from petroleum or natural gas

petrol *noun*
a liquid made from petroleum, used as a fuel for engines

petroleum *noun* (*pronounced* pi-**troh**-li-um)
an oil found underground that is purified to make petrol, diesel oil, and other fuels

petticoat *noun* (*plural* **petticoats**)
a piece of women's clothing worn under a skirt or dress

petty *adjective* (**pettier, pettiest**)
1 minor and unimportant ♦ *There are some petty regulations* **2** mean and small-minded
pettily *adverb* in a petty way **pettiness** *noun* being petty

pew *noun* (*plural* **pews**)
one of the long wooden seats in a church

pewter *noun*
a grey alloy of tin and lead

pH *noun*
a measure of the acidity or alkalinity of a solution. Pure water has a pH of 7; acids have a pH between 0 and 7, and alkalis have a pH between 7 and 14

pharaoh *noun* (*plural* **pharaohs**)
(*pronounced* **fair**-oh)
a king of ancient Egypt

pharmacy *noun* (*plural* **pharmacies**)
a shop that sells medicines

phase ➤ *noun* (*plural* **phases**)
a stage in the progress or development of something

phase ➤ *verb* (**phases, phasing, phased**)
to phase a plan or operation is to carry it out in stages ♦ *The new buildings were phased over three years*
to phase something in is to start it gradually
to phase something out is to stop it gradually

pheasant *noun* (*plural* **pheasants**)
(*pronounced* **fez**-ant)
a game bird with a long tail

phenomenal *adjective* (*pronounced* fin-**om**-in-al)
amazing or remarkable
phenomenally *adverb* in a phenomenal way

phenomenon *noun* (*plural* **phenomena**)
an event or fact, especially one that is remarkable or unusual

philately *noun* (*pronounced* fil-**at**-el-i)
collecting postage stamps
philatelist *noun* someone who collects stamps

philosophical *adjective*
1 to do with philosophy **2** calmly accepting suffering or difficulty ♦ *He was philosophical about his illness*
philosophically *adverb* in a philosophical way

philosophy *noun* (*plural* **philosophies**)
(*pronounced* fil-**os**-o-fi)
1 philosophy is the study of truths about life and human behaviour **2** a philosophy is a way of thinking or a system of beliefs
philosopher *noun* someone who studies philosophy

phobia *noun* (*plural* **phobias**) (*pronounced* **foh**-bi-a)
a great or unusual fear of something

phoenix *noun* (*plural* **phoenixes**)
(*pronounced* **fee**-niks)
a mythical bird that was said to burn itself to death on a fire and be born again from the ashes

phone ➤ *noun* (*plural* **phones**)
a telephone

phone ➤ *verb* (**phones, phoning, phoned**)
to phone someone is to telephone them

phonecard *noun* (*plural* **phonecards**)
a plastic card that you can use to work some kinds of public telephone

phone-in *noun* (*plural* **phone-ins**)
a radio or TV programme in which people telephone the studio and take part in a discussion

phosphorescent *adjective*
shining or glowing in the dark
phosphorescence *noun* being
phosphorescent

phosphorus *noun*
a yellowish substance that glows in the
dark
phosphoric *adjective* like phosphorus

photo *noun* (*plural* **photos**)
(*informal*) a photograph

photocopier *noun* (*plural* **photocopiers**)
a machine that makes photocopies

photocopy ➤ *noun* (*plural* **photocopies**)
a copy of a document or page made by a
machine that photographs it on special
paper

photocopy ➤ *verb* (**photocopies, photocopying,
photocopied**)
to photocopy a document is to make a copy
of it with a photocopier

photoelectric *adjective*
using the electrical effects of light

photograph ➤ *noun* (*plural* **photographs**)
a picture made on film, using a camera

photograph ➤ *verb* (**photographs,
photographing, photographed**)
to photograph someone or something is to
take a photograph of them
photographer *noun* someone who takes
photographs

photography *noun*
taking photographs with a camera
photographic *adjective* to do with
photography

phrase ➤ *noun* (*plural* **phrases**)
1 a group of words that form a unit
smaller than a clause, for example *in the
garden* in the sentence *The Queen was in
the garden* 2 a short section of a tune

phrase ➤ *verb* (**phrases, phrasing, phrased**)
to phrase an idea or thought is to put it
into words

physical *adjective*
1 to do with the body rather than the mind
or feelings 2 to do with things you can
touch or see
physically *adverb* in a physical way

physical education *noun*
gymnastics or other exercises that you do
to keep the body healthy

physician *noun* (*plural* **physicians**)
a doctor

physics *noun*
the study of matter and energy, including
movement, heat, light, and sound
physicist *noun* an expert in physics

physiology *noun* (*pronounced* fiz-i-ol-o-ji)
the study of the body and how it works
physiological *adjective* to do with
physiology
physiologist *noun* an expert in physiology

pi *noun* (*pronounced* pie)
a number roughly equal to 3·14159, shown
by the symbol π and used in calculating
the circumference and area of circles. The
diameter of a circle multiplied by pi gives
the circumference

pianist *noun* (*plural* **pianists**)
someone who plays the piano

piano *noun* (*plural* **pianos**)
a large musical instrument with a
keyboard

piccolo *noun* (*plural* **piccolos**)
a small high-pitched flute

pick[1] ➤ *verb* (**picks, picking, picked**)
1 to pick something or someone is to
choose them ♦ *Pick someone to dance with*
2 to pick flowers or fruit is to cut or pull
them off the plant or tree 3 to pick
someone's pocket is to steal from it 4 to
pick a lock is to open it without using a key
5 to pick bits off or out of something is to
pull them away from it
to pick holes in something is to find fault with
it
to pick on someone is to keep criticizing or
bothering them
to pick someone up is to give them a lift in a
vehicle
to pick something up 1 is to take it from the
ground or a surface 2 is to collect it ♦ *I'll
pick up my bags from the station*
to pick up is to improve or recover

pick ➤ *noun*
1 a choice ♦ *Take your pick* 2 the best
part of something

pick[2] *noun* (*plural* **picks**)
a pickaxe

pickaxe *noun* (*plural* **pickaxes**)
a heavy pointed tool with a long handle,
used for breaking up concrete or hard
ground

picket ➤ *noun* (*plural* **pickets**)
a group of strikers who try to persuade other people not to go into a place of work during a strike

picket ➤ *verb* (**pickets, picketing, picketed**)
to picket a place is to act as a picket outside it during a strike

pickle ➤ *noun* (*plural* **pickles**)
1 a strong-tasting food made of vegetables preserved in vinegar **2** (*informal*) a difficulty ♦ *Now we're in a real pickle!*

pickle ➤ *verb* (**pickles, pickling, pickled**)
to pickle food is to preserve it in vinegar or salt water

pickpocket *noun* (*plural* **pickpockets**)
a thief who steals from people's pockets or bags

pick-up *noun* (*plural* **pick-ups**)
1 an open truck for carrying small loads **2** the part of a record player that holds the stylus

picnic ➤ *noun* (*plural* **picnics**)
a meal eaten in the open air away from home

picnic ➤ *verb* (**picnics, picnicking, picnicked**)
to picnic is to have a picnic
picnicker *noun* someone who is having a picnic

pictogram *noun* (*plural* **pictograms**)
a picture that stands for a word or a phrase

pictorial *adjective*
with or using pictures
pictorially *adverb* by means of pictures

picture ➤ *noun* (*plural* **pictures**)
1 a painting, drawing, or photograph **2** a film at the cinema
in the picture having the information about something

picture ➤ *verb* (**pictures, picturing, pictured**)
1 to picture someone or something is to show them in a picture **2** to picture someone or something in your mind is to imagine them

picturesque *adjective* (*pronounced* pik-cher-**esk**)
1 attractive or charming ♦ *We drove through a picturesque village* **2** clear and vivid ♦ *They described the scene in picturesque language*

pie *noun* (*plural* **pies**)
a baked dish of meat or fruit covered with pastry

piece ➤ *noun* (*plural* **pieces**)
1 a part of something; a bit **2** a work of art or writing or music ♦ *They played a piece of piano music* **3** one of the objects used on a board to play a game ♦ *You've dropped a chess piece*
in one piece not broken; intact
piece by piece gradually; one bit at a time

piece ➤ *verb* (**pieces, piecing, pieced**)
to piece things together is to join them to make something

piecemeal *adverb*
one piece or part at a time

pie chart *noun* (*plural* **pie charts**)
a diagram in the form of a circle divided into slices, showing how a quantity or amount is divided up

pier *noun* (*plural* **piers**)
1 a long structure built out into the sea for people to walk on **2** a pillar supporting a bridge or arch

pierce *verb* (**pierces, piercing, pierced**)
to pierce something is to make a hole through it

piercing *adjective*
very strong or very loud ♦ *We heard a piercing shriek* ♦ *The wind was cold and piercing*

pig *noun* (*plural* **pigs**)
1 a fat animal with short legs and a blunt snout, kept for its meat **2** (*informal*) someone who is greedy, dirty, or unpleasant
piggy *noun* a little pig

pigeon *noun* (*plural* **pigeons**)
1 a common grey bird with a small head and large chest **2** (*informal*) someone's business or responsibility ♦ *That's his pigeon*

pigeon-hole *noun* (*plural* **pigeon-holes**)
a small compartment for holding papers and letters, for someone to collect

piggyback *noun* (*plural* **piggybacks**)
a ride on someone's back

pig-headed *adjective*
obstinate; stubborn

piglet *noun* (*plural* **piglets**)
a young pig

pigment *noun* (*plural* **pigments**)
a substance that colours something

pigmy *noun* (*plural* **pigmies**)
another spelling of **pygmy**

pigsty *noun* (*plural* **pigsties**)
1 a place for keeping pigs 2 (*informal*) a very untidy room or place

pigtail *noun* (*plural* **pigtails**)
a single plait of hair worn hanging at the back of the head

pike *noun* (*plural* **pikes**)
1 a large fish that lives in rivers and lakes 2 a heavy spear

pilchard *noun* (*plural* **pilchards**)
a small sea fish

pile¹ ➤ *noun* (*plural* **piles**)
1 a number of things on top of one another 2 (*informal*) a large amount of something, especially money

pile ➤ *verb* (**piles, piling, piled**)
to pile things is to put them into a pile
to pile up is to become very much or very many ♦ *The work was piling up*

pile² *noun* (*plural* **piles**)
a heavy beam driven vertically into the ground to support something

pilfer *verb* (**pilfers, pilfering, pilfered**)
to pilfer small or unimportant things is to steal them

pilgrim *noun* (*plural* **pilgrims**)
someone who goes on a journey to a holy place

pilgrimage *noun* (*plural* **pilgrimages**)
a journey to a holy place

pill *noun* (*plural* **pills**)
a small piece of medicine for swallowing
the pill a special kind of pill taken by a woman to prevent her from becoming pregnant

pillage *verb* (**pillages, pillaging, pillaged**)
to pillage a place is to seize things from it by force and carry them off, especially in a war

pillar *noun* (*plural* **pillars**)
a tall stone or wooden post

pillar box *noun* (*plural* **pillar boxes**)
a postbox standing in a street

pillion *noun* (*plural* **pillions**)
a seat for a passenger behind the driver's seat on a motorcycle

pillion

pillow *noun* (*plural* **pillows**)
a cushion to rest your head on, especially in bed

pillowcase *noun* (*plural* **pillowcases**)
a cloth cover for a pillow

pilot ➤ *noun* (*plural* **pilots**)
1 someone who flies an aircraft
2 someone who helps to steer a ship in and out of a port or through a difficult stretch of water

pilot ➤ *verb* (**pilots, piloting, piloted**)
to pilot an aircraft or ship is to be the pilot of it

pimple *noun* (*plural* **pimples**)
a small round swelling on the skin
pimply *adjective* having pimples

pin ➤ *noun* (*plural* **pins**)
1 a short piece of metal with a sharp point and a rounded head, used to fasten pieces of paper or cloth together 2 a pointed device for fixing or marking something
pins and needles a tingling feeling in the skin

pin ➤ *verb* (**pins, pinning, pinned**)
1 to pin something is to fasten it with a pin 2 to pin someone or something is to keep them fixed or trapped in one place
♦ *He was pinned under the wreckage for hours*

pinafore *noun* (*plural* **pinafores**)
a large apron

pincer *noun* (*plural* **pincers**)
the claw of a shellfish such as a lobster

pincers *plural noun*
a tool for gripping and pulling things, especially for pulling out nails

pinch ➤ *verb* (**pinches, pinching, pinched**)
1 to pinch something is to squeeze it tightly between two things, especially between the finger and thumb 2 (*informal*) to pinch something is to steal it

pinch ➤ *noun* (*plural* **pinches**)
1 a firm squeezing movement 2 the amount you can pick up between the tips of your finger and thumb ♦ *Take a pinch of salt*
at a pinch if it is really necessary

pincushion *noun* (*plural* **pincushions**)
a small pad into which needles and pins are stuck to keep them ready for use

pine [1] *noun* (*plural* **pines**)
an evergreen tree with leaves shaped like needles

pine [2] *verb* (**pines, pining, pined**)
1 to pine for someone or something is to feel a strong longing for them 2 to pine, or pine away, is to become weak or ill through sorrow or yearning

pineapple *noun* (*plural* **pineapples**)
a large tropical fruit with yellow flesh and prickly leaves and skin

ping-pong *noun*
table tennis

pink ➤ *adjective* (**pinker, pinkest**)
pale red

pink ➤ *noun* (*plural* **pinks**)
1 a sweet-smelling garden flower 2 a pink colour

pint *noun* (*plural* **pints**)
a measure of liquid, an eighth of a gallon or about 568 millilitres

pioneer *noun* (*plural* **pioneers**)
one of the first people to go to a place or do something new

pious *adjective*
very religious or devout
piously *adverb* in a pious way

pip *noun* (*plural* **pips**)
1 a small hard seed of a fruit such as an apple, orange, or pear 2 a short high-pitched sound ♦ *She heard the six pips of the time signal on the radio*

pipe ➤ *noun* (*plural* **pipes**)
1 a tube for carrying water, gas, or oil from one place to another 2 a short tube with a small bowl at one end, used to smoke tobacco 3 a tubular musical instrument
the pipes bagpipes

pipe ➤ *verb* (**pipes, piping, piped**)
1 to pipe something is to send it along pipes or wires 2 to pipe is to play music on a pipe or the bagpipes
to pipe down (*informal*) is to be quiet
to pipe up is to start saying something

pipe dream *noun* (*plural* **pipe dreams**)
a wish for something you are unlikely to get

pipeline *noun* (*plural* **pipelines**)
a pipe for carrying oil, water, or gas over a long distance

piper *noun* (*plural* **pipers**)
someone who plays a pipe or the bagpipes

piping ➤ *adjective*
high-pitched; shrill
piping hot very hot, ready to eat

piping ➤ *noun*
material used for making pipes; a length of pipes

pirate *noun* (*plural* **pirates**)
a sailor who attacks and robs other ships
piracy *noun* being a pirate

pistil *noun* (*plural* **pistils**)
the part of a flower that produces the seed

pistil

pistol *noun* (*plural* **pistols**)
a small gun for use with one hand

piston *noun* (*plural* **pistons**)
a disc that moves up and down inside a cylinder in an engine or pump

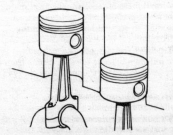

pit ➤ *noun* (*plural* **pits**)
1 a deep hole or hollow 2 a coal mine
3 the part of a race circuit where cars are
refuelled and serviced during a race

pit ➤ *verb* (**pits, pitting, pitted**)
1 to pit something is to make deep holes or
hollows in it ♦ *The ground was pitted with
craters* 2 to pit one person against another
is to arrange for them to compete with one
another ♦ *In the final he was pitted
against the champion*

pitch[1] ➤ *noun* (*plural* **pitches**)
1 a pitch is a piece of ground marked out
for cricket, football, or another game
2 pitch is how high or low a voice or
musical note is 3 intensity or strength
♦ *Excitement was at a high pitch*

pitch ➤ *verb* (**pitches, pitching, pitched**)
1 to pitch something is to throw or fling it
2 to pitch a tent is to set it up 3 to pitch
is to fall heavily ♦ *He tripped over the
doorstep and pitched headlong* 4 a ship
pitches when it moves up and down on a
rough sea 5 to pitch something is to set it
at a particular level ♦ *We are pitching our
hopes high*
to pitch in is to start working or eating
vigorously

pitch[2] *noun*
pitch is a black sticky substance like tar

pitch-black or **pitch-dark** *adjective*
completely black or dark, with no light at
all

pitched battle *noun* (*plural* **pitched battles**)
a battle between armies in regular
formation

pitcher *noun* (*plural* **pitchers**)
a large jug, usually with two handles

pitchfork *noun* (*plural* **pitchforks**)
a large fork with two prongs for lifting hay

pitfall *noun* (*plural* **pitfalls**)
an unsuspected danger or difficulty

pitiful *adjective*
1 making you feel pity ♦ *It was a pitiful
sight* 2 inadequate; feeble ♦ *He made a
pitiful attempt to make us laugh*
pitifully *adverb* in a pitiful way

pitiless *adjective*
having or showing no pity
pitilessly *adverb* in a pitiless way

pity ➤ *noun*
1 the feeling of being sorry because
someone is in pain or in trouble ♦ *I feel
pity for the homeless people* 2 something
that you regret ♦ *It's a pity we can't meet*
to take pity on someone is to help someone
who is in trouble

pity ➤ *verb* (**pities, pitying, pitied**)
to pity someone is to feel pity for them

pivot ➤ *noun* (*plural* **pivots**)
a point on which something turns or
balances

pivot ➤ *verb* (**pivots, pivoting, pivoted**)
to pivot is to turn on a pivot or balance

pixie or **pixy** *noun* (*plural* **pixies**)
a small fairy or elf

pizza *noun* (*plural* **pizzas**) (*pronounced*
peet-sa)
an Italian food made as a layer of dough
covered with cheese, vegetables, and
spices and baked

pizzicato *adverb* and *adjective* (*pronounced*
pit-si-**kah**-toh)
in music, plucking the strings of an
instrument such as a violin

placard *noun* (*plural* **placards**)
a large poster or notice put up on a wall or
carried at a demonstration

place ➤ *noun* (*plural* **places**)
1 a particular part of space, especially
where something belongs; an area or
position 2 a seat ♦ *Save me a place* 3 a
person's duty or function ♦ *It's not my
place to interfere*
in place in the proper position
in place of something or **someone** instead of
them
out of place 1 in the wrong position 2
unsuitable ♦ *Jeans and sandals are out of
place in a smart restaurant*
to take place is to happen

place ➤ *verb* (**places, placing, placed**)
to place something somewhere is to put it
in a particular place

placid *adjective*
calm and peaceful
placidity *noun* being placid **placidly** *adverb* in
a placid way

plague ➤ *noun* (*plural* **plagues**)
1 a dangerous illness that spreads very
quickly 2 a large number of pests ♦ *The
country was hit by a plague of locusts*

plague ➤ *verb* (**plagues, plaguing, plagued**)
to plague someone is to pester or annoy
them continuously ♦ *They have been
plagued with complaints*

plaice *noun* (*plural* **plaice**)
a flat sea fish used for food

plaid *noun* (*plural* **plaids**) (*pronounced* plad)
cloth with a tartan or chequered pattern

plain ➤ *adjective* (**plainer, plainest**)
1 simple; not decorated 2 not pretty
3 easy to understand or see 4 frank;
straightforward ♦ *I'll be quite plain with
you*
plainly *adverb* clearly; obviously **plainness**
noun being plain

plain ➤ *noun* (*plural* **plains**)
a large area of flat country without trees

plain clothes *plural noun*
ordinary clothes worn instead of a uniform

plaintiff *noun* (*plural* **plaintiffs**)
a person who brings a complaint against
someone else to a lawcourt

plaintive *adjective*
sounding sad ♦ *We heard a plaintive cry*
plaintively *adverb* in a plaintive way

plait ➤ *noun* (*plural* **plaits**) (*pronounced*
plat)
a length of hair or rope with several
strands twisted together

plait ➤ *verb* (**plaits, plaiting, plaited**)
(*pronounced* plat)
to plait hair or rope is to make it into a
plait

plan ➤ *noun* (*plural* **plans**)
1 a way of doing something thought out in
advance 2 a drawing showing how the
parts of something are arranged 3 a map
of a town or district

plan ➤ *verb* (**plans, planning, planned**)
to plan something is to make a plan to
do it
planner *noun* someone who plans things

plane[1] ➤ *noun* (*plural* **planes**)
1 an aeroplane 2 a tool for making wood
smooth 3 a flat or level surface

plane ➤ *verb* (**planes, planing, planed**)
to plane wood is to smooth it with a plane

plane[2] *noun* (*plural* **planes**)
a tall tree with broad leaves

planet *noun* (*plural* **planets**)
one of the bodies that move in an orbit
round the sun. The main planets of the
solar system are Mercury, Venus, Earth,
Mars, Jupiter, Saturn, Uranus, Neptune,
and Pluto
planetary *adjective* to do with planets

plank *noun* (*plural* **planks**)
a long flat piece of wood

plankton *noun*
tiny creatures that float in the sea and
lakes

plant ➤ *noun* (*plural* **plants**)
1 a living thing that grows out of the
ground, including flowers, bushes, trees,
and vegetables 2 a factory or its
equipment

plant ➤ *verb* (**plants, planting, planted**)
1 to plant something such as a tree or
flower is to put it in the ground to grow
2 to plant something is also to put it firmly
in place ♦ *He planted his feet on the
ground and took hold of the rope* 3 to
plant something such as a piece of
evidence is to put it where it will be found,

usually to mislead people or to cause
trouble

planter *noun* someone who plants trees or
shrubs

plantation *noun* (*plural* **plantations**)
an area of land where a crop such as
tobacco, tea, or rubber is planted

plaque *noun* (*plural* **plaques**) (*pronounced*
plak or plahk)
1 a plaque is a metal or porcelain plate
fixed on a wall as a memorial or an
ornament 2 plaque is a substance that
forms a thin layer on teeth, allowing
bacteria to develop

plasma *noun* (*pronounced* plaz-ma)
the colourless liquid part of blood, which
carries the corpuscles

plaster ➤ *noun* (*plural* **plasters**)
1 a plaster is a small covering put over the
skin around a wound to protect it
2 plaster is a mixture of lime, sand, and
water, used to cover walls and ceilings

plaster ➤ *verb* (**plasters, plastering, plastered**)
1 to plaster a surface is to cover it with
plaster 2 to plaster a surface with
something is to cover it thickly ♦ *The
toddlers plastered the floor with mud*
plasterer *noun* someone who plasters walls
and ceilings

plaster of Paris *noun*
a white paste used for making moulds and
for casts round a broken leg or arm

plastic ➤ *noun* (*plural* **plastics**)
a strong light synthetic substance that can
be moulded into different shapes

plastic ➤ *adjective*
made of plastic ♦ *I need a plastic bag*

Plasticine *noun*
(*trademark*) a soft and easily shaped
substance used for making models

plastic surgery *noun*
work done by a surgeon to alter or mend
parts of someone's body

plate ➤ *noun* (*plural* **plates**)
1 a dish that is flat or almost flat, used for
eating 2 a thin flat sheet of metal, glass,
or other hard material 3 one of the large
areas of rock that make up the earth's
crust 4 an illustration on a separate page
in a book

plate ➤ *verb* (**plates, plating, plated**)
to plate metal is to cover it with a thin
layer of gold, silver, tin, or other soft metal

plateau *noun* (*plural* **plateaux**) (*pronounced*
plat-oh)
a flat area of high land

plateful *noun* (*plural* **platefuls**)
as much as you can put on a plate

platform *noun* (*plural* **platforms**)
 1 a flat raised area along the side of the line at a railway station **2** a small stage in a hall

platinum *noun*
 a silver-coloured metal that does not lose its brightness

platoon *noun* (*plural* **platoons**)
 a small unit of soldiers

platypus *noun* (*plural* **platypuses**)
 an Australian animal with a beak and feet like those of a duck

play ➤ *verb* (**plays, playing, played**)
 1 to play, or play a game, is to take part in a game or other amusement **2** to play music, or a musical instrument, is to make music or sound with it **3** to play a part in a film or play is to perform it
 to play about or **around** is to have fun or be mischievous
 to play someone up is to tease or annoy them
 player *noun* someone who plays an instrument or a game

play ➤ *noun* (*plural* **plays**)
 1 a play is a story acted on a stage or broadcast on radio or television **2** play is playing or having fun

playback *noun* (*plural* **playbacks**)
 playing something that has been recorded

playful *adjective*
 1 wanting to play; full of fun **2** not serious
 playfully *adverb* in a playful way **playfulness** *noun* being playful

playground *noun* (*plural* **playgrounds**)
 a place out of doors where children can play

playgroup *noun* (*plural* **playgroups**)
 a group of very young children who play together regularly, with adults to supervise them

playing card *noun* (*plural* **playing cards**)
 each of a set of cards (usually 52) used for playing games

playing field *noun* (*plural* **playing fields**)
 a grassy field for outdoor games

playmate *noun* (*plural* **playmates**)
 someone that you play games with

play-off *noun* (*plural* **play-offs**)
 an extra match played to decide a draw or tie

playtime *noun* (*plural* **playtimes**)
 the time when young schoolchildren go out to play

playwright *noun* (*plural* **playwrights**)
 someone who writes plays

plc short for
 public limited company

plea *noun* (*plural* **pleas**)
 1 a request or appeal **2** a statement of 'guilty' or 'not guilty' made in a lawcourt by someone accused of a crime

plead *verb* (**pleads, pleading, pleaded**)
 to plead with someone is to beg them to do something
 to plead guilty or **not guilty** is to state in a lawcourt that you are guilty or not guilty of a crime

pleasant *adjective* (**pleasanter, pleasantest**)
 pleasing; nice
 pleasantly *adverb* in a pleasant way

please *verb* (**pleases, pleasing, pleased**)
 1 to please someone is to make them happy or satisfied **2** used when you want to ask something politely ♦ *Please shut the door*
 as you please as you like ♦ *Do as you please*

pleasurable *adjective*
 causing pleasure; enjoyable

pleasure *noun* (*plural* **pleasures**)
 1 pleasure is being pleased **2** a pleasure is something that pleases you
 with pleasure gladly; willingly

pleat *noun* (*plural* **pleats**)
 a fold made in the cloth of a garment
 pleated *adjective* having pleats

pledge ➤ *noun* (*plural* **pledges**)
 a solemn promise

pledge ➤ *verb* (**pledges, pledging, pledged**)
 to pledge something is to promise it

plentiful *adjective*
 large in amount
 plentifully *adverb* in a plentiful way

plenty *noun*
 a lot of something; more than enough ♦ *We have plenty of chairs*

pliable *adjective*
 easy to bend; flexible

pliers *plural noun*
pincers with flattened jaws for gripping
something or for breaking wire

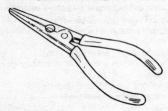

plight *noun* (*plural* **plights**)
a difficult situation

plod *verb* (**plods, plodding, plodded**)
1 to plod is to walk slowly and heavily
2 to plod, or plod away, is to work slowly
but steadily
plodder *noun* someone who works slowly
but steadily

plop ➤ *noun* (*plural* **plops**)
the sound of something dropping into
water

plop ➤ *verb* (**plops, plopping, plopped**)
to plop is to fall with a plop

plot ➤ *noun* (*plural* **plots**)
1 a secret plan, especially to do something
illegal or bad 2 what happens in a story,
film, or drama 3 a piece of land for a
house or garden

plot ➤ *verb* (**plots, plotting, plotted**)
1 to plot is to make a secret plan 2 to plot
a chart or graph is to make it, marking all
the points on it
plotter *noun* someone who takes part in a
plot

plough ➤ *noun* (*plural* **ploughs**)
(*pronounced* plow)
a device used on farms for turning over the
soil

plough ➤ *verb* (**ploughs, ploughing, ploughed**)
1 to plough the soil is to turn it over with
a plough 2 to plough through something is
to go through it with effort or difficulty
♦ *He ploughed through the book*

ploughman *noun* (*plural* **ploughmen**)
someone who uses a plough

plover *noun* (*plural* **plovers**) (*pronounced*
pluv-er)
a long-legged wading bird

pluck ➤ *verb* (**plucks, plucking, plucked**)
1 to pluck a bird is to pull the feathers
off it to prepare it for cooking 2 to pluck
a flower or fruit is to pick it 3 to pluck
something is to pull it or pull it out
♦ *I'll try and pluck out your splinter*
4 in music, to pluck a string is to pull it
and let it go again
to pluck up courage is to be brave and
overcome fear

pluck ➤ *noun*
courage or bravery

plucky *adjective* (**pluckier, pluckiest**)
brave or courageous
pluckily *adverb* in a plucky way

plug ➤ *noun* (*plural* **plugs**)
1 something used to stop up a hole 2 a
device by which an electric wire is fitted
into a socket 3 (*informal*) a piece of
publicity for something

plug ➤ *verb* (**plugs, plugging, plugged**)
1 to plug a hole is to stop it up
2 (*informal*) to plug an event or product is
to publicize it
to plug something in is to connect it to an
electric socket by means of a plug

plum *noun* (*plural* **plums**)
a soft juicy fruit with a stone in the middle

plumage *noun* (*pronounced* ploo-mij)
a bird's plumage is its feathers

plumb *verb* (**plumbs, plumbing, plumbed**)
1 to plumb a river or the sea is to measure
how deep it is 2 to plumb a mystery or
puzzle is to find out what it means

plumber *noun* (*plural* **plumbers**)
someone who fits and mends water pipes
in a building

plumbing *noun*
1 the work of a plumber 2 the water
pipes and water tanks in a building

plume *noun* (*plural* **plumes**)
1 a large feather 2 something shaped like
a feather ♦ *We saw a plume of smoke in the
distance*
plumed *adjective* decorated with plumes

plump ➤ *adjective* (**plumper, plumpest**)
rounded or slightly fat

plump ➤ *verb* (**plumps, plumping, plumped**)
to plump for something or **someone** is to choose
them

plunder ➤ *verb* (**plunders, plundering, plundered**)
to plunder a place or an enemy is to rob
them violently, especially in a time of war
or disorder
plunderer *noun* someone who plunders a
place

plunder ➤ *noun*
1 plundering a person or place 2 goods taken by plundering

plunge ➤ *verb* (**plunges, plunging, plunged**)
1 to plunge into water is to jump or dive into it with force 2 to plunge something into a liquid or something soft is to put it in with force

plunge ➤ *noun* (*plural* **plunges**)
a sudden fall or dive

plural ➤ *noun* (*plural* **plurals**)
the form of a word meaning more than one person or thing, such as *cakes* and *children*

plural ➤ *adjective*
in the plural; meaning more than one
♦ *'Mice' is a plural noun*

plus *preposition*
with the next number or thing added
♦ *2 plus 2 equals 4 (2+2=4)*

plutonium *noun* (*pronounced* ploo-**toh**-ni-um)
a radioactive element used in nuclear weapons and reactors

plywood *noun*
board made from thin sheets of wood glued together

p.m. short for Latin *post meridiem* which means 'after midday'

pneumatic *adjective* (*pronounced* new-**mat**-ik)
filled with air or worked by compressed air

pneumonia *noun* (*pronounced* new-**moh**-ni-a)
a serious disease of the lungs

poach *verb* (**poaches, poaching, poached**)
1 to poach food, especially fish or an egg taken out of its shell, is to cook it in or over boiling water 2 to poach animals is to hunt them illegally on someone else's land
poacher *noun* someone who poaches animals

pocket ➤ *noun* (*plural* **pockets**)
1 part of a piece of clothing shaped like a small bag, for keeping things in 2 a small area in which something happens ♦ *There will be pockets of rain in the south* 3 a person's pocket is their supply of money ♦ *The cost is well beyond my pocket*
to be out of pocket is to have spent more money than you got back

pocket ➤ *adjective*
small enough to carry in your pocket ♦ *Use a pocket calculator*

pocket ➤ *verb* (**pockets, pocketing, pocketed**)
(*informal*) to pocket something is to steal it

pocketful *noun* (*plural* **pocketfuls**)
an amount you can put in your pocket

pocket money *noun*
money given to a child to spend

pod *noun* (*plural* **pods**)
a long seed-container on a pea or bean plant

podgy *adjective* (**podgier, podgiest**)
short and fat

poem *noun* (*plural* **poems**)
a piece of poetry

poet *noun* (*plural* **poets**)
someone who writes poetry

poetic or **poetical** *adjective*
like poetry; using the language of poetry
poetically *adverb* in a poetic way

poetry *noun*
writing arranged in short lines, often with a particular rhythm

point ➤ *noun* (*plural* **points**)
1 the narrow or sharp end of something
♦ *Don't hold the knife by its point* 2 a dot or mark ♦ *Put in a decimal point* 3 a particular place or time ♦ *They gave up at this point* 4 a detail or special feature
♦ *He has some good points* 5 purpose or advantage ♦ *There's no point in hurrying* 6 a movable part of a railway line that allows trains to change from one track to another
to come to the point is to mention the thing you really want to say

point ➤ *verb* (**points, pointing, pointed**)
1 to point to something is to show where it is, especially by holding out your finger towards it 2 to point something is to aim it or direct it ♦ *She pointed a gun at us*
to point something out is to show it or explain it

point-blank *adjective* and *adverb*
1 close to the target 2 directly and completely ♦ *He refused point-blank*

pointed *adjective*
1 having a point at the end 2 clearly directed at a person ♦ *He made a pointed remark about working hard*
pointedly *adverb* in a pointed way

pointer *noun* (*plural* **pointers**)
1 a stick or device used to point at something 2 a dog that points with its muzzle at birds which it scents 3 a hint or piece of guidance ♦ *He gave us a few pointers on catching fish*

pointless *adjective*
having no purpose or meaning
pointlessly *adverb* in a pointless way

point of view *noun* (*plural* **points of view**)
a way of looking at something or thinking about it

poise ➤ *noun*
  1 poise is a dignified and self-confident manner 2 poise is also a state of balance

poise ➤ *verb* (**poises, poising, poised**)
  1 to poise something is to balance it or keep it steady 2 to be poised to do something is to be ready for it

poison ➤ *noun* (*plural* **poisons**)
  a substance that can kill or harm living things

poison ➤ *verb* (**poisons, poisoning, poisoned**)
  1 to poison someone is to kill or harm them with poison 2 to poison something is to put poison in it
  poisoner *noun* a person who poisons someone

poisonous *adjective*
  1 containing poison 2 able to poison someone

poke¹ ➤ *verb* (**pokes, poking, poked**)
  to poke something or someone is to push or jab them hard with a finger or pointed object
  to poke about is to rummage nosily
  to poke out is to stick out

poke ➤ *noun* (*plural* **pokes**)
  a prod or poking movement

poke² *noun*
  to buy a pig in a poke is to buy something without seeing it first

poker *noun* (*plural* **pokers**)
  1 a metal rod for poking a fire 2 a card game in which the players bet on who has the best cards

polar *adjective*
  to do with the North or South Pole, or near one of them

polar bear *noun* (*plural* **polar bears**)
  a powerful white bear living in Arctic regions

Polaroid *noun*
  (*trademark*) a type of plastic that reduces the brightness of the light. It is used in sunglasses

Polaroid camera *noun* (*plural* **Polaroid cameras**)
  (*trademark*) a camera that takes a picture and produces the finished photograph a few seconds later

pole¹ *noun* (*plural* **poles**)
  a long thin piece of wood or metal

pole² *noun* (*plural* **poles**)
  1 each of the two points at the ends of the earth's axis, the **North Pole** and the **South Pole** 2 each end of a magnet

pole vault *noun*
  an athletic contest of jumping over a high bar with the help of a long springy pole

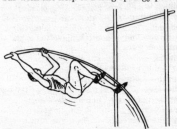

police *noun*
  the people whose job is to catch criminals and make sure that people obey the law

policeman or **policewoman** *noun* (*plural* **policemen** or **policewomen**)
  a man or woman member of the police

police officer *noun* (*plural* **police officers**)
  a member of the police

policy *noun* (*plural* **policies**)
  1 the aims or plans of a person or group of people 2 a plan of action ♦ *Honesty is the best policy*

polio *noun* (*pronounced* poh-li-oh) (*informal*) poliomyelitis

poliomyelitis *noun* (*pronounced* poh-li-oh-my-i-ly-tis)
  a disease that paralyses the body

polish ➤ *verb* (**polishes, polishing, polished**) (*pronounced* pol-ish)
  to polish something is to make its surface shiny or smooth
  to polish something off (*informal*) is to finish it quickly

polish ➤ *noun* (*plural* **polishes**) (*pronounced* pol-ish)
  1 polish is a substance used in polishing 2 a polish is a shine got by polishing

polished *adjective*
  1 shiny 2 well practised or rehearsed ♦ *The choir gave a polished performance*

polite *adjective* (**politer, politest**)
  having good manners; respectful and thoughtful towards other people
  politely *adverb* in a polite way **politeness** *noun* being polite

political *adjective*
  to do with the governing of a country
  politically *adverb* in a political way

politician *noun* (*plural* **politicians**)
  someone who is involved in politics

politics *noun*
 political matters; the business of
 governing a country

polka *noun* (*plural* **polkas**)
 a lively dance

poll *noun* (*plural* **polls**)
 1 a round of voting at an election **2** an
 opinion poll

pollen *noun*
 yellow powder found inside flowers,
 containing male seeds for fertilizing other
 flowers

pollen count *noun* (*plural* **pollen counts**)
 a measurement of how much pollen there
 is in the air, given as a warning for people
 who are allergic to pollen

pollute *verb* (**pollutes, polluting, polluted**)
 to pollute a place or thing is to make it
 dirty or impure
 pollution *noun* polluting a place or thing

polo *noun*
 a game rather like hockey, with players on
 horseback using long mallets

polo neck *noun* (*plural* **polo necks**)
 a high rounded collar that is turned over
 at the top

poltergeist *noun* (*plural* **poltergeists**)
 (*pronounced* **pol**-ter-gyst)
 a noisy mischievous ghost that damages
 things

poly- *prefix*
 meaning 'many', as in *polygon*

polygon *noun* (*plural* **polygons**)
 a figure or shape with many sides, such as
 a hexagon or octagon

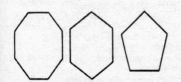

polystyrene *noun* (*pronounced*
 pol-i-**sty**-reen)
 a kind of plastic used for insulating or
 packing things

polythene *noun* (*pronounced* **pol**-i-theen)
 a lightweight plastic used to make bags
 and wrappings

pomegranate *noun* (*plural* **pomegranates**)
 a tropical fruit with many seeds

pomp *noun*
 pomp is the dignified and solemn way in
 which an important ceremony is
 conducted

pompous *adjective*
 thinking too much of your own importance
 pomposity *noun* being pompous **pompously**
 adverb in a pompous way

pond *noun* (*plural* **ponds**)
 a small lake

ponder *verb* (**ponders, pondering, pondered**)
 to ponder something is to think seriously
 about it

ponderous *adjective*
 1 heavy and awkward **2** dull and not easy
 to follow ♦ *He writes in a ponderous style*
 ponderously *adverb* in a ponderous way

pony *noun* (*plural* **ponies**)
 a small horse

ponytail *noun* (*plural* **ponytails**)
 a bunch of long hair tied at the back of the
 head

pony-trekking *noun*
 travelling across country on ponies for
 pleasure

poodle *noun* (*plural* **poodles**)
 a dog with long curly hair

pool[1] *noun* (*plural* **pools**)
 1 a pond **2** a puddle **3** a swimming pool

pool[2] *noun* (*plural* **pools**)
 1 a fund of money, especially in a
 gambling game **2** a group of things shared
 by several people
 the pools a system of gambling on the
 results of football matches

poor *adjective* (**poorer, poorest**)
 1 having very little money ♦ *He came
 from a poor family* **2** not good or adequate
 ♦ *This is poor work* **3** unfortunate ♦ *Poor
 fellow!*

poorly ➤ *adverb*
 not adequately ♦ *They arrived poorly
 dressed*

poorly ➤ *adjective*
 unwell ♦ *I'm feeling poorly today*

pop[1] ➤ *noun* (*plural* **pops**)
 1 a small explosive sound **2** a fizzy drink

pop ➤ *verb* (**pops, popping, popped**)
  1 to pop is to make a small explosive sound **2** (*informal*) to pop somewhere is to go quickly there ♦ *I'm just popping out to the shop* **3** to pop something somewhere is to put it there quickly ♦ *Will you pop the potatoes in the oven?*

pop² *noun*
  modern popular music

popcorn *noun*
  maize heated till it bursts and forms light fluffy balls for eating

Pope *noun* (*plural* **Popes**)
  the leader of the Roman Catholic Church

poplar *noun* (*plural* **poplars**)
  a tall straight tree

poppadam or **poppadom** *noun* (*plural* **poppadams** or **poppadoms**)
  a thin crisp pancake eaten with Indian food

poppy *noun* (*plural* **poppies**)
  a plant with large red flowers

popular *adjective*
  liked or enjoyed by a lot of people
  popularity *noun* being popular **popularly** *adverb* in a popular way

popularize *verb* (**popularizes, popularizing, popularized**)
  to popularize something is to make it known and liked by a lot of people

populated *adjective*
  having people living there ♦ *The land is thinly populated*

population *noun* (*plural* **populations**)
  the people who live in a particular place

populous *adjective*
  inhabited by a lot of people

porcelain *noun* (*pronounced* por-se-lin)
  a fine kind of china

porch *noun* (*plural* **porches**)
  a small roofed area outside the door of a building

porcupine *noun* (*plural* **porcupines**)
  a small animal covered with long prickles

pore¹ *noun* (*plural* **pores**)
  a tiny opening in the skin through which moisture passes

pore² *verb* (**pores, poring, pored**)
  to pore over something is to study it closely

pork *noun*
  meat from a pig

pornography *noun* (*pronounced* por-nog-ra-fi)
  obscene pictures or writings
  pornographic *adjective* to do with pornography; obscene

porous *adjective*
  allowing liquid or air to pass through ♦ *Sandy soil is porous*
  porosity *noun* being porous

porpoise *noun* (*plural* **porpoises**) (*pronounced* por-pus)
  a sea animal rather like a small whale

porridge *noun*
  porridge is a food made by boiling oatmeal to make a thick paste

port¹ *noun* (*plural* **ports**)
  1 a harbour **2** a city or town with a harbour **3** the left-hand side of a ship or aircraft when you are facing forward

port² *noun*
  a strong red Portuguese wine

portable *adjective*
  able to be carried

portcullis *noun* (*plural* **portcullises**)
  a heavy grating that can be lowered to block the gateway to a castle

porter *noun* (*plural* **porters**)
  1 someone whose job is to carry luggage or goods **2** someone whose job is to look after the entrance to a large building

porthole *noun* (*plural* **portholes**)
  a small round window in the side of a ship or aircraft

portion *noun* (*plural* **portions**)
  a part or share given to someone

portly *adjective* (**portlier, portliest**)
rather fat
portliness *noun* being portly

portrait *noun* (*plural* **portraits**)
a picture of a person

portray *verb* (**portrays, portraying, portrayed**)
1 to portray someone is to make a portrait of them **2** to portray something or someone is to describe or show them in a certain way ♦ *The play portrays the king as a kind man*
portrayal *noun* portraying or describing someone or something

pose ➤ *noun* (*plural* **poses**)
1 a way of standing or sitting for a portrait or photograph to be made of you **2** a pretence; unnatural behaviour to impress people

pose ➤ *verb* (**poses, posing, posed**)
1 to pose is to put your body into a special position **2** to pose someone is to put them in a particular position to be painted or photographed **3** to pose as someone is to pretend to be them ♦ *The man posed as a police officer* **4** to pose a question or problem is to present it ♦ *Icy weather always poses a problem to motorists*

poser *noun* (*plural* **posers**)
1 a puzzling question or problem
2 someone who behaves in an unnatural way to impress people

posh *adjective* (**posher, poshest**)
(*informal*) **1** very smart; high-class
♦ *They stayed at a posh hotel* **2** of a high social class ♦ *She spoke with a posh accent*

position *noun* (*plural* **positions**)
1 the place where something is or should be **2** the way in which someone or something is placed or arranged ♦ *He was in a sitting position* **3** a situation or condition ♦ *I am in no position to help you* **4** a regular job

positive ➤ *adjective*
1 sure or definite ♦ *I am positive I saw him* ♦ *We need positive proof* **2** agreeing or saying 'yes' ♦ *We received a positive answer* **3** a positive number is one that is greater than nought **4** a positive electric charge is one that does not carry electrons
positively *adverb* in a positive way

positive ➤ *noun* (*plural* **positives**)
a photographic print made from a negative, with light and dark parts as in real life

posse *noun* (*plural* **posses**) (*pronounced* **poss-i**)
a group of people that helps a sheriff in the USA

possess *verb* (**possesses, possessing, possessed**)
to possess something is to own it
possessor *noun* an owner

possessed *adjective*
behaving as if controlled by an outside force ♦ *He fought like a man possessed*

possession *noun* (*plural* **possessions**)
1 a possession is something that you own **2** possession is owning something ♦ *They gained possession of a piece of land*

possessive *adjective*
1 wanting to get and keep things for yourself **2** (*in Grammar*) showing that someone owns something ♦ *'His' and 'yours' are possessive pronouns*

possibility *noun* (*plural* **possibilities**)
1 possibility is being possible ♦ *Is there any possibility of changing your mind?*
2 a possibility is something that is possible ♦ *There are many possibilities*

possible *adjective*
able to exist, happen, be done, or be used

possibly *adverb*
1 in any way ♦ *That cannot possibly be right* **2** perhaps ♦ *I will arrive at six o'clock, or possibly earlier*

post[1] ➤ *noun* (*plural* **posts**)
1 an upright piece of wood, concrete, or metal fixed in the ground **2** the starting point or finishing point of a race ♦ *He was left at the post*

post ➤ *verb* (**posts, posting, posted**)
to post a notice or poster is to put it in a public place

post[2] ➤ *noun* (*plural* **posts**)
1 the post is the collecting and delivering of letters and parcels **2** post is letters and parcels carried by post; mail **3** a post is a collection or delivery of mail ♦ *The last post is at 4 p.m.*

post ➤ *verb* (**posts, posting, posted**)
to post a letter or parcel is to send it to someone by post

post[3] ➤ *noun* (*plural* **posts**)
1 a regular job **2** the place where a sentry stands **3** a place occupied by soldiers or traders

post ➤ *verb* (**posts, posting, posted**)
to post a sentry is to put a sentry on duty

post- *prefix*
meaning 'after', as in *post-war*

postage *noun*
the cost of sending something by post

postage stamp *noun* (*plural* **postage stamps**)
a stamp for putting on letters and parcels, showing the amount paid

postal *adjective*
to do with the post; by post

postal order noun (plural **postal orders**)
a voucher you buy at a post office, which can be sent by post and exchanged for money by the person receiving it

postbox noun (plural **postboxes**)
a box into which you put letters to be sent by post

postcard noun (plural **postcards**)
a card that you can write a message on and post without an envelope

postcode noun (plural **postcodes**)
a group of letters and numbers included in an address to help in sorting the post

poster noun (plural **posters**)
a large public notice having information or advertising something

postman noun (plural **postmen**)
someone who collects and delivers letters and parcels

postmark noun (plural **postmarks**)
an official mark stamped on something sent by post, showing when and where it was posted

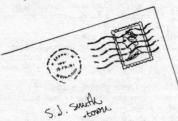

post-mortem noun (plural **post-mortems**)
an examination of a dead body to find the cause of death

post office noun (plural **post offices**)
a place where you can post letters and parcels and buy stamps, postal orders, and other official documents

postpone verb (**postpones, postponing, postponed**)
to postpone a meeting or event is to arrange for it to take place later than originally planned ♦ *The match has been postponed for two weeks*
postponement noun postponing something

postscript noun (plural **postscripts**)
something extra added at the end of a letter or book

posture noun (plural **postures**)
the way that a person stands, sits, or walks

posy noun (plural **posies**)
a small bunch of flowers

pot¹ ➤ noun (plural **pots**)
1 a deep round container 2 a flowerpot
to go to pot (*informal*) is to become bad or be ruined
pots of money (*informal*) a lot of money

pot ➤ verb (**pots, potting, potted**)
to pot a plant is to put it into a flowerpot

pot² noun
the drug marijuana

potassium noun
a soft silvery-white metallic substance that living things need

potato noun (plural **potatoes**)
a vegetable that grows underground

potent adjective
powerful
potency noun power **potently** adverb in a potent way

potential ➤ adjective
capable of happening or becoming important or useful in the future ♦ *She is a potential star*
potentially adverb as a possibility in the future

potential ➤ noun
an ability to become important or useful in the future

pothole noun (plural **potholes**)
1 a deep natural hole in the ground 2 a hole in a road

potholing noun
exploring underground potholes
potholer noun someone who goes potholing

potion noun (plural **potions**) (*pronounced* poh-shon)
a drink containing medicine or poison

potter¹ noun (plural **potters**)
someone who makes pottery

potter² verb (**potters, pottering, pottered**)
to potter, or potter about, is to work in a leisurely or casual way

pottery noun (plural **potteries**)
1 pottery is pots, cups, plates, and other things made of baked clay 2 a pottery is a place where a potter works

potty¹ adjective (**pottier, pottiest**)
(*informal*) mad or silly

potty² noun (plural **potties**)
(*informal*) a small bowl used by young children as a lavatory

pouch noun (plural **pouches**)
1 a small bag or pocket 2 a fold of skin in which a kangaroo keeps its young

poultry noun
birds such as chickens, geese, and turkeys, kept for their eggs and meat

pounce verb (**pounces, pouncing, pounced**)
to pounce on someone or something is to jump on them or attack them suddenly

pound[1] *noun* (*plural* **pounds**)
1 a unit of money, in Britain equal to 100 pence **2** a unit of weight equal to 16 ounces or about 454 grams

pound[2] *verb* (**pounds, pounding, pounded**)
1 to pound something is to hit it repeatedly to crush it **2** to pound, or pound along, is to walk with heavy steps **3** to be pounding is to make a dull thumping sound, or to beat heavily ♦ *My heart was pounding with the excitement*

pour *verb* (**pours, pouring, poured**)
1 to pour a liquid is to make it flow out of a container **2** to pour is to flow in a large amount ♦ *Blood was pouring from the wound on her leg* **3** to pour is also to rain heavily ♦ *It was pouring this morning* **4** to pour in or out is to come or go in large numbers or amounts ♦ *After the programme, letters of complaint poured in* ♦ *The fans poured out of the stadium*

pout *verb* (**pouts, pouting, pouted**)
to pout is to stick out your lips when you are annoyed or sulking

poverty *noun*
being poor

powder ➤ *noun* (*plural* **powders**)
1 a mass of tiny pieces of something dry, like flour or dust **2** make-up in the form of powder

powdery *adjective* like powder

powder ➤ *verb* (**powders, powdering, powdered**)
1 to powder a substance is to make it into powder **2** to powder a surface is to put powder on it

power *noun* (*plural* **powers**)
1 power is strength or great energy **2** the power to do something is the ability or authority to do it ♦ *Humans have the power of speech* ♦ *I do not have the power to give you permission* **3** a power is a powerful country **4** power is also electricity or another form of energy **5** (*in Mathematics*) the power of a number is the result obtained by multiplying the number by itself one or more times ♦ *27 is the third power of 3 ($3 \times 3 \times 3 = 27$)*

powered *adjective* worked by electricity or another form of power

powerful *adjective*
having a lot of power or influence

powerfully *adverb* in a powerful way

powerhouse *noun* (*plural* **powerhouses**)
a power station

powerless *adjective*
unable to act or control things

power station *noun* (*plural* **power stations**)
a building where electricity is produced

practicable *adjective*
possible or able to be done ♦ *That is not a practicable plan*

practical *adjective*
1 able to do or make useful things ♦ *She is a very practical person* **2** likely to be useful ♦ *That is a practical idea* **3** concerned with doing or making things ♦ *He has had practical experience*

practical joke *noun* (*plural* **practical jokes**)
a trick played on someone

practically *adverb*
1 in a practical way ♦ *He is practically skilled* **2** almost ♦ *It's practically ready now*

practice *noun* (*plural* **practices**)
1 practice is doing something often and regularly so as to get better at it ♦ *I must do my piano practice* **2** practice is also actually doing something rather than thinking or talking about it ♦ *It works well in practice* **3** a practice is the business of a doctor or lawyer

practise *verb* (**practises, practising, practised**)
1 to practise something is to do it often so as to get better at it **2** to practise an activity or habit is to do it regularly ♦ *Practise what you preach* **3** to practise is to work as a doctor, lawyer, or other professional person

prairie *noun* (*plural* **prairies**)
a large area of flat grass-covered land in North America

praise ➤ *verb* (**praises, praising, praised**)
to praise someone or something is to say that they are good or have done well

praise ➤ *noun* (*plural* **praises**)
words that praise someone or something

pram *noun* (*plural* **prams**)
a small open carriage for a baby, pushed by a person walking

prance *verb* (**prances, prancing, pranced**)
to prance, or prance about, is to jump about in a lively or happy way

prank *noun* (*plural* **pranks**)
a trick played on someone for mischief

prawn *noun* (*plural* **prawns**)
a shellfish like a large shrimp, used for food

pray *verb* (**prays, praying, prayed**)
1 to pray is to talk to God 2 to pray is also to ask earnestly for something ♦ *He prayed to be set free*

prayer *noun* (*plural* **prayers**)
1 prayer is praying 2 a prayer is what you say when you pray

pre- *prefix*
meaning 'before', as in *pre-war*

preach *verb* (**preaches, preaching, preached**)
to preach is to give a talk about religion or about right and wrong
preacher *noun* someone who preaches

precarious *adjective* (*pronounced* pri-kair-i-us)
not very safe or secure
precariously *adverb* in a precarious way

precaution *noun* (*plural* **precautions**)
something done to prevent future trouble or danger

precede *verb* (**precedes, preceding, preceded**)
to precede someone or something is to come or go in front of them
precedence *noun* the right to go first

precinct *noun* (*plural* **precincts**)
(*pronounced* pree-sinkt)
1 a part of a town where traffic is not allowed ♦ *The town has a large shopping precinct* 2 the area round a cathedral

precious *adjective*
very valuable or loved

precipice *noun* (*plural* **precipices**)
the steep face of a mountain or cliff

précis *noun* (*plural* **précis**) (*pronounced* pray-see)
a brief statement or summary of the main points of something

precise *adjective*
1 exact ♦ *Are your measurements precise?*
2 clearly stated ♦ *I gave them precise instructions*
precisely *adverb* in a precise way **precision** *noun* being precise

predator *noun* (*plural* **predators**)
(*pronounced* pred-a-ter)
an animal that hunts other animals
predatory *adjective* hunting other animals

predecessor *noun* (*plural* **predecessors**)
(*pronounced* pree-di-ses-er)
an earlier person or thing, such as an ancestor or someone who once did the job you do now

predict *verb* (**predicts, predicting, predicted**)
to predict something is to say that it will happen in the future
predictable *adjective* able to be predicted
prediction *noun* something that someone predicts

predominant *adjective*
most important or largest in size or number
predominance *noun* being predominant
predominantly *adverb* mostly; most importantly

predominate *verb* (**predominates, predominating, predominated**)
to predominate is to be the largest in size or number, or the most important ♦ *Girls predominate in our class*

preface *noun* (*plural* **prefaces**) (*pronounced* pref-ass)
an introduction at the beginning of a book

prefect *noun* (*plural* **prefects**)
1 a school pupil who is given authority to help to keep order 2 a local official in some countries

prefer *verb* (**prefers, preferring, preferred**)
to prefer someone or something is to like them better than another
preference *noun* preferring; something you prefer

preferable *adjective* (*pronounced* pref-er-a-bul)
better or liked more
preferably *adverb* rather; in a preferable way

prefix *noun* (*plural* **prefixes**)
a word or syllable joined to the front of a word to change or add to its meaning, as in *dis*order, *out*stretched, and *un*happy

pregnant *adjective*
having an unborn baby growing inside the womb
pregnancy *noun* being pregnant

prehistoric *adjective*
belonging to a very long time ago, before written records were kept
prehistory *noun* prehistoric times

prejudice *noun* (*plural* **prejudices**)
a prejudice is when you make up your mind about something before you have thought about it
prejudiced *adjective* having a prejudice

preliminary *adjective*
coming before something or preparing for it

prelude *noun* (*plural* **preludes**) (*pronounced* prel-yood)
1 an introduction to a play, poem, or event
2 a short piece of music

premier noun (plural **premiers**) (pronounced prem-i-er)
the leader of a government

première noun (plural **premières**) (pronounced prem-yair)
the first public performance of a play or showing of a film

premises plural noun
a building with its land

premium noun (plural **premiums**) (pronounced pree-mi-um)
an amount paid regularly to an insurance company
at a premium above the normal price; valued highly

Premium Bond noun (plural **Premium Bonds**)
a government savings certificate that gives the owner a chance to win a money prize in a draw

preoccupied adjective
thinking hard about something and not noticing other things
preoccupation noun being preoccupied

prep noun
(informal) homework

preparation noun (plural **preparations**)
1 getting something ready 2 a thing done in order to get ready for something ♦ We were making last-minute preparations

preparatory adjective (pronounced pri-pa-ra-ter-i)
preparing for something

preparatory school noun (plural **preparatory schools**)
a school that prepares pupils for a higher school

prepare verb (**prepares, preparing, prepared**)
to prepare something is to get it ready
to be prepared to do something is to be ready or willing to do it

preposition noun (plural **prepositions**)
a word put in front of a noun or pronoun to show how the noun or pronoun is connected with another word, for example on in the sentence Put the flowers on the table and with in the sentence I'd like some sauce with my food

prep school noun (plural **prep schools**)
a preparatory school

prescribe verb (**prescribes, prescribing, prescribed**)
1 to prescribe a medicine for a patient is to instruct them to take it and give them a prescription for it 2 to prescribe a method or solution is to say what must be done

prescription noun (plural **prescriptions**)
a doctor's order for a medicine to be prepared for a patient

presence noun
being at a place ♦ Your presence is expected
in the presence of someone at the place where someone is

present¹ ➤ adjective (pronounced prez-ent)
1 in a particular place; here ♦ Nobody else was present 2 existing or happening now ♦ Who is the present Queen?

present ➤ noun (pronounced prez-ent)
the time now ♦ Our teacher is away at present

present² ➤ noun (plural **presents**) (pronounced prez-ent)
something that you give to someone or receive from them

present ➤ verb (**presents, presenting, presented**) (pronounced pri-zent)
1 to present something to someone is to give it to them, especially with a ceremony ♦ Who will present the prizes this year?
2 to present a play or other entertainment is to perform it or arrange for it to be performed 3 to present a radio or television programme is to introduce it to the audience 4 to present something you have done or made is to show it formally to people ♦ We are here to present our latest products

presentation noun (plural **presentations**)
a formal talk showing or demonstrating something

presenter noun (plural **presenters**)
someone who presents something, especially a radio or television programme

presently adverb
soon; in a while ♦ I shall be with you presently

present participle noun (plural **present participles**)
a form of a verb used after am, are, is to describe an action that is happening now, or used after was, were, has been, have been, had been to describe an action that went on for some time in the past, for example looking in the sentences I am looking at the pictures and I was looking at the pictures

present tense noun
a form of a verb used to describe something that is happening now, for example likes in the sentence He likes swimming

preservative noun (plural **preservatives**)
a substance added to food to preserve it

preserve verb (**preserves, preserving, preserved**)
to preserve something is to keep it safe or in good condition
preservation noun preserving something

preside *verb* (presides, presiding, presided)
(*pronounced* pri-zyd)
to preside over a meeting or other occasion
is to be in charge of it

president *noun* (*plural* presidents)
1 the person in charge of a society,
business, or club **2** the head of a country
that is a republic
presidency *noun* being a president
presidential *adjective* to do with a president

press ➤ *verb* (presses, pressing, pressed)
1 to press something is to push hard on it
or squeeze it **2** to press clothes or soft
material is to make them flat and smooth
with an iron or press **3** to press someone
for something is to urge them to do or give
something ♦ *We must press them for more
money*

press ➤ *noun* (*plural* presses)
1 the action of squeezing or pushing on
something **2** a device for flattening and
smoothing things **3** a machine for
printing things **4** a business that prints or
publishes books **5** the press are
newspapers and journalists

press conference *noun* (*plural* press
conferences)
an interview given by a politician or other
important person with a group of
journalists

press-up *noun* (*plural* press-ups)
an exercise in which you lie face
downwards and press down with your
hands to lift your body

pressure *noun* (*plural* pressures)
1 continuous pushing or squeezing **2** the
force with which something pushes
against something or squeezes it **3** an
action that persuades or forces you to do
something

pressurize *verb* (pressurizes, pressurizing,
pressurized)
1 to pressurize a place or compartment is
to keep it at the same air pressure all the
time ♦ *The aircraft is pressurized* **2** to
pressurize someone is to try to force them
to do something

prestige *noun* (*pronounced* pres-teezh)
good reputation and influence
prestigious *adjective* having prestige

presumably *adverb*
probably; according to what you may
presume

presume *verb* (presumes, presuming, presumed)
1 to presume something is to suppose it
♦ *I presumed that he was dead* **2** to
presume to do something is to dare to do it
♦ *I wouldn't presume to advise you*
presumption *noun* presuming something

presumptuous *adjective*
too bold or confident

pretence *noun* (*plural* pretences)
an attempt to pretend something

pretend *verb* (pretends, pretending, pretended)
1 to pretend is to behave as if something
untrue or imaginary is true **2** to pretend
something is to claim it dishonestly
♦ *They pretended they were policemen*

pretender *noun* (*plural* pretenders)
someone who claims a country's throne

pretty ➤ *adjective* (prettier, prettiest)
pleasant to look at or hear; attractive
prettily *adverb* in a pretty way **prettiness**
noun being pretty

pretty ➤ *adverb*
(*informal*) quite; moderately ♦ *It's pretty
cold outside*

prevail *verb* (prevails, prevailing, prevailed)
1 to prevail is to be most frequent or
general ♦ *The prevailing view is that we
were wrong* **2** to prevail is also to be
successful in a battle, contest, or game

prevalent *adjective*
most frequent or common; widespread

prevent *verb* (prevents, preventing, prevented)
1 to prevent something is to stop it from
happening or make it impossible **2** to
prevent someone is to stop them from
doing something
prevention *noun* preventing something or
someone **preventive** *adjective* helping to
prevent something

preview *noun* (*plural* previews)
a showing of a film or play before it is
shown to the public

previous *adjective*
coming before this; preceding ♦ *I was in
London the previous week*
previously *adverb* before; earlier

prey[1] ➤ *noun* (*pronounced* pray)
an animal that is hunted or killed by
another animal for food

prey ➤ *verb* (preys, preying, preyed)
(*pronounced* pray)
to prey on something is to hunt and kill an
animal for food ♦ *Owls prey on mice and
other small animals*
to prey on your mind is to worry you a lot

price ➤ *noun* (*plural* prices)
1 the amount of money for which
something is sold **2** what you have to give
or do to get something ♦ *What is the price
of peace?*
at any price at any cost

price ➤ *verb* (prices, pricing, priced)
to price something is to decide its price

priceless *adjective*
1 very valuable 2 (*informal*) very amusing

prick ➤ *verb* (**pricks, pricking, pricked**)
1 to prick something is to make a tiny hole in it 2 to prick someone is to hurt them with something sharp or pointed
to prick up your ears is to start listening suddenly

prick ➤ *noun* (*plural* **pricks**)
a prick is a pricking feeling

prickle *noun* (*plural* **prickles**)
a sharp point on a plant or animal
prickly *adjective* feeling like prickles

pride *noun* (*plural* **prides**)
1 pride is a feeling of being proud 2 a pride is something that makes you feel proud ♦ *This stamp is the pride of my collection* 3 a pride is also a group of lions

priest *noun* (*plural* **priests**)
1 a member of the clergy 2 someone who conducts religious ceremonies; a religious leader
priesthood *noun* the position of a priest

priestess *noun* (*plural* **priestesses**)
a female priest in a non-Christian religion

prig *noun* (*plural* **prigs**)
someone who is smug and self-righteous
priggish *adjective* smug and self-righteous

prim *adjective* (**primmer, primmest**)
liking things to be correct, and not liking anything rough or rude
primly *adverb* in a prim way **primness** *noun* being prim

primary *adjective*
first; most important
primarily *adverb* most importantly

primary colour *noun* (*plural* **primary colours**)
one of the colours from which all other colours can be made by mixing: red, yellow, and blue for paint, and red, green, and violet for light

primary school *noun* (*plural* **primary schools**)
a school for the first stage of a child's education

primate *noun* (*plural* **primates**)
1 an animal of the group which includes human beings, apes, and monkeys 2 an archbishop

prime ➤ *adjective*
1 chief or most important ♦ *The weather was the prime cause of the accident* 2 of the best quality

prime ➤ *noun* (*plural* **primes**)
the best part or stage of something ♦ *He was in the prime of life*

prime ➤ *verb* (**primes, priming, primed**)
1 to prime something is to get it ready for use ♦ *Pour water into the pump to prime it* 2 to prime a surface is to put a special liquid on it before painting it

prime minister *noun* (*plural* **prime ministers**)
the leader of a government

prime number *noun* (*plural* **prime numbers**)
a number that can only be divided exactly by itself and the number one, for example 2, 3, 5, 7, and 11

primer *noun* (*plural* **primers**)
1 paint used for the first coat on an unpainted surface 2 a textbook dealing with the first or simplest stages of a subject

primeval *adjective* (*pronounced* pry-**mee**-val)
belonging to the earliest times of the world; ancient

primitive *adjective*
1 at an early stage of development or civilization ♦ *Primitive humans were hunters rather than farmers* 2 basic or simple ♦ *They used a primitive technology*

primrose *noun* (*plural* **primroses**)
a pale yellow flower that comes out in spring

prince *noun* (*plural* **princes**)
1 the son of a king or queen 2 a man or boy in a royal family
princely *adjective* like a prince

princess *noun* (*plural* **princesses**)
1 the daughter of a king or queen 2 a woman or girl in a royal family 3 the wife of a prince

principal ➤ *adjective*
chief or most important ♦ *Name the principal cities of Britain*
principally *adverb* chiefly; mainly

principal ➤ *noun* (*plural* **principals**)
the head of a college or school

principle *noun* (*plural* **principles**)
a general truth, belief, or rule ♦ *She taught me the principles of geometry*
in principle in general, not in detail

print ➤ *verb* (**prints, printing, printed**)
1 to print words or pictures is to put them on paper with a machine 2 to print letters is to write them separately and not joined together 3 to print a photograph is to make it from a negative

print ➤ *noun* (*plural* **prints**)
1 print is printed words or pictures 2 a print is a mark made by something pressing on a surface ♦ *Her thumb left a print on the glass* 3 a print is also a photograph made from a negative

printed circuit noun (plural **printed circuits**)
an electric circuit made by pressing thin
metal strips on to a board

printer noun (plural **printers**)
1 someone who prints books or
newspapers **2** a machine that prints on
paper from data in a computer

printout noun (plural **printouts**)
the information printed on paper from
data in a computer

priority noun (plural **priorities**) (pronounced
pry-o-ri-ti)
1 a priority is something that is more
urgent or important than other things
♦ Repairing the roof is a priority
2 priority is the right to be considered
before other things ♦ People in need of
urgent medical help will have priority

prise verb (**prises, prising, prised**)
to prise something open is to force or lever
it open

prism noun (plural **prisms**)
1 a piece of glass that breaks up light into
the colours of the rainbow **2** (in
Mathematics) a solid object with parallel
ends that are equal triangles or polygons

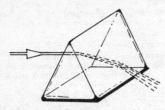

prison noun (plural **prisons**)
a place where criminals are kept as a
punishment

prisoner noun (plural **prisoners**)
someone who is kept in a prison or who is
a captive

privacy noun
being private or away from other people

private ➤ adjective
1 belonging to a particular person or
group of people ♦ This is a private road
2 meant to be kept secret ♦ These letters
are private **3** away from other people ♦ Is
there a private place to swim?
in private where only particular people can
see or hear; not in public
privately adverb separately; not with other
people

private ➤ noun (plural **privates**)
a soldier of the lowest rank

privatize verb (**privatizes, privatizing, privatized**)
to privatize a public business or
organization is to sell it to private owners
to run
privatization noun privatizing businesses
and organizations

privet noun
an evergreen shrub with small leaves,
used to make hedges

privilege noun (plural **privileges**)
a special right or advantage given to one
person or group of people
privileged adjective having a privilege

prize ➤ noun (plural **prizes**)
1 something you get for winning a game or
competition, or for doing well in an
examination **2** something taken from an
enemy

prize ➤ verb (**prizes, prizing, prized**)
to prize something is to value it highly

pro noun (plural **pros**)
(informal) a professional

pro- prefix
meaning 'in favour of' or 'supporting', as in
pro-government

probable adjective
likely to be true or to happen
probability noun being probable **probably**
adverb very likely

probation noun
testing a person's character or behaviour,
or making sure they are suitable for a job
or club
on probation being supervised by a
probation officer
probationary adjective being on probation

probation officer noun (plural **probation
officers**)
an official who supervises the behaviour of
someone convicted of a crime but not sent
to prison

probe ➤ noun (plural **probes**)
1 a long thin instrument used to look
closely at something such as a wound
2 an investigation

probe ➤ verb (**probes, probing, probed**)
1 to probe something is to look at it with a
probe **2** to probe is to investigate

problem noun (plural **problems**)
something difficult to answer or deal with

procedure noun (plural **procedures**)
a fixed or special way of doing something

proceed verb (**proceeds, proceeding, proceeded**)
(pronounced pro-**seed**)
to proceed is to go on or continue

proceedings plural noun
1 things that happen; activities **2** a
lawsuit

proceeds *plural noun* (*pronounced* proh-seedz)
the money made from a sale or event

process ➤ *noun* (*plural* **processes**)
a series of actions for making or doing something

process ➤ *verb* (**processes, processing, processed**)
to process something is to deal with it by a process

procession *noun* (*plural* **processions**)
a number of people or vehicles moving steadily forwards

proclaim *verb* (**proclaims, proclaiming, proclaimed**)
to proclaim something is to announce it officially or publicly
proclamation *noun* a public announcement

prod *verb* (**prods, prodding, prodded**)
to prod something or someone is to poke or jab them

prodigal *adjective*
wasteful or extravagant
prodigality *noun* being prodigal **prodigally** *adverb* in a prodigal way

produce ➤ *verb* (**produces, producing, produced**) (*pronounced* pro-dewss)
1 to produce something is to make or create it 2 to produce something that is hidden or put away is to bring it out so that people can see it 3 to produce a play or film or other entertainment is to organize the performance of it

produce ➤ *noun* (*pronounced* prod-yewss)
things produced, especially by farmers

producer *noun* (*plural* **producers**)
someone who produces a play or film

product *noun* (*plural* **products**)
1 something someone makes or produces for sale 2 the result of multiplying two numbers ♦ *12 is the product of 4 and 3*

production *noun* (*plural* **productions**)
1 production is the process of making or creating something ♦ *The factory is engaged in car production* 2 production is also the amount someone produces or makes ♦ *Oil production increased last year* 3 a production is a version of a play or film

productive *adjective*
producing a lot of things

productivity *noun*
the rate at which someone works or produces thing

profession *noun* (*plural* **professions**)
a type of work for which you need special knowledge and training, for example medicine or law

professional ➤ *adjective*
1 to do with a profession 2 doing a certain type of work to earn money
♦ *He became a professional tennis player*
professionally *adverb* in a professional way

professional ➤ *noun* (*plural* **professionals**)
someone doing a certain type of work to earn money

professor *noun* (*plural* **professors**)
a teacher of the highest rank in a university

proficient *adjective* (*pronounced* pro-fish-ent)
skilled; doing something well
proficiency *noun* being proficient **proficiently** *adverb* in a proficient way

profile *noun* (*plural* **profiles**)
1 a side view of a person's face 2 a short description of a person's life or character

profit ➤ *noun* (*plural* **profits**)
1 the extra money got by selling something for more than it cost to buy or make 2 an advantage or benefit

profit ➤ *verb* (**profits, profiting, profited**)
to profit from something is to get an advantage from it

profitable *adjective*
making a profit; bringing in money
profitably *adverb* so as to make a profit

profound *adjective*
1 very deep or intense ♦ *We take a profound interest in the problem*
2 showing or needing great knowledge or thought ♦ *The book she wrote was quite profound*
profoundly *adverb* in a profound way
profundity *noun* being profound

profuse *adjective* (*pronounced* pro-fewss)
large in amount; plentiful ♦ *They had profuse wealth*
profusely *adverb* in a profuse way **profusion** *noun* being profuse

program ➤ *noun* (*plural* **programs**)
a series of coded instructions for a computer to carry out

program ➤ *verb* (**programs, programming, programmed**)
to program a computer is to prepare or control it by means of a program

programme *noun* (*plural* **programmes**)
1 a show, play, or talk on radio or television 2 a list of a planned series of events 3 a leaflet or pamphlet giving details of an entertainment or activity

progress ➤ *noun* (*pronounced* proh-gress)
1 advance or forward movement; an advance ♦ *The procession made slow progress* 2 development or improvement

progress ➤ *verb* (**progresses, progressing, progressed**) (*pronounced* pro-**gress**)
1 to progress is to move forward **2** to progress is also to develop or improve
progression *noun* advancing or moving forward **progressive** *adjective* developing or moving forward

prohibit *verb* (**prohibits, prohibiting, prohibited**)
to prohibit something is to forbid it
♦ *Smoking is prohibited*
prohibition *noun* prohibiting something

project ➤ *noun* (*plural* **projects**) (*pronounced* **proj**-ekt)
1 a planned task in which you find out as much as you can about something and write about it **2** a plan or scheme

project ➤ *verb* (**projects, projecting, projected**) (*pronounced* pro-**jekt**)
1 to project is to stick out **2** to project a picture is to show it with a projector on a screen
projection *noun* projecting something; a part that sticks out

projectionist *noun* (*plural* **projectionists**)
someone who works a projector

projector *noun* (*plural* **projectors**)
a machine for showing films or photographs on a screen

prologue *noun* (*plural* **prologues**) (*pronounced* **proh**-log)
an introduction to a poem or play or long story

prolong *verb* (**prolongs, prolonging, prolonged**)
to prolong something is to make it last longer

promenade *noun* (*plural* **promenades**) (*pronounced* prom-en-**ahd**)
1 a place suitable for walking, especially beside the seashore **2** a leisurely walk

prominent *adjective*
1 easily seen; standing out **2** important
prominence *noun* being prominent
prominently *adverb* in a prominent way

promise ➤ *noun* (*plural* **promises**)
1 a promise is a statement that you will definitely do or not do something **2** promise is an indication of future success ♦ *She shows promise*

promise ➤ *verb* (**promises, promising, promised**)
to promise something is to make a promise about it

promising *adjective*
likely to be good or successful ♦ *We have several promising pupils*

promontory *noun* (*plural* **promontories**) (*pronounced* **prom**-on-ter-i)
a piece of high land sticking out into the sea

promote *verb* (**promotes, promoting, promoted**)
1 to promote someone is to give them a more senior or more important job or rank
2 to promote a product or cause is to make it do well ♦ *He has done much to promote the cause of peace*
promoter *noun* someone who promotes something

promotion *noun* (*plural* **promotions**)
1 promotion is promoting someone or something **2** a promotion is a piece of publicity or advertising

prompt ➤ *adjective* (**prompter, promptest**)
happening soon or without delay ♦ *We need a prompt reply*
promptly *adverb* soon; without delay
promptness *noun* being prompt

prompt ➤ *verb* (**prompts, prompting, prompted**)
1 to prompt someone to do something is to cause or encourage them to do it **2** to prompt an actor is to remind them of their words if they forget them
prompter *noun* someone who prompts actors

prone *adjective*
lying face downwards
to be prone to something is to be likely to do it or suffer from it ♦ *He is prone to jealousy*

prong *noun* (*plural* **prongs**)
one of the pointed spikes at the end of a fork

pronoun *noun* (*plural* **pronouns**)
a word used instead of a noun, such as *he, her, it, them, those*

pronounce *verb* (**pronounces, pronouncing, pronounced**)
1 to pronounce a word is to say it in a particular way ♦ *'Too' and 'two' are pronounced the same* **2** to pronounce something is to declare it formally ♦ *I now pronounce you man and wife*

pronounced *adjective*
noticeable; definite ♦ *This street has a pronounced slope*

pronouncement *noun* (*plural* **pronouncements**)
something said formally; a declaration

pronunciation *noun* (*plural* **pronunciations**) (*pronounced* pro-nun-si-**ay**-shon)
the way a word is pronounced

proof ➤ *noun* (*plural* **proofs**)
1 a fact which shows that something is true **2** a printed copy of something made for checking before other copies are printed

proof ➤ *adjective*
giving protection against something
♦ *They wore bullet-proof jackets*

prop[1] ➤ *noun* (*plural* props)
a support, especially one made of a long
piece of wood or metal

prop ➤ *verb* (**props, propping, propped**)
to prop something is to support it by
leaning it on something else ♦ *The ladder
was propped up against the wall*

prop[2] *noun* (*plural* props)
a piece of furniture or other object used on
stage in a theatre

propaganda *noun*
publicity intended to make people believe
something

propel *verb* (**propels, propelling, propelled**)
to propel something is to move it rapidly
forward

propellant *noun* (*plural* propellants)
liquid fuel for a rocket

propeller *noun* (*plural* propellers)
a device with blades that spin round to
drive an aircraft or ship

proper *adjective*
1 suitable or right ♦ *This is the proper
way to hold a bat* 2 respectable ♦ *You
must behave in a proper fashion*
3 (*informal*) complete; great ♦ *He's a
proper nuisance*
properly *adverb* in a proper way; correctly

proper fraction *noun* (*plural* proper fractions)
a fraction that is less than 1, such as $\frac{1}{2}$ or $\frac{3}{5}$

proper noun *noun* (*plural* proper nouns)
the name given to one person or thing,
such as *Mary* and *Tokyo*, and usually
written with a capital first letter

property *noun* (*plural* properties)
1 a thing or things that belong to someone
2 buildings or land belonging to someone
3 a quality or characteristic ♦ *Rubber has
elastic properties*

prophecy *noun* (*plural* prophecies)
(*pronounced* prof-i-si)
1 a prophecy is something that someone
has said will happen in the future
2 prophecy is saying what will happen in
the future

prophesy *verb* (**prophesies, prophesying,
prophesied**) (*pronounced* prof-i-sy)
to prophesy something is to say that it will
happen in the future

prophet *noun* (*plural* prophets)
1 someone who makes prophecies 2 a
religious teacher who is believed to speak
the word of God
the Prophet a name for Muhammad, the
founder of the Muslim faith

prophetic *adjective*
saying or showing what will happen in the
future

proportion *noun* (*plural* proportions)
1 a fraction or share 2 a ratio 3 the
correct relationship between the size,
amount, or importance of two things
proportions size or scale ♦ *It is a ship of
large proportions*

proportional or **proportionate** *adjective*
in proportion; according to a ratio
proportionally or **proportionately** *adverb* in
proportion

propose *verb* (**proposes, proposing, proposed**)
1 to propose an idea or plan is to suggest it
2 to propose to someone is to ask them to
marry you
proposal *noun* something proposed or
suggested

proprietor *noun* (*plural* proprietors)
(*pronounced* pro-pry-et-er)
the owner of a shop or business

propulsion *noun*
propelling something or driving it forward

prose *noun*
writing that is like ordinary speech, not
verse

prosecute *verb* (**prosecutes, prosecuting,
prosecuted**)
1 to prosecute someone is to make them go
to a lawcourt to be tried for a crime 2 to
prosecute something official or formal is to
carry it out
prosecution *noun* prosecuting someone
prosecutor *noun* an official who prosecutes
people

prospect ➤ *noun* (*plural* prospects)
(*pronounced* pros-pekt)
1 a possibility or hope ♦ *There are good
prospects of success* 2 a wide view ♦ *We
saw a vast prospect from the top of the hill*

prospect ➤ *verb* (**prospects, prospecting,
prospected**) (*pronounced* pro-spekt)
to prospect is to search for gold or some
other mineral
prospector *noun* someone who prospects for
minerals

prosper *verb* (**prospers, prospering, prospered**)
to prosper is to be successful or do well

prosperous *adjective*
successful or rich
prosperity *noun* being prosperous

prostitute *noun* (*plural* **prostitutes**)
someone who takes part in sexual acts for payment

protect *verb* (**protects, protecting, protected**)
to protect someone or something is to keep them safe
protection *noun* protecting someone or something **protector** *noun* a person who protects someone or something

protective *adjective*
1 a person is protective when they want to protect someone or something 2 a thing is protective when it is meant to protect something

protein *noun* (*plural* **proteins**) (*pronounced* **proh-teen**)
a substance in food that is necessary for growth and good health

protest > *noun* (*plural* **protests**) (*pronounced* **proh-test**)
something you say or do because you disapprove of someone or something

protest > *verb* (**protests, protesting, protested**) (*pronounced* **pro-test**)
to protest is to make a protest
protester *noun* someone who protests about something

Protestant *noun* (*plural* **Protestants**) (*pronounced* **prot-is-tant**)
a member of a western Christian Church other than the Roman Catholic Church

proton *noun* (*plural* **protons**)
a particle of matter with a positive electric charge

protoplasm *noun* (*pronounced* **proh-to-plazm**)
a colourless substance of which animal and vegetable cells are made

prototype *noun* (*plural* **prototypes**) (*pronounced* **proh-to-typ**)
the first example of something, used as a model for making others

protractor *noun* (*plural* **protractors**)
a device for measuring and drawing angles on paper

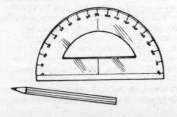

protrude *verb* (**protrudes, protruding, protruded**)
to protrude is to stick out
protrusion *noun* protruding

proud *adjective* (**prouder, proudest**)
1 very pleased with yourself or with someone else who has done well ♦ *I am proud of my sister* 2 too satisfied because of who you are or what you have done
♦ *They were too proud to ask for help*
proudly *adverb* in a proud way; with pride

prove *verb* (**proves, proving, proved**)
1 to prove something is to show that it is true 2 to prove to be something is to turn out to be that way ♦ *The forecast proved to be correct*

proverb *noun* (*plural* **proverbs**)
a short well-known saying that states a truth, for example *many hands make light work*

proverbial *adjective*
1 occurring in a proverb 2 familiar or well-known

provide *verb* (**provides, providing, provided**)
1 to provide something is to supply it 2 to provide for something is to prepare for it
♦ *They have provided for all possible disasters*
provided or **providing** on condition; on condition that ♦ *You can come providing that you pay for yourself*

province *noun* (*plural* **provinces**)
1 a part of a country 2 an area of knowledge or skill
the provinces the part of a country outside the capital
provincial *adjective* to do with the provinces

provision *noun* (*plural* **provisions**)
1 provision is providing something ♦ *the provision of free meals for old people* 2 a provision is a statement in a document

provisional *adjective*
arranged or agreed on for the time being, but likely to be changed

provisions *plural noun*
supplies of food and drink

provocative *adjective*
likely to make someone angry ♦ *That was a provocative remark*

provoke *verb* (**provokes, provoking, provoked**)
1 to provoke someone is to make them angry 2 to provoke a feeling is to arouse or cause it ♦ *His statement provoked a great deal of criticism*
provocation *noun* provoking someone

prow 339 **puff**

prow *noun* (*plural* **prows**)
the front end of a ship

prowl *verb* (**prowls, prowling, prowled**)
to prowl is to move about cautiously or
threateningly
prowler *noun* someone who prowls
threateningly

prudent *adjective* (*pronounced* **proo**-dent)
wise and careful
prudence *noun* being prudent **prudently**
adverb in a prudent way

prune[1] *noun* (*plural* **prunes**)
a dried plum

prune[2] *verb* (**prunes, pruning, pruned**)
to prune a tree or bush is to cut off
unwanted parts from it

pry *verb* (**pries, prying, pried**)
to pry is to snoop in someone else's
business

PS short for
postscript

psalm *noun* (*plural* **psalms**) (*pronounced*
sahm)
a religious song, especially one from the
Book of Psalms in the Bible

pseudonym *noun* (*plural* **pseudonyms**)
(*pronounced* s'**yoo**-do-nim)
a false name used by an author

psychiatrist *noun* (*plural* **psychiatrists**)
(*pronounced* sy-**ky**-a-trist)
a doctor who treats mental illness

psychiatry *noun* (*pronounced* sy-**ky**-a-tree)
the treatment of mental illness
psychiatric *adjective* to do with psychiatry

psychic *adjective* (*pronounced* **sy**-kik)
1 supernatural **2** having or using
telepathy or supernatural powers

psychologist *noun* (*plural* **psychologists**)
(*pronounced* sy-**kol**-o-jist)
someone who studies how the mind works

psychology *noun*
the study of the mind
psychological *adjective* to do with
psychology

PTA short for *Parent-Teacher Association*,
an organization that arranges discussions
between teachers and parents about
school business, and raises money for the
school

pub *noun* (*plural* **pubs**)
(*informal*) a building where people can
buy and drink alcoholic drinks

puberty *noun* (*pronounced* **pew**-ber-ti)
the time when a young person starts to
become an adult

public ➤ *adjective*
belonging to everyone; used or known by
everyone
publicly *adverb* in public

public ➤ *noun*
the public is all the people; everyone
in public openly; where anyone can see or
take part

publication *noun* (*plural* **publications**)
1 publication is printing and selling books
or magazines **2** a publication is a book or
magazine that is printed and sold

public house *noun* (*plural* **public houses**)
a pub

publicity *noun*
information or activity to make people
know about someone or something

publicize *verb* (**publicizes, publicizing,
publicized**) (*pronounced* pub-li-syz)
to publicize something is to make people
know about it

public school *noun* (*plural* **public schools**)
1 (*in England and Wales*) a secondary
school that charges fees **2** (*in Scotland
and America*) a school run by the State or
by a local authority

publish *verb* (**publishes, publishing, published**)
1 to publish books or magazines is to print
and sell them **2** to publish information is
to make it known publicly
publisher *noun* someone who publishes
books or magazines

puck *noun* (*plural* **pucks**)
a hard rubber disc used in ice hockey

pucker *verb* (**puckers, puckering, puckered**)
to pucker is to wrinkle

pudding *noun* (*plural* **puddings**)
1 a food made in a soft mass, especially
with a mixture of flour and other
ingredients **2** the sweet course of a meal

puddle *noun* (*plural* **puddles**)
a small pool, especially of rainwater

puff ➤ *noun* (*plural* **puffs**)
1 a small amount of breath, wind, smoke,
or steam **2** a soft pad for putting powder
on the skin **3** a light pastry cake filled
with cream

puff ➤ *verb* (**puffs, puffing, puffed**)
1 to puff smoke or steam is to blow it out
2 to puff is to breathe with difficulty **3** to
puff something, or to puff it out, is to
inflate or swell it ♦ *He puffed out his chest*

puffin *noun* (*plural* **puffins**)
a seabird with a large striped beak

pull ➤ *verb* (**pulls, pulling, pulled**)
1 to pull something is to get hold of it and make it come towards you or follow behind you **2** to pull is to move with an effort
♦ *She tried to grab the boy but he pulled away*
to pull a face is to make a strange face
to pull in 1 a car pulls in when it stops at the side of the road **2** a train pulls in when it comes into a station and stops
to pull out is to withdraw from something
♦ *Half the competitors pulled out just before the race*
to pull someone's leg is to tease them
to pull something off is to achieve it
to pull through is to recover from an illness
to pull up is to stop ♦ *A car pulled up and two men got out*
to pull yourself together is to become calm or sensible

pull ➤ *noun* (*plural* **pulls**)
a pull is an action of pulling ♦ *Give the handle a pull*

pulley *noun* (*plural* **pulleys**)
a wheel with a groove round it to take a rope, used for lifting heavy things

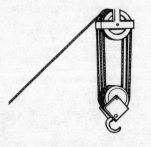

pullover *noun* (*plural* **pullovers**)
a knitted piece of clothing for the top half of your body, that you put on over your head

pulp ➤ *noun* (*plural* **pulps**)
a soft wet mass of something, especially for making paper

pulp ➤ *verb* (**pulps, pulping, pulped**)
to pulp something is to make it into a pulp

pulpit *noun* (*plural* **pulpits**)
a raised platform in a church, from which the preacher speaks to the congregation

pulse[1] *noun* (*plural* **pulses**)
1 the regular movement of blood in your arteries, which shows how fast your heart is beating **2** a regular vibration or movement ♦ *The music had a throbbing pulse*

pulse[2] *noun* (*plural* **pulses**)
the edible seed of certain plants, such as peas, beans, and lentils

pulverize *verb* (**pulverizes, pulverizing, pulverized**)
to pulverize something is to crush it into a powder

puma *noun* (*plural* **pumas**)
a large wild cat of North America

pumice *noun* (*pronounced* **pum**-iss)
pumice is a kind of soft sponge-like stone rubbed on hard surfaces to clean or polish them

pump ➤ *noun* (*plural* **pumps**)
1 a device that forces air or liquid into or out of something, or along pipes **2** a lightweight shoe ♦ *She took off her pumps*

pump ➤ *verb* (**pumps, pumping, pumped**)
to pump air or liquid is to force it into or out of something with a pump
to pump something up is to fill something like a balloon or tyre with air or gas

pumpkin *noun* (*plural* **pumpkins**)
a large round fruit with a hard yellow skin

pun ➤ *noun* (*plural* **puns**)
a joke made by using a word with two different meanings, or two words that sound the same, as in *Choosing where to bury him was a grave decision*

pun ➤ *verb* (**puns, punning, punned**)
to pun is to make a pun

punch [1] ➤ *verb* (**punches, punching, punched**)
1 to punch someone is to hit them with your fist **2** to punch a hole is to make a hole in something ♦ *The guard checked and punched our tickets* ♦ *The builder punched a hole in the wall*

punch ➤ *noun* (*plural* **punches**)
1 a punch is a blow or hit with the fist **2** a punch is also a device for making holes in paper, metal, or other things **3** punch is force or vigour ♦ *He told the story with a lot of punch*

punch [2] *noun* (*plural* **punches**)
a hot alcoholic drink

punchline *noun* (*plural* **punchlines**)
the last part of a joke or story, that makes the point

punch-up *noun* (*plural* **punch-ups**)
(*informal*) a fight

punctual *adjective*
exactly on time; not arriving late
punctuality *noun* being punctual **punctually** *adverb* in good time

punctuate *verb* (**punctuates, punctuating, punctuated**)
to punctuate a piece of writing is to put the commas, full stops, and other punctuation in it

punctuation *noun*
punctuation is a set of marks such as commas, full stops, and brackets put into a piece of writing to make it easier to understand

puncture *noun* (*plural* **punctures**)
a small hole made in a tyre by accident

punish *verb* (**punishes, punishing, punished**)
to punish someone is to make them suffer in some way because they have done wrong
punishment *noun* a way of punishing someone

punk *noun* (*plural* **punks**)
a young person who wears black or torn clothes and has spiky or unusual hairstyles, so as to shock people, and who likes punk rock

punk rock *noun*
a kind of loud, simple rock music

punt [1] ➤ *noun* (*plural* **punts**)
a flat-bottomed boat moved by pushing a pole against the bottom of a river while standing in the punt

punt ➤ *verb* (**punts, punting, punted**)
to punt is to use a pole to push a boat along

punt [2] *verb* (**punts, punting, punted**)
to punt a football is to kick it after dropping it from your hands, before it touches the ground

puny *adjective* (**punier, puniest**) (*pronounced* pew-ni)
small and weak

pup *noun* (*plural* **pups**)
a puppy

pupa *noun* (*plural* **pupae**) (*pronounced* pew-pa)
a chrysalis

pupil *noun* (*plural* **pupils**)
1 someone who is being taught by a teacher **2** the opening in the centre of the eye

puppet *noun* (*plural* **puppets**)
a kind of doll that can be made to move by fitting it over your fingers or hand or by pulling strings or wires attached to it

puppy *noun* (*plural* **puppies**)
a young dog

purchase ➤ *verb* (**purchases, purchasing, purchased**)
to purchase something is to buy it
purchaser *noun* someone who buys something

purchase ➤ *noun* (*plural* **purchases**)
1 a purchase is something you have bought **2** purchase is the fact of buying something ♦ *Keep the receipt as proof of purchase* **3** a purchase is a firm hold or grip ♦ *It was hard to get a purchase on the slippery rocks*

purdah *noun*
purdah is the Muslim or Hindu custom of keeping women from being seen by men or strangers

pure *adjective* (purer, purest)
1 not mixed with anything else ♦ *Use pure olive oil* 2 clean or clear ♦ *They washed in a pure cold mountain stream*

purely *adverb*
only, simply ♦ *They did it purely for the money*

purge ➤ *verb* (purges, purging, purged)
to purge people or things is to get rid of them when they are not wanted

purge ➤ *noun* (*plural* purges)
an act of purging

purify *verb* (purifies, purifying, purified)
to purify something is to make it pure
purification *noun* purifying something **purifier** *noun* someone or something that purifies

Puritan *noun* (*plural* Puritans)
a Protestant in the 16th or 17th century who wanted simpler religious ceremonies and strictly moral behaviour

puritan *noun* (*plural* puritans)
someone who believes in leading a strictly moral life

puritanical *adjective*
extremely strict in behaviour and morals

purity *noun*
the state of being pure

purple *noun* and *adjective*
a deep reddish-blue

purpose *noun* (*plural* purposes)
what you intend to do; your plan or aim
on purpose intentionally; not by chance

purposely *adverb*
on purpose

purr *verb* (purrs, purring, purred)
to purr is to make a gentle murmuring sound like a cat when it is pleased

purse *noun* (*plural* purses)
a small bag for holding money

pursue *verb* (pursues, pursuing, pursued)
1 to pursue someone or something is to chase them 2 to pursue an activity is to continue to do it or work at it ♦ *She pursued her studies at college*
pursuer *noun* a person who chases someone

pursuit *noun* (*plural* pursuits)
1 pursuit is the action of chasing someone
2 a pursuit is something you spend a lot of time doing

pus *noun*
pus is a thick yellowish substance produced in boils and other sore places on the body

push ➤ *verb* (pushes, pushing, pushed)
to push something is to move it away from you by applying pressure to it
to push off (*slang*) is to go away

push ➤ *noun* (*plural* pushes)
a pushing movement
to get the push (*informal*) is to be dismissed from a job

pushchair *noun* (*plural* pushchairs)
a small chair with wheels, in which a child can be pushed along

puss or **pussy** *noun* (*plural* pusses or pussies)
(*informal*) a cat

put *verb* (puts, putting, put)
1 to put something in a place is to move it there ♦ *Put it over there* ♦ *Where shall I put it?* 2 to put also means to affect someone or something in a particular way ♦ *They've put me in a bad mood* 3 to put an idea in a certain way is to express it in words of a special kind ♦ *She put it very tactfully*
to put someone off is to make them less keen on something ♦ *Seeing you eat so much has put me off my food*
to put someone up is to give them a place to sleep ♦ *Can we put them up for the night?*
to put off is to postpone it ♦ *We'll have to put off the party if you're ill*
to put something on 1 is to switch on an electrical device, for example a light or a television 2 is to start wearing a piece of clothing ♦ *I'll just put on my coat*
to put something out is to stop something like a fire or light from burning or shining
to put something up is to raise it or make it upright ♦ *Let's put up the tent*
to put up with something is to be willing to accept it although it is not welcome

putt *verb* (putts, putting, putted)
to putt a golf ball is to tap it gently towards the hole

putter *noun* (*plural* putters)
a golf club used to putt the ball

putty *noun*
putty is a soft paste that sets hard, used by builders to fit windows in their frames

puzzle ➤ *noun* (*plural* puzzles)
1 a tricky game that you have to solve
2 a difficult question; a problem

puzzle ➤ *verb* (puzzles, puzzling, puzzled)
1 to puzzle someone is to give them a problem that is hard to understand 2 to puzzle over something is to think hard about it

pygmy *noun* (*plural* **pygmies**) (*pronounced* pig-mi)
an unusually small person or animal

pyjamas *plural noun*
a loose lightweight set of jacket and trousers worn in bed

pylon *noun* (*plural* **pylons**)
a metal tower for supporting electric cables. It is made of struts and widens out nearer the ground

pyramid *noun* (*plural* **pyramids**)
1 an object with a square base and four sloping sides coming to a point **2** an ancient Egyptian monument shaped like this. They were massive and were usually built of huge stone blocks

pyramidal *adjective* (*pronounced* pir-am-id-al)
shaped like a pyramid ♦ *The house had a pyramidal roof*

python *noun* (*plural* **pythons**)
a large snake that crushes its prey

Qq

quack ⊳ *noun* (*plural* **quacks**)
the harsh loud sound made by a duck

quack ⊳ *verb* (**quacks, quacking, quacked**)
to make a quack

quad *noun* (*plural* **quads**)
(*informal*) **1** a quadrangle **2** a quadruplet

quadrangle *noun* (*plural* **quadrangles**)
a rectangular courtyard with large buildings round it

quadrant *noun* (*plural* **quadrants**)
a quarter of a circle

quadrilateral *noun* (*plural* **quadrilaterals**)
a figure with four sides

quadruple ⊳ *adjective*
1 four times as much or as many
2 having four parts

quadruple ⊳ *verb* (**quadruples, quadrupling, quadrupled**)
1 to quadruple something is to make it four times as much or as many **2** to quadruple is to become four times as much or as many

quadruplet *noun* (*plural* **quadruplets**)
each of four children born to the same mother at one time

quail [1] *noun* (*plural* **quails**)
a bird that looks like a small partridge

quail [2] *verb* (**quails, quailing, quailed**)
to quail is to feel or show fear

quaint *adjective* (**quainter, quaintest**)
attractive in an unusual or old-fashioned way

quake *verb* (**quakes, quaking, quaked**)
to quake is to tremble or shake

Quaker *noun* (*plural* **Quakers**)
a member of a religious group called the Society of Friends, founded by George Fox in the 17th century

qualification *noun* (*plural* **qualifications**)
1 something that qualifies a remark or statement **2** a skill or ability to do a job

qualify *verb* (**qualifies, qualifying, qualified**)
1 to qualify for something such as a job is to be suitable for it or have the right abilities **2** to qualify a statement or remark is to change it or add to it to make it less strong or less definite

quality *noun* (*plural* **qualities**)
1 how good or bad something is **2** what something is like ♦ *The paper had a shiny quality*

quantity *noun* (*plural* **quantities**)
how much there is of something, or how many things there are of one sort

quarantine *noun* (*pronounced* kwo-ran-teen)
a period when a person or animal is kept apart from others to prevent a disease from spreading

quarrel ➤ *noun* (*plural* **quarrels**)
a strong or angry argument

quarrel ➤ *verb* (**quarrels, quarrelling, quarrelled**)
to quarrel with someone is to argue fiercely with them

quarrelsome *adjective*
fond of quarrelling or often quarrelling

quarry *noun* (*plural* **quarries**)
1 a place where stone or slate is dug out of the ground 2 an animal that is being hunted

quart *noun* (*plural* **quarts**)
a measure of liquid, a quarter of a gallon

quarter *noun* (*plural* **quarters**)
1 each of four equal parts into which something is divided or can be divided
2 three months, one-fourth of a year
at close quarters close together ♦ *They fought at close quarters*

quarters *plural noun*
where someone lives for a time; lodgings

quartet *noun* (*plural* **quartets**) (*pronounced* kwor-tet)
1 a group of four musicians 2 a piece of music for four musicians

quartz *noun* (*pronounced* kworts)
a hard mineral

quaver ➤ *verb* (**quavers, quavering, quavered**)
to quaver is to tremble ♦ *His voice quavered with fear*

quaver ➤ *noun* (*plural* **quavers**)
1 a trembling sound 2 a musical note equal to half a crotchet, written ♪

quay *noun* (*plural* **quays**) (*pronounced* kee)
a harbour wall or pier where ships can be tied up for loading and unloading

queasy *adjective* (**queasier, queasiest**)
feeling slightly sick

queen *noun* (*plural* **queens**)
1 a woman who has been crowned as the ruler of a country 2 a king's wife 3 a female bee or ant that produces eggs 4 a piece in chess, the most powerful on the board 5 a playing card with a picture of a queen

queen mother *noun*
a king's widow who is the mother of the present king or queen

queer *adjective* (**queerer, queerest**)
1 strange or odd 2 ill or unwell ♦ *I feel a bit queer*

quench *verb* (**quenches, quenching, quenched**)
1 to quench your thirst is to drink until you are satisfied 2 to quench a fire is to put it out

query ➤ *noun* (*plural* **queries**) (*pronounced* kweer-i)
1 a question 2 a question mark

query ➤ *verb* (**queries, querying, queried**)
to query something is to question whether it is true or correct

quest *noun* (*plural* **quests**)
a long search, especially for something precious or valuable

question ➤ *noun* (*plural* **questions**)
1 something you ask ♦ *I will try to answer your question* 2 a problem or subject for discussion
out of the question impossible; not allowed

question ➤ *verb* (**questions, questioning, questioned**)
1 to question someone is to ask them questions 2 to question something is to be doubtful about it

questioner *noun* someone who asks a question

questionable *adjective*
causing doubt; not certainly true or correct

question mark *noun* (*plural* **question marks**)
the punctuation mark (?) put at the end of a question

questionnaire *noun* (*plural* **questionnaires**)
(*pronounced* kwes-chon-**air**)
a set of questions asked to get information for a survey

queue ➤ *noun* (*plural* **queues**) (*pronounced* kew)
a line of people or vehicles waiting for something

queue ➤ *verb* (**queues, queueing, queued**) (*pronounced* kew)
to queue is to wait in a queue

quibble ➤ *verb* (**quibbles, quibbling, quibbled**)
to quibble is to argue or complain about minor details

quibble ➤ *noun* (*plural* **quibbles**)
a quibble is a trivial complaint or objection

quiche *noun* (*plural* **quiches**) (*pronounced* keesh)
an open tart with a savoury filling

quick *adjective* (**quicker, quickest**)
1 taking only a short time ♦ *You were quick* 2 done in a short time ♦ *She gave a quick answer* 3 able to learn or think quickly 4 (*old use*) alive

quicken *verb* (**quickens, quickening, quickened**)
1 to quicken something is to make it quicker 2 to quicken is to become quicker

quicksand *noun* (*plural* **quicksands**)
an area of loose wet sand that sucks in anything that falls into it

quid *noun* (*plural* **quid**)
(*slang*) a pound (£1)

quiet *adjective* (**quieter, quietest**)
1 silent 2 not loud ♦ *He spoke in a quiet voice* 3 calm and peaceful ♦ *They lead a quiet life*

quieten *verb* (**quietens, quietening, quietened**)
1 to quieten something or someone is to make them quiet 2 to quieten is to become quiet

quill *noun* (*plural* **quills**)
1 a large feather 2 a pen made from a large feather

quilt *noun* (*plural* **quilts**)
a thick soft cover for a bed

quintet *noun* (*plural* **quintets**)
1 a group of five musicians 2 a piece of music for five musicians

quit *verb* (**quits, quitting, quitted** or **quit**)
1 to quit something is to leave or abandon it 2 (*informal*) to quit doing something is to stop it ♦ *Quit teasing him!*
quitter *noun* someone who quits or gives up

quite *adverb*
1 completely; truly ♦ *I am quite all right* 2 somewhat; rather ♦ *He's quite a good swimmer*

quiver[1] *verb* (**quivers, quivering, quivered**)
to quiver is to tremble ♦ *He was quivering with excitement*

quiver[2] *noun* (*plural* **quivers**)
a container for arrows

quiz ➤ *noun* (*plural* **quizzes**)
a series of questions, especially as an entertainment or competition

quiz ➤ *verb* (**quizzes, quizzing, quizzed**)
to quiz someone is to ask them a lot of questions

quoit *noun* (*plural* **quoits**) (*pronounced* koit)
a ring thrown at a peg in the game of **quoits**

quota *noun* (*plural* **quotas**) (*pronounced* **kwoh**-ta)
a fixed share or amount ♦ *Each school has its quota of equipment*

quotation *noun* (*plural* **quotations**)
1 quotation is the action of repeating words that were first written or spoken by someone else 2 a quotation is a set of words taken from a book or speech

quotation marks *plural noun*
inverted commas, used to mark a quotation

quote *verb* (**quotes, quoting, quoted**)
1 to quote words is to use them in a quotation 2 to quote someone is to quote words first used by them

quotient *noun* (*plural* **quotients**) (*pronounced* **kwoh**-shent)
the result of dividing one number by another

Rr

rabbi *noun* (*plural* **rabbis**) (*pronounced* rab-I)
a Jewish religious leader

rabbit *noun* (*plural* **rabbits**)
a furry animal with long ears that digs
burrows

rabid *adjective* (*pronounced* **rab**-id)
1 affected with rabies **2** fiercely
enthusiastic about something

rabies *noun* (*pronounced* **ray**-beez)
a fatal disease involving madness that
affects dogs and cats and can be passed to
humans

raccoon *noun* (*plural* **raccoons**)
a small North American meat-eating
animal with greyish-brown fur and a
bushy, striped tail

race¹ ➤ *noun* (*plural* **races**)
a competition to be the first to reach a
particular place or to do something

race ➤ *verb* (**races, racing, raced**)
1 to race someone is to have a race against
them **2** to race is to move very fast ♦ *The
train raced along the track*
racer *noun* a competitor in a race

race² *noun* (*plural* **races**)
a large group of people having the same
ancestors, and sharing certain physical
features such as colour of skin and hair
racial *adjective* to do with race

racecourse *noun* (*plural* **racecourses**)
a place where horse races are run

racism *noun* (*pronounced* **ray**-sizm)
1 believing that one race of people is
better than all the others **2** hostility
shown by one race of people towards
another
racist *noun* someone who practises racism

rack ➤ *noun* (*plural* **racks**)
1 a framework used as a shelf or container
2 an ancient device for torturing people by
stretching them

rack ➤ *verb* (**racks, racking, racked**)
to rack your brains is to think hard to
remember something or solve a problem

racket¹ *noun* (*plural* **rackets**)
a bat with strings stretched across a
frame, used in tennis and similar games

racket² *noun* (*plural* **rackets**)
1 a loud noise **2** (*informal*) a dishonest
business; a swindle

radar *noun* (*pronounced* **ray**-dar)
a system that uses radio waves to show
the position of objects which cannot be
seen because of distance or poor visibility

radial *adjective*
1 to do with rays or radii **2** having spokes
or lines that radiate from a central point

radiant *adjective*
1 radiating light or heat **2** looking bright
and happy
radiance *noun* brightness **radiantly** *adverb*
brightly

radiate *verb* (**radiates, radiating, radiated**)
1 to radiate heat, light, or other energy is
to send it out in rays **2** to radiate is to
spread out like the spokes of a wheel
♦ *The city's streets radiate from the central
square*

radiation *noun*
1 heat, light, or other energy given out by
something **2** energy or particles sent out
by something radioactive

radiator *noun* (*plural* **radiators**)
1 a device that gives out heat, especially a
metal container through which steam or
hot water flows **2** a device that cools the
engine of a motor vehicle

radical ➤ *adjective*
1 thorough; going right to the roots of
something ♦ *The new government made
radical changes* **2** wanting to make
changes or reforms ♦ *He is a radical
politician*
radically *adverb* in a radical way

radical ➤ *noun* (*plural* **radicals**)
someone who is radical

radii plural of **radius**

radio *noun* (*plural* **radios**)
1 radio is sending or receiving sound by
means of electrical waves **2** a radio is an
apparatus for receiving broadcast sound
programmes, or for receiving and sending
messages

radioactive *adjective*
 having atoms that break up and send out radiation which produces electrical and chemical effects
 radioactivity *noun* the state of being radioactive

radish *noun* (*plural* **radishes**)
 a small hard red vegetable, eaten raw in salads

radium *noun*
 a radioactive element

radius *noun* (*plural* **radii**)
 1 a straight line from the centre of a circle to the circumference **2** the length of this line

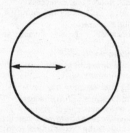

raffle ➤ *noun* (*plural* **raffles**)
 a way of raising money by selling numbered tickets, some of which win prizes

raffle ➤ *verb* (**raffles, raffling, raffled**)
 to raffle something is to give it as a prize in a raffle

raft *noun* (*plural* **rafts**)
 a floating platform of logs or barrels tied together

rafter *noun* (*plural* **rafters**)
 each of the long sloping pieces of wood that hold up a roof

rag *noun* (*plural* **rags**)
 1 an old or torn piece of cloth **2** a piece of ragtime music

rage ➤ *noun* (*plural* **rages**)
 great or violent anger
 all the rage (*informal*) very fashionable or popular

rage ➤ *verb* (**rages, raging, raged**)
 1 to rage is to be very angry **2** to rage is also to be violent or noisy ♦ *A storm was raging*

ragged *adjective* (*pronounced* **rag**-id)
 1 torn or frayed **2** wearing torn or old clothes **3** not smooth ♦ *They gave a ragged performance*

ragtime *noun*
 a kind of jazz music

raid ➤ *noun* (*plural* **raids**)
 1 a sudden attack **2** an unexpected visit from police to search a place or arrest people

raid ➤ *verb* (**raids, raiding, raided**)
 to raid a place is to make a raid on it
 raider *noun* someone who attacks a place in a raid

rail *noun* (*plural* **rails**)
 1 a bar or rod for hanging things on or forming part of a fence or banisters **2** a long metal strip that is part of a railway track
 by rail on a train

railings *plural noun*
 a fence made of metal bars

railway *noun* (*plural* **railways**)
 1 the parallel metal strips that trains travel on **2** a system of transport using rails

rain ➤ *noun*
 drops of water that fall from the sky

rain ➤ *verb* (**rains, raining, rained**)
 1 to rain is to come down like rain ♦ *After the explosion fragments of glass rained on them from above* **2** to rain something is to send it down like rain ♦ *They rained blows on him*
 it is raining rain is falling

rainbow *noun* (*plural* **rainbows**)
 a curved band of colours seen in the sky when the sun shines through rain

raincoat *noun* (*plural* **raincoats**)
 a waterproof coat

raindrop *noun* (*plural* **raindrops**)
 a single drop of rain

rainfall *noun*
 the amount of rain that falls in a particular place or time

rainforest *noun* (*plural* **rainforests**)
a dense tropical forest in an area of very heavy rainfall

raise *verb* (**raises, raising, raised**)
1 to raise something is to move it to a higher place or to an upright position **2** to raise an amount or number is to increase it ♦ *They raised our pay by 20%* **3** to raise money is to succeed in collecting it ♦ *They raised £1,000 for the appeal* **4** to raise a subject or idea is to mention it for people to think about **5** to raise young children is to bring them up and educate them **6** to raise animals is to breed them **7** to raise a laugh or smile is to make people laugh or smile **8** to raise a siege is to end it

raisin *noun* (*plural* **raisins**)
a dried grape

rake ➤ *noun* (*plural* **rakes**)
a gardening tool with a row of short spikes fixed to a long handle

rake ➤ *verb* (**rakes, raking, raked**)
1 to rake something is to move it or smooth it with a rake **2** to rake, or rake around, is to search ♦ *I raked around in my desk for the letter*
to rake something in (*informal*) is to earn it as profit

rally ➤ *noun* (*plural* **rallies**)
1 a large meeting **2** a competition to test skill in driving **3** a series of strokes and return strokes of the ball in tennis

rally ➤ *verb* (**rallies, rallying, rallied**)
1 to rally people is to bring them together for a united effort **2** to rally, or rally round, is to come together to support someone **3** to rally is to revive or recover after an illness or setback ♦ *The team rallied when they realized they could win*

RAM short for *random-access memory*, a type of computer memory with parts that can be located directly

ram ➤ *noun* (*plural* **rams**)
a male sheep

ram ➤ *verb* (**rams, ramming, rammed**)
to push one thing hard against another

Ramadan *noun* (*pronounced* ram-a-**dan**)
the ninth month of the Muslim year, when Muslims do not eat or drink during the daytime

ramble ➤ *noun* (*plural* **rambles**)
a long walk in the country

ramble ➤ *verb* (**rambles, rambling, rambled**)
1 to ramble is to go for a ramble or to wander **2** to ramble is also to say a lot without keeping to a subject

rambler *noun* someone who goes rambling in the country

ramp *noun* (*plural* **ramps**)
a slope joining two different levels

rampage ➤ *verb* (**rampages, rampaging, rampaged**) (*pronounced* ram-**payj**)
to rampage is to rush about wildly or violently

rampage ➤ *noun*
on the rampage rushing about violently

ran past tense of **run** *verb*

ranch *noun* (*plural* **ranches**)
a large cattle-farm in America

random ➤ *noun*
at random by chance; without any purpose or plan

random ➤ *adjective*
done or taken at random ♦ *They took a random sample*

rang past tense of **ring**² *verb*

range ➤ *noun* (*plural* **ranges**)
1 a line or series of things ♦ *They could see a range of mountains* **2** the limits within which things exist or are available
♦ *Supermarkets sell a wide range of things*
3 the distance that a gun can shoot, or an aircraft can fly, or a sound can be heard **4** a place with targets for shooting practice **5** a large area of land **6** a kitchen fireplace with ovens

range ➤ *verb* (**ranges, ranging, ranged**)
1 to range between two limits is to extend from one to the other ♦ *Prices ranged from £1 to £50* **2** to range people or things is to arrange them in a line ♦ *Crowds were ranged along the streets, hoping to see the Queen go by* **3** to range is to wander or move over a wide area ♦ *Hens ranged all over the farm*

Ranger *noun* (*plural* **Rangers**)
a senior member of the Guides

ranger *noun* (*plural* **rangers**)
1 someone who looks after a park or forest **2** a mounted police officer in a remote area

rank ➤ *noun* (*plural* **ranks**)
1 a position in a series of people or things
♦ *He was promoted to the rank of captain*
2 a line of people or things

rank ➤ *verb* (**ranks, ranking, ranked**)
to rank is to have a certain rank or place
♦ *She ranks among the greatest writers*

ransack *verb* (**ransacks, ransacking, ransacked**)
to ransack a place is to search it thoroughly, leaving it untidy

ransom ➤ *noun* (*plural* **ransoms**)
money paid so that a prisoner can be set free
to hold someone to ransom is to keep them prisoner and demand a ransom

ransom ➤ *verb* (**ransoms, ransoming, ransomed**)
to ransom someone is to free them by paying a ransom

rap ➤ *verb* (**raps, rapping, rapped**)
to rap is to knock quickly and loudly

rap ➤ *noun* (*plural* **raps**)
1 a rap is a rapping movement or sound 2 rap is a kind of pop music in which the words are spoken to the rhythm
to take the rap (*informal*) is to take the blame for something

rapid *adjective*
moving or working at speed
rapidity *noun* speed **rapidly** *adverb* fast; quickly

rapids *plural noun*
part of a river where the water flows very fast

rare *adjective* (**rarer, rarest**)
unusual; not often found or experienced ◆ *She died of a rare disease*
rarely *adverb* not often **rarity** *noun* being rare

rascal *noun* (*plural* **rascals**)
a dishonest or mischievous person

rash [1] *adjective* (**rasher, rashest**)
acting or done quickly without proper thought ◆ *He tends to be rash* ◆ *It was a rash decision*

rash [2] *noun* (*plural* **rashes**)
1 an outbreak of red spots or patches on the skin 2 a number of unwelcome things happening about the same time ◆ *Over the holiday there was a rash of accidents*

rasher *noun* (*plural* **rashers**)
a slice of bacon

raspberry *noun* (*plural* **raspberries**)
a small soft red fruit

Rastafarian *noun* (*plural* **Rastafarians**) (*pronounced* ras-ta-fair-i-an)
a member of a religious group that started in Jamaica

rat *noun* (*plural* **rats**)
1 an animal like a large mouse 2 a nasty or treacherous person

rate ➤ *noun* (*plural* **rates**)
1 speed ◆ *The train moved at a great rate* 2 cost or charge ◆ *What is the rate for a letter to Italy?*
at any rate anyway
at this rate if this is typical or true

rate ➤ *verb* (**rates, rating, rated**)
to rate something or someone is to regard them in a certain way or as having a certain value ◆ *Drivers rate the new car very highly* ◆ *He rated me among his best friends*

rather *adverb*
1 slightly; somewhat ◆ *It was rather dark* 2 preferably; more willingly ◆ *I would rather not come* 3 more truly ◆ *He lay down, or rather fell, on the bed*
4 (*informal*) as an answer: definitely, yes ◆ *'Will you come?' 'Rather!'*

ratio *noun* (*plural* **ratios**) (*pronounced* ray-shi-oh)
the relationship between two numbers; how often one number goes into another ◆ *In a group of 2 girls and 10 boys, the ratio of girls to boys is 1 to 5*

ration ➤ *noun* (*plural* **rations**) (*pronounced* rash-on)
an amount allowed to one person

ration ➤ *verb* (**rations, rationing, rationed**) (*pronounced* rash-on)
to ration something is to give it out in fixed amounts

rational *adjective* (*pronounced* rash-o-nal)
reasonable or sane ◆ *No rational person would do such a thing*
rationally *adverb* in a rational way

rationalize *verb* (**rationalizes, rationalizing, rationalized**)
1 to rationalize something complex is to make it logical and regular 2 to rationalize a problem or difficulty is to invent an explanation for it

rat race *noun*
a continuous struggle for success in a career or business

rattle ➤ *verb* (**rattles, rattling, rattled**)
1 to rattle is to make a series of short sharp hard sounds 2 to rattle something is to make it rattle 3 (*informal*) to rattle someone is to make them nervous and confused

rattle ➤ *noun* (*plural* **rattles**)
1 a rattling sound 2 a baby's toy that rattles

rattlesnake *noun* (*plural* **rattlesnakes**)
a poisonous American snake that makes
rattling sounds with its tail

rave ➤ *verb* (**raves, raving, raved**)
to rave is to talk or behave wildly or very
enthusiastically

rave ➤ *noun* (*plural* **raves**)
a big party with loud music and bright
lights

raven *noun* (*plural* **ravens**)
a large black bird

ravenous *adjective* (*pronounced* rav-e-nus)
very hungry
ravenously *adverb* in a ravenous way

ravine *noun* (*plural* **ravines**) (*pronounced*
ra-veen)
a very deep narrow gorge

raw *adjective* (**rawer, rawest**)
1 not cooked 2 in the natural state; not
yet processed ♦ *What raw materials do
you need?* 3 without experience ♦ *They
are just raw beginners* 4 with the skin
removed ♦ *He had a raw wound on his leg*
5 cold and damp ♦ *There was a raw wind*

raw deal *noun*
a raw deal is being treated unfairly

ray [1] *noun* (*plural* **rays**)
a thin line of light, heat, or other energy

ray [2] *noun* (*plural* **rays**)
a large sea fish with a flat body and a long
tail

razor *noun* (*plural* **razors**)
a device with a very sharp blade,
especially one used for shaving

reach ➤ *verb* (**reaches, reaching, reached**)
1 to reach a place is to go as far as it and
arrive there 2 to reach, or reach out, is to
stretch out your hand to get or touch
something

reach ➤ *noun* (*plural* **reaches**)
1 the distance you can reach with your
hand 2 a distance that you can easily
travel ♦ *My uncle lives within reach of the
sea* 3 a straight stretch of a river or canal

react *verb* (**reacts, reacting, reacted**)
to react is to act in response to another
person or thing

reaction *noun* (*plural* **reactions**)
an action or feeling caused by another
person or thing

reactor *noun* (*plural* **reactors**)
an apparatus for producing nuclear power

read *verb* (**reads, reading, read**)
1 to read something written or printed is
to look at it and understand it or say it
aloud 2 a gauge or instrument reads a
certain amount when that is what it shows
♦ *The thermometer reads 20°*
readable *adjective* able to be read

reader *noun* (*plural* **readers**)
1 someone who reads 2 a book that helps
you learn to read

readily *adverb*
1 willingly or eagerly ♦ *She readily agreed
to help* 2 quickly; without any difficulty
♦ *The system can be installed readily in
less than an hour*

reading *noun* (*plural* **readings**)
1 the action of reading a book, magazine,
or newspaper 2 an amount shown on a
gauge or instrument

ready *adjective* (**readier, readiest**)
1 able or willing to do something or to be
used at once; prepared 2 quick ♦ *He
always has ready answers*
at the ready ready for use or action
readiness *noun* being ready

ready-made *adjective*
made already, and not made specially

real *adjective*
1 true or existing; not imaginary
2 genuine; not a copy ♦ *Are those pearls
real?*

realism *noun*
seeing or showing things as they really are

realist *noun* (*plural* **realists**)
someone who tries to see things as they
really are

realistic *adjective*
true to life; seeing things as they really are
realistically *adverb* in a realistic way

reality *noun* (*plural* **realities**)
1 what is real 2 something that is real
♦ *Cold and hunger are the realities of
being homeless*

realize *verb* (**realizes, realizing, realized**)
to realize something is to understand it or
accept it as true
realization *noun* realizing something

really *adverb*
truly; certainly; in fact

realm *noun* (*plural* **realms**) (*pronounced*
relm)
1 a kingdom 2 an area of knowledge or
activity

reap *verb* (**reaps, reaping, reaped**)
1 to reap corn is to cut it down and gather it in when it is ripe **2** to reap a benefit is to gain it
reaper *noun* someone who reaps corn

reappear *verb* (**reappears, reappearing, reappeared**)
to reappear is to appear again
reappearance *noun* reappearing

rear[1] ➤ *adjective*
placed or found at the back ♦ *She had a car with a rear engine*

rear ➤ *noun* (*plural* **rears**)
the back part of something

rear[2] *verb* (**rears, rearing, reared**)
1 to rear young children or animals is to bring them up or help them grow **2** to rear, or rear up, is to rise up on the hind legs ♦ *The horse reared up in fright*

rearrange *verb* (**rearranges, rearranging, rearranged**)
to rearrange something is to arrange it differently
rearrangement *noun* rearranging something; a new arrangement

reason ➤ *noun* (*plural* **reasons**)
1 a reason is a cause or explanation for something **2** reason is reasoning or common sense ♦ *You must listen to reason*

reason ➤ *verb* (**reasons, reasoning, reasoned**)
1 to reason is to think in a logical way **2** to reason with someone is to try to persuade them of something

reasonable *adjective*
1 sensible or logical **2** fair or moderate ♦ *These are reasonable prices for what you get*

reasonably *adverb*
1 in a reasonable way; sensibly ♦ *They were behaving quite reasonably* **2** fairly; somewhat ♦ *It's reasonably warm now*

reassure *verb* (**reassures, reassuring, reassured**)
to reassure someone is to take away their doubts or fears
reassurance *noun* reassuring someone

rebel ➤ *verb* (**rebels, rebelling, rebelled**) (*pronounced* ri-bel)
to rebel is to refuse to obey someone in authority, especially the government

rebel ➤ *noun* (*plural* **rebels**) (*pronounced* reb-el)
someone who refuses to obey someone in authority

rebellion *noun* (*plural* **rebellions**)
1 rebellion is rebelling against authority **2** a rebellion is a revolt or act of rebelling

rebellious *adjective*
often refusing to obey authority; likely to rebel

rebound *verb* (**rebounds, rebounding, rebounded**)
to rebound is to bounce back after hitting something

rebuild *verb* (**rebuilds, rebuilding, rebuilt**)
to rebuild something is to build it again after it has been destroyed

recall *verb* (**recalls, recalling, recalled**)
1 to recall someone is to tell them to come back **2** to recall someone or something is to remember them

recap *verb* (**recaps, recapping, recapped**)
(*informal*) to recap is to summarize what has been said

recapture *verb* (**recaptures, recapturing, recaptured**)
to recapture something or someone is to capture them again, especially after they have escaped

recede *verb* (**recedes, receding, receded**)
to recede is to go back ♦ *The floods have receded*

receipt *noun* (*plural* **receipts**) (*pronounced* ri-seet)
1 a receipt is a written statement that money has been received **2** receipt is receiving something

receive *verb* (**receives, receiving, received**)
1 to receive something is to get it when it is given or sent to you **2** to receive visitors is to greet them formally ♦ *The President was received at Buckingham Palace*

receiver *noun* (*plural* **receivers**)
1 someone who receives something **2** someone who buys and sells stolen goods **3** an official who takes charge of a bankrupt person's property **4** a radio or television set **5** the part of a telephone that you hold to your ear

recent *adjective*
made or happening a short time ago
recently *adverb* in the recent past

receptacle *noun* (*plural* **receptacles**)
something for holding what is put into it; a container

reception *noun* (*plural* **receptions**)
1 the sort of welcome that someone gets ♦ *We were given a friendly reception* **2** a formal party to receive guests ♦ *We are going to a wedding reception* **3** a place in a hotel or office where visitors report or check in

receptionist *noun* (*plural* **receptionists**)
someone whose job is to receive and welcome visitors to a hotel or office

recess *noun* (*plural* **recesses**)
1 an alcove **2** a time when work or business is stopped for a while

recession *noun* (*plural* **recessions**)
a reduction in trade or in the wealth of a
country

recipe *noun* (*plural* **recipes**) (*pronounced*
ress-i-pi)
instructions for preparing or cooking food

reciprocal ➤ *adjective* (*pronounced*
ri-sip-ro-kal)
given and received at the same time;
mutual ♦ *They gave a reciprocal greeting*

reciprocal ➤ *noun* (*plural* **reciprocals**)
the amount by which you must multiply a
number to obtain the answer 1 ♦ *0·5 is the
reciprocal of 2 (0·5 ×2 = 1)*

recital *noun* (*plural* **recitals**) (*pronounced*
ri-sy-tal)
1 reciting something 2 a concert by a
small number of performers

recite *verb* (**recites, reciting, recited**)
to recite something such as a poem is to
say it aloud
recitation *noun* something you recite

reckless *adjective*
doing things without thinking or caring
about what might happen
recklessly *adverb* in a reckless way
recklessness *noun* being reckless

reckon *verb* (**reckons, reckoning, reckoned**)
1 to reckon something is to calculate or
count it 2 to reckon something is to think
it or have an opinion about it ♦ *I reckon it's
about to rain*

reclaim *verb* (**reclaims, reclaiming, reclaimed**)
1 to reclaim land is to make it usable
again 2 to reclaim something is to claim it
or get it back

reclamation *noun*
making land usable again

recline *verb* (**reclines, reclining, reclined**)
to recline is to lean or lie back

recognize *verb* (**recognizes, recognizing,
recognized**)
1 to recognize someone or something is to
know who they are because you have seen
them before 2 to recognize a fault or
mistake is to admit to it ♦ *We recognize
that we may have acted unfairly*
recognition *noun* recognizing someone or
something **recognizable** *adjective* able to be
recognized

recoil *verb* (**recoils, recoiling, recoiled**)
to recoil is to move backwards suddenly
♦ *He recoiled in horror*

recollect *verb* (**recollects, recollecting,
recollected**)
to recollect something is to remember it
recollection *noun* remembering something

recommend *verb* (**recommends, recommending,
recommended**)
1 to recommend something or someone is
to say that they are good or suitable ♦ *I
recommend the strawberry ice cream* 2 to
recommend an action is to advise someone
to do it ♦ *We recommend that you wear
strong shoes on the walk*
recommendation *noun* recommending
someone or something

reconcile *verb* (**reconciles, reconciling,
reconciled**)
1 to reconcile people or countries is to
restore peace or friendship between them
2 to reconcile someone to something is to
persuade them to put up with it ♦ *He soon
became reconciled to wearing glasses*
reconciliation *noun* becoming reconciled

reconstruction *noun* (*plural* **reconstructions**)
1 reconstruction is building something up
again 2 a reconstruction is acting out an
event that took place in the past ♦ *They
did a reconstruction of the bank robbery*

record ➤ *noun* (*plural* **records**) (*pronounced*
rek-ord)
1 a disc with recorded sound on it 2 the
best performance in a sport or most
remarkable event of its kind ♦ *She broke
the record for swimming 100 metres* 3 a
set of information or facts about
something or someone

record ➤ *verb* (**records, recording, recorded**)
(*pronounced* ri-kord)
1 to record music or other sound is to put
it on a tape or disc 2 to record things that
have happened is to put them down in
writing

recorder *noun* (*plural* **recorders**)
1 a tape recorder 2 a wooden musical
instrument played by blowing into one end
3 someone who records something

record player *noun* (*plural* **record players**)
a device for reproducing sound from
records

recover *verb* (**recovers, recovering, recovered**)
1 to recover is to get better after being ill
2 to recover something is to get it back after losing it
recovery *noun* recovering, or recovering something

recreation *noun* (*plural* **recreations**)
a game, hobby, or other enjoyable pastime done in your spare time
recreational *adjective* to do with recreation

recruit ➤ *noun* (*plural* **recruits**)
someone who has just joined the armed forces or a business or club

recruit ➤ *verb* (**recruits, recruiting, recruited**)
to recruit someone is to bring them in as a recruit

rectangle *noun* (*plural* **rectangles**)
a shape with four straight sides and four right angles
rectangular *adjective* in the form of a rectangle

recur *verb* (**recurs, recurring, recurred**)
to recur is to happen again
recurrence *noun* something that happens again

recycle *verb* (**recycles, recycling, recycled**)
to recycle waste material is to treat it so that it can be used again ♦ *Waste paper can be recycled to make cardboard*

red ➤ *adjective* (**redder, reddest**)
1 of the colour of blood **2** (*informal*) to do with Communists; favouring Communism

red ➤ *noun* (*plural* **reds**)
1 a red colour **2** (*informal*) a Communist
in the red in debt
to see red is to become suddenly angry

redden *verb* (**reddens, reddening, reddened**)
1 to redden something is to make it red
2 to redden is to become red

reddish *adjective*
fairly red

redeem *verb* (**redeems, redeeming, redeemed**)
1 to redeem someone is to save them from damnation, as in some religions **2** to redeem something is to get it back by paying for it
redeemer *noun* someone who redeems
redemption *noun* redeeming

red-handed *adjective*
in the act of committing a crime ♦ *They were caught red-handed*

redhead *noun* (*plural* **redheads**)
a person with reddish-brown hair

red herring *noun* (*plural* **red herrings**)
something that takes attention away from the real point or answer; a false clue

red tape *noun*
too many rules and official forms

reduce *verb* (**reduces, reducing, reduced**)
1 to reduce something is to make it smaller or less **2** to be reduced to something is to be forced to do it ♦ *He was reduced to asking for more money*

reduction *noun* (*plural* **reductions**)
1 the act of reducing something **2** the amount by which something is reduced
♦ *They gave us a reduction of £5*

redundant *adjective*
not needed, especially for a particular job
redundancy *noun* being redundant

reed *noun* (*plural* **reeds**)
1 a plant that grows in or near water **2** a thin strip that vibrates to make the sound in some wind instruments, such as a clarinet, saxophone, or oboe
reedy *adjective* making a sound like a wind instrument

reef *noun* (*plural* **reefs**)
a line of rocks near the surface of the sea

reef knot *noun* (*plural* **reef knots**)
a symmetrical double knot for tying two cords together

reek *verb* (**reeks, reeking, reeked**)
to reek is to have a strong unpleasant smell

reel ➤ *noun* (*plural* **reels**)
1 a round device on which cotton or thread is wound **2** a lively Scottish dance

reel ➤ *verb* (**reels, reeling, reeled**)
to reel is to stagger ♦ *The drunk reeled along the road*
to reel something off is to say a lot very quickly

refer *verb* (**refers, referring, referred**)
to refer a question or problem to someone else is to give it to them to deal with
to refer to something is to mention it or speak about it

referee ➤ *noun* (*plural* **referees**)
someone who makes sure that people keep to the rules of a game

referee ➤ *verb* (**referees, refereeing, refereed**)
to referee a game is to act as referee in it

reference *noun* (*plural* **references**)
1 a mention of something 2 a place in a book or file where information can be found 3 a description of the work someone has done and how well they have done it; a testimonial
in or **with reference to something** or **someone** concerning them or about them

reference book *noun* (*plural* **reference books**)
a book that gives information

referendum *noun* (*plural* **referendums**) (*pronounced* ref-er-en-dum)
a vote on a particular question by all the people in a country

refill ➤ *verb* (**refills, refilling, refilled**)
to refill something is to fill it again

refill ➤ *noun* (*plural* **refills**)
a container used to replace something that has been used up ♦ *My pen needs a refill*

refine *verb* (**refines, refining, refined**)
to refine something is to purify or improve it

refined *adjective*
cultured; having good manners

refinement *noun* (*plural* **refinements**)
1 refinement is refining something 2 a refinement is something special that improves a thing

refinery *noun* (*plural* **refineries**)
a factory for refining a product, such as oil

reflect *verb* (**reflects, reflecting, reflected**)
1 to reflect light or heat or sound is to send it back from a surface 2 to reflect something is to form an image of it, as in a mirror 3 to reflect on something is to think seriously about it

reflective *adjective*
1 sending back light ♦ *The traffic policeman wore a reflective waistcoat* 2 suggesting or showing serious thought ♦ *The music has a reflective quality*

reflex *noun* (*plural* **reflexes**) (*pronounced* ree-fleks)
a movement or action done without any conscious thought

reflex angle *noun* (*plural* **reflex angles**)
an angle of between 180 and 360 degrees

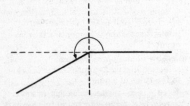

reflexive pronoun *noun* (*plural* **reflexive pronouns**) (*pronounced* ri-flek-siv)
(*in Grammar*) any of the pronouns *myself, yourself, himself, herself, itself, ourselves, themselves*, which refer back to the subject of the verb, as in *they have hurt themselves*

reform ➤ *verb* (**reforms, reforming, reformed**)
to reform a person or thing is to improve them by getting rid of their faults

reform ➤ *noun* (*plural* **reforms**)
1 reform is changing something to improve it 2 a reform is a change made for this reason

reformation *noun* reforming someone or something

Reformation *noun*
a movement for change in the Church in the 16th century, leading to the beginning of the Reformed or Protestant Churches

reformer *noun* (*plural* **reformers**)
someone who makes reforms

refract *verb* (**refracts, refracting, refracted**)
to refract a ray of light is to change its direction at a point where it enters water or glass at an angle

refraction *noun* refracting light

refrain [1] *verb* (**refrains, refraining, refrained**)
to refrain from something is to keep yourself from doing it ♦ *Please refrain from talking*

refrain [2] *noun* (*plural* **refrains**)
the chorus of a song

refresh *verb* (**refreshes, refreshing, refreshed**)
to refresh someone who is tired is to make them feel fresh and strong again

refreshments *plural noun*
food and drink

refrigerate *verb* (**refrigerates, refrigerating, refrigerated**)
to refrigerate something is to freeze it so as to keep it in good condition

refrigeration *noun* the process of refrigerating food

refrigerator *noun* (*plural* **refrigerators**)
a cabinet in which food is stored at a low temperature

refuel *verb* (**refuels, refuelling, refuelled**)
to refuel a ship or aircraft is to supply it with more fuel

refuge *noun* (*plural* **refuges**)
a place where someone is safe from pursuit or danger

refugee *noun* (*plural* **refugees**) (*pronounced* ref-yoo-jee)
someone who has had to leave their home or country because of war or persecution or disaster

refund ➤ *verb* (**refunds, refunding, refunded**)
(*pronounced* ri-**fund**)
to refund money is to pay it back

refund ➤ *noun* (*plural* **refunds**) (*pronounced*
ree-fund)
money paid back

refuse ➤ *verb* (**refuses, refusing, refused**)
(*pronounced* ri-**fewz**)
to refuse something, or to do something, is
to say that you will not accept it or do it
♦ *They refuse to help*
refusal *noun* refusing something

refuse ➤ *noun* (*pronounced* **ref**-yooss)
rubbish or waste material

regain *verb* (**regains, regaining, regained**)
1 to regain something is to get it back
2 to regain a place is to reach it again

regard ➤ *verb* (**regards, regarding, regarded**)
1 to regard someone or something is to
think of them in a certain way ♦ *I regard
her as a friend* **2** to regard someone or
something is also to look at them closely

regard ➤ *noun* (*plural* **regards**)
1 a gaze or look **2** consideration or
respect ♦ *They acted without regard for
our safety*
with regard to something about it; in
connection with it

regarding *preposition*
on the subject of; about ♦ *There are rules
regarding use of the library*

regardless *adjective*
paying no attention to something ♦ *Buy it,
regardless of the cost*

regards *plural noun*
kind wishes sent in a message ♦ *Give
them my regards*

regatta *noun* (*plural* **regattas**) (*pronounced*
ri-**gat**-a)
a meeting for boat or yacht races

reggae *noun* (*pronounced* **reg**-ay)
a West Indian style of music with a strong
beat

regiment *noun* (*plural* **regiments**)
an army unit consisting of two or more
battalions
regimental *adjective* to do with a regiment

region *noun* (*plural* **regions**)
1 a part of a country **2** a part of the world
♦ *These plants only grow in tropical
regions*
regional *adjective* to do with a region

register ➤ *noun* (*plural* **registers**)
1 an official list of names or information,
especially of people present each day at a
school **2** the range of a voice or musical
instrument

register ➤ *verb* (**registers, registering, registered**)
1 to register something or someone is to
put their names in a register or list **2** a
gauge or instrument registers a certain
amount when that is what it shows ♦ *The
thermometer registered 25°* **3** to register a
letter or parcel is to have it officially
recorded for sending with special care
registration *noun* putting information on a
register

registration number *noun* (*plural* **registration
numbers**)
the set of numbers and letters that a motor
vehicle has when it is registered

regret ➤ *noun* (*plural* **regrets**)
the feeling of being sorry or sad about
something

regret ➤ *verb* (**regrets, regretting, regretted**)
to regret something is to feel sorry or sad
about it

regretful *adjective*
feeling regret
regretfully *adverb* in a regretful way

regrettable *adjective*
likely to be regretted; unfortunate

regular *adjective*
1 always happening at certain times
♦ *You need regular meals* **2** even or
symmetrical ♦ *She has beautiful regular
teeth* **3** normal or correct ♦ *Let's go home
by the regular route* **4** belonging to a
country's permanent armed forces ♦ *He
wants to be a regular soldier*
regularity *noun* being regular **regularly**
adverb in a regular way

regulate *verb* (**regulates, regulating, regulated**)
to regulate something is to adjust or
control it
regulator *noun* a device for regulating
something

regulation *noun* (*plural* **regulations**)
1 regulation is the adjusting or controlling
of something **2** a regulation is a rule or
law

rehearse *verb* (**rehearses, rehearsing, rehearsed**)
to rehearse something is to practise it
before you perform it
rehearsal *noun* rehearsing something

reign ➤ *verb* (**reigns, reigning, reigned**)
1 to reign is to be king or queen
2 something reigns when it is the most
noticeable or important thing ♦ *Silence
reigned for a while*

reign ➤ *noun* (*plural* **reigns**)
the time when someone is king or queen

rein *noun* (*plural* **reins**)
a strap used by a rider to guide a horse

reindeer *noun* (*plural* **reindeer**)
a kind of deer that lives in Arctic regions

reinforce *verb* (**reinforces, reinforcing, reinforced**)
to reinforce something is to strengthen it

reinforcement *noun* (*plural* **reinforcements**)
a thing that strengthens something
reinforcements extra troops or equipment sent to strengthen a military force

reject ➤ *verb* (**rejects, rejecting, rejected**) (*pronounced* ri-jekt)
1 to reject something or someone is to refuse to accept them ♦ *They have rejected my offer of help* **2** to reject something is to get rid of it ♦ *Faulty parts are rejected at the factory*
rejection *noun* rejecting something

reject ➤ *noun* (*plural* **rejects**) (*pronounced* ree-jekt)
a thing that is got rid of, especially because of being faulty or poorly made

rejoice *verb* (**rejoices, rejoicing, rejoiced**)
to rejoice is to be very happy or pleased

relate *verb* (**relates, relating, related**)
1 to relate one thing with another is to compare them **2** to relate a story is to tell it

related *adjective*
belonging to the same family

relation *noun* (*plural* **relations**)
1 a relation is someone who is related to you **2** relation is the way that one thing is connected or compared with another

relationship *noun* (*plural* **relationships**)
1 the way people or things are connected with each other **2** the way people get on with one another ♦ *There is a good relationship between the teachers and the children* **3** a close friendship or connection between two people

relative ➤ *noun* (*plural* **relatives**)
someone who is related to you

relative ➤ *adjective*
1 connected or compared with something **2** compared with the average ♦ *They live in relative comfort*

relatively *adverb*
compared with other people or things; more or less ♦ *Books are relatively cheap*

relative pronoun *noun* (*plural* **relative pronouns**)
one of the words *who, what, which,* or *that,* placed in front of a clause to connect it with an earlier clause. In the sentence *we saw the man who had stolen the car,* the relative pronoun is 'who'

relax *verb* (**relaxes, relaxing, relaxed**)
1 to relax is to become less anxious or worried **2** to relax is also to rest or stop working **3** to relax a part of you is make it less stiff or tense ♦ *Try to relax your arm*
relaxation *noun* relaxing

relay ➤ *verb* (**relays, relaying, relayed**)
to relay a message or broadcast is to pass it on

relay ➤ *noun* (*plural* **relays**)
1 a fresh group taking the place of another ♦ *The firemen worked in relays* **2** a relay race **3** a device for passing on a broadcast

relay race *noun* (*plural* **relay races**)
a race between two teams in which each competitor covers part of the distance

release ➤ *verb* (**releases, releasing, released**)
1 to release something or someone is to set them free or unfasten them **2** to release a film or record is to make it available to the public

release ➤ *noun* (*plural* **releases**)
1 release is being released **2** a release is something released, especially a new film or record **3** a release is a device that unfastens something ♦ *The seatbelt has a quick release*

relegate *verb* (**relegates, relegating, relegated**) (*pronounced* rel-i-gayt)
1 to relegate something is to put it into a lower group or position than before **2** to relegate a sports team is to put it into a lower division of a league
relegation *noun* relegating something, or being relegated

relent *verb* (**relents, relenting, relented**)
to relent is to be less angry or severe than you were going to be

relentless *adjective*
1 pitiless or harsh ♦ *They faced a relentless enemy* **2** not stopping or relenting ♦ *Their criticism was relentless*
relentlessly *adverb* in a relentless way

relevant *adjective* (*pronounced* rel-i-vant)
connected with what is being discussed or dealt with
relevance *noun* being relevant

reliable *adjective*
able to be relied on; trustworthy

reliability *noun* being reliable **reliably** *adverb* in a reliable way

reliant *adjective*
relying on someone or something
reliance *noun* being reliant

relic *noun* (*plural* **relics**)
something that has survived from an ancient time

relief *noun* (*plural* **reliefs**)
1 relief is the ending or lessening of pain or suffering **2** a relief is something that causes this **3** a relief is also a person or thing that takes over or helps with a job **4** relief is also a method of making a map or design that stands out from a flat surface ◆ *The model shows hills and valleys in relief*

relieve *verb* (**relieves, relieving, relieved**)
to relieve pain or suffering is to end or lessen it
to relieve someone of something is to take it from them

religion *noun* (*plural* **religions**)
what people believe about God or gods, and how they worship

religious *adjective*
1 to do with religion **2** believing in a religion and following it carefully

religiously *adverb*
with great attention or care ◆ *They did all their work religiously*

reluctant *adjective*
not wanting to do something; not keen
reluctance *noun* being reluctant **reluctantly** *adverb* in a reluctant way

rely *verb* (**relies, relying, relied**)
to rely on someone or **something** is to trust them or need them to help or support you

remain *verb* (**remains, remaining, remained**)
1 to remain is to continue in the same place or condition ◆ *It will remain cloudy all day* **2** to remain is also to be left over ◆ *A lot of food remained after the party*
remainder *noun* something remaining

remains *plural noun*
1 something left over **2** ruins or relics **3** a dead body

remark ➤ *verb* (**remarks, remarking, remarked**)
to remark on something is to say something that you have thought or noticed

remark ➤ *noun* (*plural* **remarks**)
something said

remarkable *adjective*
so unusual that you notice or remember it
remarkably *adverb* in a remarkable way

remedial *adjective* (*pronounced* ri-mee-di-al)
1 helping to cure an illness or problem
2 helping children who learn slowly

remedy *noun* (*plural* **remedies**)
a cure or medicine

remember *verb* (**remembers, remembering, remembered**)
1 to remember something is to keep it in your mind, or bring it into your mind when you need to **2** to remember someone is to be thinking about them
remembrance *noun* remembering someone or something

remind *verb* (**reminds, reminding, reminded**)
to remind someone is to help or make them remember something
reminder *noun* something that reminds someone

reminisce *verb* (**reminisces, reminiscing, reminisced**) (*pronounced* rem-in-iss)
to reminisce is to think or talk about things you remember
reminiscence *noun* reminiscing **reminiscent** *adjective* reminding you of something

remnant *noun* (*plural* **remnants**)
a small piece of something left over

remorse *noun*
deep regret for having done wrong

remorseful *adjective*
feeling remorse
remorsefully *adverb* in a remorseful way

remorseless *adjective*
relentless; not stopping
remorselessly *adverb* in a remorseless way

remote *adjective* (**remoter, remotest**)
1 far away **2** unlikely or slight ◆ *Their chances of winning were remote*
remotely *adverb* in a remote way **remoteness** *noun* being remote

remote control *noun* (*plural* **remote controls**)
1 remote control is controlling something from a distance, usually by means of radio or electricity **2** a remote control is a device for doing this

removal *noun* (*plural* **removals**)
removing or moving something

remove *verb* (**removes, removing, removed**)
to remove something is to take it away or take it off

Renaissance *noun*
the revival of art and literature in Europe in the 14th–16th centuries

render *verb* (**renders, rendering, rendered**)
1 to render someone is to put them in a particular condition ◆ *The shock rendered her speechless* **2** to render help or a service is to provide it

rendezvous *noun* (*plural* **rendezvous**) (*pronounced* ron-day-voo)
1 a meeting with someone **2** a place for meeting

renew *verb* (renews, renewing, renewed)
to renew something is to make it as it was before or replace it with something new
renewal *noun* renewing something

renewable *adjective*
able to be renewed or replaced; never completely used up

renown *noun*
fame ♦ *He is a man of great renown*
renowned *adjective* famous

rent ➤ *noun* (*plural* rents)
a regular payment for the use of something, especially a house

rent ➤ *verb* (rents, renting, rented)
to rent something is to pay money for the use of it

repair ➤ *verb* (repairs, repairing, repaired)
to repair something is to mend it

repair ➤ *noun* (*plural* repairs)
1 repair is mending something ♦ *The car is in for repair* **2** a repair is a mended place ♦ *You can hardly see the repair*
in good repair in good condition

repay *verb* (repays, repaying, repaid)
to repay something is to pay it back
repayment *noun* something repaid

repeat ➤ *verb* (repeats, repeating, repeated)
to repeat something is to say it or do it again

repeat ➤ *noun* (*plural* repeats)
something that is repeated

repeatedly *adverb*
several times; again and again

repel *verb* (repels, repelling, repelled)
1 to repel someone or something is to drive or force them away or apart **2** to repel someone is to make them disgusted
repellent *adjective* disgusting

repent *verb* (repents, repenting, repented)
to repent is to be sorry for what you have done
repentance *noun* repenting **repentant** *adjective* feeling sorry for what you have done

repetition *noun* (*plural* repetitions)
1 repeating or doing something again
2 something repeated

repetitive *adjective*
being repeated too much

replace *verb* (replaces, replacing, replaced)
1 to replace something is to put it back in its place **2** to replace someone or something is to take their place **3** to replace something is to put a new thing in the place of it ♦ *We will have to replace the old engine with a new one*

replacement *noun* (*plural* replacements)
1 replacing something or someone
2 something used or given in place of another

replay *noun* (*plural* replays)
1 a football match played again after a draw **2** the playing or showing again of a recording

replica *noun* (*plural* replicas) (*pronounced* rep-li-ka)
an exact copy

reply ➤ *noun* (*plural* replies)
something said or written to deal with what someone else has asked or said

reply ➤ *verb* (replies, replying, replied)
to reply is to give a reply

report ➤ *verb* (reports, reporting, reported)
1 to report something is to describe something that has happened or something you have studied **2** to report someone is to complain about them to those in charge of them **3** to report to someone is to tell them you have arrived or are available

report ➤ *noun* (*plural* reports)
1 a description or account of something
2 a regular statement of how someone has worked or behaved, especially at school
3 an explosive sound ♦ *We heard the report of a gun*

reporter *noun* (*plural* reporters)
someone whose job is to collect news for a newspaper or for radio or television

repossess *verb* (repossesses, repossessing, repossessed)
to repossess goods is to take them back when someone has bought them but cannot finish paying for them

represent *verb* (represents, representing, represented)
1 to represent something or someone is to be a picture or model or symbol of them
2 to represent something is also to be a typical example of it **3** to represent someone is to support them by speaking or acting for them
representation *noun* being represented

representative ➤ *noun*
a person or thing that represents others

representative ➤ *adjective* **1** representing others **2** typical of a group

repress *verb* (represses, repressing, repressed)
to repress something or someone is to control or restrain them by force
repression *noun* being repressed **repressive** *adjective* repressing people

reprieve ➤ *noun* (*plural* **reprieves**)
(*pronounced* ri-preev)
postponing or cancelling a punishment,
especially the death penalty

reprieve ➤ *verb* (**reprieves, reprieving, reprieved**)
to reprieve someone is to cancel or
postpone their punishment

reprimand *verb* (**reprimands, reprimanding, reprimanded**)
to reprimand someone is to scold them or
tell them off

reprisal *noun* (*plural* **reprisals**) (*pronounced* ri-pry-zal)
an act of revenge

reproach *verb* (**reproaches, reproaching, reproached**)
to reproach someone is to find fault with
them

reproduce *verb* (**reproduces, reproducing, reproduced**)
1 to reproduce something is to make it be
heard or seen again ♦ *Sound can be
reproduced by discs or magnetic tapes*
2 to reproduce something is also to copy it
3 to reproduce is to have offspring
reproduction *noun* reproducing something,
or something reproduced **reproductive**
adjective to do with having offspring

reptile *noun* (*plural* **reptiles**)
an animal that creeps or crawls, such as
snakes and lizards

republic *noun* (*plural* **republics**)
a country ruled by a president and
government that are chosen by the people
republican *adjective* to do with a republic

Republican *noun* (*plural* **Republicans**)
a supporter of the Republican Party in the
USA

repulsive *adjective*
disgusting
repulsion *noun* a feeling of disgust

reputation *noun* (*plural* **reputations**)
what people think about a person or thing
♦ *He has a reputation for being honest*

request ➤ *verb* (**requests, requesting, requested**)
to request something is to ask politely or
formally for it

request ➤ *noun* (*plural* **requests**)
1 the action of asking for something
2 what someone asks for

require *verb* (**requires, requiring, required**)
1 to require something is to need or want
it **2** to require someone to do something is
to make them do it ♦ *Pedestrians are
required to walk on the pavements*
requirement *noun* something required; a
rule

reread *verb* (**rereads, rereading, reread**)
to reread something is to read it again

rescue ➤ *verb* (**rescues, rescuing, rescued**)
to rescue someone is to save them from
danger or capture

rescue ➤ *noun* (*plural* **rescues**)
the action of rescuing someone
rescuer *noun* a person who rescues
someone

research *noun* (*plural* **researches**)
careful study or investigation
researcher *noun* someone who does research

resemblance *noun* (*plural* **resemblances**)
being similar ♦ *There is a resemblance
between the brothers*

resemble *verb* (**resembles, resembling, resembled**)
to resemble someone or something is to
look or sound like them

resent *verb* (**resents, resenting, resented**)
to resent something is to feel indignant or
angry about it
resentful *adjective* resenting something
resentment *noun* a feeling of resenting

reservation *noun* (*plural* **reservations**)
1 reserving something **2** something
reserved **3** an area of land kept for a
special purpose **4** a doubt or feeling of
unease ♦ *I had reservations about the
excuses he made*

reserve ➤ *verb* (**reserves, reserving, reserved**)
to reserve something is to keep it or order
it for a particular person or for a special
use

reserve ➤ *noun* (*plural* **reserves**)
1 a person or thing kept ready to be used
if necessary **2** an area of land kept for a
special purpose ♦ *This island is a nature
reserve*

reserved *adjective*
1 kept for someone ♦ *These seats are
reserved* **2** shy or unwilling to show your
feelings

reservoir *noun* (*plural* **reservoirs**)
(*pronounced* rez-er-vwar)
a place where water is stored, especially
an artificial lake

reshuffle *noun* (*plural* **reshuffles**)
a rearrangement, especially an exchange
of jobs between people in a group ♦ *The
Prime Minister announced a Cabinet
reshuffle*

reside *verb* (**resides, residing, resided**)
to reside in a place is to live there

residence *noun* (*plural* **residences**)
a place where someone lives

resident *noun* (*plural* **residents**)
someone who lives in a particular place

resign *verb* (**resigns, resigning, resigned**)
to resign is to give up your job or position
to resign yourself to something is to accept a
difficulty without complaining or arguing

resignation *noun* (*plural* **resignations**)
1 resignation is accepting a difficulty
without complaining **2** a resignation is a
letter saying you are resigning a job or
position

resin *noun* (*plural* **resins**) (*pronounced*
rez-in)
a sticky substance that comes from plants
or is made artificially
resinous *adjective* like resin

resist *verb* (**resists, resisting, resisted**)
to resist someone or something is to
oppose them or try to stop them

resistance *noun* (*plural* **resistances**)
1 fighting or taking action against
someone or something ♦ *The troops came
up against armed resistance* **2** the ability
of a material to hold up the passage of
electric current
resistant *adjective* resisting; showing
resistance

resolute *adjective* (*pronounced* rez-o-loot)
determined or firm
resolutely *adverb* in a resolute way

resolution *noun* (*plural* **resolutions**)
1 resolution is being determined or firm
2 a resolution is something you have
decided to do

resolve *verb* (**resolves, resolving, resolved**)
1 to resolve to do something is to decide to
do it **2** to resolve doubts or disagreements
is to overcome them

resort ➤ *noun* (*plural* **resorts**)
a place where people go for holidays
the last resort the only thing you can do
when everything else has failed

resort ➤ *verb* (**resorts, resorting, resorted**)
to resort to something is to make use of it
♦ *In the end they resorted to violence*

resound *verb* (**resounds, resounding, resounded**)
to resound is to fill a place with sound or to
echo

resource *noun* (*plural* **resources**)
something that can be used ♦ *The land is
rich in natural resources*

respect ➤ *noun* (*plural* **respects**)
1 respect is admiration for someone's good
qualities or achievements **2** respect is
also consideration or concern ♦ *Have
respect for people's feelings* **3** a respect is a
detail or aspect ♦ *In some respects, he is
like his sister*
with respect to something concerning
something

respect ➤ *verb* (**respects, respecting, respected**)
to respect someone is to have respect for
them

respectable *adjective*
1 having good manners and character
2 of a good size or standard
respectability *noun* being respectable
respectably *adverb* in a respectable way

respectful *adjective*
showing respect; polite
respectfully *adverb* in a respectful way

respecting *preposition*
concerning; to do with

respective *adjective*
belonging to each one of several ♦ *We went
to our respective rooms*

respectively *adverb*
in the same order as the people or things
already mentioned ♦ *Emma and I went to
London and Paris respectively*

respiration *noun*
breathing
respiratory *adjective* to do with breathing

respirator *noun* (*plural* **respirators**)
a mask or machine for helping with
people's breathing

respond *verb* (**responds, responding, responded**)
to respond is to reply or react

response *noun* (*plural* **responses**)
a reply or reaction

responsibility *noun* (*plural* **responsibilities**)
1 responsibility is being responsible for
something **2** a responsibility is something
for which you are responsible

responsible *adjective*
1 looking after something and likely to
take the blame if anything goes wrong
2 able to be trusted **3** important and
needing trust ♦ *She has a responsible job*
4 causing something ♦ *His carelessness
was responsible for their deaths*
responsibly *adverb* in a responsible way

rest[1] ➤ *noun* (*plural* **rests**)
1 a time when you can sleep or relax
2 a support for something

rest ➤ *verb* (**rests, resting, rested**)
1 to rest is to sleep or relax **2** to rest on or
against something is to lean on it ♦ *The
ladder is resting against the wall* **3** to rest
something is to lean or support it
somewhere ♦ *Rest the ladder on the roof*

rest[2] ➤ *noun*
the rest the part that is left; the others

rest > *verb* (rests, resting, rested)
to rest with someone is to be their
responsibility
restaurant *noun* (*plural* restaurants)
a place where you can buy a meal and
eat it
restful *adjective*
giving a feeling of rest
restless *adjective*
unable to rest or keep still
restlessly *adverb* in a restless way
restlessness *noun* being restless
restore *verb* (restores, restoring, restored)
to restore something is to put it back as it
was or make it new again
restoration *noun* restoring something
restrain *verb* (restrains, restraining, restrained)
to restrain someone or something is to
hold them or keep them tightly controlled
restraint *noun* restraining someone or
something
restrict *verb* (restricts, restricting, restricted)
to restrict someone or something is to keep
them within certain limits
restriction *noun* restricting; something that
restricts **restrictive** *adjective* restricting
result > *noun* (*plural* results)
1 a thing that happens because something
else has happened **2** the score or situation
at the end of a game or competition or race
3 the answer to a sum or problem
result > *verb* (results, resulting, resulted)
to result is to happen as a result
to result in something is to have it as a result
♦ *The game resulted in a draw*
resume *verb* (resumes, resuming, resumed)
to resume, or to resume something, is to
start again after stopping
resumption *noun* resuming; starting again
resuscitate *verb* (resuscitates, resuscitating,
resuscitated) (*pronounced* ri-**suss**-it-ate)
to resuscitate someone is to revive them
after they have been unconscious
retail > *verb* (retails, retailing, retailed)
to retail goods is to sell them to the public
retail > *noun*
retail is selling to the public
retain *verb* (retains, retaining, retained)
1 to retain something is to keep it
♦ *Retain your tickets for inspection* **2** to
retain something is to hold it in place

retina *noun* (*plural* retinas) (*pronounced*
ret-i-na)
a layer at the back of the eyeball that is
sensitive to light

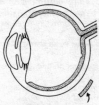

retire *verb* (retires, retiring, retired)
1 to retire is to give up regular work at a
certain age **2** to retire is also to retreat or
withdraw, or to go to bed
retirement *noun* retiring from regular work
retiring *adjective*
shy; avoiding company
retort > *verb* (retorts, retorting, retorted)
to retort is to reply quickly or angrily
retort > *noun* (*plural* retorts)
a quick or angry reply
retrace *verb* (retraces, retracing, retraced)
to retrace something is to go back over it
retreat *verb* (retreats, retreating, retreated)
to retreat is to go back when you are
attacked or defeated
retrieve *verb* (retrieves, retrieving, retrieved)
to retrieve something is to get it back or
find it again
retrievable *adjective* able to be got back
retrieval *noun* retrieving something
retriever *noun* (*plural* retrievers)
a dog that can find and bring back shot
birds and animals
return > *verb* (returns, returning, returned)
1 to return is to come or go back to a place
2 to return something is to give it or send
it back
return > *noun* (*plural* returns)
1 returning **2** something given or sent
back **3** profit ♦ *He gets a good return on
his savings* **4** a return ticket
return match *noun* (*plural* return matches)
a second match played between the same
teams as an earlier match
return ticket *noun* (*plural* return tickets)
a ticket for a journey to a place and back
again
reunion *noun* (*plural* reunions)
a meeting of people who have not met for
some time
Rev. short for **Reverend**

rev ➤ *verb* (**revs, revving, revved**)
(*informal*) to rev an engine is to make it run quickly

rev ➤ *noun* (*plural* **revs**)
(*informal*) a revolution of an engine

reveal *verb* (**reveals, revealing, revealed**)
to reveal something is to show it or make it known
revelation *noun* something surprising

revenge *noun*
harming someone because they have done harm to you

revenue *noun* (*plural* **revenues**)
(*pronounced* **rev**-e-nyoo)
income

revere *verb* (**reveres, revering, revered**)
(*pronounced* ri-**veer**)
to revere someone or something is to respect them deeply or religiously

Reverend *noun*
the title of a member of the clergy ♦ *This is the Reverend John Smith*

reverent *adjective*
feeling or showing awe or respect, especially towards God or holy things
reverence *noun* being reverent

reverse ➤ *noun*
1 the opposite way or side 2 reverse gear
in reverse going in the opposite direction

reverse ➤ *verb* (**reverses, reversing, reversed**)
1 to reverse something is to turn it round
2 to reverse is to go backwards in a vehicle
3 to reverse a decision is to cancel it
reversal *noun* reversing something **reversible** *adjective* able to be reversed

reverse gear *noun*
a gear used to drive a vehicle backwards

review ➤ *noun* (*plural* **reviews**)
1 an inspection or survey 2 a published description and opinion of a book or film or play, or a piece of music

review ➤ *verb* (**reviews, reviewing, reviewed**)
1 to review something is to inspect or survey 2 to review a book or play or film, or a piece of music, is to write a review of it
reviewer *noun* someone who writes a review

revise *verb* (**revises, revising, revised**)
1 to revise is to study work that you have already done 2 to revise something is to correct or change it
revision *noun* revising something

revive *verb* (**revives, reviving, revived**)
1 to revive something is to start using it again 2 to revive someone is to make them conscious again after fainting
revival *noun* reviving something

revolt ➤ *verb* (**revolts, revolting, revolted**)
1 to revolt is to rebel 2 to revolt someone is to disgust or horrify them

revolt ➤ *noun* (*plural* **revolts**)
a rebellion

revolution *noun* (*plural* **revolutions**)
1 a rebellion that overthrows the government 2 a complete change 3 one turn of a wheel or engine

revolutionary *adjective*
1 to do with a revolution 2 completely new or original

revolutionize *verb* (**revolutionizes, revolutionizing, revolutionized**)
to revolutionize something is to change it completely

revolve *verb* (**revolves, revolving, revolved**)
to revolve is to go round in a circle

revolver *noun* (*plural* **revolvers**)
a pistol that has a revolving store for bullets so that it can be fired several times without having to be loaded again

revue *noun* (*plural* **revues**)
an entertainment of songs and short sketches

reward ➤ *noun* (*plural* **rewards**)
something given to a person in return for something they have done

reward ➤ *verb* (**rewards, rewarding, rewarded**)
to reward someone is to give them a reward

rewarding *adjective*
pleasing or satisfying

rewind *verb* (**rewinds, rewinding, rewound**)
to rewind a cassette or videotape is to wind it back to the beginning

rewrite *verb* (**rewrites, rewriting, rewrote, rewritten**)
to rewrite something is to write it again or differently

rheumatism *noun* (*pronounced* **roo**-ma-tizm)
a disease that causes pain and stiffness in the joints and muscles
rheumatic *adjective* suffering from rheumatism

rhinoceros *noun* (*plural* **rhinoceroses** or **rhinoceros**) (*pronounced* ry-**noss**-er-os)
a large heavy animal with a horn or two horns on its nose

rhododendron *noun* (*plural* **rhododendrons**)
(*pronounced* roh-do-den-dron)
an evergreen shrub with large flowers

rhombus *noun* (*plural* **rhombuses**)
a shape with four equal sides and no right
angles, like a diamond on a playing card

rhubarb *noun*
a plant with pink or green stalks used as
food

rhyme ➤ *noun* (*plural* **rhymes**)
1 similar sounds in the endings of words,
as in *bat* and *mat*, *batter* and *matter* **2** a
short rhyming poem

rhyme ➤ *verb* (**rhymes, rhyming, rhymed**)
1 to rhyme is to have rhymes at the ends
of lines **2** to rhyme with another word is to
form a rhyme with it ♦ *Bat rhymes with
hat*

rhythm *noun* (*plural* **rhythms**)
a regular pattern of beats, sounds, or
movements in music and poetry
rhythmic or **rhythmical** *adjective* having a
rhythm **rhythmically** *adverb* with a rhythm

rib *noun* (*plural* **ribs**)
one of the curved bones above your waist

ribbon *noun* (*plural* **ribbons**)
a strip of nylon, silk, or other material

rice *noun*
white seeds from a cereal plant, used as
food

rich *adjective* (**richer, richest**)
1 having a lot of money or property **2** full
of goodness, quality, or strength **3** costly
or luxurious ♦ *The house has rich
furnishings*
richness *noun* being rich

riches *plural noun*
wealth

richly *adverb*
1 in a rich or luxurious way
2 thoroughly, completely ♦ *They richly
deserved their punishment*

rick *noun* (*plural* **ricks**)
a stack of hay or straw

rickety *adjective*
unsteady; likely to break or fall down

rickshaw *noun* (*plural* **rickshaws**)
a two-wheeled carriage pulled by one or
more people, used in the Far East

ricochet *verb* (**ricochets, ricocheting, ricocheted**)
(*pronounced* rik-o-shay)
to ricochet is to bounce off something
♦ *The bullets ricocheted off the wall*

rid *verb* (**rids, ridding, rid**)
to rid a person or place of something
unwanted is to free them from it ♦ *He rid
the town of rats*
to get rid of something or **someone** is to cause
them to go away ♦ *I wish I could get rid of
these spots*

riddance *noun*
good riddance used to show that you are glad
that something or someone has gone

riddle *noun* (*plural* **riddles**)
a puzzling question, especially as a joke

ride ➤ *verb* (**rides, riding, rode, ridden**)
1 to ride a horse or bicycle is to sit on it
and be carried along on it **2** to ride is to
travel in a vehicle
rider *noun* someone who rides a horse

ride ➤ *noun* (*plural* **rides**)
a journey on a horse or bicycle, or in a
vehicle

ridge *noun* (*plural* **ridges**)
a long narrow part higher than the rest of
something

ridicule *verb* (**ridicules, ridiculing, ridiculed**)
to ridicule someone or something is to
make fun of them

ridiculous *adjective*
extremely silly or absurd
ridiculously *adverb* in a ridiculous way

rifle *noun* (*plural* **rifles**)
a long gun. You hold it against your
shoulder to fire it

rift *noun* (*plural* **rifts**)
1 a crack or split **2** a disagreement
between friends

rig *verb* (**rigs, rigging, rigged**)
to rig a ship is to provide it with rigging,
sails, and other equipment
to rig someone out is to provide them with
clothes or equipment
to rig something up is to make it quickly

rigging *noun*
the ropes that support a ship's masts and
sails

right ➤ *adjective*
1 on or towards the east if you think of
yourself as facing north **2** correct ♦ *Is this
sum right?* **3** fair or honest ♦ *It's not right
to cheat* **4** conservative; not in favour of
political reforms
rightness *noun* being correct or fair

right ➤ *adverb*
1 on or towards the right ♦ *Turn right*
2 completely ♦ *Turn right round*
3 exactly ♦ *She stood right in the middle*
4 straight; directly ♦ *Go right ahead*
right away immediately

right ➤ *noun* (*plural* **rights**)
1 the right side 2 what is fair or just; something that people ought to be allowed ♦ *They fought for their rights*

right ➤ *verb* (**rights, righting, righted**)
1 to right something is to make it upright ♦ *They righted the boat* 2 to right something is also to put it right ♦ *The fault might right itself*

right angle *noun* (*plural* **right angles**)
an angle of 90 degrees, like angles in a rectangle

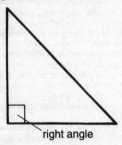

right angle

righteous *adjective*
being or doing good; obeying the law
righteously *adverb* in a righteous way
righteousness *noun* being righteous

rightful *adjective*
deserved or proper
rightfully *adverb* deservedly

right-hand *adjective*
on the right side of something

right-handed *adjective*
using the right hand more than the left hand

rightly *adverb*
correctly or fairly

rigid *adjective* (*pronounced* rij-id)
1 firm or stiff 2 strict or harsh ♦ *The rules are rigid*
rigidity *noun* being rigid **rigidly** *adverb* strictly; harshly

rim *noun* (*plural* **rims**)
the outer edge of a cup or wheel or other round object

rind *noun* (*plural* **rinds**)
the tough skin on bacon, cheese, or fruit

ring¹ ➤ *noun* (*plural* **rings**)
1 a circle 2 a thin circular piece of metal worn on a finger 3 the space where a circus performs 4 the place where a boxing match or other contest is held

ring ➤ *verb* (**rings, ringing, ringed**)
to ring something is to put a ring round it ♦ *Ring the answer that you think is the right one*

ring² ➤ *verb* (**rings, ringing, rang, rung**)
1 to ring a bell is to make it sound 2 to ring is to make a clear musical sound like a bell 3 to ring someone is to telephone them ♦ *She rang her brother last night*

ring ➤ *noun* (*plural* **rings**)
a ringing sound
to give someone a ring (*informal*) is to telephone them

ringleader *noun* (*plural* **ringleaders**)
someone who leads other people in rebellion or mischief or crime

ringlet *noun* (*plural* **ringlets**)
a long curled piece of hair

ringmaster *noun* (*plural* **ringmasters**)
the person who is in charge of a performance in the circus ring

ring road *noun* (*plural* **ring roads**)
a road that goes right round a town

ringworm *noun*
a skin disease which makes an itchy rash on the skin

rink *noun* (*plural* **rinks**)
a place made for skating

rinse ➤ *verb* (**rinses, rinsing, rinsed**)
to rinse something is to wash it in clean water without soap

rinse ➤ *noun* (*plural* **rinses**)
a process of rinsing

riot ➤ *noun* (*plural* **riots**)
wild or violent behaviour by a crowd of people

riot ➤ *verb* (**riots, rioting, rioted**)
to riot is to run wild and behave violently

riotous *adjective*
wild or unruly
riotously *adverb* in a riotous way

rip ➤ *verb* (**rips, ripping, ripped**)
to rip something is to tear it roughly
to rip someone off (*slang*) is to charge them too much or swindle them

rip ➤ *noun* (*plural* **rips**)
a torn place

ripe *adjective* (**riper, ripest**)
ready to be harvested or eaten
ripeness *noun* being ripe

ripen *verb* (**ripens, ripening, ripened**)
1 to ripen something is to make it ripe
2 to ripen is to become ripe

rip-off *noun* (*plural* **rip-offs**)
(*slang*) a cheat or swindle

ripple ➤ *noun* (*plural* **ripples**)
a small wave on the surface of water

ripple ➤ *verb* (**ripples, rippling, rippled**)
to ripple is to form small waves

rise ➤ *verb* (**rises, rising, rose, risen**)
1 to rise is to go upwards ♦ *Smoke was rising from the fire* **2** to rise is also to get larger or more ♦ *Prices rose this year* **3** a person rises when they get up from sleeping or sitting ♦ *They all rose as she came in* **4** people rise, or rise up, when they rebel ♦ *The army rose against the government* **5** in cooking, a mixture rises when it swells up by the action of yeast

rise ➤ *noun* (*plural* **rises**)
1 an increase, especially in wages **2** an upward slope
to give rise to something is to cause it

risk ➤ *verb* (**risks, risking, risked**)
to risk something is to take a chance of damaging or losing it ♦ *They risked their lives during the rescue*

risk ➤ *noun* (*plural* **risks**)
a chance of danger or loss
risky *adjective* involving risk; dangerous

risotto *noun*
an Italian dish of rice cooked with vegetables and often with meat

rissole *noun* (*plural* **rissoles**)
a fried cake of minced meat

rite *noun* (*plural* **rites**)
a ceremony or ritual

ritual *noun* (*plural* **rituals**)
a regular ceremony or series of actions

rival ➤ *noun* (*plural* **rivals**)
a person or thing that competes with another or tries to do the same thing
rivalry *noun* being rivals

rival ➤ *verb* (**rivals, rivalling, rivalled**)
to rival someone or something is to be their rival

river *noun* (*plural* **rivers**)
a large natural stream of water flowing along a channel

rivet ➤ *noun* (*plural* **rivets**)
a strong metal pin for holding pieces of metal together

rivet ➤ *verb* (**rivets, riveting, riveted**)
1 to rivet something is to fasten it with rivets **2** to rivet someone is to hold them still ♦ *She stood riveted to the spot* **3** to be riveted by something is to be fascinated by it ♦ *The children were riveted by his story*

road *noun* (*plural* **roads**)
a level way with a hard surface made for traffic to go along

road rage *noun*
angry or violent behaviour by road users

roadroller *noun* (*plural* **roadrollers**)
a heavy motor vehicle with wide metal wheels used to flatten surfaces when making roads

roadside *noun* (*plural* **roadsides**)
the side of a road

roadway *noun* (*plural* **roadways**)
the middle part of the road, used by traffic

roam *verb* (**roams, roaming, roamed**)
to roam is to wander ♦ *They roamed about the city*

roar ➤ *noun* (*plural* **roars**)
a loud deep sound of the kind that a lion makes

roar ➤ *verb* (**roars, roaring, roared**)
to roar is to make a roar
a roaring trade is a brisk selling of something

roast *verb* (**roasts, roasting, roasted**)
1 to roast food is to cook it in an oven or over a fire **2** to be roasting is to be very hot

rob *verb* (**robs, robbing, robbed**)
to rob someone is to steal something from them ♦ *He robbed me of my watch*
robber *noun* a thief **robbery** *noun* theft

robe *noun* (*plural* **robes**)
a long loose piece of clothing

robin *noun* (*plural* **robins**)
a small brown bird with a red breast

robot *noun* (*plural* **robots**)
a machine that imitates the movements of a person or does the work of a person

robust *adjective*
tough and strong

rock¹ *noun* (*plural* **rocks**)
1 a rock is a large stone **2** rock is a large mass of stone **3** rock is also a hard sweet usually shaped like a stick and sold at the seaside
rocky *adjective* having a lot of rocks

rock ² ➤ *verb* (**rocks, rocking, rocked**)
1 to rock is to move gently backwards and forwards or from side to side **2** to rock something is to make it do this

rock ➤ *noun* (*plural* **rocks**)
1 a rocking movement 2 rock music
rocky *adjective* unsteady

rock-bottom *adjective*
very low ♦ *All the goods were sold off at rock-bottom prices*

rocker *noun* (*plural* **rockers**)
1 a rocking chair 2 a curved support for a chair or cradle
off your rocker (*slang*) crazy or mad

rockery *noun* (*plural* **rockeries**)
part of a garden where flowers grow between rocks

rocket *noun* (*plural* **rockets**)
1 a firework that shoots high into the air
2 a pointed tube propelled into the air by hot gases, especially as a spacecraft or weapon

rocking chair *noun* (*plural* **rocking chairs**)
a chair which can be rocked by the person sitting in it

rock music *noun*
popular music with a heavy beat

rod *noun* (*plural* **rods**)
1 a long thin stick or bar 2 a rod with a line attached for fishing

rode past tense of **ride** *verb*

rodent *noun* (*plural* **rodents**)
an animal that has large front teeth for gnawing things, such as rats, mice, and squirrels

rodeo *noun* (*plural* **rodeos**) (*pronounced* roh-day-oh or roh-di-oh)
a display or contest of cowboys' skill in riding and in controlling cattle

rogue *noun* (*plural* **rogues**)
a dishonest or mischievous person
roguish *adjective* mischievous

role *noun* (*plural* **roles**)
1 a performer's part in a play, film, or story 2 the purpose something has
♦ *Computers have a role in teaching*

roll ➤ *verb* (**rolls, rolling, rolled**)
1 to roll is to move along by turning over and over, like a ball or wheel 2 to roll something is to make it do this 3 to roll something, or roll something up, is to form it into the shape of a cylinder or ball 4 to roll something soft is to flatten it by moving a round heavy object over it 5 to roll is to sway from side to side, as a ship does 6 drums roll when they make a long rumbling sound

roll ➤ *noun* (*plural* **rolls**)
1 a cylinder made by rolling something up
2 a small loaf of bread shaped like a bun
3 a list of names 4 the rumbling sound of drums

roller *noun* (*plural* **rollers**)
1 a cylinder-shaped object, especially one used for flattening things 2 a long swelling wave in the sea

roller skate *noun* (*plural* **roller skates**)
a device with wheels that you can fit under your shoes, so as to move smoothly over the ground

rolling pin *noun* (*plural* **rolling pins**)
a heavy cylinder rolled over pastry to flatten it

ROM short for *read-only memory*, a type of computer memory with information that can be accessed but not changed by the user

Roman ➤ *noun* (*plural* **Romans**)
an inhabitant of ancient Rome

Roman ➤ *adjective*
to do with ancient Rome

Roman candle *noun* (*plural* **Roman candles**)
a firework that shoots up coloured balls

Roman Catholic *noun* (*plural* **Roman Catholics**)
a member of the Church with the Pope in Rome at its head

Romance *adjective*
belonging to the group of languages which grew out of Latin and which includes French, Italian, Spanish, and Portuguese

romance *noun* (*plural* **romances**)
1 romance is experiences and feelings connected with love 2 a romance is a love affair or a love story

Roman numerals *plural noun*
letters that represent numbers, as used by the ancient Romans (compare *arabic figures*). I=1, V=5, X=10, L=50, C=100, and M=1000

romantic *adjective*
1 to do with love or romance 2 to do with emotions or imagination
romantically *adverb* in a romantic way

Romany *noun* (*pronounced* roh-ma-ni)
the language of the gypsies

romp ➤ *verb* (**romps, romping, romped**)
to romp is to play in a lively way

romp ➤ *noun* (*plural* **romps**)
a spell of lively play

rompers *plural noun*
a piece of clothing for a young child, covering the body and legs

roof *noun* (*plural* **roofs**)
1 the part that covers the top of a building, shelter, or vehicle **2** the upper part of the mouth

rook *noun* (*plural* **rooks**)
1 a black bird that looks like a crow **2** a piece in chess, also called a *castle*

room *noun* (*plural* **rooms**)
1 a room is a part of a building with its own walls and ceiling **2** room is space for someone or something ♦ *Is there room for me?*

roomful *adjective* (*plural* **roomfuls**)
the amount or number a room will hold

roomy *adjective* (**roomier, roomiest**)
having plenty of room or space

roost *noun* (*plural* **roosts**)
the place where a bird rests

root ➤ *noun* (*plural* **roots**)
1 the part of a plant that grows under the ground **2** a source or basis of something ♦ *People say that money is the root of all evil* **3** a number in relation to the number it produces when multiplied by itself ♦ *9 is the square root of 81*
to take root is to grow roots or to become established ♦ *The custom never took root in other countries*

root ➤ *verb* (**roots, rooting, rooted**)
1 to root is to take root in the ground **2** to root someone is to fix them firmly ♦ *Fear rooted him to the spot*
to root something out is to find it and get rid of it

rope *noun* (*plural* **ropes**)
a strong thick cord made of strands twisted together
to show someone the ropes is to show them how to do something

rose ¹ *noun* (*plural* **roses**)
a scented flower with a long thorny stem

rose ² past tense of **rise** *verb*

rosette *noun* (*plural* **rosettes**)
a large circular badge

rosy *adjective* (**rosier, rosiest**)
1 pink **2** hopeful or cheerful ♦ *The future looks rosy*

rot ➤ *verb* (**rots, rotting, rotted**)
to rot is to go soft or bad so that it is useless ♦ *This wood has rotted*

rot ➤ *noun*
1 decay **2** (*informal*) nonsense

rota *noun* (*plural* **rotas**)
a list of people who have to do tasks

rotate *verb* (**rotates, rotating, rotated**)
1 to rotate is to go round like a wheel
2 to rotate is to take turns at something
♦ *The job of treasurer rotates*
rotary *adjective* turning round **rotation** *noun* the process of turning round

rotor *noun* (*plural* **rotors**)
something that goes round, especially the large horizontal propeller of a helicopter

rotten *adjective*
1 rotted ♦ *There was rotten fruit on the ground* **2** (*informal*) nasty or very bad ♦ *We had rotten weather*
rottenness *noun* being rotten

rottweiler *noun* (*plural* **rottweilers**)
a large dog with short black and tan hair, often kept as a guard dog

rough *adjective* (**rougher, roughest**)
1 not smooth; uneven **2** violent; not gentle ♦ *He is a rough boy* **3** not exact; done quickly ♦ *It's only a rough guess*
roughly *adverb* approximately; not exactly
roughness *noun* being rough

roughage *noun*
fibre in food, which helps you to digest it

roughen *verb* (**roughens, roughening, roughened**)
1 to roughen something is to make it rough **2** to roughen is to become rough

round ➤ *adjective* (**rounder, roundest**)
1 shaped like a circle or ball or cylinder
2 full or complete ♦ *We bought a round dozen* **3** returning to the start ♦ *We made a round trip of 50 miles*

round ➤ *adverb*
1 in a circle or curve; by a longer route
♦ *Go round to the back of the house* **2** in every direction or to every person ♦ *Hand the cakes round* **3** in a new direction
♦ *Turn your chair round* **4** to someone's house or place of work ♦ *Come round at lunchtime*

round ➤ *preposition*
1 on all sides of ♦ *We'll put a fence round the field* **2** in a curve or circle about ♦ *The earth moves round the sun* **3** to every part of ♦ *Show them round the house*

round ➤ *noun* (*plural* **rounds**)
1 a round object **2** a whole slice of bread, or a sandwich made from two whole slices of bread **3** a series of visits or calls made by a doctor, postman, or other person
4 each stage in a competition ♦ *The winners go on to the next round* **5** a shot or series of shots from a gun; a piece of ammunition **6** a song in which people sing the same words but start at different times

round ➤ *verb* (**rounds, rounding, rounded**)
  1 to round something is to make it round
  2 to round is to become round **3** to round a place is to travel round it ♦ *A large car rounded the corner*
  to round a number down is to decrease it to the nearest lower number ♦ *123·4 may be rounded down to 123*
  to round a number up is to increase it to the nearest higher number ♦ *123·7 may be rounded up to 124*
  to round something off is to finish it
  to round up people or things is to gather them together

roundabout ➤ *noun* (*plural* **roundabouts**)
  1 a road junction at which traffic has to pass round a circular island
  2 a merry-go-round

roundabout ➤ *adjective*
  not using the shortest or most direct way ♦ *We went by a roundabout route*

rounders *noun*
  a game in which players try to hit a ball and run round a circuit

Roundhead *noun* (*plural* **Roundheads**)
  an opponent of King Charles I in the English Civil War of 1642–9

roundly *adverb*
  thoroughly or severely ♦ *We were roundly told off for being late*

rouse *verb* (**rouses, rousing, roused**)
  to rouse someone is to wake them up or make them excited

rout ➤ *verb* (**routs, routing, routed**) (*pronounced* rowt)
  to rout an enemy is to defeat them and chase them away

rout ➤ *noun* (*plural* **routs**) (*pronounced* rowt)
  a disorganized retreat after being defeated in a battle

route *noun* (*plural* **routes**) (*pronounced* root)
  the way you have to go to get to a place

routine *noun* (*plural* **routines**) (*pronounced* roo-**teen**)
  a regular way of doing things

rove *verb* (**roves, roving, roved**)
  to rove is to roam or wander
  rover *noun* someone who roves

row[1] *noun* (*plural* **rows**) (*rhymes with* go)
  a line of people or things

row[2] *verb* (**rows, rowing, rowed**) (*rhymes with* go)
  to row a boat is to use oars to make it move
  rower *noun* someone who rows a boat

row[3] *noun* (*plural* **rows**) (*rhymes with* cow)
  1 a great noise or disturbance **2** a quarrel; a noisy argument or scolding

rowdy *adjective* (**rowdier, rowdiest**)
  noisy and disorderly
  rowdily *adverb* in a rowdy way **rowdiness** *noun* being rowdy

rowing boat *noun* (*plural* **rowing boats**)
  a small boat that is moved forward by using oars

rowlock *noun* (*plural* **rowlocks**) (*pronounced* rol-ok)
  a device on the side of a boat to hold an oar in place

rowlock

royal *adjective*
  to do with a king or queen

royalty *noun*
  1 being royal **2** a royal person or royal people ♦ *We will be in the presence of royalty*

rub ➤ *verb* (**rubs, rubbing, rubbed**)
  to rub something is to move it backwards and forwards while pressing it on something else ♦ *He rubbed his hands together*
  to rub something off or **out** is to make it disappear by rubbing it

rub ➤ *noun* (*plural* **rubs**)
  a spell of rubbing ♦ *Give it a quick rub*

rubber *noun* (*plural* **rubbers**)
  1 a strong elastic substance used for making tyres, balls, hoses, and other things **2** a piece of rubber or soft plastic for rubbing out pencil marks
  rubbery *adjective* like rubber

rubbish *noun*
  1 things that are not wanted or needed
  2 nonsense

rubble *noun*
  broken pieces of brick or stone

ruby *noun* (*plural* **rubies**)
  a red jewel

rucksack *noun* (*plural* **rucksacks**)
  a bag with straps for carrying on the back

rudder *noun* (*plural* **rudders**)
a flat hinged device at the back of a ship or
aircraft, used for steering it

ruddy *adjective* (**ruddier, ruddiest**)
red and healthy-looking ♦ *He had a ruddy
face*

rude *adjective* (**ruder, rudest**)
1 impolite **2** indecent or improper
3 roughly made; crude
rudely *adverb* in a rude way **rudeness** *noun*
being rude

ruffian *noun* (*plural* **ruffians**)
a violent brutal person

ruffle *verb* (**ruffles, ruffling, ruffled**)
1 to ruffle something is to disturb its
smoothness ♦ *The bird ruffled its feathers*
2 to ruffle someone is to annoy them or
upset them

rug *noun* (*plural* **rugs**)
1 a thick piece of material that partly
covers a floor **2** a thick blanket

rugby or **rugby football** *noun*
a kind of football game using an oval ball
that players may kick or carry

rugged *adjective* (*pronounced* **rug**-id)
having a rough or uneven surface or
outline ♦ *His face was rugged* ♦ *It was a
rugged coast*

rugger *noun*
(*informal*) rugby football

ruin ➤ *verb* (**ruins, ruining, ruined**)
to ruin something is to spoil it or destroy it
completely

ruin ➤ *noun* (*plural* **ruins**)
1 a ruin is a building that has almost all
fallen down **2** ruin is the action of ruining
or destroying
ruinous *adjective* causing ruin

rule ➤ *noun* (*plural* **rules**)
1 a rule is something that people have to
obey **2** rule is ruling or governing ♦ *The
country used to be under French rule*
as a rule usually; normally

rule ➤ *verb* (**rules, ruling, ruled**)
1 to rule people is to govern them; to rule
is to be ruler **2** to rule something is to
make a decision ♦ *The referee ruled that it
was a foul* **3** to rule a line is to draw a
straight line with a ruler or other straight
edge

ruler *noun* (*plural* **rulers**)
1 someone who governs **2** a strip of wood,
plastic, or metal with straight edges, used
for measuring and drawing straight lines

ruling *noun* (*plural* **rulings**)
a judgement or decision ♦ *I will give my
ruling tomorrow*

rum *noun* (*plural* **rums**)
a strong alcoholic drink made from sugar
cane

rumble ➤ *verb* (**rumbles, rumbling, rumbled**)
to rumble is to make a deep heavy sound
like thunder

rumble ➤ *noun* (*plural* **rumbles**)
a rumbling sound

rummage *verb* (**rummages, rummaging,
rummaged**)
to rummage is to turn things over or move
them about while looking for something

rummy *noun*
a card game in which players try to form
sets or sequences of cards

rumour *noun* (*plural* **rumours**)
something that a lot of people are saying,
although it may not be true

rump *noun* (*plural* **rumps**)
the hind part of an animal

run ➤ *verb* (**runs, running, ran, run**)
1 to run is to move with quick steps and
with both feet off the ground for a time
2 to run is also to move or go or travel
♦ *Tears ran down his cheeks* **3** something
like a container or a tap runs when liquid
flows from it **4** an engine or machine runs
when it is working or functioning ♦ *The
engine was running smoothly* **5** to run
something is to manage it or organize it
♦ *She runs a corner shop* **6** to run
someone somewhere is to give them a lift
there
to run a risk is to take a chance
to run away is to leave a place quickly or
secretly
to run into someone is to meet them
unexpectedly
to run out of something is to have used up a
supply of it
to run someone over is to knock them down
with a car or bicycle

run ➤ *noun* (*plural* **runs**)
1 a spell of running ♦ *Go for a run* **2** a
point scored in cricket or baseball **3** a
series of damaged stitches in a pair of
tights or other piece of clothing **4** a
continuous series of events ♦ *They've had
a run of good luck* **5** a place with a fence
round it for keeping animals
on the run running away, especially from
the police

runaway *noun* (*plural* **runaways**)
someone who has run away

rung[1] *noun* (*plural* **rungs**)
each of the short crossbars on a ladder

rung[2] past participle of **ring**[2] *verb*

runner *noun* (*plural* **runners**)
1 a person or animal that runs in a race
2 the part of a sledge that slides along the ground

runner bean *noun* (*plural* **runner beans**)
a kind of climbing bean

runner-up *noun* (*plural* **runners-up**)
someone who comes second in a race or competition

runny *adjective* (**runnier, runniest**)
flowing or moving like liquid

runway *noun* (*plural* **runways**)
a long strip with a hard surface for aircraft to take off and land

rural *adjective*
to do with the countryside; in the country

rush¹ ➤ *verb* (**rushes, rushing, rushed**)
1 to rush is to hurry 2 to rush someone is to attack or capture them by surprise

rush ➤ *noun*
a rush is a hurry

rush² *noun* (*plural* **rushes**)
a plant with a thin stem that grows in wet or marshy places

rush hour *noun*
the rush hour is the time when traffic is busiest

rusk *noun* (*plural* **rusks**)
a kind of hard dry biscuit for babies to chew

rust ➤ *noun*
a red or brown substance formed on metal that is exposed to air and dampness

rust ➤ *verb* (**rusts, rusting, rusted**)
1 to rust metal is to cause rust to form on it 2 to rust is to develop rust

rustic *adjective*
rural

rustle *verb* (**rustles, rustling, rustled**)
1 to rustle is to make a gentle sound like dry leaves being blown by the wind 2 to rustle horses or cattle is to steal them
to rustle something up (*informal*) is to collect it or provide it quickly
rustler *noun* someone who rustles horses or cattle

rusty *adjective* (**rustier, rustiest**)
1 coated with rust 2 weak from lack of practice ♦ *My French is a bit rusty*

rut *noun* (*plural* **ruts**)
a deep groove made by wheels in soft ground
in a rut having a dull life with no changes
rutted *adjective* marked with ruts

ruthless *adjective*
pitiless; merciless or cruel
ruthlessly *adverb* in a ruthless way
ruthlessness *noun* being ruthless

rye *noun*
a cereal used to make bread and biscuits

Ss

sabbath *noun* (*plural* **sabbaths**)
a weekly day for rest and prayer, Saturday for Jews, Sunday for Christians

sabotage ➤ *noun* (*pronounced* **sab**-o-tah*zh*)
deliberate damage or disruption to machinery or equipment

sabotage ➤ *verb* (**sabotages, sabotaging, sabotaged**)
to sabotage something is to damage it with sabotage
saboteur *noun* someone who commits sabotage

sac *noun* (*plural* **sacs**)
any bag-like part of an animal or plant

saccharin *noun* (*pronounced* **sak**-a-rin)
a very sweet substance used as a substitute for sugar

sachet *noun* (*plural* **sachets**) (*pronounced* **sash**-ay)
a small sealed packet of something such as shampoo

sack¹ ➤ *noun* (*plural* **sacks**) (*pronounced* **sash**-ay)
a large bag made of strong material
the sack (*informal*) being dismissed from a job ♦ *He got the sack*

sack ➤ *verb* (**sacks, sacking, sacked**)
(*informal*) to sack someone is to dismiss them from their job

sack² *verb* (**sacks, sacking, sacked**)
to sack a place is to plunder and destroy it in war

sacred *adjective*
to do with God or a god; holy

sacrifice ➤ *noun* (*plural* **sacrifices**)
  1 giving or doing something that you think will please a god 2 giving up a thing that you value so that something good may happen 3 something given or done to please a god or to make something good happen
  sacrificial *adjective* to do with a sacrifice
sacrifice ➤ *verb* (**sacrifices, sacrificing, sacrificed**)
  to sacrifice something is to give it as a sacrifice, or to do without it
sad *adjective* (**sadder, saddest**)
  unhappy; showing sorrow or causing it
  sadly *adverb* in a sad way **sadness** *noun* being sad
sadden *verb* (**saddens, saddening, saddened**)
  to sadden someone is to make them sad or unhappy
saddle ➤ *noun* (*plural* **saddles**)
  1 a seat for putting on the back of a horse or other animal 2 the seat of a bicycle
saddle ➤ *verb* (**saddles, saddling, saddled**)
  to saddle an animal is to put a saddle on its back
  to be saddled with something is to have it as a burden or problem
sadist *noun* (*plural* **sadists**) (*pronounced* say-dist)
  someone who enjoys hurting other people
  sadism *noun* being a sadist **sadistic** *adjective* enjoying hurting other people
safari *noun* (*plural* **safaris**) (*pronounced* sa-far-i)
  an expedition to see wild animals or hunt them
safari park *noun* (*plural* **safari parks**)
  a park where wild animals are kept in large enclosures for visitors to see
safe ➤ *adjective* (**safer, safest**)
  1 free from danger; protected 2 not causing danger ♦ *Drive at a safe speed*
  safely *adverb* in a safe way
safe ➤ *noun* (*plural* **safes**)
  a strong cupboard or box in which valuable things can be locked safely
safeguard *noun* (*plural* **safeguards**)
  a protection
safety *noun*
  being safe; protection
safety belt *noun* (*plural* **safety belts**)
  a belt to hold someone securely in a seat

safety pin *noun* (*plural* **safety pins**)
  a curved pin made with a clip to protect the point
sag *verb* (**sags, sagging, sagged**)
  to sag is to sink slightly in the middle because something heavy is pressing on it
saga *noun* (*plural* **sagas**)
  a long story with many adventures
sago *noun*
  a starchy white food used in puddings
said past tense and past participle of **say** *verb*
sail ➤ *noun* (*plural* **sails**)
  1 a large piece of strong cloth attached to a mast to make a boat move 2 a short voyage 3 an arm of a windmill
  to set sail is to start on a voyage in a ship
sail ➤ *verb* (**sails, sailing, sailed**)
  1 to sail is to travel in a ship 2 to sail a ship or boat is to control it 3 to sail is to be moved along by means of a sail or sails
  ♦ *This boat sails beautifully*
sailboard *noun* (*plural* **sailboards**)
  a flat board with a mast and sail, used for windsurfing
sailor *noun* (*plural* **sailors**)
  1 a member of a ship's crew 2 someone who sails
saint *noun* (*plural* **saints**)
  a holy or very good person
  saintly *adjective* holy, like a saint
sake *noun*
  for the sake of something in order to do it or get it ♦ *He'll do anything for the sake of money*
  for someone's sake so as to help them or please them ♦ *She went to great trouble for his sake*
salaam *interjection*
  a word used by Muslims to greet someone
salad *noun* (*plural* **salads**)
  a mixture of vegetables eaten cold and often raw
salami *noun* (*plural* **salamis**)
  a kind of strong spicy sausage
salary *noun* (*plural* **salaries**)
  a regular wage, usually paid every month
sale *noun* (*plural* **sales**)
  1 the selling of something 2 a time when things are sold at reduced prices
  for sale or **on sale** able to be bought

salesperson *noun* (*plural* **salespersons**)
someone whose job is to sell things

saline *adjective*
containing salt

saliva *noun* (*pronounced* sa-ly-va)
the natural liquid in a person's or animal's mouth

sally *verb* (**sallies, sallying, sallied**)
to sally forth or **sally out** is to rush forward or rush ahead

salmon *noun* (*plural* **salmon**)
a large fish with pink flesh, used for food

salon *noun* (*plural* **salons**)
a room or shop where a hairdresser or a beauty specialist works

saloon *noun* (*plural* **saloons**)
1 a motor car with a hard roof **2** a bar in a public house

salt ➤ *noun*
the white substance that gives sea water its taste and is used for flavouring food
salty *adjective* tasting of salt

salt ➤ *verb* (**salts, salting, salted**)
to salt food is to use salt to flavour or preserve it

salute ➤ *verb* (**salutes, saluting, saluted**)
to salute is to raise your hand to your forehead as a sign of respect or greeting

salute ➤ *noun* (*plural* **salutes**)
1 the act of saluting **2** the firing of guns as a sign of greeting or respect

salvage *verb* (**salvages, salvaging, salvaged**)
to salvage something such as a damaged ship is to save or rescue it or parts of it

salvation *noun*
saving someone or something

same *adjective*
not different; exactly equal or alike ♦ *We are the same age*

samosa *noun* (*plural* **samosas**)
a small case of crisp pastry filled with a mixture of spicy meat or vegetables

sample ➤ *noun* (*plural* **samples**)
a small amount that shows what something is like

sample ➤ *verb* (**samples, sampling, sampled**)
1 to sample something is to take a sample of it ♦ *Scientists sampled the lake water*
2 to sample something is also to try part of it ♦ *She sampled the cake*

sanctuary *noun* (*plural* **sanctuaries**)
a safe place ♦ *We visited a bird sanctuary*

sand ➤ *noun*
the tiny grains of rock that you find on beaches and in deserts

sand ➤ *verb* (**sands, sanding, sanded**)
to sand a surface is to smooth or polish it with sandpaper or rough material

sander *noun* a machine for sanding surfaces

sandal *noun* (*plural* **sandals**)
a lightweight shoe with straps that go round your foot

sandbag *noun* (*plural* **sandbags**)
a bag filled with sand, used to build defences

sandpaper *noun*
strong paper coated with hard grains, rubbed on rough surfaces to make them smooth

sands *plural noun*
a beach or sandy area

sandstone *noun*
rock made of compressed sand

sandwich *noun* (*plural* **sandwiches**)
slices of bread with jam, meat, cheese, or some other filling between them

sandy *adjective* (**sandier, sandiest**)
1 made of sand; covered with sand
2 yellowish-red ♦ *She has sandy hair*

sane *adjective* (**saner, sanest**)
having a healthy mind; not mad
sanely *adverb* in a sane way

sang past tense of **sing**

sanitary *adjective*
free from germs and dirt; hygienic

sanitary towel *noun* (*plural* **sanitary towels**)
an absorbent pad used by a woman during menstruation

sanitation *noun*
arrangements for drainage and the disposal of sewage

sanity *noun*
being sane

sank past tense of **sink** *verb*

Sanskrit *noun*
an ancient language of India

sap ➤ *noun*
the juice inside a tree or plant

sap ➤ *verb* (**saps, sapping, sapped**)
to sap someone's strength or energy is to use it up or weaken it

sapling *noun* (*plural* **saplings**)
a young tree

sapphire *noun* (*plural* **sapphires**)
a bright blue jewel

sarcasm *noun*
mocking someone or something, especially by saying the opposite of what you mean ♦ *Saying 'Great shot!' when Ben missed the ball was a piece of sarcasm*
sarcastic *adjective* containing sarcasm
sarcastically *adverb* in a sarcastic way

sardine *noun* (*plural* **sardines**)
a small sea fish, usually sold packed tightly in tins

sari *noun* (*plural* **saris**) (*pronounced* sar-i)
a long length of cloth worn as a dress, especially by Indian women and girls

sash *noun* (*plural* **sashes**)
a strip of cloth worn round the waist or over one shoulder

sash window *noun* (*plural* **sash windows**)
a window that slides up and down

sat past tense and past participle of **sit**

satchel *noun* (*plural* **satchels**)
a bag worn over your shoulder or on your back, especially for carrying books to and from school

satellite *noun* (*plural* **satellites**)
a moon or a spacecraft that moves in an orbit round a planet

satellite dish *noun* (*plural* **satellite dishes**)
a dish-shaped aerial for receiving television signals sent by satellite

satin *noun*
a silky material that is shiny on one side

satire *noun* (*plural* **satires**)
1 using humour or exaggeration to show what is bad or weak about a person or thing, especially the government **2** a play or piece of writing that does this
satirical *adjective* to do with satire **satirist** *noun* someone who writes satire

satisfaction *noun*
1 the feeling of being satisfied **2** giving someone what they need or want

satisfactory *adjective*
good enough; sufficient
satisfactorily *adverb* in a satisfactory way

satisfy *verb* (**satisfies, satisfying, satisfied**)
1 to satisfy someone is to give them what they need or want **2** to be satisfied is to be sure of something ♦ *I am satisfied that you have done your best*

saturate *verb* (**saturates, saturating, saturated**)
1 to saturate something is to soak it with liquid ♦ *My clothes are saturated with rain* **2** to saturate a place is to make it take in as much as possible or too much of something ♦ *The town is saturated with tourists in the summer*

saturation *noun* being saturated

Saturday *noun* (*plural* **Saturdays**)
the seventh day of the week

sauce *noun* (*plural* **sauces**)
1 a thick liquid served with food to add flavour **2** (*informal*) impudence; being cheeky

saucepan *noun* (*plural* **saucepans**)
a metal cooking pan with a long handle

saucer *noun* (*plural* **saucers**)
a small curved plate on which a cup is placed

saucy *adjective* (**saucier, sauciest**)
rude or cheeky

sauna *noun* (*plural* **saunas**) (*pronounced* saw-na or sow-na)
a room or compartment filled with steam, used as a kind of bath

saunter *verb* (**saunters, sauntering, sauntered**)
to saunter is to walk about in a leisurely way

sausage *noun* (*plural* **sausages**)
a tube of edible skin or plastic stuffed with minced meat and other ingredients

sausage roll *noun* (*plural* **sausage rolls**)
a small short roll of pastry filled with meat

savage ➤ *adjective*
wild and fierce; cruel
savagely *adverb* in a savage way **savagery** *noun* being savage

savage ➤ *verb* (**savages, savaging, savaged**)
to savage someone is to attack them and bite or scratch them fiercely

savannah *noun* (*plural* **savannahs**) (*pronounced* sa-**van**-a)
a grassy plain in a hot country, with few trees

save *verb* (**saves, saving, saved**)
1 to save someone or something is to free them from danger or harm **2** to save something, especially money, is to keep it so that it can be used later **3** to save computer data is to instruct the computer to keep it on its hard disk **4** in football, to save a ball is to stop it going into your goal
saver *noun* someone who saves something, especially money

savings *plural noun*
money saved

saviour *noun* (*plural* **saviours**)
a person who saves someone
our Saviour or **the Saviour** a name for Jesus
Christ

savoury *adjective*
tasty but not sweet

saw¹ ➤ *noun* (*plural* **saws**)
a tool with sharp teeth for cutting wood or
other hard materials

saw ➤ *verb* (**saws, sawing, sawed, sawn** or
sawed)
to saw something is to cut it with a saw

saw² past tense of **see**

sawdust *noun*
powder that comes from wood when it is
cut with a saw

saxophone *noun* (*plural* **saxophones**)
a wind instrument with a tube that curves
upward and a reed in the mouthpiece

say ➤ *verb* (**says, saying, said**)
to say something is to make words with
your voice

say ➤ *noun*
someone's right to speak or to give an
opinion

saying *noun* (*plural* **sayings**)
a well-known phrase or proverb

scab *noun* (*plural* **scabs**)
a hard crust that forms over a cut or graze
while it is healing

scabbard *noun* (*plural* **scabbards**)
a cover for a sword or dagger

scaffold *noun* (*plural* **scaffolds**)
a platform on which criminals are
executed

scaffolding *noun*
a structure of poles and planks for workers
to stand on when building or repairing a
house

scald *verb* (**scalds, scalding, scalded**)
1 to scald your skin is to burn it with very
hot liquid or steam **2** to scald something
is to clean it with boiling water

scale¹ ➤ *noun* (*plural* **scales**)
1 a series of units or marks for measuring
something ♦ *This ruler has one scale in
centimetres and another in inches* **2** a
series of musical notes going up or down in
a fixed pattern **3** a proportion or ratio
♦ *The scale of this map is one inch to the
mile* **4** the relative size or importance of
something ♦ *They organize picnics on a
large scale*

scale ➤ *verb* (**scales, scaling, scaled**)
to scale something is to climb up it

scale² *noun* (*plural* **scales**)
1 one of the thin overlapping parts on the
outside of fish, snakes, and other animals
2 the coating that forms on the inside of
kettles and pans
scaly *adjective* covered in scales

scales *plural noun*
a device for weighing things

scalp ➤ *noun* (*plural* **scalps**)
the skin on top of the head

scalp ➤ *verb* (**scalps, scalping, scalped**)
to scalp someone is to cut off their scalp

scamper *verb* (**scampers, scampering,
scampered**)
to scamper is to run quickly ♦ *The rabbits
scampered for safety*

scampi *plural noun*
large prawns

scan ➤ *verb* (**scans, scanning, scanned**)
1 to scan something is to look at every
part of it **2** to scan a large area is to look
over it quickly **3** to scan poetry is to work
out its rhythm; poetry scans when it has a
fixed rhythm **4** to scan an area, or a part
of the body, is to sweep a radar or
electronic beam over it in order to find
something

scan ➤ *noun* (*plural* **scans**)
an act of scanning

scandal *noun* (*plural* **scandals**)
1 a scandal is a shameful or disgraceful
action **2** scandal is gossip that damages
someone's reputation
scandalous *adjective* to do with scandal;
shameful

Scandinavian *adjective*
to do with Scandinavia (Norway, Sweden,
and Denmark, and sometimes Finland
and Iceland)

scanner *noun* (*plural* **scanners**)
1 a machine used to examine part of the
body, using an electronic beam **2** a
machine that converts print and pictures
into data that can be read by a computer

scanty *adjective* (**scantier, scantiest**)
hardly big enough; small
scantily *adverb* without very much

scapegoat *noun* (*plural* **scapegoats**)
someone who is blamed or punished for other people's mistakes or wrongs

scar ➤ *noun* (*plural* **scars**)
a mark left on your skin by a cut or burn after it has healed

scar ➤ *verb* (**scars, scarring, scarred**)
to scar skin is to make a scar or scars on it

scarce *adjective* (**scarcer, scarcest**)
not enough to supply people ♦ *Wheat was scarce because of the bad harvest*
to make yourself scarce (*informal*) is to go away or keep out of the way
scarcity *noun* a shortage

scarcely *adverb*
hardly; only just ♦ *She could scarcely walk*

scare ➤ *verb* (**scares, scaring, scared**)
to scare someone is to frighten them

scare ➤ *noun* (*plural* **scares**)
a scare is a fright ♦ *You gave me quite a scare*

scarecrow *noun* (*plural* **scarecrows**)
a figure of a person dressed in old clothes, set up to frighten birds away from crops

scarf *noun* (*plural* **scarves**)
a strip of material worn round the neck or head

scarlet *adjective*
bright red

scary *adjective* (**scarier, scariest**)
(*informal*) frightening

scatter *verb* (**scatters, scattering, scattered**)
1 to scatter things is to throw them in all directions **2** to scatter is to move quickly in all directions ♦ *The crowd scattered when the police arrived*

scene *noun* (*plural* **scenes**)
1 the place where something happens ♦ *Here is the scene of the crime* **2** a part of a play or film **3** a view someone sees **4** an angry or noisy outburst ♦ *They made a scene about the money*

scenery *noun*
1 the natural features of an area ♦ *We were admiring the scenery* **2** things put on a stage to make it look like a place

scent ➤ *noun* (*plural* **scents**) (*pronounced* sent)
1 a perfume **2** an animal's smell, that other animals can follow
scented *adjective* having a perfume

scent ➤ *verb* (**scents, scenting, scented**)
to scent something is to discover it by its scent

sceptic *noun* (*plural* **sceptics**) (*pronounced* skep-tik)
someone who is sceptical

sceptical *adjective* (*pronounced* skep-tik-al)
not believing things easily or readily
scepticism *noun* being sceptical

schedule *noun* (*plural* **schedules**) (*pronounced* shed-yool)
a timetable of things to be done
on schedule on time; not late

scheme ➤ *noun* (*plural* **schemes**)
a plan of what to do

scheme ➤ *verb* (**schemes, scheming, schemed**)
to scheme is to make secret plans
schemer *noun* someone who schemes

scholar *noun* (*plural* **scholars**)
1 someone who studies a subject thoroughly **2** someone who has been given a scholarship

scholarly *adjective*
showing knowledge and learning

scholarship *noun* (*plural* **scholarships**)
1 a scholarship is a grant of money given to someone for their education **2** scholarship is knowledge and learning

school[1] *noun* (*plural* **schools**)
1 a place where children go to be taught **2** the children who go there ♦ *The whole school had a holiday*

school[2] *noun* (*plural* **schools**)
a group of whales or fish

schoolchild *noun* (*plural* **schoolchildren**)
a child who goes to school

schoolteacher *noun* (*plural* **schoolteachers**)
a teacher at a school

schooner *noun* (*plural* **schooners**) (*pronounced* skoo-ner)
a sailing ship with two or more masts

science *noun*
the study of objects and happenings in the world that can be observed and tested

science fiction *noun*
stories about imaginary worlds, especially in space and in the future

scientific *adjective*
1 to do with science **2** studying things carefully and logically

scientist *noun* (*plural* **scientists**)
someone who studies science or is an expert in science

scissors *plural noun*
a cutting device made of two movable
blades joined together

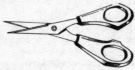

scoff *verb* (**scoffs, scoffing, scoffed**)
to scoff at someone or something is to
make fun of them

scold *verb* (**scolds, scolding, scolded**)
to scold someone is to tell them off harshly

scone *noun* (*plural* **scones**) (*pronounced*
skon or skohn)
a small plain cake, usually eaten with
butter and jam

scoop ➤ *noun* (*plural* **scoops**)
1 a deep spoon for serving soft food such as
ice cream or mashed potato 2 a deep
shovel 3 (*informal*) an important piece of
news that only one newspaper prints

scoop ➤ *verb* (**scoops, scooping, scooped**)
to scoop something, or to scoop it out, is to
take it out with a scoop

scooter *noun* (*plural* **scooters**)
1 a kind of motor cycle with small wheels
2 a toy with two wheels and a narrow
platform for riding on

scope *noun*
1 opportunity or possibility for something
♦ *There is scope for improvement* 2 the
range or extent of something ♦ *Chemistry
is outside the scope of the syllabus for this
year*

scorch *verb* (**scorches, scorching, scorched**)
to scorch something is to make it go brown
by slightly burning it

scorching *adjective*
very hot

score ➤ *noun* (*plural* **scores**)
1 the number of points or goals made in a
game 2 (*old use*) a score is twenty ♦ *He
reached the age of four-score (=80) years*

score ➤ *verb* (**scores, scoring, scored**)
1 to score a goal or point in a game is to get
it 2 to score is to keep a count of the score in
a game 3 to score a surface is to scratch it
scorer *noun* someone who scores a goal or
point

scorn ➤ *noun*
treating a person or thing with contempt

scorn ➤ *verb* (**scorns, scorning, scorned**)
to scorn someone or something is to have
contempt for them

scorpion *noun* (*plural* **scorpions**)
an animal related to the spider, with
pincers and a poisonous sting in its curved
tail

Scot *noun* (*plural* **Scots**)
a person from Scotland

Scotch *adjective*
Scottish

Scotch terrier *noun* (*plural* **Scotch terriers**)
a small terrier with rough hair

Scottish *adjective*
to do with Scotland

scoundrel *noun* (*plural* **scoundrels**)
a wicked or dishonest person

scour *verb* (**scours, scouring, scoured**)
1 to scour something is to rub it with
something hard until it is clean and bright
2 to scour an area is to search it
thoroughly

Scout *noun* (*plural* **Scouts**)
a member of the Scout Association

scout *noun* (*plural* **scouts**)
someone sent out to collect information

scowl *verb* (**scowls, scowling, scowled**)
to scowl is to look bad-tempered

scramble ➤ *verb* (**scrambles, scrambling,
scrambled**)
1 to scramble is to move quickly and
awkwardly ♦ *We scrambled up the steep
slope* 2 to scramble eggs is to cook them by
mixing them and heating them in a pan
3 to scramble for something is to struggle
to do it or get it

scramble ➤ *noun* (*plural* **scrambles**)
1 a climb or walk over rough ground 2 a
struggle to get something ♦ *There was a
scramble for the best seats* 3 a motorcycle
race across rough country

scrap [1] ➤ *noun* (*plural* **scraps**)
1 a scrap is a small piece of something
2 scrap is rubbish, especially unwanted
metal

scrap ➤ *verb* (**scraps, scrapping, scrapped**)
to scrap something is to get rid of it when
you do not want it

scrap² ➤ *noun* (*plural* **scraps**)
(*informal*) a fight

scrap ➤ *verb* (**scraps, scrapping, scrapped**)
to scrap is to fight or quarrel

scrape ➤ *verb* (**scrapes, scraping, scraped**)
1 to scrape something is to rub it with
something rough, hard, or sharp 2 to
scrape by or past or through is to move
along or get past with difficulty 3 to
scrape something together is to collect it
with difficulty ♦ *They scraped together
enough money for a holiday*
scraper *noun* a device for scraping
something clean

scrape ➤ *noun* (*plural* **scrapes**)
1 a scraping movement or sound 2 a
mark made by scraping something
3 (*informal*) an awkward situation ♦ *They
were in a bit of a scrape*

scrappy *adjective* (**scrappier, scrappiest**)
1 made of scraps or bits; not complete
2 done carelessly or untidily

scratch ➤ *verb* (**scratches, scratching, scratched**)
1 to scratch a surface is to damage it by
rubbing something sharp over it 2 to
scratch the skin is to rub it with the
fingers because it itches

scratch ➤ *noun* (*plural* **scratches**)
1 a mark made by scratching 2 the action
of scratching
to start from scratch is to begin at the very
beginning
up to scratch up to the proper standard

scrawl ➤ *noun* (*plural* **scrawls**)
a piece of untidy writing

scrawl ➤ *verb* (**scrawls, scrawling, scrawled**)
to scrawl something is to write it in a
hurried or careless way

scream ➤ *noun* (*plural* **screams**)
1 a loud cry of pain or fear or anger
2 (*informal*) something very amusing

scream ➤ *verb* (**screams, screaming, screamed**)
to scream is to give a scream

screech ➤ *noun* (*plural* **screeches**)
a harsh high-pitched sound

screech ➤ *verb* (**screeches, screeching, screeched**)
to screech is to make a screech

screen ➤ *noun* (*plural* **screens**)
1 a surface on which films or television
programmes or computer data are shown
2 a movable panel used to hide or protect
something 3 a windscreen

screen ➤ *verb* (**screens, screening, screened**)
1 to screen a film or television programme
is to show it 2 to screen something is to
hide it or protect it with a screen 3 to
screen people is to test them to find out if
they have a disease

screw ➤ *noun* (*plural* **screws**)
1 a metal pin with a spiral ridge round it,
which holds things by being twisted into
them 2 a propeller

screw ➤ *verb* (**screws, screwing, screwed**)
1 to screw something is to fix it with
screws 2 to screw something in or on is to
fit it by turning it ♦ *Screw the lid on to the
jar* ♦ *I screwed in the light-bulb*

screwdriver *noun* (*plural* **screwdrivers**)
a tool for putting in or taking out a screw

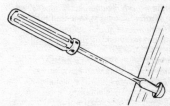

scribble *verb* (**scribbles, scribbling, scribbled**)
to scribble is to write untidily or
carelessly, or to make meaningless marks
scribbler *noun* someone who scribbles

script *noun* (*plural* **scripts**)
1 the words of a play or broadcast
2 handwriting; something handwritten

scripture *noun* (*plural* **scriptures**)
a sacred book, especially the Bible

scroll *noun* (*plural* **scrolls**)
a roll of paper or parchment with writing
on it

scrotum *noun* (*plural* **scrotums** or **scrota**)
(*pronounced* **skroh**-tum)
the pouch of skin behind the penis,
containing the testicles

scrounge *verb* (**scrounges, scrounging, scrounged**)
(*informal*) to scrounge something is to get
it without paying for it ♦ *He scrounged a
meal from us*
scrounger *noun* someone who scrounges

scrub¹ ➤ *verb* (**scrubs, scrubbing, scrubbed**)
1 to scrub something is to rub it with a
hard brush 2 (*slang*) to scrub a meeting or
performance is to cancel it

scrub ➤ *noun*
the action of scrubbing

scrub² *noun*
low trees and bushes, or land covered with
them

scruffy *adjective* (**scruffier, scruffiest**)
shabby and untidy

scrum or **scrummage** *noun* (*plural* **scrums** or **scrummages**)
(*in Rugby Football*) a group of players from each side who push against each other and try to win the ball with their feet

scrutinize *verb* (**scrutinizes, scrutinizing, scrutinized**)
to scrutinize something is to examine it or look at it closely
scrutiny *noun* scrutinizing something

scuba diving *noun*
swimming underwater, breathing air from a supply carried on your back

scuffle ➤ *noun* (*plural* **scuffles**)
a confused struggle or fight

scuffle ➤ *verb* (**scuffles, scuffling, scuffled**)
to scuffle is to fight in a confused way

scullery *noun* (*plural* **sculleries**)
a room for washing dishes and other kitchen work

sculptor *noun* (*plural* **sculptors**)
someone who makes sculptures

sculpture *noun* (*plural* **sculptures**)
1 a sculpture is something carved or shaped out of a hard material such as stone, clay, or metal **2** sculpture is the art or work of a sculptor

scum *noun*
1 froth or dirt on the top of a liquid **2** (*informal and offensive*) people who are thought to be worthless

scurry *verb* (**scurries, scurrying, scurried**)
to scurry is to run or hurry with short steps

scurvy *noun*
a disease caused by lack of fresh fruit and vegetables

scuttle¹ *noun* (*plural* **scuttles**)
a container for coal, kept by a fireplace

scuttle² *verb* (**scuttles, scuttling, scuttled**)
to scuttle a ship is to sink it deliberately

scuttle³ *verb* (**scuttles, scuttling, scuttled**)
to scuttle is to run with short quick steps

scythe *noun* (*plural* **scythes**)
a tool with a long curved blade for cutting grass or corn

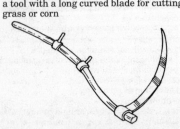

sea *noun* (*plural* **seas**)
1 the salt water that covers most of the earth's surface **2** a large lake or area of water, such as the Mediterranean Sea or the Sea of Galilee **3** a large area of something ♦ *Across the table we saw a sea of faces*
at sea 1 on the sea **2** unable to understand something or cope with it ♦ *He's completely at sea in his new job*

seabed *noun*
the bottom of the sea

seafaring *adjective* and *noun*
travelling or working on the sea
seafarer *noun* someone who works at sea

seafood *noun*
fish or shellfish from the sea eaten as food

seagull *noun* (*plural* **seagulls**)
a sea bird with long wings

sea horse *noun* (*plural* **sea horses**)
a small fish that swims upright, with a head rather like a horse's head

seal¹ *noun* (*plural* **seals**)
a furry sea animal that breeds on land

seal² ➤ *noun* (*plural* **seals**)
1 a design pressed into a soft substance such as wax or lead **2** something designed to close an opening and stop air or liquid getting in or out **3** a small decorative sticker

seal ➤ *verb* (**seals, sealing, sealed**)
to seal something is to close it by sticking two parts together ♦ *He sealed the envelope*

sea level *noun*
the level of the sea halfway between high and low tide ♦ *The mountain rises 1,000 metres above sea level*

sea lion *noun* (*plural* **sea lions**)
a large kind of seal. The male has a kind of mane

seam *noun* (*plural* **seams**)
1 the line where two edges of cloth or wood join together 2 a layer of coal in the ground

seaman *noun* (*plural* **seamen**)
a sailor

seamanship *noun*
skill in seafaring

seaplane *noun* (*plural* **seaplanes**)
an aeroplane that can land on water and take off from water

seaport *noun* (*plural* **seaports**)
a port on the coast

search ≻ *verb* (**searches, searching, searched**)
1 to search for something or someone is to look very carefully for them 2 to search a person or place is to look very carefully for something they may have
searcher *noun* someone who searches for something or someone

search ≻ *noun* (*plural* **searches**)
a very careful look for someone or something

searching *adjective*
thorough ♦ *They asked some searching questions*

searchlight *noun* (*plural* **searchlights**)
a light with a strong beam that can be turned in any direction

search party *noun* (*plural* **search parties**)
a group of people organized to look for someone or something

seashore *noun*
the land close to the sea

seasick *adjective*
sick because of the movement of a ship
seasickness *noun* feeling seasick

seaside *noun*
a place by the sea where people go for holidays

season ≻ *noun* (*plural* **seasons**)
1 one of the four main parts of the year: spring, summer, autumn, and winter
2 the time of year when a sport or other activity happens ♦ *When does the football season start?*

season ≻ *verb* (**seasons, seasoning, seasoned**)
to season food is to put salt, pepper, or other strong-tasting things on it to flavour it

seasonal *adjective*
happening only at certain times of the year ♦ *Fruit-picking is seasonal work*

seasoning *noun* (*plural* **seasonings**)
something strong-tasting like salt and pepper, used to season food

season ticket *noun* (*plural* **season tickets**)
a ticket that can be used as often as you like for a certain period

seat ≻ *noun* (*plural* **seats**)
1 a piece of furniture for sitting on 2 a place in parliament or on a council or a board of a business 3 the place where something is located ♦ *London is the seat of government* 4 a person's bottom

seat ≻ *verb* (**seats, seating, seated**)
to seat people is to have seats for them
♦ *The theatre seats 3,000*

seat belt *noun* (*plural* **seat belts**)
a strap to hold a person securely in the seat of a vehicle or aircraft

seaward or **seawards** *adverb*
towards the sea

seaweed *noun* (*plural* **seaweeds**)
plants that grow in the sea

secateurs *plural noun* (*pronounced* **sek-a-terz**)
clippers used for pruning plants

secluded *adjective*
away from large numbers of people; not crowded ♦ *They found a secluded beach for their picnic*
seclusion *noun* being secluded

second ≻ *adjective* and *noun*
the next after the first
to have second thoughts is to wonder whether your decision was really right
secondly *adverb* in the second place; as the second one

second ≻ *noun* (*plural* **seconds**)
1 a person or thing that is second
2 someone who helps a fighter in a boxing match or duel 3 something that is not of the best quality 4 a very short period of time, one-sixtieth of a minute

second ≻ *verb* (**seconds, seconding, seconded**)
1 to second a fighter is to act as second
2 to second a proposal or motion is to support it formally

secondary *adjective*
coming second; not original or essential
♦ *This is of secondary importance*

secondary colour *noun* (*plural* **secondary colours**)
a colour made by mixing two primary colours

secondary school *noun* (*plural* **secondary schools**)
a school for children more than about 11 years old

second-hand *adjective* and *adverb*
1 bought or used after someone else has used it ♦ *I can only afford a second-hand car* 2 that sells used goods ♦ *She runs a second-hand shop*

second nature *noun*
behaviour that has become a habit
♦ *Lying is second nature to him*

secrecy *noun*
being secret

secret ➤ *adjective*
1 that must not be told or shown to other people 2 that is not known by everyone
secretly *adverb* without telling other people

secret ➤ *noun* (*plural* **secrets**)
something that is secret
in secret secretly

secretary *noun* (*plural* **secretaries**)
(*pronounced* **sek**-re-tri)
1 someone whose job is to type letters, answer the telephone, and make business arrangements for a person or organization 2 the chief assistant of a government minister

secrete *verb* (**secretes, secreting, secreted**)
(*pronounced* si-**kreet**)
1 to secrete something is to hide it carefully 2 to secrete a substance in the body is to release it ◆ *Saliva is secreted in the mouth*
secretion *noun* secreting something

secretive *adjective* (*pronounced* **seek**-rit-iv)
liking or trying to keep things secret
secretively *adverb* in a secretive way
secretiveness *noun* being secretive

secret service *noun*
a government department in charge of spies and espionage

sect *noun* (*plural* **sects**)
a group of people who have special or unusual religious opinions or beliefs

section *noun* (*plural* **sections**)
a part of something
sectional *adjective* made in sections

sector *noun* (*plural* **sectors**)
part of an area or activity

secure ➤ *adjective* (**securer, securest**)
1 firm and safe ◆ *Is that ladder secure?*
2 not likely to be lost ◆ *I need a secure job*
3 made safe or protected from attack
◆ *Check that all the doors and windows are secure*
securely *adverb* in a secure way

secure ➤ *verb* (**secures, securing, secured**)
1 to secure something is to make it secure
2 to secure something is also to get hold of it ◆ *She secured two tickets for the show*

security *noun*
1 being secure or safe 2 measures taken to prevent theft or spying 3 something offered as a guarantee that a loan will be repaid

sedate *adjective* (*pronounced* si-**dayt**)
calm and dignified
sedately *adverb* in a sedate way

sedative *noun* (*plural* **sedatives**)
(*pronounced* **sed**-a-tiv)
a medicine that makes a person calm
sedation *noun* being sedated

sediment *noun*
solid matter that floats in liquid or sinks to the bottom of it

sedimentary *adjective* (*pronounced* sed-i-**ment**-er-i)
sedimentary rocks are formed from particles that have settled on a surface

see *verb* (**sees, seeing, saw, seen**)
1 to see something or someone is to use your eyes to notice them or be aware of them 2 to see someone is to meet or visit them ◆ *See me in my office* 3 to see something is to understand it ◆ *She saw what I meant* 4 to see someone as something is to imagine them being it ◆ *Can you see yourself as a teacher?* 5 to see that something happens is to make sure of it ◆ *See that the windows are shut*
6 to see someone somewhere is to escort or lead them ◆ *I'll see you to the door*
to see through something or **someone** is not to be deceived by them
to see to something is to attend to it

seed *noun* (*plural* **seeds**)
a tiny part of a plant that can grow in the ground to make a new plant

seedling *noun* (*plural* **seedlings**)
a very young plant

seek *verb* (**seeks, seeking, sought**)
1 to seek a person or thing is to try to find them ◆ *We sought him everywhere* 2 to seek something is to try to achieve it ◆ *She is seeking fame*

seem *verb* (**seems, seeming, seemed**)
to seem to be something or to have some quality is to appear that way or give that impression ◆ *They seem happy in their new house*
seemingly *adverb* so it seems

seen past participle of **see**

seep *verb* (**seeps, seeping, seeped**)
to seep is to flow slowly through or into or out of something ◆ *Water was seeping into the cellar*
seepage *noun* seeping

see-saw *noun* (*plural* **see-saws**)
a plank balanced in the middle so that people can sit at each end and make it go up and down

seethe *verb* (**seethes, seething, seethed**)
1 to seethe is to boil or bubble 2 to be seething is to be very angry or excited

segment *noun* (*plural* **segments**)
a part that is cut off or can be separated from the rest of something ♦ *He ate a few segments of an orange*
segmented *adjective* divided into segments

segregate *verb* (**segregates, segregating, segregated**) (*pronounced* seg-ri-gayt)
to segregate people of different races or religions is to separate them and make them live separately
segregation *noun* being segregated

seismograph *noun* (*plural* **seismographs**)
a device for detecting the strength of earthquakes

seize *verb* (**seizes, seizing, seized**) (*pronounced* seez)
to seize someone or something is to take hold of them suddenly or eagerly
to seize up is to become jammed or stuck

seizure *noun* (*plural* **seizures**)
1 seizing is seizing something **2** a seizure is a sudden attack of illness

seldom *adverb*
not often ♦ *I seldom cry*

select ➤ *verb* (**selects, selecting, selected**)
to select a person or thing is to choose them carefully

select ➤ *adjective*
small and carefully chosen ♦ *They have a select group of friends*

self *noun* (*plural* **selves**)
a person as an individual; a person's particular nature or interests ♦ *He always puts self first*

self-centred *adjective*
selfish; thinking about yourself too much

self-confident *adjective*
confident in what you can do
self-confidence *noun* being self-confident

self-conscious *adjective*
embarrassed or shy because you know people are watching you

self-contained *adjective*
having everything you need in one place

self-control *noun*
the ability to control your own behaviour or feelings
self-controlled *adjective* having self-control

self-defence *noun*
1 defending yourself against attack
2 skill in defending yourself

self-employed *adjective*
working independently and not for an employer

self-evident *adjective*
clear or obvious and not needing proof

self-important *adjective*
pompous or haughty

selfish *adjective*
having or doing what you want without thinking of other people
selfishly *adverb* in a selfish way **selfishness** *noun* being selfish

selfless *adjective*
thinking of other people; not selfish

self-raising flour *noun*
flour that makes cakes and pastry rise during cooking

self-respect *noun*
the feeling that you are behaving and thinking in the proper way

self-righteous *adjective*
smugly sure that you are behaving virtuously

self-service *adjective*
where customers serve themselves with goods and pay a cashier for what they have taken

self-sufficient *adjective*
able to provide what you need without help from others

sell *verb* (**sells, selling, sold**)
to sell goods or services is to offer them in exchange for money
to sell out is to sell all your stock of something

semaphore *noun*
a system of signalling by holding flags out with your arms in positions to indicate letters of the alphabet

semen *noun* (*pronounced* see-men)
white liquid produced by males and containing sperm

semi- *prefix*
meaning 'half', as in *semicircle*

semibreve *noun* (*plural* **semibreves**) (*pronounced* sem-i-breev)
the longest musical note normally used, written o

semicircle *noun* (*plural* **semicircles**)
half a circle
semicircular *adjective* in the form of a semicircle

semicolon *noun* (*plural* **semicolons**)
a punctuation mark (;), marking a more definite break in a sentence than a comma does

semi-detached *adjective*
a semi-detached house is one that is joined to another house on one side

semi-final *noun* (*plural* **semi-finals**)
a match played to decide who will take part in the final
semi-finalist *noun* a contestant in a semi-final

semitone *noun* (*plural* **semitones**)
half a tone in music

semolina *noun*
a milk pudding made with grains of wheat

senate *noun* (*pronounced* **sen**-at)
1 the governing council in ancient Rome
2 the higher-ranking section of the parliament in France, the USA, and some other countries
senator *noun* a member of a senate

send *verb* (**sends, sending, sent**)
to send something or someone somewhere is to make them go or be taken there
to send for something or **someone** is to ask for them to come to you
to send someone up (*informal*) is to make fun of them

senior ➤ *adjective*
1 older than someone else 2 higher in rank ♦ *He is a senior officer in the navy*
seniority *noun* being senior

senior ➤ *noun* (*plural* **seniors**)
someone who is older or higher in rank than you are ♦ *Steve and Laura are my seniors*

senior citizen *noun* (*plural* **senior citizens**)
an elderly person, especially a pensioner

sensation *noun* (*plural* **sensations**)
1 a feeling ♦ *We had a sensation of warmth* 2 a very exciting event or the excitement caused by it ♦ *The news caused a great sensation*

sensational *adjective*
causing great excitement or shock

sense ➤ *noun* (*plural* **senses**)
1 the ability to see, hear, smell, touch, or taste things 2 the ability to feel or appreciate something ♦ *She has a good sense of humour* 3 the power to think or make good judgements ♦ *He hasn't got the sense to come in out of the rain* 4 meaning ♦ *The word 'set' has many senses*
to make sense is to have a meaning you can understand

sense ➤ *verb* (**senses, sensing, sensed**)
1 to sense something is to feel it or be aware of it ♦ *I sensed that she did not like me* 2 to sense something is also to detect it ♦ *This device senses radioactivity*

senseless *adjective*
1 stupid; not sensible 2 unconscious

sensible *adjective*
wise; having or showing common sense
sensibly *adverb* in a sensible way

sensitive *adjective*
1 affected by the sun or chemicals or something else physical ♦ *I have sensitive skin* 2 easily offended ♦ *She is very sensitive about her age*
sensitively *adverb* in a sensitive way

sensitivity *noun* (*plural* **sensitivities**)
1 sensitivity is being sensitive 2 a sensitivity is something you are sensitive about

sensitize *verb* (**sensitizes, sensitizing, sensitized**)
to sensitize something is to make it sensitive to light or something else physical

sensor *noun* (*plural* **sensors**)
a device or instrument for detecting something physical such as heat or light

sent past tense and past participle of **send**

sentence ➤ *noun* (*plural* **sentences**)
1 a group of words that express a complete thought and form a statement or question or command 2 the punishment given to a convicted person in a lawcourt

sentence ➤ *verb* (**sentences, sentencing, sentenced**)
to sentence someone is to give them a sentence in a lawcourt ♦ *The judge sentenced them to a year in prison*

sentiment *noun* (*plural* **sentiments**)
1 a sentiment is a feeling or opinion
2 sentiment is a show of feeling or emotion

sentimental *adjective*
arousing or showing emotion, especially weak or foolish emotion ♦ *That love-story is too sentimental*
sentimentality *noun* being sentimental
sentimentally *adverb* in a sentimental way

sentinel *noun* (*plural* **sentinels**)
a sentry

sentry *noun* (*plural* **sentries**)
a soldier guarding something

separable *adjective*
able to be separated

separate ➤ *adjective* (*pronounced* **sep**-er-at)
1 not joined to anything; on its own 2 not together; not with other people ♦ *They lead separate lives*
separately *adverb* apart; by yourself or by itself

separate ➤ *verb* (**separates, separating, separated**) (*pronounced* **sep-er-ayt**)
1 to separate things or people is to take them away from others **2** to separate is to become separate **3** to separate is also when two people stop living together as a couple
separation *noun* being separated

September *noun*
the ninth month of the year

septic *adjective*
infected with harmful bacteria

sequel *noun* (*plural* **sequels**) (*pronounced* **see-kwel**)
1 a book or film that continues the story of an earlier one **2** something that results from an earlier event

sequence *noun* (*plural* **sequences**) (*pronounced* **see-kwenss**)
1 a series of things **2** the order in which things happen

sequin *noun* (*plural* **sequins**) (*pronounced* **see-kwin**)
a tiny bright disc sewn on clothes to decorate them

serene *adjective*
calm and peaceful
serenely *adverb* in a serene way **serenity** *noun* being serene

sergeant *noun* (*plural* **sergeants**) (*pronounced* **sar-jent**)
a soldier or police officer who is in charge of others

sergeant major *noun* (*plural* **sergeant majors**)
a soldier who is one rank higher than a sergeant

serial *noun* (*plural* **serials**)
a story or film that is presented in separate parts

series *noun* (*plural* **series**)
a number of things following each other or connected with each other

serious *adjective*
1 not funny; important ♦ *We need a serious talk* **2** thoughtful; solemn ♦ *His face was serious* **3** very bad ♦ *They've had a serious accident*
seriously *adverb* in a serious way **seriousness** *noun* being serious

sermon *noun* (*plural* **sermons**)
a talk given by a preacher

serpent *noun* (*plural* **serpents**)
a snake

servant *noun* (*plural* **servants**)
a person whose job is to work in someone else's house

serve ➤ *verb* (**serves, serving, served**)
1 to serve a person or organization is to work for them **2** to serve people is to sell things to them in a shop **3** to serve food is to give it to people at a meal **4** to serve is to be suitable for a purpose **5** (*in Tennis*) to serve is to start play by hitting the ball to your opponent
it serves you right you deserve it
server *noun* someone who serves

serve ➤ *noun* (*plural* **serves**)
the action of serving in tennis

service ➤ *noun* (*plural* **services**)
1 service is working for someone or something **2** a service is something that helps people or supplies what they want ♦ *There is a good bus service into town* **3** a service is also a religious ceremony in a church **4** a service, or dinner service, is a set of plates and crockery **5** a service is the servicing of a vehicle or machine **6** (*in Tennis*) a service is a serve
the services the armed forces of a country

service ➤ *verb* (**services, servicing, serviced**)
to service a vehicle or machine is to repair and maintain it

service station *noun* (*plural* **service stations**)
a place beside the road where petrol is sold

serviette *noun* (*plural* **serviettes**)
a napkin for use at meals

session *noun* (*plural* **sessions**)
1 a time spent doing one thing ♦ *They were in the middle of a recording session* **2** a meeting or series of meetings ♦ *The Queen will open the next session of Parliament*

set ➤ *verb* (**sets, setting, set**)
This word has many meanings, depending on the words that go with it: **1** to set something somewhere is to put or place it there ♦ *Set the vase on the table* **2** to set a device is to make it ready to work ♦ *Have you set the alarm?* **3** to set is to become solid or hard ♦ *The jelly has set now* **4** the sun sets when it goes down towards the horizon **5** to set someone doing something is to start them doing it ♦ *The news set me thinking* **6** to set someone a task or problem is to give it to them to do or solve ♦ *Has the teacher set your homework?*
to set about something is to start doing it
to set off or **set out** is to begin a journey
to set something out is to display it or make it known ♦ *She set out her reasons for leaving*
to set something up is to place it in position or get it started ♦ *We want to set up a playgroup*

set ➤ *noun* (*plural* **sets**)
1 a group of people or things that belong together 2 a radio or television receiver 3 (*in Mathematics*) a collection of things that have something in common, such as being odd numbers 4 a series of games in a tennis match 5 the scenery on a stage

set square *noun* (*plural* **set squares**)
a device in the shape of a right-angled triangle, used for drawing parallel lines and to draw angles

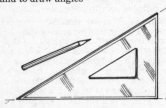

sett *noun* (*plural* **setts**)
the underground burrow of a badger

settee *noun* (*plural* **settees**)
a sofa

setting *noun* (*plural* **settings**)
1 the land and buildings around something ♦ *The house stood in a rural setting* 2 a set of cutlery or crockery for one person

settle *verb* (**settles, settling, settled**)
1 to settle a problem or difficulty is to solve it or decide about it 2 to settle, or settle down, is to become relaxed or make yourself comfortable ♦ *He settled down in the armchair* 3 to settle somewhere is to go and live there ♦ *The family settled in Canada* 4 something light such as dust or snow settles when it comes to rest on something ♦ *The dust was settling on the books* 5 to settle a bill or debt is to pay it

settlement *noun* (*plural* **settlements**)
1 settlement is settling something 2 a settlement is a group of people or houses in a new area

settler *noun* (*plural* **settlers**)
one of the first people to settle in a new area

set-up *noun* (*plural* **set-ups**)
(*informal*) the way that something is organized or arranged

seven *noun* (*plural* **sevens**)
the number 7

seventeen *noun* (*plural* **seventeens**)
the number 17
seventeenth *adjective* and *noun* 17th

seventh *adjective* and *noun*
the next after the sixth

seventhly *adverb* in the seventh place; as the seventh one

seventy *noun* (*plural* **seventies**)
the number 70
seventieth *adjective* and *noun* 70th

sever *verb* (**severs, severing, severed**)
to sever something is to cut or break it off

several *adjective*
more than two but not many

severe *adjective* (**severer, severest**)
1 strict; not gentle or kind ♦ *Their teacher was severe* 2 very bad; violent ♦ *a severe cold*
severely *adverb* in a severe way **severity** *noun* being severe

sew *verb* (**sews, sewing, sewed, sewn or sewed**) (*pronounced* so)
1 to sew cloth or other soft material is to use a needle and cotton to join it or form it into clothing 2 to sew is to work with a needle and thread or with a sewing machine

sewage *noun* (*pronounced* soo-ij)
waste matter carried away in drains

sewer *noun* (*plural* **sewers**) (*pronounced* soo-er)
an underground drain that carries away sewage

sewing machine *noun* (*plural* **sewing machines**)
a machine for sewing things

sex *noun* (*plural* **sexes**)
1 a sex is each of the two groups, male or female, that people and animals belong to 2 sex is the instinct that causes members of the two sexes to be attracted to one another 3 sex is also sexual intercourse

sexism *noun*
unfair or offensive treatment of people of a particular sex, especially women
sexist *noun* someone who practises sexism

sextet *noun* (*plural* **sextets**)
1 a group of six musicians 2 a piece of music for six musicians

sexual *adjective*
to do with sex or the sexes
sexuality *noun* being sexual **sexually** *adverb* in a sexual way

sexual intercourse *noun*
the act of physical love in which a man puts his penis into a woman's vagina and ejects seed into it

sexy *adjective* (**sexier, sexiest**)
(*informal*) 1 attractive to people of the opposite sex 2 concerned with sex ♦ *They saw a sexy film*

shabby *adjective* (**shabbier, shabbiest**)
1 very old and worn ♦ *He was wearing shabby clothes* 2 mean or unfair ♦ *What a shabby trick*
shabbily *adverb* in a shabby way **shabbiness** *noun* being shabby

shack *noun* (*plural* **shacks**)
a roughly-built hut

shade ➤ *noun* (*plural* **shades**)
1 shade is an area sheltered from bright light 2 a shade is a device that decreases or shuts out bright light 3 a shade is also a colour, or how light or dark a colour is 4 a shade of something is a slight difference ♦ *This word has several shades of meaning*

shade ➤ *verb* (**shades, shading, shaded**)
1 to shade something or someone is to shelter them from bright light 2 to shade a drawing is to make parts of it darker than the rest

shadow ➤ *noun* (*plural* **shadows**)
1 a shadow is a dark shape that falls on a surface when something is between it and the light 2 shadow is an area of shade
shadowy *adjective* having many shadows

shadow ➤ *verb* (**shadows, shadowing, shadowed**)
1 to shadow something is to cast a shadow on it 2 to shadow someone is to follow them secretly

shady *adjective* (**shadier, shadiest**)
1 giving shade ♦ *We sat under a shady tree* 2 situated in the shade ♦ *Find a shady spot* 3 dishonest or suspect ♦ *It was a shady deal*

shaft *noun* (*plural* **shafts**)
1 a long thin rod or straight part of something 2 a deep narrow hole ♦ *They found an old mine shaft* 3 a ray of light

shaggy *adjective* (**shaggier, shaggiest**)
having long untidy hair

shake ➤ *verb* (**shakes, shaking, shook, shaken**)
1 to shake something is to move it quickly up and down or from side to side ♦ *Have you shaken the bottle?* 2 to shake is to move in this way 3 to shake someone is to shock or upset them ♦ *The news shook her* 4 to shake is to tremble ♦ *His voice was shaking*
to shake hands is to clasp someone's right hand as a greeting or as a sign that you agree

shake ➤ *noun* (*plural* **shakes**)
shaking or a shaking movement ♦ *Give it a shake*
in two shakes very soon ♦ *I'll be there in two shakes*

shaky *adjective* (**shakier, shakiest**)
shaking or likely to fall down
shakily *adverb* in a shaky way

shall *verb* (*past tense* **should**)
used with *I* and *we* to refer to the future ♦ *We shall arrive tomorrow. We told them we should arrive the next day*

shallow *adjective* (**shallower, shallowest**)
not deep ♦ *They stood in shallow water*

sham *noun* (*plural* **shams**)
a person or thing that is not genuine or what they claim to be

shamble *verb* (**shambles, shambling, shambled**)
to shamble is to walk or run in a lazy or awkward way

shambles *noun*
a scene of great disorder or bloodshed; a mess

shame ➤ *noun*
1 shame is a feeling of great sorrow or guilt because you have done wrong 2 a shame is something that you regret

shame ➤ *verb* (**shames, shaming, shamed**)
to shame someone is to make them feel ashamed

shameful *adjective*
causing shame; disgraceful
shamefully *adverb* in a shameful way

shameless *adjective*
feeling or showing no shame
shamelessly *adverb* in a shameless way

shampoo ➤ *noun* (*plural* **shampoos**)
liquid soap for washing things, especially the hair or a car or a carpet

shampoo ➤ *verb* (**shampoos, shampooing, shampooed**)
to shampoo something is to wash it with shampoo

shamrock *noun*
a small plant rather like clover, with leaves divided in three

shandy *noun* (*plural* **shandies**)
a mixture of beer with lemonade or another soft drink

shan't short for *shall not*

shanty [1] *noun* (*plural* **shanties**)
a sailor's traditional song

shanty [2] *noun* (*plural* **shanties**)
a roughly-built hut

shape ➤ *noun* (*plural* **shapes**)
1 the outline of something or the way it looks 2 the proper form or condition of something ♦ *Get it into shape*

shape ➤ *verb* (**shapes, shaping, shaped**)
to shape something is to give it a shape
to shape up is to develop well

shapeless *adjective*
having no definite shape

shapely *adjective* (**shapelier, shapeliest**)
having an attractive shape

share ➤ *noun* (*plural* **shares**)
1 one of the parts into which something is divided between several people or things
2 part of a company's money, lent by someone who is then given part of the profits in return

share ➤ *verb* (**shares, sharing, shared**)
1 to share something is to divide it between several people or things 2 to share something is to use it when someone else is also using it ♦ *She shared a room with me*

shark *noun* (*plural* **sharks**)
a large sea fish with sharp teeth

sharp ➤ *adjective* (**sharper, sharpest**)
1 having an edge or point that can cut or make holes ♦ *This is a sharp knife*
2 quick to learn or notice things ♦ *She has sharp eyes* 3 sudden or severe ♦ *We came to a sharp bend in the road* 4 slightly sour ♦ *The apples taste sharp* 5 above the proper musical pitch
sharply *adverb* clearly; definitely; **sharpness** *noun* being sharp

sharp ➤ *adverb*
1 sharply ♦ *Turn sharp right*
2 punctually; exactly ♦ *Be there at six o'clock sharp*

sharp ➤ *noun* (*plural* **sharps**)
the note that is a semitone above a particular musical note; the sign # that indicates this

sharpen *verb* (**sharpens, sharpening, sharpened**)
to sharpen something is to make it sharp or pointed
sharpener *noun* a device for sharpening a pencil

shatter *verb* (**shatters, shattering, shattered**)
1 to shatter something is to break it suddenly into tiny pieces 2 to shatter is to break in this way 3 to shatter hopes or dreams is to show they are unreal 4 to be shattered is to be very upset by something ♦ *We were shattered by the news*

shave ➤ *verb* (**shaves, shaving, shaved**)
1 to shave is to scrape hair from the skin with a razor 2 to shave something is to cut or scrape a thin slice off it
shaver *noun* a device for shaving the face

shave ➤ *noun* (*plural* **shaves**)
the act of shaving the face
a close shave (*informal*) a narrow escape

shavings *plural noun*
thin strips shaved off a piece of wood or metal

shawl *noun* (*plural* **shawls**)
a large piece of material for covering the shoulders or wrapping a baby

she *pronoun*
a female person or animal: used as the subject of a verb

sheaf *noun* (*plural* **sheaves**)
1 a bundle of corn stalks tied together after reaping 2 a bundle of papers

shear *verb* (**shears, shearing, sheared, shorn or sheared**)
to shear a sheep is to cut the wool from it
to shear off is to break off under a force or stress
shearer *noun* someone who shears sheep

shears *plural noun*
a tool like a very large pair of scissors for trimming grass and bushes or for shearing sheep

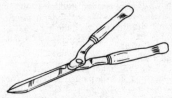

sheath *noun* (*plural* **sheaths**)
1 a cover for the blade of a sword or dagger
2 a cover that fits something closely

sheathe *verb* (**sheathes, sheathing, sheathed**)
1 to sheathe a sword is to put it into its sheath 2 to sheathe something is to put a protective covering on it

shed[1] *noun* (*plural* **sheds**)
a simply-made building used for storing things or sheltering animals, or as a workshop

shed[2] *verb* (**sheds, shedding, shed**)
to shed something is to let it fall or flow ♦ *The trees are shedding their leaves* ♦ *He was so badly hurt he was shedding blood*

she'd short for *she had, she should,* or *she would*

sheen *noun*
a shine on a surface

sheep *noun* (*plural* **sheep**)
a grass-eating animal kept by farmers for
its wool and meat

sheepdog *noun* (*plural* **sheepdogs**)
a dog trained to guard and control sheep

sheepish *adjective*
shy or embarrassed
sheepishly *adverb* in a sheepish way

sheer *adjective* (**sheerer, sheerest**)
1 complete or thorough ♦ *The mistake was
sheer stupidity* 2 vertical or perpendicular
♦ *To the right of the road there was a sheer
drop* 3 sheer material is very thin or
transparent

sheet *noun* (*plural* **sheets**)
1 a large piece of lightweight material put
on a bed 2 a whole flat piece of paper,
glass, or metal 3 a wide area of water,
snow, ice, or flame

sheikh *noun* (*plural* **sheikhs**) (*pronounced*
shayk)
the leader of an Arab tribe or village

shelf *noun* (*plural* **shelves**)
1 a flat piece of hard material fitted to a
wall or in a piece of furniture so that
things can be put on it 2 a flat level
surface that sticks out

shell ➤ *noun* (*plural* **shells**)
1 the hard outer covering round a nut or
egg, or round an animal such as a snail or
tortoise 2 a metal case filled with
explosive, fired from a large gun 3 the
walls or framework of a building or ship

shell ➤ *verb* (**shells, shelling, shelled**)
1 to shell something is to take it out of its
shell 2 to shell a building, ship, town, etc.,
is to fire explosive shells at it
to shell out (*slang*) is to pay money

she'll short for *she will*

shellfish *noun* (*plural* **shellfish**)
a sea animal that has a shell

shelter ➤ *noun* (*plural* **shelters**)
1 a shelter is a place that protects people
from danger or from the weather
2 shelter is being protected ♦ *We found
shelter from the rain*

shelter ➤ *verb* (**shelters, sheltering, sheltered**)
1 to shelter something or someone is to
protect or cover them ♦ *The hill shelters
the house from the wind* 2 to shelter is to
find a shelter ♦ *We sheltered under the
trees*

shelve *verb* (**shelves, shelving, shelved**)
1 to shelve something is to put it on a shelf
or shelves 2 to shelve an idea or piece of
work is to reject or postpone it 3 to shelve
is to slope ♦ *The river bed shelves steeply*

shepherd *noun* (*plural* **shepherds**)
someone whose job is to look after sheep

shepherd's pie *noun* (*plural* **shepherd's pies**)
a baked dish of minced meat covered with
mashed potato

sherbet *noun* (*plural* **sherbets**)
a fizzy sweet powder or drink

sheriff *noun* (*plural* **sheriffs**)
the chief judge or law officer of a county

sherry *noun* (*plural* **sherries**)
a kind of strong wine

she's short for *she is* and (before a verb in
the past tense) *she has*

shield ➤ *noun* (*plural* **shields**)
1 a large piece of metal or wood carried to
protect the body in fighting 2 a design in
the shape of a shield 3 a protection

shield ➤ *verb* (**shields, shielding, shielded**)
to shield someone is to protect them ♦ *I
was shielded from the wind*

shift ➤ *noun* (*plural* **shifts**)
1 a change of position or condition 2 a
group of workers who start work as
another group finishes; the time when
they work ♦ *He's on the night shift this
month* 3 a woman's lightweight dress that
hangs loosely

shift ➤ *verb* (**shifts, shifting, shifted**)
1 to shift something is to move it 2 to
shift is to change position
to shift for yourself is to manage without any
help

shilling *noun* (*plural* **shillings**)
an old British coin that was worth a
twentieth of a pound (now 5 pence)

shimmer *verb* (**shimmers, shimmering,
shimmered**)
to shimmer is to shine with a quivering
light ♦ *The sea shimmered in the sunlight*

shin *noun* (*plural* **shins**)
the front of your leg between your knee
and your ankle

shine ➤ *verb* (**shines, shining, shone** or, in
'polish' sense, **shined**)
1 to shine is to give out or reflect bright
light 2 to shine something is to polish it
♦ *Have you shined your shoes?* 3 to shine
is to do well or be excellent ♦ *He does not
shine in maths*

shine ➤ *noun*
1 brightness 2 the act of polishing ♦ *Give
your shoes a good shine*

shingle *noun*
pebbles on a beach

shiny *adjective* (**shinier, shiniest**)
having a shine; glossy

ship ➤ *noun* (*plural* **ships**)
a large boat, especially one that goes to sea

ship ➤ *verb* (**ships, shipping, shipped**)
to ship something is to send it on a ship

shipping *noun*
all the ships of a country

shipwreck *noun* (*plural* **shipwrecks**)
1 the wrecking of a ship in a storm or
accident at sea **2** the remains of a
wrecked ship
shipwrecked *adjective* wrecked at sea

shipyard *noun* (*plural* **shipyards**)
a dockyard

shire *noun* (*plural* **shires**)
a county

shirk *verb* (**shirks, shirking, shirked**)
to shirk a task or duty is to avoid doing it

shirt *noun* (*plural* **shirts**)
a piece of clothing worn on the top half of
the body, with a collar and sleeves
in your shirtsleeves not wearing a jacket over
your shirt

shiver ➤ *verb* (**shivers, shivering, shivered**)
to shiver is to tremble with cold or fear
shivery *adjective* shivering a lot

shiver ➤ *noun* (*plural* **shivers**)
an act of shivering

shoal [1] *noun* (*plural* **shoals**)
a large number of fish swimming together

shoal [2] *noun* (*plural* **shoals**)
a shallow place

shock [1] ➤ *noun* (*plural* **shocks**)
1 a shock is a sudden unpleasant surprise
2 a shock is also a violent knock or jolt
3 shock is weakness caused by severe pain
or injury **4** a shock, or electric shock, is a
harmful effect caused by a strong electric
current passing through the body

shock ➤ *verb* (**shocks, shocking, shocked**)
1 to shock someone is to give them a shock
2 to shock someone is also to make them
feel disgusted or appalled

shock [2] *noun* (*plural* **shocks**)
a bushy mass of hair

shoddy *adjective* (**shoddier, shoddiest**)
of poor quality ♦ *This is shoddy work*

shoe *noun* (*plural* **shoes**)
1 a strong covering for the foot **2** a
horseshoe
in someone's shoes in someone's place ♦ *I'm
glad I'm not in her shoes*

shoelace *noun* (*plural* **shoelaces**)
a cord for fastening a shoe

shoestring *noun*
on a shoestring with only a small amount of
money

shone past tense and past participle of
shine *verb*

shook past tense of **shake** *verb*

shoot ➤ *verb* (**shoots, shooting, shot**)
1 to shoot a gun or other weapon is to fire
it **2** to shoot a person or animal is to fire a
gun at them **3** to shoot somewhere is to
move very fast ♦ *The car shot past* **4** (*in
Football*) to shoot is to kick or hit a ball at
a goal **5** to shoot a film or scene is to film
or photograph it ♦ *The film was shot in
Africa*

shoot ➤ *noun* (*plural* **shoots**)
a young branch or new growth of a plant

shooting star *noun* (*plural* **shooting stars**)
a meteor

shop ➤ *noun* (*plural* **shops**)
1 a building where people buy things **2** a
workshop

shop ➤ *verb* (**shops, shopping, shopped**)
to shop is to go and buy things at shops
shopper *noun* someone who goes shopping

shopkeeper *noun* (*plural* **shopkeepers**)
someone who owns or looks after a shop

shoplifter *noun* (*plural* **shoplifters**)
someone who steals from shops

shopping *noun*
1 buying things at shops ♦ *I like shopping*
2 things that someone has bought ♦ *Will
you carry my shopping, please?*

shop steward *noun* (*plural* **shop stewards**)
a trade-union official who represents a
group of fellow workers

shore *noun* (*plural* **shores**)
1 the seashore **2** the land along the edge
of a lake

shorn past tense of **shear**

short ➤ *adjective* (**shorter, shortest**)
1 not long; occupying a small distance or
time ♦ *I went for a short walk* **2** not tall
♦ *He is a short person* **3** not sufficient;
scarce ♦ *Water is short* **4** bad-tempered
♦ *He was rather short with me* **5** short
pastry is rich and crumbly, and contains a
lot of fat
for short as a shorter form of something
♦ *William is called Will for short*
short for something a shorter form of
something ♦ *Will is short for William*
shortness *noun* being short

short ➤ *adverb*
suddenly ♦ *She stopped short*

shortage *noun* (*plural* **shortages**)
the situation when something is scarce or
insufficient

shortbread *noun*
a rich sweet biscuit made with butter

shortcake *noun* (*plural* **shortcakes**)
1 shortbread **2** a light cake usually served
with fruit

short circuit *noun* (*plural* **short circuits**)
a fault in an electrical circuit in which current flows along a shorter route than the normal one

shortcoming *noun* (*plural* **shortcomings**)
a fault or failure ♦ *He has many shortcomings*

short cut *noun* (*plural* **short cuts**)
a route or method that is quicker than the usual one

shorten *verb* (**shortens, shortening, shortened**)
1 to shorten something is to make it shorter 2 to shorten is to become shorter

shorthand *noun*
a set of special signs for writing words down as quickly as people say them

short-handed *adjective*
not having enough people to help you

shortly *adverb*
1 soon ♦ *I'll be there shortly* 2 briefly or sharply ♦ *'Go away,' she said shortly*

shorts *plural noun*
trousers with legs that stop at or above the knee

short-sighted *adjective*
1 unable to see things clearly when they are further away 2 not thinking enough about what may happen in the future

shot [1] *noun* (*plural* **shots**)
1 a shot is the firing of a gun or other weapon 2 a shot is also something fired from a gun 3 shot is lead pellets fired from small guns 4 a good or bad shot is a person judged by their skill in shooting ♦ *She is a great shot* 5 a shot is a heavy metal ball thrown as a sport 6 a shot is also a stroke in a game with a ball, such as tennis or snooker 7 in photography, a shot is a photograph or filmed sequence 8 a shot at something is an attempt to do it ♦ *Have a shot at this crossword*

shot [2] past tense and past participle of **shoot** *verb*

shotgun *noun* (*plural* **shotguns**)
a gun for firing small lead pellets over a short distance

should *verb*
used to express 1 what someone ought to do ♦ *You should have told me* 2 what someone expects ♦ *They should be here soon* 3 what might happen ♦ *If you should happen to see him, tell him to come*

shoulder ➤ *noun* (*plural* **shoulders**)
the part of your body between your neck and your arm

shoulder ➤ *verb* (**shoulders, shouldering, shouldered**)
1 to shoulder something is to put it or rest it on your shoulder or shoulders 2 to shoulder blame or responsibility is to accept it

shoulder blade *noun* (*plural* **shoulder blades**)
each of the two large flat bones at the top of your back

shout ➤ *verb* (**shouts, shouting, shouted**)
to shout is to speak or call very loudly

shout ➤ *noun* (*plural* **shouts**)
a loud cry or call

shove *verb* (**shoves, shoving, shoved**) (*pronounced* shuv)
to shove something is to push it hard
to shove off (*informal*) is to go away

shovel ➤ *noun* (*plural* **shovels**) (*pronounced* shuv-el)
a tool like a spade with the sides turned up, for lifting and moving coal, earth, sand, snow, and other things

shovel ➤ *verb* (**shovels, shovelling, shovelled**)
to shovel something is to move it or clear it with a shovel

show ➤ *verb* (**shows, showing, showed, shown**)
1 to show something is to let people see it ♦ *She showed me her new bike* 2 to show something to someone is to explain it to them ♦ *She showed me how to do it* 3 to show someone somewhere is to guide or lead them there ♦ *Please show them in* 4 to show is to be visible ♦ *That scratch won't show*
to show off is to try to impress people
to show something off is to be proud of letting people see it

show ➤ *noun* (*plural* **shows**)
1 a display or exhibition ♦ *Have you been to the flower show?* 2 an entertainment 3 (*informal*) something that happens or is done ♦ *He runs the whole show*

show business *noun*
the entertainment business; the theatre, films, radio, and television

shower ➤ *noun* (*plural* **showers**)
1 a brief fall of rain or snow 2 a lot of small things coming or falling like rain ♦ *They were met by a shower of stones* 3 a device or cabinet for spraying water to wash the body; a wash in this

shower ➤ *verb* (**showers, showering, showered**)
1 to shower is to fall like rain 2 to shower things is to send a lot of them 3 to shower is to wash under a shower

showery *adjective*
raining occasionally

showjumping *noun*
a competition in which riders make their horses jump over fences and other obstacles
showjumper *noun* someone who takes part in showjumping

showman *noun* (*plural* **showmen**)
1 someone who presents entertainments 2 someone who is good at attracting attention or at entertaining
showmanship *noun* ability in being a showman

showroom *noun* (*plural* **showrooms**)
a large room where goods are displayed for people to look at and to buy

showy *adjective* (**showier, showiest**)
likely to attract attention; bright or highly decorated
showily *adverb* in a showy way **showiness** *noun* being showy

shrank past tense of **shrink**

shrapnel *noun*
pieces of metal scattered from an exploding shell

shred ➤ *noun* (*plural* **shreds**)
a tiny strip or piece torn or cut off something

shred ➤ *verb* (**shreds, shredding, shredded**)
to shred something is to tear or cut it into shreds

shrew *noun* (*plural* **shrews**)
1 a small animal rather like a mouse 2 a bad-tempered woman

shrewd *adjective* (**shrewder, shrewdest**)
having common sense and good judgement
shrewdly *adverb* in a shrewd way **shrewdness** *noun* being shrewd

shriek ➤ *noun* (*plural* **shrieks**)
a shrill cry or scream

shriek ➤ *verb* (**shrieks, shrieking, shrieked**)
to shriek is to give a shriek

shrill *adjective* (**shriller, shrillest**)
sounding very high and loud
shrilly *adverb* in a shrill way **shrillness** *noun* being shrill

shrimp *noun* (*plural* **shrimps**)
a small shellfish

shrine *noun* (*plural* **shrines**)
an altar or chapel or other sacred place

shrink *verb* (**shrinks, shrinking, shrank, shrunk**)
1 to shrink is to become smaller ♦ *My dress has shrunk* 2 to shrink something is to make it smaller, usually by washing it ♦ *Their jeans have been shrunk* 3 to shrink from something is to avoid it from fear or embarrassment ♦ *He shrank from meeting strangers*

shrinkage *noun*
the amount that something shrinks

shrivel *verb* (**shrivels, shrivelling, shrivelled**)
to shrivel is to become wrinkled and dry

shroud ➤ *noun* (*plural* **shrouds**)
1 a sheet in which a dead body is wrapped 2 each of the ropes that support a ship's mast

shroud ➤ *verb* (**shrouds, shrouding, shrouded**)
1 to shroud a dead body is to wrap it in a shroud 2 to shroud something is to cover or conceal it ♦ *The countryside was shrouded in mist*

Shrove Tuesday *noun*
the day before Ash Wednesday, when pancakes are eaten

shrub *noun* (*plural* **shrubs**)
a bush or small tree

shrubbery *noun* (*plural* **shrubberies**)
an area full of shrubs

shrug ➤ *verb* (**shrugs, shrugging, shrugged**)
to raise your shoulders slightly as a sign that you do not care or do not know

shrug ➤ *noun* (*plural* **shrugs**)
the act of shrugging

shrunk past participle of **shrink**

shrunken *adjective*
smaller because it has shrunk

shudder ➤ *verb* (**shudders, shuddering, shuddered**)
to shudder is to shake from cold or fear

shudder ➤ *noun* (*plural* **shudders**)
the act of shuddering

shuffle ➤ *verb* (**shuffles, shuffling, shuffled**)
1 to shuffle is to drag your feet along the ground as you walk **2** to shuffle playing cards is to mix them by sliding them over each other several times

shuffle ➤ *noun* (*plural* **shuffles**)
the act of shuffling

shunt *verb* (**shunts, shunting, shunted**)
to shunt a railway train or wagons is to move them from one track to another

shunter *noun* an engine used for shunting

shut *verb* (**shuts, shutting, shut**)
1 to shut a door or window, or a lid or cover, is to move it so as to block up an opening **2** to shut is to become closed
♦ *The door shut suddenly*
to shut down is to stop work or business
to shut up (*informal*) is to stop talking
to shut something up is to close it securely

shutter *noun* (*plural* **shutters**)
1 a panel or screen that can be closed over a window **2** the device in a camera that opens and closes to let light fall on the film

shuttle *noun* (*plural* **shuttles**)
1 the part of a loom that carries the thread from side to side **2** a train or bus or aircraft that makes frequent short journeys between two places **3** a space shuttle

shuttlecock *noun* (*plural* **shuttlecocks**)
a small rounded piece of cork or plastic with a ring of feathers fixed to it, used in the game of badminton

shy *adjective* (**shyer, shyest**)
timid and afraid to meet or talk to other people

shyly *adverb* in a shy way **shyness** *noun* being shy

SI *noun*
an international system of metric units of measurement, including the metre and kilogram

Siamese *adjective*
to do with Siam (now called Thailand)

Siamese cat *noun* (*plural* **Siamese cats**)
a cat with blue eyes and short pale fur with darker patches

Siamese twins *plural noun*
twins who are born with their bodies joined together

sick *adjective* (**sicker, sickest**)
1 ill or unwell **2** vomiting or likely to vomit ♦ *I feel sick*
to be sick of something or **someone** is to be tired of them or fed up with them

sicken *verb* (**sickens, sickening, sickened**)
1 to sicken is to start feeling ill **2** to sicken someone is to disgust them

sickle *noun* (*plural* **sickles**)
a tool with a curved blade and a short handle, used for cutting tall grass and crops.

sickly *adjective* (**sicklier, sickliest**)
1 often ill; unhealthy **2** making people feel sick ♦ *There was a sickly taste*

sickness *noun* (*plural* **sicknesses**)
an illness or disease

side ➤ *noun* (*plural* **sides**)
1 a flat surface, especially one joining the top and bottom of something **2** a line that forms the edge of a shape ♦ *A triangle has three sides* **3** the outer part of something that is not the front or the back ♦ *Paint the side of the shed* **4** a group of people playing, arguing, or fighting against another group ♦ *They are on our side*

side ➤ *verb* (**sides, siding, sided**)
to side with someone is to support them in a quarrel or argument

sideboard *noun* (*plural* **sideboards**)
a long heavy piece of furniture with drawers and cupboards and a flat top

sidecar *noun* (*plural* **sidecars**)
a small compartment for a passenger, fixed to the side of a motorcycle

sideline *noun* (*plural* **sidelines**)
something that you do in addition to your normal work or activity

sideshow *noun* (*plural* **sideshows**)
a small entertainment forming part of a large show, especially at a fair

sideways *adverb* and *adjective*
1 to or from the side ♦ *Crabs walk sideways* **2** with one side facing forward ♦ *We sat sideways in the bus*

siding *noun* (*plural* **sidings**)
a short railway line leading off the main line

siege *noun* (*plural* **sieges**) (*pronounced* seej)
the action of besieging a place

sieve *noun* (*plural* **sieves**) (*pronounced* siv)
a device made of mesh or perforated metal or plastic, used to separate harder or larger parts from liquid

sift *verb* (**sifts, sifting, sifted**)
1 to sift a fine or powdery substance is to pass it through a sieve 2 to sift facts or information is to examine or select them

sigh ➤ *noun* (*plural* **sighs**)
a sound made by breathing out heavily when you are sad, tired, or relieved

sigh ➤ *verb* (**sighs, sighing, sighed**)
to sigh is to make a sigh

sight ➤ *noun* (*plural* **sights**)
1 the ability to see ♦ *She has very good sight* 2 something that you see ♦ *Our garden is a lovely sight* 3 something worth seeing ♦ *Visit the sights of Paris* 4 something silly or ridiculous to look at ♦ *What a sight you are!* 5 a device that helps you to aim a gun
at sight or **on sight** as soon as you see someone or something

sight ➤ *verb* (**sights, sighting, sighted**)
to sight something is to see it or observe it

sightseeing *noun*
going round looking at interesting places
sightseer *noun* someone who goes sightseeing

sign ➤ *noun* (*plural* **signs**)
1 a mark or board or notice that tells or shows people something 2 something that shows that a thing exists ♦ *There are signs of rust* 3 an action or signal giving information or a command ♦ *She made a sign to them to be quiet*

sign ➤ *verb* (**signs, signing, signed**)
1 to sign your name is to write your signature on something 2 to sign is to make a sign or signal 3 to sign someone is to give them a contract for a job, especially in a professional sport ♦ *We have signed three new players*

signal ➤ *noun* (*plural* **signals**)
1 a device or gesture or sound that gives information 2 a series of radio waves sent out or received

signal ➤ *verb* (**signals, signalling, signalled**)
to signal to someone is to give them a signal
signaller *noun* someone who gives a signal

signal box *noun* (*plural* **signal boxes**)
a building from which railway signals and points are controlled

signalman *noun* (*plural* **signalmen**)
a person who controls railway signals

signature *noun* (*plural* **signatures**)
your name written by yourself

signature tune *noun* (*plural* **signature tunes**)
a special tune used to introduce a well-known person on radio or television, or to begin or end a programme

significance *noun*
meaning or importance

significant *adjective*
having a meaning or importance
significantly *adverb* in a significant way

signify *verb* (**signifies, signifying, signified**)
to signify something is to mean it or indicate it

signing or **sign language** *noun*
a way of communicating by using movements of the hands instead of sounds, used by deaf people

signpost *noun* (*plural* **signposts**)
a sign at a road junction showing the names and distances of the places that each road leads to

Sikh *noun* (*plural* **Sikhs**) (*pronounced* seek)
someone who believes in **Sikhism**, a religion of India having one God and some Hindu and Islamic beliefs

silence ➤ *noun* (*plural* **silences**)
absence of sound or talk

silence ➤ *verb* (**silences, silencing, silenced**)
to silence someone or something is to make them silent

silencer *noun* (*plural* **silencers**)
a device designed to reduce the sound made by an engine or a gun

silent *adjective*
without any sound; not speaking
silently *adverb* without speaking or making any sound

silhouette *noun* (*plural* **silhouettes**) (*pronounced* sil-oo-et)
a dark outline seen against a light background

silicon *noun*
a substance found in many rocks and used in making transistors and chips for microprocessors

silk *noun*
1 a fine soft thread produced by silkworms for making their cocoons 2 smooth shiny cloth made from this thread
silken *adjective* made of silk **silky** *adjective* soft like silk

silkworm *noun* (*plural* **silkworms**)
a kind of caterpillar that covers itself with a cocoon of fine threads when it is ready to turn into a moth

sill *noun* (*plural* **sills**)
a strip of stone or wood or metal underneath a window or door

silly *adjective* (**sillier, silliest**)
foolish or unwise
silliness *noun* being silly

silver *noun*
1 a shiny white precious metal 2 coins made of this metal or a metal that looks like it 3 the colour of silver
silvery *adjective* like silver

silver wedding *noun* (*plural* **silver weddings**) the 25th anniversary of a wedding

similar *adjective*
of the same kind as someone or something else, or alike in some ways
similarity *noun* being similar **similarly** *adverb* in a similar way

simile *noun* (*plural* **similes**) (*pronounced* sim-i-li)
a kind of expression that compares one thing with another, such as *bold as brass* or *as brave as a lion*

simmer *verb* (**simmers, simmering, simmered**)
to simmer is to boil very gently
to simmer down is to become calm after being anxious or angry

simple *adjective* (**simpler, simplest**)
1 easy ♦ *That is a simple question* 2 not complicated ♦ *I have a simple idea*
3 plain ♦ *She was wearing a simple dress*
4 not having much sense or intelligence ♦ *I'm not so simple*
simplicity *noun* being simple

simplify *verb* (**simplifies, simplifying, simplified**)
to simplify something is to make it simple or easy to understand
simplification *noun* making something simple

simply *adverb*
1 in a simple way ♦ *Explain it simply*
2 completely ♦ *It's simply marvellous*
3 only or merely ♦ *It's simply a question of time*

simulate *verb* (**simulates, simulating, simulated**)
1 to simulate something is to reproduce the conditions for it ♦ *The machine simulates a space flight* 2 to simulate a feeling or state is to pretend to have it ♦ *He simulated illness*
simulation *noun* something simulated or reproduced **simulator** *noun* a machine for simulating things

simultaneous *adjective* (*pronounced* sim-ul-**tay**-ni-us)
happening at the same time
simultaneously *adverb* at the same time

sin ➤ *noun* (*plural* **sins**)
the breaking of a religious or moral law; a bad action

sin ➤ *verb* (**sins, sinning, sinned**)
to sin is to commit a sin
sinner *noun* someone who sins

since ➤ *conjunction*
1 from the time when ♦ *Where have you been since I last saw you?* 2 because ♦ *Since we have missed the bus, we must walk home*

since ➤ *preposition*
from a certain time ♦ *I have been here since Christmas*

since ➤ *adverb*
between then and now ♦ *He has not been seen since*

sincere *adjective* (**sincerer, sincerest**)
truly felt or meant; genuine ♦ *I gave them my sincere good wishes*
sincerely *adverb* in a sincere way **sincerity** *noun* being sincere

sinew *noun* (*plural* **sinews**)
strong tissue that joins a muscle to a bone

sinful *adjective*
wicked; guilty of sin
sinfully *adverb* in a sinful way **sinfulness** *noun* being sinful

sing *verb* (**sings, singing, sang, sung**)
to sing is to make musical sounds with your voice
singer *noun* someone who sings

singe *verb* (**singes, singeing, singed**) (*pronounced* sinj)
to singe something is to burn it slightly

single ➤ *adjective*
1 only one; not double 2 designed for one person ♦ *The bedroom had two single beds*
3 not married 4 for a journey in one direction only

single ➤ *noun* (*plural* **singles**)
1 a single person or thing 2 a single ticket 3 a record with one song or short piece of music on it

single ➤ *verb* (**singles, singling, singled**)
to single someone out is to pick them from other people

single file *noun*
in single file in a line, one behind the other

single-handed *adjective*
by your own efforts; without any help

single parent *noun* (*plural* **single parents**)
a person who is bringing up a child or children without a partner

single ticket *noun* (*plural* **single tickets**)
a ticket for a journey to a place but not back again

singly *adverb*
in ones; one by one

singular ➤ *noun* (*plural* **singulars**)
the form of a word meaning only one person or thing, such as *cake* and *child*

singular ➤ *adjective*
1 in the singular; meaning only one
♦ *'Mouse' is a singular noun*
2 extraordinary ♦ *She is a woman of singular courage*
singularly *adverb* in a singular way

sinister *adjective*
looking or seeming evil or harmful

sink ➤ *verb* (**sinks, sinking, sank** or **sunk, sunk**)
1 to sink is to go under water ♦ *The ship sank in a storm* 2 to sink something is to make it go under water ♦ *They fired on the ship and sank it* 3 to sink, or to sink down, is to go or fall down to the ground ♦ *He sank to his knees*
to sink in is to be gradually understood

sink ➤ *noun* (*plural* **sinks**)
a fixed basin with taps to supply water

sinus *noun* (*plural* **sinuses**) (*pronounced* **sy**-nus)
a hollow in the bones of your skull, connected with your nose ♦ *My sinuses are blocked*

sip *verb* (**sips, sipping, sipped**)
to sip a drink is to drink it slowly in small mouthfuls

siphon ➤ *noun* (*plural* **siphons**)
a bent tube for transferring liquid from one container to another at a different level

siphon ➤ *verb* (**siphons, siphoning, siphoned**)
to siphon liquid is to transfer it with a siphon

sir *noun*
a word sometimes used when speaking politely to a man, instead of his name
♦ *Can I help you, sir?*
Sir the title given to a knight ♦ *Sir Francis Drake*

siren *noun* (*plural* **sirens**)
a device that makes a loud hooting or screaming sound, usually as a warning signal

sisal *noun* (*pronounced* **sI**-sal)
a fibre made from the leaves of a tropical plant, used for making ropes

sister *noun* (*plural* **sisters**)
1 a woman or girl who has the same parents as another person 2 a senior nurse in a hospital
sisterly *adjective* like a sister

sister-in-law *noun* (*plural* **sisters-in-law**)
a person's sister-in-law is the sister of their husband or wife, or the wife of their brother

sit *verb* (**sits, sitting, sat**)
1 to sit is to rest on your bottom, as you do when you are on a chair 2 to sit someone, or to sit someone down, is to put them in a sitting position 3 to sit an examination or test is to be a candidate for it ♦ *We sit our end-of-year exam this afternoon* 4 to sit somewhere is to be situated or positioned there ♦ *The house sits on top of a hill* 5 to sit for someone is to act as a babysitter
sitter *noun* someone who is sitting; a babysitter

site ➤ *noun* (*plural* **sites**)
1 the place where something has been built or will be built ♦ *They crossed a building site* 2 a place made for some activity ♦ *We stayed at a camping site*

site ➤ *verb* (**sites, siting, sited**)
to site something somewhere is to locate or build it there

sit-in *noun* (*plural* **sit-ins**)
a protest in which people sit down or occupy a place and refuse to move

sitting room *noun* (*plural* **sitting rooms**)
a room with comfortable chairs for sitting in

situated *adjective*
in a particular place or situation ♦ *They lived in a town situated in a valley*

situation *noun* (*plural* **situations**)
1 a place or position; where something is
2 the conditions affecting a person or thing 3 a job or employment

six *noun* (*plural* **sixes**)
the number 6

sixpence *noun* (*plural* **sixpences**)
an old British coin that was worth half a shilling

sixteen *noun* (*plural* **sixteens**)
the number 16
sixteenth *adjective* and *noun* 16th

sixth *adjective* and *noun*
the next after the fifth
sixthly *adverb* in the sixth place; as the sixth one

sixty *noun* (*plural* **sixties**)
the number 60
sixtieth *adjective* and *noun* 60th

size ➤ *noun* (*plural* **sizes**)
1 how big a person or thing is 2 the measurement something is made in ♦ *I wear a size eight shoe*

size ➤ *verb* (**sizes, sizing, sized**)
to size something or **someone up** (*informal*) is to form an opinion about them

sizeable *adjective*
fairly large

sizzle *verb* (**sizzles, sizzling, sizzled**)
to sizzle is to make a crackling and hissing sound

skate[1] ➤ *noun* (*plural* **skates**)
1 a boot with a steel blade attached to the sole, used for sliding smoothly over ice
2 a roller skate

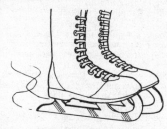

skate ➤ *verb* (**skates, skating, skated**)
to skate is to move on skates
skater *noun* someone who skates

skate[2] *noun* (*plural* **skate**)
a large flat sea fish used for food

skateboard *noun* (*plural* **skateboards**)
a small board with wheels, used for standing and riding on as a sport

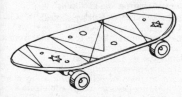

skeleton *noun* (*plural* **skeletons**)
1 the framework of bones in a person's or animal's body **2** the framework or shell of a new building
skeletal *adjective* like a skeleton

sketch ➤ *noun* (*plural* **sketches**)
1 a quick or rough drawing **2** a short amusing play

sketch ➤ *verb* (**sketches, sketching, sketched**)
to sketch something or someone is to make a sketch of them

sketchy *adjective* (**sketchier, sketchiest**)
roughly drawn or described, without any detail

skewer *noun* (*plural* **skewers**)
a long wooden or metal or plastic pin that is pushed through meat to hold it together while it is being cooked

ski ➤ *noun* (*plural* **skis**) (*pronounced* skee)
a long flat strip of wood or metal or plastic, fastened to each foot for moving quickly over snow

ski ➤ *verb* (**skis, skiing, skied** or **ski'd**)
to ski is to travel on skis
skier *noun* someone who skis

skid ➤ *verb* (**skids, skidding, skidded**)
to skid is to slide accidentally, especially in a vehicle

skid ➤ *noun* (*plural* **skids**)
a skidding movement

skilful *adjective*
having or showing a lot of skill
skilfully *adverb* in a skilful way

skill *noun* (*plural* **skills**)
the ability to do something well
skilled *adjective* having a skill or skills

skim *verb* (**skims, skimming, skimmed**)
1 to skim is to move quickly over a surface
2 to skim something is to remove it from the surface of a liquid, especially to take the cream off milk

skimp *verb* (**skimps, skimping, skimped**)
to skimp is to use or provide less than is needed for something

skimpy *adjective* (**skimpier, skimpiest**)
too little or too small

skin ➤ *noun* (*plural* **skins**)
1 the outer covering of a person's or animal's body **2** the outer covering of a fruit or vegetable **3** a thin firm layer that has formed on the surface of a liquid

skin ➤ *verb* (**skins, skinning, skinned**)
to skin something is to take the skin off it

skin diving *noun*
swimming under water with flippers and breathing equipment but without a diving suit
skin diver *noun* someone who goes skin diving

skinny *adjective* (**skinnier, skinniest**)
very thin

skint *adjective*
(*slang*) having no money left

skip [1] ➤ *verb* (skips, skipping, skipped)
1 to skip is to jump or move along by hopping from one foot to the other **2** to skip is also to jump with a skipping rope **3** to skip something is to miss it out or ignore it ♦ *You can skip the last chapter*

skip ➤ *noun* (*plural* **skips**)
a skipping movement

skip [2] *noun* (*plural* **skips**)
a large metal container for taking away builders' rubbish

skipper *noun* (*plural* **skippers**)
the captain of a ship or team

skipping rope *noun* (*plural* **skipping ropes**)
a length of rope, usually with a handle at each end, that you swing over your head and under your feet as you jump

skirt ➤ *noun* (*plural* **skirts**)
a piece of clothing for a woman or girl that hangs down from her waist

skirt ➤ *verb* (**skirts, skirting, skirted**)
to skirt something is to go round the edge of it

skirting or **skirting board** *noun* (*plural* **skirtings** or **skirting boards**)
a narrow board round the wall of a room, close to the floor

skit *noun* (*plural* **skits**)
a play or sketch or poem that makes fun of something by imitating it

skittish *adjective*
lively and excitable

skittle *noun* (*plural* **skittles**)
a piece of wood or plastic shaped like a bottle, that people try to knock down with a ball in a game of **skittles**

skull *noun* (*plural* **skulls**)
the framework of bones in the head

skunk *noun* (*plural* **skunks**)
a black furry North American animal that can make an unpleasant smell

sky *noun* (*plural* **skies**)
the space above the earth, where you can see the sun, moon, and stars

skylark *noun* (*plural* **skylarks**)
a small brown bird that sings as it hovers high in the air

skylight *noun* (*plural* **skylights**)
a window in a roof

skyscraper *noun* (*plural* **skyscrapers**)
a very tall building

slab *noun* (*plural* **slabs**)
a thick flat piece of something

slack *adjective* (**slacker, slackest**)
1 loose; not pulled tight ♦ *The rope was slack* **2** lazy; not busy or working hard
slackly *adverb* in a slack way **slackness** *noun* being slack

slacken *verb* (**slackens, slackening, slackened**)
1 to slacken something is to make it slack
2 to slacken is to become slack

slacks *plural noun*
loose-fitting casual trousers

slag heap *noun* (*plural* **slag heaps**)
a heap of waste material from a mine

slain past participle of **slay**

slam *verb* (**slams, slamming, slammed**)
1 to slam something is to shut it hard or loudly **2** to slam something is to hit it with great force ♦ *He slammed the ball into the net*

slang *noun*
a kind of colourful language used in less formal writing and speaking

slant ➤ *verb* (**slants, slanting, slanted**)
1 to slant is to slope or lean **2** to slant news or information is to present it from a particular point of view

slant ➤ *noun* (*plural* **slants**)
1 a sloping or leaning position ♦ *The caravan floor was at a slant* **2** a way of presenting news or information from a particular point of view

slap ➤ *noun* (*plural* **slaps**)
a hit with the palm of the hand or with something flat

slap ➤ *verb* (**slaps, slapping, slapped**)
1 to slap someone is to give them a slap
2 to slap something somewhere is to put it there forcefully or carelessly ♦ *We slapped paint on the walls*

slapstick *noun*
noisy lively comedy, with people hitting each other, throwing things, and falling over

slash ➤ *verb* (**slashes, slashing, slashed**)
1 to slash something is to make large cuts in it **2** to slash prices or costs is to reduce them a lot

slash ➤ *noun* (*plural* **slashes**)
1 a large cut **2** a sloping line (/) used to separate words or letters

slat *noun* (*plural* **slats**)
a thin strip of wood or plastic, usually arranged to overlap with others, for example in a blind or screen

slate *noun* (*plural* **slates**)
1 a kind of grey rock that is easily split into flat plates **2** a piece of this rock used to cover a roof
slaty *adjective* like slate

slaughter ➤ *verb* (**slaughters, slaughtering, slaughtered**) (*pronounced* **slor-**ter)
1 to slaughter an animal is to kill it for food **2** to slaughter people or animals is to kill a lot of them

slaughter ➤ *noun*
slaughtering or killing

slaughterhouse *noun* (*plural* **slaughterhouses**)
a place where animals are killed for food

slave ➤ *noun* (*plural* **slaves**)
a person who is owned by someone else and has to work for them without being paid

slave ➤ *verb* (**slaves, slaving, slaved**)
to slave is to work very hard

slavery *noun*
the system of having slaves

slay *verb* (**slays, slaying, slew, slain**)
(*old or poetical use*) to slay someone is to kill them

sledge or **sled** *noun* (*plural* **sledges** or **sleds**)
a vehicle for travelling over snow, with strips of metal or wood instead of wheels

sledgehammer *noun* (*plural* **sledgehammers**)
a very large heavy hammer

sleek *adjective* (**sleeker, sleekest**)
smooth and shiny ♦ *She has lovely sleek hair*

sleep ➤ *noun*
1 sleep is the condition in which the eyes are closed, the body is relaxed, and the mind is unconscious ♦ *You need some sleep* **2** a sleep is a time when you are sleeping ♦ *Have a sleep*

sleep ➤ *verb* (**sleeps, sleeping, slept**)
to sleep is to have a sleep

sleeper *noun* (*plural* **sleepers**)
1 someone who is asleep **2** each of the wooden or concrete beams on which a railway line rests **3** a railway carriage equipped for sleeping in

sleeping bag *noun* (*plural* **sleeping bags**)
a warm padded bag for sleeping in, especially when camping

sleepless *adjective*
unable to sleep; without sleep ♦ *We've had a sleepless night*

sleepwalker *noun* (*plural* **sleepwalkers**)
someone who walks around while asleep

sleepwalking *noun* what a sleepwalker does

sleepy *adjective* (**sleepier, sleepiest**)
feeling like sleeping; wanting to sleep
sleepily *adverb* in a sleepy way **sleepiness** *noun* being sleepy

sleet *noun*
a mixture of rain with snow or hail

sleeve *noun* (*plural* **sleeves**)
1 the part of a piece of clothing that covers your arm **2** the cover of a record
sleeveless *adjective* not having sleeves

sleigh *noun* (*plural* **sleighs**) (*pronounced* slay)
a large sledge pulled by horses

slender *adjective* (**slenderer, slenderest**)
1 slim or thin **2** slight or small ♦ *Their chances of winning are slender*

slept past tense and past participle of **sleep** verb

slew past tense of **slay**

slice ➤ *noun* (*plural* **slices**)
a thin flat piece cut off something

slice ➤ *verb* (**slices, slicing, sliced**)
to slice something is to cut it into slices

slick ➤ *adjective* (**slicker, slickest**)
quick and clever or cunning

slick ➤ *noun* (*plural* **slicks**)
a large patch of oil floating on water

slide ➤ *verb* (**slides, sliding, slid**)
1 to slide is to move smoothly over a flat or polished or slippery surface **2** to slide somewhere is to move quickly or secretly there ♦ *The thief slid behind a bush*

slide ➤ *noun* (*plural* **slides**)
1 a sliding movement **2** a smooth slope or a slippery surface on which people or things can slide **3** a type of photograph that lets light through and that can be shown on a screen **4** a small glass plate on which things are examined under a microscope **5** a fastener for keeping hair tidy

slight *adjective* (**slighter, slightest**)
very small; not serious or important

slightly *adverb*
in a slight way; not seriously ♦ *They were slightly hurt*

slim ➤ *adjective* (**slimmer, slimmest**)
1 thin and graceful **2** small; hardly enough ♦ *We have a slim chance of succeeding*

slim ➤ *verb* (**slims, slimming, slimmed**)
to slim is to try to make yourself thinner, especially by dieting
slimmer *noun* someone who is slimming

slime *noun*
unpleasant wet slippery stuff ♦ *There was slime on the pond*

slimy *adjective* like slime

sling ➤ *verb* (**slings, slinging, slung**)
1 to sling something is to throw it forcefully or carelessly ♦ *They were slinging stones at us* **2** to sling something is also to hang it up or support it so that it hangs loosely ♦ *He had slung the bag round his neck*

sling ➤ *noun* (*plural* **slings**)
1 a piece of cloth tied round the neck to support an injured arm **2** a device for throwing stones

slink *verb* (**slinks, slinking, slunk**)
to slink is to move in a stealthy or guilty way ♦ *He slunk off to bed*

slip ➤ *verb* (**slips, slipping, slipped**)
1 to slip is to slide without meaning to or to fall over **2** to slip somewhere is to move there quickly and quietly ♦ *We slipped away from the party* **3** to slip something somewhere is to put it there quickly without being seen ♦ *Slip this in your pocket* **4** to slip something is to escape from it ♦ *The dog slipped its leash*
to slip up is to make a mistake

slip ➤ *noun* (*plural* **slips**)
1 an accidental slide or fall **2** a minor mistake **3** a small piece of paper **4** a petticoat **5** a pillowcase
to give someone the slip is to escape from them or avoid them

slipper *noun* (*plural* **slippers**)
a soft comfortable shoe for wearing indoors

slippery *adjective*
smooth or wet so that it is difficult to stand on or hold

slipshod *adjective*
careless or badly done

slit ➤ *noun* (*plural* **slits**)
a long narrow cut or opening

slit ➤ *verb* (**slits, slitting, slit**)
to slit something is to make a slit in it

slither *verb* (**slithers, slithering, slithered**)
to slither is to slip or slide unsteadily

sliver *noun* (*plural* **slivers**) (*pronounced* sli-ver)
a thin strip of wood, glass, or other material

slog ➤ *verb* (**slogs, slogging, slogged**)
1 to slog something is to hit it hard or wildly **2** to slog is to work hard ♦ *I'm slogging away at my essay* **3** to slog is also to walk with effort ♦ *We slogged through the snow*

slog ➤ *noun*
a piece of hard work or effort

slogan *noun* (*plural* **slogans**)
a catchy phrase used to advertise something or to summarize an idea

slop *verb* (**slops, slopping, slopped**)
1 to slop liquid is to spill it over the edge of its container **2** liquid slops when it spills in this way

slope ➤ *verb* (**slopes, sloping, sloped**)
to slope is to go gradually downwards or upwards or to have one end higher than the other

slope ➤ *noun* (*plural* **slopes**)
1 a sloping surface **2** the amount by which a surface slopes ♦ *The hill has a slope of 10%*

sloppy *adjective* (**sloppier, sloppiest**)
1 liquid and slopping easily **2** careless or badly done ♦ *Their work is sloppy* **3** (*informal*) weak and sentimental ♦ *What a sloppy story*
sloppily *adverb* in a sloppy way **sloppiness** *noun* being sloppy

slops *plural noun*
liquid waste matter

slosh *verb* (**sloshes, sloshing, sloshed**)
1 to slosh is to splash or slop **2** to slosh liquid is to slop it carelessly **3** (*slang*) to slosh someone is to hit them hard

slot *noun* (*plural* **slots**)
a narrow opening to put things in

sloth *noun* (*plural* **sloths**) (*rhymes with* both)
1 laziness **2** a long-haired South American animal that lives in trees and moves very slowly

slot machine *noun* (*plural* **slot machines**)
a machine that is worked by putting a coin in a slot

slouch *verb* (**slouches, slouching, slouched**)
to slouch is to move or stand or sit in a lazy way, especially with your head and shoulders bent forwards

slovenly *adjective* (*pronounced* sluv-en-li)
careless or untidy

slow ➤ *adjective* (**slower, slowest**)
1 not quick; taking more time than usual
2 showing a time earlier than the correct time ♦ *Your watch is slow*

slow ➤ *adverb*
at a slow rate; slowly ♦ *Go slow*
slowness *noun* being slow

slow ➤ *verb* (**slows, slowing, slowed**)
to slow, or to slow down, is to go slower

slowcoach *noun* (*plural* **slowcoaches**)
(*informal*) someone who moves or works slowly

slowly *adverb*
at a slow rate or speed

sludge *noun*
thick sticky mud

slug *noun* (*plural* **slugs**)
1 a small slimy animal like a snail without its shell 2 a pellet for firing from a gun

slum *noun* (*plural* **slums**)
an area of dirty and crowded houses

slumber ➤ *noun*
peaceful sleep

slumber ➤ *verb* (**slumbers, slumbering, slumbered**)
to slumber is to sleep peacefully

slump ➤ *verb* (**slumps, slumping, slumped**)
to slump is to fall heavily or suddenly

slump ➤ *noun* (*plural* **slumps**)
a slump is a sudden fall in prices or trade

slung past tense and past participle of **sling** *verb*

slunk past tense and past participle of **slink**

slur *noun* (*plural* **slurs**)
something that harms a person's reputation; an insult

slush *noun*
snow that is melting on the ground
slushy *adjective* melting and wet, like slush

sly *adjective* (**slyer, slyest**)
cunning or mischievous
slyly *adverb* in a sly way **slyness** *noun* being sly

smack ➤ *verb* (**smacks, smacking, smacked**)
to smack someone is to slap them with the hand, especially as a punishment

smack ➤ *noun* (*plural* **smacks**)
a slap with the hand

small *adjective* (**smaller, smallest**)
not large; less than the normal size

smallpox *noun*
a serious disease that causes a fever and produces spots that leave scars on the skin

smart ➤ *adjective* (**smarter, smartest**)
1 neat and well dressed 2 clever 3 fast
♦ *She ran at a smart pace*
smartly *adverb* in a smart way **smartness** *noun* being smart

smart ➤ *verb* (**smarts, smarting, smarted**)
to smart is to feel a stinging pain

smarten *verb* (**smartens, smartening, smartened**)
1 to smarten something or someone is to make them smarter 2 to smarten is to become smarter

smash ➤ *verb* (**smashes, smashing, smashed**)
1 to smash is to break into pieces noisily and violently; to smash something is to break it in this way 2 to smash into something is to hit it with great force
♦ *The lorry left the road and smashed into a wall* 3 (*informal*) to smash something or someone is to destroy them or defeat them completely

smash ➤ *noun* (*plural* **smashes**)
1 the act or sound of smashing 2 a collision between vehicles

smash hit *noun* (*plural* **smash hits**)
(*informal*) something very successful or popular

smashing *adjective*
(*informal*) excellent

smear ➤ *verb* (**smears, smearing, smeared**)
1 to smear something dirty or greasy is to rub it thickly over a surface 2 to smear someone is to try to damage their reputation

smear ➤ *noun* (*plural* **smears**)
a mark made by smearing; a smudge

smell ➤ *verb* (**smells, smelling, smelt or smelled**)
1 to smell something is to use your nose to sense it 2 to smell is to give out a smell
♦ *The cheese smells funny*

smell ➤ *noun* (*plural* **smells**)
1 something you can smell, especially something unpleasant 2 the ability to smell things ♦ *I have a good sense of smell*

smelly *adjective* (**smellier, smelliest**)
having an unpleasant smell

smelt *verb* (**smelts, smelting, smelted**)
to smelt ore is to melt it so as to get metal from it

smile ➤ *noun* (*plural* **smiles**)
an expression on the face that shows pleasure or amusement, with the lips stretched and turning upwards at the ends

smile ➤ *verb* (**smiles, smiling, smiled**)
to smile is to give a smile

smith noun (plural **smiths**)
someone who makes things out of metal

smithereens plural noun
small fragments ♦ *They smashed it to smithereens*

smock noun (plural **smocks**)
a loose garment like a very long shirt

smog noun
a mixture of smoke and fog

smoke ➤ noun
1 smoke is the grey or blue mixture of gas and particles that rises from a fire 2 a smoke is a spell of smoking tobacco ♦ *He wants a smoke*
smoky adjective full of smoke

smoke ➤ verb (**smokes, smoking, smoked**)
1 to smoke is to give out smoke ♦ *The fire is smoking* 2 to smoke is also to breathe in the smoke of tobacco
smoker noun someone who smokes tobacco

smokeless adjective
burning without giving off much smoke

smooth ➤ adjective (**smoother, smoothest**)
1 having an even surface without any marks or roughness 2 moving without bumps or jolts ♦ *We had a smooth ride* 3 not harsh; flowing easily ♦ *She spoke in a smooth voice*
smoothly adverb in a smooth way; evenly
smoothness noun being smooth

smooth ➤ verb (**smooths, smoothing, smoothed**)
to smooth something is to make it smooth

smother verb (**smothers, smothering, smothered**)
1 to smother someone is to stop them from breathing 2 to smother something is to cover it thickly ♦ *He brought in a cake smothered in icing* 3 to smother a fire is to put it out by covering it

smoulder verb (**smoulders, smouldering, smouldered**)
to smoulder is to burn slowly without a flame

smudge ➤ noun (plural **smudges**)
a dirty mark made by rubbing something

smudge ➤ verb (**smudges, smudging, smudged**)
to smudge something is to make a smudge on it

smuggle verb (**smuggles, smuggling, smuggled**)
to smuggle something is to bring it into a country secretly and illegally
smuggler noun someone who smuggles goods

smut noun (plural **smuts**)
1 a smut is a small piece of soot or dirt 2 smut is something rude or indecent
smutty adjective indecent

snack noun (plural **snacks**)
a quick light meal

snag noun (plural **snags**)
an unexpected difficulty or obstacle

snail noun (plural **snails**)
a small animal with a soft body in a hard shell

snake noun (plural **snakes**)
a reptile with a long narrow body and no legs
snaky adjective winding like a snake

snap ➤ verb (**snaps, snapping, snapped**)
1 to snap is to break suddenly with a sharp noise 2 to snap is also to bite suddenly or quickly ♦ *The dog snapped at me* 3 to snap something is to say it quickly and angrily 4 to snap your fingers is to make a sharp snapping sound with them 5 to snap something or someone is to take a snapshot of them

snap ➤ noun (plural **snaps**)
1 the act or sound of snapping 2 a snapshot 3 a card game in which players shout 'Snap!' when they spot two similar cards

snappy adjective (**snappier, snappiest**)
quick and lively

snapshot noun (plural **snapshots**)
a photograph taken with a simple camera

snare ➤ noun (plural **snares**)
a trap for catching animals

snare ➤ verb (**snares, snaring, snared**)
to snare an animal is to catch it in a snare

snarl[1] ➤ verb (**snarls, snarling, snarled**)
to snarl is to growl angrily

snarl ➤ noun (plural **snarls**)
a snarling sound

snarl[2] verb to be snarled up is to become tangled or jammed ♦ *The motorway was snarled up for several miles*

snatch ➤ verb (**snatches, snatching, snatched**)
to snatch something is to grab it quickly ♦ *He snatched the bag from me*

snatch ➤ noun (plural **snatches**)
1 a short piece of speech or music 2 (*informal*) a robbery or theft

sneak ➤ verb (**sneaks, sneaking, sneaked**)
1 to sneak is to move quietly and secretly 2 (*informal*) to sneak on someone is to tell tales about them

sneak ➤ noun (plural **sneaks**)
(*informal*) a person who tells tales

sneaky *adjective* (**sneakier, sneakiest**)
dishonest or deceitful

sneer *verb* (**sneers, sneering, sneered**)
to sneer is to speak or behave in a scornful way

sneeze ➤ *verb* (**sneezes, sneezing, sneezed**)
to push air through your nose suddenly and uncontrollably ♦ *She was sneezing a lot because of her cold*
not to be sneezed at (*informal*) valuable or important

sneeze ➤ *noun* (*plural* **sneezes**)
the action or sound of sneezing

sniff ➤ *verb* (**sniffs, sniffing, sniffed**)
1 to sniff is to make a noise by drawing air in through your nose **2** to sniff something is to smell it with a sniff

sniff ➤ *noun* (*plural* **sniffs**)
the action or sound of sniffing or smelling something

snigger ➤ *verb* (**sniggers, sniggering, sniggered**)
to snigger is to give a quiet sly laugh

snigger ➤ *noun* (*plural* **sniggers**)
a quiet sly laugh

snip ➤ *verb* (**snips, snipping, snipped**)
to snip something is to cut a small piece or pieces off it

snip ➤ *noun* (*plural* **snips**)
an act of snipping something

snipe *verb* (**snipes, sniping, sniped**)
to snipe is to shoot at people from a hiding place
sniper *noun* someone who snipes at people

snippet *noun* (*plural* **snippets**)
a short piece of news or information

snivel *verb* (**snivels, snivelling, snivelled**)
to snivel is to cry or complain in a whining way

snob *noun* (*plural* **snobs**)
someone who despises people who have not got wealth or power or particular tastes or interests
snobbery *noun* being a snob **snobbish** *adjective* like a snob

snooker *noun*
a game played with long sticks (called *cues*) and 22 balls on a cloth-covered table

snoop *verb* (**snoops, snooping, snooped**)
to snoop is to pry or try to find out about someone else's business
snooper *noun* someone who snoops

snore *verb* (**snores, snoring, snored**)
to snore is to breathe noisily while sleeping

snorkel *noun* (*plural* **snorkels**)
a tube with one end above the water, worn by an underwater swimmer to get air

snort ➤ *verb* (**snorts, snorting, snorted**)
to snort is to make a loud noise by forcing air out through the nose

snort ➤ *noun* (*plural* **snorts**)
a snorting noise

snout *noun* (*plural* **snouts**)
the front projecting part of an animal's head, with its nose and mouth

snow ➤ *noun*
frozen drops of water falling from the sky as small white flakes

snow ➤ *verb* (**snows, snowing, snowed**)
it is snowing snow is falling

snowball *noun* (*plural* **snowballs**)
snow pressed into the shape of a ball for throwing

snowdrop *noun* (*plural* **snowdrops**)
a small white flower that blooms in early spring

snowflake *noun* (*plural* **snowflakes**)
a flake of snow

snowman *noun* (*plural* **snowmen**)
a figure made of snow

snowplough *noun* (*plural* **snowploughs**)
a vehicle or device for clearing snow from a road or railway track

snowshoe *noun* (*plural* **snowshoes**)
a broad frame with a mesh, attached to the feet for walking over deep snow without sinking in

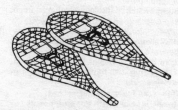

snowstorm *noun* (*plural* **snowstorms**)
a storm with snow falling

snowy *adjective* (**snowier, snowiest**)
1 with snow falling ♦ *We're expecting snowy weather* 2 covered with snow ♦ *The roofs looked snowy* 3 brightly white

snub *verb* (**snubs, snubbing, snubbed**)
to snub someone is to treat them in a scornful or unfriendly way

snub-nosed *adjective*
having a short turned-up nose

snuff *noun*
powdered tobacco that is taken into the nose by sniffing

snug *adjective* (**snugger, snuggest**)
warm and comfortable
snugly *adverb* in a snug way

snuggle *verb* (**snuggles, snuggling, snuggled**)
to snuggle is to curl up in a warm comfortable place ♦ *She snuggled down in bed*

so ➤ *adverb*
1 in this way; to such an extent ♦ *Why are you so cross?* 2 very ♦ *Cricket is so boring* 3 also ♦ *I was wrong but so were you*
and so on and other similar things ♦ *They took food, water, spare clothing, and so on*
or so or about that number ♦ *We need about fifty or so*
so as to in order to
so far up to now
so what? (*informal*) what does that matter?

so ➤ *conjunction*
for that reason ♦ *They threw me out, so I came here*

soak *verb* (**soaks, soaking, soaked**)
to soak someone or something is to make them very wet
to soak something up is to take in a liquid in the way that a sponge does

so-and-so *noun* (*plural* **so-and-so's**)
(*informal*) 1 a person or thing that need not be named ♦ *Old so-and-so told me*
2 an unpleasant person ♦ *He's a real so-and-so*

soap *noun* (*plural* **soaps**)
1 a substance used with water for washing and cleaning things 2 (*informal*) a soap opera
soapy *adjective* like soap; covered in soap

soap opera *noun* (*plural* **soap operas**)
a television serial about the day-to-day life of a group of imaginary people

soar *verb* (**soars, soaring, soared**)
1 to soar is to rise or fly high in the air
2 to soar is also to increase a lot ♦ *Prices were soaring*

sob ➤ *verb* (**sobs, sobbing, sobbed**)
to sob is to cry with gasping noises

sob ➤ *noun* (*plural* **sobs**)
a sound of sobbing

sober *adjective*
1 not drunk 2 calm and serious ♦ *She had a sober expression* 3 not bright or showy ♦ *The room was painted in sober colours*
soberly *adverb* in a sober way **sobriety** *noun* being sober

so-called *adjective*
named in what may be the wrong way
♦ *Even the so-called experts couldn't solve the problem*

soccer *noun*
Association football

sociable *adjective* (*pronounced* **soh**-sha-bul)
liking to be with other people; friendly
sociably *adverb* in a sociable way **sociability** *noun* being sociable

social *adjective* (*pronounced* **soh**-shal)
1 living in a community 2 to do with society ♦ *They were writing a social history of the area* 3 helping the people in a community ♦ *She wants to be a social worker* 4 helping people to meet one another ♦ *Let's join a social club*
socially *adverb* in a social way

socialism *noun*
a political system in which wealth is equally shared and the main industries and resources are controlled by the government

socialist *noun* (*plural* **socialists**)
someone who believes in socialism

society *noun* (*plural* **societies**)
1 a society is a community of people; society is people living together in a group or nation 2 a society is also a group of people organized for a particular purpose
♦ *He's joined a dramatic society* 3 society is also company or companionship ♦ *We enjoy the society of our friends*

sociology *noun* (*pronounced* soh-si-ol-o-ji)
the study of society or societies
sociological *adjective* to do with sociology
sociologist *noun* someone who studies sociology

sock [1] *noun* (*plural* **socks**)
a soft piece of clothing that covers your foot and the lower half of your leg
to pull your socks up (*informal*) is to try to do better

sock [2] *verb* (**socks, socking, socked**)
(*informal*) to sock someone is to hit or punch them hard ♦ *He socked me on the jaw*

socket *noun* (*plural* **sockets**)
a device or hole into which something fits, especially the place where an electric plug or bulb is put to make a connection

soda *noun*
1 a substance made from sodium, such as baking soda 2 soda water

soda water *noun*
fizzy water used in drinks

sodium *noun* (*pronounced* soh-di-um)
a soft silvery-white metal

sofa *noun* (*plural* **sofas**)
a long soft seat with sides and a back

soft *adjective* (**softer, softest**)
1 not hard or firm; easily pressed or cut into a new shape 2 smooth; not rough or stiff 3 gentle; not loud ♦ *He spoke in a soft voice*
softly *adverb* gently; quietly **softness** *noun* being soft

soft drink *noun* (*plural* **soft drinks**)
a drink that does not contain alcohol

soften *verb* (**softens, softening, softened**)
1 to soften something is to make it softer
2 to soften is to become softer

software *noun*
(*in Computing*) programs and data, which are not part of the machinery (the *hardware*) of a computer

soggy *adjective* (**soggier, soggiest**)
very wet and heavy

soil[1] *noun*
the loose earth that plants grow in

soil[2] *verb* (**soils, soiling, soiled**)
to soil something is to make it dirty

solar *adjective*
to do with the sun or powered by the sun's energy

solar system *noun*
the sun and the planets that revolve round it

sold past tense and past participle of **sell**

solder ➤ *noun*
a soft alloy that is melted to join pieces of metal together

solder ➤ *verb* (**solders, soldering, soldered**)
to solder things is to join them with solder

soldier *noun* (*plural* **soldiers**)
a member of an army

sole[1] *noun* (*plural* **soles**)
1 the bottom part of a shoe or foot 2 a flat sea fish used for food

sole[2] *adjective*
single or only ♦ *She was the sole survivor*
solely *adverb* only

solemn *adjective*
serious and dignified
solemnly *adverb* in a solemn way **solemnity** *noun* being solemn

solicitor *noun* (*plural* **solicitors**)
a lawyer who advises clients and prepares legal documents

solid ➤ *adjective*
1 not hollow; with no space inside
2 keeping its shape; not a liquid or gas
3 firm or strongly made ♦ *The house is built on solid foundations* 4 strong and reliable ♦ *They gave solid support*
solidly *adverb* in a solid way **solidity** *noun* being solid

solid ➤ *noun* (*plural* **solids**)
a solid thing or shape

solidify *verb* (**solidifies, solidifying, solidified**)
1 to solidify is to become solid 2 to solidify something is to make it solid

soliloquy *noun* (*plural* **soliloquies**)
(*pronounced* so-lil-o-kwi)
a speech expressing deep thoughts, made by an actor alone on the stage and not addressed to anyone else

solitary *adjective*
1 alone; on your own ♦ *He lived a solitary life* 2 single ♦ *This is a solitary example*

solitude *noun*
being on your own

solo *noun* (*plural* **solos**)
something sung or performed by one person

soloist *noun* (*plural* **soloists**)
someone who plays or sings a solo

solstice *noun* (*plural* **solstices**)
either of the two times in the year when the sun is at its furthest point north or south of the equator. The **summer solstice** is about 21 June, and the **winter solstice** is about 22 December, in the northern hemisphere

soluble *adjective*
1 able to be dissolved 2 able to be solved ♦ *Is the problem soluble?*
solubility *noun* being soluble

solution *noun* (*plural* **solutions**)
1 a liquid with something dissolved in it
2 the answer to a problem or puzzle

solve *verb* (**solves, solving, solved**)
to solve a problem or puzzle is to find an answer to it

solvent ➤ *noun* (*plural* **solvents**)
a liquid in which other substances can be dissolved

solvent ➤ *adjective*
having enough money to pay your debts

sombre *adjective*
gloomy or dark

some ➤ *adjective*
1 a few or a little ♦ *I'd like some biscuits and some sugar* 2 a certain amount of ♦ *Would you like some cake?* 3 an unknown person or thing ♦ *Some fool left the window open*

some ➤ *pronoun*
a certain or unknown number or amount ♦ *Some of them were late*

somebody *pronoun*
someone; some person

somehow *adverb*
in some way ♦ *We must finish the work somehow*

someone *pronoun*
some person

somersault *noun* (*plural* **somersaults**)
(*pronounced* **sum**-er-solt)
a movement in which you turn head over heels and land on your feet

something *pronoun*
a certain or unknown thing

sometime *adverb*
at some time ♦ *I saw her sometime last year*

sometimes *adverb*
at some times but not always ♦ *We sometimes walk to school*

somewhat *adverb*
to some extent; rather ♦ *He was somewhat annoyed*

somewhere *adverb*
in or to some place

son *noun* (*plural* **sons**)
a boy or man who is someone's child

sonar *noun* (*plural* **sonars**)
a system using the echo from sound waves to locate objects underwater

song *noun* (*plural* **songs**)
1 a song is a tune for singing 2 song is singing ♦ *He burst into song*
a song and dance (*informal*) a great fuss

songbird *noun* (*plural* **songbirds**)
a bird that sings sweetly

sonic *adjective*
to do with sound or sound waves

sonnet *noun* (*plural* **sonnets**)
a kind of poem with 14 lines

soon *adverb* (**sooner, soonest**)
1 in a short time from now 2 not long after something ♦ *She became ill, but was soon better* 3 early or quickly ♦ *You spoke too soon*
as soon as willingly ♦ *I'd just as soon stay at home*
sooner or later at some time in the future

soot *noun*
the black powder left by smoke in a chimney or on a building
sooty *adjective* covered in soot

soothe *verb* (**soothes, soothing, soothed**)
1 to soothe someone is to make them calm 2 to soothe a pain or ache is to ease it

sophisticated *adjective* (*pronounced* sof-**iss**-ti-kay-tid)
1 used to a fashionable or cultured life ♦ *They are sophisticated people*
2 complicated ♦ *It is a sophisticated machine*
sophistication *noun* being sophisticated

sopping *adjective*
very wet; soaked

soppy *adjective* (**soppier, soppiest**)
(*informal*) sentimental or silly

soprano *noun* (*plural* **sopranos**)
(*pronounced* so-**prah**-noh)
a singer with a high singing voice

sorcerer *noun* (*plural* **sorcerers**)
someone who can do magic; a wizard
sorcery *noun* magic or witchcraft

sorceress *noun* (*plural* **sorceresses**)
a woman who can do magic

sore ➤ *adjective* (**sorer, sorest**)
1 painful or smarting 2 (*informal*) annoyed or upset
soreness *noun* being sore

sore ➤ *noun* (*plural* **sores**)
a sore place

sorely *adverb*
seriously; very ♦ *I was sorely tempted to run away*

sorrow *noun* (*plural* **sorrows**)
sadness or regret
sorrowful *adjective* feeling sorrow **sorrowfully** *adverb* in a sorrowful way

sorry *adjective* (**sorrier, sorriest**)
1 feeling regret ♦ *I'm sorry I forgot to send you a birthday card* 2 feeling pity ♦ *She felt sorry for the lost child*

sort ➤ *noun* (*plural* **sorts**)
a group of things or people that are similar; a kind ♦ *What sort of fruit do you like?*
sort of (*informal*) rather; to some extent ♦ *I sort of wanted to go*

sort ➤ *verb* (**sorts, sorting, sorted**)
  to sort things is to arrange them in groups or kinds
  to sort something out is to organize it or arrange it
  to sort someone out (*informal*) is to deal with or punish them

SOS *noun*
  an urgent appeal for help from someone whose life is in danger

sought past tense and past participle of **seek**

soul *noun* (*plural* **souls**)
  the invisible part of a person that is believed to go on living after the body has died

sound[1] ➤ *noun* (*plural* **sounds**)
  1 sound is vibrations in the air that you can detect with your ear **2** a sound is something that can be heard

sound ➤ *verb* (**sounds, sounding, sounded**)
  1 to sound is to make a sound ♦ *A bell sounded* **2** to sound a certain way is to give that impression when heard ♦ *He sounds angry* ♦ *The car sounds as if it needs a service*

sound[2] *verb* (**sounds, sounding, sounded**)
  to sound a river or sea is to test the depth of it
  to sound someone out is to try to find out what they think or feel about something

sound[3] *adjective* (**sounder, soundest**)
  1 not damaged; in good condition **2** healthy **3** reasonable or correct ♦ *His ideas are sound* **4** reliable or secure ♦ *They made a sound investment* **5** thorough or deep ♦ *I could do with a sound sleep*
  soundly *adverb* thoroughly or completely **soundness** *noun* being sound

sound[4] *noun* (*plural* **sounds**)
  a narrow passage of water

sound barrier *noun*
  the resistance of the air to objects moving at speeds near the speed of sound

sound effects *plural noun*
  special sounds produced to make a play or film more realistic

soundtrack *noun* (*plural* **soundtracks**)
  the sound that goes with a cinema film

soup *noun* (*plural* **soups**)
  a liquid food made from vegetables or meat

sour *adjective* (**sourer, sourest**)
  1 having a sharp taste like vinegar or lemons **2** unpleasant or bad-tempered
  sourly *adverb* in a sour way **sourness** *noun* being sour

source *noun* (*plural* **sources**)
  the place where something comes from

south ➤ *noun*
  1 the direction to the right of a person facing east **2** the part of a country or city that is in this direction

south ➤ *adjective* and *adverb*
  1 towards the south or in the south **2** coming from the south ♦ *A south wind was blowing*

south-east *noun, adjective,* and *adverb*
  midway between south and east

southerly *adjective* (*pronounced* **suth**-er-lee)
  a southerly wind is one that blows from the south

southern *adjective* (*pronounced* **suth**-ern)
  from or to do with the south

southerner *noun* (*plural* **southerners**) (*pronounced* **suth**-er-ner)
  someone who lives in the south of a country

southward or **southwards** *adjective* and *adverb*
  towards the south

south-west *noun , adjective,* and *adverb*
  midway between south and west

souvenir *noun* (*plural* **souvenirs**) (*pronounced* soo-ven-**eer**)
  something that you keep to remind you of a person, place, or event

sovereign *noun* (*plural* **sovereigns**) (*pronounced* **sov**-rin)
  1 a king or a queen **2** an old British gold coin that was worth £1

sow[1] *verb* (**sows, sowing, sowed, sown** or **sowed**) (*rhymes with* go)
  to sow seeds is to put them into the ground so that they will grow into plants
  sower *noun* someone who sows seeds

sow[2] *noun* (*plural* **sows**) (*rhymes with* cow)
  a female pig

soya bean *noun* (*plural* **soya beans**)
  a kind of bean from which edible oil and flour are made

space ➤ *noun* (*plural* **spaces**)
  1 space is the whole area outside the earth, where the stars and planets are **2** space is also an area or volume ♦ *There is plenty of space for a car* **3** a space is an empty area or gap ♦ *There is a space at the back of the cupboard* **4** a space is also a period of time ♦ *They moved house twice in the space of a year*

space ➤ *verb* (**spaces, spacing, spaced**)
  to space things, or space things out, is to
  arrange them with gaps or periods of time
  between them

spacecraft *noun* (*plural* **spacecraft**)
  a vehicle for travelling in outer space

spaceman *noun* (*plural* **spacemen**)
  a man who travels in a spacecraft

spaceship *noun* (*plural* **spaceships**)
  a spacecraft

space shuttle *noun* (*plural* **space shuttles**)
  a spacecraft that can travel into space and
  return to earth

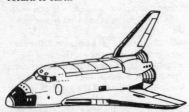

space station *noun* (*plural* **space stations**)
  a satellite which orbits the earth and is
  used as a base by scientists and
  astronauts

spacewoman *noun* (*plural* **spacewomen**)
  a woman who travels in a spacecraft

spacious *adjective*
  roomy
  spaciously *adverb* in a spacious way
  spaciousness *noun* being spacious

spade *noun* (*plural* **spades**)
  1 a tool with a long handle and a wide
  blade for digging **2** a playing card with
  black shapes like upside-down hearts
  on it

spaghetti *noun* (*pronounced* spa-**get**-i)
  pasta made in long thin strips

span ➤ *noun* (*plural* **spans**)
  1 the length from one end of something
  to the other **2** the distance between the
  tips of your thumb and little finger when
  your hand is spread out **3** a part of a
  bridge between two supports **4** a period
  of time

span ➤ *verb* (**spans, spanning, spanned**)
  to span something is to reach from one
  side or end of it to the other ♦ *A bridge
  spanned the river*

spaniel *noun* (*plural* **spaniels**)
  a breed of dog with long ears and silky fur

spank *verb* (**spanks, spanking, spanked**)
  to spank someone is to smack them
  several times on the bottom as a
  punishment

spanner *noun* (*plural* **spanners**)
  a tool for tightening or loosening a nut

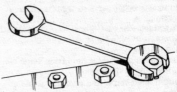

spar[1] *noun* (*plural* **spars**)
  a strong pole used for a mast or boom on a
  ship

spar[2] *verb* (**spars, sparring, sparred**)
  to spar is to practise boxing ♦ *He was my
  sparring partner*

spare ➤ *verb* (**spares, sparing, spared**)
  1 to spare something is to afford it or be
  able to give it to someone ♦ *Can you spare
  a moment?* **2** to spare someone is to be
  merciful towards them, or not harm them
  3 to spare something is to use it or treat it
  economically ♦ *No expense will be spared*

spare ➤ *adjective*
  1 not used but kept ready in case it is
  needed; extra ♦ *Where's the spare wheel?*
  2 thin or lean
  to go spare (*slang*) is to become angry

spare ➤ *noun* (*plural* **spares**)
  a spare thing or part ♦ *The local garage
  sells spares*

sparing *adjective*
  careful or economical, especially with
  money

spark ➤ *noun* (*plural* **sparks**)
  1 a tiny flash **2** a tiny glowing piece of
  something hot

spark ➤ *verb* (**sparks, sparking, sparked**)
  to spark is to give off sparks

sparking plug or **spark plug** *noun* (*plural*
  sparking plugs or **spark plugs**)
  a device that makes a spark to explode the
  fuel in an engine

sparkle *verb* (**sparkles, sparkling, sparkled**)
  to sparkle is to shine with a lot of tiny
  flashes of bright light

sparkler *noun* (*plural* **sparklers**)
  a firework that sparkles

sparrow *noun* (*plural* **sparrows**)
  a small brown bird

sparse *adjective* (**sparser, sparsest**)
  small in number or amount ♦ *Vegetation
  on the island is sparse*
  sparsely *adverb* in a sparse way **sparseness**
  noun being sparse

spastic *noun* (*plural* **spastics**)
someone born with a disability that makes it difficult for them to control their muscles

spat past tense and past participle of **spit** *verb*

spatter *verb* (**spatters, spattering, spattered**)
to spatter something is to splash it or scatter it in small drops or pieces ♦ *The lorry spattered mud all over the pavement*

spawn ➤ *noun*
the eggs of frogs, fish, and other water animals

spawn ➤ *verb* (**spawns, spawning, spawned**)
to spawn is to produce spawn

speak *verb* (**speaks, speaking, spoke, spoken**)
1 to speak is to say something ♦ *I spoke to them this morning* **2** to speak a language is to be able to talk in it ♦ *Do you speak German?*
to speak up is to say something more clearly or loudly

speaker *noun* (*plural* **speakers**)
1 a person who is speaking or making a speech **2** a loudspeaker
the Speaker the person who is in charge of debates in the House of Commons or similar parliaments

spear ➤ *noun* (*plural* **spears**)
a long pole with a sharp point, used as a weapon

spear ➤ *verb* (**spears, spearing, speared**)
to spear something is to pierce it with a spear or something pointed

special *adjective*
1 different from other people or things; unusual **2** meant for a particular person or purpose ♦ *You'll need special training*

specialist *noun* (*plural* **specialists**)
an expert in a particular subject

speciality *noun* (*plural* **specialities**)
1 something that someone specializes in **2** a special product, especially a food

specialize *verb* (**specializes, specializing, specialized**)
to specialize is to give particular attention to one subject or thing ♦ *She is specializing in biology*

specialization *noun* specializing in something

specially *adverb*
for a special purpose ♦ *I came specially to see you*

species *noun* (*plural* **species**) (*pronounced* spee-shiz)
a group of animals or plants that are very similar

specific *adjective*
1 definite or precise **2** to do with a particular thing ♦ *The money was given for a specific purpose*

specifically *adverb*
1 in a special way or for a special purpose ♦ *The car is designed specifically for the disabled* **2** clearly and precisely ♦ *I specifically said we had to go*

specification *noun* (*plural* **specifications**)
a detailed list or description of something

specific gravity *noun*
the mass of something compared with the mass of the same volume of water or air

specify *verb* (**specifies, specifying, specified**)
to specify a person or thing is to name them precisely ♦ *The recipe specified brown sugar, not white*

specimen *noun* (*plural* **specimens**)
1 a small amount or sample of something **2** an example of one kind of plant, animal, or thing ♦ *We saw a fine specimen of an oak*

speck *noun* (*plural* **specks**)
1 a tiny piece of something **2** a tiny mark or spot

speckled *adjective*
covered with small spots

spectacle *noun* (*plural* **spectacles**)
1 an exciting sight or display **2** a ridiculous sight

spectacles *plural noun*
a pair of lenses in a frame, worn over the eyes to help improve eyesight

spectacular *adjective*
exciting to see

spectator *noun* (*plural* **spectators**)
a person who watches a game or show

spectre *noun* (*plural* **spectres**) (*pronounced* spek-ter)
a ghost

spectrum *noun* (*plural* **spectra**)
1 the band of colours like those in a rainbow **2** a range of things or ideas ♦ *The library caters for a broad spectrum of interests*

speech *noun* (*plural* **speeches**)
1 speech is the action or power of speaking **2** a speech is a talk given to a group of people

speechless *adjective*
unable to speak, especially from surprise or anger

speed ➤ *noun* (*plural* **speeds**)
1 quickness; swiftness **2** the rate at which something moves or happens
at speed fast; quickly

speed ➤ *verb* (**speeds, speeding, sped** or **speeded**)
to speed is to go very fast or too fast
♦ *Drivers can be fined for speeding*
to speed up is to become quicker
to speed something up is to make it go or happen faster

speedboat *noun* (*plural* **speedboats**)
a fast motor boat

speedometer *noun* (*plural* **speedometers**) (*pronounced* spee-**dom**-it-er)
a device in a vehicle that shows its speed

speedway *noun* (*plural* **speedways**)
a track for motorcycle racing

speedy *adjective* (**speedier, speediest**)
quick or fast ♦ *We need a speedy reply*
speedily *adverb* fast or quickly

spell [1] *verb* (**spells, spelling, spelt** or **spelled**)
to spell a word is to give its letters in the right order

spell [2] *noun* (*plural* **spells**)
1 a period of time ♦ *We're having a cold spell* **2** a period of activity ♦ *I must do a spell of work now*

spell [3] *noun* (*plural* **spells**)
a saying that is supposed to have magic power

spelling *noun* (*plural* **spellings**)
the way in which letters are put together to form words

spend *verb* (**spends, spending, spent**)
1 to spend money is to use it to pay for things **2** to spend time is to pass it doing something ♦ *He spent a year in Singapore* **3** to spend something is also to use it up
♦ *She spends all her spare energy on gardening*

sperm *noun* (*plural* **sperms** or **sperm**)
the male sex cell that joins with an ovum to produce offspring

sphere *noun* (*plural* **spheres**)
1 a perfectly round solid shape; a globe or ball **2** an area of activity or interest
spherical *adjective* having the shape of a sphere

spice *noun* (*plural* **spices**)
a strong-tasting substance used to flavour food, often made from the dried parts of plants
spicy *adjective* strong-tasting, like spice

spider *noun* (*plural* **spiders**)
a small animal with eight legs that spins webs to catch insects on which it feeds

spied past tense and past participle of **spy** *verb*

spike *noun* (*plural* **spikes**)
a pointed piece of metal; a sharp point
spiky *adjective* full of spikes

spill ➤ *verb* (**spills, spilling, spilt** or **spilled**)
1 to spill something is to let it fall out of a container by accident **2** to spill is to fall out of a container ♦ *The coins came spilling out*

spill ➤ *noun* (*plural* **spills**)
1 spilling or something spilt **2** a minor accident or fall

spin ➤ *verb* (**spins, spinning, spun**)
1 to spin is to turn round and round quickly **2** to spin something is to make it spin **3** to spin is also to make pieces of wool or cotton into thread by twisting them **4** to spin a web or cocoon is to make it out of threads ♦ *The spider spun a web*

spin ➤ *noun* (*plural* **spins**)
1 a spinning movement **2** a short outing in a car

spinach *noun*
a vegetable with dark green leaves

spindle *noun* (*plural* **spindles**)
1 a thin rod on which you wind thread **2** a pin or bar that turns round, or on which something turns round

spin-drier *noun* (*plural* **spin-driers**)
a machine for drying clothes by spinning them round in a drum at high speed

spine *noun* (*plural* **spines**)
1 the line of bones down the middle of the back **2** a thorn or prickle **3** the back part of a book where the pages are joined together
spinal *adjective* to do with the spine **spiny** *adjective* prickly

spine-chilling *adjective*
frightening and exciting ♦ *We heard a spine-chilling ghost story*

spinning wheel *noun* (*plural* **spinning wheels**)
a machine for spinning thread out of wool or cotton

spin-off *noun* (*plural* **spin-offs**)
something extra produced while making something else

spinster *noun* (*plural* **spinsters**)
a woman who has not married

spiral *adjective*
going round and round a central point, getting further from it with each turn

spire *noun* (*plural* **spires**)
a tall pointed part on top of a church tower

spirit *noun* (*plural* **spirits**)
1 a person's spirit is their soul **2** a spirit is a ghost or other supernatural being **3** spirit is courage or liveliness **4** a person's spirits are their mood or the way they feel ♦ *She was in good spirits after the exam* **5** a spirit is also a strong alcoholic drink

spiritual ➤ *adjective*
1 to do with the human soul **2** to do with religion or the Church
spiritually *adverb* in a spiritual way

spiritual ➤ *noun* (*plural* **spirituals**)
a religious song originally sung by Black Americans

spiritualism *noun*
the belief that the spirits of dead people communicate with living people
spiritualist *noun* someone who practises spiritualism

spit[1] ➤ *verb* (**spits, spitting, spat**)
1 to spit is to send drops of liquid forcibly out of the mouth ♦ *He spat into the basin* **2** (*informal*) to spit is to rain lightly ♦ *It's only spitting*

spit ➤ *noun*
saliva or spittle

spit[2] *noun* (*plural* **spits**)
1 a long thin metal spike put through meat to hold it while it is roasted **2** a narrow strip of land sticking out into the sea

spite *noun*
a desire to hurt or annoy someone
in spite of something although something has happened or is happening ♦ *They went out in spite of the rain*
spiteful *adjective* showing spite **spitefully** in a spiteful way

spittle *noun*
saliva, especially when it is spat out

splash ➤ *verb* (**splashes, splashing, splashed**)
1 to splash liquid is to make it fly about, as you do when you jump into water **2** to splash is to fly about in drops ♦ *The water splashed all over me* **3** to splash someone or something is to make them wet by sending drops of liquid towards them ♦ *The bus splashed us as it went past*

splash ➤ *noun* (*plural* **splashes**)
the action or sound of splashing
to make a splash is to make a big display or effect

splashdown *noun* (*plural* **splashdowns**)
the landing of a spacecraft in the sea

splendid *adjective*
magnificent; very fine
splendidly *adverb* in a splendid way

splendour *noun*
splendour is a brilliant display or appearance

splint *noun* (*plural* **splints**)
a straight piece of wood, metal, etc. that is tied to a broken arm or leg to hold it firm

splinter ➤ *noun* (*plural* **splinters**)
a small sharp piece of wood or glass broken off a larger piece

splinter ➤ *verb* (**splinters, splintering, splintered**)
to splinter is to break into splinters

split ➤ *verb* (**splits, splitting, split**)
1 to split is to break into parts **2** to split something is to divide it into parts **3** (*slang*) to split is also to reveal a secret
to split up 1 is to divide into parts **2** is to separate after being together for some time

split ➤ *noun* (*plural* **splits**)
1 the splitting or dividing of something **2** a place where something has split
the splits a movement in gymnastics with the legs stretched widely in opposite directions

splutter *verb* (**splutters, spluttering, spluttered**)
1 to splutter is to make a quick series of spitting or coughing sounds ♦ *The smoke from the bonfire made him splutter* **2** to splutter is also to speak quickly and unclearly

spoil *verb* (**spoils, spoiling, spoilt or spoiled**)
1 to spoil something is to make it less good or useful ♦ *The rain spoilt our holiday* **2** to spoil someone is to make them selfish by always letting them have what they want

spoils *plural noun*
booty taken in war

spoilsport *noun* (*plural* **spoilsports**)
someone who spoils other people's fun

spoke[1] *noun* (*plural* **spokes**)
each of the rods or bars that go from the centre of a wheel to the rim

spoke[2] past tense of **speak**
spoken past participle of **speak**

spokesperson *noun* (*plural* **spokespersons**)
someone who speaks on behalf of a group of people

sponge ➤ *noun* (*plural* **sponges**)
1 a lump of soft material containing lots of tiny holes, used for washing **2** a sea creature from which this kind of material is made **3** a soft lightweight cake or pudding

sponge ➤ *verb* (**sponges, sponging, sponged**)
1 to sponge something is to wash it with a sponge **2** (*informal*) to sponge is to get money or help by cadging from people ♦ *He was sponging on his relatives*
sponger *noun* someone who cadges from people

spongy *adjective* (**spongier, spongiest**)
soft and absorbent like sponge

sponsor *noun* (*plural* **sponsors**)
someone who provides money or help for a person or thing, or who supports someone who sets out to do something for charity
sponsorship *noun* sponsoring someone

spontaneous *adjective* (*pronounced* spon-tay-ni-us)
happening or done without being planned; not forced or suggested by someone else ♦ *A spontaneous cheer greeted the local team*
spontaneously *adverb* in a spontaneous way
spontaneity *noun* being spontaneous

spooky *adjective* (**spookier, spookiest**)
(*informal*) frighteningly strange; haunted by ghosts

spool *noun* (*plural* **spools**)
a rod or reel for winding on something such as thread or film or tape

spoon ➤ *noun* (*plural* **spoons**)
a piece of metal or wood or plastic consisting of a small bowl with a handle, used for lifting food to the mouth or for stirring or measuring

spoon ➤ *verb* (**spoons, spooning, spooned**)
to spoon something is to lift it or take it with a spoon

spoonful *noun* (*plural* **spoonfuls**)
as much as a spoon will hold

sport *noun* (*plural* **sports**)
1 a sport is a game that exercises your body, especially a game played out of doors ♦ *What sports do you play?* **2** sport is games of this sort ♦ *Are you keen on sport?* **3** (*informal*) a sport is someone who plays or behaves fairly and unselfishly ♦ *Come on, be a sport*

sporting *adjective*
1 connected with sport; interested in sport
2 behaving fairly and unselfishly
a sporting chance a reasonable chance

sports car *noun* (*plural* **sports cars**)
an open low-built fast car

sports jacket *noun* (*plural* **sports jackets**)
a man's jacket for informal wear, not part of a suit

sportsman or **sportswoman** *noun* (*plural* **sportsmen** or **sportswomen**)
a man or woman who takes part in sport

sportsmanship *noun*
behaving fairly and generously in sport and in other ways

spot ➤ *noun* (*plural* **spots**)
1 a small round mark **2** a pimple **3** a small amount of something ♦ *We've had a spot of bother* **4** a place ♦ *This is a nice spot*
on the spot immediately; there and then ♦ *We can repair your bike on the spot*

spot ➤ *verb* (**spots, spotting, spotted**)
1 to spot someone or something is to notice them or see them **2** to spot things of interest is to go and watch them or study them ♦ *We're going to spot trains* **3** to spot something is to mark it with spots

spotless *adjective*
perfectly clean
spotlessly *adverb* in a spotless way

spotlight *noun* (*plural* **spotlights**)
a strong light with a beam that shines on a small area

spotter *noun* (*plural* **spotters**)
someone who spots things for a hobby ♦ *They are keen train-spotters*

spotty *adjective* (**spottier, spottiest**)
marked with spots

spout ➤ *noun* (*plural* **spouts**)
1 a pipe or opening from which liquid can pour **2** a jet of liquid

spout ➤ *verb* (**spouts, spouting, spouted**)
1 to spout is to come out in a jet of liquid
2 (*informal*) to spout is also to speak for a long time

sprain ➤ *verb* (**sprains, spraining, sprained**)
to sprain an ankle or wrist is to injure it by twisting it

sprain ➤ *noun* (*plural* **sprains**)
an injury by spraining

sprang past tense of **spring** *verb*

sprawl *verb* (**sprawls, sprawling, sprawled**)
1 to sprawl is to sit or lie with your arms and legs spread out **2** to be sprawled is to be spread out loosely or untidily ♦ *There were newspapers sprawled all over the floor*

spray¹ ➤ *verb* (**sprays, spraying, sprayed**)
to spray liquid is to scatter it in tiny drops over something; to spray something is to cover it with liquid in this way

spray ➤ *noun* (*plural* **sprays**)
1 tiny drops of liquid sprayed on
something 2 a device for spraying liquid

spray[2] *noun* (*plural* **sprays**)
a small bunch of flowers

spread ➤ *verb* (**spreads, spreading, spread**)
1 to spread something is to lay or stretch
it out to its full size ♦ *The bird spread its
wings* 2 to spread something over a
surface is to make it cover the surface
♦ *He spread jam on his toast* 3 to spread
news or information is to make it widely
known 4 to spread is when news or
information becomes widely known ♦ *The
story spread quickly round the village*

spread ➤ *noun* (*plural* **spreads**)
1 the action or result of spreading 2 the
breadth or extent of something
3 (*informal*) a large meal

spreadsheet *noun* (*plural* **spreadsheets**)
a computer program that allows you to set
out tables of figures, and to do complex
calculations

sprightly *adjective* (**sprightlier, sprightliest**)
lively and energetic

spring ➤ *verb* (**springs, springing, sprang,
sprung**)
1 to spring is to move quickly or suddenly
♦ *He sprang to his feet* 2 to spring, or
spring up, is to arise or happen ♦ *The
trouble has sprung from carelessness* 3 to
spring something on someone is to
surprise them with it ♦ *They sprang a new
idea on us last night*

spring ➤ *noun* (*plural* **springs**)
1 a spring is a springy coil of metal 2 a
spring is also a sudden upward movement
3 a spring is also a place were water rises
out of the ground 4 spring is the season of
the year when most plants start to grow,
between winter and summer

springboard *noun* (*plural* **springboards**)
a springy board from which people jump or
dive

spring-clean *verb* (**spring-cleans,
spring-cleaning, spring-cleaned**)
to spring-clean a house is to clean it
thoroughly, usually in spring

springtime *noun*
the season of spring

springy *adjective* (**springier, springiest**)
able to spring back to its original position
when you bend it or squeeze it and let
it go

sprinkle *verb* (**sprinkles, sprinkling, sprinkled**)
to sprinkle liquid or powder is to make
tiny drops or pieces of it fall on something
sprinkler *noun* a device for sprinkling liquid

sprint *verb* (**sprints, sprinting, sprinted**)
to sprint is to run very fast for a short
distance
sprinter *noun* someone who sprints

sprout ➤ *verb* (**sprouts, sprouting, sprouted**)
to sprout is to start to grow or to produce
leaves

sprout ➤ *noun* (*plural* **sprouts**)
a Brussels sprout

spruce[1] *noun* (*plural* **spruces**)
a kind of fir tree

spruce[2] *adjective* (**sprucer, sprucest**)
neat and smart

sprung past participle of **spring** *verb*

spud *noun* (*plural* **spuds**)
(*informal*) a potato

spun past tense and past participle of **spin**
verb

spur ➤ *noun* (*plural* **spurs**)
1 a sharp device worn on the heel of a
rider's boot to urge a horse to go faster
2 a ridge that sticks out from a mountain
on the spur of the moment on an impulse;
without planning

spur ➤ *verb* (**spurs, spurring, spurred**)
1 to spur a horse is to urge it to go faster
2 to spur someone, or to spur someone on,
is to encourage them

spurt ➤ *verb* (**spurts, spurting, spurted**)
1 to spurt is to gush out or up ♦ *Blood
spurted from the cut* 2 to spurt is also to
speed up suddenly ♦ *He spurted round the
corner*

spurt ➤ *noun* (*plural* **spurts**)
1 a jet of liquid 2 a sudden increase in
speed ♦ *He put on a spurt and caught us
up*

spy ➤ *noun* (*plural* **spies**)
someone who works secretly to find out
things about another country or person

spy ➤ *verb* (**spies, spying, spied**)
1 to spy is to be a spy or to watch secretly
♦ *He was spying on us* 2 to spy someone
or something is to see them or notice them
♦ *We spied a house in the distance*

squabble ➤ *verb* (**squabbles, squabbling,
squabbled**)
to squabble is to quarrel about something
unimportant

squabble ➤ *noun* (*plural* **squabbles**)
a minor quarrel or argument

squad *noun* (*plural* **squads**)
a small group of people working or being
trained together

squadron *noun* (*plural* **squadrons**)
part of an army, navy, or air force

squalid *adjective*
dirty and unpleasant ♦ *The houses were very squalid*
squalidly *adverb* in a squalid way **squalor** *noun* being squalid

squall *noun* (*plural* **squalls**)
1 a sudden storm or strong wind 2 a baby's loud cry
squally *adjective* windy

squander *verb* (**squanders, squandering, squandered**)
to squander money or time is to waste it

square ➤ *adjective*
1 having four equal sides and four right angles 2 forming a right angle or having right angles 3 used for units of measurement that give an area, such as a square metre and a square foot. For example, a square metre is the size of a square with each side one metre long 4 equal or even ♦ *The teams are square with six points each*
squareness *noun* being square

square ➤ *noun* (*plural* **squares**)
1 a square shape or object 2 in a town, an area surrounded by buildings 3 the result of multiplying a number by itself ♦ *9 is the square of 3*

square ➤ *verb* (**squares, squaring, squared**)
1 to square something is to make it square 2 to square a number is to multiply it by itself ♦ *3 squared is 9* 3 to square with something is to match it or agree with it ♦ *His story doesn't square with yours*

square deal *noun* (*plural* **square deals**)
a deal or agreement that is fair and honest

squarely *adverb*
directly; exactly ♦ *The ball hit him squarely in the mouth*

square meal *noun* (*plural* **square meals**)
a good satisfying meal

square root *noun* (*plural* **square roots**)
the number that gives a particular number if it is multiplied by itself ♦ *3 is the square root of 9*

squash ➤ *verb* (**squashes, squashing, squashed**)
1 to squash something is to squeeze it so that it loses its shape 2 to squash a person or thing into something is to force them into it when there is not much space ♦ *We squashed ourselves into the minibus*

squash ➤ *noun* (*plural* **squashes**)
1 a squash is a crowd or a crowded place ♦ *There was a tremendous squash outside the football ground* 2 squash is a fruit-flavoured drink 3 squash is also a game played with rackets and a small ball in a special indoor court

squat ➤ *verb* (**squats, squatting, squatted**)
1 to squat is to sit back on your heels 2 to squat in an unoccupied house is to live there without permission
squatter *noun* someone who squats in a house

squat ➤ *adjective* (**squatter, squattest**)
short and fat

squaw *noun* (*plural* **squaws**)
a Native American woman or wife

squawk ➤ *verb* (**squawks, squawking, squawked**)
to squawk is to make a loud harsh cry

squawk ➤ *noun* (*plural* **squawks**)
a squawking sound

squeak ➤ *verb* (**squeaks, squeaking, squeaked**)
to make a high-pitched sound or cry

squeak ➤ *noun* (*plural* **squeaks**)
a squeaking sound
squeaky *adjective* making squeaks

squeal ➤ *verb* (**squeals, squealing, squealed**)
to squeal is to make a long shrill sound

squeal ➤ *noun* (*plural* **squeals**)
a sound of squealing

squeeze ➤ *verb* (**squeezes, squeezing, squeezed**)
1 to squeeze something is to press it from opposite sides, especially so as to get liquid out of it 2 to squeeze somewhere is to force a way into or through a place or gap ♦ *We squeezed into the car*
squeezer *noun* a device for squeezing fruit

squeeze ➤ *noun* (*plural* **squeezes**)
1 the action of squeezing 2 a hug 3 a tight fit 4 a time when money is difficult to get or borrow

squelch ➤ *verb* (**squelches, squelching, squelched**)
to squelch is to make a sound like someone treading in thick mud

squelch ➤ *noun* (*plural* **squelches**)
a squelching sound

squid *noun* (*plural* **squid** or **squids**)
a sea animal with eight short arms and two long ones

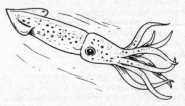

squint ➤ *verb* (**squints, squinting, squinted**)
1 to squint is to be cross-eyed 2 to squint at something is to peer at it or look at it with half-shut eyes

squint ➤ *noun* (*plural* **squints**)
a fault in someone's eyesight that makes
them squint

squire *noun* (*plural* **squires**)
1 the man who owns most of the land in a
country district **2** in the Middle Ages, a
young nobleman who served a knight

squirm *verb* (**squirms, squirming, squirmed**)
to squirm is to wriggle about, especially
when you feel awkward or embarrassed

squirrel *noun* (*plural* **squirrels**)
a small animal with grey or red fur and a
bushy tail, that lives in trees and eats nuts

squirt *verb* (**squirts, squirting, squirted**)
to squirt something is to send it out in a
strong jet of liquid; to squirt is to come out
like this ♦ *The orange juice squirted in his
eye*

St. or **St** short for **Saint** or **Street**

stab ➤ *verb* (**stabs, stabbing, stabbed**)
to stab someone is to pierce or wound them
with something sharp ♦ *She stabbed him
with a knife*

stab ➤ *noun* (*plural* **stabs**)
1 the action of stabbing **2** a sudden sharp
pain

stability *noun*
being stable or firm

stabilize *verb* (**stabilizes, stabilizing, stabilized**)
1 to stabilize something is to make it
stable **2** to stabilize is to become stable

stabilizer *noun* (*plural* **stabilizers**)
a device for keeping a vehicle or ship
steady

stable [1] *adjective* (**stabler, stablest**)
steady or firmly fixed
stably *adverb* in a stable way

stable [2] *noun* (*plural* **stables**)
a building where horses are kept

stack ➤ *noun* (*plural* **stacks**)
1 a neat pile **2** a haystack **3** a large
amount of something ♦ *I've got a stack of
work to do* **4** a single small chimney

stack ➤ *verb* (**stacks, stacking, stacked**)
to stack things is to put them in a stack or
pile

stadium *noun* (*plural* **stadiums** or **stadia**)
a sports ground surrounded by seats for
spectators

staff *noun* (*plural* **staffs**)
1 the people who work in an office or shop
2 the teachers in a school or college **3** a
thick stick for walking with **4** a set of five
lines on which music is written

stag *noun* (*plural* **stags**)
a male deer

stage ➤ *noun* (*plural* **stages**)
1 a platform for performances in a theatre
or hall **2** the point that you have reached
in a process or journey ♦ *Now for the final
stage*

stage ➤ *verb* (**stages, staging, staged**)
1 to stage a performance is to present it on
a stage **2** to stage an event is to organize it
♦ *They decided to stage a protest*

stagecoach *noun* (*plural* **stagecoaches**)
a horse-drawn coach of a kind that used to
travel regularly along the same route

stagger *verb* (**staggers, staggering, staggered**)
1 to stagger is to walk unsteadily **2** to
stagger someone is to amaze or confuse
them ♦ *I was staggered at the price* **3** to
stagger events is to arrange them so that
they do not all happen at the same time
♦ *We stagger our holidays so that someone
is always here*

stagnant *adjective*
not flowing or fresh ♦ *The pond is
stagnant*

stain ➤ *noun* (*plural* **stains**)
1 a dirty mark on something **2** something
bad in someone's character or past record

stain ➤ *verb* (**stains, staining, stained**)
1 to stain something is to make a stain on
it ♦ *The juice has stained my dress* **2** to
stain material or wood is to colour it

stainless *adjective*
without stains

stainless steel *noun*
steel that does not rust easily

stair *noun* (*plural* **stairs**)
each of a series of steps that take you from
one floor to another in a building

staircase *noun* (*plural* **staircases**)
a series of stairs

stake ➤ *noun* (*plural* **stakes**)
1 a thick pointed stick to be driven into
the ground **2** the thick post to which
people used to be tied for execution by
being burnt alive **3** an amount of money
bet on something

stake ➤ *verb* (**stakes, staking, staked**)
to stake money is to use it on a bet
to stake a claim is to claim something or get
a right to it

stalactite *noun* (*plural* **stalactites**)
a stony spike hanging like an icicle from
the roof of a cave

stalagmite *noun* (*plural* **stalagmites**)
a stony spike standing like a pillar on the
floor of a cave

stale *adjective* (**staler, stalest**)
not fresh ♦ *The bread has gone stale*

stalk[1] *noun* (*plural* **stalks**)
the main part of a plant, from which the leaves and flowers grow

stalk[2] *verb* (**stalks, stalking, stalked**)
1 to stalk someone is to hunt them stealthily **2** to stalk is to walk in a proud or dignified way

stall[1] ➤ *noun* (*plural* **stalls**)
1 a table or small open-fronted shop where things are sold, usually in the open air **2** a place for one animal in a stable or shed

stall ➤ *verb* (**stalls, stalling, stalled**)
to stall is to stop suddenly ♦ *The car engine stalled*

stall[2] *verb* (**stalls, stalling, stalled**)
to stall is to delay or hold things up to give yourself more time

stallion *noun* (*plural* **stallions**)
a male horse

stalls *plural noun*
the seats on the ground floor of a theatre or cinema

stamen *noun* (*plural* **stamens**) (*pronounced* **stay-men**)
the part of a flower that bears pollen

stamina *noun* (*pronounced* **stam-in-a**)
the ability to endure pain or hard effort over a long time

stammer ➤ *verb* (**stammers, stammering, stammered**)
to stammer is to keep repeating the sounds at the beginning of words

stammer ➤ *noun* (*plural* **stammers**)
a tendency to stammer

stamp ➤ *noun* (*plural* **stamps**)
1 a small piece of gummed paper with a special design on it; a postage stamp **2** the act of banging your foot on the ground **3** a small block with raised letters for printing words or marks on something; the words or marks made with this

stamp ➤ *verb* (**stamps, stamping, stamped**)
1 to stamp is to bang your foot heavily on the ground **2** to stamp something is to put a postage stamp on it, or to put marks on it with a stamp

stampede *noun* (*plural* **stampedes**)
a sudden rush of animals or people

stand ➤ *verb* (**stands, standing, stood**)
1 to stand is to be on your feet without moving ♦ *She stood at the back of the hall* **2** to stand something somewhere is to put it upright there ♦ *Stand the vase on the table* **3** something stands when it stays unchanged ♦ *My offer still stands* **4** to stand a difficulty or hardship is to endure it ♦ *I can't stand the heat*
it stands to reason it is reasonable or obvious
to stand by is to be ready for action
to stand for something 1 is to tolerate it or put up with it ♦ *She won't stand for any arguments* **2** is to mean something ♦ *'Dr' stands for 'Doctor'*
to stand in for someone is to take their place
to stand out is to be clear or obvious
to stand up for someone is to support them or defend them

stand ➤ *noun* (*plural* **stands**)
1 something made for putting things on ♦ *Use a music stand* **2** a stall where things are sold or displayed **3** a grandstand **4** resistance to attack ♦ *She was determined to make a stand for her rights*

standard ➤ *noun* (*plural* **standards**)
1 how good something is ♦ *They reached a high standard of work* **2** a thing used to measure or judge something else ♦ *The metre is the standard for length* **3** a special flag **4** an upright pole

standard ➤ *adjective*
of the usual or ordinary kind

standardize *verb* (**standardizes, standardizing, standardized**)
to standardize something is to make it a standard size or type

standard lamp *noun* (*plural* **standard lamps**)
a lamp on an upright pole that stands on the floor

standard of living *noun* (*plural* **standards of living**)
the level of comfort and wealth that a person or country has

standby *noun* (*plural* **standbys**)
something or someone kept to be used if they are needed

standstill *noun*
a stop; an end to movement or activity

stank past tense of **stink** *verb*

stanza *noun* (*plural* **stanzas**)
a group of lines in a poem

staple[1] *noun* (*plural* **staples**)
1 a tiny piece of metal used to fix pieces of paper together **2** a U-shaped nail
stapler *noun* a machine for putting staples in paper

staple[2] *adjective*
main or normal ♦ *Rice is their staple food*

star ➤ *noun* (*plural* **stars**)
1 a large mass of burning gas that you see as a bright speck of light in the sky at night **2** one of the main performers in a film or show; a famous entertainer **3** a shape with five or six points
starry *adjective* full of stars

star ➤ *verb* (**stars, starring, starred**)
1 to star in a film or show is to be one of the main performers **2** to star someone is to have them as a main performer

starboard *noun*
the right-hand side of a ship or aircraft when you are facing forward

starch *noun* (*plural* **starches**)
1 a white carbohydrate in bread, potatoes, and other food **2** this or a similar substance used to stiffen clothes
starchy *adjective* like starch

stare *verb* (**stares, staring, stared**)
to look continuously at someone or something without moving your eyes

starfish *noun* (*plural* **starfish** or **starfishes**)
a sea animal shaped like a star with five points

starling *noun* (*plural* **starlings**)
a noisy black or brown speckled bird

start ➤ *verb* (**starts, starting, started**)
1 to start something is to take the first steps in doing it **2** to start, or start out, is to begin a journey **3** to start is also to make a sudden movement of surprise
♦ *They all started at the noise outside*

start ➤ *noun* (*plural* **starts**)
1 the act of starting; the point or place where something starts **2** an advantage that someone starts with ♦ *We gave the young ones 10 minutes' start* **3** a sudden movement

starter *noun* (*plural* **starters**)
1 someone who starts a race **2** a device for starting the engine of a vehicle

starting pistol *noun* (*plural* **starting pistols**)
a pistol fired to signal the start of a race

startle *verb* (**startles, startling, startled**)
to startle a person or animal is to surprise or alarm them

starve *verb* (**starves, starving, starved**)
1 to starve is to suffer or die from not having enough food **2** to starve someone is to make them suffer or die in this way ♦ *The prisoners had been starved to death* **3** to starve someone of something they need is to deprive them of it ♦ *She was starved of love*
4 (*informal*) to be starving is to be very hungry
starvation *noun* starving; not having enough food

state ➤ *noun* (*plural* **states**)
1 the quality of a person or thing or their circumstances; the way they are **2** a nation **3** a division of a country **4** a government and its officials **5** a dignified or grand style ♦ *The King was buried in state* **6** (*informal*) an excited or upset condition ♦ *Don't get in a state about the burglary*

state ➤ *verb* (**states, stating, stated**)
to state something is to say it clearly or formally

stately *adjective* (**statelier, stateliest**)
grand and dignified
stateliness *noun* being stately

stately home *noun* (*plural* **stately homes**)
a large and splendid house that a noble family has owned for many years

statement *noun* (*plural* **statements**)
1 words that state something **2** a formal account of something that happened **3** a report made by a bank about the money in a person's account

statesman or **stateswoman** *noun* (*plural* **statesmen** or **stateswomen**)
someone who is important or skilled in governing a state
statesmanship *noun* skill in being a statesman or stateswoman

state school *noun* (*plural* **state schools**)
a school which gets its money from the government and does not charge fees

static *adjective*
not moving or changing

static electricity *noun*
electricity which is present in something but does not flow as a current

station ➤ *noun* (*plural* **stations**)
1 a set of buildings where people get on or off trains or buses **2** a building for police, firemen, or other workers who serve the public **3** a place from which radio or television broadcasts are made

station ➤ *verb* (**stations, stationing, stationed**)
to station a person somewhere is to place them there for a particular purpose ♦ *He was stationed at the door to take the tickets*

stationary *adjective*
not moving; still ♦ *The car was stationary when the van hit it*

stationery *noun*
paper, envelopes, and other things used for writing or word-processing

stationmaster *noun* (*plural* **stationmasters**)
the person in charge of a railway station

statistic *noun* (*plural* **statistics**)
a piece of information expressed as a number ♦ *These statistics show that the population has doubled*
statistical *adjective* to do with statistics
statistically *adverb* by means of statistics

statistician *noun* (*plural* **statisticians**)
(*pronounced* stat-is-tish-an)
an expert in statistics

statistics *noun*
the study of information that is expressed as numbers

statue *noun* (*plural* **statues**)
a model made of stone or metal to look like a person or animal

status *noun* (*plural* **statuses**)
1 a status is a person's position or rank in relation to other people ♦ *What is your status in the company?* **2** status is high rank or prestige

staunch *adjective*
firm and loyal ♦ *They are the team's most staunch supporters*

stave ➤ *noun* (*plural* **staves**)
a set of five lines on which music is written

stave ➤ *verb* (**staves, staving, staved** or **stove**)
to stave something is to make a hole or dent in it ♦ *The collision stove in the front of the ship*
to stave something off is to keep something unwelcome away ♦ *They staved off hunger by drinking a lot of water*

stay ➤ *verb* (**stays, staying, stayed**)
1 to stay somewhere is to continue to be there or to remain there **2** to stay somewhere or with someone is to spend time as a visitor

stay ➤ *noun* (*plural* **stays**)
a period of time spent somewhere ♦ *We didn't have time for a long stay*

steady ➤ *adjective* (**steadier, steadiest**)
1 not shaking or moving; firm **2** regular or continuous ♦ *They kept up a steady pace*
steadily *adverb* in a steady way; gradually
steadiness *noun* being steady

steady ➤ *verb* (**steadies, steadying, steadied**)
to steady something is to make it steady

steak *noun* (*plural* **steaks**)
a thick slice of meat or fish

steal *verb* (**steals, stealing, stole, stolen**)
1 to steal something is to take and keep it when it does not belong to you **2** to steal somewhere is to move there stealthily ♦ *He stole out of the room*

stealthy *adjective* (**stealthier, stealthiest**)
secret and quiet, so as not to be noticed
stealth *noun* being stealthy **stealthily** *adverb* in a stealthy way

steam ➤ *noun*
1 the gas or vapour that comes from boiling water **2** (*informal*) energy or power ♦ *He ran out of steam*
steamy *adjective* full of steam

steam ➤ *verb* (**steams, steaming, steamed**)
1 to steam is to give out steam **2** to steam somewhere is to move using the power of steam ♦ *The boat steamed down the river* **3** to steam food is to cook it with steam ♦ *Let's have a steamed pudding*
to steam up is to be covered with mist or condensation ♦ *The windows have steamed up*

steam engine *noun* (*plural* **steam engines**)
an engine driven by steam

steamer *noun* (*plural* **steamers**)
a steamship

steamroller *noun* (*plural* **steamrollers**)
a heavy vehicle with wide metal wheels, used to flatten surfaces when making roads

steamship *noun* (*plural* **steamships**)
a ship driven by steam

steed *noun* (*plural* **steeds**)
(*old or poetical use*) a horse

steel ➤ *noun*
a strong metal made from iron and carbon
steely *adjective* hard like steel

steel ➤ *verb* (**steels, steeling, steeled**)
to steel yourself is to find courage to do
something difficult

steel band *noun* (*plural* **steel bands**)
a West Indian band of musicians who play
instruments made from oil drums

steep *adjective* (**steeper, steepest**)
rising or sloping sharply
steeply *adverb* in a steep way **steepness** *noun*
being steep

steeple *noun* (*plural* **steeples**)
a church tower with a spire

steeplechase *noun* (*plural* **steeplechases**)
a race across country or over hedges and
fences

steeplejack *noun* (*plural* **steeplejacks**)
a person who climbs tall steeples or
chimneys to do repairs

steer[1] *verb* (**steers, steering, steered**)
to steer a vehicle or bicycle is to make it go
in the direction you want

steer[2] *noun* (*plural* **steers**)
a young bull kept for its beef

steering wheel *noun* (*plural* **steering wheels**)
a wheel for steering a vehicle

stem ➤ *noun* (*plural* **stems**)
1 the main central part of a plant or tree;
a stalk **2** the thin part of a wine glass
3 (*in Grammar*) the main part of a word,
to which different endings are attached.
For example, *call* is the stem of the words
caller, called, calls, and *calling*

stem ➤ *verb* (**stems, stemming, stemmed**)
to stem from something is to start there or
arise from it ♦ *The problem stems from
lack of money*

stench *noun* (*plural* **stenches**)
a very unpleasant smell

stencil *noun* (*plural* **stencils**)
a piece of card or metal or plastic with
pieces cut out of it, used to produce a
picture or design

step ➤ *noun* (*plural* **steps**)
1 a movement made with the foot when
walking, running, or dancing **2** the sound
of a person putting down their foot when
walking **3** each of the level surfaces on a
stair or ladder **4** each of a series of actions
to watch your step is to be careful

step ➤ *verb* (**steps, stepping, stepped**)
to step is to tread or walk
to step on it (*slang*) is to hurry
to step something up is to increase it

stepchild *noun* (*plural* **stepchildren**)
a child that someone's husband or wife has
from an earlier marriage. A boy is a **stepson**
and a girl is a **stepdaughter**

stepfather *noun* (*plural* **stepfathers**)
a man who is married to your mother but
is not your own father

stepladder *noun* (*plural* **stepladders**)
a folding ladder with flat treads

stepmother *noun* (*plural* **stepmothers**)
a woman who is married to your father but
is not your own mother

steppe *noun* (*plural* **steppes**)
a grassy plain with few trees, especially in
Russia

stepping stone *noun* (*plural* **stepping stones**)
each in a line of stones put in a river or
stream to help people walk across

steps *plural noun*
a stepladder ♦ *Have you seen my steps?*

stereo ➤ *adjective*
stereophonic

stereo ➤ *noun* (*plural* **stereos**)
1 stereo is stereophonic sound or
recording **2** a stereo is a stereophonic
radio or record player

stereophonic *adjective* (*pronounced*
ste-ri-o-**fon**-ik)
using sound that comes from two different
directions to give a natural effect

sterile *adjective*
1 not able to have children or reproduce
2 free from germs
sterility *noun* being sterile

sterilize *verb* (**sterilizes, sterilizing, sterilized**)
1 to sterilize something is to make it free
from germs **2** to sterilize a person or
animal is to make them unable to bear
young
sterilization *noun* sterilizing something or
someone

sterling *noun*
British money ♦ *Tourists paid for their
meals in sterling*

stern[1] *noun* (*plural* **sterns**)
the back part of a ship

stern[2] *adjective* (**sterner, sternest**)
strict and severe
sternly *adverb* in a stern way **sternness** *noun*
being stern

stethoscope *noun* (*plural* **stethoscopes**)
(*pronounced* **steth-o-skohp**)
a device used by doctors for listening to a
patient's heartbeat or breathing

stew ➤ *verb* (**stews, stewing, stewed**)
to stew food is to cook it slowly in liquid

stew ➤ *noun* (*plural* **stews**)
a dish of meat and vegetables cooked by
stewing
in a stew (*informal*) very worried or agitated

steward *noun* (*plural* **stewards**)
1 a man whose job is to look after the
passengers on a ship or aircraft **2** an
official who looks after the arrangements
at a public event

stewardess *noun* (*plural* **stewardesses**)
a woman whose job is to look after the
passengers on a ship or aircraft

stick¹ *noun* (*plural* **sticks**)
1 a long thin piece of wood **2** a walking
stick **3** the implement used to hit the ball
in hockey, polo, or other ball games **4** a
long thin piece of something ♦ *I must get a
stick of rock*

stick² *verb* (**sticks, sticking, stuck**)
1 to stick something sharp into a thing is
to push it in roughly or carelessly ♦ *He
stuck a pin in her finger* **2** to stick things
is to fasten or join them **3** to stick is to
become fixed or jammed ♦ *The door keeps
sticking* **4** (*informal*) to stick a difficulty or
hardship is to endure it ♦ *I can't stick it
any longer*
to stick out is to come out from a surface or
be noticeable
to stick together is to stay loyal to one
another
to stick up for someone (*informal*) is to
support them or defend them
to be stuck with someone or **something**
(*informal*) is to be unable to avoid an
unwelcome person or thing

sticker *noun* (*plural* **stickers**)
a label or sign for sticking on something

sticking plaster *noun* (*plural* **sticking plasters**)
a strip of sticky material for covering a cut

stick insect *noun* (*plural* **stick insects**)
an insect with a long thin body that looks
like a twig

stickleback *noun* (*plural* **sticklebacks**)
a small fish with sharp spines on its back

sticky *adjective* (**stickier, stickiest**)
1 able or likely to stick to things
2 (*informal*) unpleasant or nasty ♦ *He
came to a sticky end*
stickily *adverb* in a sticky way **stickiness**
noun being sticky

stiff *adjective* (**stiffer, stiffest**)
1 not able to bend or change its shape
easily **2** difficult ♦ *We had a stiff
examination* **3** formal; not friendly
4 strong or severe ♦ *There's a stiff wind
outside*
stiffly *adverb* in a stiff way **stiffness** *noun*
being stiff

stiffen *verb* (**stiffens, stiffening, stiffened**)
1 to stiffen something is to make it stiff
2 to stiffen is to become stiff

stifle *verb* (**stifles, stifling, stifled**)
1 to stifle someone is to make it difficult or
impossible for them to breathe **2** to stifle
something is to suppress it ♦ *She stifled a
yawn*

stile *noun* (*plural* **stiles**)
an arrangement of steps or bars for people
to climb over a fence

still ➤ *adjective* (**stiller, stillest**)
1 not moving **2** silent ♦ *In the night, the
streets are still* **3** not fizzy
stillness *noun* being still

still ➤ *adverb*
1 up to this or that time ♦ *He was still
there* **2** even; yet; in a greater amount
♦ *They wanted still more food* **3** however
♦ *They lost. Still, they have another game*

still ➤ *verb* (**stills, stilling, stilled**)
to still something is to make it still

stilts *plural noun*
1 a pair of poles on which you can walk
high above the ground **2** supports for a
house built over water

stimulate *verb* (**stimulates, stimulating,
stimulated**)
1 to stimulate someone is to make them
excited or interested **2** to stimulate
something is to cause it to happen ♦ *His
new book stimulated an interest in wildlife*
stimulant *noun* something that stimulates
someone **stimulation** *noun* being stimulated
or excited

stimulus *noun* (*plural* **stimuli**)
something that stimulates or produces a
reaction

sting ➤ *noun* (*plural* **stings**)
1 the part of an insect or plant that can cause pain or a wound 2 a painful area or wound caused by an insect or plant

sting ➤ *verb* (**stings, stinging, stung**)
1 to sting someone is to wound or hurt them with a sting ♦ *She was stung by a wasp* 2 to sting is to feel a sharp or throbbing pain ♦ *My back is stinging from sunburn* 3 (*slang*) to sting someone is to cheat them by charging them too much

stingy *adjective* (**stingier, stingiest**) (*pronounced* stin-ji)
mean; not generous

stink ➤ *noun* (*plural* **stinks**)
1 an unpleasant smell 2 (*informal*) an unpleasant fuss or complaint

stink ➤ *verb* (**stinks, stinking, stank** or **stunk, stunk**)
to stink is to have an unpleasant smell

stir ➤ *verb* (**stirs, stirring, stirred**)
1 to stir something liquid or soft is to move it round and round, especially with a spoon 2 to stir is to move slightly or start to move after sleeping or being still
to stir something up is to excite or arouse it ♦ *They stirred up trouble*

stir ➤ *noun* (*plural* **stirs**)
1 an act of stirring ♦ *Give it a stir* 2 a fuss or disturbance ♦ *The news caused a stir*

stirrup *noun* (*plural* **stirrups**)
a metal loop that hangs down on each side of a horse's saddle to support the rider's foot

stitch *noun* (*plural* **stitches**)
1 a loop of thread made in sewing or knitting 2 a sudden pain in your side caused by running

stoat *noun* (*plural* **stoats**)
an animal rather like a weasel, also called an ermine

stock ➤ *noun* (*plural* **stocks**)
1 a stock of things is an amount of them kept ready to be sold or used 2 stock is a collection of farm animals, also called livestock 3 a person's stock is the line of their ancestors 4 stock is liquid made by stewing meat, fish, or vegetables 5 a stock is a garden flower with a sweet smell 6 stock is also a number of shares in a company's capital

stock ➤ *verb* (**stocks, stocking, stocked**)
1 to stock goods is to keep a stock of them for sale or use 2 to stock a place is to provide it with a stock of things ♦ *The explorers stocked their base camp with tinned food*

stockade *noun* (*plural* **stockades**)
a fence made of large stakes

stockbroker *noun* (*plural* **stockbrokers**)
someone whose job is to buy and sell stocks and shares for clients

stock car *noun* (*plural* **stock cars**)
an ordinary car strengthened for use in races in which bumping is allowed

stock exchange *noun* (*plural* **stock exchanges**)
a country's central place for selling and buying stocks and shares

stocking *noun* (*plural* **stockings**)
a garment that covers the whole of someone's leg and foot

stock market *noun* (*plural* **stock markets**)
1 a stock exchange 2 the business of buying and selling stocks and shares

stockpile *noun* (*plural* **stockpiles**)
a large stock of things kept in reserve

stocks *plural noun*
a wooden framework with holes for people's legs and arms, in which criminals were locked as a punishment

stocky *adjective* (**stockier, stockiest**)
short and solidly built

stodgy *adjective* (**stodgier, stodgiest**)
1 thick and heavy; not easy to digest ♦ *The pudding's very stodgy* 2 dull and boring ♦ *What a stodgy book*

stoke *verb* (**stokes, stoking, stoked**)
to stoke a furnace or fire is to add fuel to it

stole [1] *noun* (*plural* **stoles**)
a wide piece of material worn round the shoulders by women

stole [2] past tense of **steal**

stolen past participle of **steal**

stomach ➤ *noun* (*plural* **stomachs**)
1 the part of the body where food starts to be digested 2 the abdomen

stomach ➤ *verb* (**stomachs, stomaching, stomached**)
to stomach something is to tolerate it or put up with it ♦ *I can't stomach their awful jokes*

stone ➤ *noun* (*plural* **stones** or, for the unit of weight, **stone**)
1 stone is the hard solid mineral of which rocks are made 2 a stone is a piece of this mineral 3 a stone is also a jewel 4 a stone is also the hard seed in the middle of some fruits, such as a cherry, plum, or peach 5 a stone is also a unit of weight equal to 14 pounds ♦ *She weighs 6 stone*

stone ➤ *verb* (**stones, stoning, stoned**)
1 to stone someone is to throw stones at them 2 to stone fruit is to take the stones out of it

stone-cold *adjective*
extremely cold

stone-deaf *adjective*
completely deaf

stony *adjective* (**stonier, stoniest**)
1 full of stones 2 hard like stone 3 unfriendly or hostile ♦ *Our question was met by a stony silence*

stood past tense and past participle of **stand** *verb*

stool *noun* (*plural* **stools**)
a small seat without a back

stoop *verb* (**stoops, stooping, stooped**)
to stoop is to bend your body forwards

stop ➤ *verb* (**stops, stopping, stopped**)
1 to stop something is to finish doing it, or make it finish 2 to stop is to be no longer moving or working 3 to stop something is to prevent it happening or continuing ♦ *I must go out and stop that noise* 4 to stop a hole or gap is to fill it 5 to stop at a place is to stay there briefly

stop ➤ *noun* (*plural* **stops**)
1 stopping; an end 2 a place where a bus or train stops regularly

stoppage *noun* (*plural* **stoppages**)
1 an interruption in the work of a business or factory 2 a blockage

stopper *noun* (*plural* **stoppers**)
something that fits into the top of a bottle or jar to close it

stop press *noun*
late news printed in a newspaper after printing has started

stopwatch *noun* (*plural* **stopwatches**)
a watch that can be started or stopped, used for timing races

storage *noun*
the storing of things

store ➤ *verb* (**stores, storing, stored**)
to store things is to keep them until they are needed

store ➤ *noun* (*plural* **stores**)
1 a place where things are stored 2 things kept for future use 3 a shop, especially a large one
in store that is going to happen ♦ *There is a treat in store for you*

storey *noun* (*plural* **storeys**)
one whole floor of a building

stork *noun* (*plural* **storks**)
a large bird with long legs and a long beak

storm ➤ *noun* (*plural* **storms**)
1 a period of bad weather with strong winds, rain or snow, and often thunder and lightning 2 a violent attack or outburst ♦ *There was a storm of protest*
a storm in a teacup a big fuss over something unimportant

storm ➤ *verb* (**storms, storming, stormed**)
1 to storm is to move or behave violently or angrily ♦ *He stormed out of the room* 2 to storm a place is to attack it suddenly ♦ *They stormed the castle*

stormy *adjective* (**stormier, stormiest**)
1 likely to end in a storm ♦ *The weather is stormy today* 2 loud and angry ♦ *We had a stormy meeting*

story *noun* (*plural* **stories**)
1 an account of real or imaginary events 2 (*informal*) a lie ♦ *Don't tell stories!*

stout *adjective* (**stouter, stoutest**)
1 rather fat 2 thick and strong ♦ *She carried a stout stick* 3 brave ♦ *The defenders put up a stout resistance*
stoutly *adverb* in a stout way **stoutness** *noun* being stout

stove [1] *noun* (*plural* **stoves**)
a device that produces heat for warming a room or cooking

stove [2] past tense and past participle of **stave** *verb*

stow *verb* (**stows, stowing, stowed**)
to stow something is to pack it or store it away
to stow away is to hide on a ship or aircraft so as to travel without paying

stowaway *noun* (*plural* **stowaways**)
someone who stows away on a ship or aircraft

straddle *verb* (**straddles, straddling, straddled**)
1 to straddle something is to sit or stand astride it 2 to straddle something is also to be built across it ♦ *A long bridge straddles the river*

straggle *verb* (**straggles, straggling, straggled**)
1 to straggle is to grow or move in an untidy way ♦ *Brambles straggled across the path* 2 to straggle is also to lag behind or wander on your own
straggler *noun* someone who straggles
straggly *adjective* spread out untidily

straight *adjective* (**straighter, straightest**)
1 going continuously in one direction; not curving or bending 2 tidy; in proper order 3 honest or frank ♦ *Give me a straight answer*

straighten *verb* (**straightens, straightening, straightened**)
1 to straighten something is to make it straight 2 to straighten is to become straight

straightforward *adjective*
1 easy to understand or do; not complicated 2 honest or frank

strain ➤ *verb* (**strains, straining, strained**)
1 to strain something is to stretch it or push it or pull it hard or too hard 2 to strain is to make a great effort 3 to strain liquid is to put it through a sieve to take out any lumps or other things in it

strain ➤ *noun* (*plural* **strains**)
1 straining or the force of straining 2 an injury caused by straining 3 something that uses up your strength or patience; exhaustion

strainer *noun* (*plural* **strainers**)
a device for straining liquids

strait *noun* (*plural* **straits**)
a narrow stretch of water connecting two seas

straits *plural noun*
in dire straits having severe difficulties

strand *noun* (*plural* **strands**)
1 each of the threads or wires twisted together to make a rope or cable 2 a lock of hair

stranded *adjective*
1 left on sand or rocks in shallow water ♦ *We could see a stranded ship* 2 left in a difficult or lonely position ♦ *They were stranded in the desert*

strange *adjective* (**stranger, strangest**)
1 unusual or surprising 2 not known or experienced before
strangely *adverb* in a strange way
strangeness *noun* being strange

stranger *noun* (*plural* **strangers**)
1 a person you do not know 2 a person who is in a place they do not know

strangle *verb* (**strangles, strangling, strangled**)
to strangle someone is to kill them by pressing their throat so as to prevent them breathing
strangler *noun* a person who strangles someone **strangulation** *noun* strangling someone

strap ➤ *noun* (*plural* **straps**)
a flat strip of leather or cloth or plastic for fastening things together or holding them in place

strap ➤ *verb* (**straps, strapping, strapped**)
to strap something is to fasten it with a strap or straps

strategy *noun* (*plural* **strategies**)
1 a strategy is a plan or policy to achieve something 2 strategy is planning a war or military campaign
strategic *adjective* to do with strategy
strategist *noun* an expert in strategy

stratum *noun* (*plural* **strata**) (*pronounced* strah-tum)
a layer or level ♦ *You can see several strata of rock in the cliffs*

straw *noun* (*plural* **straws**)
1 straw is dry cut stalks of corn 2 a straw is a narrow tube for drinking through

strawberry *noun* (*plural* **strawberries**)
a small red juicy fruit, with its seeds on the outside

stray ➤ *verb* (**strays, straying, strayed**)
to stray is to wander or become lost

stray ➤ *adjective*
wandering around lost ♦ *We found a stray cat*

streak ➤ *noun* (*plural* **streaks**)
1 a long thin line or mark 2 a trace or sign ♦ *They showed a streak of cruelty*

streak ➤ *verb* (**streaks, streaking, streaked**)
1 to streak something is to mark it with streaks 2 to streak somewhere is to move there very quickly

streaky *adjective* (**streakier, streakiest**)
marked with streaks

stream ➤ *noun* (*plural* **streams**)
1 a narrow river or brook 2 liquid flowing in one direction 3 a number of things moving in the same direction, such as traffic 4 a group in a school containing children of similar ability

stream ➤ *verb* (**streams, streaming, streamed**)
1 to stream is to move in a strong or fast flow ♦ *Traffic streamed across the junction* 2 to stream is also to produce a flow of liquid ♦ *Blood was streaming from her cut hand* 3 to stream schoolchildren is to organize them in groups of similar ability

streamer *noun* (*plural* **streamers**)
a long strip of paper or ribbon

streamline *verb* (**streamlines, streamlining, streamlined**)
1 to streamline a vehicle or object is to give it a smooth shape that helps it to move easily through air or water 2 to streamline an activity or operation is to make it work more efficiently

street *noun* (*plural* **streets**)
a road with houses beside it in a city or town

strength *noun* (*plural* **strengths**)
1 how strong a person or thing is 2 something that makes a person or thing useful or effective ♦ *Patience is your greatest strength*

strengthen *verb* (**strengthens, strengthening, strengthened**)
1 to strengthen something or someone is to make them stronger 2 to strengthen is to become stronger

strenuous *adjective*
needing or using great effort
strenuously *adverb* in a strenuous way

stress ➤ *noun* (*plural* **stresses**)
1 a force or pressure that pulls or pushes or twists something 2 strain, especially worry and nervous tension 3 emphasis, especially the extra force with which you pronounce part of a word or phrase

stress ➤ *verb* (**stresses, stressing, stressed**)
1 to stress someone is to put a stress on them 2 to stress part of a word or phrase is to pronounce it with extra emphasis 3 to stress a point or idea is to emphasize it ♦ *I must stress that this is an unusual problem*

stretch ➤ *verb* (**stretches, stretching, stretched**)
1 to stretch something is to pull it so that it becomes longer or wider 2 to stretch is to become longer or wider when pulled 3 to stretch somewhere is to extend or continue there ♦ *The wall stretches all the way round the park*

to stretch out is to lie down and extend your arms and legs fully

stretch ➤ *noun* (*plural* **stretches**)
1 the action of stretching something 2 a continuous period of time or area of land or water

stretcher *noun* (*plural* **stretchers**)
a framework like a light folding bed with handles at each end, for carrying a sick or injured person

strew *verb* (**strews, strewing, strewed, strewn** or **strewed**)
to strew things is to scatter them over a surface ♦ *Flowers were strewn over the path*

stricken *adjective*
overcome or strongly affected by a feeling or illness

strict *adjective* (**stricter, strictest**)
1 demanding obedience or good behaviour ♦ *The teachers are all fairly strict* 2 complete or exact ♦ *I want the strict truth*
strictly *adverb* in a strict way **strictness** *noun* being strict

stride ➤ *verb* (**strides, striding, strode, stridden**)
to stride is to walk with long steps

stride ➤ *noun* (*plural* **strides**)
a long step you take when walking or running

to get into your stride is to settle into a steady rate of work

to take something in your stride is to cope with it easily

strife *noun*
conflict; fighting or quarrelling

strike ➤ *verb* (**strikes, striking, struck**)
1 to strike something or someone is to hit them 2 to strike people or a place is to attack them suddenly ♦ *Plague struck the village* 3 to strike a match is to light it by rubbing it against something rough 4 a clock strikes (for example) seven when it rings seven chimes at seven o'clock 5 workers strike when they stop working as a protest against their pay or conditions 6 to strike oil or gold is to find it by drilling or mining 7 to strike someone in some way is to make them think that way ♦ *The film struck me as rather violent*

to strike up is to begin playing or singing

strike ➤ *noun* (*plural* **strikes**)
1 a hit 2 refusing to work, as a way of making a protest 3 a find of oil, gold, etc. underground

on strike having stopped working as a protest

striker *noun* (*plural* **strikers**)
1 a worker who is on strike **2** in football, an attacking player who tries to score goals

striking *adjective*
impressive or very interesting

string ➤ *noun* (*plural* **strings**)
1 string is thin rope or cord for tying things; a string is a piece of thin rope **2** in music, a string is a piece of stretched wire or nylon used in an instrument to make sounds **3** a string of things is a line or series of them ♦ *There was a string of buses along the High Street*

string ➤ *verb* (**strings, stringing, strung**)
1 to string something is to tie it with string **2** to string pearls or beads is to thread them on a string **3** to string beans is to remove the tough fibre from them **4** to string a racket or musical instrument is to put strings on it
to string out is to spread out in a line

stringed *adjective*
in music, stringed instruments are ones that belong to the violin family, especially members of the violin family

strings *plural noun*
the stringed instruments in an orchestra

stringy *adjective* (**stringier, stringiest**)
1 long and thin like string **2** containing tough fibres

strip[1] ➤ *verb* (**strips, stripping, stripped**)
1 to strip something is to take a covering off it **2** to strip is to undress **3** to strip someone of something is to take it away from them

strip ➤ *noun* (*plural* **strips**)
the special outfit worn by a sports team

strip[2] *noun* (*plural* **strips**)
a long narrow piece of something

strip cartoon *noun* (*plural* **strip cartoons**)
a series of drawings telling a story; a comic strip

stripe *noun* (*plural* **stripes**)
1 a long narrow band of colour **2** something worn on the sleeve of a uniform to show the rank of the wearer
striped or **stripy** *adjective* having stripes

strive *verb* (**strives, striving, strove, striven**)
to strive to do something is to try hard to do it

strobe *noun* (*plural* **strobes**)
a light that flickers on and off continuously

trode past tense of **stride** *verb*

troke[1] *noun* (*plural* **strokes**)
1 a hit; a movement or action **2** a sudden illness that often causes someone to be paralysed

stroke[2] *verb* (**strokes, stroking, stroked**)
to stroke something is to move your hand gently along it

stroll ➤ *verb* (**strolls, strolling, strolled**)
to stroll is to walk slowly

stroll ➤ *noun* (*plural* **strolls**)
a short leisurely walk

strong ➤ *adjective* (**stronger, strongest**)
1 having great power, energy, or effect **2** not easily broken or damaged ♦ *The gate was held by a strong chain* **3** having a lot of flavour or smell ♦ *Do you like your tea strong?* **4** having a particular number or size ♦ *The game had a crowd 20,000 strong*

strong ➤ *adverb*
to be going strong is to be making good progress

stronghold *noun* (*plural* **strongholds**)
a fortified place

strongly *adverb*
1 in a strong way; with strength ♦ *They fought back strongly* **2** very much ♦ *The room smelt strongly of perfume*

strove past tense of **strive**

struck past tense and past participle of **strike** *verb*

structure *noun* (*plural* **structures**)
1 something that has been built or put together **2** the way that something is built or made
structural *adjective* to do with a structure
structurally *adverb* as regards a structure

struggle ➤ *verb* (**struggles, struggling, struggled**)
1 to struggle is to move your body about violently in fighting or trying to get free **2** to struggle to do something is to make strong efforts to do it

struggle ➤ *noun* (*plural* **struggles**)
a spell of struggling; a hard fight

strum *verb* (**strums, strumming, strummed**)
to strum a guitar is to sound it by running your finger across its strings

strung past tense and past participle of **string** *verb*

strut ➤ *verb* (**struts, strutting, strutted**)
to strut is to walk proudly or stiffly

strut ➤ *noun* (*plural* **struts**)
1 a strutting walk **2** a bar of wood or metal that strengthens a framework

stub ➤ *verb* (**stubs, stubbing, stubbed**)
1 to stub your toe is to knock it against something hard **2** to stub, or to stub out, a cigarette or cigar is to extinguish it by pressing it against something hard

stub ➤ *noun* (*plural* **stubs**)
a short piece of something left after the rest has been used up or worn down

stubble *noun*
1 the short stalks of corn left in the ground after a harvest 2 short stiff hairs on a man's chin

stubborn *adjective*
not willing to change your ideas or ways; obstinate
stubbornly *adverb* in a stubborn way
stubbornness *noun* being stubborn

stuck past tense and past participle of **stick** *verb*

stuck-up *adjective*
(*informal*) unpleasantly proud or snobbish

stud *noun* (*plural* **studs**)
1 a small curved lump or knob 2 a device like a button on a stalk, used for fastening a detachable collar to a shirt

student *noun* (*plural* **students**)
someone who studies, especially at a college or university

studio *noun* (*plural* **studios**)
1 a place where radio or television broadcasts are made 2 a place where cinema or television films are made 3 the room where an artist or photographer works

studious *adjective*
fond of studying; studying hard
studiously *adverb* in a studious way

study ➤ *verb* (**studies, studying, studied**)
1 to study is to spend time learning about something 2 to study something is to look at it carefully

study ➤ *noun* (*plural* **studies**)
1 study is the process of studying 2 a study is a room used for studying or writing

stuff ➤ *noun*
1 a substance or material 2 things; possessions ♦ *Will you move your stuff off the table?*

stuff ➤ *verb* (**stuffs, stuffing, stuffed**)
1 to stuff something is to fill it tightly, especially with stuffing ♦ *She stuffed the turkey* 2 to stuff one thing inside another is to push it in carelessly ♦ *He stuffed the paper into his pocket*

stuffing *noun* (*plural* **stuffings**)
1 material used to fill the inside of something 2 a savoury mixture put into meat or poultry before cooking it

stuffy *adjective* (**stuffier, stuffiest**)
1 badly ventilated; without fresh air 2 formal and boring
stuffily *adverb* in a stuffy way **stuffiness** *noun* being stuffy

stumble *verb* (**stumbles, stumbling, stumbled**)
1 to stumble is to lose your balance or fall over something 2 to stumble is also to speak or act hesitantly or uncertainly
to stumble across something or **stumble on something** is to find it by chance

stump ➤ *noun* (*plural* **stumps**)
1 the bottom of a tree trunk left in the ground when the tree has fallen or been cut down 2 (*in Cricket*) each of the three upright sticks of a wicket

stump ➤ *verb* (**stumps, stumping, stumped**)
1 (*in Cricket*) to stump the person batting is to get them out by touching the stumps with the ball when they are not standing in the correct place 2 to stump someone is to be too difficult for them ♦ *The last question stumped everyone*

stun *verb* (**stuns, stunning, stunned**)
1 to stun someone is to knock them unconscious 2 to stun someone is also to shock or confuse them ♦ *They were stunned by the news*

stung past tense and past participle of **sting** *verb*

stunk past tense and past participle of **stink** *verb*

stunt *noun* (*plural* **stunts**)
something unusual or difficult done to attract publicity or as part of a performance

stupendous *adjective*
amazing; tremendous

stupid *adjective* (**stupider, stupidest**)
without reason or common sense; not clever or thoughtful
stupidly *adverb* in a stupid way **stupidity** *noun* being stupid

sturdy *adjective* (**sturdier, sturdiest**)
strong and vigorous or solid
sturdily *adverb* in a sturdy way **sturdiness** *noun* being sturdy

stutter ➤ *verb* (**stutters, stuttering, stuttered**)
to stutter is to keep repeating the sounds at the beginning of words

stutter ➤ *noun* (*plural* **stutters**)
a tendency to stutter; a stammer

sty [1] *noun* (*plural* **sties**)
a pigsty

sty [2] or **stye** *noun* (*plural* **sties** or **styes**)
a sore swelling on an eyelid

style ➤ *noun* (*plural* **styles**)
1 a style is the way that something is done, made, said, or written 2 style is fashion or elegance 3 a style is also a part of the pistil in a flower

style ➤ *verb* (**styles, styling, styled**)
to style something is to give it a special style

stylish *adjective*
fashionable and smart
stylishly *adverb* in a stylish way

stylus *noun* (*plural* **styluses**)
the device like a needle that travels in the grooves of a record to reproduce the sound

sub *noun* (*plural* **subs**)
(*informal*) **1** a submarine **2** a subscription **3** a substitute, especially in sports

sub- *prefix*
meaning 'below', as in *submarine* and *substandard*

subcontinent *noun* (*plural* **subcontinents**)
a large area of land that forms part of a continent

subdivide *verb* (**subdivides, subdividing, subdivided**)
to subdivide something that has already been divided is to divide it again into smaller parts

subdue *verb* (**subdues, subduing, subdued**)
1 to subdue someone is to overcome them or bring them under control **2** to subdue a person or animal is to make them quieter or gentler

subject ➤ *noun* (*plural* **subjects**)
(*pronounced* sub-jikt)
1 the person or thing that is being talked or written about **2** something that is studied **3** (*in Grammar*) the person or thing that is doing the action stated by the verb in a sentence, for example *dog* in the sentence *the dog chewed a bone*
4 someone who must obey the laws of a particular ruler or government

subject ➤ *adjective*
having to obey a ruler or government; not independent
subject to something depending on it ♦ *Our decision is subject to your approval*

subject ➤ *verb* (**subjects, subjecting, subjected**)
(*pronounced* sub-jekt)
to subject someone to something is to make them submit to it ♦ *They subjected him to a string of questions*

subjective *adjective*
1 existing only in a person's mind
2 influenced by a person's own beliefs or ideas ♦ *His account of what happened is rather subjective*

submarine *noun* (*plural* **submarines**)
a type of ship that can travel under water

submerge *verb* (**submerges, submerging, submerged**)
1 to submerge is to go under water **2** to submerge something or someone is to put them under water
submergence or **submersion** *noun* being submerged

submission *noun* (*plural* **submissions**)
1 submitting to someone **2** something submitted or offered to someone

submissive *adjective*
willing to obey

submit *verb* (**submits, submitting, submitted**)
1 to submit to someone is to let them rule or control you **2** to submit something to someone is to give it to them for their opinion or decision

subordinate ➤ *adjective* (*pronounced* sub-or-din-at)
less important, or lower in rank

subordinate ➤ *noun* (*plural* **subordinates**)
someone who is subordinate to someone else

subordinate ➤ *verb* (**subordinates, subordinating, subordinated**) (*pronounced* sub-or-din-ayt)
to subordinate something is to treat it as less important than something else
subordination *noun* subordinating something

subordinate clause *noun* (*plural* **subordinate clauses**)
a clause which is added to a main clause, for example *when you arrive* in the sentence *Let me know when you arrive*

subscribe *verb* (**subscribes, subscribing, subscribed**)
to subscribe to something is to pay money to receive it regularly or to be a member of a club or society
subscriber *noun* someone who subscribes to something

subscription *noun* (*plural* **subscriptions**)
money paid to subscribe to something

subsequent *adjective*
coming later or after something else
♦ *Subsequent events proved that she was right*
subsequently *adverb* later; afterwards

subside *verb* (**subsides, subsiding, subsided**)
1 to subside is to sink ♦ *The house has subsided over the years* **2** to subside is also to become quiet or normal ♦ *The noise subsided after midnight*
subsidence *noun* subsiding, especially into the ground

subsidize *verb* (**subsidizes, subsidizing, subsidized**)
to subsidize someone or something is to give them a subsidy

subsidy *noun* (*plural* **subsidies**)
money paid to keep prices low or to support an industry or activity

substance *noun* (*plural* **substances**)
1 something that you can touch or see; something used for making things **2** the essential part of something

substantial *adjective*
1 large or important **2** strong and solid
substantially *adverb* mostly ♦ *The two books are substantially the same*

substitute ➤ *verb* (**substitutes, substituting, substituted**)
to substitute one thing or person for another is to use the first one instead of the second ♦ *In this recipe you can substitute oil for butter*
substitution *noun* substituting something or someone

substitute ➤ *noun* (*plural* **substitutes**)
a person or thing that is used instead of another

subtle *adjective* (**subtler, subtlest**)
(*pronounced* **sut**-el)
1 slight and delicate ♦ *There was a subtle perfume in the room* **2** ingenious but not obvious ♦ *Your jokes are too subtle for me*
subtly *adverb* in a subtle way **subtlety** *noun* being subtle

subtract *verb* (**subtracts, subtracting, subtracted**)
to subtract one amount from another is to take it away ♦ *If you subtract 2 from 7, you get 5*
subtraction *noun* subtracting an amount

suburb *noun* (*plural* **suburbs**)
an area of houses on the edge of a city or large town
suburban *adjective* belonging to a suburb

suburbia *noun*
the suburbs of a place and the people who live in them

subway *noun* (*plural* **subways**)
an underground passage for pedestrians

succeed *verb* (**succeeds, succeeding, succeeded**)
1 to succeed is to do or get what you wanted or intended **2** to succeed someone is to be the next person to do what they did, especially to be king or queen

success *noun* (*plural* **successes**)
1 success is doing or getting what you wanted or intended **2** a success is a person or thing that does well ♦ *The plan was a great success*

successful *adjective*
having success
successfully *adverb* in a successful way

succession *noun* (*plural* **successions**)
1 a series of people or things **2** the act of following other people or things, especially becoming king or queen

successive *adjective*
following one after another
successively *adverb* one after another

successor *noun* (*plural* **successors**)
a person or thing that comes after another
♦ *The headteacher retired and handed over to her successor*

such *adjective*
1 of the same kind ♦ *Cakes and sweets and all such food is fattening* **2** so great or so much ♦ *It gave me such a fright!*

such-and-such *adjective*
one in particular but not now named ♦ *He promises to come at such-and-such a time but is always late*

suck ➤ *verb* (**sucks, sucking, sucked**)
1 to suck liquid or air is to take it in through your mouth ♦ *I sucked milk through a straw* **2** to suck something is to move it around inside your mouth ♦ *She was sucking a sweet* **3** to suck something is also to draw it in or absorb it ♦ *The boat was sucked into the whirlpool*

suck ➤ *noun* (*plural* **sucks**)
the action of sucking

suction *noun*
producing a vacuum so that liquid or air is drawn in ♦ *Vacuum cleaners work by suction*

sudden *adjective*
happening or done quickly and unexpectedly
suddenly *adverb* quickly and unexpectedly **suddenness** *noun* being sudden

suds *plural noun*
froth on soapy water

sue *verb* (**sues, suing, sued**)
to sue someone is to start a claim in a lawcourt to get money from them

suede *noun* (*pronounced* swayd)
leather with one side soft and velvety

suet *noun*
hard fat from cattle and sheep, used in cooking

suffer *verb* (**suffers, suffering, suffered**)
1 to suffer is to feel pain or sadness **2** to suffer something unpleasant is to have to put up with it

sufficient *adjective*
enough ♦ *Have we sufficient food?*
sufficiency *noun* being enough **sufficiently** *adverb* to a sufficient degree

suffix *noun* (*plural* **suffixes**)
a word or syllable joined to the end of a word to change or add to its meaning, as in forget*ful*, lion*ess*, and rust*y*

suffocate *verb* (**suffocates, suffocating, suffocated**)
1 to suffocate someone is to make it impossible or difficult for them to breathe **2** to suffocate is to suffer or die because you cannot breathe
suffocation *noun* suffocating someone

sugar *noun*
a sweet food obtained from the juices of various plants, such as sugar beet or sugar cane
sugary *adjective* like sugar; having a lot of sugar in it

suggest *verb* (**suggests, suggesting, suggested**)
1 to suggest something is to offer it as an idea that you think is useful **2** to suggest something is also to give an idea or impression of something ♦ *Your smile suggests that you agree with me*
suggestion *noun* something that someone suggests

suicide *noun* (*plural* **suicides**)
killing yourself deliberately ♦ *He committed suicide*
suicidal *adjective* likely to commit suicide

suit ➤ *noun* (*plural* **suits**)
1 a matching set of jacket and trousers or jacket and skirt, that are meant to be worn together **2** a set of clothing for a particular activity ♦ *He wore a diving suit* **3** each of the four sets in a pack of playing cards: spades, hearts, diamonds, and clubs **4** a lawsuit

suit ➤ *verb* (**suits, suiting, suited**)
to suit someone or something is to be suitable or convenient for them

suitable *adjective*
satisfactory or right for a particular person, purpose, or occasion
suitability *noun* being suitable **suitably** *adverb* in a suitable way

suitcase *noun* (*plural* **suitcases**)
a container with a lid and a handle, for carrying clothes and other things on journeys

suite *noun* (*plural* **suites**) (*pronounced* sweet)
1 a set of furniture **2** a set of rooms **3** a set of short pieces of music

suitor *noun* (*plural* **suitors**)
a man who is courting a woman

sulk *verb* (**sulks, sulking, sulked**)
to sulk is to be silent and bad-tempered because you are not pleased

sulky *adjective* (**sulkier, sulkiest**)
sulking or inclined to sulk
sulkily *adverb* in a sulky way **sulkiness** *noun* being sulky

sullen *adjective*
sulking and gloomy
sullenly *adverb* in a sullen way **sullenness** *noun* being sullen

sulphur *noun*
a yellow chemical used in industry and medicine

sulphuric acid *noun*
a strong colourless acid containing sulphur

sultan *noun* (*plural* **sultans**)
the ruler of certain Muslim countries

sultana *noun* (*plural* **sultanas**)
a raisin without seeds

sum ➤ *noun* (*plural* **sums**)
1 a total, or the amount you get when you add numbers together **2** a problem in arithmetic **3** an amount of money

sum ➤ *verb* (**sums, summing, summed**)
to sum up is to give a summary at the end of a discussion or talk

summarize *verb* (**summarizes, summarizing, summarized**)
to summarize something is to give a summary of it

summary *noun* (*plural* **summaries**)
a statement of the main points of something said or written

summer *noun* (*plural* **summers**)
the warm season between spring and autumn

summertime *noun*
the season of summer

summit *noun* (*plural* **summits**)
1 the top of a mountain or hill **2** a meeting between the leaders of powerful countries

summon *verb* (**summons, summoning, summoned**)
to summon someone is to order them to come or appear

to summon something up is to find it in yourself ♦ *I need to summon up all my courage for the ordeal*

summons *noun* (*plural* **summonses**)
a command to someone to appear in a lawcourt

sun ➣ *noun*
1 the star round which the earth travels, and from which it gets warmth and light
2 warmth and light from this star ♦ *Shall we sit in the sun?*

sun ➣ *verb* (**suns, sunning, sunned**)
to sun yourself is to warm yourself in the sun

sunbathe *verb* (**sunbathes, sunbathing, sunbathed**)
to sunbathe is to expose your body to the sun

sunburn *noun*
redness of the skin caused by being in the sun too long
sunburned or **sunburnt** *adjective* affected by sunburn

sundae *noun* (*plural* **sundaes**) (*pronounced* sun-day)
a mixture of ice cream with fruit, nuts, and cream

Sunday *noun* (*plural* **Sundays**)
the first day of the week

sundial *noun* (*plural* **sundials**)
a device that shows the time by a shadow made by the sun

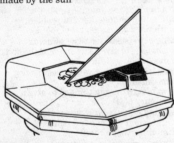

sunflower *noun* (*plural* **sunflowers**)
a tall flower with a large round yellow head

sung past participle of **sing**

sunglasses *plural noun*
dark glasses worn to protect the eyes from strong sunlight

sunk past tense and past participle of **sink** *verb*

sunlight *noun*
light from the sun
sunlit *adjective* lit by sunlight

sunny *adjective* (**sunnier, sunniest**)
1 having a lot of sunshine ♦ *It's a sunny day* 2 full of sunshine ♦ *What a sunny room*

sunrise *noun* (*plural* **sunrises**)
dawn ♦ *They left at sunrise*

sunset *noun* (*plural* **sunsets**)
the time when the sun sets

sunshade *noun* (*plural* **sunshades**)
a parasol or other device to protect people from the sun

sunshine *noun*
warmth and light that come from the sun

sunspot *noun* (*plural* **sunspots**)
1 a dark patch on the sun's surface 2 a sunny place

sunstroke *noun*
an illness caused by being in the sun for too long

suntan *noun* (*plural* **suntans**)
a brown colour of the skin caused by the sun

suntanned *adjective* having a suntan

super *adjective*
(*informal*) excellent or very good

super- *prefix*
meaning 'over' or 'beyond', as in *superhuman*

superb *adjective*
magnificent or excellent
superbly *adverb* in a superb way

superficial *adjective*
1 on the surface ♦ *It's only a superficial cut* 2 not deep or thorough ♦ *His knowledge of French is fairly superficial*
superficially *adverb* in a superficial way

superfluous *adjective* (*pronounced* soo-per-floo-us)
not necessary; no longer needed

superintend *verb* (**superintends, superintending, superintended**)
to superintend someone or something is to be in charge of them

superintendent *noun* (*plural* **superintendents**)
1 someone who is in charge 2 a police officer above the rank of inspector

superior ➣ *adjective*
1 higher or more important than someone else 2 better than another person or thing 3 conceited or proud
♦ *I don't like his superior attitude*
superiority *noun* being superior

superior ➣ *noun* (*plural* **superiors**)
someone of higher rank or position than another person

superlative ➤ *adjective* (*pronounced* soo-per-la-tiv)
of the highest quality

superlative ➤ *noun* (*plural* **superlatives**)
the form of an adjective or adverb that expresses 'most' ♦ *The superlative of 'big' is 'biggest', and the superlative of 'bad' is 'worst'*

supermarket *noun* (*plural* **supermarkets**)
a large self-service shop that sells food and other goods

supernatural *adjective*
not belonging to the natural world or having a natural explanation

supersonic *adjective*
faster than the speed of sound

superstition *noun* (*plural* **superstitions**)
a belief or action that is not based on reason or evidence ♦ *It is a superstition that 13 is an unlucky number*
superstitious *adjective* believing in superstitions

supervise *verb* (**supervises, supervising, supervised**)
to supervise someone or something is to be in charge of them
supervision *noun* supervising someone
supervisor *noun* someone who supervises

supper *noun* (*plural* **suppers**)
a meal or snack eaten in the evening

supple *adjective* (**suppler, supplest**)
bending easily; flexible, not stiff
supplely *adverb* in a supple way **suppleness** *noun* being supple

supplement *noun* (*plural* **supplements**)
1 something added as an extra **2** an extra section added to a book or newspaper
supplementary *adjective* extra; additional

supply ➤ *verb* (**supplies, supplying, supplied**)
1 to supply something is to give or sell it to people who need it **2** to supply someone is to give them what they need
supplier *noun* someone who supplies something

supply ➤ *noun* (*plural* **supplies**)
1 an amount of something kept ready to be used when needed **2** the action of supplying something

support ➤ *verb* (**supports, supporting, supported**)
1 to support something is to hold it so that it does not fall down **2** to support someone or something is to give them help or encouragement

support ➤ *noun* (*plural* **supports**)
1 support is the action of supporting **2** a support is a person or thing that supports

supporter *noun* (*plural* **supporters**)
someone who gives support, especially to a sports team

suppose *verb* (**supposes, supposing, supposed**)
to suppose something is to think that it is likely or true
to be supposed to do something is to have to do it as an order or duty
supposition *noun* something someone supposes

supposedly *adverb*
so people suppose or think ♦ *They are supposedly millionaires*

suppress *verb* (**suppresses, suppressing, suppressed**)
to suppress something is to keep it secret or stop it happening
suppression *noun* suppressing something

supreme *adjective*
highest or greatest; most important
supremacy *noun* being supreme **supremely** *adverb* to a supreme degree; very

sure ➤ *adjective* (**surer, surest**)
1 confident about something; convinced
2 very likely to happen or do something ♦ *The telephone is sure to ring*
3 completely true or known ♦ *One thing is sure: she is not here at the moment*
4 reliable ♦ *Visiting places is a sure way of getting to know them*
to make sure of something is to find out that it is true or right

sure ➤ *adverb*
(*informal*) certainly
sure enough (*informal*) certainly; in fact ♦ *I thought he'd be late, and sure enough he was*

surely *adverb*
1 certainly; definitely **2** it must be true; I feel sure ♦ *Surely I met you last year*

surf ➤ *noun*
the white foam of waves breaking on rocks or the seashore

surf ➤ *verb* (**surfs, surfing, surfed**)
1 to surf is to go surfing **2** to surf the internet is to browse through it

surface ➤ *noun* (*plural* **surfaces**)
1 the outside of something **2** each of the sides of something, especially the top part

surface ➤ *verb* (**surfaces, surfacing, surfaced**)
1 to surface a road or path is to give it a hard covering layer **2** to surface is to come up to the surface from under water ♦ *The submarine slowly surfaced*

surfboard *noun* (*plural* **surfboards**)
a board used in surfing

surfing *noun*
the sport of balancing yourself on a board or small boat that is carried towards the seashore by the waves
surfer *noun* someone who goes surfing

surge ➤ *verb* (**surges, surging, surged**)
to surge is to move forwards or upwards like waves
surge ➤ *noun* (*plural* **surges**)
the action of surging

surgeon *noun* (*plural* **surgeons**)
a doctor who deals with disease or injury by cutting or repairing the affected parts of the body

surgery *noun* (*plural* **surgeries**)
1 a surgery is a building or room where a doctor or dentist sees patients **2** surgery is the time when patients can see a doctor or dentist ♦ *Surgery will close at 6 o'clock today* **3** surgery is also the work of a surgeon

surgical *adjective*
to do with a surgeon or surgery
surgically *adverb* by means of surgery

surname *noun* (*plural* **surnames**)
the name that all members of a family have

surpass *verb* (**surpasses, surpassing, surpassed**)
to surpass someone is to do better or be better than them

surplus *noun* (*plural* **surpluses**)
an amount left over after you have spent or used what you need

surprise ➤ *noun* (*plural* **surprises**)
1 something that you did not expect **2** the feeling you have when something unexpected happens

surprise ➤ *verb* (**surprises, surprising, surprised**)
1 to surprise someone is to be a surprise to them **2** to surprise someone is also to catch or attack them unexpectedly

surrender ➤ *verb* (**surrenders, surrendering, surrendered**)
1 to surrender to an enemy is to stop fighting and put yourself under their control **2** to surrender something to someone is to give it over to them
surrender ➤ *noun*
the act of surrendering

surround *verb* (**surrounds, surrounding, surrounded**)
to surround someone or something is to be or come all round them

surroundings *plural noun*
the things or conditions around a person or place

survey ➤ *noun* (*plural* **surveys**) (*pronounced* ser-vay)
1 a general look at a topic or activity **2** a detailed inspection or examination of a building or area
survey ➤ *verb* (**surveys, surveying, surveyed**) (*pronounced* ser-**vay**)
to survey something is to inspect it or make a survey of it

surveyor *noun* (*plural* **surveyors**)
someone whose job is to survey buildings and land

survive *verb* (**survives, surviving, survived**)
1 to survive is to stay alive **2** to survive someone is to continue living after they have died **3** to survive an accident or disaster is to remain alive in spite of it
survival *noun* surviving **survivor** *noun* someone who survives

suspect ➤ *verb* (**suspects, suspecting, suspected**) (*pronounced* su-**spekt**)
1 to suspect someone is to think that they have done something wrong or are not to be trusted **2** to suspect something unwelcome is to think that it might happen

suspect ➤ *noun* (*plural* **suspects**) (*pronounced* **sus**-pekt)
someone who is thought to have done something wrong

suspend *verb* (**suspends, suspending, suspended**)
1 to suspend something that is happening is to stop it for a time **2** to suspend someone is to take away their job or position for a time ♦ *He was suspended from the team for bad behaviour* **3** to suspend something is to hang it up

suspense *noun*
an anxious or uncertain feeling while waiting for something to happen or for news about something

suspension *noun* (*plural* **suspensions**)
1 suspension is suspending something or someone 2 a vehicle's suspension is the set of springs and other devices that make the ride more comfortable

suspension bridge *noun* (*plural* **suspension bridges**)
a bridge supported by cables

suspicion *noun* (*plural* **suspicions**)
1 suspicion is suspecting someone or being suspected 2 a suspicion is a slight or uncertain feeling about something or someone

suspicious *adjective*
1 making you suspect someone or something ♦ *There are suspicious footprints along the path* 2 suspecting someone or something ♦ *I'm suspicious about what happened*
suspiciously *adverb* in a suspicious way

sustain *verb* (**sustains, sustaining, sustained**)
1 to sustain someone is to keep them alive 2 to sustain something is to keep it going ♦ *It's difficult to sustain such an effort* 3 to sustain an injury is to be injured 4 to sustain something is also to hold it up or support it

swagger *verb* (**swaggers, swaggering, swaggered**)
to walk or behave in a conceited way

swallow [1] *verb* (**swallows, swallowing, swallowed**)
to swallow something is to make it go down your throat
to find something hard to swallow is to find it difficult to believe
to swallow something up is to cover or hide it

swallow [2] *noun* (*plural* **swallows**)
a small bird with a forked tail and pointed wings

swam past tense of **swim** *verb*

swamp ➤ *verb* (**swamps, swamping, swamped**)
1 to swamp something is to flood it 2 to swamp someone is to overwhelm them with a large number of things ♦ *They have been swamped with complaints*

swamp ➤ *noun* (*plural* **swamps**)
a marsh

swampy *adjective* full of swamps

swan *noun* (*plural* **swans**)
a large white water bird with a long neck and powerful wings

swank *verb* (**swanks, swanking, swanked**)
(*informal*) to swank is to swagger or boast

swap ➤ *verb* (**swaps, swapping, swapped**)
(*informal*) to swap something is to exchange it ♦ *After the game they swapped jerseys*

swap ➤ *noun* (*plural* **swaps**)
1 an act of swapping ♦ *Let's do a swap*
2 something you swap for something else

swarm ➤ *noun* (*plural* **swarms**)
a large number of insects flying or moving about together

swarm ➤ *verb* (**swarms, swarming, swarmed**)
1 to swarm is to move in a swarm 2 to be swarming is to be crowded with people ♦ *The town is swarming with tourists in summer*

swastika *noun* (*plural* **swastikas**)
(*pronounced* swos-ti-ka)
a sign formed by a cross with its ends bent at right angles, used as a symbol by the Nazis in Germany

swat *verb* (**swats, swatting, swatted**)
(*pronounced* swot)
to swat a fly or other insect is to hit or crush it
swatter *noun* a device for swatting insects

sway *verb* (**sways, swaying, swayed**)
to sway is to move gently from side to side

swear *verb* (**swears, swearing, swore, sworn**)
1 to swear is to make a solemn promise ♦ *She swore to tell the truth* 2 to be sworn is to be made to give a solemn promise ♦ *He was sworn to secrecy* 3 to swear is also to use curses or coarse words
to swear by something is to have a lot of confidence in it

swear word *noun* (*plural* **swear words**)
a word that is coarse or shocking, used by someone who is angry or upset

sweat ➤ *verb* (**sweats, sweating, sweated**)
(*pronounced* swet)
to sweat is to give off moisture through the pores of your skin, especially when you are hot or doing exercise

sweat ➤ *noun* (*pronounced* swet)
moisture that is given off when sweating
sweaty *adjective* covered in sweat; sweating a lot

sweater *noun* (*plural* **sweaters**) (*pronounced* swet-er)
a jersey or pullover

sweatshirt noun (plural **sweatshirts**)
a thick cotton jersey

swede noun (plural **swedes**)
a large kind of turnip with purple skin and yellow flesh

sweep ➤ verb (**sweeps, sweeping, swept**)
1 to sweep a room or floor is to clean or clear it with a broom or brush ♦ *He swept the floor* 2 to sweep something away is to move or change it quickly ♦ *The flood has swept away the bridge* 3 to sweep somewhere is to go there swiftly or proudly ♦ *She swept out of the room*

sweep ➤ noun (plural **sweeps**)
1 a sweeping action or movement ♦ *Give this room a sweep* 2 a chimney sweep

sweeper noun (plural **sweepers**)
1 a machine for sweeping floors 2 (*in Football*) a defensive player at the back

sweet ➤ adjective (**sweeter, sweetest**)
1 tasting of sugar or honey 2 very pleasant ♦ *There was a sweet smell in the room* 3 charming or delightful ♦ *What a sweet little cottage*
sweetly adverb in a sweet way **sweetness** noun being sweet

sweet ➤ noun (plural **sweets**)
1 a small shaped piece of sweet food made of sugar or chocolate 2 a pudding; the sweet course in a meal

sweetcorn noun
the juicy yellow seeds of maize

sweeten verb (**sweetens, sweetening, sweetened**)
1 to sweeten something is to make it sweet 2 to sweeten is to become sweet
sweetener noun something that makes things sweet

sweetheart noun (plural **sweethearts**)
a person you love very much

sweet pea noun (plural **sweet peas**)
a climbing plant with sweet-smelling flowers

swell ➤ verb (**swells, swelling, swelled, swollen** or **swelled**)
to swell is to get bigger or louder

swell ➤ noun (plural **swells**)
the rise and fall of the sea's surface

swelling noun (plural **swellings**)
a swollen place on the body

swelter verb (**swelters, sweltering, sweltered**)
to swelter is to be uncomfortably hot

swept past tense and past participle of **sweep** verb

swerve ➤ verb (**swerves, swerving, swerved**)
to swerve is to move suddenly to one side ♦ *The car swerved to avoid the cyclist*

swerve ➤ noun (plural **swerves**)
a swerving movement

swift ➤ adjective (**swifter, swiftest**)
quick; moving quickly and easily
swiftly adverb quickly **swiftness** noun being swift

swift ➤ noun (plural **swifts**)
a small bird rather like a swallow

swill ➤ verb (**swills, swilling, swilled**)
to swill something is to rinse or flush it

swill ➤ noun
a sloppy mixture of waste food given to pigs

swim ➤ verb (**swims, swimming, swam, swum**)
1 to swim is to move yourself through the water or to be in the water for pleasure 2 to swim a stretch of water is to cross it by swimming ♦ *She has swum the Channel* 3 to be swimming in liquid or with liquid is to be covered in it or full of it ♦ *Their eyes were swimming with tears* 4 your head swims when you feel dizzy

swim ➤ noun (plural **swims**)
a spell of swimming ♦ *Let's go for a swim*

swimmer noun (plural **swimmers**)
someone who swims ♦ *Are you a good swimmer?*

swimming bath or **swimming pool** noun (plural **swimming baths** or **swimming pools**)
a specially built pool with water for people to swim in

swimming costume noun (plural **swimming costumes**)
a piece of clothing for swimming in

swimsuit noun (plural **swimsuits**)
a one-piece swimming costume

swindle ➤ verb (**swindles, swindling, swindled**)
to swindle someone is to get money or goods from them dishonestly
swindler noun someone who swindles people

swindle ➤ noun (plural **swindles**)
a trick to swindle someone

swine noun (plural **swine** or **swines**)
1 a pig 2 (*informal*) an unpleasant person or a difficult thing

swing ➤ verb (**swings, swinging, swung**)
1 to swing is to move to and fro or in a curve 2 to swing something is to turn it quickly or suddenly ♦ *He swung the car round to avoid the bus*

swing ➤ *noun* (*plural* **swings**)
1 a swinging movement **2** a seat hung on chains or ropes so that it can move backwards and forwards **3** the amount that votes or opinions change from one side to the other
in full swing full of activity; working fully

swipe ➤ *verb* (**swipes, swiping, swiped**)
1 to swipe someone or something is to give them a hard hit **2** (*informal*) to swipe something is to steal it **3** to swipe a credit card is to pass it through a special reading device when making a payment

swipe ➤ *noun* (*plural* **swipes**)
a hard hit

swirl ➤ *verb* (**swirls, swirling, swirled**)
to swirl is to move around quickly in circles; to swirl something is to make it do this

swirl ➤ *noun* (*plural* **swirls**)
a swirling movement

swish ➤ *verb* (**swishes, swishing, swished**)
to swish is to make a hissing or rustling sound

swish ➤ *noun* (*plural* **swishes**)
a swishing sound

Swiss roll *noun* (*plural* **Swiss rolls**)
a thin sponge cake spread with jam or cream and rolled up

switch ➤ *noun* (*plural* **switches**)
1 a device that you press or turn to start or stop something working, especially by electricity **2** a sudden change of opinion or methods

switch ➤ *verb* (**switches, switching, switched**)
1 to switch a device on or off is to use a switch to make it work or stop working **2** to switch something is to change it suddenly

switchboard *noun* (*plural* **switchboards**)
a panel with switches for connecting telephone lines

swivel *verb* (**swivels, swivelling, swivelled**)
to swivel is to turn round

swollen past participle of **swell** *verb*

swoon *verb* (**swoons, swooning, swooned**)
(*old use*) to swoon is to faint from fear or weakness

swoop *verb* (**swoops, swooping, swooped**)
1 to swoop is to dive or come down suddenly **2** to swoop is also to make a sudden attack or raid

swoop ➤ *noun* (*plural* **swoops**)
a sudden dive or attack

swop *verb* (**swops, swopping, swopped**)
(*informal*) to swap

sword *noun* (*plural* **swords**) (*pronounced* sord)
a weapon with a long pointed blade fixed in a handle

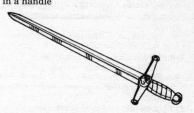

swore past tense of **swear**

sworn past participle of **swear**

swot ➤ *verb* (**swots, swotting, swotted**)
(*informal*) to swot is to study hard

swot ➤ *noun* (*plural* **swots**)
(*informal*) someone who swots

swum past participle of **swim** *verb*

swung past tense and past participle of **swing** *verb*

sycamore *noun* (*plural* **sycamores**)
a tall tree with winged seeds

syllable *noun* (*plural* **syllables**)
a word or part of a word that has one separate sound when you say it ♦ *'Cat' has one syllable, 'el-e-phant' has three syllables*
syllabic *adjective* to do with syllables

syllabus *noun* (*plural* **syllabuses**) (*pronounced* sil-a-bus)
a list of things to be studied by a class or for an examination

symbol *noun* (*plural* **symbols**)
1 a mark or sign with a special meaning **2** a thing that stands for something ♦ *The crescent is a symbol of Islam*

symbolic or **symbolical** *adjective*
acting as a symbol of something
symbolically *adverb* in a symbolic way

symbolism *noun*
the use of symbols to stand for something

symbolize *verb* (**symbolizes, symbolizing, symbolized**)
to symbolize something is to be a symbol of it ♦ *Red symbolizes danger*

symmetrical *adjective* (*pronounced* sim-et-rik-al)
able to be divided into two halves which are exactly the same but the opposite way round ♦ *Wheels and butterflies are symmetrical*
symmetrically *adverb* in a symmetrical way

symmetry *noun*
the quality of being symmetrical or well-proportioned

sympathetic *adjective*
feeling sympathy or understanding for someone
sympathetically *adverb* in a sympathetic way

sympathize *verb* (**sympathizes, sympathizing, sympathized**)
to sympathize with someone is to show or feel sympathy for them

sympathy *noun* (*plural* **sympathies**)
1 the sharing or understanding of other people's feelings or opinions **2** the feeling of being sorry for someone's unhappiness or suffering

symphony *noun* (*plural* **symphonies**)
a long piece of music for an orchestra
symphonic *adjective* to do with a symphony

symptom *noun* (*plural* **symptoms**)
a sign or clue that someone has an illness
♦ *Red spots are a symptom of measles*
symptomatic *adjective* acting as a symptom

synagogue *noun* (*plural* **synagogues**)
(*pronounced* sin-a-gog)
a building where Jews meet to worship

synchronize *verb* (**synchronizes, synchronizing, synchronized**) (*pronounced* sink-ro-nyz)
1 to synchronize things is to make them happen at the same time **2** to synchronize watches or clocks is to set them to show the same time
synchronization *noun* synchronizing things

syncopated *adjective* (*pronounced* sink-o-payt-id)
a piece of music is syncopated when the strong beats are played weak and the weak beats are played strong

synonym *noun* (*plural* **synonyms**)
(*pronounced* sin-o-nim)
a word that means the same or nearly the same as another word, such as *big* and *large*
synonymous *adjective* having the same meaning

synthesis *noun* (*plural* **syntheses**)
combining different things or parts into a whole thing or system

synthesize *verb* (**synthesizes, synthesizing, synthesized**)
to synthesize something is to make it by combining parts

synthesizer *noun* (*plural* **synthesizers**)
an electronic musical instrument that can make many different sounds

synthetic *adjective*
artificially made; not natural
synthetically *adverb* in a synthetic way

syringe *noun* (*plural* **syringes**)
a device for sucking in a liquid and squirting it out

syrup *noun* (*plural* **syrups**)
a thick sweet liquid
syrupy *adjective* like syrup

system *noun* (*plural* **systems**)
1 a set of parts or things or ideas that work together **2** a well-organized way of doing something ♦ *There is a new system of training motorcyclists*

systematic *adjective*
using a system; careful and well planned
systematically *adverb* in a systematic way

Tt

tab *noun* (*plural* **tabs**)
a small strip or flap that sticks out

tabby *noun* (*plural* **tabbies**)
a grey or brown cat with dark streaks in its fur

table *noun* (*plural* **tables**)
1 a piece of furniture with a flat top supported on legs **2** a list of facts arranged in order **3** a list of the results of multiplying a number by other numbers
♦ *Do you know your multiplication tables?*

tablecloth *noun* (*plural* **tablecloths**)
a cloth for covering a table

tablespoon *noun* (*plural* **tablespoons**)
a large spoon used for serving food

tablespoonful *noun* (*plural* **tablespoonfuls**)
as much as a tablespoon will hold

tablet *noun* (*plural* **tablets**)
1 a pill **2** a lump of soap **3** a flat piece of stone or wood with words carved or written on it

table tennis *noun*
a game played on a table divided in the middle by a net, over which you hit a small ball with bats

tack[1] ➤ *noun* (*plural* **tacks**)
1 a short nail with a flat top **2** the action of tacking in sailing; the direction you take

tack ➤ *verb* (**tacks, tacking, tacked**)
1 to tack something is to nail it with tacks **2** to tack material is to sew it together quickly with long stitches **3** to tack is to sail a zigzag course to get full benefit from the wind
to tack something on is to add it as an extra

tack[2] *noun*
equipment for horses, such as harnesses and saddles

tackle ➤ *verb* (**tackles, tackling, tackled**)
1 to tackle a task is to start doing it **2** in football or hockey, to tackle a player is to try to get the ball from them or (in rugby) to bring them to the ground

tackle ➤ *noun* (*plural* **tackles**)
1 equipment, especially for fishing **2** an act of tackling someone in football or rugby or hockey

tacky *adjective* (**tackier, tackiest**)
1 sticky or not quite dry ♦ *The paint is still tacky* **2** (*informal*) cheaply made and showing poor taste

tact *noun*
skill in not offending people

tactful *adjective*
having or showing tact
tactfully *adverb* in a tactful way

tactics *plural noun*
ways of organizing people or things to do something, especially organizing troops in a battle
tactical *adjective* to do with tactics **tactically** *adverb* in a tactical way

tactless *adjective*
likely to offend people; having no tact
tactlessly *adverb* in a tactless way

tadpole *noun* (*plural* **tadpoles**)
a young frog or toad at a stage when it has an oval head and a long tail and lives in water

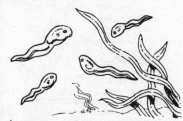

tag[1] ➤ *noun* (*plural* **tags**)
1 a label tied or stuck to something **2** the metal or plastic part at the end of a shoelace

tag ➤ *verb* (**tags, tagging, tagged**)
to tag something is to fix a tag or label on it
to tag along is to go along with other people
to tag something on is to add it as something extra

tag[2] *noun*
a game in which one person chases the others

tail ➤ *noun* (*plural* **tails**)
1 the part that sticks out from the rear end of the body of an animal or bird **2** the part at the end or rear of something, such as an aircraft **3** the side of a coin opposite the head

tail ➤ *verb* (**tails, tailing, tailed**)
1 to tail fruit is to remove the stalks from it **2** to tail someone is to follow them without them seeing you
to tail off is to become fewer or smaller

tailback *noun* (*plural* **tailbacks**)
a long line of traffic stretching back from an obstruction

tailless *adjective*
not having a tail

tailor *noun* (*plural* **tailors**)
someone whose job is to make clothes

take *verb* (**takes, taking, took, taken**)
This word has many meanings, depending on the words that go with it: **1** to take something or someone is to get hold of them or bring them into your possession ♦ *He took a cake from the plate* ♦ *Who do you think took the money?* ♦ *They took many prisoners* **2** to take someone or something somewhere is to carry or drive or convey them there ♦ *Shall I take you to the station?* ♦ *Take this parcel to the post* **3** to take something useful or pleasant is to make use of it ♦ *Do you take sugar?* ♦ *You must take a holiday this year* ♦ *Do take a seat* **4** to take someone or something is to need them for a purpose ♦ *It will take two people to lift the table* **5** to take a piece of information is to make a note of it ♦ *Take their names and addresses* **6** to take a class for a subject is to teach it to them ♦ *Who takes you for English?* **7** to take one number from another is to subtract it ♦ *Take two from ten and you get eight* **8** to take an examination is to do it ♦ *I'm taking my maths exam today* **9** to take a joke is to accept it well **10** to take a photograph or picture is to produce it with a camera
I take it I understand or assume ♦ *I take it that you agree*
to take off is to leave the ground at the beginning of a flight
to take part in something is to share in doing it
to take place is to happen
to take someone in is to fool or deceive them
to take something off is to remove it
to take something over is to take control of it
to take something up is to start doing it ♦ *I've taken up yoga*

takeaway *noun* (*plural* **takeaways**)
1 a place that sells cooked food for customers to take away **2** a meal from a takeaway

takings *plural noun*
money that has been received, especially by a shopkeeper

talc or **talcum powder** *noun*
a perfumed powder put on the skin to dry it or make it smell pleasant

tale *noun* (*plural* **tales**)
a story

talent *noun* (*plural* **talents**)
a natural ability to do something well
♦ *She has a talent for singing*
talented *adjective* having a talent

talk ➤ *verb* (**talks, talking, talked**)
to talk is to speak or have a conversation
talker *noun* someone who is talking

talk ➤ *noun* (*plural* **talks**)
1 a conversation or discussion **2** a lecture

talkative *adjective*
fond of talking; talking a lot

tall *adjective* (**taller, tallest**)
1 higher than the average ♦ *They sat under a tall tree* **2** measured from the bottom to the top ♦ *The bookcase is two metres tall*
a tall story is a story that is hard to believe

tally *verb* (**tallies, tallying, tallied**)
to tally is to correspond or agree with something else ♦ *Does your list tally with mine?*

Talmud *noun*
a collection of writings on Jewish religious law

talon *noun* (*plural* **talons**)
a strong claw

tambourine *noun* (*plural* **tambourines**)
a round musical instrument like a small drum with metal discs fixed around the edge so that it jingles when you shake it or hit it

tame ➤ *adjective* (**tamer, tamest**)
1 a tame animal is one that is gentle and not afraid of people **2** something is tame when it is dull or uninteresting
tamely *adverb* in a tame or gentle way
tameness *noun* being tame

tame ➤ *verb* (**tames, taming, tamed**)
to tame an animal is to make it tame
tamer *noun* someone who tames animals

tamper *verb* (**tampers, tampering, tampered**)
to tamper with something is to interfere with it or change it so that it will not work properly

tampon *noun* (*plural* **tampons**)
a plug of soft material that a woman puts into her vagina to absorb the blood during her period

tan ➤ *noun* (*plural* **tans**)
1 a suntan **2** a yellowish-brown colour

tan ➤ *verb* (**tans, tanning, tanned**)
1 to tan your skin is to make it brown with a suntan **2** to tan the skin of a dead animal is to make it into leather

tandem *noun* (*plural* **tandems**)
a bicycle for two riders, one behind the other

tang *noun*
a strong flavour or smell

tangent *noun* (*plural* **tangents**) (*pronounced* tan-jent)
a straight line that touches the outside of a curve or circle

tangerine *noun* (*plural* **tangerines**) (*pronounced* tan-jer-een)
a kind of small orange

tangle ➤ *verb* (**tangles, tangling, tangled**)
1 to tangle something is to make it twisted or muddled **2** to tangle is to become twisted or muddled ♦ *My fishing line has tangled*

tangle ➤ *noun* (*plural* **tangles**)
a tangled state

tank *noun* (*plural* **tanks**)
1 a large container for a liquid or gas **2** a heavy armoured vehicle used in war

tankard *noun* (*plural* **tankards**)
a large heavy mug for drinking from

tanker *noun* (*plural* **tankers**)
 1 a large ship for carrying oil **2** a large lorry for carrying a liquid

tanner *noun* (*plural* **tanners**)
 someone who tans animal skins to make leather

tantalize *verb* (**tantalizes, tantalizing, tantalized**)
 to tantalize someone is to torment them by showing them something good that they cannot have

tantrum *noun* (*plural* **tantrums**)
 an outburst of bad temper

tap[1] ➤ *noun* (*plural* **taps**)
 a device for letting out liquid or gas in a controlled flow

tap ➤ *verb* (**taps, tapping, tapped**)
 1 to tap a container is to take liquid out of it through a tap **2** to tap a source of information or supplies is to make use of it **3** to tap a telephone is to fix a device to it so that you can hear someone else's conversation

tap[2] ➤ *noun* (*plural* **taps**)
 1 a tap is a quick light hit, or the sound it makes ♦ *I gave him a tap on the shoulder* **2** tap is tapdancing

tap ➤ *verb* (**taps, tapping, tapped**)
 to tap someone or something is to give them a tap or gentle hit

tapdance *noun*
 a dance in hard shoes that make sharp tapping sounds on the floor
 tapdancing *noun* performing a tapdance
 tapdancer *noun* someone who performs a tapdance

tape ➤ *noun* (*plural* **tapes**)
 1 tape is soft material such as cloth or paper or plastic in a thin strip; a tape is a piece of this **2** a narrow plastic strip coated with a magnetic substance and used for making recordings

tape ➤ *verb* (**tapes, taping, taped**)
 1 to tape something is to fix or cover or surround it with tape **2** to tape music or sound is to record it on magnetic tape
 to get or **have something taped** (*informal*) is to know or understand it, or be able to deal with it

tape-measure *noun* (*plural* **tape-measures**)
 a long strip marked in centimetres or inches for measuring things

taper ➤ *verb* (**tapers, tapering, tapered**)
 to taper is to get narrower towards one end

taper ➤ *noun* (*plural* **tapers**)
 a piece of string thinly coated with wax, for lighting things

tape recorder *noun* (*plural* **tape recorders**)
 a machine for recording music or sound on magnetic tape and playing it back

tape recording *noun* a recording made with magnetic tape

tapestry *noun* (*plural* **tapestries**)
 (*pronounced* **tap**-i-stree)
 a piece of strong cloth with pictures or patterns woven or embroidered on it

tapeworm *noun* (*plural* **tapeworms**)
 a long flat worm that can live as a parasite in the intestines of people and animals

tapioca *noun*
 a starchy substance consisting of white grains used for making milk puddings

tar ➤ *noun*
 a thick black liquid made from coal or wood and used in making roads
 tarry *adjective* like tar or covered in tar

tar ➤ *verb* (**tars, tarring, tarred**)
 to tar something is to cover it with tar

tarantula *noun* (*plural* **tarantulas**)
 (*pronounced* ta-**ran**-tew-la)
 a large poisonous spider found in warm countries

target ➤ *noun* (*plural* **targets**)
 something that you aim at and try to hit or reach

target ➤ *verb* (**targets, targeting, targeted**)
 to target something or someone is to make them a target

tarmac *noun*
 an area covered with tarmacadam, especially on an airfield

tarmacadam *noun*
 a mixture of tar and broken stone, used for making a hard surface on roads and paths and open areas

tarnish *verb* (**tarnishes, tarnishing, tarnished**)
 1 to tarnish a metal is to make it less shiny **2** to tarnish is to become less shiny **3** to tarnish something is to spoil it ♦ *The scandal tarnished his reputation*

tarpaulin *noun* (*plural* **tarpaulins**)
 a large sheet of waterproof canvas

tart[1] *noun* (*plural* **tarts**)
 a pie containing fruit or jam

tart[2] *adjective* (**tarter, tartest**)
 sour ♦ *The apples are tart*

tartan *noun* (*plural* **tartans**)
 a woollen cloth with a special pattern of colours and stripes, especially as worn in the Scottish Highlands

task *noun* (*plural* **tasks**)
 a piece of work to be done
 to take someone to task is to tell them off for doing wrong

task force *noun* (*plural* **task forces**)
 a group of people given a special task to do

tassel *noun* (*plural* **tassels**)
 a bundle of threads tied together at the top and used to decorate something

taste ➤ *verb* (**tastes, tasting, tasted**)
1 to taste food or drink is to eat or drink a small amount to see what it is like 2 to taste a certain way is to have a particular flavour ♦ *The milk tastes sour*

taste ➤ *noun* (*plural* **tastes**)
1 a taste is the flavour something has when you taste it ♦ *The milk has a strange taste* 2 taste is the ability to taste things 3 taste is also the ability to enjoy beautiful things ♦ *Their choice of clothes shows good taste* 4 a tiny amount of food ♦ *Can I have a taste of your pudding?*

tasteful *adjective*
showing good taste
tastefully *adverb* in a tasteful way

tasteless *adjective*
showing poor taste
tastelessly *adverb* in a tasteless way

tasty *adjective* (**tastier, tastiest**)
having a strong pleasant taste

tattered *adjective*
badly torn; in rags

tatters *plural noun*
rags; badly torn pieces
in tatters badly torn

tattoo[1] ➤ *noun* (*plural* **tattoos**)
a picture or pattern made on someone's skin with a needle and dye

tattoo ➤ *verb* (**tattoos, tattooing, tattooed**)
to tattoo someone is to put a tattoo on their skin

tattoo[2] *noun* (*plural* **tattoos**)
1 a drumming sound ♦ *He beat a tattoo on the table with his fingers* 2 an outdoor entertainment including military music and marching

tatty *adjective* (**tattier, tattiest**)
ragged or shabby; untidy

taught past tense and past participle of **teach**

taunt ➤ *verb* (**taunts, taunting, taunted**)
to taunt someone is to jeer at them or insult them

taunt ➤ *noun* (*plural* **taunts**)
a taunt is a jeer or spell of taunting

taut *adjective* (**tauter, tautest**)
stretched tightly
tautly *adverb* in a taut way **tautness** *noun* being taut

tavern *noun* (*plural* **taverns**)
(*old use*) an inn or public house

tawny *adjective* (**tawnier, tawniest**)
brownish-yellow

tax ➤ *noun* (*plural* **taxes**)
an amount of money that people and businesses have to pay to the government for public use

tax ➤ *verb* (**taxes, taxing, taxed**)
1 to tax someone is to charge them a tax 2 to tax something is to charge a tax when someone buys or owns or uses it ♦ *The government taxes alcohol, tobacco, and petrol* 3 to tax something is also to pay the tax due on it ♦ *The car is taxed until June*
taxable *adjective* having a tax on it **taxation** *noun* taxing people or things

taxi or **taxicab** ➤ *noun* (*plural* **taxis** or **taxicabs**)
a car with a driver which you can hire for journeys, with a meter for recording the distance

taxi ➤ *verb* (**taxis, taxiing, taxied**)
to taxi is what an aircraft does when it moves slowly along the ground before taking off or after landing

taxpayer *noun* (*plural* **taxpayers**)
someone who pays taxes

tea *noun* (*plural* **teas**)
1 a drink made by pouring hot water on the dried leaves of an evergreen shrub 2 the dried leaves of this shrub 3 a meal eaten in the afternoon

teabag *noun* (*plural* **teabags**)
a small bag of tea for making tea in a cup

teacake *noun* (*plural* **teacakes**)
a kind of bun usually eaten toasted and buttered

teach *verb* (**teaches, teaching, taught**)
1 to teach someone is to give them knowledge or skill about something 2 to teach a subject is to give lessons in it ♦ *She taught us history last year*

teacher *noun* (*plural* **teachers**)
someone who teaches people at a school or college

tea cloth or **tea towel** *noun* (*plural* **tea cloths** or **tea towels**)
a cloth used for drying washed dishes and cutlery

teacup *noun* (*plural* **teacups**)
a cup for drinking tea

teak *noun*
a hard strong wood from Asia

team *noun* (*plural* **teams**)
1 a set of players who form one side in a game or sport 2 a group of people who work together

teapot *noun* (*plural* **teapots**)
a pot with a handle and spout, for making and pouring out tea

tear[1] ➤ *verb* (tears, tearing, tore, torn)
(*pronounced* tair)
1 to tear something is to make a split in it
or to pull it apart **2** to tear something is
also to pull or remove it with force ♦ *He
tore the picture off the wall* **3** to tear is to
become torn ♦ *Paper tears easily* **4** to tear
somewhere is to move very quickly there
♦ *He tore down the street*
tear ➤ *noun* (*plural* **tears**)
a hole or split made by tearing something

tear[2] ➤ *noun* (*plural* **tears**) (*pronounced*
teer)
a drop of water that comes from your eye
when you cry

tearful *adjective*
in tears; crying easily
tearfully *adverb* in a tearful way

tear gas *noun*
a gas that makes people's eyes water
painfully

tease *verb* (teases, teasing, teased)
to tease someone is to annoy them
playfully or joke about them

teaspoon *noun* (*plural* **teaspoons**)
a small spoon for stirring tea

teaspoonful *noun* (*plural* **teaspoonfuls**)
as much as a teaspoon will hold

teat *noun* (*plural* **teats**)
1 a nipple through which a baby drinks
milk **2** the cap of a baby's feeding bottle

tech *noun* (*plural* **techs**)
(*informal*) a technical college

technical *adjective*
to do with technology or the way things
work
technically *adverb* in a technical way

technical college *noun* (*plural* **technical
colleges**)
a college where technical subjects are
taught

technicality *noun* (*plural* **technicalities**)
a technical word or detail

technician *noun* (*plural* **technicians**)
someone whose job is to look after
scientific equipment and do practical work
in a laboratory

technique *noun* (*plural* **techniques**)
(*pronounced* tek-**neek**)
the method of doing something skilfully

technology *noun* (*plural* **technologies**)
the study of machinery and the way things
work
technological *adjective* to do with
technology

teddy bear *noun* (*plural* **teddy bears**)
a soft furry toy bear

tedious *adjective* (*pronounced* tee-di-us)
annoyingly slow or long; boring
tediously *adverb* in a tedious way **tediousness**
noun being tedious

tedium *noun*
tedium is a dull or boring time or
experience ♦ *He hated the tedium of
visiting his grandparents*

teem *verb* (teems, teeming, teemed)
1 to teem with something is to be full of it
♦ *The river was teeming with fish* **2** to
teem, or teem down, is to rain very hard

teenage or **teenaged** *adjective*
in your teens; to do with teenagers

teenager *noun* (*plural* **teenagers**)
a person in their teens

teens *plural noun*
the time of your life between the ages of 13
and 19 ♦ *They started playing chess in
their teens*

teeth plural of **tooth**

teetotal *adjective*
never drinking alcoholic drink
teetotaller *noun* someone who is teetotal

telecommunications *plural noun*
sending news and information over long
distances by telephone, telegraph, fax,
television, and radio

telegram *noun* (*plural* **telegrams**)
a message sent by telegraph

telegraph *noun* (*plural* **telegraphs**)
a way of sending messages by using
electric current along wires or by radio
telegraphic *adjective* to do with a telegraph
telegraphy *noun* the system of telegraphs

telepathy *noun* (*pronounced* til-**ep**-a-thee)
communication of thoughts from one
person's mind to another without
speaking, writing, or gestures
telepathic *adjective* to do with telepathy

telephone ➤ *noun* (*plural* **telephones**)
a device using electric wires or radio to
enable someone to speak to another
person who is some distance away

telephone ➤ *verb* (telephones, telephoning,
telephoned)
to telephone someone is to speak to them
by telephone

telephonist *noun* (*plural* **telephonists**)
(*pronounced* til-**ef**-on-ist)
someone who operates a telephone
switchboard

telescope *noun* (*plural* **telescopes**)
a tube with lenses at each end, through
which you can see distant objects more
clearly

telescopic *adjective*
1 to do with telescopes 2 folding into
itself like a portable telescope

teletext *noun*
a system for displaying news and
information on a television screen

televise *verb* (**televises, televising, televised**)
to televise a programme is to put it on
television

television *noun* (*plural* **televisions**)
1 television is a system using radio waves
to reproduce pictures on a screen 2 a
television, or a television set, is a device
for receiving these pictures

tell *verb* (**tells, telling, told**)
1 to tell something to someone is to give
them information or orders by speaking to
them 2 to tell is to reveal a secret
♦ *Promise you won't tell* 3 to tell
something is to recognize it ♦ *Can you tell
the difference between butter and
margarine?*
all told in all, altogether ♦ *There are ten of
them, all told*
to tell someone off is to scold them
to tell tales is to report someone else's bad
behaviour

telling *adjective*
having a strong effect or meaning ♦ *It was
a telling reply*

tell-tale ➤ *noun* (*plural* **tell-tales**)
someone who tells tales

tell-tale ➤ *adjective*
showing or telling something ♦ *He had a
tell-tale spot of jam on his chin*

telly *noun* (*plural* **tellies**)
(*informal*) 1 telly is television 2 a telly is
a television set

temper *noun* (*plural* **tempers**)
1 a person's mood ♦ *He is in a good temper*
2 an angry mood ♦ *She was in a temper*
to lose your temper is to become very angry

temperate *adjective*
neither extremely hot nor extremely cold
♦ *Britain has a temperate climate*

temperature *noun* (*plural* **temperatures**)
1 how hot or cold a person or thing is
2 an unusually high body temperature
♦ *She's feverish and has a temperature*

tempest *noun* (*plural* **tempests**)
(*old use*) a violent storm
tempestuous *adjective* stormy

temple [1] *noun* (*plural* **temples**)
a building where a god is worshipped

temple [2] *noun* (*plural* **temples**)
the part of the head between the forehead
and the ear

tempo *noun* (*plural* **tempos**)
the speed or rhythm of something,
especially of a piece of music

temporary *adjective*
only lasting or used for a short time
♦ *They were using a temporary classroom*
temporarily *adverb* for a short time

tempt *verb* (**tempts, tempting, tempted**)
to tempt someone is to try to make them do
something wrong or unwise
temptation *noun* being tempted **tempter** *noun*
a person who tempts someone **temptress**
noun a woman who tempts someone

ten *noun* (*plural* **tens**)
the number 10

tenant *noun* (*plural* **tenants**)
someone who rents a house or building, or
piece of land from a landlord
tenancy *noun* being a tenant

tend [1] *verb* (**tends, tending, tended**)
to tend to do something is to be inclined or
likely to do it ♦ *Prices tend to rise*

tend [2] *verb* (**tends, tending, tended**)
to tend something or someone is to look
after them ♦ *Shepherds were tending their
sheep*

tendency *noun* (*plural* **tendencies**)
the way a person or thing is likely to
behave ♦ *She has a tendency to be lazy*

tender [1] *adjective* (**tenderer, tenderest**)
1 not tough or hard; easy to chew
2 delicate or sensitive ♦ *These are more
tender plants* 3 gentle or loving ♦ *She
gave a tender smile*
tenderly *adverb* in a tender way **tenderness**
noun being tender

tender [2] *noun* (*plural* **tenders**)
a truck attached to a steam locomotive to
carry its coal and water

tender [3] ➤ *verb* (**tenders, tendering, tendered**)
to tender something is to give it or offer it
♦ *He tendered his resignation*

tender ➤ *noun* (*plural* **tenders**)
an offer to do work or supply goods at an
agreed price

tendon *noun* (*plural* tendons)
a piece of strong tissue that joins a muscle to a bone

tendril *noun* (*plural* tendrils)
the part of a climbing plant that twists round something to support itself

tennis *noun*
a game played with rackets and a ball on a court with a net across the middle

tenor *noun* (*plural* tenors)
a male singer with a high voice

tenpin bowling *noun*
a game in which you knock down sets of ten skittles with a ball

tense¹ *adjective* (tenser, tensest)
1 tightly stretched **2** nervous; excited or exciting
tensely *adverb* in a tense way

tense² *noun* (*plural* tenses)
a form of a verb that shows when something happens. The past tense of come is *came*; the present tense is *come*, and the future tense is *will come*

tension *noun* (*plural* tensions)
1 how tightly stretched a rope or wire is **2** a feeling of anxiety or nervousness about something about to happen

tent *noun* (*plural* tents)
a shelter made of canvas or cloth supported by upright poles

tentacle *noun* (*plural* tentacles)
a long bending part of the body of some animals

tenth *adjective* and *noun*
the next after the ninth
tenthly *adverb* in the tenth place; as the tenth one

tepid *adjective*
only slightly warm; lukewarm

term ➤ *noun* (*plural* terms)
1 the time when a school or college is open for teaching **2** a definite period ♦ *He was sentenced to a term of imprisonment* **3** a word or expression with a special meaning ♦ *I don't understand these technical terms* **4** a condition offered or agreed ♦ *They won't agree to our terms*
to be on good or **bad terms** is to be friendly or unfriendly with someone

term ➤ *verb* (terms, terming, termed)
to term something is to give it a special name ♦ *This music is termed jazz*

terminal *noun* (*plural* terminals)
1 the place where something ends; a terminus **2** a building where air passengers arrive or depart **3** a place where a wire is connected to a battery or electric circuit **4** a device for sending data to or from a computer

terminate *verb* (terminates, terminating, terminated)
1 to terminate something is to end it or stop it **2** to terminate is to stop or end
termination *noun* terminating something

terminus *noun* (*plural* termini)
the station at the end of a railway or bus route

termite *noun* (*plural* termites)
a small insect that eats and destroys wood in warm countries.

terrace *noun* (*plural* terraces)
1 a row of houses joined together **2** a level area on a slope or hillside **3** a paved area beside a house

terrapin *noun* (*plural* terrapins)
a kind of small turtle that lives in water

terrible *adjective*
awful; very bad
terribly *adverb* awfully; badly

terrier *noun* (*plural* terriers)
a kind of strong lively small dog

terrific *adjective*
(*informal*) **1** very great ♦ *They went at a terrific speed* **2** very good or excellent ♦ *That's a terrific idea*
terrifically *adverb* very; greatly

terrify *verb* (terrifies, terrifying, terrified)
to terrify a person or animal is to make them very frightened

territory *noun* (*plural* territories)
an area of land, especially an area that belongs to a country or person
territorial *adjective* to do with territory

terror *noun* (*plural* terrors)
great fear

terrorism *noun*
the use of violence for political purposes
terrorist *noun* someone who practises terrorism

terrorize *verb* (terrorizes, terrorizing, terrorized)
to terrorize someone is to terrify them with threats

tessellation *noun* (*plural* tessellations)
an arrangement of shapes joined together to cover a surface without gaps

test ➤ *noun* (*plural* **tests**)
1 a short set of questions to check someone's knowledge, especially in school
2 a series of questions or experiments to get information about someone or something ♦ *They gave her a test for diabetes* 3 (*informal*) a test match

test ➤ *verb* (**tests, testing, tested**)
to test someone or something is to give them a test

testament *noun* (*plural* **testaments**)
1 a written statement 2 each of the two main parts of the Bible, the **Old Testament** and the **New Testament**

testicle *noun* (*plural* **testicles**)
each of the two glands in the scrotum of a man or male animal where semen is produced

testify *verb* (**testifies, testifying, testified**)
to testify is to give evidence or swear that something is true

testimonial *noun* (*plural* **testimonials**)
a letter describing someone's abilities and character

testimony *noun* (*plural* **testimonies**)
evidence; what someone testifies

test match *noun* (*plural* **test matches**)
a cricket or rugby match between teams from different countries

test tube *noun* (*plural* **test tubes**)
a tube of thin glass closed at one end, used for experiments in chemistry

testy *adjective*
irritable or slightly bad-tempered

tether ➤ *verb* (**tethers, tethering, tethered**)
to tether an animal is to tie it so that it cannot move far

tether ➤ *noun* (*plural* **tethers**)
a rope for tying an animal
at the end of your tether unable to stand something any more

text *noun* (*plural* **texts**)
1 the words of something printed or written 2 a short extract from the Bible

textbook *noun* (*plural* **textbooks**)
a book that teaches you about a subject

textiles *plural noun*
kinds of cloth; fabrics

text message *noun* (*plural* **text messages**)
a message sent from one mobile to another and read on screen

texture *noun* (*plural* **textures**)
the way that the surface of something feels ♦ *Silk has a smooth texture*

than *conjunction*
compared with another person or thing ♦ *His sister is taller than him or than he is*

thank *verb* (**thanks, thanking, thanked**)
to thank someone is to tell them you are grateful for something they have given you or done for you
thank you words that you say when thanking someone

thankful *adjective*
feeling glad that someone has done something for you
thankfully *adverb* in a thankful way

thankless *adjective*
not very enjoyable or likely to win thanks ♦ *It was a thankless task*

thanks *plural noun*
1 words that thank someone 2 (*informal*) a short way of saying 'Thank you'
thanks to someone or **something** because of them ♦ *Thanks to you, we succeeded*

that ➤ *adjective* the one there ♦ *Whose is that book?*

that ➤ *conjunction*
used to introduce a fact or statement or result ♦ *I hope that you are well* ♦ *Do you know that it is one o'clock?* ♦ *The puzzle was so hard that no one could solve it*

that ➤ *pronoun*
1 the one there ♦ *Whose book is that?*
2 which or who ♦ *This is the book that I wanted* ♦ *Are you the person that I saw the other day?*

thatch ➤ *noun*
straw or reeds used to make a roof

thatch ➤ *verb* (**thatches, thatching, thatched**)
to thatch a roof is to make it with thatch
thatcher *noun* someone who works with thatch

thaw *verb* (**thaws, thawing, thawed**)
to melt; to stop being frozen ♦ *The ice has thawed*

the *adjective* (called the *definite article*) a particular one; that or those

theatre *noun* (*plural* **theatres**)
1 a building where people go to see plays or shows 2 a special room where surgical operations are done

theatrical *adjective*
to do with plays or acting
theatrically *adverb* in a theatrical way

thee *pronoun*
(*old use*) you, referring to one person and used as the object of a verb

theft *noun* (*plural* **thefts**)
stealing

their *adjective*
belonging to them ♦ *This is their house*

theirs *pronoun*
belonging to them ♦ *This house is theirs*

them *pronoun*
a word used for *they* when it is the object of a verb, or when it comes after a preposition ♦ *I like them* ♦ *I gave it to them*

theme *noun* (*plural* **themes**)
1 a subject for talking about **2** a short tune or melody

theme park *noun* (*plural* **theme parks**)
an amusement park with rides and activities connected with a special subject or theme

themselves *plural noun*
them and nobody else, used to refer back to the subject of a verb ♦ *They have hurt themselves*
by themselves on their own; alone ♦ *They did the work all by themselves*

then *adverb*
1 at that time ♦ *I lived in London then*
2 after that; next ♦ *Then they came home*
3 in that case; therefore ♦ *If you are going, then I can stay*

theology *noun*
the study of God and religion
theologian *noun* an expert in theology
theological *adjective* to do with theology

theorem *noun* (*plural* **theorems**)
a statement in mathematics that can be proved

theoretical *adjective*
based on theory and not on practice or experience
theoretically *adverb* in a theoretical way; in theory

theory *noun* (*plural* **theories**)
1 an idea or set of ideas suggested to explain something **2** the principles of a subject
in theory according to what should happen

therapy *noun* (*plural* **therapies**)
a way of treating an illness of the mind or the body, usually without using surgery or artificial medicines
therapist *noun* an expert in therapy

there *adverb*
1 in or to that place **2** a word that you say to call attention to someone or something or to refer to them ♦ *There's a spider in the bath* ♦ *There's a good dog!*

thereabouts *adverb*
near there ♦ *They live in York or thereabouts*

therefore *adverb*
for that reason; and so

thermal *adjective*
to do with heat; using heat

thermometer *noun* (*plural* **thermometers**)
a device for measuring temperature

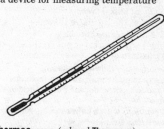

Thermos *noun* (*plural* **Thermoses**)
(*trademark*) a kind of vacuum flask

thermostat *noun* (*plural* **thermostats**)
a device that automatically controls the temperature of a room or piece of equipment
thermostatic *adjective* to do with a thermostat **thermostatically** *adverb* by means of a thermostat

thesaurus *noun* (*plural* **thesauri** or **thesauruses**)
a kind of dictionary in which words with the same meaning are listed in groups together, instead of one long list in alphabetical order

these *adjective* and *pronoun*
the people or things here

they *pronoun*
1 the people or things that someone is talking about **2** people in general ♦ *They say it's a very good film*

they'd short for *they had* or *they should* or *they would*

they'll short for *they will*

they're short for *they are*

they've short for *they have*

thick *adjective* (**thicker**, **thickest**)
1 measuring a lot from one side to the other ♦ *I'm reading a thick book*
2 measured from one side to the other ♦ *The wall is ten centimetres thick*
3 crowded or dense ♦ *The town was in thick fog* **4** (*informal*) stupid
thickly *adverb* with a thick amount

thicken *verb* (**thickens**, **thickening**, **thickened**)
1 to thicken something is to make it thicker **2** to thicken is to become thicker

thicket *noun* (*plural* **thickets**)
a group of trees and shrubs growing close together

thickness *noun* (*plural* **thicknesses**)
how thick something is

thief *noun* (*plural* **thieves**)
someone who steals things

thigh *noun* (*plural* **thighs**)
the part of the leg above the knee

thimble *noun* (*plural* **thimbles**)
a metal or plastic cover put on the end of
the finger to protect it when sewing

thin ➤ *adjective* (**thinner, thinnest**)
1 measuring a small amount from one
side to the other; not fat 2 not thick or
dense
thinly *adverb* with a thin amount **thinness**
noun being thin

thin ➤ *verb* (**thins, thinning, thinned**)
1 to thin something, or thin something
out, is to make it less thick or less crowded
2 to thin, or thin out, is to become less
dense or less crowded ♦ *The crowds had
thinned by late afternoon*

thine *adjective*
(*old use*) yours (referring to one person)

thing *noun* (*plural* **things**)
an object; anything that can be touched or
seen or thought about

think *verb* (**thinks, thinking, thought**)
1 to think is to use your mind 2 to think
something is to have it as an idea or
opinion ♦ *I think that's a good idea*
thinker *noun* someone who thinks; a
philosopher

third ➤ *adjective* and *noun*
the next after the second
thirdly *adverb* in the third place; as the
third one

third ➤ *noun* (*plural* **thirds**)
each of three equal parts into which
something can be divided

Third World *noun*
the poor or developing countries of Asia,
Africa, and South and Central America

thirst *noun*
a feeling that you need to drink
thirsty *adjective* having a thirst

thirteen *noun* (*plural* **thirteens**)
the number 13
thirteenth *adjective* and *noun* 13th

thirty *noun* (*plural* **thirties**)
the number 30
thirtieth *adjective* and *noun* 30th

this *adjective* and *pronoun*
the one here ♦ *Take this pen* ♦ *This is
the one*

thistle *noun* (*plural* **thistles**)
a wild plant with prickly leaves and purple
or white or yellow flowers

thorn *noun* (*plural* **thorns**)
a small pointed growth on the stem of
roses and other plants

thorny *adjective* (**thornier, thorniest**)
1 full of thorns; prickly 2 difficult;
causing argument or disagreement ♦ *It is
a thorny problem*

thorough *adjective*
1 done properly and carefully ♦ *This is a
thorough piece of work* 2 absolute or
complete ♦ *They've made a thorough mess*
thoroughly *adverb* in a thorough way;
completely **thoroughness** *noun* being
thorough

those *adjective* and *pronoun*
the ones there ♦ *Where are those cards?*
♦ *Those are the ones I want*

thou *pronoun*
(*old use*) you (referring to one person)

though ➤ *conjunction*
in spite of the fact that; even if ♦ *It is not
true, though he says it is*

though ➤ *adverb*
however; all the same ♦ *She's right,
though*

thought[1] *noun* (*plural* **thoughts**)
1 a thought is something that you think;
an idea or opinion 2 thought is thinking
♦ *I'll give the matter some thought*

thought[2] past tense and past participle of
think

thoughtful *adjective*
1 thinking a lot 2 thinking of other people
and what they would like
thoughtfully *adverb* in a thoughtful way
thoughtfulness *noun* being thoughtful

thoughtless *adjective*
not thinking of other people and what they
would like; reckless
thoughtlessly *adverb* in a thoughtless way
thoughtlessness *noun* being thoughtless

thousand *noun* (*plural* **thousands**)
the number 1,000
thousandth *adjective* and *noun* 1,000th

thrash *verb* (**thrashes, thrashing, thrashed**)
1 to thrash someone is to keep hitting
them hard with a stick or whip 2 to
thrash a person or team is to defeat them
in a game or sport 3 to thrash, or thrash
about, is to fling your arms and legs about
wildly

thread ➤ *noun* (*plural* **threads**)
1 a long piece of cotton, wool, nylon, or other material used for sewing or weaving 2 a long thin piece of something 3 the spiral ridge round a screw or bolt

thread ➤ *verb* (**threads, threading, threaded**)
1 to thread a needle is to put a thread through its eye 2 to thread a long and thin material is to put it through or round something 3 to thread a piece of string is to put beads on it

threadbare *adjective*
clothes are threadbare when they are worn thin with threads showing

threat *noun* (*plural* **threats**)
1 a warning that you will punish or harm someone if they do not do what you want 2 a danger

threaten *verb* (**threatens, threatening, threatened**)
1 to threaten someone is to make threats to them 2 to threaten is to be a danger to someone or something ♦ *The quarrel threatened to turn violent*

three *noun* (*plural* **threes**)
the number 3

three-dimensional *adjective*
having three dimensions: length, width, and height or depth

thresh *verb* (**threshes, threshing, threshed**)
to thresh corn is to beat it so as to separate the grain from the husks

threshold *noun* (*plural* **thresholds**)
1 a slab of stone or board under the doorway of a building; the entrance 2 the beginning of something important ♦ *We are on the threshold of a great discovery*

threw past tense of **throw** *verb*

thrift *noun*
being careful with money

thrifty *adjective* (**thriftier, thriftiest**)
careful with money
thriftily *adverb* in a thrifty way

thrill ➤ *noun* (*plural* **thrills**)
1 a sudden feeling of excitement 2 something that gives you this feeling

thrill ➤ *verb* (**thrills, thrilling, thrilled**)
to thrill someone is to give them a thrill

thriller *noun* (*plural* **thrillers**)
an exciting story or film, usually about crime

thrive *verb* (**thrives, thriving, thrived or throve, thrived or thriven**)
to thrive is to prosper or grow strongly

throat *noun* (*plural* **throats**)
1 the front of the neck 2 the tube in the neck that takes food and air into the body

throb ➤ *verb* (**throbs, throbbing, throbbed**)
to throb is to beat or vibrate with a strong rhythm

throb ➤ *noun* (*plural* **throbs**)
a throbbing sound

throne *noun* (*plural* **thrones**)
1 a special chair for a king or queen 2 the position of being king or queen ♦ *William I won the throne by conquest*

throng *noun* (*plural* **throngs**)
a crowd of people

throttle ➤ *verb* (**throttles, throttling, throttled**)
to throttle someone is to strangle them

throttle ➤ *noun* (*plural* **throttles**)
a device to control the flow of fuel to an engine; an accelerator

through ➤ *adverb* and *preposition*
1 from one end or side to the other ♦ *I can't get through* ♦ *Climb through the window* 2 because of; by means of ♦ *We'll do it through hard work* 3 (*informal*) finished ♦ *I'm through now*

through ➤ *adjective*
1 travelling all the way to a place ♦ *I'm catching a through train to Dover* 2 having a way through ♦ *This is a no through road*

throughout *preposition* and *adverb*
all the way through

throve past tense of **thrive**

throw ➤ *verb* (**throws, throwing, threw, thrown**)
1 to throw something or someone is to send them through the air 2 to throw something somewhere is to put it there carelessly ♦ *He came in and threw his coat on the chair* 3 to throw a part of your body is to move it quickly ♦ *She threw her head back and laughed* 4 to throw someone into a certain state is to put them in that state ♦ *We were thrown into confusion*
to throw something away is to get rid of it

throw ➤ *noun* (*plural* **throws**)
a throwing action or movement

thrush *noun* (*plural* **thrushes**)
a bird that has a white front with brown spots

thrust *verb* (**thrusts, thrusting, thrust**)
to thrust something is to push it hard ♦ *He thrust his hands into his pockets*

thud ➤ *noun* (*plural* **thuds**)
the dull sound of something heavy falling

thud ➤ *verb* (**thuds, thudding, thudded**)
to fall with a thud

thumb *noun* (*plural* **thumbs**)
the short thick finger at the side of each hand
to be under someone's thumb is to be controlled or ruled by them

thump ➤ *verb* (thumps, thumping, thumped)
1 to thump someone or something is to hit them heavily **2** to thump is to make a dull heavy sound

thump ➤ *noun* (*plural* thumps)
an act or sound of thumping

thunder ➤ *noun*
1 the loud noise that you hear with lightning during a storm **2** a loud heavy noise

thunder ➤ *verb* (thunders, thundering, thundered)
1 to thunder is to make the noise of thunder **2** to thunder is also to speak with a loud booming voice

thunderous *adjective*
extremely loud

thunderstorm *noun* (*plural* thunderstorms)
a storm with thunder and lightning.

Thursday *noun* (*plural* Thursdays)
the fifth day of the week

thus *adverb*
1 in this way ♦ *We did it thus* **2** therefore ♦ *Thus, we must try again*

thy *adjective*
(*old use*) your (referring to one person)

tick ➤ *noun* (*plural* ticks)
1 a small mark, usually ✓, made next to something when checking it as a sign that it is correct or has been done **2** each of the short sharp sounds that a clock or watch makes **3** (*informal*) a moment ♦ *I won't be a tick*

tick ➤ *verb* (ticks, ticking, ticked)
1 to tick something is to mark it with a tick ♦ *She ticked the correct answers* **2** to tick is to make the sound of a tick, as a clock or watch does

to tick someone off (*informal*) is to scold them or tell them off

ticket *noun* (*plural* tickets)
a piece of paper or card that allows you to do something such as see a show or travel on a bus or train

tickle *verb* (tickles, tickling, tickled)
1 to tickle someone is to keep touching their skin lightly so as to produce a tingling feeling that can make them laugh and wriggle **2** to tickle is to have a tickling or itching feeling ♦ *My throat is tickling* **3** to tickle someone is also to please or amuse them

ticklish *adjective*
1 likely to laugh or wriggle when tickled **2** awkward or difficult ♦ *This is a ticklish situation*

tidal *adjective*
to do with tides or affected by tides

tidal wave *noun* (*plural* tidal waves)
a huge sea wave moving with the tide

tiddler *noun* (*plural* tiddlers)
(*informal*) a very small fish

tiddlywink *noun* (*plural* tiddlywinks)
a small counter flipped into a cup with another counter in the game of tiddlywinks

tide ➤ *noun* (*plural* tides)
the regular rising or falling of the sea, which usually happens twice a day

tide ➤ *verb* (tides, tiding, tided)
to tide someone over is to give them what they need for the time being

tidy *adjective* (tidier, tidiest)
1 neat and orderly, with things in the right place ♦ *What a tidy room* **2** (*informal*) fairly large ♦ *That's a tidy sum of money*
tidily *adverb* in a tidy way **tidiness** *noun* being tidy

tie ➤ *verb* (ties, tying, tied)
1 to tie something is to fasten it with string or ribbon **2** to tie a knot or bow is to make one in a strip of material such as a ribbon **3** to tie a game or competition is to finish it with an equal score or position
tied up occupied or busy ♦ *I'm tied up all afternoon*

tie ➤ *noun* (*plural* ties)
1 a thin strip of material tied round the collar of a shirt with a knot at the front **2** the result of a game or competition in which more than one player or team has the same position or score **3** one of the matches in a competition

tie-break or **tie-breaker** *noun* (*plural* tie-breaks or tie-breakers)
an extra game or part of a game, played when the result so far is a tie

tiger *noun* (*plural* tigers)
a large wild animal of the cat family, with yellow and black stripes

tight *adjective* (**tighter, tightest**)
1 fitting very closely or firmly fastened
2 fully stretched **3** (*informal*) drunk
4 (*informal*) mean or stingy ♦ *He's a bit tight with his money*
tightly *adverb* in a tight way; closely or securely **tightness** *noun* being tight

tighten *verb* (**tightens, tightening, tightened**)
1 to tighten something is to make it tighter **2** to tighten is to become tighter

tightrope *noun* (*plural* **tightropes**)
a tightly stretched rope above the ground, for acrobats to perform on

tights *plural noun*
a piece of clothing that fits tightly over the lower parts of the body including the legs and feet

tigress *noun* (*plural* **tigresses**)
a female tiger

tile *noun* (*plural* **tiles**)
a thin piece of baked clay or other hard material used in rows to cover roofs, walls, or floors
tiled *adjective* covered with tiles

till[1] *preposition* and *conjunction*
until

till[2] *noun* (*plural* **tills**)
a drawer or box for money in a shop; a cash register

till[3] *verb* (**tills, tilling, tilled**)
to till land is to plough it ready for cultivation

tiller *noun* (*plural* **tillers**)
a handle used to turn a boat's rudder

tilt ➤ *verb* (**tilts, tilting, tilted**)
1 to tilt is to slope or lean **2** to tilt something is to tip it or make it slope

tilt ➤ *noun* (*plural* **tilts**)
a sloping position

timber *noun* (*plural* **timbers**)
1 timber is wood for building or making things **2** a timber is a beam of wood

time ➤ *noun* (*plural* **times**)
1 a measure of the continued existence of everything in years, months, days, and other units **2** a particular moment or period of things existing or happening
♦ *There was a time when I would have agreed with you* ♦ *Come back another time*
♦ *There were fields here in past times*
3 an occasion ♦ *This is the first time I've been here* **4** a period that is suitable or available for something ♦ *Is there time for a drink?* **5** the rhythm and speed of a piece of music
at times or **from time to time** sometimes; occasionally
in time or **on time** soon or early enough
♦ *Make sure you get to the station in time*

time ➤ *verb* (**times, timing, timed**)
1 to time something is to measure how long it takes **2** to time an event or activity is to arrange the time when it will happen

time limit *noun* (*plural* **time limits**)
a limited amount of time for doing something, or the time by which something must be done

timer *noun* (*plural* **timers**)
a device for timing things

times *plural noun*
multiplied by ♦ *5 times 3 is 15 (5×3=15)*

time scale *noun* (*plural* **time scales**)
the length of time that something takes or that you need in order to do something

timetable *noun* (*plural* **timetables**)
a list of the times when things happen, such as buses and trains leaving and arriving, and when school lessons take place

timid *adjective*
nervous and easily frightened
timidly *adverb* in a timid way **timidity** *noun* being timid

timing *noun*
the choice of time to do something
♦ *Arriving at lunchtime was good timing*

timpani *plural noun* (*pronounced* timp-a-nee)
kettledrums

tin ➤ *noun* (*plural* **tins**)
1 tin is a soft white metal **2** a tin is a metal container for preserving food

tin ➤ *verb* (**tins, tinning, tinned**)
to tin food is to preserve it in tins

tingle ➤ *verb* (**tingles, tingling, tingled**)
to tingle is to have a slight stinging or tickling feeling

tingle ➤ *noun* (*plural* **tingles**)
a tingling feeling

tinker ➤ *verb* (**tinkers, tinkering, tinkered**)
to tinker with something is to try to mend or improve it without really knowing how to

tinker ➤ *noun* (*plural* **tinkers**)
(*old use*) someone who travelled around mending pots and pans

tinkle ➤ *verb* (**tinkles, tinkling, tinkled**)
to tinkle is to make a gentle ringing sound

tinkle ➤ *noun* (*plural* **tinkles**)
a tinkling sound

tinny *adjective* (**tinnier, tinniest**)
1 like tin 2 making a thin high-pitched sound

tinsel *noun*
strips of glittering material used for decoration

tint ➤ *noun* (*plural* **tints**)
a shade of colour, especially a pale one

tint ➤ *verb* (**tints, tinting, tinted**)
to tint something is to colour it slightly

tiny *adjective* (**tinier, tiniest**)
very small

tip[1] ➤ *noun* (*plural* **tips**)
the part at the very end of something

tip ➤ *verb* (**tips, tipping, tipped**)
to tip something is to give it a tip ♦ *The parcel was tied in a red ribbon tipped with gold*

tip[2] ➤ *noun* (*plural* **tips**)
1 a small present of money given to someone who has helped you 2 a quick piece of advice

tip ➤ *verb* (**tips, tipping, tipped**)
1 to tip someone is to give them a small present of money 2 to tip someone or something is to name them as likely to win or succeed

tip[3] ➤ *verb* (**tips, tipping, tipped**)
1 to tip something is to turn it upside down or put it on to one edge 2 to tip rubbish is to leave it somewhere

tip ➤ *noun* (*plural* **tips**)
a place where rubbish is left

tiptoe ➤ *verb* (**tiptoes, tiptoeing, tiptoed**)
to tiptoe is to walk on your toes very quietly or carefully

tiptoe ➤ *noun*
on tiptoe walking or standing on your toes

tire *verb* (**tires, tiring, tired**)
1 to tire someone is to make them tired 2 to tire is to become tired

tired *adjective*
feeling that you need to sleep or rest
to be tired of something is to have had enough of it

tireless *adjective*
having a lot of energy; not tiring easily

tiresome *adjective*
annoying

tissue *noun* (*plural* **tissues**)
1 tissue, or tissue paper, is thin soft paper; a tissue is a piece of this 2 tissue is also the substance of which an animal or plant is made

tit[1] *noun* (*plural* **tits**)
a kind of small bird

tit[2] *noun*
tit for tat something equal given in return

titbit *noun* (*plural* **titbits**)
a small piece of something

title *noun* (*plural* **titles**)
1 the name of something that gives information or entertains, such as a book or film or piece of music 2 a word that shows a person's position or profession, such as ♦ *Sir, Lady, Dr, Mrs* 3 a legal right to something, especially land or property

titter *verb* (**titters, tittering, tittered**)
to titter is to giggle or laugh in a silly way

to ➤ *preposition*
1 towards ♦ *They set off to London* 2 as far as; so as to reach ♦ *I am soaked to the skin* 3 compared with; rather than ♦ *She prefers cats to dogs*

to ➤ *adverb*
to the usual or closed position ♦ *Push the door to*
to and fro backwards and forwards

toad *noun* (*plural* **toads**)
an animal like a large frog, that lives on land

toad-in-the-hole *noun*
sausages baked in batter

toadstool *noun* (*plural* **toadstools**)
a fungus that looks like a mushroom, and is often poisonous

toast ➤ *verb* (**toasts, toasting, toasted**)
1 to toast food is to cook it by heating it under a grill or in front of a fire 2 to toast someone or something is to have a drink in their honour

toast ➤ *noun* (*plural* **toasts**)
1 toast is toasted bread 2 a toast is a call to toast someone or something with a drink

toaster *noun* (*plural* **toasters**)
an electrical device for toasting bread

tobacco *noun*
the dried leaves of certain plants prepared for smoking in cigarettes, cigars, or pipes

tobacconist *noun* (*plural* **tobacconists**)
a shopkeeper who sells cigarettes, cigars, and tobacco

toboggan noun (plural **toboggans**)
a small sledge for sliding downhill
tobogganing noun using a toboggan

today ➤ noun
this day ♦ Today is Monday

today ➤ adverb
1 on this day ♦ I saw him today
2 nowadays ♦ Today we don't have slaves

toddler noun (plural **toddlers**)
a young child who is just learning to walk

toe noun (plural **toes**)
1 each of the five separate parts at the end of each foot 2 the part of a shoe or sock that covers the toes

toffee noun (plural **toffees**)
1 toffee is a sticky sweet made from butter and sugar 2 a toffee is a piece of this

toga noun (plural **togas**)
a long loose piece of clothing worn by men in ancient Rome

together adverb
with another person or thing; with each other ♦ They went to school together

toil verb (**toils, toiling, toiled**)
1 to toil is to work hard 2 to toil is also to move slowly and with difficulty ♦ The old man toiled up the hill

toilet noun (plural **toilets**)
a place for getting rid of waste from the body

toilet paper noun
paper for cleaning yourself after using a toilet

token noun (plural **tokens**)
1 a piece of metal or plastic used instead of money to pay for something 2 a card or voucher that can be exchanged for goods in a shop 3 a sign or signal of something ♦ A white flag is a token of surrender

told past tense and past participle of **tell**

tolerable adjective
able to be tolerated; bearable
tolerably adverb in a tolerable way

tolerant adjective
tolerating other people's behaviour and opinions when you don't agree with them
tolerance noun being tolerant **tolerantly** adverb in a tolerant way

tolerate verb (**tolerates, tolerating, tolerated**)
to tolerate something is to allow it although you do not approve of it

toll¹ noun (plural **tolls**)
1 a payment charged for using a bridge or road 2 an amount of loss or damage ♦ The death toll in the earthquake is rising

toll² verb (**tolls, tolling, tolled**)
to toll a bell is to ring it slowly

tom or **tomcat** noun (plural **toms** or **tomcats**)
a male cat

tomahawk noun (plural **tomahawks**)
an axe used by Native Americans

tomato noun (plural **tomatoes**)
a soft round red fruit with seeds inside it, eaten as a vegetable

tomb noun (plural **tombs**) (pronounced toom)
a place where a dead body is buried; a grave

tomboy noun (plural **tomboys**)
a girl who enjoys rough noisy games and activities

tombstone noun (plural **tombstones**)
a memorial stone set up over a grave

tommy-gun noun (plural **tommy-guns**)
a small machine-gun

tomorrow noun and adverb
the day after today

tom-tom noun (plural **tom-toms**)
a type of drum that you beat with the palms of your hands

ton noun (plural **tons**)
1 a unit of weight equal to 2,240 pounds or about 1,016 kilograms 2 (informal) a large amount ♦ There's tons of room 3 (slang) a speed of 100 miles per hour

tonal adjective
to do with tone
tonally adverb as regards tone

tone ➤ noun (plural **tones**)
1 a sound in music or speech 2 each of the five larger intervals between two notes in a musical scale 3 a shade of a colour 4 the quality or character of something

tone ➤ verb (**tones, toning, toned**)
to tone something down is to make it softer or quieter
to tone in is to blend or fit in well, especially in colour

tone-deaf adjective
unable to tell the difference between musical notes

tongs plural noun
a tool with two arms joined at one end, used to pick things up or hold them

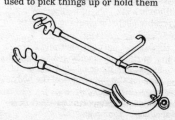

tongue *noun* (*plural* **tongues**)
1 the long soft part that moves about inside the mouth 2 a language 3 the flap of material under the laces of a shoe 4 the part inside a bell that makes it ring

tongue-tied *adjective*
feeling too shy or embarrassed to speak

tongue-twister *noun* (*plural* **tongue-twisters**)
something that is very difficult to say

tonic *noun* (*plural* **tonics**)
something that makes a person healthier or stronger

tonight *adverb* and *noun*
this evening or night

tonne *noun* (*plural* **tonnes**)
a metric ton, a unit of weight equal to 1,000 kilograms

tonsillitis *noun*
a disease that makes your tonsils extremely sore

tonsils *plural noun*
your tonsils are two small masses of soft flesh inside your throat

too *adverb*
1 also ♦ *Take the others too* 2 more than is wanted or allowed or wise ♦ *Don't drive too fast*

took past tense of **take**

tool *noun* (*plural* **tools**)
a device that you use to help you do a particular job, such as a hammer or saw

tooth *noun* (*plural* **teeth**)
1 each of the hard white bony parts that grow in the gums, used for biting and chewing 2 each in a row of sharp parts, such as those on the blade of a saw
to fight tooth and nail is to fight very fiercely
toothed *adjective* having teeth

toothache *noun*
a pain in a tooth

toothbrush *noun* (*plural* **toothbrushes**)
a small brush on a long handle, for brushing the teeth

toothpaste *noun* (*plural* **toothpastes**)
a creamy paste for cleaning the teeth

top[1] ≻ *noun* (*plural* **tops**)
1 the highest part of something 2 the upper surface of something 3 the covering or stopper of a jar or bottle 4 a piece of clothing for the upper part of the body

top ≻ *adjective*
highest or most important ♦ *They were travelling at top speed*

top ≻ *verb* (**tops, topping, topped**)
1 to top something is to put a top on it ♦ *The cake was topped with icing* 2 to top something is also to be at the top of it ♦ *She tops the list*
to top something up is to fill it to the top when it is already partly full

top[2] *noun* (*plural* **tops**)
a toy that can be made to spin on its point

top hat *noun* (*plural* **top hats**)
a man's tall stiff black or grey hat worn with formal clothes

topic *noun* (*plural* **topics**)
a subject to write or talk or learn about

topical *adjective*
to do with things that are happening now ♦ *The film we saw was very topical*
topicality *noun* being topical **topically** *adverb* in a topical way

topless *adjective*
not wearing any clothes on the top half of the body

topmost *adjective*
highest

topping *noun* (*plural* **toppings**)
food that is put on the top of a cake or pudding

topple *verb* (**topples, toppling, toppled**)
1 to topple, or topple over, is to fall over 2 to topple something is to make it fall over 3 to topple someone in power is to overthrow them

top secret *adjective*
extremely secret

topsy-turvy *adverb* and *adjective*
upside-down; muddled

torch *noun* (*plural* **torches**)
1 a small electric lamp that you hold in your hand 2 a stick with burning material on the end, used as a light

tore past tense of **tear** *verb*

toreador *noun* (*plural* **toreadors**)
a bullfighter

torment ≻ *verb* (**torments, tormenting, tormented**)
1 to torment someone is to make them suffer or feel pain 2 to torment someone is also to keep annoying them deliberately
tormentor *noun* a person who torments someone

torment ≻ *noun* (*plural* **torments**)
great suffering

torn past participle of **tear** *verb*

tornado *noun* (*plural* **tornadoes**)
(*pronounced* tor-nay-doh)
a violent storm or whirlwind

torpedo ➢ *noun* (*plural* **torpedoes**)
a long tube-shaped missile sent under
water to destroy ships and submarines

torpedo ➢ *verb* (**torpedoes, torpedoing,
torpedoed**)
to torpedo a ship is to attack it with a
torpedo

torrent *noun* (*plural* **torrents**)
a very strong stream or fall of water
torrential *adjective* like a torrent

torso *noun* (*plural* **torsos**)
the trunk of the human body

tortoise *noun* (*plural* **tortoises**) (*pronounced*
tor-tus)
a slow-moving animal with a shell over its
body

torture ➢ *verb* (**tortures, torturing, tortured**)
to torture someone is to make them feel
great pain, especially so that they will give
information

torture ➢ *noun* (*plural* **tortures**)
something done to torture a person
torturer *noun* someone who tortures
people

Tory *noun* (*plural* **Tories**)
a Conservative

toss ➢ *verb* (**tosses, tossing, tossed**)
1 to toss something is to throw it into the
air 2 to toss a coin is to spin it so as to
decide something from the side that lands
uppermost 3 to toss is to move about
restlessly in bed

toss ➢ *noun* (*plural* **tosses**)
an act of tossing

total ➢ *noun* (*plural* **totals**)
the amount you get by adding everything
together

total ➢ *adjective*
1 complete; including everything ♦ *What
is the total amount?* 2 complete ♦ *There
was total darkness outside*
totally *adverb* completely

total ➢ *verb* (**totals, totalling, totalled**)
1 to total something is to add it up
2 to total an amount is to reach it as a
total ♦ *Sales totalled over £50,000 this
month*

totalitarian *adjective* (*pronounced*
toh-tal-i-**tair**-i-an)
using a form of government with only one
political party

totem pole *noun* (*plural* **totem poles**)
a large pole carved or painted by Native
Americans

totter *verb* (**totters, tottering, tottered**)
to totter is to walk unsteadily or wobble

touch ➢ *verb* (**touches, touching, touched**)
1 to touch something is to feel it lightly
with your hand or fingers 2 to touch
something is also to come into contact with
it or hit it gently 3 to be touching
something is to be next to it so that there
is no space in between 4 to touch
something is also to interfere or meddle
with it ♦ *Don't touch anything in this room*
5 to touch an amount is to just reach it
♦ *His temperature touched 104 degrees*
6 to touch someone is to affect their
emotions ♦ *We were touched by his sad
story*

to touch down is to land in an aircraft or
spacecraft

to touch something up is to improve it by
making small changes or additions

touch ➢ *noun* (*plural* **touches**)
1 a touch is an act of touching 2 touch
is the ability to feel things by touching
them 3 a touch is also a small thing
that greatly improves something
♦ *We're just putting the finishing touches
to it* 4 touch is also communication
with someone ♦ *We have lost touch with
them* 5 touch is also the part of a football
field outside the playing area

touch and go *adjective*
uncertain or risky

touchy *adjective* (**touchier, touchiest**)
easily or quickly offended

tough *adjective* (**tougher, toughest**)
1 strong; hard to break or damage ♦ *You'll need tough shoes for the climb* **2** hard to chew **3** rough or violent ♦ *The police were dealing with tough criminals* **4** firm or severe ♦ *It's time to get tough with football hooligans* **5** difficult ♦ *It was a tough decision*
toughly *adverb* in a tough way **toughness** *noun* being tough

toughen *verb* (**toughens, toughening, toughened**)
1 to toughen someone or something is to make them tougher **2** to toughen is to become tougher

tour *noun* (*plural* **tours**)
a journey visiting several places

tourist *noun* (*plural* **tourists**)
someone who is travelling or on holiday abroad
tourism *noun* travelling or on holiday abroad

tournament *noun* (*plural* **tournaments**)
a series of games or contests

tow ➤ *verb* (**tows, towing, towed**) (*rhymes with* go)
to tow a vehicle or boat is to pull it behind you in another vehicle ♦ *They towed our car to a garage*

tow ➤ *noun*
an act of towing

toward or **towards** *preposition*
1 in the direction of ♦ *She walked towards the sea* **2** in relation to ♦ *He behaved kindly towards his children* **3** as a contribution to ♦ *Put the money towards a new bicycle*

towel *noun* (*plural* **towels**)
a piece of soft cloth used for drying things
towelling *noun* material that towels are made of

tower ➤ *noun* (*plural* **towers**)
a tall narrow building or part of a building

tower ➤ *verb* (**towers, towering, towered**)
to tower above or over things is to be taller than them ♦ *The skyscrapers towered above the city*

tower block *noun* (*plural* **tower blocks**)
a tall building containing offices or flats

town *noun* (*plural* **towns**)
a place with many houses, shops, schools, offices, and other buildings

town hall *noun* (*plural* **town halls**)
a building with offices for the local council and usually a hall for public events

towpath *noun* (*plural* **towpaths**)
a path beside a canal or river

toxic *adjective*
poisonous

toy ➤ *noun* (*plural* **toys**)
something to play with

toy ➤ *verb* (**toys, toying, toyed**)
to toy with an idea is to think about it casually or idly

toyshop *noun* (*plural* **toyshops**)
a shop that sells toys

trace ➤ *noun* (*plural* **traces**)
1 a mark left by a person or thing; a sign ♦ *There was no trace of any dog* **2** a very small amount of something ♦ *They found traces of blood on the carpet*

trace ➤ *verb* (**traces, tracing, traced**)
1 to trace someone or something is to find them after a search **2** to trace a picture or map is to copy it by drawing over it on paper you can see through

traceable *adjective*
able to be traced or found

track ➤ *noun* (*plural* **tracks**)
1 a path made by people or animals **2** marks left by a person or thing **3** a set of rails for trains or trams to run on **4** a road or area of ground prepared for racing **5** a metal belt used instead of wheels on a heavy vehicle such as a tank or tractor
to keep track of something or **someone** is to know where they are or what they are doing

track ➤ *verb* (**tracks, tracking, tracked**)
1 to track a person or animal is to follow them by the signs they leave **2** to track something is to follow or observe it as it moves
tracker *noun* someone who tracks people or animals

tracksuit *noun* (*plural* **tracksuits**)
a warm loose suit of a kind worn by athletes for jogging and warming up

tract[1] *noun* (*plural* **tracts**)
1 an area of land **2** a series of connected parts in the body

tract[2] *noun* (*plural* **tracts**)
a short pamphlet or essay, especially about religion

traction *noun*
1 the ability of a vehicle to grip the ground ♦ *The car's wheels lost traction in the mud* **2** a medical treatment in which an injured arm or leg is pulled gently for a long time by means of weights and pulleys

traction engine *noun* (*plural* **traction engines**)
a heavy steam or diesel engine used for pulling a heavy load

tractor noun (plural **tractors**)
a motor vehicle used for pulling farm machinery or heavy loads

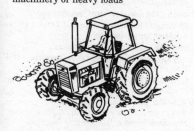

trade ➢ noun (plural **trades**)
1 trade is the business of buying or selling or exchanging things 2 a trade is a job or occupation, especially a skilled craft

trade ➢ verb (**trades, trading, traded**)
to trade is to buy or sell or exchange things to trade something in is to give it towards the cost of something new ♦ He traded in his motorcycle for a car

trademark noun (plural **trademarks**)
a sign or name that only one manufacturer is allowed to use

trader noun (plural **traders**)
someone who buys and sells things in trade

tradesman noun (plural **tradesmen**)
someone occupied in a trade; a shopkeeper

trade union noun (plural **trade unions**)
an organization of workers in a particular industry, set up to protect their interests

tradition noun (plural **traditions**)
1 tradition is the passing down of beliefs and customs from one generation to the next 2 a tradition is something passed on in this way

traditional adjective
1 passed down from one generation to the next 2 of a kind that has existed for a long time ♦ She was using a traditional rocking chair

traditionally adverb in a traditional way

traffic ➢ noun
1 vehicles, ships, or aircraft moving along a route 2 trade, especially in something illegal or wrong ♦ They were involved in traffic in drugs

traffic ➢ verb (**traffics, trafficking, trafficked**)
to traffic in something is to trade in it illegally

traffic lights plural noun
a set of coloured lights used to control traffic at road junctions and other hazards

traffic warden noun (plural **traffic wardens**)
an official whose job is to control the movement and parking of vehicles

tragedy noun (plural **tragedies**)
1 a play with unhappy events or a sad ending 2 a very sad event

tragic adjective
1 very sad or distressing 2 to do with tragedy

tragically adverb in a tragic way

trail ➢ noun (plural **trails**)
1 a path or track through the countryside or a forest 2 the scent and marks left behind by an animal as it moves 3 marks left behind by something that has passed

trail ➢ verb (**trails, trailing, trailed**)
1 to trail an animal is to follow the scent or marks it has left behind 2 to trail something is to drag it behind you; to trail, or trail behind, is to follow someone in this way 3 to trail behind someone is to follow them more slowly or at a distance ♦ A few walkers trailed behind the others 4 to trail is also to hang down or float loosely ♦ She wore a long trailing scarf

trailer noun (plural **trailers**)
1 a truck or other container that is pulled along by a car or lorry 2 a short film advertising a film or television programme that will soon be shown

train ➢ noun (plural **trains**)
1 a group of railway coaches or trucks joined together and pulled by an engine 2 a number of people or animals moving along together, especially in a desert 3 a series of things ♦ The train of events began in London 4 a long part of a dress that trails on the ground

train ➢ verb (**trains, training, trained**)
1 to train someone is to give them skill or practice in something 2 to train is to practise, especially for a sporting event ♦ She was training for the race 3 to train a plant is to make it grow in a particular direction ♦ Roses can be trained up walls 4 to train a gun is to aim it at a target ♦ He trained his rifle on the bridge

trainer noun (plural **trainers**)
1 a person who trains people or animals 2 a soft shoe with a rubber sole, worn for running and jogging

traitor noun (plural **traitors**)
someone who betrays their country or friends

tram noun (plural **trams**)
a passenger vehicle that runs along rails set in the road

tramp ➤ *noun* (*plural* **tramps**)
1 a person without a home or job who walks from place to place **2** a long walk **3** the sound of heavy footsteps

tramp ➤ *verb* (**tramps, tramping, tramped**)
1 to tramp is to walk with heavy footsteps **2** to tramp is also to walk for a long distance

trample *verb* (**tramples, trampling, trampled**)
to trample something, or to trample on it, is to crush it by treading heavily on it

trampoline *noun* (*plural* **trampolines**)
(*pronounced* tramp-o-leen)
a large piece of canvas joined to a frame by springs, used by gymnasts for jumping on

trance *noun* (*plural* **trances**)
a dreamy or unconscious condition like sleep

tranquil *adjective*
quiet and peaceful
tranquillity *noun* being tranquil

tranquillizer *noun* (*plural* **tranquillizers**)
a drug used to make a person feel calm

trans- *prefix*
meaning 'across', as in *transatlantic*

transact *verb* (**transacts, transacting, transacted**)
to transact business is to do it or carry it out

transaction *noun* (*plural* **transactions**)
a piece of business

transatlantic *adjective*
across the Atlantic Ocean or on the other side of it

transfer ➤ *verb* (**transfers, transferring, transferred**) (*pronounced* trans-**fer**)
1 to transfer someone or something is to move them to another place **2** to transfer something is to give it or pass it on to someone else

transfer ➤ *noun* (*plural* **transfers**)
(*pronounced* **trans**-fer)
1 the process of moving a person or thing to another place **2** a piece of paper with a picture or design that can be transferred to another surface by soaking or heating the paper

transferable *adjective*
able to be transferred or taken somewhere else

transference *noun*
transferring someone or something

transform *verb* (**transforms, transforming, transformed**)
to transform a person or thing is to change their form or appearance to something quite different ♦ *The caterpillar is transformed into a butterfly*
transformation *noun* being transformed

transformer *noun* (*plural* **transformers**)
a device used to change the voltage of an electric current

transfusion *noun* (*plural* **transfusions**)
putting blood taken from one person into another person's body

transistor *noun* (*plural* **transistors**)
1 a tiny electronic device that controls a flow of electricity **2** a portable radio that uses transistors to strengthen the signal it receives

transition *noun* (*plural* **transitions**)
a change from one thing to another
transitional *adjective* changing from one thing to another

transitive *adjective*
(*in Grammar*) a verb is transitive when it is used with a direct object, for example *ran* in *they ran a paper shop* (but not in *they ran away*)

translate *verb* (**translates, translating, translated**)
to translate language is to say or write it in another language
translation *noun* something translated from another language **translator** *noun* someone who translates language

translucent *adjective*
allowing light to shine through, without being fully transparent

transmission *noun* (*plural* **transmissions**)
1 transmitting something **2** the gears that transmit power from the engine to the wheels of a vehicle

transmit *verb* (**transmits, transmitting, transmitted**)
1 to transmit a broadcast or signal is to send it out **2** to transmit something is to send it or pass it from one person or place to another

transmitter *noun* (*plural* **transmitters**)
a device for transmitting radio signals

transparency *noun* (*plural* **transparencies**)
1 being transparent **2** a type of transparent photograph that is projected on a screen

transparent *adjective*
able to be seen through

transpire *verb* (**transpires, transpiring, transpired**)
1 to transpire is to become known ♦ *It transpired that she had known nothing about it* **2** to transpire is also to happen ♦ *This is what transpired* **3** plants and animals transpire when they emit moisture through their leaves or skin

transplant ➤ *verb* (**transplants, transplanting, transplanted**)
1 to transplant a plant is to move it from one place to another **2** to transplant a body organ is to remove it from one person and put it in another
transplantation *noun* transplanting something

transplant ➤ *noun* (*plural* **transplants**)
1 the process of transplanting
2 something that is transplanted

transport ➤ *verb* (**transports, transporting, transported**) (*pronounced* trans-**port**)
to transport people or things is to take them from one place to another
transportation *noun* transporting people or things

transport ➤ *noun* (*pronounced* **trans**-port)
1 the process of transporting people or things **2** vehicles used to do this

transporter *noun* (*plural* **transporters**)
a heavy vehicle for transporting large objects

trap ➤ *noun* (*plural* **traps**)
1 a device for catching and holding animals **2** a plan or trick to capture, detect, or cheat someone **3** a two-wheeled carriage pulled by a horse **4** a bend in a pipe, filled with liquid to prevent air or gas escaping

trap ➤ *verb* (**traps, trapping, trapped**)
1 to trap a person or animal is to catch them in a trap **2** to trap someone is to capture, detect, or cheat them

trapdoor *noun* (*plural* **trapdoors**)
a door in a floor, ceiling, or roof

trapeze *noun* (*plural* **trapezes**)
a bar hanging from two ropes, used as a swing by acrobats

trapezium *noun* (*plural* **trapeziums**)
a four-sided figure that has only two parallel sides, which are of different length

trapezoid *noun* (*plural* **trapezoids**)
a four-sided figure with no two sides parallel

trapper *noun* (*plural* **trappers**)
someone who traps animals, especially for their fur

trash *noun*
rubbish or nonsense
trashy *adjective* worthless

travel ➤ *verb* (**travels, travelling, travelled**)
to travel is to go from one place to another

travel ➤ *noun*
travelling ♦ *Do you enjoy travel?*

travel agent *noun* (*plural* **travel agents**)
a person or business whose job is to arrange travel and holidays for people

traveller *noun* (*plural* **travellers**)
1 someone who is travelling or who often travels **2** a gypsy, or a person who does not settle in one place

traveller's cheque *noun* (*plural* **traveller's cheques**)
a cheque for a fixed amount of money that is sold by banks and that can be exchanged for money in other countries

trawler *noun* (*plural* **trawlers**)
a fishing boat that pulls a large net behind it

tray *noun* (*plural* **trays**)
a flat piece of wood or metal or plastic, used for carrying food, cups, plates, and other household things

treacherous *adjective*
1 betraying someone; not loyal
2 dangerous or unreliable ♦ *It's been snowing and the roads are treacherous*
treacherously *adverb* in a treacherous way
treachery *noun* being treacherous or disloyal

treacle *noun*
a thick sweet sticky liquid made from purified sugar

tread ➤ *verb* (**treads, treading, trod, trodden**)
to tread on something is to walk on it or put your foot on it

tread ➤ *noun* (*plural* **treads**)
1 a sound or way of walking **2** the part of a staircase or ladder that you put your foot on **3** the part of a tyre that touches the ground

treason *noun*
betraying your country

treasure ➤ *noun* (*plural* **treasures**)
1 treasure is a collection of valuable things like jewels or money **2** a treasure is a precious thing

treasure ➤ *verb* (**treasures, treasuring, treasured**)
to treasure something is to think that it is very precious

treasure hunt *noun* (*plural* **treasure hunts**)
a game in which people try to find a hidden object

treasurer *noun* (*plural* **treasurers**)
an official who is in charge of the money of an organization or club

treasury *noun* (*plural* **treasuries**)
a place where treasure is stored
the Treasury the government department in charge of a country's income

treat ➤ *verb* (**treats, treating, treated**)
1 to treat someone or something in a certain way is to behave towards them in that way ♦ *She treats her friends very kindly* **2** to treat a person or animal is to give them medical care ♦ *He was treated for rheumatism* **3** to treat someone is to pay for their food or drink or entertainment ♦ *I'll treat you to an ice cream*

treat ➤ *noun* (*plural* **treats**)
1 something special that gives someone pleasure **2** the act of treating someone by paying for them ♦ *This is my treat*

treatment *noun* (*plural* **treatments**)
1 the way you treat someone **2** medical care

treaty *noun* (*plural* **treaties**)
a formal agreement between two or more countries

treble ➤ *adjective*
three times as much or three times as many

treble ➤ *noun* (*plural* **trebles**)
1 an amount that is three times as much or as many **2** a boy with a high singing voice

treble ➤ *verb* (**trebles, trebling, trebled**)
1 to treble something is to make it three times as big **2** to treble is to become three times as big

tree *noun* (*plural* **trees**)
a tall plant with leaves, branches, and a thick wooden stem called a trunk

trek ➤ *verb* (**treks, trekking, trekked**)
to trek is to make a long walk or journey

trek ➤ *noun* (*plural* **treks**)
a long walk or journey

trellis *noun* (*plural* **trellises**)
a framework of crossing wooden or metal bars, used to support climbing plants

tremble ➤ *verb* (**trembles, trembling, trembled**)
to tremble is to shake gently, especially with fear

tremble ➤ *noun* (*plural* **trembles**)
a trembling movement or sound

tremendous *adjective*
1 very large **2** excellent
tremendously *adverb* in a tremendous way

tremor *noun* (*plural* **tremors**)
a shaking or trembling

trench *noun* (*plural* **trenches**)
a long hole or ditch dug in the ground

trend *noun* (*plural* **trends**)
the general direction in which something is going; a tendency

trendy *adjective* (**trendier, trendiest**)
(*informal*) fashionable; trying to be up to date
trendily *adverb* in a trendy way **trendiness** *noun* being trendy

trespass *verb* (**trespasses, trespassing, trespassed**)
to trespass is to go on someone's land or property without their permission
trespasser *noun* someone who trespasses

trestle *noun* (*plural* **trestles**)
each of a set of supports on which you place a board to make a table

trial *noun* (*plural* **trials**)
1 trying something to see how well it works **2** the process of trying someone in a lawcourt
by trial and error by trying out different methods until you find one that works
on trial being tried out, or being tried in a lawcourt

triangle *noun* (*plural* **triangles**)
1 a flat shape with three straight sides and three angles **2** a percussion instrument made from a metal rod bent into a triangle
triangular *adjective* in the form of a triangle

tribe *noun* (*plural* **tribes**)
a group of families living together, ruled by a chief
tribal *adjective* to do with tribes

tribesman *noun* (*plural* **tribesmen**)
a man who belongs to a particular tribe

tributary *noun* (*plural* **tributaries**)
a river or stream that flows into a larger river or a lake

tribute *noun* (*plural* **tributes**)
1 something said or done as a mark of respect or admiration for someone
2 money that people in one country used to have to pay a powerful ruler in another country

trick ➤ *noun* (*plural* **tricks**)
1 something done to deceive or fool someone **2** a clever action **3** the winning of one round of a card game such as whist

trick ➤ *verb* (**tricks, tricking, tricked**)
to trick someone is to deceive or fool them
trickery *noun* the use of tricks **trickster** *noun* someone who plays tricks

trickle ➤ *verb* (**trickles, trickling, trickled**)
to trickle is to flow slowly and in small quantities

trickle ➤ *noun* (*plural* **trickles**)
a slow gradual flow

tricky *adjective* (**trickier, trickiest**)
1 difficult; needing skill ♦ *This is a tricky job* **2** cunning or deceitful

tricycle *noun* (*plural* **tricycles**)
a vehicle like a bicycle with three wheels

tried past tense and past participle of **try**
verb

trifle ➤ *noun* (*plural* **trifles**)
1 a pudding made of sponge cake covered with custard, fruit, and cream **2** a very small amount of something **3** something that has little importance or value

trifle ➤ *verb* (**trifles**, **trifling**, **trifled**)
to trifle with someone or something is to treat them without seriousness or respect

trifling *adjective*
very small or unimportant

trigger ➤ *noun* (*plural* **triggers**)
a lever that is pulled to fire a gun

trigger ➤ *verb* (**triggers**, **triggering**, **triggered**)
to trigger something, or trigger it off, is to cause it to happen

trillion *noun* (*plural* **trillions**)
a million million (1,000,000,000,000)

trim ➤ *adjective* (**trimmer**, **trimmest**)
neat and tidy

trim ➤ *verb* (**trims**, **trimming**, **trimmed**)
1 to trim something is to cut the edges or unwanted parts from it **2** to trim clothing is to decorate it **3** in a boat, to trim the sails is to arrange them to suit the wind

trim ➤ *noun*
an act of trimming ♦ *Give it a quick trim*
in good trim in good condition

Trinity *noun*
the Trinity in Christianity, the union of Father, Son, and Holy Spirit in one God

trio *noun* (*plural* **trios**)
1 three people or things **2** a group of three musicians **3** a piece of music for three musicians

trip ➤ *verb* (**trips**, **tripping**, **tripped**)
1 to trip is to catch your foot on something and fall or stumble **2** to trip someone is to make them fall or stumble **3** to trip, or trip along, is to move with quick gentle steps

trip ➤ *noun* (*plural* **trips**)
1 a short journey or outing **2** the action of tripping or stumbling

tripe *noun*
1 part of the stomach of an ox used as food **2** (*informal*) nonsense

triple ➤ *adjective*
1 three times as much or three times as many **2** consisting of three parts or involving three people or groups

triple ➤ *verb* (**triples**, **tripling**, **tripled**)
to triple something is to make it three times as big

triple jump *noun*
an athletics event in which athletes try to jump as far as possible with a hop, step, and jump

triplet *noun* (*plural* **triplets**)
each of three children or animals born at the same time to the same mother

tripod *noun* (*plural* **tripods**) (*pronounced* try-pod)
a stand with three legs, for supporting a camera or other instrument

triumph *noun* (*plural* **triumphs**)
1 a triumph is a great success or victory **2** triumph is a feeling of victory or success ♦ *They returned home in triumph*

triumphant *adjective*
enjoying a victory or celebrating one
triumphantly *adverb* in a triumphant way

trivial *adjective*
not important or valuable
trivially *adverb* in a trivial way **triviality** *noun* being trivial

trod past tense of **tread** *verb*

trodden past participle of **tread** *verb*

troll *noun* (*plural* **trolls**)
a creature in Scandinavian mythology, either a dwarf or a giant

trolley *noun* (*plural* **trolleys**)
1 a small table on wheels **2** a small cart or truck **3** a basket on wheels, used in supermarkets

trombone *noun* (*plural* **trombones**)
a large brass musical instrument with a sliding tube

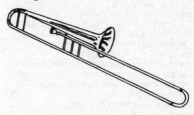

troop ➤ *noun* (*plural* **troops**)
an organized group of people, especially soldiers or Scouts

troop ➤ *verb* (**troops**, **trooping**, **trooped**)
to troop is to move along in large numbers

troops *plural noun*
soldiers

trophy *noun* (*plural* **trophies**)
a prize or souvenir for a victory or other success

tropic *noun* (*plural* **tropics**)
a line of latitude about $23\frac{1}{2}$ ° north of the
equator (**Tropic of Cancer**) or about $23\frac{1}{2}$ °
south of the equator (**Tropic of Capricorn**)
the tropics the hot regions between these
two latitudes
tropical *adjective* to do with the tropics

trot ➤ *verb* (**trots, trotting, trotted**)
1 a horse trots when it runs gently
without cantering or galloping **2** a person
trots when they run gently with short
steps

trot ➤ *noun* (*plural* **trots**)
a trotting run
on the trot (*informal*) one after another

trouble ➤ *noun* (*plural* **troubles**)
something that causes worry or difficulty
to take trouble is to take great care in doing
something

trouble ➤ *verb* (**troubles, troubling, troubled**)
1 to trouble someone is to cause them
trouble **2** to trouble to do something is to
make an effort to do it ♦ *Nobody troubled
to ask us what we wanted*

troublesome *adjective*
causing trouble or worry

trough *noun* (*plural* **troughs**) (*pronounced*
trof)
1 a long narrow box for animals to eat or
drink from **2** an area of low pressure
between two areas of high pressure

trousers *plural noun*
a piece of clothing worn over the lower half
of your body, with two parts to cover your
legs

trout *noun* (*plural* **trout**)
a freshwater fish

trowel *noun* (*plural* **trowels**)
1 a tool for digging small holes or lifting
plants **2** a tool with a flat blade for
spreading cement or mortar

truant *noun* (*plural* **truants**)
a child who stays away from school
without permission
to play truant is to stay away from school
without permission
truancy *noun* being a truant

truce *noun* (*plural* **truces**)
an agreement to stop fighting for a while

truck *noun* (*plural* **trucks**)
1 an open railway wagon for carrying
goods **2** a lorry **3** a cart

trudge *verb* (**trudges, trudging, trudged**)
to trudge is to walk slowly and heavily

true *adjective* (**truer, truest**)
1 real or correct; telling what actually
exists or happened ♦ *This is a true story*
2 genuine or proper ♦ *He was the true heir*
3 loyal and faithful ♦ *You are a true friend*

truly *adverb*
1 truthfully **2** sincerely or genuinely ♦ *We
are truly grateful* **3** loyally or faithfully

trump ➤ *noun* (*plural* **trumps**)
a playing card of a suit that ranks above
the others for one game or round of
play

trump ➤ *verb* (**trumps, trumping, trumped**)
to trump a card is to beat it by playing a
trump

trumpet ➤ *noun* (*plural* **trumpets**)
a brass musical instrument with a narrow
tube that widens at the end
trumpeter *noun* someone who plays the
trumpet

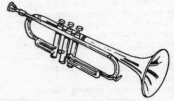

trumpet ➤ *verb* (**trumpets, trumpeting,
trumpeted**)
1 to trumpet is to make a loud sound, as
an elephant does **2** to trumpet something
is to shout it out or announce it loudly

truncheon *noun* (*plural* **truncheons**)
a short thick stick carried as a weapon by
a police officer

trundle *verb* (**trundles, trundling, trundled**)
to trundle is to move along heavily

trunk *noun* (*plural* **trunks**)
1 the main stem of a tree **2** an elephant's
long flexible nose **3** a large box with a
hinged lid, for carrying or storing clothes
and other things **4** the human body
except for the head, legs, and arms

trunk call *noun* (*plural* **trunk calls**)
a long-distance telephone call

trunk road *noun* (*plural* **trunk roads**)
a main road

trunks *plural noun*
shorts worn by men and boys for
swimming, boxing, and other activities

trust ➤ *verb* (**trusts, trusting, trusted**)
1 to trust someone or something is to
believe that they are good or truthful or
reliable **2** to trust that something is so is
to hope it ♦ *I trust that you are well*
to trust someone with something is to let them
use it or look after it

trust ➤ *noun*
1 the feeling that a person or thing can be
trusted **2** responsibility; being trusted

trustful *adjective*
trusting people
trustfully *adverb* in a trustful way

trustworthy *adjective*
able to be trusted; reliable

trusty *adjective*
trustworthy or reliable

truth *noun* (*plural* **truths**)
1 truth is the quality of being true 2 a truth is something that is true

truthful *adjective*
1 telling the truth ♦ *They are truthful children* 2 true ♦ *They gave a truthful account of what happened*
truthfully *adverb* in a truthful way
truthfulness *noun* being truthful

try ➤ *verb* (**tries, trying, tried**)
1 to try to do something is to make an effort to do it or to see if you can do it ♦ *Try to keep still* 2 to try something is to use it to see if it works ♦ *Try this can opener* 3 to try someone in a lawcourt is to find out whether they are guilty of a crime, by hearing all the evidence about it 4 to try someone is also to annoy them over a long time ♦ *You really do try me with your constant complaining*
to try something on is to put on clothes to see if they fit
to try something out is to use it to see if it works

try ➤ *noun* (*plural* **tries**)
1 a go at trying something; an attempt 2 (*in Rugby Football*) putting the ball down on the ground behind your opponents' goal so as to score points

T-shirt *noun* (*plural* **T-shirts**)
a shirt or vest with short sleeves

tub *noun* (*plural* **tubs**)
a round container for liquids or soft stuff such as ice cream

tuba *noun* (*plural* **tubas**) (*pronounced* tew-ba)
a large brass musical instrument that makes a deep sound

tube *noun* (*plural* **tubes**)
1 a long thin hollow piece of material such as metal, plastic, rubber, or glass 2 a long hollow container for something soft such as toothpaste 3 the underground railway in London ♦ *She goes to work by tube*

tuber *noun* (*plural* **tubers**)
a thick rounded plant root or stem that produces buds

tubing *noun*
a length or piece of tube

tubular *adjective*
shaped like a tube

tuck ➤ *verb* (**tucks, tucking, tucked**)
to tuck something is to push a loose edge of it somewhere so that it is tidy or hidden
to tuck in (*informal*) is to eat heartily
to tuck someone up is to put the bedclothes snugly round them

tuck ➤ *noun* (*plural* **tucks**)
1 a flat fold stitched in a piece of clothing 2 (*slang*) food, especially the kind which children enjoy eating

tuck shop *noun* (*plural* **tuck shops**)
a shop that sells tuck to children

Tuesday *noun* (*plural* **Tuesdays**)
the third day of the week

tuft *noun* (*plural* **tufts**)
a bunch of soft or fluffy things such as threads, grass, hair, or feathers, held or growing together

tug ➤ *noun* (*plural* **tugs**)
1 a hard or sudden pull 2 a small powerful boat used for towing ships

tug ➤ *verb* (**tugs, tugging, tugged**)
to tug something is to pull it hard

tug of war *noun*
a contest between two teams pulling a rope from opposite ends

tulip *noun* (*plural* **tulips**)
a large bright cup-shaped flower that grows on a tall stem from a bulb

tumble ➤ *verb* (**tumbles, tumbling, tumbled**)
1 to tumble is to fall over or fall down clumsily 2 to tumble to something is to suddenly realize it or be aware of it

tumble ➤ *noun* (*plural* **tumbles**)
a clumsy fall

tumble-drier *noun* (*plural* **tumble-driers**)
a machine that dries washing in a rotating drum with heated air passing through

tumbler *noun* (*plural* **tumblers**)
1 a drinking glass with no stem or handle 2 an acrobat

tummy *noun* (*plural* **tummies**)
(*informal*) the stomach

tumour *noun* (*plural* **tumours**) (*pronounced* tew-mer)
an abnormal growth on or in the body

tumult *noun* (*pronounced* tew-mult)
an uproar or state of great confusion

tumultuous *adjective*
noisy and excited ♦ *We got a tumultuous welcome*

tuna *noun* (*plural* **tuna** or **tunas**) (*pronounced* tew-na)
a large sea fish used for food

tundra *noun*
a large area of flat land in cold regions (especially northern Canada and Siberia) with no trees and with soil that is frozen for most of the year

tune ➤ *noun* (*plural* **tunes**)
a short piece of music; a pleasant series of musical notes
in tune at the correct musical pitch

tune ➤ *verb* (**tunes, tuning, tuned**)
1 to tune a musical instrument is to adjust it to be in tune 2 to tune a radio or television is to adjust it to receive a particular broadcasting station 3 to tune an engine is to adjust it so that it works smoothly

tuneful *adjective*
having a pleasant tune
tunefully *adverb* in a tuneful way

tunic *noun* (*plural* **tunics**) (*pronounced* tew-nik)
1 a jacket that is part of some uniforms 2 a piece of clothing

tunnel ➤ *noun* (*plural* **tunnels**)
a passage made underground or through a hill

tunnel ➤ *verb* (**tunnels, tunnelling, tunnelled**)
to tunnel is to make a tunnel

turban *noun* (*plural* **turbans**)
a covering for the head made by wrapping a long strip of cloth round it

turbine *noun* (*plural* **turbines**)
a machine or motor that is driven by a flow of water or gas

turbulent *adjective*
moving violently; heaving ♦ *The seas in March can be turbulent*
turbulence *noun* being turbulent

turf *noun* (*plural* **turfs** or **turves**)
1 short grass with the soil it is growing in 2 a piece of grass and soil cut out of the ground

turkey *noun* (*plural* **turkeys**)
a large bird kept for its meat

Turkish bath *noun* (*plural* **Turkish baths**)
a bath in steam or hot air

Turkish delight *noun*
a sweet consisting of lumps like jelly covered in powdered sugar

turmoil *noun*
a great disturbance or confusion

turn ➤ *verb* (**turns, turning, turned**)
1 to turn is to move round or move to a new direction; to turn something is to make it move in this way 2 to turn (for example) pale is to change appearance and become pale 3 to turn into something is to change into it ♦ *The frog turned into a prince* 4 to turn something into something else is to change it ♦ *You can turn milk into cheese* 5 to turn a device on or off is to use a switch to make it work or stop working; to turn (for example) a radio or television up or down is to make it louder or softer
to turn out is to happen a certain way ♦ *The weather's turned out fine*
to turn something down is to reject it or not want it
to turn something out is to empty it
to turn up is to appear or arrive suddenly or unexpectedly

turn ➤ *noun* (*plural* **turns**)
1 the action of turning; a turning movement 2 a place where a road bends; a junction 3 a task or duty that people do successively ♦ *It's your turn to wash up* 4 a short performance in a show 5 (*informal*) an attack of illness; a nervous shock ♦ *It gave me a nasty turn*
a good turn is a helpful action
in turn first one and then the other; following one after another

turncoat *noun* (*plural* **turncoats**)
someone who changes side or changes what they believe

turnip *noun* (*plural* **turnips**)
a plant with a large round white root used as a vegetable

turnover *noun* (*plural* **turnovers**)
a small pie made of pastry folded over fruit or jam

turnstile *noun* (*plural* **turnstiles**)
a revolving gate that lets one person through at a time

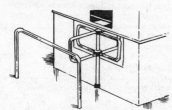

turntable *noun* (*plural* **turntables**)
a revolving platform or support, especially the part of a record player that you put the record on

turpentine *noun* (*pronounced* ter-pen-tyn)
a kind of oil used to make paint thinner and to clean paintbrushes

turquoise *noun* (*pronounced* ter-kwoiz)
1 a sky-blue or greenish-blue colour 2 a blue jewel

turret *noun* (*plural* **turrets**)
1 a small tower in a castle 2 a revolving structure containing a gun

turtle *noun* (*plural* **turtles**)
a sea animal that looks like a tortoise
to turn turtle is to capsize

tusk *noun* (*plural* **tusks**)
a long pointed tooth that sticks out of the mouth of an elephant or walrus or boar

tussle ➤ *noun* (*plural* **tussles**)
a hard struggle or fight

tussle ➤ *verb* (**tussles, tussling, tussled**)
to tussle is to struggle or fight over something

tutor *noun* (*plural* **tutors**)
a teacher who teaches one person or a small group at a time

TV short for **television**

tweak ➤ *verb* (**tweaks, tweaking, tweaked**)
to tweak something is to twist it or pull it sharply

tweak ➤ *noun* (*plural* **tweaks**)
a tweaking movement

tweed *noun*
a thick rough woollen cloth

tweezers *plural noun*
a small tool for gripping or picking up small things like stamps and hairs

twelve *noun* (*plural* **twelves**)
the number 12
twelfth *adjective* and *noun* 12th

twenty *noun* (*plural* **twenties**)
the number 20
twentieth *adjective* and *noun* 20th

twice *adverb*
1 two times; on two occasions 2 double the amount

twiddle ➤ *verb* (**twiddles, twiddling, twiddled**)
to twiddle something is to turn it round or over and over in an idle way ♦ *He was twiddling a knob on the radio*

twiddle ➤ *noun* (*plural* **twiddles**)
a twiddling movement

twig [1] *noun* (*plural* **twigs**)
a short thin branch or shoot

twig [2] *verb* (**twigs, twigging, twigged**)
(*informal*) to twig something is to realize what it means

twilight *noun*
the time of dim light just before sunrise or after sunset

twin ➤ *noun* (*plural* **twins**)
1 each of two children or animals born at the same time from one mother 2 each of two things that are exactly alike

twin ➤ *verb* (**twins, twinning, twinned**)
to twin one city or town with another is to make an arrangement involving exchange visits and other cultural events that they do together

twine *noun*
strong thin string

twinkle ➤ *verb* (**twinkles, twinkling, twinkled**)
to twinkle is to sparkle or shine with flashes of bright light

twinkle ➤ *noun* (*plural* **twinkles**)
a twinkling light

twirl ➤ *verb* (**twirls, twirling, twirled**)
to twirl is to turn round and round quickly; to twirl something is to make it do this

twirl ➤ *noun* (*plural* **twirls**)
a twirling movement

twist ➤ *verb* (**twists, twisting, twisted**)
1 to twist something is to turn its ends in opposite directions 2 to twist is to turn round or from side to side ♦ *The road twisted through the hills* 3 to twist something is to bend it out of its proper shape ♦ *My bicycle's front wheel is twisted* 4 (*informal*) to twist someone is to swindle them

twist ➤ *noun* (*plural* **twists**)
a twisting movement or action

twister *noun* (*plural* **twisters**)
(*informal*) someone who swindles people

twitch ➤ *verb* (**twitches, twitching, twitched**)
to twitch is to jerk or move suddenly and quickly; to twitch something is to make it do this

twitch ➤ *noun* (*plural* **twitches**)
a twitching movement

twitter *verb* (**twitters, twittering, twittered**)
to twitter is to make quick chirping sounds, as birds do

two *noun* (*plural* **twos**)
the number 2
to be in two minds is to be undecided about something

two-faced *adjective*
dishonest or deceitful

tying present participle of **tie** *verb*

type ➤ *noun* (*plural* **types**)
1 a group or class of similar people or things; a kind or sort **2** letters and figures designed for use in printing

type ➤ *verb* (**types, typing, typed**)
to type something is to write it with a typewriter

typewriter *noun* (*plural* **typewriters**)
a machine with keys that you press to print letters or figures on a sheet of paper
typewritten *adjective* written with a typewriter

typhoid *noun*
a serious disease caused by harmful bacteria in food or drinking water.

typhoon *noun* (*plural* **typhoons**)
a violent windy storm

typical *adjective*
1 having the qualities or features of a particular type of person or thing ♦ *They are typical schoolchildren* **2** usual in a particular person or thing ♦ *She worked with typical thoroughness*
typically *adverb* in a typical way

typist *noun* (*plural* **typists**)
a person who types, especially as their job

tyranny *noun* (*plural* **tyrannies**) (*pronounced* ti-ra-nee)
a cruel or unjust way of ruling people
tyrannical *adjective* cruel or unjust

tyrant *noun* (*plural* **tyrants**) (*pronounced* ty-rant)
someone who rules people cruelly or unjustly

tyre *noun* (*plural* **tyres**)
a covering of rubber fitted round the rim of a wheel to make it grip the road and run smoothly

Uu

udder *noun* (*plural* **udders**)
the bag-like part of a cow, goat, or ewe, from which milk is taken

UFO *noun* (*plural* **UFOs**)
short for *unidentified flying object*

ugly *adjective* (**uglier, ugliest**)
1 not beautiful; unpleasant to look at
2 threatening or dangerous ♦ *The crowd was in an ugly mood*
ugliness *noun* being ugly

ulcer *noun* (*plural* **ulcers**)
a sore on the inside or outside of the body

ultimate *adjective*
furthest in a series of things; final
ultimately *adverb* finally; eventually

ultra- *prefix*
meaning 'beyond', as in *ultraviolet*

ultraviolet *adjective*
ultraviolet light is light beyond the violet end of the spectrum

umbilical cord *noun* (*plural* **umbilical cords**)
the tube through which a baby receives nourishment in the mother's womb, connected to the baby's navel

umbrella *noun* (*plural* **umbrellas**)
a mushroom-shaped piece of cloth stretched over a folding frame, which you open to protect yourself from rain or snow

umpire *noun* (*plural* **umpires**)
a referee in cricket, tennis, and some other games

un- *prefix*
meaning 'not', as in *uncommon*, or added to verbs to make the action of the verb opposite to normal, as in *undo*

unable *adjective*
not able ♦ *She was unable to hear*

unaided *adjective*
without any help

unanimous *adjective* (*pronounced* yoo-nan-i-mus)
agreed by everyone ♦ *It was a unanimous decision*
unanimity *noun* being unanimous
unanimously *adverb* with everyone agreeing

unavoidable *adjective*
not able to be avoided; bound to happen
unavoidably *adverb* in an unavoidable way

unaware *adjective*
not aware

unawares *adjective*
unexpectedly; without someone knowing
♦ *His question caught me unawares*

unbearable *adjective*
not able to be borne or endured
unbearably *adverb* in an unbearable way

unbelievable *adjective*
1 not able to be believed **2** amazing
unbelievably *adverb* in an unbelievable way

unblock *verb* (**unblocks, unblocking, unblocked**)
to unblock something is to clear it of a block or obstruction

unborn *adjective*
not yet born

uncalled for *adjective*
not justified or necessary ♦ *Your rudeness is uncalled for*

uncanny *adjective* (**uncannier, uncanniest**)
strange and mysterious ♦ *There was an uncanny silence*

uncertain *adjective*
1 not certain ♦ *He is uncertain about what to do* 2 not reliable ♦ *The weather is uncertain at the moment*
uncertainly *adverb* in an uncertain way
uncertainty *noun* being uncertain

uncle *noun* (*plural* **uncles**)
1 the brother of your father or mother
2 your aunt's husband

uncomfortable *adjective*
not comfortable
uncomfortably *adverb* in an uncomfortable way

uncommon *adjective*
not common; unusual

unconscious *adjective*
1 not conscious 2 not aware ♦ *I was unconscious of doing anything wrong*
unconsciously *adverb* in an unconscious way
unconsciousness *noun* being unconscious

uncontrollable *adjective*
unable to be controlled
uncontrollably *adverb* in an uncontrollable way

uncountable *adjective*
unable to be counted; too many to count

uncouth *adjective* (*pronounced* un-kooth)
rude and rough in manner

uncover *verb* (**uncovers, uncovering, uncovered**)
1 to uncover something is to take the cover or top off it 2 to uncover a secret or something unknown is to discover it ♦ *The police have uncovered a huge fraud*

undecided *adjective*
not decided; uncertain

undeniable *adjective*
impossible to deny; certainly true
undeniably *adverb* certainly

under ➤ *preposition*
1 lower than; below ♦ *Hide it under the desk* 2 less than ♦ *They are under 5 years old* 3 ruled or controlled by ♦ *The army is under his command* 4 in the process of; undergoing ♦ *The road is under repair* 5 using; moving by means of ♦ *The machine moves under its own power*

under ➤ *adverb*
in or to a lower place ♦ *Slowly the diver went under*

underarm *adjective* and *adverb*
with the arm kept below shoulder level and moving forward and upwards

underclothes *plural noun* or **underclothing** *noun*
underwear

underdeveloped *adjective*
1 not fully developed or grown 2 an underdeveloped country is one that is poor and lacking modern industrial development

underdone *adjective*
not properly done or cooked

underfoot *adverb*
1 on the ground ♦ *There was a thick carpet of leaves underfoot* 2 under someone's feet ♦ *The flag fell to the ground and was trampled underfoot*

undergo *verb* (**undergoes, undergoing, underwent, undergone**)
to undergo something is to experience something or be subjected to it

undergraduate *noun* (*plural* **undergraduates**)
a student at a university who has not yet taken a degree

underground ➤ *adjective* and *adverb*
1 under the ground 2 done or working in secret

underground ➤ *noun* (*plural* **undergrounds**)
a railway that runs through tunnels under the ground

undergrowth *noun*
bushes and other plants growing closely under tall trees

underhand *adjective*
secret and deceitful

underlie *verb* (**underlies, underlying, underlay, underlain**)
1 to underlie something is to be under it or lie under it 2 to underlie a fact or circumstance is to cause or explain it
♦ *Hard work underlies the team's success this season*

underline *verb* (**underlines, underlining, underlined**)
1 to underline something you have written is to draw a line under it 2 to underline a fact is to show it clearly
♦ *Hassan's accident underlines the need to be careful*

undermine *verb* (**undermines, undermining, undermined**)
1 to undermine something is to make a hollow or tunnel beneath it 2 to undermine someone's efforts or plans is to weaken them gradually

underneath *preposition* and *adverb*
below or beneath

underpants *plural noun*
a piece of men's underwear worn under trousers

underpass *noun* (*plural* **underpasses**)
a place where one road or path goes under another

underprivileged *adjective*
not having the same rights or standard of living as most people

understand *verb* (**understands, understanding, understood**)
1 to understand something is to know what it means or how it works 2 to understand something is also to have heard about it ♦ *I understand he has measles*

understandable *adjective*
1 able to be understood 2 reasonable or normal ♦ *He replied with understandable delight*
understandably *adverb* in an understandable way

understanding ➤ *noun*
1 the power to understand or think; intelligence 2 agreement; harmony 3 sympathy or tolerance

understanding ➤ *adjective*
sympathetic and helpful ♦ *He was very understanding when I was ill*

undertake *verb* (**undertakes, undertaking, undertook, undertaken**)
to undertake something is to agree or promise to do it

undertaker *noun* (*plural* **undertakers**)
someone whose job is to arrange funerals

undertaking *noun* (*plural* **undertakings**)
something that someone agrees to do

underwater *adjective*
placed or used or done below the surface of water

underwear *noun*
clothes worn next to the skin, under other clothes

underworld *noun*
1 in legends, the place for the spirits of the dead; hell 2 people who are regularly involved in crime

undesirable *adjective*
not wanted or liked

undeveloped *adjective*
not yet developed

undo *verb* (**undoes, undoing, undid, undone**)
1 to undo a package or parcel is to unwrap it 2 to undo something already done is to cancel the effect of it ♦ *He has undone all our careful work*

undoubted *adjective*
definite or certain
undoubtedly *adverb* certainly

undress *verb* (**undresses, undressing, undressed**)
1 to undress is to take your clothes off 2 to undress someone is to take their clothes off

unearth *verb* (**unearths, unearthing, unearthed**)
to unearth something is to dig it up, or to find it by searching

unearthly *adjective*
supernatural; strange and frightening

uneasy *adjective* (**uneasier, uneasiest**)
anxious or worried
uneasily *adverb* in an uneasy way **uneasiness** *noun* being uneasy

uneatable *adjective*
not fit for eating

unemployed *adjective*
without a job
unemployment *noun* being unemployed

uneven *adjective*
not level or regular
unevenly *adverb* in an uneven way
unevenness *noun* being uneven

unexpected *adjective*
not expected; surprising
unexpectedly *adverb* without being expected; surprisingly

unfair *adjective*
not fair; unjust
unfairly *adverb* in an unfair way **unfairness** *noun* being unfair

unfaithful *adjective*
not faithful or loyal

unfamiliar *adjective*
not familiar

unfasten *verb* (**unfastens, unfastening, unfastened**)
to unfasten something is to open it when it has been fastened

unfavourable *adjective*
not favourable or helpful
unfavourably *adverb* in an unfavourable way

unfinished *adjective*
not finished

unfit *adjective*
1 not fit or fully healthy 2 not suitable
♦ *He is unfit for the job*

unfold *verb* (**unfolds, unfolding, unfolded**)
1 to unfold something is to open it or
spread it out 2 to unfold a story or plan is
to make it known gradually 3 to unfold is
to become known gradually ♦ *Listen as the
story unfolds*

unforgettable *adjective*
not able to be forgotten

unforgivable *adjective*
not able to be forgiven

unfortunate *adjective*
1 unlucky 2 unsuitable or regrettable ♦ *It
was an unfortunate remark*
unfortunately *adverb* in an unfortunate way

unfreeze *verb* (**unfreezes, unfreezing, unfroze,
unfrozen**)
1 to unfreeze something is to make it no
longer frozen 2 to unfreeze is to become no
longer frozen

unfriendly *adjective*
not friendly
unfriendliness *noun* being unfriendly

ungrateful *adjective*
not grateful
ungratefully *adverb* in an ungrateful way

unhappy *adjective* (**unhappier, unhappiest**)
1 not happy 2 regrettable or unsuitable
♦ *It was an unhappy coincidence*
unhappily *adverb* in an unhappy way
unhappiness *noun* being unhappy

unhealthy *adjective* (**unhealthier, unhealthiest**)
not healthy

unheard-of *adjective*
never known or done before; extraordinary

unicorn *noun* (*plural* **unicorns**) (*pronounced*
yoo-ni-korn)
an imaginary animal in stories, like a
horse with a long straight horn growing
out of the front of its head

uniform ➤ *noun* (*plural* **uniforms**)
the special clothes worn by members of an
army or school or organization

uniform ➤ *adjective*
always the same; not changing
uniformly *adverb* in a uniform way

uniformed *adjective*
wearing a uniform

uniformity *noun*
being uniform or the same

unify *verb* (**unifies, unifying, unified**)
to unify several things, especially
countries, is to join them into one thing; to
unify is to join together
unification *noun* being unified

unimportant *adjective*
not important
unimportance *noun* being unimportant

uninhabited *adjective*
with nobody living there

unintentional *adjective*
not intentional or deliberate
unintentionally *adverb* in an unintentional
way

uninterested *adjective*
not interested

uninteresting *adjective*
not interesting

union *noun* (*plural* **unions**)
1 the joining of things together; a united
thing 2 a trade union

Union Jack *noun* (*plural* **Union Jacks**)
the flag of the United Kingdom

unique *adjective* (*pronounced* yoo-neek)
being the only one of its kind or very
unusual ♦ *This jewel is unique*
uniquely *adverb* in a unique way **uniqueness**
noun being unique

unisex *adjective*
designed to be suitable for men and
women

unison *noun* (*pronounced* **yoo**-ni-son)
in unison 1 making the same sound together
2 agreeing

unit *noun* (*plural* **units**)
1 an amount used in measuring or
counting, such as a centimetre or a pound
2 a single person or thing 3 a group of
people or things that belong together

unite *verb* (**unites, uniting, united**)
1 to unite several people or things is to
form them into one thing or group 2 to
unite is to join together

unity *noun* (*plural* **unities**)
1 unity is being united or having
agreement 2 a unity is a complete thing

universal *adjective*
including everyone and everything
universally *adverb* in a universal way

universe *noun*
everything that exists, including the earth and living things and all the stars and planets

university *noun* (*plural* **universities**)
a place where people go to study for degrees after they have left school

unjust *adjective*
not fair or just
unjustly *adverb* in an unjust way

unkind *adjective* (**unkinder, unkindest**)
not kind
unkindly *adverb* in an unkind way **unkindness** *noun* being unkind

unknown *adjective*
not known

unleaded *adjective*
not containing lead ♦ *The car runs on unleaded petrol*

unless *conjunction*
except when; if not ♦ *We cannot go unless we are invited*

unlike ➤ *preposition*
not like ♦ *Unlike me, she enjoys sport*

unlike ➤ *adjective*
not alike; different ♦ *The two children are very unlike*

unlikely *adjective* (**unlikelier, unlikeliest**)
not likely to happen or be true

unload *verb* (**unloads, unloading, unloaded**)
to unload a container or vehicle is to take off the things it carried

unlock *verb* (**unlocks, unlocking, unlocked**)
to unlock a door or container is to open it with a key

unlucky *adjective* (**unluckier, unluckiest**)
not lucky
unluckily *adverb* in an unlucky way

unmistakable *adjective*
not likely to be mistaken for something or someone else; clear and definite
unmistakably *adverb* in an unmistakable way

unnatural *adjective*
not natural or normal
unnaturally *adverb* in an unnatural way

unnecessary *adjective*
not necessary
unnecessarily *adverb* in an unnecessary way

unoccupied *adjective*
not occupied; empty

unpack *verb* (**unpacks, unpacking, unpacked**)
to unpack a suitcase or container is to take out the things in it

unpleasant *adjective*
not pleasant
unpleasantly *adverb* in an unpleasant way
unpleasantness *noun* being unpleasant

unplug *verb* (**unplugs, unplugging, unplugged**)
to unplug an electrical device is to disconnect it by taking its plug out of the socket

unpopular *adjective*
not popular
unpopularity *noun* being unpopular

unravel *verb* (**unravels, unravelling, unravelled**)
1 to unravel something is to unwind it or disentangle it **2** to unravel a problem or mystery is to investigate it and solve it

unreal *adjective*
not real; existing only in the imagination

unreasonable *adjective*
not reasonable or fair

unrest *noun*
a discontented feeling, or trouble caused by it

unroll *verb* (**unrolls, unrolling, unrolled**)
to unroll something is to open it when it has been rolled up

unruly *adjective* (**unrulier, unruliest**)
(*pronounced* un-roo-lee)
difficult to control; behaving badly
unruliness *noun* being unruly

unscrew *verb* (**unscrews, unscrewing, unscrewed**)
to unscrew something is to undo it when it has been screwed up

unseemly *adjective*
not proper or suitable; indecent

unseen *adjective*
not seen; invisible

unselfish *adjective*
not selfish
unselfishly *adverb* in an unselfish way
unselfishness *noun* being unselfish

unsightly *adjective*
not pleasant to look at; ugly

unskilled *adjective*
not having or not needing special skill or training

unsound *adjective*
not sound or reliable; incorrect

unsteady *adjective* (**unsteadier, unsteadiest**)
not steady
unsteadily *adverb* in an unsteady way
unsteadiness *noun* being unsteady

unsuccessful *adjective*
not successful
unsuccessfully *adverb* in an unsuccessful way

unsuitable *adjective*
not suitable
unsuitably *adverb* in an unsuitable way

unthinkable *adjective*
too bad or unlikely to be worth thinking
about

untidy *adjective* (**untidier, untidiest**)
not tidy
untidily *adverb* in an untidy way **untidiness**
noun being untidy

untie *verb* (**unties, untying, untied**)
to untie something is to undo it when it
has been tied

until *preposition* and *conjunction*
up to a particular time or event ♦ *The shop
is open until 8 o'clock* ♦ *We will stay with
you until the train comes*

untimely *adjective*
happening at a bad or unsuitable time

unto *preposition*
(*old use*) to

untold *adjective*
not able to be counted or measured ♦ *They
enjoyed untold wealth*

untoward *adjective*
inconvenient or unfortunate ♦ *I hope
nothing untoward happens*

untrue *adjective*
not true

untruthful *adjective*
not telling the truth
untruthfully *adverb* in an untruthful way

unused *adjective* (*pronounced* un-**yoozd**)
not yet used
unused to something
(*pronounced* un-**yoost**)
not familiar with something ♦ *He is
unused to eating meat*

unusual *adjective*
not usual; strange or rare
unusually *adverb* in an unusual way

unwanted *adjective*
not wanted

unwell *adjective*
not well; ill

unwilling *adjective*
not willing
unwillingly *adverb* in an unwilling way
unwillingness *noun* being unwilling

unwind *verb* (**unwinds, unwinding, unwound**)
(*rhymes with* find)
1 to unwind something is to unroll it 2 to
unwind is to become unrolled
3 (*informal*) to unwind is also to relax
after hard work

unwrap *verb* (**unwraps, unwrapping, unwrapped**)
to unwrap something is to take it out of its
wrapping

unzip *verb* (**unzips, unzipping, unzipped**)
to unzip something is to undo it when it is
zipped up

up ➤ *adverb*
1 in or to a standing or upright position
♦ *Stand up* 2 in or to a high or higher
place or level ♦ *Put it up on the shelf*
♦ *Prices are going up* 3 completely ♦ *Eat
up your carrots* 4 out of bed ♦ *It's time to
get up* 5 finished ♦ *Your time is up*
6 (*informal*) happening ♦ *Something is up*
up against something faced with difficulties or
dangers
ups and downs changes of luck, sometimes
good and sometimes bad
to be up to something is to be doing
something mysterious or suspicious
♦ *What are they up to?*
up to date 1 modern or fashionable 2 having
the latest information

up ➤ *preposition*
in or to a higher position on something
♦ *Let's climb up the mountain*

update *verb* (**updates, updating, updated**)
to update something is to bring it up to
date

upgrade *verb* (**upgrades, upgrading, upgraded**)
to upgrade a machine is to improve it by
installing new parts in it

upheaval *noun* (*plural* **upheavals**)
a sudden violent change or disturbance

uphill *adjective* and *adverb*
1 sloping upwards 2 difficult ♦ *It was an
uphill job*

uphold *verb* (**upholds, upholding, upheld**)
to uphold a decision or belief is to support
it or agree with it

upholstery *noun*
covers and padding for furniture

upkeep *noun*
the cost of looking after something and
keeping it in good condition

uplands *plural noun*
the highest part of a country or region

upon *preposition*
on

upper *adjective*
higher in position or rank

upper class *noun* or **upper classes** *plural
noun*
the highest class in society, especially the
aristocracy
upper-class *adjective* belonging to the upper
class

upright ➤ *adjective*
1 standing up; vertical 2 honest

upright ➤ *noun* (*plural* **uprights**)
an upright post or support

uprising *noun* (*plural* **uprisings**)
a rebellion or revolt against the
government

uproar *noun*
a loud or angry noise or disturbance

upset ➤ *verb* (**upsets, upsetting, upset**)
(*pronounced* up-set)
1 to upset someone is to make them
unhappy or anxious **2** to upset something
is to knock it over and spill its contents

upset ➤ *noun* (*plural* **upsets**) (*pronounced*
up-set)
1 a slight illness ♦ *He's got a stomach
upset* **2** an unexpected result or setback
♦ *Losing the game on Saturday was a real
upset*

upshot *noun*
what happens in the end ♦ *The upshot
was that we had to stay behind*

upside down *adjective* and *adverb*
1 with the upper part underneath instead
of on top **2** very untidy; in disorder
♦ *Everything in the room was upside down*

upstairs *adverb* and *adjective*
to or on a higher floor in a house or other
building

upstart *noun* (*plural* **upstarts**)
someone who quickly reaches a position of
power and behaves arrogantly

upstream *adjective* and *adverb*
in the direction opposite to the flow of a
river or stream

uptake *noun*
quick on the uptake quick to understand
slow on the uptake slow to understand

uptight *adjective*
(*informal*) upset or nervous about
something

upward *adjective* and *adverb*
going towards what is higher

upwards *adverb*
towards what is higher

uranium *noun* (*pronounced* yoor-ay-ni-um)
a radioactive metal used as a source of
atomic energy

urban *adjective*
to do with a town or city

urbanize *verb* (**urbanizes, urbanizing, urbanized**)
to urbanize a place is to make it more like
a town
urbanization *noun* being urbanized

urchin *noun* (*plural* **urchins**)
a dirty or mischievous boy

Urdu *noun*
a language related to Hindi, spoken in
northern India and Pakistan

urge ➤ *verb* (**urges, urging, urged**)
1 to urge someone to do something is to try
to persuade them to do it **2** to urge people
or animals is to drive them forward

urge ➤ *noun* (*plural* **urges**)
a sudden strong desire or wish ♦ *She felt
an urge to go for a swim*

urgent *adjective*
needing to be done or dealt with
immediately
urgency *noun* being urgent **urgently** *adverb*
in an urgent way

urinate *verb* (**urinates, urinating, urinated**)
(*pronounced* yoor-i-nayt)
to urinate is to pass urine out of the body
urination *noun* urinating

urine *noun* (*pronounced* yoor-in)
waste liquid that collects in the bladder
and is passed out of the body
urinary *adjective* to do with the passing of
urine

urn *noun* (*plural* **urns**)
1 a large metal container with a tap, in
which water is heated **2** a kind of large
vase for holding the ashes of a person who
has been cremated

US or **USA** short for *United States of
America*

us *pronoun*
a word used for *we*, usually when it is the
object of a sentence, or when it comes after
a preposition ♦ *She likes us* ♦ *She gave it
to us*

usable *adjective*
that you can use

usage *noun* (*plural* **usages**) (*pronounced*
yoo-sij)
the way that something is used, especially
the way that words and language are used

use ⮞ *verb* (**uses, using, used**) (*pronounced* yooz)
to use something is to perform an action or job with it ♦ *Are you using my pen?*
used to did in the past ♦ *I used to live in Glasgow*
to be used to something or **someone** is to know them well or be familiar with them ♦ *We're used to hard work*
to use something up is to use all of it, so that none is left

use ⮞ *noun* (*plural* **uses**) (*pronounced* yooss)
1 the action of using something or being used **2** the purpose or value of something ♦ *Can you find a use for this box?* ♦ *This knife is no use to us*

used *adjective* (*pronounced* yoozd)
not new; second-hand ♦ *We're buying a used car*

useful *adjective*
able to be used a lot or do something that needs doing
usefully *adverb* in a useful way **usefulness** *noun* being useful

useless *adjective*
not having any use
uselessly *adverb* in a useless way **uselessness** *noun* being useless

user *noun* (*plural* **users**)
someone who uses something

user-friendly *adjective* (**user-friendlier, user-friendliest**)
designed to be easy to use

usher ⮞ *noun* (*plural* **ushers**)
someone who shows people to their seats in a church or cinema or theatre

usher ⮞ *verb* (**ushers, ushering, ushered**)
to usher someone is to lead them in or out of a place

usherette *noun* (*plural* **usherettes**)
a woman who shows people to their seats in a cinema or theatre

usual *adjective*
such as happens often or all the time; expected
usually *adverb* on most occasions; normally

usurp *verb* (**usurps, usurping, usurped**) (*pronounced* yoo-zerp)
to usurp power or a position is to take it by force from someone else
usurper *noun* someone who usurps power

utensil *noun* (*plural* **utensils**) (*pronounced* yoo-ten-sil)
a tool or device, especially one used in the house

uterus *noun* (*plural* **uteri**)
the womb

utilize *verb* (**utilizes, utilizing, utilized**)
to utilize something is to use it
utilization *noun* being used

utmost *adjective*
greatest ♦ *Look after it with the utmost care*

utopia *noun* (*plural* **utopias**)
an imaginary place where everyone is happy and everything is perfect

utter [1] *verb* (**utters, uttering, uttered**)
to utter something is to say it clearly, or to make a sound with your mouth ♦ *He uttered a loud yell*
utterance *noun* something that someone says

utter [2] *adjective*
complete or absolute ♦ *It was utter misery*
utterly *adverb* completely

U-turn *noun* (*plural* **U-turns**)
1 a turn a vehicle makes when it is driven round in one movement to face the opposite direction **2** a complete change of ideas or policy

Vv

vacancy *noun* (*plural* **vacancies**)
a job, or a room in a guest house, that is available and not taken

vacant *adjective*
1 empty; not filled or occupied **2** not showing any expression ♦ *He gave a vacant stare*
vacantly *adverb* in a vacant way

vacate *verb* (**vacates, vacating, vacated**)
to vacate a place is to leave it empty

vacation *noun* (*plural* **vacations**) (*pronounced* vay-**kay**-shon)
a holiday, especially between the terms at a university

vaccinate *verb* (**vaccinates, vaccinating, vaccinated**) (*pronounced* **vak**-si-nayt)
to vaccinate someone is to inoculate them with a vaccine
vaccination *noun* being vaccinated

vaccine *noun* (*plural* **vaccines**) (*pronounced* **vak**-seen)
a type of medicine injected into people to protect them from disease

vacuum *noun* (*plural* **vacuums**)
a completely empty space; a space without any air in it

vacuum cleaner *noun* (*plural* **vacuum cleaners**)
an electrical device that sucks up dust and dirt from the floor

vacuum flask *noun* (*plural* **vacuum flasks**)
a container with double walls that have a vacuum between them, for keeping liquids hot or cold

vagina *noun* (*plural* **vaginas**) (*pronounced* va-**jy**-na)
the passage in the female body that leads from the vulva to the womb

vague *adjective* (**vaguer, vaguest**)
not definite or clear
vaguely *adverb* in a vague way **vagueness** *noun* being vague

vain *adjective* (**vainer, vainest**)
1 too proud of yourself, especially of how you look 2 unsuccessful ♦ *They made vain attempts to save him*
in vain with no result; unsuccessfully
vainly *adverb* in a vain way

valentine *noun* (*plural* **valentines**)
1 a card sent on St Valentine's Day (14 February) to someone you love 2 the person you send a valentine to

valiant *adjective*
brave or courageous
valiantly *adverb* in a valiant way

valid *adjective*
able to be used or accepted; legal ♦ *Your passport is not valid*
validity *noun* being valid

valley *noun* (*plural* **valleys**)
an area of low land between hills

valour *noun*
bravery, especially in fighting

valuable *adjective*
1 worth a lot of money 2 having great value or importance ♦ *She gave me valuable advice*

valuables *plural noun*
things that are worth a lot of money

value ➤ *noun* (*plural* **values**)
1 the amount of money that something could be sold for 2 how useful or important something is
value ➤ *verb* (**values, valuing, valued**)
1 to value something is to think that it is valuable 2 to value something is also to estimate what it is worth ♦ *The estate agent is coming to value the house*
valuation *noun* an estimate of what something is worth **valuer** *noun* someone who values something

valueless *adjective*
having no value

valve *noun* (*plural* **valves**)
1 a device used to control the flow of gas or liquid 2 a device that controls the flow of electricity in older electrical equipment

vampire *noun* (*plural* **vampires**)
a mythical creature that sucks people's blood

van *noun* (*plural* **vans**)
1 a small lorry with a covered area for goods at the back 2 a railway carriage used for goods or for the train's guard

vandal *noun* (*plural* **vandals**)
someone who deliberately breaks or damages things
vandalism *noun* doing deliberate damage

vane *noun* (*plural* **vanes**)
1 a pointer that shows which way the wind is blowing 2 the blade or surface of a propeller, sail of a windmill, or other device that moves through air or water

vanilla *noun*
a flavouring made from the pods of a tropical plant

vanish *verb* (**vanishes, vanishing, vanished**)
to vanish is to disappear completely

vanity *noun*
being vain or conceited

vanquish *verb* (**vanquishes, vanquishing, vanquished**)
to vanquish someone is to win a victory over them

vaporize *verb* (**vaporizes, vaporizing, vaporized**)
to vaporize is to turn into vapour

vapour *noun* (*plural* **vapours**)
a visible gas which some liquids and solids can be turned into by heat

variable ➤ *adjective*
able or likely to change

variable ➤ *noun* (*plural* **variables**)
something that varies or can vary, especially a variable quantity

variation *noun* (*plural* **variations**)
1 the process of varying 2 the amount by which something varies 3 a different form of something

varied *adjective*
of various kinds; full of variety

variety *noun* (*plural* **varieties**)
1 a variety is a number of different kinds of things ♦ *There was a variety of cakes to choose from* 2 a variety is a particular kind of something ♦ *There are many rare varieties of butterfly* 3 variety is a situation where things are not always the same ♦ *We have a life full of variety* 4 variety is also a mixed form of light entertainment

various *adjective*
1 of different kinds ♦ *They came for various reasons* 2 several ♦ *We met various people*

variously *adverb* in different ways

varnish ➤ *noun* (*plural* **varnishes**)
a liquid that dries to form a hard shiny surface on wood or other surfaces

varnish ➤ *verb* (**varnishes, varnishing, varnished**)
to varnish a surface is to put varnish on it

vary *verb* (**varies, varying, varied**)
1 to vary something is to change it 2 to vary is to keep changing 3 to vary is also to be different ♦ *The cars are the same, although the colours vary*

vase *noun* (*plural* **vases**) (*pronounced* vahz)
a jar used for holding flowers or as an ornament

vast *adjective*
very large or wide

vastly *adverb* greatly; very **vastness** *noun* being vast

VAT short for *value-added tax*, a tax on goods and services

vat *noun* (*plural* **vats**)
a very large container for holding liquid

vault ➤ *verb* (**vaults, vaulting, vaulted**)
to vault something is to jump over it, using your hands to support you or with the help of a pole

vault ➤ *noun* (*plural* **vaults**)
1 a jump done by vaulting 2 an arched roof 3 an underground room for storing money and valuables

VCR short for **video cassette recorder**

VDU short for **visual display unit**

veal *noun*
the flesh of calves used for food

vector *noun* (*plural* **vectors**)
(*in Mathematics*) a quantity that has size and direction, such as velocity (which is speed in a certain direction)

Veda *plural noun*
the ancient writings of the Hindu religion

veer *verb* (**veers, veering, veered**)
to veer is to swerve or change direction suddenly

vegan *noun* (*plural* **vegans**) (*pronounced* vee-gan)
someone who does not use or eat any products made from animals

vegetable *noun* (*plural* **vegetables**)
a plant that can be used as food

vegetarian *noun* (*plural* **vegetarians**) (*pronounced* vej-i-tair-i-an)
someone who does not eat meat

vegetate *verb* (**vegetates, vegetating, vegetated**)
to vegetate is to lead a dull life doing nothing interesting

vegetation *noun*
plants that are growing

vehicle *noun* (*plural* **vehicles**)
a means of carrying people or things, especially on land

veil ➤ *noun* (*plural* **veils**)
a piece of thin material to cover your face or head

veil ➤ *verb* (**veils, veiling, veiled**)
1 to veil something is to cover it with a veil 2 to veil something such as a hint or a threat is to suggest it without being clear about it

vein *noun* (*plural* **veins**)
1 any of the tubes in the body that carry blood towards the heart 2 a line or streak on a leaf or rock or insect's wing 3 a long deposit of a mineral in the middle of rock

velocity *noun* (*plural* **velocities**) (*pronounced* vil-os-i-tee)
speed in a particular direction

velvet *noun*
a soft material with short furry fibres on one side

velvety *adjective* like velvet

vendetta *noun* (*plural* **vendettas**)
a long-lasting quarrel or feud

vendor *noun* (*plural* **vendors**)
someone who sells something

venerable *adjective*
worthy of respect or honour because of great age

venereal disease noun (*plural* **venereal diseases**) (*pronounced* vin-eer-i-al)
a disease that is passed on by sexual intercourse

venetian blind noun (*plural* **venetian blinds**)
a blind for a window, made of thin horizontal slats which you can move to control the amount of light that comes through

vengeance noun
revenge
with a vengeance very strongly or effectively

venison noun
the flesh of deer used for food

Venn diagram noun (*plural* **Venn diagrams**)
(*in Mathematics*) a diagram using circles to show how sets of things relate to one another

venom noun
1 the poison of snakes **2** a feeling of bitter hatred for someone
venomous *adjective* poisonous

vent noun (*plural* **vents**)
an opening in something, especially to let out smoke or gas
to give vent to something is to express your feelings openly ♦ *He gave vent to his anger*

ventilate verb (**ventilates, ventilating, ventilated**)
to ventilate a place is to let air move freely in and out of it
ventilation noun ventilating a place **ventilator** noun a device for ventilating a place

ventriloquist noun (*plural* **ventriloquists**) (*pronounced* ven-tril-o-kwist)
an entertainer who speaks without moving their lips, making it appear that a dummy is speaking
ventriloquism noun the skill of a ventriloquist

venture ➤ noun (*plural* **ventures**)
something you decide to do that is dangerous or adventurous

venture ➤ verb (**ventures, venturing, ventured**)
to venture somewhere is to do something difficult or adventurous ♦ *Shall we venture out into the snow?*

veranda noun (*plural* **verandas**) (*pronounced* ver-an-da)
an open terrace with a roof along the outside of a house

verb noun (*plural* **verbs**)
a word that shows what someone or something is doing, such as *be, go, sing, take*

verdict noun (*plural* **verdicts**)
the decision reached by a judge or jury about whether someone is guilty of a crime

verge ➤ noun (*plural* **verges**)
a strip of grass beside a road or path

verge ➤ verb (**verges, verging, verged**)
to verge on something is to be nearly something ♦ *His remark verged on the absurd*

verify verb (**verifies, verifying, verified**)
to verify something is to find or show whether it is true or correct
verification noun verifying something

vermin noun
animals or insects that damage crops or food or carry disease, such as rats and fleas

verruca noun (*plural* **verrucas**) (*pronounced* ver-oo-ka)
a kind of wart on the sole of the foot

versatile *adjective* (*pronounced* ver-sa-tyl)
able to do or be used for many different things
versatility noun being versatile

verse noun (*plural* **verses**)
1 verse is writing in the form of poetry **2** a verse is a group of lines in a poem or song **3** a verse is also each of the short numbered sections of a chapter in the Bible

version noun (*plural* **versions**)
1 someone's account of something that has happened ♦ *His version of the accident is different from mine* **2** something translated or rewritten ♦ *There are several new versions of the Bible* **3** a particular form of a thing ♦ *Do you like the new version of this car?*

versus *preposition*
against or competing with, especially in sport ♦ *The final will be Brazil versus Germany*

vertebra noun (*plural* **vertebrae**) (*pronounced* ver-ti-bra)
each of the bones that form the backbone

vertebrate noun (*plural* **vertebrates**) (*pronounced* ver-ti-brit)
an animal with a backbone

vertex noun (*plural* **vertices**)
the highest point of a hill, or of a cone or triangle

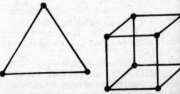

vertical *adjective*
going directly upwards, at right angles to
something level or horizontal
vertically *adverb* in a vertical direction

very ➣ *adverb*
to a great amount; extremely ♦ *It is very
cold*

very ➣ *adjective*
1 exact or actual ♦ *That's the very thing
we need!* **2** extreme ♦ *We've reached the
very end*

Vesak *noun* (*pronounced* **ves**-ak)
an important festival of Buddhism, held in
April to May

vessel *noun* (*plural* **vessels**)
1 a boat or ship **2** a container **3** a tube
inside an animal or plant, carrying blood
or some other liquid

vest *noun* (*plural* **vests**)
a piece of underwear worn on the top half
of the body

vested interest *noun* (*plural* **vested interests**)
a strong reason for wanting something to
happen, because it will help you

vestment *noun* (*plural* **vestments**)
a piece of outer clothing worn by the clergy
or choir at a church service

vestry *noun* (*plural* **vestries**)
a room in a church where the vestments
are kept and the clergy and choir prepare
for a service

vet *noun* (*plural* **vets**)
a person trained to treat sick animals

veteran *noun* (*plural* **veterans**)
a person with long experience, especially
as a soldier

veteran car *noun* (*plural* **veteran cars**)
a car made before 1916

veterinary *adjective* (*pronounced* vet-rin-ree)
to do with the medical treatment of
animals

veto ➣ *noun* (*plural* **vetoes**) (*pronounced*
vee-toh)
1 a refusal to let something happen **2** the
right to prohibit something

veto ➣ *verb* (**vetoes, vetoing, vetoed**)
to veto something is to refuse or prohibit it

vex *verb* (**vexes, vexing, vexed**)
to vex someone is to annoy them or cause
them worry
vexation *noun* vexing someone

VHF short for *very high frequency*

via *preposition* (*pronounced* **vy**-a)
going through; stopping at ♦ *This train
goes from Edinburgh to London via York*

viaduct *noun* (*plural* **viaducts**) (*pronounced*
vy-a-dukt)
a long bridge with many arches, carrying a
road or railway over low ground

vibrate *verb* (**vibrates, vibrating, vibrated**)
to vibrate is to move quickly to and fro, or
to make a quivering sound
vibration *noun* vibrating

vicar *noun* (*plural* **vicars**)
a member of the clergy who is in charge of
a parish

vicarage *noun* (*plural* **vicarages**)
the house of a vicar

vice[1] *noun* (*plural* **vices**)
1 evil or wickedness **2** an evil or bad habit

vice[2] *noun* (*plural* **vices**)
a device with jaws for holding something
tightly in place while you work on it

vice-president *noun* (*plural* **vice-presidents**)
a deputy to a president

vice versa *adverb* (*pronounced* vys-**ver**-sa)
the other way round ♦ *'We talk about them
and vice versa' means 'We talk about them
and they talk about us'*

vicinity *noun* (*plural* **vicinities**)
the neighbourhood or surrounding district
♦ *There are shops in the vicinity of their
house*

vicious *adjective* (*pronounced* **vish**-us)
1 cruel and aggressive **2** severe or violent
viciously *adverb* in a vicious way **viciousness**
noun being vicious

victim *noun* (*plural* **victims**)
1 a person who suffers from something
♦ *He is a polio victim* **2** someone who is
killed, injured, or robbed ♦ *The murderer
lay in wait for his victim*

victimize *verb* (**victimizes, victimizing, victimized**)
to victimize someone is to treat them
unfairly

victor *noun* (*plural* **victors**)
the winner of a battle or contest

Victorian *adjective*
belonging to the time when Queen Victoria reigned (1837–1901)

victory *noun* (*plural* **victories**)
success in a battle or contest or game
victorious *adjective* winning a victory

video ➤ *noun* (*plural* **videos**) (*pronounced* vid-i-oh)
1 the recording on tape of pictures and sound **2** a video recorder **3** a television programme or a film recorded on a video cassette

video ➤ *verb* (**videoes, videoing, videoed**)
to video something is to record it on videotape

video game *noun* (*plural* **video games**)
a game played on a computer, with special images on the screen

video recorder or **video cassette recorder** *noun* (*plural* **video recorders** or **video cassette recorders**)
a machine for recording television programmes and playing them back

videotape *noun* (*plural* **videotapes**)
magnetic tape used for video recording

view ➤ *noun* (*plural* **views**)
1 what you can see from one place
♦ *There's a fine view from the top of the hill*
2 someone's opinion ♦ *She has strong views about smoking*
in view of something because of it
on view shown for people to see

view ➤ *verb* (**views, viewing, viewed**)
1 to view something is to look at it carefully **2** to view something or someone in a certain way is to think about them in that way ♦ *He viewed us with suspicion*

viewer *noun* (*plural* **viewers**)
someone who views something, especially a television programme

vigilant *adjective* (*pronounced* vij-i-lant)
watching carefully for something
vigilantly *adverb* in a vigilant way **vigilance** *noun* being vigilant

vigorous *adjective*
full of strength and energy
vigorously *adverb* in a vigorous way

vigour *noun*
strength and energy

Viking *noun* (*plural* **Vikings**)
a Scandinavian pirate or trader in the 8th to 10th centuries

vile *adjective* (**viler, vilest**)
disgusting or bad ♦ *What a vile smell*

villa *noun* (*plural* **villas**)
a house, especially a large one in its own grounds, or one used for holidays abroad

village *noun* (*plural* **villages**)
a group of houses and other buildings in the country, smaller than a town
villager *noun* someone who lives in a village

villain *noun* (*plural* **villains**)
a wicked person or criminal
villainous *adjective* wicked **villainy** *noun* being wicked

vine *noun* (*plural* **vines**)
a plant on which grapes grow

vinegar *noun*
a sour liquid used to flavour food

vineyard *noun* (*plural* **vineyards**) (*pronounced* vin-yard)
an area of land where vines are grown to produce grapes for making wine

vintage *noun* (*plural* **vintages**)
1 all the grapes that are harvested in one season, or the wine made from them
2 the period from which something comes
♦ *The furniture is of 1920s vintage*

vintage car *noun* (*plural* **vintage cars**)
a car made between 1917 and 1930

vinyl *noun* (*pronounced* vy-nil)
a kind of plastic

viola *noun* (*plural* **violas**) (*pronounced* vee-oh-la)
a stringed instrument rather like a violin but slightly larger and with a lower pitch

violate *verb* (**violates, violating, violated**)
1 to violate a promise or a law is to break it **2** to violate a person or place is to treat them without respect
violation *noun* violating a law or promise
violator *noun* someone who violates a law or promise

violence *noun*
force that does harm or damage
violent *adjective* using violence **violently** *adverb* in a violent way

violet *noun* (*plural* **violets**)
1 purple **2** a small plant that usually has purple flowers

violin *noun* (*plural* **violins**)
a musical instrument with four strings,
played with a bow
violinist *noun* someone who plays a violin

VIP short for *very important person*
viper *noun* (*plural* **vipers**)
a small poisonous snake
virgin *noun* (*plural* **virgins**)
a person, especially a girl or woman, who
has not had sexual intercourse
virginity *noun* being a virgin
virtual *adjective*
amounting to the real thing in effect
♦ *His silence was a virtual admission of
guilt*
virtually *adverb*
in effect; nearly ♦ *She virtually admitted
it*
virtual reality *noun*
a computer image or environment that
imitates the real world and that you can
be part of
virtue *noun* (*plural* **virtues**)
1 virtue is moral goodness or excellence
2 a virtue is a particular kind of goodness
♦ *Honesty is a virtue*
virtuous *adjective* having virtue **virtuously**
adverb in a virtuous way
virus *noun* (*plural* **viruses**) (*pronounced*
vy-rus)
1 a microscopic creature that can cause
disease **2** a disease caused by a virus
♦ *The doctor said I had a virus* **3**
4 a hidden set of instructions in a
computer program that is designed to
destroy data
visa *noun* (*plural* **visas**)
an official mark put on someone's passport
by officials of a foreign country to show
that the holder of the passport has
permission to enter that country
visibility *noun*
the distance to which you can see clearly
♦ *Visibility is down to 20 metres*

visible *adjective*
able to be seen ♦ *The ship was visible on
the horizon*
visibly *adverb* so as to be seen
vision *noun* (*plural* **visions**)
1 vision is the power to see **2** a vision is
something that you see or imagine,
especially in a dream **3** vision is also
imagination and understanding ♦ *They
need a leader with vision*
visit ➤ *verb* (**visits**, **visiting**, **visited**)
to visit a place or person is to go to see
them or stay there
visit ➤ *noun* (*plural* **visits**)
a short stay at a place or with a person
visitor *noun* (*plural* **visitors**)
someone who is visiting or staying at a
place
visor *noun* (*plural* **visors**) (*pronounced*
vy-zer)
the part of a helmet that closes over the
face

visual *adjective*
to do with seeing; used for seeing
visually *adverb* as regards being seen
visual aid *noun* (*plural* **visual aids**)
a picture or film or video used in teaching
visual display unit *noun* (*plural* **visual display
units**)
a screen on which a computer displays
information
visualize *verb* (**visualizes**, **visualizing**, **visualized**)
to visualize something is to imagine it as
something you can see
vital *adjective*
1 connected with life; needed in order to
live **2** extremely important; essential ♦ *It
is vital that we catch the last bus*
vitally *adverb* in a vital way
vitality *noun*
liveliness or energy
vitamin *noun* (*plural* **vitamins**)
each of several substances which are
present in some foods and which you need
to stay healthy

vivid *adjective*
bright and clear ♦ *The colours are very vivid* ♦ *She gave a vivid description of the storm*
vividly *adverb* in a vivid way **vividness** *noun* being vivid

vivisection *noun*
doing surgical experiments on live animals as part of scientific research

vixen *noun* (*plural* **vixens**)
a female fox

vocabulary *noun* (*plural* **vocabularies**)
1 a list of words used in a language 2 the words that a person knows and uses

vocal *adjective*
to do with the voice; using the voice
vocally *adverb* in a vocal way

vocalist *noun* (*plural* **vocalists**)
a singer

vocation *noun* (*plural* **vocations**)
a job or activity that you feel strongly you want to do

vocational *adjective*
teaching you the skills you need for a particular job ♦ *They are going to have some vocational training*

vodka *noun* (*plural* **vodkas**)
a strong alcoholic drink especially popular in Russia

voice ➤ *noun* (*plural* **voices**)
1 the sound you make in speaking or singing 2 the power to speak or sing ♦ *She has lost her voice* 3 the right to say something ♦ *Do I get a voice in the decision?*

voice ➤ *verb* (**voices, voicing, voiced**)
to voice something is to say it clearly and strongly ♦ *He voiced their objections to the plan*

volcano *noun* (*plural* **volcanoes**)
a mountain with a hole at the top formed by molten lava which has burst through the earth's crust
volcanic *adjective* to do with volcanoes or produced by volcanoes

vole *noun* (*plural* **voles**)
a small animal rather like a rat

volley *noun* (*plural* **volleys**)
1 a number of bullets or shells fired at the same time 2 in ball games, hitting or kicking the ball back before it touches the ground

volleyball *noun*
a game in which two teams hit a large ball to and fro over a net with their hands

volt *noun* (*plural* **volts**)
a unit for measuring the force of an electric current

voltage *noun* (*plural* **voltages**)
electric force measured in volts

volume *noun* (*plural* **volumes**)
1 the amount of space filled by something 2 an amount ♦ *The volume of work has increased* 3 the strength or power of sound ♦ *Turn down the volume!* 4 a book, especially one of a set

voluntary *adjective*
done or doing something because you want to, not for pay
voluntarily *adverb* in a voluntary way

volunteer ➤ *verb* (**volunteers, volunteering, volunteered**)
1 to volunteer is to offer to do something that you do not have to do 2 to volunteer something is to provide it willingly or freely ♦ *Several people generously volunteered their time*

volunteer ➤ *noun* (*plural* **volunteers**)
someone who volunteers to do something

vomit *verb* (**vomits, vomiting, vomited**)
to vomit is to bring food back from the stomach through the mouth

vote ➤ *verb* (**votes, voting, voted**)
1 to vote for someone or something is to show which you prefer by putting up your hand or making a mark on a piece of paper 2 to vote to do something is to say that you want to do it ♦ *I vote we go away this weekend*

vote ➤ *noun* (*plural* **votes**)
1 the act of voting 2 the right to vote

voter *noun* (*plural* **voters**)
someone who votes, especially in an election

vouch *verb* (**vouches, vouching, vouched**)
to vouch for something or someone is to say they are genuine or reliable

voucher *noun* (*plural* **vouchers**)
a piece of paper showing that you have paid something or that you can get something in exchange

vow ➤ *noun* (*plural* **vows**)
a solemn promise, especially to God

vow ➤ *verb* (**vows, vowing, vowed**)
to vow is to make a vow

vowel *noun* (*plural* **vowels**)
any of the letters a, e, i, o, u, and sometimes y

voyage *noun* (*plural* **voyages**)
a long journey by ship or in space
voyager *noun* someone who goes on a voyage

vulgar *adjective*
rude; without good manners
vulgarly *adverb* in a vulgar way

vulgar fraction *noun* (*plural* **vulgar fractions**)
a fraction shown by numbers above and below a line (such as $\frac{1}{2}$ and $\frac{7}{8}$), not a decimal fraction

vulnerable *adjective*
able to be harmed or attacked easily

vulture *noun* (*plural* **vultures**)
a large bird that eats dead animals

vulva *noun* (*plural* **vulvas**)
the outer parts of the female genitals

Ww

wad *noun* (*plural* **wads**)
a pad or bundle of soft material or pieces of paper

waddle ➤ *verb* (**waddles, waddling, waddled**)
to waddle is to walk with short steps, rocking from side to side, as a duck does

waddle ➤ *noun* (*plural* **waddles**)
a waddling walk

wade *verb* (**wades, wading, waded**)
to wade through something such as water or mud is to walk with difficulty through it

wafer *noun* (*plural* **wafers**)
a thin kind of biscuit, often eaten with ice cream

wag ➤ *verb* (**wags, wagging, wagged**)
to wag is to move quickly to and fro; to wag something is to make it do this

wag ➤ *noun* (*plural* **wags**)
a wagging movement

wage ➤ *noun* or **wages** *plural noun*
the money paid to someone for the job they do

wage ➤ *verb* (**wages, waging, waged**)
to wage a war or campaign is to fight it

wager ➤ *noun* (*plural* **wagers**) (*pronounced* way-jer)
a bet

wager ➤ *verb* (**wagers, wagering, wagered**)
to wager someone is to make a bet with them

waggle *verb* (**waggles, waggling, waggled**)
to waggle something is to move it quickly to and fro

wagon *noun* (*plural* **wagons**)
1 a cart with four wheels, pulled by a horse or ox **2** an open railway truck

wagtail *noun* (*plural* **wagtails**)
a small bird with a long tail that it moves up and down when it is standing still

wail ➤ *verb* (**wails, wailing, wailed**)
to wail is to make a long sad cry

wail ➤ *noun* (*plural* **wails**)
a sound of wailing

waist *noun* (*plural* **waists**)
the narrow part in the middle of your body

waistcoat *noun* (*plural* **waistcoats**)
a close-fitting jacket without sleeves, worn over a shirt and under a jacket

wait ➤ *verb* (**waits, waiting, waited**)
1 to wait, or to wait for someone or something, is to stay in a place or situation until something happens **2** to wait is also to be a waiter

wait ➤ *noun* (*plural* **waits**)
a spell of waiting ♦ *We had a long wait for the bus*

waiter *noun* (*plural* **waiters**)
a man who serves people with food in a restaurant or hotel

waiting list *noun* (*plural* **waiting lists**)
a list of people waiting for something to become available

waiting room *noun* (*plural* **waiting rooms**)
a room provided for people who are waiting for something

waitress *noun* (*plural* **waitresses**)
a woman who serves people with food in a restaurant or hotel

waive *verb* (**waives, waiving, waived**)
to waive a right or privilege is to say you do not need it ♦ *She waived her right to a first-class seat*

wake [1] *verb* (**wakes, waking, woke, woken**)
1 to wake, or to wake up, is to stop sleeping **2** to wake someone is to make them stop sleeping ♦ *You have woken the baby*

wake [2] *noun* (*plural* **wakes**)
1 the trail left on the water by a ship
2 what is left when something is gone, or when something unusual has happened
♦ *The storm left a lot of damage in its wake*
in the wake of someone or **something** following or coming after them

waken *verb* (**wakens, wakening, wakened**)
to waken someone is to wake them

walk ➤ *verb* (**walks, walking, walked**)
to walk is to move along on your feet at an ordinary speed

walk ➤ *noun* (*plural* **walks**)
1 a journey on foot **2** the way that someone walks ♦ *He has a funny walk*
3 a path or route for walking ♦ *There are some lovely walks near here*

walkabout *noun* (*plural* **walkabouts**)
an informal stroll among a crowd by an important visitor

walker *noun* (*plural* **walkers**)
someone who goes for a walk, especially a long one

walkie-talkie *noun* (*plural* **walkie-talkies**)
a small portable radio transmitter and receiver

walking stick *noun* (*plural* **walking sticks**)
a stick carried or used as a support while walking

Walkman *noun* (*plural* **Walkmans**)
(*trademark*) a portable stereo cassette player

walk of life *noun* (*plural* **walks of life**)
a person's job or occupation

wall ➤ *noun* (*plural* **walls**)
1 a structure built of brick or stone and forming one of the sides of a building or room, or going round a garden or other space **2** the outer surface of something, such as the stomach

wall ➤ *verb* (**walls, walling, walled**)
to wall something, or wall it in, is to enclose it with a wall

wallaby *noun* (*plural* **wallabies**) (*pronounced* wol-a-bee)
a kind of small kangaroo

wallet *noun* (*plural* **wallets**)
a small flat folding case for holding banknotes, credit cards, and small documents

wallflower *noun* (*plural* **wallflowers**)
a sweet-smelling garden plant

wallop *verb* (**wallops, walloping, walloped**)
(*informal*) to wallop someone is to hit or beat them

wallow *verb* (**wallows, wallowing, wallowed**)
1 to wallow is to roll about in water or mud **2** to wallow in something is to get great pleasure from it ♦ *They are wallowing in luxury*

wallpaper *noun* (*plural* **wallpapers**)
paper used to cover the walls of rooms

walnut *noun* (*plural* **walnuts**)
a kind of nut with a wrinkled surface

walrus *noun* (*plural* **walruses**)
a large Arctic sea animal with two long tusks

waltz ➤ *noun* (*plural* **waltzes**)
a dance with three beats to a bar

waltz ➤ *verb* (**waltzes, waltzing, waltzed**)
to waltz is to dance a waltz

wand *noun* (*plural* **wands**)
a short thin rod, especially one used by a conjurer

wander *verb* (**wanders, wandering, wandered**)
1 to wander is to go about without trying to reach a particular place **2** to wander is also to stray or get lost ♦ *Don't let the sheep wander*

wanderer *noun* someone who wanders

wane *verb* (**wanes, waning, waned**)
1 the moon wanes when its bright area gets gradually smaller **2** to wane is to become less or smaller or less powerful ♦ *His popularity was waning*

wangle *verb* (**wangles, wangling, wangled**)
(*informal*) to wangle something is to get it or arrange it by trickery or clever planning

want ➤ *verb* (**wants, wanting, wanted**)
1 to want something is to feel that you would like to have it or do it **2** to want something is also to need it ♦ *Your hair wants cutting* **3** to be wanting something is to be without it or lacking it ♦ *My car is wanting one of its rear lights*

want ➤ *noun* (*plural* **wants**)
1 a wish to have something **2** a lack of something ♦ *They died for want of water*

wanted *adjective*
being looked for by the police as a suspected criminal ♦ *He was a wanted man*

war *noun* (*plural* **wars**)
1 war is fighting between nations or armies; a war is a period of fighting **2** a serious struggle or effort against an evil such as crime or disease

warble ➤ *verb* (warbles, warbling, warbled)
to warble is to sing gently, as some birds do

warble ➤ *noun* (*plural* warbles)
a warbling sound

warbler *noun* (*plural* warblers)
a kind of small bird

ward ➤ *noun* (*plural* wards)
1 a long room with beds for patients in a hospital 2 a child looked after by a guardian 3 an area of a town or city represented by a councillor

ward ➤ *verb* (wards, warding, warded)
to ward something off is to keep it away

-ward or **-wards** *suffix*
an ending for words such as *backward* and *homewards*, which show direction

warden *noun* (*plural* wardens)
1 an official in charge of a hostel or college, or who supervises something 2 a traffic warden

warder *noun* (*plural* warders)
an official in charge of prisoners in a prison

wardrobe *noun* (*plural* wardrobes)
1 a cupboard to hang clothes in 2 a stock of clothes or costumes

ware *noun* (*plural* wares)
manufactured goods, especially pottery
wares goods offered for sale

warehouse *noun* (*plural* warehouses)
a large building where goods are stored

warfare *noun*
fighting or waging war

warhead *noun* (*plural* warheads)
the explosive head of a missile

warlike *adjective*
fond of fighting; ready for war

warm ➤ *adjective* (warmer, warmest)
1 fairly hot; not cold or cool
2 enthusiastic or friendly ♦ *They gave us a warm welcome* 3 (*informal*) close to the right answer, or to something hidden ♦ *You're getting warm now*
warmly *adverb* in a warm or friendly way
warmth *noun* being warm

warm ➤ *verb* (warms, warming, warmed)
1 to warm something or someone is to make them warm 2 to warm, or warm up, is to become warm

warn *verb* (warns, warning, warned)
to warn someone is to tell them about a danger or difficulty that might affect them

warning *noun* (*plural* warnings)
something said or written to warn someone

warp ➤ *verb* (warps, warping, warped)
(*pronounced* worp)
1 to warp something is to bend or twist it out of shape because of dampness or heat; to warp is to be bent or twisted in this way
2 to warp someone's ideas or judgement is to distort them ♦ *Jealousy warped his mind*

warp ➤ *noun*
1 being warped 2 the lengthwise threads in weaving, crossed by the weft

warrant ➤ *noun* (*plural* warrants)
a document that entitles a person to do something, especially to arrest someone or search a place

warrant ➤ *verb* (warrants, warranting, warranted)
to warrant something is to justify or deserve it ♦ *Nothing warrants such rudeness*

warren *noun* (*plural* warrens)
a piece of ground where there are many rabbit burrows

warrior *noun* (*plural* warriors)
someone who fights in battles; a soldier

warship *noun* (*plural* warships)
a ship designed for use in war

wart *noun* (*plural* warts)
a small hard lump on the skin

wary *adjective* (warier, wariest)
cautious and careful
warily *adverb* in a wary way **wariness** *noun* being wary

was 1st and 3rd person singular past tense of **be**

wash ➤ *verb* (washes, washing, washed)
1 to wash something is to clean it with water 2 to wash is to flow over or against something ♦ *Waves washed over the beach* 3 to wash someone or something somewhere is to carry them along by means of moving liquid ♦ *The boxes were washed overboard* 4 (*informal*) to wash is to be accepted or believed ♦ *That story won't wash*
to wash up is to wash the dishes and cutlery after a meal

wash ➤ *noun* (*plural* washes)
1 the action of washing 2 the disturbed water behind a moving ship 3 a thin coating of colour

washable *adjective*
able to be washed without being damaged

washbasin *noun* (*plural* **washbasins**)
a small basin with taps, holding water for washing your hands and face

washer *noun* (*plural* **washers**)
1 a small ring of metal or rubber placed between two surfaces, especially under a bolt or screw, to fit them tightly together
2 a washing machine

washing *noun*
clothes that need washing or have been washed

washing machine *noun* (*plural* **washing machines**)
a machine for washing clothes

washing-up *noun*
washing the dishes and cutlery after a meal

wash-out *noun* (*plural* **wash-outs**)
(*slang*) a complete failure

wasn't short for *was not*

wasp *noun* (*plural* **wasps**)
a stinging insect with black and yellow stripes across its body

wastage *noun*
losing something by waste

waste ➤ *verb* (**wastes, wasting, wasted**)
1 to waste something is to use more of it than you need to, or to use it without getting much value from it 2 to waste something is also to fail to use it ♦ *You are wasting a good opportunity* 3 to waste is to become weak or useless

waste ➤ *adjective*
1 left over or thrown away because it is not wanted ♦ *What shall we do with all this waste paper?* 2 not used or usable ♦ *We came to an area of waste land*

waste ➤ *noun* (*plural* **wastes**)
1 a waste is wasting something or not using it well ♦ *It's a waste of time*
2 waste is things that are not wanted or used 3 a waste is also an area of desert or frozen land ♦ *We flew over the wastes of Alaska*

wasteful *adjective*
wasting things or not using them well
wastefully *adverb* in a wasteful way

watch ➤ *verb* (**watches, watching, watched**)
1 to watch someone or something is to look at them for some time 2 to watch is to be on guard or ready for something to happen ♦ *Watch for the light to change* 3 to watch something is also to take care of it ♦ *His job is to watch the sheep*
watcher *noun* someone who watches

watch ➤ *noun* (*plural* **watches**)
1 a device like a small clock, usually worn on the wrist 2 the action of watching 3 a period of duty on a ship

watchdog *noun* (*plural* **watchdogs**)
a dog kept to guard buildings

watchful *adjective*
alert and watching carefully
watchfully *adverb* in a watchful way
watchfulness *noun* being watchful

watchman *noun* (*plural* **watchmen**)
someone whose job is to guard a building at night

water ➤ *noun* (*plural* **waters**)
1 water is a transparent colourless liquid that is a compound of hydrogen and oxygen 2 a water is a sea or lake 3 water is also the state of the tide ♦ *The sea is at high water*
to pass water is to urinate

water ➤ *verb* (**waters, watering, watered**)
1 to water something is to sprinkle water over it ♦ *Have you watered the plants?*
2 to water an animal is to give it water to drink 3 to water is to produce water or tears or saliva ♦ *The smell of toast makes my mouth water*
to water something down is to dilute it or make it weaker

water closet *noun* (*plural* **water closets**)
a lavatory with a pan that is flushed by water

watercolour *noun* (*plural* **watercolours**)
1 a paint that can be mixed with water
2 a painting done with this kind of paint

watercress *noun*
a kind of cress that grows in water

waterfall *noun* (*plural* **waterfalls**)
a place where a river or stream flows over a cliff or large rock

watering can *noun* (*plural* **watering cans**)
a container with a long spout, for watering plants

waterlogged *adjective*
completely soaked or filled with water

watermark *noun* (*plural* **watermarks**)
1 a mark showing the level of water 2 a design in some types of paper, visible when held up to the light

watermelon *noun* (*plural* **watermelons**)
a large melon with a smooth green skin and red juicy flesh.

waterproof *adjective*
able to keep water out

water-skiing *noun*
the sport of skimming over the surface of water on flat boards (**water-skis**) while being towed by a motor boat

watertight *adjective*
1 made so that water cannot get into it
2 completely certain or secure ♦ *He has a watertight excuse*

waterway *noun* (*plural* **waterways**)
a river or canal that ships can travel on

waterworks *noun* (*plural* **waterworks**)
a place with pumping machinery for supplying water to a district

watery *adjective*
1 like water 2 full of water ♦ *You have watery eyes*

watt *noun* (*plural* **watts**)
a unit of electric power

wave ➤ *verb* (**waves, waving, waved**)
1 to wave is to move your hand to and fro, usually to say hello or goodbye 2 to wave something is to move it to and fro or up and down 3 to wave hair is to make it curl

wave ➤ *noun* (*plural* **waves**)
1 a moving ridge on the surface of water, especially on the sea 2 a curling piece of hair 3 a sudden build-up of something strong ♦ *There was a wave of anger* 4 (*in Science*) one of the to-and-fro movements in which sound and light and electricity travel 5 the action of waving your hand

waveband *noun* (*plural* **wavebands**)
the wavelengths between certain limits

wavelength *noun* (*plural* **wavelengths**)
the size of a sound wave or electric wave

waver *verb* (**wavers, wavering, wavered**)
1 to waver is to be unsteady or uncertain ♦ *They wavered between two choices* 2 to waver is also to move unsteadily

wavy *adjective* (**wavier, waviest**)
full of waves or curves

wax[1] ➤ *noun* (*plural* **waxes**)
a soft substance that melts easily, used for making candles, crayons, and polish
waxy *adjective* like wax

wax ➤ *verb* (**waxes, waxing, waxed**)
to wax something is to cover it with wax

wax[2] *verb* (**waxes, waxing, waxed**)
the moon waxes when its bright area gets gradually larger

waxwork *noun* (*plural* **waxworks**)
a model made of wax, especially a full-size model of a person

way *noun* (*plural* **ways**)
1 a road or path leading from one place to another 2 a route; the direction or distance to a place 3 how something is done; a method 4 a respect ♦ *It's a good idea in some ways* 5 a condition or state ♦ *Things are in a bad way*
to get your own way is to make people let you have what you want
in the way forming a hindrance or difficulty
no way (*informal*) that is impossible; that is not true

WC short for **water closet**, used especially on a plan or a sign showing where a lavatory is

we *pronoun*
a word used by someone to mean 'I and someone else' or 'I and others'

weak *adjective* (**weaker, weakest**)
not strong; easy to break, bend, or defeat
weakly *adverb* in a weak way **weakness** *noun* being weak

weaken *verb* (**weakens, weakening, weakened**)
1 to weaken something is to make it weaker 2 to weaken is to become weaker

weakling *noun* (*plural* **weaklings**)
a weak person

wealth *noun*
1 wealth is a lot of money or property 2 a wealth of something is a lot of it ♦ *The book has a wealth of illustrations*

wealthy *adjective* (**wealthier, wealthiest**)
having a lot of money or property

weapon *noun* (*plural* **weapons**)
something used to harm or kill people in a battle or fight

wear ➤ *verb* (**wears, wearing, wore, worn**)
1 to wear something is to be dressed in it
2 to wear something is to damage it by rubbing or using it; to wear is to become damaged like this ♦ *The carpet has worn thin* 3 to last ♦ *This cloth wears well*
to wear off is to become less strong or intense
to wear out is to become weak or useless
wearer *noun* someone who wears something

wear ➤ *noun*
1 what you wear; clothes ♦ *Where can I find men's wear?* 2 gradual damage done by rubbing or using something

weary *adjective* (**wearier, weariest**)
not having any more energy; tired

wearily *adverb* in a weary way **weariness** *noun* being weary

weasel *noun* (*plural* **weasels**)
a small fierce animal with a slender body

weather ➤ *noun*
the rain, snow, wind, sunshine, and temperature at a particular time or place
under the weather feeling ill or depressed

weather ➤ *verb* (**weathers, weathering, weathered**)
1 to weather is to become worn because of being exposed to the weather 2 to weather something is to make it suffer the effects of the weather ♦ *The wind and rain have weathered the cliffs* 3 to weather a difficulty is to come through it successfully ♦ *They weathered the storm*

weathercock *noun* (*plural* **weathercocks**)
a pointer, often shaped like a cockerel, that turns in the wind and shows which way the wind is blowing

weave *verb* (**weaves, weaving, wove, woven**)
1 to weave material or baskets is to make them by crossing threads or strips over and under each other 2 to weave is to twist and turn ♦ *He wove skilfully through the traffic*
weaver *noun* someone who weaves material

web *noun* (*plural* **webs**)
1 a cobweb 2 something complicated ♦ *We were caught up in a web of lies* 3 a computer network, especially the internet

webbed or **web-footed** *adjective*
having toes joined by pieces of skin, as ducks do

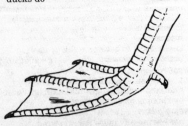

website *noun* (*plural* **websites**)
a place on the internet where you can get information.

wed *verb* (**weds, wedding, wedded** or **wed**)
to wed someone is to marry them

we'd short for *we had* or *we should* or *we would*

wedding *noun* (*plural* **weddings**)
the ceremony when a man and woman get married

wedge ➤ *noun* (*plural* **wedges**)
a piece of wood or metal or plastic that is thick at one end and thin at the other, pushed between things to force them apart or to hold them tight
the thin end of the wedge a situation which is not bad yet but might get worse

wedge ➤ *verb* (**wedges, wedging, wedged**)
to wedge something is to hold it in place, especially with a wedge

Wednesday *noun* (*plural* **Wednesdays**)
the fourth day of the week

weed ➤ *noun* (*plural* **weeds**)
a wild plant that grows where it is not wanted

weed ➤ *verb* (**weeds, weeding, weeded**)
to weed the ground is to remove weeds from it

weedy *adjective* (**weedier, weediest**)
1 full of weeds 2 weak or thin

week *noun* (*plural* **weeks**)
a period of seven days, especially from Sunday to the following Saturday

weekday *noun* (*plural* **weekdays**)
any day except Saturday and Sunday

weekend *noun* (*plural* **weekends**)
Saturday and Sunday

weekly *adjective* and *adverb*
every week

weep *verb* (**weeps, weeping, wept**)
to weep is to cry or shed tears

weeping willow *noun* (*plural* **weeping willows**)
a kind of willow tree that has drooping branches

weft *noun*
the threads on a loom that are woven across the warp

weigh *verb* (**weighs, weighing, weighed**)
1 to weigh something is to find out how heavy it is 2 to weigh a certain amount is to have that as its weight ♦ *My dad weighs ten stone*
to weigh anchor is to raise the anchor and start a voyage
to weigh someone down is to depress or trouble them
to weigh something down is to hold it down with something heavy

to weigh something up is to estimate or assess it

weight *noun* (*plural* **weights**)
1 weight is the measure of how heavy something is **2** a weight is a piece of metal of known weight, used on scales to weigh things **3** a weight is also a heavy object, used to hold things down
weightless *adjective* having no weight

weightlifting *noun*
the sport or exercise of lifting heavy weights

weighty *adjective* (**weightier, weightiest**)
1 heavy **2** important

weir *noun* (*plural* **weirs**) (*pronounced* weer)
a small dam across a river or canal to control the flow of water

weird *adjective* (**weirder, weirdest**) (*pronounced* weerd)
very strange or unnatural
weirdly *adverb* in a weird way **weirdness** *noun* being weird

welcome ➤ *noun* (*plural* **welcomes**)
a kind or friendly greeting or reception

welcome ➤ *adjective*
1 that you are glad to get or see ♦ *This is a welcome surprise* **2** allowed or free to do or take something ♦ *You are welcome to use my bicycle*

welcome ➤ *verb* (**welcomes, welcoming, welcomed**)
to welcome someone or something is to show that you are pleased when they arrive

weld *verb* (**welds, welding, welded**)
to weld pieces of metal or plastic together is to join them by using heat or pressure
welder *noun* someone who welds things together

welfare *noun*
people's health, happiness, and comfort

welfare state *noun*
a system of paying for health care and other social services from public funds

well[1] *noun* (*plural* **wells**)
a deep hole dug or drilled to get water or oil out of the ground

well[2] ➤ *adverb* (**better, best**)
1 in a good or right way ♦ *He swims well* **2** actually; probably ♦ *It may well be our last chance*
well off fairly rich or fortunate

well ➤ *adjective*
1 in good health ♦ *She is not well* **2** good or satisfactory ♦ *All is well*

we'll short for *we shall* or *we will*

well-being *noun*
health or happiness

well-disposed *adjective*
to be well-disposed towards someone is to have friendly feelings for them

wellington boots or **wellingtons** *plural noun*
rubber or plastic waterproof boots

well-known *adjective*
known to many people

well-mannered *adjective*
having good manners

went past tense of **go** *verb*

wept past tense and past participle of **weep**

were plural and 2nd person singular past tense of **be**

we're short for *we are*

werewolf *noun* (*plural* **werewolves**)
in stories, a person who sometimes changes into a wolf

west ➤ *noun*
1 the direction where the sun sets **2** the part of a country or city that is in this direction

west ➤ *adjective and adverb*
1 towards the west or in the west **2** coming from the west ♦ *There was a west wind blowing*

westerly *adjective*
a westerly wind is one that blows from the west

western ➤ *adjective*
from or to do with the west

western ➤ *noun* (*plural* **westerns**)
a film or story about the people of western America in the 19th century and early 20th century

westward or **westwards** *adjective and adverb*
towards the west

wet ➤ *adjective* (**wetter, wettest**)
1 covered or soaked in water or other liquid **2** not yet set or dry ♦ *Watch out for wet paint* **3** rainy ♦ *We're getting wet weather*
wetness *noun* being wet

wet ➤ *verb* (**wets, wetting, wetted**)
to wet something is to make it wet

wet blanket *noun* (*plural* **wet blankets**)
someone who is gloomy and who prevents other people from enjoying themselves

wet suit *noun* (*plural* **wet suits**)
a rubber suit that clings to the skin, worn by skin divers and windsurfers to keep them warm and dry

we've short for *we have*

whack ➤ *verb* (**whacks, whacking, whacked**)
to whack someone or something is to hit them hard

whack ➤ *noun* (*plural* **whacks**)
a hard hit or blow

whale *noun* (*plural* **whales**)
a very large sea animal
to have a whale of a time (*informal*) is to enjoy yourself

whaler *noun* (*plural* **whalers**)
a person or ship that hunts whales

whaling *noun*
hunting whales

wharf *noun* (*plural* **wharves** or **wharfs**)
(*pronounced* worf)
a quay where ships are loaded or unloaded

what ➤ *adjective*
1 used to ask the amount or kind of something ♦ *What kind of bike have you got?* **2** used to say how strange or great a person or thing is ♦ *What a fool you are!*

what ➤ *pronoun*
1 what thing or things ♦ *What did you say?* **2** the thing that ♦ *This is what you must do*
what's what (*informal*) what is important or useful ♦ *She knows what's what*

whatever ➤ *pronoun*
1 anything or everything ♦ *Do whatever you like* **2** no matter what ♦ *Whatever happens*

whatever ➤ *adjective*
of any kind or amount ♦ *Get whatever help you can*

wheat *noun*
a cereal plant from which flour is made

wheel ➤ *noun* (*plural* **wheels**)
1 a round device that turns on an axle passing through its centre **2** a horizontal revolving disc on which clay is made into a pot

wheel ➤ *verb* (**wheels, wheeling, wheeled**)
1 to wheel a bicycle or cart is to push it along on its wheels **2** to wheel is to move in a curve or circle ♦ *The column of soldiers wheeled to the right*

wheelbarrow *noun* (*plural* **wheelbarrows**)
a small cart with one wheel at the front and two handles at the back

wheelchair *noun* (*plural* **wheelchairs**)
a chair on wheels for a person who cannot walk

wheel clamp *noun* (*plural* **wheel clamps**)
a device that can be locked around a vehicle's wheel to immobilize it

wheeze *verb* (**wheezes, wheezing, wheezed**)
to wheeze is to make a whistling or gasping noise as you breathe

whelk *noun* (*plural* **whelks**)
a shellfish that looks like a snail

when ➤ *adverb*
at what time ♦ *When can you come to tea?*

when ➤ *conjunction*
1 at the time that ♦ *The bird flew away when I moved* **2** because; considering that ♦ *Why do you smoke when you know it is dangerous?*

whenever *conjunction*
at any time; every time ♦ *Whenever I see him, he's smiling*

where *adverb* and *conjunction*
1 in or to what place ♦ *Where have you put the glue?* **2** in or to that place ♦ *Leave it where it is*

whereabouts ➤ *adverb*
roughly where; in what area ♦ *Whereabouts is Timbuktu?*

whereabouts ➤ *noun*
the place where something is ♦ *Have you any idea of her whereabouts?*

whereas *conjunction*
but on the other hand ♦ *Some people like sailing, whereas others hate it*

whereupon *adverb*
after that; and then

wherever *adverb* and *conjunction*
in or to whatever place; no matter where

whether *conjunction*
used to introduce more than one possibility ♦ *I don't know whether they are here or not*

whey *noun* (*pronounced* way)
the watery liquid left when milk forms curds

which ➤ *adjective*
what particular ♦ *Which way did he go?*

which ➤ *pronoun*
1 what person or thing ♦ *Which is your desk?* **2** the person or thing just mentioned ♦ *Here's my book, which you asked me to bring*

whichever *pronoun* and *adjective*
that or those which; any which ♦ *Take whichever you like*

whiff *noun* (*plural* whiffs)
a puff or slight smell of something

while ➤ *conjunction*
1 during the time that; as long as ♦ *She was singing while she worked* **2** but; although ♦ *She is fair, while her sister is dark*

while ➤ *noun*
a period of time ♦ *We have waited all this while*

while ➤ *verb* (whiles, whiling, whiled)
to while away time is to pass it doing something leisurely ♦ *We whiled away the afternoon by playing cards*

whilst *conjunction*
while

whimper ➤ *verb* (whimpers, whimpering, whimpered)
to whimper is to cry with a low trembling voice

whimper ➤ *noun* (*plural* whimpers)
a sound of whimpering

whine ➤ *verb* (whines, whining, whined)
1 to whine is to make a long high piercing sound **2** to whine is also to complain in a feeble way

whine ➤ *noun* (*plural* whines)
a whining sound

whinny *verb* (whinnies, whinnying, whinnied)
to whinny is to neigh gently, as a horse does

whip ➤ *noun* (*plural* whips)
a cord or strip of leather fixed to a handle and used for hitting people or animals

whip ➤ *verb* (whips, whipping, whipped)
1 to whip a person or animal is to beat them with a whip **2** to whip cream is to beat it until it becomes thick and frothy **3** (*informal*) to whip something is to steal it

to whip something out (*informal*) is to take it out quickly or suddenly

to whip something up is to stir up people's feelings ♦ *They quickly whipped up support for their ideas*

whirl ➤ *verb* (whirls, whirling, whirled)
to whirl is to turn or spin very quickly; to whirl something is to cause it to do this

whirl ➤ *noun* (*plural* whirls)
a whirling movement

whirlpool *noun* (*plural* whirlpools)
a strong current of water going round in a circle and pulling things towards it

whirlwind *noun* (*plural* whirlwinds)
a very strong wind that whirls around or blows in a spiral

whirr ➤ *verb* (whirrs, whirring, whirred)
to whirr is to make a continuous buzzing sound

whirr ➤ *noun* (*plural* whirrs)
a whirring sound

whisk ➤ *verb* (whisks, whisking, whisked)
1 to whisk something is to move it very quickly ♦ *A waiter whisked away my plate* **2** to whisk cream or eggs is to beat them until they are thick or frothy

whisk ➤ *noun* (*plural* whisks)
1 a device for whisking eggs or cream **2** a whisking movement

whisker *noun* (*plural* whiskers)
a hair growing on the face of a person or animal

whisky *noun* (*plural* whiskies)
a kind of very strong alcoholic drink

whisper ➤ *verb* (whispers, whispering, whispered)
to whisper is to speak very softly or secretly

whisper ➤ *noun* (*plural* whispers)
a whispering voice or sound

whist *noun*
a card game usually for four people

whistle ➤ *verb* (whistles, whistling, whistled)
to whistle is to make a shrill or musical sound by blowing through your lips
whistler *noun* someone who whistles

whistle ➤ *noun* (*plural* whistles)
1 a whistling sound 2 a device that makes a shrill sound when you blow into it

white ➤ *adjective* (whiter, whitest)
1 of the very lightest colour, like snow or milk 2 having light-coloured skin 3 white coffee is coffee with milk
whiteness *noun* being white **whitish** *adjective* rather white

white ➤ *noun* (*plural* whites)
1 a white colour 2 the substance round the yolk of an egg, which turns white when it is cooked

white elephant *noun* (*plural* white elephants)
a useless possession

white-hot *adjective*
extremely hot; so hot that heated metal looks white

whiten *verb* (whitens, whitening, whitened)
1 to whiten something is to make it white
2 to whiten is to become white

whitewash ➤ *noun*
a white liquid made from lime and chalk and painted on walls and ceilings

whitewash ➤ *verb* (whitewashes, whitewashing, whitewashed)
to whitewash something is to coat it with whitewash

Whitsun *noun*
Whit Sunday, or the period around it

Whit Sunday *noun*
the seventh Sunday after Easter

whiz *verb* (whizzes, whizzing, whizzed)
1 to whiz is to move very quickly 2 to whiz is also to sound like something rushing through the air

who *pronoun*
1 which person or people ♦ *Who threw that?* 2 the person or people spoken about ♦ *These are the boys who did it*

whoever *pronoun*
any person who ♦ *Whoever comes is welcome*

whole ➤ *adjective*
complete; not broken or damaged

whole ➤ *noun* (*plural* wholes)
a complete thing
on the whole considering everything; mainly

wholefood *noun* (*plural* wholefoods)
food that has not been processed or produced with artificial fertilizers

wholemeal *adjective*
made from the whole grain of wheat

whole number *noun* (*plural* whole numbers)
a number without a fraction

wholesale *adjective* and *adverb*
1 sold in large quantities to be sold again by others 2 on a large scale; including everybody or everything ♦ *There has been wholesale destruction*

wholesome *adjective*
good for health; healthy ♦ *We all need wholesome food*

wholly *adverb*
completely or entirely

whom *pronoun*
a word used for *who* when it is the object of a verb or comes after a preposition, as in *the boy whom I saw* or *the boy to whom I spoke*

whoop *noun* (*plural* whoops) (*pronounced* woop)
a loud excited cry

whoopee *interjection* (*pronounced* wuup-ee)
a cry of joy

whooping cough *noun* (*pronounced* hoop-ing-kof)
an illness that makes you cough and gasp

who's short for *who has* or *who is*

whose *adjective* and *pronoun*
1 belonging to what person ♦ *Whose bike is that?* 2 of which; of whom ♦ *The girl whose party we went to*

why *adverb*
for what reason or purpose

wick *noun* (*plural* wicks)
1 the string that goes through the middle of a candle and is lit to give a flame 2 the strip of material that you light in a lamp or heater that uses oil

wicked *adjective* (wickeder, wickedest)
1 very bad or cruel; doing things that are wrong 2 mischievous ♦ *He gave a wicked smile* 3 (*slang*) very fine or good ♦ *He makes wicked cakes*
wickedly *adverb* in a wicked way **wickedness** *noun* being wicked

wicker or **wickerwork** *noun*
things made of reeds or canes woven together

wicket *noun* (*plural* wickets)
1 in cricket, each set of three stumps with two bails on top of them 2 the part of a cricket ground between or near the wickets

wicketkeeper *noun* (*plural* wicketkeepers)
the fielder in cricket who stands behind the batsman's wicket

wide ➤ *adjective* (**wider**, **widest**)
1 measuring a lot from one side to the other ♦ *The river was wide* 2 from one side to the other ♦ *The room is 4 metres wide* 3 covering a large range ♦ *She has wide knowledge of birds*

wide ➤ *adverb* (**wider**, **widest**)
1 completely; fully ♦ *He is wide awake*
2 far from the target ♦ *The shot went wide*
3 over a large area ♦ *She travelled far and wide*

widely *adverb*
commonly; among many people ♦ *They are widely admired*

widen *verb* (**widens**, **widening**, **widened**)
to widen something is to make it wider; to widen is to become wider

widespread *adjective*
existing in many places; common

widow *noun* (*plural* **widows**)
a woman whose husband has died

widower *noun* (*plural* **widowers**)
a man whose wife has died

width *noun* (*plural* **widths**)
how wide something is

wield *verb* (**wields**, **wielding**, **wielded**)
(*pronounced* weeld)
to wield something is to hold it and use it ♦ *He wielded a sword*

wife *noun* (*plural* **wives**)
the woman that a man has married

wig *noun* (*plural* **wigs**)
a covering of false hair worn on the head

wiggle ➤ *verb* (**wiggles**, **wiggling**, **wiggled**)
to wiggle is to move from side to side

wiggle ➤ *noun* (*plural* **wiggles**)
a wiggling movement

wigwam *noun* (*plural* **wigwams**)
the tent of a Native American

wild *adjective* (**wilder**, **wildest**)
1 living or growing in its natural state and not looked after by people 2 very foolish or unreasonable ♦ *They do have wild ideas* 3 not controlled; violent ♦ *His behaviour became more and more wild*

wildly *adverb* in a wild way **wildness** *noun* being wild

wildebeest *noun* (*plural* **wildebeest**, **wildebeests**) (*pronounced* wil-di-beest)
a gnu.

wilderness *noun* (*plural* **wildernesses**)
an area of wild country; a desert

wildlife *noun*
wild animals in their natural setting

wilful *adjective*
1 determined to do what you want ♦ *What a wilful child* 2 deliberate ♦ *This is wilful disobedience*

wilfully *adverb* in a wilful way **wilfulness** *noun* being wilful

will [1] *verb* (*past tense* **would**)
used to refer to the future ♦ *They will like this*

will [2] *noun* (*plural* **wills**)
1 will is the power to use your mind to decide and control what you do
2 someone's will is what they choose or want ♦ *The people's will must be done* 3 a will is a legal document saying what is to be done with someone's possessions after they die

willing *adjective*
ready and happy to do what is wanted

willingly *adverb* in a willing way **willingness** *noun* being willing

willow *noun* (*plural* **willows**)
a tree with thin flexible branches, often growing near water

wilt *verb* (**wilts**, **wilting**, **wilted**)
to wilt is to lose freshness and droop, as plants do

wily *adjective* (**wilier**, **wiliest**)
crafty or cunning

wiliness *noun* being wily

wimp *noun* (*plural* **wimps**)
(*informal*) a feeble or timid person

win ➤ *verb* (**wins**, **winning**, **won**)
1 to win a contest or game or battle is to do better than your opponents 2 to win something is to get it by using effort or skill ♦ *She won the prize*

win ➤ *noun* (*plural* **wins**)
a success or victory

wince *verb* (**winces**, **wincing**, **winced**)
to wince is to make a slight movement because you are in pain or embarrassed

winch ➤ *noun* (*plural* **winches**)
a device for lifting or pulling things, using a rope or cable that goes round a wheel or drum

winch ➤ *verb* (**winches**, **winching**, **winched**)
to winch something is to lift it or pull it with a winch

wind[1] *noun* (*plural* **winds**) (*rhymes with* tinned)

1 a current of air **2** gas in the stomach or intestines that makes you uncomfortable **3** breath used for a purpose, such as running **4** the wind instruments of an orchestra

to get or **have the wind up** (*slang*) is to be scared

wind[2] *verb* (**winds, winding, wound**) (*rhymes with* find)

1 to wind is to turn or go in twists or curves or circles **2** to wind, or wind up, a watch or clock is to tighten its spring so that it works

to wind up somewhere is to end up there
♦ *They wound up in gaol*

windfall *noun* (*plural* **windfalls**)

1 a fruit blown down from a tree **2** a piece of unexpected good luck, especially a sum of money

wind instrument *noun* (*plural* **wind instruments**)

a musical instrument played by blowing, such as a trumpet or clarinet

windmill *noun* (*plural* **windmills**)

a mill with four long arms called *sails* which are turned by the wind

window *noun* (*plural* **windows**)

1 an opening in a wall or roof to let in light and air, usually filled with glass **2** the glass in a window opening **3** (*in Computing*) an area on a VDU screen used for a particular purpose

window shopping *noun*

browsing in shop windows without buying anything

windpipe *noun* (*plural* **windpipes**)

the tube through which air reaches the lungs

windscreen *noun* (*plural* **windscreens**)

the window at the front of a motor vehicle

windsurfing *noun*

surfing on a board with a sail fixed to it
windsurfer *noun* someone who goes windsurfing

windward *adjective*

facing the wind, especially on a ship

windy *adjective* (**windier, windiest**)

with much wind

wine *noun* (*plural* **wines**)

1 an alcoholic drink made from grapes or other plants **2** a dark red colour

wing ➤ *noun* (*plural* **wings**)

1 each of the parts of a bird or insect used for flying **2** each of the long flat parts that stick out from an aircraft and support it in the air **3** a part of a building that extends from the main part **4** each side of a theatre stage, out of sight of the audience **5** the part of a motor vehicle's body above a wheel **6** each of the players in football and other ball games whose place is at the side of the field **7** a section of a political party, having particular views

on the wing flying
to take wing is to fly away

winged *adjective* having wings **wingless** *adjective* without wings

wing ➤ *verb* (**wings, winging, winged**)

1 to wing someone is to wound them in the side **2** a bird wings its way when it flies a long way

wingspan *noun* (*plural* **wingspans**)

the distance across the wings of a bird or aeroplane

wink ➤ *verb* (**winks, winking, winked**)

1 to wink is to close and open your eye quickly **2** to wink is also to flicker or twinkle

wink ➤ *noun* (*plural* **winks**)

1 the action of winking **2** a short period of sleep ♦ *I didn't sleep a wink*

winkle ➤ *noun* (*plural* **winkles**)

a shellfish that is used for food

winkle ➤ *verb* (**winkles, winkling, winkled**)

to winkle something out is to find it with a lot of effort

winner *noun* (*plural* **winners**)

1 a person who wins something **2** (*informal*) something very successful
♦ *Her new book is a winner*

winnings *plural noun*

money won in a game or by betting

winter *noun* (*plural* **winters**)

the coldest season of the year, between autumn and spring

wintry *adjective* cold like winter

wintertime *noun*

the season of winter

wipe ➤ *verb* (**wipes, wiping, wiped**)

to wipe something is to dry it or clean it by rubbing it

to wipe something out is to destroy it or cancel it ♦ *He's wiped out his debt*

wipe ➣ *noun* (*plural* **wipes**)
the action of wiping ♦ *Give it a quick wipe*

wiper *noun* (*plural* **wipers**)
a device for wiping something, especially on a vehicle's windscreen

wire ➣ *noun* (*plural* **wires**)
1 a thin length of covered metal used to carry electric current 2 (*informal*) a telegram

wire ➣ *verb* (**wires, wiring, wired**)
1 to wire something is to connect it with wires to carry electricity 2 to wire something is also to fasten it or strengthen it with wire

wireless *noun* (*plural* **wirelesses**)
(*old use*) a radio set

wiring *noun*
the system of wires carrying electricity in a building or in a device

wiry *adjective* (**wirier, wiriest**)
1 thin and tough like wire 2 lean and strong

wisdom *noun*
1 being wise 2 wise sayings or writings

wisdom tooth *noun* (*plural* **wisdom teeth**)
a molar tooth that may grow at the back of your jaw much later than the other teeth

wise *adjective* (**wiser, wisest**)
knowing or understanding many things
none the wiser not knowing any more about something than before
wisely *adverb* in a wise way

wish ➣ *verb* (**wishes, wishing, wished**)
1 to wish something, or to do something, is to think or say that you would like it 2 to wish someone something is to say that you hope they will get it ♦ *They wished us luck*

wish ➣ *noun* (*plural* **wishes**)
1 something you want 2 the action of wishing ♦ *Make a wish* ♦ *We send you our best wishes*

wishbone *noun* (*plural* **wishbones**)
a forked bone from the breast of a chicken or other bird

wisp *noun* (*plural* **wisps**)
a thin piece of something light or fluffy
wispy *adjective* in the form of wisps

wistful *adjective*
sadly longing for something
wistfully *adverb* in a wistful way **wistfulness** *noun* being wistful

wit *noun* (*plural* **wits**)
1 wit is intelligence or cleverness 2 wit is also a clever kind of humour 3 a wit is a witty person
to keep your wits about you is to stay alert

witch *noun* (*plural* **witches**)
a woman who is believed to use magic

witchcraft *noun*
using magic, especially to make bad things happen

witch doctor *noun* (*plural* **witch doctors**)
a magician who belongs to a tribe and is thought to heal people

with *preposition*
there are many meanings, of which the most important are: 1 having ♦ *I saw a man with a wooden leg* 2 in the company of or accompanied by ♦ *I came with a friend* 3 using ♦ *Hit it with a hammer* 4 against ♦ *They fought with each other* 5 because of ♦ *He shook with laughter* 6 towards or concerning ♦ *Be careful with that*

withdraw *verb* (**withdraws, withdrawing, withdrew, withdrawn**)
1 to withdraw something is to take it away or take it back ♦ *She withdrew her offer* 2 to withdraw is to retreat or leave ♦ *The troops have withdrawn from the frontier*
withdrawal *noun* withdrawing, or withdrawing something

wither *verb* (**withers, withering, withered**)
to wither is to shrivel or wilt

withhold *verb* (**withholds, withholding, withheld**)
to withhold something is to refuse to give it to someone ♦ *He has withheld his permission*

within *preposition* and *adverb*
inside; not beyond something ♦ *Is the top shelf within your reach?*

without *preposition*
not having; free from ♦ *It is difficult to live without money*

withstand *verb* (**withstands, withstanding, withstood**)
to withstand something is to resist it or put up with it successfully

witness *noun* (*plural* **witnesses**)
1 a person who sees something happen ♦ *There were no witnesses to the accident* 2 a person who gives evidence in a lawcourt

witty *adjective* (**wittier, wittiest**)
clever and amusing
wittily *adverb* in a witty way **wittiness** *noun* being witty

wizard *noun* (*plural* **wizards**)
1 a male witch or magician 2 an amazing person ♦ *He's a wizard on the accordion*
wizardry *noun* magic or clever things

wobble ➣ *verb* (**wobbles, wobbling, wobbled**)
to wobble is to move unsteadily from side to side; to wobble something is to make it do this

wobble ➤ *noun* (*plural* **wobbles**)
a wobbling movement
wobbly *adjective* unsteady or wobbling

woe *noun* (*plural* **woes**)
sorrow or misfortune
woeful *adjective* full of woe **woefully** *adverb* in a woeful way

wok *noun* (*plural* **woks**)
a deep round-bottomed frying-pan used in Chinese cookery

woke past tense of **wake** *verb*

woken past participle of **wake** *verb*

wolf *noun* (*plural* **wolves**)
a wild animal like a large fierce dog

woman *noun* (*plural* **women**)
a grown-up female human being

womb *noun* (*plural* **wombs**) (*pronounced* woom)
the part of a female's body where babies develop before they are born

won past tense and past participle of **win** *verb*

wonder ➤ *noun* (*plural* **wonders**)
1 wonder is a feeling of surprise and admiration **2** a wonder is something that makes you feel surprised and admiring; a marvel
no wonder it is not surprising

wonder ➤ *verb* (**wonders, wondering, wondered**)
1 to wonder about something is to be trying to decide about it ♦ *I wonder what to do next* **2** to wonder at something is to feel surprise and admiration about it

wonderful *adjective*
marvellous or excellent
wonderfully *adverb* in a wonderful way

won't short for *will not*

wood *noun* (*plural* **woods**)
1 wood is the substance that trees are made of **2** a wood is a lot of trees growing together

wooded *adjective*
covered with growing trees

wooden *adjective*
1 made of wood **2** stiff or awkward ♦ *His movements were wooden*

woodland *noun* (*plural* **woodlands**)
wooded country

woodlouse *noun* (*plural* **woodlice**)
a small crawling creature with seven pairs of legs, living in rotten wood or damp soil. It rolls itself into a ball if it is alarmed

woodpecker *noun* (*plural* **woodpeckers**)
a bird that taps tree trunks with its beak to find insects

woodwind *noun*
wind instruments that are usually made of wood or plastic, such as the clarinet and oboe

woodwork *noun*
1 making things with wood **2** things made out of wood

woodworm *noun* (*plural* **woodworm** or **woodworms**)
the larva of a beetle that bores into wood

woody *adjective* (**woodier, woodiest**)
1 like wood or made of wood **2** full of trees

wool *noun*
1 the thick soft hair of sheep or goats
2 thread or cloth made from this hair

woollen *adjective*
made of wool

woollens *plural noun*
clothes made of wool

woolly *adjective* (**woollier, woolliest**)
1 covered with wool **2** made of wool or like wool **3** vague and not clear ♦ *He has woolly ideas*
woolliness *noun* being woolly

word ➤ *noun* (*plural* **words**)
1 a set of sounds or letters that has a meaning and is written with a space before and after it **2** a promise ♦ *He cannot keep his word* **3** a command or order ♦ *Run when I give the word* **4** a message or piece of information ♦ *We sent word that we had arrived safely*

word ➤ *verb* (**words, wording, worded**)
to word something is to express it in words

word class *noun* (*plural* **word classes**)
each of the groups (also called **parts of speech**) into which words can be divided in grammar: noun, adjective, verb, pronoun, adverb, preposition, conjunction, interjection

wording *noun*
the words used to say something

word processor *noun* (*plural* **word processors**)
a computer used for writing and editing letters and documents, and for printing them out
word processing *noun* using a word processor

wordy *adjective* (**wordier, wordiest**)
using too many words ♦ *We heard a wordy speech*

wore past tense of **wear** *verb*

work ➤ *noun* (*plural* **works**)
1 something that you have to do that needs effort or energy ♦ *Digging is hard work* 2 a person's job ♦ *What work do you do?* 3 something produced by work ♦ *The teacher marked our work* 4 (*in Science*) the result of applying a force to move an object 5 a piece of writing or music or painting ♦ *The book has all the works of Shakespeare*
at work working

work ➤ *verb* (**works, working, worked**)
1 to work is to do work 2 to work is also to have a job or be employed ♦ *She works in a bank* 3 something works when it operates correctly or successfully ♦ *Is the lift working?* 4 to work something is to make it act or operate ♦ *Can you work the lift?* 5 to work (for example) loose is to become gradually loose ♦ *The screw had worked loose*
to work out is to succeed or reach the right answer
to work something out is to find the answer to it

workable *adjective*
able to be used or done ♦ *This is a workable plan*

worker *noun* (*plural* **workers**)
1 someone who works 2 a member of the working class 3 a bee or ant that does the work in a hive or colony but does not produce eggs

workforce *noun* (*plural* **workforces**)
the number of people who work for a business or factory

working class *noun* or **working classes** *plural noun*
people who do paid manual or industrial work
working-class *adjective* belonging to the working class

workman *noun* (*plural* **workmen**)
a man who does manual work

workmanship *noun*
skill in working

workout *noun* (*plural* **workouts**)
a session of physical exercise or training

works *plural noun*
1 the moving parts of a machine 2 a factory or industrial site

worksheet *noun* (*plural* **worksheets**)
a sheet of paper with a set of questions about a subject for students

workshop *noun* (*plural* **workshops**)
a place where things are made or mended

world *noun* (*plural* **worlds**)
1 the world is the earth with all its countries and peoples 2 a world is a planet ♦ *The film is about creatures from another world* 3 everything to do with a particular subject or activity ♦ *They enjoy the world of sport*

worldly *adjective* (**worldlier, worldliest**)
1 to do with life on earth 2 only interested in money and possessions
worldliness *noun* being worldly

world war *noun* (*plural* **world wars**)
a war involving many countries all over the world

worldwide *adjective* and *adverb*
over the whole world

worm ➤ *noun* (*plural* **worms**)
1 a small thin wriggling animal without legs, especially an earthworm
2 (*informal*) an unimportant or unpleasant person

worm ➤ *verb* (**worms, worming, wormed**)
to worm is to move by wriggling or crawling
to worm something out of someone is to get them to tell you something secret

worn past participle of **wear** *verb*

worry ➤ *verb* (**worries, worrying, worried**)
1 to worry someone is to make them feel anxious or troubled about something 2 to worry is to be anxious or troubled 3 an animal worries its prey when it holds it in its teeth and shakes it
worrier *noun* someone who worries a lot

worry ➤ *noun* (*plural* **worries**)
1 worry is worrying or being anxious 2 a worry is something that makes you worry

worse *adjective* and *adverb*,   comparative of **bad** and **badly**
more badly; less good or less well

worsen *verb* (**worsens, worsening, worsened**)
1 to worsen something is to make it worse
2 to worsen is to become worse

worship ➤ *verb* (**worships, worshipping, worshipped**)
to worship God or a god is to give them praise or respect
worshipper *noun* someone who worships

worship ➤ *noun*
worshipping; religious ceremonies or services

worst *adjective* and *adverb*
superlative of **bad** and **badly**
most bad or most badly; least good or least well

worth ➤ *adjective*
1 having a certain value ♦ *This stamp is worth £100* 2 deserving something; good or important enough for something ♦ *That book is worth reading*

worth ➤ *noun*
value or usefulness

worthless *adjective*
having no value; useless

worthwhile *adjective*
important or good enough to do; useful

worthy *adjective* (**worthier, worthiest**)
deserving respect or support ♦ *The sale is for a worthy cause*
worthy of something deserving something; good enough for something ♦ *This charity is worthy of your support*
worthily *adverb* in a worthy way **worthiness** *noun* being worthy

would *verb*
1 past tense of the verb will ♦ *We said we would do it* ♦ *He said he would come if he could* 2 used in polite questions or requests ♦ *Would you like some tea?*

wouldn't short for *would not*

wound[1] ➤ *noun* (*plural* **wounds**)
(*pronounced* woond)
an injury done to a part of the body or to someone's feelings

wound ➤ *verb* (**wounds, wounding, wounded**)
to wound someone is to give them a wound or hurt their feelings

wound[2] (*pronounced* wownd)
past tense and past participle of
wind *verb*

wove past tense of **weave**

woven past participle of **weave**

wrap ➤ *verb* (**wraps, wrapping, wrapped**)
to wrap something is to put paper or some other covering round it

wrap ➤ *noun* (*plural* **wraps**)
a shawl or cloak worn to keep you warm

wrapper *noun* (*plural* **wrappers**)
a piece of paper or cloth wrapped round something

wrapping *noun* (*plural* **wrappings**)
material used to wrap something

wrath *noun* (*rhymes with* cloth)
(*old-fashioned use*) anger
wrathful *adjective* angry **wrathfully** *adverb* angrily

wreath *noun* (*plural* **wreaths**) (*pronounced* reeth)
flowers and leaves and branches bound together to make a circle

wreathe *verb* (**wreathes, wreathing, wreathed**)
(*pronounced* reeth)
to be wreathed in something is to be covered in it or decorated with it ♦ *Her face was wreathed in smiles*

wreck ➤ *verb* (**wrecks, wrecking, wrecked**)
to wreck something is to damage or ruin it so badly that it cannot be used again
wrecker *noun* someone who wrecks something

wreck ➤ *noun* (*plural* **wrecks**)
a wrecked ship or car or building

wreckage *noun*
the pieces of a wreck

wren *noun* (*plural* **wrens**)
a very small brown bird

wrench ➤ *verb* (**wrenches, wrenching, wrenched**)
to wrench something is to pull or twist it suddenly or violently ♦ *He wrenched the door open*

wrench ➤ *noun* (*plural* **wrenches**)
1 a wrenching movement 2 a tool for gripping and turning bolts or nuts

wrestle *verb* (**wrestles, wrestling, wrestled**)
1 to wrestle with someone is to fight them by grasping them and trying to throw them to the ground 2 to wrestle with a problem or difficulty is to struggle to solve it
wrestler *noun* someone who wrestles for sport

wretch *noun* (*plural* **wretches**)
someone who is unhappy, poor, or disliked

wretched *adjective* (*pronounced* rech-id)
1 unhappy; miserable; poor ♦ *a wretched beggar* 2 not satisfactory or pleasant ♦ *This wretched car won't start*

wriggle ➤ *verb* (**wriggles, wriggling, wriggled**)
to wriggle is to twist and turn your body
to wriggle out of something is to avoid doing something you do not like

wriggle ➤ *noun* (*plural* **wriggles**)
a wriggling movement
wriggly *adjective* wriggling a lot

wring *verb* (**wrings, wringing, wrung**)
1 to wring something wet, or to wring it
out, is to squeeze or twist it to get the
water out of it **2** to wring something is to
squeeze it violently ♦ *I'll wring your neck!*
wringing wet very wet; soaked

wrinkle ➤ *noun* (*plural* **wrinkles**)
a small crease or line in the skin or on a
surface

wrinkle ➤ *verb* (**wrinkles, wrinkling, wrinkled**)
to wrinkle something is to make wrinkles
in it

wrist *noun* (*plural* **wrists**)
the joint that connects the hand to the arm

wristwatch *noun* (*plural* **wristwatches**)
a watch that you wear on the wrist

write *verb* (**writes, writing, wrote, written**)
1 to write words or signs is to put them on
paper or some other surface so that people
can read them **2** to write a story or play or
a piece of music is to be the author or
composer of it **3** to write to someone is to
send them a letter
to write something off is to think it is lost or
useless

writer *noun* (*plural* **writers**)
a person who writes; an author

writhe *verb* (**writhes, writhing, writhed**)
(*pronounced* ryth)
to writhe is to twist your body about
because you are in pain or discomfort

writing *noun* (*plural* **writings**)
something you write; the way you write

wrong ➤ *adjective*
1 not fair or morally right ♦ *It is wrong to
cheat* **2** incorrect ♦ *Your answer is wrong*
3 not working properly ♦ *There's
something wrong with the engine*
wrongly *adverb* in a wrong way; not
correctly

wrong ➤ *adverb*
wrongly ♦ *You guessed wrong*

wrong ➤ *noun* (*plural* **wrongs**)
something that is wrong
in the wrong having done or said something
wrong

wrong ➤ *verb* (**wrongs, wronging, wronged**)
to wrong someone is to do wrong to them

wrote past tense of **write**

wrung past tense and past participle of
write

wry *adjective* (**wryer, wryest**)
slightly mocking or sarcastic ♦ *He gave a
wry smile*

xenophobia *noun*
a strong dislike of foreigners

Xmas *noun* (*plural* **Xmases**)
(*informal*) Christmas

X-ray ➤ *noun* (*plural* **X-rays**)
a photograph of the inside of something,
especially a part of the body, made by a
kind of radiation that can pass through
something solid

X-ray ➤ *verb* (**X-rays, X-raying, X-rayed**)
to X-ray something is to make an X-ray of
it

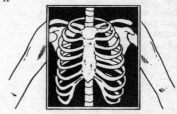

xylophone *noun* (*plural* **xylophones**)
(*pronounced* zy-lo-fohn)
a musical instrument made of wooden
bars of different lengths, that you hit with
small hammers

yacht *noun* (*plural* **yachts**) (*pronounced* yot)
1 a sailing boat used for racing or cruising
2 a private ship

yachtsman or **yachtswoman** *noun* (*plural* **yachtsmen** or **yachtswomen**)
a man or woman who sails in a yacht

yam *noun* (*plural* **yams**)
a tropical vegetable that grows underground

yank *verb* (**yanks, yanking, yanked**)
to yank something is to pull it strongly and suddenly

yap ➤ *verb* (**yaps, yapping, yapped**)
to yap is to make a shrill barking sound, as a small dog does

yap ➤ *noun* (*plural* **yaps**)
a yapping sound

yard[1] *noun* (*plural* **yards**)
a measure of length, 36 inches or about 91 centimetres

yard[2] *noun* (*plural* **yards**)
a piece of ground beside a building, or one used for a special purpose, such as a railway yard

yarn *noun* (*plural* **yarns**)
1 yarn is thread spun by twisting fibres together **2** (*informal*) a yarn is a tale or story

yawn ➤ *verb* (**yawns, yawning, yawned**)
1 to yawn is to open your mouth wide and breathe in deeply when you are tired or bored **2** to yawn is also to form a wide opening ♦ *The chasm yawned in front of them*

yawn ➤ *noun* (*plural* **yawns**)
the action of yawning

ye *pronoun*
(*old use*) you (referring to more than one person)

year *noun* (*plural* **years**)
the time that the earth takes to go right round the sun, about 365¼ days or twelve months

yearly *adjective* and *adverb*
every year

yearn *verb* (**yearns, yearning, yearned**)
to yearn for something is to long for it

yeast *noun*
a substance used in baking bread and in making beer and wine. It causes alcohol and carbon dioxide to form

yell ➤ *noun* (*plural* **yells**)
a loud cry or shout

yell ➤ *verb* (**yells, yelling, yelled**)
to yell is to cry or shout loudly

yellow ➤ *noun*
the colour of ripe lemons and buttercups

yellow ➤ *adjective* (**yellower, yellowest**)
1 yellow in colour **2** (*informal*) cowardly

yelp ➤ *verb* (**yelps, yelping, yelped**)
to yelp is to make a shrill bark or cry, as a dog does when hurt

yelp ➤ *noun* (*plural* **yelps**)
a yelping sound

yen[1] *noun* (*plural* **yens**)
a longing for something

yen[2] *noun* (*plural* **yen**)
a Japanese unit of money

yeoman *noun* (*plural* **yeomen**) (*pronounced* yoh-man)
(*old use*) a man who owns and runs a small farm

Yeoman of the Guard *noun* (*plural* **Yeomen of the Guard**)
a guard at the Tower of London; a beefeater

yes *interjection*
a word used for agreeing to something

yesterday *noun* and *adverb*
the day before today

yet ➤ *adverb*
1 up to now; by this time ♦ *Has the postman called yet?* **2** eventually ♦ *I'll get even with him yet* **3** in addition; even ♦ *She became yet more excited*

yet ➤ *conjunction*
nevertheless ♦ *It is strange, yet it is true*

yeti *noun* (*plural* **yetis**) (*pronounced* yet-ee)
a very large animal thought to live in the Himalayas

yew *noun* (*plural* **yews**)
an evergreen tree with red berries and dark leaves like needles

yield ➤ *verb* (**yields, yielding, yielded**)
1 to yield is to surrender or give in ♦ *He yielded to persuasion* **2** to yield a crop or profit is to produce it ♦ *These trees yield good apples*

yield ➤ *noun* (*plural* **yields**)
an amount produced by something ♦ *What is the yield of wheat per acre?*

yippee *interjection*
a shout of joy

yodel *verb* (**yodels, yodelling, yodelled**)
to yodel is to sing or shout with your voice going rapidly from low to high notes
yodeller *noun* someone who yodels

yoga *noun*
a Hindu system of meditation and self-control

yoghurt *noun* (*plural* **yoghurts**) (*pronounced* yog-ert)
milk made thick by the addition of bacteria, giving it a sharp taste

yoke ➤ *noun* (*plural* **yokes**)
a curved piece of wood put across the necks of animals pulling a cart

yoke ➤ *verb* (**yokes, yoking, yoked**)
to yoke animals is to harness them or link
them by means of a yoke

yolk *noun* (*plural* **yolks**) (*rhymes with* coke)
the yellow part of an egg

Yom Kippur *noun*
the Day of Atonement, an important
Jewish religious festival

yonder *adverb* and *adjective*
(*old use*) over there

Yorkshire pudding *noun* (*plural* **Yorkshire
puddings**)
a pudding made of batter and usually
eaten with roast beef

you *pronoun*
1 the person or people someone is
speaking to ♦ *Who are you?* **2** people;
anyone ♦ *You can never be too sure*

you'd short for *you had* or *you should* or *you
would*

you'll short for *you will*

young ➤ *adjective* (**younger, youngest**)
having lived or existed only a short time;
not old

young ➤ *plural noun*
children or young animals

youngster *noun* (*plural* **youngsters**)
a young person or child

your *adjective*
belonging to you

you're short for *you are*

yours *pronoun*
belonging to you ♦ *Is this house yours?*
Yours faithfully, Yours sincerely, Yours truly
formal ways of ending a letter before you
sign it

yourself *pronoun* (*plural* **yourselves**)
you (referring to one person) and nobody
else, used to refer back to the subject of a
verb ♦ *Have you hurt yourself?*
by yourself or **yourselves** on your own ♦ *Did
you do the work all by yourself?*

youth *noun* (*plural* **youths**)
1 youth is being young, or the time when
you are young **2** a youth is a young man
3 youth also means young people ♦ *What
do you think of today's youth?*
youthful *adjective* young and fresh

youth club *noun* (*plural* **youth clubs**)
a club providing leisure activities for
young people

youth hostel *noun* (*plural* **youth hostels**)
a hostel where young people can stay
cheaply when they are on holiday

you've short for *you have*

yo-yo *noun* (*plural* **yo-yos**)
a round wooden or plastic toy that moves
up and down on a string which you hold

yuppie *noun* (*plural* **yuppies**)
(*informal*) a young middle-class person
with a professional job, who earns a lot of
money and spends it on expensive things

Zz

zany *adjective* (**zanier, zaniest**)
funny in a crazy kind of way

zap *verb* (**zaps, zapping, zapped**)
(*slang*) **1** to zap something or someone is
to attack or destroy them, especially in
electronic games **2** to zap is to change
quickly from one section of a videotape to
another

zeal *noun*
keenness, especially in doing what you
believe to be right

zealous *adjective* (*pronounced* **zel**-us)
having enthusiasm; keen
zealously *adverb* in a zealous way

zebra *noun* (*plural* **zebras**)
an African animal like a horse with black
and white stripes

zebra crossing *noun* (*plural* **zebra crossings**)
part of a road marked with broad white
stripes for pedestrians to cross

zenith *noun*
1 the part of the sky directly above you
2 the highest point of something

zero *noun* (*plural* **zeros**)
nought; the figure 0

zero hour *noun* (*plural* **zero hours**)
the time when something is planned to
start

zest *noun*
great enjoyment or interest

zigzag ➤ *noun* (*plural* **zigzags**)
a line or route full of sharp turns from one
side to the other

zigzag ➤ *verb* (**zigzags, zigzagging, zigzagged**)
to zigzag is to move in a zigzag

zinc *noun*
a white metal

zip ➤ *noun* (*plural* **zips**)
1 a zip, or zip fastener, is a device with two rows of small teeth that fit together, used to join two pieces of material **2** a zip is also a sharp sound like a bullet going through the air **3** zip is liveliness or energy

zip ➤ *verb* (**zips, zipping, zipped**)
1 to zip something is to fasten it with a zip **2** to zip, or zip along, is to move quickly with a sharp sound

zodiac *noun* (*pronounced* **zoh**-di-ak)
an area of the sky divided into twelve equal parts, called **signs of the zodiac**, each named after a constellation

zombie *noun* (*plural* **zombies**)
(*informal*) someone who seems to be doing things without thinking, often through tiredness

zone *noun* (*plural* **zones**)
a special district or area ♦ *This is a no-parking zone*

zoo *noun* (*plural* **zoos**)
a place where wild animals are kept so that people can look at them or study them

zoology *noun* (*pronounced* zoh-**ol**-o-jee)
the study of animals
zoological *adjective* to do with zoology
zoologist *noun* an expert in zoology

zoom *verb* (**zooms, zooming, zoomed**)
to zoom is to move very quickly, especially with a buzzing sound

zoom lens *noun* (*plural* **zoom lenses**)
a camera lens that can be adjusted continuously to focus on things that are close up or far away

APPENDICES

Some common prefixes

Prefix	Meaning	Example
ant(i)-	against	anti-aircraft
arch-	chief	archbishop
auto-	self	autobiography
com-; con-	together; with	compare; connect
contra-	against	contradict
de-	removing something	debug
dis-	not; taking away	dishonest; disarm
em-; en-	in; into	embark; encircle
ex-	that used to be	ex-husband
extra-	more; outside	extra-special; extraterrestrial
fore-	before	foresee
il-, im-, in-, ir-	not	illegal; impossible
il-, im-, in-, ir-, etc.	in; into	illuminate; import
inter-	between	international
mis-	wrong	misbehave
mono-	one	monorail
multi-	many	multiracial
non-	not	nonsense
over-	too much	overdo
poly-	many	polygon
post-	after	postpone
pre-	before	prehistoric
pro-	supporting	pro-government
re-	again	reappear
semi-	half	semicircle
sub-	below	submarine
super-	over; beyond	supersonic
tele-	at a distance	television
trans-	across	transport
ultra-	beyond	ultraviolet
un-	not	uncertain

Some common suffixes

Suffix	Meaning	Example
-able, -ible, -uble	able (to be ...)	eatable; edible; soluble
-ant; -ent	a doer	attendant
-dom	condition; rank; territory	freedom; kingdom
-ee	one who is ...	employee
-er	a doer	baker; miner
-er	more	harder; higher
-esque	in the style of	picturesque
-ess	used to make feminine forms of words	lioness
-est	most	hardest; highest
-fold	times	threefold; fourfold
-ful	full of	trustful
-hood	state of	childhood; manhood
-ic	belonging to	historic
-ize; -ise	used to make verbs	publicize
-ish	rather like	reddish; boyish
-ism	belief; system of thought	Hinduism; Communism
-ist	a doer	artist
-itis	inflammation of	tonsillitis
-less	lacking; free from	useless; smokeless
-let	small	piglet
-ly	used to make adverbs and adjectives	bravely; kindly
-ment	used to make nouns	amusement
-ness	state of being	kindness
-oid	like	cuboid
-or	a doer	sailor; tailor
-ous	used to make adjectives	dangerous
-ship	state of being	friendship
-some	full of	troublesome
-ty	showing condition	cruelty; loyalty
-ward(s)	in a particular direction	seaward(s)

Grammar

Words can be put into sets called word classes, or parts of speech. The main ones are: **noun, pronoun, verb, adjective, adverb, preposition, conjunction, interjection**

Nouns

Nouns are words that are the names of things or persons, such as *child, danger, tree*. Nouns divide up into names (or **proper nouns**) and descriptions (or **common nouns**).

proper nouns:	[James, Africa, Dickens, Concorde...]
common nouns	[dog, stream, mystery, bone, fire, danger...]

Common nouns divide into those which stand for objects (**concrete nouns**), and those which stand for ideas (**abstract nouns**).

concrete nouns	[dog, stream, cone, fire, steel, bread, car ...]
abstract nouns	[mystery, danger, happiness, beauty ...]

Nouns also divide into those which can be made plural (**countables**), and those which cannot (**uncountables**)

countables	[dog, stream, bone, car ...]
uncountables	[bread, steel, air, clothing ...]

Pronouns

Pronouns are words used instead of a noun, such as **it, me, they**.

Verbs and their tenses

Some verbs express actions or feeling. For example:
I **came**.　She **ate**.　They **know**.

Other verbs connect words or phrases in a sentence.
It **is** late.　I **am** coming.　You **have** eaten.　They **must** not know.

Verbs have several different forms, depending on their **tense**. For example:
present tense: I speak, she speaks, they are speaking.
past tenses: I spoke, she has spoken, you had spoken, they have been speaking.
future tense: I will be speaking, they will be speaking.

The forms of verbs are given in the dictionary in the same order every time:
speak *verb* (**speaks, speaking, spoke, spoken**)
speak: present tense after I, you, and they.
speaks: present tense after he, she, or it.
speaking: present participle (used after is, are, was, has been, etc.).
spoke: simple past tense.
spoken: past participle (used after has, had, etc.).

You will see that some verbs are *regular* which means that they follow a rule in the way they form their tenses. For example:
kick *verb* (**kicks, kicking, kicked**).

But many verbs are *irregular* and have rules of their own! For example:
throw *verb* (**throws, throwing, threw, thrown**).

The connecting verb, **be**, is the most irregular of all:
be *verb* (*present tense: singular, 1st person* **am**, *2nd person* **are**, *3rd person*
is, *plural* **are**; *present participle* **being**; *past tense: singular, 1st and 3rd persons* **was**, *2nd person* **were**, *plural* **were**; *past participle* **been.**

Adjectives

Adjectives are words that describe a noun and add to its meaning, such as **happy, important, old.**

Adverbs

Adverbs are words that tell you how, when, where, or why something happens, such as **quickly, again, here, together**.

Comparison of adjectives and adverbs

Adjectives and adverbs can be made **comparative** or **superlative** in the following ways:

positive	comparative	superlative
stiff	stiffer	stiffest
quick	quicker	quickest
funny	funnier	funniest
late	later	latest

(For general rules about adding **-er** and **-est**, see **Spelling**, p. 502)

For longer adjectives, and for most adverbs, the comparative and superlative are formed by putting **more** or **most** in front of them.

positive	comparative	superlative
terrible	more terrible	most terrible
quickly	more quickly	most quickly

But watch out for exceptions:

bad	worse	worst
badly	worse	worst

If in doubt, look them up in the dictionary.

Prepositions

Prepositions are words put in front of nouns or pronouns to show how the nouns and pronouns are connected with other words, such as **against**, **in**, **on**.

Conjunctions

Conjunctions are joining words, such as **and**, **but**, **whether**.

Interjections

Interjections are words that express surprise, pain, delight, etc., such as **oh**, **ouch**, **hooray**.

Spelling Some useful rules

To make a noun plural:

Normally, just add **-s**:
   skirts, socks, ties, pianos, pieces, stars.

But watch out for some words ending in **-o**, that need **-es**:
   echoes, heroes, potatoes, tomatoes, volcanoes, etc.

To words ending in **-ch**, **-s**, **-sh**, **-x**, or **-z**, add **-es**:
   dress – dresses, box – boxes, stitch – stitches.

To words ending in **-f** and **-fe**, change to **-ves**:
   scarf – scarves, life – lives, half – halves.

But watch out for the exceptions: beliefs, proofs, roofs, etc.

To words ending in a consonant followed by **-y**, change the **y** to **i** and add **-es**:
   copy – copies, cry – cries, party – parties.

Adding -ing and -ed to verbs:

Normally, just add **-ing** or **-ed**:
   load – loading – loaded; open – opening – opened; stay – staying – stayed.

For short words ending in **-e**, usually leave off the **e**:
   race – racing – raced, blame – blaming – blamed.

For many short words that end with one consonant, double the last consonant:
   slam – slamming – slammed; tip – tipping – tipped.

For longer words ending with one consonant and having the stress on the last syllable, double the last consonant:
   compel – compelling – compelled; prefer – preferring – preferred.

For words ending **-y** after a consonant, change the **y** to an **i** before **-ed**:
   try – trying – tried.

For words ending in **-ie**, change the **ie** to **y** before adding **-ing**:
   lie – lying – lied; tie – tying – tied.

Watch out for these exceptions: *lay – laid; pay – paid; say – said.*

Adding -er and -est to adjectives:

Normally, just add **-er** and **-est**, unless the word already ends in **-e**:
   cold – colder – coldest; wide – wider – widest.

For many short words that end with one consonant, change to a double consonant:
   wet – wetter – wettest; dim – dimmer – dimmest.

If the word has two syllables and ends in **-y**, change the **y** to an **i**:

dirty – dirtier – dirtiest; happy – happier – happiest.

(See also **Grammar**, p. 499, on adjective and adverb forms.)

Adding -ly:

Adding **-ly** to an adjective makes it into an adverb:
slowly, badly, awkwardly.

If the word ends in **-ll**, just add **-y**:
full – fully.

For words ending in **-y** and with more than one syllable, leave off the **-y** and add **-ily**:
happy – happily; hungry – hungrily.

For words ending in **-le**, leave off the **e**:
idle – idly; simple – simply.

For adjectives ending in **-ic**, you usually add **-ally**:
basic – basically; drastic – drastically.

But watch out for these special ones: *public – publicly.*

List of Countries and Peoples

Country	People	Country	People
Afghanistan	Afghans	Colombia	Colombians
Albania	Albanians	Comoros	Comorans
Algeria	Algerians	Congo, Democratic Republic of the	Congolese
Andorra	Andorrans		
Angola	Angolans	Congo, Republic of the	Congolese
Antigua and Barbuda	Antiguans, Barbudans	Costa Rica	Costa Ricans
Argentina	Argentinians	Côte d'Ivoire	People of the Côte d'Ivoire
Armenia	Armenians	Croatia	Croats
Australia	Australians	Cuba	Cubans
Austria	Austrians	Cyprus	Cypriots
Azerbaijan	Azerbaijanis or Azeris	Czech Republic	Czechs
Bahamas	Bahamians	**D**enmark	Danes
Bahrain	Bahrainis	Djibouti	Djiboutians
Bangladesh	Bangladeshis	Dominica	Dominicans
Barbados	Barbadians	Dominican Republic	Dominicans
Belarus	Belorussians		
Belgium	Belgians	**E**ast Timor	East Timorese
Belize	Belizians	Ecuador	Ecuadoreans
Benin	Beninese	Egypt	Egyptians
Bhutan	Bhutanese	El Salvador	Salvadoreans
Bolivia	Bolivians	Equatorial Guinea	Equatorial Guineans
Bosnia-Herzegovina	Bosnians		
Botswana	Batswana or Citizens of Botswana	Eritrea	Eritreans
		Estonia	Estonians
		Ethiopia	Ethiopians
Brazil	Brazilians		
Brunei Darussalam	People of Brunei	**F**iji	Fijians
Bulgaria	Bulgarians	Finland	Finns
Burkina Faso	Burkinans	France	French
Burundi	People of Burundi		
		Gabon	Gabonese
Cambodia	Cambodians	Gambia, The	Gambians
Cameroon	Cameroonians	Georgia	Georgians
Canada	Canadians	Germany	Germans
Cape Verde	Cape Verdeans	Ghana	Ghanaians
Central African Republic	People of the Central African Republic	Greece	Greeks
		Grenada	Grenadians
		Guatemala	Guatemalans
Chad	Chadians	Guinea	Guineans
Chile	Chileans	Guinea-Bissau	People of Guinea-Bissau
China, People's Republic of	Chinese		
		Guyana	Guyanese

Country	People	Country	People
Haiti	Haitians	Monaco	Monégasques
Honduras	Hondurans	Mongolia	Mongolians
Hungary	Hungarians	Morocco	Moroccans
		Mozambique	Mozambicans
Iceland	Icelanders	Myanmar (Burma)	Burmese
India	Indians		
Indonesia	Indonesians	Namibia	Namibians
Iran	Iranians	Nauru	Nauruans
Iraq	Iraqis	Nepal	Nepalese
Ireland, Republic of	Irish	Netherlands	Dutch
Israel	Israelis	New Zealand	New Zealanders
Italy	Italians	Nicaragua	Nicaraguans
		Niger	Nigeriens
Jamaica	Jamaicans	Nigeria	Nigerians
Japan	Japanese	North Korea	North Koreans
Jordan	Jordanians	(People's Democratic Republic of Korea)	
Kazakhstan	Kazakhs		
Kenya	Kenyans	Norway	Norwegians
Kiribati	Kiribatians		
Kuwait	Kuwaitis	Oman	Omanis
Kyrgyzstan	Kyrgyz		
		Pakistan	Pakistanis
Laos	Laotians	Palau	Palauans
Latvia	Latvians	Panama	Panamanians
Lebanon	Lebanese	Papua New Guinea	Papua New Guineans
Lesotho	Basotho		
Liberia	Liberians	Paraguay	Paraguayans
Libya	Libyans	Peru	Peruvians
Liechtenstein	Liechtensteiners	Philippines	Filipinos
Lithuania	Lithuanians	Poland	Poles
Luxembourg	Luxembourgers	Portugal	Portuguese
Macedonia (Former Yugoslav Republic of Macedonia)	Macedonians	Qatar	Qataris
Madagascar	Malagasies	Romania	Romanians
Malawi	Malawians	Russia (Russian Federation)	Russians
Malaysia	Malaysians	Rwanda	Rwandans
Maldives	Maldivians		
Mali	Malians	St Kitts and Nevis	People of St Kitts and Nevis
Malta	Maltese		
Marshall Islands	Marshall Islanders	St Lucia	St Lucians
Mauritania	Mauritanians	St Vincent and the Grenadines	St Vincentians
Mauritius	Mauritians		
Mexico	Mexicans	Samoa	Samoans
Micronesia	Micronesians	San Marino	People of San Marino
Moldova	Moldovans		

Country	People	Country	People
São Tomé and Principe	People of São Tomé and Principe	Trinidad and Tobago	Trinidadians and Tobagans or Tobagonians
Saudi Arabia	Saudi Arabians	Tunisia	Tunisians
Senegal	Senegalese	Turkey	Turks
Seychelles	Seychellois	Turkmenistan	Turkmens
Sierra Leone	Sierra Leoneans	Tuvalu	Tuvaluans
Singapore	Singaporeans		
Slovakia	Slovaks	Uganda	Ugandans
Slovenia	Slovenes	Ukraine	Ukrainians
Solomon Islands	Solomon Islanders	United Arab Emirates	People of the United Arab Emirates
Somalia	Somalis		
South Africa	South Africans	United Kingdom	British
South Korea (Republic of Korea)	South Koreans	United States of America	Americans
Spain	Spaniards	Uruguay	Uruguayans
Sri Lanka	Sri Lankans	Uzbekistan	Uzbeks
Sudan	Sudanese		
Suriname	Surinamers	Vanuatu	People of Vanuatu
Swaziland	Swazis	Vatican City	Vatican citizens
Sweden	Swedes	Venezuela	Venezuelans
Switzerland	Swiss	Vietnam	Vietnamese
Syria	Syrians		
		Yemen	Yemenis
Taiwan	Taiwanese	Yugoslavia (Montenegro and Serbia)	Yugoslavians (Montenegrins and Serbians)
Tajikistan	Tajiks		
Tanzania	Tanzanians		
Thailand	Thais	Zambia	Zambians
Togo	Togolese	Zimbabwe	Zimbabweans
Tonga	Tongans		